PRODUCT LIABILITY LAW

EDITORIAL ADVISORS

Rachel E. Barkow
Segal Family Professor of Regulatory Law and Policy
Faculty Director, Center on the Administration of Criminal Law
New York University School of Law

Erwin Chemerinsky
Dean and Jesse H. Choper Distinguished Professor of Law
University of California, Berkeley School of Law

Richard A. Epstein
Laurence A. Tisch Professor of Law
New York University School of Law
Peter and Kirsten Bedford Senior Fellow
The Hoover Institution
Senior Lecturer in Law
The University of Chicago

Ronald J. Gilson
Charles J. Meyers Professor of Law and Business
Stanford University
Marc and Eva Stern Professor of Law and Business
Columbia Law School

James E. Krier
Earl Warren DeLano Professor of Law Emeritus
The University of Michigan Law School

Tracey L. Meares
Walton Hale Hamilton Professor of Law
Director, The Justice Collaboratory
Yale Law School

Richard K. Neumann, Jr.
Alexander Bickel Professor of Law
Maurice A. Deane School of Law at Hofstra University

Robert H. Sitkoff
Austin Wakeman Scott Professor of Law
John L. Gray Professor of Law
Harvard Law School

David Alan Sklansky
Stanley Morrison Professor of Law
Faculty Co-Director, Stanford Criminal Justice Center
Stanford Law School

ASPEN CASEBOOK SERIES

Product Liability Law

Second Edition

Mark A. Geistfeld

Sheila Lubetsky Birnbaum Professor of Civil Litigation
New York University School of Law

Copyright © 2022 CCH Incorporated. All Rights Reserved.

Published by Wolters Kluwer in New York.

Wolters Kluwer Legal & Regulatory U.S. serves customers worldwide with CCH, Aspen Publishers, and Kluwer Law International products. (www.WKLegaledu.com)

No part of this publication may be reproduced or transmitted in any form or by any means, electronic or mechanical, including photocopy, recording, or utilized by any information storage or retrieval system, without written permission from the publisher. For information about permissions or to request permissions online, visit us at www.WKLegaledu.com, or a written request may be faxed to our permissions department at 212-771-0803.

To contact Customer Service, e-mail customer.service@wolterskluwer.com, call 1-800-234-1660, fax 1-800-901-9075, or mail correspondence to:

> Wolters Kluwer
> Attn: Order Department
> PO Box 990
> Frederick, MD 21705

Printed in the United States of America.

1 2 3 4 5 6 7 8 9 0

ISBN 978-1-5438-2066-9

Library of Congress Cataloging-in-Publication Data

Names: Geistfeld, Mark, 1958- author.
Title: Product liability law / Mark A. Geistfeld, Sheila Lubetsky Birnbaum Professor of Civil Litigation, New York University School of Law.
Description: Second Edition. | New York : Wolters Kluwer, 2021. | Series: Aspen casebook series | Includes bibliographical references and index. | Summary: "Products liability casebook for law school students"– Provided by publisher.
Identifiers: LCCN 2021034783 (print) | LCCN 2021034784 (ebook) | ISBN 9781543820669 (hardback) | ISBN 9781543820676 (ebook)
Subjects: LCSH: Products liability—United States. | Products liability—United States—Cases. | LCGFT: Casebooks (Law)
Classification: LCC KF8925.P7 G45 2021 (print) | LCC KF8925.P7 (ebook) | DDC 346.7303/8—dc23
LC record available at https://lccn.loc.gov/2021034783
LC ebook record available at https://lccn.loc.gov/2021034784

About Wolters Kluwer Legal & Regulatory U.S.

Wolters Kluwer Legal & Regulatory U.S. delivers expert content and solutions in the areas of law, corporate compliance, health compliance, reimbursement, and legal education. Its practical solutions help customers successfully navigate the demands of a changing environment to drive their daily activities, enhance decision quality and inspire confident outcomes.

Serving customers worldwide, its legal and regulatory portfolio includes products under the Aspen Publishers, CCH Incorporated, Kluwer Law International, ftwilliam.com and MediRegs names. They are regarded as exceptional and trusted resources for general legal and practice-specific knowledge, compliance and risk management, dynamic workflow solutions, and expert commentary.

For my students

Summary of Contents

Contents		*xi*
Preface		*xix*
Acknowledgments		*xxi*
Chapter 1	The Big Picture	1
Chapter 2	Doctrinal Foundations of Strict Products Liability	23
Chapter 3	The Substantive Basis of Products Liability	73
Chapter 4	Manufacturing Defects and Product Malfunctions	123
Chapter 5	The "Unreasonably Dangerous" Requirement, Patent Defects, and the Element of Duty	153
Chapter 6	Design Defects	177
Chapter 7	Warning Defects	253
Chapter 8	The Relation Between Warnings and Product Design	341
Chapter 9	Medical Products and the Exemption of "Unavoidably Unsafe" Products from Strict Products Liability	365
Chapter 10	Products Liability in the "Age of Statutes"	393
Chapter 11	Factual Causation	423
Chapter 12	Scope of Liability: Proximate Cause	525
Chapter 13	Damages and the Scope of Liability as Defined by the Type of Injury	557
Chapter 14	Defenses Based on Consumer Conduct	617
Chapter 15	The Scope of Strict Products Liability as Defined by the Nature of the Transaction	667
Chapter 16	Bystander Liability	699
Chapter 17	Comparative Products Liability	725
Table of Cases		*755*
Index		*761*

Contents

Preface	*xix*
Acknowledgments	*xxi*

Chapter 1. The Big Picture — 1

- I. The Early Limitation of Tort Liability to the Contractual Relationship — 2
    - *Winterbottom v. Wright* — 2
- II. An (Extreme) Example of Strict Products Liability: The Asbestos Cases — 5
    - *Borel v. Fibreboard Paper Products Corp.* — 5
    - Asbestos Changes — 8
    - S. 3274, Fairness in Asbestos Injury Resolution Act of 2006 — 10
- III. The Social Problem of Product Accidents — 13
    - *Hammontree v. Jenner* — 15
- IV. A Reprise of Excessive Liability as a Reason for Limiting Tort Liability to the Contractual Relationship — 19
    - *Strauss v. Belle Realty Co.* — 20

Chapter 2. Doctrinal Foundations of Strict Products Liability — 23

- I. The Implied Warranty — 23
    - A. Contaminated or Unwholesome Food — 24
        - *Van Bracklin v. Fonda* — 24
        - *Jacob E. Decker & Sons v. Capps* — 27
    - B. Warranties in Nonfood Cases — 32
        - *Seixas and Seixas v. Woods* — 32
        - *Escola v. Coca Cola Bottling Co.* — 36
    - C. The *Restatement (Second)* Rule of Strict Products Liability — 42
        - Restatement (Second) of Torts — 42
- II. The Negligence Principle — 47
    - A. The Demise of the Privity Bar to Negligence Liability — 47
        - *Thomas v. Winchester* — 47
        - *Macpherson v. Buick Motor Co.* — 51
    - B. Proof of Negligence Liability — 55
        - *Escola v. Coca Cola Bottling Co.* — 56
    - C. The Evidentiary Rationale for Strict Liability — 60
        - *Cole v. Goodwin & Story* — 60

	D.	The Negligence Foundation of the *Restatement (Third)*	65
		Restatement (Third) of Torts: Products Liability	66

Chapter 3. The Substantive Basis of Products Liability — 73

I.		Controversy Over the Liability Rule	73
		Stewart, Strict Liability for Defective Product Design: The Quest for a Well-Ordered Regime	74
II.		Strict Products Liability 1.0	79
		Halliday v. Sturm, Ruger & Co.	80
		Green v. Smith & Nephew Ahp, Inc.	83
		Denny v. Ford Motor Co.	89
III.		Strict Products Liability 2.0	96
	A.	Incorporating the Risk-Utility Test into Strict Products Liability	97
		Potter v. Chicago Pneumatic	97
		Bifolck v. Phillip Morris, Inc.	102
	B.	Defining Consumer Expectations with the Risk-Utility Test	106
		Cipollone v. Liggett Group Inc.	107
		Geistfeld, The Value of Consumer Choice in Strict Products Liability	111

Chapter 4. Manufacturing Defects and Product Malfunctions — 123

I.	Rationale(s) for Strict Liability	123
	Restatement (Third) of Torts: Products Liability	123
II.	Proof of Manufacturing Defect	126
	Mckenzie v. SK Hand Tool Corp.	126
III.	Food Cases	131
	Allen v. Grafton	131
	Schafer v. JLC Food Systems, Inc.	132
IV.	Product Malfunctions	137
	Metropolitan Property & Casualty Co. v. Deere & Co.	137
	Sigler v. American Honda Motor Co.	144
V.	Autonomous Vehicles and Products Liability: Problem Set 1	149

Chapter 5. The "Unreasonably Dangerous" Requirement, Patent Defects, and the Element of Duty — 153

I.	Different Interpretations of the "Unreasonably Dangerous" Requirement	154
	Cronin v. J.B.E. Olson Corp.	154
	Luque v. Mclean	158
	Cepeda v. Cumberland Engineering Co.	161
II.	Distinguishing Patent Defects from Patent Dangers	165
III.	The Element of Duty	170
IV.	Autonomous Vehicles and Products Liability: Problem Set 2	172

Contents

Chapter 6. Design Defects — 177

- I. Emerging Consensus or Widespread Disagreement? — 178
  - A. "Exclusive" Reliance on the Consumer Expectations Test — 178
  - B. "Exclusive" Reliance on the Risk-Utility Test — 179
  - C. Combining the Two Tests — 180
    - *Soule v. General Motors Corp.* — 180
- II. The Risk-Utility Test Applied — 186
  - A. Reasonable Alternative Design — 187
    - Restatement (Third) of Torts: Products Liability — 188
  - B. Balancing the Risk-Utility Factors — 192
    - *Laplante v. American Honda Motor Corp.* — 195
    - *Dawson v. Chrysler Corp.* — 200
- III. The Role of Consumer Choice — 207
  - A. Foreseeable Product Use — 207
    - *Salazar v. Wolo Mfg. Group* — 208
  - B. Inherent Product Dangers and Categorical Liability — 210
    - *Dreisonstok v. Volkswagenwerk, A.G.* — 211
    - *In re: Depuy Orthopaedics, Inc. Pinnicale Hip Implant Product Liability Litigation* — 217
    - *Linegar v. Armour of America* — 222
  - C. Optional Safety Equipment — 228
    - *Scarangella v. Thomas Built Buses, Inc.* — 228
- IV. Limits on the Duty to Design: Technological Feasibility and "State of the Art" — 235
  - Restatement (Third) of Torts: Products Liability — 235
  - *Boatland of Houston v. Bailey* — 238
  - *Hyjek v. Anthony Industries* — 244
- V. Autonomous Vehicles and Products Liability: Problem Set 3 — 248

Chapter 7. Warning Defects — 253

- I. Information and Consumer Choice — 253
  - *Watkins v. Ford Motor Co.* — 253
- II. The Substantive Basis of the Liability Rule — 257
  - *Anderson v. Owens-Corning Fiberglass Corp.* — 257
  - *Vassallo v. Baxter Healthcare Corp.* — 261
- III. To Whom Must the Warning Be Directed? — 265
  - A. The Average or Ordinary Consumer — 266
    - *Johnson v. American Standard, Inc.* — 266
    - *Livingston v. Marie Callender's, Inc.* — 271
    - *Medina v. Louisville Ladder, Inc.* — 275
  - B. The Role of Intermediaries — 279
    - *Sowell v. American Cyanamid Co.* — 279
    - *Hoffman v. Houghton Chemical Corp.* — 282
- IV. The Type of Risks Encompassed by the Duty to Warn — 287
  - *American Tobacco Co., Inc. v. Grinnell* — 288
  - *Liriano v. Hobart Corp.* — 295
  - *Moran v. Faberge, Inc.* — 303

V.	The Adequacy of Disclosure	311
	Jones v. Amazing Products, Inc.	311
	Macdonald v. Ortho Pharmaceutical Corp.	313
	Broussard v. Continental Oil Co.	318
VI.	The Risk-Utility Test	323
	Campos v. Firestone Tire & Rubber Co.	323
	Hood v. Ryobi America Corp.	324
VII.	The Risk-Utility Test Applied	327
VIII.	The Post-Sale Duty to Warn	329
	Great Northern Insurance Co. v. Honeywell International, Inc.	329
IX.	Autonomous Vehicles and Products Liability: Problem Set 4	336

Chapter 8. The Relation Between Warnings and Product Design — 341

I.	The Duty to Warn as a Complete Substitute for the Duty to Design	341
	Skyhook Corp. v. Jasper	342
II.	Separating the Duty to Design from the Duty to Warn	344
	Klein v. Sears, Roebuck and Co.	344
	Klopp v. Wackenhut Corp.	349
III.	Incorporating Both the Design and the Warning into the Risk-Utility Test	351
	Uniroyal Goodrich Tire Co. v. Martinez	351
	Hood v. Ryobi America Corp.	358
IV.	Autonomous Vehicles and Products Liability: Problem Set 5	362

Chapter 9. Medical Products and the Exemption of "Unavoidably Unsafe" Products from Strict Products Liability — 365

I.	"Unavoidably Unsafe Products" and Design Defects	366
	Brown v. Superior Court	366
	Freeman v. Hoffman-La Roche, Inc.	372
II.	Manufacturing Defects and Product Malfunctions	381
	Rogers v. Miles Labs, Inc.	381
	Transue v. Aesthetech Corp.	385
III.	Autonomous Vehicles and Products Liability: Problem Set 6	390

Chapter 10. Products Liability in the "Age of Statutes" — 393

I.	Statutory Violations as Proof of Defect	394
	Harned v. Dura Corp.	394
II.	The Regulatory Compliance Defense	399
	Ramirez v. Plough, Inc.	400
III.	Statutory Preemption of Tort Claims	409
	Williamson v. Mazda Motor of America	410
III.	Autonomous Vehicles and Products Liability: Problem Set 7	418

Chapter 11.		**Factual Causation**	**423**
	I.	The But-For Test	424
		Crossley v. General Motors Corp.	424
		Liriano v. Hobart Corp.	429
		Daubert v. Merrell Dow Pharmaceuticals, Inc.	433
	II.	Proof of Causation in Warning Cases	440
		A. The Subjective Standard	440
		B. The Objective Standard	441
		C. The Heeding Presumption	442
		Coffman v. Keene Corp.	442
	III.	Proof of Causation in Warranty Cases	448
		Baxter v. Ford Motor Co.	449
		Baxter v. Ford Motor Co.	451
	IV.	Enhanced Injury	456
		Trull v. Volkswagen of America, Inc.	457
		Story Parchment Co. v. Paterson Parchment Paper Co.	463
		May v. Portland Jeep	465
	V.	Factual Uncertainty Regarding the Tortfeasor's Identity: Alternative and Market-Share Liability	469
		Sindell v. Abbott Laboratories	469
		Brown v. Superior Court	476
		Smith v. Eli Lilly & Co.	479
		Geistfeld, The Doctrinal Unity of Alternative Liability and Market-Share Liability	483
	VI.	The Problem of Scientific Uncertainty	493
		Rider v. Sandoz Pharmaceuticals Corp.	494
		Stevens v. Secretary of Dept. of Health and Human Services	505
		In re: Roundup Products Liability Litigation	510
		In re: Roundup Products Liability Litigation	514
	VII.	Autonomous Vehicles and Products Liability: Problem Set 8	521
Chapter 12.		**Scope of Liability: Proximate Cause**	**525**
	I.	The Foreseeability Test	526
		Stazenski v. Tennant Co.	526
		In re September 11 Litigation	531
	II.	Backward-Looking Tests	538
		Union Pump v. Albritton	538
	III.	A Reprise of Duty	547
		Jeld-Wen, Inc. v. Gamble by Gamble	547
	IV.	Autonomous Vehicles and Products Liability: Problem Set 9	553
Chapter 13.		**Damages and the Scope of Liability as Defined by the Type of Injury**	**557**
	I.	Physical Harm and the Measure of Compensation	558

	II.	Pure Economic Loss	561
		East River Steamship v. Transamerica Delavel	561
		Pfizer, Inc. v. Farsian	570
		80 South Eighth Street Limited Partnership v. Carey-Canada, Inc.	574
	III.	The Cost of Medical Monitoring	581
		Donovan v. Philip Morris USA, Inc.	581
	IV.	Stand-Alone Emotional Harms	586
		In re Methyl Tertiary Butyl Ether ("MTBE") Products Liability Litigation	587
	V.	Punitive Damages	595
		Owens-Illinois, Inc. v. Zenobia	595
		Philip Morris USA v. Williams	603
	VI.	Autonomous Vehicles and Products Liability: Problem Set 10	612

Chapter 14. Defenses Based on Consumer Conduct   **617**

	I.	Contractual Limitations of Liability	617
	II.	Assumption of Risk	618
		A. Voluntary Choice	619
		Cremeans v. Willmar Henderson Mfg. Co.	619
		Wangsness v. Builders Cashway, Inc.	625
		B. Knowledge of Risk	630
		Traylor v. Husqvarna Motor	630
		C. Primary Assumption of Risk	633
		Ford v. Polaris Indus., Inc.	633
	III.	Contributory Negligence and Comparative Responsibility	640
		A. Product Misuse Without Comparative Responsibility	641
		Bexiga v. Havir Mfg. Corp.	641
		B. Product Misuse in a System of Comparative Responsibility	643
		Daly v. General Motors Corp.	644
		Donze v. General Motors, LLC	650
		C. Forms of Product Misuse	653
		States v. R.D. Werner Co.	653
		Exxon Company, U.S.A. v. Sofec, Inc.	656
		D. Assumption of Risk and Comparative Responsibility	659
		Andren v. White-Rodgers Co.	659
	IV.	Autonomous Vehicles and Products Liability: Problem Set 11	664

Chapter 15. The Scope of Strict Products Liability as Defined by the Nature of the Transaction   **667**

	I.	Distributor and Retailer Liability	667
		Godoy v. Abamaster of Miami, Inc.	668
	II.	The "Sale" of a Product	672
		Delaney v. Towmotor Corp.	672
		New Texas Auto Auction Services, L.P. v. Gomez de Hernandez	675
		Bolger v. Amazon.com, LLC	679

	III.	The Sale of a "Product"	683
		Gorran v. Atkins Nutritionals, Inc.	683
		Cafazzo v. Central Medical Health Services, Inc.	686
	IV.	Autonomous Vehicles and Products Liability: Problem Set 12	695

Chapter 16. Bystander Liability — 699

	I.	The Extension of Strict Products Liability to Encompass Bystanders	699
		Gibberson v. Ford Motor Co.	699
		Horst v. Deere & Co.	701
	II.	Conflicts Between Consumers and Bystanders	706
		Gaines-Tabb v. ICI Explosives, USA, Inc.	706
		McCarthy v. Olin Corp.	709
	III.	Negligence Liability and the Protection of Bystanders	716
		Passwaters v. General Motors Corp.	716
	IV.	Autonomous Vehicles and Products Liability: Problem Set 13	721

Chapter 17. Comparative Products Liability — 725

A v. National Blood Authority — 728

Second Commission Report of 31 January 2001 on the Application of Directive 85/374 on Liability for Defective Products (COM (2000) 893 Final) — 741

Third Report on the Application of Council Directive on the Approximation of Laws, Regulations and Administrative Provisions of the Member States Concerning Liability for Defective Products (COM (2006) 496 Final), September 2006 — 745

Fourth Report on the Application of Council Directive 85/374/EEC (COM (2011) 547), 8 Sept. 2011 — 746

European Commission, Fifth Report on the Application of Council Directive on the Approximation of Laws, Regulations and Administrative Provisions of the Member States Concerning Liability for Defective Products (85/374/EEC) (COM/2018/246 Final), 7 May 2018 — 748

Table of Cases — 755
Index — 761

Preface

In writing this book, I have tried to accomplish three different but closely related objectives:

- The primary objective of the book, of course, is to provide a solid grounding in the fundamentals of product liability law. The basic liability rules are covered in the casebooks on tort law, but that coverage is necessarily abbreviated. Indeed, this material is often not taught in the introductory torts class because of its complexity. Regardless of whether one has previously studied products liability in a torts class, there is plenty more to learn.
- In many respects, products liability is an ideal subject for the advanced study of tort law. Extended study of products liability reveals the extent to which it is both part of tort law and yet a distinctive field. By studying products liability, one necessarily learns a great deal about tort law more generally. Product cases also pose interesting questions about evidentiary problems, strategic lawyering choices, how liability rules are applied in the courtroom, and the relation between the tort system and other institutional mechanisms for regulating product risk and compensating physical injuries. And because products liability is the most practically important field of tort law due to its far-reaching consequences within the economy, its development has generated tort-reform measures that provide further opportunity for studying the relation between tort law and statutory law. These themes are developed in the book, providing the foundation for a deeper understanding of the practice and substantive content of tort law more generally.
- Finally, products liability is an ideal subject for studying the evolutionary processes of the common law. The rapid development of products liability has attracted the attention of many scholars interested in the nature of legal reasoning and the processes of the common law, *e.g.*, Martin P. Golding, LEGAL REASONING 112-25 (1983) (using the development of early products liability doctrine culminating in the rejection of the privity requirement by courts in the early twentieth century to illustrate the nature of common-law reasoning and noting that this "*line* of cases . . . has often been used to show the technique of case law development") and Edward H. Levi, AN INTRODUCTION TO LEGAL REASONING 1-19 (1949) (illustrating the nature of common-law reasoning with this same line of cases). To develop this theme, the book repeatedly shows how many doctrinal controversies in products liability can be attributed to the evolutionary processes of the common law. Unlike other areas of the common law, the rule of strict products liability

largely originates from a common textual source adopted by virtually all the states—the rule of strict products liability in *Restatement (Second) of Torts* §402A (1965) and its accompanying commentary. This rule has been developed differently by different jurisdictions for reasons that are highlighted throughout the book. Case-by-case litigation can frame issues in a manner that influences doctrinal development within a jurisdiction, enabling one to understand why the appropriate interpretation of a legal rule often critically depends on its doctrinal lineage. This dynamic of the common law is hard to capture adequately in a casebook on tort law, but is essential for understanding products liability and the common law more generally.

In editing the cases and other secondary materials, my objective has been to simplify the exposition to the maximal extent possible. Product cases routinely involve a variety of complicated issues that require resolution by long, complicated judicial opinions. Rather than identify the omitted portions of the opinion, I have edited the material to provide a single, coherent opinion focused on the issues under study. Ellipses and so on do not ordinarily appear to acknowledge the omitted portions of the opinion. Similarly, most of the citations to cases and so on have been omitted unless acknowledgement provides useful information (either by full citation or an identification of the omission, denoted by []). I have also modified the citation form to conform to current conventions. The few footnotes that remain have their original numbering.

References to the *Restatement (Second) of Torts* (1965) are simply to the *Restatement (Second)*. Likewise, references to the *Restatement (Third) of Torts: Products Liability* (1998) are simply to the *Restatement (Third)*. Each of these important sources is quoted extensively throughout the book, and I am grateful to the American Law Institute as copyright holder for its permission. I am also grateful for permission to reprint portions of Patrick M. Hanlon & Anne Smetak, *Asbestos Changes*, 62 N.Y.U. Ann. Surv. Am. L. 525 (2007); Robert L. Rabin, *Territorial Claims in the Domain of Accidental Harm: Conflicting Conceptions of Tort Preemption*, 74 Brook. L. Rev. 987 (2009); Robert L. Rabin, *A Sociolegal History of the Tobacco Tort Litigation*, 44 Stan. L. Rev. 853, 855 (1992); and Larry S. Stewart, *Strict Liability for Defective Product Design: The Quest for a Well-Ordered Regime*, 74 Brook. L. Rev. 1039 (2009).

My students over the years have been of invaluable help in developing this book, with each subsequent iteration of the manuscript substantially benefitting from the lessons I learned in the classroom. As my students would tell you if asked, this casebook is independent of, but highly complementary to, my textbook *Principles of Products Liability* (3d ed. 2021). Each reinforces the other.

As always, Janette Sadik-Khan and our son Max have provided an amazing amount of encouragement and support. I could never thank them enough. Financial support was provided by the Filomen D'Agostino and Max E. Greenberg Research Fund of the New York University School of Law.

Mark A. Geistfeld
New York City
July 1, 2021

Acknowledgments

American Law Institute. Various sections from the Restatement of the Law, Second, Torts, copyright © 1977 by The American Law Institute. Reproduced with permission. All rights reserved.

Various sections from the Restatement of the Law, Third, Torts: Apportionment of Liability, copyright © 2000 by The American Law Institute. Reproduced with permission. All rights reserved.

Various sections from the Restatement of the Law, Third, Torts: Liability for Physical and Emotional Harm, copyright © 2010 by The American Law Institute. Reproduced with permission. All rights reserved.

American Law Institute. Various sections from the Restatement of the Law, Third, Torts: Products Liability, copyright © 1997 by The American Law Institute. Reproduced with permission. All rights reserved.

Mark A. Geistfeld. "The Doctrinal Unity of Alternative Liability and Market-Share Liability," University of Pennsylvania Law Review, Vol. 155 (2006). University of Pennsylvania Law School. Reprinted with permission from the publisher.

Gary T. Schwartz. "The Beginning and the Possible End of the Rise of Modern American Tort Law," Georgia Law Review, Vol. 26 (1992). University of Georgia School of Law.

Larry S. Stewart. "Strict Liability for Defective Product Design: The Quest for a Well-Ordered Regime," Brooklyn Law Review, Vol. 74 (2009). Brooklyn Law School. Reprinted with permission from the author.

Matthew Wansley. "The End of Accidents," UC Davis Law Review, Vol. 55 (2021). UC Davis School of Law. Reprinted with permission from the publisher.

PRODUCT LIABILITY LAW

1

The Big Picture

Products liability is a set of legal rules governing cases of product-caused injury. The rules are largely ones of tort law, with importance that would have been quite surprising to a tort lawyer in the early twentieth century. "Indeed, the subject of manufacturer or retailer liability for defective products was of minor scholarly significance during the 1930s and 1940s." George L. Priest, *The Invention of Enterprise Liability: A Critical History of the Intellectual Foundations of Modern Tort Law*, 14 J. Legal Stud. 461, 482 (1985). The category "Products Liability" appeared in the Index of Legal Periodicals "for the first time in 1965, recording entries from 1961-64." *Id.* at 497 n. 238.

In 1965, the rule of strict products liability was published by the American Law Institute in §402A of the *Restatement (Second) of Torts*, which in turn was adopted by most states within the next ten years. The dozen or so pages devoted to the problem of product defects in the *Restatement (Second)* subsequently led to a body of law requiring more than 300 pages of exposition in the *Restatement (Third) of Torts: Products Liability*, which was published by the American Law Institute in 1998.

The growth of products liability is extraordinary when compared to the slowly evolving tort rules of the common law. In light of this rapid growth, many do not find it plausible that products liability is based on well-established principles of tort law. According to one view, the growth of products liability can be attributed to "a conceptual revolution that is among the most dramatic ever witnessed in the Anglo-American legal system." Priest, *supra*, at 461.

Are the rules of strict products liability a "revolutionary" departure from fundamental tort principles, or is this body of law consistent with the important doctrines and practices of tort law more generally? And if products liability is truly a field of tort law, is there a reason for adopting special rules limited to commercially supplied products? Consider Jane Stapleton, *Bugs in Anglo-American Products Liability*, 53 S.C. L. Rev. 1225, 1255 (2002) (arguing that "the creation of special rules for injuries associated with commercially supplied products warps our laws of obligation for little if any benefit and blinkers us to important common themes that run through all personal injury cases generally"). These foundational questions frame the overarching inquiry of this chapter and of the book more generally.

I. THE EARLY LIMITATION OF TORT LIABILITY TO THE CONTRACTUAL RELATIONSHIP

The early case law largely limited liability for product-caused injuries to the parties in a contractual relationship—the *requirement of privity*, typically in reliance on the following English case. Are the reasons that the court invokes for limiting liability still relevant or persuasive?

WINTERBOTTOM v. WRIGHT
Court of Exchequer, 1842
152 E.R. 402

Case. [According to plaintiff's declaration, defendant Wright had contracted with the Postmaster-General to provide a mail-coach and maintain it in "a fit, proper, safe, and secure state and condition for the said purpose" of "conveying the mailbags from Hartford, in the county of Chester, to Holyhead." Atkinson, "having notice of the said contract," entered into a separate contract with the Postmaster-General to supply horses and coachmen and not "use or employ any other coach or carriage whatever than such as should be so provided, directed, and appointed by the Postmaster-General." Atkinson hired the plaintiff Winterbottom as a mail-coachman, who had notice of these contracts and "believ[ed] that the said coach was in a fit, safe, secure, and proper state and condition for the purpose aforesaid, and not knowing and having no means of knowing to the contrary thereof." While Winterbottom was driving the mail-coach from Hartford to Holyhead, "the said mail-coach being then in a frail, weak, and infirm, and dangerous state and condition, to wit, by and through certain latent defects in the state and condition thereof, and unsafe and unfit for the use and purpose aforesaid, and from no other cause, circumstance, matter or thing whatsoever, gave way and broke down, whereby the plaintiff was thrown from his seat, and in consequence of injuries then received, had become lamed for life." The plaintiff then alleged that his injury occurred because "the defendant so improperly and negligently conducted himself, and so utterly disregarded his aforesaid contract, and so wholly neglected and failed to perform his duty in this behalf."]

Lord ABINGER, C.B. I am clearly of opinion that the defendant is entitled to our judgment. We ought not to permit a doubt to rest upon this subject, for our doing so might be the means of letting in upon us an infinity of actions. This is an action of the first impression. Here the action is brought simply because the defendant was a contractor with a third person; and it is contended that thereupon he became liable to every body who might use the carriage. If there had been any ground for such an action, there certainly would have been some precedent of it; but with the exception of actions against innkeepers, and some few other persons, no case of a similar nature has occurred in practice. That is a strong circumstance, and is of itself a great authority against its maintenance. It is however contended, that this contract being made on the behalf of the public

I. The Early Limitation of Tort Liability to the Contractual Relationship

by the Postmaster-General, no action could be maintained against him, and therefore the plaintiff must have a remedy against the defendant. But that is by no means a necessary consequence—he may be remediless altogether. There is no privity of contract between these parties; and if the plaintiff can sue, every passenger, or even any person passing along the road, who was injured by the upsetting of the coach, might bring a similar action. Unless we confine the operation of such contracts as this to the parties who entered into them, the most absurd and outrageous consequences, to which I can see no limit, would ensue. Where a party becomes responsible to the public, by undertaking a public duty, he is liable, though the injury may have arisen from the negligence of his servant or agent. So, in cases of public nuisances, whether the act was done by the party as a servant, or in any other capacity, you are liable to an action at the suit of any person who suffers. Those, however, are cases whether the real ground of the liability is the public duty, or the commission of the public nuisance. There is also a class of cases in which the law permits a contract to be turned into a tort; but unless there has been some public duty undertaken, or public nuisance committed, they are all cases in which an action might have been maintained upon the contract. Thus, a carrier may be sued either in assumpsit or case; but there is no instance in which a party, who was not privy to the contract entered into with him, can maintain any such action. The plaintiff in this case could not have brought an action on the contract; if he could have done so, what would have been his situation, supposing the Postmaster-General had released the defendant? That would, at all events, have defeated his claim altogether. By permitting this action, we should be working this injustice, that after the defendant had done everything to the satisfaction of his employer, and after all matters between them had been adjusted, and all accounts settled on the footing of their contract, we should subject them to be ripped open by this action of tort being brought against him.

ALDERSON, B. I am of the same opinion. The contract in this case was made with the Postmaster-General alone; and the case is just the same as if he had come to the defendant and ordered a carriage, and handed it at once over to Atkinson. If we were to hold that the plaintiff could sue in such a case, there is no point at which such actions would stop. The only safe rule is to confine the right to recover to those who enter into the contract: if we go one step beyond that, there is no reason why we should not go fifty. The only real argument in favour of the action is, that this is a case of hardship; but that might have been obviated, if the plaintiff had made himself a party to the contract. Our judgment must therefore be for the defendant.

GURNEY, B., concurred.

ROLFE, B. The breach of the defendant's duty, stated in this declaration, in his omission to keep the carriage in a safe condition; and when we examine the mode in which that duty is alleged to have arisen, we find a statement that the defendant took upon himself, to wit, under and by virtue of the said contract, to keep and maintain the said mail-coach in a fit, proper, safe, and secure state and condition. The duty, therefore, is shewn to have arisen solely from the contract; and the fallacy consists in the use of that word "duty." If a duty to the Postmaster-General be meant, that is true; but if a duty to the plaintiff be intended (and in that sense the word is evidently used), there was none. This is one of those unfortunate cases in which there certainly has been damnum, but it is damnum absque injuria; it is, no doubt, a hardship upon the plaintiff to be without a remedy, but by that consideration we ought not to be influenced. Hard cases, it has been frequently observed, are apt to introduce bad law.

Judgment for the defendant.

NOTES AND QUESTIONS

1. *Excessive liability as a limitation of duty.* As the court explains, the duty relied on by the plaintiff was based solely on the contract, with the defendant's alleged negligence involving a breach of that contractual duty. If the plaintiff had been in contractual privity with the defendant, could he have recovered upon proof of the negligence? As we find in the next chapter, the rule limiting negligence liability to contractual parties—the requirement of privity—was widely adopted by courts in both England and the U.S. by the turn of the twentieth century. The influence of *Winterbottom* stems from the policy reasons the court invokes in support of such a limitation of duty. What are those reasons? Does the recognition of a tort duty outside of the contractual relationship necessarily lead to limitless liability, or are there limitations recognized by tort law?

2. *From the writ system to the modern tort system.* When *Winterbottom* was decided in the mid-nineteenth century, common-law courts still operated within the "writ system," the requirements of which limited the plaintiff to a single claim or writ as illustrated by *Winterbottom*. To determine whether the plaintiff in *Winterbottom* erred by relying on a contractual duty instead of making a single claim based on the tort duty to exercise reasonable care, it is critical to know that under the writ system, the most common rule of tort law was not one of negligence liability, but rather one of immunity from liability. *See* Robert L. Rabin, *The Historical Development of the Fault Principle: A Reinterpretation*, 15 Ga. L. Rev. 925 (1981). The reasons why the plaintiff relied on a contractual duty in *Winterbottom* are discussed more extensively in the next chapter.

Beginning with New York's adoption of the Field Code in 1848, the states abolished the writ system, replacing it with the unitary civil action that lets plaintiffs file multiple claims or causes of action. Because legal claims were no longer organized in terms of writs, this procedural reform produced tort law and the other substantive fields around which the common law is organized today.

Following abolition of the writ system, courts transformed many of the fragmented, individualized rules of the writ system into a general rule of negligence liability. Having done so, courts naturally reconsidered the issue of whether this general standard of tort liability ought to be subject to the various immunities that courts had adopted within the writ system. As illustrated by *Winterbottom*, courts had long justified immunities on grounds of public policy, but the passage of time ultimately undermined this justification. Many activities had long been exposed to tort liability without any apparent detrimental effect, making it seem highly dubious that the particular activity protected by an immunity would be unduly restricted by negligence liability. Instead, the salutary features of the fault principle would force the activity to be conducted in a socially reasonable manner, an outcome consistent with the public policy rationale for the fault principle. In hindsight, the considerable expansion of tort liability over the course of the twentieth century is largely attributable to the way in which a consolidated negligence rule of general application combined with public policy to justify eliminating many of the immunities recognized by the early common law, including *Winterbottom*'s privity requirement. *See id.* at 959-961; Gary T. Schwartz, *The Beginning and the Possible End of the Rise of Modern American Tort Law*, 26 Ga. L. Rev. 601, 605-620 (1992) (concluding that judicial tort opinions until the 1960s, "for the most part, sharpened and clarified tort doctrines that had been presented somewhat more crudely in nineteenth-century cases," and that the "vitality of negligence" then caused an expansion of tort liability lasting until the 1980s).

II. AN (EXTREME) EXAMPLE OF STRICT PRODUCTS LIABILITY: THE ASBESTOS CASES

By the mid-twentieth century, the robust growth of negligence liability produced the rule of strict products liability. This dynamic is illustrated by the following case, which substantially facilitated the litigation of asbestos cases. The case involves application of various liability rules that are reflective of the modern approach, so there is nothing particularly distinctive about the case except for its impact on the scope of tort liability faced by the suppliers of asbestos products.

BOREL v. FIBREBOARD PAPER PRODUCTS CORP.
United States Court of Appeals, Fifth Circuit, 1973
493 F.2d 1076

WISDOM, C.J. This product liability case involves the scope of an asbestos manufacturer's duty to warn industrial insulation workers of dangers associated with the use of asbestos.

Clarence Borel, an industrial insulation worker, sued certain manufacturers of insulation materials containing asbestos to recover damages for injuries caused by the defendants' alleged breach of duty in failing to warn of the dangers involved in handling asbestos. Borel alleged that he had contracted the diseases of asbestosis and mesothelioma as a result of his exposure to the defendants' products over a thirty-three year beginning in 1936 and ending in 1969. The jury returned a verdict in favor of Borel on the basis of strict liability. We affirm.

The medical testimony adduced at trial indicates that inhaling asbestos dust in industrial conditions, even with relatively light exposure, can produce the disease of asbestosis. The disease is difficult to diagnose in its early stages because there is a long latent period between initial exposure and apparent effect. This latent period may vary according to individual idiosyncrasy, duration and intensity of exposure, and the type of asbestos used. In some cases, the disease may manifest itself in less than ten years after initial exposure. In general, however, it does not manifest itself until ten to twenty-five or more years after initial exposure. This latent period is explained by the fact that asbestos fibers, once inhaled, remain in place in the lung, causing a tissue reaction that is slowly progressive and apparently irreversible. Even if no additional asbestos fibers are inhaled, tissue changes may continue undetected for decades. By the time the disease is diagnosable, a considerable period of time has elapsed since the date of the injurious exposure. Furthermore, the effect of the disease may be cumulative since each exposure to asbestos dust can result in additional tissue changes. A worker's present condition is the biological product of many years of exposure to asbestos dust, with both past and recent exposures contributing to the overall effect. All of these factors combine to make it impossible, as a practical matter, to determine which exposure or exposures to asbestos dust caused the disease.

The plaintiff introduced evidence tending to establish that the defendant manufacturers either were, or should have been, fully aware of the many articles and studies on asbestosis. The evidence also indicated, however, that during Borel's working career no manufacturer ever warned contractors or insulation workers, including Borel, of the dangers associated with inhaling asbestos dust or informed them of [suggested] threshold limit values for exposure to asbestos dust. Furthermore, no manufacturer ever tested the effect of their products on the workers using them or attempted to discover whether the exposure of insulation workers to asbestos dust exceeded the suggested threshold limits.

The plaintiff sought to hold the defendants liable for negligence, gross negligence, and breach of warranty or strict liability. The negligent acts alleged in the complaint were: (1) failure to take reasonable precautions or to exercise reasonable care to warn Borel of the danger to which he was exposed as a worker when using the defendant's asbestos insulation products; (2) failure to inform Borel as to what would be safe and sufficient wearing apparel and proper protective equipment and appliances or method of handling and using the various products; (3) failure to test the asbestos products in order to ascertain the dangers involved in their use; and (4) failure to remove the products from the market upon ascertaining that such products would cause asbestosis. The plaintiff also alleged that the defendants should be strictly liable in warranty and tort. The plaintiff contended that the defendants' products were unreasonably dangerous because of the failure to provide adequate warnings of the foreseeable dangers associated with them.

The defendants denied the allegations in the plaintiff's complaint and interposed the defenses of contributory negligence and assumption of risk.

The trial court submitted the case to the jury on general verdicts accompanied by a special interrogatory as to Borel's contributory negligence. As to the negligence count, the jury found that all [but two of] the defendants . . . were negligent but that none of the defendants had been grossly negligent. It found also, however, that Borel had been contributorily negligent.

II. An (Extreme) Example of Strict Products Liability: The Asbestos Cases

As to the strict liability count, the jury found that all the defendants were liable and determined that the total damages were $79,436.24. Since four defendants originally named in the complaint had previously settled, paying a total of $20,902.20, the trial court gave full credit for the sums paid in settlement and held the remaining six defendants jointly and several liable for the balance of $58,534.04. The defendants appealed.

Under Texas law, a manufacturer of a defective product may be liable to a user or consumer in either warranty or tort. With respect to personal injuries caused by a defective product, the Texas Supreme Court has adopted the theory of strict liability in tort as expressed in section 402A of the Restatement (Second) of Torts (1964). Section 402A provides, in relevant part: "One who sells any product in a defective condition unreasonably dangerous to the user or consumer . . . is subject to liability for physical harm thereby caused to the ultimate consumer or user."

Here, the plaintiff alleged that the defendants' product was unreasonably dangerous because of the failure to give adequate warnings of the known or knowable dangers involved.

A product must not be made available to the public without disclosure of those dangers that the application of reasonable foresight would reveal. Nor may a manufacturer rely unquestioningly on others to sound the hue and cry concerning a danger in its product. Rather, each manufacturer must bear the burden of showing that its own conduct was proportionate to the scope of its duty.

[T]he foreseeability of the danger must be measured in light of the manufacturer's status as an expert and the manufacturer's duty to test its product. In these circumstances, we think the jury was entitled to find that the danger to Borel and other insulation workers from inhaling asbestos dust was foreseeable to the defendants at the time the products causing Borel's injuries were sold.

In reaching our decision in the case at bar, we recognize that the question of the applicability of Section 402A of the Restatement to cases involving "occupational diseases" is one of first impression. But though the application is novel, the underlying principle is ancient. Under the law of torts, a person has long been liable for the foreseeable harm caused by his own negligence. This principle applies to the manufacture of products as it does to almost every other area of human endeavor. It implies a duty to warn of foreseeable dangers associated with those products. This duty to warn extends to all users and consumers, including the common worker in the shop or in the field. Where the law has imposed a duty, courts stand ready in proper cases to enforce the rights so created. Here, there was a duty to speak, but the defendants remained silent. The district court's judgment does no more than hold the defendants liable for the foreseeable consequences of their own inaction. For the reasons stated, the decision of the district court is Affirmed.

NOTES AND QUESTIONS

1. *From negligence to strict products liability.* As in *Borel*, plaintiffs in product cases often allege multiple claims of negligence liability, strict liability for breach of the implied warranty, and strict products liability.

The negligence claims are based on an "ancient" tort principle as the court observed. Indeed, the development of negligence liability for defective products is hard to distinguish from the robust growth of negligence liability that occurred throughout tort law in the twentieth century. When framed in these terms, products liability does not appear to be a revolutionary or novel form of liability.

A better candidate for this description resides in the rule of strict liability under §402A of the *Restatement (Second) of Torts*. Pursuant to this rule, manufacturers and other commercial distributors of products are strictly liable in tort for physical injuries caused by a defect in the product. The buyer, other users, and bystanders can all recover from the seller of a defective product. This rule of strict products liability more starkly contrasts with the baseline rule of negligence liability in tort law, requiring deeper inquiry into the question of whether this rule of strict products liability can be derived from established principles of the common law—the subject of Chapter 2.

2. *Whither* Winterbottom? The *Borel* court recognized that tort law has long subjected negligent actors to liability for foreseeable harms. The plaintiff's harm in *Winterbottom* was foreseeable, yet the court limited liability based on the concern of excessive liability. In deciding the novel question whether a manufacturer is subject to liability for not adequately warning about the hazards of asbestos exposure, did the court in *Borel* pay any attention to this concern about excessive liability? Should it have?

ASBESTOS CHANGES
Patrick M. Hanlon & Anne Smetak
62 N.Y.U. Ann. Surv. Am. L. 525 (2007)

Asbestos is "the big one" of American mass toxic tort litigation. From an inauspicious beginning in the late 1960s, asbestos litigation has generated over 730,000 claims, at an overall cost of at least $70 billion. Between seventy-five and eighty companies have been driven into bankruptcy, with more than half of those since the beginning of 2000. According to Nobel Laureate Joseph E. Stiglitz, these bankruptcies cost at least 60,000 jobs through 2002. The total impact on the economy is, of course, much greater. Employees displaced by such bankruptcies lose an average of $25,000 to $50,000 over their lifetimes, and may lose a significant portion of their 401(k) savings. The overall value of such losses is between $1.4 and $3.0 billion. Fewer jobs in the manufacturing industries are created as companies battling asbestos litigation have less capital to finance investments and corporate growth. Asbestos litigation is estimated to have caused an overall loss of productivity in certain manufacturing sectors that is valued at more than $300 billion. It is clear that asbestos litigation has had a profound impact on individual companies, their employees, and the economy as a whole.

If asbestos litigation had run its course, we would still be studying it for its size and historical pride of place as a mass tort, as well as for its amazing capacity to change and adapt. But, of course, asbestos litigation is not just of historical interest. Stephen Carroll and his colleagues at RAND estimate that before the

II. An (Extreme) Example of Strict Products Liability: The Asbestos Cases

litigation is over—likely in about fifty years—hundreds of thousands, and perhaps over two million, claims could be filed. The total cost from 2002 onward could ultimately be between $130 billion and $195 billion, which must be added to the $70 billion already spent by the end of 2002.

In part, the high cost of asbestos litigation results from the inherent resource intensiveness of the civil justice system. Transaction costs—especially legal fees and related expenses—are very high. According to RAND, through 2002, plaintiffs received only 42% of total spending on asbestos litigation. In other words, defendants and their insurers spent $2.38 to provide $1.00 of compensation to claimants.

Even if all the inefficiency and misallocation of resources were eliminated, the costs of compensating asbestos victims would still be enormous. Behind the asbestos litigation problem, in the U.S. and many other countries, is a public health problem. In the last forty years, thousands of people have lost their health, and often their lives, to diseases caused by asbestos. This tragedy is not over.

The widespread use of asbestos in the twentieth century, together with inadequate industrial safety precautions, led to widespread disease. This asbestos disease generated a compensation problem, which in the United States (and elsewhere) has also become a litigation problem.

Over the years, asbestos litigation has constantly changed in response to external events and, even more, its own internal logic. [There are] three phases in this historical dialectic. It starts in the 1990s, when asbestos litigation seemed under control as a result of mass litigation—and mass settlement—strategies. This era of coping came to an end in 1997, when the U.S. Supreme Court rejected a class action settlement that would have been the first step toward substituting an administrative claims process for litigation in the courts. In the succeeding period, from 1997 to 2002, asbestos litigation exploded, eventually bankrupting virtually all traditional defendants and drawing in thousands of new defendants from practically every sector of the economy. This success set off a sharp reaction. Since the beginning of 2003, defendants and insurers have succeeded in encouraging judicial rethinking of the litigation and using public opinion and the political process to transform the system. Courts and legislatures have effected dramatic tort reform in the states, while Congress has been considering legislation that would replace the tort system altogether with a comprehensive administrative claims resolution system financed by defendants and insurers and managed by the Federal Government. As a result of this pattern of action and reaction, asbestos litigation is today in a period of turmoil. We cannot know whether the pendulum will swing out again, or whether the litigation will settle into a new equilibrium after a period of instability in which liabilities and values are reestablished, or whether the litigation will cease altogether as a result of Federal legislation.

The civil justice system has, in the past several years, become much less friendly to the interests of asbestos claimants and more solicitous of defendants. This is a necessary correction. Some reforms, such as sensible medical criteria, limitations on forum shopping, and elimination of inappropriate consolidations, seem to be reasonable adjustments to a failed tort system. But the tort reform effort doesn't stop there; other reforms, such as cutting back on joint and several liability, or cutting off liability to wives exposed to asbestos dust brought home on their husband's clothing, are really aimed at making sure that claimants rather than defendants and their insurers bear the brunt of the mismatch between the harm done by asbestos and diminished responsibility of the remaining defendants. In the either-or world of the civil justice system, this struggle is to be expected.

The current asbestos litigation system is unstable. If the trends of the last two years hold up—and many of them are eminently reversible—it is likely that asbestos litigation will become more costly, more adversarial, and more focused on the seriously ill. At the same time, an intense struggle is underway as plaintiffs' lawyers seek to expand the ranks of defendants and increase the liability share of existing defendants, while defendants and insurers try to create a firebreak that limits the spread of the litigation to new defendants and new settings. As the litigation picks up in intensity, more and more defendants are likely to resort to bankruptcy to settle their liabilities and put asbestos litigation behind them. These new bankruptcies will, of course, aggravate the ongoing struggle between the plaintiffs' trial bar and the remaining solvent defendants.

In this struggle, it is important not to lose sight of the claimant. Over the next forty years, tens of thousands of people will die of mesothelioma and lung cancer due to their exposure to asbestos products. Most of the companies responsible for that exposure are already in bankruptcy, and the only assets available for compensating these people are in existing asbestos trusts or the ones that are in the process of formation. If the defense side succeeds in holding the asbestos litigation within bounds, many of the undoubted victims of asbestos exposure will not receive appropriate compensation, and some will receive no compensation at all. If the defense does not succeed, there will be compensation, but it will be paid largely by the wrong companies, with a significant adverse impact on the economy.

The only way to ensure that the sick are compensated without undue burdens on American industry is to replace the tort system altogether, as Congress has attempted to do with the [Fairness in Asbestos Injury Resolution] Act. Creation of a new compensation scheme is a huge challenge. But the alternatives are either unfairness to innocent victims or continuing with the stream of bankruptcies and the outrageous costs of the tort system forever. There should be a better way.

S. 3274, FAIRNESS IN ASBESTOS INJURY RESOLUTION ACT OF 2006
(109th Cong. 2006)

SEC. 2. FINDINGS AND PURPOSE.

(a) Findings.—Congress finds the following:

    (1) Millions of Americans have been exposed to forms of asbestos that can have devastating health effects.

    (2) Various injuries can be caused by exposure to some forms of asbestos, including pleural disease and some forms of cancer.

II. An (Extreme) Example of Strict Products Liability: The Asbestos Cases

(3) The injuries caused by asbestos can have latency periods of up to 40 years, and even limited exposure to some forms of asbestos may result in injury in some cases.

(4) Asbestos litigation has had a significant detrimental effect on the country's economy, driving companies into bankruptcy, diverting resources from those who are truly sick, and endangering jobs and pensions.

(5) The scope of the asbestos litigation crisis cuts across every State and virtually every industry.

(6) The United States Supreme Court has recognized that Congress must act to create a more rational asbestos claims system. In 1991, a Judicial Conference Ad Hoc Committee on Asbestos Litigation, appointed by Chief Justice William Rehnquist, found that the "ultimate solution should be legislation recognizing the national proportions of the problem . . . and creating a national asbestos dispute resolution scheme." The Court found in 1997 in *Amchem Products Inc. v. Windsor*, 521 U.S. 591, 595 (1997), that "[t]he argument is sensibly made that a nationwide administrative claims processing regime would provide the most secure, fair, and efficient means of compensating victims of asbestos exposure." In 1999, the Court in *Ortiz v. Fibreboard Corp.*, 527 U.S. 819, 821 (1999), found that the "elephantine mass of asbestos cases . . . defies customary judicial administration and calls for national legislation." That finding was again recognized in 2003 by the Court in *Norfolk & Western Railway Co. v. Ayers*, 123 S. Ct. 1210 (2003).

(7) This crisis, and its significant effect on the health and welfare of the people of the United States, on interstate and foreign commerce, and on the bankruptcy system, compels Congress to exercise its power to regulate interstate commerce and create this legislative solution in the form of a national asbestos injury claims resolution program to supersede all existing methods to compensate those injured by asbestos, except as specified in this Act.

(8) This crisis has also imposed a deleterious burden upon the United States bankruptcy courts, which have assumed a heavy burden of administering complicated and protracted bankruptcies with limited personnel.

NOTES AND QUESTIONS

1. *Empirical study of asbestos liability.* Much of the data on the asbestos suits comes from an influential study by the Rand Institute for Civil Justice. *See* Stephen J. Carroll et al., Rand Inst. for Civil Justice, Asbestos Litigation Costs and Compensation: An Interim Report (2002). Based on data collected by the National Cancer Institute, the incidence of mesothelioma in the U.S. has been declining since 1992, although more than 45,000 people died from the disease in the U.S. between 1999 and 2015.

2. *Products liability and tort reform.* The asbestos liabilities first recognized by courts in cases like *Borel* during the 1970s resulted in a flood of litigation by the 1980s. From 1984 to 1986, premiums for general liability insurance nearly tripled. These policies indemnify the policyholder for various forms of legal liabilities, most notably tort liability. Such insurance became unaffordable or unavailable for some, leading to the so-called "liability crisis"

that appeared in myriad forms such as the closing of day-care centers and municipal swimming pools for reasons related to operator concerns about uninsured exposure to tort liability. The perception was that the courts had created the crisis by expanding the scope of tort liability, thereby producing an excessively costly tort system.

Not surprisingly, calls for tort reform quickly followed. In 1986, 46 states held legislative sessions and 41 enacted laws designed to slow the increase in insurance rates and costs. During this period, there were also a number of federal legislative proposals aimed at products liability reform, and studies on tort and products liability reform were instituted by the U.S. Department of Justice, the American Law Institute, the American Bar Association, and others.

The asbestos cases illustrate how common-law developments, like that in *Borel*, can substantially increase the scope of tort liability that is then subsequently limited by legislative responses. This important dynamic of products liability is illustrated at various points in the ensuing chapters.

The politicized nature of products liability is also reflected in state judicial elections.

> An unprecedented number of incumbent state judges are facing a flood of special interest dollars aiming to kick them off the bench. . . . Primarily responsible for the escalating dollars are trial lawyers and business groups struggling over tort reform. In a series of John Grisham-style attempts to buy control of state courts, they have transformed the tort wars into "court wars"—and they have become the attack dogs of judicial elections: In 2008, special interests and political parties paid for 87% of all negative ads.

Susan Liss & Adam Skaggs, *Is Justice for Sale?*, Nat'l L.J., Sept. 6, 2010, 58 (paragraph structure omitted).

3. *Products liability and "mass torts."* The asbestos cases are perhaps the paradigmatic example of a *mass tort*, which is a "term of art" that is "understood not merely to involve tortious misconduct on a mass scale but, more specifically, a kind of mass tortious misconduct that is especially difficult for the legal system to address." Richard A. Nagareda, Mass Torts in a World of Settlement viii (2007). The emergence of mass tort litigation is a recent phenomenon that can be traced to the emergence of strict products liability.

> The precise theories of tort liability asserted in mass tort litigation vary somewhat from one context to another. But the most common formulation stems directly from the changes wrought by the products liability revolution. Persons exposed to a product sue its ultimate manufacturer. And the crux of their allegation typically is that the manufacturer failed to provide adequate warnings concerning some risk associated with the product.

Id. at 5.

4. *Products liability and federalism.* As the asbestos cases also illustrate, products liability sharply raises the issue of whether products liability should be a matter of state or federal law. Tort law has traditionally been virtually the exclusive province of state law, with federal tort law limited

to a few areas such as admiralty. Alteration of state tort law by federal legislation accordingly raises contested federalism issues concerning the appropriate relationship between the state and federal governments. No asbestos bill has yet been enacted into federal law. Although federal lawmakers have proposed this type of federal tort reform as illustrated by the proposed FAIR Act, this particular reform effort has apparently faded into the past. The issue of federalism is also of prominent concern regarding the question of whether federal law should displace or *preempt* state tort law. *See* Chapter 10, section III.

5. *Institutional considerations.* The FAIR Act implicates questions of relative institutional competence. Is the problem of product-caused injuries more capably addressed by administrative compensation funds of the type contemplated in the Act? Consider the data described by Hanlon and Smetak regarding the transaction costs of providing injury compensation through tort litigation. If compensation were instead wholly provided by a less costly insurance mechanism, what would give product suppliers the financial incentive to supply reasonably safe products? The safety issue, in turn, implicates further questions of institutional choice. In a case of preemption, for example, the decision to preempt effectively displaces tort regulation with legislative regulation, typically involving health-and-safety standards promulgated by administrative agencies. How does the decentralized regulation of product safety via tort liability compare to centralized regulation by administrative agencies? Aside from the issue of preemption, the question of institutional competence has broader importance. Does the difficulty of applying a tort rule provide a sufficient reason for limiting liability on the ground that the market is a better institutional mechanism for addressing these issues?

6. *Excessive liability?* Consider again the role of excessive liability that the court in *Winterbottom* relied on to limit the duty with the requirement of contractual privity. What might explain why courts no longer seem to be troubled by this concern? One possibility is that excessive liability is not a persuasive reason for limiting liability. After all, as long as liability is limited to injuries proximately caused by a defective product, how can it be excessively high? The massive liabilities incurred by the sellers of asbestos-containing products simply reflect the massive number of injuries caused by asbestos exposure. Does this reasoning imply that the widespread incidence of product-caused injuries sufficiently justifies strict products liability?

III. THE SOCIAL PROBLEM OF PRODUCT ACCIDENTS

When the modern tort system emerged in the nineteenth century following the abolition of the writ system, it had to confront a new social problem—the increased number of accidental injuries caused by industrialization. *See, e.g.*, Lawrence M. Friedman, A History of American Law 300 (2d ed. 1985) ("In pre-industrial society, there are few personal injuries, except as a result of assault and battery. Modern tools and machines, however, have a marvelous capacity to cripple and maim their servants. From about 1840 on, one specific machine, the railroad locomotive, generated, on its own steam (so to speak), more tort law than any other in the 19th century."). With the increasing industrialization of America over the course of the nineteenth century, the problem of accidental injury became an acute social concern. One particularly good study found the rate of fatal accidents in the late nineteenth century was triple the rate of today. *See* John Fabian Witt, *Toward a New History of American Accident Law: Classical Tort Law and the Cooperative First-Party Insurance Movement*, 114 Harv. L. Rev. 690, 718 (2001). Not only was accidental harm socially problematic, the highly influential nineteenth-century liberal theory of John Stuart Mill maintained that the government's primary task is to regulate conduct doing "harm to others." John Stuart Mill, ON LIBERTY 22 (E.P. Dutton 1859).

For much of the twentieth century, injuries at the workplace or on the roadways largely defined the social problem of accidental injury. By the 1960s, however, product-caused injuries were deemed to be a substantial social problem. In 1967, the U.S. Congress established a national commission to investigate the problem. In 1970, the Commission presented its final report:

> Americans—20 million of them—are injured each year in the home as a result of incidents connected with consumer products. Of the total, 110,000 are permanently disabled and 30,000 are killed. A significant number could have been spared if more attention had been paid to hazard reduction. The annual cost to the Nation of product-related injuries may exceed $5.5 billion.
>
> The exposure of consumers to unreasonable consumer product hazards is excessive by any standard of measurement.

National Commission on Product Safety, Final Report 1 (June 1970) (footnote omitted).

A heightened concern about product-caused injury helps to explain why strict products liability fully emerged in the 1960s for reasons provided by Professor Gary Schwartz:

> On some occasions, the creation of specific public programs exercised an especially clear influence on the development of tort doctrine. Consider the adoption of the National Traffic and Motor Vehicle Safety Act of 1966 and the Consumer Product Safety Act in 1972. This latter statute had been recommended by the National Commission on Product Safety, whose Final Report was submitted in 1970. The 1966 Safety Act was the consequence of a new public-policy consensus on the subject of product-related accidents—a new "legal culture." The new set of attitudes contained in this consensus also surrounded the deliberations of the National Commission (set up in 1967) and the subsequent adoption of the Consumer Product Safety Act.
>
> These attitudes enabled policymakers to recognize and affirm that the level of highway fatalities (and the number of injuries due to dangerous consumer products) were unacceptably high; the resulting losses were hence recognized as a serious social problem, inviting the development of public-policy solutions. That new consensus, moreover, brought about a reconceptualization of the basic nature of the problem of highway and product safety. No longer was this seen as a problem of driver and consumer error; rather, the problem related in a fundamental way to vehicle and product design. During the

III. The Social Problem of Product Accidents

congressional consideration of the 1966 Act, one witness posed this rhetorical question: "Which is easier, to convince 195 million drivers to habitually refrain from panic application of the brake in emergencies or to design an anti-locking braking system in the vehicle?" According to the National Commission, consumer injuries are due to the interaction between consumers and consumer products within the environment of the home. The "weak link" in the chain of causation of consumer injuries—the link that public policy could most effectively attack—was the product itself. "[Manufacturers] can accomplish more for safety with less effort and expense than any other body," including "consumers" themselves. The Commission appreciated, of course, that many consumer injuries are immediately due to the careless use of products by consumers. But the Commission viewed human error as human nature; these are the occasional lapses in attention to which all of us are inevitably prone. Indeed, in 1966, supporters of the Safety Act, having acknowledged the likelihood of driver error, were able to convert that acknowledgment into a strong argument favoring the proposed federal program: "[a] crashworthy vehicle can make [driver] failures failsafe." The Senate Commerce Committee, in reporting out the bill, certainly made clear its concern for those features of auto design that bring about auto accidents; still, the Committee was particularly impressed "by the critical distinction between the cause of the accident itself and the cause of the resulting death or injury." Improving the crashworthiness of cars was thus a major goal of the Act.

Gary T. Schwartz, *The Beginning and the Possible End of the Rise of Modern American Tort Law*, 26 Ga. L. Rev. 601, 612-613 (1992) (citations omitted).

In light of this history, the social problem of accidents might explain why the tort system adopted the rule of strict products liability in the 1960s. To test this explanation, we can look at how courts have addressed other risky activities involving widespread injury. If the mere existence of widespread injury were sufficient to justify strict products liability, then presumably courts would also adopt other rules of strict liability to deal with other types of risky activities causing extensive harm.

HAMMONTREE v. JENNER
Court of Appeal, Second District, Division 1, California, 1971
97 Cal. Rptr. 739

LILLIE, J. Plaintiffs Maxine Hammontree and her husband sued defendant for personal injuries and property damage arising out of an automobile accident. The cause was tried to a jury. Plaintiffs appeal from judgment entered on a jury verdict returned against them and in favor of defendant.

The evidence shows that on the afternoon of April 25, 1967, defendant was driving his 1959 Chevrolet home from work; at the same time plaintiff Maxine Hammontree was working in a bicycle shop owned and operated by her and her husband; without warning defendant's car crashed through the wall of the shop, struck Maxine and caused personal injuries and damage to the shop.

Defendant claimed he became unconscious during an epileptic seizure losing control of his car. He did not recall the accident but his last recollection before it, was leaving a stop light after his last stop, and his first recollection after the accident was being taken out of his car in plaintiffs' shop. Defendant testified he has a medical history of epilepsy and knows of no other reason for his loss of consciousness except an epileptic seizure; prior to 1952 he had been examined by several neurologists whose conclusion was that the condition could be controlled and who placed him on medication; in 1952 he suffered a seizure while fishing; several days later he went to Dr. Benson Hyatt who diagnosed his condition as petit mal seizure and kept him on the same medication; thereafter he saw Dr. Hyatt every six months and then on a yearly basis several years prior to 1967; in 1953 he had another seizure, was told he was an epileptic and continued his medication; in 1954 Dr. Kershner prescribed dilantin and in 1955 Dr. Hyatt prescribed phelantin; from 1955 until the accident occurred (1967) defendant had used phelantin on a regular basis which controlled his condition; defendant has continued to take medication as prescribed by his physician and has done everything his doctors told him to do to avoid a seizure; he had no inkling or warning that he was about to have a seizure prior to the occurrence of the accident.

In 1955 or 1956 the Department of Motor Vehicles was advised that defendant was an epileptic and placed him on probation under which every six months he had to report to the doctor who was required to advise it in writing of defendant's condition. In 1960 his probation was changed to a once-a-year report.

Dr. Hyatt testified that during the times he saw defendant, and according to his history, defendant "was doing normally" and that he continued to take phelantin; that "[t]he purpose of the [phelantin] would be to react on the nervous system in such a way that where, without the medication, I would say to raise the threshold so that he would not be as subject to these episodes without the medication, so as not to have the seizures. He would not be having the seizures with the medication as he would without the medication compared to taking medication"; in a seizure it would be impossible for a person to drive and control an automobile; he believed it was safe for defendant to drive.

Appellants' contentions that the trial court erred in refusing to grant their motion for summary judgment on the issue of liability and their motion for directed verdict on the pleadings and counsel's opening argument are answered by the disposition of their third claim that the trial court committed prejudicial error in refusing to give their jury instruction on absolute liability.[1]

Appellants seek to have this court override the established law of this state which is dispositive of the issue before us as outmoded in today's social and economic structure, particularly in the light of the now recognized principles imposing liability upon the manufacturer, retailer and all distributive and vending elements and activities which bring a product to the consumer to his injury, on the basis of strict liability in tort. These authorities hold that "A manufacturer [or retailer] is strictly liable in tort when an article he places on the market,

---

1. "When the evidence shows that a driver of a motor vehicle on a public street or highway loses his ability to safely operate and control such vehicle because of some seizure or health failure, that driver is nevertheless legally liable for all injuries and property damage which an innocent person may suffer as a proximate result of the defendant's inability to so control or operate his motor vehicle."

"This is true even if you find the defendant driver had no warning of any such impending seizure or health failure."

III. The Social Problem of Product Accidents

knowing that it is to be used without inspection for defects, proves to have a defect that causes injury to a human being." Greenman v. Yuba Power Products, Inc., 377 P.2d 897, 900 (Cal. 1963). Drawing a parallel with these products liability cases, appellants argue, with some degree of logic, that only the driver affected by a physical condition which could suddenly render him unconscious and who is aware of that condition can anticipate the hazards and foresee the dangers involved in his operation of a motor vehicle, and that the liability of those who by reason of seizure or heart failure or some other physical condition lose the ability to safely operate and control a motor vehicle resulting in injury to an innocent person should be predicated on strict liability.

We decline to superimpose the absolute liability of products liability cases upon drivers under the circumstances here. The theory on which those cases are predicated is that manufacturers, retailers and distributors of products are engaged in the business of distributing goods to the public and are an integral part of the over-all producing and marketing enterprise that should bear the cost of injuries from defective parts. This policy hardly applies here and it is not enough to simply say, as do appellants, that the insurance carriers should be the ones to bear the cost of injuries to innocent victims on a strict liability basis. In Maloney v. Rath, 69 Cal. 2d 442, followed by Clark v. Dziabas, 69 Cal. 2d 449, appellant urged that defendant's violation of safety provision (defective brakes) of the Vehicle Code makes the violator strictly liable for damages caused by the violation. While reversing the judgment for defendant upon another ground, the California Supreme Court refused to apply the doctrine of strict liability to automobile drivers. The situation involved two users of the highway but the problems of fixing responsibility under a system of strict liability are as complicated in the instant case as those in Maloney v. Rath, and could only create uncertainty in the area of its concern. As stated in *Maloney*: "To invoke a rule of strict liability on users of the streets and highways, however, without also establishing in substantial detail how the new rule should operate would only contribute confusion to the automobile accident problem. Settlement and claims adjustment procedures would become chaotic until the new rules were worked out on a case-by-case basis, and the hardships of delayed compensation would be seriously intensified. Only the Legislature, if it deems it wise to do so, can avoid such difficulties by enacting a comprehensive plan for the compensation of automobile accident victims in place of or in addition to the law of negligence."

The judgment is affirmed.

NOTES AND QUESTIONS

1. *The social cost of product accidents.* According to one study, the "[c]osts associated with consumer product injuries account for nearly one-third of total annual injury costs. They are estimated at nearly $517 billion (all costs in 1997 dollars) annually in the United States." Bruce A. Lawrence et al., *Estimating the Costs of Non-Fatal Consumer Product Injuries in the United States*, 7 Injury Control & Safety Promotion 97, 97, 105 (2000). Due to data limitations, this estimate excludes certain injury costs, most notably, those caused by automobiles and firearms. For motor vehicle crashes that occurred in 2017, "the cost of medical care and productivity losses

associated with occupant injuries and deaths . . . exceeded $75 billion." Centers for Disease Control and Prevention, Transportation Safety: Cost Data and Prevention Policies (accessed June 1, 2021).

2. *Negligence or strict liability?* The holding in *Hammontree* does not foreclose tort recovery altogether for motor vehicle crashes, but instead limits the plaintiff to a claim for negligence liability. If negligence liability is sufficient for dealing with the social problem of automobile accidents, what justifies a rule of strict liability for accidents caused by defective products? This particular question is perhaps the most vexing issue in all of products liability, one that courts repeatedly address across a wide range of doctrinal disputes covered in the following chapters.

3. *Deterrence and the reduction of accidents.* Motor vehicles cause more injuries than any other type of product, leading to the question of whether the existence of widespread injury is a sufficient rationale for adopting a rule of strict liability for the same policy reasons that justify strict products liability. Did the court adequately explain why the reduction of injuries—a deterrence rationale for liability—was not sufficient to establish the plaintiffs' claim? Given that the defendant owed plaintiffs a duty to exercise reasonable care, is there any way in which strict liability might further reduce risk? Whether strict liability requires such a deterrence rationale is another issue that recurs throughout our study of products liability.

4. *Insurance and the compensation of injuries.* Another plausible rationale for strict liability involves the manner in which it provides more compensation or insurance to accident victims as compared to negligence liability. Drivers are required to be insured, and so liability for motor vehicle crashes is routinely covered by this insurance. Does the court adequately explain why strict liability cannot be justified simply because it would be desirable to have insurance carriers pay for accidental harms as opposed to the injured individuals like the plaintiffs in *Hammontree?*

In justifying strict products liability, courts have often relied on this type of insurance rationale for reasons that would seem to be applicable to automobile accidents. *See, e.g.*, Dix W. Noel, *Comparison of Strict Liability in Products Area and Auto Accident Reparations, in* THE ORIGIN AND DEVELOPMENT OF THE NEGLIGENCE ACTION 67, 90 (U.S. Dept. of Transp. Automobile Insurance and Compensation Study 1970) (concluding that "arguments based on superior loss distribution, or placing the risk on the enterprise which creates it and receives benefits . . . seem to have considerable applicability to injuries from motoring as well as to injuries from defective products"). The plaintiffs' argument in *Hammontree* that "the insurance carriers should be the ones to bear the cost of injuries to innocent victims on a strict liability basis" poses another foundational policy question that we address in our study of strict products liability.

5. *Deference to the legislature.* As in *Hammontree*, courts continue to limit liability due to administrative problems that could be more capably addressed by legislative action. *See, e.g.*, RESTATEMENT (THIRD) OF TORTS: LIABILITY FOR PHYSICAL AND EMOTIONAL HARMS §7 cmt. f (2010) (recognizing that courts can limit the tort duty for reasons of "institutional competence and administrative difficulties"). Insofar as this concern provides a sufficient reason for rejecting a rule of strict liability for automobile accidents, why would

it not also defeat a claim of strict products liability? Consider the asbestos cases in this regard.

6. *Absolute and strict products liability.* The term "absolute liability" conventionally refers to a "type of strict liability based on causation alone." BLACK'S LAW DICTIONARY (11th ed. 2019). The rule of strict products liability is based on injuries caused by a defective product, as illustrated by the defective warning in *Borel*. Consequently, the term "absolute liability" in a product case refers to a rule of strict liability that is not limited by the requirement of defect. *E.g.*, Phillips v. Kimwood Mach. Co., 525 P.2d 1033, 1036 (Or. 1974) ("No one wants absolute liability where all the article has to do is to cause injury."). This form of strict liability was proposed by the plaintiffs in *Hammontree*—the crash was not caused by any defect in the motor vehicle, explaining why the court described the proposed rule as one of absolute liability.

Courts uniformly reject absolute liability and instead limit strict liability to *defective* products. What explains this limitation? Once again, the issue recurs throughout products liability and is one we address in later chapters.

7. *Motor vehicles and the development of products liability.* As *Hammontree* illustrates, courts have not relied on the rationales for strict products liability to justify a rule of strict liability governing automobile drivers involved in crashes. Strict liability requires some other rationale beyond the widespread incidence of injuries caused by actors who control the risk and are covered by an insurance policy for the associated legal liabilities. The large number of crashes, however, has provided ample opportunity for courts to develop the rules of products liability in cases involving automotive technologies. Many of the important cases we study in later chapters involve alleged defects in cars and other motor vehicles.

Due to advances in technology, motor vehicle crashes are likely to considerably influence further developments in products liability. The majority of tort cases in state courts now involve automobile crashes allegedly caused by a driver's negligence. By eliminating the human driver, autonomous vehicles will eliminate these negligence claims. Manufacturers will instead be responsible for ensuring that their autonomous vehicles can drive in a reasonably safe manner, potentially making them liable for a crash. Autonomous vehicles will alter the mix and number of tort cases, causing a massive shift from ordinary negligence claims to those based on products liability. This dynamic will put even more pressure on the doctrines of products liability for reasons we explore throughout the book.

IV. A REPRISE OF EXCESSIVE LIABILITY AS A REASON FOR LIMITING TORT LIABILITY TO THE CONTRACTUAL RELATIONSHIP

Based on the ancient principle of negligence, courts substantially expanded the scope of tort liability for most of the twentieth century. Nevertheless, courts still limit the reach of negligence liability in important contexts. This ancient principle apparently includes built-in limitations. Can this limiting principle be squared with the rule of strict products liability?

STRAUSS v. BELLE REALTY CO.
Court of Appeals of New York, 1985
482 N.E.2d 34

KAYE, J. On July 13, 1977, a failure of defendant Consolidated Edison's power system left most of New York City in darkness. In this action for damages allegedly resulting from the power failure, we are asked to determine whether Con Edison owed a duty of care to a tenant who suffered personal injuries in a common area of an apartment building, where his landlord—but not he—had a contractual relationship with the utility. We conclude that in the case of a blackout of a metropolis of several million residents and visitors, each in some manner necessarily affected by a 25-hour power failure, liability for injuries in a building's common areas should, as a matter of public policy, be limited by the contractual relationship.

Plaintiff, Julius Strauss, then 77 years old, resided in an apartment building in Queens. Con Edison provided electricity to his apartment pursuant to agreement with him, and to the common areas of the building under a separate agreement with his landlord, defendant Belle Realty Company. As water to the apartment was supplied by electric pump, plaintiff had no running water for the duration of the blackout. Consequently, on the second day of the power failure, he set out for the basement to obtain water, but fell on the darkened, defective basement stairs, sustaining injuries. In this action against Belle Realty and Con Edison, plaintiff alleged negligence against the landlord, in failing to maintain the stairs or warn of their dangerous condition, and negligence against the utility in the performance of its duty to provide electricity.

A defendant may be held liable for negligence only when it breaches a duty owed to the plaintiff. The essential question here is whether Con Edison owed a duty to plaintiff, whose injuries from a fall on a darkened staircase may have conceivably been foreseeable, but with whom there was no contractual relationship for lighting in the building's common areas.

Duty in negligence cases is defined neither by foreseeability of injury nor by privity of contract. As this court has long recognized, an obligation rooted in contract may engender a duty owed to those not in privity, for "[t]here is nothing anomalous in a rule which imposes upon A, who has contracted with B, a duty to C and D and others according as he knows or does not know that the subject-matter of the contract is intended for their use." MacPherson v. Buick Motor Co., 217 N.Y. 382, 393 (1916).

But while the absence of privity does not foreclose recognition of a duty, it is still the responsibility of courts, in fixing the orbit of duty, "to limit the legal consequences of wrongs to a controllable degree" [ ] and to protect against crushing exposure to liability. "In fixing the bounds of that duty, not only logic and science, but policy play an important role." [ ] The courts' definition of an orbit of duty based on public policy may at times result in the exclusion of some

IV. A Reprise of Excessive Liability as a Reason for Limiting Tort Liability

who might otherwise have recovered for losses or injuries if traditional tort principles had been applied.

Considerations of privity are not entirely irrelevant in implementing policy. Indeed, in determining the liability of utilities for consequential damages for failure to provide service—a liability which could obviously be "enormous," and has been described as "sui generis," rather than strictly governed by tort or contract law principles—courts have declined to extend the duty of care to noncustomers. For example, in Moch Co. v. Rensselaer Water Co., 247 N.Y. 160, a water works company contracted with the City of Rensselaer to satisfy its water requirements. Plaintiff's warehouse burned and plaintiff brought an action against the water company in part based on its alleged negligence in failing to supply sufficient water pressure to the city's hydrants. The court denied recovery, concluding that the proposed enlargement of the zone of duty would unduly extend liability.

Here, insofar as revealed by the record, the arrangement between Con Edison and Belle Realty was no different from those existing between Con Edison and the millions of other customers it serves. Thus, Con Edison's duty to provide electricity to Belle Realty should not be treated separately from its broader statutory obligation to furnish power to all other applicants for such service in New York City and Westchester County. When plaintiff's relationship with Con Edison is viewed from this perspective, it is no answer to say that a duty is owed because, as a tenant in an apartment building, plaintiff belongs to a narrowly defined class.

Additionally, we deal here with a system-wide power failure occasioned by what has already been determined to be the utility's gross negligence. If liability could be found here, then in logic and fairness the same result must follow in many similar situations. For example, a tenant's guests and invitees, as well as persons making deliveries or repairing equipment in the building, are equally persons who must use the common areas, and for whom they are maintained. Customers of a store and occupants of an office building stand in much the same position with respect to Con Edison as tenants of an apartment building. In all cases the numbers are to a certain extent limited and defined, and while identities may change, so do those of apartment dwellers. While limiting recovery to customers in this instance can hardly be said to confer immunity from negligence on Con Edison, permitting recovery to those in plaintiff's circumstances would, in our view, violate the court's responsibility to define an orbit of duty that places controllable limits on liability.

Finally, we reject the suggestion of the dissent that there should be a fact-finding hearing to establish the alleged catastrophic probabilities flowing from the 1977 blackout and prospective blackouts, before any limitation is placed on Con Edison's duty to respond to the public for personal injuries. In exercising the court's traditional responsibility to fix the scope of duty, for application beyond a single incident, we need not blind ourselves to the obvious impact of a city-wide deprivation of electric power, or to the impossibility of fixing a rational boundary once beyond the contractual relationship, or to the societal consequences of rampant liability.

In sum, Con Edison is not answerable to the tenant of an apartment building injured in a common area as a result of Con Edison's negligent failure to provide electric service as required by its agreement with the building owner.

NOTES AND QUESTIONS

1. *Social value as a limitation of liability.* As in *Strauss*, courts today will limit the tort duty for socially valuable activities. *See* Mark A. Geistfeld, *Social Value as a Policy-Based Limitation of the Duty to Exercise Reasonable Care*, 44 Wake Forest L. Rev. 899 (2009). Does this rationale explain why courts like the one in *Hammontree* haven't applied strict liability to motor vehicle crashes? If so, why doesn't this limitation of liability apply to products containing asbestos, which was classified as a strategic material during World War II and widely considered to be a "miracle mineral" due to its many favorable characteristics, including its low cost and resistance to fire, heat, and corrosion? In *Borel*, 493 F.2d at 1088, the court held that products like asbestos "possessing both unparalleled utility and unquestioned danger" are not exempt from the rule of strict products liability. Why is the provision of electricity any different?

2. *Excessive liability and the limitation of duty.* Aside from the concern over socially valuable products, *Strauss* also illustrates how courts sometimes justify a limitation of liability on the ground that the scope of liability would otherwise be excessive or unmanageable. Are these reasons for limiting the tort duty to the contractual relationship in *Strauss* substantively different from the reasons relied on by the court in *Winterbottom*? What distinguishes the asbestos cases? Is there any substantive distinction between the proposed congressional findings in the asbestos reform bill known as the FAIR Act excerpted in section II above, and the concerns about excessive liability expressed by the courts in both *Winterbottom* and *Strauss*?

3. *Looking ahead.* In light of the varied policy questions posed by the cases in this chapter, one can see why strict products liability appears to be governed by its own distinctive principles and policies that importantly differ from the more traditional limits on ordinary tort liability. This characterization explains why leading scholars have claimed that the development of strict products liability stems from "a conceptual revolution that is among the most dramatic ever witnessed in the Anglo-American legal system." George L. Priest, *The Invention of Enterprise Liability: A Critical History of the Intellectual Foundations of Modern Tort Law*, 14 J. Legal Stud. 461, 461 (1985). *See, also, e.g.*, James A. Henderson, Jr. & Aaron D. Twerski, *A Proposed Revision of Section 402A of the Restatement (Second) of Torts*, 77 Cornell L. Rev. 1512, 1526 (1992) ("If the truth be known," the rule of strict products liability in "section 402A as originally drafted was not really a restatement of existing law."); David G. Owen, *Design Defect Ghosts*, 74 Brook. L. Rev. 927, 935 (2009) ("Tort law has probably never witnessed such a rapid, widespread, and altogether explosive change in the rules and theory of legal responsibility."). To evaluate this claim, we need to understand the underlying concepts of products liability, both analytically and historically. That understanding, in turn, makes it possible to untangle the complex doctrinal issues that comprise products liability law.

2

Doctrinal Foundations of Strict Products Liability

As compared to other forms of tort liability, the regime of strict products liability appears to be novel and new. The appearance is deceptive. Strict products liability can be derived from well-established tort doctrines. The implied warranty and negligence principle each provide a sufficient, independent doctrinal basis for imposing strict liability on the seller of a product that is defective for not being able to perform one of its ordinary functions, such as a bottle of soda that explodes when opened.

I. THE IMPLIED WARRANTY

The sale of a product involves a contractual transaction, and so the substantive nature of products liability involves the legal obligations that a seller incurs in performance of the product contract. These obligations could be defined exclusively by the contract itself or implied by law as a matter of public policy.

At one extreme lies the doctrine of *caveat emptor* or "let the buyer beware." Lacking any express contractual protection, the buyer or any other party has no legal recourse against the product seller. The buyer is solely responsible for protecting her own interests through bargaining with the product seller. The failure to do so is the buyer's problem and not the seller's responsibility. Under *caveat emptor*, the substantive nature of products liability is wholly defined by the product contract in provisions commonly called *express warranties*.

Caveat emptor has strongly influenced the common law, but the doctrine has never fully specified the legal obligations running between the buyers and sellers of products. *See generally* Walton H. Hamilton, *The Ancient Maxim Caveat Emptor*, 40 Yale L.J. 1133, 1136, 1164 (1931) (finding that the expression *caveat emptor* "is not to be found among the reputable ideas of the Middle Ages" and "appears in print for the first time well along in the sixteenth century"). For centuries, purchasers of food products have been protected by the implied warranty of merchantable quality. By making food available for commercial sale, the seller makes an implied representation that the food is fit for human consumption. One who sells contaminated food that causes injury to the purchaser has breached the implied warranty and is subject to liability, even if the sales contract does not give the buyer an express right to recovery. The law implies such a right to protect the purchaser, a position contrary to the premise of *caveat emptor*— that the contractual relationship enables buyers to bargain for whatever protection they require. *See id.* at 1173 ("Thus *caveat emptor*, whatever it was, was subject to the exceptions that the seller must make good a warranty and was liable for fraud.").

In reading the following cases, identify the rationales for *caveat emptor* and those for the implied warranty. How would these rationales be affected by the change in the channels of product distribution over time? Is there any reason why the implied warranty should be limited to cases of contaminated food, or does the rationale for liability extend to any product that is unfit for its ordinary purpose? Finally, is this rationale for liability limited to the contracting parties, or does it also apply to consumers who are not in privity with the product seller?

A. Contaminated or Unwholesome Food

VAN BRACKLIN v. FONDA
Supreme Court of Judicature of New York, 1815
12 Johns. 468, 7 Am. Dec. 339

Prior History: It appeared in evidence, that Fonda purchased of Van Bracklin a quarter of beef, for his own use; that the cow had eaten, shortly before she was killed, a very large quantity of peas and oats, and that she was slaughtered for fear she would die in consequence of her having eaten them; and it was proved, also, that those who ate of the beef were generally made very sick, and that one of Fonda's servants was sick for two weeks from eating it. The jury found a verdict for the plaintiff below, for five dollars damages.

Per Curiam. The verdict settles the facts, that the beef sold was unsound and unwholesome, and that the defendant below knew the animal to be diseased, and did not communicate that fact when he sold the beef to the plaintiff below.

In 3 Black. Com. 165, it is stated as a sound and elementary proposition, that in contracts for provisions, it is always implied that they are wholesome; and if they are not, case lies to recover damages for the deceit.

In the sale of provisions for domestic use, the vendor is bound to know that they are sound and wholesome, at his peril. This is a principle, not only salutary, but necessary to the preservation of health and life.

In the present case, the concealment of the fact that the animal was diseased, is equivalent to the suggestion of a falsehood that she was sound.

Judgment affirmed.

NOTES AND QUESTIONS

1. *Industrialization and the problem of contaminated food.* The legal rules governing the sale of contaminated food can be traced back to the advent

of a market economy, with the process of industrialization then explaining the evolution of this body of law.

> In a simple agricultural society the problem of food supply devolves upon every family. Nearly every family produces its own supply, and those who do not produce it themselves obtain it from their neighbors or in the local market. The effects of neglect or carelessness in the matter of sanitation fall upon the producers themselves.
>
> This is different in an industrial society. There a large proportion of the population is entirely dependent upon the general market. People buy their food at the stores, often chain-stores, which have imported it from distant places, much of it in cans or packages. Usually only a small part of the food which is consumed in any community has been produced in that locality. Much of it has come from other states and countries. And what is true in this respect of food is also true of drugs, narcotics, and liquors. . . .
>
> The transition from an agricultural to an industrial society is a gradual process. In the United States it came about during the second half of the nineteenth century. The federal law-makers, however, were not willing to face this fact squarely—as far as the food situation was concerned—until the twentieth century was well on the way.

C.C. Regier, *The Struggle for Federal Food and Drugs Legislation*, 1 Law & Contemp. Probs. 3, 3 (1933).

The laxity of regulation produced predictable results, at least if one assumes that sellers in product markets are motivated by the desire to make profits.

> In the effort to sell food and drug commodities every human weakness and desire was exploited. . . . By suggestion, innuendo, or outright assertion one product was held up as superior to the next. The philosophy was largely based upon the old policy of *caveat emptor*—let the buyer beware. . . .
>
> In the annual report for 1869, Dr. Thonias Antisell, the chemist of the [U.S. Department of Agriculture], said that fertilizers and food were extensively adulterated, and called for the control of the purity of these products by chemical supervision. The annual report of the Department for the fiscal year 1878 contained the first official record of the Chemical Division's study of food adulteration. Minerals and organic poisons were found to be common adulterants in tea, sausage and other foods. During the following year, Peter Collier, of the Chemical Division, presented the alarming results of his analyses of butter, oleomargarine, alcoholic liquors, and lead powders used to color coffee. Collier, convinced that the adulteration of food and medicine should be a criminal offense, stated: "Where life and health are at stake no specious argument should prevent the speedy punishment of those unscrupulous men who are willing, for the sake of gain to endanger the health of unsuspecting purchasers."

Richard Curtis Litman & Donald Saunders Litman, *Protection of the American Consumer: The Muckrakers and the Enactment of the First Federal Food and Drug Law in the United States*, 36 Food Drug Cosm. L.J. 647, 647, 660 (1981).

Ultimately, both federal and state governments responded to these problems by enacting various laws regulating the purity and safety of foods, drugs, and cosmetics.

> THE PURE FOOD AND DRUG ACT of 1906 was passed [by the federal government] in response to the demand of the public for protection from the deception practiced upon consumers by manufacturers of and dealers in foods and drugs. The Act protected the public from being deceived in the foods which nourish them and in the medicines which are relied on to cure their ills, but did not deprive the public of the freedom to eat what they may choose to eat and to take such remedies as they may wish to take.

Id. at 647.

What is the public policy embodied in this legislation and related criminal regulations? Should that policy guide courts when formulating the tort duty owed by the seller of contaminated food?

2. *Misrepresentation as a basis of responsibility.* Although the defendant in *Van Bracklin* knew that the beef was unwholesome, the legal rule stated by the court does not require such knowledge. Why? To answer this question, consider the legal basis of responsibility for the implied warranty.

In the early 1940s, William Prosser found that "[b]oth as a matter of history and at the present day, . . . there are three distinct theories to be discerned as the basis of implied warranties of quality." One theory is "pure contract," another is "obviously a tort theory," and the third is "one of policy" that "partakes of the nature" of both contract and tort, "and in either case it is liability without fault." The "pure contract" theory, however, "has predominated from the very beginning; and with few exceptions it explains the decisions." This theory is based on the idea that the "warranty has in fact been agreed upon by the parties as an unexpressed term of the contract of sale." Like any other contract term, its breach triggers liability, regardless of fault. William L. Prosser, *The Implied Warranty of Merchantable Quality*, 27 Minn. L. Rev. 117, 122-125 (1943). Strict liability is also justified by the "pure tort theory" of the seller's obligation, which is based on the buyer's reasonable reliance on a material representation implied by the sales transaction—that the product is minimally capable of performing its ordinary functions. The seller's breach of this implied warranty accordingly involves "a misrepresentation of fact" that "differs from [the tort action of] deceit only in that it imposes strict liability for innocent misrepresentations." *Id.* at 122.

Which version did the court rely on in *Van Bracklin*? Note that the case was decided within the writ system, and legal rules of this era were categorized wholly in terms of the writs and not in the substantive categories commonly employed today. Does the court's substantive reasoning provide any indication of whether the implied warranty would be governed by contract law or tort law today? Does the social problem of contaminated food and adulterated drugs provide any guidance?

JACOB E. DECKER & SONS v. CAPPS
Supreme Court of Texas, 1942
164 S.W.2d 828

ALEXANDER, C.J. This suit involves the question of the liability of a manufacturer of food products to the consumer thereof for damages for personal injuries sustained by him as the result of the unwholesomeness of such food.

Jacob E. Decker & Sons, Inc., manufactured and sold certain sausage, advertised as being suitable for human consumption in the summer time, under the trade name of "Cervalet," which sausage was wrapped in a cellophane package. The sausage in question was sold on March 16, 1939, by Jacob E. Decker & Sons, Inc., to a retail merchant in Texas for resale, and was purchased by C. K. Capps on March 19, 1939. It was consumed immediately by members of Capps' family, and as a result one of the children died and other members of the family were made seriously ill. Mrs. Capps, after the death of her husband from other causes, brought suit for herself for damages for the injuries sustained by her as a result of the eating of the contaminated sausage. She also brought two other suits as next friend for her two surviving minor children for damages for the injuries suffered by them. The three suits were tried together. The jury found that at the time the sausage in question was processed and manufactured it was contaminated and poisonous to such an extent as to be unfit for human consumption; and that the eating thereof by the members of Capps' family proximately resulted in their serious illness. The jury further found, however, that Decker & Sons did not fail to properly inspect the sausage, and that the contaminated and poisonous condition of the sausage at the time it was manufactured was not due to the negligence of Decker & Sons in the manufacture and processing thereof, and that the illness suffered by Capps' family from the eating of the sausage was the result of an unavoidable accident. Judgments in favor of the plaintiffs for damages sustained by them were affirmed by the Court of Civil Appeals.

After having considered the matter most carefully, we have reached the conclusion that the manufacturer is liable for the injuries sustained by the consumers of the products in question. We think the manufacturer is liable in such a case under an implied warranty imposed by operation of law as a matter of public policy. We recognize that the authorities are by no means uniform, but we believe the better reasoning supports the rule which holds the manufacturer liable. Liability in such case is not based on negligence, nor on a breach of the usual implied contractual warranty, but on the broad principle of the public policy to protect human health and life. It is a well-known fact that articles of food are manufactured and placed in the channels of commerce, with the intention that they shall pass from hand to hand until they are finally used by some remote consumer. It is usually impracticable, if not impossible, for the ultimate consumer to analyze the food and ascertain whether or not it is suitable for human consumption. Since it has been packed and placed on the market as a food for human consumption, and marked as such, the purchaser usually eats it or causes it to be served to his family without the precaution of having it analyzed by a technician to ascertain whether or not it is suitable for human consumption. In fact, in most instances the only satisfactory examination that could be made would be only at the time and place of the processing of the food. It seems to be the rule that where food products sold for human consumption are unfit for that purpose, there is such an utter failure of the purpose for which the food is sold, and the consequences of eating unsound food are so disastrous to human health and life, that the law imposes a warranty of purity in favor of the ultimate consumer as a matter of public policy.

Since very early times the common law has applied more stringent rules to sales of food than to sales of other merchandise. It has long been a well-established rule that in sales of food for domestic use there is an implied warranty that it is wholesome and fit for human consumption. A majority of the American courts that have followed this holding have not based such warranty upon an implied term in the contract between buyer and seller, nor upon any reliance by the buyer on the representation of the seller, but have imposed it as a matter of public policy in order to discourage the sale of unwholesome food. The Supreme Court of Michigan has stated the reason for the rule in Hoover v. Peters, 18 Mich. 51 (1869), as follows:

> There may be sellers who are not much skilled, and there may be purchasers able to judge for themselves, but in sales of provisions the seller is generally so much better able than the buyer to judge of quality and condition, that if a general rule is to be adopted, it is safer to hold the vendor to a strict accountability than to throw the risk on the purchaser. The reason given by the New York authorities, in favor of health and personal safety, is much more satisfactory than the purely commercial considerations which take no account of these important interests.

In Wiedeman v. Keller, 49 N.E. 210, 211 (1897), the Supreme Court of Illinois adopted the same rule and pointed out the distinction between sales of food and other sales, saying:

> In an ordinary sale of goods, the rule of caveat emptor applies, unless the purchaser exacts of the vendor a warranty. Where, however, articles of food are purchased from a retail dealer for immediate consumption, the consequences resulting from the purchase of an unsound article may be so serious, and may prove so disastrous to the health and life of the consumer, that public safety demands that there should be an implied warranty on the part of the vendor that the article sold is sound, and fit for the use for which it was purchased.

The rule which imposes a warranty, as a matter of public policy, of the soundness of food sold for human consumption is not of modern origin. [This rule was recognized as] far back as the year 1266 A.D. the statute of Pillory and Tumbrel and of the assize of bread and ale (51 Hen. III, stat. 6). It will be noted that a clear distinction is drawn between sales of food and sales of cloth, or other articles of merchandise. In the latter case, knowledge is necessary, unless there is an express warranty, but not so in the former.

The rule above announced has been adhered to by subsequent decisions of other courts in this country and has been recognized as a distinct implied warranty peculiar to sales of food, although the obligation existed long before implied warranties were recognized. This implied warranty was not based on

I. The Implied Warranty   29

any reliance by the buyer upon the representations of the seller, or upon his skill and judgment, but was grounded squarely upon the public policy of protecting the public health [citing, among other cases, Van Bracklin v. Fonda, 12 Johns., N.Y. 468, 7 Am. Dec. 339].

While a right of action in such a case is said to spring from a "warranty," it should be noted that the warranty here referred to is not the more modern contractual warranty, but is an obligation imposed by law to protect public health. According to Prof. Williston the law of warranty is older by a century than the [writ or] action of special assumpsit, from which the modern law of contracts developed. 1 Williston on Sales, p. 368, §195; Jeanblanc, "Manufacturer's Liability to Persons Other Than Their Immediate Vendees," 24 Va. L. Rev. 134, 158, at p. 148. The action on a warranty sounded in tort was in the nature of a [writ or] action on the case for deceit, although it was not necessary to plead or prove scienter. 1 Williston on Sales, p. 371. It is believed that much of the confusion among the courts on this question is due to the failure to note this difference in the use of the term "warranty." It has led many courts to believe that in order to sustain an action under such a warranty there must be privity of contract and reliance on the representation. The doctrine of privity of contract and of the necessity therefor in order to sustain an action grew out of the later action of assumpsit. It applies only when one is seeking to enforce a contract. Here the liability of the manufacturer and vendor is imposed by operation of law as a matter of public policy for the protection of the public, and is not dependent on any provision of the contract, either expressed or implied.

It must be conceded that many courts have denied recovery against the manufacturer and have insisted strictly on the requirement of privity. [ ]

There is a growing tendency, however, to discard the requirement of privity and to hold the manufacturer liable directly to the ultimate consumer. [ ]

It is also true that there are many cases in which liability has been sustained on the ground of contractual warranty. Where there is privity of contract and there is a breach of warranty, either expressed or implied, liability can be sustained thereon, as in the case of the sale of commodities other than food. The fact, however, that liability may be sustained in some cases because of a breach of a contractual warranty does not argue against the sustaining of liability on the ground herein adhered to—warranty imposed by law as a matter of public policy. The two remedies may coexist, and liability may be sustained under either one of them that is available.

Many of the courts which have allowed a recovery where there was no direct contractual relationship between plaintiff and defendant have done so by indulging in fictions, such as presumed negligence, fraud, assignment of cause of action from dealer to consumer, third party beneficiary contract, and agency of the buyer for the consumer. Such authorities but evidence the efforts made by the courts to place absolute liability on the manufacturer and vendor of food products to the consumer for damages caused by impurities therein. Such fictions are indulged merely because it is thought necessary to do so in order to get away from the rule which requires privity of contract where recovery is sought on an implied warranty growing out of a contract. We believe the better and sounder rule places liability solidly on the ground of a warranty not in contract, but imposed by law as a matter of public policy.

Some courts have imposed upon the manufacturer and vendor an implied warranty which is said to "run with the article." [ ] While this appears to be based on sound logic, it is more a reason for the imposition of warranty by operation of law than it is an independent ground of liability in itself. There certainly is justification for indulging a presumption of a warranty that runs with the article in the sale of food products. A party who processes a product and gives it the appearance of being suitable for human consumption, and places it in the channels of commerce, expects some one to consume the food in reliance on its appearance that it is suitable for human consumption. He expects the appearance of suitableness to continue with the product until some one is induced to consume it as food. But a modern manufacturer or vendor does even more than this under modern practices. He not only processes the food and dresses it up so as to make it appear appetizing, but he uses the newspapers, magazines, billboards, and the radio to build up the psychology to buy and consume his products. The invitation extended by him is not only to the house wife to buy and serve his product, but to the members of the family and guest to eat it. In fact, the manufacturer's interest in the product is not terminated when he has sold it to wholesaler. He must get it off the wholesaler's shelves before the wholesaler will buy a new supply. The same is not only true of the retailer, but of the house wife, for the house wife will not buy more until the family has consumed that which she has in her pantry. Thus the manufacturer or other vendor intends that this appearance of suitability of the article for human consumption should continue and be effective until some one is induced thereby to consume the goods. It would be but to acknowledge a weakness in the law to say that he could thus create a demand for his products by inducing a belief that they are suitable for human consumption, when, as a matter of fact, they are not, and reap the benefits of the public confidence thus created, and then avoid liability for the injuries caused thereby merely because there was no privity of contract between him and the one whom he induced to consume the food. The mere fact that a manufacturer or other vendor may thus induce the public to consume unwholesome food evidences the soundness of the rule which imposes a warranty, as a matter of public policy on the sale of food or other products intended for human consumption.

The policy of the law to protect the health and life of the public would only be half served if we were to make liability depend on the ordinary contractual warranty. Privity of contract and reliance on the skill and judgment of the manufacturer or other vendor would be necessary to a recovery in such a case. If the main purpose of the rule is to protect the health and life of the public, there is no merit in denying relief to a consumer against the manufacturer on the ground of lack of direct contractual relation. If a man buys food and his whole family and guest eat it and all become ill, it would be arbitrary and unreasonable to say that only the man who bought the food would have a remedy for his sufferings.

It will also be noted that in many cases liability is placed on negligence in the processing of the food, and this has led some courts to conclude that proof of negligence was essential to a recovery. But it must be borne in mind that liability could be based on negligence, independent of the rule which imposes a warranty as a matter of public policy, and therefore those authorities which allow a recovery on proof of negligence are not authority for holding that a recovery

I. The Implied Warranty

cannot be had under the doctrine of a warranty imposed by an operation of law, even though there be no negligence. Since the warranty of suitableness is imposed by law as a matter of public policy, there is no need for proof of negligence.

There is no doubt about the public policy of this State with regard to the sale of impure foods. Article 706 of the Penal Code expressly provides that no person shall manufacture or offer for sale in this State any adulterated food. Article 707 of the Penal Code defines adulterated food as any food containing any added poisonous or deleterious ingredients which may render such food injurious to health, or which consists in whole or in part of a filthy, decomposed, or putrid animal or vegetable substance.

We hold that the defendant, as the manufacturer and vendor of the sausage in question, was liable to the plaintiffs, as the consumers thereof, for the injuries caused to them by the contaminated and poisonous substance in the sausage at the time the defendant manufactured and sold the same, even though the defendant was not negligent in the processing thereof.

The judgments of the Court of Civil Appeals and of the trial court in each of the three cases are affirmed.

NOTES AND QUESTIONS

1. *The tort rationale for the implied warranty.* Does the court persuasively explain why the tort version of the implied warranty is limited to food products? As indicated by the court's discussion, criminal statutes govern the sale of contaminated food and adulterated drugs, whereas that type of statutory prohibition is lacking in the sale of most other products. Is the statutory prohibition the exclusive source of the public policy promoted by the implied warranty?

Consider in this regard the reasons why the implied warranty is not exclusively a doctrine of contract law. A fundamental premise of contract law is that the terms of a contract are based "on supposedly informed assent" of the contracting parties. E. Allan Farnsworth, FARNSWORTH ON CONTRACTS §4.9 (3d ed. 2004). The implied warranty applies only to cases in which the buyer is misinformed about one or more facts basic to the transaction, rendering the premise of contract law invalid. To what extent does this informational problem factor into the court's decision in *Jacob E. Decker*? Does it justify a tort duty?

Aside from extreme cases of unconscionable terms, contract law does not address the fairness of transactions involving uninformed or unsophisticated buyers. An unconscionable term, moreover, only renders the contract (or that particular term) unenforceable. So, too, an uninformed buyer's unilateral mistake only voids the contract and perhaps generates a claim for restitution. *Id.* §9.4. Would any of these remedies adequately protect the plaintiff's expectations in *Jacob E. Decker*?

To adequately protect the expectations of poorly informed buyers, contract law could reform the terms of a contract to embody the agreement that purchasers would have made if they were adequately informed. For example, the contract for food transactions could be reformed to give the buyer a right to compensation for injuries caused by contaminated food. However, a "court will not reform a document to reflect an agreement that the court merely *thinks* the parties *would have decided to make* had they not been mistaken"; reformation instead requires "clear and convincing evidence" showing why the agreed-upon contract did not contain the language in question. E. Allan Farnsworth, ALLEVIATING MISTAKES: REVERSAL AND FORGIVENESS FOR FLAWED PERCEPTIONS 101 (2004).

Reformation is quite limited so that parties can rely on the agreed-upon terms of a contract without worrying that a court will subsequently modify the agreement to impose new obligations. But when buyers routinely lack the requisite information to strike a good bargain in the first instance, the integrity of contracting process can be undermined, potentially impeding the entire category of transactions.

Consider in this regard the problem of contaminated food and adulterated drugs addressed by federal law in the United States since the early twentieth century. By assuring compensation for injuries caused by unwholesome food, the implied warranty protects consumer expectations that the food is fit for human consumption. The buyer did not expect to be made sick by the food, and the guarantee of compensation for that injury remedies the buyer's frustrated expectation.

In this respect, the tort remedy functions no differently from the ordinary contractual remedy that bases compensation on the injured party's expectation of the benefit to be derived from the contract. But unlike a contractual remedy, the tort remedy is formulated to protect the safety expectations of poorly informed buyers.

2. *Beyond food?* Why did the early common law limit liability to food cases? Can the implied warranty be justified even if there is no criminal statute governing the sale of the defective product, thereby extending this rule of strict liability to nonfood products?

B. Warranties in Nonfood Cases

In contrast to cases involving contaminated food, the early common law did not recognize an implied warranty for nonfood products. This body of the common law was more clearly influenced by *caveat emptor*. As compared to food products, how might the rationale for *caveat emptor* be more compelling with respect to the type of products that were typically at issue in the early cases?

SEIXAS AND SEIXAS v. WOODS
Supreme Court of Judicature of New York, 1804
2 Cai. R. 48.

Prior History: THIS was an action on the case for selling peachum wood for brazilletto. The former worth hardly any thing, the latter of considerable value. The defendant had received the wood in question from a house in New-Providence, to whom he was agent, and in the invoice it was mentioned as brazilletto.

I. The Implied Warranty 33

He had also advertised it as brazilletto, had shown the invoice to the plaintiffs, and had made out the bill of parcels for brazilletto. But it was not pretended that he knew that it was peachum, nor did the plaintiffs suspect it to be so, as it was delivered from the vessel, and picked out from other wood by a person on their behalf. In short, neither side knew it to be other than brazilletto, nor was any fraud imputed. On discovery, however, of the real quality of the wood, it was offered to the defendant, and the purchase-money demanded. On his refusal to accept the one, or return the other, as he had remitted the proceeds, the present action was brought, in which a verdict was taken for the plaintiffs, subject to the opinion of the court.

THOMPSON, J. Two questions arising out of this case are presented for consideration:

1. Whether an action can be maintained to recover back the consideration money, paid under the circumstances stated in the case? and if so, then,

2. Whether the defendant, who acted only as agent or factor, can be made responsible?

From the facts stated with respect to the first point, it appears there was no express warranty by the defendant, or any fraud in the sale. The wood was sold and purchased as brazilletto wood, and a fair price for such wood paid, when in fact the wood was of a different quality, and of little or no value. The plaintiffs' agent, who made the purchase, saw the wood when unloaded and delivered, and did not discover or know that it was of a different quality from that described in the bills of parcels; neither did the defendant, who was only consignee of this cargo, know that the wood was not brazilletto. The question then arises, whether there was an implied warranty, so as to afford redress to the plaintiffs, or whether the maxim of *caveat emptor* must be applied to them. From an examination of the decisions in courts of common law, I can find no case where an action has been sustained under similar circumstances: an express warranty, or some fraud in the sale, are deemed indispensably necessary to be shown.

Fonblanque, in his valuable Treatise of Equity, 1 Fonb. 380, note h, speaking of the justice and propriety of this principle, says, "To excite that diligence which is necessary to guard against imposition, and to secure that good faith which is necessary to justify a certain degree of confidence, is essential to the intercourse of society. These objects are attained by those rules of law which require the purchaser to apply his attention to those particulars, which may be supposed to be within the reach of his observation and judgment; and the vendor to communicate those particulars and defects, which cannot be supposed to be immediately within the reach of such attention. If the purchaser be wanting of attention to those points, where attention would have been sufficient to protect him from surprise or imposition, the maxim *caveat emptor* ought to apply. But even against this maxim he may provide, by requiring the vendor expressly to warrant that which the law would not imply to be warranted. If the vendor be wanting in good faith, fides servanda is the rule of law, and may be enforced, both in equity and at law." These observations, I think, apply with peculiar force in the case before us. The agent of the plaintiffs, who made the purchase, was present at the delivery of the wood; and the defect now complained of was within the reach of his observation and judgment, had he bestowed proper attention. I am satisfied that according to the settled decisions in the English courts, either an express warranty, or some fraud or deceit on the part of the vendor, is necessary to be shown, in order to entitle the purchaser to the remedy sought after in the present case. I see no injustice or inconvenience resulting from this doctrine, but, on the contrary, think it is best calculated to excite that caution and attention which all prudent men ought to observe in making their contracts. I am therefore of opinion with the defendant, on the first point, which renders it unnecessary for me to examine the other question raised on the argument.

KENT, J. This is a clear case for the defendant. If upon a sale there be neither a warranty nor deceit, the purchaser purchases at his peril. This seems to have been the ancient, and the uniform language of the English law. By the civil law, says Lord Coke, every man is bound to warrant the thing that he selleth, albeit there be no express warranty; but the common law bindeth him not, unless there be a warranty in deed, or law. The civil law, and the law of those countries which have adopted the civil as their common law, is more rigorous towards the seller, and make him responsible in every case for a latent defect, and, if the question was res integra in our law, I confess I should be overcome by the reasoning of the Civilians. And yet the rule of the common law has been well and elegantly vindicated by Fonblanque, as most happily reconciling the claims of convenience with the duties of good faith. It requires the purchaser to apply his attention to those particulars which may be supposed within the reach of his observation and judgment, and the vendor to communicate those particulars and defects which cannot be supposed to be immediately within the reach of such attention. And even against his want of vigilance, the purchaser may provide, by requiring the vendor expressly to warrant the article.[1] The mentioning the wood as brazilletto wood, in the bill of parcels, and in the advertisement some days previous to the sale, did not amount to a warranty to the plaintiffs. To make an affirmation at the time of the sale, a warranty, it must appear by evidence to be so intended and not to have been a mere matter of judgment and opinion, and of which the defendant had no particular knowledge.[2] Here it is admitted the defendant was equally ignorant with the plaintiffs, and could have had no such intention.

I am therefore for the defendant.

LEWIS, Ch. J. contra [without dissenting opinion].

NOTES AND QUESTIONS

1. *Information costs and informed contractual exchange.* In justifying *caveat emptor*, the court makes assumptions about the buyer's ability to inspect the product. What are those assumptions? Are they valid for food products?

---

1. And in sale of provisions for domestic use, the vendor is bound to know that they are sound and wholesome at his peril; a warranty is implied. A warranty of title is also implied on the sale of chattel.

2. There are no particular words prescribed by law to make out a warranty; but it is essential that the affirmation made at the time of sale be intended by the parties as a warranty, and not as the mere expression of an opinion by the vendor.

I. The Implied Warranty

The seller, of course, can also inspect and then disclose the relevant information to the buyer. What are the relevant considerations for determining whether it is desirable to force the buyer or the seller to inspect for quality? Consider in this regard the following observations:

> Every contractual agreement is predicated upon a number of factual assumptions about the world. Some of these assumptions are shared by the parties to the contract and some are not. It is always possible that a particular factual assumption is mistaken. From an economic point of view, the risk of such a mistake (whether it be the mistake of only one party or both) represents a cost. It is a cost to the contracting parties themselves and to society as a whole since the actual occurrence of a mistake always (potentially) increases the resources which must be devoted to the process of allocating goods to their highest-valuing users. . . .
>
> Information is the antidote to mistake. Although information is costly to produce, one individual may be able to obtain relevant information more cheaply than another. If the parties to a contract are acting rationally, they will minimize the joint costs of a potential mistake by assigning the risk of its occurrence to the party who is the better (cheaper) information-gatherer. Where the parties have actually assigned the risk—whether explicitly, or implicitly through their adherence to trade custom and past patterns of dealing—their own allocation must be respected. Where they have not—and there is a resulting gap in the contract—a court concerned with economic efficiency should impose the risk on the better information-gatherer. This is so for familiar reasons: by allocating the risk in this way, an efficiency-minded court reduces the transaction costs of the contracting process itself.

Anthony T. Kronman, *Mistake, Disclosure, Information, and the Law of Contracts,* 7 J. Legal Stud. 1, 2-5 (1978) (citations omitted).

Do differences in the cost of acquiring information about product quality explain why the early common law relied on *caveat emptor* for chattels, even though that rule had been repudiated by the implied warranty in food cases?

2. *Contractual exchange in the modern economy.* Some products of this era were like food in the sense that the buyer could not adequately inspect for quality. But "if [the buyer] distrusts his own judgment, he may if he chooses require a warranty." Jones v. Just, L.R. 3 Q.B. 197 (1868). Why wouldn't this reasoning apply to food products as well?

Because buyers of food products ordinarily cannot inspect, they presumably should bargain for warranty protection in all these cases. Rather than forcing buyers to obtain such protection, the common law instead imposed the warranty obligation on all sellers. Outside of food transactions, by contrast, buyers could ordinarily inspect, and so there was no need to impose the warranty obligation on sellers in all transactions. But "[w]here there is no opportunity to inspect the commodity, the maxim of *caveat emptor* does not apply." Gardiner v. Gray, 171 E.R. 46 (1815). How would this rationale for the implied warranty be affected by increased industrialization and the associated changes in the modes of product manufacturing and distribution?

ESCOLA v. COCA COLA BOTTLING CO.
Supreme Court of California, 1944
150 P.2d 436

Plaintiff, a waitress in a restaurant, was injured when a bottle of Coca Cola broke in her hand. She alleged that defendant company, which had bottled and delivered the alleged defective bottle to her employer, was negligent in selling "bottles containing said beverage which on account of excessive pressure of gas or by reason of some defect in the bottle was dangerous . . . and likely to explode." This appeal is from a judgment upon a jury verdict in favor of plaintiff.

[The majority affirmed the judgment in an opinion excerpted in the next section of this chapter.]

TRAYNOR, J., *concurring*. I concur in the judgment, but I believe the manufacturer's negligence should no longer be singled out as the basis of a plaintiff's right to recover in cases like the present one. In my opinion it should now be recognized that a manufacturer incurs an absolute liability when an article that he has placed on the market, knowing that it is to be used without inspection, proves to have a defect that causes injury to human beings. MacPherson v. Buick Motor Co., 217 N.Y. 382 (1916), established the principle, recognized by this court, that irrespective of privity of contract, the manufacturer is responsible for an injury caused by such an article to any person who comes in lawful contact with it. In these cases the source of the manufacturer's liability was his negligence in the manufacturing process or in the inspection of component parts supplied by others. Even if there is no negligence, however, public policy demands that responsibility be fixed wherever it will most effectively reduce the hazards to life and health inherent in defective products that reach the market. It is evident that the manufacturer can anticipate some hazards and guard against the recurrence of others, as the public cannot. Those who suffer injury from defective products are unprepared to meet its consequences. The cost of an injury and the loss of time or health may be an overwhelming misfortune to the person injured, and a needless one, for the risk of injury can be insured by the manufacturer and distributed among the public as a cost of doing business. It is to the public interest to discourage the marketing of products having defects that are a menace to the public. If such products nevertheless find their way into the market it is to the public interest to place the responsibility for whatever injury they may cause upon the manufacturer, who, even if he is not negligent in the manufacture of the product, is responsible for its reaching the market. However intermittently such injuries may occur and however haphazardly they may strike, the risk of their occurrence is a constant risk and a general one. Against such a risk there should be general and constant protection and the manufacturer is best situated to afford such protection.

In the case of foodstuffs, the public policy of the state is formulated in a criminal statute, [which] prohibits the manufacturing, preparing, compounding, packing, selling, offering for sale, or keeping for sale, or advertising within the state, of any adulterated food. [It] declares that food is adulterated when "it has been produced, prepared, packed or held under insanitary conditions whereby it may have become contaminated with filth, or whereby it may have

I. The Implied Warranty

been rendered diseased, unwholesome or injurious to health." [ ] The statute imposes criminal liability not only if the food is adulterated, but if its container, which may be a bottle, has any deleterious substance, or renders the product injurious to health. The criminal liability under the statute attaches without proof of fault, so that the manufacturer is under the duty of ascertaining whether an article manufactured by him is safe. Statutes of this kind result in a strict liability of the manufacturer in tort to the member of the public injured.

The statute may well be applicable to a bottle whose defects cause it to explode. In any event it is significant that the statute imposes criminal liability without fault, reflecting the public policy of protecting the public from dangerous products placed on the market, irrespective of negligence in their manufacture. While the Legislature imposes criminal liability only with regard to food products and their containers, there are many other sources of danger. It is to the public interest to prevent injury to the public from any defective goods by the imposition of civil liability generally.

The retailer, even though not equipped to test a product, is under an absolute liability to his customer, for the implied warranties of fitness for proposed use and merchantable quality include a warranty of safety of the product. This warranty is not necessarily a contractual one, for public policy requires that the buyer be insured at the seller's expense against injury. The courts recognize, however, that the retailer cannot bear the burden of this warranty, and allow him to recoup any losses by means of the warranty of safety attending the wholesaler's or manufacturer's sale to him. Such a procedure, however, is needlessly circuitous and engenders wasteful litigation. Much would be gained if the injured person could base his action directly on the manufacturer's warranty.

The liability of the manufacturer to an immediate buyer injured by a defective product follows without proof of negligence from the implied warranty of safety attending the sale. Ordinarily, however, the immediate buyer is a dealer who does not intend to use the product himself, and if the warranty of safety is to serve the purpose of protecting health and safety it must give rights to others than the dealer. In the words of Judge Cardozo in the *MacPherson* case: "The dealer was indeed the one person of whom it might be said with some approach to certainty that by him the car would not be used. Yet the defendant would have us say that he was the one person whom it was under a legal duty to protect. The law does not lead us to so inconsequent a conclusion." While the defendant's negligence in the *MacPherson* case made it unnecessary for the court to base liability on warranty, Judge Cardozo's reasoning recognized the injured person as the real party in interest and effectively disposed of the theory that the liability of the manufacturer incurred by his warranty should apply only to the immediate purchaser. It thus paves the way for a standard of liability that would make the manufacturer guarantee the safety of his product even when there is no negligence.

This court and many others have extended protection according to such a standard to consumers of food products, taking the view that the right of a consumer injured by unwholesome food does not depend "upon the intricacies of the law of sales" and that the warranty of the manufacturer to the consumer in absence of privity of contract rests on public policy. [ ] Dangers to life and health inhere in other consumers' goods that are defective and there is no reason to differentiate them from the dangers of defective food products.

In the food products cases the courts have resorted to various fictions to rationalize the extension of the manufacturer's warranty to the consumer: that a warranty runs with the chattel; that the cause of action of the dealer is assigned to the consumer; that the consumer is a third party beneficiary of the manufacturer's contract with the dealer. They have also held the manufacturer liable on a mere fiction of negligence: "Practically he must know it [the product] is fit, or take the consequences, if it proves destructive." [ ] Such fictions are not necessary to fix the manufacturer's liability under a warranty if the warranty is severed from the contract of sale between the dealer and the consumer and based on the law of torts as a strict liability. Warranties are not necessarily rights arising under a contract. An action on a warranty "was, in its origin, a pure action of tort," and only late in the historical development of warranties was an action in assumpsit allowed. Ames, *The History of Assumpsit*, 2 Harv. L. Rev. 1, 8; 4 Williston on Contracts (1936) §970. "And it is still generally possible where a distinction of procedure is observed between actions of tort and of contract to frame the declaration for breach of warranty in tort." Williston, loc. cit.; see Prosser, *Warranty on Merchantible Quality*, 27 Minn. L. Rev. 117, 118. On the basis of the tort character of an action on a warranty, recovery has been allowed for wrongful death as it could not be in an action for breach of contract. [ ] Even a seller's express warranty can arise from a noncontractual affirmation inducing a person to purchase the goods. "As an actual agreement to contract is not essential, the obligation of a seller in such a case is one imposed by law as distinguished from one voluntarily assumed. It may be called an obligation either on a quasi-contract or quasi-tort, because remedies appropriate to contract and also to tort are applicable." 1 Williston on Sales, 2d Ed. §197; see Ballantine, *Classification of Obligations*, 15 Ill. L. Rev. 310, 325.

As handicrafts have been replaced by mass production with its great markets and transportation facilities, the close relationship between the producer and consumer of a product has been altered. Manufacturing processes, frequently valuable secrets, are ordinarily either inaccessible to or beyond the ken of the general public. The consumer no longer has means or skill enough to investigate for himself the soundness of a product, even when it is not contained in a sealed package, and his erstwhile vigilance has been lulled by the steady efforts of manufacturers to build up confidence by advertising and marketing devices such as trade-marks. Consumers no longer approach products warily but accept them on faith, relying on the reputation of the manufacturer or the trademark. Manufacturers have sought to justify that faith by increasingly high standards of inspection and a readiness to make good on defective products by way of replacements and refunds. The manufacturer's obligation to the consumer must keep pace with the changing relationship between them; it cannot be escaped because the marketing of a product has become so complicated as to require one or more intermediaries. Certainly there is greater reason to impose liability on the manufacturer than on the retailer who is but a conduit of a product that he is not himself able to test.

The manufacturer's liability should, of course, be defined in terms of the safety of the product in normal and proper use, and should not extend to injuries that cannot be traced to the product as it reached the market.

NOTES AND QUESTIONS

1. *Doctrinal evolution.* Justice Traynor's concurring opinion in *Escola* is widely recognized as one of the most important developments in strict products liability. The case of an exploding bottle of soda provided a particularly good fact pattern for this doctrinal development.

In the 1940s, these cases were common. "Every state developed case law on exploding bottle cases. In Los Angeles County, the largest, busiest trial court district in California, juries reached verdicts in an average of one to two exploding bottle cases a year during the 1950s." Benjamin T. Field, JUSTICE ROGER TRAYNOR AND HIS CASE FOR JUDICIAL ACTIVISM 157 (Doctoral Dissertation, Univ. Cal. Berkeley 2000).

The California Supreme Court decided another exploding-bottle case five years later, and it again based liability on res ipsa loquitur. Gordon v. Aztec Brewing Co., 203 P.2d 522 (Cal. 1949). As in *Escola*, Traynor thought the liability was based on "spurious application of rules developed to determine the sufficiency of circumstantial evidence in negligence cases." *Id.* at 532. Traynor again advocated that liability be based on strict liability for the reasons he gave in *Escola*. No member of the court accepted Traynor's argument for strict liability.

In 1958, the court considered another exploding-bottle case, this time finding that res ipsa loquitur was inapplicable because the plaintiff had failed to establish that the defect existed while the bottle was possessed by the defendants. Trust v. Arden Farms Co., 324 P.2d 583 (Cal. 1958). Traynor concurred with respect to the defendant manufacturer and dissented with respect to the defendant bottler, arguing that the defect probably existed while the bottler had possession. Traynor concluded that the bottler should be strictly liable for reasons given in the *Escola* concurrence. Once again, he was the lone advocate for strict liability.

Traynor was influencing the court, however. In a 1960 case, the court held that warranty liability could be imposed on the manufacturer of a defective grinding wheel that blew up in the plaintiff's face. Peterson v. Lamb Rubber Co., 353 P.2d 575 (Cal. 1960). Although the plaintiff was a worker who was not in contractual privity with the manufacturer, the whole court (except Traynor) nevertheless supported warranty liability because employees are "members of the industrial 'family' of the employer." This reasoning, of course, is consistent with Traynor's argument in *Escola* that the implied warranty does not depend on privity. Gladys Escola, after all, was also in the "industrial family" of her employer, and so the warranty between Coca Cola and her employer should also have extended to her by this reasoning. Traynor agreed with the majority that the plaintiff worker should recover for his injuries, but for the reasons he had earlier given in *Escola* and other cases.

Finally, in 1963, Traynor persuaded the entire Court to impose strict liability on the manufacturer of a defective power tool in the landmark case Greenman v. Yuba Power Products, 377 P.2d 897 (Cal. 1963). As in *Escola*, none of the parties had made an argument concerning strict liability. Three new justices had been appointed to the court, but three others adopted

Traynor's position despite their earlier refusal to do so. Writing for the Court, Traynor stated: "We need not recanvass the reasons for imposing strict liability on the manufacturer. They have been fully articulated. . . ."

The development of strict products liability can be traced to Traynor's concurrence in *Escola*, but before he had finally persuaded his colleagues about the matter, the New Jersey Supreme Court reached the same result under the implied warranty in a case involving a defective automobile:

> The limitations of privity in contracts for the sale of goods developed their place in the law when marketing conditions were simple, when maker and buyer frequently met face to face on an equal bargaining plane and when many of the products were relatively uncomplicated and conducive to inspection by a buyer competent to evaluate their quality. With the advent of mass marketing, the manufacturer became remote from the purchaser, sales were accomplished through intermediaries, and the demand for the product was created by advertising media. In such an economy it became obvious that the consumer was the person being cultivated. Manifestly, the connotation of "consumer" was broader than that of "buyer." He signified such a person who, in the reasonable contemplation of the parties to the sale, might be expected to use the product. Thus, where the commodities sold are such that if defectively manufactured they will be dangerous to life or limb, then society's interests can only be protected by eliminating the requirement of privity between the maker and his dealers and the reasonably expected ultimate consumer. In that way the burden of losses consequent upon use of defective articles is borne by those who are in a position to either control the danger or make an equitable distribution of the losses when they do occur.
>
> Most of the cases where lack of privity has not been permitted to interfere with recovery have involved food and drugs. We see no rational doctrinal basis for differentiating between a fly in a bottle of beverage and a defective automobile. The unwholesome beverage may bring illness to one person, the defective car, with its great potentiality for harm to the driver, occupants, and others, demands even less adherence to the narrow barrier of privity.
>
> Accordingly, we hold that under modern marketing conditions, when a manufacturer puts a new automobile in the stream of trade and promotes its purchase by the public, an implied warranty that it is reasonably suitable for use as such accompanies it into the hands of the ultimate purchaser.

Henningsen v. Bloomfield Motors, Inc., 161 A.2d 69 (N.J. 1960).

2. *Distinguishing the tort and contractual versions of the implied warranty.* When the common law first recognized the implied warranty for nonfood products, it did so on a purely contractual basis. The contractual obligation was limited by the requirement of privity. This limitation, for reasons given by Justice Traynor, meant that the warranty provided little or no protection to consumers in the modern economy. Like any other contractual obligation, manufacturers could also expressly disclaim the warranty obligation within the contract, as they frequently did. By the 1960s, the court in *Henningsen* observed that standardized sales documents have "metamorphosed the warranty into a device to limit the maker's liability." *Id.* at 78.

I. The Implied Warranty

The requirement of privity, coupled with the widespread use of disclaimers, typically prevented consumers from recovering under the contractual version of the implied warranty, leaving them "powerless" and in need of legal protection as Traynor put it.

For reasons previously discussed by the court in *Jacob E. Decker & Sons*, p. 27 *supra*, the tort version of the implied warranty is not based on mutual consent and therefore is not contractual. The tort duty instead is justified by the consumer's lack of information about product quality. According to Justice Traynor's concurrence in *Escola*, is there any reason to distinguish contaminated food from other defective products in this respect? What is the court's position about this matter in *Henningsen*? Lacking such a substantive distinction between food and nonfood products, is there any reason for not extending the tort version of the implied warranty to encompass all defective products? Would such a development be "revolutionary" as the materials from Chapter 1 might otherwise suggest?

3. *Analogous developments involving the express warranty.* An express warranty is created when the seller makes an affirmative representation of product quality. When that express representation is false, the seller could be liable for breach of contract regardless of whether the product was otherwise defective. The seller could also be liable under the separate tort of fraud or misrepresentation for having falsely communicated material information to the plaintiff who was harmed by reasonably relying on that information.

Despite the overlap of the express warranty as a contract doctrine and the tort of misrepresentation, the contractual conceptualization had obscured its tort counterpart by the nineteenth century, much like it had done with respect to the implied warranty.

> At common law, an action grounded on breach of warranty sounded in tort rather than in contract. Characterizing the action as trespass on the case, the English courts permitted recovery for the breach of an express warranty of a material fact, relied upon in the purchase of a chattel, that later proved to be false.
>
> By the end of the eighteenth century, however, the tort character of an express warranty action had disappeared in favor of a [contractual] cause of action.... Thereafter, claims for breach of the express warranty by the manufacturer's representation became the sole cognizable claim for product misrepresentations. Because this contractual cause of action required privity between the parties to the contract of sale, however, suits between the consumer and the manufacturer were uniformly dismissed.
>
> As the law continued to evolve, the courts increasingly rejected the necessity for a contractual relationship, recognizing that the ultimate consumer, in purchasing a product, often relied heavily upon the manufacturer's express public representations of the qualities and character of the product. Moreover, the modern approach to merchandising precipitated a judicial rejection of the contractual trappings of express warranty and a recharacterization of a publicly communicated innocent misrepresentation as tortious in nature.

American Safety Equip. Co. v. Winkler, 640 P.2d 216, 219-220 (Colo. 1982).

Liability for an express misrepresentation does not require proof of any negligence on the seller's part. In effect, a seller incurs strict liability for having expressly misrepresented product quality in a manner that foreseeably caused injury to the consumer. Like the implied warranty, the express warranty yields a rule of strict tort liability formulated to protect the consumer's expectations of product performance.

C. *The Restatement (Second) Rule of Strict Products Liability*

Organized in the 1920s by prominent lawyers, judges, and law professors, the American Law Institute strives to bring "clarity and predictability to American law through the production of a series of massive, annotated 'Restatements' of specific legal subjects" that provide black-letter formulations of the liability rules adopted by the majority of states. G. Edward White, TORT LAW IN AMERICA: AN INTELLECTUAL HISTORY 80 (rev. ed. 2003). Various state courts then often adopt specific Restatement provisions as their own law. The rule of strict products liability has been the most influential provision in a Restatement; it is the textual source of modern products liability law.

In 1961, the Institute adopted a draft rule imposing strict liability on sellers of food products, leaving open the question whether the rule should apply to other products as in *Henningsen*. In 1962, the draft extended strict liability to both food and products for "intimate bodily use," and again the draft was approved by the Institute. In 1963, the California Supreme Court accepted Traynor's argument for strict products liability in *Greenman v. Yuba Power Products*, a case not involving contaminated food. Both California and New Jersey at this point recognized a general rule of strict products liability. In 1964, the American Law Institute approved yet another draft, §402A of the *Restatement (Second) of Torts*, imposing strict liability on the sellers of defective products. By 1971, 28 states had adopted the rule of strict liability for product defects; by 1976, 41 states had adopted it. Today, only five states have formally rejected the doctrine of strict products liability, although "each applies the bulk of modern products liability jurisprudence as it has evolved across the nation." David G. Owen & Mary J. Davis, 1 OWEN & DAVIS ON PRODUCTS LIABILITY §5:6 (4th ed. 2014).

RESTATEMENT (SECOND) OF TORTS
Copyright 1965-2006 by the American Law Institute

§402A. Special Liability of Seller of Product for Physical Harm to User or Consumer

(1) One who sells any product in a defective condition unreasonably dangerous to the user or consumer or to his property is subject to liability for physical harm thereby caused to the ultimate user or consumer, or to his property, if
    (a) the seller is engaged in the business of selling such a product, and
    (b) it is expected to and does reach the user or consumer without substantial change in the condition in which it is sold.

I. The Implied Warranty

(2) The rule stated in Subsection (1) applies although

    (a) the seller has exercised all possible care in the preparation and sale of his product, and

    (b) the user or consumer has not bought the product from or entered into any contractual relation with the seller.

Comment:

a. This Section states a special rule applicable to sellers of products. The rule is one of strict liability, making the seller subject to liability to the user or consumer even though he has exercised all possible care in the preparation and sale of the product. The Section is inserted in the Chapter dealing with the negligence liability of suppliers of chattels, for convenience of reference and comparison with other Sections dealing with negligence. The rule stated here is not exclusive, and does not preclude liability based upon the alternative ground of negligence of the seller, where such negligence can be proved.

b. History. Since the early days of the common law those engaged in the business of selling food intended for human consumption have been held to a high degree of responsibility for their products. As long ago as 1266 there were enacted special criminal statutes imposing penalties upon victualers, vintners, brewers, butchers, cooks, and other persons who supplied "corrupt" food and drink. In the earlier part of this century this ancient attitude was reflected in a series of decisions in which the courts of a number of states sought to find some method of holding the seller of food liable to the ultimate consumer even though there was no showing of negligence on the part of the seller. These decisions represented a departure from, and an exception to, the general rule that a supplier of chattels was not liable to third persons in the absence of negligence or privity of contract. In the beginning, these decisions displayed considerable ingenuity in evolving more or less fictitious theories of liability to fit the case. The various devices included an agency of the intermediate dealer or another to purchase for the consumer, or to sell for the seller; a theoretical assignment of the seller's warranty to the intermediate dealer; a third party beneficiary contract; and an implied representation that the food was fit for consumption because it was placed on the market, as well as numerous others. In later years the courts have become more or less agreed upon the theory of a "warranty" from the seller to the consumer, either "running with the goods" by analogy to a covenant running with the land, or made directly to the consumer. Other decisions have indicated that the basis is merely one of strict liability in tort, which is not dependent upon either contract or negligence.

Recent decisions, since 1950, have extended this special rule of strict liability beyond the seller of food for human consumption. The first extension was into the closely analogous cases of other products intended for intimate bodily use, where, for example, as in the case of cosmetics, the application to the body of the consumer is external rather than internal. Beginning in 1958 with a Michigan case involving cinder building blocks, a number of recent decisions have discarded any limitation to intimate association with the body, and have extended the rule of strict liability to cover the sale of any product which, if it should prove to be defective, may be expected to cause physical harm to the consumer or his property.

c. On whatever theory, the justification for the strict liability has been said to be that the seller, by marketing his product for use and consumption, has undertaken and assumed a special responsibility toward any member of the consuming public who may be injured by it; that the public has the right to and does expect, in the case of products which it needs and for which it is forced to rely upon the seller, that reputable sellers will stand behind their goods; that public policy demands that the burden of accidental injuries caused by products intended for consumption be placed upon those who market them, and be treated as a cost of production against which liability insurance can be obtained; and that the consumer of such products is entitled to the maximum of protection at the hands of someone, and the proper persons to afford it are those who market the products.

d. The rule stated in this Section is not limited to the sale of food for human consumption, or other products for intimate bodily use, although it will obviously include them. It extends to any product sold in the condition, or substantially the same condition, in which it is expected to reach the ultimate user or consumer. Thus the rule stated applies to an automobile, a tire, an airplane, a grinding wheel, a water heater, a gas stove, a power tool, a riveting machine, a chair, and an insecticide. It applies also to products which, if they are defective, may be expected to and do cause only "physical harm" in the form of damage to the user's land or chattels, as in the case of animal food or a herbicide.

g. Defective condition. The rule stated in this Section applies only where the product is, at the time it leaves the seller's hands, in a condition not contemplated by the ultimate consumer, which will be unreasonably dangerous to him. The seller is not liable when he delivers the product in a safe condition, and subsequent mishandling or other causes make it harmful by the time it is consumed. The burden of proof that the product was in a defective condition at the time that it left the hands of the particular seller is upon the injured plaintiff; and unless evidence can be produced which will support the conclusion that it was then defective, the burden is not sustained.

Safe condition at the time of delivery by the seller will, however, include proper packaging, necessary sterilization, and other precautions required to permit the product to remain safe for a normal length of time when handled in a normal manner.

i. Unreasonably dangerous. The rule stated in this Section applies only where the defective condition of the product makes it unreasonably dangerous to the user or consumer. Many products cannot possibly be made entirely safe for all consumption, and any food or drug necessarily involves some risk of harm, if only from over-consumption. Ordinary sugar is a deadly poison to diabetics, and castor oil found use under Mussolini as an instrument of torture. That is not what is meant by "unreasonably dangerous" in this Section. The article sold must be dangerous to an extent beyond that which would be contemplated by the ordinary consumer who purchases it, with the ordinary knowledge common to the community as to its characteristics. Good whiskey is not unreasonably dangerous merely because it will make some people drunk, and is especially dangerous to alcoholics; but bad whiskey, containing a dangerous amount of fuel oil, is unreasonably dangerous. Good tobacco is not unreasonably dangerous merely because the effects of smoking may be harmful; but tobacco containing

I. The Implied Warranty

something like marijuana may be unreasonably dangerous. Good butter is not unreasonably dangerous merely because, if such be the case, it deposits cholesterol in the arteries and leads to heart attacks; but bad butter, contaminated with poisonous fish oil, is unreasonably dangerous.

l. User or consumer. In order for the rule stated in this Section to apply, it is not necessary that the ultimate user or consumer have acquired the product directly from the seller, although the rule applies equally if he does so. He may have acquired it through one or more intermediate dealers. It is not even necessary that the consumer have purchased the product at all. He may be a member of the family of the final purchaser, or his employee, or a guest at his table, or a mere donee from the purchaser. The liability stated is one in tort, and does not require any contractual relation, or privity of contract, between the plaintiff and the defendant.

"Consumers" include not only those who in fact consume the product, but also those who prepare it for consumption; and the housewife who contracts tularemia while cooking rabbits for her husband is included within the rule stated in this Section, as is also the husband who is opening a bottle of beer for his wife to drink. Consumption includes all ultimate uses for which the product is intended, and the customer in a beauty shop to whose hair a permanent wave solution is applied by the shop is a consumer. "User" includes those who are passively enjoying the benefit of the product, as in the case of passengers in automobiles or airplanes, as well as those who are utilizing it for the purpose of doing work upon it, as in the case of an employee of the ultimate buyer who is making repairs upon the automobile which he has purchased.

m. "Warranty." The liability stated in this Section does not rest upon negligence. It is strict liability. The basis of liability is purely one of tort.

A number of courts, seeking a theoretical basis for the liability, have resorted to a "warranty," either running with the goods sold, by analogy to covenants running with the land, or made directly to the consumer without contract. In some instances this theory has proved to be an unfortunate one. Although warranty was in its origin a matter of tort liability, and it is generally agreed that a tort action will still lie for its breach, it has become so identified in practice with a contract of sale between the plaintiff and the defendant that the warranty theory has become something of an obstacle to the recognition of the strict liability where there is no such contract. There is nothing in this Section which would prevent any court from treating the rule stated as a matter of "warranty" to the user or consumer. But if this is done, it should be recognized and understood that the "warranty" is a very different kind of warranty from those usually found in the sale of goods, and that it is not subject to the various contract rules which have grown up to surround such sales.

The rule stated in this Section does not require any reliance on the part of the consumer upon the reputation, skill, or judgment of the seller who is to be held liable, nor any representation or undertaking on the part of that seller. The seller is strictly liable although, as is frequently the case, the consumer does not even know who he is at the time of consumption.... In short, "warranty" must be given a new and different meaning if it is used in connection with this Section. It is much simpler to regard the liability here stated as merely one of strict liability in tort.

NOTES AND QUESTIONS

1. *Strict products liability and the implied warranty.* The rule of strict products liability under §402A is limited to a product defect, which in turn is defined terms of consumer expectations as per the implied warranty. According to comment g, a "defect" in a product is "a condition not contemplated by the ultimate consumer, which will be unreasonably dangerous to him." According to comment i, to be "unreasonably dangerous" the "article sold must be dangerous to an extent beyond that which would be contemplated by the ordinary consumer who purchases it, with the ordinary knowledge common to the community as to its characteristics." This method for determining a product defect is known as the *consumer expectations test*. Based on this definition of defect, the rule of strict liability for the sale of a *defective* product protects consumer expectations of product safety, the same expectation protected by the implied warranty. Consequently, comment m states that there is no substantive difference between the rule of strict products liability and the tort version of the implied warranty. *Accord* Commonwealth v. Johnson Insulation, 682 N.E.2d 1323, 1326 (Mass. 1997) (recognizing that the implied warranty "without most contractually based defenses" is "congruent in nearly all respects with the principles expressed in Restatement (Second) of Torts §402A") (internal quotes and citation omitted)).

2. *Inherent limitations of strict products liability?* How does the §402A black-letter rule apply in the case of contaminated food or an exploding soda bottle? Is the formulation of the rule implicitly limited to these types of product defects? To address this question, consider how the liability rule applies to a claim that an automobile is defective for not incorporating airbags into the design. How would the rule apply when the danger is apparent, as would be the case if the manufacturer slapped a sticker on the windshield of the vehicle proclaiming, "Warning: No airbag in vehicle"? Insofar as §402A does not clearly address these issues, is that limitation inherent in a restatement of the case law involving products like contaminated food and exploding soda bottles? These questions are addressed in Chapter 3.

3. *Strict liability and the express warranty.* The rule of strict products liability in §402A has a companion provision §402B, which provides that a seller is liable to a consumer who justifiably relies on a material misrepresentation and suffers physical harm as a result, even if the misrepresentation was innocently made and the consumer did not buy the product from the seller. Does the protection of consumer expectations justify this rule of strict liability, thereby unifying §402B with the rule of strict products liability in §402A? *See* Note 3, p. 41 *supra*.

4. *The global influence of §402A.* Countries around the world have adopted liability standards substantively similar to those in §402A of the *Restatement (Second)*. The European Economic Community Directive on Liability for Defective Products states that "[t]he producer shall be liable for damage caused by a defect in his product." A product is defective if it "does not provide the safety which a person is entitled to expect, taking all circumstances into account." Council Directive 85/374/EEC of July 25, 1985 on the Approximation of the Laws, Regulations and Administrative Provisions of

the Member States Concerning Liability for Defective Products, art. 1 & 6, 1985 O.J. (L 210) 29. The Directive, which is covered in Chapter 17, has influenced other countries. Hence the "U.S. experience with the special products liability rule stated in section 402A . . . has profound significance for the corresponding products rule that is now in place throughout the European Union and in many other countries such as Japan and Australia." Jane Stapleton, *Liability for Drugs in the U.S. and EU: Rhetoric and Reality*, 26 Rev. Litig. 991, 991-992 (2007).

II. THE NEGLIGENCE PRINCIPLE

The implied warranty is not the only doctrine capable of justifying strict products liability; the principle of negligence liability provides an independently sufficient doctrinal basis for the liability rule. The negligence principle first overturned the privity rule, subsequently provided a doctrinal rationale for strict products liability, and now largely forms the liability framework in the *Restatement (Third) of Torts: Products Liability*.

A. The Demise of the Privity Bar to Negligence Liability

The following case was decided shortly after *Winterbottom v. Wright*, p. 2 *supra*. Consider whether the court's reasoning effectively eliminates the requirement of contractual privity that the court adopted in *Winterbottom*. How does the rationale for the court's decision compare to the logic of the implied warranty?

THOMAS v. WINCHESTER
Court of Appeals of New York, 1852
6 N.Y. 397

RUGGLES, C.J. This is an action brought to recover damages from the defendant for negligently putting up, labeling and selling as and for the extract of dandelion, which is a simple and harmless medicine, a jar of the extract of belladonna, which is a deadly poison; by means of which the plaintiff Mary Ann Thomas, to whom, being sick, a dose of dandelion was prescribed by a physician, and a portion of the contents of the jar, was administered as and for the extract of dandelion, was greatly injured, &c.

The facts proved were briefly these: Mrs. Thomas being in ill health, her physician prescribed for her a dose of dandelion. Her husband purchased what was believed to be the medicine prescribed, at the store of Dr. Foord, a physician and druggist in Cazenovia, Madison county, where the plaintiffs reside.

A small quantity of the medicine thus purchased was administered to Mrs. Thomas, on whom it produced very alarming effects; such as coldness of the surface and extremities, feebleness of circulation, spasms of the muscles, giddiness of the head, dilation of the pupils of the eyes, and derangement of mind. She recovered however, after some time, from its effects, although for a short time her life was thought to be in great danger. The medicine administered was belladonna, and not dandelion. The jar from which it was taken was labeled "½ lb. dandelion, prepared by A. Gilbert, No. 108, John-street, N.Y. Jar 8 oz." The extract contained in the jar sold to Foord was not manufactured by the defendant, but was purchased by him from another manufacturer or dealer. The extract of dandelion and the extract of belladonna resemble each other in color, consistence, smell and taste; but may on careful examination be distinguished the one from the other by those who are well acquainted with these articles. Gilbert's labels were paid for by Winchester and used in his business with his knowledge and assent.

The case depends on the first point taken by the defendant on his motion for a nonsuit; and the question is, whether the defendant, being a remote vendor of the medicine, and there being no privity or connection between him and the plaintiffs, the action can be maintained.

If, in labeling a poisonous drug with the name of a harmless medicine, for public market, no duty was violated by the defendant, excepting that which he owed to his immediate vendee, in virtue of his contract of sale, this action cannot be maintained. If *A* build a wagon and sell it to *B*, who sells it to *C*, and *C* hires it to *D*, who in consequence of the gross negligence of *A* in building the wagon is overturned and injured, *D* cannot recover damages against *A*, the builder. *A*'s obligation to build the wagon faithfully, arises solely out of his contract with *B*. The public have nothing to do with it. Misfortune to third persons, not parties to the contract, would not be a natural and necessary consequence of the builder's negligence; and such negligence is not an act imminently dangerous to human life.

This was the ground on which the case of *Winterbottom v. Wright* was decided. *A* contracted with the postmaster general to provide a coach to convey the mail bags along a certain line of road, and *B* and others, also contracted to horse the coach along the same line. *B* and his co-contractors hired *C*, who was the plaintiff, to drive the coach. The coach, in consequence of some latent defect, broke down; the plaintiff was thrown from his seat and lamed. It was held that *C* could not maintain an action against *A* for the injury thus sustained. The reason of the decision is best stated by Baron Rolfe. *A*'s duty to keep the coach in good condition, was a duty to the postmaster general, with whom he made his contract, and not a duty to the driver employed by the owners of the horses.

But the case in hand stands on a different ground. The defendant was a dealer in poisonous drugs. Gilbert was his agent in preparing them for market. The death or great bodily harm of some person was the natural and almost inevitable consequence of the sale of belladonna by means of the false label.

Gilbert, the defendant's agent, would have been punishable for manslaughter if Mrs. Thomas had died in consequence of taking the falsely labeled medicine. Every man who, by his culpable negligence, causes the death of another, although without intent to kill, is guilty of manslaughter. A chemist who negligently sells laudanum in a phial labeled as paregoric, and thereby causes the death of a person to whom it is administered, is guilty of manslaughter. So highly does the law value human life, that it admits of no justification wherever life has been lost and the carelessness or negligence of one person has contributed to the death of another. And this rule applies not only where the death of one is occasioned by the negligent act of another, but where it is caused by the negligent omission of a duty of that other. Although the defendant Winchester may not be answerable criminally for the negligence of his agent, there can be no doubt of his liability in a civil action, in which the act of the agent is to be regarded as the act of the principal.

In respect to the wrongful and criminal character of the negligence complained of, this case differs widely from those put by the defendant's counsel. No such imminent danger existed in those cases. In the present case the sale of the poisonous article was made to a dealer in drugs, and not to a consumer. The injury therefore was not likely to fall on him, or on his vendee who was also a dealer; but much more likely to be visited on a remote purchaser, as actually happened. The defendant's negligence put human life in imminent danger. Can it be said that there was no duty on the part of the defendant, to avoid the creation of that danger by the exercise of greater caution? or that the exercise of that caution was a duty only to his immediate vendee, whose life was not endangered? The defendant's duty arose out of the nature of his business and the danger to others incident to its mismanagement. Nothing but mischief like that which actually happened could have been expected from sending the poison falsely labeled into the market; and the defendant is justly responsible for the probable consequences of the act.

In Longmeid v. Holliday (6 Law and Eq. Rep. 562), the distinction is recognized between an act of negligence imminently dangerous to the lives of others, and one that is not so. In the former case, the party guilty of the negligence is liable to the party injured, whether there be a contract between them or not; in the latter, the negligent party is liable only to the party with whom he contracted, and on the ground that negligence is a breach of the contract.

Judgment affirmed.

NOTES AND QUESTIONS

1. *Reconsidering* Winterbottom. In light of *Winchester*, we can now more fully understand the privity requirement adopted in *Winterbottom*. That case was decided under the writ system; the plaintiff could recover only by alleging a single claim that fit within a recognized writ or cause of action. On the alleged facts in *Winterbottom*, "[t]here simply were no precedents authorizing recovery in tort." Vernon Palmer, *Why Privity Entered Tort—An Historical Examination of* Winterbottom v. Wright, 27 Am J. Legal Hist. 85, 94 (1983).

Lacking any precedents supporting recovery in tort, the plaintiff had to argue that the contract itself provided the basis for recovery. Hence the court in *Winterbottom* merely concluded that one must be a party to the contract in order to have any contractually based rights. The case did not stand "for the proposition that the background existence of a contract in the facts operated as a broad shield against tort duties to third parties," particularly since at this time the "common law was against this proposition, having asserted from the earliest times that wrongs require no privity because they are essentially actions between strangers." *Id.* at 92-93.

During this era, courts had not formulated negligence into an independent basis of liability. Negligence was only an element of various writs rather than a tort unto itself. Shortly after *Winterbottom* was decided, another English case expressly recognized a legal duty, not dependent on contract, "when any one delivers to another without notice an instrument in its nature dangerous, or under particular circumstances, as a loaded gun which he himself loaded, and that other person to whom it is delivered is injured thereby." Longmeid v. Holliday, 6 Ex. 761, 767 (1851). Like the court in *Longmeid*, the court in *Winchester* did not reject the *Winterbottom* privity requirement; it instead recognized an independent legal duty involving the delivery of inherently or imminently dangerous products, such as the defective gun in *Longmeid* and the mislabeled poison in the case at hand. Unless the product had these characteristics, the requirement of privity limited the tort duty.

According to the court in *Winchester*, a defective gun or mislabeled poison creates a foreseeable risk of physical harm properly governed by the tort duty, whereas the defective wagon in *Winterbottom* did not create a foreseeable risk of physical harm. Is this reasoning persuasive? Consider in this respect the ability of the user to inspect the product for defects prior to use or consumption. Did the court in *Winterbottom* justify the limitation of the tort duty in these terms?

2. *Reconsidering the implied warranty.* Recall that the tort version of the implied warranty was limited to food products until the twentieth century, based on the assumption that consumers could adequately inspect nonfood products and discover any defects or otherwise bargain for protection from the seller. In addition to explaining why the plaintiff could not rely on the implied warranty to recover in *Winterbottom*, this aspect of the implied warranty also shows why the court in *Winchester* could have relied on inspection as the reason for concluding that the physical harm in *Winterbottom* was not foreseeably caused by the defect.

3. *Subsequent developments in the case law.* After the writ system was abolished in the mid-nineteenth century, courts continued to rely on the rules adopted in both *Winterbottom* and *Winchester*. By the early twentieth century, virtually all courts across the country followed the "general rule . . . that a contractor, manufacturer, or vendor is not liable to third parties who have no contractual relationship with him for negligence in the construction, manufacture, or sale of the articles he handles." Huset v. J.I. Case Threshing Machine Co., 120 F. 865, 867-868 (8th Cir. 1903). "But while this general rule is both established and settled, there are, as is usually the case, exceptions to it as well defined and settled as the rule itself." *Id.* at 870. The case law had recognized three exceptions to the requirement of privity. Under the most important exception, "an act of negligence of a manufacturer or vendor which is imminently dangerous to the life or health of mankind, and which is committed in the preparation or sale of an article intended to preserve, destroy, or affect human life, is actionable by third parties who suffer from the negligence." *Id.* (citing numerous cases, including *Thomas v. Winchester*). Inevitably, courts had to confront the question of whether the "exceptions" were in fact constitutive of a more general rule of liability.

II. The Negligence Principle

MACPHERSON v. BUICK MOTOR CO.
Court of Appeals of New York, 1916
111 N.E. 1050

CARDOZO, J. The defendant is a manufacturer of automobiles. It sold an automobile to a retail dealer. The retail dealer resold to the plaintiff. While the plaintiff was in the car, it suddenly collapsed. He was thrown out and injured. One of the wheels was made of defective wood, and its spokes crumbled into fragments. The wheel was not made by the defendant; it was bought from another manufacturer. There is evidence, however, that its defects could have been discovered by reasonable inspection, and that inspection was omitted. There is no claim that the defendant knew of the defect and willfully concealed it. The charge is one, not of fraud, but of negligence. The question to be determined is whether the defendant owed a duty of care and vigilance to any one but the immediate purchaser.

The foundations of this branch of the law, at least in this state, were laid in Thomas v. Winchester, 6 N.Y. 397 (1852). A poison was falsely labeled. The sale was made to a druggist, who in turn sold to a customer. The customer recovered damages from the seller who affixed the label. "The defendant's negligence," it was said, "put human life in imminent danger." A poison falsely labeled is likely to injure any one who gets it. Because the danger is to be foreseen, there is a duty to avoid the injury. Cases were cited by way of illustration in which manufacturers were not subject to any duty irrespective of contract. The distinction was said to be that their conduct, though negligent, was not likely to result in injury to any one except the purchaser. We are not required to say whether the chance of injury was always as remote as the distinction assumes. Some of the illustrations might be rejected today. The *principle* of the distinction is for present purposes the important thing.

Thomas v. Winchester became quickly a landmark of the law. In the application of its principle there may, at times, have been uncertainty or even error. There has never in this state been doubt or disavowal of the principle itself. The chief cases are well known, yet to recall some of them will be helpful. Loop v. Litchfield, 42 N.Y. 351 (1870), is the earliest. It was the case of a defect in a small balance wheel used on a circular saw. The manufacturer pointed out the defect to the buyer, who wished a cheap article and was ready to assume the risk. The risk can hardly have been an imminent one, for the wheel lasted five years before it broke. In the meanwhile the buyer had made a lease of the machinery. It was held that the manufacturer was not answerable to the lessee. *Loop v. Litchfield* was followed in Losee v. Clute, 51 N.Y. 494 (1873), the case of the explosion of a steam boiler. That decision has been criticised; but it must be confined to its special facts. It was put upon the ground that the risk of injury was too remote. The buyer in that case had not only accepted the boiler, but had tested it. The manufacturer knew that his own test was not the final one. The finality of the test has a bearing on the measure of diligence owing to persons other than the purchaser.

These early cases suggest a narrow construction of the rule. Later cases, however, evince a more liberal spirit. First in importance is Devlin v. Smith, 89 N.Y. 470 (1882). The defendant, a contractor, built a scaffold for a painter.

The painter's servants were injured. The contractor was held liable. He knew that the scaffold, if improperly constructed, was a most dangerous trap. He knew that it was to be used by the workmen. He was building it for that very purpose. Building it for their use, he owed them a duty, irrespective of his contract with their master, to build it with care.

From *Devlin v. Smith* we pass over intermediate cases and turn to the latest case in this court in which *Thomas v. Winchester* was followed. That case is Statler v. Ray Mfg. Co., 195 N.Y. 478, 480 (1909). The defendant manufactured a large coffee urn. It was installed in a restaurant. When heated, the urn exploded and injured the plaintiff. We held that the manufacturer was liable. We said that the urn "was of such a character inherently that, when applied to the purposes for which it was designed, it was liable to become a source of great danger to many people if not carefully and properly constructed."

The defendant argues that things imminently dangerous to life are poisons, explosives, deadly weapons—things whose normal function it is to injure or destroy. But whatever the rule in *Thomas v. Winchester* may once have been, it has no longer that restricted meaning. A scaffold is not inherently a destructive instrument. It becomes destructive only if imperfectly constructed. A large coffee urn may have within itself, if negligently made, the potency of danger, yet no one thinks of it as an implement whose normal function is destruction. We have mentioned only cases in this court. But the rule has received a like extension in our courts of intermediate appeal. We are not required at this time either to approve or to disapprove the application of the rule that was made in these cases. It is enough that they help to characterize the trend of judicial thought.

Devlin v. Smith was decided in 1882. A year later a very similar case came before the Court of Appeal in England (Heaven v. Pender, L.R. [11 Q. B. D.] 503). We find in the opinion of Brett, M., afterwards Lord Esher, the same conception of a duty, irrespective of contract, imposed upon the manufacturer by the law itself:

> Whenever one person supplies goods, or machinery, or the like, for the purpose of their being used by another person under such circumstances that every one of ordinary sense would, if he thought, recognize at once that unless he used ordinary care and skill with regard to the condition of the thing supplied or the mode of supplying it, there will be danger of injury to the person or property of him for whose use the thing is supplied, and who is to use it, a duty arises to use ordinary care and skill as to the condition or manner of supplying such thing.

He then points out that for a neglect of such ordinary care or skill whereby injury happens, the appropriate remedy is an action for negligence. The right to enforce this liability is not to be confined to the immediate buyer. The right, he says, extends to the persons or class of persons for whose use the thing is supplied. It is enough that the goods "would in all probability be used at once . . . before a reasonable opportunity for discovering any defect which might exist," and that the thing supplied is of such a nature "that a neglect of ordinary care or skill as to its condition or the manner of supplying it would probably cause danger to the person or property of the person for whose use it was supplied, and who was about to use it." On the other hand, he would

II. The Negligence Principle

exclude a case "in which the goods are supplied under circumstances in which it would be a chance by whom they would be used or whether they would be used or not, or whether they would be used before there would probably be means of observing any defect," or where the goods are of such a nature that "a want of care or skill as to their condition or the manner of supplying them would not probably produce danger of injury to person or property." What was said by Lord Esher in that case did not command the full assent of his associates. His opinion has been criticized. [ ] Perhaps it may need some qualification even in our own state. Like most attempts at comprehensive definition, it may involve errors of inclusion and of exclusion. But its tests and standards, at least in their underlying principles, with whatever qualification may be called for as they are applied to varying conditions, are the tests and standards of our law.

We hold, then, that the principle of *Thomas v. Winchester* is not limited to poisons, explosives, and things of like nature, to things which in their normal operation are implements of destruction. If the nature of a thing is such that it is reasonably certain to place life and limb in peril when negligently made, it is then a thing of danger. Its nature gives warning of the consequences to be expected. If to the element of danger there is added knowledge that the thing will be used by persons other than the purchaser, and used without new tests, then, irrespective of contract, the manufacturer of this thing of danger is under a duty to make it carefully. That is as far as we are required to go for the decision of this case. We are dealing now with the liability of the manufacturer of the finished product, who puts it on the market to be used without inspection by his customers. If he is negligent, where danger is to be foreseen, a liability will follow. We have put aside the notion that the duty to safeguard life and limb, when the consequences of negligence may be foreseen, grows out of contract and nothing else. We have put the source of the obligation where it ought to be. We have put its source in the law.

From this survey of the decisions, there thus emerges a definition of the duty of a manufacturer which enables us to measure this defendant's liability. Beyond all question, the nature of an automobile gives warning of probable danger if its construction is defective. This automobile was designed to go fifty miles an hour. Unless its wheels were sound and strong, injury was almost certain. It was as much a thing of danger as a defective engine for a railroad. The defendant knew the danger. It knew also that the car would be used by persons other than the buyer. The dealer was indeed the one person of whom it might be said with some approach to certainty that by him the car would not be used. Yet the defendant would have us say that he was the one person whom it was under a legal duty to protect. The law does not lead us to so inconsequent a conclusion. Precedents drawn from the days of travel by stage coach do not fit the conditions of travel today. The principle that the danger must be imminent does not change, but the things subject to the principle do change. They are whatever the needs of life in a developing civilization require them to be.

Subtle distinctions are drawn by the defendant between things inherently dangerous and things imminently dangerous, but the case does not turn upon these verbal niceties. If danger was to be expected as reasonably certain, there was a duty of vigilance, and this whether you call the danger inherent or imminent.

We think the defendant was not absolved from a duty of inspection because it bought the wheels from a reputable manufacturer. It was not merely a dealer in automobiles. It was a manufacturer of automobiles. It was responsible for the finished product. It was not at liberty to put the finished product on the market without subjecting the component parts to ordinary and simple tests. The obligation to inspect must vary with the nature of the thing to be inspected. The more probable the danger, the greater the need of caution.

The judgment should be affirmed with costs.

NOTES AND QUESTIONS

1. *A landmark decision.* Did the court in *MacPherson* reject the "imminently dangerous" requirement, or did it instead broaden the definition of products governed by that requirement? Following *MacPherson*, courts in New York struggled with this question, although courts in other jurisdictions quickly realized that the case effectively abolished the privity requirement for all types of defective products. This landmark case is now widely recognized as establishing the principle that a product seller's liability for negligence is not circumscribed by the requirement of contractual privity. After *MacPherson* "swept the country," it "laid the foundation for strict products liability." William L. Prosser, *The Assault on the Citadel (Strict Liability to the Consumer)*, 69 Yale L.J. 1099, 1100-1103 (1960).

2. *Reconsidering the implied warranty.* According to Judge Cardozo, what is the basis of the tort duty? Is it limited to negligence claims, or does it apply to rules of strict liability as well? Consider in this regard how Cardozo's reasoning applies to the tort version of the implied warranty of merchantable quality. Having based the tort duty on the foreseeable risk of physical harm rather than the type of product, the logic of *MacPherson* implies that there is no persuasive reason to distinguish contaminated food from other defective products. Like contaminated food, any defective product can create a foreseeable risk of physical harm governed by the tort duty. For centuries, the implied warranty had imposed a tort duty on the sellers of contaminated food. Cardozo's reasoning in *MacPherson* showed why this tort duty is not limited by the inherent characteristics of food products, enabling courts to defensibly extend the implied warranty from contaminated food to other types of defective products that foreseeably cause physical harm—the line of cases discussed in Part A *supra*.

3. *Reconsidering the concern about excessive liability.* In eliminating the privity requirement, did Judge Cardozo address the concern about excessive liability that the court in *Winterbottom* had invoked to justify this limitation of the tort duty? Is it possible to square *MacPherson*'s rejection of the privity requirement with the retention of that requirement by the New York Court of Appeals in a later case involving the negligence of a public utility, *Strauss v. Belle Realty Co.*, p. 20 *supra*? Recall that in *Strauss*, the court limited the tort duty to the contractual relationship while also recognizing that doing so would hardly "confer immunity from negligence." 482 N.E.2d

II. The Negligence Principle

at 38. Although the plaintiff in the case at hand did not satisfy the privity requirement, in numerous other cases, those injured by the utility's negligence would also have a direct contractual relationship, enabling them to sue for breach of the limited tort duty. Given the prospect of that limited but nevertheless substantial scope of liability, the public utility would still have a sufficient financial incentive for complying with the tort duty.

At the time of *Winterbottom*, a tort duty limited to the contractual relationship had these same properties: the consumer or user of the product often purchased it directly from the maker. Although limited, the potential scope of tort liability was still sufficient to render the duty meaningful. But with the onset of the industrial revolution, the channels of product distribution substantially changed. Based on Cardozo's reasoning in *MacPherson*, would a tort duty limited by the requirement of privity have much significance in the modern economy? By the twentieth century, did the privity requirement effectively result in *unduly limited liability*, thereby eliminating the now outdated concern about excessive liability that had first justified the requirement?

4. *From negligence to strict liability.* In addition to providing the logic that enabled courts to extend the implied warranty from contaminated food to other types of defective products, *MacPherson* also laid a distinctive foundation for strict products liability based on the negligence principle. To be sure, the negligence principle would seem to be flatly inconsistent with a rule of strict liability, but they can be unified by problems involving proof of negligence liability.

B. Proof of Negligence Liability

After the privity bar to negligence liability had been eliminated, the most difficult issue in product cases typically involved proof of negligence. To establish negligence liability, plaintiffs routinely invoked the doctrine *res ipsa loquitur*, a Latin phrase meaning "the thing speaks for itself." The doctrine permits proof of negligence with circumstantial evidence:

> The factfinder may infer that the defendant has been negligent when the accident causing the plaintiff's physical harm is a type of accident that ordinarily happens as a result of the negligence of a class of actors of which the defendant is the relevant member.

Restatement (Third) of Torts: Liability for Physical and Emotional Harms §17 (2010).

Given the circumstances of such an accident, the jury as fact finder can reasonably infer that the plaintiff's injury, more likely than not, was caused by the negligence of the defendant. The accident "speaks for itself" on the issue, satisfying the plaintiff's burden of proving negligence.

In a product case, does the plaintiff establish res ipsa loquitur by proving that she was injured by a defect in the product sold by the defendant? Do product defects "ordinarily happen as a result of negligence," or can they be an inevitable result of reasonable, but imperfect, manufacturing processes?

ESCOLA v. COCA COLA BOTTLING CO.
Supreme Court of California, 1944
150 P.2d 436

GIBSON, C.J. Plaintiff, a waitress in a restaurant, was injured when a bottle of Coca Cola broke in her hand. She alleged that defendant company, which had bottled and delivered the alleged defective bottle to her employer, was negligent in selling "bottles containing said beverage which on account of excessive pressure of gas or by reason of some defect in the bottle was dangerous . . . and likely to explode." This appeal is from a judgment upon a jury verdict in favor of plaintiff.

Defendant's driver delivered several cases of Coca Cola to the restaurant, placing them on the floor, one on top of the other, under and behind the counter, where they remained at least thirty-six hours. Immediately before the accident, plaintiff picked up the top case and set it upon a near-by ice cream cabinet in front of and about three feet from the refrigerator. She then proceeded to take the bottles from the case with her right hand, one at a time, and put them into the refrigerator. Plaintiff testified that after she had placed three bottles in the refrigerator and had moved the fourth bottle about 18 inches from the case "it exploded in my hand." The bottle broke into two jagged pieces and inflicted a deep five-inch cut, severing blood vessels, nerves and muscles of the thumb and palm of the hand. Plaintiff further testified that when the bottle exploded, "It made a sound similar to an electric light bulb that would have dropped. It made a loud pop." Plaintiff's employer testified, "I was about twenty feet from where it actually happened and I heard the explosion." A fellow employee, on the opposite side of the counter, testified that plaintiff "had the bottle, I should judge, waist high, and I know that it didn't bang either the case or the door or another bottle . . . when it popped. It sounded just like a fruit jar would blow up. . . ." The witness further testified that the contents of the bottle "flew all over herself and myself and the walls and one thing and another."

The top portion of the bottle, with the cap, remained in plaintiff's hand, and the lower portion fell to the floor but did not break. The broken bottle was not produced at the trial, the pieces having been thrown away by an employee of the restaurant shortly after the accident. Plaintiff, however, described the broken pieces, and a diagram of the bottle was made showing the location of the "fracture line" where the bottle broke in two.

One of defendant's drivers, called as a witness by plaintiff, testified that he had seen other bottles of Coca Cola in the past explode and had found broken bottles in the warehouse when he took the cases out, but that he did not know what made them blow up.

Plaintiff then rested her case, having announced to the court that being unable to show any specific acts of negligence she relied completely on the doctrine of res ipsa loquitur.

Defendant contends that the doctrine of res ipsa loquitur does not apply in this case, and that the evidence is insufficient to support the judgment.

Many jurisdictions have applied the doctrine in cases involving exploding bottles of carbonated beverages. [ ] Other courts for varying reasons have refused to apply the doctrine in such cases. [ ] It would serve no useful purpose to discuss the reasoning of the foregoing cases in detail, since the problem is whether

II. The Negligence Principle

under the facts shown in the instant case the conditions warranting application of the doctrine have been satisfied.

Res ipsa loquitur does not apply unless (1) defendant had exclusive control of the thing causing the injury and (2) the accident is of such a nature that it ordinarily would not occur in the absence of negligence by the defendant.

Upon an examination of the record, the evidence appears sufficient to support a reasonable inference that the bottle here involved was not damaged by any extraneous force after delivery to the restaurant by defendant. It follows, therefore, that the bottle was in some manner defective at the time defendant relinquished control, because sound and properly prepared bottles of carbonated liquids do not ordinarily explode when carefully handled.

The next question, then, is whether plaintiff may rely upon the doctrine of res ipsa loquitur to supply an inference that defendant's negligence was responsible for the defective condition of the bottle at the time it was delivered to the restaurant. Under the general rules pertaining to the doctrine, as set forth above, it must appear that bottles of carbonated liquid are not ordinarily defective without negligence by the bottling company.

An explosion such as took place here might have been caused by an excessive internal pressure in a sound bottle, by a defect in the glass of a bottle containing a safe pressure, or by a combination of these two possible causes. The question is whether under the evidence there was a probability that defendant was negligent in any of these respects. If so, the doctrine of res ipsa loquitur applies.

The bottle was admittedly charged with gas under pressure, and the charging of the bottle was within the exclusive control of defendant. As it is a matter of common knowledge that an overcharge would not ordinarily result without negligence, it follows under the doctrine of res ipsa loquitur that if the bottle was in fact excessively charged an inference of defendant's negligence would arise. If the explosion resulted from a defective bottle containing a safe pressure, the defendant would be liable if it negligently failed to discover such flaw. If the defect were visible, an inference of negligence would arise from the failure of defendant to discover it. Where defects are discoverable, it may be assumed that they will not ordinarily escape detection if a reasonable inspection is made, and if such a defect is overlooked an inference arises that a proper inspection was not made. A difficult problem is presented where the defect is unknown and consequently might have been one not discoverable by a reasonable, practicable inspection. [We have previously] refused to take judicial notice of the technical practices and information available to the bottling industry for finding defects which cannot be seen. In the present case, however, we are supplied with evidence [from the defendant] of the standard methods used for testing bottles.

A chemical engineer for the Owens-Illinois Glass Company and its Pacific Coast subsidiary, maker of Coca Cola bottles, explained how glass is manufactured and the methods used in testing and inspecting bottles. He testified that his company is the largest manufacturer of glass containers in the United States, and that it uses the standard methods for testing bottles recommended by the glass containers association. A pressure test is made by taking a sample from each mold every three hours—approximately one out of every 600 bottles—and subjecting the sample to an internal pressure of 450 pounds per square inch, which is sustained for one minute. (The normal pressure in Coca Cola bottles is less than 50 pounds per square inch.) The sample bottles are also subjected to the standard thermal shock test. The witness stated that these tests are "pretty near" infallible.

It thus appears that there is available to the industry a commonly used method of testing bottles for defects not apparent to the eye, which is almost infallible. Since Coca Cola bottles are subjected to these tests by the manufacturer, it is not likely that they contain defects when delivered to the bottler which are not discoverable by visual inspection. Both new and used bottles are filled and distributed by defendant. The used bottles are not again subjected to the tests referred to above, and it may be inferred that defects not discoverable by visual inspection do not develop in bottles after they are manufactured. Obviously, if such defects do occur in used bottles there is a duty upon the bottler to make appropriate tests before they are refilled, and if such tests are not commercially practicable the bottles should not be re-used. This would seem to be particularly true where a charged liquid is placed in the bottle. It follows that a defect which would make the bottle unsound could be discovered by reasonable and practicable tests.

Although it is not clear in this case whether the explosion was caused by an excessive charge or a defect in the glass there is a sufficient showing that neither cause would ordinarily have been present if due care had been used. Further, defendant had exclusive control over both the charging and inspection of the bottles. Accordingly, all the requirements necessary to entitle plaintiff to rely on the doctrine of res ipsa loquitur to supply an inference of negligence are present.

It is true that defendant presented evidence tending to show that it exercised considerable precaution by carefully regulating and checking the pressure in the bottles and by making visual inspections for defects in the glass at several stages during the bottling process. It is well settled, however, that when a defendant produces evidence to rebut the inference of negligence which arises upon application of the doctrine of res ipsa loquitur, it is ordinarily a question of fact for the jury to determine whether the inference has been dispelled.

The judgment is affirmed.

TRAYNOR, J., *concurring*. I concur in the judgment, but I believe the manufacturer's negligence should no longer be singled out as the basis of a plaintiff's right to recover in cases like the present one. . . . The inference of negligence may be dispelled by an affirmative showing of proper care. If the evidence against the fact inferred is "clear, positive, uncontradicted, and of such a nature that it can not rationally be disbelieved, the court must instruct the jury that the nonexistence of the fact has been established as a matter of law." An injured person, however, is not ordinarily in a position to refute such evidence or identify the cause of the defect, for he can hardly be familiar with the manufacturing process as the manufacturer himself is. In leaving it to the jury to decide whether the inference has been dispelled, regardless of the evidence against it, the negligence rule approaches the rule of strict liability. It is needlessly circuitous to make negligence the basis of recovery and impose what is in reality liability without negligence. If public policy demands that a manufacturer of goods be responsible for their quality regardless of negligence there is no reason not to fix that responsibility openly.

[Traynor then discusses the policy reasons and doctrinal rationales for strict liability in the portion of his concurring opinion excerpted in the prior section of this chapter.]

II. The Negligence Principle

NOTES AND QUESTIONS

1. *The application of res ipsa loquitur in product cases.* The mere fact that any accident occurs is not sufficient proof that the accident was caused by negligence, much less the negligence of the defendant. Instead, the circumstances of an accident sufficiently prove negligence only when the plaintiff has provided evidence satisfying the requirements of res ipsa loquitur. Did the majority's reasoning in *Escola* persuasively show that the plaintiff had satisfied this evidentiary burden?

Consider the possibility that the exploding bottle had been reused and exploded due to a nonobservable, hairline fracture in the bottle. According to the court, the existence of such a defect would establish negligence because if there were no "commercially practicable" test for detecting such defects, then it would be unreasonably dangerous to reuse or recycle bottles. Is this reasoning sound? If the mere fact of accident does not establish negligence, then reasonable care does not necessarily require the complete elimination of risk. Why, then, would it necessarily be unreasonable to recycle bottles when doing so could not be completely safe?

In general, reasonable care does not require manufacturing or quality-control procedures that completely eliminate the risk of defect. Despite the exercise of reasonable care, some defective products will inevitably enter the stream of commerce and injure consumers. Does the court ever address this possibility? Consider James M. Guiher & Stanley C. Morris, *Handling Food Product Liability Cases*, 1 Food Drug Cosm. L.Q. 109, 130-131 (1946) ("The *bona fide* claimant will usually find it well nigh impossible to prove specific negligence on the part of a food processor in the processing of a particular packaged item. . . . On the other hand, the *bona fide* processor who is using the most modern methods and equipment in his plant is generally incapable of showing more than the merits of the system, being unable to give specific evidence as to the single package allegedly occasioning injury to the consumer. The problem of resolving the rights of the parties in a manner consistent with our conception of ethics and justice is therefore unusually difficult. . . . [M]ost of the courts have resolved the problem in a manner quite harsh toward those processing and handling food products.").

As William Prosser observed, the food cases were not novel in this regard:

> When a negligence action is brought against a manufacturer, the plaintiff is faced with two initial tasks. One is to prove that his injury has been caused by a defect in the product. The other is to prove that the defect existed when the product left the hands of the defendant. . . . Once over these two hurdles, the plaintiff has a third task, to prove that the defect was there because of the defendant's negligence. This is by far the easiest of the three, and it is one in which the plaintiff almost never fails.
>
> It is true that he has the burden of proof on the issue of negligence. It is true also that he seldom, if ever, has any direct evidence of what went on in the defendant's plant. But in every jurisdiction, he is aided by the doctrine of *res ipsa loquitur*, or by its practical equivalent. In all

jurisdictions this at least gives rise to a permissible inference of the defendant's negligence, which gets the plaintiff to the jury. And in cases against manufacturers, once the cause of harm is laid at their doorstep, a jury verdict for the defendant on the negligence issue is virtually unknown.

William L. Prosser, *The Assault Upon the Citadel (Strict Liability to the Consumer)*, 69 Yale L.J. 1099, 1114-1115 (1960) (citations omitted).

If negligence liability depends solely on proof that the product was defective when it left the defendant's possession, and that the defect caused the plaintiff's harm, is the negligence rule any different from a rule of strict liability for defective products? What might be problematic about such a rule? Could it effectively turn res ipsa loquitur from a doctrine of circumstantial evidence into a device for relaxing the burden of proof? If so, what justifies doing so? Would there be any reason to limit this application of the doctrine to product cases?

2. *The difficulty of proving negligence.* In Justice Traynor's view, is it likely that plaintiffs would be able to satisfy the ordinary burden of proving negligence? Consider again the critical inference in the majority's reasoning — that bottles should not be recycled unless they are perfectly safe. Proof of this particular matter does not depend on circumstantial evidence. The plaintiff would instead have to show that there is a precaution, such as pressure testing each bottle, which would eliminate the risk. Would plaintiffs ordinarily be able to produce such evidence? Lacking sufficient evidence, plaintiffs would lose if the rule were properly applied. Does the difficulty of proving negligence provide yet another rationale for strict liability as Traynor's concurrence suggests?

C. The Evidentiary Rationale for Strict Liability

Although courts in the latter half of the nineteenth century decided to adopt negligence liability as the default rule for accidental harms, most continued to recognize the limited rules of strict liability that the early common law had recognized. Courts often justified rules of strict liability on grounds of public policy, including the policy of enabling plaintiffs to recover when problems of proof would routinely bar recovery for negligence liability.

COLE v. GOODWIN & STORY
Supreme Court of Judicature of New York, 1838
19 Wend. 251

[The defendants were stage-coach proprietors, and the plaintiff a passenger on one of their coaches. The plaintiff's trunk was lost for 11 months, and upon its return, the plaintiff discovered that some contents, including money, were missing. The judge charged the jury that the defendants were "bound to deliver the trunk to the plaintiff," and that defendants as common carriers were not excused from this obligation even though they had given notice that "all baggage was at the risk of the owner." The jury found for the plaintiff, and defendants then appealed on the ground that the jury instructions were erroneous.]

BRONSON, J. The defendants were common carriers as to the baggage; and as such were answerable for any loss of the property which was not occasioned by the act of God or the public enemies. It is wholly unimportant to inquire whether there was any actual default on their part. It is enough that the property was lost, and that the loss did not happen in either of the two ways which, according to the law of the land, will exempt the carrier from liability.

COWEN, J. It cannot be denied that the defendants are, prima facie, as much common carriers in respect to the baggage of passengers, as anything else which they convey for hire. As such they are, according to all the books, insurers against losses except such as arise from the act of God, or the public enemy. The accident in question can in no sense be called either.

What is the reason that the common law will not excuse the carrier unless he show the act of God, or the enemies of the republic, or the misconduct of the plaintiff? This, says Lord Holt, "is a politic establishment, contrived by the policy of the law for the safety of all persons the necessity of whose affairs require them to trust these sorts of persons, that they may be safe in their ways of dealing; for else these carriers might have an opportunity of undoing all persons that had any dealings with them, by combining with thieves, &c., and yet doing it in such a clandestine manner as would not be possible to be discovered." [ ] Nor was this said of a barbarous people or a barbarous age; but in the reign of Queen Anne, of morals, arts, and arms, an age distinguished as the Augustan Era of England. As late as 1828, Best, C.J., said: "If the goods should be lost or injured by the grossest negligence of the carrier or his servants, or stolen by them or by thieves in collusion with them, the owner would be unable to prove either of these causes of loss: his witnesses must be the carrier's servants, and they, knowing that they could not be contradicted, would excuse their masters and themselves." [ ] It would be arrogant in any nation to claim a state of morals superior to those of England, and especially to Scotland where the same rigor prevails; still more arrogant, not to say profane, to claim a national perfectibility so high as to rise above temptation.

NOTES AND QUESTIONS

1. *Strict liability and difficulties of proof.* According to one of the first tort treatises, "the ground on which a rule of strict obligation has been maintained and consolidated by modern authorities is the magnitude of danger, coupled with the difficulty of proving negligence as the specific cause, in the particular event of the danger having ripened into actual harm." Frederick Pollock, THE LAW OF TORTS: A TREATISE ON THE PRINCIPLES OF OBLIGATIONS ARISING FROM CIVIL WRONGS IN THE COMMON LAW 393 (1st ed. 1887). How does the difficulty of proof in *Cole* compare with the difficulty of proof in *Escola*? Recall in this regard that the likelihood of a reused soda bottle exploding depended on whether visual inspection by the defendant's employees would identify fractures in those bottles. According to the court in *Cole*, would such testimony provide a reliable foundation for the plaintiff's case?

2. *The example of workers' compensation.* In the early decades of the twentieth century, states across the country adopted workers' compensation statutes. These statutes give workers a right to compensation for injuries arising out of the workplace in exchange for the elimination of their right to sue the employer in tort law. The employee's statutory right to compensation is strict; no fault of the employer is required. The employee typically receives full compensation for the medical and rehabilitation costs of the injury and limited compensation for lost wages as determined on a scheduled basis by an administrative tribunal.

The difficulty of proving negligence provided an important rationale for workers' compensation:

> In support of the legislation, it is said that the whole common-law doctrine of employer's liability for negligence, with its defenses of contributory negligence, fellow servant's negligence, and assumption of risk, is based upon fictions, and is inapplicable to modern conditions of employment; that in the highly organized and hazardous industries of the present day the causes of accident are often so obscure and complex that in a material proportion of cases it is impossible by any method correctly to ascertain the facts necessary to form an accurate judgment, and in a still larger proportion the expense and delay required for such ascertainment amount in effect to a defeat of justice; that, under the present system, the injured workman is left to bear the greater part of industrial accident loss, which, because of his limited income, he is unable to sustain, so that he and those dependent upon him are overcome by poverty and frequently become a burden upon public or private charity; and that litigation is unduly costly and tedious, encouraging corrupt practices and arousing antagonisms between employers and employees.

New York Cent. R.R. Co. v. White, 243 U.S. 188, 197 (1917).

Because it was often not possible to identify the causes of workplace accidents due to their complexity or obscurity, employers as a practical matter were often not subject to negligence liability, encouraging corrupt practices involving unsafe work conditions. To give employers an adequate financial incentive for reducing workplace injuries while giving employees a guaranteed right to compensation, the states widely adopted workers' compensation statutes.

3. *Beyond workers' compensation.* The rule of strict liability governing workplace injuries strongly influenced how courts and scholars subsequently evaluated other forms of negligence liability, including those involving defective products. After all, if negligence liability could not effectively regulate systems of workplace safety, then presumably negligence liability was similarly incapable of regulating complex systems of product safety. Consider in this regard the extent to which the deterrence and compensation rationales for workers' compensation are reflected in the policy reasons that Justice Traynor relied on to justify strict liability in his *Escola* concurrence, p. 36 *supra*.

II. The Negligence Principle

Another good example is provided by the manner in which the Texas Supreme Court justified the rule of strict liability for contaminated food:

> [A] rule which would require proof of negligence as a basis of recovery would, in most instances, by reason of the difficulty of making such proof, be equivalent to a denial of recovery. It is well known that in many instances the product is processed in a distant state or in a foreign country many months prior to a discovery of the defect. It would be impracticable, if not impossible, for the consumer to prove the circumstances under which a particular can of beans or meat eaten by him has been processed. This can be very well illustrated by the facts involved in the case of Burkhardt v. Armour & Co., 161 A. 385 (Conn. 1932). In that case a resident of Connecticut purchased a can of meat from a local merchant. The merchant had purchased it from Armour & Company, of Illinois, who in turn had purchased it from Frigorifico Armour de la Plata, of Argentina. The latter company had purchased it from a packer in Argentina. It would have been impracticable, if not impossible, for the consumer to have proved the conditions under which the food had been packed in Argentina many months prior to the date of the injury suffered by the consumer. All this furnishes proof of the soundness of the rule . . . that in the sale of food for human consumption "the vendor is bound to know that they are sound and wholesome, at his peril." Such a rule would seem to be more desirable because it permits the placing of the ultimate loss upon the manufacturer, who is in the best position to prevent the production and sale of unwholesome food. It stimulates and induces a greater degree of precaution for the protection of human health and life than does the rule of ordinary care.

Jacob E. Decker & Sons v. Capps, 164 S.W.2d 828, 843 (Tex. 1942) (other portions of the opinion are excerpted in section I.A of this chapter); *see also, e.g.,* Cushing v. Rodman, 82 F.2d 864, 869 (D.C. Cir. 1936) ("Restricting recovery by the injured member of the public to [contaminated food] cases predicated upon negligence is a seriously inadequate means of securing the social interest in the individual safety, because of the great difficulty of proof for the plaintiff.").

4. *A negligence-based rationale for strict liability.* To understand why the difficulty of proving negligence liability can justify strict liability, we need to consider how strict liability predictably affects the behavior of a manufacturer as duty-bearer. Under a rule of strict liability, the manufacturer incurs only a compensatory duty for the injuries proximately caused by a defect in the product. The compensatory duty does not dictate how the manufacturer should behave and leaves that decision entirely to its discretion. In deciding how to proceed, a manufacturer subject to strict liability will presumably try to maximize its profits. To do so, it must minimize the total costs of selling the product. The manufacturer's expected liability costs depend on the probability that an injury will occur (denoted P) and the total amount of damages or loss caused by the injury (denoted L). Multiplying these two factors together yields the manufacturer's *expected liability costs* (PL), which measures the average amount of liability the

manufacturer will incur for each product. The manufacturer can reduce its expected liability costs by adopting quality-control measures that would reduce the incidence of defective products and thereby decrease the number of product-caused injuries. Each particular safety precaution eliminates some type of risk, such as the likelihood that a reused soda bottle will explode. Ordinarily, the manufacturer must incur a cost or burden to adopt such a precaution (denoted B). To minimize all these costs, the strictly liable manufacturer must compare the burden (B) of a safety precaution with the expected liability costs that it would otherwise incur by not taking the precaution and eliminating the associated risk of product-caused injury (PL). The manufacturer will reduce its total costs by taking any safety precaution for which

$$B < PL$$

So, too, if the costs of a precaution exceed the safety benefit or reduction in expected liability (injury) costs, the manufacturer will reduce its total costs by foregoing the safety investment and instead incurring the liabilities:

$$B > PL$$

Now consider the precautions required by the negligence standard of reasonable care. According to comment e in the *Restatement (Second)* §283, the standard of reasonable care requires a determination of "whether the magnitude of the risk outweighs the value which the law attaches to the conduct which involves it." One form of this determination is captured by Judge Learned Hand's well-known formulation of the negligence standard: "if the probability [of injury] be called P; the injury, L; and the burden [of a precaution that would eliminate this risk] B; liability depends upon whether B is less than L multiplied by P: i.e., whether $B < PL$." U.S. v. Carroll Towing Co., 159 F.2d 169, 173 (2d Cir. 1947) (Hand, J.) (italics added). This specification of reasonable care requires the same safety precautions that would be voluntarily chosen by a strictly liable actor seeking to maximize profits by minimizing costs.

If this duty of reasonable care were perfectly enforced, then the choice between negligence and strict liability would not affect risky behavior, as each liability rule either requires (negligence) or predictably induces (strict liability) the same precautions. To recover under negligence liability, however, the plaintiff must prove that the defendant manufacturer violated the standard of reasonable care. The extent to which plaintiffs can enforce the duty of reasonable care, therefore, critically depends on the difficulties of proving negligence.

Absent sufficient evidence of this type, the manufacturer will not incur liability, even if it in fact acted negligently. As one court observed:

> It is not doubted that due care might require the defendant to adopt some device that would afford [reasonable protection against the injury suffered by plaintiff]. Such a device, if it exists, is not disclosed by the record. The burden was upon the plaintiff to show its

practicability. Since the burden was not sustained, a verdict should have been directed for the defendant.

Cooley v. Public Serv. Co., 10 A.2d 673, 677 (N.H. 1940).

If the standard of reasonable care requires a particular safety precaution but the plaintiff is unable to prove as much, a defendant who unreasonably foregoes the precaution will avoid negligence liability. Without a credible threat of liability, duty-bearers like a defendant manufacturer are not effectively governed by the duty to exercise reasonable care, giving them a financial incentive to forego such a reasonable but costly safety precaution required by the duty. The duty to exercise reasonable care no longer adequately incentivizes manufacturers to actually exercise reasonable care.

In these circumstances, the desired safety incentive can be at least partially restored by strict liability. When the manufacturer is strictly liable for injuries caused by the conduct in question, the court no longer needs to evaluate the its safety decisions on the basis of the plaintiff's proof of negligence. Strict liability takes the safety decision from the court and gives it to the defendant manufacturer. As previously discussed, a strictly liable manufacturer has an incentive to make any safety investment that reduces liability (and injuries) in a cost-effective manner: $B < PL$. Insofar as the manufacturer would have foregone any of these costly precautions in a negligence regime due to problems of proof, the shift to strict liability will increase these safety investments and reduce the incidence of defects. The evidentiary difficulties of proving negligence liability, therefore, can justify strict liability as a means for inducing the safe behavior otherwise required by the duty to exercise reasonable care. *See* Steven Shavell, *Strict Liability Versus Negligence*, 9 J. Legal Stud. 1 (1980) (showing how strict liability can reduce risk by reducing "activity" levels, where "activity" is any aspect of risky behavior that is outside the ambit of negligence liability due to evidentiary limitations).

Under the common law, this type of evidentiary problem justified rules of strict liability, most notably for common carriers. The same evidentiary problem was relied on by legislatures to justify the rule of strict liability for injuries under workers' compensation statutes. As explained by Justice Traynor's concurrence in *Escola*, the same type of evidentiary problem exists with respect to complicated systems of product manufacture and distribution, yielding a negligence-based evidentiary rationale for the rule of strict products liability.

D. *The Negligence Foundation of the* Restatement (Third)

When a rule of strict liability is justified in terms of the negligence principle, it is fundamentally consistent with complementary rules of negligence liability. Strict liability applies only when evidentiary problems impair negligence liability, with negligence liability governing all other cases. Hence the *Restatement (Third)* can consistently adopt a rule of strict liability for contaminated food and exploding soda bottles, while employing rules of negligence liability for the remaining types of product defects.

RESTATEMENT (THIRD) OF TORTS: PRODUCTS LIABILITY (1998)
Copyright by the American Law Institute

§1. Liability of Commercial Seller or Distributor for Harm Caused by Defective Products

One engaged in the business of selling or otherwise distributing products who sells or distributes a defective product is subject to liability for harm to persons or property caused by the defect.

Comment:

a. History. The liability established in this Section draws on both warranty law and tort law. Historically, the focus of products liability law was on manufacturing defects. A manufacturing defect is a physical departure from a product's intended design. Typically, manufacturing defects occur in only a small percentage of units in a product line. Courts early began imposing liability without fault on product sellers for harm caused by such defects, holding a seller liable for harm caused by manufacturing defects even though all possible care had been exercised by the seller in the preparation and distribution of the product. In doing so, courts relied on the concept of warranty, in connection with which fault has never been a prerequisite to liability.

The imposition of liability for manufacturing defects has a long history in the common law. As early as 1266, criminal statutes imposed liability upon victualers, vintners, brewers, butchers, cooks, and other persons who supplied contaminated food and drink. In the late 1800s, courts in many states began imposing negligence and strict warranty liability on commercial sellers of defective goods. In the early 1960s, American courts began to recognize that a commercial seller of any product having a manufacturing defect should be liable in tort for harm caused by the defect regardless of the plaintiff's ability to maintain a traditional negligence or warranty action. Liability attached even if the manufacturer's quality control in producing the defective product was reasonable. A plaintiff was not required to be in direct privity with the defendant seller to bring an action. Strict liability in tort for defectively manufactured products merges the concept of implied warranty, in which negligence is not required, with the tort concept of negligence, in which contractual privity is not required.

Questions of design defects and defects based on inadequate instructions or warnings arise when the specific product unit conforms to the intended design but the intended design itself, or its sale without adequate instructions or warnings, renders the product not reasonably safe. If these forms of defect are found to exist, then every unit in the same product line is potentially defective. Imposition of liability for design defects and for defects based on inadequate instructions or warnings was relatively infrequent until the late 1960s and early 1970s. A number of restrictive rules made recovery for such defects, especially design defects, difficult to obtain. As these rules eroded, courts sought to impose liability without fault for design defects and defects due to inadequate instructions or warnings under the general principles of §402A of the Restatement, Second, of Torts. However, it soon became evident that §402A, created to deal with liability for manufacturing defects, could not appropriately

II. The Negligence Principle

be applied to cases of design defects or defects based on inadequate instructions or warnings. A product unit that fails to meet the manufacturer's design specifications thereby fails to perform its intended function and is, almost by definition, defective. However, when the product unit meets the manufacturer's own design specifications, it is necessary to go outside those specifications to determine whether the product is defective.

The rule developed for manufacturing defects is inappropriate for the resolution of claims of defective design and defects based on inadequate instructions or warnings. These latter categories of cases require determinations that the product could have reasonably been made safer by a better design or instruction or warning. Sections 2(b) and 2(c) rely on a reasonableness test traditionally used in determining whether an actor has been negligent. Nevertheless, many courts insist on speaking of liability based on the standards described in §§2(b) and 2(c) as being "strict."

Thus, "strict products liability" is a term of art that reflects the judgment that products liability is a discrete area of tort law which borrows from both negligence and warranty. It is not fully congruent with classical tort or contract law. Rather than perpetuating confusion spawned by existing doctrinal categories, §§1 and 2 define the liability for each form of defect in terms directly addressing the various kinds of defects. As long as these functional criteria are met, courts may utilize the terminology of negligence, strict liability, or the implied warranty of merchantability, or simply define liability in the terms set forth in the black letter.

§2. Categories of Product Defect

A product is defective when, at the time of sale or distribution, it contains a manufacturing defect, is defective in design, or is defective because of inadequate instructions or warnings. A product:

(a) contains a manufacturing defect when the product departs from its intended design even though all possible care was exercised in the preparation and marketing of the product;

(b) is defective in design when the foreseeable risks of harm posed by the product could have been reduced or avoided by the adoption of a reasonable alternative design by the seller or other distributor, or a predecessor in the commercial chain of distribution, and the omission of the alternative design renders the product not reasonably safe;

(c) is defective because of inadequate instructions or warnings when the foreseeable risks of harm posed by the product could have been reduced or avoided by the provision of reasonable instructions or warnings by the seller or other distributor, or a predecessor in the commercial chain of distribution, and the omission of the instructions or warnings renders the product not reasonably safe.

Comment:

a. Rationale. The rule for manufacturing defects stated in Subsection (a) imposes liability whether or not the manufacturer's quality control efforts satisfy standards of reasonableness. Strict liability without fault in this context is generally believed to foster several objectives. On the premise that tort law serves the instrumental function of creating safety incentives, imposing strict liability on manufacturers for harm caused by manufacturing defects encourages greater investment in product safety than does a regime of fault-based liability under which, as a practical matter, sellers may escape their appropriate share of responsibility. Some courts and commentators also have said that strict liability discourages the consumption of defective products by causing the purchase price of products to reflect, more than would a rule of negligence, the costs of defects. And by eliminating the issue of manufacturer fault from plaintiff's case, strict liability reduces the transaction costs involved in litigating that issue.

Several important fairness concerns are also believed to support manufacturers' liability for manufacturing defects even if the plaintiff is unable to show that the manufacturer's quality control fails to meet risk-utility norms. In many cases manufacturing defects are in fact caused by manufacturer negligence but plaintiffs have difficulty proving it. Strict liability therefore performs a function similar to the concept of res ipsa loquitur, allowing deserving plaintiffs to succeed notwithstanding what would otherwise be difficult or insuperable problems of proof. Products that malfunction due to manufacturing defects disappoint reasonable expectations of product performance. Because manufacturers invest in quality control at consciously chosen levels, their knowledge that a predictable number of flawed products will enter the marketplace entails an element of deliberation about the amount of injury that will result from their activity. Finally, many believe that consumers who benefit from products without suffering harm should share, through increases in the prices charged for those products, the burden of unavoidable injury costs that result from manufacturing defects.

An often-cited rationale for holding wholesalers and retailers strictly liable for harm caused by manufacturing defects is that, as between them and innocent victims who suffer harm because of defective products, the product sellers as business entities are in a better position than are individual users and consumers to insure against such losses. In most instances, wholesalers and retailers will be able to pass liability costs up the chain of product distribution to the manufacturer. When joining the manufacturer in the tort action presents the plaintiff with procedural difficulties, local retailers can pay damages to the victims and then seek indemnity from manufacturers. Finally, holding retailers and wholesalers strictly liable creates incentives for them to deal only with reputable, financially responsible manufacturers and distributors, thereby helping to protect the interests of users and consumers.

In contrast to manufacturing defects, design defects and defects based on inadequate instructions or warnings are predicated on a different concept of responsibility. In the first place, such defects cannot be determined by reference to the manufacturer's own design or marketing standards because those standards are the very ones that plaintiffs attack as unreasonable. Some sort of independent assessment of advantages and disadvantages, to which some attach the label "risk-utility balancing," is necessary. Products are not generically defective merely because they are dangerous. Many product-related accident costs can be eliminated only by excessively sacrificing product features that make products useful and desirable. Thus, the various trade-offs need to be considered in determining whether accident costs are more fairly and efficiently borne by accident victims, on the one hand, or, on the other hand, by consumers generally through the mechanism of higher product prices attributable to liability costs imposed by courts on product sellers.

Subsections (b) and (c), which impose liability for products that are defectively designed or sold without adequate warnings or instructions and are thus not reasonably safe, achieve the same general objectives as does liability predicated on negligence. The emphasis is on creating incentives for manufacturers to achieve optimal levels of safety in designing and marketing products. Society does not benefit from products that are excessively safe—for example, automobiles designed with maximum speeds of 20 miles per hour—any more than it benefits from products that are too risky. Society benefits most when the right, or optimal, amount of product safety is achieved. From a fairness perspective, requiring individual users and consumers to bear appropriate responsibility for proper product use prevents careless users and consumers from being subsidized by more careful users and consumers, when the former are paid damages out of funds to which the latter are forced to contribute through higher product prices.

In general, the rationale for imposing strict liability on manufacturers for harm caused by manufacturing defects does not apply in the context of imposing liability for defective design and defects based on inadequate instruction or warning. Consumer expectations as to proper product design or warning are typically more difficult to discern than in the case of a manufacturing defect. Moreover, the element of deliberation in setting appropriate levels of design safety is not directly analogous to the setting of levels of quality control by the manufacturer. When a manufacturer sets its quality control at a certain level, it is aware that a given number of products may leave the assembly line in a defective condition and cause injury to innocent victims who can generally do nothing to avoid injury. The implications of deliberately drawing lines with respect to product design safety are different. A reasonably designed product still carries with it elements of risk that must be protected against by the user or consumer since some risks cannot be designed out of the product at reasonable cost.

. . .

g. Consumer expectations: general considerations. Under Subsection (b), consumer expectations do not constitute an independent standard for judging the defectiveness of product designs. Courts frequently rely, in part, on consumer expectations when discussing liability based on other theories of liability. Some courts, for example, use the term "reasonable consumer expectations" as an equivalent of "proof of a reasonable, safer design alternative," since reasonable consumers have a right to expect product designs that conform to the reasonableness standard in Subsection (b). Other courts, allowing an inference of defect to be drawn when the incident is of a kind that ordinarily would occur as a result of product defect, observe that products that fail when put to their manifestly intended use disappoint reasonable consumer expectations. See §3. However, consumer expectations do not play a determinative role in determining defectiveness. Consumer expectations, standing alone, do not take into account whether the proposed alternative design could be implemented at reasonable cost, or whether an alternative design would provide greater overall safety. Nevertheless, consumer expectations about product performance and the dangers attendant to product use affect how risks are perceived and relate to foreseeability and frequency of the risks of harm, both of which are relevant under Subsection (b). See Comment *f.* Such expectations are often influenced by how products are portrayed and marketed and can have a significant impact on consumer behavior. Thus, although consumer expectations do not constitute an independent standard for judging the defectiveness of product designs, they may substantially influence or even be ultimately determinative on risk-utility balancing in judging whether the omission of a proposed alternative design renders the product not reasonably safe.

§3. Circumstantial Evidence Supporting Inference of Defect

It may be inferred that the harm sustained by the plaintiff was caused by a product defect existing at the time of sale or distribution, without proof of a specific defect, when the incident that harmed the plaintiff:

    (a) was of a kind that ordinarily occurs as a result of product defect; and

    (b) was not, in the particular case, solely the result of causes other than product defect existing at the time of sale or distribution.

Comment:

a. History. This Section traces its historical antecedents to the law of negligence, which has long recognized that an inference of negligence may be drawn in cases where the defendant's negligence is the best explanation for the cause of an accident, even if the plaintiff cannot explain the exact nature of the defendant's conduct. As products liability law developed, cases arose in which an inference of product defect could be drawn from the incident in which a product caused plaintiff's harm, without proof of the specific nature of the defect. This Section sets forth the formal requisites for drawing such an inference.

b. Requirement that the harm be of a kind that ordinarily occurs as a result of product defect. The most frequent application of this Section is to cases involving manufacturing defects. When a product unit contains such a defect, and the defect affects product performance so as to cause a harmful incident, in most instances it will cause the product to malfunction in such a way that the inference of product defect is clear. From this perspective, manufacturing defects cause products to fail to perform their manifestly intended functions. Frequently, the plaintiff is able to establish specifically the nature and identity of the defect and may proceed directly under §2(a). But when the product unit involved in the harm-causing incident is lost or destroyed in the accident, direct evidence of specific defect may not be available. Under that circumstance, this Section may offer the plaintiff the only fair opportunity to recover.

. . .

Although the rules in this Section, for the reasons just stated, most often apply to manufacturing defects, occasionally a product design causes the product to malfunction in a manner identical to that which would ordinarily be caused by a manufacturing defect. Thus, an aircraft may inadvertently be designed in such a way that, in new condition and while flying within its intended performance parameters, the wings suddenly and unexpectedly fall off, causing harm. In theory, of course, the plaintiff in such a case would be able to show how other units in the same production line were designed, leading to a showing of a reasonable alternative design under §2(b). As a practical matter, however, when the incident involving the aircraft is one that ordinarily occurs as a result of product defect, and evidence in the particular case establishes that the harm was not solely the result of causes other than product defect existing at time of sale, it should not be necessary for the plaintiff to incur the cost of proving whether the failure resulted from a manufacturing defect or from a defect in the design of the product. Section 3 allows the trier of fact to draw the inference that the product was defective whether due to a manufacturing defect or a design defect. Under those circumstances, the plaintiff need not specify the type of defect responsible for the product malfunction.

It is important to emphasize the difference between a general inference of defect under §3 and claims of defect brought directly under §§1 and 2. Section 3 claims are limited to situations in which a product fails to perform its manifestly intended function, thus supporting the conclusion that a defect of some kind is the most probable explanation. If that is not the case, and if no other provision of Chapter 1 allows the plaintiff to establish defect independently of the requirements in §2 . . . , a plaintiff is required to establish a cause of action for defect based on proof satisfying the requirements set forth in §2. See §2, Comment *b*.

NOTES AND QUESTIONS

1. *A discrete area of the law?* According to *Restatement (Third)* §1 comment a, "'strict products liability' is a term of art that reflects the judgment that products liability is a discrete area of tort law which borrows from both negligence and warranty. It is not fully congruent with classical tort or contract law." Does this interpretation adequately account for the tort version of the implied warranty? Insofar as the *Restatement (Third)* does not adequately account for the implied warranty, how might its formulation of liability rules differ from the formulation in the *Restatement (Second)*?

2. *The* Restatements *contrasted.* As is true of the *Restatement (Second)*, the provisions of the *Restatement (Third)* are the subject of extended study in the ensuing chapters. But by comparing the foregoing provisions in the *Restatement (Third)* with §402A of the *Restatement (Second)*, we can now identify a number of important issues:

- Section 1 comment a of the *Restatement (Third)* explains how strict products liability evolved from manufacturing defects (such as the exploding soda bottle in *Escola*) to cases involving defects of design or warnings as defined in §§2(b), 2(c) of the *Restatement (Third)*. According to §2 comment a, the liability rules for defective design or warnings—the most important class of cases for products liability today—"rely on a reasonableness test traditionally used in determining whether an actor has been negligent." Is a negligence rule for defective designs and warnings consistent with the rule of strict products liability in §402A of the *Restatement (Second)*?
- In §2 comment a, the *Restatement (Third)* also relies on the evidentiary rationale for strict liability to justify the liability rule for manufacturing defects: "On the premise that tort law serves the instrumental function

of creating safety incentives, imposing strict liability on manufacturers for harm caused by manufacturing defects encourages greater investment in product safety than does a regime of fault-based liability under which, as a practical matter, sellers may escape their appropriate share of responsibility." As we previously found, the evidentiary rationale for strict liability is consistent with the principle of negligence liability. Is this a sufficient basis for reconciling the negligence rule for defective designs and warnings with the rule of strict products liability in the *Restatement (Second)*?

- In §3, the *Restatement (Third)* defines product defects based exclusively on whether it malfunctioned. This inquiry does not require the plaintiff to identify the exact type of defect that caused the malfunction and appears to be the type of defect contemplated by §402A of the *Restatement (Second)*. Consider, for example, how an exploding bottle of soda would be evaluated under both formulations. Like the *Restatement (Second)* rule of strict products liability, the *Restatement (Third)* subjects manufacturers and other sellers to strict liability for product malfunctions. The *Restatement (Third)*, however, rejects consumer expectations as the test for malfunction. Liability instead depends on whether the product failed to perform in its "manifestly intended" manner. Intentionality in this context plainly refers to the manufacturer and not consumers, who only have expectations about product performance. The official commentary never mentions the implied warranty or consumer expectations, but instead states that this rule "traces its historical antecedents to the law of negligence" involving proof of liability with circumstantial evidence. The difficulty of proving negligence, in turn, justifies strict liability as a device for creating financial incentives that indirectly enforce the negligence standard of reasonable care.

- As the foregoing provisions make clear, the *Restatement (Third)* invokes the negligence heritage of strict products liability to justify its liability rules. Does this rationale cast doubt on the continued vitality of the implied-warranty heritage? According to §2 comment g, "consumer expectations do not play a determinative role in determining defectiveness." Can this conclusion be squared with the *Restatement (Second)* rule of strict products liability?

- Insofar as the *Restatement (Third)* exclusively relies on the negligence principle, the approach would be justifiable if that principle is substantively equivalent to the tort version of the implied warranty. By that same reasoning, however, the implied warranty rationale for strict products liability in the *Restatement (Second)* would also be fully capable of justifying the liability rules in the *Restatement (Third)*. The particular substantive rationale for strict products liability would not matter. Alternatively, the implied warranty and the consumer expectations test might substantively differ from the negligence principle, in which case the *Restatement (Third)* substantively diverges from the rule of strict products liability in the *Restatement (Second)*. Which interpretation is correct? This foundational issue is probably the most important question of products liability that continues to be widely litigated in the courts.

3

The Substantive Basis of Products Liability

The widely adopted rule of strict products liability can be derived from two different tort doctrines. The implied warranty and the negligence principle each independently justify the rule holding a product seller strictly liable for the physical harms proximately caused by defects that cause products to malfunction, as in cases of contaminated food or exploding soda bottles.

Are the two doctrines substantively consistent for determining defects in products that do not malfunction? Is a finding of defect under the implied warranty always matched by the same finding under the negligence principle? Even if the two doctrines determine defects in the same way, they have a different focus. The implied warranty protects consumer expectations of safe product performance, whereas the negligence principle centers on protection from the unreasonable risk of physical harm. In what respects, if any, is the framework of consumer expectations different from a negligence-based framework?

These fundamental questions are now quite prominent. The implied warranty supplies the basis for the liability rule in the *Restatement (Second)*, whereas the negligence principle underlies the liability rules in the *Restatement (Third)*. The framework of liability differs in the two *Restatements*, fueling an ongoing controversy regarding the substantive basis of products liability.

I. CONTROVERSY OVER THE LIABILITY RULE

"[M]odern products liability doctrine in most states was constructed squarely on §402A of the *Second Restatement* which, in various important respects, the *Third Restatement* largely dismantles." Most important, it "explicitly abandons the doctrine of 'strict' products liability for design and warning defects, which comprise the bulk of products liability litigation." David G. Owen & Mary J. Davis, 1 OWEN & DAVIS ON PRODUCTS LIABILITY §5:1 (4th ed. 2014). After the American Law Institute approved the *Restatement (Third)* in 1997, litigants in many cases argued that courts should adopt its liability framework and reject the *Restatement*

(Second) rule of strict products liability. This case law continues to develop, but the clear trend is summarized in the following materials.

STRICT LIABILITY FOR DEFECTIVE PRODUCT DESIGN: THE QUEST FOR A WELL-ORDERED REGIME
Larry S. Stewart
74 Brook. L. Rev. 1039 (2009)

Beginning with *Greenman v. Yuba Power Products, Inc.* and the adoption shortly thereafter of *Restatement (Second) of Torts* section 402A, "strict liability" for product defects came to replace negligence as the primary basis for products liability. Section 402A avoided the inherent proof problems of negligence by providing for liability even though the seller "has exercised all possible care in the preparation and sale of his product." Under strict liability, sellers are liable for harms caused by products that are "in a defective condition unreasonably dangerous," that is "dangerous to an extent beyond that which would be contemplated by the ordinary consumer." In the lexicon of products liability law, this came to be known as the "consumer expectations" test. As such, it mirrored implied warranty of sales law stripped of its contractual limitations and defenses. Thus, after 402A, if a product malfunctioned, sellers were liable for both the loss of the product as well as any injuries resulting from the malfunction.

The cost of rendering the product reasonably safe was not a factor in the liability equation. The manufacturer could either design out the defect or it had to bear the burden of resulting injuries.

While 402A swept the land, the idea that product defectiveness could be determined on the basis of what an ordinary consumer would expect did not meet with universal acceptance. Some believed that defectiveness should be anchored in traditional negligence concepts, a proposition championed by Dean John Wade in his article "On the Nature of Strict Tort Liability for Products."[14] Dean Wade argued for nullification of strict liability for all product defects, both manufacturing and design. He proposed instead that liability for defective products be based only on the reasonableness of the marketing decision under a reasonably prudent seller standard. Because his conceptual analysis utilized a number of risk/benefit factors, this approach came to be known as the "risk/benefit" test.

By the 1980s, what began as an academic debate became partisan as manufacturing interests began advocating that design defects should only be decided under a risk/benefit test.[16] Their argument was that while the

---

14. John W. Wade, *On the Nature of Strict Tort Liability for Products*, 44 Miss. L.J. 825 (1973). There were earlier iterations of Dean Wade's article but this is the one commonly cited as the origin of the risk/benefit test.

16. Industry interests were coordinated by the Products Liability Advisory Council (PLAC). According to its web site, PLAC was formed in the early 1980s and consists of over 130 corporate members representing a broad cross-section of product manufacturers and several hundred products liability defense attorneys that advocate for changes in products liability laws to favor manufacturers, principally through coordinating efforts across jurisdictions and filing amicus briefs. For an overview of cases tracing PLAC's role, see Larry S. Stewart, *Courts Overrule ALI "Consensus" On Products*, Trial Mag., Nov. 2003, at 18.

I. Controversy Over the Liability Rule

consumer expectation test was appropriate for manufacturing defect claims where consumers would expect that products were built according to design, it was meaningless for design defects since consumers could not know all the considerations involved in arriving at a particular product design. According to manufacturers, the only appropriate way to evaluate design defect claims was by a cost-benefit analysis that weighs the risks and benefits of the design. This was, however, different from the simple negligence standard that had been proposed by Dean Wade. What the manufacturing industry sought was an express risk/benefit test whereby juries would have to make a cost-benefit analysis to determine liability.

Conceptually, the risk/benefit approach rejected corrective justice for a law and economics theory by which product sellers would be liable only when the risks of the product, on balance, outweighed the benefits of having the product on the market.

In 1991 the American Law Institute ("ALI") undertook to draft a comprehensive new restatement of products liability law. That project proposed that products liability claims be divided into manufacturing defects, design defects, and failure to warn cases, a concept that closely paralleled the Products Liability Advisory Council ("PLAC") agenda. For manufacturing defects, the proposed new Restatement acknowledged the basic rationales for modern products liability law and urged continuance of a strict liability regime but with the twist that injured consumers could only bring a single claim, thus foreclosing the possibility of an alternative or independent claim for negligence.

For design defects, the new Restatement also followed the PLAC agenda. According to the new Restatement, the policy rationales for strict liability were not applicable to design defect cases and a different concept of responsibility was needed. As related in the new Restatement, consumer expectations of safe design were allegedly too difficult to discern because consumers cannot know all the considerations involved in product design and the focus of liability instead should be on the "trade-offs" in product design and requiring consumers to bear responsibility for proper product use. This change would be accomplished [under section 2(b)] by restricting design defect cases to a single negligence based, "risk-utility balancing" claim that required proof of an alternative design. Injured consumers would no longer have the option to bring alternative claims for both strict liability and negligence, could no longer bring design defect claims under 402A strict liability and its consumer expectation test, and, in most cases, experts would be required to present an alternative design for the product.

The deliberations over these proposals and their rationales were some of the most contentious in ALI history. Although the proposals were ultimately adopted by the ALI, many believed that the core provisions of section 2(b) were fundamentally flawed, a conclusion that was in significant part based on the rejection of the strict liability policy rationales for design defect claims.

Public policy rationales are the foundations upon which the legal rules rest. In the case of products liability, the original policy rationales that led to the adoption of strict liability were the ameliorative societal effects of risk spreading, litigation efficiencies resulting from simpler liability rules, deterrence of unsafe practices, and consumer expectations about the fitness and safety of products. But the *Restatement (Third)* took a different tact for design defects.

It found those rationales unsatisfactory and opted instead for a rationale based on "manufacturer expectations" that a reasonably designed product will still carry some risk that cannot be designed out of the product at reasonable cost, and that product users should bear some of the risk of product design.

In the end, dismissal of the policy rationales as support for a strict liability design defect regime just does not add up. Shifting to a "manufacturer expectations" rationale and a more easily defended risk/benefit regime would inevitably lead to less liability. Lost would be the fundamental purpose of strict liability—to relieve injured consumers of having to prove negligence, the societal purposes of deterrence of unsafe practices, and of having the cost of injuries borne by the manufacturers rather than consumers, who are ordinarily powerless to protect themselves.

The dismissal of modern products liability rationales for design defect cases was a harbinger for what followed in the courts. The case was not made that courts had rejected those rationales or were even open to their modification. Nor was any case made that design defect liability needed to be restricted. With no compelling rationales for section 2(b) and serious questions about its support from case law, it was not surprising that before the ink was dry, the design defect provisions of *Restatement (Third)* were in trouble and have now been largely rejected.

While still only in draft form, the Georgia Supreme Court[37] refused to mandate proof of an alternative design and the Supreme Courts of California and Connecticut[38] rejected section 2(b). The decision of the Connecticut Court in *Potter v. Chicago Pneumatic* was stunning, coming just days after final passage of *Restatement (Third)*. The *Potter* court boldly questioned the scholarship underlining section 2(b), concluding it was wrong. The court independently reviewed the law and found "that the majority of jurisdictions do not impose upon plaintiffs an absolute requirement to prove a feasible alternative design" and that such a requirement "imposes an undue burden on plaintiffs that might preclude otherwise valid claims from jury consideration." *Potter* also rejected the core principle that the consumer expectation test should not apply in design defect cases but ultimately adopted a "modified" consumer expectation test under which the test to be applied would depend on whether a product is "complex."

After *Potter*, the Supreme Courts of Missouri, Kansas, Oregon, Wisconsin, New Hampshire, and the Maryland Court of Appeals all refused to adopt section 2(b).[41] Against this parade of decisions, only Iowa has expressly adopted section 2(b), and it did so in a tobacco claim in which the plaintiff urged its adoption to prevent the defendant from relying on consumer expectations.[42]

---

37. Banks v. ICI Americas, Inc., 450 S.E.2d 671 (Ga. 1994).
38. Carlin v. Superior Court, 920 P.2d 1347 (Cal. 1996); Potter v. Chicago Pneumatic Tool Co., 694 A.2d 1319 (Conn. 1997).
41. Rodriguez v. Suzuki Motor Corp., 996 S.W.2d 47, 64-65 (Mo. 1999); Delaney v. Deere & Co., 999 P.2d 930 (Kan. 2000); McCathern v. Toyota Motor Corp., 23 P.3d 320 (Or. 2001); Green v. Smith & Nephew AHP, Inc., 629 N.W.2d 727 (Wis. 2001); Halliday v. Sturm, Ruger & Co., 792 A.2d 1145 (Md. 2002).
42. Wright v. Brooke Group Ltd., 652 N.W.2d 159, 162, 169 (Iowa 2002).

I. Controversy Over the Liability Rule

NOTES AND QUESTIONS

1. *Further developments in the case law.* The case law continues to develop along the lines described by Stewart in this article. For example, the Illinois Supreme Court in 2008 refused to adopt the *Restatement (Third)* provision requiring proof of design or warning defects with the risk-utility test, concluding that it would "change . . . the substantive law of this state." Mikolajczyk v. Ford Motor Co., 901 N.E.2d 329, 346-347 (Ill. 2008). After surveying this case law, the Supreme Court of Florida found in 2015 that "various courts have criticized" the "discussion of strict products liability" in the *Restatement (Third)*, "emphasizing that it 'goes beyond the law' because '[r]ather than taking a photograph of the law of the field,' [it] attempts to create a framework for products liability." The court agreed with this critique and rejected the "new approach" of the *Restatement (Third)* because it "is inconsistent with the rationale for strict products liability." Aubin v. Union Carbide Corp., 177 So.3d 489, 510 (Fla. 2015). This same reasoning also led the Nevada Supreme Court in 2017 to reject the *Restatement (Third)* framework: "risk-utility analysis represents a substantial departure from the underlying tenets of our strict products liability jurisprudence, which does not rest on traditional concepts of fault." Ford Motor Co. v. Trejo, 409 P.3d 649, 651 (Nev. 2017).

By contrast, the Supreme Court of South Carolina adopted the risk-utility test in the *Restatement (Third)*, in part because "[s]ome form of a risk-utility test is employed by an overwhelming majority of jurisdictions in this country." Branham v. Ford Motor Co., 701 S.E.2d 5, 14-15 (S.C. 2010). The court, however, did not acknowledge that its survey of the case law also shows that the consumer expectations test, in one form or another, is recognized by a substantial majority of jurisdictions. *Id.* at 14 n.2 (citing only 17 states that exclusively rely on the risk-utility test and do not recognize any role for consumer expectations in design cases). By contrast, a different survey of the case law addressing this issue found "no consensus with respect to application either of the consumer expectations test or the risk-utility test." Mike McWilliams & Margaret Smith, *An Overview of the Legal Standard Regarding Product Liability Design Defect Claims and a Fifty State Survey on the Applicable Law in Each Jurisdiction*, 82 Def. Couns. J. 80, 83 (2015).

2. *Efficiency versus fairness?* In this article, Stewart, a member of both the plaintiffs' bar and the American Law Institute, identifies the basis for a potentially divisive debate over products liability. A liability rule protecting consumer expectations appears to protect fairly the victims of product accidents, whereas the risk/benefit or risk-utility test is a form of cost-benefit analysis, which is the calculus of economic efficiency presumably preferred by the business community. Critics of the *Restatement (Third)* accordingly claim that its cost-benefit risk-utility test is based on a pro-business political bias instead of the fair or just tort principles that the *Restatement (Second)* invoked to justify strict products liability.

This particular dispute is part of a wider debate regarding the appropriate purpose of tort law. Many scholars have argued that tort law, including products liability, is justified by moral principles for which efficiency considerations are irrelevant. *E.g.*, Ernest Weinrib, THE IDEA OF PRIVATE LAW 132 (1995) (arguing that tort law is based on a principle of corrective justice that "rules out the economic analysis of private law"). Others argue that tort law should efficiently minimize accident costs and thereby maximize social wealth. *E.g.*, Richard A. Posner, THE ECONOMICS OF JUSTICE (1981). The wider debate about the appropriate roles of fairness and efficiency norms in tort law thus appears to encompass the doctrinal debate pitting the fair, consumer expectations standard of liability in the *Restatement (Second)* against the efficient, risk-utility test in the *Restatement (Third)*.

According to one study, opinions in product cases tend to rely on fairness norms when courts perceive a conflict between fairness and efficiency. *See* James A. Henderson, Jr., *Judicial Reliance on Public Policy: An Empirical Analysis of Products Liability Decisions*, 59 Geo. Wash. L. Rev. 1570 (1991). Professor Henderson found that judicial opinions "explicitly developed and relied upon public policy reasoning in 15% of the products liability decisions." *Id.* at 1589. "[F]airness was developed 18% more frequently than efficiency, and fairness controlled in the decision 24% more frequently." *Id.* at 1595. Do these findings support the claim that there is a deep divide between the requirements of efficiency and fairness, or that the two rationales, for the most part, overlap?

3. *Other policy rationales for strict products liability.* Aside from fairness, Stewart describes a number of other policy rationales for strict products liability. These rationales stem from the theory of enterprise liability that was first formulated by tort scholars in light of the workers' compensation statutes that most states adopted in the first part of the twentieth century. Recall that these statutes removed workplace injuries from the tort system, giving workers a right to compensation for injuries arising out of the workplace. The right to compensation is strict; no fault of the employer is required. Based on this development, scholars concluded that workplace injuries "represented a 'cost' of enterprise and that the compensation statutes served to internalize those costs to the responsible corporate decision makers. It was also accepted that businesses could bear those costs more adequately than injured workers could because businesses could pass them along to consumers in the price of their products." George L. Priest, *The Invention of Enterprise Liability: A Critical History of the Intellectual Foundations of Modern Tort Law*, 14 J. Legal Stud. 461, 463 (1985).

Relying on these same policy rationales, the theory of enterprise liability maintains that tort law should adopt rules of strict liability that internalize accident costs to the risk-creating business enterprise. A profit-maximizing business seeks to reduce costs, creating an incentive to reduce its exposure to liability by adopting safety measures that reduce injuries. The business can then spread these liability/injury costs more widely throughout society via price increases that are borne by all consumers of the product, thereby serving the social objective of risk spreading. These two objectives are most fully attained by tort rules that maximize the amount of cost internalized to the business enterprise, yielding a general rule of strict liability of the type utilized by workers' compensation. *See generally id.*; Virginia E. Nolan & Edmund Ursin, UNDERSTANDING ENTERPRISE LIABILITY: RETHINKING TORT REFORM FOR THE TWENTY-FIRST CENTURY (1995).

II. Strict Products Liability 1.0

To what extent is the theory of enterprise liability embodied in the rule of strict products liability? Consider Camacho v. Honda Motor Co., 741 P.2d 1240, 1246 (Col. 1987) ("In the final analysis, the principle of products liability contemplated by section 402A is premised upon the concept of enterprise liability for casting defective products into the stream of commerce."). Do the policies of enterprise liability justify strict liability only for injuries caused by defective products, or do they instead justify strict liability for all product-caused injuries?

The requirement of defect poses another problem for this line of policy analysis. As discussed in Chapter 2, section II.C, strict products liability creates financial incentives for manufacturers to make product-safety decisions by selecting only those precautions costing less than the associated reduction in expected liability/injury costs. In light of this property, why is it necessarily problematic to determine defect directly by a comparison of those costs and benefits—the inquiry embodied in the risk-utility test?

These questions are difficult and cannot be easily answered at this point. Doing so is the subject matter of the remainder of this chapter.

II. STRICT PRODUCTS LIABILITY 1.0

The rule of strict products liability in §402A of the *Restatement (Second)* defines defect in a monolithic manner determined by the expectations of the ordinary consumer based on ordinary knowledge common to the community. The *Restatement (Third)* §2, by contrast, employs a tripartite classification defined in terms of manufacturing defects, design defects, and warning defects. Section 3 also recognizes that defect can be defined by the circumstantial evidence of a product malfunction. Exploring the reasons for these different formulations of defect goes a long way toward identifying the differences between the two restatements.

As we found in Chapter 2, the cases that first developed the rule of strict products liability involved malfunctioning products, such as contaminated food or exploding bottles of soda. Based on ordinary knowledge common to the community, the ordinary consumer minimally expects that products can perform their basic functions: food should be edible; soda bottles should deliver the drink without exploding. Malfunctions frustrate consumer expectations and subject the seller of the defective product to strict liability. *See, e.g.*, Farmer v. International Harvester Co., 553 P.2d 1306, 1311 (Idaho 1976) ("[A] product will not ordinarily malfunction within the reasonable contemplation of a consumer in the absence of defect.").

Consequently,

> [s]ection 402A and the scholars and courts that crafted it were concerned about easy cases in which products failed in performing at a minimal level of safety.... In this era, the type of defect was not important, and the founders, although aware of the different ways in which a product might be defective, paid little attention to the matter as section 402A was being drafted.

Michael D. Green, *The Unappreciated Congruity of the Second and Third Restatements on Design Defects*, 74 Brook. L. Rev. 807, 836 (2012).

Application of this liability rule does not depend on the type of defect; the fact of malfunction instead defines the defect that triggers the rule of strict liability. For example, product malfunctions can be attributable to the product design. *E.g.*, McCabe v. L.K. Liggett Drug Co., 112 N.E.2d 254 (Mass. 1953) (upholding jury verdict finding that defendant breached the implied warranty by selling a "Lucifer Lifetime" metal coffeemaker with a design that caused it to explode while plaintiff was making coffee one morning). Presumably, however, most malfunctions involve errors in manufacture or construction, such as a hairline fracture in a soda bottle or contaminants in a food product. Regardless of the source of malfunction, the seller of the defective product incurs strict liability under §402A.

After adopting strict products liability, courts began to confront cases in which products did not malfunction but were still alleged to be defectively designed. In the next set of cases, courts apply the original formulation of §402A to resolve these allegations, after having decided to retain the consumer expectations test instead of replacing it with the risk-utility test. Consider whether the original version of strict products liability adequately protects consumer expectations in these cases.

HALLIDAY v. STURM, RUGER & CO.
Court of Appeals of Maryland, 2002
792 A.2d 1145

WILNER, J. This case arises from the tragic death of Jordan Garris. In June, 1999, Jordan shot himself while playing with his father's handgun. Jordan's mother, petitioner here, seeks to hold the manufacturer of the handgun, respondent Sturm, Ruger & Co. (Sturm Ruger), liable for Jordan's death. The Circuit Court for Baltimore City, by granting respondent's motion for summary judgment, found no liability. A divided Court of Special Appeals affirmed. We shall do likewise.

Jordan's father, Clifton Garris, purchased the gun in March, 1999, from On Target, Inc., a retail firearms store. With the purchase of the gun came an instruction manual, the offer of a free safety course, which Garris declined, a pamphlet entitled "Youth Handgun Safety Act Notice" published by the Federal Bureau of Alcohol, Tobacco and Firearms, a lock box in which to store the gun and the magazine, and a padlock for the box.

The instruction manual provided multiple warnings and instructions regarding the storage and use of the gun.

Garris disregarded virtually every one of these warnings and opportunities. He did not store either the gun or the magazine in the lock box but rather placed the gun under his mattress and kept the loaded magazine on a bookshelf in the same room, so that it was visible and accessible to Jordan. Jordan found the handgun under his father's mattress. He also found the loaded magazine. From watching television, the child knew how to load the magazine into the gun, and he did so. While playing with the gun, he apparently pulled the slide

II. Strict Products Liability 1.0 81

and thereby placed a bullet into the chamber. Either the safety lever was in the "fire" position already or Jordan moved it there. He then pulled the trigger, shot himself in the head, and died two days later. He was three years old.

Petitioner alleged that the gun was defective and unreasonably dangerous because its design "failed to incorporate reasonable devices to prevent its use by young children," in particular "one or more of the following: a grip safety, a heavy trigger-pull, a child-resistant manual safety, a built-in lock, a trigger lock, and/or personalized gun technology that would have substantially reduced the likelihood that a child could fire the gun." Citing data released by the Centers for Disease Control and Prevention to the effect that 1,641 children under ten were accidentally killed by handguns between 1979 and 1996, petitioner averred in her complaint that "[i]t was foreseeable that the gun would be found and handled by a young child, and that it would be fired by a young child, with resulting foreseeable grievous or fatal injury to the child and/or others." Petitioner contended that the handgun industry was aware of the problem of young children finding and injuring themselves with handguns and, in the 1880's, had developed a childproof grip safety, but that Sturm Ruger manufactured the gun without that, or any other, childproof device.

The essence of petitioner's case was that, when dealing with design defects in a strict liability claim, the court should apply a "risk-utility" analysis in lieu of a "consumer expectation" test and hold that the gun in question failed that preferred test because (1) the risk of excluding child safety features outweighs the utility of that exclusion, and (2) alternative safer designs could have been adopted economically. She argued to the Circuit Court that "[t]he central thing that Sturm Ruger did wrong in designing this gun . . . is to sell a gun a three year old could shoot." The court rejected that argument. . . .

The principal issue presented here is whether, in examining whether a product in general, or a handgun in particular, is defective for purposes of a strict liability action, this Court should continue to apply the "consumer expectation" test, as urged by Sturm Ruger, or should adopt instead a version of the "risk-utility" analysis, as requested by petitioner.

There has been a great deal of ferment regarding these issues, both in Maryland and elsewhere. Some of the debate is grounded in theory—whether, on the one hand, a consumer expectation test is either relevant or workable in a design defect situation, especially when the product is inherently dangerous, or, on the other, whether a departure from the consumer expectation test necessarily reintroduces negligence concepts, by focusing on the manufacturer's conduct rather than the product itself, and thus becomes inconsistent with the notion and function of strict liability. That debate has a practical significance. The concept of strict liability, especially as formulated in §402A of the *Restatement (Second)*, was regarded as an important pro-consumer advance; relieving persons injured by products from the requirement of proving negligence on the part of manufacturers or others in the distribution chain and focusing, instead, on the product itself, made it easier to obtain a recovery for a defectively designed or manufactured product. Substitution of a risk-utility analysis, however, especially as formulated in the *Restatement (Third)*, has attracted considerable criticism and has been viewed by many as a retrogression, as returning to negligence concepts and placing a very difficult burden on plaintiffs. *See* John F. Vargo, *The Emperor's New Clothes: The American Law Institute Adorns a "New Cloth" for Section 402A*

Products Liability Design Defects—A Survey of the States Reveals a Different Weave, 26 U. Mem. L. Rev. 493 (1996); [ ].

It is clear that, under the consumer expectation test no cause of action had been stated in this case. There was no malfunction of the gun; regrettably, it worked exactly as it was designed and intended to work and as any ordinary consumer would have expected it to work. The gun is a lawful weapon and was lawfully sold. What caused this tragedy was the carelessness of Jordan's father in leaving the weapon and the magazine in places where the child was able to find them, in contravention not only of common sense but of multiple warnings given to him at the time of purchase.

Given the controversy that continues to surround the risk-utility standard articulated for design defect cases in §2 of the *Restatement (Third)*, we are reluctant at this point to cast aside our existing jurisprudence in favor of such an approach on any broad, general basis. Nor is there a need to do so in this case, which deals with more specific issues that have been presented on several occasions to the General Assembly and have been considered and debated in that arena. So far, the Legislature has chosen not to place these burdens on gun manufacturers but has attempted to deal with the problem in other ways. We shall respect that policy choice.

JUDGMENT OF COURT OF SPECIAL APPEALS AFFIRMED, WITH COSTS.

NOTES AND QUESTIONS

1. *Consumer expectations and consumer interests.* As the court in *Halliday* observed, the risk-utility test has been criticized for representing an "unwanted ascendancy of corporate interests under the guise of tort reform," suggesting that the risk-utility test is more protective of corporate interests than the consumer expectations test. The plaintiff, however, argued for the risk-utility test, indicating that she found it to be more protective of her interests. In what respect is the consumer expectations test problematic in this type of case?

2. *The problem of obvious dangers.* Under §402A, a product is both defective and "unreasonably dangerous" only if it is more dangerous than would be expected by the ordinary consumer with ordinary knowledge common to the community. This inquiry would seem to necessarily bar recovery in cases like *Halliday*. The ordinary consumer would be aware of the risk that a child can misuse a handgun lacking childproof features, and so the materialization of that risk cannot cause the product to perform in an unexpectedly dangerous manner. Consequently, the court in *Halliday* emphasized both the obvious nature of the risk and the extensive product warnings about the matter.

Under the risk-utility test, by contrast, the "fact that a danger is open and obvious is relevant to the issue of defectiveness, but does not necessarily preclude a plaintiff from establishing that a reasonable alternative design should have been adopted that would have reduced or prevented injury to the plaintiff." RESTATEMENT (THIRD) OF TORTS: PRODUCTS LIABILITY §2 cmt. d. For this reason, the plaintiff in *Halliday* argued for the risk-utility test. Unlike the court in *Halliday*, most other courts have found this argument to be persuasive; their adoption of the risk-utility test provides much of the body of case law that the *Restatement (Third)* relied on in adopting the risk-utility test.

3. *Distinguishing different types of product performance.* Does it make sense to limit the liability inquiry to the question of whether the *actual* product performance was unexpected, when the plaintiff alleged that if the gun design had incorporated the safety features in question, the product *should have performed differently* by not shooting on this occasion? In the case of malfunction, the product such as an exploding coffeemaker actually performs in a manner that frustrates consumer expectations, but the source of that frustration lies in the fact that the coffeemaker *should have performed differently* by not exploding. Expectations are frustrated only if the product's actual performance diverges from the consumer's expectation of how that product should have performed. When the plaintiff claims that the product should have performed more safely in light of the relatively low costs of the safety improvement, why does the consumer expectations test foreclose such an inquiry?

4. *Cases that limit §402A to product malfunctions.* Does the court in *Halliday* effectively hold that §402A only applies to product malfunctions? Consider how it characterized the product performance: "There was no malfunction of the gun; regrettably, it worked exactly as it was designed and intended to work and as any ordinary consumer would have expected it to work." By limiting the frustration of consumer expectations to product malfunctions, the court limited §402A to the type of defect that generated this rule, such as contaminated food and exploding soda bottles. Recognizing as much, other courts have concluded that the §402A formulation of the consumer expectations test, "while illustrative of a particular problem, does not provide a satisfactory test" for identifying defective designs across all cases." Camacho v. Honda Motor Co., 741 P.2d 1240, 1246 (Col. 1987).

GREEN v. SMITH & NEPHEW AHP, INC.
Supreme Court of Wisconsin, 2001
629 N.W.2d 727

WILCOX, J. This case arises from a products liability claim brought by Linda M. Green (Green) against Smith & Nephew AHP, Inc. (S & N). Green alleged that S & N manufactured defective and unreasonably dangerous latex medical gloves, which caused her to suffer injuries arising from allergic reactions to the proteins in those gloves. Accordingly, Green claimed, S & N should be held strictly liable for these injuries.

At the close of the trial on Green's claim, the jury returned a verdict in favor of Green and against S & N. The Milwaukee County Circuit Court entered judgment on the verdict. S & N subsequently appealed, but the court of appeals affirmed the circuit court judgment in its entirety.

S & N argues that the circuit court erroneously instructed the jury that: (1) a product can be deemed defective and unreasonably dangerous based solely on consumer expectations about that product; and (2) a product can be deemed defective and unreasonably dangerous regardless of whether the manufacturer of that product knew or could have known of the risk of harm the product presented to consumers. Accordingly, S & N asks us to review the circuit court's jury instructions.

[Since 1967, Wisconsin has adhered to the rule of strict products liability set forth in the *Restatement (Second) of Torts* §402A (1965). T]his court adopted Comment g to §402A, which provides that a product is defective where the product is, at the time it leaves the seller's hands, *in a condition not contemplated by the ultimate consumer,* which will be unreasonably dangerous to him. Similarly, this court adopted Comment i to §402A, which provides in pertinent part that a defective product is unreasonably dangerous where it is *dangerous to an extent beyond that which would be contemplated by the ordinary consumer* who purchases it, with the ordinary knowledge common to the community as to its characteristics. These Comments provide that although defect and unreasonable danger are distinct elements to a claim in strict products liability, both elements are based on consumer expectations. [W]e frequently have reiterated that Wisconsin applies a consumer-contemplation test in strict products liability cases.

In the present case, the circuit court properly instructed the jury on this standard. As the court of appeals aptly noted, the circuit court's instruction was "essentially a clone of Comment g to §402A." Therefore, we hold that the circuit court did not erroneously exercise its discretion in instructing the jury.

S & N further contends that a number of policy considerations gravitate against this court's continued use of the consumer-contemplation test. S & N thus argues that this state should abandon its exclusive reliance on the consumer-contemplation test.

According to S & N, consumers do not always have expectations regarding the relevant design aspects of a product. S & N suggests that while most consumers likely have expectations about how safely a product will perform its basic functions or serve its intended use, they generally do not have expectations about—or, oftentimes, even know of—technical or mechanical design aspects of the product. Thus, in cases involving technical or mechanical matters, consumer contemplation may be an inappropriate measure for liability.

In addition, S & N posits that in many circumstances, the consumer-contemplation test may bar manufacturer liability and, therefore, contravene public safety. S & N suggests that in cases where a consumer sustains injuries caused by a product containing a patent defect, the consumer-contemplation test may prevent recovery because, due to the obvious nature of the defect, the defect—*i.e.,* the condition of the product—would not be beyond the contemplation of the ordinary consumer. Consequently, S & N argues, for manufacturers to avoid liability under a pure consumer-contemplation standard, they simply need to ensure that any unreasonably dangerous defects in their products are patent and, thus, obvious to the ordinary consumer.

We fail to see that any of these policy considerations advanced by S & N warrant this court to overrule the rest of Wisconsin products liability law.

We agree with S & N that in many instances, ordinary consumers may not know of or fully understand the technical or mechanical design aspects of the product at issue. In such instances, the technical or mechanical product design features of the product will comprise "condition[s] not contemplated by the

II. Strict Products Liability 1.0

ultimate consumer." Thus, the inquiry in those cases must focus on whether the design features present an unreasonable danger to the ordinary consumer.

A determination of "unreasonable danger," like a determination that a product is in a condition not contemplated by the ordinary consumer, does not inevitably require any degree of scientific understanding about the product itself. Rather, it requires understanding of how safely the ordinary consumer would expect the product to serve its intended purpose. If the product falls below such minimum consumer expectations, the product is unreasonably dangerous.

These standards are straightforward and may be applied even in "complex" cases. This court frequently has upheld use of the consumer-contemplation test in cases involving complex products. [ ] Additionally, this court has rejected the argument that the average jury cannot properly evaluate the often complex economic and engineering data presented at products liability trials. [ ]

Second, we acknowledge that in some cases, the open and obvious nature of a design defect may defeat claims for strict products liability. This does not mean, however, that manufacturers can avoid all liability by making unreasonably dangerous design defects open and obvious to the ordinary consumer. Wisconsin recognizes several other causes of action which may be applicable against manufacturers that produce products with open and obvious dangers. The open and obvious nature of a defective and unreasonably dangerous condition does not inherently bar claims based on, for example, negligence, breach of implied warranty, or breach of express warranty. We do not believe, as S & N suggests, that simply because strict products liability may not allow recovery in all circumstances involving defective and unreasonably dangerous products, we should abandon our current products liability standard.

For these reasons, we decline S & N's invitation to abandon or qualify this state's exclusive reliance on the consumer-contemplation test. We reaffirm that Wisconsin is committed to the consumer-contemplation test in all strict products liability cases.

We next review whether the circuit court erred in instructing the jury that a product can be deemed defective and unreasonably dangerous regardless of whether the manufacturer of that product knew or could have known of the risk of harm the product presented to consumers. S & N contends that the circuit court erroneously instructed the jury that "[a] manufacturer is responsible for the harm caused by a defective and unreasonably dangerous product even if the manufacturer had no knowledge or could [not] have known of the risk of harm presented by the condition of the product." As S & N points out, one of the primary policies underlying products liability law is to encourage manufacturers to produce safer products. To advance this policy, S & N further indicates, the law imposes liability on manufacturers who fail to eliminate from their products unreasonably dangerous defects, which present a risk of harm to consumers. However, S & N asserts that manufacturers cannot consciously eliminate potentially harmful defects from their products when the manufacturers do not and cannot know that those defects exist. Consequently, S & N argues, imposing liability on manufacturers that do not and cannot know of the risk of harm that their products present to consumers does not encourage manufacturers to produce safer products. Rather, S & N claims, imposing liability in such circumstances transforms strict products liability into absolute liability, a legal standard that this court specifically disavowed in [ ].

We reject this argument. Foreseeability of harm is an element of negligence. Negligence liability . . . hinges in large part on the defendant's conduct under circumstances involving a foreseeable risk of harm. By contrast, unlike negligence liability, strict products liability focuses not on the defendant's conduct, but on the nature of the defendant's product. In other words, strict products liability imposes liability without regard to negligence and its attendant factors of duty of care and foreseeability. Thus, regardless of whether a manufacturer could foresee potential risks of harm inherent in its defective and unreasonably dangerous product, strict products liability holds that manufacturer responsible for injuries caused by that product.

This is not to say that strict products liability is tantamount to absolute liability. Strict products liability does not impose liability in every instance that a consumer is injured while using a product. But under no circumstance must the plaintiff prove that the risk of harm presented by the product that caused his or her injury was foreseeable.

[W]hen this court recognized the cause of action for strict liability in tort, we identified several policy considerations supporting our decision to make manufacturers and other sellers of products responsible for placing defective and unreasonably dangerous products into the stream of commerce: (1) the seller of a product is "in the paramount position to distribute the costs of the risks" presented by the products by passing along costs to consumers or by purchasing insurance; (2) consumers have "the right to rely on the apparent safety of the product and . . . it is the seller in the first instance who creates the risk by placing the defective product on the market"; and (3) "the manufacturer has the greatest ability to control the risk created by [its] product since [it] may initiate or adopt inspection and quality control measures thereby preventing defective products from reaching the consumer." [ ]

S & N's argument focuses solely on one public policy underlying strict products liability while ignoring a second, more important policy consideration. Although products liability law is intended in part to make products safer for consumers, the primary "rationale underlying the imposition of strict liability on manufacturers and sellers is that the risk of the loss associated with the use of defective products should be borne by those who have created the risk and who have reaped the profit by placing a defective product in the stream of commerce." [ ] In a case where a manufacturer places an unforeseeably defective and unreasonably dangerous product on the market, the manufacturer both creates the risk of harm and reaps the profit from the defective and unreasonably dangerous product. . . . [H]olding the manufacturer accountable will serve the equitable purpose of imposing the cost of the risk on the party that created the risk. Thus, contrary to S & N's position, our policy discussion [of strict products liability] does not suggest that foreseeability is or should be an element in products liability cases.

Accordingly, we hold that current Wisconsin law does not support S & N's contention that the circuit court erred in instructing the jury that it could find S & N's gloves to be defective and unreasonably dangerous regardless of whether S & N knew or could have known of the risk of harm its latex gloves presented to consumers.

S & N and amicus curiae suggest in the alternative, however, that if Wisconsin strict products liability law currently does not include an element of foreseeability,

II. Strict Products Liability 1.0

this court should adopt the *Restatement (Third) of Torts* §2(b) (1998). Section 2(b) provides that a product:

> is defective in design when the foreseeable risks of harm posed by the product could have been reduced or avoided by the adoption of a reasonable alternative design by the seller or other distributor, or a predecessor in the commercial chain of distribution, and the omission of the alternative design renders the product not reasonably safe.

Comment a to §2 of the *Restatement (Third) of Torts* explains that §2(b) incorporates an element of foreseeability of risk of harm and a risk-benefit test. As such, §2(b) departs from the consumer-contemplation test set forth in the *Restatement (Second) of Torts* §402A (1965), and blurs the distinction between strict products liability claims and negligence claims. In this sense, for the reasons explained above, §2(b) is fundamentally at odds with current Wisconsin products liability law.

Where a manufacturer places a defective and unreasonably dangerous product into the stream of commerce, the manufacturer, not the injured consumer, should bear the costs of the risks posed by the product. Because §2(b) unduly obstructs this equitable principle, we refuse to adopt §2(b) into Wisconsin law.

The decision of the court of appeals is affirmed.

NOTES AND QUESTIONS

1. *Consumer expectations of unforeseeable risks.* In *Green*, the gloves actually performed more dangerously than expected by the ordinary consumer, thereby subjecting the seller to liability for the unforeseeable allergic reaction. As the court emphasized, this conclusion follows from a literal application of the consumer expectations test as formulated by §402A, the same reasoning employed by the court in *Halliday*.

By rejecting the foreseeability requirement, *Green* identifies one way in which the consumer expectations test can differ from the risk-utility test. *See also* Sternhagen v. Dow Co., 935 P.2d 1139, 1144 (Mont. 1997) (rejecting the "state-of-the-art defense [which] raises issues of reasonableness and foreseeability" because these concepts are "fundamental to negligence law" and would inappropriately "inject negligence principles into strict liability law and thereby sever Montana's strict products liability law from the core principles for which it was adopted"). In these cases, the §402A formulation of the consumer expectations test is more demanding of manufacturers than the risk-utility test. *See* RESTATEMENT (THIRD) OF TORTS: PRODUCTS LIABILITY §2 cmt. m (explaining that the risk-utility tests for determining defects in product designs or warnings "impose liability only when the product is put to uses that it is reasonable to expect a seller or distributor to foresee").

2. *Warnings and malfunctions.* As in *Halliday*, the court in *Green* formulates the consumer expectations test in a manner that is inherently limited to the problem of product malfunctions—the type of defect exclusively considered by the drafters of §402A. To prevent a product from being

"unreasonably dangerous" under §402A, the consumer must be sufficiently informed of all factors relevant to its safe performance, in which case the product cannot perform in an unexpectedly dangerous manner that would subject the seller to strict tort liability. Consequently, comment j of §402A obligates sellers to provide warnings about product risks that are not known by the ordinary consumer and would be material to his or her decision whether to purchase or use the product. To satisfy this warning obligation for an exploding soda bottle, the manufacturer would have to warn about the malfunction itself: "Warning: This soda bottle will explode when opened." No one would buy that particular bottle once warned. Such a warning, moreover, is not feasible. Although the manufacturer knows that some soda bottles will explode, even with the exercise of reasonable care, it will not know which particular bottles will explode. As a matter of both commercial reality and feasibility, the manufacturer cannot rely on warnings to avoid liability for malfunctions. Hence §402A subjects the manufacturer to liability for product malfunctions, "even though it has exercised all possible care in the preparation and sale of the product." Is there anything about the malfunction in *Green* that departs from this logic?

Consider the cases in Chapter 2 outlining the doctrinal development of strict products liability. Did any of them involve unforeseeable malfunctions? Did the courts in those cases ever address this issue? In restating this case law, did §402A implicitly limit the liability rule to foreseeable malfunctions?

3. *An equitable rationale for strict liability?* According to the court in *Green*, "holding the manufacturer accountable [for the unforeseeable risk] will serve the equitable purpose of imposing the cost of the risk on the party that created the risk." If the justification for liability stems from the fact that the product seller profits or benefits from the sale of the risky product, why limit strict liability to a "defective and unreasonably dangerous product"? Is this a rationale for strict products liability or absolute liability?

A related rationale is based on the risk-spreading properties of strict liability. "[M]any believe that consumers who benefit from products without suffering harm should share, through increases in the prices charged for those products, the burden of unavoidable injury costs that result from manufacturing defects" RESTATEMENT (THIRD) OF TORTS: PRODUCTS LIABILITY § cmt. a. Consider, once again, whether this rationale can be squared with the requirement of defect as reflected in the court's observation, "strict products liability does not impose liability in every instance that a consumer is injured while using a product."

4. *Consumer expectations and the occurrence of injury.* Can the holding in *Green* be justified on the ground that consumers don't expect to be injured by latex gloves? When the product is the sole cause of an injury, why doesn't that outcome frustrate consumer expectations, thereby justifying a rule that makes product sellers strictly liable for all product-caused injuries?

According to *disappointment theory*, when the actual outcome of a risky situation (such as the occurrence of a product-caused injury) is inferior to the individual's expectation, she "will experience disappointment." Philippe Delquie & Alessandra Cillo, *Disappointment Without Prior Expectation: A Unifying Perspective on Decision Under Risk*, 33 J. Risk & Uncer.

197, 197 (2006). The degree to which a consumer expects to be injured by the product (or the probability of a product-caused injury) ordinarily is quite low, and so in this respect consumers do not "expect" to be injured by the product. The occurrence of injury, therefore, can "trigger disappointment feelings when compared to better outcomes" of no injury. *Cf. id.* at 199 ("[A]ny outcome [of a risky prospect] is liable to trigger disappointment feelings when compared to better outcomes."). For this simple reason, the ordinary consumer who suffers a product-caused injury could have disappointed expectations of product performance, regardless of whether there was anything "wrong" with the product.

To be sure, no court would say that consumer expectations are frustrated simply because the product caused the plaintiff's injury. "[I]t is hornbook law that proof of a product accident alone proves neither defectiveness nor causation." David G. Owen, Products Liability Law §7.4, at 454 (3d ed. 2015). But if the liability inquiry turns only on the question of whether the product performed in a manner that frustrated consumer expectations, what explains why the unexpected occurrence of injury is not a malfunction that triggers the rule of strict liability?

DENNY v. FORD MOTOR CO.
Court of Appeals of New York, 1995
662 N.E.2d 730

Titone, J. Are the elements of New York's causes of action for strict products liability and breach of implied warranty always coextensive? If not, can the latter be broader than the former? These are the core issues presented by the questions that the United States Court of Appeals for the Second Circuit has certified to us in this diversity action involving an allegedly defective vehicle.

As stated by the Second Circuit, this action arises out of a June 9, 1986 accident in which plaintiff Nancy Denny was severely injured when the Ford Bronco II that she was driving rolled over. The rollover accident occurred when Denny slammed on her brakes in an effort to avoid a deer that had walked directly into her motor vehicle's path. Denny and her spouse sued Ford Motor Co., the vehicle's manufacturer, asserting claims for negligence, strict products liability and breach of implied warranty of merchantability.

In response to interrogatories, the jury found that the Bronco II was not "defective" and that defendant was therefore not liable under plaintiffs' strict products liability cause of action. However, the jury also found that defendant had breached its implied warranty of merchantability and that the breach was the proximate cause of Nancy Denny's injuries. Following apportionment of damages, plaintiff was awarded judgment in the amount of $1.2 million.

In this proceeding, Ford's sole argument is that plaintiffs' strict products liability and breach of implied warranty causes of action were identical and that, accordingly, a defendant's verdict on the former cannot be reconciled with a plaintiff's verdict on the latter. This argument is, in turn, premised on both the intertwined history of the two doctrines and the close similarity in their elements and legal functions. Ford's argument has much to commend it. However, in the final analysis, the argument is flawed because it overlooks the continued existence of a separate *statutory* predicate for the breach of warranty theory and the subtle but important distinction between the two theories that arises from their different historical and doctrinal root.

Although the products liability theory sounding in tort and the breach of implied warranty theory authorized by the Uniform Commercial Code ("UCC") coexist and are often invoked in tandem, the core element of "defect" is subtly different in the two causes of action. Under New York law, a design defect may be actionable under a strict products liability theory if the product is not reasonably safe. [T]he New York standard for determining the existence of a design defect has required an assessment of whether "if the design defect were known at the time of manufacture, a reasonable person would conclude that the utility of the product did not outweigh the risk inherent in marketing a product designed in that manner." [ ] [This] analysis is rooted in a recognition that there are both risks and benefits associated with many products and that there are instances in which a product's inherent dangers cannot be eliminated without simultaneously compromising or completely nullifying its benefits. In such circumstances, a weighing of the product's benefits against its risks is an appropriate and necessary component of the liability assessment under the policy-based principles associated with tort law.

The adoption of this risk/utility balance as a component of the "defectiveness" element has brought the inquiry in design defect cases closer to that used in traditional negligence cases, where the reasonableness of an actor's conduct is considered in light of a number of situational and policy-driven factors. While efforts have been made to steer away from the fault-oriented negligence principles by characterizing the design defect cause of action in terms of a product-based rather than a conduct-based analysis, the reality is that the risk/utility balancing test is a "negligence-inspired" approach.

It is this negligence-like risk/benefit component of the defect element that differentiates strict products liability claims from UCC-based breach of implied warranty claims in cases involving design defects. While the strict products concept of a product that is "not reasonably safe" requires a weighing of the product's dangers against its over-all advantages, the UCC's concept of a "defective" product requires an inquiry only into whether the product in question was "fit for the ordinary purposes for which such goods are used" (UCC 2-314[2][c]). The latter inquiry focuses on the expectations for the performance of the product when used in the customary, usual and reasonably foreseeable manners. The cause of action is one involving true "strict" liability, since recovery may be had upon a showing that the product was not minimally safe for its expected purpose—without regard to the feasibility of alternative designs or the manufacturer's "reasonableness" in marketing it in that unsafe condition.

This distinction between the "defect" analysis in breach of implied warranty actions and the "defect" analysis in strict products liability actions is explained by the differing etiology and doctrinal underpinnings of the two distinct theories. The former class of actions originates in contract law, which directs its attention to the purchaser's disappointed expectations; the latter originates in tort law, which traditionally has concerned itself with social policy and risk allocation by means other than those dictated by the marketplace.

II. Strict Products Liability 1.0

As long as that legislative source of authority exists, we are not free to merge the warranty cause of action with its tort-based sibling regardless of whether, as a matter of policy, the contract-based warranty claim may fairly be regarded as a historical relic that no longer has any independent substantive value. Rather, we must construe and apply this separate remedy in a manner that remains consistent with its *current* roots in contract law.

The current version of UCC 2-318 is not the equivalent of these uniform product liability provisions, nor does it manifest an intention by our State's Legislature to engraft a tort cause of action onto a UCC article that concerns itself principally with the contract-based obligations. Indeed, the Law Revision Commission Staff Notes, which the dissent cites, clearly state that the proposed amendments to UCC 2-318 "would . . . allow recovery by the [strict products liability] plaintiffs *on a different cause of action.*"

In any event, while the critics and commentators may debate the relative merits of the consumer-expectation and risk/utility tests, there is no existing authority for the proposition that the risk/utility analysis is appropriate when the plaintiff's claim rests on a claimed breach of implied warranty under UCC 2-314(2)(c) and 2-318. Further, the negligence-like risk/utility approach is foreign to the realm of contract law.

As a practical matter, the distinction between the defect concepts in tort law and in implied warranty theory may have little or no effect in most cases. In this case, however, the nature of the proof and the way in which the fact issues were litigated demonstrates how the two causes of action can diverge. In the trial court, Ford took the position that the design features of which plaintiffs complain, i.e., the Bronco II's high center of gravity, narrow track width, short wheel base and specially tailored suspension system, were important to preserving the vehicle's ability to drive over the highly irregular terrain that typifies off-road travel. Ford's proof in this regard was relevant to the strict products liability risk/utility equation, which required the fact finder to determine whether the Bronco II's value as an off-road vehicle outweighed the risk of the rollover accidents that could occur when the vehicle was used for other driving tasks.

On the other hand, plaintiffs' proof focused, in part, on the sale of the Bronco II for suburban driving and everyday road travel. Plaintiffs also adduced proof that the Bronco II's design characteristics made it unusually susceptible to rollover accidents when used on paved roads. All of this evidence was useful in showing that routine highway and street driving was the "ordinary purpose" for which the Bronco II was sold and that it was not "fit"—or safe—for that purpose.

Thus, under the evidence in this case, a rational fact finder could have simultaneously concluded that the Bronco II's utility as an off-road vehicle outweighed the risk of injury resulting from rollover accidents *and* that the vehicle was not safe for the "ordinary purpose" of daily driving for which it was marketed and sold. Under the law of this State such a set of factual judgments would lead to the concomitant legal conclusion that plaintiffs' strict products liability cause of action was not viable but that defendant should nevertheless be held liable for breach of its implied promise that the Bronco II was "merchantable" or "fit" for its "ordinary purpose." Importantly, what makes this case distinctive is that the "ordinary purpose" for which the product was marketed and sold to the plaintiff was *not* the same as the utility against which the risk was to be weighed. It is these unusual circumstances that give practical significance to the ordinarily theoretical difference between the defect concepts in tort and statutory breach of implied warranty causes of action.

From the foregoing it is apparent that the causes of action for strict products liability and breach of implied warranty of merchantability are not identical in New York and that the latter is not necessarily subsumed by the former. It follows that, under the circumstances presented, a verdict such as the one occurring here—in which the manufacturer was found liable under an implied warranty cause of action and not liable under a strict products cause of action—is theoretically reconcilable under New York law.

NOTES AND QUESTIONS

1. *Contrasting strict products liability with the implied warranty under the Uniform Commercial Code.* In deciding that the implied warranty claim under the UCC substantively differs from strict products liability, did the court have to conclude that the two inquiries rely on different tests for defect? The implied warranty under the UCC is the contractual version. (Although the UCC permits modifications that effectively convert the warranty into a tort rule, New York has not adopted these modifications.) By contrast, the tort version of the implied warranty is embodied in strict products liability. The contractual version of the warranty significantly differs from the tort version for reasons unrelated to the test for defect. For example, the UCC permits product sellers to disclaim liability under the implied warranty, whereas such disclaimers are not enforceable under strict products liability. *See* Chapter 14, section I. In addition, a claim of strict products liability is not ordinarily available for cases in which the defect causes only pure economic or financial losses, and so the plaintiff in such a case is limited to the contractual terms of recovery under the warranty governed by the UCC. *See* Chapter 13, section II. Finally, the contractual version of the implied warranty requires the plaintiff to notify a defendant of an alleged breach within a reasonable time after discovering the defect. *E.g.,* N.Y. U.C.C. §2-607(3). As a contractual doctrine, the implied warranty under the UCC serves a distinctive role unrelated to the definition of defect, explaining why most courts recognize that the implied warranty under the UCC utilizes the same test for defect as strict products liability. *See* Sean M. Flower, Note, *Is Strict Product Liability in Tort Identical to Implied Warranty in Contract in the Context of Personal Injuries?*, 62 Mo. L. Rev. 381, 389-390 (1997) ("Jurisdictions which adopted the majority rule . . . [have] held that verdicts which find liability for breach of implied warranty, but not for strict product liability in tort, are inconsistent.").

Instead of recognizing the other ways in which the contractual version of the implied warranty substantively differs from strict products liability, the court in *Denny* differentiated the two claims by holding that the finding of defect under the consumer expectations test substantively differs from the risk-utility test. Although the court emphasized that its analysis is limited to products with multiple uses, it upholds a divergence between consumer expectations and the risk-utility test that is not inherently limited to this class of cases. Its formulation of the consumer expectations test exclusively focuses on product performance without any consideration of the utility or cost factors in the risk-utility test—the same formulation of consumer expectations governing the claims of strict products liability in both *Halliday* and *Green*. In all three cases, the consumer expectations test is wholly based on the §402A inquiry that focuses on product malfunctions, the type of defect that rules out the type of cost considerations embodied in the risk-utility test.

2. *Vehicle rollovers as malfunctions.* Having identified the version of the consumer expectations test at issue in *Denny*, we can now more closely scrutinize the jury verdict. Did the vehicle malfunction by rolling over? The question is hard to answer because the court provides very little detail about the crash. According to the defendant's brief, the plaintiff "slammed on the brakes" and tried to avoid a deer that had "darted onto the highway in front of her while she was traveling approximately 37 m.p.h.," causing the vehicle to roll over. Brief for Respondent at *3, Denny v. Ford Motor Co., 1995 WL 17050877. On what basis could the jury determine that this was a product malfunction?

Now consider the jury verdict in a broader context. The vehicle at issue in *Denny*—the Ford Bronco II—was involved in numerous lawsuits and ultimately dubbed as the "notorious bucking Bronco II, which cost the company approximately $2.4 billion in settlements." John Greenwald, *Inside the Ford/Firestone Fight*, Time, May 29, 2001.

> In December 1980, "60 Minutes" aired a startling program which documented severe rollover problems with the Jeep CJ vehicles. Ford engineers and executives became alarmed because the Jeep CJ was the "image" for the Bronco II. Ford engineers' preliminary designs at that time showed that the stability of the Bronco II was worse than that of the Jeep CJ. In response to the "60 Minutes" program, Ford engineers presented to Ford executives five proposals to increase the stability of the Bronco II above that of the Jeep CJs since Ford engineers knew that the Jeep CJs were unstable. Ford executives chose the least expensive proposal even though they knew that with this design the Bronco II would be less stable than the Jeep CJs. The reason that Ford executives made this choice was simple—it was the least expensive proposal but, more importantly, choosing the proposals which would have made the Bronco II more stable would also have delayed Job 1 of the Bronco II and cost Ford millions of dollars. If Ford had simply spent an additional $83.00 per vehicle, or approximately 2% of the anticipated profit from the Bronco II, the Bronco II would have been a stable vehicle.

James and Belinda Watkins, Individually, as Parents of Brian Watkins, and as Administrators of the Estate of Brian Watkins, Stacy Purcell, Rachelle L. Oliver, and Joseph P. Washo, Jr., Plaintiffs and Appellants, v. Ford Motor Company, Defendant and Appellee, 1998 WL 34084747, at 10–11 (11th Cir.).

In light of these facts, it is easier to understand why the jury in *Denny* concluded that the roll over of the vehicle frustrated consumer expectations and rendered the design defective The more puzzling question is why the design passed the risk-utility test.

3. *The problem of vagueness.* Regardless of whether the vehicle in *Denny* was defectively designed, the jury's application of the consumer expectations test was opaque. According to critics of the consumer expectations test, that problem is inherent in the liability rule.

> The meaning is ambiguous and the test is very difficult of application to discrete problems. What does the reasonable purchaser contemplate? In one sense, he does not "expect" to be adversely affected by a risk or hazard unknown to him. In another sense, he does contemplate the "possibility" of unknown "side effects." In a sense the ordinary purchaser cannot reasonably expect anything more than that reasonable care in the exercise of the skill and knowledge available to design engineers has been exercised. The test can be utilized to explain most any result that a court or jury chooses to reach.

W. Page Keeton et al., PROSSER AND KEETON ON THE LAW OF TORTS §99, at 699 (5th ed. 1984) (footnote omitted). Echoing the complaints of others, the product manufacturer in one case claimed that the test is "deficient" and "unfair," in part because it "defies definition" and "focuses on the subjective, unstable and often unreasonable opinions of consumers." Soule v. General Motors Corp., 882 P.2d 298, 309 (Cal. 1994); *see also id.* at 310 (stating that "similar arguments" were made in an amicus brief filed by the Products Liability Advisory Council).

4. *The limited scope of the consumer expectations test.* Aside from the easy cases involving product malfunctions like exploding soda bottles, what do consumers actually know about how safely products should perform? The §402A formulation of the consumer expectations test is based on the consumer knowledge that is common to the community, which necessarily forecloses its application to safety questions that consumers know little or nothing about. Most courts, therefore, have concluded that "the expectations of the ordinary consumer cannot be viewed as the exclusive yardstick for evaluating design defectiveness because "[in] many situations . . . the consumer would not know what to expect, because he would have no idea how safe the product could be made." Barker v. Lull Eng'g Co., 573 P.2d 443, 455 (Cal. 1978). To address this problem, courts have adopted the risk-utility test. *E.g., id.*

5. *A minority position.* Although *Denny* continues to be recognized under New York law, the case relies on the minority rule that imputes substantively different tests for defect to the implied warranty and strict product liability. Similarly, the approach taken in *Halliday* and *Green* represents the minority position that continues to limit the rule of strict products liability to product malfunctions as per the original formulation in §402A. In jurisdictions that exclusively rely on the consumer expectations test for purposes of strict products liability, plaintiffs can still invoke the risk-utility test in pursuing claims that the manufacturer acted negligently by not adopting a reasonable alternative design — one passing the risk-utility test. *See* RESTATEMENT (SECOND) OF TORTS §402A cmt. a ("The rule stated here is not

exclusive, and does not preclude liability based on the alternative ground of negligence of the seller, where such negligence can be proved."). Hence version 1.0 of strict products liability is limited to the problem of product malfunctions, requiring plaintiffs to rely on negligence liability to recover for injuries caused by allegedly defective designs in products that did not malfunction, like the gun at issue in *Halliday*. (Note that the plaintiff in *Halliday* could not recover under negligence because the father's contributory negligence would bar recovery altogether under Maryland law.)

6. *Rethinking the implied warranty rationale for strict liability.* In developing the implied warranty rationale for strict products liability, courts have not addressed a basic question: Why does the frustration of consumer expectations justify a rule of strict liability? Insofar as the implied warranty is a doctrine of contract law, the answer is easy. Like any other term in a contract, breach of the implied warranty triggers liability, regardless of fault. But what justifies strict liability under the tort version of the implied warranty?

Consumers know that perfect quality control is often prohibitively costly and may not even be feasible. Despite the best inspection or manufacturing procedures, some defective soda bottles will be distributed in the market. The risk of defect is unavoidable. Consumers do not reasonably expect perfection.

Rather than expect perfect quality control and the complete absence of defective products, consumers minimally expect the seller to guarantee that the product has passed reasonable, though imperfect methods of quality control. For the expectation of reasonable quality to be frustrated, the product defect must be attributable to the seller's failure to exercise reasonable care in quality control. This form of consumer expectation yields a liability rule no different from ordinary negligence liability. Consider James J. White & Robert S. Summers, UNIFORM COMMERCIAL CODE §10:1 (6th ed. 2010) (observing that the implied warranty "has much . . . in common with negligence liability").

But even though consumers do not reasonably expect perfection and understand that some defective products are inevitable, they can still expect sellers to provide a guaranteed remedy for defective products. This expectation is protected by the implied warranty, which gives consumers a guaranteed remedy for defective products, regardless of whether the seller employed reasonable or unreasonable methods of quality control.

Consumers can expect a guaranteed remedy only because the guarantee of reasonable quality is too difficult to enforce. To prove that a defective product breaches a guarantee of quality, the consumer must establish the unreasonableness of the seller's quality-control measures, an issue of considerable complexity for many mass-manufacturing processes. What is the full range of reasonably safe measures that a manufacturer could adopt for monitoring the quality of a mass-manufactured product like bottled soda? The various measures are either complex (the incorporation of quality-control systems into the manufacturing process) or cannot be independently evaluated with reliable evidence (as with visual inspection by employees whose testimony about the matter might be suspect). The expectation of reasonable quality, therefore, generates important safety obligations that the consumer cannot adequately enforce. To solve this evidentiary problem, consumers can reasonably expect the seller to provide a guaranteed remedy for injuries caused by defective products.

A guaranteed remedy effectively guarantees product quality, because it gives the seller an incentive to reduce the incidence of defects by adopting reasonable quality-control measures. The logic behind this conclusion is supplied by the evidentiary rationale for strict liability. *See* Chapter 2, section II.C. This form of consumer expectation accordingly explains why the implied warranty is limited to defective products, and why this rule of strict liability can be justified by the negligence principle—it is the only practical way to enforce the obligation for sellers to adopt reasonable quality-control measures.

Hence the implied warranty does not foreclose consideration of cost in all cases, even though the §402A formulation of the liability rule excludes consideration of cost in cases of product malfunctions. We have yet to consider how the implied warranty governs products that do not malfunction—the subject of the next section. A liability rule of that type must necessarily depart from the black-letter requirements of §402A, making it possible for courts to fashion a newer, more comprehensive version of strict products liability.

III. STRICT PRODUCTS LIABILITY 2.0

To address the limitations of the consumer expectations test in the *Restatement (Second)* §402A rule of strict products liability, most courts adopted rules that depart from the textual requirements of §402A. *See* Tincher v. Omega Flex, Inc., 104 A.3d 328, 389 (Pa. 2014) (observing that many jurisdictions have adopted the risk-utility test to "vindicat[e] the salient public policy in cases in which the alleged defective condition is premised upon either an obvious danger or a danger outside the ordinary consumer's contemplation"). In light of these developments, the American Law Institute decided in the 1990s to restate the rules of products liability. As the Reporters to the *Restatement (Third)* explained in an article published at the outset of this project, a restatement was required because "doctrinal developments in products liability have placed such a heavy gloss on the original text of and comments to section 402A as to render them anachronistic and at odds with their currently discerned objectives." James A. Henderson, Jr. & Aaron D. Twerski, *A Proposed Revision of Section 402A of the Restatement (Second) of Torts*, 77 Cornell L. Rev. 1512, 1513 (1992).

According to the *Restatement (Third)* §1 comment a, the rule of strict products liability in §402A of the *Restatement (Second)* was "created to deal with liability for manufacturing defects" such as the construction flaws that cause soda bottles to explode or the contaminants that adulterate food products. Consequently, the rule "could not be appropriately applied to cases of design defects or defects based on inadequate instructions or warnings." These problems are illustrated by the cases in the last section. To address these problems, the *Restatement*

III. Strict Products Liability 2.0

(Third) followed the approach taken by most courts and adopted a different liability rule—the risk-utility test—to determine defects in product designs and in warnings. The *Restatement (Third)*, however, did not merely restate the rules that courts had adopted for determining defects in products that did not malfunction. It altered the normative framework of products liability by eliminating the protection of consumer expectations as the rationale for tort liability and by characterizing the liability rule in terms of negligence rather than strict liability. The negligence-based framework of the *Restatement (Third)* has produced the controversy over the substantive rationale for products liability discussed in section I.

We are now in a position to more fully evaluate this ongoing controversy. Rather than adopting the risk-utility test as a form of negligence liability, the majority of jurisdictions have instead incorporated that test into the framework of strict products liability. Courts could do so by extending the implied warranty from malfunctioning products—the original inquiry in §402A—to products that do not malfunction, resulting in a new framework more accurately described as strict products liability 2.0.

A. Incorporating the Risk-Utility Test into Strict Products Liability

POTTER v. CHICAGO PNEUMATIC
Supreme Court of Connecticut, 1997
694 A.2d 1319

KATZ, A.J. This appeal arises from a products liability action brought by the plaintiffs against the defendants. The plaintiffs claim that they were injured in the course of their employment as shipyard workers at the General Dynamics Corporation Electric Boat facility in Groton as a result of using pneumatic hand tools manufactured by the defendants. Specifically, the plaintiffs allege that the tools were defectively designed because they exposed the plaintiffs to excessive vibration, and because the defendants failed to provide adequate warnings with respect to the potential danger presented by excessive vibration.

The plaintiffs suffer from permanent vascular and neurological impairment of their hands, which has caused blanching of their fingers, pain, numbness, tingling, reduction of grip strength, intolerance of cold and clumsiness from restricted blood flow. As a result, the plaintiffs have been unable to continue their employment as grinders and their performance of other activities has been restricted. The plaintiffs' symptoms are consistent with a diagnosis of hand arm vibration syndrome. Expert testimony confirmed that exposure to vibration is a significant contributing factor to the development of hand arm vibration syndrome, and that a clear relationship exists between the level of vibration exposure and the risk of developing the syndrome.

After a six week trial, the trial court rendered judgment on jury verdicts in favor of the plaintiffs. Finding that the defendants' tools had been defectively designed so as to render them unreasonably dangerous, the jury awarded the plaintiffs compensatory damages [and rejected plaintiffs' claim for punitive damages].

We first address the defendants' argument that the trial court improperly failed to render judgment for the defendants notwithstanding the verdicts because there was insufficient evidence for the jury to have found that the tools had been defectively designed. Specifically, the defendants claim that, in order to establish a prima facie design defect case, the plaintiffs were required to prove that there was a feasible alternative design available at the time that the defendants put their tools into the stream of commerce. We disagree.

Products liability law has evolved to hold manufacturers strictly liable for unreasonably dangerous products that cause injury to ultimate users. Nevertheless, strict tort liability does not transform manufacturers into insurers, nor does it impose absolute liability. As the Wisconsin Supreme Court has pointed out, "from the plaintiff's point of view the most beneficial aspect of the rule is that it relieves him of proving specific acts of negligence and protects him from the defenses of notice of breach, disclaimer, and lack of privity in the implied warranty concepts of sales and contracts." [ ] Strict tort liability merely relieves the plaintiff from proving that the manufacturer was negligent and allows the plaintiff to establish instead the defective condition of the product as the principal basis of liability.

Although courts have widely accepted the concept of strict tort liability, some of the specifics of strict tort liability remain in question. In particular, courts have sharply disagreed over the appropriate definition of defectiveness in design cases. As the Alaska Supreme Court has stated: "Design defects present the most perplexing problems in the field of strict products liability because there is no readily ascertainable external measure of defectiveness. While manufacturing flaws can be evaluated against the intended design of the product, no such objective standard exists in the design defect context." [ ]

This court has long held that in order to prevail in a design defect claim, "the plaintiff must prove that the product is unreasonably dangerous." [ ] We have derived our definition of "unreasonably dangerous" from comment (i) to §402A, which provides that "the article sold must be dangerous to an extent beyond that which would be contemplated by the ordinary consumer who purchases it, with the ordinary knowledge common to the community as to its characteristics." This "consumer expectation" standard is now well established in Connecticut strict products liability decisions.

The defendants propose that it is time for this court to abandon the consumer expectation standard and adopt the requirement that the plaintiff must prove the existence of a reasonable alternative design in order to prevail on a design defect claim. We decline to accept the defendants' invitation.

In our view, the feasible alternative design requirement imposes an undue burden on plaintiffs that might preclude otherwise valid claims from jury consideration. Such a rule would require plaintiffs to retain an expert witness even in cases in which lay jurors can infer a design defect from circumstantial evidence. Connecticut courts, however, have consistently stated that a jury may, under appropriate circumstances, infer a defect from the evidence without the necessity of expert testimony. [ ] Accordingly, we decline to adopt the requirement that a plaintiff must prove a feasible alternative design as a sine qua non to establishing a prima facie case of design defect.

Although today we continue to adhere to our long-standing rule that a product's defectiveness is to be determined by the expectations of an ordinary

III. Strict Products Liability 2.0

consumer, we nevertheless recognize that there may be instances involving complex product designs in which an ordinary consumer may not be able to form expectations of safety. In such cases, a consumer's expectations may be viewed in light of various factors that balance the utility of the product's design with the magnitude of its risks. We find persuasive the reasoning of those jurisdictions that have modified their formulation of the consumer expectation test by incorporating risk-utility factors into the ordinary consumer expectation analysis. *See, e.g.,* Reed v. Tiffin Motor Homes, Inc., 697 F.2d 1192, 1196-97 (4th Cir. 1982) (applying South Carolina law); Koske v. Townsend Engineering Co., 551 N.E.2d 437, 440-441 (Ind. 1990); Aller v. Rodgers Machinery Mfg. Co., 268 N.W.2d 830, 835 (Iowa 1978); Jenkins v. Amchem Products, Inc., 886 P.2d 869 (Kan. 1994); Seattle-First National Bank v. Tabert, 542 P.2d 774 (Wash. 1975). Thus, the modified consumer expectation test provides the jury with the product's risks and utility and then inquires whether a reasonable consumer would consider the product unreasonably dangerous. As the Supreme Court of Washington stated in *Seattle-First National Bank v. Tabert,* supra, "in determining the reasonable expectations of the ordinary consumer, a number of factors must be considered. The relative cost of the product, the gravity of the potential harm from the claimed defect and the cost and feasibility of eliminating or minimizing the risk may be relevant in a particular case. In other instances the nature of the product or the nature of the claimed defect may make other factors relevant to the issue." Accordingly, under this modified formulation, the consumer expectation test would establish the product's risks and utility, and the inquiry would then be whether a reasonable consumer would consider the product design unreasonably dangerous.

In our view, the relevant factors that a jury *may* consider include, but are not limited to, the usefulness of the product, the likelihood and severity of the danger posed by the design, the feasibility of an alternative design, the financial cost of an improved design, the ability to reduce the product's danger without impairing its usefulness or making it too expensive, and the feasibility of spreading the loss by increasing the product's price. [ ] The availability of a feasible alternative design is a factor that the plaintiff may, rather than must, prove in order to establish that a product's risks outweigh its utility. [ ]

Furthermore, we emphasize that our adoption of a risk-utility balancing component to our consumer expectation test does not signal a retreat from strict tort liability. In weighing a product's risks against its utility, the focus of the jury should be on the product itself, and not on the conduct of the manufacturer.

Although today we adopt a modified formulation of the consumer expectation test, we emphasize that we do not require a plaintiff to present evidence relating to the product's risks and utility in every case. As the California Court of Appeals has stated: "There are certain kinds of accidents—even where fairly complex machinery is involved—[that] are so bizarre that the average juror, upon hearing the particulars, might reasonably think: 'Whatever the user may have expected from that contraption, it certainly wasn't that.'" [ ] Accordingly, the ordinary consumer expectation test is appropriate when the everyday experience of the particular product's users permits the inference that the product did not meet minimum safety expectations.

Conversely, the jury should engage in the risk-utility balancing required by our modified consumer expectation test when the particular facts do not reasonably permit the inference that the product did not meet the safety expectations of the ordinary consumer. Furthermore, instructions based on the ordinary consumer expectation test would not be appropriate when, as a matter of law, there is insufficient evidence to support a jury verdict under that test. In such circumstances, the jury should be instructed solely on the modified consumer expectation test we have articulated today.

In this respect, it is the function of the trial court to determine whether an instruction based on the ordinary consumer expectation test or the modified consumer expectation test, or both, is appropriate in light of the evidence presented. In making this determination, the trial court must ascertain whether, under each test, there is sufficient evidence as a matter of law to warrant the respective instruction.

With these principles in mind, we now consider whether, in the present case, the trial court properly instructed the jury with respect to the definition of design defect for the purposes of strict tort liability. The trial court instructed the jury that a manufacturer may be strictly liable if the plaintiffs prove, among other elements, that the product in question was in a defective condition, unreasonably dangerous to the ultimate user. The court further instructed the jury that, in determining whether the tools were unreasonably dangerous, it may draw its conclusions based on the reasonable expectations of an ordinary user of the defendants' tools. Because there was sufficient evidence as a matter of law to support the determination that the tools were unreasonably dangerous based on the ordinary consumer expectation test, we conclude that this instruction was appropriately given to the jury.

The jury heard testimony that Guarneri, [the industrial hygienist for one of the defendants], had performed extensive testing of tools used at the shipyard, which tests revealed that a large number of the defendants' tools violated the [American National Standards Institute's] limits for vibration exposure and exceeded the [American Conference of Governmental and Industrial Hygienists'] threshold limit. The jury also heard substantial testimony with respect to various methods, including isolation, dampening and balancing, available to reduce the deleterious effects of vibration caused by the defendants' tools. Moreover, there was expert testimony that exposure to vibration is a significant contributing factor to the development of hand arm vibration syndrome and that a clear relationship exists between the level of vibration exposure and the risk of developing the syndrome. Viewing the evidence in a light favorable to supporting the jury's verdicts, as we must, we conclude that the jury properly determined that the defendants' tools had been defectively designed.

[For other reasons, the court reversed the judgment and remanded the case for a new trial on the design defect claim and the punitive damages claim in connection with the design defect claim.]

NOTES AND QUESTIONS

1. *Defining consumer expectations with the risk-utility test.* As in *Potter*, a significant number of other courts have rejected the risk-utility test in the *Restatement (Third)* while defining the consumer expectations test in terms of the risk-utility test. For example, the Illinois Supreme Court "decline[d]

III. Strict Products Liability 2.0

defendants' invitation to adopt section 2(b) of the Products Liability Restatement" on the ground that it would "change . . . the substantive law of this state." Mikolajczyk v. Ford Motor Co., 901 N.E.2d 329, 346-347 (Ill. 2008). The court then concluded that there is no substantive difference between consumer expectations and the risk-utility test. *Id.* at 348 ("the consumer-expectation test and the risk-utility test . . . are not *theories of liability*; they are *methods of proof*") (sentence structure and quotation omitted). This type of approach is common. A substantial majority of states rely on some combination of consumer expectations and the risk-utility test, even if they have expressly rejected the framework for the risk-utility test adopted by the *Restatement (Third)*. *See* Branham v. Ford Motor Co., 701 S.E.2d 5, 14 n.12 (S.C. 2010) (citing 17 different states as exclusively relying on the risk-utility test, with the remaining states either exclusively employing the consumer test—a distinct minority—or a hybrid of the consumer expectations and risk-utility tests).

2. *Rhetorical confusion?* Did the court in *Potter* adequately explain why the consumer expectations test can be modified to incorporate the risk-utility test for evaluating defective designs? Is it enough to merely cite to cases from other jurisdictions that have taken the same approach? Based on this body of case law, it appears that "courts applying the consumer expectations test have offered in the alternative only an ill-defined doctrinal construction that seems repeatedly to collapse into the very risk-utility framework that the courts claim to reject." Douglas A. Kysar, *The Expectations of Consumers*, 103 Colum. L. Rev. 1700, 1704 (2003). After surveying the reported case law in state courts that have retained the consumer expectations test, Professor Aaron Twerski recently found that the consumer expectations test is routinely litigated by reference to the reasonable alternative design required by the risk-utility test. Aaron D. Twerski, *The Quieting of Products Liability*, 105 Cornell L. Rev. 1211, 1213-1214 (2020). What, then, is the difference between the consumer expectations and risk-utility tests?

Because the consumer expectations test appears to be both doctrinally and functionally indistinguishable from the risk-utility test, any debate about their respective merits would seem to be "hullabaloo" that for sound reasons "has faded into the past. The torrent of scholarly literature dealing with products liability has been reduced to a trickle." *Id.* at 1212-1213. Though once confused about the matter, scholars presumably now recognize that "consensus has been achieved" and "the *Restatement (Third)* reflects the consensus view." James A. Henderson, Jr. & Aaron D. Twerski, *Achieving Consensus on Defective Product Design*, 83 Cornell L. Rev. 867, 872, 919 (1998).

Professors Henderson and Twerski served as Reporters for the products liability volume of the *Restatement (Third)*. After analyzing *Potter*, which was decided while the *Restatement (Third)* was still in draft form, the Reporters in the published version of the *Restatement (Third)* concluded, "it is, in actuality, perfectly consistent with this Restatement." RESTATEMENT (THIRD) OF TORTS: PRODUCTS LIABILITY §2 Rptrs.' Notes cmt. d, sect. II.C. But if the liability rules in *Potter* are identical to those in the *Restatement (Third)*, why did the court in *Potter* expressly reject the *Restatement (Third)* formulation of the risk-utility test? Unable to discern any good answer to this question, Professors Henderson and Twerski argue that courts like the one in *Potter* are misguided by the "rhetorical confusion" engendered by the label of strict products liability that "is largely unnecessary." 83 Cornell L. Rev. at 871. Courts have been clinging to a "myth" about strict products liability first given "credence" by section 402A of the *Restatement (Second). Id.* at 870. Is it plausible that so many courts are simply confused about the matter?

BIFOLCK v. PHILLIP MORRIS, INC.
Supreme Court of Connecticut, 2016
152 A.3d 1183

McDonald, J. . . . In the present action, this court considers three substantive questions: (1) whether, for claims alleging design defects, we should abandon our dual tests based on §402A of the Restatement (Second) of Torts and adopt the standards under the Restatement (Third) of Torts, Products Liability. . . . [The facts of the case are not relevant to the resolution of this question and therefore are not recounted here — ED.]

A

PARTIES' POSITIONS

The parties and the amici supporting their respective positions take sharply divergent views on every consideration relevant to this issue. The plaintiff urges us not to abandon our dual *Restatement (Second)* tests, characterizing the *Restatement (Third)* as a significant departure from our long-standing strict liability standard and the public policies that this standard advances. Conversely, the defendant urges us to adopt the *Restatement (Third)*, characterizing it as consistent with our case law, our [products liability act], and litigation practice. To the extent that both parties acknowledge that the *Restatement (Third)* will make some change to our product liability law, they point to different effects of those changes. The plaintiff contends that these changes will have a detrimental, unfair effect on injured consumers, whereas the defendant contends that these changes will provide greater clarity and objectivity without such effects. The plaintiff contends that the task of weighing the numerous policy considerations implicated is better left to the legislature, whereas the defendant contends that the issue should be resolved by this court.

B

CURRENT STANDARD UNDER OUR LAW

. . . Whereas *Potter* established dual tests to prove that a design defect is unreasonably dangerous, our recent decision clarified the circumstances under which each test applies. Izzarelli v. R.J. Reynolds Tobacco Co., 136 A.3d 1232 (Conn. 2016). The modified consumer expectation test is our primary test. [ ] The

III. Strict Products Liability 2.0

ordinary consumer expectation test is reserved for those cases in which the product failed to meet consumers' legitimate, commonly accepted, *minimum* safety expectations. [ ] The defect in such cases is so obvious that expert testimony is not needed to establish it and the utility of the product is not an excuse for the undisclosed defect. [ ]

In sum, under either test, §402A provides the elements of a strict product liability claim [ ]; but the unreasonably dangerous element is determined by minimum safety expectations in one and by balancing risks and utility in the other.

C
STANDARD UNDER THE *RESTATEMENT (THIRD)*

[The court discusses the *Restatement (Third)* requirement that a plaintiff must ordinarily prove a defective design by identifying a reasonable alternative design that passes the risk-utility test. It then discusses the limited exception recognized by the *Restatement (Third)* §2 cmt. e for products that are so "manifestly unreasonable in that they have low social utility and high degree of danger, that liability should attach even absent proof of a reasonable alternative design." Finally, the court explains why the *Restatement (Third)*'s formulation of the risk-utility test is no different from negligence liability.]

Section 402A is a true strict liability standard. . . . Although the availability of an alternative design could be relevant under either of our tests under §402A, neither requires such proof. Indeed, under our primary modified consumer expectation test, a plaintiff may establish liability solely by reference to the product sold, upon proof that its risks outweigh its utility. It bears emphasizing that this risk-utility balancing does not limit liability to products that are of excessively low utility and exceedingly high risk, as does the "manifestly" unreasonable standard in the *Restatement (Third)*. On its face, therefore, the *Restatement (Third)* would appear to make consequential changes to our product liability law.

D
WHETHER THE *RESTATEMENT (THIRD)* SHOULD BE ADOPTED

. . . Putting aside the question of any purported advantages that could be gained from adoption of the *Restatement (Third)*, we note the following considerations that weigh against its adoption.

We have followed §402A's strict liability standard for more than five decades. We have only modified that standard to the extent that it was necessary to fill a gap in our law; *Potter*; or to clarify the field of operation of those tests to a case before us. *Izzarelli*.

In the almost two decades since this court adopted our modified consumer expectation test in *Potter*, there has been no evidence that our §402A strict liability tests have proved to be unworkable. Not a single case applying Connecticut law has been brought to our attention demonstrating either that a jury had difficulty applying our law or that a jury's verdict yielded a bizarre or unconscionable result. Indeed, we noted in *Izzarelli* that we would trust our trial courts to safeguard against any such result. [ ]

In those two decades since *Potter*, there is also no indication that any action has been undertaken to seek changes to our tests. No party has ever asked this court to modify those tests, or to reconsider the *Restatement (Third)* in light of the failure of the court in *Potter* to address its exceptions to the alternative design requirement. [ ] No interest group has sought change legislatively. Shortly before the court's decision in *Potter*, the Connecticut Business and Industry Association drafted a bill that sought to amend our act to incorporate the definition of design defect in the draft *Restatement (Third)*. [ ] That bill was not acted on by the Judiciary Committee after it heard competing views on it at a public hearing. Since *Potter*, other legislation has been proposed to amend the act; [ ]; but none that would have changed our product liability standards.

An argument that our standard is unworkable because it lacks an "objective" basis for decision-making was implicitly rejected in *Potter*, and is both circular and contradicted by experience. The presumption on which this argument rests is that failing to require proof of a reasonable alternative design in a risk-utility test deprives the fact finder of an objective basis for decision-making because it lacks an alternative against which to compare the marketed product. The flaw in this argument is that it assumes that a product cannot be unsafe unless it can be made safer. If the fact finder's task is to determine whether the defendant could have made a safer product, it necessarily follows that the absence of an alternative design makes this task impossible. If, however, the fact finder's task is to assess whether the product is unreasonably dangerous because its risks exceed its utility, no comparison to an alternative is necessary. The fact that jurors commonly engage in such a balancing test whenever they are called upon to assess reasonableness, such as in a claim of negligence, evidences that such weighing is workable. [ ] Indeed, even under the *Restatement (Third)*, the fact finder weighs the risks and utility of each respective design before comparing the alternative design to the product sold. [ ]

We also note that Connecticut's standard is hardly an outlier. It is not a fruitful exercise to attempt to obtain a precise count of how many jurisdictions have adopted or rejected the *Restatement (Third)* standard. Like every other aspect of this area of the law, parties on each side of this debate disagree about what legal standard has been adopted in the various jurisdictions and whether that determination should be made on the basis of how the court has articulated its standard or how the cases have been litigated. [ ] It suffices for our purposes that several other jurisdictions apply similar standards to ours, some for many years. [ ]

In addition to the lack of evidence that our *Restatement (Second)* standard is unworkable, we are not persuaded that the *Restatement (Third)* fully addresses all of the concerns that previously led this court to reject the draft *Restatement (Third)*. . . .

With respect to the reasonable alternative design requirement, the court in *Potter* expressed a concern that such a rule would preclude valid claims for products for which there is no alternative design. [ ] Although the *Restatement (Third)* provides some exceptions to this requirement, they are exceedingly limited in their operation. Of particular concern is the narrow scope of manifestly unreasonable designs, which excuses this requirement only for products of negligible utility. This standard will not apply "in most instances even though the plaintiff alleges that the category of product sold by the defendant is so dangerous that it

III. Strict Products Liability 2.0

should not have been marketed at all." RESTATEMENT (THIRD) OF TORTS: PRODUCTS LIABILITY §2 cmt. d. Thus, proof of a reasonable alternative design would be required even if the design creates a risk of grave injury or death, as long as the product has some appreciable utility. Moreover, the *Restatement (Third)* would seem to immunize certain classes of products, like novel products for which there is no alternative design.

The court's concerns in *Potter* are not ameliorated by the argument of the defendant and some of the amici that evidence of a reasonable alternative design is routinely presented. As the Pennsylvania Supreme Court recently explained: "[R]elying upon a confined universe of reported appellate cases to draw evidence-based (versus principle-based) rules is problematic as a general matter in our mature legal system. This is so because the small class of cases posing issues of sufficient consequence to result in reported, precedential decisions naturally tends to raise narrow unsettled issues and/or fact-sensitive applications, rather than to provide vehicles to illustrate those parts of the law that are so 'well accepted' as to reflect emergent general rules. Of course, these cases may, by analogy and distinction, illuminate general principles at issue; but, purporting to limit the general rule to the facts of those cases is anathema to the common law. Stated otherwise, simply because in cases of factually-marginal applications courts have found evidence relating to alternative designs to be particularly probative and persuasive, in our minds, does not necessarily support a thesis that adducing such evidence is dispositive of whether a plaintiff has carried his/her burden of proof. . . . And, if adopted as a broadly applicable legal regime, the Third Restatement would engender a self-fulfilling prophecy by providing for a future restatement, going forward, of only those cases that meet the evidentiary threshold the regime permits." Tincher v. Omega Flex, Inc., 104 A.3d 328, 413-14 (Pa. 2014).

. . . Having reaffirmed our allegiance to a strict liability standard under §402A of the *Restatement (Second)*, [the court then decides the remaining issues raised by the case.]

NOTES AND QUESTIONS

1. *Is the risk-utility test a form of strict products liability?* In addition to the concern about the manner in which the *Restatement (Third)* requires proof of defect with a reasonable alternative design except for a very limited class of cases, the court—in a portion of the opinion not excerpted above—also emphasized that strict products liability is not limited by the requirement of foreseeability, unlike the rule of negligence liability. Does this factor and the other arguments made by the court adequately explain why its version of the risk-utility test is a form of strict products liability? Note in this regard that a rule of strict liability does not necessarily eliminate the requirement of foreseeability for reasons we address at various points in the ensuing chapters. *See, e.g.*, Vassallo v. Baxter Healthcare Corp., 696 N.E.2d 909, 922-923 (Mass. 1992) (observing that only "a distinct minority of States" do not limit the duty to warn to foreseeable risks and adopting a foreseeability requirement within the rule of strict products liability based on the tort version of the implied warranty because the "goal of the law is to induce

conduct that is capable of being performed. The goal is not advanced by imposing liability for failure to warn of risks that were not capable of being known."). Once foreseeability is eliminated as a reason for choosing strict products liability over the negligence-based rationale for the risk-utility test, is there any meaningful substantive difference between the two formulations identified by the court in *Bifolck*?

"Such cases pose a puzzle for products liability scholars: How is one to explain the dedication of judicial authorities to a doctrine that learned observers, after considerable deliberation, have concluded is conceptually indistinguishable from the risk-utility test and its recognized exceptions?" Douglas A. Kysar, *The Expectations of Consumers,* 103 Colum. L. Rev. 1700, 1725-1726 (2003).

2. *Missing in action: the implied warranty.* As the discussion in *Bifolck* indicates, most of the controversy over the negligence-based framework of the *Restatement (Third)* centers on the narrow question whether the plaintiff must identify a reasonable alternative design to prove that the existing design is defective. Limiting the controversy to this particular issue ignores the fundamental question of whether the protection of consumer expectations under a rule of strict products liability substantively differs from a negligence-based rationale for liability. The issue turns on the implied warranty, the doctrinal basis of §402A that is surprisingly absent from this ongoing debate.

The implied warranty has largely developed as a rule of contract law governing commercial transactions, and so it has been "under-theorized in the [tort] context of products causing physical harm." Michael D. Green, *The Unappreciated Congruity of the Second and Third Restatements on Design Defects,* 74 Brook. L. Rev. 807, 823 (2012). The tort version of the implied warranty is not well understood, explaining why strict products liability is not well understood.

For example, the courts in both *Potter* and *Bifolck* affirmed the commitment to the §402 rule of strict products liability while also incorporating the risk-utility test into that framework. In neither case did the court explain how the implied warranty rationale for §402A justifies the risk-utility test. This case law accordingly leaves open a foundational doctrinal question: Can courts defensibly conclude that the risk-utility test is a substantive form of strict products liability? Or is the *Restatement (Third)* correct that the terminology is merely a "rhetorical preference" that "perpetuat[es] confusion" about the substantive basis for liability? §1 cmt. a. The answers depend on how the implied warranty applies to products that do not malfunction, an issue that has not received the attention it so clearly merits.

B. *Defining Consumer Expectations with the Risk-Utility Test*

Whether consumer expectations can be defined in terms of the unadorned risk-utility test adopted by the *Restatement (Third)* depends on whether the risk-utility test accounts for consumer interests in the manner that the ordinary consumer would reasonably expect. The risk-utility test would substantively differ

III. Strict Products Liability 2.0

from consumer expectations if the two tests depend on different factors or otherwise differently evaluate the same set of factors. Unless such a difference exists, there is no substantive reason why courts cannot define consumer expectations in terms of the risk-utility test, thereby extending strict products liability beyond its original formulation to encompass products that do not malfunction.

CIPOLLONE v. LIGGETT GROUP INC.
United States District Court, District of New Jersey, 2002
644 F. Supp. 283

SAROKIN, J. In this diversity action plaintiff Antonio Cipollone, acting individually and as the administrator of his deceased wife's estate, seeks damages against the companies that manufactured and sold cigarettes which he alleges to be the proximate cause of her lung cancer and death. At this juncture, plaintiff moves in *limine* for an order precluding the defendants from introducing evidence as to the cigarette industry's collateral benefits to the economy as part of their defense to those of his strict liability claims which are premised on "risk/utility" theory. Having examined the judicial precedent and scholarly commentary defining the scope, purpose and operation of risk/utility theory, the court concludes that plaintiffs are entirely correct and that all such collateral benefit evidence should be ordered excluded as an inappropriate consideration under risk/utility analysis.

The instant motion relates to the evidence which the parties plan to introduce with regard to plaintiff's strict liability claims. In September of 1983 plaintiff served a First Set of Interrogatories on the defendants, two of which were directed to the "risk/utility" issues which is a significant aspect of New Jersey strict liability law. Those interrogatories, and defendant Liggett Group's supplemental answers, state in relevant part as follows:

> INTERROGATORY NO. 48: Do you contend that the cigarettes which you manufacture have social utility? If so, set forth:
> (a) a full and detailed description of the factual basis for this contention. . . .
> INTERROGATORY NO. 49: If your answer to the foregoing interrogatory is in the affirmative, state whether you contend that the social utility of the cigarettes which you manufacture outweighs the health risks associated with the smoking of these cigarettes. If so, set forth:
> (a) a full and detailed description of the factual basis for this contention. . . .
> *Supplemental Answer*: Without agreeing that application of a risk/utility test is appropriate in this case, Liggett states as follows: The chief component of the social utility of cigarettes is the enjoyment that they provide the millions of individuals in this country who have chosen to smoke. Cigarette smoking was a popular practice long before the advent of the cigarette industry. The cigarette manufacturers came into existence to satisfy the preexisting demand for cigarettes.
> Liggett is unaware of any study which has sought to place some numerical value, whether a dollar figure or otherwise, upon the total enjoyment experienced as a result of smoking by those who have chosen to smoke. Although this "societal enjoyment" may defy precise measurement, its existence in a society where so many have chosen to smoke for so many years is irrefutable.

The cigarette industry is a major contributor to the nation's economy. The industry provides thousands of jobs in manufacturing and in sales. Moreover, thousands of farm families derive their livelihood from their tobacco crop. Cigarettes are an important export and as such have a favorable impact upon the nation's balance of trade. And, of course, the industry contributes substantially to the public fisc by way of its payment of federal, state and local taxes. . . .

Plaintiff now moves to preclude the defendants from attempting to introduce any and all evidence as to the social benefits that flow from the production of cigarettes, as opposed to their consumption, as a factor to be considered in the risk/utility analysis. Defendants respond that the motion should be denied because risk/utility analysis permits them to introduce evidence relating to every kind of social benefit that stems from their product in order to rebut plaintiffs' claims as to the secondary social harms that result from cigarette use.

While resolution of this issue is largely preordained by the basic theoretical underpinnings of strict liability generally, the court must look to the pronouncements of the New Jersey Supreme Court in order to frame the issue and advance its resolution in this diversity case.

[T]he New Jersey Supreme Court's decisions have never said that a product's utility may be established by looking to whether the defendant "reasonably" believed that its profits would be sufficient to maintain a livelihood, hire employees, or pay taxes by operating the company that placed a product on the market.

The New Jersey Supreme Court's silence in this regard becomes all the more deafening upon an inspection of the principles underlying strict liability theory. Defendants' proposed evidence, when distilled to its essence, aims to establish that their product is profitable, that some of those profits are disseminated to others in society, and that such benefits would be reduced or eliminated if liability were imposed. But strict liability law is, if anything, intended to temper the profit motive by making a manufacturer or marketer aware that it may be less costly in the long run to market a product more safely, or not to market it at all. To permit defendants to introduce the evidence that they here propose would undercut the very goals of strict liability law insofar as it suggests that defendants' interest in making a profit could transform an otherwise insufficient evaluation of their product's safety into a reasonable one.

Secondly, a fundamental purpose behind the imposition of strict liability is to require that a product "pay its way" by compensating for the harms it causes. [ ] For this purpose to be furthered it is of course necessary to accept that a product's profitability will be reduced as it bears the costs attendant to its use, and indeed that its true costs to society may so outweigh its usefulness that those costs, when reflected in the product's price, will ultimately lead to that product's withdrawal from the market. That some economic dislocation may thereby result in the short run is, in turn, an accepted fact of life in the operation of a free market system in which those entities who profit from the marketing of a product—rather than its individual victims, or the government, or society—are the ones who are expected to bear the risks that such products are not economically viable. Indeed, any avoidance of product liability for reasons unrelated to the inherent value of the product itself would permit the continued marketing of products that do not truly pay their way, thus discouraging the profiting entities from devoting their energies to making their product safer, or to producing products that are more socially beneficial in the long term. To permit a manufacturer or marketer to introduce evidence of a product's profitability, and to suggest that such profitability will be endangered if legal liability is found, would thus undermine these goals of greater overall economic efficiency and product safety.

In essence, defendants argue that in determining liability, a jury engaged in the risk-utility analysis may take into consideration profits made, employees hired, benefits to suppliers of goods and services, taxes generated and even charitable activities or contributions made by the defendant manufacturer. The analysis was never meant to balance the risk to the consumer against the general benefit to society. Rather, the sole question presented is whether the risk to the consumers exceeds the utility to those consumers. The manufacturer of a highly dangerous or defective product with no or limited utility to a consumer, should not escape liability by demonstrating that the manufacturer of the product makes money for stockholders, for workers, for contractors, for suppliers, for municipalities, for the IRS, etc. It is the benefit and utility to the cigarette smoker which is here in issue, and not the benefit to the cigarette industry or those in turn, who benefit from its existence.

Plaintiff's motion in *limine* to preclude the introduction of evidence of the collateral social benefit of cigarette production is firmly grounded in a proper reading of New Jersey precedent, as well as a correct interpretation of strict liability theory generally. Defendants having produced no persuasive argument to contest plaintiff's motion, it will be granted.

NOTES AND QUESTIONS

1. *The limitation of risk-utility evidence to consumer interests.* In describing the risk-utility test, the *Restatement (Third)* states that "it is not a factor . . . that the imposition of liability would have a negative effect on corporate earnings or would reduce employment in a given industry." §2 cmt. f. As the court in *Cipollone* explained, "the sole question presented is whether the risk to the consumers exceeds the utility to those consumers."

2. *Bystander injury.* An exclusive focus on the interests of consumers—those who purchase or otherwise use the product—ignores the interests of bystanders who might be injured by the product. For this reason, we leave the issue of bystander injury for separate consideration in Chapter 16 and otherwise largely address the problem of consumer injury.

3. *Two different types of consumer expectations.* Why would a risk-utility test that only considers consumer interests to evaluate reasonable product safety ever require product designs or warnings that the ordinary consumer would not reasonably expect? As this question suggests in an almost circular manner, consumer expectations ought to be capable of justifying the risk-utility test. Doing so requires us to distinguish between two different types of consumer expectations.

The §402A formulation of strict products liability is based on malfunctions that frustrate consumer expectations of safe product performance.

This form of consumer expectations is derived from the ordinary consumer with ordinary knowledge common to the community. Although the scope of this test is inherently limited by actual consumer knowledge of safe product performance, the implied warranty is not inherently limited to this type of inquiry. It also recognizes a different type of consumer expectation based on the safety performance that consumers would expect if they were sufficiently informed about the relevant factors.

The implied warranty is violated if the consumer, knowing the "true character" of the product, would either forego the purchase altogether or pay a significantly lower price commensurate with the actual quality. *See* William L. Prosser, *The Implied Warranty of Merchantable Quality*, 27 Minn. L. Rev. 117, 122 (1943); *id.* at 139 (observing that although the enforceability of a contract does not depend on adequacy of consideration, "it is difficult to escape the conviction that price cannot be left out of account" in the implied warranty). A consumer who knows the "true character" of a product is well informed about all attributes relevant to its safe performance, knowledge that is constructive rather than based on actual experience and understanding.

This requirement of the implied warranty is a direct implication of its underlying tort rationale. When consumers are not adequately informed about product risk, their expectations can be frustrated in a manner that contract law does not adequately redress. *See* Chapter 2, section I. To protect the expectation interest in these cases, tort law imposes a duty on sellers to provide the amount of product safety that would be chosen by consumers if they were adequately informed; that is, if they knew the "true character" of the product. Formulated in this manner, the theory of the implied warranty is "one of policy" that "partakes of the nature" of both contract and tort. *Id.* at 124 (identifying this theory as a basis for the implied warranty alongside the theory of "pure contract" or the alternative "tort theory"). In effect, the tort duty solves the contracting problem by obligating sellers to supply the amount of product safety that would be demanded by consumers if they were well informed.

Thus, in contrast to *ordinary* consumer expectations based on *actual* knowledge of how products should perform, the implied warranty recognizes that consumers also have *reasonable* expectations based on *constructive* knowledge of how products should perform. Having constructive knowledge of the product's "true character," the ordinary consumer can reasonably expect that a nonmalfunctioning product should nevertheless have performed more safely than it actually did, rendering the product defective in this respect. This reasoning explains why the court in *Potter* called this liability rule the "modified" consumer expectations test to distinguish it from the ordinary consumer expectations test for identifying product malfunctions based on ordinary knowledge common to the community.

For example, if consumers know that an automobile does not have any airbags, then the failure of an airbag to deploy in a crash would not be an unexpected malfunction. However, the ordinary consumer with constructive knowledge could still reasonably expect that the vehicle should have airbags. In that event, the failure of an airbag to deploy in a crash would frustrate this reasonable expectation in violation of the implied warranty, even though the automobile did not malfunction in this respect and satisfied the consumer's minimal expectations based on actual knowledge. *See* Izzarelli v. R.J. Reynolds Tobacco Co., 136 A.3d 1232, 1249 (Conn. 2016) ("If . . . one test sets the floor for recovery—a product that meets *minimum* safety expectations—then a verdict for the defendant on that test logically could be reconciled with a plaintiff's verdict on a test that sets a higher standard.").

Hence the implied warranty can be extended to cases in which products do not malfunction. The open doctrinal question is whether this modification of the consumer expectations test yields the risk-utility test, and if so, whether that formulation is substantively equivalent to the version adopted by the *Restatement (Third)*.

THE VALUE OF CONSUMER CHOICE IN STRICT PRODUCTS LIABILITY
Mark A. Geistfeld
74 Brook. L. Rev. 781 (2009)

Tort law has always recognized the principle expressed by the Latin maxim *volenti non fit injuria*, or "a person is not wronged by that to which he or she consents." The absence of consent is part of the prima facie case for tort liability, distinguishing tortious behavior from socially acceptable behavior. "For example, consent turns trespass into a dinner party; a battery into a handshake; [or] a theft into a gift."[3]

By removing informed choices from the ambit of liability, tort law allows individuals to structure their relationships in the manner that promotes their welfare as per the requirements of allocative efficiency.[4] More fundamentally, "[t]o have the ability to create and dispel rights and duties [as a matter of informed, voluntary consent] is what it means to be an autonomous moral agent."[5] The role of consent within tort law derives from the value of individual autonomy or self-determination.

Enabling individuals to make their own safety choices as a matter of self-determination is a value that tort law presumably also recognizes in product cases. In the typical product case, the individual right-holder is a consumer, making the value of individual choice equivalent to the value of consumer choice.

---

3. Heidi M. Hurd, *The Moral Magic of Consent*, 2 Legal Theory 121, 123 (1996).

4. *Cf.* R.H. Coase, *The Problem of Social Cost*, 3 J.L. & Econ. 1, 9-11, 13, 15 (1960) (showing that when individuals have full information of all the relevant factors and do not incur any other costs in bargaining with others, voluntary agreements among right-holders and duty-bearers will produce allocatively efficient outcomes).

5. Hurd, *supra* note 3, at 124. For purposes of legal analysis, a normative value such as individual autonomy is necessarily more fundamental than the instrumental objective of allocative efficiency. The computation of costs and benefits depends on how the legal system has specified the underlying legal entitlements. Consequently, neither allocative efficiency nor cost-benefit analysis can determine initial entitlements, making the substantive content of any legal rule dependent on normative justification in the first instance. *See* Mark A. Geistfeld, *Efficiency, Fairness, and the Economic Analysis of Tort Law*, in Theoretical Foundations of Law and Economics 234, 234-35 (Mark D. White ed., 2009).

In light of the consumerist orientation of contemporary society, it would be astonishing to find that products liability does not fundamentally value consumer choice. Nevertheless, the value of consumer choice in strict products liability is surprisingly unclear.

Consider the liability rules governing defects of product design or warning, the most important categories of product defect. According to the *Restatement (Third) of Torts: Products Liability*, "[t]he emphasis is on creating incentives for manufacturers to achieve optimal levels of safety in designing and marketing products."[8] The optimal level of safety has no evident connection to the amount of safety that would be chosen by consumers, because "consumer expectations do not play a determinative role in determining defectiveness."[9] Whether a product is defective in these cases instead depends on "[a] broad range of factors," including "the nature and strength of consumer expectations regarding the product."[10] In some cases, consumer expectations can be "ultimately determinative" of the liability question,[11] but it is not apparent why the liability rules exclusively rely on consumer choice in only these cases but not others.

The value of consumer choice is obscured by the way in which the *Restatement (Third)* has de-emphasized the importance of consumer expectations. Properly understood, the value of consumer choice not only justifies the liability rules in the *Restatement (Third)*, it also provides the key to understanding the important limitations of strict products liability.

I. Uninformed Consumer Choice as the Predicate for Strict Products Liability

The widely adopted rule of strict products liability law in section 402A of the *Restatement (Second) of Torts* is based on the tort doctrine of the implied warranty. "In its inception, breach of warranty was a tort. The . . . wrong was conceived to be a form of misrepresentation, in the nature of deceit. . . ."[18] The misrepresentation stemmed from the manner in which the product frustrated the reasonable safety expectations of the purchaser; liability was strict in the sense that it did not require any culpable wrongdoing on the seller's part. The rule of strict liability was instead justified by the purchaser's lack of knowledge about the product attributes in question, creating a mismatch between the product's actual qualities and the purchaser's expectation of quality.

When interpreting the rule of strict products liability, courts have continued to recognize the problem of uninformed consumer choice:

> In today's world, it is often only the manufacturer who can fairly be said to know and to understand when an article is suitably designed and safely made for its intended purpose. Once floated on the market, many articles in a very

---

8. Restatement (Third) of Torts: Prods. Liab. §2 cmt. a (1998).
9. *Id.* §2 cmt. g.
10. *Id.* §2 cmt. f.
11. *Id.* §2 cmt. g; *see also id.* §§7-8 (defining defect exclusively in terms of consumer expectations for food products and used products respectively).
18. William L. Prosser, *The Implied Warranty of Merchantable Quality*, 27 Minn. L. Rev. 117, 118 (1943).

III. Strict Products Liability 2.0

real practical sense defy detection of defect, except possibly in the hands of an expert after laborious and perhaps even destructive disassembly.[25]

The rule of strict products liability governs the designs of automobiles, for example, because "manufacturers of such complex products as motor vehicles invariably have greater access than do ordinary consumers to the information necessary to reach informed decisions concerning the efficacy of potential safety measures."[26] Thus, one of the public policy rationales for the rule of strict products liability is that "the consumer does not have the ability to investigate for himself the soundness of the product."[27]

Tort liability can be justified in these terms because of the safety problems that are created when product sellers rationally respond to the safety decisions made by uninformed consumers. Consider a manufacturer's decision about whether to install a costly safety device to eliminate an unreasonable product risk of which the ordinary consumer is unaware. By installing the safety device, the manufacturer increases the cost and the price of the product. Without the device, the product would expose consumers to the associated risk of injury. Unless consumers know about the risk, they will not be willing to pay for the safety device, leading them to purchase the lower priced product without the device. Why spend money on safety if one is unaware of the need to do so? Manufacturers will not tell consumers about these risks, as doing so would only increase consumer estimates of product cost and decrease sales. What is the point of advertising negative product attributes to the consumer? The process of price competition predictably forces manufacturers to forego these types of safety investments, resulting in unreasonably dangerous products. The ensuing safety problem both justifies the tort duty and explains why customary product safety practices can be unreasonably dangerous.[28]

During the 1920s, for example, the president of the automobile manufacturer General Motors "insisted that the company could not make windshields with safety glass because doing so would harm the bottom line."[29] The automobile manufacturers were simply responding to misinformed consumer demand. "G.M. believed that consumers weren't prepared to pay more for cars with safety glass. . . ." The same dynamic has occurred throughout the history of automotive safety. During the 1950s, "auto executives told Congress that making seat belts compulsory would slash industry profits." The industry had the same response to airbags. As the president of Chrysler Motors lamented, "safety has really killed all our business." Without the intervention of tort law or other forms of safety regulation, the market would have adopted customary practices (no safety glass, no seat belts, no airbags) that were unreasonably dangerous.

The growth of the economy and proliferation of products have also made it increasingly difficult for consumers to acquire information about product risk. Consumers now face a bewildering array of product choices. Over thirty

---

25. Micallef v. Miehle Co., 348 N.E.2d 571, 577 (N.Y. 1976) (quoting Codling v. Paglia, 298 N.E.2d 622, 627 (N.Y. 1973)).
26. Camacho v. Honda Motor Co., 741 P.2d 1240, 1247 (Colo. 1987).
27. Sternhagen v. Dow Co., 935 P.2d 1139, 1143 (Mont. 1997) (quoting Brandenburger v. Toyota Motor Sales, U.S.A., Inc., 513 P.2d 268, 273 (Mont. 1973)).
28. For a more complete analysis, including other economic rationales for the tort duty, see Mark A. Geistfeld, PRINCIPLES OF PRODUCTS LIABILITY 34-50 (2006).
29. James Surowiecki, *Fuel for Thought*, New Yorker, July 23, 2007, at 25.

thousand items are available in the typical supermarket.[33] Experience with a brand may provide the consumer with some knowledge, but even that is short-lived. For U.S. manufacturing firms that remain in operation over a manufacturing census period (every five years), almost two-thirds of the firms change their product mixes, with the product switches involving almost half of existing products.[34] The consumer's ability to evaluate risk is then made even more difficult by the increased complexity of products. Who has the time, energy and desire to evaluate each and every one of these product risks, particularly given the range of other decisions we face on a daily basis?[35]

Recognizing that consumers are simply unable to evaluate all product risks, courts and legislatures have adopted the rule of strict products liability. The associated tort duty places responsibility for the safety decision on the party most capable of making that decision on an informed basis—the manufacturer.[36]

II. Strict Products Liability as the Instantiation of Informed Consumer Choice

As we have found, the tort duty is predicated on the conclusion that the ordinary consumer does not have sufficient information about product risks, causing her to undervalue product safety. Due to the process of price competition, these uninformed consumer choices give manufacturers an incentive to supply unreasonably dangerous products. These products are more dangerous than expected by the ordinary (misinformed) consumer, and so the resultant product-caused injuries frustrate consumer safety expectations. To address this safety problem, tort law overrides these misguided contractual choices (and customary product-safety practices more generally) by subjecting product sellers to a tort duty.

The *Restatement (Second)* rule of strict products liability applies to "[o]ne who sells any product in a defective condition unreasonably dangerous to the user or consumer or to his property."[37] To be "unreasonably dangerous," the product

---

33. Gary Cross, An All-Consuming Century: Why Commercialism Won in Modern America 214 (2000).

34. *See* Andrew B. Bernard et al., *Product Choice and Product Switching* 5-6 (Nat'l Bureau of Econ. Research, Working Paper No. 9789, 2003).

35. *See id.*

36. The manufacturer has greater technical expertise and can make one thorough investigation of the product, spreading that information cost among all consumers via a price increase. The associated cost per consumer will often be less than the average amount that each consumer would otherwise incur to investigate product safety on her own. Because information acquisition depends on a comparison of costs and benefits incurred by the decision maker, a reduction in costs should increase the total amount of information acquired, assuming there is no change in the benefits of the information.

A tort duty, moreover, is likely to increase the benefits of information for the decision maker. A seller owing a duty to all consumers considers the benefit of added information in terms of that group, whereas the individual consumer acquiring information only considers her private benefit. The benefit for the group will typically exceed the benefit for the individual consumer. Because information acquisition depends on the decision maker's comparison of costs with benefits, an increase in benefits should increase the amount of information acquired, all else being equal.

For other reasons why a tort duty would improve safety decisions in situations of high information costs, see Steven P. Croley & Jon D. Hanson, *Rescuing the Revolution: The Revived Case for Enterprise Liability*, 91 Mich. L. Rev. 683, 770-92 (1993).

37. Restatement (Second) of Torts §402A(1) (1965).

III. Strict Products Liability 2.0

attribute "must be dangerous to an extent beyond that which would be contemplated by the ordinary consumer who purchases it, with the ordinary knowledge common to the community as to its characteristics."[38] Such a product attribute frustrates the ordinary consumer's actual expectations of product safety, the condition required for tort law to supplement the seller's contractual obligations with a tort duty.

Because the tort duty is based on the product attribute frustrating the actual (misinformed) safety expectations of the ordinary consumer, the separate element of defect must be defined in some other manner. Otherwise, the existence of duty would necessarily establish the existence of defect, conflating the two elements into a single requirement.

The frustration of the ordinary consumer's *actual* (misinformed) safety expectations creates the tort duty, and so the element of defect becomes a separate requirement when defined in terms of the ordinary consumer's *reasonable* (well-informed) safety expectations. Having received a product with the amount of safety that she would have chosen if adequately informed of the relevant factors, the ordinary consumer could not reasonably expect some other amount of product safety. A product satisfying the well-informed or reasonable safety expectations of the ordinary consumer is not defective.[39]

This definition of defect has a straightforward rationale. A liability rule formulated to address the safety problems created by uninformed consumer choice should require the amount of safety that would be chosen by consumers if they were fully informed. Fully informed consumers understand that products cannot always be made entirely safe for all uses. Perfection typically is either not possible or unduly expensive. Some product risk is usually inevitable, and so the mere fact that a product causes an accident does not frustrate the consumer's reasonable safety expectations. The accident must instead be caused by a defect in the product, making the definition of defect dependent on the reason why the product attribute frustrates the safety expectations of the ordinary consumer.

According to the *Restatement (Third)*, "[p]roducts that malfunction due to manufacturing defects disappoint reasonable expectations of product performance," thereby justifying strict liability.[41] A manufacturing or construction defect departs from the product's intended design. In an effort to eliminate such defects, sellers adopt procedures or systems of quality control. Perfect quality control is not reasonably expected by the ordinary consumer for the same reason that perfect product safety is not a reasonable expectation. The complete elimination of product risk typically is not feasible or desirable. Consequently, the ordinary consumer only reasonably expects that the product has passed the appropriate tests of quality control. To enforce such an implied guarantee of product quality, the consumer can reasonably expect the seller to provide a guaranteed remedy for malfunctioning products. This guarantee

---

38. *Id.* §402A cmt. i.
39. *See, e.g.*, Potter v. Chi. Pneumatic Tool Co., 694 A.2d 1319, 1333 (Conn. 1997) (holding that for safety attributes that are not well understood by the ordinary consumer, "the inquiry would then be whether a reasonable consumer would consider the product design unreasonably dangerous," and providing citations to a number of other jurisdictions that have adopted this approach).
41. RESTATEMENT (THIRD) OF TORTS: PRODS. LIAB. §2 cmt. a (1998).

makes the seller (strictly) liable for malfunctioning products, thereby creating the requisite financial incentive for reducing the incidence of these defects in a cost-effective manner.[42]

In contrast to the rule governing construction or manufacturing defects, the *Restatement (Third)* eschews consumer expectations in favor of the risk-utility test to determine whether the product is defective because of design or an inadequate warning. Doing so is unnecessary, if not counterproductive.

Excluding instances of bystander injuries, product cases only implicate consumer interests. Any tort burdens incurred by the manufacturer or other product sellers, including the cost of safety investments and liability for injury compensation, are passed on to the consumer in the form of higher prices. Consequently, the risk-utility test in the *Restatement (Third)* is formulated entirely in terms of consumer interests: "[I]t is not a factor . . . that the imposition of liability would have a negative effect on corporate earnings or would reduce employment in a given industry."[45]

The consumer's full set of interests is best protected by safety investments satisfying the cost-benefit version of the risk-utility test. For example, the *risk* of a car design without an airbag refers to the increased risk the consumer will suffer injury due to the absence of the airbag, a measure corresponding to the consumer's injury costs that would be reduced or eliminated by the airbag. The *utility* of the design without an airbag involves any savings the consumer experiences by not having the airbag, an amount equal to the total cost of the airbag. Under the cost-benefit version of the risk-utility test, the car is defective for not having an airbag if the utility of the existing design is less than the increased risk posed by the design:

added utility of design without airbag < added risk of design without airbag
total cost of airbag < injury costs eliminated by airbag

For safety investments satisfying this condition, consumer rightholders incur a cost or burden that is less than the associated benefit they derive from the enhanced product safety (the reduction of expected injury costs). A product containing the cost-benefit amount of product safety promotes consumer welfare as reasonably expected by the ordinary consumer, thereby satisfying the seller's tort obligation.[46]

Proof that a product is defectively designed usually involves a comparison of the existing design to a proposed alternative. "While a manufacturer has a duty to design a product that is reasonably safe for its foreseeable use, it is not required to design the 'best possible product,' and 'proof that technology existed, which if implemented could feasibly have avoided a dangerous condition, does not

---

42. *See id.* §2 cmt. a ("[I]mposing strict liability on manufacturers for harm caused by manufacturing defects encourages greater investment in product safety than does a regime of fault-based liability under which, as a practical matter, sellers may escape their appropriate share of responsibility.").

45. *Id.* §2 cmt. f.

46. *Cf.* 63 AM. JUR. 2D *Products Liability* §583 (2d ed. 1997) ("The reasonable expectation of the user or consumer is to be determined through consideration of a number of factors, including the relative cost of the product, the gravity of potential harm from a claimed defect, and the cost and feasibility of eliminating or minimizing risk.").

III. Strict Products Liability 2.0

alone establish a defect.'"[47] Increased product safety typically increases product costs for the consumer due to increased price or decreased functionality. The safest possible product is not preferred by a well-informed consumer whenever the benefits of such safety for the consumer are outweighed by the resultant costs borne by the consumer. A design defect, therefore, is defined by reference to a reasonable alternative design. By proving that there is a reasonable alternative to the existing product design—one that passes the risk-utility test in the usual case—the plaintiff in effect proves that the manufacturer failed to provide the design that would be chosen by well-informed consumers.[49]

To further foster informed consumer choice, strict products liability obligates the seller to warn consumers of any unknown product risks that would be material to their decisions concerning the purchase or safe use of the product. Insofar as the average or ordinary consumer is unaware of a risk, a warning to that effect allows her to make an informed risk-utility decision. The duty to warn is the most obvious instance in which strict products liability is formulated in terms of consumer choice, further confirming that this body of tort law strives to create outcomes that instantiate the value of informed consumer choice.

Conclusion

The growth of products liability has been astounding, particularly when compared to the slowly evolving tort rules of the common law. A rapidly developing body of law cannot be simply restated, and the ongoing interplay between consumer expectations and the risk-utility test has proven to be a particularly hard problem.

For reasons articulated here, courts could defensibly reject the basic approach of the *Restatement (Third)* while also adopting its liability rules. The *Restatement (Third)* has obscured the essential way in which strict products liability depends on consumer expectations, thereby creating the misleading impression that this body of law does not adequately value consumer choice. Rather than being confused about the liability rules, courts could rightly reject any approach that does not appropriately recognize the value of consumer choice in products liability.

The value of consumer choice is recognized by the *Restatement (Second)* rule of strict products liability—the textual source of contemporary products liability law. The rule has considerably evolved over a short period of time. Courts have applied it to different sets of circumstances, producing a larger number of distinct doctrines that are addressed by the *Restatement (Third)*. As the common origin of these varied doctrines, the *Restatement (Second)* rule of strict products liability ought to be substantively compatible with the liability rules in the *Restatement (Third)*. Case law that adopts the risk-utility test in the *Restatement (Third)*, for example, has often evolved from earlier decisions that defined

---

47. Robinson v. Brandtjen & Kluge, Inc., 500 F.3d 691, 696 (8th Cir. 2007) (applying South Dakota law) (citing Sexton *ex rel.* Sexton v. Bell Helmets, Inc., 926 F.2d 331, 336 (4th Cir. 1991)) (internal citation omitted).

49. *See* Restatement (Third) of Torts: Prods. Liab. §2 Reporters' Note, cmt. d (1998).

consumer expectations in risk-utility terms.[102] Like the risk-utility test, other important liability rules in the *Restatement (Third)* can be justified by the value of consumer choice. The two *Restatements* can be squared in this fundamental respect, and so the de-emphasis of consumer expectations in the *Restatement (Third)* should not prevent courts from adopting its liability rules.

NOTES AND QUESTIONS

1. *Consumer expectations and the risk-utility test.* Product cases are situated within a contractual context that causes consumers to internalize both the costs and the benefits of the manufacturer's tort duties. For the equilibrium in a market governed by tort rights and their correlative obligations, the manufacturer is entitled "to generate a sustained profit, above the cost of doing business." Tincher v. Omega Flex, Inc., 104 A.3d 328, 385 (Pa. 2014). The manufacturer's cost of doing business—of performing the product contract—includes those costs that are imposed as a matter of legal obligation. The ordinary consumer accordingly pays (via higher product prices or decreased product functionality) for both the safety investments and the injury compensation that tort law requires of the manufacturer. Leaving aside cases of bystander injuries for later discussion, the liability rule only affects consumer interests, justifying a tort duty limited to the protection of consumer expectations regarding safe product performance— the duty embodied in the rule of strict products liability.

Although the risk-utility test is clearly related to ordinary negligence liability, it can also be independently derived from the reasonable expectations of the ordinary consumer who knows the "true character" of the product. For example, by proving that the design of an automobile must incorporate airbags under the risk-utility test, a plaintiff would show that the existing design without an airbag is more dangerous than the ordinary consumer reasonably expects. The failure of an airbag to deploy frustrates this expectation of reasonably safe performance, constituting a defect that subjects the manufacturer and other product sellers to strict products liability under the tort version of the implied warranty. *See, e.g.,* Camacho v. Honda Motor Co., 741 P.2d 1240 (Colo. 1987) ("A consumer is justified in expecting that a product placed in the stream of commerce is reasonably safe for its intended use, and when a product is not reasonably safe a products liability action may be maintained.").

Because the reasonable safety expectations of the ordinary consumer are fully embodied in and protected by the risk-utility test, the inquiry is not a technocratic exercise that somehow departs from the way in which consumers evaluate products, contrary to the claims of those who

---

102. *Compare* Aller v. Rodgers Mach. Mfg. Co., 268 N.W.2d 830, 834-35 (Iowa 1978) ("'The article sold must be dangerous to an extent beyond that which would be contemplated by the ordinary consumer. . . .' Proof of unreasonableness involves a balancing process. On one side of the scale is the utility of the product and on the other is the risk of its use.") (quoting RESTATEMENT (SECOND) OF TORTS §402A cmt. i (1965)) (citation omitted), *with* Wright v. Brooke Group Ltd., 652 N.W.2d 159, 169 (Iowa 2002) (adopting the *Restatement (Third)*'s risk-utility test).

III. Strict Products Liability 2.0

have invoked this rationale for the consumer expectations test. Compare Douglas A. Kysar, *The Expectations of Consumers*, 103 Colum. L. Rev. 1700, 1789 (2003) (arguing that the risk-utility test embodies a preference for the technical expertise of engineers over the populist beliefs of consumers); Marshall S. Shapo, TORT LAW AND CULTURE 225 (2003) (equating the risk-utility test with "an exercise in balance sheets" and the consumer expectations test "with a more psychologically oriented view of law [tied] closely to the wellsprings of human behavior"). Costs and benefits are evaluated from the ordinary consumer's perspective. The ordinary consumer's valuation of the risk and safety benefits necessarily depends on all factors he or she deems to be of importance in making that decision. When derived from reasonable consumer expectations, the risk-utility test completely expresses the values of concern to consumers.

2. *Consumer expectations and the requirement of defect.* By rejecting the rule of absolute liability, all jurisdictions effectively recognize that consumers do not reasonably expect to receive tort compensation for injuries caused by nondefective products. An analysis of consumer expectations regarding nondefective products further illustrates the extent to which the entire body of products liability law depends on consumer expectations.

If liability were not limited by the requirement of defect, consumers would receive tort compensation for all product-caused injuries. Under this rule of absolute liability, consumers would effectively receive insurance covering product-caused injuries in exchange for their payment of an "insurance premium" (via increased product prices). The premium for this "tort insurance," however, would substantially increase costs for consumers relative to the alternatives, explaining why consumers do not reasonably expect product sellers to pay tort damages for injuries caused by nondefective products.

To be sure, consumers value insurance, but they need not purchase tort insurance from absolutely liable manufacturers; instead, they can purchase "ordinary" insurance from insurance companies. Ordinary insurance has many cost advantages over the tort insurance provided by product sellers. The primary reasons for the cost differential involve the scope of coverage and the cost of obtaining the insurance proceeds. For example, even when covered by tort insurance, consumers still need to purchase ordinary health insurance covering medical expenses, because not all health problems are attributable to products. Tort insurance, therefore, can be duplicative or cause problems of coordination with ordinary insurance. Given the need to purchase ordinary insurance, what added compensatory benefit is supplied by tort insurance?

The benefit is not one of reducing total insurance costs. To receive payments under an ordinary insurance policy, a policyholder typically does not need to hire a lawyer. Coverage supplied by most ordinary insurance policies is triggered by the fact of loss (like medical expenses for health insurance), which usually is easy to prove (submitting bills). By contrast, one who seeks to receive tort compensation for an injury usually must hire a lawyer. The resultant litigation expenses substantially increase the cost of tort insurance for consumers, which largely explains why even in a tort regime of absolute liability, the cost per dollar of coverage supplied by tort insurance would substantially exceed the cost of ordinary insurance. *See* Mark Geistfeld, *Should Enterprise Liability Replace the Rule of Strict Liability for Abnormally Dangerous Activities?*, 45 UCLA L. Rev. 611, 625-633, 639-646 (1998) (collecting data comparing costs of the two forms of insurance). Due to the relatively high cost of tort insurance, consumers do not reasonably expect a seller to incur liability for purely compensatory reasons. Consumers can instead obtain compensation more cheaply by purchasing ordinary insurance.

Lacking a compensatory rationale, consumers only reasonably expect a seller to incur liability when doing so would promote the objective of product safety. This safety objective explains why liability is limited to defective products, as the requirement of defect necessarily limits liability to cases involving unsafe products.

3. *Reassessing the ongoing controversy about the substantive basis for products liability.* Because the risk-utility test functions like the negligence standard of reasonable care, the *Restatement (Third)* drops the label of strict products liability for reasons captured by a leading treatise: "Whether one calls this method for determining liability 'strict' or 'popcorn,' it is at bottom negligence." David G. Owen & Mary J. Davis, 1 OWEN & DAVIS ON PRODUCTS LIABILITY §6:14 at 620 (4th ed. 2014). This change is not only one of terminology. The *Restatement (Third)* also rejects the consumer expectations test as an independent standard for liability and effectively adopts a negligence rationale for products liability.

Negligence is the default rule of modern tort law, and so it would seem to supply the most defensible rationale for products liability. However, the same property that makes the negligence principle so appealing can also make it overly general and ambiguous in product cases. Unlike the negligence principle, the implied warranty tailors the liability rules to account for the normative attributes that distinguish product cases from ordinary tort cases, giving the consumer expectations test a normative focus that is masked by the more general negligence standard.

The implied warranty exclusively protects consumer expectations of reasonably safe product performance, whereas the reasonable-person negligence standard equitably balances the conflicting interests of right-holders and duty-bearers. *See* RESTATEMENT (SECOND) OF TORTS §283 cmt. e (obligating a risky actor to "give an impartial consideration to the harm likely to be done to the interests of the other as compared with the advantages likely to accrue to his own interests, free from the natural tendency of the actor, as a party concerned, to prefer his own interests over others"). The implied warranty exclusively focuses on consumer interests because consumers effectively pay for the tort obligations incurred by manufacturers (via increased prices or decreased product functionality), and so the liability inquiry does not account for the interests of manufacturers and other duty-bearers. In this important respect, product cases normatively differ from ordinary tort cases in which right-holders (like pedestrians) do not incur the tort burdens imposed on duty-bearers (automobile drivers), requiring a negligence standard that equitably balances their conflicting interests.

III. Strict Products Liability 2.0

By framing the liability rules in the normatively appropriate manner, strict products liability sharpens the inquiry. Although the *Restatement (Third)* has adopted liability rules that are sound in most cases and often substantially clarify vexing issues, its general framework for liability can be overly vague. In our ensuing study of the important doctrines of products liability, consider whether the more general negligence-based formulation of products liability creates unnecessary confusion across the distinctive elements of the tort claim—duty, breach, and causation. Insofar as the implied warranty avoids these problems, courts can defensibly reject the negligence-based framework of the *Restatement (Third)* in favor of strict products liability 2.0.

4

Manufacturing Defects and Product Malfunctions

Courts first subjected product sellers to strict tort liability for defects that caused the product to malfunction, such as a defect in a soda bottle that caused it to explode when handled in an ordinary manner. This type of defect is usually attributable to the construction or manufacture of the product (like a hairline fracture in the bottle), although in some instances it can be caused by the design itself. In the vast majority of states, the seller of a malfunctioning product is subject to strict liability for the physical harms proximately caused by the defect.

I. RATIONALE(S) FOR STRICT LIABILITY

As discussed in Chapter 2, strict products liability can be independently derived from the tort doctrines of either the implied warranty or the negligence principle. In light of these distinct doctrinal rationales, courts have invoked a variety of policy rationales to justify strict liability. A restatement of this case law accordingly yields the full range of reasons that support strict products liability, providing another opportunity for us to assess the substantive rationale for this liability rule.

RESTATEMENT (THIRD) OF TORTS: PRODUCTS LIABILITY (1998)
Copyright by the American Law Institute

§2. Categories of Product Defect

A product is defective when, at the time of sale or distribution, it contains a manufacturing defect, is defective in design, or is defective because of inadequate instructions or warnings. A product:

(a) contains a manufacturing defect when the product departs from its intended design even though all possible care was exercised in the preparation and marketing of the product.

Comment:

a. Rationale. The rule for manufacturing defects stated in Subsection (a) imposes liability whether or not the manufacturer's quality control efforts satisfy standards of reasonableness. Strict liability without fault in this context is generally believed to foster several objectives. On the premise that tort law serves the instrumental function of creating safety incentives, imposing strict liability on manufacturers for harm caused by manufacturing defects encourages greater investment in product safety than does a regime of fault-based liability under which, as a practical matter, sellers may escape their appropriate share of responsibility. Some courts and commentators also have said that strict liability discourages the consumption of defective products by causing the purchase price of products to reflect, more than would a rule of negligence, the costs of defects. And by eliminating the issue of manufacturer fault from plaintiff's case, strict liability reduces the transaction costs involved in litigating that issue.

Several important fairness concerns are also believed to support manufacturers' liability for manufacturing defects even if the plaintiff is unable to show that the manufacturer's quality control fails to meet risk-utility norms. In many cases manufacturing defects are in fact caused by manufacturer negligence but plaintiffs have difficulty proving it. Strict liability therefore performs a function similar to the concept of res ipsa loquitur, allowing deserving plaintiffs to succeed notwithstanding what would otherwise be difficult or insuperable problems of proof. Products that malfunction due to manufacturing defects disappoint reasonable expectations of product performance. Because manufacturers invest in quality control at consciously chosen levels, their knowledge that a predictable number of flawed products will enter the marketplace entails an element of deliberation about the amount of injury that will result from their activity. Finally, many believe that consumers who benefit from products without suffering harm should share, through increases in the prices charged for those products, the burden of unavoidable injury costs that result from manufacturing defects.

An often-cited rationale for holding wholesalers and retailers strictly liable for harm caused by manufacturing defects is that, as between them and innocent victims who suffer harm because of defective products, the product sellers as business entities are in a better position than are individual users and consumers to insure against such losses. In most instances, wholesalers and retailers will be able to pass liability costs up the chain of product distribution to the manufacturer. When joining the manufacturer in the tort action presents the plaintiff with procedural difficulties, local retailers can pay damages to the victims and then seek indemnity from manufacturers. Finally, holding retailers and wholesalers strictly liable creates incentives for them to deal only with reputable, financially responsible manufacturers and distributors, thereby helping to protect the interests of users and consumers.

In contrast to manufacturing defects, design defects and defects based on inadequate instructions or warnings are predicated on a different concept of responsibility.

c. Manufacturing defects. More distinctly than any other type of defect, manufacturing defects disappoint consumer expectations.

NOTES AND QUESTIONS

1. *Is strict products liability based on a unified rationale?* According to comment a, manufacturing defects depend on a "different concept of responsibility" than defects of design or warnings. Is the difference merely that a product seller's legal responsibility for manufacturing defects is governed by a rule of strict liability, unlike defects of design or warnings that are determined by a negligence inquiry embodied in the risk-utility test? Or does the difference pertain to differing justifications for tort liability? Why does this issue matter?

If the substantive rationale for tort liability depends on the type of defect, then the precedential value of a particular rule will be limited to the type of defect governed by that rule. Strict products liability would not be a substantively unified body of law, but merely a collection of disparate rules defined by and limited to the type of defect in question.

2. *"Makeweight" rationales.* Based on the case law, the *Restatement (Third)* justifies strict liability with some rationales that are not independently sufficient to justify the liability rule. Can you identify rationales of this type?

Consider the rationale that "product sellers as business entities are in a better position than are individual users and consumers to insure against such losses." This loss-spreading rationale applies to any injury suffered by the consumer, not merely to those caused by a manufacturing defect. It justifies a rule of absolute liability. The rule of strict liability, however, is limited to defective products, implying that the loss-spreading rationale is not an independently sufficient reason for subjecting a product seller to liability. *See, e.g.,* Cafazzo v. Central Medical Health Services, Inc., 668 A.2d 521, 527 (Pa. 1995) (rejecting rationale for strict liability based solely on the defendant's "ability to pay plaintiffs and charge others" because doing so "would result in absolute rather than strict liability"). Consequently, courts have recognized that the "loss spreading" rationale provides "only the part of a makeweight argument" in favor of liability. Brody v. Overlook Hosp., 317 A.2d 392, 398 (N.J. App. Div. 1974). Loss spreading, in other words, is a positive attribute of strict products liability, but not a sufficient condition that is independently capable of justifying the liability rule; some other rationale is needed.

Now consider the *Restatement (Third)*'s claim that strict liability is justified because of the manufacturer's "element of deliberation about the amount of injury that will result from their activity." Can you prove that this is a makeweight argument? (As illustrated by the prior example, one can always prove that any rationale for strict products liability is only a "makeweight argument" if it would justify a rule of absolute liability.)

Of the varied rationales for strict liability in the *Restatement (Third)*, only one expressly invokes consumer expectations. Is this rationale a "makeweight argument," or does it provide a sufficient reason for limiting strict liability to defective products? Can you explain why the concept of consumer expectations also yields the other rationales in the *Restatement (Third)*? *See generally* Chapter 3, section III (developing the concept of consumer expectations). Because consumer expectations can also justify the risk-utility test for evaluating defective designs or warnings, this rationale unifies the full set of liability rules that comprise strict products liability.

II. PROOF OF MANUFACTURING DEFECT

Whether a product is defective implicates issues of fact that can be proven either by direct evidence or circumstantial evidence. "[D]irect evidence means evidence that directly proves a fact, without an inference or presumption, and which in itself, if true, conclusively establishes that fact." Cal. Evid. Code §410. Circumstantial evidence sufficient for proving defects is addressed by the malfunction doctrine, which is addressed in section IV. To directly prove that a product contains a manufacturing defect, the plaintiff can compare the product as manufactured to the product's design:

> [A] manufacturing defect is a departure from a product unit's design specifications.... Common examples of manufacturing defects are products that are physically flawed, damaged, or incorrectly assembled. In actions against the manufacturer, under prevailing rules concerning allocation of burdens of proof the plaintiff ordinarily bears the burden of establishing that such a defect existed in the product when it left the hands of the manufacturer.

RESTATEMENT (THIRD) OF TORTS: PRODUCTS LIABILITY §2 cmt. c.

MCKENZIE v. SK HAND TOOL CORP.
Appellate Court of Illinois, Fifth District, 1995
650 N.E.2d 612

GOLDENHERSH, J. The underlying cause of action filed by plaintiff (Ronnie McKenzie) was a products liability suit based upon strict liability in tort against defendant, SK Hand Tool Corporation, for injuries plaintiff sustained when the ratchet wrench plaintiff was using broke while he was working on a truck, causing him to fall and injure himself. The case was tried to a jury, and at the close of all evidence, the jury returned a verdict in favor of defendant.

On the day of the accident, plaintiff was to overhaul the engine on a large over-the-road truck. To overhaul the engine, plaintiff was required to remove the heads, which were held to the engine by a number of large bolts. Normally plaintiff used a ¾-inch air impact wrench to remove the bolts; however, after removing several bolts, the wrench developed a low-pressure problem. Plaintiff decided to use the ¾-inch ratchet wrench his employer had in the shop. This ¾-inch wrench was manufactured by defendant. Plaintiff broke two or three bolts loose with the ratchet wrench and removed those bolts with the wrench. Plaintiff, in attempting to remove another bolt, experienced difficulty even

II. Proof of Manufacturing Defect

though the bolt broke loose. To remove the bolt, plaintiff put an extension on the wrench. While standing on the truck, plaintiff began pulling back the wrench. The wrench came apart and plaintiff fell off the truck backwards, hitting his right side and shoulder on the concrete floor. Plaintiff sustained injuries to his neck and shoulder.

Defendant has blueprints that contain the specifications of the sizes of each component of the wrench. The components are to comply with these specifications, which have a tolerance for each measurement. The part is acceptable if its actual measurement fits within the tolerance limits. For each part there are figures that represent its upper and lower limits. If the measurement of the part does not fall between the upper and lower limits, the machinist knows the part is not acceptable for use.

The component parts of the wrench in question were measured by four individuals, and the measurements were compared to those required by the specifications.

Plaintiff's experts measured the hardness of the snap ring several times on a Rockwell C scale and got several different hardnesses ranging from 45 to 51 when the ring was measured in various places. [One of his experts, Reynolds,] concluded that the ring did not meet the hardness required in the specifications (a measurement of 48 to 52 on a Rockwell C scale) and that this failure to comply with the specifications could affect the snug fit of the ring in the grooves of the driver and thus its ability to properly hold the driver and the handle together. Reynolds also stated that the variance in hardness found in the ring was the result of manufacturing and not use. Defendant's experts did not measure the snap ring for hardness.

Upon measuring the "ears" of the snap ring compressed at .56 and .59 inches apart, plaintiff's expert got a diameter of 2.269 inches and 2.280 inches respectively. Defendant's expert's measurement for the same part was 2.315 inches. However, the measurements obtained by both plaintiff's and defendant's experts exceeded defendant's specifications.

Reynolds, one of plaintiff's experts, noticed a tapering in the radius of both the inside and outside edges of the snap ring groove in the handle. In his opinion, the tapering was done during manufacturing and did not result from use. This point was affirmed by [the] engineering manager of defendant's Ohio plant.

Regarding the possible causes of the accident, Reynolds offered two potential explanations for why the wrench came apart. First, Reynolds opined that the failure of the parts to comply with defendant's specifications would create a manufacturing defect which could contribute to an incident of the sort involved here. Specifically, the snap ring groove is not to specification, and the handle has a large radius and tapering of the edges. Reynolds suggests, as a second possible cause of the accident, improper reassembly of the snap ring either during servicing of the wrench or during assembly by the manufacturer.

At the end of direct examination, Reynolds testified that in his opinion, the wrench in question was defective and unreasonably dangerous because the snap ring groove did not comply with defendant's specifications and, in conjunction with the outward taper of the snap ring groove, this overall noncompliance with the specifications could permit the wrench to come apart.

After the conference on instructions and before closing arguments, the court instructed the jury that it had granted motions to strike the testimony of plaintiff's and defendant's experts "with respect to measurements and specifications with respect to the effect of those specifications and measurements on the wrench." The jury returned a verdict in favor of defendant and against plaintiff. The court denied plaintiff's posttrial motion, from which plaintiff appeals.

Plaintiff contends that the trial court erroneously struck all evidence relating to the measurements and specifications of the component parts of the wrench and plaintiff's expert's testimony with respect to those measurements and specifications. Plaintiff maintains that the existence of a manufacturing defect was . . . proven because the measurements of the parts of the wrench were shown not to comply with the manufacturer's specifications. We agree.

In the present case, the evidence is sufficient to establish the presence of a defect in the wrench. The wrench in question has a number of component parts, the inner body, or driver, and handle which are held together by a snap ring that fits into a groove in the handle and driver. Defendant has design specifications which set forth measurements with which the parts must comply. Each part has upper and lower limits within which a part must fall. If the part does not fall within these limits, the machinist knows the part is not acceptable for use. Plaintiff's experts measured these component parts. These experts found that the hardness of the snap ring was not uniform. When measured in various places, the hardness of the ring ranged from 45 to 51 on a Rockwell C scale. Defendant's specifications require a measurement of 48 to 52 on the Rockwell C scale. The outside diameter of the snap ring groove in the handle measured 2.3130 to 2.3125. The specifications required 2.290 inches, with a tolerance of .005 inches, so a measurement between 2.285 to 2.295 inches would be acceptable. Therefore, the outside diameter of the snap ring groove in the handle is larger than the diameter required in the specifications. Plaintiff's expert also found a tapering in the radius of both the inside and outside edges of the snap ring groove in the handle. The design specifications do not require a tapering in the radius of either edge of the ring. Moreover, Reynolds testified in direct examination that, in his opinion, the wrench was defective and unreasonably dangerous because it did not comply with the specifications, thereby creating the possibility of the wrench coming apart while being used. Furthermore, testimony by plaintiff and his coworkers indicates that the wrench had not been disassembled since its purchase, thereby eliminating a possible secondary cause. Plaintiff has established a *prima facie* case that the wrench was defective, that the defect existed when it left defendant's control, and that in the absence of abnormal use or secondary causes, the wrench failed to perform in the manner reasonably expected in light of its nature and intended function.

Plaintiff next contends that the trial court improperly admitted evidence regarding the lack of prior accidents because a sufficient foundation for such testimony was never laid. We agree.

Existing case law establishes that a party may introduce evidence of the lack of prior accidents or incidents when that party establishes as a foundation that (1) the same product was used and (2) the product was used under conditions substantially similar to those in which plaintiff used the product. [ ]

In the instant case, defendant's witness, a corporate personnel manager for defendant, testified that defendant made about 7,000 of the ¾-inch-drive ratchet wrenches each year. Defendant also manufactures approximately 350,000 smaller wrenches annually. The witness testified that he reviewed existing corporate records and found that no claim, return, allegation, or anything else indicating problems with the ¾-inch ratchet wrenches or any of the various other wrenches manufactured by defendant had ever been made. He further testified that no claims had been made with respect to the snap ring dislodging while the wrench was in use. The trial court admitted this evidence over objections from plaintiff's counsel.

In reviewing the testimony of defendant's personnel manager, it is clear that the evidence presented is without a minimal foundation. Defendant failed to establish that the same product was used. There was no evidence whether the other ¾-inch-drive ratchet wrenches complied or failed to comply with defendant's design specifications. Consequently, no evidence was presented regarding prior accidents and incidents involving nonconforming wrenches. Further, evidence with respect to prior accidents and incidents involving other wrenches is irrelevant to the functioning of the ¾-inch wrench involved here. Admission of this evidence was unduly prejudicial to plaintiff because its interjection permitted the jury to make unsupported inferences regarding the wrench in question.

Similarly, defendant's witness failed to present any evidence indicating that the absence of claims and complaints occurred when others were using the ¾-inch wrench under conditions substantially similar to those used by plaintiff (*i.e.*, removing head bolts from a truck engine, in a crouching position four feet above the floor while using an extension and socket).

For the foregoing reasons, the judgment of the circuit court of Williamson County is reversed, and the cause is remanded for a new trial.

NOTES AND QUESTIONS

1. *Expert testimony.* To determine whether the product in question deviated from the manufacturer's design or specifications, plaintiffs and defendants often employ expert witnesses. A party must rely on expert testimony to prove any fact that the ordinary juror could not otherwise adequately understand.

2. *Evidence of prior accidents.* Consider the definition of a manufacturing defect. Based on that definition, did the court correctly conclude that the defendant's proffered evidence regarding prior accidents was irrelevant? Would the relevancy of this evidence change for purposes of negligence liability? Consider Ake v. Gen. Motors Corp., 942 F. Supp. 869, 874 (W.D.N.Y. 1996) (A "large number of cases recognize that lack of other accidents may be admissible to show" either "the nonexistence of an unduly dangerous situation, or . . . want of knowledge (or of grounds to realize) the danger."). Would the relevance of such evidence change if the allegation of defect involved the product design or warning?

3. *Sufficiency of the evidence.* The plaintiff had uncontested proof of defect, so why did the court remand for a new trial? *See McKenzie*, 650 N.E.2d at 622 (Welch, J. specially concurring) ("Plaintiff's expert never testified that, in his opinion, the failure of the wrench to comply with design specifications did cause the wrench to come apart while plaintiff was using it. He testified only that it was possible that the wrench came apart because it did not comply with the specifications."). The issue of whether the defect actually caused the plaintiff's injury is discussed in Chapter 11, section I.

4. *Scope of liability.* A manufacturing defect is not limited to flaws in the construction or manufacture of the product. Such "a defect may arise after manufacture, for example, during shipment or while in storage." RESTATEMENT (THIRD) OF TORTS: PRODUCTS LIABILITY §2 cmt. c. Why are post-manufacturing defects governed by the same liability rule applicable to manufacturing defects? Would the manufacturer be liable for this type of defect?

5. *Departure from which design?* Could a defendant bottle manufacturer claim that the design of a soda bottle includes its method of production, so that a bottle does not depart from its design so long as its characteristics are within the expected parameters of the production process? Insofar as the manufacturer cannot reasonably expect perfect quality control, the expected parameters of production will allow for a certain number of bottles that might explode. Consequently, if the "design" of a soda bottle is defined in this manner, an exploding soda bottle would not necessarily satisfy the definition of a manufacturing defect. Is this a proper way to define the product "design" for purposes of evaluating manufacturing defects? Can the issue be resolved merely as a matter of definition, or does it require resort to the substantive rationale for strict liability?

In one case, plaintiff alleged "that he purchased a bag of potting soil sold by defendant, and upon opening the bag and putting his hand in to scoop out some soil, his hand was bitten by a copperhead snake." Defendant moved to dismiss the claim of strict liability on the ground that the plaintiff did not allege "facts . . . to indicate how the process of manufacturing the potting soil was defective." The court rejected this argument for the simple reason that in "a product liability case based on a manufacturing defect, . . . negligence of the manufacturer is not required." McGregor v. Scotts Co., 2011 WL 3471012 (E.D. Mo. 2011). Is this reasoning adequately persuasive or largely conclusory?

If defect were defined by reference to the process of production, then a manufacturer could effectively avoid strict liability by arguing that it exercised reasonable care in the manufacturing process. Having exercised reasonable care, the manufacturer could not avoid distributing at least some nonconforming products (i.e., those with manufacturing flaws that could not be eliminated by the exercise of reasonable care). A product could only deviate from its "design" because of negligent manufacturing or quality-control processes. In effect, a plaintiff could establish such a manufacturing defect only by proving negligence.

To maintain the integrity of strict liability, the defect cannot be defined by reference to the process of production. Instead, a product is defective for departing from the quality or characteristics that the manufacturer tried or intended to achieve in making the particular product. The manufacturer did not have the objective of producing a soda bottle that explodes or a bag of soil containing a copperhead snake, and so these products are defective for departing from this particular aspect of the product design. Compare RESTATEMENT (THIRD) OF TORTS: PRODUCTS LIABILITY §2(a) (providing that a product "contains a manufacturing defect when the product departs from its intended design even though all possible care was exercised in the preparation and marketing of the product").

III. FOOD CASES

The modern rule of strict products liability can be traced to the ancient rules that imposed a strict liability on the sellers of contaminated food. The food cases would seem to be the most simple to resolve, yet they can pose difficulties that provide another useful perspective for identifying the logic of liability.

ALLEN v. GRAFTON
Supreme Court of Ohio, 1960
164 N.E.2d 167

TAFT, J. [This case is an appeal from a judgment reversing the dismissal of plaintiff's petition for recovery. W]hether plaintiff's petition sets forth a cause of action depends upon whether the presence in one fried oyster of a serving of six of a piece of shell, such as described in the petition, will justify a legal conclusion that that serving constituted food not "reasonably fit for" eating.

It is obvious that a piece of shell such as described in the petition can be readily removed from a fried oyster by anyone who is going to eat it; and that, if it is so removed, the fried oyster would then admittedly be food that is fit for eating and that is not "adulterated." A different problem would be presented if the shell had been shattered into smaller pieces which could not be readily removed from the oyster so as to leave any substantial edible portion that was free from such pieces. In the latter instance, a contention, that the oyster would constitute "adulterated" food or food not reasonably fit for eating, might be more persuasive.

In the instant case, it is not necessary to hold, as some [cases from other jurisdictions do], that, because an oyster shell is natural to an oyster and thus not a substance "foreign" to an oyster, no liability can be predicated upon the sale of a fried oyster containing a piece of oyster shell. However, the fact, that something that is served with food and that will cause harm if eaten is natural to that food and so not a "foreign substance," will usually be an important factor in determining whether a consumer can reasonably anticipate and guard against it.

In our opinion, the possible presence of a piece of oyster shell in or attached to an oyster is so well known to anyone who eats oysters that we can say as a matter of law that one who eats oysters can reasonably anticipate and guard against eating such a piece of shell, especially where it is as big a piece as the one described in plaintiff's petition.

Judgment reversed.

SCHAFER v. JLC FOOD SYSTEMS, INC.
Supreme Court of Minnesota, 2005
695 N.W.2d 570

PAGE, J. The underlying facts of this case are relatively simple and straightforward. On January 27, 2001, Karen Schafer went to a Perkins Restaurant in St. Cloud, Minnesota, with a friend and their daughters. At the restaurant, Schafer ordered a pumpkin muffin. She unwrapped the muffin and, using her fork, placed a piece of the muffin in her mouth. Upon swallowing, she immediately felt a "sharp pain" in her throat and "a choking sensation." After drinking some water and still feeling as though there was something stuck in her throat, Schafer went directly to a hospital emergency room. Before leaving the restaurant, Schafer's friend notified a Perkins employee that, as a result of swallowing a piece of the muffin, Schafer was going to the emergency room. The rest of the muffin was not saved.

At the hospital, a doctor told Schafer that she had a cut on her throat, but the doctor did not observe any object that would have caused the cut. Schafer was prescribed a painkiller and released. Two days later, she returned to the emergency room where she was diagnosed with a throat infection and was hospitalized for three days. According to Schafer, it took her about three months to fully recover. Although Schafer is not able to identify what was in the muffin that caused the problems with her throat, she speculated in her deposition that "it had to have been something sharp and hard."

Schafer sued Perkins, alleging that the pumpkin muffin was in a defective condition unreasonably dangerous to consumers, the defective condition was a direct cause of the injury to her throat, and, as a result of the injury, she suffered damages in the form of medical expenses, loss of earnings, pain, disability, and emotional distress. Perkins, in turn, asserted a third-party claim for contribution against Foxtail Foods, the company that manufactured the muffin mix Perkins used to make the pumpkin muffin.

After some discovery, Perkins and Foxtail moved for summary judgment, arguing that Schafer had failed to establish a prima facie case of negligence because she could not identify the object in the muffin that caused her injury. The district court granted summary judgment on that basis and the court of appeals affirmed.

Schafer argues that circumstantial evidence should be available to a plaintiff in a defective food products case for purposes of establishing liability when no harm-causing object can be identified. Schafer further urges us to adopt section 7 of the *Restatement (Third) of Torts: Products Liability* (1998), which recognizes reasonable consumer expectations in food products liability cases. Respondents, while conceding that circumstantial evidence should be available in defective food products cases for purposes of establishing liability in cases when the harm-causing object cannot be identified, argue that the circumstantial evidence available in this case is insufficient to support Schafer's claim that the muffin in question was defective.

To determine the viability of Schafer's claim, we must first establish the proper standard for assessing whether a food product is defective. We note that courts across the country have diverged on the proper test to apply in determining whether food containing an injurious object is actionable. Some courts

III. Food Cases

follow what has been referred to as the "foreign-natural" test, while others have adopted what has become known as the "reasonable expectation" test.

The foreign-natural test draws a distinction between the "foreign" and "natural" characteristics of a food product ingredient. Under the test, if an object or substance in a food product is natural to any of the ingredients of the product, there is no liability for injuries caused; if the object or substance is foreign to any of the ingredients, the seller or manufacturer of the product may be liable for any injury caused.

Comparatively, the reasonable expectation test focuses on what is reasonably expected by the consumer in the food product as served, not what might be foreign or natural to the ingredients of that product before preparation. As applied to common-law negligence, the reasonable expectation test is related to the foreseeability of harm on the part of the defendant; that is, the defendant has the duty of ordinary care to eliminate or remove in the preparation of the food served such harmful substance as the consumer of the food, as served, would not ordinarily anticipate and guard against. The majority of jurisdictions that have dealt with the defective food products issue have adopted some formulation of the reasonable expectation test. *See* RESTATEMENT (THIRD) OF TORTS: PRODUCTS LIABILITY §7 rep. n.1 to cmt. b (1998).

Recognizing the majority view, the *Restatement*'s approach to food products liability cases considers reasonable consumer expectations. The *Restatement* provides:

> One engaged in the business of selling or otherwise distributing food products who sells or distributes a food product that is defective . . . is subject to liability for harm to persons or property caused by the defect. [A] harm-causing ingredient of the food product constitutes a defect if a reasonable consumer would not expect the food product to contain that ingredient.

Under the *Restatement* approach, consumer expectations are based on culturally defined, widely shared standards allowing a seller's liability to be resolved by judges and triers of fact based on their assessment of what consumers have a right to expect from preparation of the food in question. The Reporters to the *Restatement* note that the majority view is unanimously favored by law review commentators.

Having considered the two tests and the approach taken by the *Restatement*, we conclude that the reasonable expectation test is the more appropriate test to follow. Instead of drawing arbitrary distinctions between foreign and natural substances that caused harm, relying on consumers' reasonable expectations is likely to yield a more equitable result. After all, an unexpected natural object or substance contained in a food product, such as a chicken bone in chicken soup, can cause as much harm as a foreign object or substance, such as a piece of glass in the same soup. Therefore, we agree with the majority view and expressly adopt the reasonable expectation test as the standard for determining defective food products liability claims in Minnesota. Accordingly, when a person suffers injury from consuming a food product, the manufacturer, seller, or distributor of the food product is liable to the extent that the injury-causing object or substance in the food product would not be reasonably expected by an ordinary consumer. Whether the injury-causing object or substance in the food product is reasonably expected by an ordinary consumer presents a jury question in most cases.

Having identified the test to be applied for determining liability in defective food products cases, we now turn to the primary question presented by this case: whether circumstantial evidence may be used to establish a prima facie defective food products claim in cases in which the specific harm-causing object or substance cannot be identified. At oral argument, Schafer argued and Perkins and Foxtail conceded that circumstantial evidence should be available for such purposes. Perkins and Foxtail argued, however, that the circumstantial evidence available in this case was insufficient to permit Schafer's claim to go forward.

We agree with the parties that when the specific harm-causing object is not known circumstantial evidence should be available, if such evidence is sufficient and other causes are adequately eliminated, for purposes of submitting the issue of liability to the jury in defective food products cases.

The use of circumstantial evidence, however, is not without limits, nor should it be. In order to address defendants' legitimate concerns about a lack of boundaries for such claims, we hold that in defective food products cases a plaintiff may reach the jury, without direct proof of the specific injury-causing object or substance, when the plaintiff establishes by reasonable inference from circumstantial evidence that: (1) the injury-causing event was of a kind that would ordinarily only occur as a result of a defective condition in the food product; (2) the defendant was responsible for a condition that was the cause of the injury; and (3) the injury-causing event was not caused by anything other than a food product defect existing at the time of the food product's sale. In order to forestall summary judgment, each of the three elements must be met.

Finally, we must apply the test set out above to the facts presented in this case to determine whether Schafer's claim can withstand summary judgment. The record presented here establishes that Schafer purchased a pumpkin muffin at a Perkins restaurant, began eating the muffin while at the restaurant, and experienced a sharp pain and choking sensation immediately after swallowing her first bite of the muffin. According to Schafer, the pain must have been caused by a hard, sharp object. Such an occurrence is not the kind of event that an ordinary consumer would anticipate and guard against. Although the harm-causing object was never identified, Schafer immediately reported her experience to a Perkins employee and went directly to a hospital emergency room. Moreover, the events leading to Schafer's injury occurred in the presence of witnesses, Schafer's friend and their daughters. At the hospital, the doctor who examined Schafer found a cut on her throat. There is no allegation that Schafer had any throat-related ailment immediately preceding her swallowing the first bite of the muffin.

Viewing the circumstantial evidence in the record before us in the light most favorable to Schafer, we conclude that a jury could reasonably infer that Schafer's alleged injury is of a kind that would ordinarily only occur as a result of a defective condition in the pumpkin muffin served by Perkins, that Perkins was responsible for making the pumpkin muffin that caused Schafer's throat injury, and that Schafer's injury was not caused by anything other than a defect in the pumpkin muffin existing at the time of the muffin's sale.

Reversed and remanded to the district court.

III. Food Cases

NOTES AND QUESTIONS

1. *The ongoing problem of contaminated food.* The federal government estimates "that there are about 48 million cases of foodborne illness annually—the equivalent of sickening 1 in 6 Americans each year. And each year these illnesses result in an estimated 128,000 hospitalizations and 3,000 deaths." U.S. Dept. Health & Human Services, Foodsafety.gov/foodpoisoning (last visited Feb. 1, 2021). Based on a data set containing all food-safety incidents in all states between 1990 and 2000, one empirical study found "that the application of strict liability joined with punitive damages decreases the number of food safety cases and consequently increases the applied rate of care by firms." Maria L. Loureiro, *Liability and Food Safety Provision: Empirical Evidence from the US*, 28 Int'l Rev. L. & Econ. 204, 210 (2008).

2. *Negligence liability in a world of strict products liability.* The plaintiff's claim in *Schafer* was based on negligence and not strict products liability. (Minnesota has adopted a tort-reform statute that exempts nonmanufacturing product sellers from claims of strict liability under certain conditions. *See* Minn. Stat. Ann. §544.41.) Does the court's analysis differ in any important respect from the analysis that a court would employ when applying the rule of strict products liability? Consider Chapter 2, section II (discussing how circumstantial proof of negligence liability for manufacturing defects can effectively operate like a regime of strict liability).

Even for cases expressly governed by strict products liability, the plaintiff will often claim negligence liability as well. Under modern pleading rules, the plaintiff can pursue any legal claim that would provide recovery for the injuries in question. Consequently, the plaintiff can make one claim based on the rule of strict liability for manufacturing defects, and then make an additional negligence claim that the defect was caused by the defendant's unreasonable care in the manufacture or distribution of the product. *See* RESTATEMENT (THIRD) OF TORTS: PRODUCTS LIABILITY §2 cmt. c. Given the availability of strict products liability, why would a plaintiff make an additional claim of negligence liability and incur the added evidentiary burden of proving unreasonable care?

To prove negligence liability, the plaintiff can offer evidence concerning the defendant's conduct—evidence that is otherwise irrelevant to (and inadmissible for) the claim of strict liability. The claim of negligence liability, therefore, gives the plaintiff the opportunity to introduce evidence that impugns the defendant's conduct. Insofar as the plaintiff can show that the defendant behaved in a questionable manner, the jury is more likely to exercise any discretion in favor of the plaintiff. *See* Richard L. Cupp, Jr. & Danielle Polage, *The Rhetoric of Strict Products Liability versus Negligence: An Empirical Analysis*, 77 N.Y.U. L. Rev. 874 (2002) (finding higher pain and suffering damage awards when jury instructions are framed in terms of negligence rather than strict liability).

Plaintiffs are also well advised to allege negligence liability for another reason. Some defects are exempt from the rule of strict products liability when the product is "unavoidably unsafe." *See* Chapter 9. If the court concludes that the product in question is governed by the exemption, then a plaintiff who relies exclusively on a claim of strict liability no longer has a substantive basis for recovery, unlike the plaintiff who also alleges negligence liability in addition to the claim of strict products liability.

3. *Implications for defective design.* Although the food cases involve manufacturing defects, they have important implications for the liability rule governing defective design. The "design" of a food product is the recipe. For objects that are natural to the food sources in question, the recipe is often silent. Does a pumpkin muffin contain any pumpkin seeds? Does a chicken enchilada contain any chicken bones? Absent any express guidance from the recipe (or design), how can the court determine that the food product is defectively made because it departs from its intended specifications? Food cases pose the interesting question of how courts should evaluate product design absent express guidance from the seller or manufacturer.

By defining the incomplete components of product design in terms of reasonable consumer expectations, courts effectively equate reasonable product design with reasonable consumer expectations. A food product, in other words, defectively departs from its (incomplete) design by departing from the consumer's reasonable expectations of the product.

With respect to the problem of incomplete design, food cases do not comprise a special product category; the issue arises in other product cases as well. Any product design is likely to be incomplete in important respects, much like a food recipe ordinarily does not fully specify every characteristic or component of the ingredients (like the size of chicken bones). A tire manufacturer can describe the components and proper assembly of the tire, but not specify how long the tire is intended to function. What if the tire fails after 2,000 miles? As one federal district court found, "[c]ommon experience indicates that no owner of a tire expects it to fail with less than 2,000 miles on its treads." McCann v. Atlas Supply Co., 325 F. Supp. 701, 704 (W.D. Pa. 1971). The tire had a manufacturing defect, not because the manufacturer's design stated that the tire would perform for more than 2,000 miles, but because the ordinary consumer reasonably expected the tire to perform for at least that long. The problem of incomplete product design is not limited to food products; it potentially applies to any product. *But see* James A. Henderson, Jr. & Aaron D. Twerski, *Achieving Consensus on Defective Product Design*, 83 Cornell L. Rev. 867, 890 (1998) (arguing that the liability standard in food cases does "not apply to products generally [and therefore does not] support the thesis that the general design standard is based on consumer expectations").

As illustrated by these cases, incomplete product designs create a gap filled by reasonable consumer expectations. To serve this function, reasonable consumer expectations must be the *default* or background definition of defect. The default definition is not required whenever there is a more concrete or particularized definition available, such as a departure from express design requirements or a violation of the risk-utility test. These more particularized definitions of defect flesh out the requirements of the more abstract default definition in particular sets of circumstances; they do not otherwise provide independent bases of liability that are substantively different from consumer expectations. The definition of defect, therefore, always depends on reasonable consumer expectations, even for tort rules that do not expressly define defect in those terms.

For this reason, the *Restatement (Third)* can consistently define defective food products in terms of consumer expectations while also maintaining that consumer expectations do not provide an "independent standard for judging the defectiveness of product designs." §2 cmt. g. As the default definition of defect, consumer expectations appropriately fill the gap of incomplete product designs in food and other cases—a foundational role that does not make consumer expectations independent of the more particularized definitions, such as the risk-utility test, that are capable of resolving the defect question in other cases.

IV. PRODUCT MALFUNCTIONS

The plaintiff is not always able to establish a manufacturing defect with direct evidence showing that that the product departed from its intended design. In many cases, for example, the product was destroyed in the accident and cannot be compared to its intended design. In these cases, plaintiffs can only rely on proof that "is called circumstantial and will be seen to require further processes of inference. Typically it involves proof of fact *A* (which is not itself a fact in issue) as the basis of an inference of the existence of fact *B* (which is an issue)." Fleming James, Jr., *Proof of Breach in Negligence Cases (Including Res Ipsa Loquitur)*, 37 Va. L. Rev. 179, 181 (1951). Can the circumstantial facts of a product malfunction sufficiently prove that the defendant commercially distributed a defective product?

METROPOLITAN PROPERTY & CASUALTY CO. v. DEERE & CO.
Supreme Court of Connecticut, 2011
25 A.3d 571

ZARELLA, J. This appeal arises from a product liability action brought by the plaintiff, Metropolitan Property and Casualty Insurance Company, against the named defendant, Deere and Company, in which the plaintiff claimed that a lawn tractor manufactured by the defendant contained a manufacturing defect in its electrical system that caused a fire resulting in the destruction of the home of the plaintiff's insureds. [Having paid for the damage under a homeowner's policy to the insureds, the plaintiff insurer acquired subrogation rights with respect to the insured's tort claims against defendant.] The defendant appeals from the judgment of the trial court rendered in favor of the plaintiff, following a jury verdict for the plaintiff. On appeal, the defendant claims that the trial court improperly denied the defendant's motions for a directed verdict and to set aside the verdict, in which the defendant claimed that the plaintiff had failed to present sufficient evidence to establish liability. The plaintiff responds that it presented sufficient evidence to sustain the jury's verdict pursuant to the "malfunction theory" of products liability, which permits a plaintiff to prove its case on the basis of circumstantial evidence. Although we agree that a plaintiff may base a product liability action on the "malfunction theory," we conclude that the plaintiff's evidence in the present case was insufficient to establish its products liability claim, and, therefore, we reverse the judgment of the trial court.

Although most product liability cases are based on direct evidence of a specific product defect, there are cases in which such evidence is unavailable. For example, a product malfunction may result in an explosion, a crash or a fire that damages or destroys much, if not all, of the product's components. The product also may be lost when it has been discarded or destroyed after the incident such that the parties are no longer able to examine it.

The absence of direct evidence of a specific product defect is not, however, fatal to a plaintiff's claims, and a plaintiff, under certain circumstances, may establish a prima facie case using circumstantial evidence of a defect attributable to the manufacturer. In addition, a plaintiff need not present evidence to establish a specific defect, "[as] long as there is evidence of some unspecified dangerous condition." [ ]

Most states have adopted some form of the malfunction theory. Although this theory does not relieve a plaintiff of the burden to prove all elements of a product liability claim, it does help to establish a prima facie product liability case by permitting the jury to infer the existence of a defect attributable to the manufacturer. According to §3 of the *Restatement (Third) of Torts, Products Liability*, in a product liability action, the malfunction theory permits a jury to infer "that the harm sustained by the plaintiff was caused by a product defect existing at the time of sale or distribution, without proof of a specific defect, when the incident that harmed the plaintiff . . . was of a kind that ordinarily occurs as a result of product defect . . . and . . . was not, in the particular case, solely the result of causes other than product defect existing at the time of sale or distribution." This theory is based on the same principles underlying the doctrine of res ipsa loquitur, which permits a fact finder to infer negligence from the circumstances of the incident, without resort to direct evidence of a specific wrongful act.

Although the malfunction theory is based on the principle that the fact of an accident can support an inference of a defect, proof of an accident alone is insufficient to establish a manufacturer's liability. The fact of a product accident does not necessarily establish either the existence of a defect or that the manufacturer is responsible, both of which must be proven in product liability cases. . . . When the product is out of the control of the manufacturer, the likelihood of other potential causes of the accident that are not attributable to the manufacturer necessarily increases. Additionally, product accidents often occur for a variety of reasons that do not indicate the existence of a defect. . . . Therefore, the plaintiff's evidence must support a chain of inferences sufficient to link the plaintiff's injury to a product defect and to link the defect to the manufacturer.

For these reasons, it is important that appropriate limitations be placed on the application of the malfunction theory, and, when the evidence presented by the plaintiff does not remove the case from the realm of speculation, courts must intervene to prevent such cases from reaching a jury. Before permitting a case to go to the jury on the basis of the malfunction theory, a court must be

IV. Product Malfunctions

satisfied that the plaintiff's evidence is sufficient to establish the probability, and not the mere possibility, that the plaintiff's injury resulted from a product defect attributable to the manufacturer.

With these concerns in mind, we conclude that, when direct evidence of a specific defect is unavailable, a jury may rely on circumstantial evidence to infer that a product that malfunctioned was defective at the time it left the manufacturer's or seller's control if the plaintiff presents evidence establishing that (1) the incident that caused the plaintiff's harm was of a kind that ordinarily does not occur in the absence of a product defect, and (2) any defect most likely existed at the time the product left the manufacturer's or seller's control and was not the result of other reasonably possible causes not attributable to the manufacturer or seller. These two inferences, taken together, permit a trier of fact to link the plaintiff's injury to a product defect attributable to the manufacturer or seller. A plaintiff may establish these elements through the use of various forms of circumstantial evidence, including evidence of (1) the history and use of the particular product, (2) the manner in which the product malfunctioned, (3) similar malfunctions in similar products that may negate the possibility of other causes, (4) the age of the product in relation to its life expectancy, and (5) the most likely causes of the malfunction. If lay witnesses and common experience are not sufficient to remove the case from the realm of speculation, the plaintiff will need to present expert testimony to establish a prima facie case.

Evidence supporting the first element permits the trier of fact to infer that the plaintiff's injury resulted from a defect in the product rather than from some other cause of the accident, such as operator error. In most cases, the evidence easily will establish that a product malfunctioned as a result of a defect and thereby caused the plaintiff's injury. *See, e.g.,* Liberty Mutual Ins. Co. v. Sears, Roebuck & Co., 35 Conn. Supp. 687, 691 (1979) (inference of defect in television set permitted when witness saw flames emanating from television set because "television sets, in normal use, do not self-ignite"). This may also be established with circumstantial evidence of a malfunction, such as difficulties with the product at or near the time of the accident, or the "failure [of] a relatively inaccessible part integral to the structure of the product and not generally required to be repaired, replaced or maintained." [ ] When, however, a plaintiff cannot establish that an accident involving a product is of the type that normally occurs when a product is defective, the plaintiff fails to establish a sufficient cause of action.

Evidence as to the second element supports an inference that the defect in the product existed when the product left the manufacturer's control and was not introduced by any other reasonably possible cause outside of its control. Even if a plaintiff presents sufficient evidence to establish that a product defect most likely caused the plaintiff's harm, there remains the possibility that the defect resulted from something not attributable to the manufacturer, such as the age of the product, abuse or improper maintenance. The plaintiff therefore must present sufficient evidence to negate a reasonable possibility that something or someone besides the manufacturer caused the defect in the product. A plaintiff need not conclusively eliminate all possible causes of a product defect but must only negate reasonably possible secondary causes.

The age of the product in relation to its life expectancy is another important factor that may weaken any inference that a product defect is attributable to the manufacturer. This inference is more speculative when the manufacturer has lacked control of the product for a substantial period of time, thereby increasing the possibility of other, possibly unknown and undetectable causes of the defect. When a product malfunctions when it is new, the inference that the malfunction resulted from a defect attributable to the manufacturer is likely to be stronger than when the product is older because of the diminished possibility of other causes in the case of the newer product. The age of a product should not, however, present an absolute bar to recovery in those cases in which the product that malfunctioned had not outlived its expected lifespan because consumers should reasonably expect to benefit from the use of a product for the length of its expected useful life.

Even though the age of a product is not a complete bar to recovery in a malfunction theory case, courts often require more evidence from a plaintiff to overcome a presumption that something other than a defect attributable to the manufacturer caused the malfunction when the product is not new or nearly new. If a product is not new or nearly new when it allegedly malfunctioned, and the product functioned without problems indicative of a defect before the malfunction, the plaintiff must present some evidence to explain how the product could have operated without incident for a time and then have failed on this particular occasion. In the absence of such evidence, any link between the product failure and a defect attributable to the manufacturer is simply too attenuated to serve to establish liability on the part of the manufacturer.

Although the trier of fact may draw inference upon inference to find liability on the part of the manufacturer, it is essential that the trial court ensure that the plaintiff has presented sufficient evidence to support each inference by a preponderance of the evidence before submitting a case to the jury, in order to prevent liability on the basis of speculation. Furthermore, not only must there be sufficient evidence to support each required inference, but the evidence also must be sufficient for the trier of fact to conclude, after considering all of the evidence presented and all reasonable inferences to be drawn therefrom, that the manufacturer is more likely than not responsible for the plaintiff's harm. When the evidence is not sufficient to support such a finding, and such a finding essentially would require speculation by the trier of fact, the case cannot properly be submitted to the jury.

Applying the foregoing principles to the present case, we conclude that the plaintiff did not present sufficient evidence to support a finding of liability against the defendant, and, therefore, the trial court should have granted the defendant's motion for a directed verdict on the ground that the plaintiff's evidence was insufficient, as a matter of law, to implicate the malfunction theory. Although we conclude that the plaintiff's evidence was sufficient to permit the jury to infer that the fire started within the tractor and that the fire most likely started as a result of a failure in the tractor's electrical system, the plaintiff's evidence did not support an inference that any defect existed in the electrical system when the tractor left the defendant's manufacturing facilities or at the time it was sold, as the plaintiff alleged.

Viewing the evidence in the light most favorable to the plaintiff, we conclude that the jury reasonably could have found that the fire originated from the tractor's electrical system [while the tractor was located in the garage of plaintiff's insureds]. Although the defendant argues that it presented evidence of other

IV. Product Malfunctions 141

possible causes of the fire apart from the tractor, the testimony of the plaintiff's experts was sufficient to rule out other possible causes. The plaintiff's experts testified that they ruled out other potential causes in the garage and that the burn patterns in the garage pinpointed the tractor as the origin of the fire. Furthermore, the plaintiff's vehicle fire expert testified that he was able to rule out all other possible causes of a fire in the tractor except for the electrical system. Although thin, we conclude that this evidence was sufficient to support a finding that the tractor's electrical system started the fire.

Furthermore, the plaintiff presented sufficient evidence to establish that the fire most likely resulted from a defect in the tractor, satisfying the first requirement of the malfunction theory. Because common experience informs us that a tractor's electrical system does not ordinarily ignite, especially when not in operation, the evidence provided a reasonable basis on which the jury could have concluded that the tractor malfunctioned as a result of some defect in the electrical system.

We further conclude, however, that the plaintiff failed to present sufficient evidence to eliminate other reasonably possible secondary causes of the defect and to establish that the fire in the tractor most likely resulted from a defect attributable to the defendant. First, the plaintiff's own evidence pointed to the possibility of other causes of an electrical failure not attributable to the defendant, namely, the possibility of improper maintenance and improper use. The evidence at trial established that the tractor operated without issue for more than four years and that the reported problems, which, according to the plaintiff's evidence, could have stemmed from an electrical problem, did not develop until *after* the dealer performed a tune-up on the tractor. Although the plaintiff presented the testimony of the dealer's technician, who testified that he did not alter or modify the electrical system, no evidence was presented that the work performed on the tractor could not have damaged or caused problems with the tractor's electrical system, resulting in the problems of which the homeowners complained and, ultimately, the failure of the electrical system. Furthermore, although the evidence established that the homeowners continued to operate the tractor while the tractor was having problems, no evidence was presented that this was a proper use of the tractor or that this could not have resulted in damage or excessive wear and tear to the tractor's components, including the electrical system.

In addition, the plaintiff's evidence failed to link an electrical failure in the tractor to a defect attributable to the defendant. The evidence presented at trial clearly established that there were no problems reported with the tractor's electrical system during the first four years of use and that the tractor functioned properly during that time, weakening any inference that the tractor's electrical system was defective at the time it was manufactured or when it was sold to the homeowners. The evidence further established that, prior to the fire, the tractor had been inspected by a technician and that he identified no problems with the tractor's electrical systems, further weakening any inference that the electrical system was in a defective condition before it was serviced, let alone when it left the defendant's control several years earlier.

Furthermore, because the evidence established that the tractor was not new or nearly new when it malfunctioned, the plaintiff was required to present additional evidence to explain how the tractor could have had a defect in the electrical system when it left the defendant's manufacturing facilities yet function without problems for several years before failing. The plaintiff did not present any such evidence. Moreover, the plaintiff's own vehicle fire expert testified that he had no opinion as to whether the fire resulted from a defect attributable to the defendant and that he would have to speculate as to the cause of the fire. When the plaintiff's own expert concedes that speculation would be required to determine whether the fire resulted from anything attributable to the defendant, and there is no other evidence to link the defect to the defendant, a reasonable juror would have to resort to speculation to infer liability on the part of the defendant by a preponderance of the evidence.

The judgment is reversed and the case is remanded with direction to grant the defendant's motion for a directed verdict and to render judgment for the defendant.

NOTES AND QUESTIONS

1. *The malfunction doctrine and res ipsa loquitur.* The malfunction doctrine is usefully contrasted with the tort doctrine of *res ipsa loquitur*, a Latin phrase meaning "the thing speaks for itself." Res ipsa loquitur permits the plaintiff to establish the prima facie case of negligence liability on the basis of circumstantial evidence:

> The factfinder may infer that the defendant has been negligent when the accident causing the plaintiff's physical harm is a type of accident that ordinarily happens as a result of the negligence of a class of actors of which the defendant is the relevant member.

RESTATEMENT (THIRD) OF TORTS: LIABILITY FOR PHYSICAL AND EMOTIONAL HARM §17.

Res ipsa loquitur requires proof showing that most accidents of the type at issue are caused by negligence or legal fault, with the implication that less than 50 percent of these accidents are unavoidable or caused by no-fault:

F region:	NF region:
Accidents caused by some form of legal fault or failure to exercise reasonable care	Unavoidable accidents

Given the circumstances of such an accident, the jury as fact finder can reasonably infer that the plaintiff's injury, more likely than not, was caused by negligence. The plaintiff must then connect the negligence to the defendant, a burden that can be satisfied with proof showing that the defendant had exclusive control of the instrumentality at the time the risk in question was created. Having provided such evidence, the plaintiff does not have to identify the specific manner in which the defendant acted unreasonably. The accident "speaks for itself" on the negligence question, satisfying the plaintiff's burden of proof.

IV. Product Malfunctions 143

So, too, the malfunction doctrine does not require the plaintiff to identify the specific defect. The malfunction "speaks for itself" on the liability question when most accidents of the type at issue are caused by a product defect of some sort:

> **Defective region:** Accidents caused by some type of defect | Nondefective region

Having established this fact, the plaintiff must then prove that the defendant is responsible for the defect in question, an inquiry analogous to the exclusivity requirement of res ipsa loquitur. When properly applied, the malfunction doctrine merely permits proof of the prima facie case of liability on the basis of circumstantial evidence without otherwise relaxing the plaintiff's burden of proof.

2. *Spoliation of evidence.* In some cases, courts can draw inferences about the issue of defect based on the reasons why the product was unavailable for inspection. For example, suppose the plaintiff intentionally destroyed the product following the accident. What kind of inference could a court draw from such conduct? As a matter of fairness or public policy, what kind of inference should a court draw from such conduct?

As one court explained,

> To permit claims of defective products where a purchaser of the product has simply thrown it away after an accident, would both encourage false claims and make legitimate defense of valid claims more difficult. It would put a plaintiff (or plaintiff's attorney) in the position of deciding whether the availability of the item would help or hurt his or her case. Where producing the product for defense inspection would weaken rather than strengthen a case, we unfortunately are obliged to conclude that some plaintiffs and attorneys would be unable to resist the temptation to have the product disappear.

Dansak v. Cameron Coca-Cola Bottling Co., 703 A.2d 489, 492 (Pa. Super. 1997). When the plaintiff voluntarily disposed of the product, courts can draw the inference that the plaintiff did so because the product was not defective, justifying summary judgment for the defendant.

If, however, the plaintiff was not at fault for disposing of the product, then disposal of the product does not create any inferences about the nondefectiveness of the product, enabling the plaintiff to proceed under the malfunction theory. *E.g., id.* at 495 ("[F]ailure to produce the product is not fatal to [plaintiff's] claim if she can proceed with circumstantial evidence under a malfunction theory, and [plaintiff] was in no way at fault for disposing or failing to preserve the product. Summary judgment to [defendant] based on the spoliation doctrine was therefore unwarranted.").

3. *Reconsidering the evidentiary rationale for strict liability.* The outcome in *Deere & Co.* is not exceptional. "[T]he law reports brim with decisions that recite the propriety of the [malfunction] doctrine as a general proposition but hold it inapplicable to the facts. The opinions in such cases frequently

note that . . . the law will not allow plaintiffs or juries to rely on guess, conjecture, or speculation." David G. Owen, *Manufacturing Defects*, 53 S.C. L. Rev. 851, 878 (2002).

Why do courts insist that the plaintiff must sufficiently rule out other causes, even if doing so would be practically impossible in some cases? Apparently, courts are unwilling to reduce the plaintiff's burden of proving defect, regardless of any difficulties of proof that the plaintiff might face in trying to satisfy this burden. Can these cases be squared with the evidentiary rationale for strict liability, which utilizes strict liability to overcome the evidentiary difficulties that plaintiffs would otherwise confront in trying to prove that the defect was attributable to the defendant's negligence? Does the evidentiary rationale for strict liability apply to any difficulty of proof, or only to cases in which the plaintiff has otherwise sufficiently proven defect? Why does this distinction matter?

To see why the distinction matters, consider the following observation from *Deere & Co.* in a part of the opinion not excerpted above: "To allow such a speculative inference solely from the fact of an accident, when manufacturers and sellers no longer have exclusive control of the product, would essentially convert them into insurers of their products; this is contrary to the purposes of our product liability laws." 25 A.3d at 582. The requirement of defect distinguishes strict products liability from absolute liability and prevents manufacturers and sellers from being insurers of their products, explaining why courts do not relax the plaintiff's burden of proving defect, even if doing so would be practically impossible in some cases.

4. *Identifying malfunctions.* Like a soda bottle that explodes, a tractor that catches fire obviously malfunctioned. What about closer cases in which it is unclear whether the product malfunctioned? For example, in *McKenzie*, p. 126 *supra*, the plaintiff hired expert witnesses to establish that the wrench contained a manufacturing defect. By contrast, circumstantial proof of malfunction would not have required such direct evidence. Why might it have been difficult for the plaintiff to prove a malfunction in that case?

SIGLER v. AMERICAN HONDA MOTOR CO.
United States Court of Appeals, Sixth Circuit, 2008
532 F.3d 469

MOORE, KAREN NELSON, C.J. . . . On September 23, 2004, Sigler was involved in a single-car accident while traveling northbound on Interstate 75 in Bradley County, Tennessee. According to Sigler's recollection and an affidavit filed by Terry Williams, a motorist who was driving his car seventy-five to one hundred yards behind Sigler, Sigler was driving at approximately seventy miles per hour immediately prior to the accident. Sigler's vehicle, a 1999 Honda Accord EX (the "Accord"), then "veered off the road, drove down an embankment and through a small wire fence, and hit a tree." "The tree, approximately six inches in diameter, was uprooted by the collision." Williams's declaration states that

IV. Product Malfunctions

when he saw Sigler's vehicle "suddenly veer off the roadway [he] did not see any brake lights or blinkers" and that "[t]he car then went down the embankment and into a clump of trees." Sigler's Accord was a "certified pre-owned" vehicle equipped with a driver's side airbag, which did not deploy.

[After describing Sigler's injuries, the court describes various contested evidentiary rulings made by the district court in its decision to grant defendant's summary judgment motion. The district court provided two grounds for its decision, the first being that Sigler "failed to circumstantially show a defect in the Accord's airbag because [Sigler] has offered insufficient evidence to suggest that a defect is the 'more probable hypothesis' as to why the airbag did not deploy." Sigler appealed this ruling and other evidentiary rulings.]

As the district court noted, under Tennessee law, establishing a prima facie products-liability claim requires that "the plaintiff must show: (1) the product was defective and/or unreasonably dangerous, (2) the defect existed at the time the product left the manufacturer's control, and (3) the plaintiff's injury was proximately caused by the defective product." [ ] The parties do not contest the second element, and in this section we consider the first element.

As the district court noted, "[a] plaintiff may demonstrate that a product was defective or unreasonably dangerous through direct evidence, circumstantial evidence, or a combination." [ ] Tennessee law provides two tests for determining whether a product is unreasonably dangerous. Under the "consumer expectation test," bringing a successful claim "simply requires a showing that the product's performance was below reasonable minimum safety expectations of the ordinary consumer having ordinary, 'common' knowledge as to its characteristics." [ ] Further, "'[t]he general rule in Tennessee is that the issue of whether a product is defective or unreasonably dangerous is one for the jury.'" [ ]

Honda vigorously contests that the consumer-expectation test is the proper test to apply in this case, but its argument [that the test does not apply to complex products like airbags] is unpersuasive.... Sigler's claim involves an airbag, a federally required component of new automobiles, 49 U.S.C. §30127, and alleges only that the particular airbag in her vehicle was defective and failed to deploy in what she alleges was a high-speed collision that uprooted a tree. Sigler submitted a sworn affidavit stating her expectation that the airbag would deploy in an accident like the high-speed crash that she alleges occurred, and Honda's own brochure created an expectation that an airbag should deploy in a high-speed, frontal crash like that which Sigler alleged (Honda Brochure at 7) (stating that "when a car traveling 30 mph crashes head-on into a parked vehicle or other solid, stationary object, its speed will change very quickly" and that the vehicle's "sensors will detect the rapid decrease in speed and immediately signal the airbags to deploy"). The Tennessee Supreme Court stated that satisfying the consumer-expectation test "entails a showing by the plaintiff that... familiarity of the product's performance by consumers is sufficient to allow consumers to form reasonable expectations of the product's safety." [ ] Sigler offered evidence that an airbag is such a familiar product and that consumers—and, indeed, manufacturers like Honda—have expectations about the product's performance and safety. As a result, we hold that the consumer-expectation test is an acceptable standard by which to evaluate Sigler's claim.

Analyzing Sigler's claim under the consumer-expectation test—and without considering Honda's hearsay expert reports [deemed inadmissible in a prior portion of the opinion]—we hold that the district court inappropriately granted summary judgment on the ground that Sigler failed to present a genuine issue of material fact as to the existence of a defect in the airbag. Because none of Honda's hearsay expert reports should have been considered, the only evidence in the record regarding the nature of the accident is the circumstantial evidence that Sigler presented: that prior to her seizure she was driving at a speed of approximately seventy miles an hour; that the Accord suddenly veered off the road; that an eye witness did not see any brake lights; that the Accord collided with and uprooted a tree located some distance downhill from the Interstate; and that Sigler's insurance company declared the vehicle a "total loss" and paid the Siglers over $11,000 on their insurance claim, showing that the vehicle sustained significant damage and giving rise to an inference that her vehicle was traveling at a high speed when it collided with the tree.

Shorn of its expert reports concluding that the collision was a relatively low-speed accident, Honda has essentially no evidence to counter Sigler's circumstantial evidence that the Accord struck the tree at a high speed, in which case according to Honda's own brochure the airbag likely should have deployed. "Where a plaintiff is dependent upon circumstantial evidence [to prove a defect in a product], it is sufficient if he makes out the more probable hypothesis, and the evidence need not arise to that degree of certainty which would exclude every other reasonable conclusion." [ ] Under this standard, Sigler's claim should survive summary judgment because the only evidence in the record, viewed according to our obligation to draw all reasonable inferences in her favor, supports her hypothesis that the airbag in her Accord was defective because her accident more likely than not involved conditions in which the airbag should have deployed

NOTES AND QUESTIONS

1. *Source of the malfunction.* Did the airbag fail to deploy because of a manufacturing defect, or because of defective design? Does it matter when the plaintiff proves defect with the circumstantial evidence of malfunction?

2. *Complex products and consumer expectations.* Recall that one rationale for the risk-utility test is the "reality that ordinary consumers know little about how safe the complex products they use can or should be made." Soule v. General Motors Corp., 882 P.2d 298, 309 (Cal. 1994). Relying on this rationale for the risk-utility test, defendants often argue that the consumer expectations test does not apply to complex products. Though many courts still struggle with the issue, *Sigler* illustrates the common approach—an airbag, after all, is a complex product. Similarly, courts have applied the consumer expectations test to the performance of a newly purchased automobile tire that failed under normal driving conditions, because "[a]lthough the manufacturing process may be complex, the general driving populace understands the basic function and purpose of a tire." Tatham v. Bridgestone Americas Holding, 473 S.W.3d 734, 751

IV. Product Malfunctions

(Tenn. 2015); *see also* McCabe v. American Honda Motor Corp., 123 Cal. Rptr.2d 303, 313 (Ct. App. 2002) ("The critical question, in assessing the applicability of the consumer expectation test, is not whether the product, when considered in isolation, is beyond the ordinary knowledge of the consumer, but whether the product, *in the context of the facts and circumstances of its failure,* is one about which the ordinary consumers can form minimum safety expectations.").

3. *Airbags and malfunctions.* The mere fact that an airbag failed to deploy in a crash does not necessarily constitute a malfunction. In one case involving a fatal crash in which the airbag in front of the decedent driver did not deploy, the defendant's expert provided the following reconstruction of the event:

> "As the vehicle left the right side of the roadway, the left side wheels firmly struck and jumped the asphalt curb and the clockwise yaw continued as the vehicle traveled onto the grassy shoulder. The front portion of the left side of the vehicle engaged a rising dirt embankment which accelerated its clockwise yaw and caused the vehicle to roll toward the driver's side. Now travelling in a rearward and a driver's side leading direction, the rear bumper, fender and upper rear portion of the occupant compartment struck a large boulder on the right-hand side shoulder. This impact redirected the vehicle back out toward the paved roadway and continued its clockwise rotation. Its front end and hood contacted a lamp post as it passed by, rotating to rest in the breakdown lane. . . ."
>
> The accident reconstruction expert concluded that "given the direction and magnitude of this impact, it is neither surprising nor unexpected that the driver's side front airbag did not deploy in this accident sequence. The vehicle struck [a] boulder with the rear driver's side leading, and the angle and direction of this impact would not deploy the driver's front airbag which is designed and intended to deploy only in a frontal impact of significant magnitude. Given the force and angle of this impact, the airbag system functioned appropriately by deploying the side airbags and curtain shield airbags on the driver's side."

Koutsoukos v. Toyota Motor Sales, U.S.A., Inc., 49 A.3d 302, 306 (Conn. App. 2012). The court concluded that the plaintiff could not prove defect under the consumer expectations test, because "[t]his is not an accident 'so bizarre that the average juror, upon hearing the particulars, might reasonably think: Whatever the user may have expected from that contraption, it certainly wasn't that.'" *Id.* (quoting Potter v. Chicago Pneumatic Tool Co., 694 A.2d 1319 (Conn. 1990)).

4. *Source of consumer expectations.* As *Sigler* illustrates, consumer expectations of how a product should minimally perform can be based on the manufacturer's portrayal of the product. For this reason, courts justify the liability rule on the ground that "[t]he consumer expectations test intrinsically recognizes a manufacturer's central role in crafting the image of a product and establishing the consumer's expectations for that product—a portrayal which in turn motivates consumers to purchase that particular product." Aubin v. Union Carbide Corp., 177 So.3d 489, 507 (Fla. 2015).

Consumer expectations are also based on common knowledge of how a product should perform. For example, both food and soda bottles minimally perform certain functions that are both widely understood and expected by consumers who purchase or use them—that is what makes them "food" or "soda bottles." Based on this ordinary knowledge common to the community, the ordinary consumer does not expect that commercially purchased "food" is unfit for human consumption, nor does he or she expect that instead of delivering the beverage, a "soda bottle" will explosively shatter when opened. Products that fail to function in the manner minimally expected by the ordinary consumer are defective and violate the implied warranty.

To be sure, the malfunction in these cases can be derived by a simple comparison of how the performance of one product (an exploding bottle of Coca Cola) compares to the performance of other products in the same line (Coca Cola bottles that do not explode)—the same type of inquiry appropriate for manufacturing defects. But malfunctions are not limited to manufacturing defects, and it is not always possible to compare the product in the case at hand to others in the same line—the product can be destroyed in the accident. When the performance of the entire product line cannot serve as the benchmark, consumer expectations must instead be defined in relation to the market as a whole.

Consider a case in which employees of American Airlines alleged that a new line of uniforms caused them within weeks to suffer "skin rashes, respiratory problems, vertigo, and other ailments." Zurbriggen v. Twin Hill Acquisition Co., 338 F.Supp.3d 875, 878 (N.D. Ill. 2018). The problems allegedly stemmed from the design of the uniforms: they were made "from synthetic materials and contain '[d]etectable amounts' of several chemicals, including known and possible carcinogens, as well as chemicals known to cause the type of 'auto-immune' conditions experienced by American employees." In denying the defendant manufacturer's motion to dismiss the tort claims based on the consumer expectations test, the court held that "[a]n ordinary American employee would not expect company-issued uniforms to give rise to any health problems—let alone skin, respiratory, and auto-immune issues—through normal wear." This expectation was not derived from the line of uniforms manufactured by the defendant—they were all made from the same material. Consumer expectations were instead based on the product market as a whole: "[C]ompanies outfit their employees in uniforms every day that do not create the sort of health issues alleged in this case." *Id.* at 900. *See also* Wilson Sporting Goods Co. v. Hickox, 59 A.3d 1267, 1276-1277 (D.C. 2013) (citing other cases in support of holding that the jury could have reasonably relied on "the existence of safer, commercially available alternatives" and "industry practice" to "draw inferences about the level of safety an ordinary user would expect").

Thus, to determine whether a product like an airbag malfunctioned in a particular case, the jury must compare (1) the actual performance of the airbag that injured the plaintiff, with (2) the performance of an "airbag" that minimally functions in the manner that the ordinary consumer actually expects based on knowledge of how other airbags in the market perform. For purposes of this inquiry, the other airbags in the market include both those in the same product line and airbags in the vehicles of competing brands or models. Because the malfunction necessarily involves either the product's failure to perform like others in the same line (manufacturing defects), or its failure to perform like others in the same market (design defects), proof of malfunction does not require the plaintiff to identify the particular type of defect.

5. *Consumer expectations versus manufacturer intentions.* Having rejected the consumer expectation test for nonfood products, the *Restatement (Third)* instead limits product malfunctions "to situations in which a product fails to perform its manifestly intended function." §3 cmt. b. The *Restatement (Third)* does not explain why malfunctions are appropriately determined by the manufacturer's intentions and not consumer expectations, even though the Reporters recognized elsewhere that a standard of intentionality regarding defective product design is problematic because it "makes no reference to foreseeable-but-not-intended functions for which users might nevertheless reasonably have a right to expect the design to perform safely." James A. Henderson, Jr. & Aaron D. Twerski, *Achieving Consensus on Defective Product Design*, 83 Cornell L. Rev. 867, 8723 (1998) (explaining why the tort duty is based on foreseeable risks rather than intended product use). The two tests overlap when the malfunction is attributable to manufacturing defects. (Can you see why?) But insofar as the product design embodies the manufacturer's "manifest intentions," malfunctions attributable to the design might be problematic for reasons illustrated by the following materials.

V. AUTONOMOUS VEHICLES AND PRODUCTS LIABILITY: PROBLEM SET 1

The majority of tort cases in state courts now involve automobile crashes allegedly caused by a driver's negligence. By eliminating the human driver, autonomous vehicles will eliminate these negligence claims. Manufacturers will instead be responsible for ensuring that their autonomous vehicles can drive in a reasonably safe manner, potentially making them liable for a crash. Autonomous vehicles will alter the mix and number of tort cases, causing a massive shift from ordinary negligence claims to those based on products liability.

Although the technology is new and fully autonomous vehicles have yet to be commercially distributed into the market, they present a range of issues that provide a useful basis for assessing your understanding of products liability. When appropriate, our study of individual doctrines throughout the remainder of the book will conclude with an application of those doctrines to liability issues implicated by the crash of an autonomous vehicle. Try your hand at solving each problem. An analysis of each issue is then provided for your review. Most of these issues are more comprehensively addressed in Mark A. Geistfeld, *A Roadmap for Autonomous Vehicles: State Tort Liability, Automobile Insurance, and Federal Safety Regulation*, 105 Cal. L. Rev. 1611 (2017), which provides much of the material on autonomous vehicles throughout the book.

A vehicle is autonomous in the sense that it can drive without human assistance (or indeed, any human in the vehicle at all). When the vehicle's occupant is no longer executing the dynamic driving task, human driving error is no longer the cause of an accident. Instead, the manner in which the vehicle executed the driving task becomes the focus of inquiry. For obvious reasons, we will use the term "operating system" to refer to the hardware and software that determines how an autonomous vehicle executes the dynamic driving task. Consider Hod Lipson & Melba Kurman, DRIVERLESS: INTELLIGENT CARS AND THE ROAD AHEAD 66-67 (2016) (adopting this term and explaining the similarities and differences between the operating system of a driverless vehicle and the operating system of a computer).

Autonomous vehicles will not be perfectly safe; they will inevitably fail at times. Given the complexity of driving and the inherent limitations of coding that behavior, can courts reliably determine whether the crash of an autonomous vehicle was caused by a defect that subjects the manufacturer to liability? In evaluating these issues, consider whether this emerging technology can be adequately addressed by existing doctrine or instead requires a new liability regime.

AV Problem 1.1

Once the operator has properly deployed an autonomous vehicle, the manufacturer becomes primarily responsible for the vehicle's driving performance. Suppose that the operating system has a programming bug that causes the operating system to "freeze," which in turn causes the vehicle to crash. Does this problem involve a manufacturing defect or a design defect? Could the plaintiff instead prove a defect under the malfunction doctrine? If so, would it matter whether the malfunction is defined in terms of consumer expectations or the manufacturer's manifest intentions?

Analysis of AV Problem 1.1

Programming is complex and routinely contains numerous bugs or coding errors, as you've undoubtedly experienced. Even if a bug is caused by a typo, that coding is still part of the operating system, making it part of the vehicle's design. *All* vehicles with this operating system would contain the coding error, unlike manufacturing defects that affect only particular products within the entire product line. A manufacturer's liability for manufacturing defects will be largely limited to quality-control problems with the hardware of the operating system, including the cameras, lidar (laser scanning), radar, and other physical components of the system that do not perform according to design.

When a programming error or bug in the software causes the operating system to crash, in turn causing the vehicle to crash, the plaintiff would not have to identify the specific coding error and could instead prove defective design solely based on the manner in which the operating system malfunctioned. The coding error prevented the operating system from performing its expected and manifestly intended function of executing the dynamic driving task, subjecting the manufacturer to liability for the crash under any formulation of the malfunction doctrine.

V. Autonomous Vehicles and Products Liability: Problem Set 1

AV Problem 1.2

The "abstract definition of the task" to be obtained by the coding of an operating system includes arriving safely at the specified destination along with other factors such as minimizing the time or length of trip. *See* Scott D. Pendleton & Hans Andersen et al., *Planning, Control, and Coordination for Autonomous Vehicles*, *Machines* (2017), https://www.mdpi.com/2075-1702/5/1/6. Suppose a fully functioning autonomous vehicle crashes before arriving at its specified destination. Is the crash itself a malfunction? Does it matter for this purpose whether the malfunction is defined by reference to consumer expectations or the manufacturer's manifest intentions?

Analysis of AV Problem 1.2

The coding objective shows that the manufacturer manifestly intended for the vehicle to arrive safely at the programmed destination, and so the crash literally satisfies the definition of a malfunction in the *Restatement (Third)*. Moreover, the manufacturer cannot avoid liability by adequately warning about the inherent risk of crash, as that disclosure would not evince a different intent about product performance. The warning instead would be relevant for determining the expectations of either the manufacturer or consumers, neither of which disproves defect defined in relation to the manufacturer's intentions. This formulation of the malfunction doctrine accordingly subjects the manufacturer to liability only because it is striving to achieve safe driving outcomes, a perverse result from a safety perspective.

The consumer expectations test yields a different result. To the extent that consumers have expectations about how this new technology will perform, they will not expect perfect safety. After all, automated driving technologies have already caused fatalities, and so these vehicles do not malfunction simply because they crash. *Editors Note: See* Mark A. Geistfeld, *Why the Next Person Hit by a Driverless Car Might Not Be Able to Sue*, Time, March 30, 2018 (discussing these crashes and proposing that during the period of premarket testing, manufacturers be obligated to pay no-fault compensation to injured bystanders). However, consumer expectations about the matter might be influenced by the manner in which manufacturers market the new technology. "'We want customers to trust we've done a really good job,' said Anders Eugensson, Volvo's director of government affairs. 'That's why we say if anything happens, we assume liability.'" Keith Naughton & Margaret Cronin Fisk, *Driverless Cars Give Lawyers Bottomless List of Defendants*, Ins. J. (Dec. 22, 2015). Will statements like these lead consumers to expect perfect safety? Only time will tell.

AV Problem 1.3

For reasons discussed in the analysis of Problem 1.1, a manufacturer's liability for manufacturing defects will be largely limited to quality-control problems with the hardware of the operating system, including the cameras, lidar (laser scanning), radar, and other physical components of the system that do not perform according to design. Suppose there is such a defect in the hardware of the operating system that causes the vehicle to crash. Could the plaintiff recover under the malfunction theory, or must the plaintiff instead identify the manufacturing defect?

Analysis of AV Problem 1.3

Unless the hardware defect caused the operating system to "freeze," the circumstances of such a crash simply show that the vehicle could not safely execute the dynamic driving task. Nevertheless, an inference of malfunction would be created if the crash occurred under conditions that are safely managed by a fully functioning operating system. Absent these circumstances, the crash would be indistinguishable from other crashes governed by the analysis of Problem 1.2. To recover in such a case, the plaintiff must identify the manufacturing defect in the vehicle that caused the crash. If the plaintiff can do so, then strict liability applies even though consumers do not have well-formed expectations about this aspect of product performance (again, see the analysis of Problem 1.2). These defects still frustrate consumer expectations, however, because consumers reasonably expect that manufacturers will guarantee that their products pass quality-control measures and do not contain manufacturing defects.

5

The "Unreasonably Dangerous" Requirement, Patent Defects, and the Element of Duty

For any tort claim, duty refers to the tort obligation owed by one party (the duty-bearer) to another (right-holder). Without an antecedent tort obligation, there is no legal basis for subjecting the defendant to tort liability for the plaintiff's injuries. *See, e.g.*, Cipollone v. Liggett Group, Inc., 505 U.S. 504, 522 (U.S. 1992) (holding that "common-law damage actions of the sort raised by petitioner"—involving strict products liability, negligence, express warranty, and intentional tort claims—"are premised on the existence of a legal duty"); Graff v. Beard, 858 S.W.2d 918, 919 (Tex. 1993) ("It is fundamental that the existence of a legally cognizable duty is a prerequisite to all tort liability.").

Once duty has been established, the liability rule must then specify the substantive obligations imposed upon the duty-bearer: What must be done to satisfy the tort duty? Negligence liability, for example, requires duty-bearers to exercise reasonable care, and so the substantive content of the negligence rule is supplied by the behavioral requirements of reasonable care.

How do these distinctive elements of a tort claim factor into the rule of strict products liability? Under the *Restatement (Second)* §402A formulation, a product seller violates the duty and is subject to strict liability for selling a product with a defect that is unreasonably dangerous and causes physical harm to a consumer. What is the element of duty in strict products liability? What is the substantive content of that duty? Neither element is expressly identified as such by §402A, but each element is necessarily embodied within that rule.

Courts describe the duty in general terms. As one court put it, "In order to establish a prima facie case in strict products liability for design defects, the plaintiff must show that the manufacturer breached its duty to market safe products. . . ." Voss v. Black & Decker Mfg. Co., 450 N.E.2d 204, 208 (N.Y. 1983). Is the duty distinct from defect, or is the duty instead wholly defined by the obligation not to commercially distribute a defective product that proximately causes physical harm?

The issue thus far has been of little or no concern. After courts eliminated the requirement of contractual privity, the tort duty was firmly established. The duty was then obviously breached when the defendant commercially distributed a malfunctioning product that proximately caused the plaintiff's physical harm, as in the cases of contaminated food or exploding soda bottles. But outside of products that unexpectedly malfunction—the type of defect that largely defines the §402A rule of strict products liability—the role of duty, and its relation to the requirement of defect, can be of decisive importance, particularly in cases alleging defective design.

The exact formulation of duty within §402A is surprisingly elusive. The liability rule requires that the product must be both defective and "unreasonably dangerous." However, the defect itself is defined in terms of the "unreasonably dangerous" requirement. *See* RESTATEMENT (SECOND) OF TORTS §402A cmt. g (defining "defective condition" of a product as "a condition not contemplated by the ultimate consumer, which will be unreasonably dangerous to him"). The "unreasonably dangerous" requirement, in turn, is defined by the expectations of the ordinary consumer based on ordinary knowledge common to the community. This requirement is simply the consumer expectations test—the method §402A employs to determine whether the product is defective. Hence §402A first defines a "defect" in terms of the "unreasonably dangerous" requirement, and then §402A effectively uses the "unreasonably dangerous" requirement for determining "defect." The relation between the two requirements appears to be circular and has created considerable confusion, resulting in disagreement about their proper formulations.

The role of each requirement can be clarified by considering the patent-defect rule under the implied warranty. This rule shows why §402A requires a defect that is also "unreasonably dangerous"; it gives each requirement an independent meaning that fully structures the two elements of duty and breach within products liability.

I. DIFFERENT INTERPRETATIONS OF THE "UNREASONABLY DANGEROUS" REQUIREMENT

In the following pair of cases, the California Supreme Court develops the rule of strict products liability for defective design in a manner that shows why the ambiguity of the "unreasonably dangerous" requirement in §402A is related to the problem of patent dangers. The third case underscores this connection while also interpreting the "unreasonably dangerous" requirement in a different manner, illustrating the range of meanings that courts have imputed to this requirement in their efforts to deal with the problem of patent dangers.

CRONIN v. J.B.E. OLSON CORP.
Supreme Court of California, 1972
501 P.2d 1153

SULLIVAN, J. On October 3, 1966, plaintiff, a route salesman for Gravem-Inglis Bakery Co. (Gravem) of Stockton, was driving a bread delivery truck along a

I. Different Interpretations of the "Unreasonably Dangerous" Requirement

rural road in San Joaquin County. While plaintiff was attempting to pass a pick-up truck ahead of him, its driver made a sudden left turn, causing the pick-up to collide with the plaintiff's truck and forcing the latter off the road and into a ditch. As a result, plaintiff was propelled through the windshield and landed on the ground. The impact broke an aluminum safety hasp which was located just behind the driver's seat and designed to hold the bread trays in place. The loaded trays, driven forward by the abrupt stop and impact of the truck, struck plaintiff in the back and hurled him through the windshield. He sustained serious personal injuries.

The truck, a one-ton Chevrolet stepvan with built-in bread racks, was one of several trucks sold to Gravem in 1957 by defendant Chase Chevrolet Company (Chase), not a party to this appeal. Upon receipt of Gravem's order, Chase purchased the trucks from defendant J.B.E. Olson Corporation (Olson), which acted as sales agent for the assembled vehicle, the chassis, body, and racks of which were manufactured by three subcontractors. The body of the van contained three aisles along which there were welded runners extending from the front to the rear of the truck. Each rack held ten bread trays from top to bottom and five trays deep; the trays slid forward into the cab or back through the rear door to facilitate deliveries.

Plaintiff brought the present action against Chase, Olson and General Motors Corporation alleging that the truck was unsafe for its intended use because of defects in its manufacture, in that the metal hasp was exceedingly porous, contained holes, pits and voids, and lacked sufficient tensile strength to withstand the impact. Defendants' answers denied the material allegations of the complaint and asserted the affirmative defense of contributory negligence.

At the trial, plaintiff's expert testified, in substance, that the metal hasp broke, releasing the bread trays, because it was extremely porous and had a significantly lower tolerance to force than a non-flawed aluminum hasp would have had. The jury returned a verdict in favor of plaintiff and against Olson in the sum of $45,000 but in favor of defendant Chase and against plaintiff. Judgment was entered accordingly. This appeal by Olson followed.

Defendant attacks the sufficiency of the evidence to support the verdict and the trial court's instruction on strict liability. The challenge to the evidence is multi-pronged, claiming in effect that plaintiff produced no evidence on several essential issues.

[Defendant contends that] plaintiff's evidence failed to show any condition of the hasp which could be considered defective. The gist of the argument on this point appears to be that "defectiveness" cannot be properly determined without proof of some standard set by knowledgeable individuals for the manufacture and use of the particular part under scrutiny and that plaintiff's expert applied "his own unilateral standard" in giving his opinion that the hasp was defective. In the absence of an appropriate standard, so it is argued, all proof must fail.

The argument lacks merit. Gravem purchased the van and its bread racks from Chase as a unit. Since there were no standard bread racks available, Chase in turn ordered them from Olson according to the latter's blueprint, and left to Olson the manufacture of a safe set of bread racks.

Olson admitted through the testimony of its vice president that the purpose of the locking device on the bread rack (of which the hasp was a part) was to hold the trays in place and that it knew that the van was to be driven on public highways. In short, the evidence shows that the intended purpose of the locking device was to keep the bread trays from moving forward into the driver's compartment as a result of any foreseeable movements of the van in highway travel.

The record shows that the hasp, because it was defective, did not fulfill this purpose. Plaintiff's expert testified that the broken hasp was "extremely porous and extremely defective" as it was full of holes, voids and cracks. These flaws were in the metal itself and resulted in the hasp's lowered tolerance to force. He further stated that this condition could not be attributed to prolonged use. This conclusion was buttressed by the expert's testimony that the break in the hasp was a tensile fracture caused by sudden force rather than a fatigue fracture, which is by nature progressive. The hasp failed because "[it] was just a very, very bad piece of metal. Simply would not stand any force — reasonable forces at all."

Defendant's remaining contention requires us to probe the essential elements of products liability. It is claimed that in instructing the jury as to the issues upon which plaintiff had the burden of proof the trial court erred by submitting a definition of strict liability which failed to include, as defendant requested, the element that the defect found in the product be "unreasonably dangerous." It is urged that without this element, for which Olson finds support in section 402A of the *Restatement Second of Torts* (1965) and in recent decisions of this court, a seller would incur absolute liability for any injury proximately caused by an intended use of a product, regardless of the insignificance of the risk posed by the defect or the fortuity of the resulting harm.

The history of strict liability in California indicates that the requirement that the defect made the product "unreasonably dangerous" crept into our jurisprudence without fanfare after its inclusion in section 402A of the *Restatement Second of Torts* in 1965. The question raised in the instant matter as to whether the requirement is an essential part of the plaintiff's case is one of first impression.

We begin with section 402A itself. According to the official comment g to the section, a "defective condition" is one "not contemplated by the ultimate consumer, which will be unreasonably dangerous to him." Comment i, defining "unreasonably dangerous," states, "The article sold must be dangerous to an extent beyond that which would be contemplated by the ordinary consumer who purchases it, with the ordinary knowledge common to the community as to its characteristics." Examples given in comment i make it clear that such innocuous products as sugar and butter, unless contaminated, would not give rise to a strict liability claim merely because the former may be harmful to a diabetic or the latter may aggravate the blood cholesterol level of a person with heart disease. Presumably such dangers are squarely within the contemplation of the ordinary consumer. Prosser, the reporter for the Restatement, suggests that the "unreasonably dangerous" qualification was added to foreclose the possibility that the manufacturer of a product with inherent possibilities for harm (for example, butter, drugs, whiskey and automobiles) would become "automatically responsible for all the harm that such things do in the world." William L. Prosser, *Strict Liability to the Consumer in California,* 18 Hastings L.J. 9, 23 (1966).

The result of the limitation, however, has not been merely to prevent the seller from becoming an insurer of his products with respect to all harm generated by their use. Rather, it has burdened the injured plaintiff with proof of an element which rings of negligence. Of particular concern is the susceptibility of *Restatement* section 402A to a literal reading which would require the finder of

I. Different Interpretations of the "Unreasonably Dangerous" Requirement

fact to conclude that the product is, first, defective and, second, unreasonably dangerous. A bifurcated standard is of necessity more difficult to prove than a unitary one. But merely proclaiming that the phrase "defective condition unreasonably dangerous" requires only a single finding would not purge that phrase of its negligence complexion. We think that a requirement that a plaintiff also prove that the defect made the product "unreasonably dangerous" places upon him a significantly increased burden and represents a step backward in the area pioneered by this court.

We recognize that the words "unreasonably dangerous" may also serve the beneficial purpose of preventing the seller from being treated as the insurer of its products. However, we think that such protective end is attained by the necessity of proving that there was a defect in the manufacture or design of the product and that such defect was a proximate cause of the injuries. Although the seller should not be responsible for all injuries involving the use of its products, it should be liable for all injuries proximately caused by any of its products which are adjudged "defective."

We can see no difficulty in applying [our] formulation of strict products liability in *Greenman v. Yuba Power Products, Inc.* to the full range of products liability situations, including those involving "design defects." A defect may emerge from the mind of the designer as well as from the hand of the workman. Although it is easier to see the "defect" in a single imperfectly fashioned product than in an entire line badly conceived, a distinction between manufacture and design defects is not tenable.

The most obvious problem we perceive in creating any such distinction is that thereafter it would be advantageous to characterize a defect in one rather than the other category. It is difficult to prove that a product ultimately caused injury because a widget was poorly welded—a defect in manufacture—rather than because it was made of inexpensive metal difficult to weld, chosen by a designer concerned with economy—a defect in design. The proof problem would, of course, be magnified when the article in question was either old or unique, with no easily available basis for comparison. We wish to avoid providing such a battleground for clever counsel. Furthermore, we find no reason why a different standard, and one harder to meet, should apply to defects which plague entire product lines. We recognize that it is more damaging to a manufacturer to have an entire line condemned, so to speak, for a defect in design, than a single product for a defect in manufacture. But the potential economic loss to a manufacturer should not be reflected in a different standard of proof for an injured consumer.

We conclude that the trial court did not err by refusing to instruct the jury that plaintiff must establish that the defective condition of the product made it unreasonably dangerous to the user or consumer.

The judgment is affirmed.

NOTES AND QUESTIONS

1. *Is it always necessary to distinguish among the different types of defects?* As the court in *Cronin* observed in an omitted portion of the opinion, "throughout the development of the *Greenman* rule we have said very little to explain

what we meant in that case by a 'defect' which would give rise to liability if injury were proximately caused thereby." The requirement of defect is an element of strict products liability, so how could the court develop this liability rule without discussing the concept? Once again, the answer involves the implicit limitation of the original formulation of strict products liability to products that malfunction. Consider Michael D. Green, *The Unappreciated Congruity of the Second and Third Tort Restatements on Design Defects,* 74 Brook. L. Rev. 807, 836 (2009) ("In this era, the type of defect was not important, and the founders, although aware of the different ways in which a product might be defective, paid little attention to the matter as section 402A was being developed."). Recall that product malfunctions can be caused by either manufacturing defects or design defects, and in these cases the plaintiff does not need to identify the actual defect. Does this rule adequately explain why the court in *Cronin* concluded that "a distinction between manufacture and design defects is not tenable"?

2. *A liability rule limited to malfunctioning products?* To what extent does the *Cronin* court's implicit focus on malfunctioning products influence its interpretation of the "unreasonably dangerous" requirement in §402A? In the cases we have studied that involve malfunctioning products, did courts ever require the plaintiff to show that the defect was also "unreasonably dangerous"? The apparent circularity of the two requirements is particularly pronounced in cases of malfunction. The aluminum hasp at issue in *Cronin* had a latent defect that caused it to break and thereby release the bread tray into the driver's seat—a malfunction or product performance more dangerous than expected by the ordinary consumer. The same fact that establishes defect—the unexpected product malfunction—also makes the product "unreasonably dangerous."

Aside from the "dual burden" problem identified by the court in *Cronin*, are there any other problems posed by the "unreasonably dangerous" requirement? Consider this question in the context of the next case, which was decided by the California Supreme Court in tandem with *Cronin*. The court issued its decisions for the two cases on the same day.

LUQUE v. MCLEAN
Supreme Court of California, 1972
501 P.2d 1163

SULLIVAN, J. Plaintiff Celestino Luque lived in Millbrae with his cousins, Harry and Laura Dunn, who purchased from defendant Rhoads Hardware (Rhoads) a rotary power lawn mower manufactured by defendant Air Capital Manufacturing Company (Air Capital). The record discloses that the basic principle of a rotary mower is the rotation at extreme speed of a single blade which cuts the grass like a machete and ejects it through an unguarded hole in the front of the mower. In the machine used by plaintiff, the blade revolved at a speed of 175 miles per hour, passing the unguarded hole 100 times a second. Adjacent to this hole, the word 'caution' was printed on the appliance. Although Air Capital, the manufacturer, presented evidence that it customarily included safety instructions

I. Different Interpretations of the "Unreasonably Dangerous" Requirement

with every lawn mower shipped from its factory, Mr. Dunn denied receiving any. According to the manufacturer, the safety leaflet warned against leaving the mower without turning off the motor. There was also evidence that plaintiff had been instructed by Mr. Dunn on the operation of the mower and on the danger of putting a hand in the unguarded hole.

On December 4, 1965, a friend of the Dunns asked plaintiff to cut her lawn. With the help of Mr. Dunn, plaintiff took the Dunns' mower to the friend's residence a few blocks away. Plaintiff testified that as he was cutting the grass, which was wet, he noticed a small carton in the path of the mower. He left the mower in a stationary position with its motor running and walked over to remove the carton. As he did so, he suddenly slipped on the grass and fell backward. His left hand went into the unguarded hole of the mower, was caught in the revolving rotary blade and was severely mangled and lacerated.

Plaintiff brought this action against Air Capital, Rhoads, and the distributor Garehime Corporation on the theories of strict liability, negligence and breach of warranty. At trial, plaintiff's expert witness testified that the lawn mower, because of the unguarded hole, was very hazardous and was not designed with safety in mind; that even in 1961, when this mower was designed and manufactured, this type of injury was foreseeable; and that such an injury could have been prevented by a simple piece of additional equipment costing less than one dollar per machine. Defendant's expert, on the other hand, testified that the mower was not defective since it surpassed the safety standards for lawn mowers prescribed by the American Standards Association, an organization composed of representatives from industry and government; and that the design improvements suggested by plaintiff's witness were not feasible.

At the close of all the evidence, plaintiff withdrew his counts based upon theories of negligence and breach of warranty and the case was submitted to the jury only on the count based upon the theory of strict liability. The trial judge concluded that there was insufficient evidence to warrant the giving of an instruction on assumption of risk and accordingly withdrew that issue from the jury. A verdict was returned in favor of defendants. Judgment was entered accordingly. This appeal followed.

Plaintiff contends that the court erred in instructing the jury at Air Capital's request that plaintiff had the burden of proving that he was not aware of the defect in the lawn mower at the time of the accident. Plaintiff argues that the jury was told that general awareness of a defect by an injured party bars recovery and that, therefore, the effect of the instruction was virtually to direct a verdict for defendants.

Defendants take the position that under California law a manufacturer is strictly liable in tort only for products which have latent defects. However, they have not called to our attention, nor has our independent research disclosed, any reported decisions in this state which have made a distinction between latent and patent defects in applying the doctrine of strict liability. It is true that, as defendants note, the great majority of reported decisions dealing with products liability have involved defects classifiable as latent. But none of these cases limit this type of liability to hidden defects.

Indeed, we believe that if a latent-patent distinction ever had any vitality, it was laid to rest in Pike v. Frank G. Hough Co., 467 P.2d 229, 234-35 (Cal. 1970): "Defendant contends that the danger of being struck by the paydozer was a patent peril and, therefore, that it had no duty to install safety devices to protect against an obvious danger. We do not agree. Even if the obviousness of the peril is conceded, the modern approach does not preclude liability solely because the danger is obvious." This language is found in our discussion of the manufacturer's liability for negligence in the design of the piece of construction equipment involved in that case. Immediately thereafter, however, we upheld the sufficiency of a second count based on the theory of strict liability.

Furthermore, the policy underlying the doctrine of strict liability compels the conclusion that recovery should not be limited to cases involving latent defects. "The purpose of such liability is to insure that the costs of injuries resulting from defective products are borne by the manufacturers that put such products on the market rather than by the injured persons who are powerless to protect themselves." [ ] Requiring the defect to be latent would severely limit the cases in which the financial burden would be shifted to the manufacturer. It would indeed be anomalous to allow a plaintiff to prove that a manufacturer was negligent in marketing an obviously defective product, but to preclude him from establishing the manufacturer's strict liability for doing the same thing. The result would be to immunize from strict liability manufacturers who callously ignore patent dangers in their products while subjecting to such liability those who innocently market products with latent defects.

[On the other hand,] a person urging strict liability must not have assumed the risk of the defective product. Plaintiff argues that assumption of the risk is a defense and that it was therefore improper to instruct the jury that he had the burden of proving that he had not assumed the risk. We agree. "For such a defense to arise, the user or consumer must become aware of the defect and danger and still proceed unreasonably to make use of the product." [ ]

Applying the foregoing rationale to the instant case we conclude that it was error to instruct the jury that plaintiff had the burden of proving that he was not aware of the defect in the lawn mower at the time of the accident. As we have explained, such an instruction in effect told the jury either that plaintiff was required to prove that the defect was latent or that plaintiff was required to prove that he had not assumed the risk of the defect. Under either interpretation, the instruction was an incorrect statement of the law.

Since the defect in this case was patent, it seems probable that the jury may have based its verdict upon the instruction erroneously requiring that plaintiff prove that the defect was latent. Accordingly, we conclude that the court committed prejudicial error and that the judgment must be reversed.

NOTES AND QUESTIONS

1. *Consumer expectations and patent dangers.* As illustrated by the *Halliday* case, p. 80 *supra,* the original formulation of the consumer expectations test in §402A bars recovery for patent dangers. When a risk is open and obvious—such as the lack of child-proof features on the handgun at issue in *Halliday*—the materialization of that risk cannot constitute a product performance that was unexpected by the ordinary consumer with ordinary knowledge common to the community. The product is not "unreasonably dangerous," thereby barring recovery under §402A. To what extent

I. Different Interpretations of the "Unreasonably Dangerous" Requirement

does this particular problem explain the court's approach in both *Cronin* and *Luque*? Consider Barker v. Lull Eng'g Co., 573 P.2d 443, 451 (Cal. 1978) ("[O]ur decision in *Luque v. McLean*—decided the same day as *Cronin*—aptly reflects our disagreement with the restrictive implications of the Restatement formulation, for in *Luque* we held that a power rotary lawn mower with an unguarded hole could properly be found defective, in spite of the fact that the defect in the product was patent and hence in all probability within the reasonable contemplation of the ordinary consumer.").

2. *Beyond malfunctions.* Is there a difference between the types of defect at issue in *Cronin* and *Luque*? As previously discussed, the defective hasp in *Cronin* malfunctioned. Did the lawnmower in *Luque* malfunction? How about the handgun at issue in *Halliday*? A comparison of *Cronin* and *Luque* illustrates a common dynamic: courts have interpreted §402A without clearly distinguishing between malfunctioning products and those that do not malfunction but are allegedly defective in design. Because §402A implicitly defines defect in the monolithic terms of unexpected malfunctions, the "unreasonably dangerous" requirement presumably addresses that type of defect. When this requirement is applied to products that do not malfunction, it can bar recovery for reasons unrelated to the plaintiff's allegation of defect. A patent danger cannot cause an unexpected malfunction, as *Halliday* tragically illustrates, but the plaintiff's allegation is that the patent danger could be eliminated by a reasonable redesign of the product. The plaintiff in *Luque* made a similar claim. Barring recovery merely because the danger is patent, therefore, is problematic for the substantive reasons the court recognized in *Luque*. By extending §402A beyond malfunctioning products, courts inevitably put pressure on the meaning of the "unreasonably dangerous" requirement for cases involving patent dangers in products that did not malfunction. The court in *Cronin* attempted to solve this problem by eliminating the requirement. Consider how this problem influences the court's reasoning in the next case, which provides an alternative way to handle the "unreasonably dangerous" requirement.

CEPEDA v. CUMBERLAND ENGINEERING CO.
Supreme Court of New Jersey, 1978
386 A.2d 816

CONFORD, J.A.D. The action, brought by a workman operating a "pelletizing" machine, was for negligence and breach of warranty against the manufacturer of the machine, for damages consequent upon the loss of four fingers of the left hand resulting from an accident in the course of such operation in 1968. Although the machine came from the manufacturer with a bolted guard which would have prevented the accident, the guard had apparently been removed before plaintiff came to work on the day of the accident.

The theory of plaintiff's action was that the machine was defectively designed from a safety standpoint, in that the guard was required to be removed frequently in the normal course of the operation of the machine; that it could have been expected that on some such occasion the guard would not be replaced before resumption of operations, whether inadvertently or otherwise; and that therefore the defendant manufacturer should have equipped it with an electronic "interlock" mechanism, readily available and capable of installation, which would have automatically prevented the operation of the machine when the guard was off. The defense was that the machine was not defectively designed as it met general standards of safety as of the date of its sale to plaintiff's employer, 1956, and as it was reasonably contemplated that the machine would not be operated with the guard off. It was further contended that plaintiff was guilty of contributory negligence in operating the machine with the guard off and that such negligence barred recovery, being a substantial factor in bringing about the accident.

[After finding that the machine was defective in design when sold, and that the plaintiff's contributory negligence was not a proximate cause of the accident, the jury] awarded plaintiff $125,000 damages, for which judgment was entered against defendant.

The Appellate Division found that the evidence compelled the conclusion as a matter of law that the machine as delivered was free of design defect. The manufacturer was "entitled to expect normal use" of its product, and if a safety device provided with the machine was not used, the manufacturer "cannot be held responsible for unforeseeable negligence on the part of third parties in operating or permitting operation of the equipment without the device."

We have concluded that the Appellate Division did not, as it was required to do, give the plaintiff the benefit of all the proofs and of all legitimate inferences therefrom favorable to plaintiff, before deciding the fact-issues in the case against him as a matter of law. The best view of the evidence from the plaintiff's standpoint would permit an inference that it was indeed foreseeable that in view of the frequent occasion for removal of the guard during operations someone would permit the plaintiff to use the machine without the guard or that he would do so ignorantly or inadvertently. In such circumstances, moreover, authoritative interpretation of *Restatement (Second)* Sec. 402A, to which provisions this Court has broadly committed itself in this area, justifies our adopting the rule that knowledge of the dangerous potentiality of a machine design as reflected by the evidence at trial is imputable to the manufacturer, and that the remaining determinative question as to affirmative liability is whether a reasonably prudent manufacturer with such foreknowledge would have put such a product into the stream of commerce after considering the hazards as well as the utility of the machine, the ease of incorporating a remedial interlock, the likelihood *vel non* that the machine would be used only with the guard, and such other factors as would bear upon the prudence of a reasonable manufacturer in so deciding whether to market the machine.

The heart of the approach we take toward resolution of the matter of defendant's affirmative liability in this case calls for a careful distinction between ordinary manufacturing defects and defects of design. The present case is an example of the latter, where the product is made as intended, but is asserted to be dangerous in some way. The distinction has been frequently drawn in the literature. [ ] However, there has not been uniformity in the views as to what, if anything, should be the difference in the criteria for strict liability in tort in the respective types of "defects" mentioned.

I. Different Interpretations of the "Unreasonably Dangerous" Requirement

The black letter of *Restatement (Second)* §402A does not draw the stated distinction, the requirement that the product be "in a defective condition unreasonably dangerous to the user or consumer" being facially applicable to both kinds of defects. However, Comment I of the section explains that the qualification "unreasonably dangerous" was meant to negate the notion that products normally useful, such as sugar, whiskey, tobacco, or butter, could be regarded as defective because, if used improperly, excessively or in an adulterated condition, they could also be harmful. The requisite of "unreasonably dangerous," however, also extends to other manufactured objects whose utility in ordinary use outweighs the potentiality of their harmfulness. As stated in Prosser, Torts (1971), p. 659: "An ordinary pair of shoes does not become unreasonably unsafe merely because the soles become somewhat slippery when wet; nor is there unreasonable danger in a hammer merely because it can mash a thumb. Knives and axes would be quite useless if they did not cut."

In the case of a defect of a product in the sense of an abnormality unintended by the manufacturer, there would appear to be prima facie liability for physical harm proximately resulting from the defect to a user or consumer without any need for showing of unreasonable danger in any other sense. "The product would be unreasonably dangerous as a matter of law and this would be true of virtually any fabrication or construction defect." [ ]

Our present decisional concern, however, is with the design defect aspect of a manufacturer's strict liability in tort. At this point of the discussion, the point to be made is that in design defect liability analysis the §402A criterion of "unreasonably dangerous" is an appropriate one if understood to render the liability of the manufacturer substantially coordinate with liability on negligence principles.

A most useful formulation of the foregoing principles, for purposes of practical judicial implementation in design defect cases, . . . has recently been described as "the risk/utility analysis as developed by Deans Wade and Keeton." [ ] Our study of the decisions satisfies us that this risk/utility analysis rationalizes what the great majority of the courts actually do in deciding design defect cases where physical injury has proximately resulted from the defect. Several recent cases have expressly referred to and applied the stated analysis [ ].

. . .

In concluding this phase of the discussion of the law, we take notice of the fact that [an earlier decision could require a different result insofar as it relied on Cronin v. J.B.E. Olson Corp., 501 P.2d 1153 (Cal. 1972)]. *Cronin* has been widely criticized as providing no useful definition of an actionable defect, particularly in relation to a case of a product of unsafe design. As stated by Dean Keeton, "the difficulty is that no content was given [by *Cronin*] to the concept of defect and this is vitally important when a plaintiff's theory is that a product, although fabricated and constructed as it was intended to be, subjected users or others to an inherent risk of harm that made the product defective." [ ] . . .

It should be apparent from our discussion above . . . that we approve the *Restatement (Second)* §402A criterion of "unreasonably dangerous" if understood conformably therewith. It is probable, as intimated in the said discussion, that liability could be premised on the fact of defect alone, where that defect is the result of an unintended manufacturing error or mischance, and proximately related to the personal injury. In such case, the added *Restatement* requirement that the defect be unreasonably dangerous could either be discarded or held satisfied in such instance as a matter of law. We may leave definitive resolution of the matter to a case calling for it. It will suffice for purposes of the case at bar, which is clearly a situation of alleged design defect, that the *Restatement* criterion of "unreasonably dangerous" remains soundly applicable thereto.

[The court then found that the jury had reached an inconsistent verdict regarding contributory negligence and proximate cause.]

The judgment of the Appellate Division is reversed, and the cause is remanded to the Law Division for a limited new trial, subject to the conditions stated hereinabove.

NOTES AND QUESTIONS

1. *The majority rule.* In contrast to the ruling in *Cronin*, the court's decision in *Cepeda* to retain the "unreasonably dangerous" requirement reflects the majority approach. "Under the doctrine of strict liability, in most jurisdictions, liability for injuries resulting from a defective product can arise only where the defective condition of the product is unreasonably dangerous to the user or consumer." 72A C.J.S. Products Liability §13 (2021 update). *See, e.g.,* Corder v. Ethicon, Inc., 473 F. Supp. 3d 749, 761 (E.D. Ky. 2020) ("Kentucky holds manufacturers strictly liable for injuries stemming from products distributed 'in a defective condition unreasonably dangerous to the user or consumer.'").

2. *The patent-danger rule as a rationale for the risk-utility test.* By redefining the "unreasonably dangerous" requirement in terms of the risk-utility test, courts like the one in *Cepeda* could avoid having to dismiss the claim under the consumer expectations test as originally formulated in §402A. These cases, as *Cepeda* further illustrates, involved alleged defects of design in products that did not malfunction because the risk in question was open and obvious. Redefining the "unreasonably dangerous" requirement to solve the problem of patent dangers accordingly provided one method for courts to adopt the risk-utility test, thereby extending products liability beyond the limited problem of product malfunctions.

The problem of patent dangers also helps to explain why so many courts like the one in *Cepeda* conceptualized the risk-utility test as a negligence rule. In contrast to the rule of strict products liability in §402A, the patent-danger rule is easier to repudiate in a negligence case, and courts increasingly did so during the 1970s:

> The bottom does not logically drop out of a negligence case against the maker when it is shown that the purchaser knew of the dangerous condition. Thus if the product is a carrot-topping machine with exposed moving parts, or an electric clothes wringer dangerous to the limbs of the operator, and if it would be feasible for the maker of the product to install a guard or safety release, it should be a question for the jury whether reasonable care demanded such a precaution, though its absence is obvious. Surely reasonable men might find here a great danger, even to one who knew the condition; and since it was so readily avoidable they might find the maker negligent.

Micallef v. Miehle Co., 348 N.E.2d 571, 576 (N.Y. 1976) (internal quotations and citation omitted). The patent-danger rule is not defensible in negligence cases, nor is liability for open-and-obvious risks precluded by the risk-utility test. The risk-utility test is also functionally indistinguishable from a negligence inquiry, so why not interpret the liability rule as a form of negligence?

3. *Missing in action yet again: the implied warranty.* While agreeing upon the need to retain the "unreasonably dangerous" requirement, courts disagree about its meaning. As illustrated by *Cepeda*, numerous courts interpret the "unreasonably dangerous" requirement by reference to its ordinary negligence meaning, producing the negligence-based rationale for the risk-utility test adopted by the *Restatement (Third)*. Other courts, by contrast, have used the "unreasonably dangerous" requirement to incorporate the risk-utility test into the rule of strict products liability, effectively extending liability beyond the black-letter rule of §402A to encompass defects in products that do not malfunction. *E.g.*, Bifolck v. Phillip Morris, Inc., 152 A.3d 1183, 1193 (Conn. 2016) ("Under either test, §402A provides the elements of a strict product liability claim; but the unreasonably dangerous element is determined by minimum safety expectations in one and by balancing risks and utility in the other").

How can the "unreasonably dangerous" requirement justify the risk-utility test as a rule of strict products liability? Consider this question in relation to the problem of patent dangers that has largely shaped the judicial interpretation of the "unreasonably dangerous" requirement. If a patent danger always bars recovery under §402A, would this formulation of strict products liability be consistent with its underlying rationale based on the implied warranty? Did any of the courts in the preceding cases ask how the implied warranty evaluates patent dangers? Once §402A is fully situated within this doctrinal context, an alternative meaning of the "unreasonably dangerous" requirement becomes apparent that fully explains why patent dangers do not necessarily prevent plaintiffs from establishing defective designs under the risk-utility test in a regime of strict products liability.

II. DISTINGUISHING PATENT DEFECTS FROM PATENT DANGERS

In arguing that the lawn mower in *Luque* was not defective because the risk was open and obvious,, the defendant was invoking the patent-defect rule that bars recovery for cases in which the plaintiff was aware of the defect and voluntarily chose to use the product anyway. This rule originated in cases involving a product malfunction that allegedly breached the implied warranty.

> A warranty is implied, upon a sale by a manufacturer of his own product, or freedom from latent defects affecting fitness or merchantability. Different courts phrase the thought in varying terms but there is harmony upon the general principle. The common law traced the reason for the implication of a

warranty to the deceit or fraud of the vendor. At first we see the action treated as sounding in tort. Now, while recognizing its origin, the law conceives of the implied warranty as a term of the contract; but if the vendee has an opportunity of inspection he is not protected against patent defects, for then he knows the defects and does not need protection. This is the doctrine everywhere.

Anderson v. Van Doren, 172 N.W. 117, 117 (Minn. 1919).

The tort version of the implied warranty applies only to cases in which the buyer is unaware of the defect, as with the defects latent in contaminated food or exploding soda bottles. But when the defect is patent, "the warranty is ineffective. The reason is that [the buyer] must understand that the seller is offering for sale what is before him, as it appears to be; and even express language, at least in any form other than an explicit reference to the defect itself, will not entitle him to expect anything different." William L. Prosser, *The Implied Warranty of Merchantable Quality*, 27 Minn. L. Rev. 117, 153 (1943).

As illustrated by *Luque* and *Cepeda*, courts over time have conflated patent *defects* with patent *dangers*. Courts continue to do so. *E.g.*, Farkas v. Addition Mfg. Techs., LLC, 952 F.3d 944, 949 (8th Cir. 2020) ("[T]he manufacturer may be held liable if the defect or danger is latent or concealed, but where the danger is open, obvious and apparent, or the user has actual knowledge of the defect or danger, there is no liability on the manufacturer."). Patent defects, however, importantly differ from patent dangers. In *Luque*, for example, no one disputed that the risk was open and obvious, yet the expert witnesses for the plaintiff and defendant disagreed about whether the design was defective. As this disagreement illustrates, the issue of defect implicates questions beyond the mere obviousness of risk. Consequently, the patent-defect rule does not apply to all cases in which the danger is patent. In addition to explaining why patent dangers do not automatically bar recovery under the implied warranty, the patent-defect rule supplies the original meaning of the "unreasonably dangerous" requirement in §402A.

To identify the relation between the patent-defect rule and patent dangers under the implied warranty, we need to define consumer expectations in risk-utility terms. Doing so clearly shows why the consumer's decision to use a product with a patent defect involves an expectation that is fundamentally different from the decision to use a product with a patent danger.

The meaning of a "defect" under §402A is implicitly limited to product malfunctions. In deciding to purchase a product with such a known defect, the consumer presumably expected that she would use the product for a particular purpose that, on balance, would be beneficial. To eliminate the known risk of malfunction (denoted $PL_{malfunction}$), the consumer would have to forego this use of the product altogether, a burden consisting of the lost net benefit or utility of the product use ($B_{lost\ use}$). Her purchase or subsequent use of the product accordingly involved an adequately informed decision that the total burden of lost product use *exceeds* the risk of malfunction, making it worthwhile to use the product despite the patent defect:

$$B_{lost\ use} > PL_{malfunction}$$

The plaintiff's informed risk-utility decision is inconsistent with her allegation that the product breached the implied warranty. According to that allegation,

II. Distinguishing Patent Defects from Patent Dangers

this particular product should not have been sold. *See* Prosser, *supra*, at 137 (stating rule that "any latent condition, such as a pin inside of a loaf of bread, which would prevent purchase if it were known, is enough" to breach the warranty"). This requirement is satisfied only if the consumer would conclude that the product was not worth using because the burden of lost product use is *less than* the risk of malfunction:

$$B_{lost\,use} < PL_{malfunction}$$

Because the plaintiff had already decided to use the product despite knowledge of the patent defect, she cannot now claim that knowledge of the defect would prevent her from purchasing or using the product as required by the implied warranty. The logic of the implied warranty bars recovery under these conditions — the result attained by the patent-defect rule.

As this example shows, the patent-defect rule is based on the principle that the consumer's informed risk-utility choice absolves the seller of responsibility for that identical risk-utility decision (compare the prior two risk-utility equations). Having decided to purchase or use the product with the known defect, the consumer's informed risk-utility decision eliminates the seller's duty to make the identical safety decision in a contrary manner by not offering to sell the product in the first instance. Without an antecedent duty, there can be no liability.

The patent-defect rule is based on the implied warranty, and so §402A should bar recovery in these cases. In the foregoing example, the product is defective, patently so. To prevent the plaintiff from recovering for the patent defect, §402A also requires that the product must be "unreasonably dangerous." This requirement is *not* satisfied when the defect is patent—the product in this respect is *not* more dangerous than expected by the ordinary consumer with ordinary knowledge common to the community. When considered in relation to the patent-defect rule, the "unreasonably dangerous" requirement bars liability because the defendant owes no duty for the defect in question—an issue discussed more fully in section III below.

The patent-defect rule accordingly explains why the §402A rule of strict products liability applies only if the product is both defective and "unreasonably dangerous." The two requirements pertain to different elements common to any tort claim, with one defining duty and the other defining the substantive obligations the duty entails. A defendant owes a duty with respect to any attribute of the product that is "unreasonably dangerous." By definition, the ordinary consumer does not adequately know about such a risk, creating the type of contracting problem that justifies the tort duty under the implied warranty. *See* Chapter 2, section I. If the "unreasonably dangerous" product is also defective, then the seller breaches the duty and is subject to strict liability when the defect proximately causes a consumer to suffer physical harm.

This reasoning also shows why both requirements are necessarily satisfied by latent defects that cause the product to malfunction. By definition, a latent defect is not known by the consumer and so it is necessarily "unreasonably dangerous." In these cases, the two requirements overlap and are hard to distinguish.

Based on this overlap, many courts and commentators have erroneously concluded that requiring these "two separate showings . . . is decidedly problematic, if not downright wrong." David G. Owen & Mary J. Davis, 1 OWEN & DAVIS ON

PRODUCTS LIABILITY §5:14 (4th ed. 2014 & 2020 update). For reasons established by the patent-defect rule, the two requirements are not duplicative. Liability does not solely depend upon the existence of a defect; the defect must instead be latent or otherwise unexpected, in which case the defective product is also "unreasonably dangerous" in violation of the implied warranty. Consider Willis Mining, Inc. v. Noggle, 509 S.E.2d 731, 733 (Ga. 1998) ("Undisclosed latent defects . . . are the very evil that the implied warranty of merchantability was designed to remedy.").

The failure to account adequately for the patent-defect rule also underlies the mistaken conclusion that the implied warranty is necessarily satisfied by a patent danger. The consumer's decision whether to purchase or use a product in light of a known defect is fundamentally different from most safety decisions involving the apparent dangers of a product design.

Consider a vehicle that obviously does not have an airbag, either because its absence is apparent or because the manufacturer clearly warned about the matter. If there were no automobiles equipped with airbags, consumers would still use these products. The only way to eliminate the risk is by not using the car, and the burden of this lost product use vastly exceeds the risk that would be eliminated by an airbag:

$$B_{lost\,use} > PL_{airbag}$$

A plaintiff's allegation that an automobile is defectively designed, by contrast, claims that the cost (or disutility) of the airbag is less than the safety benefit (or extent to which the airbag reduces the risk of injury):

$$B_{airbag} < PL_{airbag}$$

In contrast to cases in which the patent-defect rule properly applies, the plaintiff's safety decision depends on risk-utility factors that differ from those implicated by the allegation of defective design. Both involve the same risk or patent danger, but knowledge of the risk (PL_{airbag}) is not tantamount to knowledge of defect ($B_{airbag} < PL_{airbag}$). In the case of a product malfunction, the plaintiff's knowledge of the risk of malfunction implies that she knew the product was defective in this respect, explaining why her decision to use the patently defective product turns on the same risk-utility factors implicated by the allegation of defect. The absence of an airbag, however, does not cause the vehicle to malfunction. Knowledge of risk no longer equates with knowledge of defect, explaining why the consumer's decision to use the product with a patent danger does not necessarily bar recovery under the patent-defect rule.

Because the plaintiff's risk-utility decision to use the automobile with this patent danger fundamentally differs from the risk-utility decision implicated by the allegation of defective design, those different decisions generate two types of consumer expectations. In commercially distributing a product, the seller impliedly represents that it will perform in a reasonably safe manner. *See* Chapter 3, section II. The average or ordinary consumer who is aware of a patent danger, therefore, expects that the risk is inherent in the product and cannot be reduced or eliminated by cost-effective redesign. Consequently, the plaintiff's proof of a reasonable alternative design shows that the existing design

II. Distinguishing Patent Defects from Patent Dangers

is "dangerous to an extent beyond that which would be contemplated by the ordinary consumer who purchases it, with ordinary knowledge common to the community," making the design "unreasonably dangerous" under §402A. In addition to frustrating consumer expectations based on actual knowledge, the existing design also frustrates consumer expectations based on constructive knowledge (by violating the risk-utility test), making it defective and subject to strict products liability.

When applied to the design of products that do not malfunction, the patent-defect rule does not bar recovery simply because the danger is patent. To satisfy the implied warranty, products "must be marketable with their true character known." Prosser, *supra*, at 128-129. For complex products, it is difficult for consumers to discern the true character of apparent product risks. Are they inherent in the product or could they be eliminated by cost-effective changes in product design? "Whether a danger is open and obvious depends not just on what people can see with their eyes but also on what they know and believe about what they see." Corbin v. Coleco Indus., 748 F.2d 411, 417-418 (7th Cir. 1984). A consumer who is aware of an open or obvious danger can reasonably expect that such a risk is inherent in the product and cannot be eliminated by cost-effective safety investments. If such a risk could be eliminated in this manner and the seller failed to do so, the product design frustrates consumer expectations and is defective in that respect. Outside of malfunctioning products, knowledge of risk is not necessarily the same as knowledge of defect.

Indeed, courts had already recognized this limitation of the patent-defect rule prior to the formulation of §402A. In the years leading up to the adoption of strict products liability, courts were increasingly willing to find that the implied warranty can govern apparent dangers that were inspected by the purchaser, turning these otherwise open or obvious dangers into latent defects not subject to the patent-defect rule:

> [T]he emphasis has been shifted to the actual understanding of the parties, with the result that there has been a strong tendency to find a warranty as to latent defects even in the face of inspection. This has proved to be all the more necessary as goods have become more highly specialized, marketing processes more complex, and buyers more helpless to form any intelligent estimate of the character of the goods on the basis of their own examination or tests.

Prosser, *supra*, at 156. Unless the plaintiff knew that the risk in question also rendered the product defective (as in the case of open and obvious risks that would cause the product to malfunction), courts did not bar recovery simply because the consumer could inspect the product and observe the risk. These cases establish the principle that if the consumer cannot make an "intelligent estimate" of all the factors required by the determination of defect, consumer expectations can be frustrated by risks that are otherwise open or obvious, subjecting the seller to tort liability.

This principle was established by warranty cases that were all decided before the 1960s, making them part of the doctrinal foundation for the §402A rule of strict products liability. This principle accordingly justifies the rule adopted by *Luque*, *Cepeda*, and the numerous other cases holding that the plaintiff is not barred from recovery under strict products liability merely because the danger was apparent. Liability instead is properly foreclosed only under the limited conditions identified by the patent-defect rule. For more extended discussion, see Mark A. Geistfeld, *The Value of Consumer Choice in Strict Products Liability*, 74 Brook. L. Rev. 781, 792-799 (2009).

III. THE ELEMENT OF DUTY

According to William Prosser—the Reporter for the *Restatement (Second)*—the "unreasonably dangerous" requirement in §402A was "undoubtedly" added to foreclose liability based solely on a product's inherent dangers, which he illustrated with automobiles, butter, drugs, and whiskey. William L. Prosser, *Strict Liability to the Consumer in California*, 18 Hastings L.J. 9, 23 (1966). As the California Supreme Court subsequently observed in *Cronin*, "Presumably such dangers are squarely within the contemplation of the ordinary consumer." 501 P.2d at 1161.

Unlike the patent dangers discussed in the last section, inherent dangers cannot be eliminated by a reasonable redesign of the product. Assuming that the ordinary consumer is aware of these inherent dangers, the "unreasonably dangerous" requirement forecloses liability by embodying the logic of the patent-defect rule. To eliminate an inherent danger (denoted $PL_{inherent}$), the consumer would have to forego using of the product altogether, a burden consisting of the lost net benefit or utility of the product use ($B_{lost\ use}$). Her purchase or subsequent use of the product accordingly involved an adequately informed decision that the total burden of lost product use *exceeds* the inherent risk of injury, making it worthwhile to purchase or use the product:

$$B_{lost\ use} > PL_{inherent}$$

The plaintiff's informed risk-utility decision would be inconsistent with her allegation that because of the product's inherent dangers, it breaches the implied warranty and should not have been sold in the first instance. This requirement is satisfied only if the consumer would conclude that the product is not worth using because the burden of lost product use is *less than* the risk of malfunction:

$$B_{lost\ use} < PL_{inherent}$$

As in the cases properly governed by the patent-defect rule, the plaintiff's informed safety decision involves the same risk-utility factors implicated by the allegation of liability. The plaintiff knows the "true character" of the product in this respect, and so the associated product performance does not frustrate her expectations. The logic of the implied warranty bars recovery under these conditions—the result attained by the patent-defect rule. So, too, the product in this respect is not "unreasonably dangerous" because it is not more dangerous than expected by the ordinary consumer with ordinary knowledge common to the community. The "unreasonably dangerous" requirement limits liability for the same reasons embodied in the patent-defect rule.

III. The Element of Duty

This limitation of liability affirms the value of informed consumer choice within products liability. The tort duty protects uninformed consumers by obligating sellers to provide the amount of safety that would be chosen by consumers if they were well informed or knew the "true character" of the product, a rationale not applicable to informed consumer choices. "Consumers are entitled to consider the risks and benefits of different designs and choose among them." Hernandez v. Tokai Corp., 2 S.W.3d 251, 259 (Tex. 1999). When the ordinary consumer can make an informed risk-utility choice, the "unreasonably dangerous" requirement respects that choice by preventing a plaintiff from establishing liability on the ground that the manufacturer was obligated to make the identical risk-utility decision in a contrary manner—the principle embodied in the patent-defect rule.

Applied in this manner, the "unreasonably dangerous" requirement effectively defines the element of duty within a claim of strict products liability. Like the element of duty, this requirement is distinct from the requirement of defect and serves as an independent limitation of liability. So construed, §402A embodies the conventional elements of a tort claim: (1) a duty owed by the defendant product seller to the plaintiff with respect to "unreasonably dangerous" attributes that cause a product to perform more dangerously than expected by the ordinary consumer with ordinary knowledge common to the community; (2) the defendant's breach of that duty by commercially distributing a product containing a defect (3) that proximately caused the plaintiff to suffer (4) compensable damages.

The full meaning of these different elements, however, only becomes apparent once the rule of strict products liability is extended beyond the problem of product malfunctions that implicitly defines the original inquiry in §402A. In cases of malfunction, the "unreasonably dangerous" requirement differs from the requirement of defect only when the plaintiff used the product with a patent defect, an issue that rarely arises. But as applied to the designs of products that do not malfunction, the plaintiff's awareness of risk does not mean that she knows the product is defective. The logic of the implied warranty does not bar recovery in these cases; it instead justifies the risk-utility test, resulting in a more comprehensive liability regime—what we call "strict products liability 2.0"—that most jurisdictions have now adopted. *See* Chapter 3, section III.

Thus, our study of design defects—the subject of the next chapter—necessarily depends on both consumer expectations and the risk-utility test. Any test for defect must be based on a predicate tort duty obligating the defendant to satisfy that test. Instead of being competing conceptions of liability, the ordinary consumer expectations test establishes duty (the "unreasonably dangerous" requirement), and the risk-utility test then determines whether the defendant breached that duty by selling a product that did not malfunction but was nevertheless defective. Rather than being rivals, the consumer expectations and the risk-utility tests are complementary components of strict products liability 2.0.

Tying the consumer expectations test to the element of duty also helps to explain how the case law has developed. The element of duty was once the paramount question of products liability (recall the privity requirement), but over the years the issue of duty receded in importance, much like in other areas of tort law. *See* John C.P. Goldberg & Benjamin C. Zipursky, *The Moral of*

MacPherson, 146 U. Pa. L. Rev. 1733 (1998) (describing the decline of duty in torts jurisprudence over much of the twentieth century). Once duty ceases to be of any obvious concern, the expectations of the ordinary consumer based on ordinary knowledge no longer seem so significant, particularly in an era when the prominent and controversial product cases involved allegations of design or warning defects in products that did not malfunction. A focus on these cases highlights the importance of risk-utility considerations, explaining why the *Restatement (Third)* gives primary importance to the risk-utility test while relegating the ordinary consumer expectations test to a secondary role.

But by deemphasizing consumer expectations and ignoring the implied-warranty rationale for strict products liability, the negligence-based framework in the *Restatement (Third)* obscures this rationale for the tort duty. To be sure, the element of duty is not at issue in most cases. The inquiry only becomes important if there is some reason for limiting the duty. In these cases, the implied-warranty rationale for strict products liability provides guidance that is lacking from a negligence-based inquiry.

Under the implied warranty, there is no duty—and no need to engage in risk-utility analysis—when the product is not "unreasonably dangerous" because its performance satisfies consumer expectations based on ordinary knowledge common to the community. As a matter of general negligence liability, by contrast, the duty to exercise reasonable care in cases of physical harm is limited only in "exceptional cases, when an articulated countervailing principle or policy warrants denying or limiting liability in a particular class of cases." RESTATEMENT (THIRD) OF TORTS: LIABILITY FOR PHYSICAL AND EMOTIONAL HARM §7 (2010). What is that policy in product cases? The question is not expressly addressed by the *Restatement (Third)*, which apparently contemplates that courts will limit the tort duty in product cases for the same policy reasons applicable to negligence cases. Without adequate recognition of consumer expectations, can the negligence-based framework of the *Restatement (Third)* adequately identify the conditions under which liability for defective product designs should be limited? We address this question in the next chapter.

IV. AUTONOMOUS VEHICLES AND PRODUCTS LIABILITY: PROBLEM SET 2

Autonomous vehicles can be developed in two different ways. "The first involves gradually improving the automated driving systems available in conventional vehicles so that human drivers can shift more of the dynamic driving task to these systems. The second involves deploying vehicles without a human driver and gradually expanding this operation to more contexts." OECD Int'l Transp. Forum, Automated and Autonomous Driving: Regulation Under Uncertainty 13 (2015), https://perma.cc/K6F8-FZ79.

The first approach relies on driver-assistance systems (DAS) that are incorporated into conventional vehicles and are capable of taking over one or more functions of the dynamic driving task under certain operating conditions. Examples of DAS currently on the market include antilock braking systems (first introduced in 1978), electronic stability control (1995), parking-assistance systems (mid-1990s), adaptive cruise control (1999), lane-departure warning systems (2001), and forward-collision prevention systems (both long range, introduced in 2003-2006, and short range, 2010). "Other extensions of current DAS are soon to come. Examples include an assistant for collision avoidance by evasive steering, assistants for the detection of oncoming traffic and pedestrians under adverse vision (weather) conditions, or assistants for improved intersection safety." Klaus Bengler et al., *Three Decades of Driver Assistance Systems: Review and Future Perspectives*, 6 IEEE Intelligent Transp. Sys. Mag. 6, 7-9 (2014).

Automated driving technologies can be classified by the extent to which they reduce the role of the human driver. The most widely adopted classification scheme ranges from no vehicle autonomy (level 0) to full vehicle autonomy under all conditions in which a human could otherwise perform the driving task (level 5). Levels 2 and 3 involve limited autonomous driving that requires the human operator to monitor conditions and assume control if necessary, and level 4 involves full vehicle autonomy only within certain operating conditions. Both level 2 and level 3 DAS create an interface between automated driving and conventional driving—the point at which the human takes over the dynamic driving task from the automated vehicle. The switch from one driving mode to the other presents a safety problem that does not exist in conventional vehicles lacking this technology.

The sustained autonomous operation of these vehicles can make the person behind the wheel complacent or otherwise overly reliant on the DAS. What if road conditions suddenly change and require human intervention, but the driver is not sufficiently attentive to quickly take over the wheel?

Manufacturers currently disagree about the best approach for addressing this problem. Waymo (the automated driving division of Google) and Volvo have separately concluded that the safest route is to bypass levels 2 and 3 DAS altogether in favor of fully autonomous vehicles (levels 4 and 5) that by definition do not rely on DAS and instead eliminate any chance for human driving error. Tesla and other manufacturers are instead taking the incremental approach, relying on levels 2 and 3 DAS to enable the operating system to gain driving experience that will someday allow it to become fully autonomous. In the interim, a human driver must take over the driving task, creating the potential safety problem of driver complacency.

AV Problem 2.1

This safety issue arose in an accident that occurred in May 2016 when Joshua Brown was killed while behind the wheel of a Tesla Model S electric sedan in self-driving mode (level 2)—the first known fatal accident involving a self-driving car. According to Tesla, "the vehicle was on a divided highway with Autopilot engaged when a tractor trailer drove across the highway perpendicular to the Model S. Neither Autopilot nor the driver noticed the white side of the tractor trailer against a brightly lit sky, so the brake was not applied." Tesla, *A Tragic Loss* (June 30, 2016), https://perma.cc/P3NA-DJAR. According to news reports, Brown was watching a Harry Potter movie at the time of the crash.

Suppose instead that Brown had simply become inattentive after turning on the self-driving mode and then watching the vehicle safely navigate the freeway for an hour or so, at which point the fatal crash occurred. In a suit against Tesla, the plaintiff in a wrongful-death suit claims that the design of the Tesla Model S electric sedan is defective for having adopted level 2 DAS instead of waiting for further technological developments that would have allowed the vehicle to employ level 4 DAS that would entirely eliminate the risk of driver inattention. Does the claim turn on the issue of defectiveness, or can Tesla instead argue that the design is not "unreasonably dangerous" for purposes of strict products liability? In formulating your answer, see if you can explain whether the logic of the patent-defect rule would apply to this claim (in other words, try to formulate your answer in terms of the risk-utility analysis of inherent dangers in section III). In a jurisdiction that has eliminated the "unreasonably dangerous" requirement, how would this claim proceed? To answer this question, review the court's reasoning in *Luque*.

Analysis of AV Problem 2.1

To evaluate the allegation of defective design under the risk-utility test, the court must compare the disutility or cost of the proposed design change with the risk that would be eliminated by the redesign. Level 4 DAS is not currently commercially available, unlike the level 2 DAS embodied in the existing design. Hence the cost or burden of not incorporating level 2 DAS into the design involves the lost use of this particular driving feature (denoted $B_{lost\ use}$). The inherent risk that would be eliminated is the possibility that the self-driving vehicle will crash because the driver had become insufficiently complacent or inattentive (denoted $PL_{inattention}$). The allegation of defect accordingly requires proof showing:

$$B_{lost\ use} < PL_{inattention}$$

The risk presumably was either known by the plaintiff or otherwise disclosed in the product warning; otherwise there would be an allegation that the warning was defective in this respect. In deciding to engage the self-driving mode in the vehicle, the decedent presumably made the following risk-utility decision:

$$B_{lost\ use} > PL_{inattention}$$

By comparing the allegation of defect with the plaintiff's safety decision, it becomes apparent that the plaintiff's claim is barred by the patent-defect rule: in both cases, the consumer's safety decision depends on the same risk-utility factors implicated by the allegation of defect. Not only was the inherent risk obvious or otherwise known by the plaintiff, but he also had the knowledge—the lost benefits of using the self-driving mode—required to determine whether the risk rendered the design defective. Plaintiff had sufficient knowledge of the defect, so his decision to use the product with this known defect bars recovery under the logic of the patent-defect rule. This bar to recovery is achieved by the "unreasonably dangerous" requirement in §402A: The product in this respect was not more dangerous than would be expected by the ordinary consumer with ordinary knowledge common to the community.

In a jurisdiction like California that has eliminated the "unreasonably dangerous" requirement, the defendant would instead argue that the plaintiff assumed the risk and is barred from recovery. As the California Supreme Court in *Luque* observed:

> a person urging strict liability must not have assumed the risk of the defective product. Plaintiff argues that assumption of the risk is a defense and that it was therefore improper to instruct the jury that he had the burden of proving that he had not assumed the risk. We agree. "For such a defense to arise, the user or consumer must become aware of the defect and danger and still proceed unreasonably to make use of the product."

As discussed, the plaintiff's decedent was aware of the defect and danger. According to the plaintiff's allegation of defect, the risk of inattention exceeds the disutility or lost benefits of foregoing the self-driving mode. Hence the reasonable person would not use the self-driving mode, and so the plaintiff's decedent was "aware of the defect and danger and still proceed[ed] unreasonably to make use of the product." Assumption of risk would bar recovery for the same reasons embodied in the "unreasonably dangerous" requirement.* In effect, the assumed risk rule in these jurisdictions substitutes for the "unreasonably dangerous" requirement.

---

*As we find later in our study of assumption of risk, this version of the rule eliminates the tort duty and therefore is part of the plaintiff's prima facie case, even though courts routinely call it an affirmative defense.

6

Design Defects

A commonly shared design is the defining characteristic of a product line. Consequently, an allegation of defective design implicates the entire product line, substantially expanding the manufacturer's liability exposure as compared to product-specific defects attributable to manufacturing flaws or mishandling. One aspect of design can be the subject of numerous lawsuits, potentially subjecting a manufacturer to aggregate liabilities of an amount that could cause bankruptcy.

Not only does the potential scope of liability vastly exceed that involved with product-specific defects, but the liability rules governing defective product design are also more complex and ambiguous than those governing manufacturing defects. As many courts have observed, "the determination of when a product is actionable because of its design" is one of "the most agitated controversial questions . . . in products liability law." Pritchett v. Cottrell, Inc., 512 F.3d 1057, 1063 (8th Cir. 2008).

To be sure, tort liability for defective product design is neither new nor necessarily dependent on unsettled rules. When the *Restatement (Second)* §402A rule of strict products liability was promulgated in the 1960s, there already was "a thriving trade in cases confronting the question under negligence law of how safe a product should be designed. The idea of liability for a manufacturer whose design is negligent is even ensconced in a black letter section of the first Restatement of Torts." Michael D. Green, *The Unappreciated Congruity of the Second and Third Torts Restatements*, 74 Brook. L. Rev. 807, 814 (2009) (citing RESTATEMENT OF TORTS §398 (1934)). Manufacturers had also incurred strict liability under the implied warranty for designs that caused the product to malfunction. *E.g.*, McCabe v. L.K. Liggett Drug Co., 112 N.E.2d 254 (Mass. 1953). The difficulties posed by allegations of defective design do not pertain to these established bases of liability, but instead involve the question of how defective design should be governed by the rule of strict products liability.

The issue turns on numerous issues we have already addressed, putting us in a position to fully understand the different ways in which courts evaluate allegations of defective design.

I. EMERGING CONSENSUS OR WIDESPREAD DISAGREEMENT?

After surveying how courts evaluate defective designs, the Supreme Court of South Carolina concluded that "[s]ome form of a risk-utility test is employed by an overwhelming majority of jurisdictions in this country." Branham v. Ford Motor Co., 701 S.E.2d 5, 14-15 (S.C. 2010). The court's survey also shows that the consumer expectations test, in one form or another, is recognized by a substantial majority of jurisdictions. *Id.* at 14 n.2 (citing only 17 states that exclusively rely on the risk-utility test and do not recognize any role for consumer expectations in design cases). By contrast, a different survey conducted a few years later found that there is "no consensus with respect to application either of the consumer expectations test or the risk-utility test." Mike McWilliams & Margaret Smith, *An Overview of the Legal Standard Regarding Product Liability Design Defect Claims and a Fifty State Survey on the Applicable Law in Each Jurisdiction*, 82 Def. Couns. J. 80, 83 (2015). Indeed, throughout the drafting process of the *Restatement (Third)*, there was deep disagreement about the extent to which the case law supports either the consumer expectations test or the risk-utility test. After recounting this debate, the Connecticut Supreme Court concluded that it is not a "fruitful exercise to obtain a precise count" because "parties on each side of this debate disagree about what legal standard has been adopted in the various jurisdictions." Bifolck v. Phillip Morris, Inc., 152 A.3d 1183, 1198 (Conn. 2016).

To identify the extent to which courts actually disagree about the liability rules, we will analyze the three different approaches that courts now employ for evaluating claims of defective product design. Approaches that apparently treat the consumer expectations and risk-utility tests in fundamentally different manners turn out to be surprisingly similar once analyzed across the full range of cases. The substantive similarity across the apparently different sets of liability rules explains the position reached by the *Restatement (Third)* as subsequently described by its Reporters: "although a widely shared belief persists that the general standard for defective product design is unsettled ... thousands upon thousands of design defect decisions ... demonstrate[ ] that ... [c]onsensus has been achieved." James A. Henderson, Jr. & Aaron D. Twerski, *Achieving Consensus on Defective Product Design*, 83 Cornell L. Rev. 867, 868-869 (1998) (sentence structure omitted). The consensus about the risk-utility test, however, does not extend to its underlying rationale: Is the liability rule a form of negligence or strict liability?

A. *"Exclusive" Reliance on the Consumer Expectations Test*

A few states use only the consumer expectations test to determine defective designs for purposes of strict products liability. This approach, however, does not mean that risk-utility analysis has no role to play in product cases. The risk-utility test instead is relegated to claims of negligence liability.

As we found in Chapter 3, section I, this formulation of the consumer expectations test is based on the black-letter rule of §402A. Because this inquiry is implicitly limited to product malfunctions, it bars recovery for patent dangers and otherwise forecloses consideration of costs as required by the risk-utility test. But for cases in which the product did not malfunction and the plaintiff alleges that the design is nevertheless defective, the plaintiff can still rely on the risk-utility test to prove that the defendant acted negligently by not adopting this reasonable alternative design. *See, e.g.,* Green v. Smith & Nephew AHP, Inc., 629 N.W.2d 727, 743 (Wis. 2001) ("[W]e acknowledge that in some cases, the open and obvious nature of a design defect may defeat claims for strict products liability. This does not mean, however, that the manufacturer can avoid all liability [in these cases]. The open and obvious nature of a defective or unreasonably dangerous condition does not inherently bar claims, for example, based on negligence. . . ."). When applied in this manner, the risk-utility test is substantively identical to the formulation adopted by the *Restatement (Third),* which bases the liability rule on the negligence principle. *See* Chapter 2, section II.

Across the full set of cases, jurisdictions that "exclusively" rely on the consumer expectations test effectively limit strict products liability to malfunctioning products. The negligence-based, risk-utility test governs the designs of products that do not malfunction.

B. *"Exclusive" Reliance on the Risk-Utility Test*

Concerned that the consumer expectations test necessarily bars recovery for patent dangers, a minority of states have rejected that test altogether in favor of the risk-utility test for evaluating defective product designs. *See* Branham, 701 S.E.2d at 14 n.12, 15 (identifying 17 different states that exclusively rely on the risk-utility test). To do so, courts had to reject or otherwise reinterpret the "unreasonably dangerous" requirement in the *Restatement (Second)* liability rule so that it permits proof of defect under the risk-utility test. *See* Chapter 5, section I.

Although exclusively relying on the risk-utility test to determine defects in the designs of products that do not malfunction, these jurisdictions presumably still rely on the consumer expectations test to identify product malfunctions. A design can be defective for causing a malfunction, and so courts must still determine what type of performance constitutes a malfunction. Is it defined exclusively by what the manufacturer manifestly intended, or does a malfunction involve a product's failure to minimally perform one of its ordinary functions as expected by the ordinary consumer based on ordinary knowledge common to the community? *See* Chapter 4, section IV (comparing these two formulations of a product malfunction). In a jurisdiction that has adopted §402A, the adoption of the risk-utility test for evaluating the designs of products that do not malfunction presumably does not entail rejection of all other components of §402A. Consequently, a court that uses the risk-utility test for evaluating the designs of products that do not malfunction presumably still employs the consumer expectations test for identifying product malfunctions. *Compare* Branham, 701 S.E.2d at 14 (adopting the *Restatement (Third)* formulation of risk-utility test for defective design), *with* Grubbs v. Walmart Stores, Inc., 2021 WL 168427 at *3 (D.S.C. 2021) (concluding that *Branham* "did not overrule the incorporation of the *Restatement (Second) of Torts* into South Carolina's product liability statute").

Although such a jurisdiction would count as one that "exclusively" relies on the risk-utility test, its liability rules across the full set of cases are no different from those in a jurisdiction that "exclusively" relies on the consumer expectations test. The two apparently disagree only because their "exclusive" liability rule applies to different types of design defects (those attributable to products that do not malfunction, as contrasted to those only attributable to malfunctions).

C. Combining the Two Tests

Most states follow the remaining approach, which incorporates the risk-utility test into the implied-warranty framework that protects consumer expectations. The approach adopted by the California Supreme Court is both instructive and highly influential. Its adoption of strict products liability in Greenman v. Yuba Power Products, 377 P.2d 897 (Cal. 1963), provided critical doctrinal support for the *Restatement (Second)* §402A rule of strict products liability. When courts in other jurisdictions adopted §402A, they routinely cited *Greenman* as a "seminal" or "landmark" case.

SOULE v. GENERAL MOTORS CORP.
Supreme Court of California, 1994
882 P.2d 298

BAXTER, J. On the early afternoon of January 16, 1984, plaintiff was driving her 1982 Camaro in the southbound center lane of Bolsa Chica Road, an arterial street in Westminster. There was a slight drizzle, the roadway was damp, and apparently plaintiff was not wearing her seat belt. A 1972 Datsun, approaching northbound, suddenly skidded into the path of plaintiff's car. The Datsun's left rear quarter struck plaintiff's Camaro in an area near the left front wheel. Estimates of the vehicles' combined closing speeds on impact vary from 30 to 70 miles per hour.

The collision bent the Camaro's frame adjacent to the wheel and tore loose the bracket that attached the wheel assembly (specifically, the lower control arm) to the frame. As a result, the wheel collapsed rearward and inward. The wheel hit the underside of the "toe pan"—the slanted floorboard area beneath the pedals—causing the toe pan to crumple, or "deform," upward into the passenger compartment.

Plaintiff received a fractured rib and relatively minor scalp and knee injuries. Her most severe injuries were fractures of both ankles, and the more serious of these was the compound compression fracture of her left ankle. This injury never healed properly. In order to relieve plaintiff's pain, an orthopedic surgeon fused the joint. As a permanent result, plaintiff cannot flex her left ankle. She walks with considerable difficulty, and her condition is expected to deteriorate.

I. Emerging Consensus or Widespread Disagreement? 181

Plaintiff sued General Motors (GM) for her ankle injuries, asserting a theory of strict tort liability for a defective product. She claimed the severe trauma to her ankles was not a natural consequence of the accident, but occurred when the collapse of the Camaro's wheel caused the toe pan to crush violently upward against her feet. Plaintiff attributed the wheel collapse to a manufacturing defect, the substandard quality of the weld attaching the lower control arm bracket to the frame. She also claimed that the placement of the bracket, and the configuration of the frame, were defective designs because they did not limit the wheel's rearward travel in the event the bracket should fail.

The available physical and circumstantial evidence left room for debate about the exact angle and force of the impact and the extent to which the toe pan had actually deformed. The issues of defect and causation were addressed through numerous experts produced by both sides in such areas as biomechanics, metallurgy, orthopedics, design engineering, and crash-test simulation.

Over GM's objection, the court gave the standard design defect instruction without modification. This instruction advised that a product is defective in design "if it fails to perform as safely as an ordinary consumer would expect when used in an intended or reasonably foreseeable manner *or* if there is a risk of danger inherent in the design which outweighs the benefit of the design." (Italics added.)

The jury was also told that in order to establish liability for a design defect under the "ordinary consumer expectations" standard, plaintiff must show (1) the manufacturer's product failed to perform as safely as an ordinary consumer would expect, (2) the defect existed when the product left the manufacturer's possession, (3) the defect was a "legal cause" of plaintiff's "enhanced injury," and (4) the product was used in a reasonably foreseeable manner.

In a series of special findings, the jury determined that the Camaro contained a defect (of unspecified nature) which was a "legal cause" of plaintiff's "enhanced injury." The jury further concluded that although plaintiff was guilty of comparative fault, her conduct was not a legal cause of her enhanced injuries. Plaintiff received an award of $1.65 million.

GM appealed. Among other things, it argued that the trial court erred by instructing on ordinary consumer expectations in a complex design-defect case.

In Barker v. Lull Engineering Co., 573 P.2d 443 (Cal. 1978), we offered two alternative ways to prove a design defect, each appropriate to its own circumstances. The purposes, behaviors, and dangers of certain products are commonly understood by those who ordinarily use them. By the same token, the ordinary users or consumers of a product may have reasonable, widely accepted minimum expectations about the circumstances under which it should perform safely. Consumers govern their own conduct by these expectations, and products on the market should conform to them.

In some cases, therefore, "ordinary knowledge . . . as to . . . [the product's] characteristics" (RESTATEMENT (SECOND) OF TORTS, §402A, cmt. i) may permit an inference that the product did not perform as safely as it should. *If* the facts permit such a conclusion, and *if* the failure resulted from the product's design, a finding of defect is warranted without any further proof. The manufacturer may not defend a claim that a product's design failed to perform as safely as its ordinary consumers would expect by presenting expert evidence of the design's relative risks and benefits.[3]

However, as we noted in *Barker*, a complex product, even when it is being used as intended, may often cause injury in a way that does not engage its ordinary consumers' reasonable minimum assumptions about safe performance. For example, the ordinary consumer of an automobile simply has "no idea" how it should perform in all foreseeable situations, or how safe it should be made against all foreseeable hazards. [ ]

An injured person is not foreclosed from proving a defect in the product's design simply because he cannot show that the reasonable minimum safety expectations of its ordinary consumers were violated. Under *Barker*'s alternative test, a product is still defective if its design embodies "excessive preventable danger," that is, unless "the benefits of the . . . design outweigh the risk of danger inherent in such design." [ ] But this determination involves technical issues of feasibility, cost, practicality, risk, and benefit which are "impossible" to avoid. [ ] In such cases, the jury *must* consider the manufacturer's evidence of competing design considerations, and the issue of design defect cannot fairly be resolved by standardless reference to the "expectations" of an "ordinary consumer."

As we have seen, the consumer expectations test is reserved for cases in which the *everyday experience* of the product's users permits a conclusion that the product's design violated *minimum* safety assumptions, and is thus defective *regardless of expert opinion about the merits of the design*. It follows that where the minimum safety of a product is within the common knowledge of lay jurors, expert witnesses may not be used to demonstrate what an ordinary consumer would or should expect. Use of expert testimony for that purpose would invade the jury's function, and would invite circumvention of the rule that the risks and benefits of a challenged design must be carefully balanced whenever the issue of design defect goes beyond the common experience of the product's users.[4]

By the same token, the jury may not be left free to find a violation of ordinary consumer expectations whenever it chooses. Unless the facts actually permit an inference that the product's performance did not meet the minimum safety

---

3. For example, the ordinary consumers of modern automobiles may and do expect that such vehicles will be designed so as not to explode while idling at stoplights, experience sudden steering or brake failure as they leave the dealership, or roll over and catch fire in two-mile-per-hour collisions. If the plaintiff in a product liability action proved that a vehicle's design produced such a result, the jury could find forthwith that the car failed to perform as safely as its ordinary consumers would expect, and was therefore defective.

4. Plaintiff insists that manufacturers should be forced to design their products to meet the "objective" safety demands of a "hypothetical" reasonable consumer who is fully informed about what he or she should expect. Hence, plaintiff reasons, the jury may receive expert advice on "reasonable" safety expectations for the product. However, this function is better served by the risk-benefit prong of *Barker*. There, juries receive expert advice, apply clear guidelines, and decide accordingly whether the product's design is an acceptable compromise of competing considerations.

On the other hand, appropriate use of the consumer expectations test is not necessarily foreclosed simply because the product at issue is only in specialized use, so that the general public may not be familiar with its safety characteristics. If the safe performance of the product fell below the reasonable, widely shared minimum expectations of those who do use it, perhaps the injured consumer should not be forced to rely solely on a technical comparison of risks and benefits. By the same token, if the expectations of the product's limited group of ordinary consumers are beyond the lay experience common to all jurors, expert testimony on the limited subject of what the product's actual consumers do expect may be proper.

I. Emerging Consensus or Widespread Disagreement?

expectations of its ordinary users, the jury must engage in the balancing of risks and benefits required by the second prong of *Barker*.

Accordingly, as *Barker* indicated, instructions are misleading and incorrect if they allow a jury to avoid this risk-benefit analysis in a case where it is required. [ ] Instructions based on the ordinary consumer expectations prong of *Barker* are not appropriate where, as a matter of law, the evidence would not support a jury verdict on that theory. Whenever that is so, the jury must be instructed solely on the alternative risk-benefit theory of design defect announced in *Barker*.

GM suggests that the consumer expectations test is improper whenever "crashworthiness," a complex product, or technical questions of causation are at issue. Because the variety of potential product injuries is infinite, the line cannot be drawn as clearly as GM proposes. But the fundamental distinction is not impossible to define. The crucial question in each individual case is whether the circumstances of the product's failure permit an inference that the product's design performed below the legitimate, commonly accepted minimum safety assumptions of its ordinary consumers.

GM argues at length that the consumer expectations test is an "unworkable, amorphic, fleeting standard" which should be entirely abolished as a basis for design defect. In GM's view, the test is deficient and unfair in several respects. First, it defies definition. Second, it focuses not on the objective condition of products, but on the subjective, unstable, and often unreasonable opinions of consumers. Third, it ignores the reality that ordinary consumers know little about how safe the complex products they use can or should be made. Fourth, it invites the jury to isolate the particular consumer, component, accident, and injury before it instead of considering whether the whole product fairly accommodates the competing expectations of all consumers in all situations. Fifth, it eliminates the careful balancing of risks and benefits which is essential to any design issue.

We fully understand the dangers of improper use of the consumer expectations test. However, we cannot accept GM's insinuation that ordinary consumers lack any legitimate expectations about the minimum safety of the products they use. In particular circumstances, a product's design may perform so unsafely that the defect is apparent to the common reason, experience, and understanding of its ordinary consumers. In such cases, a lay jury is competent to make that determination.

When use of the consumer expectations test is limited as *Barker* intended, the principal concerns raised by GM are met. Within these limits, the test remains a workable means of determining the existence of design defect. We therefore find no compelling reason to overrule the consumer expectations prong of *Barker* at this late date, and we decline to do so.

Applying our conclusions to the facts of this case, however, we agree that the instant jury should not have been instructed on ordinary consumer expectations. Plaintiff's theory of design defect was one of technical and mechanical detail. It sought to examine the precise behavior of several obscure components of her car under the complex circumstances of a particular accident. The collision's exact speed, angle, and point of impact were disputed. It seems settled, however, that plaintiff's Camaro received a substantial oblique blow near the left front wheel, and that the adjacent frame members and bracket assembly absorbed considerable inertial force.

An ordinary consumer of automobiles cannot reasonably expect that a car's frame, suspension, or interior will be designed to remain intact in any and all accidents. Nor would ordinary experience and understanding inform such a consumer how safely an automobile's design should perform under the esoteric circumstances of the collision at issue here. Indeed, both parties assumed that quite complicated design considerations were at issue, and that expert testimony was necessary to illuminate these matters. Therefore, injection of ordinary consumer expectations into the design defect equation was improper.

We are equally persuaded, however, that the error was harmless, because it is not reasonably probable defendant would have obtained a more favorable result in its absence. [T]he case was tried on the assumption that the alleged design defect was a matter of technical debate. Virtually all the evidence and argument on design defect focused on expert evaluation of the strengths, shortcomings, risks, and benefits of the challenged design, as compared with a competitor's approach.

Neither plaintiff's counsel nor any expert witness on her behalf told the jury that the Camaro's design violated the safety expectations of the ordinary consumer. Nor did they suggest the jury should find such a violation regardless of its assessment of such competing design considerations as risk, benefit, feasibility, and cost. The jury never made any requests which hinted it was inclined to apply the consumer expectations test without regard to a weighing of risks and benefits.

Under these circumstances, we find it highly unlikely that a reasonable jury took that path. We see no reasonable probability that the jury disregarded the voluminous evidence on the risks and benefits of the Camaro's design, and instead rested its verdict on its independent assessment of what an ordinary consumer would expect. The error in presenting that theory to the jury provides no basis for disturbing the trial judgment.

Accordingly, the judgment of the Court of Appeal, upholding the trial court judgment in favor of plaintiff, is affirmed.

NOTES AND QUESTIONS

1. *The relation between consumer expectations and the risk-utility test.* Does the court in *Soule* clearly explain why the consumer expectations test is appropriate in some cases but not others? Consider the design defect at issue in *Luque*, p. 158 *supra*, which involved a lawn mower with an unguarded hole that the plaintiff alleged could have been covered "by a simple piece of additional equipment costing less than one dollar per machine." 501 P.2d at 1166. Under the guidelines in *Soule*, is this allegation governed by the consumer expectations test or the risk-utility test?

2. *Locating malfunction.* According to *Soule*, the consumer expectations test is limited to cases in which the consumer has "reasonable minimum safety expectations." To what extent does this formulation implicitly limit application of the consumer expectations test to malfunctioning products? At minimum the ordinary consumer reasonably expects that the product will not malfunction, although the consumer can also have reasonable

expectations of safe perrformance for products that do not malfunction—an issue requiring risk-utility analysis. Consequently, the consumer expectations test determines whether the product malfunctioned and is subject to strict liability, explaining why the risk-utility test would not be a defense against this type of claim, rendering such evidence inadmissible as per the reasoning in *Soule.*

Is this component of the liability rule any different from §402A? Would the ordinary consumer expectations test ever be appropriate for cases in which the product did not malfunction? Consider in this regard the examples the *Soule* court provided in footnote 3 of the opinion, which illustrates cases in which the consumer expectations test would be appropriate.

3. *Beyond malfunctions.* A product that does not malfunction would satisfy the consumer's minimal expectations, but could still frustrate reasonable expectations and be defective for failing the risk-utility test. *See, e.g.,* Calles v. Scripto-Tokai Corp., 864 N.E.2d 249, 258-259 (Ill. 2007) (holding that the plaintiff could not prove that a cigarette lighter was defectively designed under the consumer expectations test because the lighter "produced a flame when used in a reasonably foreseeable manner, *i.e.* by a child," but concluding that the jury should be permitted to determine whether the risk-utility test required the design to incorporate child-resistant safety devices); O'Brien v. Muskin, 463 A.2d 298 (N.J. 1983) (holding that the plaintiff could not prove that a pool was defectively designed under the consumer expectations test because the "pool fulfilled its function as a place to swim," but concluding that the jury should be permitted to evaluate the design under the risk-utility test), *superseded in part on other grounds by statute,* N.J. Stat. Ann. §2A:58c-3 (West 2000). Within this liability framework, the risk-utility test extends the rule of strict products liability to encompass allegations of defective design for products that do not malfunction.

4. *Deriving the risk-utility test from consumer expectations.* Recall that the California Supreme Court rejected the "unreasonably dangerous" requirement in *Cronin*, p. 154 *supra.* Having eliminated this requirement, the court could not subsequently reinterpret "unreasonably dangerous" to embody the negligence principle capable of justifying the risk-utility test, the approach taken by some courts. *See* Chapter 5, section I. What, then, is the doctrinal basis for incorporating the risk-utility test into the California rule of strict products liability?

Recall that the risk-utility test can be derived from the implied warranty. To evaluate the designs of products that do not malfunction, the ordinary consumer with constructive knowledge of the relevant issues would choose designs that satisfy the risk-utility test. *See* Chapter 3, section III. Does this rationale adequately explain why California has incorporated the risk-utility test into the framework of strict products liability? Consider the reasoning of the *Soule* court in footnote 4 of the opinion. *See also* Evans v. Lorillard Tobacco Co., 990 N.E.2d 997, 1020 (Mass. 2013) (holding in a case involving cigarettes that were alleged to be defectively designed, the reasonable alternative design must "be evaluated through the eyes of a rational, informed consumer, whose freedom of choice is not substantially impaired by addiction").

5. *Characterizing the liability rule.* In contrast to the other approaches that "exclusively" rely on either the consumer expectations test or the risk-utility test, the approach of combining the two tests accounts for the full range of design cases. A defective design must cause the product either to malfunction (the ordinary consumer expectations test) or otherwise to perform in an excessively dangerous manner that frustrates the reasonable safety expectations of the ordinary consumer (by violating the risk-utility test). The comprehensive scope of this approach explains why it appears to be different from the other, less comprehensive approaches that "exclusively" rely on one test or the other for determining only one type of defective design.

6. *Reassessing the case law.* Once defective designs are comprehensively analyzed in relation to both malfunctioning and nonmalfunctioning products, the purportedly different approaches all involve strict liability for product malfunctions coupled with a risk-utility analysis for evaluating the design of products that do not malfunction. In this respect, courts have attained consensus about the risk-utility test. Disagreement instead centers on the question whether the risk-utility test is a form of strict products liability or negligence liability, with most jurisdictions deciding in favor of strict products liability. *See* Chapter 3, section I (discussing this debate).

II. THE RISK-UTILITY TEST APPLIED

Across the country, the risk-utility test determines whether a product that did not malfunction is defectively designed. The triumph of the risk-utility test in this respect, however, masks a more fundamental issue. The *Restatement (Second)* rule of strict products liability is based on the implied warranty, whereas the *Restatement (Third)* rejects strict products liability and conceptualizes the risk-utility test as "a reasonableness test traditionally used in determining whether an actor has been negligent." §1 cmt. a. Both approaches rely on the risk-utility test, yet each one rests on a different doctrinal foundation. Is the risk-utility test best justified by the implied warranty or the negligence principle? To address this question, we need to examine in greater detail how the risk-utility test is applied.

Under the risk-utility test, "the primary, but not the exclusive, test for defective design" "is whether a reasonable alternative design would, at reasonable cost, have reduced the foreseeable risks of harm posed by the product and, if so, whether the omission of the alternative design by the seller or a predecessor in the distributive chain rendered the product not reasonably safe." Restatement (Third) of Torts: Products Liability §2 cmt. d. Proof of a reasonable alternative design is not the exclusive test for two reasons. First, the plaintiff can establish defect by proof of a product malfunction. *See* Chapter 4, section III. In addition, the plaintiff may be able to prove that the product is defective no matter how it is designed — the category itself is inherently defective, regardless of the particular design. *See* section III.B *infra*. Aside from these exceptions, proof of defective design requires proof of a reasonable alternative design.

A. Reasonable Alternative Design

When courts first adopted the risk-utility test, they often employed "the risk-utility analysis as developed by Deans Wade and Keeton," which involves "balanced consideration" of the following factors:

(1) The usefulness and desirability of the product—its utility to the user and to the public as a whole.
(2) The safety aspects of the product—the likelihood that it will cause injury, and the probable seriousness of the injury.
(3) The availability of a substitute product which would meet the same need and not be as unsafe.
(4) The manufacturer's ability to eliminate the unsafe character of the product without impairing its usefulness or making it too expensive to maintain its utility.
(5) The user's ability to avoid danger by the exercise of care in the use of the product.
(6) The user's anticipated awareness of the dangers inherent in the product and their avoidability, because of general public knowledge of the obvious condition of the product, or of the existence of suitable warnings or instructions.
(7) The feasibility, on the part of the manufacturer, of spreading the loss by setting the price of the product or carrying liability insurance.

Cepeda v. Cumberland Eng'g Co., 386 A.2d 816 (N.J. 1978) (citing John W. Wade, *On the Nature of Strict Tort Liability for Products*, 44 Miss. L.J. 825 (1973)). Courts have refined the risk-utility test over time. But the original Wade-Keeton test still shapes the most commonly employed formulation that "may be summarized as follows: A design is defective if the product's risks exceed its utility." David G. Owen, *Toward a Proper Test for Design Defectiveness: "Micro-Balancing" Costs and Benefits*, 75 Tex. L. Rev. 1661, 1672 (1997).

How would this formulation apply to the claim that a motor vehicle is defectively designed for not incorporating an airbag? The total risks of a vehicle without an airbag clearly do not exceed the total utility of the vehicle. The same is true for most risks in many other products.. Formulated in this manner, the risk-utility test would foreclose liability for defective design in a wide swath of cases. Though courts often describe the inquiry in this manner, it does not accurately describe how they actually apply the risk-utility test.

Instead of "macro-balancing" total risk and total utility, courts focus on the particular risks and the particular burdens or costs associated with the proposed reasonable alternative design. *See generally id.*; *see also, e.g.*, Ake v. Gen. Motors Corp., 942 F. Supp. 869, 874 (W.D.N.Y. 1996) ("[T]he defect alleged here is not that the design of the truck made it likely to crash, but that a fuel-fed fire was likely to occur in the event that it did crash. Therefore, evidence of its 'overall' safety or the number of accidents in which these trucks were involved, is too tangential to the defect alleged here, and should be excluded . . . on the ground that it would be confusing to the jury, a waste of time, and of minimal relevance.").

To more clearly identify the components of risk-utility analysis, consider again the claim that an automobile is defectively designed for not having airbags (assuming, as we have done repeatedly, that there is no statutory obligation to install airbags into motor vehicles). Whether the design is defective in this respect requires a comparison of the existing design with the proposed alternative (the "substitute product" in factor (3) of the Wade-Keeton formulation). That comparison can be expressed in two different ways.

First, the risk-utility test can be expressly defined in terms of the existing design, with the proposed alternative design providing the benchmark for measurement purposes. When this version is applied to our airbag problem, the *risk* of the existing car design refers to the increased risk that the ordinary consumer will suffer injury due to the absence of the airbags, defined by the probability P that an accident will cause an amount of injury or loss L. The *utility* of the existing design involves any savings or reduced burden B for the ordinary consumer stemming from the omission of the airbags. The existing design would *fail* the risk-utility test and be defective if the risk exceeds the utility:

$$\text{Increased Risk} = PL_{no\ airbag} > B_{no\ airbag} = \text{Increased Utility or Decreased Cost of Design}$$

The existing design fails the risk-utility test because it does not incorporate an airbag. Hence the design with an airbag passes the risk-utility test, a conclusion that becomes fully apparent when the risk-utility inquiry is expressly defined in terms of the proposed alternative design, with the existing design instead providing the benchmark for measurement purposes. Under this formulation, the *risk* of the alternative design (PL) is the extent to which a design incorporating airbags would reduce risk relative to the existing design. This redesign would change the product's *utility* by adding the cost or burden B of incorporating the airbag into the design. The redesign would be a *reasonable alternative design* if it passes the risk-utility test:

$$\text{Decreased Utility or Increased Cost of Design} = B_{airbag} < PL_{airbag} = \text{Reduced Risk}$$

Both formulations reach the same result: The existing design fails the risk-utility test and is defective because there is a reasonable alternative design that passes the risk-utility test. Either formulation is appropriate, leading to the question of what type of proof is required by this inquiry.

RESTATEMENT (THIRD) OF TORTS: PRODUCTS LIABILITY (1998)
Copyright by the American Law Institute

§2. Comment f. *Design defects: factors relevant in determining whether the omission of a reasonable alternative design renders a product not reasonably safe*

A broad range of factors may be considered in determining whether an alternative design is reasonable and whether its omission renders a product not reasonably safe. The factors include, among others, the magnitude and probability of the foreseeable risks of harm[;]. . . . the likely effects of the alternative design on production costs; the effects of the alternative design on product longevity, maintenance, repair, and esthetics; and the range of consumer choice among products are factors that may be taken into account.... On the other hand, it is not a factor ... that the imposition of liability would have a negative effect on corporate earnings or would reduce employment in a given industry.

. . .

While a plaintiff must prove that a reasonable alternative design would have reduced the foreseeable risks of harm, ... the plaintiff [does not have] to produce expert testimony in every case. Cases arise in which the feasibility of a reasonable alternative design is obvious and understandable to laypersons and therefore expert testimony is unnecessary to support a finding that the product should have been designed differently and more safely. For example, when a manufacturer sells a soft stuffed toy with hard plastic buttons that are easily removable and likely to choke and suffocate a small child who foreseeably attempts to swallow them, the plaintiff should be able to reach the trier of fact with a claim that buttons on such a toy should be an integral part of the toy's fabric itself (or otherwise be unremovable by an infant) without hiring an expert to demonstrate the feasibility of an alternative safer design. Furthermore, other products already available on the market may serve the same or very similar function at lower risk and at comparable cost. Such products may serve as reasonable alternatives to the product in question.

In many cases, the plaintiff must rely on expert testimony.... [Q]ualified expert testimony on the issue suffices, even though the expert has produced no prototype, if it reasonably supports the conclusion that a reasonable alternative design could have been practically adopted at the time of sale.

Given inherent limitations on access to relevant data, the plaintiff is not required to establish with particularity the costs and benefits associated with adoption of the suggested alternative design.

NOTES AND QUESTIONS

1. *The foundation for expert testimony.* When product cases are tried in federal courts, the admissibility of expert testimony depends on a variety of factors (the so-called "*Daubert* test") that are discussed in Chapter 11, section VI. Based on these requirements, courts often reject the plaintiff's proffered expert testimony that a product is defectively designed if the expert did not test the alleged reasonable alternative design:

> While testing is not an "absolute prerequisite" for an expert's theory of causation or alternative design to be admissible in a design defect case, it is usually critical to show that an expert adhered to the same standards of intellectual rigor that are demanded in their professional work. Adherence to engineering standards of intellectual rigor almost always requires testing of a hypothesis if the expert cannot point to an existing design in the marketplace. The presence of this factor in a design defect case also ensures that the focus of the jury's deliberation is on whether the manufacturer could have designed a safer product, not on whether an expert's proposed but untested hypothesis might bear fruit.

Colon *ex rel.* Molina v. BIC USA, Inc., 199 F. Supp. 2d 53, 76-77 (S.D.N.Y. 2001). In addition to relying on existing designs in the market, the expert can rely on "published data generated by another expert in the pertinent field." Wilson Sporting Goods Co. v. Hickox, 59 A.3d 1267, 1272-1273 (D.C. 2013). Merely identifying "older, long-standing designs" is not sufficient, however, unless the expert also provides data showing that those designs reduce risk relative to the existing design. Nease v. Ford Motor Co., 848 F.3d 219, 234 (8th Cir. 2017). If the court excludes the expert testimony and the plaintiff has no other evidence of a reasonable alternative design, the court will dismiss the plaintiff's claim. *E.g., id.* (A potential exception involves the allegation that the entire category is inherently defective, regardless of the particular design—a distinctive type of claim discussed in section III.B *infra.*)

2. *Statutory safety standards.* Rather than develop a prototype that incorporates the alleged reasonable alternative design, the plaintiff in some cases can rely on a safety statute (or the regulations promulgated thereunder) that specifies design requirements for the product. A design that fails to comply with such a requirement can be deemed defective. *See* Chapter 10, section I. In effect, the statutory safety requirements define a reasonable alternative design. In a case of preemption, the statutory requirements specify the only reasonable design. *See* Chapter 10, section III.

3. *Shifting the burden of proof.* Courts justify strict products liability as a means for ameliorating the difficult problems of proving negligence liability. Proof of defective design under the risk-utility test can be onerous and complicated for reasons underscored by the role of expert testimony. Does this evidentiary burden justify shifting the burden of proof to the defendant for purposes of strict products liability?

Relying on this reasoning, the California Supreme Court in the well-known case *Barker v. Lull Engineering Company* adopted such a rule:

> Because most of the evidentiary matters which may be relevant to the determination of the adequacy of a product's design under the "risk-benefit" standard—e.g., the feasibility and cost of alternative designs—are similar to issues typically presented in a negligent design case and involve technical matters peculiarly within the knowledge of the manufacturer, we conclude that once the plaintiff makes a prima facie showing that the injury was proximately caused by the product's design, the burden should appropriately shift to the defendant to prove, in light of the relevant factors, that the product is not defective.

573 P.2d 443, 455 (Cal. 1978); *see also* Soule v. General Motors Corp., 882 P.2d 298, 311 n.8 (Cal. 1994) (affirming the *Barker* burden-shifting rule).

This ruling has attracted a great deal of attention, although only a few other jurisdictions have adopted it. In the vast majority of states, the plaintiff bears the burden of proving that the product was defectively designed. By identifying the reasons why most jurisdictions could defensibly reject the *Barker* burden-shifting rule, we can better understand the evidentiary rationale for strict liability and its limitations.

Under the *Barker* rule, the mere fact of injury is not sufficient for the plaintiff to get to the jury. A party bearing the burden of proof can receive

II. The Risk-Utility Test Applied

a directed verdict in its favor, so a manufacturer can satisfy its burden of proof and keep the case from the jury. In effect, the *Barker* burden-shifting rule operates as a rebuttable presumption. The fact of injury creates a presumption of defective design that the manufacturer can rebut by presenting sufficient risk-utility evidence. *See* Gary T. Schwartz, *Foreword: Understanding Products Liability*, 67 Cal. L. Rev. 435, 467 (1979) (concluding that "both the court's articulation of its rule and the court's reference to section 605 of the Evidence Code verify that the rule does amount to a presumption") (citations omitted). If the manufacturer's evidence is sufficiently persuasive and the plaintiff offers nothing in rebuttal, the court can direct a verdict for the manufacturer.

For cases in which the plaintiff has persuasive risk-utility evidence to establish defect, she is unlikely to invoke the presumption for reasons articulated by Professor Schwartz:

> [M]y discussions with plaintiffs' attorneys make clear that in a typical case, a plaintiff who has satisfactory facts will choose to ignore this aspect of *Barker*. *Barker* allows the plaintiff, having shown that the product's design caused his injury, to close his case and wait for the manufacturer to explain to the jury why that design is sensible after all; once the manufacturer has presented its pro-product evidence, the plaintiff can then bring forward his own evidence in an effort to counter the defense's presentation. Yet it would entail very poor trial strategy for a plaintiff to rely on this sequence, since it puts him on the defensive by allowing the manufacturer to get to the jury first with its explanation of the product's design, and why that design is a good one. If his facts are good, the plaintiff has a clear tactical interest in getting the jury to consider *his* version of the design issue first, before the manufacturer has a chance to tell its side of the story. Wishing to convey to the jury the strength of his case, the plaintiff will want to come out "with all guns blazing," presenting his strongest evidence as to the impropriety of the product's design.

Id. at 469.

Because plaintiffs with sufficient evidence are unlikely to rely on the *Barker* rule, shifting the burden of proof onto the defendant will ordinarily only affect cases in which the plaintiff is unable to sufficiently prove defective design. The question, then, is whether it makes sense to shift the burden of proof to benefit a class of cases for which the evidence of defect is weak.

As we have found, this evidentiary rationale for strict liability promotes product safety by enabling plaintiffs with meritorious claims to overcome the evidentiary difficulties that they would otherwise face in proving negligence liability. An exploding soda bottle often is the result of negligent bottling procedures, but adequate proof of negligence is beyond the capabilities of virtually all plaintiffs, those with meritorious claims and those without. Strict liability applies to manufacturing defects, therefore, because the rule is the only principled way to permit recovery for the substantial number of meritorious claims. *See* Chapter 2, section II. So, too, the appeal of strict liability diminishes considerably when those who benefit are mostly plaintiffs with weak cases. As applied to such cases, strict liability is unlikely to promote safety—plaintiffs with strong claims can recover without reliance on the burden-shifting rule, giving product sellers an adequate incentive to distribute nondefective products. Burden-shifting instead will have the primary effect of increasing litigation costs (to defeat weak claims). Lacking justification with a safety rationale, the increased litigation costs cannot be justified—they largely increase product prices for consumers without an offsetting safety benefit. For these reasons, the majority of courts could defensibly conclude that the evidentiary rationale for strict liability does not justify shifting the burden of proof onto the defendant.

Consequently, the evidentiary rationale for strict liability is limited to cases in which the plaintiff has otherwise adequately proven the element of defect. In the case of contaminated food or an exploding soda bottle, the defect is easily proven; strict liability instead reduces the plaintiff's evidentiary burden by eliminating the need to show that the defect is attributable to the manufacturer's neglect. For products that do not malfunction, plaintiffs often face difficulty in proving that the design is defective—expert testimony is expensive, prototypes hard to develop, and so on. Lacking adequate proof of defect, however, the rule of strict products liability does not apply.

In considering the plaintiff's evidentiary burden of proving defect, recall the material, quoted earlier, from the *Restatement (Third)* §2 cmt. f: "Given inherent limitations on access to relevant data, the plaintiff is not required to establish with particularity the costs and benefits associated with adoption of the suggested alternative design." To what extent, if at all, does this relax the plaintiff's ordinary burden of proof? In a negligence case governed by the Hand formula of reasonable care—the same type of inquiry embodied in the risk-utility test—"[o]rdinarily . . . the parties do not give the jury the information required to quantify the variables that the Hand formula picks out as relevant. That is why the formula has greater analytic than operational significance." McCarty v. Pheasant Run, Inc., 826 F.2d 1554, 1557 (7th Cir. 1987) (Posner, J.).

B. Balancing the Risk-Utility Factors

The widespread adoption of the risk-utility test does not necessarily mean that courts are applying the same liability rule. Based on a national survey, Professor David Owen found wide variation in how courts have formulated the risk-utility test:

> First, there is no single clearly accepted view as to how the design defect balancing test should be described or formulated. A related finding is that there is considerable variation in how the balancing test is formulated among the states, among decisions within the same state, and often even within the same judicial opinion. Another finding is that courts today quite typically cobble together a variety of separate and often conflicting formulations of balancing tests borrowed, without analysis, from earlier opinions. Further, many courts acknowledge that a variety of factors should be balanced but neither

II. The Risk-Utility Test Applied

discriminate between the various factors nor explain how they should be balanced or otherwise interrelate.

David G. Owen, *Risk-Utility Balancing in Design Defect Cases*, 30 U. Mich. J.L. Reform 239, 242 (1997).

The prior section addressed proof of the risk-utility factors. We now consider the problem of variable tests that "neither discriminate between the various factors nor explain how they should be balanced or otherwise interrelate." In balancing risks and utility, must the jury give equal weight to them as required by cost-benefit analysis? Consider Smith v. Louisville Ladder Co., 237 F.3d 515, 530 (5th Cir. 2001) (holding that Texas law "permits strict liability parties to direct their evidence to the various balancing criteria" in the risk-utility test, "while the jury can be instructed only in general terms and cannot be required to perform a balancing of enumerated factors").

Although the *Restatement (Third)* provides some guidance about the matter, it does not specify how the risk-utility test should be applied in the courtroom. *Compare* §2 cmt. f ("This Restatement takes no position regarding the specifics of how a jury should be instructed. So long as jury instructions are generally consistent with the rule of law set forth in subsection (b), their specific form and content are matters of local law."), *with* §2 cmt. d ("[T]he test is whether a reasonable alternative design would, at reasonable cost, have reduced the foreseeable risks of harm posed by the product...."). Does an inquiry into "reasonable cost" necessarily require the jury to apply the risk-utility test as a form of cost-benefit analysis—the type of inquiry assumed by our prior discussions of this test?

How jurors actually apply the risk-utility test depends on how they understand the problem. "The psychological research . . . makes clear that risk-utility balancing in the strictest sense does not completely capture the nature of decision making about risk." Jennifer K. Robbennolt & Valerie P. Hans, THE PSYCHOLOGY OF TORT LAW 41 (2016). As the COVID-19 pandemic has made clear, we all make risk-utility decisions on a daily basis, often balancing these factors quite differently from each other. Recognizing as much, litigants in any case will try to find jurors who are likely to make safety decisions in the manner most favorable to their position: "Understanding how each potential juror assesses risks is key to selecting a sympathetic jury, and presenting a case appropriately tailored to the audience." Jill Leibold et al., *COVID-19 and Design Defect Jurors' Risk Evaluations: Part 2*, Law360.com (July 29, 2020). In addition to recognizing that individuals assess risks differently, sophisticated litigants also know that different types of triggers can cause any individual to undertake a particular form of risk-utility assessment. For example, a juror might be influenced by the presence of safety protocols for combating the spread of COVID-19 in the courtroom. "Each jury will be intimately familiar with risk-utility balancing. Reminders of the risk-utility analysis in a juror's own life will permeate the courtroom, in light of the safety processes implemented by the courts." *Id. Part 3* (July 30, 2020).

What, then, are the factors that affect how lay individuals like jurors make risk-utility decisions?

> Research on risk perception indicates that lay people want risk decisions to be based on additional considerations besides expected damages, injuries and dollar costs. These considerations include voluntariness of exposure to the

hazard; the degree to which the risks are dread, controllable or catastrophic; the degree of uncertainty surrounding the risk estimates; and the possible inequities in the distribution of benefits among persons who bear the risks.

Paul Slovic, THE PERCEPTION OF RISK 199-200 (2000) (citations omitted).

All of these considerations can easily influence how jurors evaluate a manufacturer's product safety decisions. A powerful corporate actor is pursuing its own economic interests by unilaterally imposing a catastrophic risk of physical harm on vulnerable consumers who do not share in the corporate profits, cannot control the risk, and do not make an informed choice to face it. To rectify this type of distributive inequity, jurors can reject cost-benefit analysis and instead require corporate actors to exercise extraordinary care above the cost-justified amount. Doing so can result in a finding of defect, with the resultant damages award equitably distributing the plaintiff's injury costs to the profit-making corporate actor, even though the design would otherwise pass the cost-benefit version of the risk-utility test.

Perhaps the most well-known example of this type of risk-utility reasoning involved a judgment against Ford Motor Corporation for the defective design of one of its automobiles—the Pinto—which caused fatal burn injuries when the vehicle exploded after being hit in a rear-end collision:

> Through the results of the crash tests Ford knew that the Pinto's fuel tank and rear structure would expose consumers to serious injury or death in a 20- to 30-mile-per-hour collision. There was evidence that Ford could have corrected the hazardous design defects at minimal cost but decided to defer correction of the shortcomings by engaging in a cost-benefit analysis balancing human lives and limbs against corporate profits. Ford's institutional mentality was shown to be one of callous indifference to public safety. There was substantial evidence that Ford's conduct constituted "conscious disregard" of the probability of injury to members of the consuming public.

Grimshaw v. Ford Motor Co., 119 Cal. App. 3d 757, 813 (Ct. App. 1981) (upholding a substantial punitive damages award based on these facts).

The Ford Pinto case is not exceptional for reasons fully illustrated by the litigation experience of General Motors. In 1999, the company settled numerous lawsuits involving fuel-tank fires in its vehicles, with sources saying the settlement was in "the mid eight figures." The settlement occurred shortly after the jury rendered a verdict of $4.9 billion in damages, later reduced to $1.2 billion, in a case involving a horrific fuel-tank fire caused by a rear-end collision. In upholding the jury verdict, the trial judge concluded that there was "clear and convincing evidence" that that the defendant made this design decision "in order to maximize profits—to the disregard of public safety." What was this evidence? An internal document written by a "low-level engineer in 1973" concluding that the cost of redesigning the fuel tank exceeded the cost of fatal burn injuries that General Motors would otherwise incur. *See* Milo Geyelin, *How a Memo Written 26 Years Ago Is Haunting General Motors Dearly*, Wall St. J., Sept. 29, 1999.

Consider how this type of jury decision-making relates to a manufacturer's assessment of whether a particular design is required by the risk-utility test.

> Making precise assessments of costs and benefits of safety actions is often feasible through the application of the developing science of benefit-cost

II. The Risk-Utility Test Applied

analysis. For example, Ford Motor Company and General Motors routinely make explicit calculations regarding the costs and benefits of providing various safety devices, such as shielded gas tanks, reinforcing struts, anti-skid brakes, etc. (for example, the Ford Pinto; the Oldsmobile Cutlass). Making such calculations appears to offend some jurors' sensibilities. Post-trial interviews with jurors provide evidence that the plaintiff's introduction of corporations' calculations and benefit-cost memos provokes hostility and punitive attitudes.

Reid Hastie & W. Kip Viscusi, *What Juries Can't Do Well: The Jury's Performance as a Risk Manager*, 40 Ariz. L. Rev. 901, 914 (1998) (footnotes omitted).

"With this attitude widespread among the public who make up juries, how can trial lawyers defend a design case by pointing to a risk-benefit analysis performed by the manufacturer? The short answer is that they can't and don't." Michael D. Green, *The Schizophrenia of Risk-Benefit Analysis in Design Defect Litigation*, 48 Vand. L. Rev. 609, 626-627 (1995). Rather than openly defending their risk-utility calculations in the courtroom, defendants instead defend the existing design on other grounds:

> There are several kinds of arguments that defense counsel can make which juries are willing to take seriously. One argument is that the design itself is not really improper, in that an alternative design would significantly impair the usefulness of the product itself. In addition, "state of the art" is a liability-limiting idea that adequately appeals to the jury's common sense. You can also argue that the accident was really caused by the victim's own faulty conduct, or the faulty conduct of some third party. Here your argument can be strengthened by showing that the product was being misused or used in an abnormal way. When the facts are right, it can also make sense to argue that the victim assumed the risk — that the victim knew what he was getting. However, one argument that you should almost never make is that the manufacturer deliberately included a dangerous feature in the product's design because of the high monetary cost that the manufacturer would have incurred in choosing another design. If you do argue this, you're almost certain to lose on liability, and you can expose yourself to punitive damages as well.

Gary T. Schwartz, *The Myth of the Ford Pinto Case*, 43 Rutgers L. Rev. 1013, 1038 (1991).

The problem illustrated by the *Grimshaw* case thus "raises serious questions about the operational viability of the risk-benefit standard itself." *Id.* at 1067. This particular problem is easy to understand as a matter of juror psychology but more puzzling as a matter of law. Recall that for purposes of the risk-utility test, the manufacturer's profits are not relevant to the inquiry. *See* Chapter 3, section III.B. On what basis, then, can plaintiffs argue that risk-utility balancing pits human lives against corporate profits?

LAPLANTE v. AMERICAN HONDA MOTOR CORP.
United States Court of Appeals, First Circuit, 1994
27 F.3d 471

BOWNES, SENIOR C.J. [While riding on a three-wheeled all-terrain vehicle (ATV) on a mountain trail, plaintiff "fell over a steep embankment and broke his neck, resulting in permanent paralysis from the neck down." He filed claim against the manufacturer Honda, alleging six different causes of action, including negligent failure to warn and strict liability design defect.]

A twenty-three day trial on liability and compensatory damages began in July 1993. At the close of plaintiff's case Honda moved for judgment as a matter of law. Only the claims for negligent failure to warn and strict liability design defect survived the motion. Ultimately the jury found Honda liable on these two claims, and awarded plaintiff $3,652,000 for medical expenses and lost wages, and $6,000,000 for physical injuries and pain and suffering. The jury also found that plaintiff was comparatively negligent, and reduced his award by fifteen percent. The district court denied Honda's motions for postjudgment relief.

The punitive damages phase of this action commenced on September 16, 1993. On the same day, at the close of plaintiff's evidence, the district court granted Honda's motion for judgment as a matter of law. These cross-appeals ensued.

[The court then decided to order a retrial for various reasons.] Because we vacate and remand for a new trial on both the strict liability and negligence claims, ... it is unnecessary for us to address Honda's remaining arguments regarding these matters. But in order to expedite the retrial, we have considered one such argument.

Evidence of Honda's Profits from ATV Sales

Plaintiff's counsel was permitted, over Honda's objection, to read the following interrogatory and answer to the jury in connection with his negligent failure to warn claim:

Q. Please state the total gross revenues, profits and net income from the sale of the all-terrain vehicles for the years 1970 through 1989 in each and every country where ATVs are or were offered for sale to the public. ...

A. [I]n 1987 it was calculated for the period January 21, 1979 to June 25, 1985, gross receipts for ATVs approximated $1,722,881,000. Although American Honda does not keep records of net profit by ATV product line it allocated expenses pursuant to reasonable accounting principles to obtain a sum comparable to pre-tax net profits in the approximate sum of $73,371,000.

Honda argues that the evidence of its profits from ATV sales was irrelevant and therefore inadmissible. Assuming the evidence was relevant, Honda argues that its probative value was substantially outweighed by its prejudicial effect.

"Evidence is relevant if it has any tendency to make the existence of any fact consequential to the determination of the action more or less probable." [ ] After plaintiff's counsel read the interrogatory and answer, the trial judge explained to the jury that

> [t]he evidence [of Honda's profits] is being presented only to assist you in determining what Honda may have known or not known about the particular vehicle that's the subject of this case. In other words, it's to assist you in understanding or reaching conclusions as to what Honda may have known or believed about the ATC 200 or why it acted as it did and so forth. ... [Y]ou're not being asked to be Robin Hoods here and take money from Honda simply because they may have made money on the sale of this vehicle. The only purpose of this evidence is, as I said, to assist you in reaching whatever conclusions

II. The Risk-Utility Test Applied

you think are warranted about whether the vehicle as used had means to be dangerous or what Honda may have known about the vehicle or what it might have believed about the safety of the vehicle.

Near the end of the trial the court commented that the records of Honda's ATV profits "seemed to be probative of the, shall we say, the credibility of the explanation by Honda; and the Court gave a limit[ing] instruction to the jury at that time."

The first question is whether the challenged evidence was relevant to plaintiff's negligent failure to warn claim. In Rhode Island, a defendant has a duty to warn if he knew or should have known about the product's dangerous propensities which caused plaintiff's injuries. Failure to properly perform this duty as a reasonably prudent manufacturer would have under the same or similar circumstances, constitutes actionable negligence.

A defendant's motive for its action or inaction is, generally speaking, immaterial to the question of whether the defendant acted negligently. [ ] This is because the negligence inquiry measures behavior against an objective standard, without reference to the defendant's state of mind. [ ]. Here, however, whether or not Honda had a duty to warn plaintiff of the ATV's dangerous propensities depended upon its subjective knowledge of those dangers. Consequently, the evidence of Honda's profits from ATV sales was, as we demonstrate in the ensuing paragraph, relevant to plaintiff's negligent failure to warn claim.

With respect to his negligence claim plaintiff alleged that, prior to his accident, Honda knew that its ATVs would "plow" (*i.e.*, continue in a straight line even when the handlebars are turned) under normal riding conditions unless the rider shifted his or her weight in a counterintuitive manner. Honda denied that it had any knowledge of this danger. Honda's profits from ATV sales was introduced as evidence that Honda's failure to provide adequate warnings about plowing resulted from greed, not from lack of knowledge. Therefore, proof of profits as evidence of motive, while not material to any element of the failure to warn claim, was probative of an issue relevant to the case: the credibility of Honda's explanation for its inaction.

Generally speaking, "[a]ll relevant evidence is admissible." Fed.R.Evid. 402. Under Rule 403, however, relevant evidence may be excluded if the probative value of the evidence "is substantially outweighed by the danger of unfair prejudice" to the party against whom it is offered. [ ] Although the evidence of Honda's profits from ATV sales was of some probative value, we believe the danger that this evidence would unfairly prejudice the jury was overwhelming.

The evidence was, at best, marginally relevant and of scant probative value to plaintiff's failure to warn claim. On the other hand, the risk that the jury would be prejudiced by this reference to the enormous profitability of Honda's ATVs was almost inescapable. The potentially prejudicial nature of this "motive" evidence in the liability phase of the trial was one of the factors that prompted the district court to try the issue of punitive damages separately. While the court did give a limiting instruction to the jury warning against equalizing wealth between rich and poor, it did not alert the jury to the impropriety of punishing Honda for an unsavory motive. The inadequacy of the limiting instruction coupled with the highly attenuated relevance of the evidence leads us to believe that the district court miscalibrated its Rule 403 scales.

Honda argues that the admission of this evidence was reversible error, as it skewed the jury's allocation of fault, and infected its liability determinations. Because we have already ordered a new trial on both of these matters, we need not decide whether the district court's error in admitting the evidence of Honda's profits from ATV sales warrants a new trial. Nevertheless, we hold that this material should not be admitted on retrial. In addition, any references to that information, such as the one made by plaintiff at closing argument, should not be allowed.

NOTES AND QUESTIONS

1. *Relevance of profits and the profit motive.* For reasons discussed by the court in *LaPlante*, evidence about the defendant's total profits from a product line can be deemed inadmissible for proving the claim of defective design. *See also* Ake v. Gen. Motors Corp., 942 F. Supp. 869, 876 (W.D.N.Y. 1996) ("Plaintiff . . . is precluded from offering evidence of defendant's profits during her case-in-chief. Although the cost of using a certain design should be considered in the context of the cost of manufacturing the entire product, GM's profits are much less relevant and much more prejudicial.").

Although these rulings address the relevance of the manufacturer's total profits, do they also call into question the reason for allowing a plaintiff to argue that in relying on cost considerations, the defendant elevated corporate profits over human lives? As the court in *LaPlante* explained, a "defendant's motive for its action or inaction is, generally speaking, immaterial to the question of whether the defendant acted negligently." Why is the defendant's motive to make profits any different? Consider how courts commonly distinguish negligence liability from strict products liability: "Strict products liability, unlike negligence doctrine, focuses on the nature of the product, and not the nature of the manufacturer's conduct." Kim v. Toyota Motor Corp., 424 P.3d 290, 298 (Cal. 2018). Under strict products liability, risk-utility analysis of a product design exclusively focuses on the product and not the manufacturer's conduct. Moreover, that analysis does not include any consideration of how the redesign would affect the manufacturer's profits. On what basis, then, is the manufacturer's profit motive relevant?

The relevance of the profit motive is called into further question by the safety decision contemplated by the risk-utility test. The test permits the manufacturer to forego a redesign of the product that would reduce risk whenever this safety benefit is less than the associated cost. The increased costs would be borne by the ordinary consumer, who does not reasonably expect that the product be redesigned in an overly costly manner. *See* Chapter 3, section III.B. By cutting these costs, the manufacturer can promote consumer demand and corporate profits at the expense of those fatalities or other injuries that would have been avoided by the safer but overly costly redesign. The manufacturer's profit motive can be fully squared with its decision to design products in a manner that would satisfy the risk-utility test, making it even harder to discern why that motive is relevant for proving that the design violates the test.

II. The Risk-Utility Test Applied

2. *Punitive damages and bifurcated trials.* The plaintiff in *LaPlante* was pursuing a claim of punitive damages in a separate proceeding. Unlike the liability phase of the case, the inquiry into punitive damages routinely depends on the defendant's motives for engaging in the tortious conduct—a manufacturer that knows the product is defective and nevertheless decides to sell it in the hope of making profits will be punished accordingly. *See* Chapter 13, section V. Consequently, when there is only a single proceeding to determine both liability and damages, the defendant's motivation to make profits by cutting costs can be highly relevant for assessing whether that conduct merits a punitive response. But if the liability phase of the case is bifurcated from the damages phase, then evidence about total profits and the profit motive are subject to the concerns about relevance and prejudice discussed above. Compare Palmer v. A.H. Robins Co., 684 P.2d 187, 215 (Colo. 1984) ("When an adequate showing is made by the defendant, the court might consider granting a bifurcated trial on the issue of punitive damages in order to avoid any prejudice to the defendant on the issue of liability.").

3. *More contextualized cost-cutting decisions.* In the *Kim* case cited in note 1, the plaintiffs alleged that a 2005 Tundra pickup truck manufactured by defendant Toyota was defectively designed because "its standard configuration did not include a particular safety feature, known as vehicle stability control (VSC)." Instead, "Toyota offered VSC—then a relatively new technology—as part of an optional package, including various enhanced features." 424 P.3d at 293. One of plaintiffs' experts "estimated that the incremental cost to Toyota of adding the VSC to the 2005 Toyota Tundra would have been approximately $300 to $350 per vehicle." The product planning manager for Toyota testified that the company was trying to "produce a vehicle that met the customer's needs based on price, based on future availability, and at the time we felt like optional VSC was the best option." This witness "noted that Toyota's market research indicated that pickup truck customers were price sensitive and uninterested in VSC." *Id.* at 294. But according to the plaintiffs, "Toyota designed the Tundra without the standard VSC because it valued profits over safety." *Id.* at 299. The jury found for the defendant, concluding that the vehicle was not defectively designed under the risk-utility test. *Id.* at 295. As this case illustrates, plaintiffs do not necessarily prevail by arguing that the manufacturer's reduction of costs reprehensibly elevated corporate profits over human lives. Is there anything about the facts of this case that might explain why the jury accepted this type of cost-cutting argument?

4. *Risk-risk trade-offs.* Not all design cases reduce to questions of monetary cost. Often, the design trade-off is one of risk. To reduce or eliminate one set of risks, the design will often have to create or increase a different set of risks. "It is not sufficient that the alternative design would have reduced or prevented the harm suffered by the plaintiff if it would also have introduced into the product other dangers of equal or greater magnitude." RESTATEMENT (THIRD) OF TORTS: PRODUCTS LIABILITY §2 cmt. f. For cases involving such a *risk-risk trade-off*, is there any reason why jurors would give greater weight to one set of risks over the other, assuming that each is of equal magnitude and threatens equally severe injuries?

DAWSON v. CHRYSLER CORP.
United States Court of Appeals, Third Circuit, 1980
630 F.2d 950

ADAMS, J. On September 7, 1974, Richard F. Dawson, while in the employ of the Pennsauken Police Department, was seriously injured as a result of an automobile accident that occurred in Pennsauken, New Jersey. As Dawson was driving on a rain-soaked highway, responding to a burglar alarm, he lost control of his patrol car a 1974 Dodge Monaco. The car slid off the highway, over a curb, through a small sign, and into an unyielding steel pole that was fifteen inches in diameter. The car struck the pole in a backwards direction at a forty-five degree angle on the left side of the vehicle; the point of impact was the left rear wheel well. As a result of the force of the collision, the vehicle literally wrapped itself around the pole. The pole ripped through the body of the car and crushed Dawson between the seat and the "header" area of the roof, located just above the windshield. The so-called "secondary collision" of Dawson with the interior of the automobile dislocated Dawson's left hip and ruptured his fifth and sixth cervical vertebrae. As a result of the injuries, Dawson is now a quadriplegic. He has no control over his body from the neck down, and requires constant medical attention.

Dawson, his wife, and their son brought suit in the Court of Common Pleas of Philadelphia against the Chrysler Corporation, the manufacturer of the vehicle in which Dawson was injured. The plaintiffs' claims were based on theories of strict products liability and breach of implied warranty of fitness. They alleged that the patrol car was defective because it did not have a full, continuous steel frame extending through the door panels, and a cross-member running through the floor board between the posts located between the front and rear doors of the vehicle. Had the vehicle been so designed, the Dawsons alleged, it would have "bounced" off the pole following relatively slight penetration by the pole into the passenger space.

Expert testimony was introduced by the Dawsons to prove that the existing frame of the patrol car was unable to withstand side impacts at relatively low speed, and that the inadequacy of the frame permitted the pole to enter the passenger area and to injure Dawson. The same experts testified that the improvements in the design of the frame that the plaintiffs proposed were feasible and would have prevented Dawson from being injured as he was. According to plaintiffs' expert witnesses, a continuous frame and cross-member would have deflected the patrol car away from the pole after a minimal intrusion into the passenger area and, they declared, Dawson likely would have emerged from the accident with only a slight injury.

In response, Chrysler argued that it had no duty to produce a "crashproof" vehicle, and that, in any event, the patrol car was not defective. Expert testimony for Chrysler established that the design and construction of the 1974 Dodge Monaco complied with all federal vehicle safety standards, and that deformation of the body of the vehicle is desirable in most crashes because it absorbs the impact of the crash and decreases the rate of deceleration on the occupants of the vehicle. Thus, Chrysler's experts asserted that, for most types of automobile accidents, the design offered by the Dawsons would be less safe than the existing design. They also estimated that the steel parts that would be required

II. The Risk-Utility Test Applied

in the model suggested by the Dawsons would have added between 200 and 250 pounds to the weight, and approximately $300 to the price of the vehicle. It was also established that the 1974 Dodge Monaco's unibody construction was stronger than comparable Ford and Chevrolet vehicles.

After all testimony had been introduced, Chrysler moved for a directed verdict, which the district judge denied. The jury thereupon returned a verdict in favor of the plaintiffs. The jury awarded Mr. Dawson $2,064,863.19 for his expenses, disability, and pain and suffering, and granted Mrs. Dawson $60,000.00 for loss of consortium and loss of services.

Our examination of the record persuades us that the district court did not err in denying Chrysler's motion for judgment notwithstanding the verdict. The Dawsons demonstrated that the frame of the 1974 Dodge Monaco was noncontinuous, that is, it consisted of a front portion that extended from the front of the car to the middle of the front passenger seat, and a rear portion that ran from the middle of the rear passenger seat to the back end of the vehicle. Thus, there was a gap in the seventeen-inch side area of the frame between the front and rear seats. The plaintiffs also proved that, after colliding with the pole, the car slid along the left side portion of the rear frame until it reached the gap in the frame. At that point, the pole tore through the body of the vehicle into the passenger area and proceeded to push Dawson into the header area above the windshield.

Three experts—a design analyst, a mechanical engineer, and a biochemical engineer—also testified on behalf of the Dawsons. These witnesses had examined the patrol car and concluded that it was inadequate to withstand side impacts. They testified that there was an alternative design available which, had it been employed in the 1974 Monaco, would have prevented Dawson from sustaining serious injuries. The substitute design called for a continuous frame with an additional cross member running between the so-called B-posts, the vertical posts located at the side of the car between the front and rear seats. According to these witnesses, this design was known in the industry well before the accident and had been tested by a number of independent testing centers in 1969 and in 1973.

The mechanical engineer conducted a number of studies in order to ascertain the extent to which the alternative design would have withstood the crash. On the basis of these calculations, he testified that the pole would have penetrated only 9.9 inches into the passenger space, and thus would not have crushed Dawson. Instead, the engineer stated, the car would have deflected off the pole and back into the highway. Under these circumstances, according to the biochemical engineer, Dawson would have been able to "walk away from the accident" with but a bruised shoulder.

Also introduced by the Dawsons were reports of tests conducted for the United States Department of Transportation, which indicated that, in side collisions with a fixed pole at twenty-one miles per hour, frame improvements similar to those proposed by the experts presented by the Dawsons reduced intrusion into the passenger area by fifty percent, from sixteen inches to eight inches. The study concluded that the improvements, "in conjunction with interior alterations, demonstrated a dramatic increase in occupant protection." There was no suggestion at trial that the alternative design recommended by the Dawsons would not comply with federal safety standards. On cross-examination, Chrysler's attorney did get the Dawsons' expert witnesses to acknowledge that the alternative design would add between 200 and 250 pounds to the vehicle and would cost an additional $300 per car. The Dawsons' experts also conceded that the heavier and more rigid an automobile, the less able it is to absorb energy upon impact with a fixed object, and therefore the major force of an accident might be transmitted to the passengers. Moreover, an expert for Chrysler testified that, even if the frame of the patrol car had been designed in conformity with the plaintiffs' proposals, Dawson would have sustained injuries equivalent to those he actually incurred. Chrysler's witness reasoned that Dawson was injured, not by the intrusion of the pole into the passenger space, but as a result of being thrown into the header area of the roof by the vehicle's initial contact with the pole, that is, prior to the impact of the pole against the driver's seat.

On the basis of the foregoing recitation of the evidence presented respectively by the Dawsons and by Chrysler, we conclude that the record is sufficient to sustain the jury's determination, in response to the interrogatory, that the design of the 1974 Monaco was defective. The jury was not required to ascertain that all of the factors enumerated by the New Jersey Supreme Court in Cepeda v. Cumberland Eng'g, 386 A.2d 216 (N.J. 1978), weighed in favor of the Dawsons in order to find the patrol car defective. Rather, it need only to have reasonably concluded, after balancing these factors, that, at the time Chrysler distributed the 1974 Monaco, the car was "not reasonably fit, suitable and safe for its intended or reasonably foreseeable purposes." [ ] We are admonished to review the record in this case in the light most favorable to the nonmoving party, the Dawsons, and to affirm the judgment of the district court denying the motions unless the record is critically deficient of that minimum quantum of evidence from which a jury might reasonably afford relief. We hold that it is not.

Although we affirm the judgment of the district court, we do so with uneasiness regarding the consequences of our decision and of the decisions of other courts throughout the country in cases of this kind.

Congress, in enacting the National Traffic and Motor Vehicle Safety Act, provided that compliance with the Act does not exempt any person from liability under the common law of the state of injury. The effect of this provision is that the states are free, not only to create various standards of liability for automobile manufacturers with respect to design and structure, but also to delegate to the triers of fact in civil cases arising out of automobile accidents the power to determine whether a particular product conforms to such standards. In the present situation, for example, the New Jersey Supreme Court has instituted a strict liability standard for cases involving defective products, has defined the term "defective product" to mean any such item that is not "reasonably fit, suitable and safe for its intended or reasonably foreseeable purposes," and has left to the jury the task of determining whether the product at issue measures up to this standard.

The result of such arrangement is that while the jury found Chrysler liable for not producing a rigid enough vehicular frame, a factfinder in another case might well hold the manufacturer liable for producing a frame that is too rigid. Yet, as pointed out at trial, in certain types of accidents like head-on collisions it is desirable to have a car designed to collapse upon impact because the deformation would absorb much of the shock of the collision, and divert the force of deceleration away from the vehicle's passengers. In effect, this permits

II. The Risk-Utility Test Applied

individual juries applying varying laws in different jurisdictions to set nationwide automobile safety standards and to impose on automobile manufacturers conflicting requirements. It would be difficult for members of the industry to alter their design and production behavior in response to jury verdicts in such cases, because their response might well be at variance with what some other jury decides is a defective design. Under these circumstances, the law imposes on the industry the responsibility of insuring vast numbers of persons involved in automobile accidents.

Equally serious is the impact on other national social and economic goals of the existing case-by-case system of establishing automobile safety requirements. As we have become more dependent on foreign sources of energy, and as the price of that energy has increased, the attention of the federal government has been drawn to a search to find alternative supplies and the means of conserving energy. More recently, the domestic automobile industry has been struggling to compete with foreign manufacturers which have stressed smaller, more fuel-efficient cars. Yet, during this same period, Congress has permitted a system of regulation by ad hoc adjudications under which a jury can hold an automobile manufacturer culpable for not producing a car that is considerably heavier, and likely to have less fuel efficiency.

In sum, this appeal has brought to our attention an important conflict that implicates broad national concerns. Although it is important that society devise a proper system for compensating those injured in automobile collisions, it is not at all clear that the present arrangement of permitting individual juries, under varying standards of liability, to impose this obligation on manufacturers is fair or efficient. Inasmuch as it was the Congress that designed this system, and because Congress is the body best suited to evaluate and, if appropriate, to change that system, we decline today to do anything in this regard except to bring the problem to the attention of the legislative branch.

Bound as we are to adjudicate this appeal according to the substantive law of New Jersey, and because we find no basis in that law to overturn the jury's verdict, the judgment of the district court will be affirmed.

NOTES AND QUESTIONS

1. *State tort law and national product markets.* A manufacturer supplying the national market usually cannot feasibly redesign the product to comply with the particular requirements of each jurisdiction. For some design issues, the manufacturer could satisfy the most demanding liability rule in the country and thereby satisfy all remaining (and less demanding) liability rules in other states. Is it desirable to set national safety standards in this manner? Would this type of approach work for design attributes that involve a risk-risk trade-off like the one at issue in *Dawson*? These issues largely explain the appeal of federal safety regulations that preempt tort claims, the subject of Chapter 10, section III.

2. *Juror evaluation of risk.* To apply the risk-utility test, the jury needs to evaluate the degree of risk posed by the design attribute in question. In trying to understand the social psychology of jury decision-making, scholars typically rely on the "voluminous research" showing that individuals use

judgmental heuristics to draw inferences about how to reduce complex information when making decisions. Neil Feigenson, LEGAL BLAME: HOW JURORS THINK AND TALK ABOUT ACCIDENTS 7-9 (2000). Although these common-sense intuitions ordinarily work well, heuristics nevertheless are "simplifying strategies [that] often lead to errors in judgment." Michael J. Saks & Robert F. Kidd, *Human Information Processing and Adjudication: Trial by Heuristics*, 15 Law & Soc'y Rev. 123, 127 (1980-81).

Heuristics shape an individual's processing of information when making a complex decision; they do not otherwise dictate what the individual is trying to decide. In cases of risk-risk trade-offs, jurors presumably have no reason to favor one set of risks over another. By giving the two equal treatment, they will be applying the risk-utility test in the manner required by cost-benefit analysis. Their reliance on heuristics, however, can still distort that reasoning.

The problem discussed by the court in *Dawson* implicates the "hindsight bias," a heuristic that psychologists have "demonstrated repeatedly":

> In hindsight, people consistently exaggerate what could have been anticipated in foresight. They not only tend to view what has happened as having been inevitable but also to view it as having appeared "relatively inevitable" before it happened. People believe that others should have been able to anticipate events much better than was actually the case.

Jeffry J. Rachlinski, *A Positive Psychological Theory of Judging in Hindsight*, 65 U. Chi. L. Rev. 571, 571 (1998) (quotation omitted). How might this bias affect a juror's application of the risk-utility test? Consider *id.* ("The defendant's level of care will be reviewed by a judge or jury who already knows that it proved inadequate to avoid the plaintiff's injury. Consequently, the defendant's level of care will seem less reasonable in hindsight than it did in foresight.").

A related problem with assessing risk at the time of trial involves the so-called "availability heuristic," another form of decision-making that has been demonstrated repeatedly by psychologists. "[P]eople tend to perceive that a particular harm is more likely when examples of that type of harm are easier to call to mind." Jennifer K. Robbennolt & Valerie P. Hans, THE PSYCHOLOGY OF TORT LAW 43 (2016).

In hindsight, the risk that injured the plaintiff in *Dawson* can appear to be more substantial than it really was, leading the jury to conclude that the product is defectively designed for not reducing that risk. To be sure, that determination involved a risk-risk trade-off, but the availability heuristic draws the jury's attention to the injury in the case at hand and increases its perception of that salient risk as compared to the other, more abstract risk involving parties not before the court.

But once the manufacturer redesigns the car with a more rigid body, someone will be injured because the design's reduced flexibility reduces its capacity to absorb energy on impact. In such a case, the hindsight bias and availability heuristic would render this risk more salient and could result in a jury verdict finding that the design's failure to absorb energy on

II. The Risk-Utility Test Applied

impact is a defect that could be remedied by a more flexible design. These dynamics could yield inconsistent jury verdicts, the concern the court in *Dawson* identified.

Other courts have also recognized this problem. In a product case involving an alleged defect in the design of a stopping device for a department-store escalator, Judge Frank Easterbrook made the following observations in a concurring opinion:

> The *ex post* perspective of litigation exerts a hydraulic force that distorts judgment. Engineers design escalators to minimize the sum of construction, operation, and injury costs. Department stores, which have nothing to gain from maiming their customers and employees, willingly pay for cost-effective precautions. . . .
>
> Come the lawsuit, however, the passenger injured by a stop presents himself as a person, not a probability. Jurors see today's injury; persons who would be injured if buttons were harder to find and use [as required by the plaintiff's proposed alternative design] are invisible. Although witnesses may talk about them, they are spectral figures, insubstantial compared to the injured plaintiff, who appears in the flesh.

Carroll v. Otis Elevator Co., 896 F.2d 210, 215-216 (7th Cir. 1990) (Easterbrook, J., concurring).

3. *Reframing the risk-utility test.* For reasons revealed by both decision-making heuristics and a plaintiff's emphasis on the defendant's profit motive, how jurors perceive the safety problem can shape their application of the risk-utility test. In general, studies have repeatedly found that the manner in which a decision is "framed" significantly influences how individuals think about the matter. An otherwise substantively identical decision can be resolved differently when framed differently. *E.g.,* Edward McCaffery, Daniel J. Kahneman & Matthew L. Spitzer, *Framing the Jury: Cognitive Perspective on Pain and Suffering Awards*, 81 Va. L. Rev. 1341 (1995).

Under the risk-utility test, "[n]o point of view is imposed on the balancing inquiry." Sheila L. Birnbaum, *Unmasking the Test for Design Defect: From Negligence [to Warranty] to Strict Liability to Negligence*, 33 Vand. L. Rev. 593, 631 (1980). To what extent are the difficulties of applying the risk-utility test attributable to the absence of any point of view or frame for analysis?

Without a point of view, how will the jury evaluate the issue of cost in relation to the plaintiff's injury? Consider W. Kip Viscusi, *Corporate Risk Analysis: A Reckless Act?*, 52 Stan. L. Rev. 547, 570 (2000) ("Jurors have a tendency to compare the often very small per-unit safety cost with the costs borne by the injured victim. Rather than examine the entire market and the associated benefits and costs, jurors will be offended by, or will not fully understand, a comprehensive risk-analysis approach and will focus their assessment more narrowly on the identified victim and the costs of preventing that injury. The fact that these costs would also have been incurred for thousands of consumers who were not injured will not loom as large. . . .").

Without a point of view, jurors will reflexively focus on the particular (tragic) facts of the case at hand. Without a point of view, what prevents the plaintiff's attorney from arguing that the manufacturer's failure to adopt a costly design change reprehensibly elevates "corporate profits over human lives"? A point of view is provided by the consumer expectations test, leading to the question whether application of the risk-utility test would be improved if jury instructions on the risk-utility test were framed in terms of reasonable consumer expectations.

Consider the pattern jury instructions from New York, which describe the risk-utility inquiry in the negligence terms embraced by the *Restatement (Third)*'s rationale for this liability rule. When these instructions are reframed in terms of consumer expectations, they could take the following form:

> A product is defectively designed if a reasonable ~~person~~ consumer who knew ~~or should have known~~ of the product's potential for causing injury and of the feasible alternative design would have concluded that the product should not have been marketed in that condition. Whether the product should have been marketed in that condition depends upon a balancing of ~~the risks involved in using the product against (1) the product's usefulness and its costs, and (2)~~ the risks, usefulness, and costs of the alternative design as compared to the product the defendant did market. <u>All costs of the alternative design would be incurred by the ordinary consumer in the form of higher product prices, decreased functionality, diminished product performance, or any newly created risks. The ordinary consumer would also benefit from the enhanced safety performance of the alternative design. After balancing these factors, the ordinary consumer would reasonably expect the defendant to have marketed the alternative design only if its increased costs are less than the reduction of risk.</u>

New York Pattern Jury Instructions—Civil 2:120 (Dec. 2020 update).

This instruction does not tell jurors how they must balance the risk-utility factors; it only frames the problem by reference to the decision-making of the ordinary consumer. By emphasizing that consumers are the ones who both benefit from product safety and pay for it, courts would explain to jurors why the risk-utility test does not inherently pit corporate profits against human lives. An emphasis on the ordinary consumer might also help to direct attention away from the undeniably compelling facts of the case at hand involving the injury of a particular consumer. All of these factors importantly influence the decision-making of lay individuals, but none of them are addressed by the negligence-based jury instructions on the risk-utility test.

The viability of the risk-utility test might ultimately depend on whether it is derived from consumer expectations or instead is treated as a stand-alone form of negligence liability without any point of view or evident connection to consumer interests. The reason why a jurisdiction has adopted the risk-utility test may end up being the most important determinant of how the risk-utility test is applied in the courtroom. Compare RESTATEMENT (THIRD) OF TORTS: PRODUCTS LIABILITY §2 cmt. d Rptrs' N., at 74 ("[S]ome courts talk of reasonable consumer expectations as the test for liability but define consumer expectations in risk-utility terms. This is merely terminological variance and is consistent with the rule of this Section.").

III. THE ROLE OF CONSUMER CHOICE

Strict products liability addresses the safety problems stemming from consumers' uninformed product decisions. An exclusive focus on cases involving the absence of informed consumer choice creates the misleading appearance that consumer choice is largely irrelevant for products liability. These liability rules are shaped by consumer choice. The risk-utility test, for example, requires the type of product designs that well-informed or reasonable consumers would choose. Similarly, consumer choice can explain other rules governing defective design, including important limitations of liability.

A. *Foreseeable Product Use*

Products liability originated with malfunctioning products for which the defect could be easily defined by the product's failure to minimally perform one of its intended functions. A soda bottle is not intended to explode during normal use. Based on these cases, courts initially limited a manufacturer's duty regarding product design to the product's intended use, but then subsequently expanded the duty to encompass foreseeable risks of physical harm. *See, e.g.*, Evans v. General Motors Corp., 359 F.2d 822, 823-825 (7th Cir. 1966) (dismissing claim that an automobile was defectively designed for not adequately protecting the driver from side-impact collisions, because "[t]he intended purpose of an automobile does not include its participation in collisions with other objects, despite the manufacturer's ability to foresee the possibility that such collisions may occur"), *overruled by* Huff v. White Motor Corp., 565 F.2d 104, 109 (7th Cir. 1977) (holding that "our previous decision in *Evans*" is inconsistent with "the expanding extension of protection for consumers in products liability cases" where courts have found that "manufacturers must anticipate and take precautions against reasonably foreseeable risks in the use of their products"). What does this reformulation of the duty suggest about its underlying rationale? Consider James A. Henderson, Jr. & Aaron D. Twerski, *Achieving Consensus on Defective Product Design*, 83 Cornell L. Rev. 867, 8723 (1998) (explaining why a tort duty limited to intended product use is problematic because it "makes no reference to foreseeable-but-not-intended functions for which users might nevertheless reasonably have a right to expect the design to perform safely.").

In a design case, the element of duty determines the risks that factor into the risk-utility test. An unforeseeable risk is outside of the duty and therefore plays no part in the determination of defect. *See, e.g.*, Woods v. A.R.E. Accessories, LLC, 815 S.E.2d 205, 210 (Ga. App. 2018) ("As part of the risks of harm that manufacturers must foresee in choosing a product design, there is no requirement that a product be made safe for a use that is unintended and unforeseeable."); RESTATEMENT (THIRD) OF TORTS: PRODUCTS LIABILITY § 2 cmt. p ("[L]iability for defective design attaches only if the risks of harm related to foreseeable product use could have been reduced by the adoption of a reasonable alternative design."). What determines whether a risk is foreseeable?

SALAZAR v. WOLO MFG. GROUP
Court of Appeals of Texas, Fourteenth District, Houston, 1998
983 S.W.2d 87

MCKEE FOWLER, J. On December 18, 1994, the Salazars were standing behind their pickup truck in a restaurant parking lot when a car struck them. At the time of the accident, Leticia Martinez, the fourteen year old driver of the car, was receiving driving lessons from her uncle. The Salazars contend their injuries resulted because Martinez lost control of the car when an anti-theft device known as "The Club" slid from beneath Martinez's seat and lodged itself between the floorboard and the brake pedal, allegedly preventing Martinez from applying the brakes. "The Club" attaches to the steering wheel of a car when the car is not in use.

The Salazars sued Martinez, Vasquez, and Wolo, the manufacturers and designers of "The Club," to recover for their injuries. According to the Salazars, Wolo's product contained a marketing defect and was defectively designed. Allegedly, "The Club" was defectively marked because it did not come with any warnings instructing consumers on how to store "The Club" when it was not in use. The Salazars contend "The Club" was defectively designed because when Wolo made the product, a safer alternative design existed. Had this design been used, it could have prevented this accident. In addition to the marketing and design defects, the Salazars contend Wolo was negligent for failing to warn consumers not to store "The Club" under the driver's seat. Wolo filed a motion for summary judgment. The trial court originally denied this motion, but after Wolo filed a motion for reconsideration, the trial court granted it. A short time later, the trial court severed the cause against Wolo, making the judgment final.

In their third point of error, the Salazars contend the trial court erred in granting Wolo's motion for summary judgment because the question of [product] use is a fact question which must be determined by the jury. In its motion for summary judgment, Wolo maintained that the Salazars could not maintain a strict products liability claim because "The Club" was not being used for the purpose for which it was manufactured. In support of this contention, Wolo refers us to the *Restatement (Second) of Torts* §402A(1) and case law which say that the *Restatement* imposes liability for products sold "in a defective condition *unreasonably* dangerous to the user or consumer." According to Wolo, "for liability to attach under 402A of the *Restatement*, the product must be in a defective condition which renders its *use* unreasonably dangerous." Wolo also stated in its motion for summary judgment, "Plaintiffs seek to require WOLO to warn of possible consequences which may arise, not from regular or even improper use, but from scenarios completely unrelated to use of the product such as storage."

III. The Role of Consumer Choice

Wolo has not cited us a single case holding that §402A does not apply when the product is not being used and/or is only being stored. For that matter, the Salazars have not cited us a case holding that §402A does cover the storage of a product. Nonetheless, our reading of the case law leads us to conclude that §402A has been applied even when the product was not being used. For example, a court has held that §402A applied to a case in which an electrician repairing a fuse on a transformer was fatally electrocuted. The fuse was not being used for the purpose for which it was designed, it was simply being repaired. [ ] Another court applied §402A when a shopper slipped on liquid leaking from a bottle of liquid soap she put in her shopping cart. The bottle apparently had a small slit in it that allowed the liquid to leak onto the floor. Here again, the soap was not being "used." Nonetheless, §402A was applied. [ ]

Our reading of these and other cases is that the use or nonuse of the product is not the real issue. Instead of looking only at whether the product was being used or not being used, the cases appear to look at whether the product was unreasonably dangerous as designed or marketed, and whether the use was intended or foreseeable. In short, based on the case law we could find, we are unwilling to say as a matter of law, that the Salazars cannot maintain a §402A cause of action for a design defect and marketing defect simply because the Club was not on the steering wheel when the injury occurred. Thus, for the reasons we have stated, we sustain the Salazars' third point of error and reverse and remand the case to the trial court for further proceedings.

NOTES AND QUESTIONS

1. *What must be foreseeable?* As *Salazar* illustrates, a duty defined in terms of foreseeable product use does not fully address the safety problem of concern to products liability. Would it be more accurate to define duty in terms of the foreseeable risks created by the manner in which consumers interact with the product? Consider Jones v. Nordictrack, Inc., 550 S.E.2d 101, 103 (Ga. 2001) ("The 'heart' of a design defect case is the reasonableness of selecting from among alternative product designs and adopting the safest feasible one. Consequently, the appropriate analysis does not depend on the use of the product, as that may be narrowly or broadly defined, but rather includes the consideration of whether the defendant failed to adopt a reasonable alternative design which would have reduced the foreseeable risks of harm presented by the product.").

2. *Foreseeable misuse.* Consumers who foreseeably misuse a product create a foreseeable risk governed by the duty. See RESTATEMENT (THIRD) OF TORTS: PRODUCTS LIABILITY § 2 cmt. p ("Foreseeable product misuse, alteration, and modification must also be considered in deciding whether an alternative design should have been adopted."). The rationale for the duty is made clear by cases involving motor vehicle crashes, which are frequently caused by different types of misuse (inattention, excessive speed, intoxication, and so on). This formulation of the duty, however, raises questions of fairness across consumers. Why should someone who has misused the product be able to recover for the ensuing injuries? These costs are ultimately passed onto all consumers of the product, including those who do

not misuse the product. As these questions suggest, issues pertaining to product misuse will be relevant to other aspects of the legal inquiry, including the apportionment of damages under comparative responsibility.

3. *The standard of foreseeability.* What determines whether a particular risk is foreseeable and ought to factor into the manufacturer's design decision? Foreseeability refers to the types of risks that the manufacturer either knew or should have known about when making the safety decision in question. For example, the "economics and utility" of a particular type of product use determine whether it is foreseeable (consider a driver's decision to exceed the speed limit). Indian Brand Farms, Inc. v. Novartis Crop Protection, Inc., 617 F.3d 207, 226 (3d Cir. 2010) (basing finding of foreseeability in part on practices that "save time and expense"). More obviously, common or well-known forms of product use are foreseeable, as are industry practices. *Id.* The foreseeability standard, however, "does not affix responsibility for future events that are only theoretically, remotely, or just possibly foreseeable.... Rather it applies to those future occurrences that, in light of the general experience within the industry when the product was manufactured, objectively and reasonably could have been anticipated." *Id.* (internal quotations and citation omitted). The foreseeability of risk is also central to the determination of proximate cause, and so we largely defer discussion of the matter until then.

B. Inherent Product Dangers and Categorical Liability

In some cases, the plaintiff claims that the inherent dangers of a product category render the entire category defective, regardless of the particular design. By establishing such an allegation of *categorical liability*, the plaintiff also proves that any design within the category is inherently defective. An allegation of categorical liability would seem to eliminate the requirement that the plaintiff must establish defect by reference to a reasonable alternative design, and several courts "have suggested" as much in dicta. RESTATEMENT (THIRD) OF TORTS: PRODUCTS LIABILITY § 2 cmt. e. Despite appearances to the contrary, an allegation of categorical liability necessarily requires some baseline for evaluating the category in question—the same role played by the requirement of a reasonable alternative design.

For example, in Parish v. Jumpking, Inc., 719 N.W.2d 540 (Iowa 2006), the plaintiff was badly injured while attempting a somersault on a trampoline in his backyard. According to the plaintiff's allegation, "a trampoline is so inherently dangerous that a reasonable design alternative is not available." The court recognized that proof of categorical liability still requires risk-utility analysis, asking whether the entire category of trampolines is "manifestly unreasonable" because it has "low social utility and high degree of danger." The court concluded that the category of trampolines is not inherently defective largely because of its social utility: "Trampolining obviously provides valuable exercise and entertainment." *Id.* at 543-545. Although the court's analysis did not expressly reference a reasonable alternative design, its conclusion still depended on some baseline for comparison. For example, the social utility of trampolining would

III. The Role of Consumer Choice

be substantial if there were no other ways to get cardiovascular exercise. But of course one can get such exercise in many other ways that do not run the risks of trampolining, although these activities also have different entertainment values. Any evaluation of social utility depends on the reasonably available alternatives and how they compare to trampolining. Is this inquiry any different from the one involving an expressly identified reasonable alternative design?

The properties of categorical liability come more fully into focus when the plaintiff attempts to prove that one category is inherently defective because a different category is the reasonable alternative design. A finding of defect on this basis would be no different from a finding of categorical liability, because any particular design within the inherently defective category would also be defective. A plaintiff can prove categorical liability, therefore, by relying on a reasonable alternative design defined by a different category. As compared to other cases involving proof of defect by reference to a reasonable alternative design, do these claims raise any distinctive issues?

DREISONSTOK v. VOLKSWAGENWERK, A.G.
United States Court of Appeals, Fourth Circuit, 1975
489 F.2d 1066

RUSSELL, J. The plaintiff, along with her mother, sues a car manufacturer for so-called "enhanced" injuries sustained by her when the Volkswagen microbus in which she was riding crashed into a telephone pole. The bus hit the pole on its right front. The plaintiff was seated in the center of the seat, next to the driver, with her left leg under her. As a result of the impact, her right leg was caught between the back of the seat and the dashboard of the van and she was apparently thrown forward. She sustained severe injuries to her ankle and femur. She seeks to recover for her injuries, and her mother for medical expenses, from the vehicle manufacturer, contending that the latter was guilty of negligent design in the location of the gearshift in its vehicle and in the want of crashworthiness of its vehicle. The action was [governed by Virginia law and] tried without a jury. The District Court dismissed the claim relating to the gearshift but concluded that the defendant manufacturer had been guilty of negligence in failing to use due care in the design of its vehicle by providing "sufficient energy-absorbing materials or devices or 'crush space,' if you will, so that at 40 miles an hour the integrity of the passenger compartment would not be violated," and that, as a result, the injuries of the plaintiff were enhanced "over and above those injuries which the plaintiff might have incurred." [ ] From judgment entered on the basis of that conclusion in favor of the plaintiff and her mother, the defendants have appealed. We reverse.

In arguing in favor of liability, the appellees stress the foreseeability in this mechanical age of automobile collisions, as affirmed in numerous authorities, and would seemingly deduce from this a duty on the car manufacturer to design its vehicle so as to guard against injury from involvement of its vehicle in any such anticipated collisions. The mere fact, however, that automobile collisions are frequent enough to be foreseeable is not sufficient in and of itself to create a duty on the part of the manufacturer to design its car to withstand such collisions *under any circumstances*. Foreseeability, it has been many times repeated, is not to be equated with duty; it is, after all, but one factor, albeit an important one, to be weighed in determining the issue of duty. [ ]

Applying the foregoing principles to the facts of this particular case, it is clear that there was no violation by the defendant of its duty of ordinary care in the design of its vehicle. The defendant's vehicle, described as "a van type multipurpose vehicle," was of a special type and particular design. This design was uniquely developed in order to provide the owner with the maximum amount of either cargo or passenger space in a vehicle inexpensively priced and of such dimensions as to make possible easy maneuverability. To achieve this, it advanced the driver's seat forward, bringing such seat in close proximity to the front of the vehicle, thereby adding to the cargo or passenger space. This, of course, reduced considerably the space between the exact front of the vehicle and the driver's compartment. All of this was readily discernible to any one using the vehicle; in fact, it was the unique feature of the vehicle. The usefulness of the design is vouchsafed by the popularity of the type. It was of special utility as a van for the transportation of light cargo, as a family camper, as a station wagon and for use by passenger groups too large for the average passenger car. It was a design that had been adopted by other manufacturers, including American. It was a design duplicated in the construction of the large trucking tractors, where there was the same purpose of extending the cargo space without unduly lengthening the tractor-trailer coupling. There was no evidence in the record that there was any practical way of improving the "crashability" of the vehicle that would have been consistent with the peculiar purposes of its design.

The only theory on which the plaintiffs posited their claim of negligent design was, to quote the language of their brief in this Court, that "The 1968 Volkswagen station wagon did not provide the protection for the front seat passengers as did the 'normal' or standard passenger car." The "normal or standard passenger car," to which, under the plaintiffs' argument, the vehicle was required to conform if it was to meet the test of reasonable design, was defined by the plaintiffs on one occasion as "a standard American made vehicle, which is a configuration with the passengers in the middle and the motor in the front" and on another as "a passenger car with an engine in front and with a long hood." And all of their expert testimony was to this point. These experts offered by the plaintiffs concededly made no attempt to compare for safety of design or for any other purpose defendant's special type of vehicle with similar types made by other manufacturers or indicated any way in which safety in such vehicles could have been improved, given the peculiar purpose of the vehicle. In short, the plaintiffs' theory of negligent design and the thrust of all their expert testimony on such point was that, to meet the test of ordinary care in design so as to avoid "unreasonable risk" of injury, the vehicle of the defendant had to conform with the configuration of the standard American passenger car, vintage 1966, *i.e.*, its motor must be in front, not in the rear; its passenger compartment must be "in the middle"; and the space in front of the passenger compartment must be approximately the same as that in a "standard American passenger car." Under this standard, any rear engine car would be "inherently dangerous"; any microbus or front-end tractor—both in wide use in 1968 and now—would be declared

III. The Role of Consumer Choice

"inherently dangerous." To avoid liability for negligent design, no manufacturer could introduce any innovative or unique design, even though reasonably calculated to provide some special advantage such as greater roominess. Such a strait-jacket on design is not imposed [under any of the existing formulations of duty].

If a person purchases a convertible, he cannot expect—and the Court may not impose on the manufacturer the duty to provide him with—the exact kind of protection in a roll-over accident as in the "standard American passenger car." The situation is similar when he purchases a microbus: The distance between the front and the passenger compartment is minified in order to provide additional cargo or passenger space just as the convertible is designed to provide openness. It is entirely impermissible to predicate a conclusion of negligent design simply because a vehicle, having a distinctive purpose, such as the microbus, does not conform to the design of another type of vehicle, such as a standard passenger car, having a different nature and utility.

In determining whether a vehicle has been negligently designed so far as safety is concerned, the special purpose and character of the particular type of vehicle must be considered, and a microbus is no more to be compared with a standard 1966 passenger type car than the convertible is to be compared with a standard hard-top passenger car. Both the plaintiffs and the District Court employed an improper standard in determining whether the defendant had been guilty of negligent design.

Reversed and remanded with directions to the District Court to enter judgment in favor of the appellants-defendants.

NOTES AND QUESTIONS

1. *Categorical liability in practice and theory.* Virginia is one of the few jurisdictions that have not adopted strict products liability, which is why the plaintiffs' claim was based on negligence. But because the negligence standard of reasonable care is functionally equivalent to the risk-utility test, the case has important implications for the jurisprudence of design defects. In rejecting plaintiffs' claim that the category of minibuses is unreasonably dangerous no matter how designed, *Dreisonstok* is fully illustrative of the case law: "[M]ost courts that have considered product-category liability claims have rejected them out of hand. And of the very few decisions that have embraced the notion, each has been reversed by its respective state legislature." James A. Henderson, Jr. & Aaron D. Twerski, *Closing the American Products Liability Frontier: The Rejection of Liability Without Defect*, 66 N.Y.U. L. Rev. 1263, 1329 (1991). Is the rationale for these decisions obvious? "After all, if strict liability attaches to products with unreasonably dangerous features how can it not reasonably attach to unreasonably dangerous products?" Carl T. Bogus, *The Third Revolution in Products Liability*, 72 Chi.-Kent L. Rev. 3, 11 (1996).

2. *Limits of adjudication.* Cases like *Dreisonstok* can be interpreted in two distinct ways. On one view, courts reject categorical liability because they recognize the limits of adjudication and the concomitant need to leave these matters for legislative determination.

To see why, consider how the plaintiffs' negligence claim in *Dreisonstok* would be framed in terms of the risk-utility test. The cost or burden of the alternative design (standard passenger car) equals the total net benefits or inherent utility that consumers derive from the microbus as compared to the conventional motor vehicle design. The risk that would be reduced by the alternative design consists of the total increased risks inherent in the design of the microbus. Hence a standard passenger car would be a reasonable alternative design for any type of microbus if:

$$B_{inherent\ utility\ of\ microbus} < PL_{inherent\ risk\ of\ microbus}$$

Although this allegation of defect can be evaluated with the risk-utility test, the nature of that evaluation is considerably more difficult than it is for defects involving marginal improvements within an existing category (such as the inclusion of airbags within a microbus).

> Quite literally, the question asked in product-category liability cases is: "taking all relevant considerations into account, is the product category in question appropriate for use and consumption in society?" To be answered rationally, the question... would require extended legislative or administrative hearings and investigations. Even if courts attacked these problems incrementally, on a case-by-case basis, it is unrealistic to hope that courts could adjudicate their ways to intelligent, consistent solutions. Bearing in mind the magnitude of the stakes involved—imposing absolute liability might tax [the minibus] off the market—it is hardly surprising that most courts have refused to get involved.

Henderson & Twerski, *supra*, at 1305-1306 (paragraph structure omitted); *see also* Adamo v. Brown & Williamson Tobacco Corp., 900 N.E.2d 966, 969 (N.Y. 2008) ("To hold, as plaintiffs ask, that every sale of regular cigarettes exposes the manufacturer to tort liability would amount to a judicial ban on the product. If regular cigarettes are to be banned, that should be done by legislative bodies, not by courts."). To what extent is this reasoning reflected in *Dreisonstok*?

3. *The satisfaction of consumer expectations.* An alternative interpretation of *Dreisonstok* involves the manner in which the design of the microbus satisfied the safety expectations of the ordinary consumer based on ordinary knowledge common to the community—the "unreasonably dangerous" requirement in §402A. In *Dreisonstok*, the court rejected the allegation of defective design on the ground that the defendant owed no duty to adopt the alternative design advocated by plaintiffs. Recall that the "unreasonably dangerous" requirement also eliminates a defendant's duty for reasons embodied in the patent-defect rule, thereby preventing plaintiffs from using inherent product risks to prove defects. *See* Chapter 5, sections II-III. Can the "unreasonably dangerous" requirement persuasively explain the no-duty holding in *Dreisonstok*?

To evaluate this rationale, recall that the tort duty effectively guarantees that the product contains no manufacturing defects. By relying on the tort

III. The Role of Consumer Choice

duty, the consumer can also assume that each product design within any category is reasonably safe. Together, these two duties guarantee the reasonable safety of all products within any category, enabling the ordinary consumer to focus on the risk-utility comparisons across product categories. In making choices across product categories, the ordinary consumer also benefits from the duty to warn, which guarantees that the product warning provides the ordinary consumer with the material information required for informed safety decisions. *See* Chapter 7. Once the information already held by the ordinary consumer is supplemented by the information provided by the product warning, she presumably is able to make an informed categorical choice.

The ordinary consumer presumably then makes the categorical risk-utility assessment in deciding what type of product to purchase. In making the categorical decision to purchase a microbus rather than a standard passenger car, the consumer concluded

$$B_{inherent\ utility\ of\ microbus} > PL_{inherent\ risk\ of\ microbus}$$

The plaintiff's allegation of defect is based on the same factors, but reaches the opposite conclusion about the risk-utility balancing:

$$B_{inherent\ utility\ of\ microbus} < PL_{inherent\ risk\ of\ microbus}$$

Under these conditions, the patent-defect rule bars recovery for reasons embodied in the "unreasonably dangerous" requirement. *See* Chapter 5 section III (explaining why the consumer's informed risk-utility choice absolves the manufacturer of any responsibility for that same risk-utility decision). Having made an informed choice to purchase a microbus instead of a standard passenger vehicle, the ordinary consumer would not expect the microbus to perform as safely as the conventional passenger design. The microbus in this respect performed as the ordinary consumer would expect based on ordinary knowledge common to the community, and so the product was not "unreasonably dangerous" for purposes of strict products liability. *See* House v. Armour of Am., Inc., 929 P.2d 340, 344 (Utah 1996) (holding that consumer expectations are satisfied by risks that are "inherent in the product, completely within the cognition of a reasonable user, and incapable of being economically alleviated").

This rationale for the absence of duty does not rule out the related concern about the difficulty that courts would face in trying to adjudicate claims of categorical liability. These consumer choices may not satisfy the idealized conditions described above, but the difficulty presumably would be even more pronounced for courts that would have to evaluate both the total net benefits or inherent utility of the product category (presumably known by the consumer) and the inherent categorical risks (a potential source of error for both consumers and courts). So conceptualized, the judicial resistance to categorical liability fosters informed consumer choice across product categories while avoiding the pitfalls of applying the risk-utility test to an entire category.

4. *The approach adopted by the* Restatement (Third). Having rejected the consumer expectations test as embodied in the "unreasonably dangerous" requirement, the *Restatement (Third)* had to adopt a different approach for addressing allegations of categorical liability. Based on cases like *Dreisonstok* in which courts have rejected claims of categorical liability, the *Restatement (Third)* in §2 comment d concludes that "courts generally have concluded that legislatures and administrative agencies can, more appropriately than courts, consider the desirability of commercial distribution of some categories of widely used and consumed, but nevertheless dangerous, products." Consequently, the *Restatement (Third)* requires that for "common and widely distributed products," the plaintiff must prove defect by identifying a reasonable alternative design within the same category, "even though the plaintiff alleges that the entire category of product sold by defendant is so dangerous that it should not have been marketed at all."

To apply this rule, courts must distinguish one product category from another in order to determine whether the plaintiff is arguing that one category (such as standard passenger vehicles) is a reasonable alternative to the allegedly defective category (microbuses). In cases like *Dreisonstok*, the issue is easy to resolve. The same is true for cases in which the plaintiff does not allege that there is any reasonable alternative design at all. *See* Parish v. Jumpking, Inc., 719 N.W.2d 540 (Iowa 2006) (adopting the *Restatement (Third)*'s approach and rejecting the claim that all trampolines are inherently defectively designed because these products are "commonly and widely distributed").

What about cases in which it is not easy to determine whether the plaintiff is trying to use one product category as the reasonable alternative design for another category? According to §2 comment e of the *Restatement (Third)*,

> In large part the problem is one of how the range of relevant alternative designs is described. For example, a toy gun that shoots hard rubber pellets with sufficient velocity to cause injury to children could be found to be defectively designed. Toy guns unlikely to cause injury would constitute reasonable alternatives to the dangerous toy. Thus, toy guns that project ping-pong balls, soft gelatin pellets, or water might be found to be reasonable alternative designs to a toy gun that shoots hard pellets. However, if the realism of the hard-pellet gun, and thus its capacity to cause injury, is sufficiently important to those who purchase and use such products to justify the court's limiting consideration to toy guns that achieve realism by shooting hard pellets, then no reasonable alternative will, by hypothesis, be available.

Is a product category clearly defined by asking whether the attribute in question is "sufficiently important" to consumers? Consider how this approach would apply in the following case.

III. The Role of Consumer Choice

IN RE: DEPUY ORTHOPAEDICS, INC. PINNICALE HIP IMPLANT PRODUCT LIABILITY LITIGATION
United States Court of Appeals, Fifth Circuit, 2018
888 F.3d 753

JERRY E. SMITH, C.J. These appeals and cross-appeal are from the second in a series of bellwether trials from the Pinnacle Hip multidistrict litigation ("MDL"), in which several thousand plaintiffs claim injuries from Pinnacle hips manufactured and sold by DePuy Orthopaedics, Incorporated ("DePuy"). The five plaintiffs in this consolidated action received Pinnacle's metal-on-metal ("MoM") design, suffered complications, and required revision surgery. They sued DePuy and its parent corporation, Johnson & Johnson ("J & J"), and secured a half-billion-dollar jury verdict.

. . .

At trial, plaintiffs claimed DePuy defectively designed and marketed its MoM implant and that J & J was liable, as a "nonmanufacturer seller," for aiding and abetting and for negligent undertaking. At the heart of the claims lay the contested science of modern hip prosthetics, and we begin with the narrow points of agreement. As outlined in both sides' briefs, prosthetic hips are designed to replicate the hip's ball-and-socket function and typically consist of four components: a *stem* inserted into the femur, a femoral *head* attached to the stem (the hip "ball"), a *cup* implanted into the hip socket (the acetabulum), and a metal *liner* that fits into the cup and against which the ball articulates.

The liner can be made from metal, polyethylene, or ceramic. The product at issue is Pinnacle's MoM design, in which both head and liner (Ultamet) are made of metal. Plaintiffs received the Ultamet but, several years later, required revision to metal-on-plastic ("MoP") or metal-on-ceramic designs.

The briefs and trial transcripts present competing histories on hip-implant technology. Both sides agree the story begins in the 1960s with "first-generation" MoMs, the earliest models to achieve widespread use. The parties further agree that these early MoMs carried certain health risks and were quickly displaced by Sir John Charnley's metal-on-plastic ("MoP") design, long described as the industry's "gold standard."

Here, we reach a fork. Defendants suggest that, in the 1990s, MoP was viewed as the industry's "weak link" because of its tendency to cause osteolysis, bone loss in the area surrounding the implant. When the metal ball articulates against the plastic liner, it generates debris from plastic wear that can cause dissolving of the surrounding bone, which, in turn, can require revision surgery. Defendants, along with several other manufacturers, promoted MoMs in the early 2000s to address this Achilles' heel and offer high-activity patients an alternative that would wear out more slowly than plastic.

Plaintiffs meanwhile tell a less rosy story. They claim defendants hastily reintroduced Ultamet to market, without conducting any clinical tests, for the sole purpose of increasing market share. Medical science had long discovered that plastic-wear debris, and the attendant risk of osteolysis, could be reduced considerably if the plastic liner was "cross-linked," that is, sterilized through radiation. Yet, the theory goes, defendants lured surgeons away from cross-linked plastic's proven success through an intricate misinformation campaign of false advertisements and DePuy-authored academic papers.

On the core issue of marketing and design, the parties waged a war of the experts. Plaintiffs elicited testimony from engineers and medical scientists that Ultamet's MoM design was a producing cause of their injuries and that cross-linked MoP was a safer alternative. They also offered evidence that defendants, before bringing the product to market, were made aware of the considerable, and arguably unjustifiable, risks of MoM. Defendants' experts countered that, although MoP might be better suited to older patients, the risk-benefit calculus for younger, more active patients might still favor MoM. Defendants further maintained they had always been forthcoming with treating physicians about this risk calculus. . . .

The jury found for plaintiffs . . . and returned a $502 million verdict. It awarded just $500,000 in economic compensatory damages and $141.5 million in non-economic compensatory damages, and DePuy and J & J were assessed exemplary damages of $120 million and $240 million, respectively. [The trial court denied defendants' motion to vacate the verdict and enter judgment for them as a matter of law (JMOL), a ruling that defendants now appeal along with almost 20 other attacks on the jury verdict.]

JMOL is warranted only if "a reasonable jury would not have a legally sufficient evidentiary basis" to find for the nonmovant. [ ] We review the denial of JMOL *de novo*, applying "the same standard . . . the district court used in first passing on the motion." [ ] DePuy claims plaintiffs' design and marketing claims fail categorically. . . .

To establish a design defect, plaintiffs had to prove that "(1) the product was defectively designed so as to render it unreasonably dangerous; (2) a safer alternative design existed; and (3) the defect was a producing cause of the injury for which the plaintiff seeks recovery." [ ] Texas law defines a safer alternative design as one that "would have prevented or significantly reduced the risk of the claimant's personal injury . . . without substantially impairing the product's utility." Consistent with this risk-utility framework, a plaintiff "must show the safety benefits from [the] proposed design are foreseeably greater than the resulting costs, including any diminished usefulness or diminished safety." [ ] The Texas Supreme Court and intermediate courts have held that a "substantially different product" cannot constitute a safer alternative design. [ ]

. . .

Defendants' first contention—that MoP is a different product from MoM—implicates thorny questions of identity and definition, practically impossible to settle in the abstract. In select instances, nonidentity will be obvious: For example, a proposal to add two additional wheels to a motorcycle or to "fully enclos[e] the cab" of a convertible. [ ] But this case does not lend itself to such straightforward resolution, as the parties dispute how to characterize the relevant product: Is it a "high-stability, low-wear" implant, of which MoP and MoM are merely two alternative iterations? Or is it the discrete MoM design, in which case MoP is a completely different beast? Hewing carefully to guidance provided by Texas courts, we conclude, based on the record, that MoP is a viable alternative design to MoM.

The alternative-design/different-product distinction emerges from two Texas cases, both distinguishable from the present. In Caterpillar Inc. v. Shears, Inc.,

III. The Role of Consumer Choice 219

911 S.W.2d 379 (Tex. 1995), the Texas Supreme Court considered whether a front-end loader with a removable rollover-protection structure ("ROPS") was defectively designed. [ ] The court rejected the plaintiff's proposed alternative—in which the ROPS was rendered non-removable—because the non-removable structure would thwart the ROPS's "intended" function of enabling access to "low clearance areas." [ ] The court refused to "impose liability in such a way as to eliminate whole categories of *useful products* from the market." [ ]

In Brockert v. Wyeth Pharm. Inc., 287 S.W.3d 760 (Tex. App. 2009), the Texas Court of Appeals applied this principle in the pharmaceutical context to conclude that an estrogen-only drug was not a safer alternative design to Prempro, a combination of estrogen and progestin, despite that both served "the same general purpose" of treating menopausal symptoms. [ ] The plaintiff claimed her estrogen-only alternative eliminated the risk of breast cancer introduced by Prempro. [ ] The court rejected the argument, explaining that progestin helped "reduce the incidence of endometrial hyperplasia, [ ], and that the plaintiff had failed to "explain how Prempro could have been modified or improved" without compromising that function, [ ]. Thus plaintiff's theory was rejected as a "categorical attack" on the relevant product.

Doctrinally, it is notable that both *Caterpillar* and *Brockert* rejected a plaintiff's proposed alternative for failing to perform the discrete *kinds* of functions for which the alleged defective was designed—*e.g.*, accessing low clearance areas or reducing incidence of endometrial hyperplasia. But neither case clearly supports the proposition that a slight difference in *degree*—that is, that the alternative does all of the things for which the allegedly defective product was designed, but does not do one of them quite as well—automatically renders the plaintiff's proposed alternative an entirely different product. Though this kind/degree distinction cannot dispel the underlying problem of characterization, it finds direct support in the above caselaw and coheres with the overall structure of Texas design-defect law.

Texas's risk-utility test plainly contemplates that a proposed alternative design might reduce a product's utility—that is, its capacity to perform a function for which it was designed—without rendering the alternative an entirely different product. [ ] If any distinction in degree rendered the proposed alternative a different product as a matter of law, that would effectively moot the substantive balancing test for liability. Where the distinction is one of degree only, the risk-utility framework provides the proper mode of analysis.

Defendants claim to have identified two relevant functional distinctions between MoM and MoP: (a) Metal is more durable than plastic and, therefore, more suitable to younger patients "who often seek not just pain relief but also the ability to resume an active lifestyle"; and (b) metal remedies osteolysis by "*eliminat[ing]* plastic debris entirely." Neither purported distinction, however, shows MoP to be an "entirely different product" under the above, proper framework. [ ] To the first: Durability is a distinction in degree rather than kind. All hip implants—plastic, metal, or ceramic—are designed with the twin goals of minimizing wear debris and affording maximal longevity. Defendants' own promotional materials characterize both their MoP (AltrX LD) and their MoM (Ultamet XL) as "high stability, low wear" hip implants; they never suggest the latter enables the implantee to perform discrete tasks otherwise impossible with the former. *Brockert* and *Caterpillar* are thus distinguishable.

The question then is whether plastic substantially impairs the hip implant's utility along the durability axis. [ ] And though defendants presented evidence that metal was an "attractive option" for younger patients, plaintiffs presented contrary evidence that cross-linked plastic was preferable "a hundred times out of a hundred" and that it outperformed metal along the survivorship dimension by a wide margin. On this evidentiary record, we cannot conclude, as a matter of law, that MoP substantially impairs the implant's utility in terms of stability and rate of wear.

As for reduction of osteolysis, plaintiffs rightly observe that cross-linked polyethylene was intended to do the same thing. The question then is whether the risk of osteolysis from cross-linked MoP substantially reduces MoM's utility, and the record says not. A DePuy executive conceded that MoM, too, can cause osteolysis, and DePuy seems to have known, when it sold Ultamet, that cross-linked plastic significantly reduced the relevant risk. Thus, defendants have not identified a sufficiently discrete functional advantage to prove MoP is fundamentally a different product.

. . .

Defendants draw our attention to several other cases applying the alternative-design/different-product, but none disturbs the above conclusion.

First is Theriot v. Danek Medical, Inc., 168 F.3d 253 (5th Cir. 1999), in which the plaintiff alleged a design defect in pedicle screws used for spinal stability. The plaintiff identified "external neck braces or internal systems that use hooks or wires" as potential alternative designs, [ ], and, applying Louisiana law, we rejected that theory as "tak[ing] issue with the choice of treatment [i.e., the use of pedicle screws] made by Theriot's physician, not with a specific fault of the pedicle screw sold by [the defendant]," [ ]. As the facts of that case make clear, Theriot's proposed alternatives were obviously of a different categorical and structural ilk. Any analogy from that case to this one flatly begs the underlying issue of characterization. [ ]

Defendants also cite Hosford v. BRK Brands, Inc., 223 So.3d 199 (Ala. 2016), holding that ionization smoke alarms and dual-sensor smoke alarms are different products. The plaintiffs argued ionization alarms were defective because they "fail to provide adequate warning" of a fire that "begins as . . . slow [and] smoldering," [ ], and they identified the "more expensive" dual-sensor alarms, which incorporate both ionization and "photoelectric technology," as a safer alternative, [ ]. Applying *Brockert* and *Caterpillar*, the court deemed them two different products, based primarily on the wide disparity in price. [ ] That court feared liability would drive the "less expensive [option] from the market . . . [,] result[ing] in no smoke alarm being present" in homes like the plaintiffs." [ ]

Here, that empirical judgment is obviously inapposite, given that several plaintiffs were revised to the very alternative they propose. None of defendants' cases counsels reversal on our facts.

[The court also upheld the jury verdict finding that the warning for the MoM implant was defective because it "failed to describe with reasonable specificity the source of the wear-debris problem, the conditions to which it gives rise, and the magnitude of the risk." Having upheld the jury verdict on these products liability claims, the court "remanded for a new trial consistent with this opinion" because of the district court's "serious evidentiary errors and [plaintiffs'] counsel's misrepresentations."]

III. The Role of Consumer Choice

NOTES AND QUESTIONS

1. *The new locus of mass-tort actions.* The consolidation of claims in *DePuy* was based on 28 U.S.C. §1407 (2018), which authorizes the Judicial Panel on Multidistrict Litigation to transfer all civil actions that are pending in federal district courts into a single transferee court if those actions involve "one or more common questions of fact." At the conclusion of the consolidated pretrial proceedings, the suits are then remanded to the transferor courts—a process called multidistrict litigation or MDL.

> Once second fiddle to Rule 23 class actions, MDLs . . . are enjoying their star turn. As recently as 1991, MDLs accounted for only about 1 percent of pending civil cases. Now, that figure has swelled to 37 percent, and mass-tort MDLs . . . comprise a staggering 95 percent of that total and encompass some 124,000 individual lawsuits.

Nora Freeman Engstrom, *The Lessons of* Lone Pine, 129 Yale L.J. 1, 6-7 (2019). Most of these consolidated actions involve allegedly defective products. The "asbestos liability litigation, for example, consolidated over 192,000 individual lawsuits." *Id.* at 7. A "bellwether" trial involves one of these cases, presumably selected as a representative case that would provide general information about the merits that might facilitate settlement of the mass-tort claims. *See generally* Elizabeth Chamblee Burch, MASS TORT DEALS (2019).

2. *Identifying different product categories.* In determining whether the plaintiffs' proposed alternative design was based on a different product category, did the court in *DePuy* employ an analysis significantly different from the inquiry adopted by the *Restatement (Third)*? Are you persuaded by the court's rationale for placing the MoM implant within the same category as the MoP implant? Compare Adamo v. Brown & Williamson Tobacco Corp., 900 N.E.2d 966, 969 (N.Y. 2008) (holding that a light cigarette cannot be a reasonable alternative design of a regular cigarette); Niedner v. Ortho-McNeil Pharm., Inc., 58 N.E.3d 1080, 1087 (Mass. App. 2016) ("Here, [plaintiff] contends that oral contraceptives, which are taken daily, are a feasible and safer alternative design to the patch, which is applied once per week for three weeks, with the fourth week being patch-free. While both products are hormonal contraceptives that prevent pregnancy, the difference in the drug delivery method, each of which has its own advantages and disadvantages, makes the pill fundamentally different from the patch.").

To be sure, the court in *DePuy* simply held that the issue cannot be decided as a matter of law and requires jury resolution. Faced with similarly difficult issues of whether the plaintiff's proposed design is in the same category as the allegedly defective product, other courts have taken this same approach. *E.g.*, In Re: Davol, Inc./C.R. Bard, Inc., Polypropylene Hernia Mesh Products Liability Litigation, 2020 WL 5223363 (S.D. Ohio 2020) (reaching the same conclusion and citing to other cases that have done the same). What type of instructions would be required to adequately apprise the jury of the factors it must consider to resolve this issue?

3. *Reframing the inquiry in terms of consumer expectations.* To explain why a compact automobile is not defectively designed when considered in

relation to a full-sized vehicle, the *Restatement (Third)* does not conclude that the proof of defect inappropriately attempts to compare one category (full-sized vehicles) with another (compacts). It instead asserts that the costs of the proposed redesign "are unacceptably great," and "eliminating smaller vehicles from the market would unduly restrict the range of consumer choice among automobile designs." §2 cmt. f, illus. 9. Why are the costs of redesign "unacceptably great" as a matter of law, and why does consumer choice limit liability if "consumer expectations do not define an independent standard for judging the defectiveness of product designs"? *Id.* cmt. g. By resorting to this type of reasoning, does the *Restatement (Third)* implicitly recognize the difficulty of determining whether the proposed alternative design is in a category different from the allegedly defective product?

These issues are usefully considered in relation to *DePuy*. As the court held, the warning did not adequately describe the risks of the MoM implant. Due to this warning defect, consumers could not make an informed risk-utility comparison of that design with the MoP design. Hence the logic of the patent-defect rule does not apply. But if the warning had been adequate, how would the design defect claim be evaluated under the implied warranty? Notice that the defendant made both the MoM and MoP versions of the implant available to consumers (branded, respectively, as Ultamet XL and AltrX LD). An adequate warning would have enabled consumers to make an informed risk-utility decision in selecting one design over the other, thereby barring recovery for the reasons embodied in the patent-defect rule and fully illustrated by *Dreisonstok*. (Can you see why? First identify the consumer's risk-utility choice to purchase the MoM implant rather than the MoP implant, and then compare that decision to the allegation of defective design.) Insofar as the finding of defective design depends on the lack of informed consumer choice about the risk-utility properties of the MoM implant, does the true source of liability in *DePuy* involve the defective warning rather than the design?

More generally, consider all the cases discussed by the court in *DePuy*. Assuming that the warning was adequate in those cases, could the ruling in each case be explained by the logic of the patent-defect rule? Would that approach be easier than one that attempts to distinguish one product "category" from another?

LINEGAR v. ARMOUR OF AMERICA
United States Court of Appeals, Eighth Circuit, 1990
909 F.2d 1150

BOWMAN, J. Armour of America, Inc. (Armour) appeals a judgment based on a jury verdict in favor of the widow and children of Jimmy Linegar, a Missouri State Highway Patrol trooper who was killed in the line of duty. The jury found that the bullet-resistant vest manufactured by Armour and worn by Linegar at the time of the murder was defectively designed, and it awarded his family $1.5 million in damages. We reverse.

III. The Role of Consumer Choice

On April 15, 1985, as part of a routine traffic check, Linegar stopped a van with Nevada license plates near Branson, Missouri. The van's driver produced an Oregon operator's license bearing the name Matthew Mark Samuels. Linegar ascertained from the Patrol dispatcher that the name was an alias for David Tate, for whom there was an outstanding warrant on a weapons charge. Linegar did not believe the driver matched the description the dispatcher gave him for Tate, so he decided to investigate further.

A fellow trooper, Allen Hines, who was working the spot check with Linegar, then approached the passenger's side of the van while Linegar approached the driver's side. After a moment of questioning, Linegar asked the driver to step out of the van. The driver, who was in fact David Tate, brandished an automatic weapon and fired at the troopers first from inside and then from outside the van. By the time Tate stopped firing, Hines had been wounded by three shots and Linegar, whose body had been penetrated by six bullets, lay dead or dying. None of the shots that hit the contour-style, concealable protective vest Linegar was wearing — there were five such shots — penetrated the vest or caused injury. The wounds Linegar suffered all were caused by shots that struck parts of his body not protected by the vest.

The Missouri State Highway Patrol issued the vest to Linegar when he joined the Patrol in 1981. The vest was one of a lot of various sizes of the same style vest the Patrol purchased in 1979 directly from Armour. The contour style was one of several different styles then on the market. It provided more protection to the sides of the body than the style featuring rectangular panels in front and back, but not as much protection as a wrap-around style. The front and back panels of the contour vest, held together with Velcro closures under the arms, did not meet at the sides of the wearer's body, leaving an area along the sides of the body under the arms exposed when the vest was worn. This feature of the vest was obvious to the Patrol when it selected this vest as standard issue for its troopers and could only have been obvious to any trooper who chose to wear it. The bullet that proved fatal to Linegar entered between his seventh and eighth ribs, approximately three-and-one-fourth inches down from his armpit, and pierced his heart.

The theory upon which Linegar's widow and children sought and won recovery from Armour was strict liability in tort based on a design defect in the vest. Because we hold that, as a matter of law, the evidence was insufficient to present a submissible products liability case, we need not and do not reach any of Armour's other claims of error. We conclude that, as a matter of law, the contour vest Trooper Linegar was wearing when he was murdered was not defective and unreasonably dangerous.

Under the Missouri law of strict liability in tort for defective design, before a plaintiff can recover from the seller or manufacturer he must show "that the design renders the product unreasonably dangerous." [ ] Ordinarily, that will be a jury question, and the concept of unreasonable danger, which is determinative of whether a product is defective in a design case, is presented to the jury as an ultimate issue without further definition, as it was here. In this case, however, there was simply no evidence that the vest's design made it unreasonably dangerous, and the District Court should have declared that, as a matter of law, the vest was not defective, and directed a verdict or granted judgment for Armour notwithstanding the verdict.

The Missouri cases leave the meaning of the phrase "unreasonably dangerous" largely a matter of common sense, the court's or the jury's. The Missouri Supreme Court has stated, however, that a product is defectively designed if it "creates an unreasonable risk of danger to the consumer or user when put to normal use." [ ] Among the factors to be considered are "the conditions and circumstances that will foreseeably attend the use of the product." [ ] The conditions under which a bullet-resistant vest will be called upon to perform its intended function most assuredly will be dangerous, indeed life-threatening, and Armour surely knew that. It defies logic, however, to suggest that Armour reasonably should have anticipated that anyone would wear its vest for protection of areas of the body that the vest obviously did not cover.

Courts applying Missouri law also have applied what has become known as the "consumer expectation" test for unreasonable dangerousness: "The article sold must be dangerous to an extent beyond that which would be contemplated by the ordinary consumer who purchases it, with the ordinary knowledge common to the community as to its characteristics." RESTATEMENT (SECOND) OF TORTS §402A comment i (1965).

The consumer expectation test focuses attention on the vest's wearer rather than on its manufacturer. The inherent limitations in the amount of coverage offered by Armour's contour vest were obvious to this Court, observing a demonstration from the bench during oral argument, as they would be to anyone with ordinary knowledge, most especially the vest's wearer. A person wearing the vest would no more expect to be shielded from a shot taken under the arm than he would expect the vest to deflect bullets aimed at his head or neck or lower abdomen or any other area not covered by the vest.

Plaintiff insists that the user's expectations should not be considered by us, since doing so would effectively afford Armour the benefit of the "open and obvious" defense, inappropriate, they say, in a defective design strict products liability action. We disagree. Although not conclusive, "the obviousness of a defect or danger is material to the issue whether a product is 'unreasonably dangerous.'" [ ] Here, the vest's purported dangerous defect—its lack of closure at the sides—could not have been more open and obvious. An otherwise completely effective protective vest cannot be regarded as dangerous, much less unreasonably so, simply because it leaves some parts of the body obviously exposed.

We have no difficulty in concluding as a matter of law that the product at issue here was neither defective nor unreasonably dangerous. Trooper Linegar's protective vest performed precisely as expected and stopped all of the bullets that hit it. No part of the vest nor any malfunction of the vest caused Linegar's injuries. The vest was designed to prevent the penetration of bullets where there was coverage, and it did so; the amount of coverage was the buyer's choice. The Missouri Highway Patrol could have chosen to buy, and Armour could have sold the Patrol, a vest with more coverage; no one contests that. But it is not the place of courts or juries to set specifications as to the parts of the body a bullet-resistant garment must cover. A manufacturer is not obliged to market only one version of a product, that being the very safest design possible. If that were so, automobile manufacturers could not offer consumers sports cars, convertibles, jeeps, or compact cars. All boaters would have to buy full life vests instead of choosing a ski belt or even a flotation cushion. Personal safety devices, in

III. The Role of Consumer Choice 225

particular, require personal choices, and it is beyond the province of courts and juries to act as legislators and preordain those choices.

In this case, there obviously were trade-offs to be made. A contour vest like the one here in question permits the wearer more flexibility and mobility and allows better heat dissipation and sweat evaporation, and thus is more likely to be worn than a more confining vest. It is less expensive than styles of vests providing more complete coverage. If manufacturers like Armour are threatened with economically devastating litigation if they market any vest style except that offering maximum coverage, they may decide, since one can always argue that more coverage is possible, to get out of the business altogether. Or they may continue to market the vest style that, according to the latest lawsuit, affords the "best" coverage. Officers who find the "safest" style confining or uncomfortable will either wear it at risk to their mobility or opt not to wear it at all. Law enforcement agencies trying to work within the confines of a budget may be forced to purchase fewer vests or none at all. How "safe" are those possibilities? "The core concern in strict tort liability law is safety." [ ] We are firmly convinced that to allow this verdict to stand would run counter to the law's purpose of promoting the development of safe and useful products, and would have an especially pernicious effect on the development and marketing of equipment designed to make the always-dangerous work of law enforcement officers a little safer.

The death of Jimmy Linegar by the hand of a depraved killer was a tragic event. We keenly feel the loss that this young trooper's family has suffered, and our sympathies go out to them. But we cannot allow recovery from a blameless defendant on the basis of sympathy for the plaintiffs. To hold Armour liable for Linegar's death would cast it in the role of insurer for anyone shot while wearing an Armour vest, regardless of whether any shots penetrated the vest. That a manufacturer may be cast in such a role has been soundly rejected by courts applying Missouri law.

The judgment of the District Court is reversed. The District Court shall enter a final judgment in favor of Armour.

NOTES AND QUESTIONS

1. *What about categorical liability?* How would *Linegar* be resolved under the *Restatement (Third)*, which prevents the plaintiff from trying to prove defect by reference to a reasonable alternative design that is in a product category different from the allegedly defective design? Is a bullet-resistant contour-style vest in a category different from a bullet-resistant wrap-around vest, or are both within the same category of bullet-resistant vests? For discussion of the difficulties of defining product categories in the manner proposed by the *Restatement (Third)*, see Richard L. Cupp, Jr., *Defining the Boundaries of "Alternative Design" Under the* Restatement (Third) *of Torts: The Nature and Role of Substitute Products in Design Defect Analysis*, 63 Tenn. L. Rev. 329 (1996).

Instead of addressing these issues, the *Restatement (Third)* avoids them by relying on consumer choice. After analyzing an illustration based on *Linegar*, the *Restatement (Third)* concludes that "the availability of a wrap-around vest does not render defective the vest that provides only front-and-back coverage. Although the wrap-around design is somewhat safer, it is also more costly to buy and use." Because "the differences in advantages and disadvantages are sufficiently understood by consumers," the greater protection afforded by "the wrap-around feature does not render the front-and-back design not reasonably safe. To subject sellers to liability based on that design would unduly restrict the range of consumer choice among products." §2 cmt. f, Illus. 10. Rather than foreclosing liability based on the plaintiff's inappropriate attempt to prove defect by using one product category (wrap-around vests) as a reasonable alternative design for another category (front-and-back coverage vests), the *Restatement (Third)* invokes consumer choice. Why rely on consumer choice in this case but not others like *DePuy* in which courts must figure out whether the proposed reasonable alternative design is in the right product "category"?

Lacking clear guidance on the relation between categorical liability and the role of consumer choice, courts can effectively apply categorical liability without asking whether doing so is contrary to informed consumer expectations and thereby unduly restricts consumer choice. In Eghnayem v. Boston Scientific Corp., 873 F.3d 1304, 1320 (11th Cir. 2017), the plaintiff claimed that defendant's transvaginal mesh implant was defective because the design "increased both the potential for degradation and the difficulty for removal." The plaintiff did not show that the implant could be reasonably redesigned in a manner that would reduce these risks, but the court upheld the jury verdict for plaintiff because the jury could have reasonably concluded that "these [inherent] risks outweighed the [implant's inherent] benefits"—a ruling of categorical liability. *See also* Campbell v. Boston Scientific Corp., 882 F.3d 70, 79 (4th Cir. 2018) (affirming jury verdict that the same type of transvaginal mesh implant made by a different manufacturer was defectively designed for these same reasons and observing that plaintiffs "were not necessarily required to demonstrate that [defendant's mesh implant] was different from other [implants]. It is possible for an entire class of products to suffer from the same or similar design defects"). In affirming the jury verdicts of defect, the courts in *Eghnayem* and *Campbell* never used the term "choice."

2. *Consumer choice and the patent-defect rule.* By relying on the satisfaction of consumer expectations to limit liability, did the court in *Linegar* inappropriately bar recovery simply because the danger was open and obvious? Or did it instead properly apply the patent-defect rule? To address these questions, we need to identify the risk-utility decision made by the ordinary consumer in choosing a contour-style vest instead of the wrap-around style. As the court observed, the wrap-around style offers greater coverage that would obviously reduce the risk of gunshot wound (denoted $PL_{wrap\text{-}around\ vest}$), but the wrap-around vest is also more costly in terms of decreased mobility, comfort, and its higher price (a total cost or burden denoted $B_{wrap\text{-}around\ vest}$). In choosing to purchase the contour-style vest instead of the wrap-around vest, the consumer made an informed decision that the added burden of using the wrap-around vest exceeds the extent to which it would reduce risk relative to the contour-style vest:

$$B_{wrap\text{-}around\ vest} > PL_{wrap\text{-}around\ vest}$$

III. The Role of Consumer Choice

The allegation of defect, by contrast, would be successful only if the plaintiff could prove that the added burden of using the wrap-around vest is less than the extent to which it would reduce risk as compared to the contour-style vest:

$$B_{wrap-around\ vest} < PL_{wrap-around\ vest}$$

The consumer's choice to purchase the contour-style vest is based on the same risk-utility factors implicated by the allegation of defect. For reasons established by the patent-defect rule, a decision of this type absolves the seller of responsibility for that particular safety decision—the product in this respect is not "unreasonably dangerous" as defined by §402A.

3. *Categorical liability, inherent dangers, and the element of duty.* Inherent product risks, when combined with inherent utility, are constitutive of a product category. For motor vehicles, the inherent risks of a microbus differ from the inherent risks of an ordinary passenger vehicle, a difference attributable to the different utilities that inhere in the two categories. Consequently, the concern about categorical liability is simply the concern that liability for defective product designs should not be based on inherent product risks. For reasons discussed in Chapter 5, section III, this limitation of liability is embodied in the "unreasonably dangerous" requirement of §402A.

> To the scholars crafting the doctrine of strict products liability in tort in the early 1960s, particularly as they molded and debated §402A of the *Restatement Second, Torts*, it was clear that manufacturers of unavoidably hazardous products could only be expected to ensure that their products were free of production defects and contained warnings of hidden dangers they could foresee. To avoid the possibility that the new "strict liability" doctrine might be stretched further, to prevent it from being misconstrued as permitting a challenge to the *design* of products possessing such inherent dangers, Dean Prosser and the [American Law Institute] explicitly excluded such an obligation from the new strict tort regime. In particular, comments *i, j,* and *k* to §402A of the *Restatement Second, Torts* made clear that the only duties of manufacturers of inherently dangerous products—such as alcoholic beverages, prescription drugs, cigarettes, certain foods, and other products whose dangers cannot be designed away—are to avoid manufacturing defects and to warn consumers of hidden dangers.

David G. Owen & Mary J. Davis, 1 OWEN & DAVIS ON PRODUCTS LIABILITY §10:7 (4th ed. 2014 & 2020 update). The limitation of liability for inherent product risks is nothing other than a rule against categorical liability, justified by the manner in which informed consumer choice negates the tort duty and renders the product not "unreasonably dangerous" in this respect.

When applied in this manner,

> the "unreasonably dangerous" requirement serves the useful function of balancing safety considerations against a policy which favors product diversity and consumer choice. Automobiles, and numerous other types of products, vary considerably in their safety features

and characteristics. However, the law does not require that manufacturers produce only the safest product feasible in order to avoid being exposed to liability. Rather it requires them to avoid placing on the market products that are rendered "unreasonably dangerous" because of a defect in design or manufacture.

Camacho v. Honda Motor Co., 701 P.2d 628, 632 (Col. App. 1985), *rev'd on other grounds*, 741 P.2d 1240 (Col. 1987).

4. *Is there any role for categorical liability?* Only a few cases have actually imposed categorical liability on the defendant, and many were subsequently overruled by legislation. Nevertheless, "several courts have suggested in dictum that in rare instances where the product has low social utility and very high risk that they might be willing to impose liability without proof of a reasonable alternative design." RESTATEMENT (THIRD) OF TORTS: PRODUCTS LIABILITY §2 Rptrs' N. cmt. e. Consequently, the *Restatement (Third)* limits categorical liability to "manifestly unreasonable" products with low social utility and high risk that are not "commonly and widely distributed." *Id.* §2 cmt. e.

If informed consumer choice—the satisfaction of consumer expectations based on ordinary knowledge common to the community—is a sufficient reason for limiting liability, why does it matter whether the product is manifestly unreasonable and not widely distributed? How could *any* application of categorical liability be squared with the value of informed consumer choice?

The analysis so far has been confined to the *consumer*, a concept including the buyer and other users of the product. Deference to consumer choice is not necessarily compelling when the product threatens injury to complete strangers (or "bystanders" within the parlance of products liability). Consumers who make safety decisions by reference to their own interests can make product choices that are unreasonably dangerous for others. In these cases, the value of consumer choice does not justify a limitation of liability, explaining why courts have recognized that categorical liability could be appropriate if the product has "low social value" (for the consumer) that is outweighed by the "high degree of danger" (largely faced by bystanders). We consider this issue more extensively in Chapter 16.

C. Optional Safety Equipment

Whether consumer choice can limit the seller's liability is the central issue posed by cases involving optional safety equipment. In reading the next case, consider whether the role of consumer choice is analytically different from its role in cases of categorical liability.

SCARANGELLA v. THOMAS BUILT BUSES, INC.
Court of Appeals of New York, 1999
717 N.E.2d 679

LEVINE, J. A school bus being operated in reverse by a coemployee struck and severely injured plaintiff Concetta Scarangella, a school bus driver for

III. The Role of Consumer Choice

third-party defendant Huntington Coach Corp., Inc. The accident occurred in Huntington's bus parking yard on September 26, 1988. The vehicle was one of 10 new school buses that defendant Thomas Built Buses, Inc., sold Huntington in 1988. At that time, Thomas offered buyers as an optional safety feature a back-up alarm that would automatically sound when a driver shifted the bus into reverse gear, but Huntington chose not to purchase this optional equipment.

After plaintiff and her husband commenced this action for negligence, breach of warranty and products liability, Thomas made a motion to preclude plaintiff from submitting to the jury her claim that the lack of a back-up alarm was a design defect. In support of its motion, Thomas submitted a memorandum of law and excerpts from the deposition of Huntington's president and chief operating officer, Kevin Clifford.

According to Clifford's deposition testimony, Huntington owned and operated 190 school buses and had 300 employees. Clifford had worked for the company for over 30 years and had been a president of the New York State School Bus Owners Association. Clifford explained that he was aware that the back-up alarms were available but made a considered decision not to purchase them. He opted against the alarm because "it screams" when a bus is put in reverse gear, and he intended to park the buses at a bus yard in the middle of a residential neighborhood where his company had been experiencing problems with neighbors concerning noise pollution. When the buses were being parked in the bus yard, there "had to be a tremendous amount of backing up," and Clifford believed it was unnecessary to equip all 100 buses in the lot with the "screaming" alarms. Instead, Clifford instructed the drivers to be cautious and to use the bus's ordinary horn before backing up.

In response to Thomas's motion, plaintiff proffered no specific evidence. She based her design defect claim entirely on the proposition that, because a school bus driver always has a substantial blind spot when operating the vehicle in reverse, a school bus must invariably be equipped with an automatically engaged back-up alarm. [The Trial Court] concluded that there was no triable issue of fact on this design defect claim. It thus granted defendant's motion to preclude plaintiff from presenting any evidence on the issue to the jury.

Plaintiff proceeded to trial on the theory that the bus was defectively designed because it did not have proper mirrors. At the conclusion of plaintiff's case, the Trial Judge directed a verdict for defendant and dismissed the complaint. The Appellate Division affirmed.

The only issue before us is whether, based upon the submissions on the motion to preclude, plaintiff was properly barred from presenting to a jury her claim that the bus was defectively designed by Thomas because it did not incorporate the back-up alarm as standard equipment. Because we conclude that in the procedural context framed by the parties the preclusion was not erroneous as a matter of law, we affirm.

Biss v. Tenneco, Inc., 64 A.D.2d 204 (N.Y. App. Div. 4th Dep't 1978), and Rainbow v. Elia Bldg. Co., 79 A.D.2d 287 (N.Y. App. Div. 4th Dep't 1981), applied New York's design defect jurisprudence to fact patterns in which the buyer of a product elected not to purchase an optional safety device to accompany it. *Biss* held that a manufacturer of a loader vehicle could not be found liable for negligent design where an employee of the purchaser was injured due to the absence of an optional roll-over protection structure the purchaser chose not to have included when the vehicle was acquired. The opinion reasoned that

> defendants had fulfilled their duty to exercise reasonable skill and care in designing the product as a matter of law when they advised the purchaser that an appropriate safety structure . . . was available. . . . If knowledge of available safety options is brought home to the purchaser, the duty to exercise reasonable care in selecting those appropriate to the intended use rests upon him. He is the party in the best position *to exercise an intelligent judgment to make the trade-off between cost and function,* and it is he who should bear the responsibility if the decision on optional safety equipment presents an unreasonable risk to users.

In *Rainbow*, plaintiff claimed that a motorcycle without an optional safety feature, side crash bars, was unreasonably dangerous. The plaintiff was "an *experienced motorcyclist* [who] . . . had been a *successful motorcycle racer* for many years [and] . . . had removed crash bars mounted on a previously owned motorcycle." The Court dismissed plaintiff's complaint, holding that the buyer "was in the best position to exercise an intelligent judgment in making the trade-off between cost and function and thus to decide whether crash bars were reasonably necessary on his motorcycle for his purposes." [ ]

In contrast, in Rosado v. Proctor & Schwartz, 66 N.Y.2d 21 (1985), a manufacturer who sold a textile machine with completely exposed massive gears, chains and pulleys, with no safety disconnect switches, could not escape responsibility for a user's injury by inserting boilerplate language in its sales contract that required the buyer to install any necessary safety devices. In contrast to the instant case, the manufacturer there did not give the buyer the choice of a machine that was already equipped with the safety equipment. We held that

> where, as here, *the manufacturer is in the best position to know the dangers inherent in its product,* and the *dangers do not vary depending on jobsite,* it is also in the best position to determine what safety devices should be employed. . . . To allow a manufacturer . . . which sells a product . . . with no safety devices, to shift the ultimate duty of care to others through boilerplate language in a sales contract, would erode the economic incentive manufacturers have to maintain safety and give sanction to the marketing of dangerous, stripped down, machines.

We can thus distill some governing principles for cases where a plaintiff claims that a product without an optional safety feature is defectively designed because the equipment was not standard. The product is not defective where the evidence and reasonable inferences therefrom show that: (1) the buyer is thoroughly knowledgeable regarding the product and its use and is actually aware that the safety feature is available; (2) there exist normal circumstances of use in which the product is not unreasonably dangerous without the optional equipment; and (3) the buyer is in a position, given the range of uses of the product, to balance the benefits and the risks of not having the safety device in the specifically contemplated circumstances of the buyer's use of the product. In such a case, the buyer, not the manufacturer, is in the superior position to make the risk-utility assessment, and a well-considered decision by the buyer to dispense with the optional safety equipment will excuse the manufacturer from

III. The Role of Consumer Choice 231

liability. When the factors are not present, there is no justification for departure from the accepted rationale imposing strict liability upon the manufacturer because it "is in the superior position to discover any design defects." [ ]

Applying the foregoing principles, plaintiff failed to make a prima facie showing that the lack of a back-up alarm on the bus that injured her was a design defect. First, Huntington was a highly knowledgeable consumer. Huntington and its management had owned and operated school buses serving a number of school districts for decades and certainly were aware that a bus driver had a blind spot when a bus was operated in reverse. It is also undisputed that when it purchased the bus, Huntington knew that the back-up alarm was available. The product was in the exact condition contemplated and selected by Huntington at the time of purchase.

Second, the uncontradicted evidence showed that, in the actual circumstances of the operation of the buses in reverse by Huntington, the risk of harm from the absence of a back-up alarm was not substantial. In his pretrial deposition, Huntington's president indicated that the only significant incidence of operating buses in reverse was in positioning buses in and backing them out of the yard. Plaintiff submitted no evidence regarding Huntington buses backing up under any other circumstances, e.g., while transporting children to and from school or outside the parking yard. Indeed, at the trial plaintiff herself testified that, because of the blind spot, Huntington drivers were instructed as part of their training not to operate buses in reverse except in the yard. Drivers were also instructed to exercise caution and sound their regular horns when backing up.

Thus, the individuals at risk from the absence of back-up alarm equipment on Huntington buses were almost exclusively its drivers and other employees at its parking yard. It was readily inferable from the only evidence submitted on the motion that these persons at risk, including plaintiff, were fully aware of a bus driver's blind spot in backing up a bus and the resultant hazard, and could be expected to exercise special care whenever positioned in proximity to the rear of any bus that was idling or moving in reverse in the yard. Again, plaintiff made no factual showing to the contrary that school children, other pedestrians or occupants of other vehicles were exposed to any hazards of the operation of Huntington buses in reverse, without back-up alarms.

Third, Huntington was in a position to balance the benefits and the dangers of not having the safety device, given the contemplated use of the bus. After weighing the risks against the costs, Huntington made a considered decision not to buy the back-up alarm. Only Huntington knew how it would instruct and train its drivers and when and how the buses would be operated in reverse. Huntington and not Thomas was in a position to assess the efficacy of alternative safety measures in its operational rules and training of drivers. The buyer had the ability to understand and weigh the significance of costs associated with noise pollution and neighborhood relations, given the particular suburban location of the parking lot, against the anticipated, foreseeable risks of operating buses in a parking lot without a back-up alarm device or safeguard.

As shown above, plaintiff was confronted with proof that brought this case within the *Biss-Rainbow* three-factor analysis of the sophisticated consumer's knowledge of the safety feature, the existence of reasonably safe circumstances of normal use and the superior vantage point of the buyer in risk-utility balancing with respect to its own individualized use of the product. Plaintiff failed to submit, in opposition to the preclusion motion, any proof negating any of these three factors. Thus, plaintiff created no triable issues for the jury in connection with her claim that the absence of a back-up alarm was a design defect, and preclusion was warranted here.

Accordingly, the order of the Appellate Division should be affirmed, with costs.

NOTES AND QUESTIONS

1. *The "optional equipment doctrine."* The rule that a "manufacturer is, under certain circumstances, not negligent if a purchaser fails to buy optional safety equipment that would have prevented the accident" originated in the line of New York cases that the court in *Scarangella* synthesized. *See* Parks v. Ariens Co., 829 F.3d 655, 657-658 (8th Cir. 2016) (describing this line of cases). A "variety of courts have since followed some variation of this 'optional equipment doctrine.'" *Id.* at 658-659 ("The Iowa Supreme Court has not yet considered the optional equipment doctrine," but "policy reasons" and "the popularity of the doctrine lead us to conclude that the court would adopt it.").

2. *Categorical liability and optional safety equipment.* The "optional equipment doctrine" does not implicate any question of categorical liability—a bus without or without a back-up alarm is still a bus. Although the rules governing these two types of claims have different doctrinal labels, is the substantive rationale for denying liability with respect to optional safety features comparable to the reasons why courts have roundly rejected categorical liability? As *Scarangella* illustrates, the seller makes a safety feature optional when the value of that option varies for different types of consumers. The same point is illustrated by the different types of bullet-resistant vests at issue in *Linegar* and the different types of motor vehicles at issue in *Dreisonstok*. When the value of a safety option differs across consumers, each one presumably makes some sort of categorical risk-utility decision when considering whether to purchase one type of product rather than another (micribus or standard passenger vehicle?). Having decided which category of product to purchase, the ordinary consumer is unlikely to consider the entire range of safety issues implicated by that decision. (Is the steering wheel appropriately configured, the seat belts of adequate strength, and so on?) Resolving all these decisions is simply too time consuming. For these types of discrete or "noncategorical" safety decisions, the manufacturer is in the best position to make the risk-utility decision. But if the particular safety choice is brought to the consumer's attention as in the case of optional safety equipment, then the consumer is in the best position to make the risk-utility decision, assuming that he or she is otherwise adequately informed of the risk-utility factors. The liability inquiry in these cases accordingly depends on the question of whether the ordinary consumer was able to make an informed risk-utility choice, thereby eliminating the seller's duty *with respect to that identical risk-utility decision.* In this respect, the consumer's choice of optional safety features is wholly analogous to the choice of product categories—the denial of liability in both contexts is based on the logic of the patent-defect rule.

III. The Role of Consumer Choice

3. *Availability of the safety option.* Does the rationale for limiting liability with respect to optional safety equipment depend on whether the option was actually available somewhere in the marketplace, or must the optional equipment be reasonably available to the ordinary consumer? Consider Wagner v. International Harvester Co., 611 F.2d 224, 231 (8th Cir. 1979) (concluding that although defendant offered the optional safety equipment, doing so did not foreclose the allegation of defective design because the nature of defendant's marketing of the option made "it . . . unrealistic to expect" that a purchaser of the product would have been aware of that option).

Does it matter whether the safety feature was available for other products within the same category, but not for the particular brand that is allegedly defective for not incorporating that feature? In Camacho v. Honda Motor Co., Ltd., 741 P.2d 1240 (Colo. 1987), plaintiff was injured in a motorcycle crash and claimed that the design was defective for not incorporating crash bars to protect the driver's legs. To prove that the design was feasible or within the state of the art (discussed in the next section), the plaintiff showed that several other manufacturers offered the crash bars as optional safety equipment. In reversing the rulings by the lower courts that dismissed the claim based on the patent-danger rule, the court rejected the consumer expectations test and adopted the risk-utility test. *Id.* at 1245-1248. Do consumer expectations necessarily bar recovery on these facts?

Resolution of this issue reveals one important difference between a claim of categorical liability and one involving optional safety equipment. If the entire product category is defective regardless of design, then the particular attributes of any brand within the category do not factor into the risk-utility calculus—each brand is inherently defective. By contrast, an allegation involving optional safety equipment takes place within a product category that is not inherently defective, making the particular attributes of any brand relevant to the risk-utility decision.

In deciding to purchase the motorcycle at issue in *Camacho*, the plaintiff decided that this particular brand more closely matched his preferences than the other competing brands. Indeed, differences of this type are advertised and promoted by manufacturers seeking to gain a competitive advantage within the market. Even if the plaintiff wanted crash bars because of the extent to which they reduce risk ($PL_{crash\,bar}$), he could only get them by choosing a less desirable brand, in which case he would have lost the added benefit of his preferred choice ($B_{inferior\,brand}$). His choice of the preferred brand accordingly involves a risk-utility decision:

$$B_{inferior\,brand} > PL_{crash\,bar}$$

The allegation of defect, by contrast, is that the cost or burden of the crash bar is less than the risk that would thereby be eliminated:

$$B_{crash\,bar} < PL_{crash\,bar}$$

As a comparison of these two risk-utility decisions reveals, the plaintiff's choice to purchase the brand as marketed by the defendant did not absolve the defendant from the obligation to install the crash bars as required by the risk-utility test. The patent danger itself is not a sufficient reason for dismissing the plaintiff's claim because the logic of the patent-defect rule does not apply. *See* Chapter 5, section II. By contrast, if the defendant manufacturer had made the crash bars an optional safety feature for the brand selected by the plaintiff, who then decided not to purchase them, recovery would be barred under the patent-defect rule. Can you explain why?

Consider how this reasoning applies to cases in which a component-part supplier offers optional safety equipment to the manufacturer of the final product. If the manufacturer rejects that option, should the component-part supplier be obligated to make that option available to the consumer instead?

> When safety features are offered, the final manufacturer is in the best position to decide which features are necessary—and which are not—for the environment in which the integrated product will be used. *See* Parks v. Ariens Co., 829 F.3d 655, 657-58 (8th Cir. 2016) (collecting cases). And so, we hold that . . . a component-part manufacturer has no duty to include optional safety features that were offered to, and rejected by, the final manufacturer.

Brewer v. Paccar, Inc., 124 N.E.3d 616, 625 (Ind. 2019). By rejecting the optional safety feature, the manufacturer does not face the increased risk of physical injury. Should this factor affect the analysis?

4. *Who faces the risk?* In the *Camacho* case discussed in the preceding note, the plaintiff purchased and used the motorcycle. In *Scarangella*, by contrast, the plaintiff's employer was the purchaser who made the risk-utility decision, whereas the plaintiff and other employees faced the risk. Should that difference matter? In Fasolas v. Bobcat of New York, Inc., 128 N.E.3d 627 (N.Y. 2019), the buyer of a loader decided not to purchase an optional safety feature. The buyer leased the loader to the plaintiff, who was injured while using the product and claimed that it was defectively designed for not incorporating the optional safety feature. In rejecting the plaintiff's claim based on the *Scarangella* rule, the court held that a purchaser who rejects optional safety equipment need not be subject to a "risk of personal harm requirement." The "*Scarangella* purchaser undoubtedly took the safety of his employees into account when he made the 'considered decision' not to purchase the back-up alarm." Recognizing that the lessor was obligated to exercise reasonable care in selecting and leasing the equipment—and was in fact held liable for plaintiff's injury—the court concluded that there is no "rental market exception" to the *Scarangella* rule—the lessor "retains a pecuniary interest in ensuring the safety of the products rented to its customers." *Id.* at 635. How would this reasoning apply to optional safety features in a component part that was rejected by the manufacturer of the finished product, discussed in the preceding note? What if the optional equipment would largely protect strangers, as would be the case if the back-up alarm in *Scarangella* largely protected pedestrians on public roads

IV. LIMITS ON THE DUTY TO DESIGN: TECHNOLOGICAL FEASIBILITY AND "STATE OF THE ART"

rather than employees in the company parking lot? *See* Note 4, p. 228 *supra* (discussing potential for categorical liability in cases involving bystanders).

Proof of a reasonable alternative design is necessarily constrained by what is technologically feasible. Courts frequently make this determination by asking whether the plaintiff's proposed design was within the "state of the art," although the term has other connotations as well.

RESTATEMENT (THIRD) OF TORTS: PRODUCTS LIABILITY (1998)
Copyright by the American Law Institute

§2. Comment d . . . Defendants often seek to defend their product designs on the ground that the designs conform to the "state of the art." The term "state of the art" has been variously defined to mean that the product design conforms to industry custom, that it reflects the safest and most advanced technology developed and in commercial use, or that it reflects technology at the cutting edge of scientific knowledge. The confusion brought about by these various definitions is unfortunate. This Section states that a design is defective if the product could have been made safer by the adoption of a reasonable alternative design. If such a design could have been practically adopted at time of sale and if the omission of such a design rendered the product not reasonably safe, the plaintiff establishes defect. . . . When a defendant demonstrates that its product design was the safest in use at the time of sale, it may be difficult for the plaintiff to prove that an alternative design could have been practically adopted. The defendant is thus allowed to introduce evidence with regard to industry practice that bears on whether an alternative design was practicable. Industry practice may also be relevant to whether the omission of an alternative design rendered the product not reasonably safe. While such evidence is admissible, it is not necessarily dispositive. If the plaintiff introduces expert testimony to establish that a reasonable alternative design could practically have been adopted, a trier of fact may conclude that the product was defective notwithstanding that such a design was not adopted by any manufacturer, or even considered for commercial use, at the time of sale.

NOTES AND QUESTIONS

1. *The relation between custom and the tort duty.* Practices that are customary within a market are obviously feasible, and so "state of the art" implicates

customary market practices. To fully identify the relation between the two, we must first understand why a design that complies with customary market practices can nevertheless be defective. As the *Restatement (Third)* puts it, such evidence is "not necessarily dispositive." Rather than defer to these market practices, judges and juries independently evaluate the reasonableness of customary product designs. Why?

In any market, customs are created by the voluntary agreements between buyers and sellers that consistently reach the same outcome. To employ the language of economics, custom is a *market equilibrium*. By rejecting custom as a complete defense, courts have essentially concluded that the product contracts generating market equilibria do not necessarily produce reasonably safe products.

Can you derive this conclusion from the rationale for the tort duty? In order for the duty to exist, the ordinary consumer with ordinary knowledge common to the community must be unable to make an adequately informed risk-utility decision about the safety matter in question. *See* Chapter 5, section III. In such a market, sellers have a financial incentive to forego cost-effective investments in product safety, yielding customary designs that can be unreasonably dangerous. This market failure justifies the tort duty and also explains why compliance with custom does not decisively prove that a design is reasonably safe.

Similarly, compliance with custom is not proof of reasonable care in an ordinary negligence case. *See* The T.J. Hooper, 60 F.2d 737, 740 (2d Cir. 1932) ("[A] whole calling may have unduly lagged in the adoption of new and available devices. It never may set its own tests, however persuasive be its usages. Courts must in the end say what is required.").

2. *The relevance of custom.* A design's compliance with customary practices does not foreclose a finding of defect, but the evidence is still admissible and relevant for resolving the tort claim.

a. *Custom as a shield.* Evidence that the design complies with custom can provide some proof that the design is not defective. In ordinary negligence cases, for example, such evidence is admissible for reasons equally applicable to product cases:

> Evidence that the actor has complied with custom in adopting certain precautions may bear on whether there were further precautions available to the actor, whether these precautions were feasible, and whether the actor knew or should have known of them. In assessing such evidence, the jury can take into account the fact that almost all others have chosen the same course of conduct as has the actor: "ordinary care" has at least some bearing on "reasonable care." Furthermore, if the actor's conduct represents the custom of those engaging in a certain line of activity, the jury should be aware of this, for it cautions the jury that its ruling on the particular actor's negligence has implications for large numbers of other parties.

RESTATEMENT (THIRD) OF TORTS: LIABILITY FOR PHYSICAL AND EMOTIONAL HARMS §13 cmt. b.

Does this rule mean that evidence of industry custom should be admitted to help jurors understand the risk-utility balancing itself? In Kim

IV. Limits on the Duty to Design

v. Toyota Motor Corp., 424 P.3d 290, 298 (Cal. 2018), the court ruled that "[d]epending on the circumstances, evidence of other manufacturers' design decisions may aid the jury's understanding of these complexities and trade-offs, and thus may provide some assistance in determining whether the manufacturer has balanced the relevant considerations correctly." In a concurring opinion that agreed with the final disposition of the case, five justices took issue with this aspect of the majority's opinion:

> The majority opinion appears to endorse admission of a defendant's industry custom-and-practice evidence as a proxy for the foundational risks and benefits that a manufacturer should be evaluating in making product design decisions. That is a little like permitting evidence that an allegedly defective product received a J.D. Power award or the Good Housekeeping Seal of Approval—without anyone testifying about the criteria for that particular honor—because awards of this type may reflect a reasonable balancing of safety risks and benefits. Jurors should not be left to guess.

Id. at 303 (Dato, J., concurring). A customary practice could emerge from manufacturers trying to satisfy their tort obligations, or it could emerge from the type of market failures that justify the tort duty. What evidence, if any, would enable jurors to distinguish one type of custom from the other?

b. *Custom as a sword.* As compared to cases in which the defendant uses conformance with custom to defend the reasonableness of the design, the role of custom is more decisive for cases in which the plaintiff alleges that the design is defective because it does not incorporate a customary safety device.

> Conformity evidence only raises questions, but sub-conformity evidence tends to answer questions. If virtually all other members of the defendant's craft follow safer methods, then those methods are practical; the defendant has heedlessly overlooked or consciously failed to adopt common precautions. Super-cautious industrial usages are conceivable, but the self-interest of businessmen checks milquetoastish fears.

Clarence Morris, *Custom and Negligence,* 42 Colum. L. Rev. 1147, 1155 (1942).

Just as price competition can predictably force businesses to cut costs by foregoing reasonable safety precautions when consumers are not aware of the associated risks, the same dynamic forces businesses to adopt only those designs that are justified by cost-benefit analysis—the "self-interest of businessmen checks milquetoastish fears." A design lacking customary safety devices, therefore, presumably has less safety than is required by the risk-utility test. Consider *Kim,* 424 P.3d at 299 ("In what may be a more common scenario [in which evidence of custom is relevant], plaintiffs might legitimately seek to inform the jury that the defendant has not implemented a safety feature that is standard in the industry.").

To avoid liability in these circumstances, a defendant could argue that the custom is inapplicable to the product in question. In an ordinary negligence case, for example, the defendant can avoid liability by showing "its operation poses different or less serious risks than those occasioned by others engaging in seemingly similar activities, or by showing that it has adopted an alternative method for reducing or controlling risks that is at least as effective as the customary method." Morris, *supra* at 1163. After all, "[w]hen the defendant must practice his craft under conditions significantly different from others in the same business, there is no customary way of acting-under-the-circumstances." *Id.* at 1164. The same logic applies to product markets.

c. *Evidence of feasibility or "state of the art."* "To establish a prima facie case of defect, the plaintiff must prove the availability of a technologically feasible and practical alternative design that would have reduced or prevented the plaintiff's harm." RESTATEMENT (THIRD) OF TORTS: PRODUCTS LIABILITY §2 cmt. f. Like any other existing practice within the product market, a customary practice provides evidence of feasible safety options for the design in question. Should feasibility and practicality be wholly defined by existing practices in the market, or would such a definition of "state of the art" effectively make custom a defense in some cases?

BOATLAND OF HOUSTON v. BAILEY
Supreme Court of Texas, 1980
609 S.W.2d 743

McGEE, J. This is a product defect case involving an alleged defect in the design of a 16-foot bass boat. The plaintiffs were the widow and adult children of Samuel Bailey, who was killed in a boating accident in May of 1973. They sued under the wrongful death statute, alleging that Samuel Bailey's death occurred because the boat he was operating was defectively designed. The boat had struck a partially submerged tree stump, and Bailey was thrown into the water. With its motor still running, the boat turned sharply and circled back toward the stump. Bailey was killed by the propeller, but it is unclear whether he was struck when first thrown out or after the boat circled back toward him.

Bailey's wife and children sought damages under a strict liability theory from the boat's seller, Boatland of Houston, Inc. At trial, they urged several reasons why the boat was defectively designed, including inadequate seating and control area arrangement, unsafe stick steering and throttle design, and the failure of the motor to automatically turn off when Bailey was thrown from the boat.

The trial court rendered a take-nothing judgment based on the jury's failure to find that the boat was defective and findings favorable to Boatland on several defensive issues. The court of civil appeals, with one justice dissenting, reversed and remanded the cause for a new trial because of errors in the admission of evidence and the submission of the defensive issues. We reverse the judgment of the court of civil appeals and affirm that of the trial court.

Whether a product was defectively designed must be judged against the technological context existing at the time of its manufacture. Thus, when the plaintiff alleges that a product was defectively designed because it lacked a specific feature, attention may become focused on the feasibility of that feature—the capacity to provide the feature without greatly increasing the product's cost or

IV. Limits on the Duty to Design

impairing usefulness. This feasibility is a relative, not an absolute, concept; the more scientifically and economically feasible the alternative was, the more likely that a jury may find that the product was defectively designed. A plaintiff may advance the argument that a safer alternative was feasible with evidence that it was in actual use or was available at the time of manufacture. Feasibility may also be shown with evidence of the scientific and economic capacity to develop the safer alternative. Thus, evidence of the actual use of, or capacity to use, safer alternatives is relevant insofar as it depicts the available scientific knowledge and the practicalities of applying that knowledge to a product's design. This method of presenting evidence of defective design is not new to the Texas law of product liability.

As part of their case-in-chief, the Baileys produced evidence of the scientific and economic feasibility of a design that would have caused the boat's motor to automatically shut off when Bailey fell out. According to the Baileys, the boat's design should have incorporated an automatic cut-off system or the boat should have been equipped with a safety device known as a "kill switch."

The deposition of J.C. Nessmith, president of Boatland, was read, in which he stated that there were presently several types of "kill switches" available, and that they were now installed by Boatland when it assembled and sold bass boats.

The deposition of Bill Smith, who was a passenger in the boat with Bailey at the time of the accident, was also read. Smith had not heard of automatic kill switches before the accident, but afterwards he got one for his own boat.

The deposition testimony of George Horton, the inventor of a kill switch designed for open-top carriers, was also introduced. Horton began developing his "Quick Kill" in November of 1972 and applied for a patent in January of 1973. According to Horton, his invention required no breakthroughs in the state of the art of manufacturing or production. He stated that his invention was simple: a lanyard connects the operator's body to a device that fits over the ignition key. If the operator moves, the lanyard is pulled, the device rotates, and the ignition switch turns off. When he began to market his "Quick Kill," the response by boat dealers was very positive, which Horton perceived to be due to the filling of a recognized need. He considered the kill switch to be a necessary safety device for a bass boat with stick steering. If the kill switch were hooked up and the operator thrown out, the killing of the motor would prevent the boat from circling back where it came from. Horton also testified that for 30 years racing boats had been using various types of kill switches. Thus, the concept of kill switches was not new.

Robert Swint, a NASA employee who worked with human factors engineering, testified that he had tested a bass boat similar to Bailey's. He concluded that the boat was deficient for several reasons and that these deficiencies played a part in Bailey's death. According to Swint, when the boat struck a submerged object and its operator became incapacitated, the seating and control arrangement caused the boat to go into a hard turn. If the operator were thrown out, the boat was capable of coming back and hitting him. Swint also stated that a kill switch would have cut off the engine and the motor would not have been operative when it hit Bailey.

Boatland elicited evidence to rebut the Baileys' evidence of the feasibility of equipping boats with kill switches or similar devices in March of 1973, when the boat was assembled and sold. The Baileys had been granted a running objection to all evidence of this nature. In response to the Baileys' evidence that kill switches were presently used by Boatland, Nessmith testified that he did not know of kill switches until the spring of 1973, and first began to sell them a year later.

In response to the Baileys' evidence that the "Quick Kill" was readily available at the time of trial, Horton stated on cross-examination that until he obtained the patent for his "Quick Kill" in 1974 he kept the idea to himself. Before he began to manufacture them, he investigated the market for competitive devices and found none. The only applications of the automatic engine shut-off concept in use at the time were homemade, such as on racing boats. He first became aware of competitive devices in August of 1974.

Boatland introduced other evidence to show that kill switches were not available when Bailey's boat was sold. Willis Hudson, who manufactured the boat operated by Bailey, testified that he first became aware of kill switches in 1974 or 1975 and to his knowledge no such thing was available before then. Ralph Cornelius, the vice-president of a marine appliance dealership, testified that kill switches were not available in 1973. The first kill switch he saw to be sold was in 1974, although homemade "crash throttles" or foot buttons had long been in use.

Apart from evidence of the feasibility of an automatic motor cut-off design, evidence was introduced pertaining to whether such a design would have prevented Bailey's injuries. After considering the feasibility and effectiveness of an alternative design and other factors such as the utility and risk, the jury found that the boat was not defective. The trial court rendered judgment for Boatland. The Baileys complained on appeal that the trial court erred in admitting Boatland's evidence that kill switches were unavailable when Bailey's boat was assembled and sold. The court of civil appeals agreed, holding that the evidence was material only to the care exercised by Boatland and thus irrelevant in a strict liability case.

In its appeal to this court, Boatland contends that the court of civil appeals misconstrued the nature and purpose of its evidence. According to Boatland, when the Baileys introduced evidence that kill switches were a feasible safety alternative, Boatland was entitled to introduce evidence that kill switches were not yet available when Bailey's boat was sold and thus were not a feasible design alternative at that time.

The primary dispute concerning the feasibility of an alternative design for Bailey's boat was the "state of the art" when the boat was sold. The admissibility and effect of "state of the art" evidence has been a subject of controversy in both negligence and strict product liability cases. In negligence cases, the reasonableness of the defendant's conduct in placing the product on the market is in issue. Evidence of industry customs at the time of manufacture may be offered by either party for the purpose of comparing the defendant's conduct with industry customs. An offer of evidence of the defendant's compliance with custom to rebut evidence of its negligence has been described as the "state of the art defense." In this connection, it is argued that the state of the art is equivalent to industry custom and is relevant only to the issue of the defendant's negligence and irrelevant to a strict liability theory of recovery.

In our view, "custom" is distinguishable from "state of the art." The state of the art with respect to a particular product refers to the technological environment at the time of its manufacture. This technological environment includes the

IV. Limits on the Duty to Design

scientific knowledge, economic feasibility, and the practicalities of implementation when the product was manufactured. Evidence of this nature is important in determining whether a safer design was feasible. The limitations imposed by the state of the art at the time of manufacture may affect the feasibility of a safer design. Evidence of the state of the art in design defect cases has been discussed and held admissible in other jurisdictions. [ ] In this case, the evidence advanced by both parties was relevant to the feasibility of designing bass boats to shut off automatically if the operator fell out, or more specifically, the feasibility of equipping bass boats with safety switches.

The Baileys offered state of the art evidence to establish the feasibility of a more safely designed boat: They established that when Bailey's boat was sold in 1973, the general concept of a boat designed so that its motor would automatically cut off had been applied for years on racing boats. One kill switch, the "Quick Kill," was invented at that time and required no mechanical breakthrough. The Baileys were also allowed to show that other kill switches were presently in use and that the defendant itself presently installed them.

Logically, the plaintiff's strongest evidence of feasibility of an alternative design is its actual use by the defendant or others at the time of manufacture. Even if a safer alternative was not being used, evidence that it was available, known about, or capable of being developed is relevant in determining its feasibility. In contrast, the defendant's strongest rebuttal evidence is that a particular design alternative was impossible due to the state of the art. Yet the defendant's ability to rebut the plaintiff's evidence is not limited to showing that a particular alternative was impossible; it is entitled to rebut the plaintiff's evidence of feasibility with evidence of limitations on feasibility. A suggested alternative may be invented or discovered but not be feasible for use because of the time necessary for its application and implementation. Also, a suggested alternative may be available, but impractical for reasons such as greatly increased cost or impairment of the product's usefulness. When the plaintiff has introduced evidence that a safer alternative was feasible because it was used, the defendant may then introduce contradictory evidence that it was not used.

Thus in response to the Baileys' evidence of kill switch use in 1978, the time of trial, Boatland was properly allowed to show that they were not used when the boat was sold in 1973. To rebut proof that safety switches were possible and feasible when Bailey's boat was sold because the underlying concept was known and the "Quick Kill," a simple, inexpensive device had been invented, Boatland was properly allowed to show that neither the "Quick Kill" nor any other kill switch was available at that time.

It could reasonably be inferred from this evidence that although the underlying concept of automatic motor cut-off devices was not new, kill switches were not as feasible an alternative as the Baileys' evidence implied. Boatland did not offer evidence of technological impossibility or absolute nonfeasibility; its evidence was offered to show limited availability when the boat was sold. Once the jury was informed of the state of the art, it was able to consider the extent to which it was feasible to incorporate an automatic cut-off device or similar design characteristic into Bailey's boat. The feasibility and effectiveness of a safer design and other factors such as utility and risk, were properly considered by the jury before it ultimately concluded that the boat sold to Bailey was not defectively designed.

When the Baileys introduced evidence of the use of kill switches, Boatland was entitled to introduce rebuttal evidence of nonuse at the time of manufacture due to limitations imposed by the state of the art. Evidence offered under these circumstances is offered to rebut plaintiff's evidence that a safer alternative was feasible and is relevant to defectiveness. It was not offered to show that a custom existed or to infer the defendant's compliance therewith. We would be presented with a different question if the state of the art in 1973 with respect to kill switches had not been disputed and Boatland had attempted to avoid liability by offering proof that Bailey's boat complied with industry custom.

For the reasons stated above the judgment of the court of civil appeals is reversed. The judgment rendered by the trial court, that the Baileys take nothing against Boatland, is affirmed.

NOTES AND QUESTIONS

1. *Distinguishing state of the art from compliance with customary practices.* After ruling that the defendant's evidence was relevant to state of the art, the court observed, "We would be presented with a different question if the state of the art in 1973 with respect to kill switches had not been disputed and Boatland had attempted to avoid liability by offering proof that Bailey's boat complied with industry custom." Why would this be a different question? Although compliance with custom is not a complete defense, the evidence is still relevant and admissible. Why would it matter whether the defendant instead introduced the evidence to dispute state of the art? When a safety device like the kill switch is not within the state of the art, the defendant properly avoids liability because it could not have incorporated the device into the product design — it had no choice about the matter. By contrast, a defendant has a choice whether to comply with industry custom, and can be held liable for having made that choice when the customary practice is unreasonably dangerous.

2. *Commercial availability, state of the art, and custom.* Although the court in *Boatland* distinguished state of the art from custom, did it nevertheless define "state of the art" in terms of custom? To be sure, the defendant did not have a choice to purchase the kill switch when manufacturing the boat in 1973 — it was not commercially available. But was the absence of choice attributable to the existing state of the art or to customary market practices?

The court recognized that the kill switch is based on a concept that was "not new" and did not require any breakthroughs in engineering or scientific knowledge. The only issue was one of commercial availability, and the court concluded that the kill switch would not have been commercially available if "it was impractical for reasons such as greatly increased cost or impairment of the product's usefulness." Why wouldn't the concern for practicality and cost be fully resolved by a risk-utility analysis of the device? The kill switch would not have been commercially practical if its costs exceeded its benefits; that is, if the device failed the risk-utility test. A determination regarding state of the art, by contrast, is an entirely separate inquiry that forecloses the plaintiff from showing that the proposed

IV. Limits on the Duty to Design

alternative design (incorporating a kill switch) passes the risk-utility test because that design was not technologically feasible or could not otherwise have been practically manufactured within the existing set of production constraints. Was the defendant's evidence about the kill switch's commercial unavailability relevant to the issues of technological feasibility or manufacturing constraints?

Assuming that a safety device such as a kill switch is technologically feasible, such knowledge is imputed to the manufacturer.

> [T]he manufacturer is held to the knowledge and skill of an expert. . . . The manufacturer's status as expert means that at minimum he must keep abreast of scientific knowledge, discoveries, and advances and is presumed to know what is imparted thereby. But even more importantly, a manufacturer has a duty to test and inspect his product. The extent of research and experiment must be commensurate with the dangers involved.

Borel v. Fibreboard Paper Products Corp., 493 F.2d 1076, 1089-1090 (5th Cir. 1973).

As an expert on the matter, the manufacturer in *Boatland* should have known about a kill switch years before it finally began to incorporate these devices into its boats. As the inventor acknowledged, the concept was "not new"; kill switches had been used on racing boats for 30 years. If the manufacturers of bass boats, including the defendant in *Boatland,* had sought out a kill switch when it was first technically feasible or scientifically known, that device presumably would have been commercially available at the time when the defendant manufactured the allegedly defective boat in 1973. Under these conditions, the kill switch was practical and within state of the art, even though it was not commercially available at the time of manufacture. Compare Genie Indus. v. Matak, 462 S.W.3d 1, 7 (Tex. 2015) ("This design need not be actually built and tested; a plaintiff must show only that the alternative design was 'capable of being developed.'"); In Re: Davol, Inc./C.R. Bard, Inc., Polypropylene Hernia Mesh Products Liability Litigation, 2020 WL 5223363 (S.D. Ohio 2020) (rejecting defendant's argument "that Plaintiff's alternative designs must be a single, specific product already on the market embodying all of the qualities Plaintiff's expert has offered as safer alternatives").

When no manufacturer expresses any interest in a safety device, there is no demand for the product and it will not be commercially available in the market. The absence of demand could stem from the fact that the device was not technically feasible or scientifically known at the time of manufacture, but neither of these facts applied to *Boatland*. The commercial unavailability of the kill switch, therefore, can be explained only by the customary practice of not incorporating this device into the design of bass boats. In effect, the *Boatland* court permitted the defendant to use custom as a complete defense by recharacterizing the evidence about commercial unavailability as being relevant to state of the art.

3. *Component-part suppliers.* Presumably the manufacturer in *Boatland* would have purchased the kill switch from a component-part supplier, if one had been commercially available. Are there reasons why the liability

rules governing these suppliers should differ from those applicable to manufacturers? According to the *Restatement (Third)*, one who sells a component part, such as "raw materials, bulk products, and other constituent products sold for integration into other products," is not subject to liability unless "the component is defective in itself" or "the seller or distributor of the component substantially participates in the integration of the component into the design of the product." §5 & cmt. a. The component-part supplier is obviously responsible for the inherent qualities of the component part, subjecting it to liability if "the component is defective in itself." But unless the supplier substantially participates in the decision of how to integrate the component into the final design, it has no meaningful ability to influence that safety decision, explaining why it has no duty to ensure that the final product is reasonably designed. Consider Crossfield v. Quality Control Equip. Co., 1 F.3d 701, 704 (8th Cir. 1993) ("To impose responsibility on the supplier of a chain in the context of larger defectively designed machine would simply extend liability too far.... Mere suppliers cannot be expected to guarantee the safety of other manufacturers' machinery.").

4. *Evidence of subsequent remedial measures.* In *Boatland*, the plaintiff introduced evidence regarding use of the kill switch on boats that were sold after 1973, when the boat that injured the plaintiff's decedent was assembled and sold. Frequently, the defendant or others in the industry adopted a safer design subsequent to the sale of the product at issue in the suit. Can the plaintiff use a subsequently adopted design as the reasonable alternative to the allegedly defective design?

HYJEK v. ANTHONY INDUSTRIES
Supreme Court of Washington, 1997
944 P.2d 1036

MADSEN, JUSTICE. Plaintiff Gary Hyjek brought an action claiming design defect against Anthony Industries' subsidiary, K2 Corporation (K2), as a result of an injury he sustained while using a K2 snowboard. Plaintiff contends the trial court's decision excluding evidence of subsequent remedial measures relating to the binding retention system of K2's snowboards was error. [The year after plaintiff purchased the snowboard, defendant began to design a new binding system that plaintiff alleges was a reasonable alternative design for the binding system on the board that he had purchased and then used in the injury-causing accident.] We affirm.

...

The issue in this case is whether Evidence Rule 407, which provides that a party may not introduce evidence of subsequent remedial measures to establish culpable conduct or negligence, applies in products liability cases where strict liability is alleged. ER 407 provides:

When, after an event, measures are taken which, if taken previously, would have made the event less likely to occur, evidence of subsequent measures is

IV. Limits on the Duty to Design

not admissible to prove negligence or culpable conduct in connection with the event. This rule does not require the exclusion of evidence of subsequent measures when offered for another purpose, such as proving ownership, control, or feasibility of precautionary measures, if controverted, or impeachment.

Washington's Evidence Rule is identical to former Federal Evidence Rule 407 and codifies the common law doctrine which excludes evidence of subsequent remedial measures as a proof of an admission of fault. [ ]

Courts justify the exclusion of such evidence because it is not relevant and it may discourage development of safety measures. Regarding relevancy, courts have found that evidence of a subsequent repair is of little probative value, since the repair may not be an admission of fault. [ ] Rule 407 is a rejection of the notion that "'because the world gets wiser as it gets older, therefore it was foolish before.'" [ ] A manufacturer may change a product's design for many other reasons besides the existence of a defect. . . .

While the historical use of relevancy as the basis for excluding evidence of subsequent remedial measures as evidence of negligence is well established, the more widely accepted basis for exclusion appears to be the social policy rationale of encouraging safety precautions. The Federal Advisory Committee Note to Rule 407 specifically indicates a distinct preference for this rationale. [ ]. The expressed concern is that the introduction of such evidence may provide a disincentive for people to take safety precautions. Rule 407 seeks to advance the public policy of encouraging people to take steps in furtherance of added safety by freeing them from the fear that such steps will be used against them in a future lawsuit.

Although the rule clearly applies in products liability actions based in negligence, where the claim seeks recovery under theories of strict liability, the applicability of Rule 407 varies from state to state and across the federal circuits. . . .

Plaintiff asks this court to adopt the reasoning of those courts finding that ER 407 does not apply to strict products liability actions and find that the trial court erred in excluding evidence of subsequent remedial measures. Finding the majority of federal courts holding that ER 407 applies to actions based in strict liability persuasive and considering the recent amendment to the Federal Rule, we decline to reverse the trial court's decision.

Plaintiff relies primarily on the California Supreme Court's decision in Ault v. International Harvester Co., 528 P.2d 1148 (Cal. 1974), which was one of the first to admit evidence of subsequent remedial measures in a strict liability action. The *Ault* court reasoned that the public policy considerations underling the rule were not valid in strict products liability cases, and held that a plaintiff may use evidence of a subsequent remedial measure to prove a defect. The court found inapplicable the goal of encouraging repairs in the case of mass produced products. [ ] A mass producer, the court reasoned, would not "risk innumerable additional lawsuits and the attendant adverse effect upon its public image" merely to avoid admission of the evidence in the first lawsuit. [ ] The threat of future increased liability for failure to remedy a product defect is a sufficient impetus to encourage the mass producer to take remedial actions. [ ] Therefore, the court concluded, exclusion of subsequent remedial actions only provides "a shield against potential liability." [ ]

. . .

Expanding on the courts' reasoning in *Ault*, the Nevada Supreme Court held that the rule "comes into play only where negligence or other 'culpable' conduct is alleged." [ ] Strict liability, the court stated, does not include either of those issues. [ ] In a products liability case the focus is on the defect in the product, not on any culpable acts of the manufacturer. [ ] Because there is no negligent conduct to influence in strict products liability cases the rule does not apply.

We, however, agree with the majority of the federal circuits rejecting these arguments and applying the exclusionary rule to actions brought under a theory of strict products liability. The reasoning employed by the Fourth Circuit in Werner v. Upjohn Co., 628 F.2d 848 (4th Cir. 1980), exemplifies the rationale followed by the majority. In *Werner*, the court found that, regardless of the theory used to require a manufacturer to pay damages, the deterrent to taking remedial measures is the same, namely, the fear that the evidence may ultimately be used against the defendant. [ ]

. . . The rationale behind the rule, the court explained, is that people generally will not take actions that can be used against them. [ ] The court recognized the difference between negligence and strict liability: in negligence the focus is on the defendant and in strict liability it is on the product. [ ] Nevertheless, the *Werner* court found this distinction "hypertechnical" because the suit is against the manufacturer, *not* against the product, "regardless of theory." (Emphasis added.) Therefore, the court concluded, the policy of encouraging remedial measures by excluding repair evidence will be served as effectively in strict liability as in negligence. In neither case does the manufacturer want to be liable, and the assumption that he will not take steps which can be used against him remains undisturbed. [ ]

The *Werner* court went on to explain that the fallacy in the *Ault* court's mass producer rationale is it assumes a defect in the product. [ ] Furthermore, it completely ignores the situation where a manufacturer decides to improve his nondefective product. [ ] Where the earlier version of the product is not defective, the court said, the manufacturer who takes the precautionary measure of improving his product after an accident risks the imposition of liability as a result of that decision. [ ] Clearly, this would violate Rule 407's public policy of not deterring remedial action.

. . .

Additionally, the language of Washington's Product Liability Act (WPLA) supports our conclusion that ER 407 applies to strict products liability actions. The proper application of a state's equivalent of Federal Rule 407 to strict liability actions should be consistent with the state's law regarding determination of the point in time for assessing liability for a defective product. To do otherwise could impact the substantive law. *See* Randolph L. Burns, Note, *Subsequent Remedial Measures and Strict Products Liability: A New — Relevant — Answer to an Old Problem*, 81 Va. L Rev. 1141, 1146 (1995).

If the time of product distribution or manufacture is the point selected by the Legislature for determining liability in strict liability cases, then the substantive law makes any product knowledge acquired after the point of distribution irrelevant. *See id.* By contrast, if the law assigns the time of trial as the point at which to measure the product against the legal standard for defectiveness, subsequent repairs may be relevant to determining liability. *See id.*

IV. Limits on the Duty to Design

Admitting evidence of subsequent remedial measures when the time of distribution is selected, therefore, means the manufacturer is held responsible for product knowledge outside the ambit of the strict liability scheme. In other words, the evidence rule shapes the substantive law by expanding the scope of liability.

Id.

Washington's Products Liability Act explicitly provides that products are to be evaluated "at the time of manufacture" when examining a design defect or a failure to warn claim. [ ] . . . Thus, the focus in a strict products liability action brought under the WPLA is whether the product was defective at the time it left the manufacturer's control. The introduction of evidence of subsequent remedial modifications may confuse the jury by diverting its attention from whether the product was defective at the time the product was manufactured to some later point in time. For this reason, as well as those discussed above, we find that evidence of subsequent remedial measures should not be admitted in a strict products liability action absent an exception under ER 407.

In this case, none of the exceptions listed in the Rule was offered to support admission of K2's later modifications. Therefore, evidence of subsequent remedial measures was correctly excluded in this case.

NOTES AND QUESTIONS

1. *Amended Federal Rule 407.* While this case was pending, Federal Rule 407 was amended so that it now also excludes evidence of subsequent remedial measures "to prove . . . a defect in a product's design, or a need for a warning or instruction." Although this amendment has resolved the split among federal circuit courts concerning the admissibility of such evidence, state courts continue to disagree about the matter for the reasons discussed in *Hyjek*.

2. *Timing.* For reasons also discussed by the court in *Hyjek*, the evidentiary rule regarding subsequent remedial measures has implications for how courts should determine timing questions involving state of the art and foreseeability. Consistent with the reasoning in *Hyjek*, the majority approach defines state of the art at the time when the product was sold. *E.g.*, Robinson v. Brandtjen & Kluge, Inc., 500 F.3d 691 (8th Cir. 2007) (holding that consumer expectations regarding the design of defendant's printing press must be evaluated at the time when the product was sold in the 1940s, despite the considerable changes in consumer use and technology that occurred in the decades preceding trial). In contrast, the minority approach defines state of the art by reference to the state of knowledge at the time of trial, thereby preventing the manufacturer from introducing evidence that the design in question was not available at the time of sale. *E.g.*, Barker v. Deere and Co., 60 F.3d 158, 167 (3d Cir. 1995) ("Pennsylvania's public policy is to encourage manufacturers to make their products as safe as possible, as soon as possible. It is the jury's prerogative to hold a manufacturer responsible for not more aggressively researching and implementing safety devices."). Courts taking this

approach reason that "state of the art evidence has no bearing on the outcome of a strict liability claim; the sole subject of inquiry is the defective condition of the product and not the manufacturer's knowledge, negligence or fault." Elmore v. Owens-Illinois, Inc, 673 S.W.2d 434, 438 (Mo. 1984). Based on this same reasoning, the minority approach defines warning defects by reference to risks that were known at the time of trial, even if those risks were unforeseeable at the time of sale. *E.g.*, Green v. Smith & Nephew AHP, Inc., 629 N.W.2d 727 (Wis. 2001) (holding that consumer expectations can be frustrated by unforeseeable risks because "foreseeability of harm is an element of negligence") (excerpted in Chapter 3, section II). To what extent are these policy rationales similar to the ones that underlie the divided case law concerning the admissibility of subsequent remedial measures?

3. *The duty to design and the duty to warn.* Another factor relevant to risk-utility analysis involves "the instructions and warnings that accompany the product." RESTATEMENT (THIRD) OF TORTS: PRODUCTS LIABILITY §2 cmt. f. To determine the appropriate relation between the duty to design and product instructions and warnings, we must first address the duty to warn—the subject of the next chapter.

V. AUTONOMOUS VEHICLES AND PRODUCTS LIABILITY: PROBLEM SET 3

AV Problem 3.1

Consider again the facts in AV Problem 2.1, p. 174 *supra*, involving Joshua Brown who was not paying attention while his Tesla Model S electric sedan was in self-driving mode (level 2), leaving him unable to take over the controls to avoid fatally crashing into a tractor trailer that had driven across the highway perpendicular to the Model S. Suppose that when Brown purchased the vehicle, other manufacturers offered autonomous vehicles that required no driver assistance while navigating on highways (level 4). In a suit against Tesla, the plaintiff in a wrongful-death suit claims that the design of the Tesla Model S electric sedan is defective for having adopted level 2 standards because level 4 is a reasonable alternative design. Is the plaintiff's proposed reasonable alternative design improper simply because it relies on one category (level 4) to prove that another category (level 2) of autonomous vehicles is defective? Can you explain why such a denial of liability would further the substantive policies of strict products liability?

Analysis of AV Problem 3.1

As a practical matter, a court would reject the plaintiff's proposed proof because the alternative design, by definition, involves a different category of driver-assistance system (DAS). Any lawyer could make this type of argument.

More skillful lawyering would explain why this outcome finds justification in the substantive policies of strict products liability.

Because both level 2 and level 4 DAS were available at the time when the allegedly defective vehicle was purchased, the decision to purchase the level 2 vehicle is based on the conclusion that the level 4 vehicle has an added cost or burden ($B_{level\ 4}$) that exceeds the extent to which that design would reduce risk by eliminating the chance of driver error ($PL_{level\ 4}$). The plaintiff's allegation of defective design, by contrast, is that this burden is less than the reduction of risk.

Consumer's risk-utility decision: $B_{level\ 4} > PL_{level\ 4}$
Plaintiff's risk-utility allegation: $B_{level\ 4} < PL_{level\ 4}$

For reasons established by the patent-defect rule, the imposition of liability under these circumstances would not adequately value informed consumer choice—perhaps the most important substantive value furthered by strict products liability. When this resolution of the liability question is coupled with the resolution of the liability question posed in AV Problem 2.1, p. 174 *supra*, it becomes apparent that this limitation of liability enables manufacturers to develop different types of safety technologies without incurring liability for having pursued one type of product development over the other.

AV Problem 3.2

The design of an autonomous vehicle includes the software or coding that executes the dynamic driving task for the vehicle—what we have been calling the vehicle's operating system. Having previously analyzed the potential liability for the malfunction of an autonomous vehicle, you are now in a position to analyze a manufacturer's liability in the event that a fully functioning operating system causes the vehicle to crash.

The risk that a vehicle will not safely arrive at its programmed destination depends on the coding that determines how the vehicle executes the dynamic driving task. In trying to develop this technology, researchers first tried to pre-program the operating system with rule-based or symbolic artificial intelligence, consisting of IF-THEN commands, such as "IF a pedestrian is sensed to be within 75 feet on the road ahead, THEN action X will be executed." The complexity of driving behavior ultimately rendered this approach infeasible.

The coding of the operating system now involves the artificial intelligence generated by machine learning. This type of programming employs statistical algorithms "that have been 'trained' to drive by analyzing examples of safe driving, and automatically generalizing about the core patterns that constitute effective driving from these examples." Harry Surden & Mary-Anne Williams, *Technological Opacity, Predictability, and Self-Driving Cars*, 38 Cardozo L. Rev. 121, 148 (2016). Rather than relying on a fixed set of behavioral rules (which characterize symbolic artificial intelligence), the operating system "learns" by adapting or changing the program to incorporate newly acquired information about the best way to execute the dynamic driving task. Consequently, as Tesla explained in a press release addressing the first fatal crash of a self-driving vehicle, "[a]s more real-world miles accumulate and the software logic accounts for increasingly rare events, the probability of injury will keep decreasing." Tesla, *A Tragic Loss*, (June 30, 2016), https://perma.cc/P3NA-DJAR.

Once a manufacturer has commercially distributed a level 4 autonomous vehicle into the market, the operating system will have attained a certain level of machine learning based on the amount of its premarket testing. More extensive testing allows for more machine learning and continued improvement in the vehicle's safe driving performance.

Machine learning, however, is like a "black box." Aside from inputting the learning algorithm, the coding is limited to rules that constrain or guide the machine learning, such as coding that instructs the vehicle to always stop at stop signs and otherwise obey traffic rules. The algorithm then adapts in light of its learning experience in ways that might not be possible to discern by inspection of the coding itself. After a crash occurs in a specific set of circumstances, the coding of the operating system will adapt—perhaps after being prodded with certain inputs by the programmers. Nevertheless, the vehicle's performance in any given context cannot be wholly predicted—at best, the operating system can be evaluated only in terms of its systematic driving performance across its intended operating domain. For example, the premarket testing data could show that the vehicle can drive 100,000 miles under the specified conditions and be involved in no more than four crashes, albeit in contexts that cannot be determined in advance. Consequently, during premarket testing of level 4 vehicles on public roads, manufacturers like Waymo have a human driver sit behind the wheel, ready to take over if the autonomous operation threatens a crash. More extensive premarket testing would then further reduce the crash risk.

Suppose that a manufacturer comes to you seeking advice. It plans to market a level 4 autonomous vehicle and is concerned about its exposure to liability for defective design in the event that the fully functioning vehicle crashes. Assume that each newly manufactured autonomous vehicle would replace a conventional vehicle with a human driver. Available data show that over the course of 100,000 miles under the specified conditions, human drivers are involved in four crashes. Explain in general how the risk-utility factors will be formulated to evaluate the design of the autonomous vehicle's operating system. Will it matter for purposes of this inquiry whether a particular crash is one that would have been avoided by a human driver?

Analysis of AV Problem 3.2

For reasons discussed in section II.B of this chapter, risk-utility analysis requires a baseline of comparison. Unless the manufacturer is the first entrant in the market, other autonomous vehicles will be on the road gaining more extensive learning experience that will continually improve their safe driving performance. To satisfy the duty to design, however, manufacturers do not have to supply the safest possible product. Consequently, a defensible baseline of comparison involves the performance of the autonomous vehicle with the safety performance of conventional vehicles with human drivers—the type of vehicle that will be replaced by the autonomous vehicle in question.

Relative to this baseline, the autonomous vehicle must perform at least as safely as conventional vehicles for reasons embodied in the type of risk-risk trade-off involved in *Dawson*, p. 200 *supra*. If human drivers are involved in four crashes

V. Autonomous Vehicles and Products Liability: Problem Set 3

every 100,000 miles, then an autonomous vehicle that replaces human drivers would not increase the risk of a crash if the premarket testing shows that it also is involved in four crashes for every 100,000 miles under the same driving conditions. Such a design apparently satisfies the risk-utility test.

However, this conclusion is contestable in a few respects. For example, it only considers the safety benefits of autonomous vehicles and ignores other important benefits, such as the ability of individuals in the vehicle to do something other than pay attention to the road, greater mobility for individuals who are unable to drive conventional vehicles, and so on. Adding these benefits enhances the utility of the autonomous vehicle and decreases the extent to which it must reduce risk relative to human drivers in order to pass the risk-utility test. For example, inclusion of these benefits might mean that the autonomous vehicle passes the risk-utility test even though it causes five crashes every 100,000 miles, as compared to a conventional vehicle that has four crashes every 100,000 miles.

Putting this issue aside, the foregoing risk-utility analysis also ignores the ability of the manufacturer to reduce risk further by subjecting the operating system to more extensive premarket testing. When the autonomous vehicle performs as safely as human drivers, further premarket testing has no safety costs—the delayed deployment means that a human will be driving, a different mode of operation that is equally safe. Further testing, however, has a safety benefit stemming from the more extensive learning of the operating system. Accounting for this factor might mean, for example, that the autonomous vehicle only passes the risk-utility test if it causes three crashes every 100,000 miles, as compared to a conventional vehicle that has four crashes every 100,000 miles.

Fully accounting for these variations in both the utility and risk factors is obviously complicated and depends on empirical data. Recall in this regard that the primary value of the risk-utility test is analytical and not operational—plaintiffs do not have to quantify either the risk or utility of the design in question.

Regardless of how the risk-utility test is formulated, the performance of the operating system cannot be evaluated by simply asking how a human driver would have responded in the case at hand. That type of inquiry would not account for the crashes caused by human drivers that are avoided by the autonomous vehicle. When the fully functioning operating system was engaged in systemized driving behavior, its performance in any given case must be evaluated with aggregate driving data that compare its systemic performance to that of conventional vehicles. Whereas crashes caused by human drivers turn on the specifics of each case, the crashes of fully functioning autonomous vehicles properly depend on its systematic safety performance across the entire operating domain.

Editors Note: The analytical value of the risk-utility test can have operational implications. By adopting assumptions about the risk-utility factors, one can construct the analysis to bias the analysis in favor of a finding of defective design. Doing so identifies the full extent to which the design of the operating system would have to reduce risk to ensure it passes the risk-utility test. *See* Mark A. Geistfeld, *A Roadmap for Autonomous Vehicles: State Tort Liability, Automobile Insurance, and Federal Safety Regulation*, 105 Cal. L. Rev. 1611, 1651-1654 (2017) (showing why premarket testing that halves the risk of crash relative to human drivers of conventional vehicles will necessarily satisfy the risk-utility test when these vehicles are first introduced into the commercial market and replace human drivers in conventional vehicles).

7

Warning Defects

All products in the same line come with the same warnings, which provide instructions for safe use and disclosures of residual risks that are inherent in well-designed, safely used products. As compared to claims of defective design, plaintiffs usually face an easier task in proving that the product defect involves an inadequate warning. Indeed, some critics claim that plaintiffs are given a free pass: "In most cases, the elements of the warnings cause of action require plaintiffs to do little more than mouth empty phrases. . . . From a broader social perspective, . . . such a tort is too lawless to be fair or useful." James A. Henderson, Jr., and Aaron D. Twerski, *Doctrinal Collapse in Products Liability: The Empty Shell of Failure to Warn*, 65 N.Y.U. L. Rev. 265, 285 (1990). Consider this critique as you study the liability rules governing defective warnings. While doing so, also consider your own behavior. How often do you read product warnings? What is your reason for not doing so? What implications, if any, does this type of behavior have for the liability rules?

I. INFORMATION AND CONSUMER CHOICE

When the average or ordinary consumer is unaware of a risk, a warning to that effect allows him or her to make an informed risk-utility decision. The duty to warn is the most obvious instance in which strict products liability furthers the value of informed consumer choice.

WATKINS v. FORD MOTOR CO.
United States Court of Appeals, Eleventh Circuit, 1999
190 F.3d 1213

FAY, J. This is a products liability action stemming from an automobile accident that occurred on November 18, 1994. Plaintiff-appellant Joseph Washo ("Washo") was operating his pre-owned 1986 Ford Bronco II en route to a restaurant after a high school football game. Accompanying him were plaintiffs-appellants Stacy Purcell, Rachelle Oliver and plaintiffs'-appellants' decedent Brian Watkins.

While traveling in an eastward direction, the right side tires of Washo's Bronco II traveled a short distance off the road. Attempting to bring the vehicle back onto the road, Washo steered to the left and lost control. In an effort to regain control of the Bronco II, he steered the vehicle back to the right. At this time the Bronco II flipped, rolling over approximately two and one half times.

As a result of the accident, Brian Watkins sustained a severe head injury and died. Rachelle Oliver sustained severe head injuries with bleeding on the brain, and fractured her hip, ankle, and clavicle. Joseph Washo and Stacy Purcell were also injured in the accident.

On November 14, 1996, the plaintiffs filed suit against Ford Motor Company alleging, among other things, that Ford failed to warn of the known rollover hazards. The district judge granted Ford's motion for summary judgment, finding the plaintiffs' negligence claims were barred by the statute of repose [in Georgia]. The plaintiffs filed this appeal.

[The court first concluded that the statute of repose did not bar the plaintiffs' claims.]

Ford also argues, in the alternative, that summary judgment was warranted because even had a more complete warning been given it could not have prevented the accident. This argument is based on the deposition testimony of the appellants' warning expert, Dr. Edward Karnes. In his deposition, Dr. Karnes stated that once a user made the decision to drive the Bronco II, no warning could guard against the dangers of rollover. Ford submits that if no warning is sufficient to prevent the risk of rollover, there can be no causation.

We find this reasoning unpersuasive, as it misinterprets what is required to advance a failure to warn claim. Although a warning may have the net effect of preventing an accident, that is not what is required by the law. The law merely requires the warning to inform the consumer of the nature and existence of the hazard, allowing him to make an informed decision whether to take on the risks warned of. *See* [ ]; RESTATEMENT (THIRD) OF TORTS: PRODUCTS LIABILITY §10 (1997) ("Whether or not many persons would, when warned, nonetheless decide to use or consume the product, warnings are required to protect the interest of those reasonable foreseeable users or consumers who would, based on their own reasonable assessments of the risks and benefits, decline product use or consumption.").

In this case, Dr. Karnes' statement does not negate the contention that the warning on the Bronco II did not properly apprize the consumer of the risk associated with operating the vehicle. It simply expresses his belief that nothing may be done to protect the consumer from risk of rollover once the consumer decides to take on the risk warned of. The question that must be answered by the fact finder is whether the warning given was sufficient or was inadequate because it did not provide a complete disclosure of the existence and extent of the risk involved." [ ]

Because adequate evidence exists to advance appellants' failure to warn claim, the district court's grant of summary judgment was error. Accordingly, we reverse.

NOTES AND QUESTIONS

1. *Rationales for the duty to warn.* As *Watkins* illustrates, the duty to warn can be justified as a means for protecting the consumer's right to make an informed decision concerning her own safety. *E.g.*, Borel v. Fibreboard Paper Products Corp., 493 F.2d 1076, 1106 (5th Cir. 1973) ("Any . . . product user has a right to decide whether to expose himself to the risk"). Alternatively, the duty to warn can be justified in terms of its ability to reduce product accidents by ensuring that consumers have enough information to use products safely. *E.g.*, Pavildes v. Galveston Yacht Basin, Inc., 727 F.2d 330, 338 (5th Cir. 1984) ("Strict liability for failure-to-warn is founded on twin principles of social utility and the right of the individual to determine his own fate."). Are these two rationales for the duty different, or do they express different reasons why the ordinary consumer reasonably expects to be warned about unknown dangers?

2. *Inadequate warnings and deceptive trade practices.* The failure to warn about the dangerous characteristics of a product can be a form of false advertising or a deceptive trade practice that violates consumer protection statutes. *See, e.g.*, Marc G. Perlin, 1 MASSACHUSETTS PROOF OF CIVIL CASES §30:4 (Dec. 2020 update) ("The Massachusetts consumer protection statute is applicable to a products liability action, since a defendant who is found liable for negligence and breach of the implied warranty of merchantability has thereby committed an unfair or deceptive trade practice."). For example, in Aspinall v. Philip Morris Cos., Inc., 813 N.E.2d 476, 479 (Mass. 2004), plaintiff smokers filed a class-action suit alleging that defendants had violated the state's "consumer protection statute by misleading the public into believing that their product, Marlboro Lights, would deliver lower levels of tar and nicotine, when the defendant companies knew the truth to be otherwise and, in fact, intentionally designed the product so that most smokers of Marlboro Lights would receive as much, or more, tar and nicotine than if they had smoked regular cigarettes." By relying on the statute, the plaintiffs could recover damages based on the difference in the price they actually paid for the cigarettes and the true market value of the "misrepresented" cigarettes they actually received. Because the plaintiffs were "similarly situated" with respect to their claims, the court upheld certification of the class. *Id.* at 485. A tort claim for these damages, by contrast, would be barred by the economic loss rule discussed in Chapter 13, section II.

The interplay between a tort claim of defective warning and a claim of deceptive practices is further illustrated by Pelman v. McDonald's Corp., 237 F. Supp. 2d 512, 516 (S.D.N.Y. 2003), in which plaintiffs "alleged that the practices of McDonalds in making and selling their [fast food] products are deceptive and that this deception has caused the minors who have consumed McDonald's products to injure their health by becoming obese." The court initially dismissed these claims for reasons that should by now be familiar:

> As long as a consumer exercises free choice with appropriate knowledge, liability for negligence will not attach to a manufacturer. It is

only when that free choice becomes but a chimera—for instance, by the masking of information necessary to make the choice, such as the knowledge that eating McDonalds with a certain frequency would irrefragably cause harm—that manufacturers should be held accountable. Plaintiffs have failed to allege in the Complaint that their decisions to eat at McDonalds several times a week were anything but a choice freely made and which now may not be pinned on McDonalds.

Id. at 533. The plaintiffs subsequently amended their complaint and alleged that McDonald's employed deceptive advertising practices. McDonald's moved to dismiss the amended complaint, and prior to oral argument, plaintiffs dropped their negligent failure-to-warn claim, leaving only statutory claims based on alleged deceptive practices in violation of New York State's Consumer Protection Act. *See* Pelman v. McDonald's Corp., 2003 WL 22052778 (S.D.N.Y. Sept. 3, 2003), *vacated in part*, 396 F.3d 508 (2d Cir. 2005). Why do you think the plaintiffs in *Pelman* dropped the failure-to-warn claim? Consider Chapter 11, section II (discussing causation in warning cases). For extensive discussion of the case, see Mary Marshall Hodges, Comment, *The Hamburglar, Friend or Foe: What Is the Best Solution for Lawsuits Alleging Obesity Caused by Fast Food Outlets When No Causal Link Between Consumption and Obesity Can Be Found?*, 10 J. Food & Law Pol'y 281 (2014).

3. *The interplay between litigation, the media, and legislation.* The *Pelman* case discussed in the preceding note caught the media's attention and inspired the documentary *Super Size Me* (Kathbur Pictures 2004). Following this media attention, a number of other lawsuits were filed against players in the fast-food industry. *See* Theodore Frank, *A Taxonomy of Obesity Litigation*, 28 U. Ark. Little Rock L. Rev. 427 (2006). At least 23 states have responded by enacting legislation that immunizes food manufacturers from liability for obesity lawsuits, and the U.S. House of Representatives passed similar legislation, titled "Personal Responsibility in Food Consumption Act," widely known as the "cheeseburger bill." *See* David Burnett, *Fast-Food Lawsuits and the Cheeseburger Bill: Critiquing Congress' Response to the Obesity Epidemic*, 14 Va. J. Social Pol'y & L. 357 (2007).

Is this legislation required because fast-food sellers would otherwise incur extensive liability for their failure to warn about the adverse health consequences of eating fast food, or does the legislation instead reflect a concern that the civil justice system is not doing an adequate job of weeding out "frivolous" claims? Consider Melissa Mortazavi, *Tort as Democracy: Lessons from the Food Wars*, 57 Ariz. L. Rev. 929, 932 (2015) ("Lawsuits over labeling 'evaporated cane juice' as sugar or McDonald's use of beef fat in french fries or granola bars that are 'all natural' often seem futile and even silly. But whether these cases are litigated to a verdict or settled, these suits serve important purposes in American civil society: they inform public discourse, spur administrative and legislative bodies into active (or reactive) action, and push public opinion and private industry to contemplate new and conflicting ideas.").

II. THE SUBSTANTIVE BASIS OF THE LIABILITY RULE

As is true in cases involving defects of product design, courts often disagree about the substantive basis of the duty to warn. Is the liability rule one of strict liability or instead a form of negligence liability?

ANDERSON v. OWENS-CORNING FIBERGLASS CORP.
Supreme Court of California, 1991
810 P.2d 549

PANELLI, J. In this case we consider the issue whether a defendant in a products liability action based upon an alleged failure to warn of a risk of harm may present evidence of the state of the art, i.e., evidence that the particular risk was neither known nor knowable by the application of scientific knowledge available at the time of manufacture and/or distribution. As will appear, resolution of this evidentiary issue requires an examination of the failure-to-warn theory as an alternate and independent basis for imposing strict liability and a determination of whether knowledge, actual or constructive, is a component of strict liability on the failure-to-warn theory. It is manifest that, if knowledge or knowability is a component, state-of-the-art evidence is relevant and, subject to the normal rules of evidence, admissible.

We conclude that California courts, either expressly or by implication, have to date required knowledge, actual or constructive, of potential risk or danger before imposing strict liability for a failure to warn. The state of the art may be relevant to the question of knowability and, for that reason, should be admissible in that context. Exclusion of state-of-the-art evidence, *when the basis of liability is a failure to warn*, would make a manufacturer the virtual insurer of its product's safe use, a result that is not consonant with established principles underlying strict liability.

Defendants are or were manufacturers of products containing asbestos. Plaintiff Carl Anderson filed suit in 1984, alleging that he contracted asbestosis and other lung ailments through exposure to asbestos and asbestos products while working as an electrician at the Long Beach Naval Shipyard from 1941 to 1976. Plaintiff allegedly encountered asbestos while working in the vicinity of others who were removing and installing insulation products aboard ships. The complaint stated causes of action for negligence, breach of warranty, and strict liability and, inter alia, prayed for punitive damages. Pursuant to stipulation entered at the time of trial, plaintiff proceeded only on his cause of action for strict liability and did not seek punitive damages.

Plaintiff moved before trial to prevent defendants from presenting state-of-the-art evidence. The trial court granted the motion, citing the "Hawaii cases" which held that state-of-the-art evidence is irrelevant to any theory of strict liability. The defendants then moved to prevent plaintiff from proceeding on the failure-to-warn theory on grounds of waiver and fairness. With no statement of reasons, the trial court granted defendants' motion. After a four-week trial, the jury returned a verdict for defendants.

Plaintiff moved for a new trial, asserting that the court erred in precluding proof of liability on a failure-to-warn theory. The court granted the motion. The Court of Appeal, in a two-to-one decision, upheld the order granting a new trial. The appellate court added that, "in strict liability asbestos cases, including those prosecuted on a failure to warn theory, state of the art evidence is not admissible since it focuses on the reasonableness of the defendant's conduct, which is irrelevant in strict liability." We granted review.

"From its inception, strict liability has never been, and is not now, *absolute* liability. Under strict liability the manufacturer does not thereby become the insurer of the safety of the product's use." [ ] Our task in the case before us is to shape the doctrine insofar as it is applicable to a product whose *only* defect may be that the manufacturer or distributor failed to warn of inherent dangers.

[W]e hereby adopt the requirement, as propounded by the Restatement Second of Torts and acknowledged by the lower courts of this state and the majority of jurisdictions, that knowledge or knowability is a component of strict liability for failure to warn.

One of the guiding principles of the strict liability doctrine was to relieve a plaintiff of the evidentiary burdens inherent in a negligence cause of action. Indeed, it was the limitations of negligence theories that prompted the development and expansion of the doctrine. The proponents of the minority rule, including the Court of Appeal in this case, argue that the knowability requirement, and admission of state-of-the-art evidence, improperly infuse negligence concepts into strict liability cases by directing the trier of fact's attention to the conduct of the manufacturer or distributor rather than to the condition of the product. Similar claims have been made as to other aspects of strict liability, sometimes resulting in limitations on the doctrine and sometimes not. In Cronin v. J.B.E. Olson Corp. (1972), for example, we concluded that the "unreasonably dangerous" element, which the Restatement Second of Torts had introduced into the definition of a defective product, should not be incorporated into a plaintiff's burden of proof in a product liability action because it "rings of negligence." [ ]

However, the claim that a particular component "rings of" or "sounds in" negligence has not precluded its acceptance in the context of strict liability. [I]n Barker v. Lull Engineering Co. (1978), this court rejected the claim that the risk/benefit test was unacceptable because it introduced an element which "rings of negligence" into the determination of design defect. Consequently, we held that the risk/benefit test was not inconsistent with our decision in *Cronin*. [ ]

As these cases illustrate, the strict liability doctrine has incorporated some well-settled rules from the law of negligence and has survived judicial challenges asserting that such incorporation violates the fundamental principles of the doctrine. It may also be true that the warning defect theory is rooted in negligence to a greater extent than are the manufacturing or design-defect theories. The warning defect relates to a failure extraneous to the product itself. Thus, while a manufacturing or design defect *can be* evaluated without reference to the conduct of the manufacturer (see *Barker*), the giving of a warning cannot. The latter necessarily requires the communicating of something to someone.

II. The Substantive Basis of the Liability Rule

How can one warn of something that is unknowable? If every product that has no warning were defective per se and for that reason subject to strict liability, the mere fact of injury by an unlabelled product would automatically permit recovery. That is not, and has never been, the purpose and goal of the failure-to-warn theory of strict liability.

We therefore reject the contention that every reference to a feature shared with theories of negligence can serve to defeat limitations on the doctrine of strict liability. Furthermore, despite its roots in negligence, failure to warn in strict liability differs markedly from failure to warn in the negligence context. Negligence law in a failure-to-warn case requires a plaintiff to prove that a manufacturer or distributor did not warn of a particular risk for reasons which fell below the acceptable standard of care, i.e., what a reasonably prudent manufacturer would have known and warned about. Strict liability is not concerned with the standard of due care or the reasonableness of a manufacturer's conduct. The rules of strict liability require a plaintiff to prove only that the defendant did not adequately warn of a particular risk that was known or knowable in light of the generally recognized and prevailing best scientific and medical knowledge available at the time of manufacture and distribution. Thus, in strict liability, as opposed to negligence, the reasonableness of the defendant's failure to warn is immaterial.

Stated another way, a reasonably prudent manufacturer might reasonably decide that the risk of harm was such as not to require a warning as, for example, if the manufacturer's own testing showed a result contrary to that of others in the scientific community. Such a manufacturer might escape liability under negligence principles. In contrast, under strict liability principles the manufacturer has no such leeway; the manufacturer is liable if it failed to give warning of dangers that were known to the scientific community at the time it manufactured or distributed the product. Whatever may be reasonable from the point of view of the manufacturer, the user of the product must be given the option either to refrain from using the product at all or to use it in such a way as to minimize the degree of danger. Davis v. Wyeth Laboratories, Inc., 399 F.2d 121, 129-130 (9th Cir. 1968), described the need to warn in order to provide "true choice": "When, in a particular case, the risk qualitatively (e.g., of death or major disability) as well as quantitatively, on balance with the end sought to be achieved, is such as to call for a true choice judgment, medical or personal, the warning must be given." Thus, the fact that a manufacturer acted as a reasonably prudent manufacturer in deciding not to warn, while perhaps absolving the manufacturer of liability under the negligence theory, will not preclude liability under strict liability principles if the trier of fact concludes that, based on the information scientifically available to the manufacturer, the manufacturer's failure to warn rendered the product unsafe to its users.

The foregoing examination of the failure-to-warn theory of strict liability in California compels the conclusion that knowability is relevant to imposition of liability under that theory. Our conclusion not only accords with precedent but also with the considerations of policy that underlie the doctrine of strict liability.

We recognize that an important goal of strict liability is to spread the risks and costs of injury to those most able to bear them. However, it was never the intention of the drafters of the doctrine to make the manufacturer or distributor the insurer of the safety of their products. It was never their intention to impose *absolute* liability.

Therefore, a defendant in a strict products liability action based upon an alleged failure to warn of a risk of harm may present evidence of the state of the art, i.e., evidence that the particular risk was neither known nor knowable by the application of scientific knowledge available at the time of manufacture and/or distribution. The judgment of the Court of Appeal is affirmed with directions that the matter be remanded to the trial court for proceedings in accord with our decision herein.

NOTES AND QUESTIONS

1. *Strict products liability v. negligence liability.* For largely the same reasons that courts disagree about whether the liability rule governing defective design is best characterized as a rule of strict products liability or negligence liability, the same is true for the liability rule governing defective product warnings. Did the court in *Anderson* persuasively explain why strict products liability is substantively different from negligence liability? Would a defendant manufacturer be exempt from negligence liability for engaging in the type of behavior that the court claimed would otherwise be subject to strict liability? Recall in this regard that negligence liability depends on an objective standard—defined by the conduct of a reasonably prudent manufacturer—pursuant to which the manufacturer is deemed to be an expert in the field. *E.g.,* Owens-Illinois v. Zenobia, 601 A.2d 633, 639 (Md. 1992) (holding that "the manufacturer is held to the knowledge and skill of an expert. . . . The manufacturer's status as expert means that at a minimum he must keep abreast of scientific knowledge, discoveries, and advances and is presumed to know what is imparted thereby."). Based on this definition of reasonable care, could a manufacturer reasonably decide not to warn of a risk based solely on its own scientific studies that are contrary to the conclusions reached by other experts? If not, are there any other differences between negligence and strict liability for failure to warn? Consider David G. Owen & Mary J. Davis, 1 Owen & Davis on Products Liability §6:14 (4th ed. 2014) ("Whether one calls this method for determining liability 'strict' or 'popcorn,' it is at bottom negligence.").

2. *Absolute liability and the evidentiary rationale for strict liability.* In justifying the limitation of liability to foreseeable risks, the court in *Anderson* observed that "strict liability has never been, and is not now, *absolute* liability." Does the court explain why the liability rule proposed by the plaintiff would be a form of absolute liability? Unlike a case of absolute liability in which there is no proof of defect, the plaintiff showed that the warning was defective based on knowledge available at the time of trial. Why wouldn't the evidentiary rationale for strict products liability apply, absolving the plaintiff of the need to prove the manufacturer should have known about the risk when the product was commercially distributed—a negligence inquiry? Recall in this regard that California, unlike most jurisdictions, relies on the evidentiary difficulties of proving negligence to shift the burden of proof onto defendants in cases of defective design. *See* Barker v. Lull Engineering Co., 573 P.2d 443, 455 (Cal. 1978).

II. The Substantive Basis of the Liability Rule

VASSALLO v. BAXTER HEALTHCARE CORP.
Supreme Judicial Court of Massachusetts, 1998
696 N.E.2d 909

GREANEY, J. Our current law, regarding the duty to warn under the implied warranty of merchantability, presumes that a manufacturer was fully informed of all risks associated with the product at issue, regardless of the state of the art at the time of the sale, and amounts to strict liability for failure to warn of these risks. This rule has been justified by the public policy that a defective product, unreasonably dangerous due to lack of adequate warnings, is not fit for the ordinary purposes for which it is used regardless of the absence of fault on a defendant's part.

At trial, the defendants requested a jury instruction that a manufacturer need only warn of risks "known or reasonably knowable in light of the generally accepted scientific knowledge available at the time of the manufacture and distribution of the device." The judge declined this request. While the judge's instruction was a correct statement of our law, we recognize that we are among a distinct minority of States that applies a hindsight analysis to the duty to warn.

The majority of States, either by case law or by statute, follow the principle expressed in *Restatement (Second) of Torts* §402A comment j (1965), which states that "the seller is required to give warning against [a danger], if he has knowledge, or by the application of reasonable, developed human skill and foresight should have knowledge, of the . . . danger." At least three jurisdictions that previously applied strict liability to the duty to warn in a products liability claim have reversed themselves, either by statute or by decision, and now require knowledge, or reasonable knowability as a component of such a claim. [ ]

The thin judicial support for a hindsight approach to the duty to warn is easily explained. The goal of the law is to induce conduct that is capable of being performed. This goal is not advanced by imposing liability for failure to warn of risks that were not capable of being known.

The *Restatement (Third) of Torts: Products Liability* §2(c) (1998) reaffirms the principle expressed in *Restatement (Second) of Torts* §402A comment j, by stating that a product "is defective because of inadequate instructions or warnings when the foreseeable risks of harm posed by the product could have been reduced or avoided by the provision of reasonable instructions or warnings . . . and the omission of the instructions or warnings renders the product not reasonably safe." The rationale behind the principle is explained by stating that "[u]nforeseeable risks arising from foreseeable product use . . . by definition cannot specifically be warned against." RESTATEMENT (THIRD) OF TORTS: PRODUCTS LIABILITY, §2 comment m, at 34. However, comment m also clarifies the manufacturer's duty "to perform reasonable testing prior to marketing a product and to discover risks and risk-avoidance measures that such testing would reveal. A seller is charged with knowledge of what reasonable testing would reveal."

We have stated that liability under the implied warranty of merchantability in Massachusetts is "congruent in nearly all respects with the principles expressed in *Restatement (Second) of Torts* §402A." [ ] The main difference has been our application of a hindsight approach to the duty to warn of (and to provide adequate instructions regarding) risks associated with a product.

In recognition of the clear judicial trend regarding the duty to warn in products liability cases, and the principles stated in *Restatement (Third) of Torts: Products Liability* §2(c) and comment m, we hereby revise our law to state that a defendant will not be held liable under an implied warranty of merchantability for failure to warn or provide instructions about risks that were not reasonably foreseeable at the time of sale or could not have been discovered by way of reasonable testing prior to marketing the product. A manufacturer will be held to the standard of knowledge of an expert in the appropriate field, and will remain subject to a continuing duty to warn (at least purchasers) of risks discovered following the sale of the product at issue.

NOTES AND QUESTIONS

1. *The triumph of negligence?* In subsequent cases, the Massachusetts Supreme Judicial Court made clear "that negligent failure to warn and failure to warn under breach of warranty are to be judged by the same standard." Carrel v. National Cord & Braid Corp., 852 N.E.2d 100, 109 n.12 (Mass. 2006). The majority of courts have reached the same conclusion. *E.g.*, Matter of New York City Asbestos Litigation, 59 N.E.3d 458, 469 (N.Y. 2016). Consequently, the *Restatement (Third)* "adopts a reasonableness test for judging the adequacy of product instructions. It thus parallels Subsection (b), which adopts a similar standard for judging the safety of product designs." §2 cmt. i. Both rules "achieve the same general objectives as does liability predicated on negligence." *Id.* cmt. a.

The triumph of negligence, however, is not complete. As illustrated by *Anderson*, p. 257 *supra*, most courts continue to insist that the rule is one of strict products liability, not negligence liability, even if they have not persuasively explained why. A few jurisdictions continue to subject product sellers to liability for the failure to warn of risks known at the time of trial that were not reasonably foreseeable at the time of sale. *E.g.*, Green v. Smith & Nephew AHP, Inc., 629 N.W.2d 727 (Wis. 2001) (excerpted in Chapter 3, section II); Sternhagen v. Dow Co., 935 P.2d 1139, 1144 (Mont. 1997).

A similar split has occurred among the members of the European Union. The European Economic Community Directive on Liability for Defective Products allows the producer to avoid liability by showing "that the state of scientific or technical knowledge at the time he put the product into circulation was not such as to enable the existence of the defect to be discovered." Council Directive 85/374/EEC of July 25 1985 on the Approximation of the Laws, Regulations and Administrative Provisions of the Member States Concerning Liability for Defective Products, art. 7(e), 1985 O.J. (L 210) 29. This article, known as the *development risk defense*, has been adopted by a great majority of the countries in the European Union. *See generally* Mark Mildred, *The Development Risks Defense, in* PRODUCTS LIABILITY LAW IN COMPARATIVE PERSPECTIVE 167 (Duncan Fairgrieve ed. 2005) ("Only Finland and Luxembourg have chosen to omit the defense," and France, Germany, and Spain have rejected the defense for only a few types of products, such as medicinal or food products).

II. The Substantive Basis of the Liability Rule

2. *Reconsidering the evidentiary rationale for strict liability.* Is there any response to the *Vassallo* court's conclusion that a rule of strict liability for unforeseeable risks cannot promote the safety objective? What about the evidentiary rationale for strict liability? That rationale is potentially applicable only when the plaintiff has otherwise proven defect, and in these cases the plaintiff has provided such proof, at least if defect is defined by reference to knowledge available at the time of trial. The evidentiary question is whether the proof of defect should be limited to knowledge available at the time of sale, an issue involving state-of-the-art knowledge that is distinguishable from the risk-utility determination of defect. *See* Chapter 6, section IV (explaining why issues involving state-of-the-art technology are different from those implicated by the risk-utility test for defective design). Could the difficulties of proving state-of-the-art safety knowledge at the time of sale justify a rule of strict liability?

Manufacturers are subject to negligence liability for failing to discover risks that a reasonable research program would have identified. Do problems of proof render such a duty practically unenforceable? The New Jersey Supreme Court thought so in one of the leading cases that rejected state-of-the-art evidence in warning cases:

> Scientific knowability, as we understand it, refers not to what in fact was known at the time, but to what *could have been* known at the time. In other words, even if no scientist had actually formed the belief that asbestos was dangerous, the hazards would be deemed "knowable" if a scientist could have formed that belief by applying research or performing tests that were available at the time. Proof of what could have been known will inevitably be complicated, costly, confusing and time-consuming. Each side will have to produce experts in the history of science and technology to speculate as to what knowledge was feasible in a given year. We doubt that juries will be capable of even understanding the concept of scientific knowability, much less be able to resolve such a complex issue. Moreover, we should resist legal rules that will so greatly add to the costs both sides incur in trying a case.
>
> The concept of knowability is complicated further by the fact, noted above, that the level of investment in safety research by manufacturers is one determinant of the state-of-the-art at any given time. Fairness suggests that manufacturers not be excused from liability because their prior inadequate investment in safety rendered the hazards of their product unknowable. Thus, a judgment will have to be made as to whether defendants' investment in safety research in the years preceding distribution of the product was adequate. If not, the experts in the history of technology will have to testify as to what would have been knowable at the time of distribution if manufacturers had spent the proper amount on safety in prior years. To state the issue is to fully understand the great difficulties it would engender in a courtroom.

Beshada v. Johns-Manville Products Corp., 447 A.2d 539, 548 (N.J. 1982).

Without a credible threat of negligence liability, manufacturers do not have an adequate financial incentive for engaging in safety research. That incentive is restored by a rule of strict liability that makes manufacturers legally responsible for risks that have been discovered by the time of trial, even if they were not reasonably foreseeable at the time of sale.

> Defendants have treated the level of technological knowledge at a given time as an independent variable not affected by defendants' conduct. But this view ignores the important role of industry in product safety research. The "state-of-the-art" at a given time is partly determined by how much industry invests in safety research. By imposing on manufacturers the costs of failure to discover hazards, we create an incentive for them to invest more actively in safety research.

Id.

The court's reasoning is no different from that which supplies the evidentiary rationale for strict liability in the context of manufacturing defects. *See* Chapter 2, section II. Is there any reason to apply different logic to warning defects? (Note that *Beshada* has since been restricted under New Jersey law "to the circumstances giving rise to its holding." Feldman v. Lederle Labs., 479 A.2d 374, 388 (N.J. 1984).)

3. *The insurability of risk.* Recall that the California Supreme Court in *Anderson* limited liability to foreseeable risks to prevent manufacturers from becoming "insurers" of their products. Could the difficulty of insuring against liability for unforeseeable risks provide a reason for limiting the duty to foreseeable risks? Consider Randi W. v. Muroc Jt. Unified Sch. Dist., 929 P.2d 582, 588 (Cal. 1997) (explaining that under California law, whether courts will recognize a tort duty depends on "the availability, cost, and prevalence of insurance for the risk involved").

The insurability of a risk depends on the quality of actuarial data regarding the probability and the severity of loss. Insurers usually do not have difficulty collecting such data for manufacturing defects. For example, the sales volume of a soda manufacturer can provide a solid statistical basis for determining the probability that a particular bottle will explode. The extent of liability for any given defect is also largely predictable because each malfunction is typically an isolated incident. For these reasons, manufacturing defects and product malfunctions ordinarily have the actuarial characteristics required for insurability. (An important counterexample is provided by the class of "unavoidably unsafe" medical products discussed in Chapter 9.)

By contrast, the unforeseeable risks potentially governed by a duty to warn do not have the properties of an insurable risk. The appropriate insurance premium depends on the probability and magnitude of loss. How can the insurer calculate the probability of a risk that by definition is unknown? The insurability problem is then exacerbated by the potential scope of liability. A warning defect involves the entire product line, whereas a manufacturing defect usually involves a limited number of aberrations from the product line. The potential scope of liability for warning defects is vast, as starkly illustrated by the asbestos cases. The magnitude of the liability exposure, coupled with the intractable difficulty of estimating the likelihood of liability, makes it extraordinarily hard to insure against unforeseeable risks. *See generally* Mark A. Geistfeld, *Legal Ambiguity, Liability*

Insurance, and Tort Reform, 60 DePaul L. Rev. 539 (2011) (explaining in general why uncertainty about the extent of liability exposure disrupts the market for liability insurance by significantly increasing insurance premiums and reducing supply).

An instructive example is provided by terrorism insurance. Following the September 11, 2001 terrorist attacks on the World Trade Center, insurers became understandably concerned about the difficulty of estimating the probability of future terrorist attacks and the potential severity of those attacks. Rather than try to insure these unpredictable liabilities, insurers simply excluded such risks from coverage.

> Faced with a significant increase in uncertainty about the frequency and severity of future terrorist events, international reinsurers responded to the event by excluding or significantly restricting terrorism coverage from most reinsurance policies. This in turn motivated primary insurers to exclude terrorism coverage from most commercial lines insurance policies.

J. David Cummins & Christopher M. Lewis, *Catastrophic Events, Parameter Uncertainty and the Breakdown of Implicit Long-Term Contracting: The Case of Terrorism Insurance*, 26 J. Risk & Uncertainty 153, 153-154 (2003).

When liability insurance is not available or is otherwise exceedingly expensive, manufacturers might not enter into the most vulnerable product markets (like those involving new drugs) or otherwise substantially increase product price in the hope of covering the unknown liability costs. In either event, consumers incur these costs. If these costs exceed the safety benefit that would be created by strict liability, consumers reasonably expect that warning liability is limited to the risks that were reasonably foreseeable at the time of sale.

Without data that would conclusively resolve the risk-utility issue, we cannot determine which liability rule is in the best interest of consumers. This indeterminacy, however, explains why courts can reach different conclusions about the appropriate liability rule while still relying on substantively equivalent conceptions of products liability.

III. TO WHOM MUST THE WARNING BE DIRECTED?

According to *Restatement (Second)* §402A cmt. j, "In order to prevent the product from being unreasonably dangerous, the seller may be required to give directions or warning, on the container, as to its use." A product is "unreasonably dangerous" when it is "dangerous to an extent beyond that which would be contemplated by the ordinary consumer who purchases it, with ordinary knowledge common to the community as to its characteristics." *Id.* cmt. i. The warning, therefore, must be formulated by reference to the informational needs of the ordinary consumer, making the duty to warn dependent on the characteristics of the ordinary consumer and the sources of information otherwise available to him or her.

A. The Average or Ordinary Consumer

JOHNSON v. AMERICAN STANDARD, INC.
Supreme Court of California, 2008
179 P.3d 905

CHIN, J. Plaintiff William Keith Johnson is a trained and certified heating, ventilation, and air conditioning (HVAC) technician. He began working in the HVAC field in 1996 when he first received training at ITT Technical Institute, where he completed a year-long course on HVAC systems. Plaintiff continued to work as an HVAC technician until 2002. He received additional training and certifications, both on and off the job, including an Environmental Protection Agency (EPA) "universal" certification after he passed a five-part exam. "Universal" certification is the highest certification an HVAC technician can obtain from the EPA, and it allows those certified to work on, and purchase, refrigerant for large commercial air conditioning systems. "Universally" certified technicians are trained professionals, and their tasks include brazing (welding) and part replacement.

Large air conditioning systems commonly use R-22, a hydrochlorofluorocarbon refrigerant. The refrigerant can decompose into phosgene gas when exposed to flame or high heat, as could happen while a technician is brazing air conditioner pipes containing residual refrigerant. Exposure to phosgene gas may cause numerous health problems, and manufacturers and HVAC technicians have generally known of the dangers this exposure could cause since as early as 1931. The dangers and risks associated with R-22 are noted on Material Safety Data Sheets (MSDS's). The purpose of MSDS's is to inform those who may come into contact with potentially hazardous chemicals about their dangers. Employers are required to use the MSDS to train and educate their employees about the chemicals and dangers to which they may be exposed on the job. Among other things, employers are required to tell employees where they can find the MSDS's, how to read them, how to detect the presence of dangerous materials, and how to protect against possible health hazards from those materials. Beginning in 1997, every time he purchased the refrigerant R-22, plaintiff received, and sometimes read, an MSDS.

In June 2003, plaintiff filed his first amended complaint, suing various chemical manufacturers, chemical suppliers, and manufacturers of air conditioning equipment, including defendant American Standard, Inc. Plaintiff specifically alleged that he brazed refrigerant lines on an evaporator defendant manufactured in 1965 that contained R-22 refrigerant, creating and exposing him to phosgene gas. Plaintiff alleged that the maintenance and repairs he performed on air conditioning units in the normal course of his job created and exposed him to phosgene gas, causing him to develop pulmonary fibrosis. The causes of action against defendant are based on its alleged failure to warn of the potential hazards of R-22 exposure. They include negligence, strict liability failure to warn, strict liability design defect, and breach of implied warranties.

In each cause of action, plaintiff's theory was that defendant knew that servicing the evaporator would create harmful phosgene gas, but defendant failed to provide plaintiff with an adequate warning. As the Court of Appeal observed, plaintiff contended that "a warning would be adequate if it informed users that

III. To Whom Must the Warning Be Directed?

brazing refrigerant lines can result in creation of phosgene, that phosgene inhalation can result in potentially fatal lung disease, that phosgene can be detected through its fresh-cut-grass smell, changes in flame color during brazing, or physical symptoms like burning eyes or shortness of breath, and that users should wear respiratory protection while brazing and stop brazing on detection of phosgene."

In May 2004, defendant moved for summary judgment. Defendant claimed it had no duty to warn about the risks of R-22 exposure because it could assume that the group of trained professionals to which plaintiff belonged, and plaintiff himself, were aware of those risks. As the Court of Appeal observed, "the undisputed facts were that under federal law, HVAC technicians who work on commercial equipment must be certified by the EPA with 'universal' certification, which is granted after an exam. They are 'trained professionals.' Most HVAC technicians also have some kind of trade or professional training. [Plaintiff] had universal certification and had completed a one-year course of study in HVAC systems at ITT Technical Institute." In September 2004, the trial court granted defendant's motion for summary judgment and entered judgment in its favor on both grounds. The Court of Appeal affirmed the trial court's judgment on the sole ground that the sophisticated user defense applies in California. The court held that "a manufacturer cannot be liable to a sophisticated user of its product for failure to warn of a risk, if a sophisticated user should reasonably know of that risk." The Court of Appeal held that because plaintiff's theory was the same in all causes of action, i.e., product liability through the failure to warn, the sophisticated user defense should apply to plaintiff's complaint in its entirety.

The Court of Appeal next addressed whether defendant was entitled to summary judgment "on the theory that there was no duty to warn because the danger at issue was one generally known to members of the profession, one which [plaintiff] 'could reasonably have been expected to know' or . . . [that defendant] had 'reason to expect' that HVAC technicians would know of the risk." The court observed that there was "undisputed evidence that HVAC technicians could reasonably be expected to know of the hazard of brazing refrigerant lines." Despite plaintiff's testimony that he had read the MSDS for R-22, but did not understand that he should avoid heating it, the Court of Appeal concluded that there was undisputed evidence from the relevant declarations and depositions of HVAC technicians that the EPA requires those professionals "to understand the decomposition products of refrigerants at high temperatures." The court noted that "the study guide informed users that refrigerant in contact with high heat can form dangerous substances, and the Material Safety Data Sheet for R-22 informed technicians that the product can decompose when in contact with heat, releasing toxic gases." The court affirmed the summary judgment in defendant's favor. We granted review to determine whether the sophisticated user defense should apply in California.

The sophisticated user defense exempts manufacturers from their typical obligation to provide product users with warnings about the products' potential hazards. The defense is considered an exception to the manufacturer's general duty to warn consumers, and therefore, in most jurisdictions, if successfully argued, acts as an affirmative defense to negate the manufacturer's duty to warn.

As we explain further below, the sophisticated user defense evolved out of the *Restatement (Second) of Torts*, section 388 and the obvious danger rule, an accepted principle and defense in California. In addition, as we explain, the defense applies equally to strict liability and negligent failure to warn cases. The duty to warn is measured by what is generally known or should have been known to the class of sophisticated users, rather than by the individual plaintiff's subjective knowledge.

Section 388 provides that a supplier of goods is liable for physical harm the goods cause if the supplier knows, or should know, the items are likely to be dangerous, fails to reasonably warn of the danger, and "has no reason to believe that those for whose use the chattel is supplied will realize its dangerous condition." Comment k to section 388, subdivision (b), is entitled "When warning of defects unnecessary," and it emphasizes this point. It declares that although the condition may be one that only specialists would perceive, the supplier is only required to inform the users of the risk if the manufacturer has "no reason to believe that those who use it will have such special experience as will enable them to perceive the danger[.]" Courts have interpreted section 388(b) to mean that if the manufacturer reasonably believes the user will know or should know about a given product's risk, the manufacturer need not warn that user of that risk. [ ]

Other jurisdictions that have adopted the sophisticated user defense have cited section 388 and the obvious danger rule as a basis for doing so. [ ] California law also recognizes the obvious danger rule, which provides that there is no need to warn of known risks under either a negligence or strict liability theory. [ ]

Although the Court of Appeal was aware that no California court has squarely adopted the sophisticated user doctrine, the court observed that "it is a natural outgrowth of the rule that there is no duty to warn of known risks or obvious dangers." As the Court of Appeal reasoned, the sophisticated user defense simply recognizes the exception to the principle that consumers generally lack knowledge about certain products, for example, heavy industrial equipment, and hence the dangers associated with them are not obvious. For those individuals or members of professions who do know or should know about the product's potential dangers, that is, sophisticated users, the dangers should be obvious, and the defense should apply. Just as a manufacturer need not warn ordinary consumers about generally known dangers, a manufacturer need not warn members of a trade or profession (sophisticated users) about dangers generally known to that trade or profession.

Requiring manufacturers to warn their products' users in all instances would place an onerous burden on them and would "invite mass consumer disregard and ultimate contempt for the warning process." Twerski et al., *The Use and Abuse of Warnings in Products Liability-Design Defect Litigation*, 61 Cornell L. Rev. 495, 521 (1976). The sophisticated user defense fits into this understanding of the role of warnings; it helps ensure that warnings will be heeded.

In addition, numerous generally safe products exist that can become hazardous when the proper precautions are not followed. Although manufacturers are responsible for products that contain dangers of which the public is unaware, they are not insurers, even under strict liability, for the mistakes or carelessness of consumers who should know of the dangers involved. Accordingly, we adopt the defense in California. We now examine the defense's exact contours.

III. To Whom Must the Warning Be Directed?

1. A "Should Have Known" Standard

A manufacturer is not liable to a sophisticated user of its product for failure to warn of a risk, harm, or danger, if the sophisticated user knew or should have known of that risk, harm, or danger. It would be nearly impossible for a manufacturer to predict or determine whether a given user or member of the sophisticated group actually has knowledge of the dangers because of the infinite number of user idiosyncrasies. For example, given users may have misread their training manuals, failed to study the information in those manuals, or simply forgotten what they were taught. However, individuals who represent that they are trained or are members of a sophisticated group of users are saying to the world that they possess the level of knowledge and skill associated with that class. If they do not actually possess that knowledge and skill, that fact should not give rise to liability on the part of the manufacturer.

Under the "should have known" standard there will be some users who were actually unaware of the dangers. However, the same could be said of the currently accepted obvious danger rule; obvious dangers are obvious to most, but are not obvious to absolutely everyone. The obvious danger rule is an objective test, and the courts do not inquire into the user's subjective knowledge in such a case. In other words, even if a user was truly unaware of a product's hazards, that fact is irrelevant if the danger was objectively obvious. Thus, under the sophisticated user defense, the inquiry focuses on whether the plaintiff knew, or should have known, of the particular risk of harm from the product giving rise to the injury.

2. Applicability to Negligence and Strict Liability Causes of Action

Although California law recognizes the differences between negligence and strict liability causes of action (Anderson v. Owens-Corning Fiberglas Corp., 810 P.2d 549 (1991)), the sophisticated user defense is applicable to both. [O]ur *Anderson* holding recognizes there is little functional difference between the two theories in the failure to warn context.

In the context of sophisticated user defense, because the intended users are deemed to know of the risks, manufacturers have no obligation to warn, and providing no warning is appropriate. The focus of the defense, therefore, is whether the danger in question was so generally known within the trade or profession that a manufacturer should not have been expected to provide a warning specific to the group to which plaintiff belonged. Consequently, there is no reason why the sophisticated user defense should not be as available against strict liability causes of action as it is for negligence causes of action. In both instances, the sophisticated user's knowledge eliminates the manufacturer's need for a warning.

3. Determining User Sophistication

The relevant time for determining user sophistication for purposes of this exception to a manufacturer's duty to warn is when the sophisticated user is injured and knew or should have known of the risk. As amicus curiae Product Liability Advisory Counsel observe, the Court of Appeal "correctly understood the defense to eliminate any duty to warn when the expected user population is generally aware of the risk at issue, and correctly rejected the argument that a manufacturer's duty to warn should turn on the individual plaintiff's actual understanding of the risk. Legal duties must be based on objective general predictions of the anticipated user population's knowledge, not case-by-case hindsight examinations of the particular plaintiff's subjective state of mind." As the Court of Appeal pointed out, "[t]he sophisticated user defense will always be employed when a sophisticated user should have, but did not, know of the risk. Otherwise, the issue would be actual knowledge and causation." Therefore, the sophisticated user's knowledge of the risk is measured from the time of the plaintiff's injury, rather than from the date the product was manufactured. The timeline focuses on the general population of sophisticated users and conforms to the defense's purpose to eliminate any duty to warn when the expected user population is generally aware of the risk at issue.

We conclude that there is no triable issue of fact regarding applicability of the sophisticated user defense in this case. We therefore affirm the Court of Appeal's judgment.

NOTES AND QUESTIONS

1. *Warnings and the overlap of negligence and strict products liability.* Instead of relying on the warning requirement contained in the §402A rule of strict products liability, the court analyzed the duty to warn in relation to §388 of the *Restatement (Second)*, which is a negligence rule. Does the court's analysis undermine its holding in *Anderson*, p. 257 *supra*, that "in strict liability, as opposed to negligence, the reasonableness of the defendant's failure to warn is immaterial"?

2. *When the ordinary consumer is sophisticated.* To what extent is the sophisticated user defense a direct implication of the principle that the duty to warn is formulated to address the informational needs of the ordinary consumer? The characteristics of the ordinary consumer often depend on the product. For example, the ordinary consumer of a surgical instrument is a surgeon with specialized knowledge. Does the sophisticated user defense simply recognize that for the product in question, the ordinary consumer is "sophisticated" about the safety issue in question and accordingly doesn't require a warning about the matter?

3. *Limiting the duty to the informational needs of the ordinary consumer.* Why formulate the liability rule by reference to the informational needs of the ordinary consumer if the plaintiff can prove that she did not understand the risk? Even if such a warning would be informative for only a few consumers, why is that safety benefit insufficient for justifying the duty to warn? According to the court in *Johnson*, such a warning, on balance, would presumably create a greater safety problem by inviting "mass consumer disregard" of the warning. What reasoning does the court implicitly rely on to reach this conclusion?

4. *The ordinary consumer and individual differences.* How can a duty formulated by reference to the needs of the ordinary consumer account for differences among consumers based on physical characteristics, intellectual

III. To Whom Must the Warning Be Directed?

abilities, or proficiency with English? Insofar as a plaintiff is not like most everyone else, is that difference necessarily irrelevant to the adequacy of the product warning?

LIVINGSTON v. MARIE CALLENDER'S, INC.
Court of Appeal, Second District, California, 1999
72 Cal. App. 4th 830; 85 Cal. Rptr. 2d 528

TURNER, J. The question in this case is whether a restaurant offering vegetable soup "made from the freshest ingredients, from scratch, . . . every day," has an affirmative obligation to warn customers the soup contains monosodium glutamate (MSG). Plaintiff alleged that on July 12, 1993, he went to a Marie Callender's restaurant in Toluca Lake for lunch. He reviewed the menu and was interested in ordering a bowl of vegetable soup. He told the waitress he had asthma and he wanted to know if the soup contained MSG. The waitress assured plaintiff the soup did not contain MSG. Plaintiff ordered and consumed the soup. In fact, the soup did contain MSG. As a result of consuming the soup, plaintiff suffered MSG Symptom Complex including, but not limited to, respiratory arrest, hypoxia, cardiac arrest, and brain damage. In his first cause of action, for strict liability, plaintiff alleged the presence of MSG in the soup rendered it defective and unfit for human consumption. Plaintiff also asserted causes of action for negligence, breach of implied warranty, breach of express warranty, negligent misrepresentation, and intentional spoliation of evidence.

The trial court struck plaintiff's causes of action with the exception of his negligence claim and dismissed all defendants except Marie Callender's # 24, the restaurant. The trial court concluded "there was nothing wrong with the soup, or the MSG in the soup."

The case proceeded to trial on defendant's negligence cause of action against the restaurant. A special verdict form was submitted to the jury. The first question asked, "Was the defendant negligent?" The jury responded in the negative. A judgment was entered on the special verdict. This appeal followed.

The failure to warn contention in the present case arises in the context of a person with an allergy to a particular food additive, MSG. California has adopted the *Restatement (Second) of Torts*, section 402A, comment j application of strict tort liability failure to warn in the case of allergies.

Restatement (Second) of Torts, section 402A, comment j states:

Directions or warning. In order to prevent the product from being unreasonably dangerous, the seller may be required to give directions or warning, on the container, as to its use. The seller may reasonably assume that those with common allergies, as for example to eggs or strawberries, will be aware of them, and he is not required to warn against them. Where, however, the product contains an ingredient to which a substantial number of the population are allergic, and the ingredient is one whose danger is not generally known, or if known is one which the consumer would reasonably not expect to find in the product, the seller is required to give warning against it, if he has knowledge, or by the application of reasonable, developed human skill and foresight should have knowledge, of the presence of the ingredient and the danger.

Likewise in the case of poisonous drugs, or those unduly dangerous for other reasons, warning as to use may be required.

The recently adopted *Restatement Third of Torts: Products Liability*, section 2, comment k, similarly states: "Cases of adverse allergic or idiosyncratic reactions involve a special subset of products that may be defective because of inadequate warnings. . . . [¶] The general rule in cases involving allergic reactions is that a warning is required when the harm-causing ingredient is one to which a substantial number of persons are allergic." Further, comment k notes: "The ingredient that causes the allergic reaction must be one whose danger or whose presence in the product is not generally known to consumers. . . . When the presence of the allergenic ingredient would not be anticipated by a reasonable user or consumer, warnings concerning its presence are required."

Those issues not having been tried, it was error to strike plaintiff's strict liability cause of action. The matter is remanded for a limited retrial on the issue of whether any defendant is liable for failure to warn of an ingredient to which a substantial number of the population are allergic within the meaning of comment j to section 402A of the *Restatement Second of Torts*.

NOTES AND QUESTIONS

1. *Warnings and the overlap of negligence and strict products liability yet again.* Unlike the *Johnson* case, p. 266 *supra*, in which the California Supreme Court analyzed the duty to warn by relying on §388 of the *Restatement (Second)*, the California appellate court in *Livingston* analyzed the duty under §402A. Would the outcome have been any different if the court had analyzed the issue under §388?

2. *The "substantial number" requirement.* How should a court determine what constitutes a "substantial number of the population" that must be allergic to establish the duty to warn? In one case, the court made the following observations with respect to the risk of an allergic reaction from mold exposure:

> [Defendant] cites several products liability cases in which it was found that an insignificant number of persons were affected by the ingredient [thereby negating the seller's duty to warn]. In each case the number is extremely small: one out of 1,000,000 products sold (which would be the equivalent of .0001%), 3 instances out of 225,000,000 sold (.0000013%), reactions in .6 to 1.9 out of 100,000 persons in the general population (.0006 to .0019%), and four reported complaints out of 7,000,000 applications of the product sold (.0000571%). [However,] 5% is not an insignificant proportion of people to become clinically ill from mold exposure. *See* Green v. Smith & Nephew AHP, Inc., 629 N.W.2d 727, 752-55 (Wis. 2001) (holding that latex gloves could be deemed a defective and unreasonably dangerous product when they caused an allergic reaction in 5 to 17% of consumers); Ray v. Upjohn Co., 851 S.W.2d 646, 655 (Mo. Ct. App. 1993) (finding Plaintiff sufficiently established chemical manufactured by defendant was unreasonably dangerous when 5% of the population exposed to

III. To Whom Must the Warning Be Directed?

the isocyanates in the chemical will acquire permanent asthma); *see also* Stinson v. DuPont de Nemours and Co., 904 S.W.2d 428, 431 (Mo. Ct. App. 1995) (relevant number was 7% of the population).

Brandt v. Rokey Realty Co., 2006 WL 1942314, at *24 (Del. Super. 2006).

According to the *Restatement (Third)* §2 comment k, the substantiality requirement depends both on the number of consumers vulnerable to the allergic reaction and the severity of injury:

> The degree of substantiality is not precisely quantifiable. Clearly the plaintiff in most cases must show that the allergic predisposition is not unique to the plaintiff. In determining whether the plaintiff has carried the burden in this regard, however, the court may properly consider the severity of the plaintiff's harm. The more severe the harm, the more justified is a conclusion that the number of persons at risk need not be large to be considered "substantial" so as to require a warning. Essentially, this reflects the same risk-utility balancing undertaken in warnings cases generally. But courts explicitly impose the requirement of substantiality in cases involving adverse allergic reactions.

Does this reasoning provide sufficient guidance for the trial court in *Livingston* to determine, on remand, whether a "substantial number" of consumers are allergic to MSG?

3. *Allergic reactions and foreseeability.* In analyzing the duty to warn about allergic reactions, courts often frame the inquiry in terms of foreseeability. "The reason most often quoted to support the general rule denying recovery to unusually allergic users of products was articulated by the Supreme Court of Utah: 'Every substance, including food which is daily consumed by the public, occasionally becomes anathema to him peculiarly allergic to it. To require insurability against such an unforeseeable happenstance would weaken the structure of common sense, as well as present an unreasonable burden on the channels of trade.'" Adelman-Tremblay v. Jewel Companies, Inc., 859 F.2d 517, 524 (7th Cir. 1988) (quoting Bennett v. Pilot Prods. Co., 235 P.2d 525, 527 (Utah 1951)). Is an allergic reaction only foreseeable when it would affect a "substantial number" of consumers? Or does the substantiality requirement impose an additional limitation of liability?

4. *Whither the ordinary consumer?* The duty to warn is formulated by reference to the informational needs of the ordinary consumer, regardless of whether the individual plaintiff required a warning. Nevertheless, courts recognize that there is a duty to warn about allergic reactions if a "substantial number" of consumers have the allergy. Is there a way to square the duty involving allergic reactions with the duty defined by the informational needs of the ordinary consumer?

One way to incorporate individual differences within the "average or ordinary" consumer standard is by the following approach:

> The average consumer wants the warning to contain any disclosures that would significantly [or materially] affect her decisions

about product purchases or use. By definition, the average consumer has the average amount of information. To understand what this means, consider a case in which 50% of all consumers fully understand a risk and the remaining 50% do not adequately comprehend the risk. A consumer with the average amount of information can be thought of as someone who knows there is a 50% chance that he fully understands the risk and a 50% chance that he does not. The average consumer would want the warning to disclose the risk if the 50% chance of benefitting from the disclosure exceeds the cost of reading the disclosure. Materiality therefore depends upon the chance that an individual will benefit from disclosure (that is, the proportion of uninformed consumers in the group) and the amount of benefit an uninformed individual derives from the disclosure.

Mark Geistfeld, *Inadequate Product Warnings and Causation*, 30 U. Mich. J.L. Reform 309, 323-324 (1997).

Consider how this reasoning applies to allergic reactions. Anyone is potentially vulnerable to suffering an allergic reaction of some sort. Some are allergic to peanuts, others to MSG or even to allergens of which they are unaware. Individuals can also develop allergies over time. Consequently, the average or ordinary consumer can be conceptualized as someone who is aware that he or she could be vulnerable to an allergic reaction. For this reason, the average or ordinary consumer would want to be apprised of allergic risks posed by products.

How much information does the consumer want? The answer depends on the likelihood that the consumer would benefit from the warning in addition to the severity of injury. In risk-utility terms, this amount equals the risk of allergic reaction (the *PL* term), which can be defined by the probability (P) that an individual consumer is vulnerable to allergic reactions and would benefit from the warning by avoiding the reaction and suffering injury or loss (L). This safety benefit must then be compared to the cost of the warning for the consumer. In some cases, the warning could be formulated so that the ordinary consumer without allergies would not have to read that portion of the warning and incur the associated costs of doing so. When the cost for the ordinary consumer is minimal ($B \approx 0$), the possibility that a small fraction (say 1% or .01) would definitely suffer a severe allergic reaction would justify a warning ($B \approx 0 < .01L$). But as the cost of disclosure (B) increases, or as the risk of allergic reaction (*PL*) decreases, then all else being equal, a larger proportion of consumers must have the allergic predisposition to satisfy the "substantial number" requirement.

For these reasons, the requirement that a "substantial number" of consumers must be vulnerable to the allergic reaction is "not precisely quantifiable.... The more severe the harm, the more justified is a conclusion that the number of persons at risk need not be large to be considered 'substantial' so as to require a warning. Essentially, this reflects the same risk-utility balancing undertaken in warnings cases generally." RESTATEMENT (THIRD) OF TORTS: PRODUCTS LIABILITY §2 cmt. k.

5. *Does the plaintiff have to know about the allergic condition?* What if the seller knows that a substantial number of consumers will suffer an allergic

III. To Whom Must the Warning Be Directed?

reaction, but none of the consumers know in advance whether they would have such a reaction? Consider Merrill v. Beaute Vues Corp., 235 F.2d 893 (10th Cir. 1956) (concluding that such a warning would be ineffective and need not be given by the seller). Suppose that 1 percent of the entire population would suffer a fatal allergic reaction if they used the product. Would the ordinary consumer want to know of an inherent 1 percent risk that he or she might be killed by an allergic reaction of which she is otherwise unaware? Would the consumer evaluate that risk any differently than other types of inherent product risks, such as the likelihood that one will suffer a side effect from a drug or vaccine she has never previously used?

6. *Allergic reactions and other types of individual differences.* If a "substantial number" of consumers are different from the ordinary consumer in some important respect other than an allergic reaction, is there any reason to analyze the duty question differently?

MEDINA v. LOUISVILLE LADDER, INC.
United States District Court, Middle District of Florida, 2007
496 F. Supp. 2d 1324

CONWAY, J. This is a product liability/personal injury case. Plaintiffs Arnaldo Medina and his wife, Luz Lopez, sue Defendants Louisville Ladder, Inc. and Home Depot U.S.A., Inc., for injuries Medina suffered when he fell from a wooden attic ladder and impacted his elbow. Louisville Ladder manufactured the ladder; Home Depot sold it to Medina. The Complaint asserts theories of strict product liability and negligence. The Defendants seek summary judgment.

The product involved in the accident is an 11-step, ceiling-mounted wooden attic ladder, designated as Model L224P. The ladder has a rated load capacity of 250 pounds. It consists of three separate sections that are attached with steel hinges, thereby allowing the product to fold up. Louisville Ladder manufactured the ladder in December 2004. Home Depot sold it to Medina in the Spring of 2005. The point of sale was Osceola County, Florida. The ladder carried a warning label in English and was supplied with an English-only instruction manual.

After he bought the ladder, Medina says he was going to try to install it himself, but he noticed that the installation instructions were in English. Medina has, at best, a very limited ability to read English. Medina hired a local handyman, Ismael Gonzales, to help him install the ladder. Apparently, Gonzales also cannot read English very well, or at all. In any event, neither man read the installation instructions. Medina and Gonzales improperly installed the ladder in that they failed to trim its legs as directed in the installation instructions. Consequently, the legs were not flush with the floor, and gaps existed at the ladder's joints. Prior to the accident, Medina and his sons used the ladder 25-40 times without incident. On January 2, 2006, while Medina was on the ladder, the ladder collapsed and Medina fell to the floor, injuring his elbow. Upon inspection, it was discovered that the bottom folding section of the ladder had separated from the middle section, and the rivets securing the hinges connecting the bottom and middle sections had failed.

The gravamen of the Complaint is that the ladder was defective because it lacked warnings and instructions in Spanish, and that the Defendants were negligent in failing to include warnings and instructions in that language. As support for that proposition, Plaintiffs rely on the case of Stanley Indus., Inc. v. W.M. Barr & Co., Inc., 784 F. Supp. 1570 (S.D. Fla. 1992).

Stanley arose from a fire at an industrial plant, allegedly caused by the spontaneous combustion of rags soaked in linseed oil. The two employees who used the linseed oil were brothers from Nicaragua. Their primary language was Spanish. The labeling on the linseed oil can was in English. "Both employees testified that they would have sought more information on how to use the product if the label contained warnings in Spanish concerning the flammability of the product." 784 F. Supp. at 1573. Prior to the date of the fire, the defendants, acting cooperatively, regularly and actively advertised in Spanish in the Miami market. Additionally, the retailer (ironically, Home Depot) "employed a translator service to convert English instructions to Spanish for several of its product lines, including between forty and seventy products, which it marketed with bilingual instructions." *Id.*

The property owner sued Home Depot and the manufacturer of the linseed oil (Barr), asserting claims of negligent failure to warn, strict liability, and breach of warranty of fitness for a particular purpose. The inadequate warning theory was premised on the notion, among others, that

> the language on the backside of the product label was in English only and contained no pictographs or symbols, and therefore was inadequate to fairly, appropriately and comprehensively warn Spanish-speaking, monolingual product users of the dangers likely to be encountered with the product's use[,] especially the dangers associated with the risk of fire due to spontaneous combustion in linseed oil soaked rags.

Id. (alteration added). The defendants sought summary on causation grounds.

Judge Moreno of the Southern District determined as a threshold matter that issues regarding warning adequacy and proximate cause were "inextricably intertwined." *Id.* at 1574. Turning to the adequacy issue, Judge Moreno began by noting: "The issue of adequacy of a warning that does not include multilingual warnings or universally accepted pictographs or symbols, in view of defendants' active marketing of their products in the Hispanic media in the Miami market, is a question of first impression in this district." *Id.* at 1575. After observing that under Florida law warning adequacy issues "are for the jury to resolve," and citing "the defendants' joint advertising in Miami's Hispanic media and the nature of the product," and the fact that "a large portion of the unskilled or semi-skilled Miami workforce is comprised of foreign nationals whose native tongue is not English," Judge Moreno then concluded that genuine issues of material fact existed regarding "the adequacy of the warning label, the duty to warn and proximate cause." *Id.* at 1575-76. On the specific subject of warning adequacy, Judge Moreno stated: "Given the advertising of defendants' product in the Hispanic media and the pervasive presence of foreign-tongued individuals in the Miami workforce, it is for the jury to decide whether a warning, to be adequate, must contain language other than English or pictorial warning symbols." *Id.* at 1576.

III. To Whom Must the Warning Be Directed?

Respectfully, this Court disagrees with *Stanley* and declines to follow it. On the issue of whether bilingual instructions may be necessary in Florida, the decision represents isolated precedent. According to Westlaw, in the more than 15 years since *Stanley* was decided, not a single published Florida case (state or federal) has relied on the decision to conclude that bilingual warnings and instructions may be necessary under Florida law.

More fundamentally, there is no indication that Florida law imposes a duty on manufacturers and sellers to provide bilingual warnings on consumer products, and this Court is unwilling to extend the concept of duty that far. Similarly, apart from *Stanley*, there is no indication that a product may be found unreasonably dangerous under Florida law merely because it lacks bilingual warnings and instructions. Again, this Court is unwilling to extend the bounds of strict product liability law and negligence that far. Further, the Court is unpersuaded that the circumstances Plaintiffs rely on to bring their case within the ambit of *Stanley*—that Home Depot advertises in Spanish in a state having a roughly 20% Hispanic population, that its store aisle-ways have English and Spanish signs, and that Louisville Ladder provides bilingual instructions to assemblers and purchasers in other countries—mandate a different conclusion.

In sum, Plaintiffs have not presented evidence from which a reasonable jury could conclude that the subject ladder was unreasonably dangerous, or that the Defendants were negligent.

Defendants' Dispositive Motion for Summary Judgment is GRANTED.

NOTES AND QUESTIONS

1. *Multilingual warnings.* In Farias v. Mr. Heater, Inc., 684 F.3d 1231 (11th Cir. 2012), the court followed the reasoning in *Medina* and held that the defendant had no duty to warn in Spanish because there was no evidence that it had "specifically marketed" the product "in any way to Spanish-speaking customers through the use of Hispanic media." If a substantial number of consumers are only fluent in Spanish, should the duty to warn be limited by the manufacturer's marketing efforts? Consider Crawfordsville Town & Country Center v. Cordova, 119 N.E.3d 119, 130 (Ind. Ct. App. 2019) (holding that there was no duty to provide bilingual warnings, in part, because there was "no evidence" that defendant had marketed the product "specifically to non-English speakers").

By contrast, the New Jersey Supreme Court reached a different conclusion about the duty to warn: "In view of the unskilled or semi-skilled nature of the work and the existence of many in the work force who do not read English, warnings in the form of symbols might have been appropriate." Campos v. Firestone Tire & Rubber Co., 485 A.2d 305, 309 (N.J. 1984); *see also* Hubbard-Hall Chemical Co. v. Silverman, 340 F.2d 402 (1st Cir. 1965) ("We are of opinion that the jury could reasonably have believed that defendant should have foreseen that its admittedly dangerous product would be used by, among others, persons like plaintiffs' intestates, who were farm laborers, of limited education and reading ability, and that a warning . . . would not, because of its lack of a skull and bones or other comparable symbols or hieroglyphics, be adequate instructions or warnings of [the product's] dangerous condition."). Is foreseeability the test for determining whether there is a duty to warn in more than one language or format?

2. *The problem of illiteracy.* As implied by the cases discussed in the preceding note, courts must also determine the appropriate form of communication when a substantial number of consumers are illiterate. Should the seller have a duty to warn with universally understood symbols, like a skull and crossbones? Or should an illiterate user be obligated to have someone else read the warning? Consider Henry v. General Motors Corp., 60 F.3d 1545 (11th Cir. 1995) (noting that the illiterate plaintiff was aware of the warning and "did not ask anyone to read it to him," and then rejecting warning claim on ground that "if the user is aware of a warning but ignores its language, the manufacturer's negligence in drafting the warning ceases as a matter of law to be a cause of the injury"); *see also* Farias v. Mr. Heater, Inc., 757 F. Supp. 2d 1284, 1293 (S.D. Fla. 2010) ("It would be improper to find such clear warnings inadequate because Plaintiff here was not well-versed in English and did not investigate the danger to which she had been alerted in the use of the [product]."), *aff'd*, 684 F.3d 1231 (11th Cir. 2012).

3. *Reconsidering the relevance of individual differences.* Can *Medina* be squared with the duty to warn of allergic reactions? In each type of case, the average or ordinary consumer does not actually have the trait in question (most do not suffer from the allergy, and most are literate in English). In other cases courts have imposed a duty to warn of a serious allergic reaction when 5 percent of the exposed consumer population was vulnerable to that reaction. The evidence in *Medina* showed that approximately 20 percent of the relevant consumer population was Hispanic. Why is there a duty to warn in the former case, but not the latter? Are allergic reactions any different from other types of individual differences? Consider Crawfordsville Town & Country Center, 119 N.E.3d at 129 (concluding that there was no duty to provide a bilingual warning by analogizing to a case holding that "the seller had no obligation to provide additional warnings regarding the airbags even though it was aware of the plaintiff's short stature" that exposed the plaintiff to a risk of being injured by the deployment of the airbag).

To analyze these issues, we need to look more closely at the risk-utility issues implicated by the duty to warn. Assuming that the average or ordinary consumer speaks and reads English, would he or she be significantly burdened by symbols or warnings written in another language? Does the issue depend on whether the warnings in question are in a manual, which can contain separate sections written in different languages, as opposed to on the product itself, where a warning of one type has the potential to "crowd out" warnings of another type? We explore this issue in further detail in section V. If the warning could be placed in a separate section of an instruction manual, the burden of providing a bilingual warning is insignificant (ink and paper). Under these conditions, such a warning would benefit the average or ordinary consumer for essentially the same reasons that apply to allergic reactions: When the burden or cost is minimal for the ordinary consumer ($B \approx 0$), then on average the disclosure would benefit consumers if a substantial number of them (20 percent in *Medina*) would thereby be able to prevent serious physical injury ($B \approx 0 < PL$).

III. To Whom Must the Warning Be Directed?

B. The Role of Intermediaries

In *Johnson*, p. 266 *supra*, the manufacturer provided warnings to the employer, who was then legally obligated to convey them to employees with Material Safety Data Sheets (MSDS's). If such a warning is defective, the employee or other end user can recover from the manufacturer directly—the failure to adequately warn the intermediary foreseeably caused the end user's injury. But even if the manufacturer satisfies its duty to adequately warn the intermediary, in some cases it can still owe an independent duty to the end user.

SOWELL v. AMERICAN CYANAMID CO.
United States Court of Appeals, Eleventh Circuit, 1989
888 F.2d 802

ALLEN, J. In this product liability and negligence suit, plaintiff Sowell is appealing the judgment notwithstanding the verdict entered by the trial court for American Cyanamid Company and J.B. Converse Company, Inc., which set aside a jury verdict of $1,200,000.00 for the plaintiff.

Plaintiff was an employee of the Public Works Department at the Naval Air Station in Pensacola, who was assigned the task of welding a tank at the Naval Air Base. The tank was designed by Converse and contained sulfuric acid supplied by American Cyanamid. The tank exploded while plaintiff was performing his welding job, causing him serious and permanent injuries.

The tank exploded as a result of the tendency of sulfuric acid, when combined with hydrogen, to cause an explosion. No warning signs were placed on the tank; but in order for plaintiff to begin his welding job, he had to secure what is known as a burn permit from the Navy. An individual defendant, Sidney J. Harrison, had given permission to plaintiff to commence the welding. The jury returned a verdict against Harrison upon a theory of negligence, which the trial court upheld.

In the trial court's opinion, it stated that plaintiff was not a user of the product and that the intervening negligence of the Navy defeated plaintiff's right to recover. The trial court's holding that plaintiff was not a user was clearly in contravention of Florida law, which has adopted the *Restatement (Second) of Torts* §402A. Section 402A protects not only purchasers of dangerous products, but also bystanders and ultimate users. Here, plaintiff was the ultimate user and was entitled to the protection afforded by §402A.

As to the question of intervening negligence, the Court is of the opinion that a jury question was presented with respect to the corporate defendants' exercise of reasonable care under the *Restatement (Second) of Torts* §388. Section 388 provides that liability arises when the seller, having reason to know that its product is likely to be dangerous for its intended use, and having no reason to believe that the intended user will realize its dangerous condition, nevertheless fails to exercise reasonable care to inform the user of the dangerous condition.

Comment *n* to §388 states, in part, as follows:

> [W]hile it may be proper to permit a supplier to assume that one through whom he supplies a chattel which is only slightly dangerous will communicate

the information given him to those who are to use it unless he knows that the other is careless, it may be improper to permit him to trust the conveyance of the necessary information of the actual character of a highly dangerous article to a third person of whose character he knows nothing. It may well be that he should take the risk that this information may not be communicated. . . . [I]f the danger involved in the ignorant use of a particular chattel is very great, it may be that the supplier does not exercise reasonable care in entrusting the communication of the necessary information even to a person whom he has good reason to believe to be careful. Many such articles can be made to carry their own message to the understanding of those who are likely to use them by the form in which they are put out, by the container in which they are supplied, or by a label or other device, indicating with a substantial sufficiency their dangerous character. Where the danger involved in the ignorant use of their true quality is great and such means of disclosure are practicable and not unduly burdensome, it may well be that the supplier should be required to adopt them.

Florida also has adopted §388. [ ] Here, the basic issue is whether the corporate defendants discharged their duty to warn the plaintiff. Even though Converse supplied a manual to the Navy regarding the dangers posed by the use of the product, "[t]he determination of whether that method of warning was sufficient depends upon a balancing of considerations, including, among other factors, the dangerous nature of the product, the form in which it is used, the intensity and form of the warnings given, the burdens to be imposed by requiring warnings, and the likelihood that the particular warning will be adequately communicated to those who will foreseeably use the product. The determination as to whether these duties have been reasonably discharged comes within the function of the trier of fact." [ ]

Plaintiff presented to the jury an expert who testified that in light of the potential danger posed by the presence of sulfuric acid in the tank, a visual and dramatic warning should have been afforded by the corporate defendants. He also was of the opinion that although Converse had supplied a manual to the Navy, this did not meet Converse's duty to adequately warn ultimate users. The expert also testified that American Cyanamid could have required its drivers to deliver to the manager of the Navy plant information which they were required by the Department of Transportation to carry on route as to the hazards presented by the sulfuric acid.

The testimony of the expert presented an issue of fact as to whether the corporate defendants had complied with their duties under §338. Therefore, the trial court erred in entering a judgment notwithstanding the verdict for the corporate defendants, and we reverse and direct the trial court to reinstate the jury verdict in the amount of $1,200,000.

NOTES AND QUESTIONS

1. *When can the manufacturer reasonably rely on warning only the intermediary?* What made the defendant's disclosure to the intermediary unreasonable in *Sowell?* Was the intermediary in question—the U.S. Navy—unreliable? Rather than focus on the issue of reliability, which can be a loaded term,

consider how the issue can be analyzed in risk-utility terms. Having provided the relevant information to the intermediary (such as an employer), any product seller can foresee that the information will not always be fully communicated to, or otherwise known by, the end user. Mistakes are inevitable and consumers can forget about risks of which they were once aware. Suppose that such an outcome would occur only 1 percent of the time in a case like *Sowell.* Without knowledge of the risk, the consumer faces a high likelihood of suffering severe physical injury or death. What is the cost of the requested warning? The defendant could have easily affixed a warning on the tank, which apparently contained no other warnings. The cost of such a warning is minimal and in a few cases (assumed to be only 1 percent) would prevent serious bodily injury. So conceptualized, the failure to warn the end user is unreasonable ($B \approx 0 < PL \approx .01 \bullet$ death), regardless of whether the intermediary is ordinarily (99 percent of the time) reliable in conveying the information to the end user.

2. *The "sophisticated intermediary."* In Webb v. Special Elec. Co., 370 P.3d 1022 (Cal. 2016), the court observed that "[t]he duty to warn applies to all entities in a product's chain of distribution." Consequently, "a supplier that places a hazardous raw material in the stream of commerce has a duty to warn about the material's inherent risks. The supplier clearly has a duty to warn the material's immediate purchaser unless the purchaser is a sophisticated user and presumably already aware of the relevant risks." *Id.* at 1033. Is this formulation of the inquiry any different from the sophisticated-user rule?

The manufacturer does not have to warn the sophisticated intermediary, but could it nevertheless have a duty to warn the end user directly? "The supplier's duty also logically extends to others who encounter the hazardous raw material, for example, after it has been incorporated into a finished product." *Id.* Are these circumstances any different from the issue addressed by the court in *Sowell?* Consider Gray v. Badger Mining Corp., 676 N.W.2d 268, 277-278 (Minn. 2004) (using "comment n to section 388 of the *Restatement (Second) of Torts*" to explain why "[t]he sophisticated intermediary defense is generally only available where the supplier can show that it used reasonable care in relying upon the intermediary to give the warning to the end user"). By recognizing a distinct doctrine called the "sophisticated intermediary" defense, have courts sharpened the analysis or potentially created confusion by focusing on the sophistication of the intermediary rather than on the reliability of the intermediary in conveying the information directly to the end user?

3. *The burden of communication.* In adopting the sophisticated intermediary doctrine, the court in *Webb* recognized that "circumstances may make it extremely difficult, or impossible, for a raw material supplier to provide warnings directly to the consumers of finished products." 370 P.3d at 1033. How would this factor affect the determination of whether the supplier could reasonably rely on the intermediary to convey the information to the end user? Consider again the risk-utility analysis in note 1 addressing the warning obligation in *Sowell.* Can you imagine cases in which the cost of warning the end user might be unreasonably high?

HOFFMAN v. HOUGHTON CHEMICAL CORP.
Supreme Judicial Court of Massachusetts, 2001
751 N.E.2d 848

MARSHALL, C.J. On March 6, 1989, an explosion and fire ripped through Gotham Ink of New England, Inc. (Gotham), an ink manufacturer in Marlborough. The blast killed two workers and severely injured several others. The plaintiffs commenced these personal injury and wrongful death actions against three manufacturers and suppliers of the chemicals allegedly involved in the conflagration: Exxon Company, U.S.A. (Exxon); Unocal Chemicals Division, Union Oil Company of California (Unocal); and Houghton Chemical Corporation (Houghton). After nearly six weeks of testimony at a consolidated trial on the plaintiffs' claims for negligence and breach of warranty for faulty product design and failure to warn, the jury returned special verdicts in favor of all defendants, and the complaints were dismissed. The plaintiffs filed a motion for a new trial that was denied. The plaintiffs have appealed. A pivotal question in this appeal concerns the duty of a bulk supplier to warn all foreseeable users of the risks associated with a product's use. We adopt the "bulk supplier doctrine" as an affirmative defense in products liabilities actions, and affirm the judgments.

The defendants manufacture and supply chemical products in bulk. Unocal supplied Gotham with acetone and methanol in fifty-five-gallon drums. Unocal and Houghton supplied Gotham with toluene, which was delivered by tanker truck and stored in Gotham's large underground storage tanks. All three chemicals, which were involved in the tragic explosion, are highly volatile, flammable solvents.

There was extensive testimony concerning the nature and extent of instructions and warnings given by the defendants to Gotham. Prior to the date of the explosion and in the course of their dealings with Gotham, both Unocal and Houghton periodically supplied Gotham with documents detailing the properties and safe handling of the chemicals. Houghton gave Gotham material safety data sheets (MSDS) for toluene that had been supplied by the manufacturer, Exxon. The MSDS warned the company, among other things, to keep toluene away from sparks and static electricity. The MSDS also contained "empty drum warnings," advising Gotham of the specific dangers relating to the reuse of empty containers. Houghton also provided its own empty drum warnings to Gotham.

Unocal gave Gotham MSDS for acetone and methanol that had similar warnings about product flammability, the need to avoid contact with ignition sources, and the importance of not storing the product in unreconditioned drums. Additionally, Unocal issued drum label warnings with its methanol and acetone products, and its drum labels indicated in words and pictorially that the drum contents were flammable.

The defendants had ample reason to believe that Gotham was a knowledgeable purchaser of their products, able to understand the product warnings and to pass appropriate safety warnings on to their employees. As an ink manufacturer for the industrial market, Gotham annually purchased thousands of gallons of flammable chemicals. In compliance with Occupational Safety and Health Administration (OSHA) regulations, the company had grounding

III. To Whom Must the Warning Be Directed?

devices in its receiving and production areas designed to dissipate any static charge accumulated in the transfer of chemical solvents from one container to another.

Gotham also had an independent obligation under OSHA regulations to train employees about workplace safety. The evidence established that, although the company was not in full compliance with an OSHA-mandated hazard communication program for training and providing safety information to employees, Gotham periodically conducted safety meetings with its employees. Additionally, its supervisors and laboratory personnel often reminded employees of the importance of bonding and grounding when transferring solvents. For Portuguese-speaking workers, such as the plaintiffs' decedents Hoffman and Sobrinho, whose knowledge of English was limited, the warnings were given in Portuguese by a bilingual foreman and his son.

The evidence established that, prior to the explosion, Gotham had on hand a small library of books and other materials by the defendants, other suppliers, and noted authorities concerning the safe transfer of flammable solvents. In December, 1987, Gotham issued its own MSDS to its customers of "press wash," a cleaning solvent composed of equal parts of acetone, methanol, and toluene. The Gotham MSDS correctly advised that press wash was an OSHA 1B flammable liquid that was 100% volatile and that required special precautions in handling, including avoiding exposure to sparks and grounding all vessels when pouring from one container to another.

The jury reasonably could have found that Gotham, although aware of its obligations to provide a safe workplace and able to carry out those obligations, was lax in its safety procedures. Of relevance here, the company allowed workers to use unreconditioned drums to transfer chemical solvents and to place containers of flammable solvents on dollies with nonconductive wheels. There was no evidence that the defendants were aware that Gotham had not enforced the safety precautions as advised by Houghton and Unocal.

On the day in question, the decedent Remolindo Hoffman, who had been instructed to prepare a batch of press wash, was transferring toluene from a grounded pump in the production area to a rusty, unreconditioned drum containing residue from a previous batch of press wash. A jury reasonably could have found that Hoffman used an ungrounded dolly to place the "empty" drum on the grounded weighing scale, and that he dispensed the toluene without attaching back-up grounding clips to the drum. The ungrounded solvent transfer created a static spark that ignited vapors in and around the drum, causing the blast.

At the close of the evidence, the trial judge, over the plaintiffs' objection, instructed the jury on the so-called "bulk [supplier] doctrine." To evaluate this challenged instruction for error, we must inquire whether the instruction should have been given. [W]e answer in the affirmative.

The bulk supplier doctrine allows a manufacturer-supplier (supplier) of bulk products, in certain circumstances, to discharge its duty to warn end users of a product's hazards by reasonable reliance on an intermediary. For the bulk supplier doctrine to apply, a product must be delivered in bulk to an intermediary vendee. The relevant inquiry turns on the intermediary's knowledge of a product's hazard and its ability to pass on appropriate warnings to end users. [ ]

The bulk supplier doctrine originates in the *Restatement (Second) of Torts* §388 comment n (1965). Comment n addresses the duty to warn in that wide array of commercial contexts in which products are supplied to an intermediary, who in turn supplies the products, often repackaged or reformulated, to others. In such circumstances, the supplier's duty to warn may be discharged by informing the intermediary of the product's character and the care required to use the product safely. To avoid liability for failure to warn, however, the supplier must have "reasonable assurance that the information will reach those whose safety depends upon their having it." *Id.*

The reasonableness inquiry is fact intensive; no bright-line rule can "automatically determine when reliance on the intermediary is reasonable. *Id.* Among the factors that may determine reasonable reliance are "(1) the dangerous condition of the product; (2) the purpose for which the product is used; (3) the form of any warnings given; (4) the reliability of the third party as a conduit of necessary information about the product; (5) the magnitude of the risk involved; and (6) the burden imposed on the supplier by requiring that he directly warn all users." [ ]

We can imagine few more appropriate circumstances in which to apply these principles than in the context of bulk sales. First, as a practical matter, the nature and function of bulk products are different from those of many other consumer and industrial goods and thus require separate consideration. Bulk products often are delivered in tank trucks, box cars, or large industrial drums, and stored in bulk by the intermediary, who generally repackages or reformulates the bulk product. Even if the product could be labeled by the supplier, any label warnings provided to the intermediary would be unlikely to reach the end user. Often, too, the bulk product has multitudinous commercial uses. Toluene, for instance, is used in gasoline, as well as printing ink; acetone is an ingredient of both nail polish remover and press wash; methanol, another press wash component, commonly known as "wood alcohol," is used in antifreeze. To impose on bulk suppliers a duty to warn all foreseeable end users directly where the product cannot readily be labeled for such users (if it can be labeled at all); where the intermediary is often in a different industry from that of the supplier, with different means of production; and where the end users themselves are a remote and varied lot would be unduly, indeed crushingly, burdensome.

Second, the intermediary vendee, particularly the large industrial company, has its own independent obligation to provide adequate safety measures for its end users, an obligation on which bulk suppliers should be entitled to rely. The bulk supplier rarely has any control over the intermediary's personnel policies or day-to-day safety operations. Thus, the bulk supplier simply is "not in a position to constantly monitor the turnover of an employer's workforce or to provide the good housekeeping measures, training and warnings to the intermediary's workers on a continuous and systemic basis." [ ] In the oft-quoted words of the authors of comment n: "Modern life would be intolerable unless one were permitted to rely to a certain extent on others' doing what they normally do, particularly if it is their duty to do so." RESTATEMENT (SECOND) OF TORTS, *supra*.

The goal of products liability law is to "induce conduct that is capable of being performed." Vassallo v. Baxter Healthcare Corp., 696 N.E.2d 909 (Mass. 1998). The bulk supplier doctrine advances that goal by permitting a bulk supplier to satisfy its duty to warn by reasonable reliance on an intermediary who understands the product's risks and is able to pass on to end users warnings about the product's hazards. Under the bulk supplier doctrine, the bulk supplier is

III. To Whom Must the Warning Be Directed?

by no means absolved of its duty either to supply adequate warnings to the intermediary or to ensure that its reliance on the intermediary is reasonable, but is permitted to discharge its duty to warn in a responsible and practical way that equitably balances the realities of its business with the need for consumer safety. We adopt the bulk supplier doctrine as an affirmative defense to products liability negligence claims.

In *Vassallo*, we implicitly recognized that negligent failure to warn and failure to warn under breach of warranty are to be judged by the same standard: the reasonableness of the defendant's actions in the circumstances. [ ] We expressly recognize that convergence now. Under our holding in *Vassallo*, then, an instruction on the bulk supplier doctrine may apply to both a claim of negligent failure to warn and a claim of breach of warranty failure to warn in products liability actions.

For all of the foregoing reasons, we affirm the judgments for the defendants.

NOTES AND QUESTIONS

1. *The mode of inquiry.* Does the bulk supplier defense provide a method of analysis or merely a conclusion that the duty to warn does not extend to the end users of the product? Consider again the costs and benefits of the disclosure requested by plaintiffs. As the court in *Hoffman* observed, a bulk supplier distributes a product with "multitudinous commercial uses" that "cannot readily be labeled for such users (if it can be labeled at all)." The bulk supplier would need to formulate a wide array of different warnings (for different uses of the product) and would then have a hard time communicating that warning to the end user. The varied warnings could not ordinarily be affixed to the final product (unlike the propane tank in *Sowell*), so how could the information be communicated effectively? These warnings "would be unduly, indeed crushingly, burdensome" as the *Hoffman* court concluded. To be sure, the warning might have some safety benefit (if some end users receive and remember that information), but the general ineffectiveness of such a warning in conjunction with its "crushing" cost explains why there is no duty to warn the end user ($B \gg PL$).

To what extent is this mode of inquiry made evident by the *Hoffman* court's description of the various factors that determine whether a bulk supplier may reasonably rely on warning only the intermediary? Compare Victor E. Schwartz & Christopher E. Appel, *Effective Communication of Warnings in the Workplace: Avoiding Injuries in Working with Industrial Materials*, 73 Mo. L. Rev. 1, 39 (2008) ("Courts have, in most instances, appropriately addressed the difficulties faced by industrial material suppliers ill-positioned to effectively warn and prevent injury. Greater uniformity and certainty in application, however, is still necessary.").

2. *Component parts and product combinations.* The bulk supplier defense can apply to the seller of a component part of the final product. Does the defense apply to all component parts, or only to those with "multitudinous commercial uses"? Consider James A. Henderson, Jr., *Sellers of Safe Products Should Not Be Required to Rescue Users from Risks Presented by Other, More Dangerous Products*, 37 Sw. U. L. Rev. 595, 611 (2008) ("[C]ourts

generally refuse to impose responsibility on component part suppliers to monitor the end-uses of their components and to rescue, via warnings, those exposed to risks created by the integration of those components into dangerous end-products."). Monitoring the end uses of a component part is extraordinarily difficult for components with multitudinous commercial uses, and so in this respect the limited liability of component-part sellers can be explained by the bulk supplier defense.

In asbestos cases, the issue is known as the "bare metal defense."

> The defense's basic idea is that a manufacturer who delivers a product "bare metal"—that is without the insulation or other material that must be added for the product's proper operation—is not generally liable for injuries caused by asbestos in later-added materials. A classic scenario would be if an engine manufacturer ships an engine without a gasket, the buyer adds a gasket containing asbestos, and the asbestos causes injury to a worker. May the manufacturer be held liable?

In re Asbestos Products Liability Litigation (No. VI), 873 F.3d 232, 234 (3d Cir. 2017) (holding that foreseeability is the "touchstone" of the bare metal defense). In addressing this issue, the U.S. Supreme Court held that a manufacturer has a duty to warn when its product requires incorporation of other parts or components, and the manufacturer knows or has reason to know that the integrated final product is likely to be dangerous for its intended uses. Air & Liquid Systems Corp. v. DeVries, 139 S. Ct. 986 (2019) (applying federal maritime law, which incorporates the common law of torts). To what extent does this inquiry depend on whether the "bare metal" product has multitudinous commercial uses?

3. *Prescription drugs and medical devices.* Under the *learned intermediary doctrine,* a drug or medical device manufacturer ordinarily satisfies the duty to warn by disclosing the information to the prescribing physician (or learned intermediary), who in turn conveys that information to the patient (consumer) when prescribing the drug or medical device. *See* Chapter 9, section I. Is the logic of this rule any different from the one governing the duty to provide warnings to intermediaries for other types of products?

In at least one respect, the distribution of prescription drugs offers a novel twist on the intermediary doctrine. Pursuant to federal law, the warning on a brand-name drug must be identical to the warning on a generic drug (one identical in active ingredients, safety, and efficacy). The brand-name manufacturer is responsible for the accuracy and adequacy of its label and is obligated to strengthen the warning when it acquires new information indicating that the prior warning is inadequate. Because generic-drug manufacturers must use the same warning as the brand-name drug, they are obligated by federal law to disclose any new information to the FDA, which is also empowered to change the label on the brand-name drug (thereby requiring an identical change on the warning for the generic drug). In Pliva, Inc. v. Mensing, 564 U.S. 604 (2011), the Court held that this statutory scheme preempts tort claims based on a generic-drug manufacturer's failure to disclose newly acquired information to the FDA. Under state law, the manufacturer would be obligated to warn consumers about the newly acquired information, whereas federal law prohibits the manufacturer from changing the warning on the generic drug in any manner that differs from the warning on the brand-name drug. The impossibility of complying with both duties means that the federal scheme entirely displaces or preempts tort law in this respect. *Id.* at 624.

Does this holding adequately recognize the intermediary doctrine? If the generic-drug manufacturer had supplied the newly acquired risk information directly to the brand-name manufacturer, the regulatory scheme would then obligate that manufacturer to change the warning on its (brand-name) drug, which in turn would obligate the generic-drug manufacturer to change on the warning on its product. Within this regulatory framework, is the brand-name manufacturer the appropriate intermediary for the generic-drug manufacturer? If so, tort law could impose a disclosure obligation on the generic-drug manufacturer that would not inherently conflict with the federal regulatory scheme and be preempted. Having adequately warned the brand-name manufacturer about the newly acquired risk information, the generic-drug manufacturer would not be liable. Consider Borel v. Fibreboard Paper Prods. Corp., 493 F.2d 1076, 1091 (5th Cir. 1973) ("In general, of course, a manufacturer is not liable for miscarriages in the communication process that are not attributable to his failure to warn or the adequacy of the warning. This may occur, for example, where some intermediate party is notified of the danger, or discovers it for himself, and proceeds deliberately to ignore it and to pass on the product without a warning."). Under this formulation, the brand-name manufacturer would then incur liability for failure to warn, even though the plaintiff used the generic drug. *See* T.H. v. Novartis Pharm. Corp., 407 P.3d 18, 32 (Cal. 2017) (permitting generic drug user to recover from brand-name manufacturer for the failure to update the product warning, in part because "a duty of care on behalf of all those who consume the brand-name drug or its bioequivalent ensures that the brand-name manufacturer has sufficient incentive to prevent a known or reasonably knowable harm").

IV. THE TYPE OF RISKS ENCOMPASSED BY THE DUTY TO WARN

To identify the types of risk that must be disclosed in an adequate warning, we need to consider more closely the rationale for the duty to warn—the promotion of informed consumer decision-making via disclosure of the seller's superior knowledge of product risk. *See* section I, *supra*. A fundamental premise of economic analysis is that consumers seek to maximize their welfare or utility when making product decisions. Consumers maximize their utility by purchasing products that provide the greatest net benefit, which is the difference between the various benefits and costs of the product. To determine a product's expected net benefit, consumers must often estimate these benefits and costs on the basis of limited information. As a result, consumer demand is based on consumer expectations of the product's net benefit, giving sellers an incentive to supply products that conform to these expectations, even when sellers know that consumers are mistaken about the matter. Of course, a seller might let consumers know about the mistake, but that is unlikely if the disclosure would increase consumer estimates of cost, which would reduce demand and the seller's profits. The ensuing market failure is addressed by the tort duty, which imposes an obligation on the product seller to disclose its superior knowledge (actual or constructive) of product risk in the warning. *See* Lovick v. Wil-Rich, 588 N.W.2d 688, 693 (Iowa 1999) ("This duty is predicated upon superior knowledge, and arises when one may reasonably foresee danger of injury or damage to another less knowledgeable unless warned of the danger."). Hence an adequate product warning—that is, a warning which best promotes consumer welfare—is one that enables the ordinary consumer to make the best estimate of the product's net benefit by conveying information about product risk that is not possessed by the consumer but reasonably available to the product seller.

AMERICAN TOBACCO CO., INC. v. GRINNELL
Supreme Court of Texas, 1997
951 S.W.2d 420

CORNYN, J. In this wrongful death case, we confront an issue with profound health and public policy consequences: whether "common knowledge" of the health risks of cigarette smoking relieves tobacco companies of any duty to warn smokers of those risks. Applying our usual summary judgment standard, we conclude that the defendant has conclusively established the defense of common knowledge with regard to the general health risks of smoking. We also conclude, however, that the defendant has not conclusively established the common knowledge defense with regard to the addictive nature of cigarettes.

In 1952, nineteen-year-old Wiley Grinnell began smoking Lucky Strikes, cigarettes manufactured by the American Tobacco Company. Almost a year later, Grinnell changed to Pall Malls, also manufactured by American. After smoking for approximately thirty-three years, Grinnell was diagnosed with lung cancer in July 1985. Shortly thereafter, he filed this lawsuit. He died less than a year later. Grinnell's family continued this suit after his death, adding wrongful death and survival claims. The family alleges that American failed to warn of, and actively concealed, facts that it knew or should have known, including the facts that Grinnell could quickly become addicted to cigarettes and that his smoking could result in injury or death from the cancer-causing ingredients if he used the cigarettes as American intended. They also allege that, even though American knew or should have known that its cigarettes were dangerous and could not be used safely, American represented to consumers that cigarettes were not harmful, dangerous, or capable of causing injury. The gravamen of their complaint is that Grinnell began smoking because American did not warn him of the potential dangers of smoking, and once he began smoking he could not stop because he became addicted to cigarettes.

The Grinnells allege that cigarettes are both defective and unreasonably dangerous under section 402A of the *Restatement (Second) of Torts*. They assert that American's cigarettes are defectively marketed, because the cigarette packages

IV. The Type of Risks Encompassed by the Duty to Warn

contain inadequate warnings. In his deposition taken one month before his death, Grinnell testified that had he known of the dangers inherent in cigarettes he would never have started smoking in the first place.

A defendant's failure to warn of a product's potential dangers when warnings are required is a type of marketing defect. Generally, a manufacturer has a duty to warn if it knows or should know of the potential harm to a user because of the nature of its product. Nevertheless, this Court has recognized that there is no duty to warn when the risks associated with a particular product are matters "within the ordinary knowledge common to the community." [ ] American argues that it had no duty to warn Grinnell of the risks associated with smoking its cigarettes because the dangers of smoking were common knowledge when Grinnell began smoking in 1952.

Common knowledge [for this purpose] connotes a general societal understanding of the risks inherent in a specific product or class of products. [T]he standard for finding common knowledge as a matter of law is a strict one [and] encompasses "those facts that are so well known to the community as to be beyond dispute." [ ] Thus, common knowledge is an extraordinary defense that applies only in limited circumstances.[3]

For example, we do not find the dangers of alcohol and cigarettes, or the public's awareness of those respective dangers, to be commensurate. Unlike [the liquor industry], which did not dispute the health dangers of prolonged alcohol use, the tobacco industry, including American, actively disputed that cigarettes posed any health risk at the time Grinnell began smoking in 1952. Indeed, the industry continues to dispute the health risks of smoking and the addictive nature of cigarettes, before Congress, in the national press, and even at oral argument before the Court in this case. Despite this ongoing "dispute," we are bound to apply the rule that whether knowledge has become common to the community is an objective determination.

The party asserting the common-knowledge defense must establish that the dangers attributable to alcohol, tobacco, or other products were a matter of common knowledge when the consumer began using the product. Based on the summary judgment record, we hold American established that the general ill-effects of smoking were commonly known when Grinnell started smoking in 1952. However, we also hold that American did not establish that the addictive quality of cigarettes was commonly known when Grinnell began smoking in 1952.

Regarding the general health risks associated with smoking, the Tennessee Supreme Court held as early as 1898 that these risks were "generally known." [ ] Other early courts also recognized the harmful effects of smoking cigarettes. [ ] More recently, courts have similarly acknowledged that the inherent dangers of smoking cigarettes are within the community's common knowledge. [ ] Not only does historical evidence illustrate the public's pre-1952 awareness of smoking's dangerous effects, but the Grinnells' experts also confirmed that the health hazards of smoking were common knowledge when Grinnell began smoking.

---

3. Whether the risks associated with a product are common knowledge is one factor courts consider when determining the existence of a duty to warn. Common knowledge is referred to as a defense because the product user has the burden to prove that the seller had a duty warn of a product's danger, while the product seller may assert that no such duty existed because of the common knowledge regarding such danger.

We conclude that the general health dangers attributable to cigarettes were commonly known as a matter of law by the community when Grinnell began smoking. *See* [ ] (common knowledge is usually determined as a matter of law). We cannot conclude, however, that the specific danger of nicotine addiction was common knowledge when Grinnell began smoking. Addiction is a danger apart from the direct physical dangers of smoking because the addictive nature of cigarettes multiplies the likelihood of and contributes to the smoker's ultimate injury, in Grinnell's case, lung cancer. This Court has also recognized the seriousness of addiction and the need for manufacturers to warn of this danger in the context of prescription drugs.

We acknowledge that some authorities support the proposition that some members of the community associated addiction with smoking cigarettes earlier in this century. But we cannot simply assume that common knowledge of the general health risks of tobacco use naturally includes common knowledge of tobacco's addictive quality. Indeed, as David Kessler, former head of the FDA, has pointed out:

> Before 1980, when FDA last considered its jurisdiction over tobacco products, no major public health organization had determined that nicotine was an addictive drug. Today, however, *all* major public health organizations in the United States and abroad with expertise in tobacco or drug addiction recognize that the nicotine delivered by cigarettes and smokeless tobacco is addictive.

Kessler et al., *The Legal and Scientific Basis for FDA's Assertion of Jurisdiction over Cigarettes and Smokeless Tobacco*, 277 JAMA 405, 406 (1997) (emphasis added). The FDA based its 1996 assertion of jurisdiction on "a wealth of epidemiologic and laboratory data establishing that tobacco users display the clinical symptoms of addiction and that nicotine has the characteristics of other addictive drugs." *Id.* Thus, unlike the general dangers associated with smoking, as late as 1988 and certainly in 1952, the danger of addiction from smoking cigarettes was not widely known and recognized in the community in general, or, particularly, by children or adolescents.

Because the community's knowledge concerning the danger of nicotine addiction associated with cigarettes was not beyond dispute in 1952, the standard for finding common knowledge as a matter of law has not been met. Because we conclude that American did not conclusively establish that the danger of addiction to nicotine was common knowledge, the Grinnells may maintain their strict liability marketing defect claims to the extent they are based on the addictive qualities of cigarettes, if no other defenses defeat those claims.

Accordingly, we reverse in part and affirm in part the judgment of the court of appeals, and remand the Grinnells' surviving claims to the trial court for further proceedings.

NOTES AND QUESTIONS

1. *No duty or no defect?* In holding that common knowledge negated the duty to warn about the general risks of smoking, did the court in *Grinnell* conclude that there simply was no duty, or did it instead conclude that

IV. The Type of Risks Encompassed by the Duty to Warn

the warning could not have been defective for not disclosing commonly known risks? *See* Chapter 5, section III (explaining why the "unreasonably dangerous" requirement in §402A effectively negates duty for cases in which the product is not more dangerous than expected by the ordinary consumer based on ordinary knowledge common to the community).

2. *An affirmative defense?* In warning cases, courts describe a number of doctrines as affirmative defenses, including those pertaining to common knowledge, sophisticated users, and bulk suppliers. An affirmative defense does not negate any element of the plaintiff's prima facie case as set forth in the complaint, but instead provides a reason why the prima facie case does not necessarily entitle the plaintiff to full recovery. *See* BLACK'S LAW DICTIONARY 482 (11th ed. 2019) (defining "affirmative defense" as "[a] defendant's assertion of facts and arguments that, if true, will defeat the plaintiff's . . . claim, even if all the allegations in the complaint are true."). Do the doctrines pertaining to common knowledge and the like function as an affirmative defense?

By arguing that the risk is commonly known, a defendant is rebutting plaintiff's prima facie case—there is no duty—and so the doctrine is not a true affirmative defense. The doctrine only has that appearance for reasons identified by the *Grinnell* court in footnote 3: "Common knowledge is referred to as a defense because the product user has the burden to prove that the seller had a duty to warn of a product's danger, while the product seller may assert that no such duty existed because of the common knowledge regarding such danger." The same is true of the so-called defenses pertaining to sophisticated users and bulk suppliers—they rebut the plaintiff's prima facie case and therefore are not true affirmative defenses.

3. *Common knowledge and the presumption of duty.* Regardless of its definitional accuracy, the judicial characterization of common knowledge as an affirmative defense has an important substantive implication. Unless the defendant invokes the common knowledge defense, the court will presume that the risk is not commonly known.

The presumption that the risk is not commonly known implies that the product is "dangerous to an extent beyond that which would be contemplated by the ordinary consumer who purchases it, with ordinary knowledge common to the community as to its characteristics," thereby satisfying the "unreasonably dangerous" requirement in *Restatement (Second)* §402A. A product that is "unreasonably dangerous," in turn, is subject to the tort duty, because if a risk is not commonly known, then the ordinary consumer cannot make a well-informed safety decision with respect to that risk, thereby justifying the tort duty. The presumption that a risk is not commonly known, therefore, presumptively establishes the factual predicate for the tort duty.

Unlike the earlier era when duty was limited by the requirement of privity, courts now presume that the duty exists and will not evaluate this element of the prima facie case unless the defendant invokes one of the so-called "affirmative defenses," such as common knowledge, that effectively question whether there is a duty in the case at hand. Products liability is not distinctive in this respect. "In cases involving physical harm, courts ordinarily need not concern themselves with the existence or content of this ordinary duty [to exercise reasonable care]. They may proceed directly to the [other] elements of liability. . . ." RESTATEMENT (THIRD) OF TORTS: LIABILITY FOR PHYSICAL AND EMOTIONAL HARM §6 cmt. f (2010).

4. *Evaluating commonly known risks.* When a risk is commonly known, a disclosure of that risk in the product warning would not improve the decision-making of the average or ordinary consumer. A warning about these risks cannot be justified by the rationale for the tort duty, explaining why the duty excludes commonly known risks.

Does the inquiry in *Grinnell* reduce to the question whether the warning would improve the decision-making of the average or ordinary consumer? Is the inquiry simply one of determining whether the majority of consumers knew about the risk at the time of the product use in question, or does *Grinnell* suggest a more demanding standard?

The issue can be resolved by the same reasoning that explains why there is a duty to warn about an allergic reaction that would be suffered by a "substantial number" of consumers. *See* section III.A, *supra* (discussing the issue). For example, suppose that 60 percent of consumers fully understand a risk that is not adequately understood by the remaining 40 percent. Before reading the product warning, any consumer does not know whether she is informed or uninformed about the risk. Each consumer finds that out only by reading the warning. The ordinary consumer, therefore, can be conceptualized as someone who knows there is a 60 percent chance that she fully understands the risk and a 40 percent chance that she does not. The ordinary consumer would want to be warned about the risk if the 40 percent chance of benefitting from the disclosure exceeds the cost of reading and remembering the disclosure. Consequently, even if most consumers know about the risk, the ordinary consumer would still prefer to be warned when the expected safety benefit exceeds the cost, explaining why a "commonly known" risk is not necessarily one that is understood by a simple majority of consumers.

5. *The tobacco litigation.* A smoker in the 1950s presumably would know other smokers who had struggled to quit. How could the court in *Grinnell* so readily conclude that the risk of addiction was not commonly known at that time? A complete answer requires more background on the history of tobacco litigation.

Since the 1950s, tort litigation involving tobacco has occurred in "waves" reflective of the continuing evolution of products liability law and social mores regarding smoking.

> Today, it is difficult to recapture fully the allure of smoking in American life at mid-[twentieth] century. Numbers tell part of the story. Nearly one out of two Americans could be counted as a regular smoker in 1950. [This cultural dynamic started to shift in 1953, which] brought news of specific health risks—scientific findings establishing a relationship between smoking and lung cancer—that would generate an unprecedented assault on tobacco use.
>
> Not by chance, the first wave of cigarette litigation was launched as well, in 1954. Only a handful of the first wave cases actually came to trial. None resulted in a plaintiff's victory. Foreseeability, rather than causation, emerged as the central doctrinal theme in the early

cases. [A]s the court announced in one of the leading cases, the manufacturer "is an insurer against foreseeable risks—but not against unknowable risks" or "the harmful effects of which no developed skill or foresight can avoid." The principal defense argument throughout this series of cases was that the cigarette company (let alone the smokers) had no knowledge of lung cancer risk associated with smoking.

By 1983, the era of first wave litigation seemed light-years in the past. In the interim, the landmark Surgeon General's Report of 1964 was published, followed by the enactment of major legislation requiring warning labels on cigarette packages and banning broadcast advertising of tobacco products. Smoking, which had seemed such a natural accoutrement of the good life, was now regarded with disdain by many—as an unhealthy sign of weak character.

By the early 1980s, in light of the continuing evolution of products liability law, plaintiffs' lawyers had reason to believe that the shift in focal point from warranty to tort, which had then been fully effected under the influence of Section 402A, would bring to fruition a version of strict liability that focused on the intrinsically dangerous nature of the product, rather than on the foreseeability-based approach of the 1950s. [T]he emerging emphasis on risk-utility analysis, however vaguely defined, was a powerful incentive to potential tobacco litigators seeking assurance that a *prima facie* case could be established. After all, reputable studies indicated that cigarettes were killing tens of thousands annually and the intangible benefits of smoking would not be similarly quantifiable. Strict liability had a second, equally important attraction: it was not at all clear that a fault-based defense would apply to a claim based on risk-utility analysis. And so the second wave cases began to be filed.

The most salient theme in the second wave litigation has been freedom of choice. The sophisticated tobacco plaintiffs' lawyers . . . recognized that consumer awareness would be a linchpin of defense strategy in the post-labeling act era. But they counted on the advent of comparative fault, buttressed by their ability to depict a socially irresponsible industry overpromoting a highly dangerous product, to counter—or, at least, blunt—the personal choice argument. In doing so, they simply failed to grasp how intensely most jurors would react to damage claims by individuals who were aware of the risks associated with smoking and nonetheless chose to continue the activity over a long time period.

The obvious tactic for countering the freedom of choice defense is a head-on rebuttal based on the addictive character of tobacco—a tactic that has come to be a central feature of the second wave litigation. But the claim is confounded by common observation. Notwithstanding extensive expert testimony available on the physiological and psychological effects of nicotine, everyone knows some number of ex-smokers, and the data indicate that about one-half of long-term smokers have managed to quit. Finally, in a demonstration of its continuing ingenuity on all fronts, once the second wave emerged, the industry lobbied in a number of states for legislation creating a common knowledge defense in litigation involving products that are inherently unsafe. This legislation has effectively eliminated tobacco litigation in California, where tobacco product is mentioned by name in the statute, and, barring heroic statutory construction, has cut off the prospect of future lung cancer claims in the other states as well.

> Thus, after thirty-five years of litigation, the tobacco industry could still maintain the notable claim that it had not paid out a cent in tort awards.

Robert L. Rabin, *A Sociolegal History of the Tobacco Tort Litigation*, 44 Stan. L. Rev. 853, 855 (1992) (sentence and paragraph structures omitted).

In light of this history, the *Grinnell* court's decision to permit the warning claim regarding addiction would be anomalous, except that the case was decided during the "third wave" of tobacco litigation.

> The third wave of tobacco litigation began in 1994. In this wave, the fundamental nature of the claims against the tobacco industry changed. No longer was the litigation limited to individual claims by individual smokers. For the first time, states sued the tobacco industry seeking wide-scale injunctive relief and to recover the costs to the states for medical care for injured smokers.
>
> The third wave of litigation was ignited by new revelations in 1994 about the tobacco industry's conduct. They show us how this industry has managed to spread confusion by suppressing, manipulating, and distorting the scientific record. They also make clear how the tobacco industry has been able to avoid paying a penny in damages and how it has managed to remain hugely profitable from the sale of a substance long known by scientists and physicians to be lethal. The . . . documents also contained disclosures on the role of industry counsel in fostering research that perpetuated a "controversy" as to whether smoking caused disease and in suppressing research that established the causal link.

Roberta B. Walburn & Tara D. Sutton, *Decades of Deceit: Document Discovery in the Minnesota Tobacco Litigation*, 25 Wm. Mitchell L. Rev. 477, 487-489 (1999) (sentence and paragraph structures omitted).

In the 1990s, the tobacco industry suffered its first adverse tort judgment in a case brought by an individual smoker. Similar judgments followed.

> Putting aside the outcomes in individual cases, what, if any, were the critical differences in the single-plaintiff tobacco tort suits being brought in the 1990s from those brought earlier? In short, the distinction is in the documents. By the late 1990s, a tobacco litigator could build a case against the industry on the voluminous document discovery in the state health care cost recovery suits and the class action litigation, as well as the earlier caches of whistleblower revelations. A narrative could be woven beginning with tobacco officials discussing, in clandestine fashion, the targeting of teenagers before they had developed to maturity and the retention of the adult market through the addictive powers of nicotine.
>
> But as the returns to date indicate, if massive liability awards now seem a possibility as never in the past, the industry still remains armed with effective weapons. Relying on the strongly individualistic strand in American culture, freedom of choice can still be mustered as a powerful defense. This is especially true as the industry shifts ground and confesses to its past machinations—arguing, instead, that it has now reformed its ways under new "enlightened leadership." If the documents eventually come to be viewed as a matter of only historical

IV. The Type of Risks Encompassed by the Duty to Warn

interest, and if the industry concedes that addiction means it is very hard but nonetheless possible to quit—and this plaintiff, unlike so many other ex-smokers knowledgeable of the health risks, did not demonstrate the requisite will power—it may be that a freedom of choice defense will be newly energized.

Robert L. Rabin, *The Tobacco Litigation: A Tentative Assessment*, 51 DePaul L. Rev. 331, 345-346 (2001) (paragraph structures omitted).

In Engle v. Liggett Group, Inc., 945 So.3d 1246 (Fla. 2006), plaintiffs filed a class action against major tobacco companies for damages allegedly caused by smoking. The jury considered issues common to the entire class. After a year-long trial, it returned a verdict for the class on all counts. On appeal, the court concluded that a number of the jury

> findings were entitled to res judicata effect: (1) smoking cigarettes causes certain enumerated diseases, including lung cancer; (2) nicotine is addictive; (3) the *Engle* "defendants placed cigarettes on the market that were defective and unreasonably dangerous"; (4) the *Engle* defendants "concealed or omitted material information not otherwise known or available knowing that the material was false or misleading or failed to disclose a material fact concerning the health effects or addictive nature of smoking cigarettes or both"; (5) the *Engle* "defendants agreed to conceal or omit information regarding the health effects of cigarettes or their addictive nature with the intention that smokers and the public would rely on this information to their detriment"; (6) "all of the [*Engle*] defendants sold or supplied cigarettes that were defective"; (7) "all of the [*Engle*] defendants sold or supplied cigarettes that, at the time of sale or supply, did not conform to representations of fact made by said defendants"; and (8) "all of the [*Engle*] defendants were negligent.

R.J. Reynolds Co. v. Marotta, 214 So.3d 590, 593 (Fla. 2017) (quoting from *Engle*, 945 So.3d at 1276-1277). This decision has spawned a long line of cases (so-called *Engle*-progeny suits), which often result in substantial verdicts for plaintiffs. *E.g., id.* (affirming jury verdict of $6 million, which was reduced to $3.48 million to reflect comparative fault assessments, while reversing trial court's decision to preclude the jury from considering plaintiff's claim for punitive damages).

Like the issue of addiction, any warning claim clearly implicates the consumer's freedom of choice. The manner in which a court evaluates a warning claim, therefore, critically depends on how the choice in question has been framed.

LIRIANO v. HOBART CORP.
United States Court of Appeals, Second Circuit, 1999
170 F.3d 264

CALABRESI, J. Luis Liriano was severely injured on the job in 1993 when his hand was caught in a meat grinder manufactured by Hobart Corporation ("Hobart") and owned by his employer, Super Associated ("Super"). The meat grinder had been sold to Super with a safety guard, but the safety guard was removed while the machine was in Super's possession and was not affixed to the meat grinder at the time of the accident. The machine bore no warning indicating that the grinder should be operated only with a safety guard attached.

Liriano sued Hobart under several theories, including failure to warn. Hobart brought a third-party claim against Super. The United States District Court for the Southern District of New York dismissed all of Liriano's claims except the one based on failure to warn, and the jury returned a verdict for Liriano on that claim. It attributed five percent of the liability to Hobart and ninety-five percent to Super. The district court then held a partial retrial limited to the issue of whether and to what extent Liriano was responsible for his own injury. On that retrial, the jury assigned Liriano one-third of the fault.

Hobart and Super appealed.

Hobart makes two arguments challenging the sufficiency of the evidence. The first concerns the obviousness of the danger that Liriano faced, and the second impugns the causal relationship between Hobart's negligence and Liriano's injury. Each of these arguments implicates issues long debated in the law of torts.

With respect to the asserted clarity of the danger, the question is when a danger is so obvious that a court can determine, as a matter of law, that no additional warning is required. The obviousness question was the subject of an important but now generally rejected opinion by Justice Holmes, then on the Massachusetts Supreme Judicial Court. *See* Lorenzo v. Wirth, 170 Mass. 596 (1898). More than a hundred years ago, a Boston woman named Maria Wirth profited from an argument about obviousness as a matter of law that is very similar to the one Hobart urges today. Wirth was the owner of a house on whose property there was a coal hole. The hole abutted the street in front of the house, and casual observers would have no way of knowing that the area around the hole was not part of the public thoroughfare. A pedestrian called Lorenzo fell into the coal hole and sued for her injuries. Writing for a majority of the Supreme Judicial Court of Massachusetts, Oliver Wendell Holmes, Jr., held for the defendant. He noted that, at the time of the accident, there had been a heap of coal on the street next to the coal hole, and he argued that such a pile provided sufficient warning to passers-by that they were in the presence of an open hole. "A heap of coal on a sidewalk in Boston is an indication, according to common experience, that there very possibly may be a coal hole to receive it." [ ] And that was that.

It was true, Holmes acknowledged, that "blind men, and foreigners unused to our ways, have a right to walk in the streets," [ ] and that such people might not benefit from the warning that piles of coal provided to sighted Bostonians. But Holmes wrote that coal-hole cases were simple, common, and likely to be oft repeated, and he believed it would be better to establish a clear rule than to invite fact-specific inquiries in every such case. "In simple cases of this sort," he explained, "courts have felt able to determine what, in every case, however complex, defendants are bound at their peril to know." [ ] With the facts so limited, this was an uncomplicated case in which the defendant could, as a matter of law, rely on the plaintiff's responsibility to know what danger she faced.

Justice Knowlton disagreed. His opinion delved farther into the particular circumstances than did Holmes's opinion for the majority. In so doing, he

IV. The Type of Risks Encompassed by the Duty to Warn

showed that Lorenzo's failure to appreciate her peril might have been foreseen by Wirth and hence that Wirth's failure to warn might constitute negligence. He noted, for example, that the accident occurred after nightfall, when Lorenzo perhaps could not see, or recognize, the heap of coal for what it was. There was "a throng of persons" on the street, such that it would have been difficult even in daylight to see very far ahead of where one was walking. [ ] And the plaintiff was, in fact, a foreigner unused to Boston's ways. "She had just come from Spain, and had never seen coal put into a cellar through a coal hole." [ ] In sum, the case was not the "simple" one that Holmes had made it out to be. What is more, none of the facts he recited was either unusual or unforeseeable by Wirth. "What kind of conduct is required under *complex* conditions, to reach the usual standard of due care, namely, the ordinary care of persons of common prudence, is a question of fact . . . [and thus] a question for a jury." [ ] Even cases involving "obvious" dangers like coal holes, Knowlton believed, might not be resolvable as matters of law when viewed in the fullness of circumstances that rendered the issue less clear than it would be when posed in the abstract.

Holmes commanded the majority of the Supreme Judicial Court in 1898, but Knowlton's position has prevailed in the court of legal history. "'The so-called Holmes view—that standards of conduct ought increasingly to be fixed by the court for the sake of certainty—has been largely rejected. . . . The tendency has been away from fixed standards and towards enlarging the sphere of the jury.'" Fowler V. Harper, Fleming James, Jr., & Oscar S. Gray, The Law of Torts §15.3, at 358-59 n.16 (2d ed. 1986) (hereinafter Harper & James) (quoting Nuckoles v. F.W. Woolworth Co., 372 F.2d 286, 289 (4th Cir. 1967)).

The courts of New York have several times endorsed Knowlton's approach and ruled that judges should be very wary of taking the issue of liability away from juries, even in situations where the relevant dangers might seem obvious, and especially when the cases in question turn on particularized facts. [ ]

But the secular decline of the Holmes position and the concomitant tendency of the New York Court of Appeals to permit issues of obviousness to go to the jury do not fully dispose of the question before us. After all, as Holmes himself might have cautioned, general trends are far from conclusive in concrete cases. And it is not surprising that there have been situations in which New York state courts have deemed dangers to be sufficiently clear so that warnings were, as a matter of law, not necessary. [ ]

If the question before us were, therefore, simply whether meat grinders are sufficiently known to be dangerous so that manufacturers would be justified in believing that further warnings were not needed, we might be in doubt. On one hand, just as a coal hole was deemed a danger appreciated by most Bostonians in 1898, so most New Yorkers would probably appreciate the danger of meat grinders a century later. Any additional warning might seem superfluous. On the other hand, Liriano was only seventeen years old at the time of his injury and had only recently immigrated to the United States. He had been on the job at Super for only one week. He had never been given instructions about how to use the meat grinder, and he had used the meat grinder only two or three times. And the mechanism that injured Liriano would not have been visible to someone who was operating the grinder. It could be argued that such a combination of facts was not so unlikely that a court should say, as a matter of law, that the defendant could not have foreseen them or, if aware of them, need not have guarded against them by issuing a warning. That argument would draw strength from the [New York] Court of Appeals' direction that the question of whether a warning was needed must be asked in terms of the information available to the injured party rather than the injured party's employer, and its added comment that "in cases where reasonable minds might disagree as to the extent of the plaintiff's knowledge of the hazard, the question is one for the jury." [ ]

Nevertheless, it remains the fact that meat grinders are widely known to be dangerous. Given that the position of the New York courts on the specific question before us is anything but obvious, we might well be of two minds as to whether a failure to warn that meat grinders are dangerous would be enough to raise a jury issue.

But to state the issue that way would be to misunderstand the complex functions of warnings. As two distinguished torts scholars have pointed out, a warning can do more than exhort its audience to be careful. It can also affect what activities the people warned choose to engage in. *See* James A. Henderson, Jr., and Aaron D. Twerski, *Doctrinal Collapse in Products Liability: The Empty Shell of Failure to Warn*, 65 N.Y.U. L. Rev. 265, 285 (1990). And where the function of a warning is to assist the reader in making choices, the value of the warning can lie as much in making known the existence of alternatives as in communicating the fact that a particular choice is dangerous. It follows that the duty to warn is not necessarily obviated merely because a danger is clear.

To be more concrete, a warning can convey at least two types of messages. One states that a particular place, object, or activity is dangerous. Another explains that people need not risk the danger posed by such a place, object, or activity in order to achieve the purpose for which they might have taken that risk. Thus, a highway sign that says "Danger—Steep Grade" says less than a sign that says "Steep Grade Ahead—Follow Suggested Detour to Avoid Dangerous Areas."

If the hills or mountains responsible for the steep grade are plainly visible, the first sign merely states what a reasonable person would know without having to be warned. The second sign tells drivers what they might not have otherwise known: that there is another road that is flatter and less hazardous. A driver who believes the road through the mountainous area to be the only way to reach her destination might well choose to drive on that road despite the steep grades, but a driver who knows herself to have an alternative might not, even though her understanding of the risks posed by the steep grade is exactly the same as those of the first driver. Accordingly, a certain level of obviousness as to the grade of a road might, in principle, eliminate the reason for posting a sign of the first variety. But no matter how patently steep the road, the second kind of sign might still have a beneficial effect. As a result, the duty to post a sign of the second variety may persist even when the danger of the road is obvious and a sign of the first type would not be warranted.

One who grinds meat, like one who drives on a steep road, can benefit not only from being told that his activity is dangerous but from being told of a safer way. As we have said, one can argue about whether the risk involved in grinding meat is sufficiently obvious that a responsible person would fail to warn of that risk, believing reasonably that it would convey no helpful information. But if it is also the case—as it is—that the risk posed by meat grinders can feasibly be reduced by attaching a safety guard, we have a different question. Given that attaching guards is feasible, does reasonable care require that meat workers

IV. The Type of Risks Encompassed by the Duty to Warn

be informed that they need not accept the risks of using unguarded grinders? Even if most ordinary users may—as a matter of law—know of the risk of using a guardless meat grinder, it does not follow that a sufficient number of them will—as a matter of law—also know that protective guards are available, that using them is a realistic possibility, and that they may ask that such guards be used. It is precisely these last pieces of information that a reasonable manufacturer may have a duty to convey even if the danger of using a grinder were itself deemed obvious.

Consequently, the instant case does not require us to decide the difficult question of whether New York would consider the risk posed by meat grinders to be obvious as a matter of law. A jury could reasonably find that there exist people who are employed as meat grinders and who do not know (a) that it is feasible to reduce the risk with safety guards, (b) that such guards are made available with the grinders, and (c) that the grinders should be used only with the guards. Moreover, a jury can also reasonably find that there are enough such people, and that warning them is sufficiently inexpensive, that a reasonable manufacturer would inform them that safety guards exist and that the grinder is meant to be used only with such guards. Thus, even if New York would consider the danger of meat grinders to be obvious as a matter of law, that obviousness does not substitute for the warning that a jury could, and indeed did, find that Hobart had a duty to provide. It follows that we cannot say, as a matter of law, that Hobart had no duty to warn Liriano in the present case. We therefore decline to adopt appellants' argument that the issue of negligence was for the court only and that the jury was not entitled, on the evidence, to return a verdict for Liriano.

[The court then found that the proof of causation was sufficient to satisfy the plaintiff's burden in a portion of the opinion excerpted in Chapter 11.]

The district court did not err. We affirm its decision in all respects.

NEWMAN, J., *concurring*. The Court's opinion offers the example of a steep road marked in one instance with a sign that warns "Danger—Steep Grade" and in another instance with a more informative sign indicating the option of an alternate route that avoids the steep grade. The example is not precisely analogous to our case because the record gives no indication that an alternate machine with a safety guard was as readily available as an alternate driving route. Moreover, the option of a driver to choose an indicated alternate driving route immediately available is more realistic than the option of a supermarket employee to insist on a machine the availability of which is entirely uncertain. Nevertheless, the Court's analogy usefully indicates a circumstance common to both the Court's example and our case: the alternate means of proceeding more safely is an option known to the entity that bears a relationship to the dangerous condition and is not known to the person encountering the danger. When that disparity of knowledge exists, may liability be imposed by a fact-finder for failure to warn of the alternative?

This becomes the critical question in this case, and we have no firm basis on which to predict the answer New York's highest court would give to it. An injury occurring as a result of a rather obvious danger but one that might have been avoided by an alternative known to a product manufacturer and not known to a likely user of the product has not been considered by the New York Court of

Appeals, and appears not to have been directly confronted by other New York courts. I am not sure that reasonable minds could differ as to the extent of a store employee's knowledge of the hazard of placing his hand in the open spout of a meat-grinder, but I think it likely that the Court of Appeals would rule that reasonable minds might differ on the closely related question concerning the extent of the employee's knowledge of a safer alternative, i.e., avoiding use of a machine from which a safety guard had been removed and requesting a machine with the guard in place. For that reason, and in the absence of the clear answer we requested from the Court of Appeals, I agree that Liriano's case was properly submitted to a jury for its decision.

NOTES AND QUESTIONS

1. *The two types of risk disclosure.* The warning requested by the plaintiff involves safety precautions that the consumer should take while using the product. In addition to warning about safe product use, a warning can also provide information about risks that are inherent in the product even when used safely, the type of disclosure at issue in *Grinnell* (involving the unavoidable risks of smoking tobacco). Each implicates the consumer's safety decision in a manner that justifies the duty to warn.

Safe product use. Consumers benefit from precautions that enable them to reduce the risk of product-caused injury in a cost-effective manner. Consumers who are not aware of the risk, however, will not be aware of the need to take a precaution. Other consumers who are aware of the risk may not know that it can be avoided by certain precautions. But even when a substantial number of consumers would prefer to know about such precautions, if using the product in a safe manner is costly for the consumer, the product seller may choose not to disclose this information. By making consumers aware of the desirable precaution, the warning also makes consumers aware of a cost that they would not otherwise recognize. The warning reduces the desirability of the product (by increasing consumer estimates of product cost), thereby reducing consumer demand. Sellers are accordingly incentivized to withhold information about the need for consumers to take costly safety precautions that would reduce the risk of product-caused injury. This safety problem is addressed by the duty to warn: "Commercial product sellers must provide reasonable instructions [that] inform persons how to use and consume products safely." RESTATEMENT (THIRD) OF TORTS: PRODUCTS LIABILITY §2 cmt. i, at 29 (sentence structure omitted). Pursuant to this duty, any disclosure pertaining to the safe use of the product is required only if it would be reasonable for the consumer to use the product in that manner (as with an instruction, "Use meat grinder only when guard is attached").

Inherent or residual product risks. Often, products that are designed, manufactured, and used properly still present a risk of injury to the consumer. Drugs, for example, can produce side effects for users. Similarly, many products contain chemicals (such as carcinogens) that are hazardous to human health. If the seller is not liable for the injuries (such as cancer) that inevitably occur to some people who use these products, consumers need to account for the costs they will incur if injured. For example, suppose there is an unavoidable 1-in-10,000 risk that the product will cause the consumer to suffer $100,000 in damages. At the time of purchase, the risk of injury imposes a cost on each consumer at least equal to $10 per product (the expected value *PL* of the risk), so consumers should incorporate this cost into their estimate of the product's net benefit. Consumers who are unaware of the risk will not account for this cost, however, thereby inflating their estimate of the product's net benefit by $10. These consumers will buy more of the product than they would if they had known about the unavoidable risk. By disclosing information about the unavoidable product risk, sellers would reduce sales and profits, giving them an incentive not to make the disclosure. This safety problem is addressed by the duty to warn. *See id.* §2 cmt. i., at 30 ("Such warnings allow the user or consumer to avoid the risk warned against by making an informed decision not to purchase or use the product at all and hence not to encounter the risk. In this context, warnings must be provided for inherent risks that reasonably foreseeable product users and consumers would reasonably deem material or significant in deciding whether to use or consume the product.").

2. *The relation between obvious and commonly known risks.* In at least one respect, the rule regarding obvious risks is a direct implication of the rule that there is no duty to warn of commonly known risks—an obvious risk will also be commonly known by product users. Consequently, the seller has no duty to warn of either type of risk for the same reason: Disclosure of these risks would not improve the safety decisions of the ordinary consumer, and the provision of useless information could lead the ordinary consumer to disregard the warning altogether.

Not all consumers, however, necessarily have knowledge of commonly known risks, and the same is true for obvious risks. Foreseeable "users will, of course, encompass a spectrum of persons with widely varying abilities and experience bearing on their perception of the hazards at hand. Some may be practiced and skilled operators, while others may be novices, or may use the machine in adverse conditions that, though atypical, are still foreseeable." Burke v. Spartanics, Ltd., 252 F.3d 131, 138 (2d Cir. 2001). "So long as the relevant risks are not obvious to *some* members of the class of foreseeable users, a reasonable manufacturer might well be expected to warn." *Id.* Does this statement accurately describe the appropriate inquiry, or does the issue require a determination that there was a "substantial number" of such consumers as per the rule regarding the duty to warn about allergic reactions?

Despite their evident similarities, the two types of risks are not entirely analogous. Common knowledge does not depend on the particular facts of the case (e.g., would the ordinary smoker want to be warned about the risk of addiction?), whereas the obviousness of risk will often turn on case-specific facts (e.g., the particular manner in which the product was being used). Categorical determinations are ordinarily made by judges as a matter of law, whereas the jury as finder of fact ordinarily makes case-specific determinations. Consequently, the court in *Grinnell* concluded that judges usually resolve the issue of common knowledge as a matter of law, whereas the *Liriano* court concluded that the obviousness of a risk is ordinarily a jury question.

3. *The logic of* Liriano. If the plaintiff in *Liriano* had alleged that the warning was defective simply because it did not alert users to the risk of being injured by the unguarded blade, would the court have dismissed the claim? *See Burke*, 252 F.3d at 137-138 (concluding that the reasoning in *Liriano* did not apply because the plaintiff "made clear that his contention is that [defendant] should have placed a warning, at the rear approach to the machine, about the dangers of placing one's hand in the cutting plane. His argument was *expressly not* that [defendant] should have warned that the (perhaps obvious) dangers associated with access to the machine from the back could be obviated by use of" another device).

4. *Reconsidering patent dangers.* A risk that is obvious would also be a patent danger that does not necessarily bar recovery in a case of defective design. Considering the issue in this context provides another opportunity for us to see why courts permit recovery for patent dangers. For reasons identified by the court in *Liriano*, the fact that a consumer is aware of an obvious risk ("Steep Grade Ahead") does not imply that she had knowledge of all factors relevant to the safety choice ("Follow Suggested Detour to Avoid Dangerous Areas"). A fully informed safety decision instead requires knowledge of both the risk (the term *PL* in the risk-utility test) and the reasonable precautions for avoiding it (described by the term *B*). Consequently, when both the risk *and* the associated safety precaution are obvious or commonly known, a warning about the "obvious danger" would not improve consumer decision-making and is not required by the duty. The mere fact that a danger is patent does not necessarily eliminate the duty to warn—the same outcome achieved by the rule that a patent danger does not necessarily bar recovery for defective design.

Hence, the obvious-danger rule in warning cases is based on the same rationale that explains why courts have roundly rejected the patent-danger rule in design cases. *See* Chapter 5, section II (explaining why mere awareness of risk does not imply that the design satisfies the consumer's risk-utility expectations). For these same reasons, courts have roundly rejected claims of categorical liability with respect to product design. *See* Chapter 6, section III.B (explaining why recovery is barred when the ordinary consumer makes an informed safety decision based on the same risk-utility factors implicated by the allegation of defect). Finally, this analysis also shows why the defendant cannot always defend the reasonableness of the existing design on the ground that the product was accompanied by a warning that rendered the risk open and obvious. *See* Chapter 8 (discussing rule that a warning does not always substitute for the elimination of risk by alteration of design).

Based on these doctrines, each of which is recognized by New York law, would you be able to respond to Judge Newman's concern that "we have no firm basis on which to predict the answer New York's highest court would give" to the liability question in *Liriano*?

5. *Foreseeability.* Like the duty to design, the duty to warn is based on foreseeable risks of harm—the risks that the manufacturer either knew or should have known at the time of the safety decision. "When dealing with

the foreseeability of a product's misuse in particular, the crucial inquiry is whether, at the time the product was manufactured, the manufacturer was aware, or should have been aware, of that misuse." Iliades v. Dieffenbacher North America Inc., 915 N.W.2d 338, 344 (Mich. 2018). The following case illustrates how courts conceptualize this inquiry.

MORAN v. FABERGE, INC.
Court of Appeals of Maryland, 1975
332 A.2d 11

DIGGES, J. On the fateful night of June 8, 1969, Nancy Moran, then 17 years old, visited the home of Mr. and Mrs. Louis P. Grigsby in Hillcrest Heights, Maryland, to meet with a number of friends, including Randy Williams, a young lady of 15 years, who was residing with the Grigsbys at the time. The group congregated in the basement which was being maintained partly as a family clubroom and partly as a laundry room. After listening to music for some time on that warm summer night (estimated to be 72-73 degrees F.), everyone left the basement, except Nancy and Randy. Apparently these two girls were at a loss for entertainment as eventually they centered their attention on a lit Christmas-tree-shaped candle which was positioned on a shelf behind the couch in the clubroom. Possibly because "the idle mind knows not what it is it wants" the girls began to discuss whether the candle was scented. After agreeing that it was not, Randy, while remarking "Well, let's make it scented," impulsively grabbed a "drip bottle" of Faberge's Tigress cologne, which had been placed by Mrs. Grigsby in the basement for use as a laundry deodorant, and began to pour its contents onto the lower portion of the candle somewhat below the flame. Instantaneously, a burst of fire sprang out and burned Nancy's neck and breasts as she stood nearby watching but not fully aware of what her friend was doing.

During the trial the petitioner introduced evidence, which was not disputed, tending to show that, though no warning of the fact was attached to the bottle or otherwise given, Faberge's Tigress cologne was highly flammable and, therefore, inherently dangerous. To demonstrate this the petitioner produced scientific experimental evidence revealing that this cologne, composed of, by volume, 82.06% alcohol, 5.1% perfume and oils, and 12.84% water, is a dangerously combustible product with a flash point of 73 degrees Fahrenheit, approximately room temperature.

Additionally, the petitioner evoked testimony from two Faberge officials, Carl Mann, its Vice President and Chief Perfumer, and Stephen Shernov, a company aerosol chemist, which indicated that not only was the manufacturer aware of this hazardous quality but also Faberge foresaw that its product might well be dangerous when placed near flame.

Having produced evidence as to this inherently dangerous characteristic of Tigress cologne, which was known to the company though not to the public generally, as well as the fact that the manufacturer knew it might come in contact with fire and be hazardous in that circumstance, the petitioner contends that a jury question was presented as to whether Faberge was negligent for failing to warn against its product's latent flammability characteristic. Consequently, the petitioner asserts that when the Judge granted the motion for judgment n.o.v., saying, "there wasn't sufficient evidence in this case to indicate to the court, and I don't think reasonable minds should differ on this issue, that when this product was used in its intended fashion with ordinary care, that it was inherently dangerous," he improperly invaded the province of the jury.

Faberge, on the other hand, argues that the trial judge acted properly when he granted the n.o.v. motion because, in respondent's words, "the plaintiff did not present legally sufficient proof of negligence on the part of Faberge, Inc." In support of this position, Faberge urges that the Court of Special Appeals was correct when, in considering this matter, it opined:

> There was a total absence of any evidence in this case which would tend to show or would support a rational inference that Faberge foresaw or should have foreseen that its cologne would be used in the manner which caused the injuries to Nancy Moran. Since Faberge did not foresee the use, it had no duty to warn against it.

To begin with we note that a manufacturer's duty to produce a safe product, with appropriate warnings and instructions when necessary, is no different from the responsibility each of us bears to exercise due care to avoid unreasonable risks of harm to others. Whether any such unreasonable risk exists in a given situation depends on balancing the probability and seriousness of harm, if care is not exercised, against the costs of taking appropriate precautions. However, we observe that in cases such as this the cost of giving an adequate warning is usually so minimal, amounting only to the expense of adding some more printing to a label, that this balancing process will almost always weigh in favor of an obligation to warn of latent dangers, if the manufacturer is otherwise required to do so.

Since the cost factor here undisputedly would be of minimal consequence, the question then needing to be answered is, when does the responsibility to warn arise? As most courts and legal authors agree, the duty of the manufacturer to warn of latent dangers inherent in its product goes beyond the precise use contemplated by the producer and extends to all those which are reasonably foreseeable. Examples of what these foreseeable uses are and are not can be found in Comments j and k to Section 395 of the *Restatement (Second) of Torts*.

Comment j states:

> *Unforeseeable use or manner of use.* The liability stated in this Section is limited to persons who are endangered and the risks which are created in the course of uses of the chattel which the manufacturer should reasonably anticipate. In the absence of special reason to expect otherwise, the maker is entitled to assume that his product will be put to normal use, for which the product is intended or appropriate; and he is not subject to liability when it is safe for all such uses, and harm results only because it is mishandled in a way which he has no reason to expect, or is used in some unusual and unforeseeable manner. Thus a shoemaker is not liable to an obstinate lady who suffers harm because she insists on wearing a size too small for her, and the manufacturer of a bottle of cleaning fluid is not liable when the purchaser splashes it into his eye.

IV. The Type of Risks Encompassed by the Duty to Warn 305

In contrast, Comment k explains:

Foreseeable uses and risks. The manufacturer may, however, reasonably anticipate other uses than the one for which the chattel is primarily intended. The maker of a chair, for example, may reasonably expect that some one will stand on it; and the maker of an inflammable cocktail robe may expect that it will be worn in the kitchen in close proximity to a fire.

Even though there is a vast middle ground of product uses about which reasonable minds could disagree as to whether they are or should be foreseeable to the manufacturer, thus requiring resolution by the trier of fact, from these *Restatement* elaborations it can be seen that there are extremes, abutting this wide in-between group, about which reasonable minds would not differ as to whether there is a duty to warn, making the determination of this issue one of law. In this light it would be totally unreasonable to require that a manufacturer warn against every injury which might ensue from a mishap in the use of its product, no matter how the consumer utilizes the chattel or how obvious or well known is the danger. For instance, a supplier of shoes is not liable for failing to warn that, when a woman knowingly wears shoes which are two sizes too small, they will injure her feet, and a producer should not be required to warn that a knife will cut or a hammer will mash a thumb or a stove will burn a finger. While on the other side of the spectrum the manufacturer will be deemed, as a matter of law, to be aware of and required to warn against latent dangers which might reasonably follow from a foreseeable use of its product:

Hair dye will be applied to hair and will touch the skin; cosmetics will be applied to faces; underclothes will be worn next to the skin; tractors will get mired; food will be eaten; and so on.

2 Harper & James, THE LAW OF TORTS, §28.6 (1956).

A review of the many cases on this subject discloses that courts have not had an easy time agreeing as to which uses by consumers require submission to the trier of fact for determination of the foreseeability issue, and those about which reasonable minds would not disagree, so that the foreseeability issue can be decided as a matter of law; not only have they applied differing ratiocinations but they have also arrived at apparently inconsistent determinations. For example, some courts have ruled that a jury may hold a manufacturer to a duty to warn because it is foreseeable that a baby might consume furniture polish; that a body rub gives off a vapor which could be ignited under a user's clothing as he attempted to light a cigarette; that a boy of fifteen might dive into a vinyl lined swimming pool thirty inches deep; that paint might in some way be splashed into the eye of a painter's helper; or that use of an automobile includes involvement in collisions. [ ] On the other hand, there are courts which have decided that certain uses in which dangers arose (often uses very similar to those which other courts have submitted to the jury) are as a matter of law not foreseeable by the manufacturer so that he is not liable for failing to warn the consumer of the hazard involved. Cases of this ilk have included those where the court held that the manufacturer could not, as a matter of law, foresee that a housewife would splash cleaning fluid into her eye; that the magnesium alloy legs of its product, a bathinette, when made hot by a fire in a residence would begin to blaze intensely, sending flames across a hallway and thereby greatly increasing the danger to the property and persons present; that an automobile would participate in collisions; or that a window casement with steel crossbars might be used either as a handrest or as a ladder by iron and steel workmen. [ ]

We can glean from this small sampling of the many products liability cases concerning the foreseeability of various consumer uses that the standard for determining whether a given consumer use is reasonably foreseeable by the producer so as to require a warning of latent danger is, to say the least, quite vague.[7] Probably because of development on a case-by-case basis with an eye on achieving a desired result in the individual case, without following logic and applying consistent definitions, the decisions often seem to be thrashing about in a semantic and subjective morass in their attempts to apply negligence concepts in products liability litigation. The reason for this confusion is that many cases have failed to recognize that when a product liability suit sounds in tort, rather than in contract as is frequently permissible, the action is based on a negligent breach of duty owed by the manufacture to the plaintiff and, consequently the settled principles of law pertaining to negligence, including the terms used in explaining that law and their definitions, are appropriately applicable. When these well-established negligence concepts are applied the dense fog which seems to have surrounded litigation concerning the manufacturer's duty to warn will largely dissipate.

In determining what is contemplated by the foreseeability requirement in products liability cases, we obtain guidance from the many Maryland cases which dealt with this same concept in the general negligence context. "Whether foreseeability is being considered from the standpoint of negligence or proximate cause, the pertinent inquiry is not whether the actual harm was of a particular kind which was expectable. Rather, *the question is whether the actual harm fell within a general field of danger which should have been anticipated.*" [ ]

This foreseeability negligence test is consistent with the one provided by Professor Harper:

> the courts are perfectly accurate in declaring that there can be no liability where the harm is unforeseeable, if *"foreseeability" refers to the general type of harm sustained*. It is literally true that there is no liability for damage that falls entirely outside the *general threat of harm* which made the conduct of the actor negligent. *The sequence of events, of course, need not be foreseeable*. The manner in which the risk culminates in harm may be unusual, improbable and highly unexpected, from the point of view of the actor at the time of his conduct. And yet, if the harm suffered falls within the general danger area, there may be liability, provided other requisites of legal *causation are present.*

Harper, A Treatise on the Law of Torts, §7 (1933) (emphasis added).

---

7. It should be noted that there are respected authorities who suggest that the concept of foreseeable use has never been adequately defined because it cannot be. In the words of Professor Prosser: "In one sense, almost nothing is entirely unforeseeable, since there is a very slight mathematical chance, recognizable in advance, that even the most freakish accident which is possible will occur, particularly if it has ever happened in history before. In another, no event whatever is entirely foreseeable, since the exact details of a sequence never can be predicted with complete omniscience and accuracy." Prosser, The Law of Torts, §43 (4th ed. 1971).

IV. The Type of Risks Encompassed by the Duty to Warn

And, once the product is used in this "general field of danger," if the manufacturer's conduct is a significant factor in causing harm to another, the fact that the manufacturer neither foresaw nor should have foreseen the severity of the harm or the exact manner in which it occurred, does not prevent it from being liable. As Justice Cardozo reiterated in the celebrated case of Palsgraf v. Long Island R. Co., 248 N.Y. 339, 162 N.E. 99 (1928): "It was not necessary that the defendant should have had notice of the particular method in which an accident would occur, if the possibility of an accident was clear to the ordinarily prudent eye."

Based on this negligence law we think that in the products liability domain a duty to warn is imposed on a manufacturer if the item it produces has an inherent and hidden danger about which the producer knows, or should know, could be a substantial factor in bringing injury to an individual or his property when the manufacturer's product comes near to or in contact with the elements which are present normally in the environment where the product can reasonably be expected to be brought or used. Under this analysis the unusual and bizarre details of accidents, which human experience shows are far from unlikely, are only significant as background facts to the individual case; it is not necessary that the manufacturer foresee the exact manner in which accidents occur. Thus, in the context of this case, it was not necessary for a cologne manufacturer to foresee that someone would be hurt when a friend poured its product near the flame of a lit candle; it was only necessary that it be foreseeable to the producer that its product, while in its normal environment, may be brought near a catalyst, likely to be found in that environment, which can untie the chattel's inherent danger. For example while seated at a dressing table, a woman might strike a match to light a cigarette close enough to the top of the open cologne bottle so as to cause an explosion, or that while seated in a similar manner she might turn suddenly and accidentally bump the bottle of cologne with her elbow, splashing some cologne on a burning candle placed on the vanity. So, in the words of the Supreme Court of Missouri: "If there is some probability of harm sufficiently serious that ordinary men would take precautions to avoid it, then failure so to do is negligence." [ ]

In applying this test here, we hold that it was unnecessary, to support a verdict in favor of the petitioner, that there be produced evidence, as demanded by the Court of Special Appeals, "which would tend to show or support a rational inference that Faberge foresaw or should have foreseen that its [Tigress] cologne would be used in the manner [(pouring the cologne on the lower portion of a lit candle in an attempt to scent it)] which caused the injuries to Nancy Moran"; rather, it was only necessary that the evidence be sufficient to support the conclusion that Faberge, knowing or deemed to know that its Tigress cologne was a potentially dangerous flammable product, could reasonably foresee that in the environment of its use, such as the home of the Grigsbys, this cologne might come close enough to a flame to cause an explosion of sufficient intensity to burn property or injure bystanders, such as Nancy.

It is our opinion then, that the totality of the evidence presented in this case, viewed most favorably toward the petitioner, was legally sufficient to enable the jury to find that Faberge's failure to place a warning on its Tigress cologne "drip bottle" constituted actionable negligence. We say this because there was evidence presented at trial which, if accepted as true, tends to show that Faberge's Tigress cologne possessed a latent danger of flammability; that Faberge, through its officials, knew or should have known of this danger; that it is normal to find in the home environment both flame and cologne; that it was reasonably foreseeable to Faberge that the flame and the cologne may well come in contact, one with the other, so as to cause an explosion which injures a person who happens to be standing nearby—Nancy; and that a reasonably prudent manufacturer, knowing of its product's characteristics and propensities, should have warned consumers of this latent flammability danger.

Of course, regardless of whether the defendant is negligent, a plaintiff's own conduct may constitute a bar to recovery if that plaintiff is determined, either as a matter of law or by the trier of fact, to also be guilty of negligence which was a direct contributing cause of the injury. But such is not the result here as the jury specifically absolved Nancy of contributory negligence.

Whatever may be our personal persuasion if we stand in the shoes of the jury, as to whether recovery should be permitted in this specific case, we cannot close our eyes to the fact that, although reasonable foreseeability, generally a jury question, still does not encompass the far reaches of pessimistic imagination, the outer limits, within which reasonable minds may differ so that jurors are permitted to find liability in a manufacturer's negligence case based on a failure to warn, are broad in this jurisdiction as in others. Therefore, we are constrained to believe and hold that, in the instant case, especially considering the economic and social climate of our day, the issue of Faberge's negligence was for the jury and that (the) Judge should not have granted the motion for judgment n.o.v.

Judgment of the Court of Special Appeals reversed.

O'DONNELL, J., *dissenting*. When a use is made of a product so remote from that intended as to be unforeseeable, the manufacturer is relieved of liability from such use. Assuming, *arguendo*, that Faberge may have a duty to warn of a general risk because of a latent danger of flammability of its cologne—where its vapors might be brought within one-quarter of an inch of an open flame—it does not follow that this duty to warn is owed to everyone, howsoever the product might be used or abused. It may well be true that the manufacturer owes a duty to warn of the general risk of fire to a young lady who, while applying the cologne, accidentally should knock over the container and spill it upon a burning candle, but such are not the facts here.

NOTES AND QUESTIONS

1. *Reasonable foreseeability.* Is the concept of foreseeability inherently indeterminate? The problem, as one court memorably put it, is that "there are clear judicial days on which a court can foresee forever and thus determine liability but none on which that foresight alone provides a socially and judicially acceptable limit on recovery." Thing v. La Chusa, 771 P.2d 814, 830 (Cal. 1989). Does this fairly describe the court's reasoning in *Moran*?

The issue is not whether a risk or the associated harm is foreseeable if one had unlimited time and resources to consider the matter; the inquiry is whether the risk is reasonably anticipatable—whether the

IV. The Type of Risks Encompassed by the Duty to Warn

defendant knew or should have known about the risk. "The term should have known . . . is one way of saying that the reasonable person standard governs the question of unreasonable risk and foreseeability . . . ." Dan B. Dobbs, Paul T. Hayden & Ellen M. Bublick, THE LAW OF TORTS §159 (2d ed. 2014 & 2020 update). Whether a risk is reasonable "involves some manner of balancing the costs or burdens of mitigating it against the likelihood and severity of the injuries it threatens." Grubb v. Smith, 523 S.W.3d 409, 417 (Ky. 2017) (observing that this attribute of a reasonable risk has been "widely understood" from "*United States v. Carroll Towing Co.*, 159 F.2d 169 (2nd Cir. 1947) to the *Restatement (Third) of Torts: Phys. & Emot. Harm* (2010)"). Whether a risk is reasonably foreseeable also turns on a balancing of these factors.

Reasonable foreseeability depends on costs or burdens for another reason: risky actors do not have unlimited time and resources to consider every possible consequence of their behavior. What is reasonably foreseeable, therefore, depends on the cost or burden of acquiring that information. For example, the "seller bears responsibility to perform reasonable testing prior to marketing a product and to discover risks and risk-avoidance measures that such testing would reveal. A seller is charged with [constructive] knowledge of what reasonable testing would reveal." RESTATEMENT (THIRD) OF TORTS: LIABILITY FOR PHYSICAL AND EMOTIONAL HARM §29 cmt. m. Whether a seller should have known about a product risk—whether the associated harm is foreseeable—accordingly depends on whether it would be discovered by "reasonable testing," a form of reasonable care that depends on the costs and safety benefits of acquiring information about product risk. Thus, reasonable foreseeability does not require sellers to expend unlimited time and resources to consider every possible way in which their products might cause harm.

The concept of reasonableness, however, does not independently limit the concept of foreseeability. Within a negligence claim, a foreseeable risk is one that a reasonable person would account for when making the safety decision in question. Such a risk is necessarily reasonably foreseeable. Adding the proviso of reasonableness simply underscores the behavioral idea that risky actors are not omniscient and cannot realistically make safety decisions by considering every potential outcome, no matter how far-fetched.

2. *Conceptualizing foreseeability.* In the ordinary negligence case, a risk is foreseeable when it factored or should have factored into the safety decision of the actor.

> To establish the actor's negligence, it is not enough that there be a likelihood of harm; the likelihood must be foreseeable to the actor at the time of conduct. Foreseeability often relates to practical considerations concerning the actor's ability to anticipate future events or to understand dangerous conditions that already exist. In such cases, what is foreseeable concerns what the actor "should have known."

RESTATEMENT (THIRD) OF TORTS: LIABILITY FOR PHYSICAL AND EMOTIONAL HARM §3 cmt. g.

A behavioral conception of foreseeability explains why the defendant does not have to foresee the precise circumstances of the accident. "Categorization is one of the most basic cognitive functions." James E. Corter & Mark A. Gluck, *Explaining Basic Categories: Feature Predictability and Information*, 111 Psych. Bull. 291, 291 (1992). "It is well established that causal knowledge plays an important role in adult categorization. Adults are more likely to assign an object to a category if it has the same causal features as known category members." Brett K. Hayes & Bob Rehder, *The Development of Causal Categorization*, 36 Cognitive Sci. 1102, 1102 (2012). Consequently, individuals make safety decisions by considering categories of causally related features that abstract away from, or do not consider, precise details that are not necessary for predictive purposes.

An automobile driver, for example, does not make safety decisions by contemplating all of the particular circumstances that could be involved in a crash, such as the identity of the affected parties or the details of the threatened injuries (like a broken right arm as opposed to the left leg). Instead, a driver considers the categories or general classes of accident victims (other drivers, pedestrians, and nearby property owners) in relation to the general risk of crash for the circumstances at hand. Because the reasonable person makes safety decisions by reference to the general types of accidents that threaten general types of harms to general classes of people, foreseeability does not require knowledge of the particular details of the accident. These reasons explain why the court in *Moran* concluded that a risk is foreseeable if it is of the general type that factors into the safety decision of the reasonably prudent actor.

3. *Foreseeability and duty*. What is the relation between a foreseeable risk and duty?

> Foreseeability does not create a duty but sets limits once a duty is established. Once this initial determination of legal duty is made, the jury's function is to decide the foreseeable range of danger, therefore limiting the scope of that duty.

Simonetta v. Viad Corp., 197 P.3d 127, 131 n.4 (Wash. 2008). If the duty is not created by a foreseeable risk, what is the source of duty? *See* Chapter 5, section III (explaining why the tort duty is justified by the inability of the ordinary consumer to adequately comprehend the safety decision for addressing foreseeable risks of product-caused harm).

Because the element of duty is defined independently from a foreseeable risk, the duty does not have to encompass every foreseeable risk of harm. We discuss this issue in future chapters addressing limitations of duty based on the type of harm.

4. *The varied roles of foreseeability*. The concept of foreseeability can affect the tort claim in different ways, and so the meaning that a court ascribes to the term must be understood in context.

<u>Duty</u>. A risk must be foreseeable to be included within the tort duty. The inquiry is categorical and not limited to the circumstances of the case. In *Moran*, for example, the plaintiff introduced evidence showing that the cologne was highly flammable when placed near a flame. The particular ways in which the cologne might come into contact with fire are irrelevant for this purpose.

Causation. The defendant's breach of duty—sale of a defective product—must injure the plaintiff in a foreseeable manner. This issue is addressed by the element of proximate cause. *See* Chapter 12. The particular circumstances of the injury, including the particular manner in which the product was misused, are the focus of this inquiry. For example, the foreseeable risk of fire posed by the perfume in *Moran* encompasses situations in which the perfume is placed near an open flame on a table or next to a burning cigarette, but this general risk of harm does not necessarily encompass cases in which the perfume is intentionally poured onto a burning candle. The issue is not categorical (like the element of duty), but instead turns on case-specific facts. The concerns expressed by the dissent in *Moran*, therefore, are relevant to the issue of proximate cause (a jury question) and not duty.

Contributory Negligence. Finally, a plaintiff whose misuse of the product caused the injury is subject to the affirmative defense of contributory negligence. The issue is discussed at greater length in Chapter 14, section III. The foreseeability of the misuse can affect the amount of recovery, further illustrating how foreseeability can affect the tort claim in different ways.

5. *Materiality*. The duty to warn makes sellers responsible for conveying their superior knowledge (actual or constructive) via disclosures in the product warning to improve consumer decision-making about product safety. In light of this rationale for the duty, would it be more straightforward to define the risks encompassed by the duty in terms of materiality? Under this formulation, the seller has a duty to warn about (1) reasonable precautions for safely using the product, and (2) any remaining inherent, foreseeable product risks, if the disclosure would materially improve the relevant safety decision of the ordinary consumer. This formulation, for example, straightforwardly explains why there is no duty to warn about risks that are already known by the consumer or are otherwise insignificant ("remote"). Disclosure of these risks would not materially improve the consumer's safety decision and therefore are not required by the tort duty.

V. THE ADEQUACY OF DISCLOSURE

The adequacy of a warning depends on both the content and format of the disclosure. Even if a warning discloses all information the tort duty requires, it can still be defective for not adequately conveying that information. If a different format of disclosure would materially improve consumer decision-making, the existing format can render the warning defective.

JONES v. AMAZING PRODUCTS, INC.
United States District Court, Northern District of Georgia, 2002
231 F. Supp. 2d 1228

CARNES, J. This is a product liability action. Plaintiff Robert Jones ("Mr. Jones") and his wife Almarie Jones ("Mrs. Jones") (collectively "plaintiffs") filed suit alleging that a drain line clearer called "Liquid Fire" is unreasonably dangerous, improperly packaged, and accompanied with inadequate instructions under strict liability, negligence and gross negligence theories. Mr. Jones was severely injured when the product spilled on him [after he had transferred the liquid to another container, contrary to instructions in the product warning]. Currently before the Court is defendant's Motion for Summary Judgment.

In a products liability case, whether or not grounded in a strict liability or negligence theory, a manufacturer's duty to warn depends on the foreseeability of the use in question, the type of danger involved, and the foreseeability of the user's knowledge of the danger. Where a duty to warn arises, the duty may be breached by (1) failing to adequately communicate the warning to the ultimate user or (2) failing to provide an adequate warning of the product's potential risk.

A failure to read the warning will bar the plaintiff from recovering on the second prong of this test, which is based on the adequacy of the warning. The reason for this result is that if the plaintiff failed to read the warning, the inadequacy of the warning can no longer be the cause of the injury; instead plaintiff's failure to read the warning becomes the cause of the injury.

A plaintiff's failure to read a warning will not, however, bar recovery as to the first prong of the test: namely, where the plaintiff is challenging the *adequacy* of the defendant's efforts to communicate the dangers of the product to the user, not the substance of those warnings. Failure to communicate an adequate warning involves such questions as the location and presentation of the warning.

Despite the fact that plaintiffs fail to specifically articulate this argument, they do refer often to the fact that Mr. Jones attempted to read the label, but failed to read the entire label because the small print size prevented him from doing so. Moreover, it appears to this Court that the part of the cautionary instruction that directed the user not to transfer the product to another container was buried in the middle of a long paragraph, in a very small print size. Indeed, even though looking for this specific language, the undersigned had to read through the label twice to find this particular sentence. *See* Stapelton v. Kawasaki Heavy Indust., Ltd., 608 F.2d 571, 573 (5th Cir. 1979) (where the manufacturer placed a warning concerning the danger of ignition from undetected gas leakage on page 13 of a motorcycle manual, a jury could conclude that the danger posed by this leakage was sufficiently great that the warning should have been presented in a way that was immediately obvious to even a casual reader).

Accordingly, the Court concludes that plaintiff has presented a jury question as to whether the defendant adequately communicated the prohibition against transferring the liquid and the Court therefore DENIES the defendant's Motion for Summary judgment as to this part of the duty to warn claim.

NOTES AND QUESTIONS

1. *Evaluating the form of disclosure.* According to a leading formulation, an adequate warning "must (1) be designed so it can reasonably be expected to catch the attention of the consumer; (2) be comprehensible and give a fair indication of the specific risks involved with the product; and (3) be of an intensity justified by the magnitude of the risk." Pavlides

V. The Adequacy of Disclosure

v. Galveston Yacht Basin, Inc., 727 F.2d 330, 338 (5th Cir. 1984); *see also, e.g.,* In Re: Davol, Inc./C.R. Bard, Inc., Polypropylene Hernia Mesh Products Liability Litigation, 2020 WL 5223363 (S.D. Ohio 2020) (applying this formulation).

2. *Why the form of disclosure matters.* When a warning is defective due to the form of disclosure, it otherwise contains the requisite information. Given that the warning already discloses the necessary information, what precisely explains why the warning is defective?

In *Jones*, plaintiffs claimed that Mr. Jones attempted to read the warning but was unable to do so because of its "very small print size." Why not require the consumer to use a magnifying glass? If Mr. Jones had done so, he could have gained the requisite information. What is problematic about such a warning?

The cost of reading a warning is a type of *information cost* or burden that the ordinary consumer must incur to read and process the information contained in the warning. To what extent does the court's reasoning in *Jones* reflect the importance of information costs? Was the warning defective simply because the information cost of using a magnifying glass exceeds the information cost of reading a warning with ordinary print size? What problem would be created by a warning with unnecessarily high information costs? Has this problem been consistently addressed by other cases excerpted in this chapter? Consider, for example, whether it would be reasonable to require Spanish-speaking consumers to ask their English-speaking neighbors to read a warning to them. How does this burden compare to the one faced by Mr. Jones? Consider whether information costs influence the reasoning of the court in the next case.

MACDONALD v. ORTHO PHARMACEUTICAL CORP.
Supreme Judicial Court of Massachusetts, 1985
475 N.E.2d 65

ABRAMS, J. In September, 1973, the plaintiff Carole D. MacDonald (MacDonald), who was twenty-six years old at the time, obtained from her gynecologist a prescription for Ortho-Novum contraceptive pills, manufactured by Ortho. As required by the then effective regulations promulgated by the United States Food and Drug Administration (FDA), the pill dispenser she received was labeled with a warning that "oral contraceptives are powerful and effective drugs which can cause side effects in some users and should not be used at all by some women," and that "[t]he most serious known side effect is abnormal blood clotting which can be fatal." The warning also referred MacDonald to a booklet which she obtained from her gynecologist, and which was distributed by Ortho pursuant to FDA requirements. The booklet contained detailed information about the contraceptive pill, including the increased risk to pill users that vital organs such as the brain may be damaged by abnormal blood clotting. The word "stroke" did not appear on the dispenser warning or in the booklet.

MacDonald's prescription for Ortho-Novum pills was renewed at subsequent annual visits to her gynecologist. The prescription was filled annually. On July 24,

1976, after approximately three years of using the pills, MacDonald suffered an occlusion of a cerebral artery by a blood clot, an injury commonly referred to as a stroke. The injury caused the death of approximately twenty per cent of MacDonald's brain tissue, and left her permanently disabled. She and her husband initiated an action in the Superior Court against Ortho, seeking recovery for her personal injuries and his consequential damages and loss of consortium.

MacDonald testified that, during the time she used the pills, she was unaware that the risk of abnormal blood clotting encompassed the risk of stroke, and that she would not have used the pills had she been warned that stroke is an associated risk. The case was submitted to a jury on the plaintiffs' theories that Ortho was negligent in failing to warn adequately of the dangers associated with the pills and that Ortho breached its warranty of merchantability. These two theories were treated, in effect, as a single claim of failure to warn. The jury found that Ortho was negligent and in breach of warranty because it failed to give MacDonald sufficient warning of such dangers. The jury further found that MacDonald's injury was caused by Ortho's pills, that the inadequacy of the warnings to MacDonald was the proximate cause of her injury, and that Ortho was liable to MacDonald and her husband.

The common law duty to warn . . . necessitates a warning "comprehensible to the average user and conveying a fair indication of the nature and extent of the danger to the mind of a reasonably prudent person." [ ] Whether a particular warning measures up to this standard is almost always an issue to be resolved by a jury; few questions are "more appropriately left to a common sense lay judgment than that of whether a written warning gets its message across to an average person." [ ] A court may, as a matter of law, determine "whether the defendant has conformed to that standard, in any case in which the jury may not reasonably come to a different conclusion," RESTATEMENT (SECOND) OF TORTS §328B (d) and comment *g* (1965), but judicial intrusion into jury decision making in negligence cases is exceedingly rare.

Ortho argues that reasonable minds could not differ as to whether MacDonald was adequately informed of the risk of the injury she sustained by Ortho's warning that the oral contraceptives could cause "abnormal blood clotting which can be fatal" and further warning of the incremental likelihood of hospitalization or death due to blood clotting in "vital organs, such as the brain." We disagree. "The fact finder may find a warning to be unreasonable, hence inadequate, in its factual content, its expression of the facts, or the method or form in which it is conveyed. The adequacy of such warnings is measured not only by what is stated, but also by the manner in which it is stated. A reasonable warning not only conveys a fair indication of the nature of the dangers involved, but also warns with the degree of intensity demanded by the nature of the risk. A warning may be found to be unreasonable in that it was unduly delayed, reluctant in tone or lacking in a sense of urgency." [ ] We cannot say that this jury's decision that the warning was inadequate is so unreasonable as to require the opposite conclusion as a matter of law. The jury may well have concluded, in light of their common experience and MacDonald's testimony, that the absence of a reference to "stroke" in the warning unduly minimized the warning's impact or failed to make the nature of the risk reasonably comprehensible to the average consumer. Similarly, the jury may have concluded that there are fates worse than death, such as the permanent disablement suffered by MacDonald, and that the mention of the risk of death did not, therefore, suffice to apprise an average consumer of the material risks of oral contraceptive use.

We reverse the judgment, which the judge ordered notwithstanding the verdict, and remand the case to the Superior Court for the entry of judgment for the plaintiffs.

NOTES AND QUESTIONS

1. *Multiple duties to warn.* In addition to the warning provided to consumers of the drug, the defendant drug manufacturer in *MacDonald* also provided warnings to the prescribing physician, who owed a separate tort duty to the patient of ensuring that she could make an informed decision whether to use the drug (the doctrine of informed consent). For discussion of the circumstances in which the drug manufacturer must give the consumer a direct warning in addition to warning the physician, see Chapter 9, section I.

2. *The rhetoric of liability.* In a case like *MacDonald*, the plaintiff's attorney can make a compelling argument for liability: the damages award would provide compensation to someone who was badly harmed by the product, and the plaintiff testified that she would have avoided injury if she had been specifically warned about the possibility of a stroke, so the more detailed warning might prevent at least a few injuries in the future.

To understand the force of this argument, consider the plaintiff's closing argument to the jury in a case involving the claim that a "pump jack" did not adequately warn of the risks involved in raising or lowering a scaffold at a construction site:

> Your decision is going to be extremely important, not only to [this young man], but also to the defendant and to the other people who make and sell these products. They're listening to what you're going to say. You've heard about the associations, the scaffolding associations, the ladder associations, and the newsletters that go out. These people in this industry listen. The information goes out. It speaks to them and they will be interested in what you have to say in this verdict that you return.
>
> They want to know whether they can keep on selling these products just like this. They want to know can we keep on selling them, without any warnings, or should we, must we, put a warning on here that people who use these will know that they are subjected to a severe risk of personal injury if they use them without adequate bracing....
>
> It will be important to the defendant, and it will be important to the other manufacturers and people who sell pump jacks. You will tell them by your decision whether they should modify and correct the pieces of paper that they put on these things ... or will they continue to sell them just like they are and send them out into commerce for people to use.
>
> They will be listening to what you have to say, these associations, these trade associations that make and sell these products. But, you know, your decision is going to be important to somebody else. It's going to be important to some other young man that's out there,

some other twenty-two year old young man who's got a wife and child who's out there working on somebody else's project.

Precise Eng'g, Inc. v. LaCombe, 624 So. 2d 1339, 1342-1343 (Ala. 1993).

If a little more detail in the warning might save someone's life, how can the product seller persuasively defend the adequacy of the disclosure in question?

3. *The problem of limited focus.* Critics of legally mandated disclosures argue that the obligation has an unduly narrow focus that does not adequately account for the range of decisions we all must make on a daily basis:

> The disclosure paradigm . . . mistakenly asks whether people making a decision would be better off with more information. If they had nothing else in life but that decision, perhaps so. But since information that could be useful in a single-decision world becomes useless in the constant-decision world, the answer is generally no.

Omri Ben-Shahar & Carl E. Schneider, *The Failure of Mandated Disclosure*, 159 U. Penn. L. Rev. 647, 709 (2011).

In evaluating the adequacy of the product warning in *Moran*, why might the jury have focused on this particular safety decision to the exclusion of others? Consider in this regard the plaintiff's testimony that if she had known that the drug would cause a stroke, she would not have used it and thereby have avoided the injury.

4. *The problem of added detail.* An overly general warning can be inadequate as illustrated by an extreme example: WARNING—*Product can cause injury.* More detail is required, but how much? According to the *Restatement (Third)* §2 comment i:

> It is impossible to identify anything approaching a perfect level of detail that should be communicated in product disclosures. For example, educated or experienced product users and consumers may benefit from inclusion of more information about the full spectrum of product risks, whereas less-educated or unskilled users may benefit from more concise warnings and instructions stressing only the most crucial risks and safe-handling practices. In some contexts, products intended for special categories of users, such as children, may require more vivid and unambiguous warnings. In some cases, excessive detail may detract from the ability of typical users and consumers to focus on the important aspects of the warnings, whereas in others reasonably full disclosure will be necessary to enable informed, efficient choices by product users. Product warnings and instructions can rarely communicate all potentially relevant information, and the ability of a plaintiff to imagine a hypothetical better warning in the aftermath of an accident does not establish that the warning actually accompanying the product was inadequate. No easy guideline exists for courts to adopt in assessing the adequacy of product warnings and instructions. In making their assessments, courts must focus on various factors, such as content and comprehensibility, intensity of expression, and the characteristics of expected user groups.

V. The Adequacy of Disclosure

Consider the warning in *MacDonald*, which stated on the pill dispenser that the use of oral contraceptives could cause "abnormal blood clotting which can be fatal." The added detail requested by plaintiff would seem to be minimal: ". . . abnormal blood clotting, *such as a stroke*, which can be fatal." The issue is not so simple, however. Would the required alteration be limited to the added detail of a stroke, or would added detail also be required for other severe injuries that could be caused by abnormal blood clotting? Should a warning that specifically mentions strokes also mention heart attacks and clots that lodge in the lungs? Added detail of one type of risk (strokes) in principle should require added detail for other risks that are at least equally severe.

Including these added details could make the warning too lengthy to be contained on the pill dispenser, requiring their placement in the booklet accompanying the oral contraceptive. The booklet has the space for lengthier disclosures, but the problem of detail is no easier to solve. What about other risks the drug poses? Insofar as they are discussed in general terms, the logic of plaintiff's argument could mean that these disclosures also require more detail. Once reformulated in this manner, the booklet could contain much more detailed information, but it would also be much longer, considerably increasing information costs consumers incur to read and understand the warning in its entirety.

This reasoning is not fanciful. The average drug label lists 70 possible side effects, with some drugs containing warnings of more than 500 side effects. Jon Duke et al., *Prescription Drug Label Adverse Events: A Call for Prioritization*, 71 Arch. Internal Med. 946 (2011). According to some medical professionals, the problem is one of "linguistic toxicity." Jerry Avorn & William Shrank, *Highlights and a Hidden Hazard—The FDA's New Labeling Regulations*, 354 New Eng. J. Med. 2409 (2006).

Warning claims involving added detail can involve difficult trade-offs between increasing the amount of information and increasing the cost that consumers must incur to gain that information. In principle, a warning would be inadequate if the added detail would materially improve the safety decision of the ordinary consumer. Warnings that are too long, however, can be ignored. Too much detail can reduce the effectiveness of the warning.

Did the court in *MacDonald* acknowledge these trade-offs? Compare Robinson v. McNeil Consumer Healthcare, 615 F.3d 861, 869 (7th Cir. 2010) ("The plaintiff argues that the label on the bottle of Children's Motrin should have added 'rash' to the other allergic reactions warned against and should have mentioned SJS/TEN as one of the possible allergic reactions and (since virtually no consumer who was not a physician would have heard of the disease) recited its horrific consequences. But then the label would have had to describe as well every other serious disease that might, however infrequently, be caused, or even just arguably caused (for it is unclear whether ibuprofen can cause SJS/TEN), by ibuprofen. And it would have to recite the symptoms of the disease if it was rare. The resulting information overload would make label warnings worthless to consumers.").

5. *Subsequent remedial measures.* In Yates v. Ortho-McNeil-Janssen Pharmaceuticals, Inc. 808 F.3d 281 (6th Cir. 2015), plaintiff suffered a stroke

while using a birth control patch. The plaintiff claimed that the defendant manufacturer did not adequately warn about the risk. The patch had warning inserts that the Food and Drug Administration (FDA) required. The plaintiff argued "that the fact that the FDA subsequently required defendants to change [the] warning regarding the risk of stroke is evidence of the insufficiency of the label in effect when she was prescribed" the patch. The court dismissed the argument by relying on Federal Rule of Evidence 407, which bars evidence of subsequent remedial measures. *Id.* at 292. Does the rationale for this evidentiary rule apply to cases in which the remedial measure in question is mandated by federal regulation? For extended discussion of those rationales, see Hyjek v. Anthony Industries, p. 244 *supra*.

6. *A closer look at the problem of detail.* In *Yates*, the court affirmed summary dismissal of the plaintiff's warning claim on the ground that the warning adequately disclosed the risk: "Hormonal contraceptives . . . may increase the risk of developing strokes (blockage or rupture of blood vessels in the brain) and angina pectoris and heart attacks (blockage of blood vessels in the heart). Any of these conditions can cause death or serious disability." 808 F.3d at 289. How does this warning compare to the one in *MacDonald*? What does a comparison of the two suggest about the merits of the plaintiff's claim in *MacDonald* and the difficulty of determining how much detail is required in any given case?

In *Yates*, the plaintiff admitted that she knew about the risk of stroke, but claimed that the warning did not adequately convey the level of risk of stroke because it did not "state[ ] that the risk of stroke was higher than other methods of birth control, namely than birth control pills." The court rejected this argument, concluding that the duty to warn about "comparative risks extends to patients with different underlying risk factors, not to different drugs treating the same ailment." *Id.* at 291-292. Is this distinction persuasive? In Barron v. Abbott Labs., Inc., 529 S.W.3d 795, 800 (Mo. 2017), the court upheld a jury verdict that the warning was defective based on plaintiffs' evidence that defendant was aware of multiple studies showing that its antiepileptic drug created a considerably higher risk of overall birth defects than other antiepileptic drugs on the market, having an overall risk of 10 percent or even greater. Because the drug label did not disclose this information, it "was not complete and accurate and, therefore, did not adequately warn." The court then upheld a substantial punitive damages award based on defendant's deliberate disregard of the plaintiffs' tort rights.

Unlike the warnings contained on package inserts or manuals, sometimes the warning can be placed directly on the product itself. How might this difference affect the amount of detail that must be disclosed in the warning?

BROUSSARD v. CONTINENTAL OIL CO.
Court of Appeal of Louisiana, Third Circuit, 1983
433 So. 2d 354

STOKER, J. This is a personal injury suit by Mildredge T. Broussard against Black & Decker (U.S.), Inc. and The Home Insurance Company. Plaintiff-appellant

V. The Adequacy of Disclosure

(Broussard) was badly burned in an explosion of natural gas sparked by a Black & Decker hand drill. Broussard was using the drill while working at a Continental Oil Company (Conoco) plant at Grand Chenier, Louisiana. The verdict of the jury at trial was that Black & Decker was not at fault for failure to adequately warn in connection with the accident. Judgment was for the defendants and against plaintiff.

Plaintiff was directly employed by Crain Brothers Construction Company. On the day of the accident, plaintiff and four other men, including Sanders Miller, were in the process of building a sump box enclosure at the end of a natural gas vent line (pipe) at the Grand Chenier plant. Plaintiff was a carpenter's helper and Miller was a carpenter. Upon arriving at the site, both men noticed that natural gas could be heard and smelled coming from the vent line. Miller immediately notified Conoco's relief plant foreman about the escaping gas and asked if it could be shut off. The foreman refused to do so because the whole plant would have had to be shut down to prevent the gas from being vented at the location of the sump box. After Miller requested a shut down a second time, the foreman talked to Mr. Leeman, another Conoco employee and the plant supervisor. Miller was again told nothing could be done.

Miller testified that he recognized the danger of working around the flammable natural gas. The workers took what precautions they could to minimize the risk of igniting the natural gas fumes. Cigarettes, cigarette lighters and matches were left in the work vehicles. The vehicles were parked some distance away from the site. A gasoline powered electricity generator was placed at the end of two 50-foot extension cords. Miller warned the plaintiff to be careful not to cause a spark while hammering, especially when the fumes were heavy.

The explosion occurred as plaintiff was standing inside a plywood box loosely held together and being constructed as a concrete form. He was positioned inside the form to drill holes in its sides through which rods were to be inserted. It is not seriously contested that sparks from the drill plaintiff was using ignited the natural gas fumes coming from the vent line. Such sparks are normally emitted from this and similar type drills when the "brushes" inside the armature of the drill contact and slide along the inside surface of the rapidly spinning cylinder in which the brushes sit. There is no evidence, nor is the issue before this Court, that the design which allows the creation and emission of these sparks constitutes a design defect. Rather, the issues relate to the failure to warn on the part of the defendant manufacturer of the hazard of explosion.

Both the plaintiff Broussard and Sanders Miller testified that they were unaware at the time of the accident that sparks from electrical power drills could ignite gaseous atmospheres. Allen Nunez, the relief foreman, likewise testified that neither he nor anyone at the Conoco plant knew of the potential of explosion in a like situation before the accident occurred. However, a warning that would have informed the users of the drill of the precise cause and effect encountered appears in the owner's manual. Black & Decker claim that a copy of this manual is placed in every box containing one of their drills as it leaves the manufacturer's control.

The owner's manual is not attached to the drill but is loosely placed in the box. Thus, unless the box with the owner's manual inside (or the owner's manual itself, with the safety warnings inside its folded pamphlet form) is kept with the drill, the warning is not available to users other than the buyer. In addition to the owner's manual warning, there is a small notice on the side of the drill which simply reads, "CAUTION: For Safe Operation See Owner's Manual." This notice is approximately one-eighth inch high and one inch long.

Sanders Miller received the drill at the office of the Crain Brothers Construction Company from the secretary who worked in the office. The secretary asked Miller if he wanted the box the drill came in. Miller replied he had no use for it, and the box was thrown away. Neither Miller nor the plaintiff saw the owner's manual.

With reference to adequacy of warning of the danger from the emission of sparks, Black & Decker contends item eighteen in the owner's manual was sufficient. Plaintiff Broussard contends that it was not. Broussard contends that Black & Decker was guilty of fault in not putting the warning on the drill itself. Item eighteen reads as follows:

> 18. DO NOT OPERATE portable electric tools in gaseous or explosive atmospheres. Motors in these tools normally spark, and the sparks might ignite fumes.

The warning set forth in these words is adequate; the question is whether it was sufficient to put it in the owner's manual or whether it was unreasonable under the circumstances not to put this warning on the drill itself. As noted above there was a warning on the drill which read, "CAUTION: For Safe Operation See Owner's Manual." Knowledge of the risk is not a problem here for Black & Decker knew of the risk. The question is what was adequate warning.

Plaintiff's own expert witness unwittingly pointed up the difficulty in putting warnings on the drill itself. This expert demonstrated the use of warnings through symbols as opposed to words. The expert devised a series of symbols of his own creation based on international symbols which he suggested could have been placed on the drill itself. The symbols purportedly represent ten of the eighteen warnings Black & Decker set forth in the owner's manual.

While we think the use of symbols as suggested by plaintiff's expert merits no consideration, we note that the expert deemed at least ten of the warnings represented by the symbols were worthy of being noted on the drill. The fact that numerous risks other than sparking explosions or fires merit notice is a significant factor. The suggested use of symbols is also significant because the reason for it is the recognition that the space on the drill is not large enough to contain extensive warnings and cautions in words. This factor will be discussed later, but at this point we will state our opinion relative to the efficacy of symbols in lieu of words.

Plaintiff's expert testified that the symbols he proposed are neither standard nor easily recognizable by the general public. Further, the testimony indicates that the symbols are unclear and subject to different interpretations. The symbols fail in one aspect of sufficiency according to expert (as distinguished from legal) standards in that they do not inform why the activities are dangerous, just that they are dangerous. Above all, however, we are convinced that the use of symbols would require users of the drill to refer to an owner's manual or other written material to discover what the symbols meant. This would be no more efficacious than what Black & Decker did when it put a caution on the drill directing users to consult the owner's manual for safe operation.

V. The Adequacy of Disclosure

We think counsel for plaintiff recognized lack of merit in the suggested use of symbols. On plaintiff's behalf Exhibit P-17 was introduced in evidence. On the side of this exhibit a label measuring approximately $2\frac{5}{8}$ inches by $1\frac{4}{3}$ inches was affixed on which the following words were typed:

Safety Rules

- Don't abuse cord
- Wear proper apparel
- Don't use in damp areas
- Use proper extension cords outdoors
- Don't touch metal parts when drilling near any electrical wiring
- Remove tightening key
- Unplug to change bits
- Use safety glasses
- Avoid gaseous areas
- Secure work

SEE MANUAL FOR COMPLETE TEXTS

The whole of the above quoted material is typed in small letter characters in a slant-wise or diagonal fashion on the label in order to fit. It will be noted that the only reference to the risk of igniting gas from emission of sparks is contained in the three words, "Avoid gaseous areas."

We are not impressed with plaintiff's Exhibit P-17. The most important failing of the exhibit is that the mere words, "Avoid gaseous areas" does not explain or point out the precise risk of injury posed by use in gaseous areas. Moreover, this exhibit graphically illustrates the problem of attempting to put multiple warnings on a hand drill of the size and nature involved.

Defendant considers that more than ten warnings should be given. Nevertheless, if only ten are selected, deficiencies in any scheme for putting them all on the drill become apparent. As a practical matter, the effect of putting at least ten warnings on the drill would decrease the effectiveness of all of the warnings. A consumer would have a tendency to read none of the warnings if the surface of the drill became cluttered with the warnings. Unless we should elevate the one hazard of sparking to premier importance above all others, we fear that an effort to tell all about each hazard is not practical either from the point of view of availability of space or of effectiveness. We decline to say that one risk is more worthy of warning than another.

We conclude that defendant acted reasonably toward plaintiff and all persons who might use its hand drill. In view of the numerous risks which a manufacturer of a hand drill must explicitly describe, the most practical and effective thing which the manufacturer could do is to direct the user to the owner's manual as Black & Decker did.

For the reasons we have given we hold that the jury's finding of no fault on the part of Black & Decker was correct.

AFFIRMED.

NOTES AND QUESTIONS

1. *The location and intensity of a warning.* The adequacy of a warning depends on the degree to which the "intensity of expression" reflects the seriousness of the risk. RESTATEMENT (THIRD) OF TORTS: PRODUCTS LIABILITY §2 cmt. i. The intensity of expression involves both the language in and placement of the warning.

> For example, the warning "harmful if swallowed" is less intense than the warning, "swallowing will result in death"; however, the former, less intense warning, when displayed prominently in block letters on the front label of a product, may be ultimately more effective than the latter, more intense warning, when displayed unobtrusively in small letters in the middle of a 10–page package insert.

Johnson v. Johnson Chem. Co., Inc., 588 N.Y.S.2d 607, 611 (N.Y. App. 1992). What type of consumer behavior is contemplated by this rule? Does it involve the role of information costs? Consider AM. L. PROD. LIAB. 3d §33:8 (Feb. 2021 update) ("[A] manufacturer may be liable for failure to adequately warn where its warning is not prominent or not calculated to attract the user's attention due to its position, size or coloring, if it can reasonably be concluded that a more prominently displayed warning would have been read.").

2. *Does the placement of the warning affect the plaintiff's ability to recover?* The conspicuousness of a warning depends on both its location and level of detail, making it useful to compare a case involving the appropriate location of a warning (e.g., *Broussard*) with one involving the appropriate amount of detail (e.g., *MacDonald*). In a case like *Broussard*, the plaintiff's proposed warning creates a visible "crowding out" effect due to the limited amount of space for placing a warning on the product. If the proposed warning would "crowd out" warnings pertaining to more serious risks, it would create an unreasonable risk-risk trade-off that the defendant could rely on to defend the adequacy of its warning. In principle, this same logic applies to cases like *MacDonald* in which the plaintiff claims that the warning does not provide an adequate amount of detail, because the resultant, lengthier warning increases information costs that can "crowd out" other warnings the consumer might otherwise have read or remembered. *See, e.g.,* Wesley A. Magat & W. Kip Viscusi, INFORMATIONAL APPROACHES TO REGULATION 87-105 (1992) (describing a study finding that a cost is created by any new item of information on a product warning, due to the effect that additional information has on the consumer's ability to recall other information contained in the warning). The risk-risk trade-off created by this "crowding out" effect, though, is much more abstract because it stems from limitations of time and memory, not from visibly obvious space limitations on the product itself. For this reason, it may be harder to defend the warning when the alleged defect involves the amount of detail as compared to the location or conspicuousness of the warning, even though both issues involve a risk-risk trade-off created by the "crowding out" effect. Compare Todd v. Societe BIC, S.A., 9 F.3d 1216, 1218-1219 (7th Cir. 1993) ("Extended warnings present several difficulties, first among them

that, the more text must be squeezed onto the product, the smaller the type, and the less likely is the consumer to read or remember any of it.").

VI. THE RISK-UTILITY TEST

In most jurisdictions, the risk-utility test determines the adequacy of a warning—the same standard that determines whether the design is defective. Unlike design cases, the disutility or cost of a warning can be harder to identify. For example, if the ordinary consumer is not aware of the need to wear gloves while using a chemical cleaner, then adding such an instruction to the existing warning would reduce the risk of chemically induced skin burns (denoted PL_{burn}). This precaution would be reasonable if the burden or cost of wearing gloves were less than the risk that would thereby be reduced ($B_{gloves} < PL_{burn}$). This proof establishes that it would be reasonable for the ordinary consumer to wear gloves while using the cleaner, and that the ordinary consumer was not aware of the need to do so. Is this proof sufficient for proving that a warning without this instruction is defective? What about the costs of the warning itself? Are they defined wholly by the increased cost of adding the warning in question—ink and paper—or does the adequacy of a warning also depend on information costs or the burden that the ordinary consumer must incur to read and remember the warning ($B_{information\ costs} + B_{gloves} < PL_{burn}$)?

CAMPOS v. FIRESTONE TIRE & RUBBER CO.
Supreme Court of New Jersey, 1984
485 A.2d 305

SCHREIBER, J. Whether a duty exists "involves a weighing of the relationship of the parties, the nature of the risk, and the public interest in the proposed solution." [ ] The additional cost of a warning will in most cases have but a slight impact on the risk-utility analysis, since such cost would generally have little, if any, effect on a product's utility. [ ] More relevant questions in the warning context include the following. Is the lack of the warning consonant with the duty to place in the stream of commerce only products that are reasonably safe, suitable, and fit? Will the absence of a duty encourage manufacturers to eliminate warnings or to produce inadequate warnings? Is the danger so basic to the functioning or purpose of the product—for example, the fact that a match will burn—that a warning would serve no useful purpose?

... We have no difficulty in holding that under the facts and circumstances of this case defendant had a duty to warn plaintiff.

NOTES AND QUESTIONS

1. *What is the cost of disclosure?* The adequacy of a warning depends on the simple idea that information is good, which in turn has made warning

cases deceptively simple. "[I]n failure-to-warn cases the common assumption is that warnings can often be improved upon but can never be made worse; that is, the issue at stake is always whether the defendant ought to have supplied consumers with more, and by definition better, information about product risks." James A. Henderson, Jr. & Aaron D. Twerski, *Doctrinal Collapse in Products Liability: The Empty Shell of Failure to Warn*, 65 N.Y.U. L. Rev. 265, 269-270 (1990). More information is always better when the cost of a warning largely consists of ink and paper, the formulation of cost that courts adopted when initially formulating the warning doctrine as illustrated by *Campos*. For example, in *Moran v. Faberge, Inc.* (excerpted on p. 303 *supra*), Maryland's highest court "observe[d] that in cases such as this the cost of giving an adequate warning is usually so minimal, amounting only to the expense of adding some more printing to a label, that this balancing process will almost always weigh in favor of an obligation to warn of latent dangers, if the manufacturer is otherwise required to do so." 332 A.2d 11, 15 (Md. 1975).

HOOD v. RYOBI AMERICA CORP.
United States Court of Appeals, Fourth Circuit, 1999
181 F.3d 608

WILKINSON, C.J. In deciding whether a warning is adequate, Maryland law asks whether the benefits of a more detailed warning outweigh the costs of requiring the change. Moran v. Faberge, Inc., 332 A.2d 11 (Md. 1975). [Plaintiff] assumes that the cost of a more detailed warning label is minimal in this case, and he claims that such a warning would have prevented his injury. But the price of more detailed warnings is greater than their additional printing fees alone. Some commentators have observed that the proliferation of label detail threatens to undermine the effectiveness of warnings altogether. [ ] As manufacturers append line after line onto product labels in the quest for the best possible warning, it is easy to lose sight of the label's communicative value as a whole. Well-meaning attempts to warn of every possible accident lead over time to voluminous yet impenetrable labels—too prolix to read and too technical to understand.

NOTES AND QUESTIONS

1. *What does precedent require?* Based on cases like *Campos* and *Moran*, some commentators have argued that courts "have refused to regard the time of the consumer's increased label reading as a 'cost' in the calculus of liability." Paul D. Rheingold & Susan B. Feinglass, *Risk-Utility Analysis in the Failure to Warn Context*, 30 U. Mich. J.L. Reform 353, 356 (1997). By contrast, the court in *Hood* concluded that information costs—the burden that consumers incur to read, process, and remember the disclosures in a warning—are part of the risk-utility inquiry employed in *Moran*. Which interpretation is correct? When applying the risk-utility test to product warnings, do courts consider information costs?

VI. The Risk-Utility Test

The court in *Hood* distinguished *Moran* on the ground that it was a case in which "the manufacturer . . . failed to include any warnings at all with its product." 181 F.3d at 611. Does this distinction adequately explain why information costs are relevant in the one case but not the other? Would the inclusion of a single warning on the product in *Moran* have made a difference in the court's analysis? Is there a better way to distinguish *Moran*?

2. *Why is there any issue about the relevance of information costs?* As we have found, the various doctrines throughout this chapter can all be justified by the manner in which they minimize information costs for consumers. Indeed, the duty to warn is based on the problem of information costs. If information were free, then presumably everyone would be perfectly informed about product risk, eliminating any need for a product warning. The cost an individual consumer faces to acquire information, therefore, creates the need for disclosure in the first instance. The duty to warn is a consequence of information costs.

For this reason, the duty to warn can be fully understood only in relation to information costs. Any limitation on the duty to warn implicitly recognizes that more information is not always desirable, presumably because of information costs. For example, there is no duty to warn of risks known by the ordinary consumer, even if the plaintiff can prove that not everyone knew about the risk in question. If information costs were irrelevant, the slight safety benefit of such a warning for a few consumers would outweigh its virtually nonexistent cost (of ink and paper). The seller, however, does not have a duty to disclose these risks, presumably because these disclosures would create unnecessary information costs for the ordinary consumer that can lead to the widespread disregard of warnings. Similarly, the characteristics of an adequate warning often depend on information costs. After all, if information costs did not exist, then consumers would necessarily read and digest all disclosures in the warning, regardless of its format. Without information costs, there is no reason for concluding that a warning can be inadequate for "burying" disclosures in the operator's manual rather than placing them prominently on the product itself. The varied rules governing the duty to warn only make sense in a world where consumers must incur costs to acquire and retain information.

Regardless of whether a jurisdiction has expressly recognized the importance of information costs, it has done so implicitly by adopting the duty to warn. But why were information costs only implicitly relevant and not expressly recognized by courts in cases like *Campos* and *Moran*?

3. *The emergent problems of "information overload" and the proliferation of mandated disclosures.* To see why cases like *Campos* and *Moran* contain no discussion of information costs, one must recognize that courts first formulated the warning doctrine before the Internet had become widely available. In light of the ensuing proliferation of easily accessible information, is it realistic to assume that more information is always better?

> The consensus in the literature is that we live in a climate of *infoglut* or we are surrounded by *data smog*, an expression for the muck and druck of the information age. Two other terms found in the literature that are aptly used to describe the problem of information overload are *analysis paralysis* and *information fatigue*

syndrome. . . . We can all recognise the condition of information overload. However, there is no universally agreed definition of information overload—it can mean several things, such as having more relevant information than one can assimilate or it might mean being burdened with a large supply of unsolicited information, some of which may be relevant. A large amount and high rate of information act like noise when they reach overload: a rate too high for the receiver to process efficiently without distraction, stress, increasing errors and other costs making information poorer. However the term is defined, there cannot be many people who have not experienced the feeling of having too much information which uses up too much of their time, causing them to feel stressed which, in turn, affects their decision-making.

Angela Edmunds & Anne Morris, *The Problem of Information Overload in Business Organizations: A Review of the Literature*, 20 Int'l J. Info. Mgmt. 17, 18-19 (2000).

The information supplied by a product warning is only one of the many disclosures that sellers provide to consumers. "Disclosures are so ubiquitous that we tend to be unaware of them, and when the implicit is made explicit, one cannot help but be struck that it would be impossible for people to attend to even a fraction of the disclosures to which they are exposed." George Lowenstein, Cass R. Sunstein & Russell Golman, *Disclosure: Psychology Changes Everything*, 6 Ann. Rev. Econ. 391, 399 (2014). Relatedly, courts today could be influenced by the proliferation of detail in product warnings. Compare Forbes, *In Pictures: 24 Stunningly Dumb Warning Labels*, Feb. 23, 2011.

Like any other form of communication, an adequate product warning must account for the information cost of reading, evaluating, and remembering information. All else being equal, more information is good. But consumers must incur costs to acquire new information. "There are serious limitations on the amount of information to which people can attend at any point in time. Bounded attention renders many disclosures useless because consumers ignore them." Lowenstein, Sunstein & Golman, *supra*, at 398-399. A warning that does not account for information costs can be self-defeating.

This reasoning of the court in *Hood*, therefore, reflects the changed social conditions since cases like *Campos* and *Moran*. In addition to the *Hood* court, many others have recognized the importance of information costs. *See, e.g.,* Air and Liquid Sys. Corp. v. DeVries, 139 S. Ct. 986, 998 (U.S. 2019) (Gorsuch, J., dissenting) ("As the Court today recognizes, encouraging manufacturers to offer warnings about other people's products risks long, duplicative, fine print, and conflicting warnings that will leave consumers less sure about which to take seriously and more likely to disregard them all."); Finn v. G.D. Searle & Co., 677 P.2d 1147, 1153 (Cal. 1984) (observing that if manufacturers were required to warn of "every . . . possible risk," then the decision-maker would be "inundate[d] . . . indiscriminately with notice of any and every hint of danger, thereby inevitably diluting the force of any specific warning given").

VII. THE RISK-UTILITY TEST APPLIED

According to *Restatement (Third)* §2(b), the plaintiff must prove that the defendant did not provide a specific warning or instruction that satisfies the risk-utility test. In evaluating the "disutility" or cost of the plaintiff's requested disclosure, the finder of fact can consider whether it would detract from other, more important disclosures in the warning. The cost of disclosure must then be compared to the reduced risk or benefit that the additional information would create by enabling consumers to make better decisions about product safety. By showing that the defendant's warning does not contain a disclosure that satisfies the risk-utility test, the plaintiff in effect shows that the warning is inadequate because it does not make a disclosure with a cost less than its benefit.

The risk-utility test can also determine whether the warning was properly designed. A poorly designed warning does not emphasize risks in proportion to their significance. A new design alters the emphasis given to risk disclosures in the warning, creating a benefit from the greater emphasis of some risks along with a cost due to the reduced emphasis of other risks. Thus, an alternative design that properly emphasizes risks in relation to their significance will pass the risk-utility test, because greater emphasis of more significant risks necessarily creates a benefit that exceeds the cost stemming from the reduced emphasis of less significant risks.

Even though the risk-utility test can be applied to an allegation of warning defect in a manner conceptually similar to its application with respect to a design defect, "the defectiveness concept is more difficult to apply in the warnings context." *Id.* cmt. i. Does the difficulty of application stem from the abstract nature of information costs?

How courts actually apply the risk-utility test depends on how the jury is instructed about the matter. The following pattern jury instructions are not particularly distinctive in terms of the guidance, or lack thereof, they provide on warning defects. Do you think the instructions adequately inform jurors of the relevant considerations?

California Civil Jury Instructions (BAJI 9.00.7) (Sept. 2020 update)

A [manufacturer] [_____] has a duty to warn if (1) the use of the product in a manner that is reasonably foreseeable by the (manufacturer, etc.) involves a substantial danger that would not be readily recognized by the ordinary user of the product, and (2) this danger was known or knowable in light of the generally recognized and prevailing best scientific [and medical] knowledge available at the time of the manufacture and distribution.

A [manufacturer] [_____] has a duty to provide an adequate warning to the user on how to use the product if a reasonably foreseeable use of the product involves a substantial danger of which the manufacturer either is aware or should be aware, and that would not be readily recognized by the ordinary user.

A [manufacturer] [_____] of a product has a duty to warn of potential allergic reactions to the product if (1) the product contains an ingredient to which a substantial number of the population are allergic, (2) the ingredient is one whose danger is not generally known, or if known, is one which the consumer would not reasonably expect to find in the product, and (3) the [defendant] [ ] knew or by the application of reasonable, developed human skill and foresight should have known of the ingredient and the danger.

NOTES AND QUESTIONS

1. *Whither the risk-utility test?* Do the California pattern jury instructions define the attributes of an "adequate" warning? Consider in this respect the standard instructions in a negligence case that ask the jury to determine whether the defendant violated a behavioral norm defined by the conduct of the hypothetical reasonably careful person. *See, e.g.,* 7A Mich. Civ. Prac. Forms §127:30 (Sept. 2020 update) ("The law does not say what a reasonably careful person would do or not do under the circumstances. That is for you to decide."). Do courts formulate jury instructions for product warnings by relying on this same concept of reasonableness? Consider N.Y. Pattern Jury Instr.—Civil 2:120 (Dec. 2020 update) ("The manufacturer of a product which is reasonably certain to be harmful if used in a way that the manufacturer should reasonably foresee is under a duty to use reasonable care to give adequate warning of any danger known to it or which in the use of reasonable care it should have known and which the user of the product ordinarily would not discover. Reasonable care means that degree of care which a reasonably prudent person would use under the same circumstances.").

By contrast, jury instructions for defective designs describe the risk-utility factors. *See id.* ("A product is defectively designed if a reasonable person who knew or should have known of the product's potential for causing injury and of the feasible alternative design[s] would have concluded that the product should not have been marketed in that condition. Whether the product should have been marketed in that condition depends upon a balancing of the risks involved in using the product against (1) the product's usefulness and its costs, and (2) the risks, usefulness and costs of the alternative design[s] as compared to the product the defendant did market."). In light of these instructions for defective design, why don't jury instructions describe the risk-utility factors for evaluating an adequate warning?

2. *The problem of "polycentricity."* Even if jurors evaluate the adequacy of a product warning by relying on risk-utility reasoning, application of that standard can be difficult due to the intertwined or interrelated issues implicated by the various disclosures in an adequate product warning—a problem of *polycentricity*. "The characteristic of most legal problems that renders them adjudicable is the unique manner in which the various issues presented in a case are logically related to each other." When "the parties are able to take up and consider each issue separately, in an orderly sequence," each litigant "will be able to isolate analytically any given issue in the case . . . and to talk of a favorable decision in relation to that issue without simultaneously considering all of the others." In contrast, adjudication is poorly suited for resolving "polycentric" problems "in which each point for decision is related to all others," because as the litigant "moved from the first point of his argument to the second and then the third, he would find his arguments regarding the earlier points shifting beneath him." James A. Henderson, Jr., *Judicial*

Review of Manufacturers' Conscious Design Choices: The Limits of Adjudication, 73 Colum. L. Rev. 1531, 1535-1536 (1973). The problem of polycentricity could plague warning claims due to the interrelationships among the disclosures in a warning. The information costs created by some disclosures can affect the consumer's willingness to read other disclosures. The prominence of some disclosures has the effect of deemphasizing others. The adequacy of a product warning depends on how all of its constituent parts work together, creating the potential for a polycentric problem in which "each point for decision is related to all others."

3. *Jury instructions and the problem of polycentricity.* Do the pattern jury instructions from California adequately address the problem of polycentricity? The instructions define the "adequacy" of the warning solely in terms of a particular risk involving a "substantial danger" that would not be "readily recognized" by the user. This risk is the one that injured the plaintiff; otherwise the absence of such a warning could not have caused the plaintiff's injury. By focusing the jury's attention on one salient risk, do the instructions obscure or ignore the way in which that single risk disclosure affects the consumer's evaluation of other aspects of the warning? Can jury instructions be formulated to avoid this problem? *See* Mark Geistfeld, *Inadequate Product Warnings and Causation*, 30 U. Mich. J.L. Reform 309, 329-335 (1997) (proposing set of pattern jury instructions for inadequate warnings that tries to obviate the problem of polycentricity by expressly requiring the jury to consider the proposed alteration of the warning in relation to other aspects of the warning).

VIII. THE POST-SALE DUTY TO WARN

Each of the doctrines we have studied so far involves liability for defects in the product that existed at the time of sale or distribution. A product seller can also incur liability for defects that it discovers or should have discovered after the product has been commercially distributed. The manufacturer, for example, can have a post-sale duty to recall or repair the product. *See* RESTATEMENT (THIRD) OF TORTS: PRODUCTS LIABILITY §11 (limiting the post-sale duty to recall to cases in which the measure is required by statute or regulation, or the manufacturer voluntarily recalls the product and commits negligence in the course of doing so). The manufacturer can also incur a post-sale duty to warn.

GREAT NORTHERN INSURANCE CO. v. HONEYWELL INTERNATIONAL, INC.
Supreme Court of Minnesota, 2018
911 N.W.2d 510

CHUTICH, J. [One of the defendants, McMillan Electric Company, manufactured the motor that was a component part in a heat-recovery ventilator for a home located in Eden Prairie, Minnesota. Sixteen years after the ventilator was installed, a fire started in the ventilator and caused substantial property damage to the home. After paying its insured's losses, the insurer of the homeowners brought this subrogation action against McMillan and others. It asserted tort, negligence, and warranty claims, including a claim for breach of a post-sale duty to warn. The district court granted summary judgment to McMillan, concluding in part that it did not have such a duty—a ruling subsequently reversed by the court of appeals. Plaintiff appealed that decision in addition to one involving application of a statute of repose. After deciding that the statute did not bar plaintiff's claims, the court addressed the alleged post-sale duty to warn.]

II. A

We have established that manufacturers have a duty to warn of a safety hazard that is present at the time of sale. [ ] This pre-sale duty to warn attaches when "the manufacturer or the seller of the product has actual or constructive knowledge of danger to users." [ ] We have also recognized that a manufacturer can have a post-sale duty to warn when a manufacturer discovers a hidden defect *after* the time of sale. Hodder v. Goodyear Tire & Rubber Co., 426 N.W.2d 826, 833 (Minn. 1988). But unlike the pre-sale duty to warn, we have not established a general rule to describe the circumstances under which the post-sale duty to warn arises. [ ]

. . .

We now consider a general rule. Specifically, we consider two different rules for when a post-sale duty to warn arises: (1) a [five-factor] balancing test set forth and applied by federal courts interpreting the factual circumstances in *Hodder*, and (2) the rule set forth in the RESTATEMENT (THIRD) OF TORTS: PRODUCTS LIABILITY §10 (Am. Law Inst. 1998). . . . To better limit the post-sale duty to warn to "special cases," as required by *Hodder*, we adopt this rule. Section 10 provides:

> (a) One engaged in the business of selling or otherwise distributing products is subject to liability for harm to persons or property caused by the seller's failure to provide a warning after the time of sale or distribution of a product if a reasonable person in the seller's position would provide such a warning.
>
> (b) A reasonable person in the seller's position would provide a warning after the time of sale if:
>
>> (1) the seller knows or reasonably should know that the product poses a substantial risk of harm to persons or property; and
>> (2) those to whom a warning might be provided can be identified and can reasonably be assumed to be unaware of the risk of harm; and
>> (3) a warning can be effectively communicated to and acted on by those to whom a warning might be provided; and
>> (4) the risk of harm is sufficiently great to justify the burden of providing a warning.

Under this rule, the post-sale duty to warn is a negligence standard, which outlines conjunctive factors for when a reasonable person in the same situation would provide a warning. *Id.* cmt. b.

VIII. The Post-Sale Duty to Warn

We decide to adopt the *Restatement* rule for several reasons. First, the rule's factors are conjunctive, and a plaintiff must establish all the requirements for the duty to attach. *Id.* The rule therefore promotes consistency, as compared to the weighing of five factors on a case-by-case basis [under the *Hodder* test]. The conjunctive standard will also help clarify any confusion that has developed about how to weigh particular factors. [ ]

Second, the *Restatement* rule avoids the "undertaking a warning" consideration from *Hodder* that may incent potential defendants to forego a warning in hopes of avoiding a post-sale duty to warn. [ ] The logic from *Hodder* that gave rise to this consideration seems to be that, if the defendant believed it necessary to provide a warning to its customers, that action shows that the defect was deserving of a legal duty to warn. But the reverse of this logic could result in a perverse incentive: a manufacturer may well decide *not* to issue a warning because it believes that inaction will improve its chances of a court concluding that no post-sale duty exists. The Restatement rule avoids this potential problem by omitting consideration of whether a manufacturer voluntarily undertook a duty to warn. It instead focuses on a manufacturer's ability to contact consumers or purchasers and on the reasonableness of the manufacturer's actions in light of all the factors. These considerations are more appropriate and avoid creating an incentive that may undermine consumer safety.

Third, the *Restatement* rule's reasonableness standard also provides guidance on how courts can address various entities in a product's chain of distribution. Cases interpreting *Hodder* have not clarified *whom* a manufacturer must warn when that manufacturer had no contact with the ultimate purchasers or consumers. The Restatement rule, however, does clarify that the rule's "reasonableness standard" applies to each member of the chain of distribution, and "it is possible that one party's conduct may be reasonable and another's unreasonable." RESTATEMENT (THIRD) OF TORTS: PRODUCTS LIABILITY §10, cmt. b.

This reasonableness standard parallels our general law regarding warnings, in which the duty to warn may depend upon a product user's knowledge and a party's connection to product consumers. For example, "there is no duty to warn if the user knows or should know of potential danger." [ ] Nor does the duty to warn extend to manufacturers who "had no opportunity or duty to warn the ultimate consumer." [ ] The reasonableness standard therefore allows a flexible analysis that accommodates for parties acting at different levels of the chain of distribution.

Finally, the *Restatement* rule is consistent with our conclusion that a post-sale duty existed in *Hodder*. Like *Hodder*, the *Restatement* rule requires that a defendant must have had knowledge of the product's defect, the defect must have been hidden, and the defect must have had the potential to cause significant harm. [ ] Also similar to *Hodder*, the *Restatement* rule requires that "those to whom a warning might be provided can be identified and can reasonably be assumed to be unaware of the risk of harm" and that "a warning can be effectively communicated to and acted on by those to whom a warning might be provided." [ ] The *Restatement* rule's requirements therefore correspond to the circumstances in *Hodder* regarding continuation in the business and undertaking a duty to warn.

II. B

The duty to warn analysis at the point of sale essentially focuses on the foreseeability of a defective product. This standard does not, however, identify the special burdens which may exist for manufacturers to discharge this duty. Thus, if used in a post-sale case, it restricts the jury's consideration to the danger of the product and the manufacturer's foreseeability of the danger. It excludes numerous critical factors identified by the *Restatement*. The jury is not told to consider the manufacturer's ability to identify users, the likelihood the risk of harm is unknown, the ability to effectively communicate a warning, and any other burden in providing a warning compared to the risk of harm. These factors are critical to understanding the reasonableness of the conduct.

Applying the *Restatement* rule to the undisputed facts here, we conclude as a matter of law that McMillan, the manufacturer of the ventilator's motor, did not have a post-sale duty to warn. Although McMillan's actions satisfy two of the *Restatement*'s requirements, McMillan does not meet them all. First, McMillan knew that the product posed a substantial risk of harm to persons or property because Nutech [the manufacturer that incorporated the motor into the ventilator] informed McMillan of fires in the ventilators sometime after 2003. *See* RESTATEMENT (THIRD) OF TORTS: PRODUCTS LIABILITY §10(b)(1). When the fire at the Eden Prairie home occurred, around 10 other fires had occurred in other ventilators containing McMillan motors. In 2006, Nutech further informed McMillan that it was conducting a voluntary inspection program for its ventilators through the Canadian Standards Association. At the time, the cause of the fires was uncertain, but Nutech's fire investigation report theorized that it may be possible for a motor failure to cause a fire within an excessively oiled motor. After reports of more fires, Nutech conducted a Canadian recall in June 2010, but Nutech did not pursue a recall in the United States. McMillan took no part in either recall, and it did not allow Nutech to use its name in the Canadian recall. Based on these facts, we conclude, and McMillan does not dispute, that McMillan knew that the product posed a risk of harm to persons or property.

Second, the "risk of harm [was] sufficiently great to justify the burden of providing a warning." *Id.* §10(b)(4). The fires linked to the ventilators did not cause any deaths, but the fires caused substantial property damage. McMillan concedes that fires causing substantial property damage are serious injuries.

But McMillan could not identify "those to whom a warning might be provided," nor could it effectively communicate a warning to consumers using the ventilators containing McMillan's motors. *Id.* §10(b)(2)-(3). McMillan did not have any records regarding the ventilators' distribution or the consumers using the ventilators because McMillan's only customer was Nutech, the ventilator's manufacturer. Nutech received motors from McMillan, assembled the ventilators, and distributed them to Canadian consumers and [defendant] Honeywell, which then distributed the ventilators to consumers in the United States. McMillan therefore could not reasonably predict where and by whom the ventilators containing its motors would be purchased or used. Moreover, McMillan knew that Nutech was aware of the fires and was actively warning of the product's danger, at least in Canada.

Therefore, because the *Restatement* rule that we adopt here is conjunctive and [plaintiff] has not proven all four criteria, McMillan did not have a post-sale duty to warn about the risks associated with its motors that were installed into Nutech's ventilators.... Concluding that McMillan had no post-sale duty to warn of potential hazards with its motors, we reverse the court of appeals' decision regarding that claim.

NOTES AND QUESTIONS

1. *The special burdens of the post-sale duty.* The post-sale duty to warn depends both on knowledge—either actual or constructive—of a risk that was not known at the time of sale, and the manufacturer's ability to convey that information to consumers at reasonable cost. As illustrated by *Great Northern Insurance Co.*, the cost of the post-sale duty can be decisive.

> For a post-sale duty to warn to arise, the seller must reasonably be able to communicate the warning to those identified as appropriate recipients. When original customer sales records indicate which individuals are probably using and consuming the product in question, direct communication of a warning may be feasible. When direct communication is not feasible, it may be necessary to utilize the public media to disseminate information regarding risks of substantial harm. As the group to whom warnings might be provided increases in size, costs of communicating warnings may increase and their effectiveness may decrease.

RESTATEMENT (THIRD) OF TORTS: PRODUCTS LIABILITY §10 cmt. g.

Based on this rule, the post-sale duty is harder for the plaintiff to establish if the defendant did not keep records identifying its customers. Does this rule unduly diminish the incentive of product sellers to maintain customer records, or do sellers otherwise have sufficiently strong financial reasons for collecting this information?

2. *Jury instructions.* In Lovick v. Will-Rich, 588 N.W.2d 688, 694 (Iowa 1999), the trial court "recognized the existence of a post-sale duty to warn but only submitted a general reasonableness standard of care instruction to the jury." The Iowa Supreme Court remanded for a new trial because the jury instructions focused on knowledge of risk without identifying "the special burdens which may exist for manufacturers to discharge this duty." Consequently, the instructions did not satisfy the requirement that they "must thoroughly and fairly convey the applicable law to the relevant issues." *Id.* at 695. Is this standard satisfied by the jury instructions described in the last section, none of which expressly identify the costs of the proposed warning?

3. *The knowledge requirement.* To satisfy the "should have known" requirement, how closely must product sellers monitor the performance of their products to acquire information about product risk? Compare RESTATEMENT (THIRD) OF TORTS: PRODUCTS LIABILITY §10 cmt. c (stating that "constantly monitoring product performance in the field is usually too burdensome" to support a post-sale duty, while recognizing that this reasoning does not apply to prescription drugs and medical devices), *with* Kenneth Ross & J. David Prince, *Post-Sale Duties: The Most Expansive Theory*

in Products Liability, 74 Brook. L. Rev. 963, 986 (2009) ("Manufacturers must act now to put into place an appropriate post-sale monitoring system and establish appropriate committees or trained personnel who can analyze the gathered information to determine whether post-sale actions might be appropriate.").

As a practical matter, does the knowledge requirement effectively reduce a manufacturer's liability exposure for the failure to provide a post-sale warning? For cases in which the manufacturer did not actually know of the post-sale risk, would the plaintiff have access to the type of evidence required to prove that a reasonable system of monitoring would have discovered the risk? Recall in this regard the materials in section II *supra* that discuss the difficulty plaintiffs can face in proving constructive knowledge of risks that are known at the time of trial but were not known at the time of sale.

When evidentiary limitations make it hard for plaintiffs to enforce the "should have known requirement," product sellers have a diluted financial incentive to adopt reasonable systems for monitoring product risk. An ongoing monitoring system is not costly to operate, and it could uncover risks that the manufacturer might then be obligated to disclose in a post-sale warning. However, the failure to adopt such a system would not ordinarily be subject to tort liability because of plaintiffs' inability to prove that the defendant would have discovered the risk by implementing reasonable post-sale monitoring. Insofar as ignorance is the cost-effective strategy for manufacturers, the post-sale duty to warn will have limited practical application.

Does the threat of punitive damages deter manufacturers from engaging in this behavior? Consider Michael Rustad, *In Defense of Punitive Damages in Products Liability: Testing Tort Anecdotes with Empirical Data*, 78 Iowa L. Rev. 1, 66 (1992) (finding that almost 75 percent of punitive awards in product cases are based on the failure of a manufacturer to take appropriate post-sale actions). Punitive damages are the subject of Chapter 13, section V.

4. *How many consumers must be reached?* Does the *Restatement (Third)*'s formulation of the post-sale duty require that the seller be able to reach *all* consumers? If not, how many consumers are sufficient for this purpose?

5. *Product recalls.* According to *Restatement (Third)* §11, a seller's post-sale duty to recall a defective product is limited to cases in which the measure is required by statute or regulation, or the seller voluntarily recalls the product and commits negligence in the course of doing so. Perhaps the most common product recall involves motor vehicles. The National Highway Traffic Safety Administration (NHTSA) possesses the authority to mandate a recall of motor vehicles that do not comply with federal regulations or are defective and unsafe. 49 U.S.C.A. §30118(b). The agency has been reluctant to exercise this authority and has not ordered a recall in the last three decades. Ralph Vartabedian & Ken Bensinger, *Auto Safety Agency Labors to Keep Pace*, L.A. Times, Dec. 31, 2009, at B1. Instead, it relies on "voluntary" recalls that generally proceed without any agency involvement. Kevin M. McDonald, SHIFTING OUT OF PARK: MOVING AUTO SAFETY FROM RECALLS TO REASON 72 (2006) ("Historically, nearly 80% of recalls are

VIII. The Post-Sale Duty to Warn

conducted without any NHTSA involvement. The remaining 20%, again conducted voluntarily, are what insiders euphemistically call 'NHTSA-influenced.'"). This strategy has not hindered the growth of recalls, and in recent years, the number of vehicles recalled has exceeded the number of vehicles sold. *Id.* at 1-3.

NHTSA's situation is not unique. The Consumer Product Safety Commission (CPSC) also has authority to force a recall of most consumer products when there is a "substantial product hazard" or when a regulation is violated. 15 U.S.C.A. 2064 (West 2010). But "the vast majority of product recalls have been conducted by manufacturers and importers without the CPSC having to commence or even threaten a lawsuit based on a product safety violation." John B. O'Loughlin, Jr., *Consumer Product Safety Improvement Act: Not the Last Word on Preemption*, Prod. Safety & Liab. Rep. (BNA), at 1037 (Oct. 20, 2008). The CPSC orders less than one mandatory recall per year. J. Gibson Mullan, Gen. Counsel, CPSC, Reporting Safety Problems: U.S. Perspective (Nov. 30, 2006). Criticism of the agency's performance led to it being overhauled in 2008. *See* Anita Bernstein, *Implied Reverse Preemption*, 74 Brook. L. Rev. 669, 691-700 (2009).

Some parties have petitioned courts to order recalls. *See, e.g.*, Ford Motor Co. v. Reese, 684 S.E.2d 279, 283-284 (Ga. App. 2009) (concluding "that absent special circumstances, no common law duty exists under Georgia law requiring a manufacturer to recall a product after the product has left the manufacturer's control"). One scholar has argued that tort regulation is appropriate when the federal government abrogates its regulatory authority. *See generally* Bernstein, *supra*.

Is the desirability of a tort-mandated recall program enhanced or diminished by the regulatory experience?

> The most remarkable thing about recalls is how few people respond to them. . . . Publicity is not always the solution. One of the most publicized of all recent recalls was for Firestone tires on Ford Explorers. Despite the media attention, only about 60 percent of owners took their vehicles to the dealer. ([According to one estimate,] 6.5 million defective tires are still in or on vehicles.) Only half the Pintos, the infamous compact car that exploded, were ever retrieved.
>
> In most recall cases, manufacturers simply do not know who bought their products unless consumers filled out a warranty card. But because companies ask all sorts of marketing questions on those cards like age, income and where they saw the product advertised, many consumers do not bother.
>
> The consumer advocates insist that forcing makers to include simple registration cards for nearly every product over $10 in value would help solve the problem.

Damon Darlin, *Reluctance and Silence on Recalls*, N.Y. Times, Oct. 28, 2006, at C1, C4 (paragraph structure omitted). Could a "simple registration card" be required by the tort duty?

An internal study conducted by the CPSC analyzed 865 closed cases from FY 2014-2016 and found that there was an overall correction rate of

65 percent. The data also show that the most effective recalls involve those made directly to the consumer. An open forum conducted by the CSPC addressed this particular issue:

> Over the past 20 years, the means of communicating recalls has changed substantially and continues to change rapidly as technology evolves. Widespread use of the Internet, email, social media, and other forms of instant communication have changed the ways companies can reach consumers. This session focused on communication channels, the use of marketing strategies, language in recall notices, recall best practices, and limitations and barriers to effective communication. It appeared from the discussions that very few firms develop a marketing strategy for recalls.

Office of Compliance and Field Operations, Recall Effectiveness Workshop Report, CSPC in Cooperation with Stakeholders (Feb. 22, 2018). To what extent does the ease of communicating directly to consumer via the Internet or social media affect a manufacturer's post-sale duty to warn?

6. *Post-sale warnings as a cure for defects at the time of sale.* If the product was defective when sold, could the manufacturer absolve itself of liability for the defect by issuing a post-sale warning of the defect? *See* RESTATEMENT (THIRD) OF TORTS: PRODUCTS LIABILITY §10 cmt. j (post-sale warnings do not exculpate the seller from liability for a design defect). What does this rule suggest about the ability of product sellers to avoid liability for defective design by issuing warnings at the time of sale? This issue is the subject of the next chapter.

IX. AUTONOMOUS VEHICLES AND PRODUCTS LIABILITY: PROBLEM SET 4

AV Problem 4.1

A manufacturer is planning to introduce a level 4 DAS autonomous vehicle into the commercial market. It is concerned that in jurisdictions where defects are determined by the consumer expectations test, juries might conclude that the crash of a fully functioning autonomous vehicle is a malfunction subject to strict liability. Based on in-house legal research, the manufacturer has discovered that sellers cannot avoid liability for a manufacturing defect by warning about the possibility. For example, if a bottle of soda contained a warning, "This bottle might explode," the seller would still be strictly liable in the event that the bottle did explode. The manufacturer has been unable to determine whether it would face similar liability if it warned consumers that the operating system of the autonomous vehicle is not perfectly safe, so there is an inherent risk that it will crash and injure the users. The manufacturer now seeks your legal advice about this matter. Would a warning about the inherent risk of crash foreclose liability for a malfunction under the consumer expectations test?

IX. Autonomous Vehicles and Products Liability: Problem Set 4

Analysis of AV Problem 4.1

The consumer expectations test is based on the implied warranty, which requires that products be marketable with their "true character" known. Consequently, a manufacturer cannot avoid liability for manufacturing defects by warning that the product might contain such a defect. Each product either contains the defect or it does not, and so the warning would not reveal the true character of *any* product. For example, a warning that a soda bottle *might* explode due to a manufacturing defect would not exculpate the manufacturer from tort liability under the implied warranty—it does not fully convey the true character of the particular product that actually exploded and injured the plaintiff. The warning for that particular product would instead have to say, "This bottle will explode if one attempts to open it." In contrast, an adequate warning about design-related performance conveys the true character of *every* product embodying the design. The operating system is part of the autonomous vehicle's design; it determines how this class of vehicles will execute the dynamic driving task. An adequate warning about the inherent risk that the fully functioning operating system can cause the autonomous vehicle to crash, therefore, would show that this particular vehicle is marketable with its true character known. Having been adequately warned about the inherent risk of crash, the ordinary consumer cannot have frustrated expectations in the event that the risk materializes, thereby preventing such a crash from being a malfunction subject to strict liability.

AV Problem 4.2

Based on your analysis in Problem 4.1, the manufacturer would now like to know what types of information it must disclose for the warning to be adequate as required by the duty to warn. Please advise.

Analysis of AV Problem 4.2

An adequate warning will need to let the ordinary consumer know how to safely deploy the autonomous vehicle. However, insofar as the operating system is programmed to prevent the vehicle from operating in conditions that the programming cannot safely address, such as extreme weather events and so on, then the importance of these warnings will be reduced. If, for example, the consumer only needs to input the destination, and the vehicle at point fully takes over, then there is no apparent role for any further instructions about how to use the product.

An adequate warning must also apprise consumers about the inherent risk of crash. Merely warning consumers, "This vehicle is not perfectly safe and can crash," would not be adequate if the manufacturer knows or should know about the magnitude of the risk in question. This type of warning is not required for conventional vehicles because the behavior of the human driver largely determines the risk of crash. Having eliminated the human driver, the operating system of the autonomous vehicle largely determines the risk.

The manufacturer will either know or should know the inherent risk of crash. To satisfy premarket testing standards, the manufacturer will need to know the vehicle's aggregate driving performance. Across the intended operating domain, how often is the vehicle involved in a crash? How does that performance compare to human drivers or perhaps to other autonomous vehicles already on the road? The manufacturer needs to answer these questions to ensure that the operating system is not defectively designed. *See* AV Problem 3.2, p. 249 *supra*.

To make this information easily understandable, the warning could tell consumers about how safely the autonomous vehicle performs in relation to conventional vehicles; for example, "This vehicle on average performs twice as safely as a conventional motor vehicle with an ordinary driver." A warning of that type might be deemed sufficient as compared to one that simply describes the probability of a crash, such as 1/10,000 per 1 million miles. Warnings that are too technical or complex can be deemed defective if a simpler warning would adequately convey the information.

AV Problem 4.3

Some manufacturers of automated driving technologies already use wireless updates for software systems in their vehicles, and federal regulators "envision[ ] that manufacturers and other entities will likely update the vehicle's software through over-the-air updates or other means." Nat'l Highway Traffic Safety Admin., FEDERAL AUTOMATED VEHICLES POLICY: ACCELERATING THE NEXT REVOLUTION IN ROADWAY SAFETY 16 (2016). Indeed, manufacturers will have wireless connections with their autonomous vehicles so that the driving experience of each vehicle can provide the "learning" that will factor into the algorithms that program the operating system for the entire fleet. Will this type of connectivity subject them to a post-sale duty to warn? How about a post-sale duty to redesign?

Analysis of AV Problem 4.3

The burden of a post-sale warning largely depends on the cost of communicating with consumers after the product has been sold. As applied to conventional products, such a warning obligation can be quite burdensome. That will not be the case with autonomous vehicles. The wireless connection with the vehicle makes it virtually costless to convey new warnings to consumers. The substantially reduced burden of complying with a post-sale duty to warn makes that obligation quite reasonable for autonomous vehicles as compared to conventional products. In all likelihood, manufacturers will have a post-sale duty to warn about newly discovered risks.

Historically, product recalls have been "voluntarily" undertaken by manufacturers operating in the shadow of statutes that give regulatory agencies the authority to mandate recalls. Autonomous vehicles require a different analysis. Although a recall is required to repair defects in the hardware of motor vehicles, it is not necessarily needed to update or redesign the operating system

IX. Autonomous Vehicles and Products Liability: Problem Set 4

of an autonomous vehicle. Based on the "proximity" afforded by automated driving technologies, courts will most likely conclude that manufacturers must make post-sale design modifications of this type. Like the duty to warn, the duty to design will be an ongoing obligation for the manufacturers of autonomous vehicles, in this instance to provide software updates of the operating system. *Editor's Note:* For further discussion, see Bryant Walker Smith, *Proximity-Driven Liability*, 102 Geo. L.J. 1777 (2014).

8

The Relation Between Warnings and Product Design

Safety measures can take different forms. For example, courts in some cases must determine whether the most desirable safety precaution involves a warning directed to an intermediary instead of the ultimate user. *See* Chapter 7, section III. More frequently, the choice among safety alternatives implicates the decision whether the risk is best reduced by a product warning or design change. Consumers could be warned to avoid the risk by taking safety precautions, or the risk could instead be reduced by a redesign. Which of these two alternative safety measures should the tort duty require?

I. THE DUTY TO WARN AS A COMPLETE SUBSTITUTE FOR THE DUTY TO DESIGN

As is so frequently true in products liability, the case law addressing the relation between a warning and product redesign has been deeply influenced by the manner in which the *Restatement (Second)* formulates the rule of strict products liability.

> *j. Directions or warning.* In order to prevent the product from being unreasonably dangerous, the seller may be required to give directions or warning, on the container, as to its use. . . .
>
> Where warning is given, the seller may reasonably assume that it will be read and heeded; and a product bearing such a warning, which is safe for use if it is followed, is not in defective condition, nor is it unreasonably dangerous.

RESTATEMENT (SECOND) OF TORTS §402A cmt. j.

When a warning would make the product "safe for use," could the manufacturer always invoke comment j to avoid liability for defective design? If so, then the satisfaction of the warning obligation would necessarily satisfy the design obligation. Are the two duties inherently related in this manner?

SKYHOOK CORP. v. JASPER
Supreme Court of New Mexico, 1977
560 P.2d 934

OMAN, C.J. This cause is before us on a writ of certiorari directed to the New Mexico Court of Appeals, which reversed a judgment entered by the district court in favor of defendant (Skyhook) upon a directed verdict.

This is an action for claimed wrongful death brought by plaintiff (Jasper), as administrator of the estate and personal representative of Malvin Mack Brown, deceased. Decedent was employed by Electrical Products Signs, Inc. (Signs, Inc.) as an apprentice sign installer. On January 11, 1973, he was assisting a journeyman installer of signs (Pulis), also employed by Signs, Inc., to install a Phillips 66 sign at a service station near Springer, New Mexico.

A hole had been dug in the ground in which to place the heavy signpost, a metal pipe, in an upright position. Pulis and decedent were using a 100 foot telescoping crane rig to lift and place the signpost in the hole. This crane was manufactured by Skyhook and sold by it to Signs, Inc., in January 1968. A clearly visible written warning appeared on the boom. In this warning it was stated: "All equipment shall be so positioned, equipped or protected so no part shall be capable of coming within ten feet of high voltage lines."

Pulis was aware of and had read the warning, and the evidence is to the effect that decedent also had seen and was aware of the warning, since it was clearly visible and decedent had previously worked on and had operated the rig. Both Pulis and decedent knew of the presence of overhead high voltage lines, since they had been warned of the presence of these lines by the operator of the Phillips 66 station at which the sign was being installed. The station operator had warned them that they should operate the equipment ten feet from these high voltage lines.

Pulis and decedent positioned the crane so that, in the judgment of Pulis, the crane was ten or twelve feet from the power lines. However, no measurements were made to assure that the positioned distance of the crane from the power lines was sufficient to prevent any portion of the equipment from coming within ten feet of these lines, even though a tape measure was kept in the cab of the rig for the purpose of making these measurements. Pulis then hoisted the signpost with the crane and began swinging it toward the hole in which it was to be positioned. As he was swinging the signpost toward the hole, he heard decedent scream. Decedent, who was guiding the signpost by hand toward the hole, was electrocuted when the lift cable came in contact with the overhead power line.

Plaintiff sought recovery from Skyhook on the theory of strict tort liability for failing to equip its crane, at the time of its sale to Signs, Inc. in January 1968, with either an "insulated link" or a "proximity warning device." An insulated link is a device installed on a crane to isolate the lifting hook from the lifting line or cable, so that there is no electrical continuity between the crane boom or lifting cable and the load being lifted. In January 1968, no crane manufacturer installed insulated links as standard equipment, but they were available to a purchaser of a crane at an additional cost of $300 to $400, depending on the size of the link.

A proximity warning device is an alarm warning system activated by the electrostatic field of overhead power lines. The use of this device requires that the crane be positioned at the minimum distance desired from the power line and

I. The Duty to Warn as a Complete Substitute for the Duty to Design 343

the device then set for operation. If properly set, it will warn the operator by sound and lights when the equipment encroaches on the minimum preset distance from the power line. At the time of the sale of the crane to Signs, Inc., no crane manufacturer offered this device as either standard or optional equipment, but it could be purchased for approximately $700.

Since Skyhook was the seller, as well as the manufacturer of the crane involved in this case, we need only consider whether the evidence adduced at trial required the submission to the jury by the trial court of the issue of Skyhook's liability under *Restatement (Second) of Torts* §402A (1965). Thus, the question to be resolved is whether the evidence created an issue of fact as to liability of Skyhook under §402A, which should have been submitted to the jury. The only issue under §402A which must be determined is whether the crane was in a defective condition which made it unreasonably dangerous to the user.

The crane rig had been used by Signs, Inc. for five years, had performed well, and no injury had resulted. Obviously, it was not unreasonably dangerous within the contemplation of the ordinary consumer or user of such a rig when used in the ordinary ways and for the ordinary purposes for which such a rig is used. *See* §402A, comment i. Furthermore, even though Skyhook had knowledge that the rig might be used in areas where overhead high voltage lines were present, it placed on the boom a clearly visible written warning that "all equipment shall be so positioned, equipped or protected so that no part shall be capable of coming within ten feet of high voltage lines." There is no contention that this warning was inadequate, had it been heeded. Skyhook, as the seller, could reasonably assume that the warning would be read and heeded. And had it been heeded, the crane rig was not in a defective condition nor unreasonably dangerous. *See* §402A, comment j.

Since we hold that there was no defective condition in the crane rig which was unreasonably dangerous to the decedent as a user thereof, we need not consider the other issues raised in the appeal.

The decision of the Court of Appeals is reversed and this cause is remanded to that court with directions to affirm the judgment of the district court.

NOTES AND QUESTIONS

1. *Another manifestation of the patent-danger rule.* Are the court's reasons for denying plaintiff's claims of defective design any different from those that a court would use to deny the claims pursuant to the version of the patent-danger rule that bars recovery simply because the risk in question was open and obvious? Does the court's reasoning in *Jasper* extend this rule beyond those risks that are rendered open and obvious by the design itself?

Based on the *Jasper* court's interpretation, §402A gives the manufacturer the option of using a warning instead of redesigning the product. According to comment j, the manufacturer can "reasonably assume" that the warning "will be read and heeded." If the product would then be "safe for use," comment j is literally satisfied—the product is not "unreasonably dangerous," nor is it defective. Based on this reasoning, a number of courts exempted manufacturers from liability for defective design in these circumstances. *See* Howard Latin, *Good Warnings, Bad Products, and Cognitive Limitations*, 41 UCLA L. Rev. 1193, 1259-1275 (1994). This interpretation of comment j lets manufacturers avoid design-defect liability by relying on the product warning to make a risk open and obvious. So interpreted, comment j is a manifestation of the now discredited version of the patent-danger rule that bars recovery for any open and obvious danger.

2. *The patent-defect rule.* As we found in Chapter 5, section III, the "unreasonably dangerous" requirement in §402A, when properly applied, is based on the logic of the patent-defect rule. Would this rationale justify rejecting the plaintiff's claim in *Klopp* that the crane should have been redesigned to incorporate an insulated link?

3. *A transitional period.* During the 1970s, a number of courts rejected the patent-danger rule in design cases, so *Jasper* was decided during a transitional period. Insofar as comment j effectively reintroduces this version of the patent-danger rule under the guise of a product warning, it must either be rejected or reinterpreted. Does comment j necessarily imply that a product warning always forecloses an allegation that a more reasonable method for reducing the risk involves a design change?

II. SEPARATING THE DUTY TO DESIGN FROM THE DUTY TO WARN

KLEIN v. SEARS, ROEBUCK AND CO.
Court of Special Appeals of Maryland, 1992
608 A.2d 1276

BLOOM, J. Appellant Joseph W. Klein purchased from appellee Sears, Roebuck and Company, Incorporated, a 10-inch radial arm saw that had been manufactured for Sears by appellee Emerson Electric Company, Incorporated (Emerson). Several months later, while Klein was using the saw, four fingers of his left hand were amputated by the saw blade.

Klein brought an action in the Circuit Court against Sears and Emerson, seeking to recover compensatory and punitive damages for breach of warranty and strict liability in tort. The case then proceeded to trial before a jury on the claim for strict liability, based upon allegations that the absence of a lower blade guard was a design defect making the saw unreasonably dangerous.

The first witness for the plaintiff was Mr. Klein himself. Through him, five exhibits (the saw, the saw table, his receipt for the purchase of the saw, the owner's manual that came with the saw, and a diagram of the garage in which he was working at the time of the injury) were introduced in evidence. During the course of his testimony, Mr. Klein demonstrated what he was doing and how he was using the saw at the time he was hurt. At the conclusion of Klein's testimony on direct examination, appellees moved for summary judgment, which the court eventually granted after hearing extensive argument.

II. Separating the Duty to Design from the Duty to Warn 345

The defense to the strict liability claim that was raised by appellees in their motion for summary judgment was based upon the proposition that with or without additional safety features their 10-inch radial arm saw presents obvious hazards if handled improperly but is not unreasonably dangerous if used with care and in accordance with appellees' warnings and instructions. They rely upon Simpson v. Standard Container Co., 527 A.2d 1337 (Md. App. 1987), in which this Court held that misuse of the product and failure to read or follow the product's warnings and instructions are defenses to strict product liability.

Appellees' reliance on *Simpson* is misplaced. In that case, Ramesh Oza, a neighbor of the Simpsons, purchased from K-Mart a new 1 and ½ gallon gasoline can manufactured by Standard Container Company. He filled the can with gasoline, used it once, and then stored the can on his basement floor. Some time thereafter, four-year-old Lorenzo Simpson Jr. visited the Oza house to play with four-year-old Summit Oza. The children went into the basement, unscrewed the cap from the gasoline can, and spilled gasoline on the floor. The gasoline vapors ignited, fatally burning the Oza child and severely injuring the Simpson child. The product liability claim against the manufacturer and seller of the can was based upon the theory that the can was unreasonably dangerous and thus defective in that it lacked a child-proof cap. On the basis of the pleadings and certain proffers, including photographs of the four vertical sides of the can, the Circuit Court for Baltimore City dismissed the complaint. We affirmed, basing our decision both on the theory of misuse and on Comment *j* to §402A of the *Restatement (Second) of Torts*, which states:

> Where warning is given, the seller may reasonably assume that it will be read and heeded; and a product bearing such a warning, which is safe for use if it is followed, is not in a defective condition, nor is it unreasonably dangerous.

The gasoline can had warnings on two of its four sides proclaiming, "Keep Out of Reach of Children" and "Do Not Store in Vehicle or Living Space." Unquestionably, had those warnings been heeded the can would have been safe for its intended use.

Attempting to bring their case within the holding of *Simpson*, appellees pointed to warnings and instructions on the saw itself and in the owner's manual, which Mr. Klein acknowledged that he had received and read before using the saw, that would have made the saw safe for its intended use had they been heeded:

-NEVER LEAVE TOOL RUNNING UNATTENDED. Turn power off. Do not leave tool until it comes to a complete stop. [Instruction No. 22.]

-MINIMIZE ACCIDENT POTENTIAL [heading on page three of the manual followed by specific instructions for avoiding accidents, including]:

Avoid awkward hand positions where a sudden slip could cause a hand to move into the saw blade or other cutting tool. Never reach in back or around the cutting tool with either hand to hold down the work piece for any other reason. Do not place fingers or hands in the path of the saw blade.

Never leave the saw with power "ON" or before the cutting tool has come to a complete stop. Lock the motor switch and put away the key when leaving the saw.

DO NOT perform layout, assembly, or set up work while the cutting tool is rotating.

-[Warning on the top blade guard, at the out-feed side] DANGER, TO AVOID INJURY, DO NOT FEED MATERIAL INTO THE TOOL AT THIS END.

-[Warning on the saw motor] DANGER FOR YOUR OWN SAFETY [followed by nine warnings, including]

NEVER REACH AROUND THE SAW BLADE [No. 6].

Appellees asserted that Mr. Klein disregarded the warnings and instructions pertaining to not having the saw running while not actually cutting, i.e., leaving the saw running unattended, leaving the saw with power on before it came to a complete stop, and performing layout, assembly, or setup work with the blade running. They also asserted that he disregarded or failed to heed instructions pertaining to putting his hands near the out-feed side of the rotary blade, i.e., reaching in back or around the moving blade.

What appellees (and the trial court) failed to appreciate is that although the warnings and instructions on the gasoline can in the *Simpson* case were clear, direct, simple, unequivocal, unmistakable, definite, and easy to understand and obey, the meanings of the warnings and instructions on the saw and in the owner's manual are too general to be unmistakable or undebatable.

The parties disagree as to what the warnings or instructions about not leaving the tool running unattended, turning the power off, never leaving the saw with power on, mean. Appellants insist that those instructions do not mean that the saw motor should be turned off and the key put away after each cut. Nor do they agree as to the meanings of the warnings or instructions about keeping one's hands away from the blade while it is in motion, about not reaching around the blade, and about avoiding awkward hand positions. Questions are raised as to how far away from the blade one must always keep one's hands. What constitutes an awkward hand position? What is meant by the instruction about reaching around the blade? Appellees contend but appellants deny that Mr. Klein, contrary to the warnings and instructions, was performing layout, assembly, or setup work when he was injured. It is arguable that the instructions are so general that they really mean nothing more than "be careful not to run your hand into the rotating blade" while ripcutting and "be careful not to pull the rotating saw blade into your hand" while crosscutting. If so, they are far too general to justify reliance in this case upon the holding in *Simpson*, because reasonable minds may differ as to whether the existence of such warnings, if heeded, would make the saw safe for its intended use. There can be no doubt about what conduct would constitute either heeding or disregarding the warnings on the gasoline can in *Simpson*; it is not so clear exactly what conduct would constitute compliance with the warnings on appellees' saw and in their owner's manual.

It was submitted that Dr. Keith [appellants' expert] would have testified that it was not the custom of the trade to turn off the saw during repetitive ripcutting. Further, it was submitted that the manner in which Mr. Klein testified he was using the saw (placing the finished board within its designated place within the garage, retrieving a new work piece from its designated place several feet

II. Separating the Duty to Design from the Duty to Warn

from the saw in the garage, and returning to the saw table) was not leaving the saw unattended with the motor running, as proscribed by the owner's manual. Dr. Keith also would have testified that Mr. Klein was not performing layout, assembly, or setup work and did not violate any instructions or warnings pertaining to positioning himself properly while operating the saw.

In sum, the evidence presented to the trial court, together with the proffered testimony of Dr. Keith and reasonable inferences that might be drawn from that testimony, generated a genuine issue of material fact as to whether Mr. Klein was operating the saw in accordance with the owner's manual or in disregard of the warnings and instructions contained in the manual and on the saw. Accordingly, summary judgment was improper; it was for the trier of fact to resolve the factual issues.

Judgment reversed and case remanded for further proceedings.

NOTES AND QUESTIONS

1. *Whither comment j?* Did the court persuasively explain why the design claim was not foreclosed by comment j? Consider the court's conclusion that the warnings basically exhort the consumer to "be careful not to run your hand into the rotating blade" while ripcutting, and to "be careful not to pull the rotating saw blade into your hand" while crosscutting. If the consumer perfectly complies with these warnings, why would the product not be "safe for use"? In that event, comment j states that the product would not be unreasonably dangerous or defective. How, then, could the *Klein* court conclude that comment j did not bar plaintiff's claim of defective design?

2. *The meaning of comment j.* In Hickerson v. Yamaha Motor Corp., 882 F.3d 476, 483 (4th Cir. 2018), the court observed that South Carolina's Defective Product Act "codified §402A of the Restatement (Second) of Torts, whose comments the South Carolina General Assembly also adopted as the expression of its legislative intent for the Act." Relying on comment j, the court ruled that an adequate warning can "cure . . . alleged design defects" if compliance with the warning would eliminate the risks, because "a product manufacturer is entitled to assume that its warnings will be read and heeded." In a jurisdiction like South Carolina, courts have no choice but to apply comment j, which leads to the question of what that comment actually means.

As illustrated by both *Jasper* and *Klein*, when evaluating the relation between a warning and the product design, courts focus on the following language from comment j: "Where warning is given, the seller may reasonably assume that it will be read and heeded; and a product bearing such a warning, which is safe for use if it is followed, is not in defective condition, nor is it unreasonably dangerous." This language appears in the last paragraph of comment j. The comment itself is the source of the duty to warn under §402A and must be understood within that broader context.

Recall that §402A restated the case law involving product malfunctions, which is why it does not distinguish between manufacturing defects and design defects. The comments in §402A preceding comment j address the varied rules for determining whether the product malfunctioned and is subject to strict liability. As comment j then recognizes, a product that does not malfunction could still perform more dangerously than expected by the ordinary consumer with ordinary knowledge common to the community. If the consumer were not warned about the unknown risks, the product would be "unreasonably dangerous" and defective under §402A. Hence comment j begins with a statement of the duty to warn: "In order to prevent the product from being unreasonably dangerous, the seller may be required to give directions or warning, on the container, as to its use." Regardless of whether consumers actually comply with the warning, if by reading and following the instructions they could safely use the product, then the warning would not be defective and the product in this respect would not be "unreasonably dangerous." The failure to follow such a warning would be the consumer's problem, not the manufacturer's responsibility. And so comment j understandably concludes, "Where warning is given, the seller may reasonably assume that it will be read and heeded; and a product bearing such a warning, which is safe for use if it is followed, is not in defective condition, nor is it unreasonably dangerous."

When placed in context, comment j only creates a duty to warn that supplements the duty to supply a product that does not malfunction, a monolithic concept that encompasses both manufacturing and design defects. The warning obligation is a direct implication of the implied warranty rationale for §402A, which requires the seller to provide a product that consumers would purchase or use if they knew its "true character." *See* Chapter 2, section I. Knowledge of the product's "true character" requires knowledge of any defects in design, regardless of whether the product would be safe for use if consumers followed the warning. Consequently, if the plaintiff shows that the design is defective, a warning about safe use does not bar recovery under the implied warranty, and by extension, under comment j.

This interpretation of comment j becomes even more plausible when the allegation of defective design involves a product that did not malfunction. As we found in Chapter 3, section I, some courts still rely on the black letter of §402A to bar recovery for patent dangers. To solve this problem, most courts have adopted the risk-utility test, thereby extending the §402A rule of strict products liability to govern products that do not malfunction. The black letter of §402A does not recognize the risk-utility test, making it even harder to understand why the black letter of comment j necessarily bars recovery for allegations of defective design based on the risk-utility test. Doing so would essentially resurrect the patent-danger rule under the guise of product warnings, an outcome inconsistent with the reason why so many courts adopted the risk-utility test in the first instance.

In light of this reasoning, did the court in *Hickerson* properly apply comment j? Compare Branham v. Ford Motor Co., 701 S.E.2d 5, 14-15 (S.C. 2010) ("The Legislature has expressed no intention to foreclose court consideration of developments in products liability law. For example, this Court's approval of the risk-utility test in [a prior case] yielded no legislative response. We thus believe the adoption of the risk-utility test in design defect cases in no manner infringes on the Legislature's presence in this area.").

3. *Evaluating the design.* To see why comment j does not necessarily foreclose a finding of defective design despite a warning about the risk in question, consider the allegations in *Klein*. For reasons identified by

II. Separating the Duty to Design from the Duty to Warn

plaintiff's expert, a user of the saw would find it quite burdensome to comply perfectly with the express or literal content of the warnings: the saw would need to be unplugged anytime the user stopped touching it, the user would need to be constantly on guard, and so on. Suppose that a user perfectly complies with the warnings as contemplated by comment j, thereby incurring a cost of complying with the warning (added time, attention, and so on) denoted by $B_{warning}$ to safely use the product and eliminate the risk of injury PL. An adequate warning for purposes of comment j, therefore, has the following risk-utility characteristics:

$$B_{warning} < PL$$

As a substitute for the warning, the plaintiff in *Klein* alleged that the risk could have been reasonably eliminated by a relatively inexpensive guard. Denote the burden or cost of this design change by B_{design}. Due to the difficulty of perfectly complying with the warning, the cost of redesign (computed on a per-use basis) could be less than the consumer's cost of complying with the warning ($B_{design} < B_{warning}$). Under these conditions, the risk-utility characteristics of the warning do not prevent the design from being defective within the logic of comment j:

$$B_{design} < B_{warning} < PL$$

When the warning instructs consumers on how to safely use a product, the ordinary consumer expects that the risk is otherwise inherent in the design. By proving that a redesign would be a less costly method for reducing the risk, the plaintiff shows that the risk is not inherent in the design. The existing design frustrates consumer expectations, even though consumers could eliminate the risk by following the more costly alternative of complying with the warning. Consider Delaney v. Deere and Co., 999 P.2d 930, 946 (Kan. 2000) ("The fact that a hazard is open and obvious or has been warned against are factors to be considered in analyzing whether a product is defective or unreasonably dangerous. The ultimate determination remains whether the product is defective and dangerous beyond a reasonable consumer's expectations.").

4. *The assumption of perfect compliance with a product warning.* The foregoing interpretation of *Klein* assumes that consumers always follow product warnings. Is this assumption realistic? If not, what are the implications for the duty to design?

KLOPP v. WACKENHUT CORP.
Supreme Court of New Mexico, 1992
824 P.2d 293

RANSOM, C.J. On February 27, 1988, [plaintiff Nancy Klopp] was proceeding through the Albuquerque International Airport to board an airplane when she passed through an airport security station. The station consisted of an upright metal detector, to the side of which was a baggage table. The station was operated by Wackenhut under contract with TWA. The latter owned the equipment and had arranged its particular configuration. The alarm sounded as Klopp stepped through the metal detector. Having activated the alarm, Klopp removed her bracelets, placed them on a tray on the table, and stepped through the detector again. The alarm was not triggered, and she moved to the left to retrieve her bracelets. In so doing, she tripped over the protruding stanchion base of the metal detector. She fell, injuring her left leg and right knee. The stanchion base protruded approximately eighteen inches. Preoccupied with retrieving her belongings, Klopp's attention was distracted from this base.

In their motions for directed verdict, TWA and Wackenhut argued that the stanchion base of the metal detector was open and obvious and, because there was no reason to believe it constituted a danger, no duty of care was owed to Klopp. [The motions were granted and judgment entered for defendants. For the following reasons, we reverse the judgment and directed verdict in favor of TWA, the only party that had control over the choice of equipment and its configuration at the checkpoint.]

Simply by making hazards obvious to reasonably prudent persons, the occupier of premises cannot avoid liability to a business visitor for injuries caused by dangers that otherwise may be made safe through reasonable means. A risk is not made reasonable simply because it is made open and obvious to persons exercising ordinary care. Cases that appear to have held the duty to avoid unreasonable risk of injury to others is satisfied by an adequate warning are overruled by us today. *E.g.*, Skyhook Corp. v. Jasper, 560 P.2d at 939 (no duty to make product safe when risk is obvious, known, and specifically warned against). Moreover, we think that some degree of negligence on the part of all persons is foreseeable, just like the inquisitive propensities of children, and thus, should be taken into account by the occupant in the exercise of ordinary care.

In response to the alarm that sounded when she stepped through the metal detector, Klopp was required to remove her jewelry and place it in a tray on a table open to the public. As Klopp re-entered the metal detector her jewelry was most readily accessible to her on a line across the stanchion base. Despite the safety record, the fact that Klopp was distracted from the presence of the stanchion base appears to us not so extraordinary as to be unforeseeable. We conclude that TWA owed Klopp a duty to use ordinary care to protect her from tripping over the stanchion base while preoccupied with recovering her jewelry.

NOTES AND QUESTIONS

1. *The duty to exercise reasonable care and the duty to warn.* Why did the court's holding *Klopp* require it to reverse *Jasper*? By holding that the risk of inattentive behavior can be foreseeable, *Klopp* requires duty-bearers to consider such a foreseeable risk when exercising reasonable care. Like the plaintiff in *Klopp*, the plaintiff's decedent in *Jasper* was not adequately attentive. The holding in *Jasper*, however, effectively eliminated the manufacturer's duty to consider this form of foreseeable, inattentive behavior. To obligate sellers to consider the foreseeable risk that inattentive consumers

will not always comply with a warning, *Klopp* had to overrule *Jasper*. The duty to design accordingly encompasses the foreseeable risk that consumers will misuse the product by not always following the warning.

2. *Reasons why consumers do not always follow warnings.* In evaluating the efficacy of product warnings, Professor Howard Latin has identified a number of reasons why consumers do not always follow warnings. First, consumers will not always read the warning (due to functional illiteracy; incompetence; inattention; misplaced or unavailable directions; reliance on explanations by intermediaries; reliance on general knowledge and experience; information overload; or competing demands on time and attention). Second, consumers will not always understand "good" warnings (due to imperfect trade-offs among detail, clarity, and impact; textual ambiguity; uncertainty about the consequences of misuse; inadequate evaluative expertise; individual variations in capabilities, motivations, and beliefs; cognitive heuristics and biases; and competing demands on time and attention). Finally, consumers could understand a "good" warning but still not always follow it (due to imperfect memory, overconfidence, reflexive actions during emergencies, disregard of low-probability risks, or because they assume that the warning only serves to limit the manufacturer's liability and is not really required for safe use of the product). See Howard Latin, *Good Warnings, Bad Products, and Cognitive Limitations,* 41 UCLA L. Rev. 1193, 1206-1249 (1994).

Although consumers do not always fully comply with product warnings, it does not follow that warnings are entirely ineffective. How should the limited effectiveness of a warning affect a claim that the product should have been redesigned to reduce the risk in question?

III. INCORPORATING BOTH THE DESIGN AND THE WARNING INTO THE RISK-UTILITY TEST

UNIROYAL GOODRICH TIRE CO. v. MARTINEZ
Supreme Court of Texas, 1998
977 S.W.2d 328

PHILLIPS, C.J. Roberto Martinez, together with his wife and children, sued Uniroyal Goodrich Tire Company ("Goodrich"), The Budd Company, and Ford Motor Company for personal injuries Martinez suffered when he was struck by an exploding 16" Goodrich tire that he was mounting on a 16.5" rim. Attached to the tire was a prominent warning label containing yellow and red highlights and a pictograph of a worker being thrown into the air by an exploding tire. The label stated conspicuously:

DANGER
NEVER MOUNT A 16" SIZE DIAMETER TIRE ON A 16.5" RIM. Mounting a 16" tire on a 16.5" rim can cause severe injury or death. While it is possible to pass a 16" diameter tire over the lip or flange of a 16.5" size diameter rim, it

cannot position itself against the rim flange. If an attempt is made to seat the bead by inflating the tire, the tire bead will break with explosive force.

NEVER inflate a tire which is lying on the floor or other flat surface. Always use a tire mounting machine with a hold-down device or safety cage or bolt to vehicle axle.

NEVER inflate to seat beads without using an extension hose with gauge and clip-on chuck.

NEVER stand, lean or reach over the assembly during inflation.

Failure to comply with these safety precautions can cause the bead to break and the assembly to burst with sufficient force to cause serious injury or death.

Unfortunately, Martinez ignored every one of these warnings. While leaning over the assembly, he attempted to mount a 16" tire on a 16.5" rim without a tire mounting machine, a safety cage, or an extension hose. Martinez explained, however, that because he had removed a 16" tire from the 16.5" rim, he believed that he was mounting the new 16" tire on a 16" rim. Moreover, the evidence revealed that Martinez's employer failed to make an operable tire-mounting machine available to him at the time he was injured, and there was no evidence that the other safety devices mentioned in the warning were available.

In their suit, the Martinezes did not claim that the warnings were inadequate, but instead alleged that Goodrich, the manufacturer of the tire, Budd, the manufacturer of the rim, and Ford, the designer of the rim, were each negligent and strictly liable for designing and manufacturing a defective tire and rim. Budd and Ford settled with the Martinezes before trial, and the case proceeded solely against Goodrich.

At trial, the Martinezes claimed that the tire manufactured by Goodrich was defective because it failed to incorporate a safer alternative bead (the portion of the tire that holds the tire to the rim when inflated) design that would have kept the tire from exploding. This defect, they asserted, was the producing cause of Martinez's injuries. Further, they alleged that Goodrich's failure to adopt this alternative bead design was negligence that proximately caused Martinez's injury.

The jury found that the tire manufactured by Goodrich was defective, while the wheel rim designed by Ford and manufactured by Budd was not defective. The jury allocated 100% of the producing cause of Martinez's injuries to the acts and omissions of Goodrich. The jury awarded the Martinezes $5.5 million in actual damages and $11.5 million in punitive damages. After reducing the award of actual damages by $1.4 million pursuant to a settlement agreement between the Martinezes, Ford, and Budd, reducing the punitive damages to the amount of actual damages pursuant to a pretrial agreement between Goodrich and the Martinezes, and awarding prejudgment interest, the trial court rendered judgment for the Martinezes for $10,308,792.45.

The court of appeals affirmed the award of actual damages. The court rejected Goodrich's argument that Martinez's failure to heed the product's warnings was a complete defense to the product defect claim. However, the court of appeals reversed the award of punitive damages, holding that there was no evidence to support the jury's finding of gross negligence.

III. Incorporating Both the Design and the Warning into the Risk-Utility Test

As in the court of appeals, Goodrich's principal argument here is that no evidence supports the jury finding that the tire was defective because "the tire bore a warning which was unambiguous and conspicuously visible (and not claimed to be inadequate); the tire was safe for use if the warning was followed; and the cause of the accident was mounting and inflating a tire in direct contravention of those warnings."

This Court has adopted the products liability standard set forth in section 402A of the *Restatement (Second) of Torts*. [ ] To prove a design defect, a claimant must establish, among other things, that the defendant could have provided a safer alternative design. [ ] Implicit in this holding is that the safer alternative design must be reasonable, i.e., that it can be implemented without destroying the utility of the product.

To determine whether a reasonable alternative design exists, and if so whether its omission renders the product unreasonably dangerous (or in the words of the new *Restatement*, not reasonably safe), the finder of fact may weigh various factors bearing on the risk and utility of the product. One of these factors is whether the product contains suitable warnings and instructions. The new *Restatement* [§2 cmt. f] likewise carries forward this approach:

> A broad range of factors may be considered in determining whether an alternative design is reasonable and whether its omission renders a product not reasonably safe. The factors include, among others, the magnitude and probability of the foreseeable risks of harm, the instructions and warnings accompanying the product, and the nature and strength of consumer expectations regarding the product, including expectations arising from product portrayal and marketing. . . . The relative advantages and disadvantages of the product as designed and as it alternatively could have been designed may also be considered. Thus, the likely effects of the alternative design on production costs; the effects of the alternative design on product longevity, maintenance, repair, and esthetics; and the range of consumer choice among products are factors that may be taken into account.

Goodrich urges this Court to depart from this standard by following certain language from Comment j of the *Restatement (Second) of Torts*. The new *Restatement*, however, expressly rejects the Comment j approach:

> Reasonable designs and instructions or warnings both play important roles in the production and distribution of reasonably safe products. In general, when a safer design can reasonably be implemented and risks can reasonably be designed out of a product, adoption of the safer design is required over a warning that leaves a significant residuum of such risks. For example, instructions and warnings may be ineffective because users of the product may not be adequately reached, may be likely to be inattentive, or may be insufficiently motivated to follow the instructions or heed the warnings. However, when an alternative design to avoid risks cannot reasonably be implemented, adequate instructions and warnings will normally be sufficient to render the product reasonably safe. *Compare* Comment *e*. *Warnings are not, however, a substitute for the provision of a reasonably safe design.*

The Reporters' Notes in the new *Restatement* refer to Comment j as "unfortunate language" that "has elicited heavy criticism from a host of commentators."

Similarly, this Court has indicated that the fact that a danger is open and obvious (and thus need not be warned against) does not preclude a finding of product defect when a safer, reasonable alternative design exists. [ ]

The drafters of the new *Restatement* provide the following illustration for why courts have overwhelmingly rejected Comment j:

> Jeremy's foot was severed when caught between the blade and compaction chamber of a garbage truck on which he was working. The injury occurred when he lost his balance while jumping on the back step of the garbage truck as it was moving from one stop to the next. The garbage truck, manufactured by XYZ Motor Co., has a warning in large red letters on both the left and right rear panels that reads "DANGER—DO NOT INSERT ANY OBJECT WHILE COMPACTION CHAMBER IS WORKING—KEEP HANDS AND FEET AWAY." The fact that adequate warning was given does not preclude Jeremy from seeking to establish a design defect under Subsection (b). The possibility that an employee might lose his balance and thus encounter the shear point was a risk that a warning could not eliminate and that might require a safety guard. Whether a design defect can be established is governed by Subsection (b).

In fact, Goodrich recognized at trial that warnings are an imperfect means to remedy a product defect. In response to a question posed by the Martinezes' attorney, Goodrich engineer Stanley Lew answered:

Q: Is that why designs of a product are more important than warnings on a product because people may not see warnings but they are always going to encounter the design?
A: Yes, that's correct. It's the products they deal with.

For these reasons we refuse to adopt the approach of Comment j of the superseded *Restatement (Second) of Torts* section 402A.

We do not hold, as the dissenting justices claim, that "a product is defective whenever it could be more safely designed without substantially impairing its utility," or that "warnings are irrelevant in determining whether a product is reasonably safe." Rather, as we have explained, we agree with the new *Restatement* that warnings and safer alternative designs are factors, among others, for the jury to consider in determining whether the product as designed is reasonably safe. While the dissenting justices say that they also agree with the *Restatement*'s approach, they would, at least in this case, remove the balancing process from the jury. Instead, they would hold that Goodrich's warning rendered the tape bead design reasonably safe as a matter of law.

The dissenting justices first argue that Goodrich's warning was clear and that it could have been followed, and consequently Martinez was injured only by "ignoring . . . his own good sense." Even if this were true, it is precisely because it is not at all unusual for a person to fail to follow basic warnings and instructions that we have rejected the superseded Comment j. The dissent also notes that there have been few reported mismatch accidents involving tires with this particular warning label. While this is certainly relevant, and perhaps would persuade many juries, we cannot say that it conclusively establishes that the tire is reasonably safe when weighed against the other evidence. The jury heard

III. Incorporating Both the Design and the Warning into the Risk-Utility Test 355

firsthand how an accident can occur despite the warning label, and how a redesigned tire would have prevented that accident. The jury also heard evidence that Goodrich's competitors had incorporated the single strand programmed bead by the early 1980s, and that Goodrich itself adopted this design in 1991, a year after manufacturing the tire that injured Martinez. Under these circumstances, there is at least some evidence supporting the jury's finding of product defect.

For the foregoing reasons, we affirm the judgment of the court of appeals.

HECHT, J., *dissenting*. Having changed about a thousand tires in his life, Roberto Martinez admits he knew better than to lean over a tire while inflating it. Besides, he had seen the pictographic warning on the very tire he was changing which showed a worker being hurt by an exploding tire and warned: "NEVER stand, lean or reach over the assembly during inflation." Ignoring this warning and his own good sense, Martinez was leaning over the tire, inflating it, when it exploded in his face.

The 16" tire exploded because it would not fit the 16.5" wheel on which Martinez was trying to mount it. Martinez knew it was very dangerous to try to mount a 16" tire on a 16.5" wheel, and he would never knowingly have tried to do it, but the size of the wheel was not marked where he could find it. He understood that his co-worker had taken a 16" tire off the wheel, and he was simply trying to put the same size tire back on. The Budd Company, which manufactured the wheel to Ford Motor Company's specifications, knew, as did Ford, that people sometimes try to mount 16" tires on 16.5" wheels, not realizing that tire and wheel are mismatched. To minimize the risk of such mistakes, Budd and Ford could have changed the design of the wheel to prevent mounting mismatched tires, but they did not do so. Budd could also have simply stamped the size in plain view on the outboard side of the wheel near the valve stem where it was almost sure to be seen, but it did not do that, either. Instead it encoded the size in small letters on the inboard side, where it was hard to find if the wheel was clean, and indecipherable if the wheel was dirty, as it was in this case.

Although a 16.5" wheel can be designed so that a 16" tire cannot be mounted on it, a 16" tire cannot be designed so that it cannot be mounted on a 16.5" wheel. A tire manufacturer's only options to reduce the risk of injury from attempting to mount a 16" tire on a 16.5" wheel are to place a warning on the tire or to design the bead wire so that it will withstand higher inflation pressure before exploding. The Uniroyal Goodrich Tire Company, which made the tire Martinez was using, chose to put a prominent, pictographic label on it, which, as I have said, Martinez actually saw but did not heed. Had he done so, he would not have been injured. In fact, according to the record, only one other person has ever claimed to have been injured attempting to mount a 16" tire with a warning label like Goodrich's on a 16.5" wheel, although thousands of labeled tires and more than thirty million 16.5" wheels have been manufactured in the past two decades.

Now as among Martinez, the wheel manufacturers, and Goodrich, how should responsibility for Martinez's accident be apportioned? The reader may be surprised at the answer in this case. Martinez, though negligent by his own admission, is held to bear no responsibility for the accident. The wheel manufacturers, too, are held to be free of responsibility (they settled with Martinez before trial) although the undisputed testimony by both Martinez's and Goodrich's experts is that Budd and Ford defectively designed the wheel. Only Goodrich is held liable—and for providing a warning on the tire that would have prevented Martinez's accident altogether instead of redesigning the bead wire so that the accident would only have been less likely. This aberrant result flows from serious flaws in the Court's opinion which, even more importantly, misstate the law that will be applied in other cases.

First, the Court holds that a product can be found to be defective whenever it could be more safely designed without substantially impairing its utility. This is not, and should not be, the law. As the *Restatement (Third) of Torts: Products Liability* advises, a "broad range of factors" besides the utility of a reasonable alternate design should be considered in determining whether its use is necessary to keep the product reasonably safe, including "the magnitude and probability of the foreseeable risks of harm [and] the instructions and warnings accompanying the product." [ ] When the undisputed evidence is that the magnitude and probability of a risk are low, an alternative design could reduce but not eliminate that risk, and the instructions and warnings given do eliminate the risk, the product should be determined not to be defective as a matter of law.

Since it is human nature to disregard instructions, a rule that any product is reasonably safe as long as it bears an adequate warning of the risks of its use is not feasible. Such behavior, however, does not warrant the opposite rule that warnings are irrelevant in determining whether a product is reasonably safe. I agree with the Court that comment *l* to Section 2 of the *Restatement (Third) of Torts: Products Liability* now has it about right.

I do not agree, however, that the Court correctly reads or follows comment *l*. Comment *l* limits but does not foreclose the role of warnings in making products reasonably safe, even when there is a safer alternative design. The Court stresses the last sentence of comment *l* and brushes past the first sentence. Taken as a whole, the comment says, correctly, I think, that a safer alternative design that eliminates a risk is required over a warning that leaves a significant residuum of risk because product users may not get the warning, may be inattentive, or may not be motivated to heed the warning. The illustration accompanying comment *l* is of a worker whose foot is severed by a garbage truck's blade and compaction chamber when he loses his balance jumping onto the back of the truck. A warning on the truck, "keep hands and feet away," does little to protect against a worker's foreseeable inadvertence or misstep in the usual discharge of his job. But the warning might well be adequate admonishment to the merely curious, even if the garbage truck could be designed to be safer, if the residuum of risk were insignificant. Even if the risk that a worker will lose his balance and slip is significant enough to warrant designing additional protections in the truck, the risk that someone will intentionally stick his hand in a place where it obviously may be hurt when he is effectively warned not to do so may not warrant design changes.

There are two components to this rule: the possibility of a safer, reasonable alternative design, and a product that is not reasonably safe without that design. Both are required. Even if a reasonable alternative design would make a product safer, the product is not defective unless the omission of the design makes the product not reasonably safe. The comparison is not between the two designs, but between the product alternatively designed and the product including any warning.

III. Incorporating Both the Design and the Warning into the Risk-Utility Test

The Reporters' Note gives an example of how factors other than a safer alternative design affect the determination whether a product is defective:

> Comment f lists among the factors a court may consider in determining whether an alternative design is reasonable and whether its omission renders a product not reasonably safe the following: (1) magnitude and probability of the foreseeable risks of harm; (2) the instructions and warnings accompanying the product; and (3) the nature and strength of consumer expectations. A recent California case is in agreement. In Hansen v. Sunnyside Products, Inc., 55 Cal. App. 4th 1497 (1997), the court held that in a claim alleging defective design of a household cleaner containing hydrofluoric acid, the availability of an alternative safer design was not dispositive of liability. The factfinder could consider the warnings on the bottle describing the danger of exposing a user's skin to the cleaner in risk-utility balancing to decide whether the product was unreasonably dangerous.

Hansen explained its rationale as follows:

> We do not think that the risk to the consumer of the design of many household products can be rationally evaluated without considering the product's warnings. Thus, for example, what is the risk of the design of a power saw, or other power tools or equipment, without considering the product's directions and warnings? We dare say that the risk would be astronomically, and irrationally, high. The same could be said about common garden pesticides, or even the household microwave oven. In our view, were we to ask jurors to evaluate the risks of the design of many household products without considering their directions or warnings, the practical result would be the withdrawal from the market of many useful products that are dangerous in the abstract but safe when used as directed.

The Court protests that it has not disregarded the effect of warnings in determining whether the possibility of a safer alternative design makes a product defective but has merely left the matter to the jury. But the question remains: can any product be shown not to be defective as a matter of law if a reasonable alternative design could have avoided plaintiff's injury?

In the Court's view, a product manufacturer may be liable for failing to make any feasible design change that does not significantly impair a product's utility, if only to prevent rare mishaps from conscious disregard of adequate warnings. That is all the evidence in this case shows. The Court appropriately rejects one extreme position—comment *j* to Section 402A of the *Restatement (Second) of Torts*—but then adopts the opposite and equally extreme position. In so doing, the Court swings toward strict liability.

Because the Court denies Goodrich any relief, I respectfully dissent.

NOTES AND QUESTIONS

1. *The risk-utility test applied.* To illustrate how the product warning affects the risk-utility analysis of a proposed design change—the issue discussed by the dissent—consider how the test would apply to the case at the outset of this chapter involving an electrocuted worker, *Skyhook Corp. v. Jasper.*

Due to the complexity of the issues, we need to be precise about the risk-utility factors. Let $PL_{warning}$ denote the risk of being electrocuted when the product is accompanied by a warning, and $B_{warning}$ the average burden or cost that the ordinary consumer incurs by attempting to comply with the warning. The plaintiff alleged that the design was defective for not containing an insulated link. The total cost of the design change—allegedly $400 for the insulated link—must be translated into a cost for each product use (such as $1 over a lifetime of 400 uses). Denote this burden or cost of the proposed design change by B_{design}. In formulating the risk-utility test, the court would not assume that warning necessarily eliminates the risk of electrocution ($0 = PL_{warning}$). The court would instead determine the magnitude of the foreseeable risk stemming from imperfect compliance with the warning. If that foreseeable risk were significant or substantial ($0 < PL_{warning}$) as required by the *Restatement (Third)*, the plaintiff could potentially prove that the proposed design change satisfies the risk-utility test:

$$0 < B_{design} < PL_{warning}$$

Because the design change would eliminate the need for workers to comply with the warning, it would also eliminate this cost for consumers (the burden $B_{warning}$), thereby reducing the total burden of the design change:

$$B_{design} - B_{warning} < PL_{warning}$$

This type of proof would establish a reasonable alternative design that renders the existing design defective, despite a warning about the risk. The inquiry, as the dissent explained, "is not between the two designs, but between the product alternatively designed and the product including any warning."

Is this inquiry foreclosed by the majority's reasoning in *Martinez*? Does this formulation adequately capture the various factors identified by the *Restatement (Third)*? Under this approach, will a warning ever be a reasonable substitute for a design change?

HOOD v. RYOBI AMERICA CORP.
United States Court of Appeals, Fourth Circuit, 1999
181 F.3d 608

WILKINSON, C.J. Wilson M. Hood lost part of his thumb and lacerated his leg when he removed the blade guards from his new Ryobi miter saw and then used the unguarded saw for home carpentry. Hood sued Ryobi, alleging that the company failed adequately to warn of the saw's dangers and that the saw was defective. Applying Maryland products liability law, the district court granted summary judgment to Ryobi on all claims.

The saw and owner's manual bore at least seven clear, simple warnings not to operate the tool with the blade guards removed. The warnings were not required to spell out all the consequences of improper use. Nor was the saw

III. Incorporating Both the Design and the Warning into the Risk-Utility Test 359

defective—Hood altered and used the tool in violation of Ryobi's clear warnings. Thus we affirm the judgment.

The day after his purchase, Hood began working with the saw in his driveway. While attempting to cut a piece of wood approximately four inches in height Hood found that the blade guards prevented the saw blade from passing completely through the piece. Disregarding the manufacturer's warnings, Hood decided to remove the blade guards from the saw. Hood first detached the saw blade from its spindle. He then unscrewed the four screws that held the blade guard assembly to the frame of the saw. Finally, he replaced the blade onto the bare spindle and completed his cut.

Rather than replacing the blade guards, Hood continued to work with the saw blade exposed. He worked in this fashion for about twenty minutes longer when, in the middle of another cut, the spinning saw blade flew off the saw and back toward Hood. The blade partially amputated his left thumb and lacerated his right leg.

Hood asserts that Ryobi failed adequately to warn of the dangers of using the saw without the blade guards in place. Hood also contends that the design of the saw was defective. We disagree on both counts.

Hood admits that Ryobi provided several clear and conspicuous warnings not to operate the saw without the blade guards. He contends, however, that the warnings affixed to the product and displayed in the operator's manual were inadequate to alert him to the dangers of doing so. In addition to Ryobi's directive "never" to operate a guardless saw, Hood would require the company to inform of the actual consequences of such conduct. Specifically, Hood contends that an adequate warning would have explained that removing the guards would lead to blade detachment.

We disagree. Maryland does not require an encyclopedic warning. Instead, "a warning need only be one that is reasonable under the circumstances." [ ] A clear and specific warning will normally be sufficient—"the manufacturer need not warn of every mishap or source of injury that the mind can imagine flowing from the product." [ ] In deciding whether a warning is adequate, Maryland law asks whether the benefits of a more detailed warning outweigh the costs of requiring the change. Moran v. Faberge, Inc., 332 A.2d 11, 15 (Md. 1975).

Hood assumes that the cost of a more detailed warning label is minimal in this case, and he claims that such a warning would have prevented his injury. But the price of more detailed warnings is greater than their additional printing fees alone. Some commentators have observed that the proliferation of label detail threatens to undermine the effectiveness of warnings altogether. *See* James A. Henderson, Jr. & Aaron D. Twerski, *Doctrinal Collapse in Products Liability: The Empty Shell of Failure to Warn*, 65 N.Y.U. L. Rev. 265, 296-97 (1990). As manufacturers append line after line onto product labels in the quest for the best possible warning, it is easy to lose sight of the label's communicative value as a whole. Well-meaning attempts to warn of every possible accident lead over time to voluminous yet impenetrable labels—too prolix to read and too technical to understand.

By contrast, Ryobi's warnings are clear and unequivocal. Three labels on the saw itself and at least four warnings in the owner's manual direct the user not to operate the saw with the blade guards removed. Two declare that "serious injury" could result from doing so. Ryobi provided warnings sufficient to apprise the ordinary consumer that it is unsafe to operate a guardless saw—warnings which, if followed, would have prevented the injury in this case.

It is apparent, moreover, that the vast majority of consumers do not detach this critical safety feature before using this type of saw. Indeed, although Ryobi claims to have sold thousands of these saws, Hood has identified only one fifteen-year-old incident similar to his. Hood has thus not shown that these clear, unmistakable, and prominent warnings are insufficient to accomplish their purpose. Nor can he prove that increased label clutter would bring any net societal benefit. We hold that the warnings Ryobi provided are adequate as a matter of law.

Hood's defective design claim is likewise unpersuasive. Hood's injuries were the direct result of the alterations he made to the saw—alterations that directly contravened clear, unambiguous warnings. And such alterations defeat a claim of design defect.

Hood admits that he altered the table saw by removing the blade guards from the unit's frame, and he acknowledges that the alteration led directly to his injuries. Hood asserts, however, that Ryobi should have foreseen that consumers might operate its saws with the guards removed. Hood notes that the operation of equipment without safety guards is a frequently cited OSHA violation. And, as noted, Ryobi itself has faced litigation on one other occasion for the same type of accident that befell Hood. In short, Hood contends that Ryobi should have designed its saw to operate equally well with the guards in place or removed.

We disagree. Maryland imposes no duty to predict that a consumer will violate clear, easily understandable safety warnings such as those Ryobi included with this product.

We recognize that the American Law Institute has recently underscored the concern that comment j of the Second Restatement, read literally, would permit a manufacturer of a dangerously defective product to immunize itself from liability merely by slapping warning labels on that product. *See* Restatement (Third) of Torts: Products Liability §2 cmt. l & Reporters' Note. We are all afflicted with lapses of attention; warnings aimed simply at avoiding consumer carelessness should not absolve a manufacturer of the duty to design reasonable safeguards for its products. The Maryland courts have already made clear, however, that warnings will not inevitably defeat liability for a product's defective design. *See* Klein v. Sears, Roebuck & Co., 608 A.2d 1276, 1282-83 (Ct. Spec. App. 1992) (such warnings as "never leave tool running unattended" and "do not place fingers or hands in the path of the saw blade" are too vague to defeat manufacturer's liability for failing to include blade guards on its saws). Maryland has thus sought to encourage manufacturers to rid their products of traps for the unwary, while declining to hold them responsible for affirmative consumer misuse.

This case involves much more than a consumer's inevitable inattention. Rather, Hood took affirmative steps to remove the safety guards from his saw and—in contravention of warnings which were "clear, direct, simple, unequivocal, unmistakable, definite, and easy to understand and obey"—then used the saw to cut several pieces of wood. *Klein*. Hood's own conduct thus caused his injury and defeats any claim that the saw is defective in design.

Affirmed.

NOTES AND QUESTIONS

1. *Evaluating the warning.* For any case involving the interplay between a warning and design change, the threshold inquiry ordinarily is whether

III. Incorporating Both the Design and the Warning into the Risk-Utility Test

the warning is adequate. A defective warning, after all, usually subjects the seller to liability, regardless of how the product is designed. Are the court's reasons for rejecting the warning claim persuasive? Consider Chapter 7, section V (discussing how the adequacy of a warning depends on the specificity of the risk disclosure). Did the information costs of the additional disclosure so clearly outweigh the safety benefits that the court could defensibly dismiss the warning claim as a matter of law?

In removing the blade guard from the saw, the ordinary consumer would be aware of the obvious risk of being cut by the unguarded blade. Would the consumer know that the blade could also become detached and fly off the saw? Is this risk so insubstantial or unforeseeable that a warning about it is not required as a matter of law? Consider, in this regard, the plaintiff's reasons for removing the guard, the incidence of such behavior according to OSHA, and the number of similar accidents that had occurred in the past. Insofar as the plaintiff's foreseeable misuse ought to limit the defendant's liability, the behavior could reduce the plaintiff's recovery under principles of comparative responsibility rather than defeat recovery altogether. *See* Chapter 14, section III.

To be sure, the plaintiff deliberately disregarded the warnng. Must a product misuse be inadvertent to be foreseeable? If so, why does the duty of automobile manufacturers extend to the foreseeable risk that drivers will frequently (and intentionally) exceed the speed limit, a clear instance of deliberate, unreasonable behavior? Liability is not necessarily foreclosed simply because the plaintiff deliberately disobeyed the warning.

Insofar as the removal of the blade guard creates a significant, foreseeable risk of injury, wouldn't the plaintiff's proposed warning have eliminated a significant risk of injury? How many consumers would remove the guard once warned that doing so would enable the blade to fly off? Sometimes the best way to prevent misuse is to make consumers adequately aware of the dire consequences that can ensue. Did the *Hood* court seriously consider this possibility?

2. *The problem of deliberate product misuse.* For cases in which the plaintiff can establish that the risk of intentional misuse was foreseeable—that some consumers will deliberately disregard the warning—the risk-utility analysis of the proposed design change can be expressed by the same approach we previously employed, which asks whether

$$B_{design} - B_{warning} < PL_{warning}$$

The analysis, however, can be more complicated for reasons illustrated by *Hood*. In *Hood*, if the product were redesigned to make it safer for consumers to remove the guard, then this proposed alternative design would facilitate product misuse and *increase* the risk posed by the unguarded blade, explaining why the plaintiff's claim of defective design failed as a matter of law (a reasonable alternative design cannot increase risk relative to the existing design). Hence the consumer's decision whether to follow a warning, which determines whether there is a significant residuum of risk that exists despite the warning ($PL_{warning}$), can depend on how the product is designed.

The interplay between warnings and product design is complicated. Typically the product warning complements the existing design by enabling the consumer to make a well-informed decision about whether and how to use the product, the type of issue addressed in Chapter 7. For many product attributes, however, a design modification can be a reasonable substitute for a warning. For yet another type of product attribute of the type at issue in *Hood*, the design can promote the behavior reasonably required by the warning (if the blade flies off, presumably no one will remove the guard). Each type of product attribute involves a different form of risk-utility analysis, underscoring the importance of formulating these problems in risk-utility terms.

IV. AUTONOMOUS VEHICLES AND PRODUCTS LIABILITY: PROBLEM SET 5

AV Problem 5.1

Recall that for motor vehicles equipped with level 2 or level 3 DAS, the human driver must be ready to take over the driving task. In the first two fatal crashes involving Tesla vehicles with level 2 DAS, the driver did not do so. After an investigation into these crashes, the National Transportation Safety Board attributed responsibility in both instances to the design of the vehicle and to the human drivers. The investigators urged federal regulators to more "thoroughly assess the effectiveness of Tesla's driving monitoring system" due to the "foreseeable misuse and risks of it being used in ways it wasn't designed to handle." Tim Higgins & Ben Foldy, *Tesla System Is Cited in Fatal Crash*, Wall St. J., Feb. 26, 2020.

In defending its monitoring system, Tesla explained that

> [w]hen drivers activate Autopilot, the acknowledgment box explains, among other things, that Autopilot "is an assist feature that requires you to keep your hands on the steering wheel at all times," and that "you need to maintain control and responsibility for your vehicle" while using it. Additionally, every time that Autopilot is engaged, the car reminds the driver to "Always keep your hands on the wheel. Be prepared to take over at any time." The system also makes frequent checks to ensure that the driver's hands remain on the wheel and provides visual and audible alerts if hands-on is not detected. It then gradually slows down the car until hands-on is detected again.
>
> We do this to ensure that every time the feature is used, it is used as safely as possible.

Tesla, *A Tragic Loss* (June 30, 2016).

In wrongful-death suits involving the two fatalities caused by crashes of the Tesla vehicles being operating in Autopilot mode (level 2 DAS), could the plaintiffs argue that despite the warnings, the vehicle was defectively designed because a reasonable alternative design would entirely eliminate the risk of driver error—the result attained by level 4 or level 5 DAS?

IV. Autonomous Vehicles and Products Liability: Problem Set 5

Analysis of AV Problem 5.1

Even if Tesla's warnings were adequate, the duty to design is independent from the duty to warn. Consequently, Tesla has a duty to adopt a reasonably safe design features that would reduce the risk of driver attention while the vehicle is engaged in Autopilot mode. However, the plaintiffs' proposed alternative design is based on a different product category and would fail for that reason alone. *See* AV Problem 3.1, p. 248 *supra*.

AV Problem 5.2

Suppose that the operating system of the vehicle can be redesigned so that if sensors show that the driver is not paying attention, the vehicle will safely pull over to the side of the road. Would this redesign of the operating system be required instead of the type of warning provided by Tesla in the previous problem?

Analysis of AV Problem 5.2

Under the *Restatement (Third)*, manufacturers must adopt product designs that account for the inability of consumers to perfectly comply with warnings. Manufacturers cannot merely warn drivers to "stay alert" to take over the driving responsibilities when necessary; they must instead adopt fault-tolerant designs that would be a cost-effective method for reducing the "significant residuum" of foreseeable risk that consumers will not always follow the warning to "stay alert."

The proposed alternative design would reduce the risk that consumers will not always comply with the warning to stay alert and instead will be overly inattentive, denoted $PL_{inattentive}$. The cost of the redesign, B_{design}, appears to be minimal, because it largely involves initial coding that is then executed by the operating system at virtually no cost (assuming that the operating system can safely guide the vehicle off the road). In that event, the redesign of the operating system would be required by the risk-utility test: $B_{design} < PL_{inattentive}$.

AV Problem 5.3

After the fatal crashes discussed in AV Problem 5.1, Tesla updated its operating system "to further reinforce the need for driver engagement through a 'strike out' strategy. Drivers that do not respond to visual cues in the driver monitoring system alerts may 'strike out' and lose Autopilot function for the remainder of the drive cycle." Nat'l Highway Traffic Safety Admin., ODI Resume, PE 16-007, at 12 (June 19, 2017). Similarly, General Motors announced that it will design its operating system so that if "the [driver] alerts don't work, a representative [of the manufacturer] will activate the vehicle's intercom and communicate with the car's operator. If the driver still doesn't respond, the car will pull over on the side of the freeway and stop." Gauthem Nagesh, *GM's Eye-Tracking Tech Aims to Keep Drivers Alert*, Wall. St. J., Sept. 12, 2016. Identify the conditions under which the GM system would be a reasonable alternative design to the Tesla system, assuming that each vehicle also warns drivers to "stay alert" in the event that they need to take over the driving task.

Analysis of AV Problem 5.3

The risk that drivers will not stay alert is presumably the same for both the GM vehicles and Tesla vehicles. For reasons discussed in the last problem, either of the two monitoring systems would be required as compared to a warning "stay alert." The question now is which of these two systems would be required by the risk-utility test.

Because the GM system is the proposed alternative design, the risk-utility factors are appropriately defined by the manner in which that design affects both the risk and utility of the motor vehicle as compared to the Tesla design. The GM system requires the participation of someone at GM who will communicate with the driver, unlike the Tesla system that only relies on coding, which is costless once embedded in the operating system. This attribute of monitoring will increase the cost of the GM system relative to the Tesla system, denoted B_{GM}. The GM system has the potential to reduce risk because it will always force the vehicle to safely pull over and stop driving if the human driver does not respond, whereas the Tesla system does not necessarily do so (the driver who does not response "may 'strike out' "). Define this reduction as PL_{GM}. Hence the GM system would be required if $B_{GM} < PL_{GM}$

9

Medical Products and the Exemption of "Unavoidably Unsafe" Products from Strict Products Liability

There has been an explosion of products liability claims filed against the manufacturers of drugs and medical devices. "More than 71,000 drugs lawsuits have been filed in federal courts since 2001 and . . . now account for more than a third of all product liability filings." Lisa Girion, *State Vioxx Trial Is Set as Drug Suits Boom: An Explosion in Litigation Spurs Calls for Legal Reform and Regulatory Changes*, L.A. Times, June 27, 2006, at C1. "The pharmaceutical industry [is] the nation's No. 1 target of products liability lawsuits." *Id.* In 2018, "health care/pharmaceutical cases surged 59 percent (up 12,710 cases [from 2017]), largely because of multidistrict litigation related to the anticoagulant drug Xarelto." United States Courts, *Federal Judicial Caseload Statistics 2018*. With the notable exception of asbestos products, the history of mass-tort claims is largely comprised of litigation involving allegedly defective drugs or medical devices.

These lawsuits often turn on hard issues. Under *Restatement (Second)* §402A, drugs and medical devices are addressed by the "unavoidably unsafe products" exemption from strict liability in comment k, a confusing provision that has produced a confusing body of case law. These cases can also raise questions concerning the appropriate relation between product warnings, intermediaries (the prescribing physician), and the reasonableness of a product design. The issue of malfunction can even be surprisingly vexing, further illustrating the potential complexities of pharmaceutical litigation. What are the characteristics of prescription drugs and medical devices that explain why they generate so many distinctive issues?

I. "UNAVOIDABLY UNSAFE PRODUCTS" AND DESIGN DEFECTS

BROWN v. SUPERIOR COURT
Supreme Court of California, 1988
751 P.2d 470

Mosk, J. A number of plaintiffs filed actions in the San Francisco Superior Court against numerous drug manufacturers which allegedly produced diethylstilbestrol (DES), a substance plaintiffs claimed was used by their mothers to prevent miscarriage. They alleged that the drug was defective and they were injured *in utero* when their mothers ingested it.

The trial court determined that defendants could not be held strictly liable for the alleged defect in DES but only for their failure to warn of known or knowable side effects of the drug. The Court of Appeal upheld the trial court's determination. We granted review to examine the issue of strict liability of a drug manufacturer for a defect in the design of a prescription drug.

[I]n considering whether to adopt a rule of strict liability, [the American Law Institute] pondered whether the manufacturer of a prescription drug should be subject to the doctrine. During a rather confusing discussion of a draft of what was to become section 402A, a member of the institute proposed that drugs should be exempted from strict liability on the ground that it would be "against the public interest" to apply the doctrine to such products because of "the very serious tendency to stifle medical research and testing." [ ] Dean Prosser, who was the reporter for the *Restatement (Second) of Torts*, responded that the problem was a real one, and that he had it in mind in drafting section 402A. A motion to exempt prescription drugs from the section was defeated on the suggestion of Dean Prosser that the problem could be dealt with in the comments to the section.

The comment provides that the producer of a properly manufactured prescription drug may be held liable for injuries caused by the product only if it was not accompanied by a warning of dangers that the manufacturer knew or should have known about. It declares:

> k. *Unavoidably unsafe products.* There are some products which, in the present state of human knowledge, are quite incapable of being made safe for their intended and ordinary use. These are especially common in the field of drugs. An outstanding example is the vaccine for the Pasteur treatment of rabies, which not uncommonly leads to very serious and damaging consequences when it is injected. Since the disease itself invariably leads to a dreadful death, both the marketing and use of the vaccine are fully justified, notwithstanding the unavoidable high degree of risk which they involve. Such a product, properly prepared, and accompanied by proper directions and warning, is not defective, nor is it *unreasonably* dangerous. The same is true of many other drugs, vaccines, and the like, many of which for this very reason cannot legally be sold except to physicians, or under the prescription of a physician. It is also true in particular of many new or experimental drugs as to which, because of lack of time and opportunity for sufficient medical experience, there can be no assurance of safety, or perhaps even of purity of ingredients, but such

I. "Unavoidably Unsafe Products" and Design Defects

experience as there is justifies the marketing and use of the drug notwithstanding a medically recognizable risk. The seller of such products, again with the qualification that they are properly prepared and marketed, and proper warning is given, where the situation calls for it, is not to be held to strict liability for unfortunate consequences attending their use, merely because he has undertaken to supply the public with an apparently useful and desirable product, attended with a known but apparently reasonable risk.

Comment k has been analyzed and criticized by numerous commentators. While there is some disagreement as to its scope and meaning, there is a general consensus that, although it purports to explain the strict liability doctrine, in fact the principle it states is based on negligence.

Comment k has been adopted in the overwhelming majority of jurisdictions that have considered the matter. [ ] Most cases have embraced the rule of comment k without detailed analysis of its language. A few have conditioned application of the exemption stated therein on a finding that the drug involved is in fact "unavoidably dangerous," reasoning that the comment was intended to exempt only such drugs from strict liability. [ ]

We shall conclude that (1) a drug manufacturer's liability for a defectively designed drug should not be measured by the standards of strict liability; (2) because of the public interest in the development, availability, and reasonable price of drugs, the appropriate test for determining responsibility is the test stated in comment k; and (3) for these same reasons of policy, we disapprove [of the rule] that only those prescription drugs found to be "unavoidably dangerous" should be measured by the comment k standard and that strict liability should apply to drugs that do not meet that description.

[T]here is an important distinction between prescription drugs and other products such as construction machinery, a lawnmower, or perfume, the producers of which were held [in other cases to be] strictly liable. In the latter cases, the product is used to make work easier or to provide pleasure, while in the former it may be necessary to alleviate pain and suffering or to sustain life. Moreover, unlike other important medical products (wheelchairs, for example), harm to some users from prescription drugs is unavoidable. Because of these distinctions, the broader public interest in the availability of drugs at an affordable price must be considered in deciding the appropriate standard of liability for injuries resulting from their use.

Perhaps a drug might be made safer if it was withheld from the market until scientific skill and knowledge advanced to the point at which additional dangerous side effects would be revealed. But in most cases such a delay in marketing new drugs—added to the delay required to obtain approval for release of the product from the Food and Drug Administration—would not serve the public welfare. Public policy favors the development and marketing of beneficial new drugs, even though some risks, perhaps serious ones, might accompany their introduction, because drugs can save lives and reduce pain and suffering.

If drug manufacturers were subject to strict liability, they might be reluctant to undertake research programs to develop some pharmaceuticals that would prove beneficial or to distribute others that are available to be marketed, because of the fear of large adverse monetary judgments. Further, the additional expense of insuring against such liability—assuming insurance would be available—and of research programs to reveal possible dangers not detectable by available scientific methods could place the cost of medication beyond the reach of those who need it most.

The possibility that the cost of insurance and of defending against lawsuits will diminish the availability and increase the price of pharmaceuticals is far from theoretical. Defendants cite a host of examples of products which have greatly increased in price or have been withdrawn or withheld from the market because of the fear that their producers would be held liable for large judgments.

For example, according to defendant E.R. Squibb Sons, Inc., Bendectin, the only antinauseant drug available for pregnant women, was withdrawn from sale in 1983 because the cost of insurance almost equalled the entire income from sale of the drug. Before it was withdrawn, the price of Bendectin increased by over 300 percent. [ ]

Drug manufacturers refused to supply a newly discovered vaccine for influenza on the ground that mass inoculation would subject them to enormous liability. The government therefore assumed the risk of lawsuits resulting from injuries caused by the vaccine. One producer of diphtheria-tetanus-pertussis vaccine withdrew from the market, giving as its reason "extreme liability exposure, cost of litigation and the difficulty of continuing to obtain adequate insurance." [ ] There are only two manufacturers of the vaccine remaining in the market, and the cost of each dose rose a hundredfold from 11 cents in 1982 to $11.40 in 1986, $8 of which was for an insurance reserve. The price increase roughly paralleled an increase in the number of lawsuits from one in 1978 to 219 in 1985.

There is no doubt that, from the public's standpoint, these are unfortunate consequences. And they occurred even though almost all jurisdictions follow the negligence standard of comment k. It is not unreasonable to conclude in these circumstances that the imposition of a harsher test for liability would not further the public interest in the development and availability of these important products.

We decline to hold, therefore, that a drug manufacturer's liability for injuries caused by the defective design of a prescription drug should be measured by the standard set forth in Barker v. Lull Engineering Co., 20 Cal. 3d 413 (1978).

For these same reasons of policy, we reject plaintiff's assertion that a drug manufacturer should be held strictly liable for failure to warn of risks inherent in a drug even though it neither knew nor could have known by the application of scientific knowledge available at the time of distribution that the drug could produce the undesirable side effects suffered by the plaintiff.

One further question remains. Comment k, as we have seen, provides that the maker of an "unavoidably unsafe" product is not liable for injuries resulting from its use if the product is "properly prepared, and accompanied by proper directions and warning." With the few exceptions noted above, the courts which have adopted comment k have viewed all prescription drugs as coming within its scope.

[Under an alternative approach,] not all drugs are "unavoidably dangerous" so as to merit the protection of the negligence standard of comment k. [This test] gives the manufacturer a chance to avoid strict liability. But the eligibility of each drug for favorable treatment must be tested at a trial. In order to vindicate the public's interest in the availability and affordability of prescription drugs, a manufacturer must have a greater assurance that his products will not be measured by a strict liability standard than is provided by the test. Therefore, we

I. "Unavoidably Unsafe Products" and Design Defects

disapprove the [rule requiring] that comment k should not be applied to a prescription drug unless the trial court first determines that the drug is "unavoidably dangerous."

In conclusion, and in accord with almost all our sister states that have considered the issue, we hold that a manufacturer is not strictly liable for injuries caused by a prescription drug so long as the drug was properly prepared and accompanied by warnings of its dangerous propensities that were either known or reasonably scientifically knowable at the time of distribution.[12]

The judgment of the Court of Appeal is affirmed.

NOTES AND QUESTIONS

1. *The vaccine problem.* According to one study, the liability risk borne by manufacturers of the diphtheria-tetanus-pertussis (DTP) vaccine substantially increased from the late 1970s (three suits, on average, filed annually against the manufacturers) to the late 1980s (when the average number of annual suits was 217). Nevertheless, the DTP "vaccine currently in use in this country is essentially the same today as it has been for many years." Richard L. Manning, *Changing Rules in Tort Law and the Market for Childhood Vaccines*, 37 J.L. & Econ. 247, 259 (1994). What might explain this development? Recall that during this same period, there was a substantial increase in the number of asbestos cases as well.

2. *The National Vaccine Act.* To address problems in the market for vaccines linked to liability concerns, the U.S. Congress in 1986 enacted the National Childhood Vaccine Injury Act, 42 U.S.C. §§300aa-1 through 300aa-34.

> The National Childhood Vaccine Injury Act represents an effort to provide compensation to those harmed by childhood vaccines outside the framework of traditional tort law. Congress passed the law after hearing testimony 1) describing the critical need for vaccines to protect children from disease, 2) pointing out that vaccines inevitably harm a very small number of the many millions of people who are vaccinated, and 3) expressing dissatisfaction with traditional tort law as a way of compensating those few victims. Injured persons (potential tort plaintiffs) complained about the tort law system's uncertain recoveries, the high cost of litigation, and delays in obtaining compensation. They argued that government had, for all practical purposes, made vaccination obligatory, and thus it had a responsibility to ensure that those injured by vaccines were compensated. Vaccine manufacturers (potential tort defendants) complained about litigation expenses and occasional large recoveries, which caused insurance premiums and vaccine prices to rise, and which ultimately threatened the stability of the vaccine supply.

---

12. Our conclusion does not mean, of course, that drug manufacturers are free of all liability for defective drugs. They are subject to liability for manufacturing defects, as well as under general principles of negligence, and for failure to warn of known or reasonably knowable side effects.

The Vaccine Act responds to these complaints by creating a remedial system that tries more quickly to deliver compensation to victims, while also reducing insurance and litigation costs for manufacturers. The Act establishes a special claims procedure involving the Court of Federal Claims and special masters (a system that we shall call the "Vaccine Court"). A person injured by a vaccine may file a petition with the Vaccine Court to obtain compensation (from a fund financed by a tax on vaccines). He need not prove fault. Nor, to prove causation, need he show more than that he received the vaccine and then suffered certain symptoms within a defined period of time. The Act specifies amounts of compensation for certain kinds of harm (e.g., $250,000 for death, up to $250,000 for pain and suffering). And, it specifies other types of harm for which compensation may be awarded (e.g., medical expenses, loss of earnings).

At the same time, the Act modifies, but does not eliminate, the traditional tort system, which Congress understood to provide important incentives for the safe manufacture and distribution of vaccines. The Act requires that a person injured directly by a vaccine *first* bring a Vaccine Court proceeding. Then, it gives that person the choice either to accept the Court's award and abandon his tort rights (which the Act transfers to the federal government), or to reject the judgment and retain his tort rights. (He can also keep his tort rights by withdrawing his Vaccine Court petition if the Court moves too slowly.)

The Act additionally helps manufacturers by providing certain federal modifications of state tort law. For example, it forbids the award of compensation for injuries that flow from "unavoidable side effects"; it frees the manufacturer from liability for not providing direct warnings to an injured person (or his representative); it imposes a presumption that compliance with Food and Drug Administration requirements means the manufacturer provided proper directions and warnings; it limits punitive damage awards; and it requires that the trial of any tort suit take place in three phases (liability; general damages; punitive damages). The upshot is a new remedial system that interacts in a complicated way with traditional tort lawsuits.

Schafer v. American Cyanamid Co., 20 F.3d 1, 2-3 (1st Cir. 1994) (Breyer, J.).

The Vaccine Act expressly preempts (forecloses) any tort claim "if the injury or death resulted from side effects that were unavoidable even though the vaccine was properly prepared and was accompanied by proper directions and warnings." 42 U.S.C. § 300aa-22. In Bruesewitz v. Wyeth LLC, 562 U.S. 223 (2011), the Court held that the express language of the Act preempts all claims of defective vaccine design to effectuate the statutory purpose of encouraging the development of new vaccines. If a vaccine can be reasonably redesigned to reduce the risk of side effects, why is that claim barred by statutory language addressing "*unavoidable* side effects"? The issue of preemption is the subject of Chapter 10, section III.

How does the Act's express limitation of liability compare to comment k? What does it suggest about the degree of liability protection that comment k was affording to the producers of vaccines and other medical products?

3. *The Public Readiness and Emergency Preparedness (PREP) Act.* Pursuant to its statutory authority under the PREP Act, the Secretary of Health

and Human Services can issue a Declaration that provides immunity to manufacturers and other distributors against "any claim for loss that has a 'causal relationship' to medical countermeasures that diagnose, prevent or treat a declared pandemic, epidemic or security threat, except for claims involving 'willful misconduct.'" 42 U.S.C. §247d-6d. The Act also creates a compensation fund. *Id.* §247d-6e. On March 17, 2020, the Secretary issued a Declaration that COVID-19 vaccines are a medical countermeasure. 85 FR 15198. Consequently, individuals who are seriously injured by these vaccines can seek recovery only from the Countermeasures Injury Compensation Fund.

The COVID-19 vaccines illustrate the dual nature of the regulatory problem created by vaccines. Liability is limited to facilitate the rapid development and widespread distribution of these vaccines, but if those who suffer serious injury are not guaranteed adequate compensation, some individuals might decide to forego the vaccinations. The reduced number of vaccinated individuals, in turn, reduces immunity within the community, making it harder to stop the virus from spreading. To address both problems, the PREP Act decouples liability from compensation, immunizing manufacturers and distributors from liability while also guaranteeing compensation to those who are seriously injured by the vaccines.

4. *Social value as a limitation of liability.* Does the legislative response to vaccine-caused injuries help to explain the logic of comment k? Consider how the threat of strict liability led to a twenty-fold increase in the price of the DTP vaccine, which reduced by more than 1 million the number of preschool-age children who were vaccinated. Manning, *supra* note 1, at 248 n.5 & 273. Strict products liability is supposed to improve safety, so it would be self-defeating if that rule led to significantly increased prices or the withdrawal of prescription drugs and medical devices that left society, on balance, less safe than it would be without the liability rule. The safety rationale for strict products liability, therefore, can justify the immunity from strict liability for products that promote public health and safety. Is this rationale clearly expressed by comment k? Did the court in *Brown* expressly say as much, or only impliedly do so by the manner in which it distinguished medical products from other products like lawnmowers and perfume?

5. *Restating the case law on comment k.* Courts have interpreted comment k in the different manners described in *Brown.* After an extensive study of this case law, Professors James Henderson and Aaron Twerski concluded that it "is unintelligible." They attributed the problem to the fact that comment k "is poorly drafted and internally inconsistent." The ensuing interpretive problems are then exacerbated when courts try to apply comment k "to resolve problems that no one even contemplated at the time of its adoption." James A. Henderson, Jr. & Aaron D. Twerski, *A Proposed Revision to Section 402A of the* Restatement (Second) of Torts, 77 Cornell L. Rev. 1512, 1537 (1992). In their role as Reporters to the *Restatement (Third),* Professors Henderson and Twerski formulated a different approach to the problem: "Case law that is unintelligible cannot be intelligibly restated. There is a need in this area to clarify the issues and to provide direction

to the courts as to how this very special genre of cases can be sensibly approached." *Id.* at 1545.

FREEMAN v. HOFFMAN-LA ROCHE, INC.
Supreme Court of Nebraska, 2000
618 N.W.2d 827

CONNOLLY, J. In this appeal, we reconsider our approach to products liability for defects in prescription drugs in light of changes in the law and the release of *Restatement (Third) of Torts: Products Liability* §§1 to 21 (1997) (*Third Restatement*). The appellant, Aimee Freeman, filed a petition alleging seven theories of recovery against the appellee pharmaceutical company, Hoffman-La Roche, Inc. (Hoffman). She seeks damages for injuries she sustained following her use of the prescription drug Accutane. Hoffman demurred on the basis that the petition failed to state a cause of action. The district court dismissed with leave to amend. Freeman stood on her petition, and the action was dismissed with prejudice.

Freeman's operative petition alleged the following facts: On or about September 23, 1995, Freeman presented herself to her physician for treatment of chronic acne. After examination, her physician prescribed 20 milligrams daily of Accutane. Hoffman is the designer, manufacturer, wholesaler, retailer, fabricator, and supplier of Accutane.

Freeman took the Accutane daily from September 27 through October 2, 1995, and from October 4 through November 20, 1995. Hoffman alleged that as a result of taking the Accutane, she developed multiple health problems. These problems included ulcerative colitis, inflammatory polyarthritis, nodular episcleritis OS, and optic nerve head drusen. As a result, Freeman alleged that she sustained various damages. Freeman contends that she has stated a cause of action for products liability under a variety of theories of recovery.

In dealing with products other than prescription drugs, this court has recognized a manufacturer's liability in tort for design defects. [I]n regard to nonprescription drug products, we have generally followed the rule as set out in §402A of the *Second Restatement*. Prescription drugs, however, have been treated differently both by this court and by *the Second Restatement.*

Under the *Second Restatement*, prescription drugs are treated specially under §402A, comment k. Comment k provides an exception from strict liability when a product is deemed to be "unavoidably unsafe." Comment k, however, has been interpreted in a variety of ways in other jurisdictions, and there has been a wide range of disagreement regarding its application. [ ]

Only a few jurisdictions have interpreted comment k in a manner that strictly excepts all prescription drugs from strict liability. Under the minority view, a drug that is properly manufactured and accompanied by an adequate warning of the risks known to the manufacturer at the time of sale is not defectively designed as a matter of law. Brown v. Superior Court (Abbott Laboratories), 44 Cal. 3d 1049 (1988); [ ]. These jurisdictions are commonly described by legal commentators as providing manufacturers with a "blanket immunity" from

I. "Unavoidably Unsafe Products" and Design Defects

strict liability for design defects in prescription drugs. Our [case law] generally falls under this category of interpretation of comment k.

The majority of jurisdictions that have adopted comment k apply it on a case-by-case basis, believing that societal interests in ensuring the marketing and development of prescription drugs will be adequately served without the need to resort to a rule of blanket immunity. [ ] A few courts have not specifically adopted comment k and have instead either fashioned their own rules or treated prescription drugs in the same manner as that of all other products. [ ]

Although a variety of tests are employed among jurisdictions that apply comment k on a case-by-case basis, the majority apply the comment as an affirmative defense, with the trend toward the use of a risk-utility test in order to determine whether the defense applies. [ ] When a risk-utility test is applied, the existence of a reasonable alternative design is generally the central factor. Because the application of comment k is traditionally viewed as an exception and a defense to strict liability, courts generally place the initial burden of proving the various risk utility factors on the defendant. [ ] Thus, under these cases, the plaintiff's burden of proof for his or her prima facie case remains the same as it is in any products liability case in the given jurisdiction.

On further reflection, we now believe that societal interests in ensuring the marketing and development of prescription drugs can be served without resorting to a rule which in effect amounts to a blanket immunity from strict liability for manufacturers. Accordingly, we overrule [prior case law] to the extent it applies comment k to provide a blanket immunity from strict liability for prescription drugs. Accordingly, we must address how, or if, comment k should be applied, or whether we should consider adopting provisions of the *Third Restatement*.

Section 6 of the *Third Restatement* pertains specifically to prescription drugs, with §6(c) applying to design defects. Section 6 at 144-45 states in part:

(a) A manufacturer of a prescription drug or medical device who sells or otherwise distributes a defective drug or medical device is subject to liability for harm to persons caused by the defect. A prescription drug or medical device is one that may be legally sold or otherwise distributed only pursuant to a health-care provider's prescription.

(b) For purposes of liability under Subsection (a), a prescription drug or medical device is defective if at the time of sale or other distribution the drug or medical device:

(1) contains a manufacturing defect as defined in §2(a); or

(2) is not reasonably safe due to defective design as defined in Subsection (c); or

(3) is not reasonably safe due to inadequate instructions or warnings as defined in Subsection (d).

(c) A prescription drug or medical device is not reasonably safe due to defective design if the foreseeable risks of harm posed by the drug or medical device are sufficiently great in relation to its foreseeable therapeutic benefits that reasonable health-care providers, knowing of such foreseeable risks and therapeutic benefits, would not prescribe the drug or medical device for any class of patients.

In addition, §6, comment b at 146-47, states in part:

> The traditional refusal by courts to impose tort liability for defective designs of prescription drugs and medical devices is based on the fact that a prescription drug or medical device entails a unique set of risks and benefits. What may be harmful to one patient may be beneficial to another. Under Subsection (c) a drug is defectively designed only when it provides no net benefit to any class of patients. Courts have concluded that as long as a drug or medical device provides net benefits to some persons under some circumstances, the drug or device manufacturer should be required to instruct and warn health-care providers of the foreseeable risks and benefits. Courts have also recognized that the regulatory system governing prescription drugs is a legitimate mechanism for setting the standards for drug design. In part, this deference reflects concerns over the possible negative effects of judicially imposed liability on the cost and availability of valuable medical technology. This deference also rests on two further assumptions: first, that prescribing health-care providers, when adequately informed by drug manufacturers, are able to assure that the right drugs and medical devices reach the right patients; and second, that governmental regulatory agencies adequately review new prescription drugs and devices, keeping unreasonably dangerous designs off the market.
>
> Nevertheless, unqualified deference to these regulatory mechanisms is considered by a growing number of courts to be unjustified. An approved prescription drug or medical device can present significant risks without corresponding advantages. At the same time, manufacturers must have ample discretion to develop useful drugs and devices without subjecting their design decisions to the ordinary test applicable to products generally under §2(b). Accordingly, Subsection (c) imposes a more rigorous test for defect than does §2(b), which does not apply to prescription drugs and medical devices.
>
> ... Subsections (c) and (d) recognize common-law causes of action for defective drug design and for failure to provide reasonable instructions or warnings, even though the manufacturer complied with governmental standards.

Section 6, comment f at 149, states in part:

> A prescription drug or device manufacturer defeats a plaintiff's design claim by establishing one or more contexts in which its product would be prescribed by reasonable, informed health-care providers. That some individual providers do, in fact, prescribe defendant's product does not in itself suffice to defeat the plaintiff's claim. Evidence regarding the actual conduct of health-care providers, while relevant and admissible, is not necessarily controlling. The issue is whether, objectively viewed, reasonable providers, knowing of the foreseeable risks and benefits of the drug or medical device, would prescribe it for any class of patients. Given this very demanding objective standard, liability is likely to be imposed only under unusual circumstances. The court has the responsibility to determine when the plaintiff has introduced sufficient evidence so that reasonable persons could conclude that plaintiff has met this demanding standard.

There are several criticisms of §6(c), which will be briefly summarized. First, it does not accurately restate the law. It has been repeatedly stated that there is no support in the case law for the application of a reasonable physician standard in which strict liability for a design defect will apply only when a product

I. "Unavoidably Unsafe Products" and Design Defects 375

is not useful for any class of persons. Rather, as illustrated by the discussion of the treatment of comment k under the *Second Restatement* in other jurisdictions, the majority of courts apply some form of risk-utility balancing that focuses on a variety of factors, including the existence of a reasonable alternative design. The few cases that the *Third Restatement* cites to as support for the reasonable physician test also apply a risk-utility test. Thus, §6(c) does not restate the law and instead seeks to formulate new law with no precedential support. [ ]

Second, the reasonable physician test is criticized as being artificial and difficult to apply. The test requires fact finders to presume that physicians have as much or more of an awareness about a prescription drug product as the manufacturer. The test also ignores concerns of commentators that physicians tend to prescribe drugs they are familiar with or for which they have received advertising material, even when studies indicate that better alternatives are available. [ ]

A third criticism of particular applicability to Freeman's case is that the test lacks flexibility and treats drugs of unequal utility equally. For example, a drug used for cosmetic purposes but which causes serious side effects has less utility than a drug which treats a deadly disease, yet also has serious side effects. In each case, the drugs would likely be useful to a class of patients under the reasonable physician standard for some class of persons. Consequently, each would be exempted from design defect liability. But under a standard that considers reasonable alternative design, the cosmetic drug could be subject to liability if a safer yet equally effective design was available. As a result, the reasonable physician standard of §6(c) of the *Third Restatement* has been described as a standard that in effect will never allow liability. [ ] However, a standard applying a risk-utility test that focuses on the presence or absence of a reasonable alternative design, although also rarely allowing liability, at least allows the flexibility for liability to attach in an appropriate case.

Fourth, the test allows a consumer's claim to be defeated simply by a statement from the defense's expert witness that the drug at issue had some benefit for any single class of people. Thus, it is argued that application of §6(c) will likely shield pharmaceutical companies from a wide variety of suits that could have been brought under comment k of the *Second Restatement*. [ ] As the *Third Restatement*, §6(c), comment f at 149, states in part: "Given this very demanding objective standard, liability is likely to be imposed only under unusual circumstances." Thus, even though the rule is reformulated, any application of §6(c) will essentially provide the same blanket immunity from liability for design defects in prescription drugs as did the application of comment k in the few states that interpreted it as such.

We conclude that §6(c) has no basis in the case law. We view §6(c) as too strict of a rule, under which recovery would be nearly impossible. Accordingly, we do not adopt §6(c) of the *Third Restatement*.

We [further] conclude that §402A, comment k, of the *Second Restatement* should be applied on a case-by-case basis and as an affirmative defense in cases involving prescription drug products. Under this rule, an application of the comment does not provide a blanket immunity from strict liability for prescription drugs. Rather, the plaintiff is required to plead the consumer expectations test, as he or she would be required to do in any products liability case. The defendant may then raise comment k as an affirmative defense. The comment will apply to except the prescription drug product from strict liability when it is shown that (1) the product is properly manufactured and contains adequate warnings, (2) its benefits justify its risks, and (3) the product was at the time of manufacture and distribution incapable of being made more safe.

In this case, because the application of comment k is an affirmative defense, Freeman was only required to plead that the Accutane she took was unreasonably dangerous under a consumer expectations test. Freeman alleged that Accutane was unreasonably dangerous for use, that it was not fit for its intended purpose, that the risks inherent in the design outweighed the benefits of its use, and that Accutane was more dangerous to Freeman than was anticipated due to undisclosed side effects. As facts supporting her allegations, Freeman alleged that Accutane is sold as an acne medication and that the side effects of Accutane present life-threatening conditions. Thus, Freeman alleged facts that the Accutane was dangerous to an extent beyond that which would be contemplated by the ordinary consumer who purchases it, with the ordinary knowledge common to the community as to its characteristics. Accordingly, we conclude that Freeman has stated a theory of recovery based on a design defect.

Freeman alleges that Hoffman was negligent in failing to warn of dangers associated with the use of Accutane. Freeman also alleges that Hoffman failed to warn that Accutane was not adequately tested. Pharmaceutical products have historically been treated differently in regard to a duty to warn. Although in ordinary product cases, a manufacturer's duty to warn runs directly to the consumer of the product, in cases involving prescription drugs, it is widely held that the duty to warn extends only to members of the medical profession and not to the consumer. This concept, known as the learned intermediary doctrine, . . . is provided for in §6(d) of the *Third Restatement*:

> A prescription drug or medical device is not reasonably safe due to inadequate instructions or warnings if reasonable instructions or warnings regarding foreseeable risks of harm are not provided to:
> (1) prescribing and other health-care providers who are in a position to reduce the risks of harm in accordance with the instructions or warnings; or
> (2) the patient when the manufacturer knows or has reason to know that health-care providers will not be in a position to reduce the risks of harm in accordance with the instructions or warnings.

We have not specifically adopted the learned intermediary doctrine as the applicable test for determining whether a manufacturer may be liable for a warning defect in prescription drug cases. However, with a few exceptions for instances where special facts require a direct warning to the consumer, the doctrine is followed in virtually all jurisdictions that have considered whether to adopt it. [ ] The doctrine as stated in the *Third Restatement* has also been adopted in other jurisdictions. [ ] We adopt §6(d) of the *Third Restatement*. Accordingly, we apply the learned intermediary doctrine to Freeman's case.

The section of Freeman's petition devoted to factual allegations alleges that Hoffman failed to warn of Accutane's dangers in the package insert provided to physicians, including Freeman's physician. Freeman makes further allegations regarding Hoffman's failure to provide her with warnings under the section specifically devoted to her theory of recovery for a failure to warn. Thus, we

I. "Unavoidably Unsafe Products" and Design Defects

conclude that Freeman has stated a theory of recovery for liability based on a warning defect.

Applying the allegations in Freeman's petition to the legal tests, we conclude that Freeman did state theories of recovery for liability based on a design defect [and] warning defect. Accordingly, the district court erred in sustaining Hoffman's demurrer. We reverse, and remand for further proceedings to allow Freeman to amend her petition.

NOTES AND QUESTIONS

1. *The learned intermediary doctrine.* Most jurisdictions have adopted the learned intermediary doctrine. *See* In re Zimmer, NextGen Knee Implant Products Liability Litigation, 884 F.3d 746 (7th Cir. 2018) (making *Erie* prediction that the Wisconsin Supreme Court would follow "the vast majority of State Supreme Courts" and adopt the doctrine). Is this rule a distinctive doctrine with its own particular rationale, or is it simply a particular application of the more general rule for determining whether the manufacturer can provide the warning only to an intermediary, like an employer, rather than warning the consumer directly? *See* Chapter 6, section III.B.

2. *Exceptions to the learned intermediary doctrine.* Under the learned intermediary doctrine, the manufacturer is obligated to provide a warning only to the prescribing physician, although some courts have adopted limited exceptions for particular types of medical products and require an additional warning directly to the end user. *Compare* Ortho-McNeil-Janssen Pharmaceuticals, Inc., 808 F.3d 281, 293 (6th Cir. 2015) (rejecting an exception to the learned intermediary rule for birth control pills because plaintiff "was counseled meaningfully by her prescribing medical provider," while also recognizing that "[t]here may be cases in which a prescriber of birth control medication does not function as a learned intermediary, but this is not such a case"), *with* MacDonald v. Ortho Pharmaceutical Corp., 475 N.E.2d 65 (Mass. 1985) ("At her annual checkup, the patient receives a renewal prescription for a full year's supply of the pill. Thus, the patient may only seldom have the opportunity to explore her questions and concerns about the medication with the prescribing physician. Even if the physician, on those occasions, were scrupulously to remind the patient of the risks attendant on continuation of the oral contraceptive, the patient cannot be expected to remember all of the details for a protracted period of time."). Another exception involves prescription drugs that are directly advertised to consumers. In Perez v. Wyeth Labs., Inc., 734 A.2d 1245, 1257 (N.J. 1999), the court held that "prescription drug manufacturers that market their products directly to consumers should be subject to claims by consumers if their advertising fails to provide an adequate warning of the product's dangerous propensities." For a period, this advertising exception appeared as if it would be more widely adopted, but that development so far has not occurred. Do these exceptions conform to the general rule that determines whether a manufacturer can satisfy the duty to warn by disclosing the requisite information to an intermediary, such as an employer, instead of to the end user?

3. *The reasonable physician standard.* According to the court in *Freeman*, the *Restatement (Third)* rule for defectively designed drugs has "no basis in the case law" and inappropriately presumes "that physicians have as much or more of an awareness about a prescription drug product as the manufacturer." As *Freeman* illustrates, courts have not adopted the *Restatement (Third)*'s formulation of the reasonable physician standard for evaluating defective drug designs. In Tersigni v. Wyeth, 817 F.3d 364, 369 (1st Cir. 2016), the court rejected plaintiff's argument that when faced with the issue, Massachusetts courts would adopt §6(c): "This is a bridge too far, and we decline to cross it."

To evaluate whether the *Restatement (Third)* rule has any basis in the case law, we need to consider the role of the prescribing physician. The learned intermediary doctrine obligates the manufacturer to provide the physician with the information needed to make an informed decision of whether to prescribe the drug. The patient can decide otherwise, but the physician still makes the initial decision of whether the product should be used at all. Courts have recognized as much: "In light of this, we conclude that a prescription drug is defectively designed and strict liability should be imposed on its manufacturer if the prescription drug failed to perform as safely as an ordinary doctor would expect, when used by the patient in an intended and reasonably foreseeable manner." Shanks v. Upjohn Co., 835 P.2d 1189, 1195 (Alaska 1992). *See also* Reyes v. Wyeth Labs., 498 F.2d 1264, 1276 (5th Cir. 1974) ("As a medical expert, the prescribing physician can take into account the propensities of the drug, as well as the susceptibilities of [the] patient. [The physician's] task [is to weigh] the benefits of any medication against its potential dangers. The choice [the physician] makes is an informed one, an individualized medical judgment bottomed on a knowledge of both patient and palliative.").

Assuming that the manufacturer has adequately warned the physician, suppose that the physician would reasonably prescribe the drug to at least one class of patients as required by the *Restatement (Third)*. Recall that when the ordinary consumer can make an informed risk-utility decision, there is no claim for defective product design based on the same risk-utility factors. *See* Chapter 6, section III.B (discussing categorical liability and related rules). Thus, if a reasonable (or well-informed) physician would prescribe the drug for at least one class of patients, this informed risk-utility choice should exempt the manufacturer from liability with respect to the claim that this version of the product should not have been marketed at all — the outcome attained by the *Restatement (Third)* rule for defectively designed drugs. Once conceptualized in relation to the learned intermediary doctrine, the *Restatement (Third)* rule can be derived from established doctrine that forecloses claims of categorical liability.

To be sure, this rationale for the reasonable physician standard assumes that the physician properly utilizes the information the manufacturer adequately disclosed in the product warning. What if the physician does not convey the information to the patient? Or what if the physician erroneously prescribes the drug to a patient for whom the drug is unreasonably dangerous? Consider Janice Neumann, *Doctors Don't Always Tell You About Side Effects, and That's a Problem,* Wash. Post, July 29, 2017; Andrea

Petersen, *How Drug Alerts Trickle Down to Your Doctor: Amid Flurry of Red Flags About Serious Side Effects, Prescribing Turns Trickier*, Wall St. J., Sept. 15, 2004 ("[R]esearch underscores how difficult it is for doctors to stay on top of the mass of drug information, and decide how and whether to act. The number of drugs has exploded in recent years, so there are simply more side effects and potential drug-to-drug interactions to keep track of."). Is the problem solved by the liability that the physician would incur for having committed malpractice by not obtaining the patient's informed consent or by recommending the wrong prescription?

Medical malpractice liability will not necessarily solve these problems for at least one reason: There is "strong evidence" that consumers can obtain many drugs without a prescription from their physician by purchasing them from pharmacies on the Internet. Anita Bernstein, *(Almost) No Bad Drugs: Near-Total Products Liability Immunity for Prescription Drugs*, 77 Wash. & Lee L. Rev. 3, 40-44 (2020). Without the physician as a gate keeper, consumers can use the drug in disregard of a warning. How is the duty to design affected by the fact that consumers do not always comply with product warnings? How does this rule compare to the reasonable physician standard adopted by the *Restatement (Third)*?

4. *The example of thalidomide.* We can evaluate these issues by considering thalidomide, a drug that has caused so many serious birth defects that it motivated European countries to adopt strict products liability. The drug is not safe for use by pregnant women, but has significant health benefits for individuals with leprosy. The drug, in other words, is unreasonably dangerous for a very large class of potential users and beneficial for only an extremely small group.

The drug cannot be redesigned to eliminate the risk of birth defects while retaining the therapeutic benefits for those with leprosy. *See* Eric W. Martin, HAZARDS OF MEDICATION 24 (2d ed. 1978) ("[S]eparation of both toxic and side effects from therapeutic effects within a drug series is never easy and can never be accomplished."). Because thalidomide cannot be redesigned, the risk-utility analysis of the design necessarily takes the form of categorical liability: Do the inherent therapeutic benefits of the drug outweigh its inherent risks?

If the design were evaluated by reference to the full class of potential users (pregnant women and those with leprosy), it would be defective. The risk of birth defects faced by the much larger class of potential victims (the offspring of pregnant women) vastly exceeds the utility for a much smaller class (those with leprosy). But this analysis does not account for the product warning that pregnant women should not take the drug, which would significantly reduce the risk of birth defects. Assuming (unrealistically) that some pregnant women would use thalidomide despite the warning, there is a foreseeable risk that the drug will be misused and cause birth defects ($PL_{birth\ defects}$). To attain this safety benefit, however, thalidomide must be withdrawn from the market, in which case those with leprosy would lose the therapeutic benefits, creating a cost or burden ($B_{leprosy\ treatment}$). Hence thalidomide would fail the risk-utility test if

$$B_{leprosy\ treatment} < PL_{birth\ defects}$$

Under the reasonable physician standard in the *Restatement (Third)*, the mere fact that thalidomide benefits one class of patients—those with leprosy—is sufficient to defeat the claim of defective design. As discussed in the previous note, the rule implicitly assumes the prescribing physician always channels the drug to the right class of users, in which case pregnant women would never ingest thalidomide and the drug would never cause birth defects ($PL_{birth\ defects} = 0$). Under these conditions, thalidomide necessarily passes the risk-utility test:

$$B_{leprosy\ treatment} > PL_{birth\ defects} = 0$$

Unlike the reasonable physician standard, the risk-utility test recognizes that some users might improperly take the drug, despite the warning, creating a foreseeable risk of injury ($PL_{birth\ defects} > 0$). The inquiry in this regard conforms to the risk-utility analysis of whether a design change should substitute for a warning that leaves a significant residuum of risk due to lack of full compliance with the warning. *See* Chapter 8. However, a finding that the drug is defectively designed will drive it from the market (due to the threat of punitive damages discussed in a later chapter). In that event, the class of individuals who would benefit from the drug (those with leprosy) would be burdened to protect other consumers (pregnant women) who misuse the drug by not following the warning. Is it fair to deny therapeutic benefits to one class to protect another class from deliberate misuse? Does this problem help to explain why in practice, plaintiffs rarely prevail in cases alleging defective drug design? *See* Bernstein, *supra* note 3, at 12-20 (discussing the paucity of reported cases of this type).

5. *"Lifestyle" drugs.* Insofar as comment k is limited to products for which strict products liability would create a safety problem (via product withdrawals or reduced consumption), then its application should be limited to drugs having a therapeutic safety benefit. Did the drug at issue in *Freeman* satisfy this requirement? To what extent is the court's concern about the problems of "blanket immunity" limited to the way in which it would apply to "lifestyle" or cosmetic drugs?

6. *The puzzle of comment k.* Despite the *Restatement (Third)*'s wholesale rejection of comment k, courts continue to apply it in the manner discussed by the court in *Freeman*. *See, e.g.*, Burningham v. Wright Medical Technology, 448 P.3d 1283 (Utah 2019) (deciding to apply comment k on a case-by-case basis to any medical device that gains regulatory approval only because it is "substantially similar" to another medical device that had previously been approved).

The manner in which courts characterize the comment k inquiry, however, is puzzling. By treating comment k as an affirmative defense, the majority rule places the burden of proof on the defendant manufacturer to show that the design of the drug or medical device passes the risk-utility test. For all other products, however, the plaintiff in the vast majority of jurisdictions bears the burden of proving that the product design fails the risk-utility test. *See* Chapter 7, section II. Instead of providing an affirmative defense, comment k would seem to subject the manufacturers of pharmaceuticals to an evidentiary burden *more* onerous than the one they bear for other types of products, a rather baffling attribute for an affirmative defense that is supposed to benefit manufacturers.

To understand why comment k is an affirmative defense, we need to place it within its historical context. Recall that the §402A rule of strict products liability restates the case law involving defects defined by a self-defeating product malfunction, such as contaminated food or an exploding bottle of soda. Because § 402A was formulated by reference to product malfunctions, the comment k exemption from this rule of strict liability presumably applies to this type of defect. The manufacturer is subject to strict liability under §402A for defects (malfunctions) even if it "has exercised all possible care in the preparation and sale of the product." Strict products liability forecloses any defense based on risk-utility evidence in the case of a malfunction. By allowing the manufacturer to employ risk-utility evidence to avoid liability for a malfunction, comment k provides a true affirmative defense that exempts the manufacturer from strict products liability. When applied to product malfunctions, comment k makes evident sense.

As illustrated by *Freeman*, courts do not limit comment k to malfunctioning products for reasons that seem unassailable. Comment k states that an "unavoidably unsafe" product is not "unreasonably dangerous" if "properly prepared, and accompanied by proper directions and warning." Relying on this language, most courts and commentators assume that comment k does not apply to manufacturing defects. Because a manufacturing defect can cause a product to malfunction, as in the case of an exploding soda bottle, it would seem to follow that comment k does not apply in these cases: How could it coherently eliminate strict liability for malfunctions while still recognizing that strict liability applies to products that are not "properly prepared"?

Although this reasoning seems sound, it rests on some unexamined premises that require further analysis. We need to consider how comment k might apply to manufacturing defects and product malfunctions more generally.

II. MANUFACTURING DEFECTS AND PRODUCT MALFUNCTIONS

Are there any types of product malfunctions for which the rule of strict liability might create the type of policy problem addressed by comment k, thereby justifying a limitation of strict liability in order to further the safety objective of §402A?

ROGERS v. MILES LABS, INC.
Supreme Court of Washington, 1991
802 P.2d 1346

CALLOW, C.J. Jeremy Rogers was born January 16, 1980, with severe hemophilia type B. Persons with this type of hemophilia lack a blood clotting factor known as factor IX. To control the spontaneous hemorrhaging caused by the disease, hemophiliacs such as Jeremy must use factor IX concentrates on an average of once a week throughout their lives.

The production of factor concentrates is regulated and licensed by the Food and Drug Administration's Center for Biologics Evaluation and Research. Since April 1985, defendants have employed the test known as the Enzyme-Linked Immunosorbent Assay (ELISA) to detect the presence of antibodies to the HIV virus. However, prior to April 1985, no test was available to defendants in order to test plasma for the HIV virus. Moreover, it is unclear whether it will ever be possible to screen with 100 percent accuracy for the presence of the AIDS virus in blood. *See, e.g.,* Comment, *Blood Donation: A Gift of Life or a Death Sentence?*, 22 Akron L. Rev. 623, 629 (1989).

Factor concentrates possess several major advantages over other available forms of treatment for hemophilia. Factor concentrates are highly purified and thus result in fewer adverse reactions. They make it possible reliably to determine the appropriate level of clotting factor necessary to stop bleeding. Finally, they are easily stored and can be given quickly if prompt treatment is necessary.

For most of his life, Jeremy has used factor IX concentrates manufactured by defendants to treat his hemophilia. In November 1985, Jeremy tested positive for the presence of human immunodeficiency virus (HIV) antibodies. In February 1988, he was diagnosed as suffering from acquired immune deficiency syndrome (AIDS).

Plaintiff Kimberly Rogers filed this action in federal court on behalf of herself and as guardian ad litem for Jeremy against defendants Miles Laboratories and Baxter Healthcare on the tort theories of negligence and strict liability. Plaintiffs allege that Jeremy contracted AIDS as a result of using defendants' products. Defendants moved for partial summary judgment seeking dismissal of those claims brought under strict liability, and the United States District Court granted defendants' motion. Plaintiffs then filed a motion for reconsideration seeking a stay of the court's order and requested certification on the issue of strict liability.

The federal court then entered an order to stay the original holding dismissing the strict liability claim and certified the issue to this court. This opinion, therefore, addresses only the issue of whether strict liability applies to defendants in this case. Both parties recognize that the negligence claim is still available to plaintiffs.

[The court first discusses prior cases in which it adopted the *Restatement (Second)* §402A rule of strict products liability and comment k.]

Comment k justifies an exception from strict liability by focusing on the product and its relative value to society, rather than on the manufacturer's position in the stream of commerce. Some products are necessary regardless of the risks involved to the user. The alternative would be that a product, essential to sustain the life of some individuals, would not be available — thus resulting in a greater harm to the individual than that risked through use of the product. Blood and blood products fall into this category. In [a prior case], after a detailed examination of this state's law regarding blood and blood products, we unanimously concluded that "[t]he purposes of strict liability are not furthered when applied to blood and blood products." Howell v. Spokane & Inland Blood Bank, 785 P.2d 815 (Wash. 1990). We noted three policy reasons against subjecting blood and blood products to attack under strict liability:

II. Manufacturing Defects and Product Malfunctions

First, the societal need to ensure an affordable, adequate blood supply furnishes a persuasive reason for distinguishing between victims of defective blood and victims of other defective products. Second, strict liability cannot provide an incentive to promote all possible accident prevention at a time when there was no possible means of screening the blood for HIV. Third, while the producers may be in a better position to spread the costs, it is not in society's best interest to have the price of a transfusion reflect its true costs.

Id. at 53-54. These reasons apply equally to the facts before us. Therefore, we hold that strict liability does not apply to blood and blood products, including factor concentrates.

The same issue was addressed in Miles Labs. Inc. v. Jane Doe, 556 A.2d 1107 (Md. 1989), in which the court reasoned:

The singular medical utility of blood and blood products, together with the compelling necessity for their use when medically indicated, ordinarily outweighs the known risk in all blood transfusions that these products may contain some impurities. Strict tort liability principles are not applicable under Comment k when, at the time of distribution of such products, they contained a then unknown and unknowable infectious agent undetectable by any available scientific test. In such circumstances, the seller would not under then applicable common law precepts, including the substance of Comment k, be held strictly accountable in tort because the product was not free of the unknown contaminant which caused injury to the recipient; manifestly, the seller was not in a better position than the victim, or the victim's physician, to take precautions against the unknowable defect in the product.

We find this reasoning persuasive.

Numerous other jurisdictions are in accord with our decision not to apply the theory of strict liability to suppliers of blood and manufacturers of blood products. [ ]

We hold that the proper tort standard for manufacturers of blood and blood products is that of negligence, not strict liability; and the applicable law is set forth in comment k to the *Restatement (Second) of Torts* §402A. The plaintiffs have a negligence cause of action which is still before the federal district court.

NOTES AND QUESTIONS

1. *The problem of impure blood.* According to one of the founders of strict products liability, Justice Traynor of the California Supreme Court, blood is a "classic example" of an "unavoidably unsafe product" under comment k. Roger Traynor, *The Ways and Meanings of Defective Products and Strict Liability*, 32 Tenn. L. Rev. 363, 367 (1965). To see why, consider the problem posed by cases such as *Rogers* involving blood contaminated by a virus that was unknown at the time of sale. As in the case of contaminated food, the presence of such a virus in the blood is a contaminant that constitutes a manufacturing defect—it departs from the "design" or specification for the "pure" blood products the manufacturer intends to produce and the consumer expects to receive. As in a case of contaminated food, the seller can be subject to strict liability regardless of whether the contaminant

(virus) could have been discovered by the exercise of reasonable care. *See, e.g.,* Cunningham v. MacNeal Mem'l Hosp., 266 N.E.2d 897, 903 (Ill. 1970) ("[W]e believe that whether or not defendant can, even theoretically, ascertain the existence of serum hepatitis virus in whole blood employed by it for transfusion purposes is of absolutely no moment. Any other ruling would be entirely inconsistent with the concept of strict tort liability."), *overruled by statute,* 745 Ill. Comp. Stat. Ann. 4012, enacted in 1971; *see also* Jay M. Zitter, Annotation, *Liability of Blood Supplier for Injury or Death Resulting from Blood Transfusion,* 24 A.L.R. 4th 508, §2[a] (1983) ("[I]n several blood transfusion cases wherein injury or death resulted from blood which was contaminated with serum hepatitis, a theory was asserted that since the blood was impure and unfit for its intended uses, the blood bank in the sale of the blood had breached an implied warranty under a sales act or the Uniform Commercial Code, or should be held liable under strict liability in tort for the sale of an unreasonably dangerous product.").

The application of strict liability in these cases would result in blood suppliers facing extensive liability, with a resultant disruption in the supply of blood that could cause a substantial loss of social value. In one case,

> the experts for both sides all agreed that in December 1966 (when the blood was transfused) there was no known scientific or medical test for determining whether blood drawn from a donor contained serum hepatitis virus. Further, Dr. Robert Goodman, a pathologist and medical director of County Blood Bank, testified that as of that date the overall incidence of transfusion hepatitis was "about 1.3 in a hundred cases transfused" and that "the carrier rate, the people who remain with residual virus after infection, is five percent."

Brody v. Overlook Hosp., 317 A.2d 392, 395 (N.J. App. Div. 1974). Based on these facts, a blood supplier ordinarily would incur strict liability for hepatitis injuries for every one consumer out of 100, an amount that vastly exceeds the liabilities typically generated by manufacturing defects (such as the occasional bottle of soda that explodes).

The potential scope of strict liability for blood suppliers was then made even greater by the AIDS epidemic. The first AIDS diagnosis occurred in 1981, and so any tests or warnings regarding the virus were not feasible for all blood products sold prior to then. "By this time, however, a large number of hemophiliacs had become infected. The plaintiffs have presented evidence that 2,000 hemophiliacs have died of AIDS and that half or more of the remaining U.S. hemophiliac population of 20,000 may be HIV-positive." *In re* Rhone-Poulenc Rorer, Inc., 51 F.3d 1293, 1296 (7th Cir. 1995) (en banc). Liability for these injuries would "hurl the industry into bankruptcy." *Id.* at 1300.

2. *Blood shield statutes and the product/service distinction.* Due to the extensive liability that blood suppliers would face for any viral contamination of the blood supply that could not be reasonably detected at the time of sale, virtually all state legislatures have adopted *blood shield statutes* that exempt the sellers of blood products from strict liability. Rather than rely on the "unavoidably unsafe" exemption provided by comment k, the

legislation "in almost all jurisdictions" limits liability for these products to negligence, typically on the ground that human blood and tissues are not "products" or their provision is a "service" not governed by strict *products* liability. RESTATEMENT (THIRD) OF TORTS: PRODUCTS LIABILITY §19 cmt. c. This approach is adopted by the *Restatement (Third)* §19(c) ("Human blood and human tissue, even when provided commercially, are not subject to the rules of this Restatement.").

Does it make sense to provide an exemption to strict products liability by treating the sale of blood products as a service?

> So far as the transfusion itself is concerned, it has been regarded by most courts as a service, and not a sale, so that in the absence of negligence there is no liability of the hospital which gives it. But a blood bank which supplies the blood is certainly to be regarded as a seller [of a product]; and the general refusal [by courts] to hold it strictly liable has gone on the basis of the unavoidability of the danger.

William L. Prosser, LAW OF TORTS, §19 at 661-662 (4th ed. 1971). By relying on the product/service distinction to immunize blood products from strict products liability, does the rule adopted by the *Restatement (Third)* obscure the logic of comment k that is developed in *Rogers* and similar cases? Consider Belle Bonfils Mem'l Blood Bank v. Hansen, 665 P.2d 118, 124 (Colo. 1983) ("[L]ike contaminated blood, Pasteur vaccine [discussed in comment k] is impure, and its use may have adverse consequences which cannot be predicted or avoided.").

TRANSUE v. AESTHETECH CORP.
United States Court of Appeals, Ninth Circuit, 2003
341 F.3d 911

PREGERSON, J. Plaintiff-Appellant Lana Transue ("Transue") appeals the district court's decision not to give jury instructions on strict liability in her suit against Defendants-Appellees Bristol-Myers Squibb Company and Medical Engineering Corporation, Inc. alleging a defective breast implant. The district court instead gave instructions on negligence, and the jury found for appellee. We find the jury instructions to be reversible error.

In 1985, Transue received silicone-gel filled breast implants manufactured by Medical Engineering Corporation, Inc., a wholly owned subsidiary of Bristol-Myers Squibb Company (collectively, "BMS"). Transue alleges that the implants ruptured inside of her body, causing tissue death, scarring, pain, and permanent silicone contamination of her body. In 1995, Transue underwent explant surgery to remove the implants and replaced them with saline implants, which she currently uses. Transue alleges that her injuries are permanent and that she will have to undergo periodic implant and explant surgery for her lifetime.

Transue's claims arise under the Washington Product Liability Act, which consolidated the previously used common law theories of product liability.

Specifically, the surviving claims were the standard product liability claims, alleging manufacturing defects, design defects, and a failure to adequately warn, as well as a claim alleging that BMS breached express and implied warranties.

After a ten-day jury trial, the jury returned a verdict for the defendants on all of Transue's claims. Instructed on negligence, and not strict liability, the jury found that (1) BMS manufactured Transue's breast implants; (2) BMS did not fail to use ordinary care in designing the implants; (3) BMS did not fail to use ordinary care in manufacturing the implants; and (4) BMS did not fail to use ordinary care in issuing warnings or instructions.

Transue contends that the district court committed reversible error by failing to issue strict liability jury instructions, and instead issuing negligence jury instructions with regard to the manufacturing and design defect claims. BMS contends that comment k to the *Restatement (Second) of Torts* §402A governs manufacturing and design defect claims in this case, and exempts from strict liability medical devices, such as breast implants, that are available only through a prescribing physician.

Transue contends that the comment k exemption to strict liability "does *not* include claims of manufacturing defects for drugs, which are still governed by strict liability." Transue essentially argues that comment k does not apply to breast implant devices, and, even if it does, it does not provide blanket immunity from strict liability, but only exempts design defect claims. Transue states that the district court "did not give Plaintiff a chance to prove her manufacturing defect claim under the correct law," which is strict liability, and that the negligence instruction misdirected the jury.

Despite Transue's argument to the contrary, "[t]here is no debate that Washington courts have expressly adopted the comment k exception to strict liability in the case of unavoidably unsafe products." [ ]

Despite the conclusion above that comment k applies to breast implants, comment k should not be construed to provide protection for manufacturing defect claims based on unavoidably unsafe products. For the purposes of manufacturing defects, the relevant portion of comment k states: "Such a product, *properly prepared*, and accompanied by proper directions and warning, is not defective, nor is it unreasonably dangerous. . . . The seller of such products, again with the qualification that they are *properly prepared* and marketed, and proper warning is given, where the situation calls for it, is not to be held to strict liability" (emphasis added). At trial, Transue argued that the proper standard for a manufacturing defect, even under comment k, is strict liability. The district court, however, read the word "properly," italicized above, to indicate that a negligence standard is appropriate.

In commenting on the district court's conclusion, BMS states:

> The district court was right. The cases and comment k do say "properly prepared," and it is a negligence standard. To say a product was "properly prepared" is to say it was made with "proper care." As this Court has said, "proper care" is analogous to "due care" and "reasonable care under the circumstances"—that is, the standard for negligence.

BMS does not cite any authority for its crucial statement, "To say a product was 'properly prepared' is to say it was made with 'proper care.'"

II. Manufacturing Defects and Product Malfunctions

Indeed, a number of authorities from other jurisdictions persuasively indicate that such a jump is not warranted and that, in fact, comment k is not intended to apply a negligence standard to manufacturing defect claims in the context of unavoidably unsafe products. [ ]. As the Idaho Supreme Court wrote:

> By its terms, comment k excepts unavoidably unsafe products from strict liability only where the plaintiff alleges a design defect, and not where the plaintiff alleges a manufacturing flaw or an inadequate warning. Comment *k* intends to shield from strict liability products which cannot be designed more safely; however, if such products are mismanufactured or unaccompanied by adequate warnings, then the seller may be liable even if the plaintiff cannot establish the seller's negligence. Courts and commentators universally agree to this limitation on comment k's grant of immunity from strict liability.

Toner v. Lederle Labs., 732 P.2d 297 at 305 (Idaho 1987).

This understanding of comment k is further supported by commentary in the *Restatement (Third) of Torts: Product Liability*, discussing a section analogous to §402A of the *Restatement (Second) of Torts*. "Limitations on the liability for prescription drug and medical-device designs do not support treating drug and medical-device manufacturers differently from commercial sellers of other products with respect to manufacturing defects. Courts have traditionally subjected manufacturers of prescription products to liability for harm caused by manufacturing defects." RESTATEMENT (THIRD) OF TORTS: PRODUCTS LIABILITY §6 cmt. c.

BMS cites *Rogers v. Miles Laboratories, Inc.*, 802 P.2d 1346 (Wash. 1991) (en banc) in support of its argument that, under Washington law, comment k immunizes a manufacturer from strict liability on a manufacturing defect claim. However, a review of *Rogers* reveals that it was not a manufacturing defect case as there was apparently no allegation that the blood products at issue were improperly produced.

Therefore, the district court erred in denying Transue's request that a strict liability jury instruction be given with respect to her claim alleging a manufacturing defect. Based on the erroneous jury instructions given by the district court, the case is reversed and remanded.

NOTES AND QUESTIONS

1. *Confusion in the case law?* Cases like *Transue* provide strong support for the proposition that comment k is inapplicable to manufacturing defects, whereas the contaminated blood cases such as *Rogers* provide strong support for the contrary proposition. Both *Rogers* and *Transue* were decided under Washington law. What explains the different holdings?

According to the court in *Transue*, the holding in *Rogers* is distinguishable because it does not pertain to a manufacturing defect. If the contaminated blood in *Rogers* were not a manufacturing defect, then what type of defect could it possibly have been? A design defect? Compare RESTATEMENT (THIRD) OF TORTS: PRODUCTS LIABILITY §2 cmt. c ("[A] manufacturing defect is a departure from a product unit's design specifications."). Did the design specifications for blood include the virus?

Is there any other way to distinguish *Transue* from *Rogers*? Do breast implants implicate the same type of public safety issues as blood products or vaccines? In a portion of the opinion that was not excerpted above, the court in *Transue* concluded that "breast implants fall within the rationale . . . for providing comment k immunity for medical devices and products. The rationale emphasizes the presence of physicians as intermediaries between manufacturers and consumers" by relying on the physician's ability to make an informed risk-utility decision. 341 F.3d at 916. Is this a persuasive rationale for comment k?

2. *The problem of product malfunction.* The rule of strict products liability in §402A was promulgated by reference to performance-based defects or product malfunctions. For those products that have a primary purpose of promoting health or safety, the mere fact of injury could be sufficient for establishing a malfunction subject to strict liability. After all, if a product's primary purpose is to promote health and safety, hasn't it performed in a self-defeating manner by causing injury? Consider RESTATEMENT (THIRD) OF TORTS: PRODUCTS LIABILITY §3 cmt. b (defining product malfunctions as "situations in which a product fails to perform its manifestly intended function"). For example, the Sabin oral polio vaccine uses an attenuated or weakened form of the viral agent to immunize the recipient, which in turn can cause vaccine-associated paralytic polio in either recipients or close contacts. In these cases, the design or formulation of the vaccine causes it to perform in a self-defeating manner, the paradigmatic example of a product malfunction that subjects the product seller to strict liability. *E.g.,* Grinnell v. Charles Pfizer & Co., 79 Cal. Rptr. 369, 373 (Ct. App. 1969) ("[I]t is clearly the law in California that the theory of strict liability in tort is available in cases where the vaccinated individual contracts the disease the vaccine was designed to protect against."); *see also, e.g.,* Allison v. Merck and Co., 878 P.2d 948, 952 (Nev. 1994) (holding that a measles, mumps, and rubella vaccine "malfunctioned" and was subject to strict liability because an unavoidable side effect allegedly caused plaintiffs' son to suffer blindness, deafness, and mental retardation). The rule of strict liability could subject vaccine sellers to strict liability for unavoidable side effects, making it understandable why the industry claimed that it was particularly vulnerable to tort liability and required protection under the federal Vaccine Act discussed in section I, *supra.*

3. *Rethinking comment k.* Cases involving vaccines and contaminated blood most clearly reveal the policy reasons why comment k immunizes manufacturers from strict liability for malfunctions or manufacturing defects. Both types of products, however, are no longer governed by strict products liability due to legislative interventions. Consequently, the judicial development of comment k has largely occurred outside of contexts in which the rationale for the immunity is clear.

By its own terms, comment k can apply to products that malfunction because of a manufacturing defect. According to comment k, an "outstanding example" of an "unavoidably unsafe" product is the Pasteur rabies vaccine. The first version of this vaccine "in some cases led to recipients possibly developing rabies from the vaccination." D.J. Hicks et al., *Developments in Rabies Vaccine,* 169 Clinical & Experimental Immunology

II. Manufacturing Defects and Product Malfunctions

199, 200 (2012). When a vaccine with the intended purpose of preventing rabies actually caused rabies, it performed in a self-defeating manner—a malfunction subject to strict liability. By expressly invoking the Pasteur rabies vaccine, comment k clearly recognizes that strict liability for such a malfunction can create a policy problem that justifies an immunity from such liability.

This particular side effect was eliminated by a reformulation of the rabies vaccine that would still subject the manufacturer to strict liability for a different reason. According to the court in *Miles*, even when the reformulated vaccine had been "properly prepared," it could still be contaminated with brain tissue, creating dangerous side effects for the user. 802 P.2d at 1350-1351. This attribute of the rabies vaccine is accounted for by comment k when it recognizes that "unavoidably unsafe" products may have "no assurance . . . of purity of ingredients," because these "products . . . in the present state of human knowledge, are quite incapable of being made safe for their intended and ordinary use." Impurities, like those in contaminated food, are a common form of manufacturing defects subject to strict liability. Under comment k, however, the seller of a "properly prepared" rabies vaccine accompanied by a "proper warning" is not subject to strict liability for the injuries caused by impurities that cannot be eliminated from the vaccine.

The requirement that the rabies vaccine be "properly prepared," therefore, only means that the seller must have produced the vaccine with state-of-the-art processes. Any manufacturing defects that cannot be eliminated by such processes are not subject to strict liability. The vaccine treats a disease that "invariably leads to a dreadful death," so the seller should not incur liability for supplying "the public with an apparently useful and desirable product, attended with a known but apparently reasonable risk." As illustrated by the rabies vaccine, a "properly prepared" product for purposes of comment k can contain manufacturing defects that cannot be eliminated by state-of-the-art production or quality-control processes.

Under this interpretation, comment k hews to the safety rationale for strict products liability. If strict liability would unduly increase price or decrease the availability of a safety-enhancing drug or medical device, then comment k immunizes the seller from strict liability. Comment k does not bar negligence liability, which necessarily targets excessively dangerous products to promote the safety objective. Similarly, comment k does not bar application of strict liability when the medical product was not "properly prepared" because it was adulterated or contaminated with substances that could have been detected by state-of-the-art quality-control measures at the time of sale. But when a medical product is "unavoidably unsafe," strict liability would not improve safety; instead, it could create the unsafe outcome in which liability reduces the supply and use of the drug or vaccine within society.

4. *Another reprise of the rationale for strict products liability*. Regardless of how one interprets comment k, the issue provides another context in which courts have recognized that the primary purpose of strict products liability is to promote product safety. *E.g.*, Miles Labs v. Doe, 556 A.2d 1107, 1121 (Md. Ct. App. 1989) ("[T]he fundamental purpose underlying the theory

of strict tort liability is to force hazardous products from the market. That rationale plainly has no application to blood or blood products where the manufacturer had no way of knowing that its products—so essential to the life and health of the people—were contaminated by an indetectable virus."); Belle Bonfils Mem'l Blood Bank v. Hansen, 665 P.2d 118, 124 (Colo. 1983) (en banc) ("[T]he *raison d'etre* of strict liability is to force some hazardous products out of the market. The same rationale does not apply to blood or vaccines which are life-saving and which have no known substitutes.").

III. AUTONOMOUS VEHICLES AND PRODUCTS LIABILITY: PROBLEM SET 6

AV Problem 6.1

"While comment k could be read to apply to other products, it does not really give us any examples or suggest other areas where the policy balancing is precisely the same. For this reason, the courts and most commentators have assumed that comment *k* relates to pharmaceuticals." Victor E. Schwartz, *Unavoidably Unsafe Products: Clarifying the Meaning and Policy Behind Comment k*, 42 Wash. & Lee L. Rev. 1139, 1141 (1985). In particular,

> Motor vehicles and motor vehicle parts have generally been held not to be unavoidably unsafe products. Thus, the contention that a golf cart was an unavoidably unsafe product was rejected by one court, since, in the court's opinion, golf carts were not incapable of being made safe for their intended use. Likewise, courts have held or recognized that motorcycles were not unavoidably unsafe products. Additionally, where the record indicated that a truck was defective with respect to its airbrakes, such brakes were held not to constitute an unavoidably dangerous product.

Joanne Rhoton Galbreath, *Products Liability: What Is an "Unavoidably Unsafe" Product*, 70 A.L.R.4th 16, at §5 (1989 & Supp. 2021).

Because of this case law, the manufacturer of an autonomous vehicle comes to you seeking advice. Based on the manufacturer's projections, which are consistent with other industry estimates, the technology of automated driving could reduce crash frequency per vehicle by 80 percent. However, an autonomous vehicle would malfunction if it were operated by an unauthorized third party who "hacked" into the operating system and gained control of the vehicle. By definition, a manufacturer does not intend for the vehicle to be operated in this manner, and consumers actually expect that one of the ordinary functions of an autonomous vehicle is that its operating system—and not an unauthorized third party—fully executes the dynamic driving task. Regardless of how a malfunction is exactly specified, it applies to an autonomous vehicle being operated by an unauthorized third party, potentially subjecting the manufacturer to strict liability for any injuries caused by such a malfunction.

III. Autonomous Vehicles and Products Liability: Problem Set 6

These liabilities could be extensive. The hacker could subject the owner to a "ransom" demand to make the vehicle fully operational once again. "It is also feasible that driving could be maliciously interfered with, causing a physical danger to passengers. There is potential for cyber terrorism, too—for example, a large-scale immobilisation of cars on public roads could throw a country into chaos." Gillian Yeomans, Lloyd's, *Autonomous Vehicles: Handing Over Control: Opportunities and Risks for Insurance* 16 (2014), https://perma.cc/7SV2-PVZT.

The problem is difficult to solve. The varied "computers, sensors, and other components" required for autonomous driving "will expand the possible entry points for attackers and the things they can do—for example, self-driving cars rely on laser scanners and other sensors, which could be made to send false data." Tom Simonite, *Your Future Self-Driving Car Will Be Way More Hackable*, MIT Tech. Rev. (Jan. 26, 2016), https://perma.cc/9FEW-8JV6. Like the arcade game Whac-A-Mole, each time the manufacturer patches the operating system to protect against vulnerabilities hackers have previously exploited, the range of other attack points could enable hackers to pop up somewhere else by exploiting a different vulnerability.

The difficult question in this context is not whether a manufacturer has a duty to protect its motor vehicles against illegal cyberattacks like hacking, but rather the substantive content of that duty. What are the manufacturer's obligations with respect to crashes caused by cyberattacks? In particular, the manufacturer would like your advice whether comment k can be plausibly interpreted to provide an immunity from strict liability for malfunctions caused by hacking for cases in which the manufacturer exercised reasonable care in adopting cyber security measures for addressing that threat.

Analysis of AV Problem 6.1

Comment k expressly states that "unavoidably unsafe" products "are especially common in the field of drugs"; it does not otherwise limit the doctrine to only those products. Although prior case law has uniformly rejected the application of comment k to motor vehicles, autonomous vehicles have different properties. Moreover, the policy balancing that justifies the immunity in comment k is not necessarily limited to drugs and vaccines. The immunity is based on the policy conclusion that strict liability could disrupt the supply of drugs and vaccines, thereby limiting the potential for these products to promote public health and safety. Like drugs and vaccines, autonomous vehicles are safety-enhancing products; they will reduce crashes relative to conventional motor vehicles by up to 80 percent. Like drugs and vaccines, autonomous vehicles could face extensive liabilities caused by systemically occurring malfunction; the contamination of the blood supply with reasonably undetectable viruses could be analogous to widespread injuries caused by malicious hacking of the vehicle. The extent of liability has the potential for disrupting the market, either through substantial price increases or product delays and withdrawals, in which case strict liability could actually *increase* risk by reducing the availability of this life-saving technology. For these reasons, courts could conclude that autonomous vehicles—like blood and pharmaceutical products—are "unavoidably unsafe" products with respect to the risk of hacking. In that event, manufacturers would be subject not to strict liability, but to ordinary negligence liability for these malfunctions.

This conclusion, though, depends on questions that cannot be fully answered right now. The immunity under comment k requires that the product be "properly prepared" and accompanied by a "proper warning," so manufacturers remain strictly liable for lapses of quality control like an inadequately sterile environment that contaminates a blood product. To fall under the comment k exemption, the defect must instead threaten the entire product line with a substantial, correlated (systemic) risk that cannot be sufficiently reduced by the exercise of reasonable care. For example, HIV was undetectable when it first contaminated the blood supply, creating a systemic risk that could not be eliminated by reasonably safe methods of quality control. Is the risk of hacking analogous to the risk posed by new blood-borne diseases? Would strict liability for hacking result in extensive, largely unavoidable liabilities like those faced by the manufacturers of blood products contaminated with undetectable viruses? Or is hacking instead analogous to an ordinary lapse of quality control like inadequately sterile environments, involving a risk that can be sufficiently reduced by the exercise of reasonable care?

The disruptive effect of strict liability further depends on the extent to which manufacturers will be able to purchase insurance covering liabilities for hacked vehicles, as illustrated by the rule that limits the duty to warn to foreseeable risks. The availability of insurance for terrorism-related cyberattacks could be particularly problematic due to the difficulty that insurers might face in trying to predict the full scope of liability. What if terrorists hack into the vehicle and cause widespread crashes? If manufacturers cannot procure liability insurance or if their liability exposure is sufficiently systemic such that it would otherwise unduly threaten bankruptcy, then there is a strong case for immunizing this type of malfunction from strict products liability.

10

Products Liability in the "Age of Statutes"

Tort law has been increasingly shaped by legislatively enacted statutes and the administrative regulations promulgated thereunder.

> We live in the "Age of Statutes." Even the venerable common law area of torts is not immune from the pervasive influence of statutes. For example, in Oregon, statutes control civil liability areas including wrongful death, caps on damages, comparative negligence, products liability, informed consent, and landlord/tenant issues. . . . Such statutes may create, modify, or prohibit tort actions, or be the basis for courts providing or changing common law tort actions. Statutes may relate to one or more of the elements that are required for tort liability: a duty to act in a particular way, a standard of conduct (intent, recklessness, negligence, or liability without fault) that determines whether the duty is violated, the nature of the interest that must be invaded (physical injury, economic harm, etc.), causation, and the kind of remedy provided (compensatory damages, punitive damages, injunctive relief, etc.).

Caroline Forell, *Statutory Torts, Statutory Duty Actions, and Negligence Per Se: What's the Difference?*, 77 Or. L. Rev. 497, 497-498 (1998) (quoting Guido Calabresi, A COMMON LAW FOR THE AGE OF STATUTES (1982)).

A statute can create a cause of action or legal basis of recovery under a given set of facts. Some state statutes, for example, have codified rules of products liability. *E.g.*, Ind. Code §§34-6-2-29 to 34-20-9-1 (2020) (specifying the rules governing all actions brought by a user or consumer against a manufacturer or seller for physical harm caused by a product). Even if a statute does not expressly provide for civil liability, it can still create an implied cause of action under certain conditions. *See* RESTATEMENT (THIRD) OF TORTS: LIABILITY FOR PHYSICAL AND EMOTIONAL HARM §14 cmt. b (2010). For either type of statute, the cause of action as alleged in the plaintiff's complaint is based directly on the statute and not the common law of torts.

Regardless of whether a statute creates its own cause of action, it can preempt a tort claim. A statute, for example, can prohibit any tort claims that seek to impose safety requirements that are different from, or additional to, those required by the statute. Due to the supremacy of legislative law over the common law of torts, such a statute (or any regulations promulgated thereunder) wholly defines the legally mandated safety features for the product in question.

A statute does not need to preempt state tort law to be relevant for resolving a tort dispute. Proof that a product violates a statutory safety standard can establish defect, whereas proof that a product complies with such a standard can provide a partial or complete defense for the product seller under the regulatory compliance defense.

I. STATUTORY VIOLATIONS AS PROOF OF DEFECT

HARNED v. DURA CORP.
Supreme Court of Alaska, 1983
665 P.2d 5

RABINOWITZ, J. Charles Harned (Harned) filed suit against Dura Corporation (Dura) seeking compensation for injuries he sustained when a portable compressed air tank allegedly manufactured by Dura's predecessor in interest, Electronics, Inc., exploded and severed his left arm. The jury unanimously entered a defense verdict, and Harned appealed.

On July 25, 1977, Harned was working as a general mechanic at A & M Motors, a Winnebago dealership. As he filled a portable air tank from a compressor, the tank exploded and a piece of it severed his left arm at the elbow. Harned sued Dura, corporate successor to the manufacturer of the tank, alleging that the explosion was caused by the defective design and manufacture of the tank. He asserted that the tank should have contained a valve at the bottom which could be opened to drain moisture accumulating inside. Since it did not, water remained inside, causing the tank to corrode and finally explode when the weakened walls were unable to withstand the pressure of the compressed air.

Dura conceded at trial that the tank which exploded and injured Harned did not comply with applicable design and construction standards set out in the American Society of Mechanical Engineers (ASME) Code. The Code had been incorporated by reference into Alaska law at the time the tank was manufactured.

Harned requested a jury instruction stating that a violation of the ASME standard constituted negligence per se. The superior court rejected this instruction, advising the jury that noncompliance by Dura should be deemed "mere evidence" of negligence. In this appeal Harned argues that the jury should have been instructed that a violation of the ASME Code by Dura constituted negligence per se.

In assessing the merits of Harned's contention that the superior court erred in refusing to instruct the jury that a violation of the ASME Code would constitute negligence per se, we have applied the analytical scheme set out in State Mechanical, Inc. v. Liquid Air, Inc, 665 P.2d 15 at 18-19 (Alaska 1983). As we observed in *State Mechanical*, the superior court should conduct a two-step inquiry in determining whether a negligence per se instruction is appropriate. First, it must decide whether the conduct at issue lies within the ambit of the statute or regulation in question, by applying the four criteria set out in

I. Statutory Violations as Proof of Defect

the *Restatement (Second) of Torts* §286 (1971).[22] This threshold determination is strictly a legal conclusion, and we will exercise our independent judgment in deciding whether the superior court interpreted the scope of the statute or regulation correctly.

Once it has concluded that the enactment applies to the allegedly negligent conduct, the superior court may exercise its discretion to refuse to give the negligence per se instruction. Such discretion is extremely limited, being confined to those "highly unusual cases" in which "laws may be so obscure, oblique or irrational that they could not be said as a matter of law" to provide an adequate standard of due care, or to those where the enactment amounts to little more than a duplication of the common law tort duty to act reasonably under the circumstances. [ ]

Applying this analysis to the case at bar, we conclude that the trial court erred in declining to instruct the jury that Dura's failure to manufacture the tank in accordance with ASME standards constituted negligence per se. Our threshold determination that the ASME code governed Dura's conduct in manufacturing the tank which exploded and injured Harned, was based on an independent analysis under §286 of the *Restatement (Second) of Torts* of the scope of pertinent statutory and regulatory provisions. Dura concedes on appeal that Alaska law should be applied to determine the applicable standard of care, and does not contest the fact that the ASME Code was incorporated by reference into Alaska law at the time the tank was manufactured. However, Dura claims that the legislature did not intend to regulate the manufacture of pressure vessels under [the relevant state statutory provision] and that Harned was not within the class of persons protected by those provisions. We have recast and considered these contentions within the analytical framework delineated by the Restatement.

Dura's principal argument is that the "hazard" which the legislature intended to prevent by enacting these provisions was the installation and utilization—not the manufacture—of unfired pressure vessels which did not comply with the ASME Code. Thus, Dura concludes, a negligence per se instruction would have been inappropriate under §286(d) of the Restatement. In support of this contention, Dura cites numerous provisions within [the statute] which specifically regulate only the installation and operation of boilers and unfired pressure vessels.

We find this argument without merit. The introductory provision [of the statute], which expressly enables regulatory authorities to adopt the "Boiler Construction Code," specifically commands them to formulate "rules and regulations for the safe and proper construction of unfired pressure vessels."

---

22. Section 286 of the *Restatement (Second) of Torts* (1971) provides:

The court may adopt as the standard of conduct of a reasonable man the requirements of a legislative enactment or an administrative regulation whose purpose is found to be exclusively or in part

    (a) to protect a class of persons which includes the one whose interest is invaded, and

    (b) to protect the particular interest which is invaded, and

    (c) to protect that interest against the type of harm which has resulted, and

    (d) to protect that interest against the particular hazard from which the harm results.

We adopted these principles in [a prior case].

The Code itself was clearly promulgated to establish nationwide construction standards. Dura's contention that the utilization, but not the manufacture, of unfired pressure vessels is subject to [the state statute] is patently illogical. How can the manufacture of unsafe vessels be permissible if their utilization is not? Thus, we conclude that the manufacture of vessels whose design does not conform to standards set out in the ASME Code is the type of "hazard," for purposes of §286(d), which the legislature intended to curtail by enacting [the statute].

Dura's second argument against the propriety of a negligence per se instruction rests upon §286(a). Dura contends that the tank which injured Harned fell within the exemption set forth in [the statutory scheme] for "unfired pressure vessels having a volume of five cubic feet or less when not located in places of public assembly" and that Harned was not within the "class" of persons protected by the statute since he was not working in a "place of public assembly" at the time the explosion occurred. It is uncontroverted that the tank which exploded and injured Harned had a capacity of somewhat under 1.18 cubic feet. However, considerable dispute exists regarding the question of whether or not the A & M Motors repair shop was a "place of public assembly" for purposes of [the statute].

We do not find it necessary to reach this issue since we conclude that manufacturers should not be permitted to rely upon [this statutory provision]. Manufacturers have a duty under [the statute] to construct pressure vessels in accordance with ASME standards. As a rule, they have no control over where the tanks they produce will be utilized. From Dura's standpoint, it was a fortuity that this vessel arguably fell within the scope of [the statutory exemption regarding a "place of public assembly.]" Dura's duty to comply with ASME construction standards arose during the manufacture of the tank in question; it should not be diminished retrospectively because it happened to be utilized at A & M Motors. Thus, Dura did have a duty to Harned under §286(a) to manufacture the tank in accordance with the ASME Code, regardless of where he was at the time the explosion occurred.

Therefore, we conclude as a matter of law that under [the statute] Dura was impressed with a duty to manufacture the tank in question in accordance with ASME standards. Furthermore, we find it unnecessary to permit the superior court on remand to use its discretion to decide whether the ASME Code was too obscure, vague or arcane to serve as an appropriate standard of care. As it is both extremely precise and nationally recognized we conclude, as a matter of law, that it should be adopted as the relevant standard of care on retrial.

REVERSED and REMANDED for a new trial.

NOTES AND QUESTIONS

1. *Negligence per se and strict products liability.* In addition to establishing negligence per se, the violation of a safety statute or regulation can establish a defect per se. *See* RESTATEMENT (THIRD) OF TORTS: PRODUCTS LIABILITY §4(a) ("[A] product's noncompliance with an applicable product safety statute or administrative regulation renders the product defective with respect to the risks sought to be reduced by the statute or regulation."). This rule can be quite important for determining design or warning defects, but rarely has relevance for manufacturing defects. Can you explain why?

I. Statutory Violations as Proof of Defect

2. *Legal effect of a statutory or regulatory violation.* In ordinary tort cases, a statutory or regulatory violation does not conclusively prove negligence because the defendant can avoid liability by establishing that the violation was excused.

> Unless the enactment or regulation is construed not to permit such excuse, its violation is excused when
>
> (a) the violation is reasonable because of the actor's incapacity;
> (b) he neither knows or should know of the occasion for compliance;
> (c) he is unable after reasonable diligence or care to comply;
> (d) he is confronted with an emergency not due to his own misconduct;
> (e) compliance would involve a greater risk of harm to the actor or to others.

RESTATEMENT (SECOND) OF TORTS §288A(2).

Are there any excuses of relevance in product cases? *See* RESTATEMENT (THIRD) OF TORTS: PRODUCTS LIABILITY §4 cmt. d ("In connection with the adequacy of product designs and warnings, . . . design and marketing decisions are made before distribution to users and consumers. The product seller therefore has the option of deferring sale until statutory or regulatory compliance is achieved. Consequently, justification or excuse of the sort anticipated in connection with negligence claims generally does not apply in connection with failure to comply with statutes or regulations governing product design or warnings.").

3. *Rationale for the liability rule.* In cases like *Harned*, the statute does not give the plaintiff an express or implied right to compensatory damages for the injuries caused by the violation. But as *Harned* illustrates, courts will permit the plaintiff to rely on the statutory violation to establish tort liability. The judicial decision to do so is fully discretionary as made clear by the California Supreme Court in a leading case:

> The significance of the statute in a civil suit for negligence lies in its formulation of a standard of conduct that the court adopts in the determination of such liability. The decision as to what the civil standard should be still rests with the court, and the standard formulated by a legislative body in a police regulation or criminal statute becomes the standard to determine civil liability only because the court accepts it.

Clinkscales v. Carver, 136 P.2d 777, 778 (Cal. 1943) (citations omitted).

Courts "accept" or defer to these legislative safety standards for compelling reasons. Most obviously, "it would be awkward for a court in a tort case to commend as reasonable that behavior that the legislature has already condemned as unlawful." Moreover, "when the legislature has addressed the issue of what conduct is appropriate, the judgment of the legislature, as the authoritative representative of the community, takes precedence over the views of any one jury." RESTATEMENT (THIRD) OF TORTS: LIABILITY FOR PHYSICAL & EMOTIONAL HARM §14 cmt. c.

4. *Risks regulated by the statute.* According to the black-letter rule, a plaintiff seeking recovery for the defendant's violation of a safety statute must (1) be in the class of persons the statute was intended to protect, and

(2) have been injured by a type of risk the statute was intended to prevent. In permitting recovery for an injury that did not occur in a place of "public assembly," *Harned* departed from this rule. Adherence to the rule would have obligated the court to ignore the statutory violation. Would that make sense? Why should the determination of defect be limited to only those risks that the statute contemplates? Does the statute itself require this outcome?

> So far as there is now any recognized theory at all, it is that the statute itself has no tort law effects. Rather, (unless the statute itself provides otherwise) the courts are free to create tort law rules and to adopt and import rules from statutes about other matters if they wish to do so.

Dan B. Dobbs, Paul T. Hayden & Ellen M. Bublick, THE LAW OF TORTS §150 (2d ed. 2020 update).

The doctrines of negligence per se and defect per se are each based on the policy decision that courts ought to defer to legislative safety decisions as a matter of institutional comity. Courts can do so without being bound by statutory purpose. Instead, they can "import" the safety decision from the statute and use it in whatever manner is necessary for resolution of the tort claim.

To see why courts can defer to a legislative safety determination without being bound by statutory purpose, consider the common-law duty of design governing the product at issue in *Harned*. The common-law duty encompasses the foreseeable risks of physical harms. The statute addresses the risk of physical harm to those in a "place of public assembly" (to be denoted $PL_{public\ assembly}$). The statute requires that the product design must conform to the ASME code to eliminate these risks (to be denoted B_{ASME}). Deference to this legislative safety determination yields the following risk-utility conclusion:

$$B_{ASME} < PL_{public\ assembly}$$

The common-law duty, however, is not limited to the risks contemplated by the statute. It also includes anyone else who was foreseeably threatened by the product (to be denoted $PL_{other\ foreseeable\ victims}$). The statutory violation with respect to a smaller set of risks contemplated by the legislature implies a violation of a broader common-law duty encompassing a larger set of risks:

$$B_{ASME} < PL_{public\ assembly} + PL_{other\ foreseeable\ victims}$$

As the court in *Harned* explained, the "[defendant's] duty to comply with ASME construction standards arose during the manufacture of the tank in question; it should not be diminished retrospectively because it happened to be utilized at A & M Motors." At the time of manufacture, the common-law duty encompassed all foreseeable victims, not merely those in places of public assembly. This duty, therefore, was not "diminished retrospectively" because the product was used in a private workplace. *Harned* illustrates how "courts might adopt a statutory rule and give it any scope appropriate under the common law, even if the legislature had a much more limited scope in mind." Dobbs et al., THE LAW OF TORTS, *supra*.

As illustrated by this case, one must be careful when applying a black-letter rule. The black-letter rule of negligence per se identifies the conditions under which an unexcused statutory violation necessarily establishes the prima facie case of liability. The black-letter rule, however, implicitly assumes that the scope of the defendant's duty is defined entirely by the statute, an assumption that is not valid for cases in which the statute operates within a more expansive, previously established common-law duty (like the duty of design in *Harned*). Recognizing this limitation of the black-letter rule makes it possible to explain why a case like *Harned* can conclude that a statutory violation constitutes negligence per se, even though the black-letter rule is not fully satisfied. When properly formulated, black-letter rules work well for the vast majority of cases, but to properly apply these rules across the full spectrum of cases, one must have a clear understanding of the principles from which these rules are derived.

II. THE REGULATORY COMPLIANCE DEFENSE

"Compliance with a legislative enactment or an administrative regulation does not prevent a finding of negligence where a reasonable man would take additional precautions." RESTATEMENT (SECOND) OF TORTS §288C. This established tort principle applies to products liability claims:

> A product's compliance with an applicable product safety statute or administrative regulation is properly considered in determining whether the product is defective with respect to the risks sought to be reduced by the statute or regulation, but such compliance does not preclude as a matter of law a finding of product defect.

RESTATEMENT (THIRD) OF TORTS: PRODUCTS LIABILITY §4(b).

Regulatory compliance does not ordinarily preclude liability due to the "traditional view that the standards set by most product safety statutes or regulations generally are only minimum standards." *Id.* cmt. e. When a statute or regulation merely sets a floor or minimum safety requirement, a design or warning that violates the regulation is presumptively defective (as per the doctrine of negligence per se), whereas a design or warning that satisfies the regulation may still be defective when evaluated by the more demanding tort standard. *Id.* ("Thus, most product safety statutes or regulations establish a floor of safety below which product sellers fall only at their peril, but they leave open the question of whether a higher standard of product safety should be applied.").

Critics contend that regulatory compliance should conclusively establish that the product is not defective in this respect:

> Once [a safety] determination has been made by an expert licensing agency, the courts should respect it. Regulatory agencies are equipped to make the

risk comparisons on which all progressive transformation of the risk environment must be based. The courts are simply not qualified to second-guess such decisions; when they choose to do so they routinely make regressive risk choices. Requiring—or at least strongly encouraging—the courts to respect the comparative risk choices made by competent, expert agencies would inject a first, small measure of rationality into a judicial regulatory system that currently runs quite wild.

Peter Huber, *Safety and the Second Best: The Hazards of Public Risk Management in the Courts*, 85 Colum. L. Rev. 277, 334-335 (1985); *see also* Richard C. Ausness et al., *Providing a Safe Harbor for Those Who Play by the Rules: The Case for a "Strong" Regulatory Compliance Defense*, 2008 Utah L. Rev. 115, 132 (2008) (providing a range of reasons for making regulatory compliance a complete defense).

This critique assumes that the regulatory compliance defense is not adequately deferential to legislative safety determinations. In limited circumstances, however, regulatory compliance renders the product nondefective as a matter of law. The question, then, is whether this formulation of the regulatory compliance defense adequately defers to "the comparative risk choices made by competent, expert agencies."

RAMIREZ v. PLOUGH, INC.
Supreme Court of California, 1993
863 P.2d 167

KENNARD, J. We granted review in this case to determine whether a manufacturer of nonprescription drugs may incur tort liability for distributing its products with warnings in English only. Recognizing the importance of uniformity and predictability in this sensitive area of the law, we conclude that the rule for tort liability should conform to state and federal statutory and administrative law. Because both state and federal law now require warnings in English but not in any other language, we further conclude that a manufacturer may not be held liable in tort for failing to label a nonprescription drug with warnings in a language other than English.

Plaintiff Jorge Ramirez, a minor, sued defendant Plough, Inc., alleging that he contracted Reye's syndrome as a result of ingesting a nonprescription drug, St. Joseph Aspirin for Children (SJAC), that was manufactured and distributed by defendant. Plaintiff sought compensatory and punitive damages on theories of negligence, products liability, and fraud. The trial court granted summary judgment for defendant. On plaintiff's appeal, the Court of Appeal reversed.

In March 1986, when he was less than four months old, plaintiff exhibited symptoms of a cold or similar upper respiratory infection. To relieve these symptoms, plaintiff's mother gave him SJAC. Plaintiff thereafter developed Reye's syndrome, resulting in severe neurological damage, including cortical blindness, spastic quadriplegia, and mental retardation.

The cause of Reye's syndrome was unknown in 1986 (and apparently remains unknown), but by the early 1980's several studies had shown an association between ingestion of aspirin during a viral illness, such as chicken pox or influenza, and the subsequent development of Reye's syndrome. These studies

II. The Regulatory Compliance Defense

prompted the United States Food and Drug Administration (FDA) to propose a labeling requirement for aspirin products warning of the dangers of Reye's syndrome. The FDA published a regulation to this effect on March 7, 1986. In 1988, the FDA revised the required warning to state explicitly that Reye's syndrome is reported to be associated with aspirin use, and it made the regulation permanent.

Even before the federal regulation became mandatory, packages of SJAC displayed this warning: "Warning: Reye Syndrome is a rare but serious disease which can follow flu or chicken pox in children and teenagers. While the cause of Reye Syndrome is unknown, some reports claim aspirin may increase the risk of developing this disease. Consult doctor before use in children or teenagers with flu or chicken pox." The package insert contained the same warning, together with this statement: "The symptoms of Reye syndrome can include persistent vomiting, sleepiness and lethargy, violent headaches, unusual behavior, including disorientation, combativeness, and delirium. If any of these symptoms occur, especially following chicken pox or flu, call your doctor immediately, even if your child has not taken any medication. REYE SYNDROME IS SERIOUS, SO EARLY DETECTION AND TREATMENT ARE VITAL."

These warnings were printed in English on the label of the SJAC that plaintiff's mother purchased in March 1986. At that time, plaintiff's mother, who was born in Mexico, was literate only in Spanish. Because she could not read English, she was unable to read the warnings on the SJAC label and package insert. Yet she did not ask anyone to translate the label or package insert into Spanish, even though other members of her household could have done so.

Plaintiff, by and through his mother as guardian ad litem, filed suit against defendant in August 1989, alleging causes of action for fraud, negligence, and product liability, all premised on the theory of failure to warn about the dangers of Reye's syndrome.

Defendant moved for summary judgment, submitting uncontradicted evidence of the facts as stated above. The court granted summary judgment. In its order granting the motion, the court stated that there was "no duty to warn in a foreign language" and no causal relationship between plaintiff's injury and defendant's activities. Plaintiff appealed from the judgment for defendant.

The Court of Appeal reversed. Given the evidence of defendant's knowledge that SJAC was being used by non-English-literate Hispanics, and the lack of evidence as to the costs of Spanish language labeling, the reasonableness of defendant's conduct in not labeling SJAC with a Spanish language warning was, the court concluded, a triable issue of fact.[3]

The issue presented, then, is not the existence of a duty to warn as such, or the class of persons to whom the duty extends, but the nature and scope of the acknowledged duty. Specifically, the issue is whether defendant's duty to warn required it to provide label or package warnings in Spanish. Issues such as this,

---

3. In its opinion, the Court of Appeal cited and relied upon cases involving the labeling of pesticides and solvents and cases imposing requirements on employers to communicate warnings effectively to non-English-speaking employees. We here consider neither the question of foreign-language warnings (or the use of symbols or pictorial warnings) for products other than nonprescription drugs, nor the scope of an employer's duty to warn non-English-speaking employees of workplace hazards.

which concern the scope of an established duty, are resolved by reference to the governing standard of care.

The formulation of the standard of care is a question of law for the court. Once the court has formulated the standard, its application to the facts of the case is a task for the trier of fact if reasonable minds might differ as to whether the defendant's conduct has conformed to the standard.

In most cases, courts have fixed no standard of care for tort liability more precise than that of a reasonably prudent person under like circumstances. "But the proper conduct of a reasonable person under particular situations may become settled by judicial decision or be prescribed by statute or ordinance." [ ]

Justice Traynor explained the rationale for using a statute to define the standard of care in the following way:

> The significance of a statute in a civil suit for negligence lies in its formulation of a standard of conduct that the court adopts in the determination of such liability. The decision as to what the civil standard should be still rests with the court, and the standard formulated by a legislative body in a police regulation or criminal statute becomes the standard to determine civil liability only because the court accepts it.

Clinkscales v. Carver, 136 P.2d 777 (Cal. 1943).

Less common is the use of a statutory standard of conduct by a defendant to establish that no breach of duty occurred. Courts have generally not looked with favor upon the use of statutory compliance as a defense to tort liability. But there is some room in tort law for a defense of statutory compliance. Where the evidence shows no unusual circumstances, but only the ordinary situation contemplated by the statute or administrative rule, then "the minimum standard prescribed by the legislation or regulation may be accepted by the triers of fact, or by the court as a matter of law, as sufficient for the occasion. . . ." RESTATEMENT (SECOND) OF TORTS §288C cmt. a, p. 40.

Here, defendant manufacturer argues, in substance, that the standard of care for packaging and labeling nonprescription drugs, and in particular the necessity or propriety of foreign-language label and package warnings, has been appropriately fixed by the dense layer of state and federal statutes and regulations that control virtually all aspects of the marketing of its products. To evaluate this argument, we proceed to review the applicable statutes and regulations.

The federal government regulates the labeling of nonprescription drugs through section 502 of the Food, Drug, and Cosmetic Act. The FDA has adopted detailed regulations to implement this federal statute. [ ] The FDA regulations specify both the subject matter of required warnings and the actual words to be used. Aspirin products must also carry a warning to keep the product out of the reach of children and a warning about Reye's syndrome. Thus, the FDA comprehensively regulates the cautionary labeling of aspirin and other nonprescription medications.

The FDA has stated that it "encourages the preparation of labeling to meet the needs of non-English speaking or special user populations so long as such labeling fully complies with agency regulations." [ ] But the controlling regulation requires only that manufacturers provide full English labeling for all nonprescription drugs except those "distributed solely in the Commonwealth

II. The Regulatory Compliance Defense 403

of Puerto Rico or in a Territory where the predominant language is one other than English. . . ." The regulation further states that if the label or packaging of any drug distributed in the 50 states contains "any representation in a foreign language," then all required "words, statements, and other information" must appear in the foreign language as well as in English. Finally, the regulation states that "use of label space for any representation in a foreign language" is not a basis to exempt a manufacturer from the general obligation to make required language prominent and conspicuous. [ ]

California law parallels and reinforces federal law on the points discussed here. The Health and Safety Code mandates conspicuous English language warnings in section 25900, which provides: "Cautionary statements which are required by law, or regulations adopted pursuant to law, to be printed upon the labels of containers in which dangerous drugs, poisons, and other harmful substances are packaged shall be printed in the English language in a conspicuous place in type of conspicuous size in contrast to the typography, layout, or color of the other printed matter on the label." Although warnings in English are expressly required, no California statute requires label or package warnings in any other language.

Defining the circumstances under which warnings or other information should be provided in a language other than English is a task for which legislative and administrative bodies are particularly well suited. Indeed, the California Legislature has already performed this task in a variety of different contexts, enacting laws to ensure that California residents are not denied important services or exploited because they lack proficiency in English. [ ] In defining the circumstances under which a foreign language must be used, the Legislature has drawn clear lines so that affected persons and entities, in both the private and public spheres, know exactly what is expected of them. [ ] When the Legislature has extended a mandate to languages other than English and Spanish, it has provided a means to determine which languages are included. Often, the Legislature has used a numerical threshold of affected or potentially affected persons speaking a given language to define the scope of the relevant duty to provide information in that language. [ ]

These statutes demonstrate that the Legislature is able and willing to define the circumstances in which foreign-language communications should be mandated. Given the existence of a statute expressly requiring that package warnings on nonprescription drugs be in English, we think it reasonable to infer that the Legislature has deliberately chosen not to require that manufacturers also include warnings in foreign languages. The same inference is warranted on the federal level. The FDA's regulations abundantly demonstrate its sensitivity to the issue of foreign-language labeling, and yet the FDA regulations do not require it. Presumably, the FDA has concluded that despite the obvious advantages of multilingual package warnings, the associated problems and costs are such that at present warnings should be mandated only in English.

On this point, the FDA's experience with foreign-language patient package inserts for prescription drugs is instructive. Recognizing that "the United States is too heterogeneous to enable manufacturers, at reasonable cost and with reasonable simplicity, to determine exactly where to provide alternative language inserts," the FDA for a time required manufacturers, as an alternative to multilingual or bilingual inserts, to provide Spanish language translations of their patient package inserts on request to doctors and pharmacists. [ ] But the FDA later noted that manufacturers were having difficulty obtaining accurate translations, and eventually it abandoned altogether the patient package insert requirement for prescription drugs. [ ]

A legislative body considering the utility of foreign-language label warnings for nonprescription medications would no doubt gather pertinent data on a variety of subjects, including the space limitations on nonprescription drug labels and packages, the volume of information that must be conveyed, the relative risks posed by the misuse of particular medications, the cost to the manufacturer of translating and printing warnings in languages other than English, the cost to the consumer of multilingual package warnings in terms of higher prices for, or reduced availability of, products, the feasibility of targeted distribution of products with bilingual or multilingual packaging, the number of persons likely to benefit from warnings in a particular language, and the extent to which non-prescription drug manufacturers as a group have used foreign-language advertisements to promote sales of their products. Legislation and regulations would no doubt reflect findings on these and other pertinent questions.

Lacking the procedure and the resources to conduct the relevant inquiries, we conclude that the prudent course is to adopt for tort purposes the existing legislative and administrative standard of care on this issue. The feasibility and advisability of foreign-language labeling for nonprescription drugs will, no doubt, be reviewed periodically by the FDA and other concerned agencies. Indeed, we are conscious that our decision here may prompt review of this issue by the California Legislature. That is as it should be, for further study might persuade the Legislature, the FDA, or any other concerned agency to revise the controlling statutes or regulations for nonprescription drugs.

For these reasons, we reject plaintiff's attempt to place on nonprescription drug manufacturers a duty to warn that is broader in scope and more onerous than that currently imposed by applicable statutes and regulations. The FDA has stressed that "it is in the best interest of the consumer, industry, and the marketplace to have uniformity in presentation and clarity of message" in the warnings provided with nonprescription drugs. [ ] To preserve that uniformity and clarity, to avoid adverse impacts upon the warning requirements mandated by the federal regulatory scheme, and in deference to the superior technical and procedural lawmaking resources of legislative and administrative bodies, we adopt the legislative/regulatory standard of care that mandates nonprescription drug package warnings in English only.

The judgment of the Court of Appeal is reversed with directions to affirm the summary judgment for defendant.

NOTES AND QUESTIONS

1. *Regulatory compliance as a complete defense.* Like the court in *Ramirez,* other courts have concluded that in the absence of special circumstances, compliance with a statutory or regulatory safety standard renders the product nondefective as a matter of law. *See, e.g.,* Beatty v. Trailmaster Prods., Inc., 625 A.2d 1005, 1014 (Md. 1993) ("[W]here no special circumstances require extra caution, a court may find that conformity to the statutory standard amounts to due care as a matter of law."); Jones v. Hittle Service,

II. The Regulatory Compliance Defense

Inc., 549 P.2d 1383, 1390 (Kan. 1976) ("[C]ompliance is evidence of due care and that the conforming product is not defective, and may be conclusive in the absence of a showing of special circumstances."). These cases are recognized by the *Restatement (Third)*'s formulation of the regulatory compliance defense in §4 comment e:

> Occasionally, after reviewing relevant circumstances, a court may properly conclude that a particular product safety standard set by statute or regulation adequately serves the objectives of tort law and therefore that the product that complies with the standard is not defective as a matter of law. Such a conclusion may be appropriate when the safety statute or regulation was promulgated recently, thus supplying currency to the standard therein established; when the specific standard addresses the very issue of product design or warning presented in the case before the court; and when the court is confident that the deliberative process by which the safety standard was established was full, fair, and thorough and reflected substantial expertise.

2. *Deference and regulatory compliance.* We can now determine whether the regulatory compliance defense adequately defers to the specialized expertise of administrative regulatory agencies. Suppose the common-law duty of design or warning encompasses two types of foreseeable risks, yielding a risk-utility test of the following form:

$$B < PL_1 + PL_2$$

Suppose the safety regulation contemplates only one type of risk (say PL_1) and requires product manufacturers to eliminate that risk by incorporating a particular safety precaution into the product (a warning or safety feature denoted by the precaution B_1). As established by the doctrine of negligence per se, courts will defer to this legislative safety determination, yielding the following risk-utility conclusion:

$$B_1 < PL_1$$

Such a regulation merely establishes a safety floor, because deference to the legislative safety determination ($B_1 < PL_1$) does not foreclose a court from concluding that the full set of risks encompassed by the common-law duty could require an even greater amount of safety investments (denoted B_2):

$$B_2 < PL_1 + PL_2$$

For example, the regulators might have only considered one particular side effect (PL_1) in requiring a warning (B_1), whereas the common-law duty requires a more extensive warning (B_2) covering the full set of foreseeable side effects ($PL_1 + PL_2$). Cases like this explain why regulatory compliance does not ordinarily preclude liability due to the "traditional view that the standards set by most product safety statutes or regulations generally are only minimum standards." RESTATEMENT (THIRD) OF TORTS: PRODUCTS LIABILITY §4 cmt. e.

3. *Unifying the regulatory compliance defense with the doctrine of defect per se.* Consider again the risk-utility reasoning in *Harned* from section I *supra*, which showed why a statutory violation can establish defect per se with respect to a risk that the legislature did not contemplate. Can you see how that conclusion follows from the logic of the regulatory compliance defense? When regulations only set a minimal standard or floor ($B_1 < PL_1$), then the violation of such a safety statute is necessarily proof of defect with respect to the full set of risks encompassed by the common-law duty ($B_1 < PL_1 + PL_2$). In both cases, the statutory standard only sets a minimal safety requirement, the violation of which necessarily establishes negligence per se with respect to all risks the common-law duty encompasses.

A safety regulation only establishes a floor or minimal safety requirement when it does not account for the full range of risks governed by the common-law tort duty. Deference to this type of legislative safety decision does not foreclose courts from concluding that the common-law duty required a defendant to make safety expenditures in excess of the amount required by the regulators. So, too, a defendant's unexcused failure to comply with such a minimal safety requirement conclusively establishes negligence per se with respect to all risks encompassed by the common-law duty, including those that the regulators did not expressly contemplate. Deference fully explains the manner in which regulatory compliance and noncompliance affect the tort claim.

Within tort law more generally, courts will defer to any legislative policy decision that is relevant to the resolution of a tort claim. The regulatory compliance defense and the doctrine of defect per se illustrate this type of deference without fully exhausting the various ways in which this principle of common-law deference shapes tort law. *See generally* Mark A. Geistfeld, *Tort Law in the Age of Statutes*, 99 Iowa L. Rev. 957 (2014). Much of the discussion in this chapter is drawn from this article.

4. *Regulatory compliance as a complete defense.* Instead of merely establishing minimal safety requirements, statutes can fully specify the safety obligations for reasons illustrated by *Ramirez*. As the court explained, unless the FDA (or state legislature) mandated a bilingual warning, it had concluded that it would be too costly ($B_{bilingual}$) to make disclosures in both English (with a safety benefit $PL_{English}$) and Spanish ($PL_{Spanish}$). Under these conditions, deference to this legislative safety determination yields the conclusion that the bilingual disclosure is not required by the risk-utility test:

$$PL_{English} + PL_{Spanish} < B_{bilingual}$$

If a plaintiff alleges that the common-law duty requires the defendant to adopt a bilingual warning, the defendant could invoke regulatory compliance as a complete defense. To prove defect, the plaintiff must rely on a risk-utility conclusion ($B_{bilingual} < PL_{English} + PL_{Spanish}$) that directly contradicts the regulatory safety determination. By deferring to this legislative policy decision, the court will reject the plaintiff's claim and conclude that a product complying with the regulation passes the risk-utility test as a matter of law.

Can the holding in *Ramirez* be plausibly justified in this manner? Is it plausible that each time the FDA or legislature did not require a

II. The Regulatory Compliance Defense

foreign-language warning, it concluded that the cost of such a warning was unreasonably high in relation to the safety benefit? Or is it possible that they simply did not think about the issue in this particular instance? How should legislative or regulatory inaction affect the determination of statutory or regulatory purpose for purposes of resolving the tort claim? Should courts require some affirmative evidence of what the legislators or regulators were thinking about with respect to a particular safety question before concluding that inaction implies a decision about this question? These issues are discussed in notes following the next main case.

5. *The conditions under which regulatory compliance is a complete defense.* Leaving aside the hard questions about the conclusions one can draw from inaction coupled with silence, we can identify the conditions under which regulatory compliance will be a complete defense. Doing so explains why cases of this type are exceptional.

a. Changes in technology. Suppose that the regulators considered the full set of risks encompassed by the common-law duty and concluded that it would be too costly to require that all products in the market must incorporate a particular safety device for eliminating these risks ($PL_1 + PL_2 < B_{existing\ device}$). Subsequently, developments in science or technology created a new precaution (with a burden denoted $B_{new\ device}$) that could be incorporated into the design to eliminate these risks. Courts that defer to the regulator's safety decision could still conclude that the defendant must take the newly developed precaution instead of the precaution that the regulators considered when promulgating the safety standard:

$$B_{new\ device} < PL_1 + PL_2 < B_{existing\ device}$$

b. Changes in cost. Regulatory compliance would also not necessarily be a complete defense if subsequent to the regulatory determination, a precaution that the regulators had rejected as being too costly significantly decreased in cost ($B_{current} < B_{outdated}$). A good example is provided by airbags, which have considerably decreased in cost over time. In these circumstances, the risk-utility test could require the design or warning to incorporate the precaution even though the regulators had previously concluded otherwise:

$$B_{current} < PL_1 + PL_2 < B_{outdated}$$

c. Changes in knowledge of risk. Finally, regulatory compliance would not necessarily be a complete defense if the regulatory safety decision was based on risks known at that time (PL_1), and it subsequently became evident that the product (like a drug) creates additional risks (PL_2). In these cases, the regulatory safety decision functions like a safety floor and does not foreclose a court from finding that the defendant was required to take an additional precaution. Returning to the earlier example of product warnings, the regulators might have only considered one risk of side effect (PL_1) in requiring a warning (B_1), whereas the common-law duty requires a more extensive warning (B_2) covering the full set of foreseeable side effects ($PL_1 + PL_2$).

The principle of common-law deference to legislative safety determinations accordingly makes regulatory compliance a complete defense only under certain conditions: The regulation must address the full set of risks encompassed by the common-law tort duty based on a state of technology, cost structure, and knowledge of risk governing the safety decision at issue in the tort claim.

6. *Assessing regulatory compliance.* What is the best way to characterize the regulatory compliance defense? Is compliance ordinarily only a partial defense that is relevant to, but not dispositive of, the defect question, or does compliance typically provide a complete defense with exceptions based on "special circumstances"? To employ the language of the *Restatement (Third)* in §4 comment e, the issue turns on the empirical question of how often regulators use their "substantial expertise" to resolve by a "full, fair, and thorough" "deliberative process" the risk-utility question implicated by the tort claim. A regulatory regime that routinely provided rules of this type would routinely enable product sellers to invoke regulatory compliance as a complete defense. Consequently, the appropriate characterization of the regulatory compliance defense depends on the extent to which regulators can effectively regulate product risk.

Consider the regulations promulgated by the U.S. Food and Drug Administration (FDA), which present the "strongest case" for making regulatory compliance a complete defense because "the prescription drug industry is the most heavily regulated industry (for safety purposes) in this country today." Michael D. Green, *Statutory Compliance and Tort Liability: Examining the Strongest Case,* 30 U. Mich. J. L. Reform 461, 463 (1997). FDA regulations govern "approximately $1 trillion in consumer products or 25 cents of every consumer dollar expended in this country annually." Due to the staggering number of products in the marketplace, the FDA is hard-pressed to examine thoroughly every aspect of every different product within its jurisdiction, a problem that is then exacerbated by rapidly changing technologies and evolving medical knowledge of the health hazards posed by prescription drugs and medical devices. Indeed, the FDA has concluded that it has "serious scientific deficiencies and is not positioned to meet current or emerging regulatory responsibilities." FDA Subcomm. on Sci. & Tech., FDA Science and Mission at Risk 1, 2 (2007). In most cases, regulators are only able to partially address the safety issue posed by a tort claim, yielding a minimal safety requirement. Consider In re Zypexa Prods. Liab. Litig., 493 F. Supp.2d 571, 575 (E.D.N.Y. 2007) ("[L]awyers and their clients often find themselves serving as drug safety researchers of last resort." (quotation omitted)).

By treating regulatory compliance as a partial defense, the majority rule presumes that FDA regulations establish only a safety floor. The presumption rests on the empirical judgment that comprehensive safety regulation is extraordinarily difficult. For these same reasons, a different empirical judgment — that regulations ordinarily are sufficiently comprehensive to resolve tort claims — would presumptively make regulatory compliance a complete defense, requiring the plaintiff to overcome the presumption by showing that the regulation does not fully resolve the safety decision required by the tort duty. The substantive logic of the regulatory compliance defense, therefore, is not altered by the tort-reform legislation enacted in some states that presumptively makes regulatory compliance a complete defense. *See, e.g.,* Colo. Rev. Stat. Ann. §13-21-403(1)(b) (current through 2020) (creating a rebuttable presumption that a product is not defective if it complied with a federal or Colorado state statute or administrative regulation). The apparently different treatments of regulatory compliance simply rest on different empirical judgments about the frequency of comprehensive safety regulations.

Under the majority rule, compliance is only a partial defense that is based on a factual presumption regarding the regulatory process. Like any other factual presumption, this one can be overcome with proof—in this instance, that deference to the regulation in question fully resolves the safety decision required by the tort duty. Because regulatory compliance is an affirmative defense, the defendant bears the burden of proof. Lacking such proof, the presumption applies and courts will not treat compliance as a complete defense.

III. STATUTORY PREEMPTION OF TORT CLAIMS

Due to the supremacy of legislative law over the common law, a statute can modify or altogether preempt (foreclose) a common-law tort claim. State legislation that codifies tort law, for example, displaces the associated doctrines of the common law. *E.g.,* Rev. Code Wash. Ann. §7.72.020(1) (current through 2020) ("The previous existing applicable law of this state on product liability is modified only to the extent set forth in this chapter."). The most heavily litigated issues in this area involve cases in which a federal statute arguably preempts the state law of products liability, whether based on state legislation or the common law. In a case of preemption, compliance with the federal statute provides a complete defense to the (preempted) tort claim.

The federal preemption of state law is based on the Supremacy Clause of the U.S. Constitution, which commands that the laws of the United States "shall be the supreme Law of the Land; . . . any Thing in the Constitution or Laws of any state to the Contrary notwithstanding." U.S. Const. art. VI, cl. 2. Consequently, the judicial "inquiry into the scope of a [federal] statute's pre-emptive effect is guided by the rule that the purpose of Congress is the ultimate touchstone in every pre-emption case." Altria Group, Inc. v. Good, 555 U.S. 70, 76 (2008). The preemptive effect of a federal statute extends to regulations promulgated by agencies pursuant to such statutory authority.

One area of the law in which the doctrine of preemption has been especially difficult to interpret has been tort law, and particularly product liability law. State product liability law operates in fields that are entwined with federal regulation. Cigarettes, medical devices, pesticides, and motor vehicles are examples of the many products that traditionally have been subjects of both federal regulation and state common law actions. Federal statutes and regulations often incorporate measures to assure product safety, but the statutes rarely include provisions to compensate for personal injuries or other damages associated with the regulated products. Rather, federal law and state common law exist in a sometimes uncomfortable balance in our federalist society. This discomfort is enhanced by the lack of clear direction from Congress in its statutory enactments and from federal agencies in their administrative regulations. Since the 1990s, product sellers have argued with increasing frequency that plaintiffs' product liability actions under state common law are preempted by the existence of federal regulation governing the alleged injurious product. In most of these cases, the proponent of the preemption defense has asked the court to preclude the plaintiffs' claims without explicit direction from Congress.

Jean Macchiaroli Eggen, *The Normalization of Product Preemption Doctrine*, 57 Ala. L. Rev. 725, 725-726 (2006) (paragraph structure added).

Because "Congress repeatedly punts, leaving unresolved the key question of the extent to which federal standards and regulations preempt state common-law remedies," the resulting ambiguity and high stakes have made preemption "the fiercest battle in products liability litigation today." Catherine M. Sharkey, *Products Liability Preemption: An Institutional Approach*, 76 Geo. Wash. L. Rev. 449, 450 (2008).

WILLIAMSON v. MAZDA MOTOR OF AMERICA
Supreme Court of the United States, 2011
562 U.S. 323

BREYER, J. Federal Motor Vehicle Safety Standard 208 (1989 version) requires, among other things, that auto manufacturers install seatbelts on the rear seats of passenger vehicles. They must install lap-and-shoulder belts on seats next to a vehicle's doors or frames. But they have a choice about what to install on rear inner seats (say, middle seats or those next to a minivan's aisle). There they can install either (1) simple lap belts or (2) lap-and-shoulder belts. The question presented here is whether this federal regulation pre-empts a state tort suit that, if successful, would deny manufacturers a choice of belts for rear inner seats by imposing tort liability upon those who choose to install a simple lap belt.

In 2002, the Williamson family, riding in their 1993 Mazda minivan, was struck head on by another vehicle. Thanh Williamson was sitting in a rear aisle seat, wearing a lap belt; she died in the accident. Delbert and Alexa Williamson were wearing lap-and-shoulder belts; they survived. They, along with Thanh's estate, subsequently brought this California tort suit against Mazda. They claimed that Mazda should have installed lap-and-shoulder belts on rear aisle seats, and that Thanh died because Mazda equipped her seat with a lap belt instead.

The California trial court dismissed this tort claim on the basis of the pleadings. And the California Court of Appeal affirmed. The appeals court noted that in *Geier v. American Honda Motor Co.*, 529 U.S. 861 (2000), this Court considered whether a different portion of (an older version of) Federal Motor Vehicle Safety Standard 208 (FMVSS 208)—a portion that required installation of passive restraint devices—pre-empted a state tort suit that sought to hold an auto

III. Statutory Preemption of Tort Claims

manufacturer liable for failure to install a particular kind of passive restraint, namely, airbags. We found that the federal regulation intended to assure manufacturers that they would retain a choice of installing any of several different passive restraint devices. And the regulation sought to assure them that they would not have to exercise this choice in favor of airbags. For that reason we thought that the federal regulation pre-empted a state tort suit that, by premising tort liability on a failure to install airbags, would have deprived the manufacturers of the choice that the federal regulation had assured them. By requiring manufacturers to install airbags (in order to avoid tort liability) the tort suit would have deprived the manufacturers of the choice among passive restraint systems that the federal regulation gave them.

We divided this basic pre-emption question into three subsidiary questions. First, we asked whether the statute's express pre-emption provision preempted the state tort suit. That statutory clause says that "no State" may "establish, or . . . continue in effect . . . *any safety standard* applicable to the same aspect of performance" of a motor vehicle or item of equipment "which is not identical to the Federal standard." We had previously held that a word somewhat similar to "standard," namely, "requirements" (found in a similar statute) included within its scope state "common-law duties," such as duties created by state tort law. [ ] But we nonetheless held that the state tort suit in question fell outside the scope of this particular pre-emption clause. That is primarily because the statute also contains a saving clause, which says that "[c]ompliance with" a federal safety standard "does not exempt any person *from any liability under common law*." Since tort law is ordinarily "common law," we held that "the presence of the saving clause," makes clear that Congress intended state tort suits to fall outside the scope of the express pre-emption clause.

Second, we asked the converse question: The saving clause at least removes tort actions from the scope of the express pre-emption clause. But does it do more? Does it foreclose or limit "the operation of ordinary pre-emption principles insofar as those principles instruct us to read" federal statutes as pre-empting state laws (including state common-law standards) that "actually conflict" with the federal statutes (or related regulations)? We concluded that the saving clause does not foreclose or limit the operation of "ordinary pre-emption principles, grounded in longstanding precedent." [*Geier*]

These two holdings apply directly to the case before us. We here consider (1) the same statute; (2) a later version of the same regulation, FMVSS 208; and (3) a somewhat similar claim that a state tort action conflicts with the federal regulation. In light of *Geier*, the statute's express pre-emption clause cannot pre-empt the common-law tort action; but neither can the statute's saving clause foreclose or limit the operation of ordinary conflict pre-emption principles. We consequently turn our attention to *Geier*'s third subsidiary question, whether, in fact, the state tort action conflicts with the federal regulation.

Under ordinary conflict pre-emption principles a state law that "stands as an obstacle to the accomplishment and execution of the full purposes and objectives" of a federal law is pre-empted. [ ] In *Geier*, we found that the state law stood as an "'obstacle' to the accomplishment" of a significant federal regulatory objective, namely, the maintenance of manufacturer choice. We must decide whether the same is true here.

At the heart of *Geier* lies our determination that giving auto manufacturers a choice among different kinds of passive restraint devices was a significant objective of the federal regulation. We reached this conclusion on the basis of our examination of the regulation, including its history, the promulgating agency's contemporaneous explanation of its objectives, and the agency's current views of the regulation's pre-emptive effect.

The history showed that the Department of Transportation (DOT) had long thought it important to leave manufacturers with a choice.... DOT's contemporaneous explanation of its 1984 regulation made clear that manufacturer choice was an important means for achieving its basic objectives. The 1984 regulation gradually phased in passive restraint requirements, initially requiring manufacturers to equip only 10% of their new fleets with passive restraints. DOT explained that it intended its phasing period partly to give manufacturers time to improve airbag technology and to develop "other, better" passive restraint systems. DOT further explained that it had rejected an "all airbag" system. It was worried that requiring airbags in most or all vehicles would cause a public backlash.... DOT also had concerns about the safety of airbags, for they could injure out-of-place occupants, particularly children. And, given the cost of airbags, vehicle owners might not replace them when necessary, leaving occupants without passive protection. The regulation therefore "deliberately sought variety—a mix of several different passive restraint systems." [*Geier*] DOT hoped that this mix would lead to better information about the devices' comparative effectiveness and to the eventual development of "alternative, cheaper, and safer passive restraint systems." [*Id.*]

Finally, the Solicitor General told us that a tort suit that insisted upon use of airbags, as opposed to other federally permissible passive restraint systems, would "stan[d] as an obstacle to the accomplishment and execution of these objectives."

Taken together, this history, the agency's contemporaneous explanation, and the Government's current understanding of the regulation convinced us that manufacturer choice was an important regulatory objective. And since the tort suit stood as an obstacle to the accomplishment of that objective, we found the tort suit pre-empted.

We turn now to the present case. Like the regulation in *Geier*, the regulation here leaves the manufacturer with a choice. And, like the tort suit in *Geier*, the tort suit here would restrict that choice. But unlike *Geier*, we do not believe here that choice is a significant regulatory objective.

We concede that the history of the regulation before us resembles the history of airbags to some degree. In 1984, DOT rejected a regulation that would have required the use of lap-and-shoulder belts in rear seats. Nonetheless, by 1989 when DOT promulgated the present regulation, it had "concluded that several factors had changed."

DOT then required manufacturers to install a particular kind of belt, namely, lap-and-shoulder belts, for rear outer seats. In respect to rear inner seats, it retained manufacturer choice as to which kind of belt to install. But its 1989 reasons for retaining that choice differed considerably from its 1984 reasons for permitting manufacturers a choice in respect to airbags. DOT here was not concerned about consumer acceptance; it was convinced that lap-and-shoulder belts would increase safety; it did not fear additional safety risks arising from use of those belts; it had no interest in assuring a mix of devices; and, though it was concerned about additional costs, that concern was diminishing....

Why then did DOT not require lap-and-shoulder belts in these seats? We have found some indication that it thought use of lap-and-shoulder belts in rear aisle seats could cause "entry and exit problems for occupants of seating positions to the rear" by "stretch[ing] the shoulder belt across the aisleway." [ ] However, DOT encouraged manufacturers to address this issue through innovation. And there is little indication that DOT considered this matter a significant safety concern.

The more important reason why DOT did not require lap-and-shoulder belts for rear inner seats was that it thought that this requirement would not be cost-effective. The agency explained that it would be significantly more expensive for manufacturers to install lap-and-shoulder belts in rear middle and aisle seats than in seats next to the car doors. *Ibid.* But that fact—the fact that DOT made a negative judgment about cost effectiveness—cannot by itself show that DOT sought to forbid common-law tort suits in which a judge or jury might reach a different conclusion.

For one thing, DOT did not believe that costs would remain frozen. Rather it pointed out that costs were falling as manufacturers were "voluntarily equipping more and more of their vehicles with rear seat lap/shoulder belts." For another thing, many, perhaps most, federal safety regulations embody some kind of cost-effectiveness judgment. While an agency could base a decision to pre-empt on its cost-effectiveness judgment, we are satisfied that the rulemaking record at issue here discloses no such pre-emptive intent. And to infer from the mere existence of such a cost-effectiveness judgment that the federal agency intends to bar States from imposing stricter standards would treat all such federal standards as if they were *maximum* standards, eliminating the possibility that the federal agency seeks only to set forth a *minimum* standard potentially supplemented through state tort law. We cannot reconcile this consequence with a statutory saving clause that foresees the likelihood of a continued meaningful role for state tort law.

Finally, the Solicitor General tells us that DOT's regulation does not pre-empt this tort suit.

In *Geier*, then, the regulation's history, the agency's contemporaneous explanation, and its consistently held interpretive views indicated that the regulation sought to maintain manufacturer choice in order to further significant regulatory objectives. Here, these same considerations indicate the contrary. We consequently conclude that, even though the state tort suit may restrict the manufacturer's choice, it does not "stan[d] as an obstacle to the accomplishment... of the full purposes and objectives" of federal law. [*Geier.*] Thus, the regulation does not pre-empt this tort action.

The judgment of the California Court of Appeal is reversed.

NOTES AND QUESTIONS

1. *Types of preemption.* In a case of *express preemption*, the statute (or regulation promulgated thereunder) by its express terms displaces tort law. The preemption question turns entirely on the words of the statute, requiring

the court to apply the statute as written. Although important, express preemption is guided by principles of statutory interpretation and therefore is largely outside the scope of our studies. In contrast, *Geier* involves *implied preemption,* which involves a statute that displaces state tort law by implication. The inquiry concerning implied preemption depends on a finding that the statutory purpose would be frustrated by the imposition of tort liability, an analysis that obviously depends on the tort inquiry and therefore is something we can usefully explore. Implied preemption can take different forms. *Field preemption* refers to a statutory scheme that is so pervasive or of such fundamental federal importance that it implies a legislative purpose to "occupy the field," leaving no room for the operation of state tort law. *Conflict preemption* refers to cases in which it is impossible to comply with both the statute and the tort rule, or when the tort rule poses an obstacle to the goals of the statutory scheme. *See* Rice v. Santa Fe Elevator Corp., 331 U.S. 218, 230-231 (1947). The issue in *Geier* involved conflict preemption.

2. *The rise of preemption and decline of the regulatory compliance defense.* From a defendant's perspective, what are the advantages and disadvantages of federal preemption as compared to the regulatory compliance defense? A defendant can effectively make regulatory compliance a complete defense by instead claiming that the statute preempts the tort claim. Having complied with a statute that preempts tort law, the defendant is not subject to tort liability. Rather than invoke the regulatory compliance defense, defendants can avoid liability by instead arguing that the tort claim is preempted.

A defendant will ordinarily prefer preemption for a further reason. The regulatory compliance defense is based on judicial deference to a regulation or statute, whereas statutory preemption is a constitutional obligation, requiring courts to follow the supreme will of the legislature. Rather than let courts exercise their common-law discretion, defendants in these cases understandably prefer to eliminate the discretionary component by instead pursuing the constitutionally grounded claim of statutory preemption. Consider Catherine M. Sharkey, *Federalism in Action: FDA Regulatory Preemption in Pharmaceutical Cases in State Versus Federal Courts,* 15 J.L. & Pol'y 1013, 1019 (2007) (finding that "state courts, which by and large have previously rejected any absolute regulatory compliance defense . . . are now willing to entertain preemption arguments"). Although there had been "fervent interest in the regulatory compliance defense on the part of academics, policymakers, courts and legislatures over the last quarter of the 20th century," the "federal preemption of state tort liability has replaced regulatory compliance as a dominant issue for the 21st century." *Id.* at 1020-1021.

The increased reliance on preemption is altering the doctrinal landscape of products liability. For example, the Court's preemption analysis either does bar or most likely will bar most design-defect claims involving drugs, medical devices, and vaccines. *See* Riegel v. Medtronic, Inc., 552 U.S. 312, 330 (2008) (holding that the FDA's premarket approval process for medical devices preempts state-law claims of defective design and only permits tort damages "for claims premised on a violation of FDA regulations"); Bruesewitz v. Wyeth, LLC, 562 U.S. 223, 232 (2011) (holding that the National Childhood Injury Vaccine Act preempts state-law design-defect claims "[p]rovided that there was proper manufacture and warning"); Aaron D. Twerski, *The Demise of Drug Design Litigation*, 68 Am. U. L. Rev. 281, 303 (2018) (concluding that the Court's preemption analysis creates "a substantial likelihood that federal preemption will bar most common law drug design cases"). Tort claims alleging that medical products are defectively designed implicate the "unavoidably unsafe" product exemption from strict products liability, and so preemption will render that doctrine largely irrelevant unless courts extend the exemption to other types of life-saving products. And for reasons previously discussed, the rise of preemption has substantially reduced the need for defendants to invoke the regulatory compliance defense, making it largely irrelevant.

3. *Is there a rule of implied preemption?* Regardless of its impact on common-law developments, the increased emphasis on preemption has created other problems. Courts have struggled with the issue of whether a statute that does not expressly preempt tort law does so by implication, resulting in a body of law that scholars generally consider "a muddle." Caleb Nelson, *Preemption*, 86 Va. L. Rev. 225, 232 (2000).

The problem in large part involves striking the right balance between federal and state law—the problem of federalism. To account for this problem, federal courts often invoke a presumption against federal preemption of state tort law: "Preemption analysis starts with the assumption that the historic police powers of the States are not to be superseded unless that was the clear and manifest purpose of Congress. This assumption provides assurance that 'the federal-state balance' will not be disturbed unintentionally by Congress or unnecessarily by the courts." *Riegel*, 552 U.S. at 334. This presumption against federal preemption, however, "breaks down in the products liability realm, rearing its head with gusto in some cases, but oddly quiescent in others." Catherine M. Sharkey, *Products Liability Preemption: An Institutional Approach*, 76 Geo. Wash. L. Rev. 449, 449 (2008).

In contrast, some scholars have argued that there is an identifiable rule regarding implied preemption, at least in product cases. According to Professor Sharkey,

> Behind agency decisions to regulate or to refrain from regulating is a rich body of empirical cost-benefit (or increasingly risk-risk) analyses. These analyses made by the agency at the time of its action (or inaction), as well as the nature of the agency action and the contemporaneous reasons given by the agency to justify it, can guide courts' judgments regarding the need for, and equally significantly, the present feasibility of, uniform national regulatory standards.

Id. at 453. Or as Professor Robert Rabin put it, the "critical factor in determining conflict preemption" under the Court's jurisprudence is "an analysis of whether the agency directive was grounded in the same evidence-based risk-benefit inquiry as the tort process would entail." Robert L. Rabin, *Territorial Claims in the Domain of Accidental Harm: Conflicting Conceptions of Tort Preemption*, 74 Brook. L. Rev. 987, 995 (2009). "Under this narrowly framed preemption defense, what are the principal types of tort claims that survive? Most importantly, claims should survive that are based on substantial new evidence of risk arising after a product design has been approved if the agency has failed to weigh in on the new findings in a determinate manner at the time of product use by the injury victim." *Id.* at 1002. Is this reasoning consistent with *Williamson*?

4. *Rethinking preemption in terms of the regulatory compliance defense.* When the preemptive effect of federal law is limited to cases in which the safety regulation resolves the same risk-utility question that is implicated by the plaintiff's allegation of defect, the outcome is no different from that produced by the regulatory compliance defense in a case like *Ramirez v. Plough, Inc.* (excerpted in section II, *supra*). Would the regulatory compliance defense in *Restatement (Third)* §4 have provided a complete defense for the defendant in *Williamson*?

Consider the discussion in *Williamson* concerning the Court's earlier decision in *Geier*. According to the plaintiffs' allegation of defective design in *Geier*, an airbag was a reasonable alternative to the existing design that relied only on lap-and-shoulder belts. To recover under such a risk-utility claim, the plaintiffs would have had to prove that the disutility or burden of the airbag (denoted B_{airbag}) is less than the risk that an airbag would eliminate (denoted PL_{airbag}):

$$B_{airbag} < PL_{airbag}$$

As the Court in *Geier* concluded, this identical risk-utility issue had been fully considered by the U.S. Department of Transportation (DOT) when it promulgated the regulation in question. The risk addressed by the regulation—the foreseeable risk that an occupant in the vehicle would be physically injured in a crash (PL_{airbag})—encompasses the full set of risks governed by the common-law duty (other than the occupants of the vehicle, no one else is foreseeably affected by the presence or absence of an airbag). When DOT evaluated the risk that would be eliminated by airbags, it considered the burden of mandatory airbags (B_{airbag}), concluding that

> airbags brought with them their own special risks to safety, such as the risk of danger to out-of-position occupants (usually children) in small cars.
>
> ... [A]irbags were expected to be significantly more expensive than other passive restraint devices, raising the average cost of a vehicle price $320 for full frontal airbags over the cost of a car with manual lap and shoulder seatbelts (and potentially much more if production volumes were low).... [T]he high replacement cost—estimated to be $800—could lead car owners to refuse to replace [airbags] after deployment.... [And] the public, for reasons of cost, fear, or physical intrusiveness, might resist installation or use of any of the then-available passive restraint devices—a particular concern with respect to airbags.

Geier v. Am. Honda Motor Co., 529 U.S. 861, 877-878 (2000) (citations omitted).

III. Statutory Preemption of Tort Claims

Due to these varied costs, DOT "had rejected a proposed . . . 'all airbag' standard because of safety concerns (perceived or real) associated with airbags, which concerns threatened a 'backlash' more easily overcome 'if airbags' were 'not the only way of complying.'" *Id.* at 879. Thus, with respect to the full set of risks encompassed by the common-law duty to design, DOT reached a considered conclusion that

$$PL_{airbag} < B_{airbag}$$

Deference to this regulatory decision would lead courts to find as a matter of law that a plaintiff cannot recover for any tort claim requiring a risk-utility conclusion contrary to the one reached by the regulators. A defendant, therefore, could invoke regulatory compliance as a complete defense for any allegation of liability requiring such a contrary conclusion ($B_{airbag} < PL_{airbag}$), the same claim made by the plaintiffs in *Geier*.

To be sure, regulatory compliance is not a complete defense when advances in technology, increased knowledge of risk, or reductions in cost alter the risk-utility calculus. The regulators, however, also expressly considered these factors and concluded that "a mix of devices would help develop data on comparative effectiveness, would allow the industry time to overcome the safety problems and the high production costs associated with airbags, and would facilitate the development of alternative, cheaper, and safer passive restraint systems. And it would thereby build public confidence." *Id.* at 879. If an agency has decided that a regulation is integral to the development of safety technology or knowledge of risk, then deference to this aspect of the regulatory decision rules out any tort claim based on the contrary proposition that the regulators did not adequately account for such change.

The regulatory standard at issue in *Geier*, therefore, fully satisfies the conditions under which regulatory compliance is a complete defense. The federal regulatory agency had used its "substantial expertise" to resolve by a "full, fair, and thorough" "deliberative process" the "very issue of product design . . . presented in the case before the court," making regulatory compliance a complete defense under the rule adopted by the *Restatement (Third)* in §4 comment e. The regulatory compliance defense yields the same case outcome as the finding of implied preemption in *Geier*.

In *Williamson*, by contrast, the regulators did not make such a conclusive risk-utility determination when promulgating the federal regulation that gave manufacturers a choice to install either a simple lap belt or a lap-and-shoulder belt in the rear inner seats of automobiles. Under those conditions, would regulatory compliance be a complete defense to the tort claim?

5. *Regulatory inaction and implied preemption.* If federal regulators decide not to require a safety feature on a product, would that decision impliedly preempt any tort claim that the manufacturer was obligated to do so? In Sprietsma v. Mercury Marine, 537 U.S. 51 (2002), plaintiff's decedent fell out of a boat and was fatally injured when struck by the boat's propeller. The plaintiff sued the boat's designer, alleging that the boat was unreasonably dangerous because it did not have a propeller guard. The Federal

Boat Safety Act ("FBSA") authorizes the Coast Guard to regulate the matter. The defendant argued that the Coast Guard's decision not to adopt a regulation requiring propeller guards on motorboats preempted the plaintiff's claim. The Court rejected this argument: "It is quite wrong to view th[e] decision" not to adopt a regulation requiring propeller guards "as the functional equivalent of a regulation prohibiting all States and their political subdivisions from adopting such a regulation." The Court recognized that the Coast Guard had conducted significant research into propeller guards and made an "undoubtedly intentional and carefully considered" decision not to implement a regulation. Because the Coast Guard's explanation for its decision not to promulgate a rule "d[id] not convey an 'authoritative' message of a federal policy against propeller guards," the Court did not give that decision preemptive effect. *Id.* at 65-67. Compare Butler v. Daimler Trucks North American LLC, 433 F. Supp. 3d 1216, 1245 (D. Kan. 2020) ("*Geier* and *Williamson* instruct courts to consider an agency's reasoning for implementing a regulation; if the reason is not tied to a significant regulatory objective, even compliance with a federal regulation is not sufficient to insulate a manufacturer from state law tort claims based on a vehicle's design."). In these cases, would the defendant have a stronger argument by relying on the regulatory compliance defense rather than preemption? Consider in this respect the presumption against preemption discussed in note 3 *supra*.

6. *Implied preemption and federalism.* Insofar as federal preemption fully replicates the outcome that would otherwise be attained by the regulatory compliance defense, the approach has important federalism implications. For products sold in the national market like prescription drugs and medical devices, there is a distinct federal interest in uniformity and a distinct state interest in health and safety. The two interests apparently conflict, however, whenever state tort law diverges from the federally mandated safety standard, creating the federalism problem that has garnered so much attention. But if implied preemption only occurs when compliance with the federal regulation would render regulatory compliance a complete defense under state law, this conflict is eliminated—states defer to federal law as a matter of state law, and so there is no conflict between the two bodies of law. To what extent has this solution to the federalism problem been masked by the manner in which the preemption question has eclipsed the regulatory compliance defense, thereby focusing attention on the one doctrine to the exclusion of the other?

III. AUTONOMOUS VEHICLES AND PRODUCTS LIABILITY: PROBLEM SET 7

AV Problem 7.1

As of this writing, federal legislation has been proposed that would create a comprehensive framework for regulating autonomous vehicles. Although

III. Autonomous Vehicles and Products Liability: Problem Set 7

such legislation enjoyed considerable bipartisan support, it was derailed by the COVID-19 pandemic and the 2020 presidential election. Like the statute discussed in *Williamson*, the proposed federal legislation contains both an express preemption clause and a savings clause. Assuming that this framework is ultimately enacted, it presumably will give a federal motor vehicle safety standard (FMVSS) the same preemptive effect as the standards at issue in both *Geier* and *Williamson*. *See* Mark A. Geistfeld, *The Regulatory Sweet Spot for Autonomous Vehicles*, 53 Wake Forest L. Rev. 337, 341-350 (2018), which provides much of the material in this section.

Based on the Court's reasoning in *Geier*, any federal standard (FMVSS) that regulates autonomous vehicles will displace state tort law only if enforcement of the tort obligation would frustrate the federal regulatory objective—an issue of implied preemption. For example, a federal regulation that establishes only a floor or minimal safety standard contemplates that the states may impose more demanding safety requirements. In these scenarios, national uniformity is not an evident regulatory objective, enabling the states to enforce their common-law tort requirements governing this aspect of motor vehicle performance—the same outcome in *Williamson*. This interpretation of the federal statute harmonizes federal law and state tort law by ensuring that the federal regulatory purpose will be uniformly followed across the country while permitting state tort law to govern safety issues not fully resolved by federal regulations (both minimum and nonexistent standards). As the Court in *Williamson* explained, the "saving clause . . . foresees the likelihood of a continued meaningful role for state tort law." 562 U.S. at 335.

Suppose that federal regulators simply proclaimed that the regulatory objective of national uniformity requires that an FMVSS applicable to autonomous vehicles preempts state tort law. Would courts necessarily conclude that the FMVSS must have this preemptive effect?

Analysis of AV Problem 7.1

If the mere invocation of "uniformity" were always sufficient for preemption purposes, then the statute's saving clause would not have the independent meaning that the Court in *Geier* ascribed to it. The regulatory invocation of "uniformity" would effectively function as a form of express preemption, but the saving clause bars the application of express preemption to state tort claims. To preserve a "meaningful" role for state tort law as required by the saving clause, federal regulators cannot obtain preemptive effect by engaging in such administrative fiat.

Editor's Note: This reasoning explains why the Court in *Geier* concluded that in answering the preemption question, "[w]e place *some* weight upon [the agency's] interpretation of [the FMVSS at issue] and its conclusion, as set forth in the Government's brief, that a tort suit such as this one would 'stan[d] as an obstacle to the accomplishment and execution' of those objectives." 529 U.S. at 883. If the agency's interpretation of a regulation's preemptive effect is only given "some weight," then its mere invocation of the need for uniformity will not decisively establish that the FMVSS preempts state tort law.

AV Problem 7.2

Consider whether the savings clause in the federal AV statute might have further implications for the federal regulatory process. To what extent does it require federal regulators to account for state tort law when promulgating an FMVSS applicable to autonomous vehicles? Does the regulatory compliance defense provide any guidance for resolving this issue?

Analysis of AV Problem 7.2

As previously discussed, by giving federal recognition to the preservation of state tort law, the saving clause prevents federal regulators from simply invoking the federal interest in uniformity as a reason to wholly override another federal interest in preserving a meaningful role for state tort law. The one federal interest does not necessarily trump the other within the statutory scheme. Preemptive effect is instead limited to federal performance standards that adequately account for *both* federal interests, one in national uniformity and the other in preserving a meaningful role for state tort law.

Regulators could further both purposes by attempting to attain national uniformity in a manner that minimizes the displacement of state tort law via the doctrine of implied preemption. Federal regulations of this type preserve state tort law to the maximal extent that is consistent with the objective of national uniformity, thereby harmonizing these two purposes of the federal legislation.

Federal regulators would fully harmonize these two federal objectives when the FMVSS is based on the associated tort requirement enforced by the majority of states. In the majority of states, this type of FMVSS is no different from the associated tort obligation. By complying with the federal performance standard, the manufacturer also necessarily satisfies its corresponding tort obligation, thereby avoiding liability for the associated tort claim under the regulatory compliance defense. Tort law in these states fully determines the liability question, so the FMVSS attains uniformity without displacing state tort law. In the remaining minority of states, the federal constitutional doctrine of statutory preemption ensures that the FMVSS uniformly applies. The tort rules in these states impose safety requirements on manufacturers that differ from the performance required by both the FMVSS and the majority of states. Permitting this minority of states to impose different safety requirements on manufacturers would not only frustrate the statutory objective of national uniformity, but it would also elevate the interests of these states over the substantially larger number of other states that defer to federal regulations, thereby frustrating the statutory purpose of maximally preserving state tort law. Consequently, the application of tort law in these states would be impliedly preempted by the FMVSS.

At least some displacement of state tort law is ordinarily inherent in a regulatory regime that requires national uniformity, but federal regulators can minimize that outcome by deriving the FMVSS from the tort obligation enforced by most states. Federal regulations of this type do not simply substitute for or wholly displace state tort law; the two bodies of law instead complement each other. Under this approach, federal regulators would maximally preserve the traditional role of state tort law while ensuring uniformity across the national market.

AV Problem 7.3

How would this regulatory approach apply to an FMVSS that determines the minimal safety performance required of an autonomous vehicle, the issue discussed in AV Problem 3.2 in Chapter 6, p. 249?

Analysis of AV Problem 7.3

In promulgating the FMVSS for ensuring that the autonomous vehicle's operating system can systemically perform in a reasonably safe manner across its intended operating domain, federal regulators must initially resolve two important components of the safety problem. First, what are the appropriate testing conditions that would reliably establish the safety performance of a fully functioning autonomous vehicle? Once this question has been answered, the federal regulators must then define the appropriate benchmark against which that safety performance ought to be measured. Is it conventional vehicles, or instead other commercially distributed autonomous vehicles that are already on the road? Faced with this decision, the majority of states will not clearly reach the same conclusion in tort cases. Federal regulation has a comparative institutional advantage and should resolve these issues without resort to the associated rules of state tort law.

In contrast, state tort systems are better situated than federal regulators to resolve the hard policy issue of how much manufacturers should be required to expend (on more extensive testing) to reduce the risk of physical harm and make the product reasonably safe. This tort question is clearly resolved by a majority of states in the same manner—the risk-utility test, requiring that AV manufacturers test the vehicle until the costs of more extensive testing exceed the safety benefits. As a matter of comparative institutional advantage, federal regulators should defer to this policy conclusion and use the majoritarian tort standard as the minimal safety performance required by the FMVSS.

This regulatory approach for resolving the federalism problem has obvious appeal. NHTSA can promulgate the FMVSS for adequate premarket testing based on the safety standard (risk-utility test) adopted by the majority of states, while drawing on its comparative expertise to determine other policy and technical issues for which state tort law does not offer a comparative institutional advantage. This type of regulation would fully further the federal interest in uniformity while also maximally accounting for the historic state interest in tort law—the regulatory sweet spot.

11

Factual Causation

Whether the tort claim is based on negligence, strict liability, or the implied warranty, the prima facie case of liability requires the plaintiff to prove that his or her injury was caused by a product defect for which the defendant is legally responsible. The element of causation ties the violation of the plaintiff's tort right to the defendant's breach of duty, entitling the plaintiff to receive compensation from the defendant wrongdoer.

The element of causation involves two distinctive issues that courts have traditionally lumped together under the rubric of *proximate cause*. Today these issues are treated separately, with one pertaining to the factual cause of the injury, and the other to a policy-based determination of legal or proximate cause that defines the appropriate scope of liability (the subject of Chapter 12).

Ordinarily, the element of causation is compatible with the safety objective of products liability. A manufacturer that incurs liability for the injuries caused by its defective products has a sufficient financial incentive to supply nondefective products. In some cases, however, plaintiffs face insurmountable evidentiary problems and cannot prove causation. In these cases, the element of causation bars recovery, effectively immunizing the seller of a defective product from tort liability. Due to evidentiary problems, the element of causation can undermine safety incentives and conflict with the safety objective of products liability.

Eliminating the element of factual causation would solve this deterrence problem. Rather than base liability on the plaintiff's harm, liability could be set at the amount necessary to give product sellers a sufficient financial incentive to supply nondefective products; the promotion of product safety does not require proof that the defect caused the plaintiff (or anyone else) to suffer injury. *See* Guido Calabresi, *Concerning Cause and the Law of Torts: An Essay for Harry Kalven, Jr.*, 43 U. Chi. L. Rev. 69, 85 (1975) ("One could do away with the *but for* test and employ other methods to [decide whether accident avoidance is worthwhile]. For example, one could simply guess at the size of injury costs that will be associated in the future with behavior causally linked to such injury costs.").

Eliminating the element of causation or even reducing the plaintiff's burden of proof is highly controversial. When the defendant's breach of duty caused injury to the plaintiff, tort liability remedies the violation of the plaintiff's tort right. Without such a causal requirement, tort law would no longer be a system of *private law* that enforces individual rights and their correlative duties. Tort law would instead be a system of *public law* designed to further a public objective, in this instance one of product safety.

For these reasons, some of the most controversial product cases involve the question whether the plaintiff's burden of proof should be shifted or otherwise relaxed when the circumstances prevent proof of causation under ordinary evidentiary rules. In a few recurring sets of circumstances, courts have adopted special causal rules that appear to ease the plaintiff's evidentiary burden. Do these rules unduly relax the plaintiff's burden of proof and tend to show that tort law is a form of public law designed to further the important social objective of product safety? Or do these rules instead adhere to the requirement of causation that ties the violation of the plaintiff's tort right to the defendant's breach of duty?

"Whether a product defect caused harm to persons or property is determined by the prevailing rules and principles governing causation in tort." RESTATEMENT (THIRD) OF TORTS: PRODUCTS LIABILITY §15. Unlike our earlier inquiries that addressed how liability rules are shaped by the concern for product safety, we must now consider whether the general tort principle of causation tempers liability rules that might otherwise further the safety objective.

I. THE BUT-FOR TEST

CROSSLEY v. GENERAL MOTORS CORP.
United States Court of Appeals, Seventh Circuit, 1994
33 F.3d 818

Harlington WOOD, JR., J. After a one vehicle automobile accident in which Richard Crossley, the driver, was seriously injured, onlookers discovered that one of the axle shafts on his Chevrolet S-10 Blazer was fractured. Crossley sued General Motors, the manufacturer of the Blazer, seeking compensation for his injuries. The central question at trial in this diversity suit in which California law controlled was whether the axle fractured before the crash, constituting the cause of the accident, or as a result of the crash, which was caused by Crossley's negligence.

Three eyewitnesses testified that on July 23, 1988, Crossley was driving his 1987 Chevrolet S-10 Blazer on a banked, curved two-lane connector ramp linking two interstate freeways near Ontario, California, when he lost control of the Blazer. He was travelling at approximately 70 miles per hour in a 55 miles per hour zone, and was passing other vehicles on the curved connector ramp. Accident reconstructionists for both Crossley and General Motors placed Crossley's speed at or above 70 miles per hour at the time of the accident. Additionally, experts for both sides agreed that Crossley's tires were in poor condition: they were mismatched in both size and brand, worn, and had nails, screws, and plugs in them. All three eyewitnesses noticed generally that the tires looked substandard, and specifically that the left rear tire was low on air pressure.

One of the eyewitnesses noticed the left rear tire begin to buckle as Crossley veered in front of him to pass. Immediately thereafter, Crossley lost control and

I. The But-For Test

began to fishtail back and forth across both lanes of traffic. The Blazer rotated 360 degrees and flew off the side of the connector ramp passenger side first. During those moments, none of the eyewitnesses could recall witnessing signs of an axle shaft breaking—they did not notice the undercarriage of the Blazer contacting the ground, sparks flying, or the wheels detaching.

After the Blazer flew off of the connector, it sailed 40 to 50 feet in the air at approximately 60 miles per hour before hitting the ground. The eyewitnesses further noted that the initial point of impact upon landing was on the right rear tire of the Blazer. The vehicle then rolled over several times over a distance of 287 feet. Through the cloud of dust caused by the impact, one of the witnesses saw Crossley ejected from the Blazer 50 to 60 feet in the air. Crossley suffered a closed head injury, and as a result is a spastic quadriplegic.

Officer Trinidad Gonzales of the California Highway Patrol investigated the accident. He found the right rear wheel and axle stub resting ten feet from where the Blazer stopped. Officer Gonzales began inspecting the pavement on the highway where Crossley lost control for gouges, abrasions, or any other marks that would indicate that the tire came off while the Blazer was on the roadway. After 30 minutes of investigation, neither Officer Gonzales, who previously had investigated over 100 rollover accidents, nor Officer Ellen Conley, who assisted in investigating the accident, found any irregular marks on the highway.

As part of its defense, General Motors intended to call as a witness Kenneth Orlowski, an expert in assessing rollover accidents, to explain the dynamics of rollovers to the jury. To assist Orlowski in explaining those concepts to the jury, General Motors sought to introduce a videotape of a study of rollover sequences that involved a 1982 Malibu (the Malibu tape). Crossley objected to the presentation of the Malibu tape because it depicted a different model vehicle, the test was conducted in a controlled setting during which the automobile was propelled from a dolly at 31 miles per hour, and the road surfaces were different. The district court allowed General Motors to play the Malibu tape for the purpose of demonstrating "general scientific and engineering principles."

Crossley presented an entirely different picture of causation. Crossley contended that the axle shaft cracked before he lost control of his Blazer, and that the crack occurred because of a manufacturing defect for which he sought to hold General Motors strictly liable. Professor David Flebeck, Crossley's metallurgy expert, testified that General Motors was supposed to heat treat the axle so that the outer case had high hardness and the inner core was softer, or ductile. Flebeck further stated that the individual grains of metal in the axle of Crossley's Blazer were damaged during the hardening process, causing the outer case and inner core of the axle to become brittle. The brittle nature of the axle could cause the axle to fracture under even normal operating loads. Flebeck opined that the axle embrittlement caused Crossley to lose control of his vehicle and therefore caused his injuries. Professor Roland Ruhl, Crossley's accident reconstruction expert, concurred in Flebeck's assessment of what caused the accident, and added that there was no substantial damage to the right rear quarter of the Blazer, as would be consistent with the vehicle hitting the ground with sufficient force to break the axle.

After having been exposed to both theories of causation, the jury deliberated and returned the following signed special verdict form:

Question No. 1: Was there a defect in manufacture of the product involved?
Answer: YES
Question No. 2: Did the defect exist when it left the possession of the defendant?
Answer: YES
Question No. 3: Was the defect a cause of injury to plaintiff?
Answer: NO

The district court therefore entered judgment on the verdict in favor of General Motors, and subsequently denied Crossley's post-trial motion for a new trial. Crossley now appeals from the judgment of the district court and its denial of his motion for a new trial.

Crossley argues that the evidence presented at trial was insufficient to support the jury verdict against him, and therefore suggests that the district court erred in failing to grant his motion for a new trial. Appellate review of such a denial, however, is extremely limited. The decision whether to grant a new trial is committed to the discretion of the district court, and we therefore will not disturb that decision except under exceptional circumstances showing a clear abuse of discretion.

We find no abuse of discretion in the decision of the district court not to grant a new trial. General Motors elicited the testimony of three eyewitnesses to the accident, a metallurgist, and an accident reconstructionist, among others, all of whom presented ample evidence suggesting that Crossley's negligence caused his accident, not a cracked axle shaft. Crossley would have us reweigh all of the trial testimony based solely on the cold record, but we are not inclined to so cavalierly disregard the reasoned decision of twelve men and women who observed the demeanor of the witnesses and analyzed the evidence accordingly.

Crossley also argues that the special verdict form reveals an inconsistency in the jury verdict. The supposed inconsistency is based on the jury concluding that there was a manufacturing defect in the Blazer, but that the defect did not cause Crossley's accident. Our duty is to attempt to reconcile an apparently inconsistent jury verdict, if doing so is possible.

Reconciling the jury verdict in this instance is an easy task. Causation clearly is a distinct element under California law, which controls in this diversity action. The mere existence of a defect does not prove that the defect was responsible for subsequent injuries — if a person intentionally drives a defective Blazer off a cliff, the driver's estate cannot recover against General Motors because the vehicle in which the injuries occurred was defective. In this case, the jury concluded that although Crossley's Blazer was improperly manufactured, Crossley's negligence caused him to lose control of his vehicle and crash, and it was not until the impact of the crash that the already brittle axle broke. That assessment of events, whether accurate or not, certainly is internally consistent.

The judgment of the district court therefore is AFFIRMED.

I. The But-For Test

NOTES AND QUESTIONS

1. *Different types of causal questions.* To establish factual causation, the plaintiff must prove, by a preponderance of the evidence, that the defect (1) can cause the general type of injury in question, an issue called *general causation*; (2) did cause the specific injury in question, an issue of *specific causation*; and (3) was in a product that was commercially distributed by the defendant, an issue of *individualized causation*. What was the type of causal question at issue in *Crossley*?

2. *The but-for test of factual causation.* In most cases, the cause-in-fact inquiry can be simply expressed as requiring proof that but for the defect, the accident would not have occurred. In *Crossley*, for example, the jury presumably concluded that even if the plaintiff's vehicle had not been defective, his negligent driving or poorly maintained tires would still have caused the accident. The defect, therefore, was not a but-for cause of the accident.

When fully analyzed, the but-for test involves four steps that are necessary to frame the causal question properly. In the ordinary negligence case, the inquiry takes the following form:

> First, one must identify the injury or injuries for which redress is sought. This step rarely presents any difficulty. . . .
>
> Second, one must identify the defendant's wrongful conduct. Care is required here. It is not enough for the plaintiff to show that her injuries would not have occurred if the defendant had never been born; the plaintiff must show that her injuries probably would not have occurred if the defendant had not engaged in the particular conduct alleged (and ultimately proved) in the lawsuit to have been wrongful. . . .
>
> The third step is the trickiest. It involves using the imagination to create a counterfactual hypothesis. One creates a mental picture of a situation identical to the actual facts of the case in all respects save one: the defendant's wrongful conduct is now "corrected" to the minimal extent necessary to make it conform to the law's requirements. . . .
>
> The fourth step asks the key question whether the injuries that the plaintiff suffered would probably still have occurred had the defendant behaved correctly in the sense indicated.

David W. Robertson, *The Common Sense of Cause in Fact*, 75 Tex. L. Rev. 1765, 1770-1771 (1997).

In a product case, the defendant's tortious or wrongful conduct involves the commercial distribution of a defective product. Under the next step of the causal inquiry, the court must consider the "counterfactual hypothesis" involving a hypothetical "situation identical to the actual facts of the case in all respects save one": the defect in the product is eliminated. (Can you see why this is the only tortious aspect of the defendant's conduct?) The final step of the inquiry then asks whether the injury would have occurred if the nondefective product had been used in the counterfactual world; if the nondefective product would still have caused the injury (as in *Crossley*), the defect was not a but-for cause of the harm.

3. *Multiple tortious causes.* Courts do not use the but-for test in cases involving multiple tortious causes. In product cases, this situation occurs

> frequently in cases in which persons have been exposed to multiple doses of a toxic agent. When a person contracts a disease such as cancer, and sues multiple actors claiming that each provided some dose of a toxic substance that caused the disease, the question of the causal role of each defendant's toxic substance arises. Assuming that there is some threshold dose sufficient to cause the disease, the person may have been exposed to doses in excess of the threshold before contracting the disease. Thus, some or all of the person's exposures may not have been but-for causes of the disease.

RESTATEMENT (THIRD) OF TORTS: LIABILITY FOR PHYSICAL AND EMOTIONAL HARM §27 cmt. g.

In many asbestos cases, for example, the plaintiff can prove that his lung cancer was caused by exposure to different asbestos products that different defendants had supplied. Based on this evidence, each defendant asbestos supplier can argue that the cancer, more likely than not, was caused by the other defendants' asbestos products. This defense, when employed by each defendant asbestos supplier, would deny the plaintiff's recovery altogether even though no defendant disputes the plaintiff's proof that his lung disease was caused by cumulative exposure to the defendants' asbestos products. Recognizing that each defendant's evidentiary argument does not rebut the plaintiff's proof of causation, courts permit recovery:

> In products liability involving asbestos, where the plaintiff has sufficiently demonstrated both lung disease resulting from exposure to asbestos and that the exposure was to the asbestos products of many different, but identified, suppliers, no supplier enjoys a causation defense solely on the ground that the plaintiff would probably have suffered the same disease from inhaling fibers originating from the products of other suppliers.

Eagle-Picher Indus. Inc. v. Balbos, 604 A.2d 445, 449 (Md. 1992). According to the *Restatement (Third) of Torts: Liability for Physical and Emotional Harm* §27 comment g, this rule applies in all cases involving toxic substances that cause disease.

Because the but-for test does not work in these cases, courts determine factual causation by asking whether the defendant's tortious conduct was "a substantial factor in bringing about the harm." RESTATEMENT (SECOND) OF TORTS §431. In asbestos and other toxic tort cases involving dose-responsive diseases, "[b]are proof of some *de minimus* exposure to a defendant's product is insufficient to establish substantial-factor causation." Howard ex rel. Estate of Ravert v. A.W. Chesterton Co., 78 A.3d 605, 608 (Pa. 2013). *See also, e.g.*, Rutherford v. Owens-Ill. Inc., 941 P.2d 1203, 1214 (Cal. 1997) (describing insubstantial factors as those having only an "infinitesimal" or "theoretical" role in causing the injury). If a substantial factor attributable to one defendant, when combined with the substantial factors attributable to other tortfeasors, more likely than not caused the plaintiff's injury, then the plaintiff can recover from the single defendant under the rule of joint and several liability.

As these cases illustrate, courts rely on the *substantial-factor test* to determine factual causation in cases involving multiple tortious causes. In some jurisdictions, courts apply the substantial-factor test in all cases, including those in which there was only a single tortfeasor. *E.g., id.* at 1214 (explaining that the substantial-factor test applies in all negligence and products liability cases because it is "a clearer rule of causation—one which subsumes the 'but for' test while reaching beyond it to satisfactorily address other situations, such as those involving independent or concurrent causes in fact"). In cases involving a single tortfeasor, could the substantial-factor test function in a manner that reduces the plaintiff's ordinary burden of proof?

4. *Another class of hard causal questions.* The counterfactual nature of the causal inquiry can be puzzling when the course of events in the counterfactual world depends on human behavior that differs from what actually occurred. This problem was not present in *Crossley*, because the causal question turned solely on physical forces (the speed of the vehicle and condition of the tires), not on any changes in behavior (the elimination of the defective part would not have affected how the plaintiff drove the vehicle). In other cases, however, the plaintiff could have behaved differently if the product had not been defective. How should the court evaluate this counterfactual inquiry? What evidence would be sufficient to prove causation in these cases?

LIRIANO v. HOBART CORP.
United States Court of Appeals, Second Circuit, 1999
170 F.3d 264

CALABRESI, J. Luis Liriano was severely injured on the job in 1993 when his hand was caught in a meat grinder manufactured by Hobart Corporation ("Hobart") and owned by his employer, Super Associated ("Super"). The meat grinder had been sold to Super with a safety guard, but the safety guard was removed while the machine was in Super's possession and was not affixed to the meat grinder at the time of the accident. The machine bore no warning indicating that the grinder should be operated only with a safety guard attached.

Liriano sued Hobart under several theories, including failure to warn. Hobart brought a third-party claim against Super. The United States District Court for the Southern District of New York dismissed all of Liriano's claims except the one based on failure to warn, and the jury returned a verdict for Liriano on that claim.

Hobart and Super appealed.

Hobart makes two arguments challenging the sufficiency of the evidence. The first concerns the obviousness of the danger that Liriano faced, and the second impugns the causal relationship between Hobart's negligence and Liriano's injury. Each of these arguments implicates issues long debated in the law of torts.

[The portion of the opinion addressing the obviousness of the risk is excerpted in Chapter 7, section IV.]

In this argument, Hobart raises the issue of causation. It maintains that Liriano "failed to present any evidence that Hobart's failure to place a warning [on the machine] was causally related to his injury." Whether or not there had been a warning, Hobart says, Liriano might well have operated the machine as he did and suffered the injuries that he suffered. Liriano introduced no evidence, Hobart notes, suggesting either that he would have refused to grind meat had the machine borne a warning or that a warning would have persuaded Super not to direct its employees to use the grinder without the safety attachment.

Hobart's argument about causation follows logically from the notion that its duty to warn in this case merely required Hobart to inform Liriano that a guard was available and that he should not use an unguarded grinder. The contention is tightly reasoned, but it rests on a false premise. It assumes that the burden was on Liriano to introduce additional evidence showing that the failure to warn was a but-for cause of his injury, even after he had shown that Hobart's wrong greatly increased the likelihood of the harm that occurred. But Liriano does not bear that burden. When a defendant's negligent act is deemed wrongful precisely because it has a strong propensity to cause the type of injury that ensued, that very causal tendency is evidence enough to establish a *prima facie* case of cause-in-fact. The burden then shifts to the *defendant* to come forward with evidence that its negligence was *not* such a but-for cause.

We know, as a general matter, that the kind of negligence that the jury attributed to the defendant tends to cause exactly the kind of injury that the plaintiff suffered. Indeed, that is what the jury must have found when it ruled that Hobart's failure to warn constituted negligence. In such situations, rather than requiring the plaintiff to bring in more evidence to demonstrate that his case is of the ordinary kind, the law presumes normality and requires the defendant to adduce evidence that the case is an exception. Accordingly, in a case like this, it is up to the defendant to bring in evidence tending to rebut the strong inference, arising from the accident, that the defendant's negligence was in fact a but-for cause of the plaintiff's injury. *See* Zuchowicz v. United States, 140 F.3d 381, 388 nn.6-7, 390-91 (2d Cir. 1998).

This shifting of the *onus procedendi* has long been established in New York. Its classic statement was made more than seventy years ago, when the Court of Appeals decided a case in which a car collided with a buggy driving after sundown without lights. *See* Martin v. Herzog, 228 N.Y. 164, 170 (1920). The driver of the buggy argued that his negligence in driving without lights had not been shown to be the cause-in-fact of the accident. Writing for the Court, Judge Cardozo reasoned that the legislature deemed driving without lights after sundown to be negligent precisely because not using lights tended to cause accidents of the sort that had occurred in the case. The simple fact of an accident under those conditions, he said, was enough to support the inference of but-for causal connection between the negligence and the particular accident. The inference, he noted, could be rebutted. But it was up to the negligent party to produce the evidence supporting such a rebuttal. The words that Judge Cardozo applied to the buggy's failure to use lights are equally applicable to Hobart's failure to warn: "If nothing else is shown to break the connection, we have a case, prima facie sufficient, of negligence contributing to the result."

I. The But-For Test

Under that approach, the fact that Liriano did not introduce detailed evidence of but-for causal connection between Hobart's failure to warn and his injury cannot bar his claim. His *prima facie* case arose from the strong causal linkage between Hobart's negligence and the harm that occurred. And, since the *prima facie* case was not rebutted, it suffices.

The district court did not err. We affirm its decision in all respects.

NOTES AND QUESTIONS

1. *The ordinary burden of proof.* The ordinary evidentiary standard "requires the trier of fact to believe that the existence of a fact is more probable than its nonexistence before he may find in favor of the party who has the burden to persuade the judge of the fact's existence." Concrete Pipe and Prod. v. Constr. Laborers Pension Trust, 508 U.S. 602, 622 (1993). Put somewhat differently, the "preponderance standard is a more-likely-than-not rule, under which the trier of fact rules for the plaintiff if it thinks the chance greater than 0.5 that the plaintiff is in the right." Brown v. Bowen, 847 F.2d 342, 345 (7th Cir. 1988). Under this standard, errors are inevitable. After all, if the plaintiff wins because there is a 50.1 percent chance she is in the right, there is also a 49.9 percent chance that the defendant's denial of liability is true. The evidentiary standard, therefore, addresses the inevitable risk of error in a world of factual uncertainty, trying to balance "false positives" (plaintiff winning when, in fact, defendant should have prevailed) against "false negatives" (defendant prevailing when, in fact, plaintiff should have won). When evaluated in this manner, the "preponderance-of-the-evidence standard results in a roughly equal allocation of the risk of error between litigants." Grogan v. Garner, 498 U.S. 279, 286 (1991).

2. *The liberal rule of but-for causation.* Did the court in *Liriano* find that the plaintiff satisfied the ordinary evidentiary standard? The court applied a causal rule that it had explained and then adopted in a prior case:

> The problem of linking defendant's negligence to the harm that occurred is one that many courts have addressed in the past. A car is speeding and an accident occurs. That the car was involved and was a cause of the crash is readily shown. The accident, moreover, is of the sort that rules prohibiting speeding are designed to prevent. But is this enough to support a finding of fact, in the individual case, that *speeding* was, in fact, more probably than not, the cause of the accident? . . . To put it more precisely — the defendant's negligence was strongly causally linked to the accident, and the defendant was undoubtedly a *but for* cause of the harm, but does this suffice to allow a fact finder to say that the defendant's *negligence* was a *but for* cause?
>
> At one time, courts were reluctant to say in such circumstances that the wrong could be deemed to be the cause. They emphasized the logical fallacy of *post hoc, ergo propter hoc*, and demanded some direct evidence connecting the defendant's wrongdoing to the harm.
>
> All that has changed, however. And, as is so frequently the case in tort law, Chief Judge Cardozo in New York and Chief Justice Traynor

in California led the way. In various opinions, they stated that: if (a) a negligent act was deemed wrongful *because* that act increased the chances that a particular type of accident would occur, and (b) a mishap of that very sort did happen, this was enough to support a finding by the trier of fact that the negligent behavior caused the harm. Where such a strong causal link exists, it is up to the negligent party to bring in evidence denying *but for* cause and suggesting that in the actual case the wrongful conduct had not been a substantial factor.

Zuchowicz v. United States, 140 F.3d 381, 390-391 (2d Cir. 1998) (Calabresi, J.); *see also* Dan B. Dobbs, Paul T. Hayden & Ellen M. Bublick, THE LAW OF TORTS §191 (2d ed. 2014 & 2020 update) (observing that if "the defendant's conduct is deemed negligent for the very reason that it creates a core risk of the kind of harm suffered by the plaintiff," then "[c]ourts are avowedly liberal with such causation issues").

For ease of exposition, define this as the *liberal rule of but-for causation.* The liberality of the rule is most apparent in tort cases involving the defendant's negligent failure to provide emergency equipment, such as a lifesaving device on board a boat. In one representative case, the court let the jury decide whether this type of negligence caused the decedent to drown, even though the failure to install the device could have caused the death only if "there was time for a crew member to go to the hypothetical storage location, obtain the hypothetical line-throwing appliance, move it to the appropriate firing location, and fire the appliance—all before [the decedent] went limp in the water." Reyes v. Vantage S.S. Co., 609 F.2d 140, 144 (5th Cir. 1980). How could the jury determine whether the hypothetical line-throwing device, more likely than not, would have prevented the drowning? Given the exigencies of an emergency situation, the likelihood of a successful lifesaving operation would often seem to be far less than 50 percent. Courts nevertheless submit these cases to the jury if there was any chance of survival. Consequently, the liberal rule of but-for causation would seem to relax the plaintiff's burden of proof by effectively presuming causation in these cases.

What justifies the liberal rule of but-for causation?

> The reason seems fairly obvious. It would be futile for the courts to recognize a duty to provide emergency equipment and to impose an obligation to proceed promptly to the rescue if the defendant could successfully seize upon the uncertainty which nearly always attends the rescue operation as a reason for dismissing the claim. In such situations an insistence on proof by probabilities or better has no place. The ever-present chance that the rescue might fail is a part of the risk against which the rule protects.

Wex S. Malone, *Ruminations on Cause-in-Fact*, 9 Stan. L. Rev. 60, 77 (1956).

Does this reasoning prove too much? To benefit from the liberal rule of but-for causation, the plaintiff must first prove that the product was defective and that she suffered injury of the type threatened by the defect. In these circumstances, the objective of deterrence would justify a *conclusive* or *irrebuttable* presumption of causation because liability in these cases would ordinarily further the objective of deterring the distribution of defective products. A conclusive presumption, however, would effectively eliminate the element of causation from the plaintiff's prima facie case. *See* RESTATEMENT (THIRD) OF TORTS: LIABILITY FOR PHYSICAL AND EMOTIONAL HARM §28 cmt. b ("If nothing further were required [other than proof of tortious conduct and the concomitant increase in risk], the plaintiff's burden of proof on causation would always be satisfied. Thus, only when the tortious conduct reasonably could be found, after the fact, to have increased the risk of harm to a greater extent than the risk posed by all other potential causes would an inference from tortious conduct alone be permissible."). If the liberal rule of but-for causation effectively eliminates the element of factual causation, do you think courts would approve of the rule?

3. *Do courts regularly presume causation?* As formulated in *Liriano*, the liberal rule of but-for causation appears to be quite general, applicable to any case in which the plaintiff suffered injury of the type threatened by the defect. Did the court presume causation in *Crossley*? The issue cannot be easily answered because both parties presented evidence on factual causation, creating a jury question that was resolved in favor of the defendant. A court needs to expressly invoke the presumption only if the plaintiff otherwise provides insufficient evidence of causation, as in *Liriano*. In these cases, the presumption provides a basis for submitting the causal issue to the jury, which may or may not then find for the plaintiff on the issue. To determine whether the liberal rule of but-for causation is generally applicable to product cases, one must look for cases in which the court refused to submit the causal issue to the jury, even though the plaintiff proved that the defect increased the risk of injury and that she suffered injury of the type threatened by the defect. The existence of such cases would cast doubt on the proposition that the liberal rule of but-for causation can be generally applied without being subject to some limiting principle not identified by the court in *Liriano*.

DAUBERT v. MERRELL DOW PHARMACEUTICALS, INC.
United States Court of Appeals, Ninth Circuit, 1995
43 F.3d 1311

KOZINSKI, J. Two minors brought suit against Merrell Dow Pharmaceuticals, claiming they suffered limb reduction birth defects because their mothers had taken Bendectin, a drug prescribed for morning sickness to about 17.5 million pregnant women in the United States between 1957 and 1982. This appeal deals with an evidentiary question: whether certain expert scientific testimony is admissible to prove that Bendectin caused the plaintiffs' birth defects.

For the most part, we don't know how birth defects come about. We do know they occur in 2-3% of births, whether or not the expectant mother has taken Bendectin. Limb defects are even rarer, occurring in fewer than one birth out of every 1000. But scientists simply do not know how teratogens (chemicals known to cause limb reduction defects) do their damage: They cannot reconstruct the biological chain of events that leads from an expectant mother's ingestion of a teratogenic substance to the stunted development of a baby's limbs. Nor do they know what it is about teratogens that causes them to have this effect. No doubt, someday we will have this knowledge, and then we will be able to tell precisely whether and how Bendectin (or any other suspected teratogen) interferes with limb development; in the current state of scientific knowledge, however, we are ignorant.

Not knowing the mechanism whereby a particular agent causes a particular effect is not always fatal to a plaintiff's claim. Causation can be proved even when we don't know precisely *how* the damage occurred, if there is sufficiently compelling proof that the agent must have caused the damage *somehow*. One method of proving causation in these circumstances is to use statistical evidence. If 50 people who eat at a restaurant one evening come down with food poisoning during the night, we can infer that the restaurant's food probably contained something unwholesome, even if none of the dishes is available for analysis. This inference is based on the fact that, in our health-conscious society, it is highly unlikely that 50 people who have nothing in common except that they ate at the same restaurant will get food poisoning from independent sources.

It is by such means that plaintiffs here seek to establish that Bendectin is responsible for their injuries. They rely on the testimony of three groups of scientific experts. One group proposes to testify that there is a statistical link between the ingestion of Bendectin during pregnancy and limb reduction defects. These experts have not themselves conducted epidemiological (human statistical) studies on the effects of Bendectin; rather, they have reanalyzed studies published by other scientists, none of whom reported a statistical association between Bendectin and birth defects. Other experts proffered by plaintiffs propose to testify that Bendectin causes limb reduction defects in humans because it causes such defects in laboratory animals. A third group of experts sees a link between Bendectin and birth defects because Bendectin has a chemical structure that is similar to other drugs suspected of causing birth defects.

California tort law requires plaintiffs to show not merely that Bendectin increased the likelihood of injury, but that it more likely than not caused *their* injuries. [ ] In terms of statistical proof, this means that plaintiffs must establish not just that their mothers' ingestion of Bendectin increased somewhat the likelihood of birth defects, but that it more than doubled it—only then can it be said that Bendectin is more likely than not the source of their injury. Because the background rate of limb reduction defects is one per thousand births, plaintiffs must show that among children of mothers who took Bendectin the incidence of such defects was more than two per thousand.

None of plaintiffs' epidemiological experts claims that ingestion of Bendectin during pregnancy more than doubles the risk of birth defects. To evaluate the relationship between Bendectin and limb reduction defects, an epidemiologist would take a sample of the population and compare the frequency of birth defects in children whose mothers took Bendectin with the frequency of defects in children whose mothers did not. The ratio derived from this comparison would be an estimate of the "relative risk" associated with Bendectin. [ ] For an epidemiological study to show causation under a preponderance standard, "the relative risk of limb reduction defects arising from the epidemiological data will, at a minimum, have to exceed 2." [ ] That is, the study must show that children

I. The But-For Test

whose mothers took Bendectin are more than twice as likely to develop limb reduction birth defects as children whose mothers did not.[16] While plaintiffs' epidemiologists make vague assertions that there is a statistically significant relationship between Bendectin and birth defects, none states that the relative risk is greater than two. These studies thus would not be helpful, and indeed would only serve to confuse the jury, if offered to prove rather than refute causation. A relative risk of less than two may suggest teratogenicity, but it actually tends to *dis*prove legal causation, as it shows that Bendectin does not double the likelihood of birth defects.

As the district court properly found below, "the strongest inference to be drawn for plaintiffs based on the epidemiological evidence is that Bendectin could *possibly* have caused plaintiffs' injuries." The same is true of the other testimony derived from animal studies and chemical structure analyses—"these experts testify to a possibility rather than a probability." [ ] Plaintiffs do not quantify this possibility, or otherwise indicate how their conclusions about causation should be weighted, even though the substantive legal standard has always required proof of causation by a preponderance of the evidence.[19]

The district court's grant of summary judgment is *AFFIRMED*.

NOTES AND QUESTIONS

1. *Situating the case.* The court was deciding the case on remand from the U.S. Supreme Court, Daubert v. Merrell Dow Pharmaceuticals, Inc., 509 U.S. 579 (1993). That case is discussed in section VI *infra*, which contains extended discussion of whether plaintiffs must always prove causation in these circumstances with epidemiologic evidence showing a doubling of the risk. For present purposes, the case is primarily of interest to us insofar as it sheds light on the liberal rule of but-for causation.

The liberal rule of but-for causation that the court applied in *Liriano* is recognized under California law, the body of law governing the tort claims in *Daubert*. The liberal rule presumes causation when the plaintiff proves defect and suffered injury of the type threatened by the defect.

---

16. A statistical study showing a relative risk of less than two could be combined with other evidence to show it is more likely than not that the accused cause is responsible for a particular plaintiff's injury. For example, a statistical study may show that a particular type of birth defect is associated with some unknown causes, as well as two known potential causes—e.g., smoking and drinking. If a study shows that the relative risk of injury for those who smoke is 1.5 as compared to the general population, while it is 1.8 for those who drink, a plaintiff who does not drink might be able to reanalyze the data to show that the study of smoking did not account for the effect of drinking on the incidence of birth defects in the general population. By making the appropriate comparison—between nondrinkers who smoke and nondrinkers who do not smoke—the teetotaller plaintiff might be able to show that the relative risk of smoking for her is greater than two. Here, however, plaintiffs' experts did not seek to differentiate these plaintiffs from the subjects of the statistical studies. The studies must therefore stand or fall on their own.

19. Several circuits have conducted a similar analysis in finding plaintiffs' expert testimony insufficient to prove causation as a matter of law. *See* Elkins v. Richardson-Merrell, Inc., 8 F.3d 1068, 1071-72 (6th Cir. 1993); Turpin v. Merrell Dow Pharmaceuticals, Inc., 43 F.3d 1311, 1359-61 (6th Cir. 1992); Ealy v. Richardson-Merrell, Inc., 897 F.2d 1159, 1163 (D.C. Cir. 1990); Brock v. Merrell Dow Pharmaceuticals, Inc., 874 F.2d 307, 311-15 (5th Cir. 1989); Lynch v. Merrell-Nat'l Labs., 830 F.2d 1190, 1195-97 (1st Cir. 1987).

Both conditions were satisfied in *Daubert*, yet the court concluded that plaintiffs had not proven causation because they had not shown that the defective drug, more likely than not, caused the harms in question. *Daubert* is contrary to our so-called liberal rule of but-for causation, indicating that there is some limitation of the causal rule that its black-letter formulation does not expressly recognize. What might explain why the rule applied in *Liriano* and not *Daubert*?

2. *Statistical proof of causation.* "Judges generally have refused to accept naked statistics or *ex ante* causal probabilities as evidence of what actually happened on a particular occasion." Richard W. Wright, *Causation, Responsibility, Risk, Probability, Naked Statistics, and Proof: Pruning the Bramble Bush by Clarifying the Concepts*, 73 Iowa L. Rev. 1001, 1050-1051 (1988). Instead of rejecting plaintiffs' statistical proof on this basis, the court in *Daubert* held that the proffered statistics did not establish the increase in risk necessary to show that Bendectin, more likely than not, caused the plaintiffs' birth defects. But if plaintiffs had provided such evidence, then their statistical proof would have been sufficient for proving causation. What explains why the court in *Daubert* relied on "naked statistics" to determine the causal question, even though judges generally refuse to rely on this type of evidence to determine causation?

Statistical proof is presumptively unreliable when more probing particularistic proof was otherwise reasonably available. As Judge Richard Posner explained:

> Suppose . . . that a person is hit by a bus, and it is known that 51 percent of the buses on the road where he was hit are owned by Bus Company *A* and 49 percent by Bus Company *B*. He sues *A* and asks for judgment on the basis of this statistic alone; he presents no other evidence. If the defendant also presents no evidence, should a jury be permitted to award judgment for the plaintiff? The law answers "no." But this is not because of doubt about the evidentiary value of statistical evidence. The true source of disquiet in the example, we believe, is the tacit assumption that the statistic concerning the ownership of the buses is the only evidence the plaintiff can obtain. If it is his only evidence, the inference to be drawn is not that there is a 51 percent probability that it was a bus owned by *A* that hit him but that he either investigated and discovered that it was actually a bus owned by *B* (which might be judgment-proof and so not worth suing), or that he has simply not bothered to conduct an investigation. In either event he should lose, in the first case obviously and in the second because a court should not be required to expend any of its scarce resources of time and effort on a case until the plaintiff has conducted a sufficient search to indicate that an expenditure of public resources is reasonably likely to yield a social benefit.

U.S. v. Veysey, 334 F.3d 600, 605 (7th Cir. 2003) (Posner, J.).

The hypothetical posed by Judge Posner provides another reason for rejecting statistical proof of causation. In the hypothetical, the plaintiff's statistical proof inappropriately assumes that any bus from either company is equally likely to have tortiously caused the harm. However, if Bus Company *A* adopted safety procedures that considerably reduced the risk of negligent driving as compared to the procedures employed by Bus Company *B*, then the fact that Company *A* had 51 percent of the buses in town does not establish that it created a 51 percent chance of tortiously causing the harm. The relative proportion of buses owned by the two companies does not translate into a reliable measure of proportional risk, rendering the proof inadmissible.

Do any of these reasons for rejecting statistical evidence apply to *Daubert*? Ordinarily, the statistical findings of epidemiologic study are the only reliable way to establish a causal link between a substance and an injury with unknown etiology, like birth defects or cancer. "Carcinogens, reproductive toxicants, and neurotoxicants are invisible and undetectable intruders.... When they harm humans they typically leave no signature effects (the adverse effects are identical in most cases to diseases resulting from other causes)." Carl Cranor, TOXIC TORTS: SCIENCE, LAW, AND THE POSSIBILITY OF JUSTICE 92 (2006). For cancers and birth defects with unknown etiologies, any particular injury cannot be traced to any particular carcinogen or teratogen. The only way to prove causation is with general statistics showing how exposure to the substance increases the risk of cancer or birth defects. As long as the statistics were generated from the study of a population with characteristics sufficiently similar to those of the plaintiff, courts routinely recognize that statistical evidence is relevant for proof of causation in these so-called *toxic tort* cases. These issues are addressed extensively in section VI *infra*.

3. *Rethinking the liberal rule of but-for causation.* According to *Daubert*, the background risk of birth defects involving limb reduction is 1 in 1,000 births, and the plaintiffs, at most, only proved that Bendectin increases this risk but does not double it. Suppose the evidence showed that Bendectin increases the risk to 1.5 in 1,000 births. For every 2,000 births, on average three individuals who were exposed to Bendectin would have birth defects involving limb reductions. Two of the three would have had these birth defects anyway (due to the background risk), and so there is only a one in three chance that Bendectin caused any particular injury. No plaintiff can show that her injury, more likely than not, was caused by the defective drug, which is why the court in *Daubert* concluded that the evidence bars plaintiffs' recovery in all cases.

By uniformly barring recovery, the ordinary evidentiary standard makes it futile for courts to recognize the duty to warn in these cases. The foregoing analysis assumes that one-third of the individuals with birth defects were injured by Bendectin, a risk sufficient to establish a duty to warn. Nevertheless, none of these individuals could recover because none could prove that Bendectin, more likely than not, caused her injury. If no plaintiff can ever enforce the tort right, what is the point of recognizing such a duty in the first instance?

To resolve this problem, courts purportedly rely on the liberal rule of but-for causation. *See* Wex S. Malone, *Ruminations on Cause-in-Fact*, 9 Stan. L. Rev. 60, 77 (1956) (justifying the liberal rule of but-for causation to ensure that it would not be "futile" for courts to recognize the duty). But as *Daubert* illustrates, even if it would otherwise be futile to recognize the duty, courts can still bar recovery under the ordinary evidentiary standard.

Daubert is not exceptional in this regard (as illustrated by footnote 19 of the opinion). These cases show that the concern for deterrence does not adequately explain why courts apply the liberal rule of but-for causation in some cases (*Liriano*) but not others (*Daubert*).

4. *The relative plausibility theory of proof.* The foregoing analysis of the liberal rule of but-for causation has assumed that the ordinary burden of proof requires evidence that would enable a reasonable juror to conclude that there is at least a 50.1 percent chance that the plaintiff is correct. However, the probabilistic interpretation of the ordinary evidentiary standard produces a number of anomalies that have led scholars to explore alternative accounts.

> Experimental research has yielded the insight that jurors do not, by and large, estimate probabilities when determining the events that transpired in a case; rather, they draw conclusions based on whether information assembles into plausible narratives. Narrative provides a deep structure inside the courtroom just as it does outside of it, not only so that triers of fact can "organize and reorganize large amounts of constantly changing information," but also so that they can decide what it means. In order to reach a verdict, jurors construct a story, learn of their decision alternatives and the "verdict category attributes," and then classify the story "into the best fitting verdict category." At this last step—the selection of the "best" account—jurors rely on coverage (whether the story can accommodate all the evidence), coherence (whether the story makes sense), and uniqueness (whether there are other plausible explanations).

Lisa Kern Griffin, *Narrative, Truth, and Trial*, 101 Geo. L.J. 281, 293 (2013).

This process of jury decision-making informs the relative plausibility theory of evidence, which posits that the ordinary evidentiary standard is best interpreted as a requirement that the jury must determine whether "the best available explanation" favors the plaintiff or defendant. "A number of general criteria affect the strength or quality of an explanation. These criteria include considerations such as consistency, coherence, fit with background knowledge, simplicity, absence of gaps, and the number of unlikely assumptions that need to be made." Ronald J. Allen & Michael S. Pardo, *Relative Plausibility and Its Critics*, 23 Int'l J. Evidence & Proof 5, 16 (2019). This application of the ordinary evidentiary standard "fits the underlying goals" of the evidentiary standards such as accuracy and allocation of the risk of legal error. *Id.* at 17-19.

In *Daubert*, does the "relative plausibility" of the evidence turn on anything other than risk of injury identified by epidemiologic study? What about cases involving lifesaving equipment and the like that generated the liberal rule of but-for causation? Consider Dobbs et al., THE LAW OF TORTS, at §191 ("If the defendant is negligent in failing to provide a fire escape in an apartment building, a lifeguard at a hotel swimming pool, or a warning about dangers of a product, the risks are all too great that someone will die in a fire, drown, or suffer product injury, so juries may be permitted in such cases to infer that the defendant's negligent conduct was a factual cause of the harms suffered in each case, even though it is perfectly

I. The But-For Test

possible that the precautions required would have availed nothing in the particular case.").

5. *Reconceptualizing the liberal rule of but-for causation.* In justifying the liberal rule of but-for causation, courts and commentators have recognized that the rule is somehow related to the nature of the duty. The deterrence justification maintains that causation must be presumed to make the duty practically enforceable. Another interpretation is available: The liberal rule simply recognizes that the jury can make the causal determination by constructing a narrative based on the nature of the underlying tort duty.

The but-for causal test requires a counterfactual inquiry that frequently involves assumptions about human behavior. Would the plaintiff in *Liriano* have read the warning and thereby avoided the injury? Would a lifesaving device have helped someone on the boat save someone else who had fallen overboard from drowning? In each of these cases, the duty to take the precaution in question—to supply an adequate warning or to have lifesaving devices on boats—assumes that the precaution would enable the relevant actors to prevent a significant number of accidents. This attribute of the duty can provide guidance on the assumptions about human behavior that the jury can reasonably adopt in constructing the counterfactual inquiry for determining causation.

In the drowning cases, for example, the required safety precaution would enable the relevant actors to prevent a significant number of injuries. Relying on the substantive nature of the duty, a jury could reasonably construct a narrative in which the lifesaving device would have made a difference by helping those on board to save the decedent from drowning. Such a finding would not involve conjecture or speculation, as it stems from the reasonable behavioral assumption embodied in the duty to install lifesaving devices on boats. As implied by the duty, the relevant actors could use the precaution to prevent injury in a significant number of cases. If that outcome could have occurred in the present case, the jury has a reasonable basis (the duty) for concluding that the precaution would have prevented the injury in this case (but-for causation). To be sure, the evidence also supports an alternative narrative in which the lifesaving device would not have made a difference. Each narrative is reasonable, explaining why these cases create a jury question about causation, even though the result is hard to explain under the probabilistic interpretation of the ordinary evidentiary standard. Consider Cipollone v. Liggett Group, Inc., 893 F.2d 541, 561 n.17 (3d Cir. 1990), *aff'd in part, rev'd in part on other grounds*, 505 U.S. 504 (1992) ("We are not convinced that when a jury determines that 'but for' a defendant's conduct, the injury would not have occurred, it is determining that the chances of that injury being the result of defendant's conduct are 50% or greater. Traditionally, jury instructions have been in words, not numbers.").

A judge who submits such an issue of factual causation to the jury is applying our so-called liberal rule of but-for causation. So conceptualized, this causal rule turns out to be liberal only insofar as it permits the jury to construct a causal narrative based on the nature of the underlying duty.

When interpreted in this manner, the liberal rule of but-for causation in a case like *Liriano* can be squared with the ordinary evidentiary rule applied in *Daubert*. In some cases, the causal question does not implicate any changes in human behavior, such as the issue of whether Bendectin causes birth defects. A behavioral inference would not help the plaintiff prove that Bendectin caused his or her injuries, explaining why the liberal rule of but-for causation does not apply to cases like *Daubert*. A behavioral inference would also not help the plaintiff in *Crossley* prove that the defective axle in his motor vehicle caused the crash. By contrast, any behavioral inference supplied by the duty will be critical in warning cases like *Liriano*—would the plaintiff have read the adequate warning and changed his behavior? The behavioral component of the causal inquiry can explain why the liberal rule of but-for causation applies in *Liriano* but not in *Daubert*.

II. PROOF OF CAUSATION IN WARNING CASES

To resolve the causal question for warning defects, courts have adopted different rules for addressing this distinctive evidentiary question.,

> Proving causation in a failure-to-warn case has peculiar difficulties. Proof that a collision between two cars would not have happened had defendant swerved or braked or driven within the speed limit is mostly a matter of physics. Proof that an accident would not have occurred if defendant had provided adequate warnings concerning the use of a product is more psychology and does not admit of the same degree of certainty.

General Motors Corp. v. Saenz, 873 S.W.2d 353, 357 (Tex. 1993). The causal issue in *Crossley*, p. 424 *supra*, was mostly a matter of physics—did the vehicle crash because of the driving speed coupled with bad tires, or because of the defective axle? Warning cases, by contrast, are more "psychology" in the sense that causation depends on the plaintiff's behavior—how she would have responded to an adequate warning if one had been given. In evaluating the different evidentiary rules for determining causation in warning cases, consider whether they are consistent with the liberal rule of but-for causation.

A. *The Subjective Standard*

In many jurisdictions, the plaintiff can establish causation by testifying that if she had been adequately warned of the risk, she would have changed her behavior and avoided the injury in question. *See, e.g.*, MacDonald v. Ortho Pharmaceutical Corp., 475 N.E.2d 65, 72 (Mass. 1985) (causation established by plaintiff's testimony that she would not have taken birth control pills if she had been adequately warned about the risk of stroke, in which case she would not have suffered the stroke) (excerpted on p. 313 *supra*).

The logic of this evidentiary standard is readily apparent, but making the liability determination turn on the plaintiff's testimony is problematic. The

II. Proof of Causation in Warning Cases

plaintiff is testifying about her own hypothetical behavior in a counterfactual world where the defendant complied with the duty to warn. How can the jury decide whether the plaintiff is telling the truth? Consider General Motors Corp. v. Saenz, 873 S.W.2d 353, 357 (Tex. 1993) ("In the best case a plaintiff can offer evidence of his habitual, careful adherence to all warnings and instructions. In many cases, however, plaintiff's evidence may be little more than the self-serving assertion that whatever his usual practice may have been, in the circumstances critical to his claim for damages he would have been mindful of an adequate warning had it been given.").

The defendant could try to undermine the plaintiff's testimony by attacking the plaintiff's credibility. In deciding whether to adopt this strategy, what are the various considerations that the defendant's attorney should account for in arguing that despite the plaintiff's testimony to the contrary, she would have used the product even if adequately informed? In thinking about this question, consider the posture of the case at the point where the causal question would be of decisive relevance. The *MacDonald* case provides a useful reference. Given the nature of plaintiff's proof at this point—the warning did not adequately disclose the risk of stroke, and the plaintiff took the birth-control pills and suffered a stroke as a result—could this strategy backfire on the defendant?

B. The Objective Standard

The obvious alternative to a subjective standard is an objective standard, which determines causation by asking whether an adequate warning would have changed the behavior of a reasonable person in a manner that would have avoided the injury.

> Such an approach would not be new to tort law. In the area of informed consent to medical treatment, for example, a significant number of courts have decided that the better method of resolving the causation question is to ask "what a prudent person in the patient's position would have decided if suitably informed of all perils bearing significance."
>
> An objective method of establishing causation in warnings cases would arguably have all of the advantages usually attributed to objectivity. Instead of relying on the post-injury testimony of an inevitably biased, seriously injured plaintiff, . . . the objective approach would concentrate on the course of conduct that would have been taken before the injury by a hypothetical reasonable person. . . .
>
> [T]he objective approach might appear to offer factfinders a neutral way of resolving the causation issue. For all practical purposes, however, its adoption would not change or unravel the causation dilemma in any meaningful way. The hypothetical reasonable person will always read and obey an adequate warning label. This truism would always end the causation inquiry, perhaps more decisively in plaintiff's favor than either of the [alternative] two openly pro-plaintiff approaches.

Michael S. Jacobs, *Toward a Process-Based Approach to Failure-to-Warn Law*, 71 N.C. L. Rev. 121, 163-164 (1992) (paragraph structure omitted).

C. The Heeding Presumption

A third approach effectively presumes causation without requiring the plaintiff to testify about the matter. "Courts in more than half the states have now adopted the heeding presumption, where a defendant did not warn at all, to help a plaintiff prove causation in warning claims." David G. Owen, PRODUCTS LIABILITY LAW, §11.4, at 743 (3d ed. 2015). What might justify this approach?

COFFMAN v. KEENE CORP.
Supreme Court of New Jersey, 1993
628 A.2d 710

HANDLER, J. In this case, plaintiff, a former naval electrician, was exposed to various quantities of asbestos during his work inside the close quarters of naval vessels. He sued defendant, Keene Corporation, and others for injuries allegedly contracted from exposure to defendant's products in the workplace.

Plaintiff claimed that defendant had violated its duty to warn consumers of the health hazards associated with asbestos products. Defendant took the position that the absence of such a warning did not proximately contribute to plaintiff's injuries because there was no evidence proffered that plaintiff would have followed such a warning, and therefore no proof that the failure to warn had contributed to plaintiff's injuries. At trial, the court instructed the jury to presume that plaintiff would have followed a warning had one been provided. That presumption, in the absence of any evidence to the contrary from defendant, allowed plaintiff to meet his burden of proof that the lack of a warning on defendant's products had caused his ailments.

The jury [awarded plaintiff damages]. Defendant filed a motion for a new trial or in the alternative for a judgment notwithstanding the verdict. The trial court denied defendant's motions, and defendant appealed.

The Appellate Division affirmed the trial court's judgment, ruling that a plaintiff in a failure-to-warn case may rely on a "heeding presumption" in order to prove that the absence of a warning proximately caused his or her injury. The Court granted certification to review that ruling.

Causation is a fundamental requisite for establishing any product-liability action. The plaintiff must demonstrate so-called product-defect causation — that the defect in the product was a proximate cause of the injury. When the alleged defect is the failure to provide warnings, a plaintiff is required to prove that the absence of a warning was a proximate cause of his harm.

The Appellate Division, in adopting the use of a heeding presumption in failure-to-warn cases, found support for such a presumption in comment j to Section 402A of the *Restatement (Second) of Torts* (1965). Referring to comment j, the Appellate Division stated that if an adequate warning exists, a product is no longer considered defective, because when a manufacturer provides a warning, "the seller may reasonably assume that it will be read and heeded." The Appellate Division concluded that because a manufacturer or seller would benefit when a warning was provided, "a logical corollary of Comment j is that the buyer or user should benefit where a warning is *not* given." Consequently, "if a

II. Proof of Causation in Warning Cases

seller or manufacturer is entitled to a presumption that an adequate warning will be read and heeded, plaintiff should be entitled to the same presumption when no warning is given."

Defendant takes issue with the premise underlying comment j. It claims that one cannot *logically* assume, based on objectively determined facts, that consumers or product users will heed warnings if they are provided. Defendant has provided a plethora of data and studies in its pleadings to bolster its point that with the proliferation of warnings in our society, it is nearly impossible to go through a day without consciously ignoring warnings designed to protect our health and safety. Hence, defendant asserts, there is no common experience on which we can premise the creation of a presumption that the general public reads and heeds warnings.

We can agree with defendant that the heeding presumption is not firmly based on empirical evidence. It is not therefore a "natural" or "logical" presumption. Nevertheless, the creation of a presumption can be grounded in public policy. [ ] Although empirical evidence may not demonstrate the soundness of a heeding presumption, an examination of the strong and consistent public policies that have shaped our laws governing strict products liability demonstrates the justification for such a presumption.

The use of presumptions grounded in public policy in relation to a product-liability claim is not novel. We have often adopted or used presumptions in that context in order to advance our goals of fostering greater product safety and enabling victims of unsafe commercial products to obtain fair redress.

The heeding presumption . . . serves to reinforce the basic duty to warn—to encourage manufacturers to produce safer products, and to alert users of the hazards arising from the use of those products through effective warnings. The duty to warn exists not only to protect and alert product users but to encourage manufacturers and industries, which benefit from placing products into the stream of commerce, to remain apprised of the hazards posed by a product. The use of the heeding presumption provides a powerful incentive for manufacturers to abide by their duty to provide adequate warnings. [ ]

One of the policy considerations for imposing strict product liability has been to ease the burden of proof for an injured plaintiff, a policy achieved by eliminating the requirement that a plaintiff prove the manufacturer's negligence. As the Appellate Division recognized, "in a failure to warn case, establishing that the absence of a warning was a substantial factor in the harm alleged to have resulted from exposure to the product itself is particularly difficult." The heeding presumption thus serves to lighten a plaintiff's burden of proof concerning proximate causation.

The Appellate Division also observed that a jury determination of whether, if a warning had been provided, it would have been followed would most likely be highly speculative. A jury, in effect, would be invited to imagine whether a plaintiff, given the various facets of his or her personality and employment situation, would have heeded a warning. Like the Appellate Division, other courts have found that the excessively speculative nature concerning whether the plaintiff would follow a warning impelled the use of a heeding presumption. Similarly, the use of the presumption can discourage resort to evidence that is likely to be self-serving and unreliable. Thus, the effect of the heeding presumption will be to direct factual inquiries to the real causes of injury in a failure-to-warn case.

The use of the presumption will be conducive to determinations of causation that are not based on extraneous, speculative considerations and unreliable or self-serving evidence.

A great many jurisdictions have adopted the heeding presumption in failure-to-warn cases. Most jurisdictions have done so with explicit reference to comment j as the basis for such a presumption. [ ] Several other jurisdictions have adopted the presumption without a specific reference to comment j. [ ]

We conclude that the heeding presumption in failure-to-warn cases furthers the objectives of the strong public policy that undergirds our doctrine of strict products liability. The heeding presumption accords with the manufacturer's basic duty to warn; it fairly reduces the victim's burden of proof; and it minimizes the likelihood that determinations of causation will be based on unreliable evidence. Consequently, we now hold that with respect to the issue of product-defect causation in a product-liability case based on a failure to warn, the plaintiff should be afforded the use of the presumption that he or she would have followed an adequate warning had one been provided, and that the defendant in order to rebut that presumption must produce evidence that such a warning would not have been heeded.

The use of a rebuttable heeding presumption will serve to shift plaintiff's burden of proof on the issue of causation as it relates to the absence of a warning. Evidence that a plaintiff would have disregarded an adequate warning would tend to demonstrate that the plaintiff's conduct, rather than the absence of a warning, was the cause in fact of the resultant injury.

We hold that to overcome the heeding presumption in a failure-to-warn case involving a product used in the workplace, the manufacturer must prove that had an adequate warning been provided, the plaintiff-employee with meaningful choice would not have heeded the warning. Alternatively, to overcome the heeding presumption, the manufacturer must show that had an adequate warning been provided, the employer itself would not have heeded the warning by taking reasonable precautions for the safety of its employees and would not have allowed its employees to take measures to avoid or minimize the harm from their use or exposure to the dangerous product.

The judgment of the Appellate Division is affirmed.

NOTES AND QUESTIONS

1. *Procedural effect of the presumption.* For reasons given by the *Coffman* court, the heeding presumption does not conclusively establish causation. "In this instance, the term 'presumption' is used to mean 'makes a prima facie case,' i.e., creates a submissible case that the warning would have been heeded." Tune v. Synergy Gas Corp., 883 S.W.2d 10, 14 (Mo. 1994). Consequently, the defendant can try to rebut this presumption with evidence showing that the inadequate warning did not cause the plaintiff's injuries.

In many cases, the defendant tries to rebut the presumption by proving that the plaintiff does not follow product warnings as a matter of habit.

> [I]n order for evidence to be admissible to rebut the heeding presumption and demonstrate that plaintiff is the type of person that is

II. Proof of Causation in Warning Cases 445

> indifferent to safety warnings, the defendant must adduce evidence, either from the plaintiff or other witnesses, that the plaintiff has in the past failed to heed safety warnings as construed by the reasonable user, and that the plaintiff's indifference to the warning rose to the level of habit. Only under such circumstances will the evidence be admissible to rebut the heeding presumption and give rise to a jury question as to whether plaintiff would have followed a safety warning in the circumstances of a particular case had it been given.

Sharpe v. Bestop, Inc., 713 A.2d 1079, 1091 (N.J. App. Div. 1998). *See also, e.g.,* Kirkbride v. Terex USA, LLC, 798 F.3d 1343, 1351 (10th Cir. 2015) (concluding that defendant "conclusively rebutted the presumption" because plaintiff "[n]ot only had not read the warning that was in the manual but he expressed a negative view of manuals" with his testimony, "Why would you read a manual?").

2. *Comment j and the heeding presumption.* As the court in *Coffman* observed, the most common rationale for the heeding presumption is based on comment j of §402A in the *Restatement (Second)*, which states that "[w]here warning is given, the seller may reasonably assume that it will be read and heeded; and a product bearing such a warning, which is safe for use if it is followed, is not in a defective condition, nor is it unreasonably dangerous." The same interpretation of comment j that justifies the heeding presumption would also enable manufacturers to rely on product warnings as a substitute for reasonably redesigning the product. *See* Chapter 8. The majority of courts no longer rely on comment j to enable manufacturers to rely on the heeding presumption to avoid redesigning the product when required by the risk-utility test. These cases, in turn, call into question the earlier case law that had relied on comment j to adopt the heeding presumption for proving causation. *See* Ackerman v. Wyeth Pharm., 526 F.3d 203, 212-213 (5th Cir. 2008) (recognizing that the Texas Supreme Court had adopted the heeding presumption in a 1972 case but then refusing to apply the presumption to a pharmaceutical case involving a learned intermediary in part because "Texas has explicitly rejected the *Restatement (Second) of Torts* §402A cmt. j's 'read and heed' presumption for policy reasons [in cases alleging defect design]"). Insofar as the heeding presumption is based on such a shaky foundation, its support is likely to crumble over time.

3. *The deterrence rationale for the heeding presumption.* Instead of relying on comment j, the court in *Coffman* concluded that the heeding presumption furthers the public policy of product safety. Other courts have adopted the heeding presumption for this reason. *E.g.,* Golonka v. General Motors Corp., 65 P.3d 956, 969 (Ariz. Ct. App. 2003) ("[U]se of the heeding presumption in strict liability failure-to-warn cases furthers Arizona's policy of protecting the public from defective and unreasonably dangerous products. The presumption is also procedurally desirable to ensure that legitimate claims of information defect are fairly addressed. For these reasons, the heeding presumption is viable in Arizona.").

The heeding presumption undoubtedly promotes product safety, but wouldn't this rationale justify more extensive liability rules than courts have recognized? As a matter of deterrence, why would courts recognize *any* limitation of liability once the plaintiff has proven that the defendant sold a defective product? Any rule that limits the liability of such a defendant can undermine safety incentives, implying that the public policy of deterrence is not a sufficient justification for tort liability. What, then, justifies the heeding presumption?

4. *Does the heeding presumption reduce the plaintiff's burden of proof?* Lacking any other apparent rationale, the presumption of causation apparently relaxes the plaintiff's burden of proof, which many find to be problematic. On this view, "the heeding presumption . . . is not logical; in fact, people commonly ignore warnings and instructions, no matter how good they may be." David G. Owen, PRODUCTS LIABILITY LAW, §11.4, at 744 (3d ed. 2015). If consumers commonly ignore warnings, there is no evident logic for the presumption that the plaintiff, more likely than not, would have read and followed an adequate warning if one had been given. Without a logical foundation, such "a presumption makes no good sense on the merits." James A. Henderson, Jr. & Aaron D. Twerski, *Doctrinal Collapse in Products Liability: The Empty Shell of Failure to Warn*, 65 N.Y.U. L. Rev. 265, 278 (1990). Concerned that the presumption unjustifiably relaxes the plaintiff's burden of proof, some courts have rejected the doctrine. *E.g.*, Rivera v. Philip Morris, Inc., 209 P.3d 271, 276-277 (Nev. 2009) (rejecting the heeding presumption because "[i]t is a firmly rooted part of Nevada law that the plaintiff in a strict product liability case bears the burden of proving all the elements of his case, including causation").

5. *The heeding presumption and the liberal rule of but-for causation.* One alternative rationale remains to be considered: the heeding presumption could be based on the liberal rule of but-for causation. This rationale was arguably invoked by the court in *Coffman* when it observed that "[t]he heeding presumption accords with the manufacturer's basic duty to warn." For reasons discussed in section I *supra*, the jury can reasonably resolve a causal question by relying on the behavior presumed by the duty, leading to the question of whether doing so would justify the heeding presumption.

Consider a case in which the plaintiff proves that a product is defective for not adequately instructing the consumer of the need to take a particular precaution while using the product. To establish the defect, the plaintiff must prove that a reasonable alternative warning would have provided the safety instruction. This proof should establish that (1) the ordinary consumer would find it worthwhile to follow the instruction; (2) the ordinary consumer was not otherwise sufficiently aware of the need to take the precaution; and (3) the information costs created by the warning would not prevent the ordinary consumer from reading the warning to gain the information. *See* Chapter 7. The proof of defect establishes that the ordinary consumer would read and heed a warning that disclosed the safety instruction. Presumably, the plaintiff is like the ordinary consumer in these respects. Proof of defect, therefore, presumptively proves that the plaintiff—like the average or ordinary consumer—would have read and followed the safety instruction, thereby avoiding injury. *See* Thomas v. Hoffman-LaRoche, Inc., 949 F.2d 806, 813 (5th Cir. 1992) ("Typically, the choice facing the user in the preventable risk situation is between

II. **Proof of Causation in Warning Cases**   447

using the product safely and using the product unsafely. Because the precautions are typically minimal . . . we have little trouble with a rebuttable presumption that a reasonable product user will choose to use the product safely.").

Hence the heeding presumption does not reduce the plaintiff's burden of proof because it "accords with the manufacturer's basic duty to warn" as the court in *Coffman* observed. Was the court's reasoning about this matter sufficiently clear? Consider its observation that the heeding presumption is not a logical or empirical assumption that can be derived from an empirically demonstrable probability. By relying on policy reasons rather than the empirical assumptions embodied in the duty to warn, the *Coffman* court defended the heeding presumption in a manner that relaxes the plaintiff's ordinary burden of proving causation, explaining why other courts have rejected the presumption.

6. *The problem of inherent product risks.* Does the nature of the duty also explain the heeding presumption for cases in which the warning is defective because it does not adequately warn about a residual product risk, such as the risk that a prescription drug could cause an injurious side effect? To establish such a defect, the plaintiff must prove that (1) the ordinary consumer would find the risk to be material in deciding whether to buy the product; (2) the ordinary consumer was not otherwise sufficiently aware of the risk; and (3) the information costs created by the warning would not prevent the ordinary consumer from reading the warning to gain the information. *See* Chapter 7. Once again, proof of defect presumptively establishes that the plaintiff, like the average or ordinary consumer, would read and heed the adequate warning if one had been given.

The heeding presumption, however, does not obviously establish causation in these cases. Despite the risk of side effects posed by most drugs, the vast majority of consumers still find the drugs, on balance, to be beneficial. Even if he or she had been adequately warned of the risk, the ordinary consumer would still use the product. The plaintiff presumably is like the ordinary consumer, so what justifies the presumption of causation for cases in which the ordinary consumer would have used the product and still faced the risk of injury in question?

This problem has troubled courts:

> The choice presented by an unavoidable risk warning is not between the safe use and the unsafe use of a product, but between using and not using the product. The consumer can choose to use the product and face its risks, or choose not to use the product and lose its potential benefits. Generally, using the product will present the less risky of these two alternatives. Consider the polio vaccine. . . . There is a risk of contracting polio if a person uses the vaccine, and there is a risk if the person decides not to use the vaccine. Presumably, the risk of contracting polio is less with the vaccine than without it. If we assume that the average user will take the less risky alternative, the average user will choose to take the vaccine, and a warning detailing the unavoidable risks of the polio vaccine, whether given or not, would not change that decision. Unless the plaintiff can establish that using the product is, for the average consumer, the more risky alternative,

>the . . . rule that the consumer will act to minimize his level of risk, if applied in the context of an unavoidable risk, would seem to establish a rebuttable presumption that the consumer would not have changed his decision to use the product if warned of the unavoidable risk.

Thomas v. Hoffman-LaRoche, Inc., 949 F.2d 806, 813-814 (5th Cir. 1992).

Now consider this causal problem in relation to the underlying duty. The duty assumes that an adequate warning about inherent product risks would cause some consumers to forego use of the product, even if most would continue to use the product and face the risk. *See* RESTATEMENT (THIRD) OF TORTS: PRODUCTS LIABILITY §10 ("Whether or not many persons would, when warned, nonetheless decide to use or consume the product, warnings are required to protect the interest of those reasonable foreseeable users or consumers who would, based on their own reasonable assessments of the risks and benefits, decline product use or consumption."). Does the behavior recognized by this duty provide a reasonable basis for the jury to conclude that the plaintiff is someone who would have declined product use if she had been warned about the risk in question? Is this causal issue any different from the one posed by cases, such as those involving lifesaving devices, in which courts apply the liberal rule of but-for causation?

7. *A role for strict liability?* In framing the causal inquiry, have we been relying on negligence or strict liability? Does negligence liability employ the same causal inquiry required by strict products liability? Consider this issue in relation to the manner in which warranty law resolves issues of factual causation.

III. PROOF OF CAUSATION IN WARRANTY CASES

In addition to making claims of negligence and strict products liability, plaintiffs frequently allege that the product breached contractual warranties of quality. To establish liability on this basis, the plaintiff must prove that the breach of warranty caused the injuries for she seeks compensation. Warranty law, however, resolves the causal question differently from negligence law. The causal rule governing warranty cases is a form of strict liability, leading to the question whether it ought to apply to claims of strict products liability based on the tort version of the implied warranty.

Like negligence liability, strict liability requires proof of causation. However, the causal inquiry differs for the two liability rules. For purposes of negligence liability, the plaintiff must prove that the defendant's unreasonable behavior caused the injury, proof involving a counterfactual inquiry into whether the injury would have occurred if the defendant had exercised reasonable care. As applied to warning cases, this inquiry requires the plaintiff to prove that if the defendant had acted reasonably and provided a nondefective warning, the plaintiff would have read the warning and avoided the injury—the causal problem discussed in the prior section. When governed by a rule of strict liability, the causal inquiry instead asks whether the tortious risk for which the

III. Proof of Causation in Warranty Cases

defendant is strictly responsible caused the plaintiff's injury. In a warning case, the tortious risk is the risk that was not adequately disclosed in the warning. If this risk caused the plaintiff's injury, she is entitled to compensation regardless of whether she would have used the product anyway.

This causal rule is illustrated by the following case. Consider whether this rule can justifiably be extended to the rule of strict products liability. If so, does it plausibly explain why courts recognize that the risk-utility test "in design and warning cases is really nothing more than negligence," yet "still call liability 'strict'"? David G. Owen, PRODUCTS LIABILITY LAW §2.6, at 104 (3d ed. 2015).

BAXTER v. FORD MOTOR CO.
Supreme Court of Washington, 1932
12 P.2d 409

HERMAN, J. During the month of May, 1930, plaintiff purchased a Model A Ford town sedan from defendant St. John Motors, a Ford dealer, who had acquired the automobile in question by purchase from defendant Ford Motor Company. Plaintiff claims that representations were made to him by both defendants that the windshield of the automobile was made of nonshatterable glass which would not break, fly or shatter.

October 12, 1930, while plaintiff was driving the automobile through Snoqualmie pass, a pebble from a passing car struck the windshield of the car in question, causing small pieces of glass to fly into plaintiff's left eye, resulting in the loss thereof. Plaintiff brought this action for damages for the loss of his left eye, and for injuries to the sight of his right eye. The case came on for trial, and, at the conclusion of plaintiff's testimony, the court took the case from the jury and entered judgment for both defendants. From that judgment, plaintiff appeals.

Appellant's second assignment of error is that the court refused to admit in evidence certain catalogues and printed matter furnished by respondent Ford Motor Company to respondent St. John Motors for distribution and assistance in sales. Contained in such printed matter were statements which appellant maintains constituted representations or warranties with reference to the nature of the glass used in the windshield of the car purchased by appellant. A typical statement, as it appears in appellant's exhibit for identification No. 1, is here set forth:

> Triplex Shatter-Proof Glass Windshield. All of the new Ford cars have a Triplex shatter-proof glass windshield—so made that it will not fly or shatter under the hardest impact. This is an important safety factor because it eliminates the dangers of flying glass—the cause of most of the injuries in automobile accidents. In these days of crowded, heavy traffic, the use of this Triplex glass is an absolute necessity. Its extra margin of safety is something that every motorist should look for in the purchase of a car—especially where there are women and children.

Respondent Ford Motor Company contends that there can be no implied or express warranty without privity of contract, and warranties as to personal property do not attach themselves to, and run with, the article sold.

In the case at bar, the automobile was represented by the manufacturer as having a windshield of nonshatterable glass "so made that it will not fly or shatter under the hardest impact." An ordinary person would be unable to discover by the usual and customary examination of the automobile whether glass which would not fly or shatter was used in the windshield. In that respect, the purchaser was in a position similar to that of the consumer of a wrongly labeled drug, who has bought the same from a retailer, and who has relied upon the manufacturer's representation that the label correctly set forth the contents of the container. For many years, it has been held that, under such circumstances, the manufacturer is liable to the consumer, even though the consumer purchased from a third person the commodity causing the damage. Thomas v. Winchester, 6 N.Y. 397, 57 Am. Dec. 455. The rule in such cases does not rest upon contractual obligations, but rather on the principle that the original act of delivering an article is wrong, when, because of the lack of those qualities which the manufacturer represented it as having, the absence of which could not be readily detected by the consumer, the article is not safe for the purposes for which the consumer would ordinarily use it.

Since the rule of *caveat emptor* was first formulated, vast changes have taken place in the economic structures of the English speaking peoples. Methods of doing business have undergone a great transition. Radio, bill boards and the products of the printing press have become the means of creating a large part of the demand that causes goods to depart from factories to the ultimate consumer. It would be unjust to recognize a rule that would permit manufacturers of goods to create a demand for their products by representing that they possess qualities which they, in fact, do not possess; and then, because there is no privity of contract existing between the consumer and the manufacturer, deny the consumer the right to recover if damages result from the absence of those qualities, when such absence is not readily noticeable.

We hold that the catalogues and printed matter furnished by respondent Ford Motor Company for distribution and assistance in sales (appellant's exhibits for identification Nos. 1, 2, 3, 4 and 5) were improperly excluded from evidence, because they set forth representations by the manufacturer that the windshield of the car which appellant bought contained Triplex nonshatterable glass which would not fly or shatter. The nature of nonshatterable glass is such that the falsity of the representations with reference to the glass would not be readily detected by a person of ordinary experience and reasonable prudence. Appellant, under the circumstances shown in this case, had the right to rely upon the representations made by respondent Ford Motor Company relative to qualities possessed by its products, even though there was no privity of contract between appellant and respondent Ford Motor Company.

The trial court erred in taking the case from the jury and entering judgment for respondent Ford Motor Company. It was for the jury to determine, under proper instructions, whether the failure of respondent Ford Motor Company to equip the windshield with glass which did not fly or shatter, was the proximate cause of appellant's injury.

We have considered the other assignments of error, and find them to be without merit.

Reversed, with directions to grant a new trial with reference to respondent Ford Motor Company; affirmed as to respondent St. John Motors.

III. Proof of Causation in Warranty Cases 451

BAXTER v. FORD MOTOR CO.
Supreme Court of Washington, 1934
35 P.2d 1090

HOLCOMB, J. This case has been in this court before. For the issues, see the former opinion.

The action was instituted against Ford Motor Company, a corporation, and the St. Johns Motors, a corporation, and upon the previous trial, at the conclusion of the evidence on behalf of plaintiff, a judgment of dismissal was entered in favor of both defendants. That judgment was appealed from by the plaintiff and resulted in an affirmance as to St. John Motors, thereby releasing it from liability, and reversal as to the present appellant.

The case was retried on June 27 and 28, 1933. The jury returned a verdict in favor of the present respondent [the plaintiff] upon which, after a denial of motions for judgment non obstante veredicto, or for a new trial, judgment was entered.

In the former decision we held that it was for the jury to determine, under proper instructions, whether the failure of respondent Ford Motor Company to equip the windshield with glass which did not fly or shatter, was the proximate cause of appellant's (now respondent's) injury.

A new point, arising out of the last trial, claimed as error, was in excluding testimony of an expert witness on behalf of appellant to the effect that there was no better windshield made than that used in respondent's car and in sustaining the objection to appellant's offer of proof on that point.

No authorities are cited by appellant to sustain this claim, and we know of none. Indeed, it would seem that whether there was any better make of shatter-proof glass manufactured by any one at that time would be wholly immaterial, under the law as decided by us on the former appeal, since it was the duty of appellant to know that the representations made to purchasers were true. Otherwise it should not have made them. If a person states as true material facts susceptible of knowledge to one who relies and acts thereon to his injury, if the representations are false, it is immaterial that he did not know they were false, or that he believed them to be true. [ ]

There was no error of which appellant may rightfully complain, and the judgment is affirmed.

NOTES AND QUESTIONS

1. *The reliance requirement.* For warranty claims, the element of causation is addressed by the requirement of reliance: To be injured by a misrepresentation in violation of the warranty, the plaintiff must have reasonably relied on the misrepresentation. How exactly did the plaintiff in *Baxter* rely on the manufacturer's express representation that the windshield was made of shatterproof glass? Did he drive differently or travel on rocky roads that he might otherwise have avoided? Was there any other way in which the misrepresentation altered his behavior in a manner that caused the injury? Was there any evidence of this type discussed by the court? As these questions suggest, warranty law requires a type of reliance that establishes causation in a distinctive manner.

The provision in the Uniform Commercial Code addressing the express warranty "incorporates a reliance element, providing that a seller's statement that is 'part of the basis of the bargain' creates an express warranty." Compaq Computer Corp. v. Lapray, 135 S.W.2d 657, 676 (Tex. 2004). The buyer, in other words, relies on any express representation that is "part of the basis of the bargain." Indeed, the official comments to this provision in the UCC provide that "no particular reliance on such statements need be shown in order to weave them into the fabric of the agreement." *Id.*

Reliance does not need to be an independent element of the warranty claim because it is adequately accounted for by the requirement that the misrepresentation must be material. By definition, a material representation is relevant to the decision-making of the buyer—it is "part of the basis of the bargain." Consequently, a material *misrepresentation* necessarily causes harm to the purchaser by frustrating her reasonable expectations of product quality, obviating the need for a separate inquiry regarding reliance. Compare McGee v. S-L Snacks Natl., 982 F.3d 700, 706 (9th Cir. 2020) (holding that plaintiff's "benefit of the bargain theory falls short" because she did not allege that defendant had "made false representations about [product] safety"); In re Johnson & Johnson Talcum Powder Prod. Mktg., Sales Prac. & Liab. Litig., 903 F.3d 278, 298 (3d Cir. 2018) (Fuentes, J., dissenting) ("Estrada alleges that she paid for a product based, in part, on Johnson & Johnson's representation of its safety. That representation was part of the benefit of her bargain. Because that representation was false, Estrada did *not* receive the benefit of her bargain.").

In *Baxter*, no one disputed that the defendant's misrepresentation was material to the plaintiff's decision about whether to purchase or use the vehicle. Why else would the defendant advertise this attribute of the vehicle's quality? To be sure, the plaintiff might have made the same decision if he had known the truth, but a material representation only factors into the plaintiff's decision and does not have to change the decision—it need only be "part of the basis of the bargain" and not the decisive basis of the bargain.

2. *The remedy.* Having established that the defendant violated the express warranty, the plaintiff can recover the amount of damages that would adequately compensate the frustrated expectation of product quality. In *Baxter*, the plaintiff did not reasonably expect to be injured by a shattered windshield, and the tort award of compensatory damages for these unexpected injuries compensated the frustrated expectation. The rationale for this remedy does not depend on whether the defendant could in fact have supplied a shatterproof windshield. If a manufacturer creates a reasonable expectation of product safety, it incurs the obligation to satisfy that expectation by paying compensatory damages for the unexpected injury suffered by the consumer.

3. *Reliance and the implied warranty.* Although the express warranty is sometimes relevant in a products case, the implied warranty is far more important for our purposes. Like the UCC provision governing the express warranty, its provision governing the implied warranty does not contain an independent requirement of reliance—the misrepresentation must only be material. And like the claim based on the defendant's

III. Proof of Causation in Warranty Cases

express misrepresentations in *Baxter*, a claim under the implied warranty can allege that the defect involves misrepresentations or omissions in the product warning. *See, e.g.*, Smith v. E.R. Squibb & Sons, Inc., 273 N.W.2d 476, 479 (Mich. 1979) ("It is commonly accepted that inadequate warnings alone can constitute a product defect, whether the theory be implied warranty or strict liability in tort.").

4. *The implied warranty and the causal inquiry for strict products liability.* We are now in a position to determine whether the causal inquiry under the implied warranty can be utilized to formulate the causal inquiry under strict products liability. Consider a case in which the defendant failed to warn adequately of an injurious side effect that is an inherent risk of a prescription drug, such as the risk of stroke. If the disclosure would have been material to the consumer's decision-making, then the failure to warn about the risk is a misrepresentation that breaches the implied warranty. Once the plaintiff has established these facts, she can then recover by proving that her injury (a stroke) was caused by the undisclosed product risk (of stroke) that she did not reasonably expect to face, just like the plaintiff in *Baxter* could recover by proving that his injuries were caused by a product risk (of being injured by a shattered windshield) that he did not reasonably expect to face. By relying on the causal rule governing the implied warranty, courts can adopt a causal rule for strict products liability that simply asks whether the tortious product risk (of stroke) caused the plaintiff's injury.

When the ordinary consumer purchases a product, she reasonably expects that the warning discloses all of the information required for an informed safety decision. If the warning does not adequately disclose a material product risk, the ordinary consumer purchased the product on the mistaken expectation that the risk did not exist. The consumer's reasonable expectation of safety is then frustrated when the unexpected risk causes injury. This expectation is frustrated regardless of whether the consumer would have purchased the product (and faced the risk) had she known the truth. A tort rule that protects consumer expectations accordingly subjects the seller to liability for an inadequately disclosed product risk that materializes and causes the plaintiff's injury, regardless of whether the plaintiff would still have used the product—and faced the risk of injury—if she had been adequately warned. Compare Watkins v. Ford Motor Co., 190 F.3d 1213, 1219 (11th Cir. 1999) ("Although a warning may have the net effect of preventing an accident, that is not what is required by the law. The law merely requires the warning to inform the consumer of the nature and existence of the hazard, allowing him to make an informed decision whether to take on the risks warned of.").

This causal inquiry differs from the one employed in a negligence claim, which determines but-for causation by asking whether the injury would have occurred if the defendant had exercised reasonable care. In our prior example, if the defendant drug manufacturer had provided a reasonable warning of the risk, and if the plaintiff would have used the drug anyway, then the inadequate warning did not cause the plaintiff's injury. Similarly, if the defendant in *Baxter* had reasonably told the truth about the windshield, then the plaintiff would still have bought a car with a windshield that could shatter (no other type was available) and would have subsequently suffered the identical injury. As a matter of negligence liability, the defendant in both cases was not a factual cause of the plaintiff's injury, yet the plaintiff in each case could recover under the warranty. The causal rule required by negligence liability, therefore, differs from a causal rule of strict products liability, which simply asks whether the consumer was injured by the misrepresented risk that rendered the warning defective. *See* Frankel v. Lull Eng'g Co., 334 F. Supp. 913, 925–26 (E.D. Pa. 1971), *aff'd sub nom.* Frankel v. Lull Eng'g Co., Inc., 470 F.2d 995 (3d Cir. 1973) ("Once the jury found that the loader, taken with the warnings and instructions that accompanied it, was unreasonably dangerous, the only causation issue for them to resolve was whether the danger they found was a substantial factor in bringing about the accident. Accordingly, whether or not plaintiff proved that inadequate warnings or instructions caused the accident is not controlling."); *see also* Colter v. Barber-Greene Co., 525 N.E.2d 1305, 1314 (Mass. 1988) ("[W]arranty liability focuses on whether the product was defective and unreasonably dangerous and not on the conduct of the user or the seller.").

5. *Strict products liability and the heeding presumption in warning cases.* When the implied warranty supplies the causal rule for claims of strict products liability, courts can adopt the heeding presumption in warning cases without departing from general tort principles and the ordinary evidentiary rules for proving causation. The characteristics of an adequate warning imply that it would be read and followed by the ordinary consumer, and so the heeding presumption merely recognizes that the plaintiff is presumably like the ordinary consumer in this respect. See section II *supra*. The court, therefore, can presume that the plaintiff reasonably expected that the product's safety characteristics would conform to those described in the warning. (The presumption can be rebutted by showing that the plaintiff had no such expectation because she did not read the warning.) The plaintiff's reasonable safety expectations would then be frustrated if the warning failed to adequately disclose a risk that materialized and caused her injury. As in *Baxter*, it does not matter for this purpose whether the plaintiff would otherwise have faced the risk had she known the truth. Damages for the unexpected injury provide compensation for the plaintiff's frustrated expectations of safety, the interest protected by the rule of strict products liability.

6. *Strict liability, the heeding presumption, and medical products.* Some courts have held that the heeding presumption does not establish causation in cases involving drugs prescribed by physicians (or learned intermediaries):

> We are willing to assume that the failure to give an adequate warning of a known risk entitles the plaintiff to a rebuttable presumption that the learned intermediary would have read and heeded a proper warning. But "heed" in this context means only that the learned intermediary would have incorporated the "additional" risk into his decisional calculus. The burden remains on the plaintiff to demonstrate that the additional nondisclosed risk was sufficiently high that it would have changed the treating physician's decision to prescribe the product for the plaintiff.

Thomas v. Hoffman-LaRoche, Inc., 949 F.2d 806, 813-814 (5th Cir. 1992); *see also* Ackerman v. Wyeth Pharmaceuticals, 526 F.3d 203, 212-213 & n.16 (5th Cir. 2008) (holding that the heeding presumption does not establish causation in pharmaceutical cases involving a learned intermediary, even though it has that effect in ordinary product cases).

Can you explain why the courts in these cases are applying a rule of negligence liability to determine factual causation? When the heeding presumption functions as a causal rule of strict liability, should the sellers of medical products be immune from that form of strict liability? Consider Chapter 9 (discussing the "unavoidably unsafe product" exemption from strict liability for medical products).

7. *Negligence, strict liability, and consumer expectations.* Does the causal rule depend on whether defect is determined by the risk-utility test, which is functionally equivalent to negligence liability? Under strict products liability, the element of defect is separate from the element of causation. A court can consistently use the risk-utility test to determine defect while relying on strict liability to determine causation, because each rule is formulated to protect consumer expectations of product safety. Consider Carlin v. Superior Court, 920 P.2d 1347, 1351 (Cal. 1996) (holding that strict products liability is not equivalent to negligence liability merely because the liability rule "incorporate[s] certain negligence concepts into the standard of strict liability for failure to warn").

8. *Causation in cases of defective design.* To prove factual causation, the plaintiff must show that but for the defect, the injury would not have occurred. In cases of strict products liability, how does this inquiry work in cases of defective design?

Consider a motor vehicle that is defectively designed for not containing an airbag. The vehicle would perform as reasonably expected by the ordinary consumer if it had an airbag when the plaintiff crashed. The counterfactual inquiry, therefore, asks whether an airbag would have prevented the plaintiff's injuries. This inquiry is no different from the causal inquiry in a case of negligence liability, which asks whether the injury would still have occurred if the defendant had exercised reasonable care and installed an airbag in the vehicle.

For example, in Evans v. Lorillard Tobacco Co., 990 N.E.2d 997 (Mass. 2013), the jury found that defendant's Newport cigarettes were defectively designed in violation of the implied warranty. The reasonable alternative design involved a cigarette with lower levels of tar and nicotine. On appeal, defendant Lorillard argued that "no reasonable jury could have found that any design defect in Newport cigarettes caused" the death of plaintiff's mother, Marie, "because the evidence at trial was that she tried and rejected a brand of cigarettes with lower tar and nicotine." The court was not persuaded:

> In making this argument, Lorillard misunderstands the meaning of causation in products liability. Where a plaintiff proves that a product is defective, she may establish causation by proving that the defect caused her injury; the plaintiff need not prove that she would have

used a reasonable alternative design had one been available. [ ]; RESTATEMENT (THIRD) OF TORTS: PRODUCTS LIABILITY §1, at 5 (product manufacturer "who sells or distributes a defective product is subject to liability for harm to persons or property *caused by the defect*" [emphasis added]).

Here, the plaintiff submitted sufficient evidence for a reasonable jury to conclude that the combined effect of the nicotine and tar consumed by smokers of Lorillard's Newport cigarettes was a substantial factor in bringing about Marie's addiction, lung cancer, and wrongful death, and that her injury would have been reduced or avoided had she smoked cigarettes with a reasonable alternative design that would have resulted in a nonaddictive level of nicotine and a reasonably safe level of carcinogenic tar being consumed by the smoker.

Id. at 1020-1021.

As this discussion reveals, the causal inquiry in design defect cases closely matches the inquiry in a negligence case, with one potentially significant difference. Causation is established in a negligence case if the defendant's exercise of reasonable care would have prevented the injury. In the airbag example above, we assumed that the plaintiff would have used the same vehicle if it had been equipped with an airbag, in which case the causal inquiry is no different under a rule of strict liability. But as *Evans* shows, in some cases the plaintiff might have switched products if the defendant had exercised reasonable care. As the court in *Evans* concluded, that possibility is irrelevant in a case of strict products liability. Causation only depends on whether the defect created a risk that caused the plaintiff's injury, not on whether the plaintiff might have used a different product and thereby suffered the same injury—the argument rejected by the court in *Baxter*. In most cases like the airbag example, however, the plaintiff would not plausibly switch products, making the causal rule under strict products liability indistinguishable from a negligence inquiry in cases of defective design.

IV. ENHANCED INJURY

The problem of enhanced injury typically involves defects in motor vehicles that render them unreasonably dangerous in the event of a crash—a class of defects defined by the doctrine of *crashworthiness*, illustrated by designs that do not incorporate airbags into the vehicle or seatbelts that malfunction. In most of these cases, the plaintiff would have suffered some injury from the underlying crash even if the vehicle had been crashworthy. If the plaintiff can prove the extent to which the defect enhanced her injuries, she can recover damages for the aggravated harms. What if the plaintiff is unable to prove the extent to which the defect enhanced her injury? Can she still recover?

IV. Enhanced Injury

TRULL v. VOLKSWAGEN OF AMERICA, INC.
Supreme Court of New Hampshire, 2000
761 A.2d 477

NADEAU, J. In February 1991, the plaintiffs, David and Elizabeth Trull, and their two sons, Nathaniel and Benjamin, were traveling in New Hampshire when their Volkswagen Vanagon slid on black ice and collided with an oncoming car. Both parties agree that Nathaniel and Benjamin were seated in the rear middle bench seat of the Vanagon, which was equipped with lap-only seatbelts, and were wearing the available lap belts. Benjamin died in the accident, and both Elizabeth and Nathaniel suffered severe brain injuries.

In this diversity products liability action, the plaintiffs sought damages from the defendants on the ground that defects in the design of the Vanagon made their injuries more severe than they otherwise would have been. Plaintiffs had two primary theories of recovery: (1) the Vanagon was defective because it was a forward control vehicle constructed in such a way that it lacked sufficient protection against a frontal impact, and (2) the Vanagon was defective because the rear bench seats, on which Nathaniel and Benjamin were seated, did not have shoulder safety belts as well as lap belts. The plaintiffs contend that the defendants are liable in negligence and strict liability because the automobile was not crashworthy.

The United States District Court for the District of New Hampshire granted summary judgment for the defendants on a breach of warranty claim, and both Elizabeth and David Trull's claims were dismissed with prejudice. The trial proceeded with Nathaniel's and Benjamin's claims, and the jury found for the defendants.

The plaintiffs appealed to the United States Court of Appeals for the First Circuit, arguing, among other things, that the district court "improperly imposed on plaintiffs the burden of proving the nature and extent of the enhanced injuries attributable to the Vanagon's design." Recognizing that the question "of who, under New Hampshire law, should bear the burden in a so-called 'crashworthiness' case, poses sophisticated questions of burden allocation involving not only a choice of appropriate precedent but also an important policy choice," the court of appeals granted the plaintiffs' motion to certify the question to this court.

The plaintiffs' theory of liability for defective design is commonly referred to as the "crashworthiness," "second collision," or "enhanced injury" doctrine. The crashworthiness doctrine "extends the scope of liability of a manufacturer to the situations in which the construction or design of its product has caused separate or enhanced injuries in the course of an initial accident brought about by an independent cause." [ ] The doctrine is implicated, not because the design caused the accident, but because, as a result of the second collision, the plaintiffs suffered either a more severe injury or an injury they otherwise would not have received due to the defective design. Consequently, the plaintiffs seek damages from the defendants for at least a portion of their injuries.

"In a crashworthiness case, a manufacturer should be liable for that portion of the damage or injury caused by the defective design over and above the damage or injury that probably would have occurred as a result of the impact or collision absent the defective design." [ ]

Thus, in crashworthiness cases, "where the injuries sustained are separate and divisible, the burden of proof remains solely upon the plaintiffs, including the burden of proving 'enhancement,' i.e., the plaintiffs must prove which of the several injuries are attributable to the manufacturer's defective product and the degree of 'enhancement' occasioned by the product as distinguished from the injuries flowing from the third party's acts of negligence." [ ] The question of actual apportionment of damages among several causes is one of fact for the jury. In essence, the normal principles of torts apply.

When, however, the plaintiffs receive injuries that are indivisible, courts are split as to whether the plaintiffs or the defendants bear the burden of segregating the injuries caused by the automobile's defect. RESTATEMENT (THIRD) OF TORTS: PRODUCTS LIABILITY §16 comment d at 243-53 (1998).

The defendants urge us to adopt the minority approach referred to as the "*Huddell-Caiazzo*" approach, which places the burden on the plaintiffs to prove the nature and extent of their enhanced injuries. *See* Huddell v. Levin, 537 F.2d 726, 737-38 (3d Cir. 1976) (applying New Jersey law); Caiazzo v. Volkswagenwerk A.G., 647 F.2d 241, 250 (2d Cir. 1981) (applying New York law).

Under the *Huddell-Caiazzo* approach,

> first, in establishing that the design in question was defective, the plaintiffs must offer proof of an alternative safer design, practicable under the circumstances. Second, the plaintiffs must offer proof of what injuries, if any, would have resulted had the alternative, safer design been used. Third, the plaintiffs must offer some method of establishing the extent of enhanced injuries attributable to the defective design.

Caiazzo, 647 F.2d at 250 (ellipses and quotation omitted).

The plaintiffs, conversely, urge us to adopt the majority approach referred to as the "*Fox-Mitchell*" approach, derived from Fox v. Ford Motor Co., 575 F.2d 774, 786-88 (10th Cir. 1978) (applying Wyoming law), and Mitchell v. Volkswagenwerk, AG, 669 F.2d 1199, 1206-08 (8th Cir. 1982) (applying Minnesota law). *See* RESTATEMENT (THIRD) OF TORTS: PRODUCTS LIABILITY §16 reporter's note at 244 (noting that *Fox-Mitchell* approach is adopted in majority of jurisdictions).

Under the *Fox-Mitchell* approach, the plaintiffs must "prove only that the design defect was a substantial factor in producing damages over and above those which were probably caused as a result of the original impact or collision." [ ] This approach provides that once the plaintiffs carry the burden of proving that the defective design of the car was a substantial factor in causing the enhanced injury, the burden of proof shifts to the tortfeasors to apportion the damages between them.

The principles that guide our answer to the question of which approach New Hampshire should adopt are derived from products liability law grounded in both negligence and strict liability. In crashworthiness cases involving indivisible injuries, we conclude that the plaintiffs must prove that a "design defect was a substantial factor in producing damages over and above those which were probably caused as a result of the original impact or collision. Once the plaintiffs

IV. Enhanced Injury

make that showing, the burden shifts to the defendants to show which injuries were attributable to the initial collision and which to the defect." [ ]

This answer is supported by our treatment of products liability actions, where we have, based upon a "compelling reason of policy," abandoned the higher burden of proof of negligence actions in lieu of adopting the less stringent burden of proof of strict liability. [ ] Our rationale has been that the plaintiff's burden had proven to be, and would continue to be, a practically impossible burden. Similar policy reasons compel us to allocate the burden of apportionment to the defendants once the plaintiffs prove causation.

In contrast, "[a]doption of the *Huddell-Caiazzo* position takes away the incentive of automobile manufacturers to design their products in a responsible fashion." [ ] Furthermore, "application of the *Huddell-Caiazzo* standard might impair the promotion of safer products design by weakening the deterrent value of products action." [ ]

We agree with the *Mitchell* court's rejection of *Huddell* on the basis that a plaintiff would be "relegated to an almost hopeless state of never being able to succeed against a defective designer," and that the *Huddell-Caiazzo* approach "requires obvious speculation and proof of the impossible." [ ] To hold otherwise would result in the implicit adoption of the view that

> it is better that a plaintiff, injured through no fault of his own, take nothing, than that a wrongdoer pay more than his theoretical share of the damages arising out of a situation which his wrong has helped to create. In other words, the rule is a result of a choice made as to where a loss due to failure of proof shall fall—on an innocent plaintiff or on defendants who are clearly proved to have been at fault.

Mitchell, 669 F.2d at 1208; *see* RESTATEMENT (THIRD) OF TORTS: PRODUCTS LIABILITY §16 cmt. d at 240. We have adopted similar reasoning in holding that two or more tortfeasors may be jointly and severally liable where their negligence, through their independent acts, produces a single, indivisible injury. Consequently, the defendants should bear the burden of apportioning their respective liability once the plaintiffs have made a *prima facie* showing that the defendants' conduct contributed as a proximate cause to the harm suffered.

"The *Fox-Mitchell* approach does not relieve a plaintiff of the threshold obligation of proving causation, and thus liability; it is only after a plaintiff has demonstrated that the design defect was a substantial factor in producing damages over and above those that otherwise would have occurred that the burden shifts to the defendant to apportion damages." [ ]

The defendants contend that because a manufacturer will normally defend a crashworthiness claim by arguing that no defect in the vehicle existed, or that the plaintiffs' injuries could not have been prevented due to the severity of the accident, requiring them to apportion the plaintiffs' injuries would illogically "require the manufacturer to prove what it vehemently denies, that the plaintiff[s'] injuries were enhanced by a defect which the manufacturer claims does not exist."

This argument misses the mark. Defendants regularly contest the extent of plaintiffs' injuries while at the same time denying liability for the underlying causes. Requiring the defendants to apportion the plaintiffs' injuries does not require them to prove that which they deny. The burden of proving causation is on the plaintiffs. The only burden on the defendants is to apportion the plaintiffs' injuries between those caused by the first collision, by the alleged design defect, and by another source, if any.

In summary, the *Fox-Mitchell* approach and subsequent burden shifting is necessary only where the plaintiffs' injuries are indivisible. Whether the plaintiffs' injuries are indivisible or divisible is a question of law for the trial judge. If the plaintiffs' injuries are established or are stipulated to as indivisible, the plaintiffs must prove only that a design defect was a substantial factor in producing damages over and above those which were probably caused as a result of the original impact or collision. If the plaintiffs meet this burden, the burden of proof shifts to the defendants to apportion the damages between them.

Remanded.

NOTES AND QUESTIONS

1. *The crashworthiness doctrine.* Why does the duty to design encompass enhanced injuries? "[A]ccidents are natural, foreseeable consequences of using certain products." Hence "some products, although not made for certain purposes—such as accidents—should nevertheless be reasonably designed to minimize the injury-producing effect of an accident." Malen v. MTD Prods., Inc., 628 F.3d 296, 311 (7th Cir. 2010). Can you explain why this formulation of the doctrine is not necessarily limited to motor vehicles, even though its name suggests as much?

2. *The evidentiary rationale for strict liability?* Cases of enhanced injury provide yet another type of evidentiary problem that most courts solve by imposing liability on the seller of a product that has been proven to be defective. As the court in *Trull* explained, a contrary rule "takes away the incentive of ... manufacturers to design their products in a responsible fashion." How persuasive is this justification when considered in relation to the other causal rules we have studied in this chapter?

The element of factual causation limits liability when the plaintiff is unable to prove that the defect, more likely than not, caused the injury in question. Due to this limitation of liability, the seller of a defective product routinely avoids liability when the defect in its product does not at least double the risk of injury. *See* section I *supra.* Why does the plaintiff's difficulty of proving causation justify liability in cases of enhanced injury, but not in the other seemingly similar cases in which plaintiff also proves defect but cannot show that the defect, more likely than not, caused the injury?

3. *Indivisible injuries and multiple tortfeasors.* In a case of *indivisible injury,* a portion of the harm is attributable to one cause and the remainder of the harm to another cause, but evidentiary limitations prevent an apportionment of the injury between the respective causes. Once the plaintiff shows that a tortiously caused injury is indivisible, the defendant bears the burden of proving apportionment. Proof of apportionment, however, is not possible—the injury is indivisible. Consequently, the defendant is jointly and severally liable with the other tortfeasor(s) for the entire indivisible injury. *See* RESTATEMENT (THIRD) OF TORTS: APPORTIONMENT OF LIABILITY §A18

IV. Enhanced Injury

("If the independent tortious conduct of two or more persons is a legal cause of an indivisible injury, each person is jointly and severally liable for the recoverable damages caused by the tortious conduct."). "This was true whether the injury was one that was truly indivisible (such as two vehicles colliding and breaking the plaintiff's leg) or was theoretically divisible, but, because of problems of proof, could not be apportioned based on the causal roles of each defendant (e.g., marauding cattle belonging to several defendants who destroy a field of crops)." *Id.* Rptrs' N. cmt. a. Does this rule justify the majority rule on enhanced injury as the court in *Trull* concluded?

Consider an automobile accident that was caused by a drunk driver, and suppose that the plaintiff's injuries were enhanced by a defect in the automobile. When the injuries are indivisible (as in *Trull*), both the drunk driver and the automobile manufacturer are jointly and severally liable for the entirety of plaintiff's harm. Reasoning that the defendant manufacturer in such a case would have been jointly and severally liable for the entire indivisible injury, most courts have concluded that the manufacturer's liability should not depend on the fortuitous presence of another tortfeasor (such as a drunk driver).

Does this reasoning adequately explain why the logic of liability for multiple tortfeasors extends to the case of a single tortfeasor? In our hypothetical case involving a drunk driver, the plaintiff's proof shows that the *entire* injury was caused by the combined tortious conduct of the two defendants. The plaintiff has established an entitlement to receive tort compensation for the entire injury, and requiring the plaintiff to prove apportionment would be unjust. Otherwise, each defendant could escape liability merely because the other defendant also caused harm, the nature of which makes apportionment impossible. The plaintiff would receive no tort damages, even though she has proven that the entire injury was caused by the tortious conduct of the two defendants. To avoid this injustice, each defendant must be liable for the entire indivisible injury. The fair or just outcome can be achieved—the plaintiff is fully compensated and the defendant tortfeasors incur responsibility for the harm—only if the burden of apportionment is placed on the defendants. This rationale clearly depends on the fact that the entire injury was tortiously caused by the multiple defendants, a fact absent from cases like *Trull* in which a single defendant caused only a portion of the plaintiff's harm. How, then, does the rule governing the joint and several liability of multiple tortfeasors for an indivisible injury justify the majority rule on enhanced injury for cases involving a single tortfeasor?

4. *Implications for cumulative toxic torts.* The identical problem of enhanced injury can exist in other product cases, with a leading example provided by the thousands of cases in which plaintiffs have recovered for asbestosis, one of the injuries caused by exposure to asbestos products.

> Asbestosis is a cumulative and therefore, at least in theory, "divisible" disease: the more asbestos dust that is inhaled, the worse the disablement of the victim. Where a plaintiff has undergone a sequence of asbestos exposures and sues the party responsible for the first

exposure, orthodox common law rules would only support the plaintiff recovering for the degree of disablement that would have resulted from that exposure alone: the plaintiff simply cannot prove that this defendant was a factual cause of the aggravation of his condition due to later exposures. . . .

But, since the first successful products liability claim in 1973 in the case *Borel v. Fibreboard Paper Products Corp.*, U.S. courts have absolved asbestosis plaintiffs from the requirement of proving the portion of the total injury for which each culpable exposer was responsible and have thereby, in effect, proceeded on the fiction that asbestosis is an indivisible injury. . . . Any defendant responsible for a significant early exposure is held jointly and severally liable for the total disablement of the plaintiff, as it is known at the time of trial. Similarly, a defendant responsible only for a late period of exposure is held liable for the total disablement: the plaintiff does not have to establish the degree to which the tort of this defendant enhanced his disability.

Jane Stapleton, *The Two Explosive Proof-of-Causation Doctrines Central to Asbestos Claims*, 74 Brook. L. Rev. 1011, 1013 (2009).

Because the causal rule regarding enhanced injury in the asbestos cases has not been adequately justified, Professor Stapleton concludes that it is a "radical proof doctrine" that in principle generalizes to the following rule governing all cumulative toxic tort cases: "[W]henever a plaintiff sues a defendant for a cumulative condition and the court is satisfied that it is not 'reasonably capable of being divided' on the available evidence, a rule of joint and several liability, tantamount to a fiction of the injury being indivisible, will be imposed on the defendant[.]" *Id.* at 1021.

Like the crashworthiness cases involving enhanced injury, courts have imposed liability on the sellers of defective asbestos products without adequately explaining how the plaintiff has proven causation. The causal rule is "radical" insofar as it implies that the plaintiff's burden of proving causation can be relaxed or shifted to the defendant simply because evidentiary difficulties would bar plaintiff's recovery and enable the sellers of defective products to avoid liability. Such a deterrence rationale could radically alter tort law by effectively eliminating the plaintiff's burden of proving causation once the product has been shown to be defective. To have such radical implications, however, the majority rule on enhanced injury must depart from established tort principles governing causation.

5. *Enhanced injury as a damages rule.* The majority rule on enhanced injury requires proof of the prima facie case for liability — the plaintiff must show by a preponderance of the evidence that the defect enhanced or proximately caused some compensable injury. As the court in *Trull* explained, "If the plaintiffs' injuries are established or are stipulated to as indivisible, the plaintiffs must prove only that a design defect was a substantial factor in producing damages over and above those which were probably caused as a result of the original impact or collision." Having established the prima facie case for liability — the breach of a duty that proximately caused some compensable harm — the plaintiff must then prove the extent of damages: Did the defect cause all of the injuries for which the plaintiff seeks compensation? The issue of enhanced injury is a

IV. Enhanced Injury

damages question that does not implicate the plaintiff's proof of the prima facie case for liability.

By defining the problem as a damages question, we can consider an alternative rationale for the majority rule on enhanced injury. In a case of enhanced injury, courts must either deny *all* recovery for a plaintiff who has proven the defendant tortiously caused some injury, or impose *full* liability on a defendant for a product defect that only caused some of the harm. Given this either/or choice, which outcome is more fair or just? As the court in *Trull* explained, the minority rule that denies recovery for enhanced injury is based on the indefensible premise that "it is better that a plaintiff, injured through no fault of his own, take nothing, than that a wrongdoer pay more than his theoretical share of the damages arising out of a situation which his wrong has helped to create" (quoting Mitchell v. Volkswagenwerk, AG, 669 F.2d 1199, 1208 (8th Cir. 1982)). As a matter of damages law, is the *Trull* court correct that liability is not fairly apportioned by denying the plaintiff's recovery altogether? If so, courts have a sound reason for rejecting the minority rule that is based on damages law, unlike the arguments discussed above that rely on the prima facie case, such as whether enhanced injuries are sufficiently analogous to cases in which multiple tortfeasors incur joint and several liability for an indivisible injury.

The tort rules for determining damages are not unique to product cases, so we can look more widely to identify the relevant principles.

STORY PARCHMENT CO. v. PATERSON PARCHMENT PAPER CO.
Supreme Court of the United States, 1931
282 U.S. 555

SUTHERLAND, J. This is an action arising under the Sherman Anti-Trust Act to recover damages resulting from an alleged conspiracy between respondents and West Carrollton Parchment Company, not joined for lack of jurisdiction, to monopolize interstate trade and commerce in vegetable parchment, exclude the petitioner therefrom, and destroy its business in such trade and commerce. A jury returned a verdict for petitioner in the sum of $65,000, but in the alternative for the respondents "if, as a matter of law, the plaintiff is not entitled to a verdict." The trial court approved the verdict and rendered judgment for treble the amount of the damages in accordance with section 7 of the act. On appeal to the Circuit Court of Appeals, the judgment was vacated and the case remanded to the trial court, with directions to enter judgment for respondents upon the ground that petitioner had not sustained the burden of proving that it had suffered recoverable damages.

The verdict of the jury and the judgment thereon of the District Court have the effect of a finding in favor of petitioner upon that issue; and to that extent the verdict and judgment were sustained by the court below. There is enough evidence in the record to preclude an interference on our part with these concurrent findings. That the petitioner was injured in its business and property as a result of this unlawful combination we think also finds sufficient support in the evidence. Questions in respect of the liability of the wrongdoers to respond in damages alone remain to be considered.

[We cannot] accept the view of that court that the verdict of the jury cannot stand because it was based upon mere speculation and conjecture. This characterization of the basis for the verdict is unwarranted. It is true that there was uncertainty as to the extent of the damage, but there was none as to the fact of damage; and there is a clear distinction between the measure of proof necessary to establish the fact that petitioner had sustained some damage and the measure of proof necessary to enable the jury to fix the amount. The rule which precludes the recovery of uncertain damages applies to such as are not the certain result of the wrong, not to those damages which are definitely attributable to the wrong and only uncertain in respect of their amount.

Where the tort itself is of such a nature as to preclude the ascertainment of the amount of damages with certainty, it would be a perversion of fundamental principles of justice to deny all relief to the injured person, and thereby relieve the wrongdoer from making any amend for his acts. In such case, while the damages may not be determined by mere speculation or guess, it will be enough if the evidence show the extent of the damages as a matter of just and reasonable inference, although the result be only approximate. The wrongdoer is not entitled to complain that they cannot be measured with the exactness and precision that would be possible if the case, which he alone is responsible for making, were otherwise. [ ] As the Supreme Court of Michigan has forcefully declared, the risk of the uncertainty should be thrown upon the wrongdoer instead of upon the injured party. That was a case sounding in tort, and the court, speaking through Christiancy, J., said:

> But shall the injured party in an action of tort, which may happen to furnish no element of certainty, be allowed to recover no damages (or merely nominal), because he can not show the exact amount with certainty, though he is ready to show, to the satisfaction of the jury, that he has suffered large damages by the injury? Certainty, it is true, would thus be attained; but it would be the certainty of injustice.
>
> Juries are allowed to act upon probable and inferential as well as direct and positive proof. And when, from the nature of the case, the amount of the damages can not be estimated with certainty, or only a part of them can be so estimated, we can see no objection to placing before the jury all the facts and circumstances of the case, having any tendency to show damages, or their probable amount; so as to enable them to make the most intelligible and probable estimate which the nature of the case will permit.

Allison v. Chandler, 11 Mich. 542, 555.

As was said by Judge Anderson in his dissenting opinion below, there are many cases in which damages are allowed where the element of uncertainty is at least equal to that in the present case—as, for example, copyright and trade-mark cases, cases of unfair competition, and many cases of personal injury. Numerous decisions support the statement that the constant tendency of the courts is to find some way in which damages can be awarded where a wrong has been done. Difficulty of ascertainment is no longer confused with right of recovery.

IV. Enhanced Injury

The judgment of the Court of Appeals is reversed, and that of the District Court affirmed.

NOTES AND QUESTIONS

1. *Evidentiary requirements for proving damages.* The evidentiary rule adopted in *Story Parchment* is an established principle of tort law. *See* RESTATEMENT (SECOND) OF TORTS §912 (requiring the plaintiff to prove "the extent of the [tortiously caused] harm and the amount of money representing adequate compensation with as much certainty as the nature of the tort and the circumstances permit"). The reasonably available evidence, for example, can show that the tortious injury will cause the plaintiff to incur medical expenses of $1 million over a 25-year period. This proof does not show that the damages, more likely than not, are $1 million. If that degree of certainty were required to prove damages extending far into the future, the plaintiff's award would be substantially reduced, thereby enabling the defendant to benefit from the uncertainty inherent in a damages calculation that is only required because of the defendant's wrongdoing. To prevent this injustice, the evidentiary standard for determining damages is less demanding than the standard that governs the liability phase of the case.

2. *Distinguishing between the two types of causal rules in tort cases.* It should now be apparent that causal inquiries in tort law have an element of complexity that is masked by the statement that the plaintiff bears the burden of proving causation. The first type of causal inquiry determines liability: Did the defendant's breach of duty proximately cause an injury for which the plaintiff is entitled to compensation? Once the plaintiff has established the prima facie case for liability, a different causal question arises in the damages phase of the case: Did the defendant's breach cause the full extent of damages claimed by the plaintiff? For each of these causal inquiries, the plaintiff bears the burden of proof. The two types of causal issues, though, are not governed by the same evidentiary standard.

As illustrated by *Trull*, courts have not adequately distinguished between these two causal rules in discussing the plaintiff's burden of proof in cases of enhanced injury. Does this evidentiary rule governing the determination of damages justify the majority rule on enhanced injury? No court has expressly justified the rule in this manner, but there are cases in which the court apparently analyzed the problem in this manner.

MAY v. PORTLAND JEEP
Supreme Court of Oregon, 1973
509 P.2d 24

HOLMAN, J. This is a products liability action brought under Restatement (Second) of Torts §402A for damages suffered as a result of injuries inflicted in a one-vehicle accident. Plaintiff claims his injuries were caused by a defective vehicle which was sold to him by defendant. Defendant appealed from a judgment for plaintiff which was entered pursuant to a jury verdict.

Because plaintiff received the verdict, the facts will be recounted in a manner as favorable to him as the evidence will permit. Plaintiff purchased from defendant a new Jeep upon which was installed a roll bar. Thereafter, while driving the vehicle, plaintiff upset it upon a sand dike adjacent the Columbia River. He attempted to climb the landward side of the dike with five passengers in the Jeep, but became bogged down because of the loose sand. Two of his passengers disembarked, and plaintiff made a second attempt which was successful. The momentum carried the Jeep across the top of the dike and the vehicle started down the other side at a speed of from eight to ten miles per hour. The descent was much steeper on the river side than plaintiff had anticipated, for, on the way down, the front end of the Jeep buried itself in the sand and the vehicle flipped forward, landing upside down.

The roll bar had been installed by bolting it through the tops of the wheel wells which covered the rear wheels. The wheel wells were welded to the sides of the body by spot welds. The pressure of the impact of the overturning vehicle tore bits of metal from the body at the points where the wheel wells were spot welded to it. As a result, the wheel wells collapsed upon the tires of the vehicle, bringing the roll bar down with them.

The roll bar came down across the back of the neck of plaintiff, who was strapped into his seat with a seat belt, and the impact thrust his head forward, causing his face to be pinned against the steering wheel while his head rested upon the ground. He received injuries to his teeth, mouth, neck, back, chest, and one leg.

As [one] ground for its nonsuit, defendant contends there was insufficient evidence that plaintiff's injury was caused by the collapse of the roll bar. Defendant argues that there was no evidence from which a jury could reasonably conclude that plaintiff's injuries probably would not have occurred in the absence of the claimed defect. Plaintiff's testimony concerning what happened at the time of the accident was as follows:

> "Q: Now, Mr. May, after the jeep rolled over, as you have described it, what do you recall next?
> "A: Well, I was unconscious about five or ten minutes and, when I came to, I was bundled up underneath the jeep, still strapped in my seatbelt. I managed to get my seatbelt undone. I got dug out from under the jeep and went to see if everybody else was all right.
> "Q: Were you located in an upside-down position?
> "A: Yes.
> "Q: Where was the roll-bar?
> "A: It was on the back of my neck. I was pinned between the steering wheel and the top of the roll bar.
> "Q: Did it have you squeezed?
> "A: The top of my head was on the ground, my face in the steering wheel and the roll-bar on the back of my neck.
> "Q: Did you cause any physical damage to the steering wheel when you struck it, Mr. May?'
> "A: Yes, it broke the steering wheel. I had to replace it."

IV. Enhanced Injury

From the above narration of what occurred, we believe a jury could reasonably conclude that a major portion of plaintiff's injuries would not have occurred in the absence of the collapse of the bar. There is no way of determining, of course, what the exact extent of plaintiff's injuries would have been had the roll bar not collapsed. However, we allow juries to make somewhat similar inexact determinations, such as the extent of pain and suffering and its value in money. We do so because we believe such pain and suffering should be compensable, and there is no way of determining its extent and value other than to allow the jury to use its best judgment. The only alternative in this case is to say that plaintiff probably was additionally injured by the collapse of the bar, but that, because we cannot determine exactly what his injuries would have been if it had not collapsed, he cannot recover at all. This is not an acceptable alternative, and it is usual to allow the jury to use its judgment in similar inexact situations. It was proper to allow the jury to make its best estimate of that portion of plaintiff's injuries attributable to the collapse of the bar.

The judgment of the trial court is affirmed.

NOTES AND QUESTIONS

1. *Rethinking the problem of enhanced injury.* Consider the court's reasoning in *May* in relation to the court's reasoning in *Trull*. According to the *Trull* court, the majority rule on enhanced injuries requires the plaintiff to "prove only that the design defect was a substantial factor in producing damages over and above those which were probably caused as a result of the original impact or collision." The plaintiff, in other words, must prove by a preponderance of the evidence that the defect caused some compensable injury ("over and above those which" probably would have occurred even if the automobile had not been defective). The plaintiff in *May* relied on similar evidence. This proof, when combined with the plaintiff's proof establishing all other elements of the prima facie case for liability, entitles the plaintiff to receive compensation from the defendant. The court must then determine the amount of compensatory damages caused by the defect. To satisfy this burden, the plaintiff must prove "the extent of the [tortiously caused] harm and the amount of money representing adequate compensation with as much certainty as the nature of the tort and the circumstances permit." RESTATEMENT (SECOND) OF TORTS §912. Having proven the full extent of an indivisible injury (one not capable of apportionment) that was at least partially caused by the defect, the plaintiff has satisfied the evidentiary burden with respect to the entire indivisible injury. The rationale, according to the Court in *Story Parchment Co.*, is that "the risk of the uncertainty should be thrown upon the wrongdoer instead of upon the injured party." The alternative, as the court in *May* explained, is "unacceptable" because it would bar the plaintiff from any recovery simply "because we cannot determine exactly what his injuries would have been" if the vehicle had not been defective. As a matter of fairness or justice the defendant bears the inherent burden of factual uncertainty in the determination of damages. Unless the defendant can eliminate the uncertainty with proof of apportionment, it bears the burden of that uncertainty by incurring

liability for the entire indivisible injury—the result attained by the majority rule adopted in *Trull.*

2. *Enhanced injury and joint and several liability.* In *Trull* and other cases, courts have concluded that recovery for enhanced injury is somehow justified by the rule that makes jointly and severally liable defendants bear the burden of proving apportionment in cases of indivisible injury. As part of tort reform, numerous states have abolished the doctrine of joint and several liability, causing at least one court to reject the majority rule on enhanced injury. *See* Egbert v. Nissan Motor Corp., 228 P.3d 737, 745-746 (Utah 2010) (rejecting the majority rule on enhanced injury because it depends on joint and several liability, which has been statutorily eliminated in Utah). Does the rationale for the enhanced-injury rule depend on the logic of joint and several liability?

Consider an automobile accident that was negligently caused by another driver, and suppose that the plaintiff's injuries were enhanced by a defect in the automobile. When the injuries are indivisible, both the negligent driver and the automobile manufacturer are jointly and severally liable for the entirety of plaintiff's harm. This outcome makes it look like the rule regarding liability for an indivisible injury somehow depends on the logic of joint and several liability. It does not. Consider the plaintiff's claim against the manufacturer. By proving that the manufacturer tortiously caused some compensable harm that contributed to an indivisible injury, the plaintiff has established an entitlement to compensation for the entire injury with the reasonably available evidence. The manufacturer can be held liable for the entire injury, regardless of whether anyone else (the negligent driver) can also be held accountable. The liability in these cases is justified by the damages principle that places the inherent burden of factual uncertainty on the defendant rather than the plaintiff; it has nothing to do with the logic of joint and several liability, which addresses the apportionment of liability across multiple tortfeasors who have each independently caused the injury in question.

3. *Enhanced injury and the burden of proof.* We can now determine whether the majority rule on enhanced injury unduly relaxes the plaintiff's burden of proving causation as proponents of the minority rule claim. To recover for enhanced injuries, the plaintiff must prove by a preponderance of the evidence that the defendant is legally responsible for a defect that caused at least some compensable portion of an (indivisible) injury not capable of apportionment. This rule does not reduce the plaintiff's burden of proving causation in the prima facie case, nor does it relax the plaintiff's ordinary evidentiary burden for proving damages. Contrary to the manner in which courts depict the doctrine, the causal rule governing cases of enhanced injury—like the liberal rule of but-for causation and the heeding presumption discussed in the prior sections of this chapter—satisfies the fundamental tort requirement that the plaintiff must adequately prove that the defendant's breach of duty caused the injuries for which the plaintiff seeks compensation. The burden then shifts to the defendant to prove apportionment, but only because the plaintiff has already satisfied her burden. Consequently, the rule "does not formally shift any burden of proof to the defendant" as the *Restatement (Third)* recognizes in §16, Rptrs' N. cmt. d.

V. FACTUAL UNCERTAINTY REGARDING THE TORTFEASOR'S IDENTITY: ALTERNATIVE AND MARKET-SHARE LIABILITY

Product cases have produced one of the most interesting causal issues in tort law. When generic, mass-produced products cause widespread injury due to identical defects in each unit, and a plaintiff is unable to identify which of the large number of manufacturers sold the product that caused her injury, can the plaintiff establish liability against the group of manufacturers? An affirmative answer is supplied by the doctrine of market-share liability, which is an extension of the widely adopted doctrine of alternative liability according to some courts.

Courts first adopted market-share liability in cases involving the drug known as DES, but they have not applied it to many other types of products. Even in the context of DES, a strong plurality of courts has rejected market-share liability. As a practical matter, the doctrine has been narrowly applied and might be interesting largely as a matter of tort theory.

When fully developed, however, the logic of market-share liability might have more widespread application than has been commonly recognized. The doctrine could be critical for resolving issues of causal uncertainty that are likely to be increasingly confronted by courts in the decades to come.

SINDELL v. ABBOTT LABORATORIES
Supreme Court of California, 1980
607 P.2d 924

MOSK, J. This case involves a complex problem both timely and significant: may a plaintiff, injured as the result of a drug administered to her mother during pregnancy, who knows the type of drug involved but cannot identify the manufacturer of the precise product, hold liable for her injuries a maker of a drug produced from an identical formula?

Plaintiff Judith Sindell brought an action against eleven drug companies and Does 1 through 100, on behalf of herself and other women similarly situated. The complaint alleges as follows:

> Between 1941 and 1971, defendants were engaged in the business of manufacturing, promoting, and marketing diethylstilbesterol (DES), a drug which is a synthetic compound of the female hormone estrogen. The drug was administered to plaintiff's mother and the mothers of the class she represents, for the purpose of preventing miscarriage. In 1947, the Food and Drug Administration authorized the marketing of DES as a miscarriage preventative, but only on an experimental basis, with a requirement that the drug contain a warning label to that effect.

DES may cause cancerous vaginal and cervical growths in the daughters exposed to it before birth, because their mothers took the drug during pregnancy. The form of cancer from which these daughters suffer is known as adenocarcinoma, and it manifests itself after a minimum latent period of 10 or 12 years. It is a fast-spreading and deadly disease, and radical surgery is required to prevent it from spreading. DES also causes adenosis, precancerous vaginal and cervical growths which may spread to other areas of the body. Thousands of women whose mothers received DES during pregnancy are unaware of the effects of the drug.

In 1971, the Food and Drug Administration ordered defendants to cease marketing and promoting DES for the purpose of preventing miscarriages, and to warn physicians and the public that the drug should not be used by pregnant women because of the danger to their unborn children.

During the period defendants marketed DES, they knew or should have known that it was a carcinogenic substance, that there was a grave danger after varying periods of latency it would cause cancerous and precancerous growths in the daughters of the mothers who took it, and that it was ineffective to prevent miscarriage. Nevertheless, defendants continued to advertise and market the drug as a miscarriage preventative. They failed to test DES for efficacy and safety; the tests performed by others, upon which they relied, indicated that it was not safe or effective. In violation of the authorization of the Food and Drug Administration, defendants marketed DES on an unlimited basis rather than as an experimental drug, and they failed to warn of its potential danger.

Because of defendants' advertised assurances that DES was safe and effective to prevent miscarriage, plaintiff was exposed to the drug prior to her birth. She became aware of the danger from such exposure within one year of the time she filed her complaint. As a result of the DES ingested by her mother, plaintiff developed a malignant bladder tumor which was removed by surgery. She suffers from adenosis and must constantly be monitored by biopsy or colposcopy to insure early warning of further malignancy.

[The complaint alleges numerous causes of action, including negligence, strict products liability, and breach of the implied warranty.] Each cause of action alleges that defendants are jointly liable because they acted in concert, on the basis of express and implied agreements, and in reliance upon and ratification and exploitation of each other's testing and marketing methods.

Defendants demurred to the complaint. [T]he trial court sustained the demurrers of these defendants without leave to amend on the ground that plaintiff did not and stated she could not identify which defendant had manufactured the drug responsible for her injuries. Thereupon, the court dismissed the action.

This case is but one of a number filed throughout the country seeking to hold drug manufacturers liable for injuries allegedly resulting from DES prescribed to the plaintiffs' mothers since 1947. According to a note in the Fordham Law Review, estimates of the number of women who took the drug during pregnancy range from 1½ million to 3 million. Hundreds, perhaps thousands, of the daughters of these women suffer from adenocarcinoma, and the incidence of vaginal adenosis among them is 30 to 90 percent. Comment, *DES and a Proposed Theory of Enterprise Liability*, 46 Fordham L. Rev. 963, 964-967 (1978). Most of the cases are still pending. With two exceptions [currently under appeal], those that have been decided resulted in judgments in favor of the drug company defendants because of the failure of the plaintiffs to identify the manufacturer of the DES prescribed to their mothers.

V. Factual Uncertainty Regarding the Tortfeasor's Identity

We begin with the proposition that, as a general rule, the imposition of liability depends upon a showing by the plaintiff that his or her injuries were caused by the act of the defendant or by an instrumentality under the defendant's control. The rule applies whether the injury resulted from an accidental event or from the use of a defective product.

There are, however, exceptions to this rule. Plaintiff's complaint suggests several bases upon which defendants may be held liable for her injuries even though she cannot demonstrate the name of the manufacturer which produced the DES actually taken by her mother. [One of] these theories, classically illustrated by Summers v. Tice, 199 P.2d 1 (Cal. 1948), places the burden of proof of causation upon tortious defendants in certain circumstances. We shall conclude that [this doctrine of alternative liability], as previously interpreted, may not be applied to hold defendants liable under the allegations of this complaint. However, we shall propose and adopt a [new] basis for permitting the action to be tried, grounded upon an extension of the *Summers* doctrine.

In *Summers*, the plaintiff was injured when two hunters negligently shot in his direction. It could not be determined which of them had fired the shot which actually caused the injury to the plaintiff's eye, but both defendants were nevertheless held jointly and severally liable for the whole of the damages. We reasoned that both were wrongdoers, both were negligent toward the plaintiff, and that it would be unfair to require plaintiff to isolate the defendant responsible, because if the one pointed out were to escape liability, the other might also, and the plaintiff-victim would be shorn of any remedy. In these circumstances, we held, the burden of proof shifted to the defendants, "each to absolve himself if he can."

The rule developed in *Summers* has been embodied in the *Restatement (Second) of Torts*.[11]

[P]laintiff may not prevail in her claim that the *Summers* rationale should be employed to fix the whole liability for her injuries upon defendants, at least as those principles have previously been applied.[16] Defendants maintain that, while in *Summers* there was a 50 percent chance that one of the two defendants was responsible for the plaintiff's injuries, here since any one of 200 companies which manufactured DES might have made the product which harmed plaintiff, there is no rational basis upon which to infer that any defendant in this action caused plaintiff's injuries, nor even a reasonable possibility that they were responsible. While we propose, *infra*, an adaptation of the rule in *Summers*

---

11. Section 433(B), subsection (3) of the *Restatement* provides: "Where the conduct of two or more actors is tortious, and it is proved that harm has been caused to the plaintiff by only one of them, but there is uncertainty as to which one has caused it, the burden is upon each such actor to prove that he has not caused the harm." The reason underlying the rule is "the injustice of permitting proved wrongdoers, who among them have inflicted an injury upon the entirely innocent plaintiff, to escape liability merely because the nature of their conduct and the resulting harm has made it difficult or impossible to prove which of them has caused the harm." Rest. 2d Torts §433B, com. f, p. 446.

16. According to the *Restatement*, the burden of proof shifts to the defendants only if the plaintiff can demonstrate that all defendants acted tortiously and that the harm resulted from the conduct of one of them. Rest. 2d Torts §433B, com. g. It goes on to state that the rule thus far has been applied only where all the actors involved are joined as defendants and where the conduct of all is simultaneous in time, but cases might arise in which some modification of the rule would be necessary if one of the actors is or cannot be joined, or because of the effects of lapse of time, or other circumstances. *Id.*, com. h.

which will substantially overcome these difficulties, defendants appear to be correct that the rule, as previously applied, cannot relieve plaintiff of the burden of proving the identity of the manufacturer which made the drug causing her injuries.[18]

If we were confined to the theor[y] of *Summers*, we would be constrained to hold that the judgment must be sustained. Should we require that plaintiff identify the manufacturer which supplied the DES used by her mother or that all DES manufacturers be joined in the action [as required by the *Summers* rule of alternative liability], she would effectively be precluded from any recovery. As defendants candidly admit, there is little likelihood that all the manufacturers who made DES at the time in question are still in business or that they are subject to the jurisdiction of the California courts. There are, however, forceful arguments in favor of holding that plaintiff has a cause of action.

The most persuasive reason for finding plaintiff states a cause of action is that advanced in *Summers*: as between an innocent plaintiff and negligent defendants, the latter should bear the cost of the injury. Here, as in *Summers*, plaintiff is not at fault in failing to provide evidence of causation, and although the absence of such evidence is not attributable to the defendants either, their conduct in marketing a drug the effects of which are delayed for many years played a significant role in creating the unavailability of proof.

Where, as here, all defendants produced a drug from an identical formula and the manufacturer of the DES which caused plaintiff's injuries cannot be identified through no fault of plaintiff, a modification of the rule of *Summers* is warranted. As we have seen, an undiluted *Summers* rationale is inappropriate to shift the burden of proof of causation to defendants because if we measure the chance that any particular manufacturer supplied the injury-causing product by the number of producers of DES, there is a possibility that none of the five defendants in this case produced the offending substance and that the responsible manufacturer, not named in the action, will escape liability.

But we approach the issue of causation from a different perspective: we hold it to be reasonable in the present context to measure the likelihood that any of the defendants supplied the product which allegedly injured plaintiff by the percentage which the DES sold by each of them for the purpose of preventing miscarriage bears to the entire production of the drug sold by all for that purpose. Plaintiff asserts in her briefs that Eli Lilly and Company and 5 or 6 other companies produced 90 percent of the DES marketed. If at trial this is established to be the fact, then there is a corresponding likelihood that this comparative handful of producers manufactured the DES which caused plaintiff's

---

18. Garcia v. Joseph Vince Co., 84 Cal. App. 3d 868, 148 Cal. Rptr. 843 (1978), relied upon by defendants, presents a distinguishable factual situation. The plaintiff in *Garcia* was injured by a defective saber. He was unable to identify which of two manufacturers had produced the weapon because it was commingled with other sabers after the accident. In a suit against both manufacturers, the court refused to apply the *Summers* rationale on the ground that the plaintiff had not shown that either defendant had violated a duty to him. Thus in *Garcia*, only one of the two defendants was alleged to have manufactured a defective product, and the plaintiff's inability to identify which of the two was negligent resulted in a judgment for both defendants. Here, by contrast, the DES manufactured by all defendants is alleged to be defective, but plaintiff is unable to demonstrate which of the defendants supplied the precise DES which caused her injuries.

V. Factual Uncertainty Regarding the Tortfeasor's Identity

injuries, and only a 10 percent likelihood that the offending producer would escape liability.

If plaintiff joins in the action the manufacturers of a substantial share of the DES which her mother might have taken, the injustice of shifting the burden of proof to defendants to demonstrate that they could not have made the substance which injured plaintiff is significantly diminished. While 75 to 80 percent of the market is suggested by the Fordham Comment [in its proposal for a theory of "enterprise liability" that the court had previously rejected in an omitted portion of the opinion], we hold only that a substantial percentage is required.

The presence in the action of a substantial share of the appropriate market also provides a ready means to apportion damages among the defendants. Each defendant will be held liable for the proportion of the judgment represented by its share of that market unless it demonstrates that it could not have made the product which caused plaintiff's injuries. In the present case, one DES manufacturer was dismissed from the action upon filing a declaration that it had not manufactured DES until after plaintiff was born.

Under this approach, each manufacturer's liability would approximate its responsibility for the injuries caused by its own products. Some minor discrepancy in the correlation between market share and liability is inevitable; therefore, a defendant may be held liable for a somewhat different percentage of the damage than its share of the appropriate market would justify. It is probably impossible, with the passage of time, to determine market share with mathematical exactitude. But just as a jury cannot be expected to determine the precise relationship between fault and liability in applying the doctrine of comparative fault [ ] or partial indemnity [ ], the difficulty of apportioning damages among the defendant producers in exact relation to their market share does not seriously militate against the rule we adopt. As we said in *Summers* with regard to the liability of independent tortfeasors, where a correct division of liability cannot be made "the trier of fact may make it the best it can."

We are not unmindful of the practical problems involved in defining the market and determining market share.

The judgments are reversed.

NOTES AND QUESTIONS

1. *Alternative liability.* According to the court in *Sindell*, market-share liability is "grounded upon an extension of the *Summers* doctrine." The court was referring to the rule of alternative liability it had adopted in the famous case of Summers v. Tice, 199 P.2d 1 (Cal. 1948). "The vast majority of jurisdictions to have considered the issue have adopted the doctrine" of alternative liability. Conn. Interlocal Risk Management Agency v. Jackson, 214 A.3d 841, 846 (Conn. 2019). Alternative liability requires the plaintiff to prove that "all defendants have acted tortiously toward her" and that each defendant could have caused the harm. Kinnett v. Mass. Gas & Elec. Co., 716 F. Supp. 695, 698 (D.N.H. 1989). For the doctrine to apply, "all the parties who were or could have been responsible for the harm to the plaintiff [must be] joined as defendants." Goldman v. Johns-Manville Sales Corp., 514 N.E.2d 691 (Ohio 1987). Consequently, alternative liability applies to

DES cases in which the plaintiff satisfies all these requirements. *E.g.*, Abel v. Eli Lilly & Co., 343 N.W.2d 164, 173-174 (Mich. 1984) ("approving a new DES-unique version of alternative liability" for case in which "plaintiffs claim they have sued all known manufacturers of stilbene derivatives who promoted the drugs to the medical profession in Michigan for use in pregnancy during the period between 1947 and 1964"). But as *Sindell* illustrates, DES plaintiffs ordinarily cannot satisfy the joinder requirement, resulting in the widespread dismissal of these claims. Rather than permit recovery under alternative liability, the court in *Sindell* developed the doctrine of market-share liability. Did the court adequately explain how market-share liability is derived from the rule of alternative liability?

2. *Liability for the imposition of tortious risk?* When a product defect does not double the risk of injury, the element of causation can create a deterrence problem by enabling the seller of a known defective product to routinely avoid liability because a plaintiff can never prove that the defect, more likely than not, caused the injury in question. Could this type of problem be solved by the doctrine of market-share liability?

As the court in *Sindell* recognized, a DES manufacturer's market share measures the likelihood that it caused the plaintiff's harm. The plaintiff's mother could have purchased the DES from any manufacturer in the relevant market, and so a manufacturer that had a 10 percent market share also had a 10 percent chance of selling the DES that caused plaintiff's injury. Indeed, such a manufacturer presumably caused 10 percent of the total number of DES injuries in the entire market. Nevertheless, the manufacturer could avoid liability in all cases on the ground that its product was not the probable cause of plaintiff's injury, the same type of defense available to the manufacturer with a defective product that does not double the risk of injury.

By enabling the plaintiff to recover in the DES cases, the doctrine of market-share liability could provide a basis for solving the deterrence problem posed by defects that do not double the risk of injury. To see why, suppose the plaintiff sues a "substantial share" of the market involving six defendant manufacturers. According to the preponderance of the evidence, each individual manufacturer did not cause the plaintiff's harm; the evidence only establishes that each manufacturer created a 1 in 10 chance of causing the injury. Nevertheless, *Sindell* subjects the manufacturers to liability, suggesting that market-share liability might be based on a principle that the seller of a defective product is subject to liability for having imposed a tortious risk on the plaintiff who then suffered an injury of that type. Such a principle would permit recovery in other cases involving defects that increase but do not double the risk of harm, because liability turns on the imposition of tortious risk and not its magnitude.

Market-share liability is commonly understood in precisely this fashion. In a series of influential articles, leading torts scholars argued that market-share liability is based on an emergent risk-based conception of tort liability that is formulated to promote deterrence in a fair manner. *See, e.g.*, Glen O. Robinson, *Multiple Causation in Tort Law: Reflections on the* DES *Cases*, 68 Va. L. Rev. 713, 749 (1982) (concluding that *Sindell* "point[s] toward a rule that imposes liability for the creation of a risk and apportions liability according to the magnitude of that risk"); David Rosenberg, *The Causal Connection in Mass Exposure Cases: A "Public Law" Vision of the Tort System*, 97 Harv. L. Rev. 849, 866-868 (1984) (identifying market-share liability as a form of proportional liability based upon the risk that the defendant caused injury); *see also* Joseph H. King, Jr., *Causation, Valuation, and Chance in Personal Injury Torts Involving Preexisting Conditions and Future Consequences*, 90 Yale L.J. 1353, 1381 (1981) (arguing that the *Sindell* decision "is an important signal of the increased willingness of courts to integrate chance into its resolution of torts cases").

A risk-based conception of liability need not abandon the requirement that the plaintiff must suffer physical harm in order to recover. Instead, such a rule can limit recovery to those individuals who were both exposed to the tortious risk *and* suffered the type of physical harm threatened by the risk. For example, suppose there is a background or environmental risk that 2 in 10,000 individuals will get cancer, and that individuals who used the defective product face a total risk of 3 in 10,000. On average, for every 10,000 individuals exposed to the defective product, three will contract cancer. The three cancer victims could each recover proportional damages equal to one-third of the total damages for the cancer. Even though the defect subjected each plaintiff to a small risk of injury (1 in 10,000), given that she has been physically harmed, there is a one-third likelihood that the defendant manufacturer caused the harm (two out of every three cancers are caused by the background risk). Conditioning risk-based liability on the occurrence of physical harm, therefore, still compensates the plaintiff for risk exposure and not for the injury itself—the evidence only establishes that the plaintiff was exposed to the tortious risk and suffered injury of the type threatened by the risk; it does not prove that the tortious risk (a one in three chance in our example) actually caused the injury.

If the market-share doctrine is such a liability rule, can a plaintiff recover 10 percent of total damages against a single manufacturer that had a 10 percent chance of causing the injury? How would such a rule apply in *Daubert*, p. 433 *supra*, in which plaintiffs were denied recovery because they could not prove that the defect in the drug at least doubled the risk of injury? Recall that the court in *Daubert* was applying California law, the same body of law that generated *Sindell*. Is there anything about the court's reasoning in *Sindell* that would bar recovery in a case like *Daubert*?

3. *The "substantial share" requirement.* In Murphy v. E.R. Squibb & Sons, Inc., 710 P.2d 247 (Cal. 1985), the plaintiff filed a claim of market-share liability against a single DES manufacturer that had 10 percent of the national market. The trial court dismissed the claim on the ground that the defendant did not supply a "substantial percentage" of the market as required by *Sindell*. Plaintiff appealed to the California Supreme Court.

> We must determine . . . whether [defendant's] 10 percent market share is a substantial percentage of the market for the application of the rule laid down in *Sindell*. Plaintiff, relying on general definitions of the word "substantial" asserts that the term must be defined in the context of a particular case, and since [defendant] was alleged to be the second largest seller of DES in the country, its 10 percent market share must be deemed substantial in the framework of DES litigation.

We reject this contention because it is contrary to the theoretical justification underlying the market share doctrine. We held [in *Sindell*] that if the plaintiff joined in the action the manufacturers of a substantial share of the DES which her mother might have taken, the injustice of shifting the burden of proof to defendants to exonerate themselves would be significantly diminished. We declined to declare a specific percentage of the market which would satisfy application of the doctrine, but stated only that it must be substantial.

Since [defendant] had only a 10 percent share of the DES market, there is only a 10 percent chance that it produced the drug causing plaintiff's injuries, and a 90 percent chance that another manufacturer was the producer. In this circumstance, it must be concluded that she failed to meet the threshold requirement for the application of the market share doctrine. The trial court was justified in ruling, therefore, that she could not proceed to trial on th[is] cause of action.

Id. at 255-256.

What implications does *Murphy* have for the interpretation of market-share liability as a form of risk-based liability that permits recovery for those who were exposed to the tortious risk and suffered physical harm as a result? Under this liability rule, the plaintiff's recovery would be 10 percent of the total damages for the cancer itself. As a matter of risk-based liability, why does it matter that there is "a 90 percent chance that another manufacturer was the producer"? Is the problem that satisfaction of the "substantial share" requirement entitles the plaintiff to full recovery, contrary to the logic of risk-based liability? Consider Martin v. Abbott Labs., 689 P.2d 368, 380-381 (Wash. 1984) ("Although the court in *Sindell* was unclear on this point, the decision arguably requires that defendants pay 100 percent of the plaintiff's damages even though these defendants may represent less than 100 percent of the market.").

The difficulty of interpreting the rule of market-share liability in *Sindell* not only pertains to the ambiguity surrounding the "substantial share" requirement, it also involves the extent of liability that should be incurred by any defendant subject to this liability rule.

BROWN v. SUPERIOR COURT
Supreme Court of California, 1988
751 P.2d 470

MOSK, J. In current litigation several significant issues have arisen relating to the liability of manufacturers of prescription drugs for injuries caused by their products. The questions relate to the scope of liability of producers of diethylstilbestrol (DES) under the market share theory enunciated in Sindell v. Abbott Laboratories, 607 P.2d 924 (Cal. 1980) (hereafter *Sindell*). Specifically, we shall determine whether the manufacturers joined in the action are jointly and severally liable for any damages that may be awarded, or whether their liability is confined to their share of the relevant market for DES.

[In a pretrial ruling, the trial court rejected joint and several liability, and the appellate court affirmed.]

V. Factual Uncertainty Regarding the Tortfeasor's Identity

The consequences of these methods of determining liability are markedly different. If such defendants are jointly and severally liable, a plaintiff may recover the entire amount of the judgment from any of the defendants joined in the action. Since the plaintiff is required under *Sindell* to join the manufacturers of only a substantial share of the appropriate market for DES, it follows that if joint liability were the rule, a defendant could be held responsible for a portion of the judgment that may greatly exceed the percentage of its market share. Under several liability, in contrast, because each defendant's liability for the judgment would be confined to the percentage of its share of the market, a plaintiff would not recover the entire amount of the judgment (except in the unlikely event that all manufacturers were joined in the action) but only the percentage of the sum awarded that is equal to the market shares of the defendants joined in the action. In the one case, it would be the plaintiff who would bear the loss resulting from the fact that some producers of DES that might have been found liable under the market share theory were not joined in the action (or if a defendant became insolvent), whereas in the other such losses would fall on the defendants. Since, as we pointed out in *Sindell*, there is little likelihood that all manufacturers of DES in the appropriate market would be amenable to suit, the adoption of one or the other basis for liability could significantly affect the amount of a plaintiff's recovery and, concomitantly, a defendant's liability.

Instead of endeavoring to draw inferences from the language of *Sindell* as to an issue that the case did not decide, in determining whether defendants should be held jointly liable we look to the purposes underlying the market share principle and whether joint liability will promote those purposes.

We explained the basis of the doctrine as follows: In order to decrease the likelihood that a manufacturer of DES would be held liable for injuries caused by products not of its making, and to achieve a reasonable approximation of its responsibility for injuries caused by the DES it produced, the plaintiff should be required to join in the action the manufacturers of a substantial share of the relevant DES market. If this were done, the injustice of shifting the burden of proof to defendants to exonerate themselves of responsibility for the plaintiff's injuries would be diminished. Each defendant would be held liable for the proportion of the judgment represented by its market share, and its overall liability for injuries caused by DES would approximate the injuries caused by the DES it manufactured. A DES manufacturer found liable under this approach would not be held responsible for injuries caused by another producer of the drug. The opinion acknowledged that only an approximation of a manufacturer's liability could be achieved by this procedure, but underlying our holding was a recognition that such a result was preferable to denying recovery altogether to plaintiffs injured by DES.

It is apparent that the imposition of joint liability on defendants in a market share action would be inconsistent with this rationale. Any defendant could be held responsible for the entire judgment even though its market share may have been comparatively insignificant. Liability would in the first instance be measured not by the likelihood of responsibility for the plaintiff's injuries but by the financial ability of a defendant to undertake payment of the entire judgment or a large portion of it. A defendant that paid a larger percentage of the judgment than warranted by its market share would have the burden of seeking indemnity from other defendants, and it would bear the loss if producers of DES that might have been held liable in the action were not amenable to suit, or if a codefendant was bankrupt. In short, the imposition of joint liability among defendant manufacturers in a market share action would frustrate *Sindell*'s goal of achieving a balance between the interests of DES plaintiffs and manufacturers of the drug.

Finally, plaintiff proposes an alternate means to apportion liability among defendants. She suggests that if we conclude that joint liability is not appropriate, each defendant's liability should be "inflated" in proportion to its market share in an amount sufficient to assure that plaintiff would recover the entire amount of the judgment. While this ingenious approach would not be as unjust to defendants as joint liability, we decline to adopt the proposal because it would nonetheless represent a retreat from *Sindell*'s attempt to achieve as close an approximation as possible between a DES manufacturer's liability for damages and its individual responsibility for the injuries caused by the products it manufactured.

The judgment of the Court of Appeal is affirmed.

NOTES AND QUESTIONS

1. *The substantive basis of liability?* A defendant subject to joint and several liability is legally responsible for the entirety of the plaintiff's damages. By holding a defendant manufacturer severally liable for its share of the market, *Brown* ensures that the liability of each defendant is proportionate to the risk posed by its products. Assuming that the plaintiff has otherwise joined a substantial share of the market in the case, a defendant manufacturer with a 10 percent market share would incur several liability for only 10 percent of the plaintiff's injuries. If this defendant were then sued by all injured consumers in the market, it would incur liability for 10 percent of the total injuries in the entire market, the total amount of harm presumably caused by its products. For this reason, *Brown* makes it easier to interpret the market-share doctrine as a form of liability for the tortious imposition of risk that is conditional on the occurrence of injury.

Can this interpretation of market-share liability be squared with *Murphy*, note 3, p. 475 *supra*, which held that a suit filed against a single manufacturer that had 10 percent of the market does not satisfy the "substantial share" requirement? Would it be defensible to limit a rule of risk-based liability by such a "substantial share" requirement to ensure that the plaintiff's total damages are sufficiently high to justify the litigation and other transaction costs of the rule, particularly those pertaining to the determination of market share? If so, why wouldn't 10 percent of the market be substantial enough for that purpose?

2. *Beyond California.* In the decade or so after *Sindell* was decided, other jurisdictions adopted market-share liability in DES cases. Each decision adopted a rule of market-share liability that differed partially or substantially from *Sindell*. Like *Sindell*, the Washington Supreme Court justified market-share liability as "a modification of the alternative liability theory," but concluded that "plaintiff need commence suit against only one defendant and allege the following elements: [1] that the plaintiff's mother took DES; [2] that DES caused the plaintiff's subsequent injuries; [3] that the

defendant produced or marketed the type of DES taken by the plaintiff's mother; [4] and that the defendant's conduct in producing or marketing the DES constituted a breach of a legally recognized duty to the plaintiff." Martin v. Abbott Labs., 689 P.2d 368, 377 (Wash. 1984). The New York Court of Appeals, by contrast, adopted a rule of market-share liability based on the national market, thereby preventing a manufacturer from exculpating itself from liability by proving that it did not sell the DES that injured the plaintiff. *See* Hymowitz v. Eli Lilly & Co., 539 N.E.2d 1069, 1078 (N.Y. 1989) (justifying the national market to apportion liability because it represents "the amount of risk of injury each defendant created to the public-at-large"). The rule of market-share liability in Wisconsin is also based on the national product market and permits the DES plaintiff to recover full damages for the entire injury from a single manufacturer in the national market, although a defendant could escape liability if "it prove[d] by a preponderance of evidence" that "the DES it produced or marketed could not have reached the plaintiff's mother." Collins v. Eli Lilly & Co., 342 N.W.2d 37, 52 (Wis. 1984). Allowing defendants to avoid liability on this basis "will result in a pool of defendants which it can reasonably be assumed could have caused the plaintiff's injuries." *Id.*

What do the varied formulations of market-share liability suggest about the underlying substantive rationale for the doctrine? Is the best interpretation of market-share liability one of risk-based liability? Is this formulation of the tort claim consistent with the fundamental principle that tort compensation is for injury and not risk?

SMITH v. ELI LILLY & CO.
Supreme Court of Illinois, 1990
560 N.E.2d 324

RYAN, J. The plaintiff in this appeal alleges that she was injured by the drug diethylstilbestrol (DES), which her mother ingested during pregnancy. She seeks relief against defendant DES manufacturers. The issue is whether, in a negligence and strict liability cause of action, Illinois should substitute for the element of causation in fact a theory of market share liability when identification of the manufacturer of the drug that injured the plaintiff is not possible. [The lower courts denied the defendants' summary judgment motion to dismiss the claim for strict products liability, holding instead that the claim is governed by market share liability.] We granted defendants' petition for leave to appeal.

A fundamental principle of tort law is that the plaintiff has the burden of proving by a preponderance of the evidence that the defendant caused the complained-of harm or injury; mere conjecture or speculation is insufficient proof. [ ] Besides assigning blame-worthiness to culpable parties, [the element of causation] also limits the scope of potential liability and thereby encourages useful activity that would otherwise be deterred if there were excessive exposure to liability.

Although proof of causation in fact is ordinarily an indispensable ingredient of a *prima facie* case, the plaintiff points out that competing tort interests have compelled courts to create exceptions to the causation requirement. These exceptions to the rule have allowed a plaintiff to shift to a defendant or a group of defendants the burden of proof on the causation issue. Included within the exceptions are "alternative liability" and "market share liability."

Currently, four States [California, New York, Washington, and Wisconsin] have adopted some form of this theory when confronted with the issue of imposing liability on drug manufacturers for injuries caused to women whose mothers ingested DES while pregnant. [ ] However, none of these States agree on the remedy or its application.

Other than these cases, the concept of market share liability has not received strong support. The supreme courts of two of our sister States have outrightly rejected its application in DES daughter cases. The Iowa Supreme Court rejected the doctrine "on a broad policy basis." Mulcahy v. Eli Lilly & Co., 386 N.W.2d 67, 75 (Iowa 1986). The Missouri Supreme Court found that *Sindell* had not sufficiently articulated the concepts involved. The court concluded that there was insufficient public policy justification to support abandonment of so fundamental a concept of tort law as the requirement that a plaintiff prove, at a minimum, a nexus between wrongdoing and injury. Zafft v. Eli Lilly & Co., 676 S.W.2d 241, 246 (Mo. 1984). Most of the Federal courts which have addressed the issue of applying market share liability in a DES case have declined to adopt such a radical departure from the common law of the State in which each sits without a clearer direction from that State's supreme court [ ]. Plaintiffs have pursued the application of market share liability with minimal success in areas other than DES cases [citing cases involving vaccines and asbestos products].

We conclude that market share liability is not a sound theory, is too great a deviation from our existing tort principles and should not be applied in cases brought by plaintiffs who were exposed to DES while in utero.

The appellate court supported its conclusion that market share liability should be adopted based in part on analogies to [alternative liability]. Every court which has addressed the issue has held, for a number of reasons, that alternative liability does not apply to DES cases.

On the surface, cases utilizing these concepts and market share liability seem similar in that the plaintiff in each lacks evidence to establish the identity of the responsible defendant and as a result the court shifts the burden of proof to the defendants. However, though there exist some similarities, the analogy is too tenuous to rely on alternative liability as a sound basis for adopting the theory.

In . . . alternative liability situations, all parties who could have been the cause of the plaintiff's injuries are joined as defendants. This helps to preserve the identification element because liability will surely fall on the actual wrongdoer. By contrast, market share liability merely requires the plaintiff to name as defendants either a substantial share of those in the market or, in some theories, only one manufacturer who was in the market. As a result, there is a real possibility that the defendant actually responsible for the injuries is not before the court. Indeed, it is inevitable that some defendants wholly innocent of wrongdoing towards the particular plaintiff will shoulder part or all of the responsibility for the injury caused.

Plaintiff next claims that certain underlying principles of products liability laws dictate that we should impose liability on the manufacturers. We agree with the idea that liability based on tort law should be shouldered by the responsible manufacturer or manufacturers. However, we do not believe that we should abrogate a fundamental precept of tort law to reach this goal and ignore the effects of adopting market share liability.

The concept that liability may be imposed based merely on a breach of duty, without causation being established, has long been rejected in American tort law. [ ] Though it has been suggested that the DES manufacturers' creation of risk is sufficient to impose liability, Robinson, *Multiple Causation in Tort Law: Reflections on the DES Cases*, 68 Va. L. Rev. 713, 755 (1982) (damages imposed under market share liability will equal the risks created), we have held that creation of risk or breach of a duty alone is not sufficient in imposing liability. [ ] These principles should not be ignored merely because the defendants are members of the drug industry.

The market share liability theory disregards these precedents and turns manufacturers into insurers of their own products and products made by others in the industry. [S]uch a solution is an unreasonable over-reaction in attempting to achieve what is perceived as a socially satisfying result.

The plaintiff contends that by not recognizing a market share liability theory we will be abdicating our responsibility in the development of Illinois common law. We have not in the past been hesitant to develop new tort concepts; however, in this instance we decline to do so because of the infirmities in the proposed theory. Furthermore, this is too great a deviation from a tort principle which we have found to serve a vital function in the law, causation in fact, especially when market share liability is a flawed concept and its application will likely be only to a narrow class of defendants.

Reversed and remanded.

NOTES AND QUESTIONS

1. *The current status of market-share liability.* A "number of courts" have adopted market-share liability in DES cases, but a "roughly equal number of courts have declined to craft a new theory for DES plaintiffs, expressing concern that to do so would rend too great a chasm in the tort-law requirement of factual causation." RESTATEMENT (THIRD) OF TORTS: LIABILITY FOR PHYSICAL HARM AND EMOTIONAL §28 Rptrs. N. cmt. p (collecting cases showing that no more than 20 jurisdictions have decided the issue, with 9 rejecting market-share liability).

2. *Proportional liability as a rationale for market-share liability.* As illustrated by *Smith*, many courts do not find market-share liability to be justifiable insofar as it provides compensation for exposure to a tortious risk, conditional on the occurrence of injury—the rule known as proportional liability. Even those jurisdictions that have adopted market-share liability have sharply limited its application, typically by requiring that the risk in question be "fungible" or easily translated into market shares, as in the DES context. *See* Allen Rostron, *Beyond Market Share Liability: A Theory of Proportional Share Liability for Nonfungible Products*, 52 UCLA L. Rev. 151, 153 (2004) ("Courts have curtailed the reach of this theory beyond DES by emphasizing the notion that market share liability can apply only when a product is perfectly 'fungible.'"). Limiting the market-share doctrine in this manner makes no sense if the liability is for the tortious imposition of

risk. *See generally id.* Consequently, the risk-based interpretation of market-share liability apparently has little or no support in the case law. *Compare* Hymowitz v. Eli Lilly & Co., 539 N.E.2d 1069, 1075 (N.Y. 1989) (adopting market-share liability in DES cases because "the ever-evolving dictates of justice and fairness, which are the heart of our common-law system, require formation of a remedy for injuries caused by DES"), *with* Caronia v. Phillip Morris USA, Inc., 5 N.E.3d 11, 14 (N.Y. 2013) ("A threat of future harm is insufficient to impose liability against a defendant in a tort context. The requirement that a plaintiff sustain physical harm before being able to recover in tort is a fundamental principle of our state's tort system.").

3. *Factual causation as a constraint on the pursuit of product safety.* The issue of market-share liability illustrates the important limitation of tort liability that inheres in the element of factual causation. The objective of deterrence can be frustrated by the cause-in-fact requirement when the product defect does not at least double the risk of injury; the manufacturer avoids liability altogether, even though its products cause substantial injury (say one-in-three cancers). This deterrence problem is solved by subjecting the manufacturer to liability for the tortious imposition of risk, conditional on the occurrence of injury (making the manufacturer liable for one-third of each cancer victim's total damages). As the market-share cases show, however, courts are unwilling to reformulate the tort claim in this manner. The plaintiff must prove that the defect caused the physical harm for which she seeks compensation, even if this evidentiary burden effectively immunizes the sellers of defective products from tort liability and creates a deterrence problem.

4. *Rethinking the substantive basis of market-share liability.* So far we have only seriously considered the interpretation of the market-share doctrine as a form of liability for the tortious imposition of risk, conditional on the occurrence of injury. Did the California Supreme Court ever expressly justify the doctrine in these terms or otherwise disavow the fundamental tort principle of causation?

> Courts adopting market share liability have not said that causation itself, conceived of in a broader sense than the individual victim/individual manufacturer link, is irrelevant to liability. Market share liability remains an attempt to hold each manufacturer liable, in an aggregate sense, for the amount of harm caused by its products within the relevant market (whatever that may be), even if the harm caused by a specific manufacturer cannot be linked to a particular victim. No court has acknowledged that it is functionally imposing a targeted tax on manufacturers, unrelated to the fundamental tort concept of causation, and then using the proceeds of the tax as a social welfare spending measure to alleviate the financial needs of those with a related product-caused disease.

Donald G. Gifford, *The Death of Causation: Mass Products Torts' Incomplete Incorporation of Social Welfare Principles,* 41 Wake Forest L. Rev. 943, 985 (2006). If market-share liability is not justified as a form of risk-based or proportional liability, what, if anything, might justify the doctrine?

V. Factual Uncertainty Regarding the Tortfeasor's Identity

5. *Whither alternative liability?* Prior to *Smith*, it was an open question whether Illinois would recognize alternative liability. Did the court in *Smith* implicitly accept alternative liability or merely explain why this doctrine could not justify liability in the case at hand? After thoroughly analyzing the opinion, an intermediate appellate court concluded that *Smith* "provides us with no clear expression of the views of the majority on the merits of alternative liability other than the fact that it lacks some of the flaws of market share liability." Wysocki v. Reed, 583 N.E.2d 1139, 1143 (Ill. Ct. App. 1991). Consequently, the court "conclude[d] that we must decide for ourselves whether the doctrine of alternative liability should be applied *in this case*." The court decided to adopt alternative liability, after recognizing that "*Summers v. Tice* has been cited and followed in the great majority of jurisdictions that have considered it in cases where all possible tortfeasors have been before the court. We know of only one case that has rejected it." *Id.* at 1143-1145. Can a jurisdiction consistently adopt alternative liability while rejecting market-share liability?

Consider in this regard the reasons why the court in *Smith* rejected *Sindell*'s rationale for market-share liability based on an "extension" of alternative liability. As in *Summers*, suppose there are two actors who are each equally likely of having tortiously caused plaintiff's injury, and that plaintiff sues both of them. Having satisfied the joinder requirement, the plaintiff could recover under the doctrine of alternative liability against both defendants, even though one of them definitely did not cause the harm. In such a case, it is "inevitable" that "some defendants wholly innocent of wrongdoing towards the particular plaintiff will shoulder part or all of the responsibility for the injury caused," and so this problem—one that the *Smith* court attributes to market-share liability—clearly applies to alternative liability as well.

If market-share liability is merely an "extension" of alternative liability, what makes market-share liability such a radical departure from the fundamental tort principle of causation? Rather than representing conflicting views about the tort principle of causation, the sharply divided case law on market-share liability most plausibly stems from disagreement about whether the *Summers* doctrine of alternative liability properly extends to market-share liability.

THE DOCTRINAL UNITY OF ALTERNATIVE LIABILITY AND MARKET-SHARE LIABILITY
Mark A. Geistfeld
155 U. Pa. L. Rev. 447 (2006)

[A]lternative liability is easy to understand when liability is based upon the tortious infliction of risk. The plaintiff in *Summers* proved, by a preponderance of the evidence, that each defendant tortiously created a fifty percent risk of causing the harm in question. Neither defendant could provide causal proof to the contrary. Each defendant incurred liability for fifty percent of the plaintiff's total damages, an amount exactly corresponding to the probability that he caused the harm. The plaintiff received full compensation for the injury from the two defendants, but the liability of each defendant was based upon risk and not the tortious infliction of injury.

This rationale for alternative liability is problematic. It implies that the widespread acceptance of alternative liability should make market-share liability widely acceptable. However, by rejecting market-share liability, a strong plurality of courts have shown that they are not willing to make a defendant liable for merely exposing the plaintiff to a tortious risk of causing the harm. The widespread judicial acceptance of alternative liability must rest upon some other rationale.

In light of the case law, alternative liability most plausibly involves compensation for physical harm without relaxing the plaintiff's burden of proving causation. To operate in this manner, alternative liability must apply the plaintiff's causal proof to the group of defendants rather than to each defendant individually. In *Summers*, for example, the plaintiff proved that the two defendants, considered together, more likely than not caused the physical harm. As the *Summers* court concluded, "we believe it is clear that the [trial] court sufficiently found on the issue that defendants were jointly liable and that thus the negligence of both was the cause of the injury or to that legal effect."[1] By applying the plaintiff's causal proof to the group of defendants, alternative liability does not reduce the plaintiff's burden of proving causation with respect to the tortious infliction of physical harm.

According to a leading torts treatise, the doctrine of alternative liability can be expressed in terms of such a causal rule:

> When the conduct of two or more actors is so related to an event that their combined conduct, viewed as a whole, is a but-for cause of the event, and application of the but-for rule to them individually would absolve all of them, the conduct of each is a cause in fact of the event.[2]

[This causal rule] has never been adequately developed, however. As another leading treatise observes:

> [I]t depends on a decision to group various acts of various defendants together, and on a decision about what acts should be treated in this collective manner. At least to some extent, the decision to aggregate conduct of different defendants, and the decision to include or exclude specific acts in that aggregate unit, is likely to be a policy decision, or merely an intuitive selection. In either case, it may generate further legal issues, this time over the criteria for the policy decisions.[3]

Nevertheless, solving the causal problem by grouping the defendants has obvious appeal. It is the only rationale capable of explaining how alternative liability does not relax the plaintiff's burden of proving causation or otherwise provide compensation for the tortious exposure to risk. Others have solved the

---

1. Summers v. Tice, 199 P.2d 1, 2 (Cal. 1948).
2. W. Page Keeton et al., Prosser and Keeton on the Law of Torts §41, at 268 (5th ed. 1984).
3. Dan B. Dobbs, The Law of Torts §171, at 411 (2000).

V. Factual Uncertainty Regarding the Tortfeasor's Identity

causal problem in this manner, and their failure to specify its underlying rationale does not mean it lacks one. To understand adequately the rule of alternative liability, we need to determine whether there is a principle that justifies grouping a number of independent tortfeasors for the purpose of establishing causation.

Evidential Grouping and Alternative Liability

When one tortfeasor is responsible for the conduct of another, tort law groups the two together for liability purposes. A co-conspirator is liable for the tortious injuries caused by other co-conspirators in furtherance of the conspiracy. One who aids and abets a tortfeasor is liable for the resultant injuries. An employer is vicariously liable for the torts committed by an employee within the scope of her employment. In each type of case, one tortfeasor incurs joint and several liability for an injury that was caused by another tortfeasor's conduct. The two have acted as a group in causing the plaintiff's injury, either in terms of the tortious conduct itself, as in cases of conspiracy or aiding and abetting, or in terms of a preexisting relationship, as in cases of vicarious liability. By joining the group, each defendant tortfeasor becomes responsible for the tortious injuries proximately caused by the group, regardless of whether the defendant directly caused the harm.

In contrast to liability grouping, tort law can rely upon less demanding forms of grouping for evidentiary purposes. Unlike liability grouping, evidential grouping does not make a defendant responsible for the conduct of other tortfeasors, because there is nothing about any defendant's conduct that warrants such responsibility. One of the defendant shooters in *Summers* is simply not responsible for the conduct of the other defendant shooter; otherwise the case would involve a concert of action governed by liability grouping. But, even if each defendant is not responsible for the conduct of the other defendants, it may still be justifiable to group their conduct for evidentiary purposes. The evidential grouping only supports the plaintiff's prima facie case of liability, without making each defendant responsible or liable for the tortious conduct of the other defendants.

[In a case of evidential grouping,] the plaintiff's evidence shows that she was injured by the group of defendant tortfeasors, and that each defendant is a member of that group. Unless a defendant rebuts this evidence, she cannot reasonably deny that the plaintiff was harmed by one of the defendants, including herself. The defendant, therefore, cannot avoid liability merely by arguing that the other defendants, more likely than not, caused the harm, *if that same argument would enable every other defendant to avoid liability*. In these circumstances, the defendant's argument effectively denies that the plaintiff was harmed by *any* of the defendants, including herself, [and that form of argument is ruled out by] the defendant's failure to rebut the plaintiff's proof [that one of the defendants actually harmed the plaintiff.]

When every defendant attempts to avoid liability by relying upon the negligence of other defendants, they are resorting to "naked statistics" rather than particularistic proof. "Judges generally have refused to accept naked statistics or *ex ante* causal probabilities as evidence of what actually happened on a particular occasion."[4] The plaintiff has provided particularistic evidence showing that each defendant belongs to the group of tortfeasors that caused the harm, whereas each defendant only relies upon "quantitative probability" or "the greater chance" that the other defendants caused the injury. That statistical evidence, however, is not probative of what actually happened on this particular occasion, since the evidence, when relied upon by each defendant, establishes that no one caused the harm, and that outcome is inconsistent with the plaintiff's uncontested particularistic proof that she was, in fact, injured by one of the defendants. To avoid liability, a defendant must instead provide evidence rebutting the plaintiff's particularized proof. [For example, a defendant in a products case must show that it did not sell a defective product, or that its defective product could not have caused the plaintiff's harm.]

To invoke this principle, the plaintiff must satisfy the ordinary burden of proving that each defendant is responsible for a tortious risk that may have actually caused or contributed to the harm. In order for this proof to establish the plaintiff's prima facie case, each defendant must also be subject to liability in the event that her tortious conduct actually caused or contributed to the harm. With respect to the element of causation, the plaintiff must satisfy the ordinary burden of proof against the *group* of defendants. Once the plaintiff has satisfied this burden of proof, she has established a prima facie case of liability, enabling courts to shift the burden of disproving causation to each individual defendant.

The California Supreme Court did not expressly adopt evidential grouping in *Summers v. Tice*, but its rationale for alternative liability clearly depends upon the principle of evidential grouping. [As the court explained in a later case: "In *Summers*, . . . [w]e reasoned that both [defendants] were wrongdoers, both were negligent toward the plaintiff, and that it would be unfair to require plaintiff to isolate the defendant responsible, because if the one pointed out were to escape liability, the other might also, and the plaintiff-victim would be shorn of any remedy."[5] This reasoning clearly reflects the logic of evidential grouping.]

The *Summers* court's reliance on evidential grouping is more clearly reflected in its description of the evidence: "[W]e believe it is clear that the [trial] court sufficiently found on the issue that defendants were jointly liable and that thus the negligence of both was the cause of the injury or to that legal effect."[6]

From Alternative Liability to Market-Share Liability

To establish alternative liability, the plaintiff must join all potential tortfeasors in the lawsuit, as in *Summers*. The joinder requirement is not plausibly attributable to the concern about unfairly reducing the plaintiff's burden of proof. Suppose the plaintiff sues a group of six DES manufacturers, each of which had ten percent of the relevant market, and can prove, by a preponderance of the evidence, that each individual defendant sold a defective product (DES) that could have caused her injury. This evidence does not prove that any individual

---

4. Richard W. Wright, *Causation, Responsibility, Risk, Probability, Naked Statistics, and Proof: Pruning the Bramble Bush by Clarifying the Concepts*, 73 Iowa L. Rev. 1001, 1050-1051 (1988) (citations omitted).
5. Sindell v. Abbott Labs., 607 P.2d 924, 928 (Cal. 1980) (sentence structure omitted).
6. *Summers*, 199 P.2d at 2.

V. Factual Uncertainty Regarding the Tortfeasor's Identity

defendant, more likely than not, was the actual injurer. The evidence does show, however, that the *group* of DES manufacturers, more likely than not, caused the injury. When considered in relation to the group of defendants, the plaintiff has established causation by a preponderance of the evidence, the amount of evidence ordinarily required by tort law.

This form of causal proof can be justified by the principle of evidential grouping. The evidence shows that each DES manufacturer may have tortiously caused the plaintiff's harm and would be subject to liability if it actually caused the harm, and that the group of defendants, more likely than not, actually caused the harm. On these facts, the combined conduct of the defendants, viewed as a whole, is a but-for cause of the event, and application of the but-for rule to them individually would absolve all of them. Tort law has ruled out this type of exculpatory causal proof in analogous contexts, and can do so here [based on the principle of evidential grouping]. A DES manufacturer cannot avoid liability by "hiding behind" the tortious conduct of other DES manufacturers when doing so would bar a deserving plaintiff from recovery altogether. The manufacturer must instead prove that it was not a member of the group that tortiously caused the plaintiff's harm.

Liability in our hypothetical DES case therefore does not require any reduction in the plaintiff's burden of proof, leaving the problem of excessive liability as the only persuasive reason for requiring the plaintiff to join all potential tortfeasors in the lawsuit. If our hypothetical DES plaintiff could establish alternative liability by joining sixty percent of the market, then the group of manufacturers would be jointly liable for the entirety of the plaintiff's injury. Such liability would result in each of the six defendants incurring liability for one-sixth of the plaintiff's injury, whereas each had only ten percent of the market. A defendant would incur excessive liability, then, if its liability should be limited by the ten percent likelihood that it actually caused the plaintiff's injury.

In deciding upon the fair amount of liability, the court must compare the interest of the DES plaintiff who has established a right to receive compensation for the injury from the group of defendants, and the interest of each individual defendant as a member of the group. The compensatory demands that the plaintiff can fairly place upon each member of the group depend upon that individual defendant's relation to the group. An individual who is responsible for the group's conduct can be held liable for the entire injury caused by the group, as in cases involving a concert of action among the defendants. But in the DES cases, each individual manufacturer is not responsible for the group's conduct; the sale of DES by one manufacturer does not make it responsible for the sales made by other DES manufacturers. Consequently, the group is defined exclusively in causal terms — the likelihood that it caused the plaintiff's injury. Each individual defendant is a member of the causal group only by virtue of its responsibility for an independent tortious risk that may have injured the plaintiff. Each defendant's contribution to the total risk of injury created by the group, therefore, defines the extent of its responsibility for the group's conduct. In apportioning damages for the plaintiff's injury, the court can accordingly limit the liability of each defendant to the probability that its tortious conduct actually injured the plaintiff. Under this method of apportionment, the interest of the DES plaintiff who has established a right to receive compensation for the injury from the group of defendants exactly corresponds to the interest of each individual defendant as a member of the causal group.[7]

This reasoning explains why courts insist that alternative liability requires joinder of all the potential tortfeasors. Alternative liability gives the plaintiff one hundred percent compensation for the injury from the defendants. When the joinder requirement has been satisfied, the proportional liability of each defendant adds up to one hundred percent. The imposition of joint liability on the group of all potential tortfeasors lets the plaintiff receive full compensation for the injury without requiring any individual defendant to incur liability in excess of the probability that it actually caused the injury.

We are now in a position to see how the California Supreme Court could defensibly "ground[ ]" market-share liability "upon an extension of the *Summers* doctrine" by modifying alternative liability to account for the problem of excessive liability.[8] The issue is complicated, and the court's reasoning is often not fully developed, but its opinions provide the necessary logic for the argument.

Since the plaintiff could not join all potential tortfeasors as required by alternative liability, the court held that the plaintiff must instead join a "substantial share" of the market in order to establish market-share liability. Properly applied, this requirement ensures that the group of DES defendants, more likely than not, caused the plaintiff's injury.[9] Once the plaintiff has satisfied this requirement and all of the other remaining requirements for alternative liability, she has established a right to receive compensation for the injury from the group of defendants. Alternative liability would make the defendants jointly liable for the entire injury, resulting in an unfairly excessive amount of liability for each individual defendant.[10] Each of the DES defendants in our hypothetical case had only ten percent of the market, and so each should be liable for ten percent of the plaintiff's injury—the amount representing each defendant's responsibility (individual risk creation) for the group's conduct (the total tortious risk imposed on the plaintiff). To "protect . . . defendants against excessive liability," the court in a later case concluded that market-share liability involves several liability, with the liability of each DES defendant being limited by the probability that it actually caused the plaintiff's injury—an amount defined by its market share.[11] Each of the DES defendants in our hypothetical case had ten percent of the market, making each severally liable for ten percent of the plaintiff's injury.

---

7. *See* Brown v. Superior Court, 751 P.2d 470, 487 (Cal. 1988) (identifying the "goal of achieving a balance between the interests of DES plaintiffs and manufacturers of the drug").

8. *See* Sindell v. Abbott Labs., 607 P.2d 924, 928, 936-37 (Cal. 1980).

9. *Sindell* says that the substantial-share requirement "significantly diminishe[s]" the "injustice of shifting the burden of proof to defendants to demonstrate that they could not have made the substance which injured plaintiff." *Id.* Insofar as the substantial-share requirement means that the plaintiff must satisfy the ordinary burden of proof regarding causation against the group of defendants, then the satisfaction of this requirement makes it fair to shift the burden of proof to the defendants. *Cf.* Murphy v. E.R. Squibb & Sons, Inc., 710 P.2d 247, 255 (Cal. 1985) (concluding that the substantial-share requirement is not satisfied by ten percent of the market); *Sindell*, 607 P.2d at 937 (indicating that the substantial-share requirement is less than seventy-five to eighty percent of the market).

10. *See* Brown v. Superior Court, 751 P.2d 470, 487 (Cal. 1988) (describing joint liability as frustrating the "goal of achieving a balance between the interests of DES plaintiffs and manufacturers of the drug").

11. *Id.* at 486.

V. Factual Uncertainty Regarding the Tortfeasor's Identity

Having altered the rule of alternative liability in these two respects, the court could defensibly conclude that market-share liability is "an adaptation of the rule in *Summers* which will substantially overcome [the] difficulties" faced by a plaintiff who cannot join every potential tortfeasor in the lawsuit.[12] Market-share liability does not fully overcome this difficulty, since the plaintiff receives compensation for only sixty percent of the injury in our hypothetical case. The plaintiff's recovery is limited by the rule of several liability, which makes the individual manufacturer responsible only for the defective products it actually sold. This limitation of liability is required, according to the court, in order to avoid the unfairness that would arise if "one manufacturer would be held responsible for the products of another or for those of all other manufacturers if plaintiff ultimately prevails."[13] The plaintiff can prove causation by reference to the group of manufacturers, but the extent of each defendant's responsibility for the group's conduct is limited by its contribution to the total risk of injury created by the group—the same outcome achieved by alternative liability.

Evidential Grouping and the Requirements of Market-Share Liability

In a case of market-share liability, the liability of each defendant need not depend upon its share of the product market, nor must the case involve a fungible product, as neither of these factors was present in *Summers*. The plaintiff must prove that each defendant created a tortious risk that is fungible only in the sense that the risk may have actually caused the plaintiff's injury, and would subject the defendant to liability if it did cause the harm.

For example, a plaintiff who contracted AIDS from either a tortfeasor who failed to disclose the condition prior to sexual relations or from defective (contaminated) blood purchased from multiple blood suppliers over a period of time, should be able to establish alternative liability against both the sexual partner and the blood suppliers if no individual defendant is a but-for cause of the disease. Each defendant exposed the plaintiff to a tortious risk that may have caused the injury, and one of them actually caused the harm and would be subject to liability for having done so.[14] The fact that some defendants otherwise engaged in entirely different forms of behavior is irrelevant. Once the other requirements for evidential grouping have been satisfied, each defendant's liability depends only upon the amount of tortious risk for which it is responsible. Liability does not always require market shares, and so a more descriptively apt name for the liability rule might be "risk-adjusted" liability.

In applying this rule, the *Restatement (Third)* expresses concern about the litigation costs of determining the amount of risk attributable to each defendant

---

12. *Sindell*, 607 P.2d at 931.
13. *Id.* at 938.
14. If the defendant blood suppliers in this example were immune from liability due to a blood-shield statute, the plaintiff would lose. Rather than relying exclusively upon the other defendants' tortious conduct—the only form of exculpatory proof barred by evidential grouping—the blood suppliers instead invoke the blood-shield statute. Once these defendants are removed from the case, the plaintiff can proceed only against the sexual partner, who on these facts did not create more than a fifty percent chance of injuring the plaintiff.

and "the existence and accuracy" of such data.[15] These concerns are alleviated by evidential grouping.

The plaintiff must establish liability by a preponderance of the evidence with respect to the issues of duty and breach. The plaintiff must also prove that the group of defendants, more likely than not, tortiously caused the injury. This proof is sufficient to establish the prima facie case of liability against each of the defendant tortfeasors. Under evidential grouping, the remaining issue involves the extent of liability for each defendant, an issue of damages that does not generate the evidentiary concerns expressed by the *Restatement (Third)*. To avoid injustice, tort law reduces the plaintiff's burden of proof regarding causal questions in the damages phase. The plaintiff is only required to establish the amount of damages with "as much certainty as the nature of the tort and the circumstances permit."[16] Having established a right to compensation with sufficiently reliable evidence, the plaintiff faces a reduced evidentiary burden regarding the exact amount of risk attributable to each defendant. That issue is only relevant for determining the amount of a defendant's liability—a damages question. The proof may be difficult to procure, unavailable or inaccurate, but the same problem routinely exists in the damages phase of tort cases. As is true in other tort cases, the difficulty of determining the exact amount of damages is not a compelling reason for denying the plaintiff recovery altogether. The plaintiff must instead prove the amount of damages, or the amount of tortious risk created by each defendant, with "as much certainty" as can be reasonably expected in the circumstances of the case. Once the plaintiff has proven the prima facie case with sufficiently reliable evidence, the difficulty of quantifying the causal contribution of each defendant does not provide a persuasive reason for denying the plaintiff recovery altogether.

NOTES AND QUESTIONS

1. *From alternative liability to market-share liability.* In a jurisdiction that has both adopted alternative liability and rejected market-share liability, would evidential grouping require courts to reconsider their position on these matters? *Compare* Spaur v. Owens-Corning Fiberglass Corp., 510 N.W.2d 854, 858 (Iowa 1994) ("[W]hen the conduct of two or more persons is so related to an event that their combined conduct, viewed as a whole, is a but-for cause of the event, and application of the but-for rule to them individually would absolve all of them, the conduct of each is a cause in fact of the event."), *with* Mulcahy v. Eli Lilly & Co., 386 N.W.2d 67, 75-76 (Iowa 1986) ("We reject the market share liability theory on a broad policy basis. We acknowledge that plaintiff in a DES case with an unidentified product manufacturer presents an appealing claim for relief. Endeavoring to provide relief, courts have developed theories which in one way or another provided plaintiffs recovery of loss by a kind of court-constructed insurance

---

15. Restatement (Third) of Torts: Liab. for Physical Harm §28 cmt. o (Proposed Final Draft No. 1, 2005).

16. Restatement (Second) of Torts §912 (1979).

plan. The result is that manufacturers are required to pay or contribute to payment for injuries which their product may not have caused.").

Other than the risk-based interpretation, evidential grouping is the only interpretation that attempts to explain how the logic of alternative liability can justify the rule of market-share liability. Compare Arthur Ripstein & Benjamin C. Zipursky, *Corrective Justice in an Age of Mass Torts*, in PHILOSOPHY AND THE LAW OF TORTS 214, 235 (Gerald Postema ed., 2001) (arguing that *Sindell* effectively "estopped" the defendants from an argument that would both "concede and deny their liability to each plaintiff" and explaining that their account of market-share liability "requires a completed wrong," making it inapplicable to alternative liability); Richard L. Wright, *Liability for Possible Wrongs: Causation, Statistical Probability, and the Burden of Proof*, 41 Loyola L.A. L. Rev. 1295, 1298 (2008) (rejecting evidential grouping and risk-based liability and instead justifying alternative and market-share liability as "second-best solutions that impose full or proportionate liability on a defendant who behaved tortiously and whose tortious conduct may well have caused the plaintiff's injury").

When the requirements for evidential grouping are satisfied, the group of defendants incurs liability for having caused the plaintiff's physical harm, but each defendant's liability is limited to the tortious risk for which it is responsible—a factor not necessarily dependent on market shares. The liability rule accordingly provides many of the benefits of risk-based or proportional liability that have been lauded by torts scholars. The justification for liability, however, is based upon established tort principles, not on a profound change in the nature of tort liability based on the tortious imposition of risk than on tortiously caused physical harm.

2. *Administrative costs*. Regardless of the merits of market-share liability, it could be rejected on the ground that the rule is simply too costly for the courts to administer. Following *Sindell*, for example, "a rancorous and protracted hearing ensued" on the determination of each defendant's market share, a problem that has plagued other DES cases:

> For starters, not all manufacturers subject to jurisdiction could provide their sales figures for the relevant years. Even Lilly, an extraordinarily sophisticated defendant, a company that could provide the number of DES units it had made between 1942 to 1971—that would be 716 million—could not count the number of those units that went to pregnant women. So much for the numerator of the fraction [that defines market share]. The denominator remains even more elusive. Without the central recordkeeping that a patent license would have created, courts had trouble counting the total number of DES units sold.

Anita Bernstein, Hymowitz v. Eli Lilly and Co.: *Markets for Mothers*, in TORT STORIES 151, 170 (Robert L. Rabin & Stephen D. Sugarman eds., 2003).

To what extent is the problem ameliorated by evidential grouping, which treats the determination of a defendant's market share as an issue pertaining to the extent of damages governed by a less demanding evidentiary rule? Consider *Sindell*, 607 P.2d at 145 ("It is probably impossible, with the passage of time, to determine market share with mathematical exactitude.

But just as a jury cannot be expected to determine the precise relationship between fault and liability in applying the doctrine of comparative fault [ ] or partial indemnity [ ], the difficulty of apportioning damages among the defendant producers in exact relation to their market share does not seriously militate against the rule we adopt."). Because market share only determines the extent of damages rather than liability in the first instance, the plaintiff must only prove damages (market share) with the reasonably available evidence. *See* section IV *supra*. Would evidential grouping help to make the formulation of market-share liability more uniform across the jurisdictions that have adopted this doctrine? Consider Collins v. Eli Lilly & Co., 342 N.W.2d 37, 48 (Wis. 1984) ("The primary factor which prevents us from following *Sindell* is the practical difficulty of defining and proving market share."); Hymowitz v. Eli Lilly & Co., 539 N.E.2d 1069, 1077 (N.Y. 1989) ("Turning to the structure to be adopted in New York, we heed both the lessons learned through experience in other jurisdictions and the realities of the mass litigation of DES claims in this State. Balancing these considerations, we are led to the conclusion that a market share theory, based upon a national market, provides the best solution. As California discovered, the reliable determination of any market smaller than the national one likely is not practicable.").

3. *Evaluating causation*. Like the DES cases, the asbestos cases are based on a causal doctrine that could be interpreted as a form of risk-based liability that radically transforms the nature of tort liability. *See* Jane Stapleton, *The Two Explosive Proof-of-Causation Doctrines Central to Asbestos Claims*, 74 Brook. L. Rev. 1011, 1013 (2009) (interpreting the causal rule in asbestos cases as a "special proof of causation doctrine resting on exposure-to-risk"). Unlike the DES cases, the causal issue in the asbestos cases has received relatively little attention. According to Professor Stapleton, the reason could be that "in the context of other well-settled, broad-brush, plaintiff-friendly proof-of-causation rules such as that in *Summers v. Tice*, the market share approach, and the heeding presumption in the area of products liability, the . . . proof-of-causation doctrines in asbestos cases may not even seem all that remarkable to U.S. practitioners." *Id.* at 1033.

Each of the causal rules identified by Professor Stapleton do indeed raise hard questions about the element of factual causation. The conventional rationales for these doctrines make it easy to characterize them as "plaintiff-friendly" rules that somehow depart from established tort principles.

This characterization of these causal rules, however, does not explain why courts adhere to the principle of causation in other cases. Are courts merely being inconsistent in this respect, favoring plaintiffs in some cases and defendants in others?

As we have found, each of these causal rules does not need to be interpreted either as a form of risk-based liability or an unprincipled relaxation of the plaintiff's burden of proving causation. Indeed, the case law on market-share liability rather clearly shows that courts are unwilling to justify a causal rule on either of these two bases. Like other causal rules that do not obviously adhere to the ordinary evidentiary standard, the viability of market-share liability depends on whether it can be plausibly interpreted in a manner that conforms to widely accepted tort principles.

4. *The ongoing relevance of market-share liability.* Today, many injuries such as cancer or birth defects are caused by unknown factors, which are commonly called the "background" or "environmental" risk to which everyone is exposed. Advances in scientific knowledge will presumably identify a much larger number of carcinogens and teratogens. *See* Jamie A. Grodsky, *Genomics and Toxic Torts: Dismantling the Risk-Injury Divide*, 59 Stan. L. Rev. 1671, 1673-1674 (2007) (describing how "the application of new genomic technologies since the 1990s are enabling progressively fine-tuned observation of the effects of toxic substances on the body"). A cancer that is now attributed to the background or environmental risk could subsequently be attributed to a number of known carcinogens to which the individual had been exposed. Must the carcinogen at least double the risk of injury in order to subject the product seller to tort liability, or do the principles of tort law permit a plaintiff to establish liability by proving that a group of different carcinogens supplied by a group of different product sellers, more likely than not, caused the cancer for which the plaintiff seeks compensation? The issue is likely to be increasingly faced by the courts, potentially turning market-share liability into a doctrine of extraordinary practical significance.

VI. THE PROBLEM OF SCIENTIFIC UNCERTAINTY

Whereas alternative liability and market-share liability address a hard problem of individualized causation—Which defendant actually caused the harm?—other cases turn on knotty issues of general causation—Is the product in general capable of causing the harm? The issue is particularly vexing in toxic tort cases involving chemicals or drugs for which there is no conclusive scientific evidence of toxicity.

In the paradigmatic case of scientific uncertainty, the available evidence provides a reasonable basis for concluding that the product contains a substance that *might* be carcinogenic, but the evidence does not adequately establish that the substance *is* a carcinogen. When presented with such evidence, a court must decide whether the plaintiff has adequately proven that the defective product caused her cancer, an issue that also implicates the issue of specific causation—Did the product or some other carcinogen cause the plaintiff's harm?

This causal issue potentially arises whenever we do not fully understand how a substance interacts with the body and produces an adverse health outcome. We as a society do not, for example, understand the etiologies of most birth defects or cancers, each of which can be caused by genetic factors, environmental conditions, exposure to toxic substances in products, or some combination thereof. Unable to determine why someone has such a birth defect or cancer, scientists must instead use other methods that often are unable to conclusively resolve the matter.

The ideal study or "gold standard" for assessing toxicity involves controlled studies comparing the outcomes for individuals who are randomly given the substance but are otherwise physically comparable in the relevant respects. Michael D. Green et al., *Reference Guide on Epidemiology*, in FED. JUDICIAL CTR., REFERENCE MANUAL ON SCIENTIFIC EVIDENCE 551, 555 (3d ed. 2011). Purposefully exposing individuals to potential toxins is unethical, however, forcing scientists to rely on other types of evidence.

A carcinogen or teratogen can be identified with *epidemiologic evidence* produced by a large-scale study comparing the incidence of adverse health outcomes in groups of exposed and nonexposed human beings, or comparing the incidence of exposure across injured and healthy groups. These studies are expensive, time-consuming, and require that a large number of people be exposed to the substance. Numerous investigations are typically needed, as illustrated by the large number of epidemiologic studies that were required to support the conclusion that asbestos and cigarettes are carcinogens. The cost and duration of these studies explain why "there is good epidemiological evidence for only about half or less of the known or likely human carcinogens assessed by national or international scientific bodies." Carl Cranor, TOXIC TORTS: SCIENCE, LAW, AND THE POSSIBILITY OF JUSTICE 225 (2006).

Although epidemiologic study can identify carcinogens and teratogens, its failure to find that a substance does not cause cancer or birth defects does not mean that the substance is benign. Unable to reliably "detect comparatively rare diseases or subtle effects," epidemiologic study "too frequently . . . cannot detect an adverse effect, even if it is present." *Id.* at 9.

Due to the inherent limitations of epidemiologic investigations, scientists must rely on other types of toxicological evidence. To assess whether a substance may cause birth defects or cancer, scientists observe health outcomes in populations of animals exposed to large amounts of the substance, compare the substance's chemical composition to other substances that are known to cause injuries of this type, and study the biochemical effects of the substance on cells, organs, and embryos. Could this evidence be sufficient for establishing general causation? This issue is inextricably tied to questions concerning the types of scientific evidence that are admissible in a tort case. What are the appropriate evidentiary criteria for admitting scientific evidence in cases of scientific uncertainty? Is the issue merely a matter of evidence law, or does it turn on substantive tort principles?

RIDER v. SANDOZ PHARMACEUTICALS CORP.
United States Court of Appeals, Eleventh Circuit, 2002
295 F.3d 1194

RONEY, J. Bridget Siharath and Bonnie Rider both took the drug Parlodel to suppress lactation after childbirth. The active ingredient in Parlodel is bromocriptine, an ergot alkaloid compound. Both women subsequently suffered hemorrhagic strokes.

VI. The Problem of Scientific Uncertainty

Siharath and Rider filed suit against Sandoz, alleging that Parlodel caused their hemorrhagic strokes. After discovery, Sandoz moved, *in limine*, to exclude the opinions and testimony of the plaintiffs' experts on causation, and for summary judgment. Because the motions, documentary evidence, experts, and issues were the same in both cases, the district court addressed the motions together.

The district court, in a three-day hearing, examined the evidence presented in great detail and found that the plaintiffs' claims were based on speculation and conjecture rather than the scientific method. The court drew a careful distinction between clinical process, in which conclusions must be extrapolated from incomplete data, and the scientific method, in which conclusions must be drawn from an accepted process, and concluded that the plaintiffs' experts were relying on the former. Accordingly, the district court excluded the evidence and granted summary judgment in favor of Sandoz. This appeal followed.

Toxic tort cases, such as this one, are won or lost on the strength of the scientific evidence presented to prove causation. For many years the standard for admissibility of such evidence was the "general acceptance" test set forth in Frye v. United States, 54 App. D.C. 46 (D.C. Cir. 1923). When the Federal Rules of Evidence were enacted in 1975, a question arose as to whether the "general acceptance" test had been supplanted by the reliability test articulated in Rule 702. The question was resolved in three cases decided by the Supreme Court. Daubert v. Merrell Dow Pharms., 509 U.S. 579 (1993); GE v. Joiner, 522 U.S. 136 (1997); Kumho Tire Co., Ltd. v. Carmichael, 526 U.S. 137 (1999). These cases are commonly referred to as the *Daubert* trilogy.

Since *Daubert*, courts are charged with determining whether scientific evidence is sufficiently reliable to be presented to a jury. The *Daubert* court made it clear that the requirement of reliability found in Rule 702 was the centerpiece of any determination of admissibility. The Supreme Court identified four factors used to determine the reliability of scientific evidence: 1) whether the theory can and has been tested; 2) whether it has been subjected to peer review; 3) the known or expected rate of error; and 4) whether the theory or methodology employed is generally accepted in the relevant scientific community.

In *Joiner*, the Supreme Court established the standard for reviewing trial court rulings of admissibility, and held that such rulings would be made under an abuse of discretion standard. The *Joiner* court also established the important test of analytical "fit" between the methodology used and the conclusions drawn. The court reasoned that just because a methodology is acceptable for some purposes, it may not be acceptable for others, and a court may not admit evidence when there is "simply too great an analytical gap between the data and the opinion proffered."

In *Kumho Tire*, the Supreme Court made it clear that testimony based solely on the experience of an expert would not be admissible. The expert's conclusions must be based on sound scientific principles and the discipline itself must be a reliable one. The key consideration is whether the expert "employs in the courtroom the same level of intellectual rigor that characterizes the practice of an expert in the relevant field." The court emphasized that judges have considerable leeway in both how to test the reliability of evidence and determining whether such evidence is reliable.

The *Daubert* trilogy, in shifting the focus to the kind of empirically supported, rationally explained reasoning required in science, has greatly improved the quality of the evidence upon which juries base their verdicts. Although making determinations of reliability may present a court with the difficult task of ruling on matters that are outside of its field of expertise, this is "less objectionable than dumping a barrage of scientific evidence on a jury, who would likely be less equipped than the judge to make reliability and relevance determinations."
[ ] The district court did not abuse its discretion in holding that the evidence presented by plaintiffs' experts does not meet the standard of reliability.

Plaintiffs sought to introduce the testimony of five experts. All five possessed impressive credentials and were found to be well qualified by the district court, three over the defendants' objection. The experts presented a detailed argument for the cause of the plaintiffs' hemorrhagic strokes that may be summarized as follows:

1) The active ingredient in Parlodel is bromocriptine, a member of the class of drugs known as ergot alkaloids.
2) Other ergot alkaloids can cause vasoconstriction, which suggests that bromocriptine causes vasoconstriction.
3) Animal studies also suggest that bromocriptine causes vasoconstriction.
4) Vasoconstriction can cause high blood pressure and ischemic stroke (stroke caused by decreased blood flow to the brain).
5) If vasoconstriction and high blood pressure can cause ischemic stroke, it can also cause hemorrhagic stroke (stroke caused by a rupturing of a blood vessel).
6) Thus, Parlodel caused the plaintiffs' hemorrhagic strokes.

The Evidence Presented

The scientific evidence presented by plaintiffs in support of their theory of causation may be grouped into six categories: 1) epidemiological studies that, on the whole, may point weakly toward causation; 2) case reports in which injuries were reported subsequent to the ingestion of Parlodel; 3) dechallenge/rechallenge tests that implied a relationship between Parlodel and stroke; 4) evidence that ergot alkaloids (a class of drug that includes bromocriptine) may cause ischemic stroke; 5) animal studies indicating that under some circumstances, bromocriptine may cause vasoconstriction in dogs and other animals; and, 6) the FDA statement withdrawing approval of Parlodel's indication for the prevention of lactation.

A. Epidemiology

Epidemiology, a field that concerns itself with finding the causal nexus between external factors and disease, is generally considered to be the best evidence of causation in toxic tort actions. Plaintiffs presented four epidemiological studies. Three of the four appear to have found no relationship or a negative relationship between Parlodel and stroke. Another may suggest a positive relationship. Nonetheless, both parties agree that none of the studies present

VI. The Problem of Scientific Uncertainty

statistically significant results and that the epidemiological evidence in this case is inconclusive.

Plaintiffs argue that the district court erred by requiring epidemiological studies, effectively ruling against them because they could not produce sufficient epidemiological evidence linking Parlodel to stroke. Having carefully reviewed the record, we conclude that the district court did not require epidemiological studies.

It is well-settled that while epidemiological studies may be powerful evidence of causation, the lack thereof is not fatal to a plaintiff's case. [ ] This Court has long held that epidemiology is not required to prove causation in a toxic tort case. *See* Wells v. Ortho Pharm. Corp., 788 F.2d 741, 745 (11th Cir. 1986) (holding that "a cause-effect relationship need not be clearly established by animal or epidemiological studies."). Accordingly, this case presents the difficult question of whether the evidence submitted to prove causation, in the absence of epidemiology, was sufficient to meet the requirements of *Daubert*.

B. CASE REPORTS

Much of the plaintiffs' expert testimony relied on case reports in which patients suffered injuries subsequent to the ingestion of Parlodel. Although a court may rely on anecdotal evidence such as case reports, courts must consider that case reports are merely accounts of medical events. They reflect only reported data, not scientific methodology. Some case reports are a very basic form report of symptoms with little or no patient history, description of course of treatment, or reasoning to exclude other possible causes. The contents of these case reports were inadequate, even under the plaintiffs' expert's standards, to demonstrate a relationship between a drug and a potential side effect.

Some case reports do contain details of the treatment and differential diagnosis. Even these more detailed case reports, however, are not reliable enough, by themselves, to demonstrate the causal link the plaintiffs assert that they do because they report symptoms observed in a single patient in an uncontrolled context. They may rule out other potential causes of the effect, but they do not rule out the possibility that the effect manifested in the reported patient's case is simply idiosyncratic or the result of unknown confounding factors. As such, while they may support other proof of causation, case reports alone ordinarily cannot prove causation. The record demonstrates that the district court carefully considered the case reports and properly concluded that the case reports did not by themselves provide reliable proof of causation.

C. DECHALLENGE/RECHALLENGE DATA

Plaintiffs' experts provided dechallenge/rechallenge data that they argue suggests a link between Parlodel and stroke. A test is a "dechallenge" test when a drug that is suspected of causing a certain reaction is withheld to see if the reaction dissipates. The drug may then be reintroduced in a "rechallenge" to see if the reaction reoccurs. These reports, which may be analogized to controlled studies with one subject, can be particularly useful in determining whether a causal relationship exists. Nonetheless, because none of the studies involved a patient with the particular injury suffered by the plaintiffs, they do not provide data useful in determining whether Parlodel caused the plaintiffs' injuries.

D. CHEMICAL ANALOGIES

Bromocriptine is one of many drugs in a class known as ergot alkaloids. Plaintiffs sought to introduce evidence that because other ergot alkaloids cause vasoconstriction, then it is proper to conclude bromocriptine must do so as well. There is an insufficient basis in the record for this Court to hold that the district court abused its discretion by not drawing such a conclusion. Ergot alkaloids encompass a broad class of drugs with great chemical diversity, and "even minor deviations in chemical structure can radically change a particular substance's properties and propensities." [ ] The district court, after a detailed review of the properties of ergot alkaloids, concluded that plaintiffs failed to come forward with even a theory as to why the mechanism that causes some ergot alkaloids to act as vasoconstrictors would more probably than not be the same mechanism by which bromocriptine acts to cause vasoconstriction. The district court did not abuse its discretion in doing so.

E. ANIMAL STUDIES

Plaintiffs offered evidence of animal studies in which bromocriptine demonstrated vasoconstrictive properties in dogs and certain other animals. Plaintiffs did not offer any animal studies that suggest that bromocriptine causes stroke, or even high blood pressure. The district court discussed each of these studies and was within its discretion in concluding that plaintiffs offered insufficient evidence on which that court could base a conclusion that the effect of bromocriptine would be the same on humans as it is on animals.

F. FDA FINDINGS

Plaintiffs presented evidence that the FDA issued a statement withdrawing approval of Parlodel's indication for the prevention of lactation. The district court concluded that the language in the FDA statement itself undermined its reliability as proof of causation. In the statement, the FDA did not purport to have drawn a conclusion about causation. Instead, the statement merely states that possible risks outweigh the limited benefits of the drug. This risk-utility analysis involves a much lower standard than that which is demanded by a court of law. A regulatory agency such as the FDA may choose to err on the side of caution. Courts, however, are required by the *Daubert* trilogy to engage in objective review of evidence to determine whether it has sufficient scientific basis to be considered reliable. The district court did not abuse its discretion in concluding that the FDA actions do not, in this case, provide scientific proof of causation.

APPLYING THE EVIDENCE TO THE PLAINTIFF'S THEORY OF CAUSATION

The deficiencies in the evidence reveal three gaps in the causal argument advanced by the plaintiffs. First, plaintiffs suggest that because bromocriptine is an ergot alkaloid, it causes vasoconstriction. Although some other ergot alkaloids do cause vasoconstriction, plaintiffs offered insufficient evidence for the

VI. The Problem of Scientific Uncertainty

district court to find that bromocriptine does so as well. This is not a case where the Court finds the evidence offered to be unreliable. In this case the record contains no evidence at all of this hypothesis. Instead, it contains principally speculation and conjecture.

Because the ergot alkaloid class of drugs has a wide range of effects, it is not obvious that bromocriptine should have the same effects as other drugs in that class. Indeed, two widely reported symptoms associated with bromocriptine are vasodilation and hypotension, precisely the opposite of what the plaintiffs allege. Plaintiffs did offer a theory as to why the drug might cause either vasodilation or vasoconstriction, depending on the vascular characteristics of the patient, a theory that the defendants concede the district court did not correctly explain in its opinion. This minor error does not affect the correctness of the district court's conclusion however, because the plaintiffs did not offer sufficiently reliable evidence to support their theory.

Second, the plaintiffs urge the Court to extrapolate the results of animal studies to humans. As with the plaintiffs' evidence of chemical properties, the district court did not err in finding no basis for doing so. Plaintiffs' experts admitted that with respect to animal studies generally, what happens in an animal would not necessarily happen in a human being. Accordingly, it is necessary for plaintiffs to offer some rationale for the suggestion that the vascular structures of humans and animals are sufficiently similar in this context to conclude that bromocriptine's effects on animals may be extrapolated to humans. Plaintiffs have not done so.

As the Supreme Court held in *Joiner*, scientific evidence must "fit" the plaintiff's theory of causation. In this case, neither the chemical compound evidence nor the animal study evidence "fits" as evidence relevant to the cause of plaintiffs' injuries.

Third, plaintiffs argue that because there is some evidence that bromocriptine causes ischemic stroke, it also causes hemorrhagic stroke. This is the most untenable link in the causal chain. Strokes are broadly classified into two categories: ischemic and hemorrhagic. Ischemic strokes occur as a result of lack of blood flow to the brain. Hemorrhagic strokes occur as a result of bleeding within the brain. Thus, although the two conditions share a name, they involve a wholly different biological mechanism. The evidence that suggests that Parlodel may cause ischemic stroke does not apply to situations involving hemorrhagic stroke. This is a "leap of faith" supported by little more than the fact that both conditions are commonly called strokes. Plaintiffs argue that as a result of the vasoconstriction caused by Parlodel, blood pressure may increase to the point that blood vessels in the brain rupture. Plaintiffs have offered no reliable evidence that Parlodel increases blood pressure to such dangerous levels. Even if they had, they failed to offer proof of how such an increase in blood pressure can precipitate a hemorrhagic stroke.

In the absence of epidemiology, plaintiffs may still prove medical causation by other evidence. In the instant case, however, plaintiffs simply have not provided reliable evidence to support their conclusions. To admit the plaintiffs' evidence, the Court would have to make several scientifically unsupported "leaps of faith" in the causal chain. The *Daubert* rule requires more. Given time, information, and resources, courts may only admit the state of science as it is. Courts are cautioned not to admit speculation, conjecture, or inference that cannot be supported by sound scientific principles. The courtroom is not the place for scientific guesswork, even of the inspired sort. Law lags science; it does not lead it.

Plaintiffs argue that the district court erred in requiring a checklist of types of evidence to prove causation. This argument misinterprets the district court's opinion. The district court, after finding that the plaintiffs' evidence was unreliable, noted that certain types of other evidence may have been considered reliable, including peer-reviewed epidemiological literature, a predictable chemical mechanism, general acceptance in learned treatises, or a very large number of case reports. In so doing, the district court was not compiling a list of required types of evidence. Rather, it was highlighting the plaintiffs' failure to present evidence in any of several categories that would have been persuasive.

We hold that the district court did not abuse its discretion in concluding that the Plaintiffs' scientific proof of causation is legally unreliable and inadmissible under the standards set by the *Daubert* trilogy.

AFFIRMED.

NOTES AND QUESTIONS

1. *The* Daubert *standard in state courts.* Although federal courts must apply the Federal Rules of Evidence, state courts are not obligated to do so. Nevertheless, "[t]wenty-five states have affirmatively adopted the *Daubert* or similar tests for use in their courts, or had previously abandoned *Frye* and had developed a similar test; fifteen states and the District of Columbia adhere to *Frye*; six states have not rejected *Frye* in toto but apply the *Daubert* factors; and four states have developed their own tests." Alice B. Lustre, *Post* Daubert *Standards for Admissibility of Scientific and Other Expert Evidence in State Courts*, 90 A.L.R. 5th 453 (2020 update).

2. *Scientific uncertainty and the potential for legal error.* When there is scientific uncertainty about whether a substance can cause a particular type of injury like cancer, any rule that permits recovery faces the obvious problem that the substance, in fact, does not cause injuries of this type. The potential for error can be pronounced in product cases, because the defect in question (either of design or warning) implicates the entire product line and potentially involves extensive liability. An erroneous finding of causation has the potential for creating error costs of a staggering magnitude.

The problem is fully illustrated by litigation over silicone gel breast implants, in which plaintiffs argued that silicone leaking from their implants caused connective-tissue disease. A couple of early suits resulted in multimillion-dollar verdicts. *E.g.*, Hopkins v. Dow Corning Corp., 33 F.3d 1116 (3d Cir. 1994) (upholding 1991 award of $840,000 in compensatory damages and $6.5 million in punitive damages). At this time, there were no epidemiologic studies showing that the implants cause connective-tissue disease, but courts nevertheless permitted the plaintiff to prove causation with "the types of scientific data and . . . the types of scientific techniques relied upon by medical experts in making determinations regarding toxic causation where there is no solid body of epidemiological data to review." *Id.* at 1124. "The evidence presented at trial [also] indicated that Dow [the defendant manufacturer] rushed development of the silicone gel

VI. The Problem of Scientific Uncertainty

implants, failed to adequately test the implants, and ignored knowledge of adverse health consequences associated with the implants." *Id.* at 1119. These cases gained national media attention, and the federal Food and Drug Administration imposed a moratorium on sales of the implants.

> Within two years of the FDA moratorium and the revelations of the manufacturer's behavior, approximately 16,000 women filed lawsuits nationwide. . . . Later in 1994, the contending forces attempted to resolve all present and future implant claims through a $4.2 billion class action settlement. The legal basis for such a class action aside, the settlement fell apart for a much more practical reason. An unexpectedly large number of claims—by then, some 440,000—quickly made it apparent that the fixed sum of $4.2 billion set by manufacturers for the class settlement would be insufficient to fund the compensation payments described therein. Shortly before the collapse of the settlement, Dow Corning sought protection under Chapter 11 of the bankruptcy code. . . . Dow Corning ultimately garnered judicial approval for a corporate reorganization plan [that] contemplated substantial payments to implant recipients with connective tissue disease.
>
> The content of the Dow Corning reorganization plan is all the more striking when one considers what happened in the meantime on the scientific front. A wealth of epidemiological research failed to show an elevated incidence of connective tissue disease in women with implants as compared to those without. The overwhelming scientific consensus behind that conclusion ultimately included a review of the scientific literature by FDA scientists in 1996, a panel of neutral scientific experts appointed by [a] federal court . . . in 1998, and the National Academy of Sciences in 2000.
>
> The civil justice system is unlikely to witness a replay of the process that made immature litigation over breast implants into mature mass tort litigation. The reason why lies in the consequences of the Supreme Court's 1993 evidentiary decision in *Daubert*.

Richard A. Nagareda, MASS TORTS IN A WORLD OF SETTLEMENT 35-36 (2007) (paragraph structure omitted). When placed within this historical context, *Daubert* can be interpreted as a direct response to the problem of scientific uncertainty in product cases: It "reduc[es] the likelihood" that "inaccurate information from early lawsuits" will determine "the merits" of subsequent, mass tort litigation. *Id.* at 39.

3. *Application of the* Daubert *standard.* As *Rider* illustrates, federal judges have been relying on *Daubert* to exclude expert testimony proffered by plaintiffs. One empirical study of federal district court opinions from 1980 to 1999 found that after *Daubert*, there was a proportionate increase of cases involving challenges to the admissibility of expert evidence and rulings that such evidence was unreliable. Rulings regarding the admissibility of expert testimony "increasingly resulted in summary judgment after *Daubert*," with "nearly 90 percent" going "against plaintiffs." Lloyd Dixon & Brian Gill, CHANGES IN THE STANDARDS FOR ADMITTING EXPERT EVIDENCE IN FEDERAL CIVIL CASES SINCE THE *DAUBERT* DECISION 61-62 (2001). For a summary of other empirical studies, see David M. Flores et al., *Examining the Effects of the* Daubert *Trilogy on Expert Evidence Practices in Federal Civil Court: An Empirical Analysis*, 34 S. Ill. U. L.J. 533 (2010).

4. *Daubert and proof of causation with epidemiologic studies.* Recall that the problem of scientific uncertainty involves a substance for which there is a reasonable scientific basis for concluding that it could cause the harm in question, but the causal mechanism or etiology is unknown (as with cancer or birth defects) and the substance has not been subjected to epidemiologic study. How is the problem of scientific uncertainty affected by *Daubert*?

> Vigorously exercising their role as evidentiary "gatekeepers"—a task assigned to them by the United States Supreme Court in *Daubert v. Merrell Dow Pharmaceuticals, Inc.*—federal trial judges in products liability cases have been doing far more than screening proposed expert testimony to determine admissibility. The *Daubert* gatekeeper power has become a potent tool of tort lawmaking. Under the guise of admissibility determinations, federal judges have been making significant substantive legal rules on causation by substantially raising the threshold of scientific proof plaintiffs need to get their expert causation testimony admitted, and thus survive summary judgment. While the decisions purport to be no more than deferential nods to the criteria of science, judges have actually been making legal rules about what types and strengths of scientific evidence are necessary in order to prove causation. The emerging legal rule is that plaintiffs' experts must be able to base their opinions about causation on epidemiological studies, and that these studies standing alone must show that the population-wide risk of developing the disease in question, if exposed to defendants' products, is at least double the risk without exposure.

Lucinda M. Finley, *Guarding the Gate to the Courthouse: How Trial Judges Are Using Their Evidentiary Screening Role to Remake Tort Causation Rules*, 49 DePaul L. Rev. 335, 335 (1999).

Is this trend illustrated by *Daubert* itself? Recall that on remand, the U.S. Court of Appeals for the Ninth Circuit rejected plaintiffs' expert testimony because the epidemiologic evidence did not show that the defendant's product at least doubled the risk of injury, citing numerous other appellate decisions in support of such a rule. (That opinion is excerpted in section I *supra*.)

Even if *Daubert* initiated a trend in which courts had increasingly required epidemiologic proof of causation in toxic tort cases, that trend has subsided.

> Occasionally, courts have suggested or implied that a plaintiff cannot meet the burden of production on causation without epidemiologic evidence. Those cases [like *Daubert* itself] often confronted a substantial body of epidemiologic evidence introduced by the defendant that tended to exonerate the agent as causal. Circumstances in individual cases, however, are sufficiently varied that almost all courts employ a more flexible approach to proof of causation—except in those cases with a substantial body of exonerative epidemiologic evidence. Epidemiologic studies are expensive and can take considerable time to design, conduct, and publish. For disease processes

VI. The Problem of Scientific Uncertainty

with long latency periods, valid studies cannot be performed until the disease has manifested itself. As a consequence, some plaintiffs may be forced to litigate long before epidemiologic research is available. Indeed, sometimes epidemiologic evidence is impossible to obtain, which may explain why neither the plaintiff nor the defendant is able to proffer supportive epidemiology. Thus, most courts have appropriately declined to impose a threshold requirement that a plaintiff always must prove causation with epidemiologic evidence. . . .

RESTATEMENT (THIRD) OF TORTS: LIABILITY FOR PHYSICAL AND EMOTIONAL HARM §28 cmt. c(3).

For cases in which epidemiologic evidence does not sufficiently rule out the defendant's product as a cause of the plaintiff's harm, the plaintiff can try to establish causation with different types of evidence, many of which are discussed in *Rider*. Consequently, the *Restatement (Third)* adopts a "flexible approach" that does not require epidemiologic proof to establish causation for diseases with unknown etiologies.

5. *Evidence permitted by the flexible approach.* To fully understand the flexible approach, we need to consider more closely the types of evidence, other than epidemiologic study, that scientists employ for evaluating the toxicity of chemicals and drugs. Recall that the "gold standard" for toxicological research involves controlled studies that expose a group of individuals to the substance and compare their health outcomes to another unexposed group, or compare the same group when they are initially not exposed and then subsequently exposed—the dechallenge/rechallenge data discussed by the *Rider* court. Outside of cases in which the product, like a drug or vaccine, might have beneficial therapeutic benefits that merit exposure, it is unethical to expose individuals to potential carcinogens or teratogens simply to find out whether they get cancers or birth defects. Like epidemiologic studies, controlled studies are not ordinarily available for evaluating the toxicity properties of a substance, requiring resort to the other types of scientific evidence the *Rider* court discusses.

a. *Animal studies.* "[R]esearchers regard animal studies as especially important for inferring that substances cause adverse effects in humans." Carl Cranor, TOXIC TORTS: SCIENCE, LAW, AND THE POSSIBILITY OF JUSTICE 106 (2006). Despite their palpable differences, certain mammals share genetic and other important similarities with humans. Consequently, "the pathological development of tumors in [these] mammals is believed to resemble that in humans." *Id.* at 10.

Although informative, these studies only offer limited evidence of toxicity. Like epidemiologic studies, animal studies are not easily undertaken and can be hard to interpret. They "take at least five years to conduct and interpret, many person-hours of effort, and are also expensive." *Id.* at 111. To reduce costs, researchers expose a few animals such as mice to extremely high doses of the substance. Consequently, the fact that large quantities of a chemical increase the incidence of cancer for mice does not mean that the substantially lower quantity of the chemical in the product subjects humans to the same risk, or to even any risk at all. Often the evidence is only indicative of carcinogenicity. And as the court in *Rider* emphasized, a substance can affect animals differently from humans. Humans "may process (i.e., metabolize, store, excrete) the agent in question in a different manner and are much more genetically heterogeneous. These differences often receive greater attention than the similarities." *Id.* at 107 (quotation omitted).

b. *The relation between chemical structure and biological activity.* The chemical structure of a substance is related to its biological effects on humans. Evidence of toxicity, therefore, exists when the substance has a chemical structure similar to a known carcinogen or teratogen. Once again, however, this toxicological evidence can be hard to interpret for various reasons.

> The first is that chemicals often change within the body as they go through various routes to eventual elimination. Thus absorption, distribution, metabolism, and excretion are central to understanding the toxicology of an agent. The second is that human sensitivity to chemical and physical agents can vary greatly among individuals, often as a result of differences in absorption, distribution, metabolism, or excretion, as well as target organ sensitivity—all of which can be genetically determined. The third major source of complexity is the need for extrapolation . . . across doses, because human toxicological and epidemiological data often are limited to specific dose ranges that differ from the dose suffered by a plaintiff alleging a toxic tort impact.

Bernard D. Goldstein & Mary Sue Henifen, *Reference Guide on Toxicology, in* FED. JUDICIAL CTR., REFERENCE MANUAL ON SCIENTIFIC EVIDENCE 636 (3d ed. 2011).

c. *Signature diseases.* The difficulty of determining whether a substance is toxic or not also depends on the type of disease or injury. "Identifying cause-and-effect relationships in toxicology can be relatively straightforward; for example, when placed on the skin, concentrated sulfuric acid will cause massive tissue destruction . . . ." Similarly, "the relatively rare lung cancer known as mesothelioma is almost always caused by asbestos." The same is true for the cancers involved in the DES cases. Outside of these *signature diseases*, cancers and birth defects are not easily attributed to a particular substance. "[F]or many diseases, there are few if any known causes, for example, pancreatic cancer. Even when there are known causes of a disease, most individual cases are often not ascribable to any of the known causes, such as with leukemia." Diseases and injuries of this type pose a "particular challenge" for toxicological research. *Id.* at 635.

6. *Is the "flexible" approach a reliable approach?* For a disease with unknown etiology, how can plaintiffs adequately prove causation without epidemiologic evidence or controlled clinical studies? Is the flexible approach described by the *Restatement (Third)* effectively limited to signature diseases or those identified by controlled clinical studies, in which case there is no need for epidemiologic study? If not, how could a plaintiff's scientific evidence pass muster in light of inherent limitations of toxicological evidence not based on epidemiologic study? To what extent does the court's reasoning in *Rider* shed light on these questions?

VI. The Problem of Scientific Uncertainty

These issues can be usefully explored in relation to the experience that courts have had with the National Vaccine Act, which is discussed in Chapter 9, section I. The Act establishes a special claims procedure, involving the Court of Federal Claims and special masters, enabling a person injured by a vaccine to file a petition to obtain compensation from a fund financed by a tax on vaccines. A claimant can receive compensation by proving that she had been inoculated with a listed vaccine and then suffered a listed or "Table" injury within a prescribed time frame. Such proof relieves a claimant from the need to prove cause-in-fact. To recover for an unlisted or "off-Table" injury, the claimant must prove that the vaccine caused the injury. Claims of this type are particularly interesting for present purposes—the same set of judges (the special masters) face a large number of similar cases that require them to determine whether the claimant has proven causation by a preponderance of the evidence, the same issue posed by an ordinary tort claim. *See* National Vaccine Act, 42 U.S.C. §§300aa-11(c), 300aa-13(a)(1)(A) (requiring proof of causation by a preponderance of the evidence); Moberly v. Sec'y of Health & Human Servs., 592 F.3d 1315, 1322 (Fed. Cir. 1991) ("[T]his court has regularly used th[e] term [causation in fact] to describe the causal requirement for off-Table injuries and has made clear that the applicable level of proof is not certainty, but the traditional tort standard of 'preponderant evidence.'").

STEVENS v. SECRETARY OF DEPT. OF HEALTH AND HUMAN SERVICES
United States Court of Federal Claims, Office of the Special Masters, 2001
2001 WL 387418 (unpublished opinion)

GOLKIEWICZ, Chief Special Master. On August 4, 1999, petitioner, Jane Stevens, filed a claim under the National Vaccine Injury Compensation Program. Petitioner alleged that she suffered permanent neurologic deficits, including transverse myelitis, as a result of the hepatitis B vaccines she received on November 29, 1994 and January 13, 1995. On March 8, 2000, respondent filed her Rule 4 Report recommending that compensation be denied. Thereafter, on July 13, 2000, petitioner filed Petitioner's Motion for Summary Judgment arguing, *inter alia*, that petitioner is entitled to summary judgment based upon her proposed standard of proof for a causation-in-fact claim which consists of a showing of scientific plausibility, absence of alternative causes, appropriate temporal relationship, and a treating physician's clinical assessment of vaccine causation. Respondent filed her opposition to petitioner's motion on August 31, 2000, contending, *inter alia*, that petitioner's proposed standard of proof is contrary to the law of the Federal Circuit and accepted scientific principles. The court, after reviewing the arguments and for the reasons stated below, denies Petitioner's Motion for Summary Judgment. However, in so ruling, the court takes the opportunity to discuss in detail the appropriate standards for weighing a causation-in-fact claim.

The parties' respective briefs raise legitimate legal issues which the court and the parties wrestle with on a daily basis in their attempts to resolve fairly these vaccine cases. The overarching issue is what is the appropriate analytical framework for evaluating off-Table, so-called causation-in-fact, claims? Frequently two or three experts per side grapple with questions of epidemiology, neurology, immunology and virtually every other medical discipline. Extensive legal arguments concerning the sufficiency of the evidence follow the medical testimony. The cases take longer to prepare, longer to present, and longer to decide. Even though the same vaccines and injuries are represented in the cases, clear answers have proven elusive to the numerous causation-in-fact issues presented over the twelve-year history of the Program. Decisional law has not, as of yet, provided the answers. In short, litigating causation cases has proven the antithesis of Congress's desire for the Program. Instead of speed, certainty, and fairness, costly lengthy case presentations, inconsistent outcomes, and disparate treatment of similarly situated litigants has resulted.

Given that causation entails showing that the vaccine actually caused the injury, can one avoid the lengthy, costly litigation outlined above? Twelve years of experience has shown that while the vaccines and injuries differ from case to case, the nature of the evidence is essentially the same. Experts agree, with few undisputed exceptions, that vaccines do not leave "footprints," or pathological markers, on the body that prove causation. The next best evidence, epidemiologic studies, is rarely available. Where it is available it is utilized. Thus, unless one is prepared to argue, as respondent appears to do, that in the absence of either of these two types of evidence petitioner loses, the court is left to evaluate several pieces of clinically supportive, but not definitive, circumstantial evidence in ruling on the causation claim. Neither the special masters nor the reviewing courts have accepted respondent's narrow interpretation of what constitutes sufficient causation-in-fact evidence. Thus, each case proceeds with circumstantial clinical evidence weighed against uncertain, ill-defined, and often times differing evidentiary standards. It is the inconsistent weighing of this clinical evidence that results in disparate treatment of petitioners.

The special masters have undertaken efforts to apply the broad principles of causation articulated by the Federal Circuit. To that end, the court routinely evaluates causation claims through a two-prong approach, assessing first whether the vaccine can cause the injury alleged (whether it is medically possible for the vaccine to cause the alleged injury), and, if so, then whether it did in the particular case. Not infrequently, the special masters' efforts result in inconsistent findings and disparate treatment of similarly situated petitioners. While factual differences in each case partly account for this, the more appreciable factor is the various legal standards that the special masters employ. The resulting disparity involves not only what type or combination of evidence supports petitioner's claims, but the scope of petitioner's burden as well.

For the most part, petitioners submit the same type of evidence in almost every vaccine claim. Generally, experts testify to the petitioner's pre-vaccination medical history, the timing and characteristics of the symptoms suffered subsequent to the vaccination, the extent of any permanent damage, the support from the medical community or literature for opining that the vaccine caused the acute and chronic injuries alleged, and the treating physician's efforts to eliminate alternate causes. In rebuttal, respondent usually offers expert testimony

VI. The Problem of Scientific Uncertainty

that petitioner's evidence is scientifically deficient since no epidemiological or pathological evidence exists. It would seem logical and equitable then, that in cases where the vaccinee received the same vaccine, suffered the same or similar injury, and supported her claim with the same type and/or amount of evidence, including the same expert testimony, the court would render uniform results. Unfortunately, this has not always been the case, as shall be seen, regardless of whether the court is evaluating direct or circumstantial evidence.

When evaluating petitioner's causation evidence, the special masters initially look for direct evidence linking the vaccine to the alleged injury. Vaccine and traditional tort case law is replete with references to "direct evidence," "hard science," and "circumstantial evidence." In this court's discussion, "direct evidence" refers to that evidence which experts on both sides routinely accept as sufficient medical proof of causation. In the twelve years the undersigned has listened to expert testimony, numerous highly credentialed experts have accepted that the vaccine directly caused the alleged injury when the proof is based on an epidemiologic study demonstrating a relative risk greater than two (assuming the vaccinee meets the study's parameters) or dispositive clinical or pathological markers evidencing a direct causal relationship (for example, the presence of anterior horn cells on autopsy as evidence of polio contracted from the oral polio vaccine or the presence of the rubella virus in synovial fluid taken from the joints as evidence of a rubella-related arthropathy). Stated another way, direct evidence is that which moves the physician or the factfinder closer to a "scientifically certain" determination of vaccine causation.

In vaccine claims, the most desirable direct evidence is epidemiology. Where it is available, the special masters find it highly probative. While supportive epidemiology is not a prerequisite to compensation, evidence indicating a relative risk greater than two suffices to prove causation in a particular case more probable than not. Thus, a petitioner may successfully demonstrate actual causation by providing a reliable and relevant epidemiologic study and establishing that she falls within the parameters of the group associated with the statistically significant relative risk (assuming, of course, respondent fails to prove a factor unrelated).

The other desirable direct evidence is dispositive clinical or pathological markers evidencing a direct causal relationship. The presence of such "vaccine footprints" leaves little doubt in the mind of the experts and the factfinder that the vaccination is the likely cause of the injury. Unfortunately, most petitioners cannot benefit from the introduction of such evidence because it is unavailable. On this point, the competing experts agree. Its absence may be due to certain tests not being conducted in the particular case or simply science's failure to identify or even accept certain markers. Where petitioners have relied on credible footprint evidence, the government usually and rightfully concedes the claims. For example, in some OPV and rubella cases, post-vaccinal testing confirms the vaccine reaction. However, the availability of footprint evidence is simply *very limited* in vaccine litigation.

In sum, in most instances a petitioner may successfully prosecute her claim by relying on dispositive epidemiology or vaccine footprints which scientifically and legally demonstrate that the vaccine is the more likely cause of the injury alleged. Unfortunately, few petitioners are afforded this evidentiary luxury since epidemiology and footprints are rarely available — such is the nature of science.

This lack of direct evidence leaves petitioners no other recourse than to corroborate their causation claim with circumstantial evidence. Such proof presents evidentiary quandaries, as the following explains.

In the absence of epidemiology or direct clinical or pathological evidence linking the vaccine to the alleged injury, the court faces an even more perplexing causation analysis. *With few exceptions, the special masters encounter the absence of dispositive epidemiology or vaccine footprints in the vast majority of causation-in-fact cases under the Program.* The reasons for this are several. First, relevant research regarding causation is often extremely limited. A number of factors restrict the medical community's efforts to conduct such studies including the costliness of the research and the rarity of the illnesses studied. Second, most vaccines simply leave no unique markers, footprints, or clinical and/or pathological patterns of injury which would enable one to specifically identify the vaccine as the causative agent or otherwise distinguish the injury from one caused by another factor, such as a viral or bacterial infection or other illness. Physicians have accepted this medical fact in a number of cases. In the absence of supportive literature and clinical markers then, petitioners typically rely on "circumstantial evidence." This circumstantial evidence includes: epidemiology (evidencing a relative risk less than two), animal studies, case reports/case series studies, anecdotal reports, manufacturing disclosures, Physician Desk Reference citations, journal articles, institutional findings (such as those reported by the Institute of Medicine), novel medical theories, treating physician testimony, and non-dispositive but inferential clinical and laboratory findings. Not surprisingly, the petitioners' use of this evidence is met with varying success depending on the particular evaluative standard the special master utilizes.

For instance, some special masters remain largely skeptical of whether animal studies can be extrapolated to humans. Similarly, the special masters have debated the utility of case reports. To be sure, the special masters have articulated a number of general approaches to evaluating circumstantial evidence. In essence, the court considers whether the methodology used to formulate the minority opinion, rather than the expert's opinion itself, is generally accepted. But, the consequence of these and other analyses is that special masters have been both reluctant and conversely willing to award compensation in cases where the vaccine cannot be positively identified or otherwise distinguished from competing causes. The struggle is to weigh the scientific certainty of the evidence against the court's obligation to find the evidence only legally sufficient.

In addition to the evaluative inconsistencies already mentioned, the special masters must grapple with the frequently presented question of how much weight to accord a *treating physician's* opinion when it is based on clinical medicine rather than hard science.

But, a treater's assessments of the cause of the injury, just as any other expert's in the case, may be probative if the opinions expressed are relevant, rational, cogent, and well-supported. In vaccine cases, just as in civil tort cases, petitioners present contemporaneous medical records and reports from treating physicians. The treating physicians may also testify at a hearing and the records and testimony often offer a mechanism for injury or identify the vaccination as the cause of the injury alleged. The opinions are generally grounded in the *clinical* perspective and arrived at following a process of differential diagnosis which involves patient examination and laboratory testing to exclude alternate

VI. The Problem of Scientific Uncertainty

causes. The causal relationship may be identified numerous times throughout the medical records and even accepted by a number of interdisciplinaried treating physicians. When the claim proceeds to trial, however, this evidence is then pitted against opinions from respondent's experts hired in the course of litigation who most often neither examined the patient nor talked with the treating physicians. Instead, the hired experts rely on the medical records as their source of information about petitioner's medical condition. Respondent's experts then combine their knowledge of the case with their views of causation, gleaned from relevant medical or scientific literature (or the lack thereof), to render an opinion that is most often grounded in the *scientific* perspective. Based on the lack of epidemiological support and vaccine footprints, respondent's experts usually contest not only that the vaccine caused the injury in the particular case, but more basically, based on the available scientific information, that the vaccine can even cause the injury alleged generally. The court's duty then is to weigh the scientifically based opinions against those clinically grounded in the context of an Act meant to compensate vaccine-injured persons, but without concrete criteria explaining how to achieve this. It is a constant and confounding balancing problem.

The special masters' efforts to create standards for evaluating circumstantial evidence have not fared well. The difficulties stem largely from the less scientific, more clinical, nature of the evidence submitted. The special masters want petitioners to present a claim rooted in scientific or medical principles, as *Daubert* commands, but the court is not wholly convinced of how that is successfully effected when petitioners can only rely on circumstantial evidence. There simply exists no consensus about what circumstantial evidence, if any, sufficiently supports petitioner's claim. The result is confusing and inconsistent standards.

[The special master then developed an "analytical framework" for evaluating the evidence and used it to deny Petitioner's motion for summary judgment.]

NOTES AND QUESTIONS

1. *Relevance of the case.* On appeal, the Federal Court of Claims rejected the analytical framework the special master adopted in *Stevens*. *See* Althen v. Secretary of Health and Human Servs., 58 Fed. Cl. 270, 282 (2003). The ongoing importance of *Stevens* is instead supplied by its discussion of how different special masters have evaluated causal proof in vaccine cases.

2. *Different conceptions of the evidentiary rule?* According to *Stevens*, the cases often reach inconsistent outcomes due to the lack of "consensus about what circumstantial evidence, if any, sufficiently supports petitioner's claim" when there is not dispositive evidence such as epidemiologic study. The inconsistent outcomes presumably reflect different conceptions of the evidence required for adequate proof of causation.

Under the most obvious conception, the element of causation requires the plaintiff to prove that the vaccine doubled the risk of injury. For injuries without a known cause, the required proof would seem to involve epidemiologic study or other types of noncontroversial evidence. As *Stevens* explained, for some injuries, the vaccine leaves "footprints," or "pathological markers, on the body that prove causation," and no one seriously doubts this "direct evidence" satisfies the plaintiff's burden of proving causation without epidemiologic study.

This conception of the evidentiary rule, however, effectively rules out proof of causation by the types of controversial or "circumstantial evidence" discussed by *Stevens*, such as animal studies and so on. For example, the fact that a substance is carcinogenic for animals only suggests that it *might* be a human carcinogen, and so this evidence does not show that the substance, more likely than not, caused the plaintiff's cancer. The same conclusion applies to the other types of "circumstantial evidence." A plaintiff who attempts to recover by relying on such proof has not shown that the substance, more likely than not, caused the harm in question. Hence this conception of the evidentiary rule would seem to require a verdict for the defendant for cases in which there is no epidemiologic or other noncontroversial evidence of causation — an outcome illustrated by *Rider*. See also, *e.g.*, In re Neurontin Marketing, Sales Practices, and Prods. Liab. Litig., 612 F. Supp. 2d 116, 132 (D. Mass. 2010) ("While an epidemiological study is not per se required, establishing general causation without some 'confirmatory' evidence of an association between the drug and the negative effect can be an uphill battle.").

An alternative conception of the evidentiary rule is suggested by the flexible approach articulated by the *Restatement (Third)* that does not always require epidemiologic proof or other forms of "direct evidence" such as the "footprints" or other "pathological markers" discussed by *Stevens*. According to the *Restatement (Third)*,

> Factors such as a good biological-mechanism explanation of how the agent could have caused the plaintiff's disease, a differential etiology ruling out other known causes, a reasonable explanation for the lack of general-causation evidence (and no contrary evidence of an absence of general causation), a short latency period and acute response, and the appropriate disease response to dechallenge (removal from exposure) to the agent, if combined and consistent, provide a persuasive basis for excusing the plaintiff from providing other proof of general causation.

RESTATEMENT (THIRD) OF TORTS: LIABILITY FOR PHYSICAL AND EMOTIONAL HARM §28 cmt. c(4). With the exception of the dechallenge data obtained from controlled studies, this evidence comprises most of the "circumstantial evidence" discussed in *Stevens*.

Consider how these evidentiary problems apply in the following set of cases. To what extent is the court willing to rely on the types of "circumstantial evidence" of causation discussed in *Stevens*?

IN RE: ROUNDUP PRODUCTS LIABILITY LITIGATION
United States District Court, Northern District of California, 2018
390 F. Supp. 3d 1102

VINCE CHHABRIA, District Judge. The question at this early phase in the proceedings — the "general causation" phase — is whether a reasonable jury could conclude that glyphosate, a commonly used herbicide, can cause Non-Hodgkin's

VI. The Problem of Scientific Uncertainty

Lymphoma ("NHL") at exposure levels people realistically may have experienced. If the answer is yes, the case moves to the next phase, which addresses whether each particular plaintiff's NHL was caused by glyphosate. If the answer is no, none of the plaintiffs' cases may proceed. And the answer must be no unless the plaintiffs can present at least one reliable expert opinion in support of their position.

There are two significant problems with the plaintiffs' presentation, which combine to make this a very close question. First, the plaintiffs (along with some of their experts) rely heavily on the decision by the International Agency for Research on Cancer ("IARC") to classify glyphosate as "probably carcinogenic to humans." This classification is not as helpful to the plaintiffs as it might initially seem. To render a verdict for a plaintiff in a civil trial, a jury must conclude, applying the "preponderance of the evidence" standard, that the plaintiff's NHL was more likely than not caused by exposure to glyphosate. And at this general causation phase, the question is whether a reasonable jury could conclude by a preponderance of the evidence that glyphosate can cause NHL at exposure levels people realistically could have experienced. The IARC inquiry is different in kind—it is a public health assessment, not a civil trial. Public health assessments generally involve two steps: (1) an effort to identify *hazards*; and (2) an evaluation of the *risk* that the hazard poses at particular exposure levels. The first step essentially asks whether a substance is cause for concern, while the second step asks how concerned we should be. As IARC takes pains to point out, its decision that a substance is "probably carcinogenic to humans" is a hazard assessment—merely the first step in determining whether the substance currently presents a meaningful risk to human health. IARC leaves the second step—risk assessment—to other public health entities. Moreover, even with its hazard assessment, IARC makes clear that although it uses the word "probably," it does not intend for that word to have any quantitative significance. Therefore, the public health inquiry does not map nicely onto the inquiry required by civil litigation. And the hazard assessment IARC undertakes is too limited and too abstract to fully serve the plaintiffs' purposes here. A substance could be cause for concern, such that it can and should trigger preventive public health measures and further study, even when it is not so clearly dangerous as to allow a verdict in favor of a plaintiff.

The second problem with the plaintiffs' presentation is that the evidence of a causal link between glyphosate exposure and NHL in the human population seems rather weak. Some epidemiological studies suggest that glyphosate exposure is slightly or moderately associated with increased odds of developing NHL. Other studies, including the largest and most recent, suggest there is no link at all. All the studies leave certain questions unanswered, and every study has its flaws. The evidence, viewed in its totality, seems too equivocal to support any firm conclusion that glyphosate causes NHL. This calls into question the credibility of some of the plaintiffs' experts, who have confidently identified a causal link.

However, the question at this phase is not whether the plaintiffs' experts are right. The question is whether they have offered opinions that would be admissible at a jury trial. And the case law—particularly Ninth Circuit case law—emphasizes that a trial judge should not exclude an expert opinion merely because he thinks it's shaky, or because he thinks the jury will have cause to question the expert's credibility. So long as an opinion is premised on reliable scientific principles, it should not be excluded by the trial judge; instead the weaknesses in an unpersuasive expert opinion can be exposed at trial, through cross-examination or testimony by opposing experts.

The three expert opinions most helpful to the plaintiffs at this phase in the proceedings were offered by Dr. Christopher Portier, Dr. Beate Ritz, and Dr. Dennis Weisenburger. A jury may well reject these opinions at trial, finding the opinions too results-driven or concluding that the evidence behind those opinions is too weak. But applying the standard set forth in the case law for admission of expert testimony, the Court cannot go so far as to say these experts have served up the kind of junk science that requires exclusion from trial. And the testimony of these three experts is directly on topic, because they (in contrast to some other experts) went beyond the inquiry conducted by IARC, offering independent and relatively comprehensive opinions that the epidemiological and other evidence demonstrates glyphosate causes NHL in some people who are exposed to it. Accordingly, their opinions are admissible, which means the plaintiffs have presented enough evidence to defeat Monsanto's summary judgment motion. These proceedings thus move on to the next phase, which will involve an attempt by individual plaintiffs to present enough evidence to warrant a jury trial on whether glyphosate caused the NHL they developed. Given how close the question is at the general causation phase, the plaintiffs appear to face a daunting challenge at the next phase. But it is a challenge they are entitled to undertake.

[The court then extensively analyzed the admissibility of plaintiffs' scientific evidence.]

VIII. Conclusion

It's a close question whether to admit the expert opinions of Dr. Portier, Dr. Ritz, and Dr. Weisenburger that glyphosate can cause NHL at human-relevant doses. Therefore, it's a close question whether to grant or deny Monsanto's motion for summary judgment. But the Court concludes that the opinions of these experts, while shaky, are admissible. They have surveyed the significant body of epidemiological literature relevant to this question; identified at least a few statistically significant elevated odds ratios from case-control studies and meta-analyses; identified what they deem to be a pattern of odds ratios above 1.0 from the case-control studies, even if not all are statistically significant; emphasized that studies of glyphosate have focused on many different types of cancer but found a link only between glyphosate and NHL; given legitimate reasons to question the results of the primary study on which Monsanto relies; and concluded, in light of all the available evidence, that a causal interpretation is appropriate. Their opinions may be bolstered by Dr. Jameson's narrower opinions regarding glyphosate's ability to cause cancer in animals. Therefore, the plaintiffs have presented evidence from which a reasonable jury could conclude that glyphosate can cause NHL at human-relevant doses. Monsanto's motion for summary judgment is denied.

NOTES AND QUESTIONS

1. *History of the litigation.* In 2015, the International Agency for Research on Cancer (IARC) — the well-respected specialized cancer agency of the World Health Organization — concluded that epidemiologic study only provides "*limited evidence* in humans for the carcinogenicity of glyphosate."

VI. The Problem of Scientific Uncertainty 513

It also found that there is "*sufficient evidence* in experimental animals" stemming from "strong evidence that glyphosate can operate through two key characteristics of known human carcinogens," leading the agency to classify glyphosate as "*probably carcinogenic to humans.*" International Agency for Research on Cancer, 112 IARC MONOGRAPHS ON THE EVALUATION OF CARCINOGENIC RISKS TO HUMANS: SOME ORGANOPHOSPATE INSECTICIDES AND HERBICIDES 323, 398 (2017). Following this report, Austria banned glyphosate, a court in France banned a Roundup brand, and Germany will ban the use of Roundup beginning in 2024. Ruth Bender, *Bayer's Roundup Woes Deepen as Germany Bans Key Chemical*, Wall St. J., Nov. 18, 2019 (noting also that "[o]ther countries have adopted total and partial glyphosate bans in the past"). Based on the IARC report, California added glyphosate to its official list of known carcinogens as required by state law. The ensuing developments led to the consolidated proceeding governed by the court's ruling in the *Roundup Products Liability Litigation*:

> After IARC classified glyphosate as a probable carcinogen, a wave of lawsuits followed. These lawsuits, which now number in the hundreds, were dispersed among state and federal courts across the country, but the claims against Monsanto raised similar issues. In particular, a central question in all these cases is whether Monsanto's glyphosate-based herbicides can cause NHL.
>
> The Judicial Panel on Multidistrict Litigation, a panel of judges empowered to coordinate proceedings in federal cases where doing so "will be for the convenience of parties and witnesses and will promote the just and efficient conduct" of the cases, determined that coordination in these cases was warranted. [ ] The Panel therefore created this Multidistrict Litigation to centralize management of all the federal cases, and assigned to this Court all pretrial proceedings in the Multidistrict Litigation. As is common in such proceedings, the Court appointed a group of plaintiffs' counsel to serve as leaders and to represent all the plaintiffs' interests. [ ] Many additional cases have since been transferred to this district as part of the Multidistrict Litigation, and more than 400 cases are now pending.
>
> The Court decided to bifurcate the pretrial proceedings. [ ] The motions at issue here arise during the first phase, which addresses "general causation." As noted, the question at the general causation phase is whether glyphosate is capable of causing NHL at exposure levels humans might have experienced. The second phase will involve, among other things, the issue of "specific causation." The specific causation inquiry focuses on whether individual plaintiffs' exposure to glyphosate-based herbicides caused the NHL they developed.

390 F. Supp. 3d at 1110-1111.

2. *The evidentiary standard.* The federal district court in the *Roundup* case evaluated the admissibility of plaintiffs' expert testimony under the standards embodied in the *Daubert* trilogy discussed by the court in *Rider*. Based on the *Roundup* court's evidentiary ruling, will plaintiffs be able to provide general causation? If so, does the evidence fit within the "flexible approach" adopted by the *Restatement (Third)*? Even if plaintiffs can prove general causation, would this evidence enable a reasonable juror to conclude that glyphosate, more likely than not, caused the cancer suffered by

an individual plaintiff? Recall in this regard the *Daubert* case on remand, which held that the only relevant evidence for proving specific causation involves epidemiologic studies showing at least a doubling of risk.

IN RE: ROUNDUP PRODUCTS LIABILITY LITIGATION
United States District Court, Northern District of California, 2019
358 F. Supp. 3d 956

VINCE CHHABRIA, District Judge. The Court previously denied Monsanto's motion for summary judgment on general causation, concluding that the opinions of the plaintiffs' experts were shaky but admissible. The question now is whether the plaintiffs have cleared the specific causation hurdle—that is, whether they have presented evidence from which a reasonable jury could conclude that exposure to glyphosate caused the non-Hodgkin's lymphoma of the three bellwether plaintiffs: Edwin Hardeman, Sioum Gebeyehou, and Elaine Stevick. To defeat Monsanto's motion for summary judgment on this issue, the plaintiffs must present at least one admissible expert opinion to support their specific causation argument. It is again a close question, but the plaintiffs have barely inched over the line. All three of the plaintiffs' specific causation experts may testify at trial, although, as discussed below, some aspects of their opinions will not be admitted.

I.

The plaintiffs' specific causation experts use a "differential diagnosis" as the basis for their opinion that exposure to glyphosate caused these plaintiffs' NHL. A differential diagnosis is simply a framework for identifying the most probable cause of a disease. [ ] To conduct a differential diagnosis, a physician "rules in" all potential causes of a disease, "rules out" those for "which there is no plausible evidence of causation, and then determines the most likely cause among those that cannot be excluded." [ ] The Ninth Circuit has repeatedly approved the use of a differential diagnosis under *Daubert*, provided, of course, that it is applied reliably. [ ] Monsanto does not dispute that the plaintiffs' experts may use a differential diagnosis as the basis for their opinions, but instead argues that both their "ruling in" and "ruling out" were unreliable.

A.

At the ruling-in stage, the question is "which of the competing causes are *generally* capable of causing the" disease. [ ] And here, the Court already determined that the plaintiffs offered admissible expert opinions that glyphosate is capable of causing NHL. Thus, Monsanto's primary criticism of the ruling-in process—namely, that the specific causation experts improperly ruled in glyphosate exposure by cherry-picking favorable epidemiological studies—is off point. As this Court has previously ruled, the specific causation experts are permitted to build from the plaintiffs' admissible general causation opinions. And the admissible general causation opinions grappled with the full body of

VI. The Problem of Scientific Uncertainty 515

evidence. Thus, it does not matter that the specific causation experts mentioned only a subset of the epidemiological studies in their reports; at trial, their basis for ruling in glyphosate will be the general causation opinions. This result is the byproduct of the decision to bifurcate pretrial proceedings between general and specific causation—a decision that Monsanto urged.

On a related note, Monsanto complains that the specific causation experts ruled in glyphosate exposure as a risk factor without presenting epidemiological evidence that it has an adjusted odds ratio above 2.0 [that is, whether glyphosate at least doubles the risk of NHL]. But the inquiry for this step of the differential diagnosis is whether a risk factor is a *potential* cause, not whether it is in fact the cause. [ ] Indeed, as discussed further in Section II of this ruling, there is not even a categorical requirement that an expert present a study identifying an adjusted odds ratio above 2.0 to justify a decision not to rule out a risk factor. And in any event, the general causation opinions on which the specific causation experts may build are based significantly on De Roos (2003), which reported an adjusted odds ratio of 2.1 with a 95% confidence interval of 1.1 to 4.0. [ ] The specific causation experts cite De Roos as well, but, again, the important point is that these experts will not be repeating the analysis of the general causation experts, but rather relying on them to rule in glyphosate.

B.

The next question is whether the experts adequately assessed all of the potential causes of the plaintiffs' NHL, and properly ruled out factors other than glyphosate, while at the same time declining to rule out glyphosate itself.

The biggest concern, which affects all three plaintiffs, is how the experts account for idiopathy—that is, the possibility that a plaintiff's NHL is attributable to an unknown cause. Imagine 100 people who develop NHL after using Roundup. Imagine further that they had no other significant risk factors for NHL. Assuming for argument's sake that the plaintiffs' general causation opinions are correct, glyphosate was a substantial factor in causing NHL for *some* of those 100 people. But the experts cannot automatically assume that glyphosate caused all 100 people's NHL. For some, the cause of their NHL may not be determinable with the degree of certainty necessary to prevail in court (perhaps because their exposure to glyphosate was just too low, or perhaps for some other reason). The question for any particular plaintiff, then, is whether there is evidence from which a jury could conclude by a preponderance of the evidence that the plaintiff falls into the category of people whose NHL was caused by glyphosate. To assist the jury in making this assessment, an expert must have a way to differentiate Roundup users who developed NHL because they used the product from Roundup users who would have developed NHL regardless.

One way for an expert to do this is to point to a biomarker or genetic signature associated with a particular risk factor. [ ] But as the plaintiffs themselves note, that is not possible here, nor is there any evidence suggesting that NHL presents differently when caused by exposure to glyphosate. Under a strict interpretation of *Daubert*, perhaps that would be the end of the line for the plaintiffs and their experts (at least without much stronger epidemiological evidence). But in the Ninth Circuit, that is clearly not the case. [ ] Recognizing that "[m]edicine partakes of art as well as science," the Ninth Circuit's recent decisions reflect a view that district courts should typically admit specific causation opinions that lean strongly toward the "art" side of the spectrum. [ ]; Wendell v. GlaxoSmithKline LLC, 858 F.3d 1127, 1237 (9th Cir. 2017) ("The first several victims of a new toxic tort should not be barred from having their day in court simply because the medical literature, which will eventually show the connection between the victims' condition and the toxic substance, has not yet been completed."). . . . [T]he opinions are impossible to read without concluding that district courts in the Ninth Circuit must be more tolerant of borderline expert opinions than in other circuits. [ ] Of course, district judges still must exercise their discretion, but in doing so they must account for the fact that a wider range of expert opinions (arguably much wider) will be admissible in this circuit.

Under Ninth Circuit caselaw, doctors enjoy wide latitude in how they practice their art when offering causation opinions. *See Wendell,* 858 F.3d at 1237 ("Where, as here, two doctors who stand at or near the top of their field and have extensive clinical experience with the rare disease or class of disease at issue, are prepared to give expert opinions supporting causation, we conclude that poses no bar based on their principles and methodology."). It is sufficient for a qualified expert, in reliance on his clinical experience, review of a plaintiffs' medical records, and evaluation of the general causation evidence, to conclude that an "obvious and known risk factor [ ]" is the cause of that plaintiff's disease. [ ] Here, the specific causation experts did that. Relying on the plaintiffs' admissible general causation opinions—which assert a robust connection between glyphosate and NHL—the experts concluded that glyphosate was a substantial factor in causing the plaintiffs' NHL.

Moreover, the experts relied heavily on the plaintiffs' exposure levels in drawing their conclusions. All three experts noted the plaintiffs' extensive Roundup usage, and further explained—as did the plaintiffs' general causation opinions—that [two epidemiologic] studies showed a dose-response relationship between glyphosate and NHL. [ ] Thus, consistent with Ninth Circuit caselaw, the experts provided a basis for their conclusion that these plaintiffs fall into the category of Roundup users who developed NHL. The Court may be skeptical of their conclusions, and in particular of the assumption built into their opinions from the general causation phase about the strength of the epidemiological evidence. But their core opinions—that the plaintiffs had no other significant risk factors and were exposed to enough glyphosate to conclude that it was a substantial factor in causing their NHL—are admissible.

II.

During cross-examination at the *Daubert* hearings, Monsanto asked the plaintiffs' specific causation experts several hypothetical questions. These questions typically did not go directly to whether there was a sound basis for concluding that one of the plaintiffs' NHL was caused by glyphosate, but rather to whether the expert would maintain his conclusion if the plaintiffs' exposure was far less severe. In other words, returning to the previously mentioned scenario of 100 NHL patients with glyphosate exposure but no other risk factors, how, precisely, would they draw the line between those whose NHL was caused by glyphosate and those whose NHL is idiopathic? The primary response of the plaintiffs' experts—which, as discussed above, falls within the range of admissible expert

VI. The Problem of Scientific Uncertainty

testimony—was that, however they draw the line, the exposure for these three plaintiffs was so significant that their NHL should not be considered idiopathic. When further pressed, however, these experts sometimes crossed into the realm of junk science [when they concluded that various epidemiologic studies finding an adjusted odds ratio of less than 2.0 in fact implied a ratio exceeding 2.0 for the plaintiffs due to their extensive exposure]. These aspects of their opinions will be excluded, unless of course Monsanto chooses to use them as impeachment material.

. . .

IT IS SO ORDERED.

NOTES AND QUESTIONS

1. *Subsequent developments.* In the bellwether trial for plaintiff Edwin Hardeman, the jury awarded the plaintiff approximately $5 million in compensatory damages and $75 million for punitive damages. The trial court upheld both the jury verdict and the damages award for compensatory damages, but reduced the punitive damages award to $20 million for constitutional reasons (discussed in Chapter 13, section V). In upholding the punitive damages award, the court observed that

> the evidence presented at trial about Monsanto's behavior betrayed a lack of concern about the risk that its product might be carcinogenic. Despite years of colorable claims in the scientific community that Roundup causes NHL, Monsanto presented minimal evidence suggesting that it was interested in getting to the bottom of those claims. [ ] While Monsanto repeatedly intones that it stands by the safety of its product, the evidence at trial painted the picture of a company focused on attacking or undermining the people who raised concerns, to the exclusion of being an objective arbiter of Roundup's safety. For example, while the jury was shown emails of Monsanto employees crassly attempting to combat, undermine or explain away challenges to Roundup's safety, not once was it shown an email suggesting that Monsanto officials were actively committed to conducting an objective assessment of its product. Moreover, because the jury was aware that Monsanto has repeatedly sold—and continues to sell—Roundup without any form of warning label, it was clear that Monsanto's "conduct involved repeated actions," rather than "an isolated incident." [ ]

In Re: Roundup Products Liability Litigation, 385 F. Supp. 3d 1082, 1047 (N.D. Cal. 2019).

Could the jury's evaluation of the plaintiff's causal proof have been influenced by the defendant's misconduct? Should it have been? Recall in this regard the outrage expressed by jurors concerning the defendant's lack of testing and indifference to product safety in the mass-tort litigation over silicone-gel implants, which involved massive liabilities in the absence of epidemiologic evidence and arguably motivated the U.S. Supreme Court's ruling in *Daubert. See* note 2, p. 500 *supra*.

In June 2020, Bayer—a German corporation that acquired Monsanto—agreed "to pay more than $10 billion to settle tens of thousands of claims while continuing to sell the product without adding warning labels about its safety." Patricia Cohen, *Roundup Maker to Pay $10 Billion to Settle Cancer Suits*, N.Y. Times, June 24, 2020. The settlement occurred even though the U.S. Environmental Protection Agency (EPA) had reaffirmed its assessment that glyphosate is not a carcinogen despite the IARC's contrary conclusion. Relying on a larger data set than the IARC had considered, the EPA concluded that the animal and epidemiologic studies identifying some evidence of carcinogenicity "were contradicted by studies of equal or higher quality," leading it to conclude that glyphosate is "not likely to be carcinogenic to humans." U.S. Environmental Protection Agency Office of Pesticide Programs, *Revised Glyphosate Issue Paper: Evaluation of Carcinogenic Potential* 143 (Dec. 12, 2017). In 2019, the EPA said it would not approve product labels with cancer warnings about glyphosate. Moving forward, this regulatory decision is likely to preempt any tort claims alleging that the Roundup weed killer should contain a warning about the ongoing scientific dispute concerning the product's potential carcinogenicity. *See* Carson v. Monsanto Co., 2020 WL 7497385 (S.D. Ga. 2020) ("Thus, success for Plaintiff under Georgia's failure to warn tort would require the imposition of a duty upon Monsanto that is different—and in direct conflict—with the requirements set up under the [federal] statutory scheme. Accordingly, Plaintiff's failure to warn claim is preempted."). This rationale for preemption did not apply to the claims settled in the *Roundup* litigation, all of which involved warnings that could have been modified before the EPA's 2019 ruling.

2. *Reconsidering the plaintiffs' proof of causation.* To what extent was the plaintiffs' scientific evidence in the Roundup litigation based on the flexible approach adopted by the *Restatement (Third)*? As the court ruled, the plaintiffs could establish both general and specific causation based on the De Roos 2003 study, which reported an adjusted odds ratio of 2.1 with a 95 percent confidence interval. In other words, for every 4.1 cancers in the community, 2.1 would be attributable to glyphosate exposure and 2.0 would be attributable to the background risk, and so any plaintiff's cancer, more likely than not, could be attributed to glyphosate once the plaintiffs' expert sufficiently ruled out other known carcinogens—the "differential diagnosis" method discussed by the *Roundup* court. Importantly, the court also ruled that there is no "categorical requirement" of epidemiologic proof showing a doubling of the risk. These studies only identify average outcomes, creating the possibility that an individual plaintiff faced a higher than average risk due to more extensive exposure or other elevated risk factors. The court, however, then ruled that the experts' efforts to extrapolate such a conclusion from various studies was "junk science," effectively limiting the proof of general causation to a single epidemiologic study finding an adjusted odds ratio of 2.1.

That evidence, however, was quite "shaky" as the court explained in its earlier evidentiary rulings. The De Roos study pooled data from three earlier studies that found no causal relation; the larger data set instead allowed for a more robust statistical finding capable of identifying such a relation. But a subsequent study pooled these same three studies in addition to a

VI. The Problem of Scientific Uncertainty

fourth, and did not find any adjusted odds ratio exceeding the 2.0 threshold. 390 F. Supp. 3d at 1119-1120. This problem presumably explains why the *Roundup* court observed that its evidentiary ruling might have been different under the caselaw from a different federal circuit. Compare In re Lipitor (Atorvastatin Calcium) Mktg., Sales Practices and Products Liab. Litig., 150 F. Supp. 3d 644, 652 (D.S.C. 2015) (rejecting plaintiff's expert's testimony on specific causation based on the "most reliable" evidence of general causation suggesting an adjusted odds ratio of "around 1.6"), *aff'd*, 892 F.3d 624 (4th Cir. 2018).

Why even require such epidemiologic evidence? After all the IARC conclusion found that this evidence was "inconclusive" and instead relied on animal studies coupled with "strong evidence that glyphosate can operate through two key characteristics of known human carcinogens." Are you persuaded by the court's reasoning that the IARC finding is not relevant for resolving the causal issue? Why wouldn't that type of evidence be sufficient under the "flexible approach" endorsed by the *Restatement (Third)*?

3. *The deterrence problem.* If plaintiffs must always prove causation in toxic tort cases by showing that the substance, more likely than not, caused the harm, would manufacturers of these products have a sufficient incentive to study their hazardous properties? "A manufacturer that conducts no research can generally avoid liability because plaintiffs and government research programs are unlikely to conduct scientific research on their own. Voluntary safety research, on the other hand, might reveal a long-term risk associated with a product. . . ." Wendy E. Wagner, *Choosing Ignorance in the Manufacture of Toxic Products*, 82 Cornell L. Rev. 773, 774-775 (1997). Having voluntarily discovered a risk, the manufacturer would then be obligated to warn about the risk, which ordinarily will reduce consumer demand. Consequently, "it is only rational for manufacturers to choose ignorance. Studies documenting the paucity of testing available for most products confirm that manufacturers are making this rational choice." *Id.*

Consistent with this reasoning, the vast majority of potentially hazardous substances have not been subjected to epidemiologic study or even the basic toxicity studies.

> [S]ome eighty-two thousand chemicals are registered for use in commerce in the United States, with about seven hundred new chemicals introduced each year. In 1998, the [Environmental Protection Agency] found that, among chemicals produced in quantities of more than a million pounds per year, only seven percent had undergone the full slate of basic toxicity studies.

Jerome Groopman, *The Plastic Panic: How Worried Should We Be About Everyday Chemicals?*, The New Yorker, May 31, 2010, at 26, 30.

Even when toxicity evidence exists, manufacturers often question its validity.

> Affected companies and industry groups, protecting their products, have developed identifiable patterns using legal procedures under public health laws to slow improved postmarket health protections. They follow the lead of the tobacco industry: "Doubt is our product since it is the best means of competing with the 'body of fact'

that exists in the minds of the general public. It is also the means of establishing a controversy." Consistent with this, some companies claim to support the ideal of protecting the public, but they argue "at the moment" that the science is "too doubtful" (or perhaps not sufficiently "ideal" to support legal action.

Carl Cranor, Tragic Failures: How and Why We Are Harmed by Toxic Chemicals 53 (2017) (citations omitted).

In light of the paucity of manufacturer research and ongoing disputes about the existing evidence, should manufacturers be able to rely on this uncertainty to avoid liability in all cases? Is the deterrence of willful manufacturer ignorance a sufficient reason for relaxing the plaintiff's burden of proving causation in cases of scientific uncertainty? To what extent has a concern for deterrence justified other rules for relaxing the plaintiff's burden of proving causation?

4. *Rethinking the substantive basis of liability.* In cases of scientific uncertainty, courts regularly evaluate causal evidence without first considering the issue of defect, as illustrated by *Daubert*, *Rider*, and the *Roundup* litigation. Would resolution of the defect issue help to solve the causal problem? Recall in this regard how the proof of a warning defect also establishes the heeding presumption for causation in warning cases.

To evaluate the adequacy of the warnings in cases of scientific uncertainty, consider your own behavior. If you were considering whether to use the drug in *Rider*, would you want to know about the FDA's decision to withdraw approval? When considering whether to use the weed killer Roundup, would you want to know whether a leading European cancer agency has concluded that it might be carcinogenic?

In the cases under consideration, the available scientific evidence provides a reasonable foundation for concluding that the product might be a carcinogen. A consumer who has been warned of the reasonable indicators of carcinogenicity would have much lower confidence in her assessment of the injury costs she expects to incur by using the product. The difference in confidence may not matter if the consumer must use the product right now, but typically that is not the case. Consumers often have the option of waiting to consume or use a product. Delayed consumption is costly for the consumer—she cannot derive any present benefit from the product—but the cost of delayed consumption can be less than the benefit of waiting to find out whether the product really is carcinogenic. Information about possible carcinogenicity, therefore, can influence the consumer's decision of whether to purchase or use the product. Such a disclosure would increase the consumer's estimate of the injury costs she might incur by using the product and could induce her to wait until further study has been done. In these cases, disclosure of the scientific uncertainty would be material to the ordinary consumer's decision of whether to purchase or use the product. The absence of such a disclosure renders the warning defective.

Does this proof of defect affect the causal inquiry? Consider how the substantive nature of the tort duty can guide the causal inquiry, as illustrated by the liberal rule of but-for causation discussed in section I *supra*. The manufacturer has a duty to warn about scientific uncertainty concerning the product's toxicity, so why should it be able to effectively deny that legal obligation by relying on the uncertainty to dismiss the plaintiff's claim in each and every case? To ensure that the duty to warn is meaningful under these conditions, should the manufacturer be prevented from relying on the uncertainty to bar recovery in all cases? Consider in this regard the evidentiary reasons why courts reject defendants' causal arguments based on the more-likely-than-not standard in cases of alternative liability and market-share liability discussed in section V *supra*. Can those reasons be extended to cases of scientific uncertainty to explain why plaintiffs can recover under the flexible evidentiary standard?

Finally, consider the causal rule of strict liability that protects consumer expectations discussed in section III *supra*. In the case under consideration, the plaintiff has proven that the warning is defective for not disclosing that the existing scientific evidence reasonably indicates that the product might be a carcinogen. This proof accordingly shows that the defective warning created the mistaken expectation that the product does not cause cancer. The plaintiff now has cancer and has proven that the product is a reasonably identifiable cause. In these circumstances, the plaintiff has proven by a preponderance of the evidence that the warning defect frustrated her reasonable expectations of product safety, the interest protected by the rule of strict products liability. Hence the warning's failure to disclose scientific uncertainty can violate the tort right of a plaintiff who has cancer. Once the causal question is moved to the damages phase of the case, can the plaintiff satisfy the ordinary evidentiary standard, discussed in section IV *supra*, with the type of evidence permitted by the flexible approach to scientific evidence adopted by the *Restatement (Third)*? In determining damages, does the plaintiff—someone who will get cancer—have the same life expectancy as other individuals, or should her life expectancy be reduced by the likelihood her cancer is caused by the background risk rather than by exposure to the defective product?

These questions are difficult and require extended analysis involving the full range of causal rules covered in this chapter. But as these questions reveal, there are substantive rationales for liability in cases of scientific uncertainty that are masked by apparent logic of the need to prove causation with epidemiologic evidence showing that the product at least doubles the underlying risk of injury. In light of those substantive rationales, is it surprising that some courts have adopted a more flexible approach, while others effectively require such epidemiologic proof in the absence of signature diseases or controlled clinical studies?

VII. AUTONOMOUS VEHICLES AND PRODUCTS LIABILITY: PROBLEM SET 8

AV Problem 8.1

Even when subject to adequate premarket testing and properly deployed, a fully functioning operating system can still cause an autonomous vehicle to crash. The circumstances in which this might occur will be opaque to consumers, and so the underlying tort obligations require the manufacturer to adequately warn about the inherent, foreseeable risk that the fully functioning autonomous vehicle might crash. How can the manufacturer adequately warn consumers about this risk?

"Warnings alert users and consumers to the existence and nature of product risks so that they can prevent harm either by appropriate conduct during use or consumption or by choosing not to use or consume." RESTATEMENT (THIRD) OF TORTS: PRODUCTS LIABILITY §2 cmt. i. For example, suppose there is an unavoidable 1-in-1,000 risk that a safely used product will cause the ordinary consumer to suffer $10,000 in damages. The inherent risk of injury imposes a cost on the consumer at least equal to $10 per product use (the expected value of the injury), so consumers should factor this $10 cost into their estimate of the net benefit that they expect to derive from the product. Consumers who are unaware of the risk will not account for this cost, however, thereby inflating their estimate of the product's net benefit and causing them to purchase or use more of the product than they would choose if well informed. The excessive purchase or use of the product then creates excessive risk, resulting in too many injuries. To address this safety problem, tort law imposes a duty on the manufacturer to warn about any foreseeable risks of physical harm that are unknown by the ordinary consumer and would be material to his or her decision-making. By satisfying the duty to warn, the manufacturer enables consumers to make informed safety decisions. *See* Chapter 7, section I.

The systemized driving behavior of autonomous vehicles determines the inherent risk that the fully functioning operating system will be in a crash. The manufacturer knows or should know of this inherent risk—it determines whether the operating system has been subject to an adequate amount of pre-market testing. *See* AV Problem 3.2, p. 249 *supra.* At minimum, the manufacturer must disclose this risk in a product warning, analogous to a drug manufacturer that discloses the known, inherent risk that the drug might cause a side-effect like a stroke.

Such a warning, however, would not be adequate if the information could be conveyed more clearly in a different format. A different form of disclosure could involve the premium for insuring the autonomous vehicle. The aggregate driving performance of the fleet provides the requisite data for auto insurers to calculate the cost of insuring the vehicle. This insurance premium is based on the inherent, foreseeable risk that the vehicle will crash, and so manufacturers could also warn about this risk by disclosing the premium.

For example, suppose a consumer is deciding whether to purchase either Brand A or Brand B of an autonomous vehicle, each of which is otherwise identical except for their respective operating systems. Suppose Brand A costs $30,000 and has an annual, risk-adjusted insurance premium of $2,500, whereas Brand B costs $31,000 and has a risk-adjusted premium of $1,000. The consumer can readily determine that the safety decision favors Brand B because it has a lower total cost ($32,000 in the first year alone) than Brand A ($32,500). The simple price comparison enables the consumer to make good decisions about the relative risks inherent in the reasonably safe designs of different autonomous vehicles, producing a market dynamic that incentivizes manufacturers to reduce the inherent risk of crash and the corresponding cost of insurance. By enabling the ordinary consumer to make an informed safety decision about the matter, this type of disclosure satisfies the manufacturer's tort obligation to warn about the inherent, foreseeable risk that the autonomous vehicle will crash.

Hence the manufacturer could be liable for not warning about the inherent risk of crash, or it could instead be liable because an adequate warning discloses the insurance premium and not merely the underlying risk of crash. For either type of warning defect, how would the plaintiff prove that the defect caused the crash in question?

Analysis of AV Problem 8.1

The causal question involves an inherent product risk discussed in sections II-III *supra*. As we found, the causal inquiry is complicated because the ordinary consumer, when apprised of the inherent risk, would still probably use the autonomous vehicle. Hence a causal inquiry based on negligence would bar the plaintiff's recovery: More likely than not, the plaintiff would still use the autonomous vehicle once warned about the inherent risk of crash and then suffer the ensuing injury caused by such a crash, and so the warning defect did not cause the injury.

To be sure, the plaintiff might testify otherwise, but that evidence is self-serving, largely unverifiable, and therefore questionable.* To avoid this problem, courts have adopted the heeding presumption. But what does it mean for a consumer to read and heed a warning about an inherent product risk that would not prevent the consumer from nevertheless using the product? The only solution to this causal question is to rely on a causal rule of strict liability that protects consumer expectations of safe product performance. *See* section III *supra*.

The ordinary consumer who reads and heeds the product warning would expect that it adequately discloses any unknown risks of foreseeable injury. By not adequately warning about the inherent risk of crash, the manufacturer becomes strictly responsible for the risk. In the case at hand, the plaintiff was injured by the inherent risk that the fully functioning autonomous vehicle would be in a crash. The injury frustrated consumer expectations of safe product performance, entitling the plaintiff to compensation for the injuries caused by the crash.

In defense, the manufacturer could argue that the ordinary consumer knows that autonomous vehicles are not perfectly safe and have some inherent risk of

---

* *Editor's Note:* In one case, for example, the plaintiff was a passenger in an automobile that rolled over and injured her. Plaintiff alleged that if the defendant manufacturer had adequately warned about the inherent risk, the driver would not have purchased the vehicle. The court rejected this claim for lack of evidence.

> The fine line between "conjecture" on the one hand, and "reasonable inference" on the other, is sometimes hard to draw.... [I]t is reasonable to infer that a simple warning such as "Do not operate [grinding wheel] in excess of 6,000 revolutions per minute" would be followed. It is an inference that arises from the factual situation.... There are no proven facts in this record which would lend the dignity of an inference as opposed to a guess, that [the driver] would not have purchased the [vehicle] in the face of a warning.

Greiner v. Volkswagenwerk Aktiengesellschaft, 429 F. Supp. 495, 498 (E.D. Pa. 1977).

crash. Because the consumer has some expectation of being injured by a fully functioning autonomous vehicle, the mere occurrence of a crash does not necessarily frustrate consumer expectations. The plaintiff must instead show that the crash in question was caused by the elevated risk not adequately disclosed in the warning, rather than by the inherent risk in its entirety. The causal problem now looks like the problem of enhanced risk discussed in section VI *supra*, in which the defect only increases the risk above a "background" or nontortious risk. Must the plaintiff prove that the defect at least doubles the background risk of crash to recover? As the toxic tort cases have shown, courts struggle with this issue. Under the demanding approach, the manufacturer would win this argument in each and every case, with the net result that this particular duty to warn would be effectively negated.

AV Problem 8.2

Now consider the causal question in cases involving autonomous vehicles with operating systems that are defectively designed because the system was not subjected to a sufficient amount of premarket testing. *See* AV Problem 3.2, p. 249 *supra*. A defectively designed operating system has a higher inherent risk of crash than a reasonably designed system. How can a plaintiff prove that such a defective design caused the crash in question?

Analysis of AV Problem 8.2

The causal question is identical to the one posed by the previous problem. Importantly, the details of the particular crash do not solve the causal problem.** *See* AV Problem 3.2. Whether an autonomous vehicle "behaved" or performed reasonably depends on whether the operating system has had sufficient learning experience to drive the vehicle in a reasonably safe manner across its intended operating domain—a problem of inherent risk. Thus, if the defect does not at least double the inherent risk of crash—unlikely in these cases—then the plaintiff could never prove that the design defect, more likely than not, caused the particular crash in question.

Outside of cases in which the autonomous vehicle malfunctions, tort liability turns on the inherent risk that a fully functioning vehicle will crash. Like the duty to warn, the duty to design could be effectively eliminated by the element of causation if courts insist upon proof that the defect at least doubled the risk of crash. The evidentiary problems now characteristic of the toxic-tort litigation could plausibly extend to the crashes of autonomous vehicles.

** *Editor's Note*. Aside from the algorithm that enables the operating system to figure out how to drive based on machine learning, the coding of the system is limited to rules that constrain or guide the machine learning, such as coding that instructs the vehicle to always stop at stop signs. Aside from these rules, the operating system is like a "black box" in the sense that programmers do not specify its exact coding and "it's virtually impossible to reverse-engineer the steps the software program takes as it generates output." Hod Lipson & Melba Kurman, DRIVERLESS: INTELLIGENT CARS AND THE ROAD AHEAD 228 (2016). The driving behavior of an autonomous vehicle is based on repeated driving or learning experience, making it virtually impossible to figure out why the vehicle performed in a specific way in a specific set of circumstances. The causal problem accordingly depends on aggregate risk measures, not the particulars of the case at hand.

12

Scope of Liability: Proximate Cause

An old proverb illustrates how an isolated instance of wrongdoing can have widespread consequences:

> For want of a nail, the shoe was lost; for want of a shoe, the horse was lost; for want of a horse, the rider was lost; for want of a rider, the battle was lost; for want of a battle, the kingdom was lost; and all for the want of a horseshoe nail.

The defendant who negligently put the shoe on the horse was a factual cause of the kingdom being lost. Should he or she be liable for that loss? The question is not factual, but instead involves a policy judgment concerning the appropriate scope of liability for injuries that were factually caused by the defendant's tortious conduct.

Tort law has determined that some limitation of liability is warranted. To recover, the plaintiff must prove that the defendant's tortious act or omission was both a factual and a legal or *proximate* cause of the injuries in question. The plaintiff's failure to prove proximate cause will exculpate the defendant product seller from liability, even if the plaintiff has proven that the defect was a cause-in-fact of her injuries.

Courts have struggled to identify the policy rationales for this limitation of liability. "There is perhaps nothing in the entire field of law which has called forth more disagreement, or upon which the opinions are in such a welter of confusion." William L. Prosser, HANDBOOK OF THE LAW OF TORTS §45, at 311 (1st ed. 1941).

The difficulty stems from the interrelationships between proximate cause and other elements of the tort claim. Like the element of duty, the element of proximate cause is defined in terms of foreseeable risks. Are the two elements redundant in this regard, or does foreseeability play a distinct role in each element? And like the element of proximate cause, the element of damages requires a causal inquiry that must somehow limit the scope of the defendant's liability. Are the policy reasons for limiting the scope of liability in the prima facie case the same as those for limiting the scope of liability with respect to the determination of damages? The questions are difficult, but distinguishing among them helps to untangle the problem of proximate cause. See generally Mark A. Geistfeld, *Proximate Cause Untangled*, 80 Md. L. Rev. 419 (2021), which provides more extensive analysis of the issues this chapter addresses.

In defining the appropriate scope of liability for purposes of proximate cause, two types of approaches are possible. One is forward looking and determines proximate cause from the perspective of the reasonable person at the time of the tortious misconduct. The other approach relies on hindsight to trace the causal sequence directly backward from the injury to the defendant's misconduct. Each approach has substantial support in the case law. Should the choice between them depend on whether the cause of action is based on negligence or strict products liability?

I. THE FORESEEABILITY TEST

It is easy to understand why proximate cause should be defined in terms of foreseeable harms. As one court explained,

> it is well settled that a manufacturer has a duty to protect users of its products from foreseeable dangers. But if the danger is not foreseeable, there is no duty. In determining whether a danger is foreseeable, courts look at whether the specific danger was objectively reasonable to expect, not simply whether it was within the realm of any conceivable possibility. That which is not objectively reasonable to expect is too remote to create liability on the part of the manufacturer.

Whiteford by Whiteford v. Yamaha Motor Corp., U.S.A., 582 N.W.2d 916, 918 (Minn. 1998). Unforeseeable harms are too "remote" and therefore not proximately caused by the defect, explaining why the foreseeability test is commonly used to determine proximate cause. The harder question is how courts make that determination in a particular case.

STAZENSKI v. TENNANT CO.
Court of Appeal of Florida, First District, 1993
617 So. 2d 344

WOLF, J. Joseph Stazenski and Virginia Stazenski, his wife, appeal from a final summary judgment in favor of Tennant Company, the defendant in the trial court. The issue is whether the trial court erred in determining that the undisputed facts in the record established that there was no defect in the design or manufacture of the appellee's industrial sweeper which was the proximate cause of the accident which resulted in appellant's injuries. We find that the trial court erred in this determination; we, therefore, reverse the final summary judgment.

While employed by Fleming & Sons, the appellant, Joseph Stazenski, was involved in an industrial accident when he fell from an elevated platform/forklift

I. The Foreseeability Test

and struck his wrist on the sharp edge of an industrial sweeper which was manufactured by the appellee. The nature of the injury was a deep laceration to the wrist, injuring nerves and tendons. The appellant sued, alleging that the defect in the sweeper (the sharp edges) was a proximate cause of his injuries and that the appellee was liable for those injuries. The appellee moved for summary final judgment on the claim.

[I]t is undisputed that appellant fell from a forklift in the warehouse and eventually fell on the sweeper, cutting his wrist. The trial court also considered the affidavit and resume of a professor in mechanical engineering which indicated that the professor would qualify as an expert in product safety. The professor performed an examination of the sweeper in question and reached the following conclusions: (1) The sweeper was in essentially the same condition when it left the manufacturer as at the time of the accident; (2) the corners of the sweeper were in an unreasonably dangerous condition when it left the manufacturer; (3) the sharp edges served no utilitarian purpose and should have been rounded to reduce the foreseeable risk of serious injury. Further, he found that the exposed corner of the sweeper (location of accident/injury) was sufficiently sharp to lacerate skin upon impact and, when coupled with the fact that important tendons and nerves are in close proximity to the skin surface, within one centimeter, he opined that an injury similar to Mr. Stazenski's was reasonably foreseeable due to the defect in the machine. After hearing [this evidence], the trial court granted summary judgment, finding that there was no defect in design or manufacture which was the proximate cause of the accident which resulted in appellant's injuries.

In cases involving recovery of damages as a result of a defective product, the plaintiff must demonstrate a defect, that the party responsible for the defect owed a duty to the injured party, and the existence of a proximate causal connection between the defective condition and the injuries or damages suffered by the plaintiff. Here, the affidavit of the professor clearly created an issue of material fact concerning whether the industrial sweeper manufactured and designed by the appellee was defective. The remaining issues related to the existence of a duty and the existence of proximate causal connection.

In McCain v. Florida Power Corp., 593 So. 2d 500, 502 (Fla. 1992), the supreme court discussed the appropriate legal analysis in determining the existence of a duty and determining whether the breach of duty involved was a proximate cause of the injuries suffered by the plaintiff:

> The duty element of negligence focuses on whether the defendant's conduct foreseeably created a broader "zone of risk" that poses a general threat of harm to others. The proximate causation element, on the other hand, is concerned with whether and to what extent the defendant's conduct foreseeably and substantially caused the specific injury that actually occurred. In other words, the former is a minimal threshold *legal* requirement for opening the courthouse doors, whereas the latter is part of the much more specific *factual* requirement that must be proved to win the case once the courthouse doors are open.

The duty issue is resolved by determining whether the defendant created a generalized and foreseeable risk of harming others. [ ] If the defendant creates no greater risk by reason of his actions, then no duty of care arises. [ ] Where a product is defective, however, and that defect rises to the level of a dangerous condition, the manufacturer or designer has created a zone of risk to all parties who may come in contact with the product. [ ]

In the instant case, the affidavit of appellants' expert states that the sweeper had sharp edges which constituted an unreasonably dangerous condition for all parties who might come in contact with the edges. Much like the situation in *McCain*, where the power-generating equipment created a zone of risk for people who might foreseeably come into contact with the equipment, a zone of risk in the instant case was created for all those who might foreseeably come into contact with the sweeper's sharp edges. Tennant Company owed a duty to the appellant in this case.

The issue of proximate cause is generally one of fact which should be determined by a jury. In determining whether the action of the defendant is a proximate cause of the injury, the test is to what extent the defendant's conduct foreseeably and substantially caused the specific injury that actually occurred. As the supreme court stated in *McCain*:

> [I]t is immaterial that the defendant could not foresee the *precise* manner in which the injury occurred or its *exact* extent. RESTATEMENT (SECOND) OF TORTS §435 (1965). In such instances, the true extent of the liability would remain questions for the jury to decide.

In the instant case, it was not necessary that appellants prove that appellee should reasonably foresee that appellant would fall from a forklift onto the sharp edges, it was only necessary that it was foreseeable that a person might come into contact with the exposed sharp edges and thereby be injured. It was, therefore, up to the fact finder to determine whether the specific injury was generally foreseeable or merely an improbable freakish occurrence. The summary judgment is reversed.

NOTES AND QUESTIONS

1. *Terminology.* Courts often use the terms "legal cause" or "proximate cause" to encompass the requirements of both factual and proximate cause, creating the potential for confusion. To clarify matters, the *Restatement (Third)* rejects the label of "proximate cause" because "it is an especially poor one to describe the idea to which it is connected. . . . 'Scope of liability' . . . more accurately describes the concerns" addressed by this element. The *Restatement (Third)* then "separates factual cause from scope-of-liability limitations and, to further that end, no longer employs an umbrella term [of legal cause] to encompass both concepts." RESTATEMENT (THIRD) OF TORTS: LIABILITY FOR PHYSICAL HARM AND EMOTIONAL, CH. 6, SPECIAL NOTE ON PROXIMATE CAUSE.

2. *Behavioral underpinnings of the foreseeability test.* Why do courts define foreseeability in terms of a "zone of risk" as the *Stazenski* court put it? Consider also *Moran v. Faberge, Inc.*, p. 303 *supra*, which asked "whether the actual harm fell within a general field of danger which should have been anticipated." As the notes following the *Moran* case more fully explain, this

definition of foreseeability relies on behavioral concepts. When individuals make safety decisions concerning risky outcomes, they consider categories of causally related injuries or general fields of danger to make meaningful predictions. Consequently, a foreseeable risk refers to a general category of accidental harms or a "zone of risk" that the duty-bearer should account for when making the safety decision implicated by the allegation of liability. As one court explained in a product case, "Ostensibly, this [allegedly foreseeable risk] would suggest that [defendant] should have foreseen these events and, therefore, should have foreseen the need for [the safety precaution in question] at the time of manufacture. . . ." Gay v. O.F. Mossberg & Sons, Inc., 2009 WL 1743939, at *14 (Ohio Ct. App. 2009). By definition, a manufacturer could not account for an unforeseeable risk at the time of the safety decision, and so the tort duty excludes the risks of unforeseeable harm and absolves the manufacturer of responsibility for those harms.

3. *Foreseeability and the risk standard.* Despite its behavioral underpinnings, the meaning of "foreseeability" can be confusing for historical reasons. The early common law, for example, denied recovery for stand-alone emotional harms and pure economic losses on the ground that these injuries were too "remote" and therefore not proximately caused by the defendant's negligence. The rationale for doing so was based on policy reasons, not causal reasons. Today these policy reasons for categorically limiting liability justify a limitation of duty. The duty to exercise reasonable care, for example, now excludes certain emotional harms and pure economic losses. To avoid the historical ambiguities that linger in the concept of foreseeability, the *Restatement (Third)* drops the label "foreseeability test" in favor of the *risk standard*: "An actor's liability is limited to those harms that result from the risks that made the actor's conduct tortious." RESTATEMENT (THIRD) OF TORTS: LIABILITY FOR PHYSICAL HARM AND EMOTIONAL §29. "When properly understood and framed, the foreseeability standard is congruent with the risk standard. . . ." *Id.* cmt. e. Nevertheless, the risk standard "is preferable because it provides greater clarity, facilitates clearer analysis in a given case, and better reveals the reason for its existence." *Id.* cmt. j.

Would the *Stazenski* court's analysis of proximate cause have been more clear if it had relied on the risk standard rather than the foreseeability test? The risk standard requires courts to answer the predicate question: What are the risks that made the defendant's conduct tortious? That question is answered by the *Stazenski* court's formulation of the foreseeability test: The duty-bearer must account for the categories of accidental harms foreseeably threatened by the risky behavior, and so those are the risks that made the defendant's conduct tortious. When foreseeability is defined in this more limited, behavioral manner, it clarifies the inquiry. For good reason, most courts describe the inquiry in terms of foreseeability.

4. *The role of foreseeability in duty and proximate cause.* Duty is defined by "relatively clear, categorical, bright-line rules of law applicable to a general class of cases." *Id.* §7 cmt. a. Rules applicable to a general class of cases are questions of law decided by judges, including the rule that the duty is limited to the risks of foreseeable harm for *all* cases governed by the duty. Foreseeability in this respect is only a general limitation of liability that

fundamentally differs from its case-specific application. Individual cases turn on their particular facts, requiring case-by-case determinations of whether the plaintiff suffered a foreseeable harm that is within the general class of foreseeable harms governed by the duty. The prima facie case of liability accordingly depends on a case-specific inquiry into foreseeability, explaining why "virtually all jurisdictions employ a foreseeability (or risk) standard for some range" of proximate cause issues. *Id.* §29 cmts. e, j.

As applied to the forklift in *Stazenski*, for example, the general category of foreseeable accidental harm was "that a person might come into contact with the exposed sharp edges and thereby be injured" by the defect. This foreseeable risk of harm is then encompassed by the duty to design—it defines the "risk" term in the risk-utility test for evaluating this aspect of the product design. Once the plaintiff proved that the forklift design was defective for not having reduced or eliminated this foreseeable risk, he then needed to show that a risk of this type caused his injury. This proof depended on the particular circumstances of the accident, explaining why proximate cause is a case-specific issue to be resolved by the jury.

5. *Foreseeable harms and coincidental harms.* What types of contacts, if any, would be excluded from the foreseeable risk "that a person might come into contact with the exposed sharp edges and thereby be injured" by the defect? In Whiteford by Whiteford v. Yamaha Motor Corp., U.S.A., 582 N.W.2d 916 (Minn. 1998), a five-year-old child tobogganed head first down a hill and slammed into "the leading edge of a metal bracket on the underside" of a Snoscoot snowmobile manufactured by defendant Yamaha, causing him severe facial injuries. After citing numerous cases in which courts had dismissed similar claims involving plaintiffs who crashed into stationary vehicles, the court dismissed plaintiffs' claims, including those alleging defective design and warnings:

> Yamaha's duty was to protect the Snoscoot's users, along with those who might be injured by its use or misuse, from foreseeable danger. Here, [plaintiff] was not using the Snoscoot. Further, while the Snoscoot was in "use" in the limited sense that [plaintiff's older brother] had been riding it on the afternoon in question and had placed it in the spot where [plaintiff] slid into it, the Snoscoot was stationary and not being operated at the time of the accident.... As in [prior cases involving similar circumstances], the danger here was too remote to impose a duty on Yamaha and was not one which Yamaha was required to anticipate or protect against.

Id. at 919.

The dissent took issue with the majority's characterization of the crash:

> In contrast to the parked car precedents... on which the majority relies, this junior-size snowmobile was not parked and unattended. It is undisputed that the driver was still sitting on the snowmobile at the time of the accident, although there is disputed evidence as to whether the Snoscoot's engine was on or off at the time of the accident. It was quite foreseeable that other winter recreational activities such as tobogganing may have been taking place near the snowmobile.

Id. at 920 (Gilberg, J., dissenting).

I. The Foreseeability Test

Was the defective industrial sweeper in *Stazenski* being used at the time of the accident? Does foreseeability depend on that fact alone? Consider Salazar v. Wolo Mfg. Co., 983 S.W.2d 87, 89 (Tex Ct. App. 1998) ("Instead of looking only at whether the product was being used or not being used, the cases appear to look at whether the product was unreasonably dangerous as designed or marketed, and whether the use was intended or foreseeable.").

Although the opinions did not frame the issue in this manner, the disagreement between the majority and the dissent in *Whiteford* centers on the question whether the allegedly defective design was only coincidentally connected to the plaintiff's injury instead of significantly increasing the risk of such injury. *See* Dan B. Dobbs, Paul T. Hayden & Ellen M. Bublick, THE LAW OF TORTS §205 (2d ed. 2020 update) ("When courts say that such a risk is unforeseeable what they mean is that it is not a risk enhanced or created by the defendant's conduct.").

This issue often arises in cases where a third-party's negligence or other form of tortious behavior caused the plaintiff's injuries. For example, in Simler v. Dubuque Paint Equip. Servs., 942 F.3d 448 (8th Cir. 2019), the defendant negligently caused a crash. Traffic then backed up on the freeway, and eight minutes later and one-half mile down the road, a third-party who was negligently speeding crashed into the rear of plaintiff's vehicle. Was this crash coincidentally connected to the defendant's earlier negligence? The court concluded that the negligent speeding by the other driver was not foreseeable. It then recognized that "[t]he analysis is different, however, if the initial act increases the likelihood that others will act negligently." *Id.* at 451. Could a defective product ever increase the risk that third parties will engage in negligent or other forms of tortious behavior?

IN RE SEPTEMBER 11 LITIGATION
United States District Court, Southern District of New York, 2003
280 F. Supp. 2d 279

HELLERSTEIN, J. The injured, and the representatives of the thousands who died from the terrorist-related aircraft crashes of September 11, 2001, are entitled to seek compensation. By act of Congress, they may seek compensation by filing claims with a Special Master established pursuant to the Air Transportation Safety and System Stabilization Act of 2001 (codified at 49 U.S.C. §40101). Or they may seek compensation in the traditional manner, by alleging and proving their claims in lawsuits, with the aggregate of their damages capped at the limits of defendants' liability insurance.

Approximately seventy of the injured and representatives of those who died, and ten entities which sustained property damage, have chosen to bring lawsuits against defendants whom they claim are legally responsible to compensate them[, including the Boeing Company, the manufacturer of the "757" jets that were flown into the Pentagon (on American Flight 77) and the field near Shanksville, Pennsylvania (on United Flight 93). The claims against Boeing allege strict products liability, negligence, and breach of warranty for failing to design the cockpit doors and accompanying locks in a manner that would prevent hijackers and/or passengers from accessing the cockpit. These claims are respectively governed by Virginia and Pennsylvania law, the location of the two crashes.]

[With respect to the claims based on American Airlines Flight 77,] Virginia does not permit recovery on a strict liability theory in product liability cases. Boeing moves to dismiss both the claims of negligent design and breach of warranty, arguing that it did not owe a duty to prevent the use of the plane as a weapon, and that the independent and supervening acts of the terrorists, not Boeing's acts, caused the injuries of the plaintiffs.

Boeing argues that its design of the cockpit was not unreasonably dangerous in relation to reasonably foreseeable risks, and that the risk of death to passengers and ground victims caused by a terrorist hijacking was not reasonably foreseeable. The record at this point does not support Boeing's argument. There have been many efforts by terrorists to hijack airplanes, and too many have been successful. The practice of terrorists to blow themselves up in order to kill as many people as possible has also been prevalent. Although there have been no incidents before the ones of September 11, 2001 where terrorists combined both an airplane hijacking and a suicidal explosion, I am not able to say that the risk of crashes was not reasonably foreseeable to an airplane manufacturer. Plaintiffs have alleged that it was reasonably foreseeable that a failure to design a secure cockpit could contribute to a breaking and entering into, and a takeover of, a cockpit by hijackers or other unauthorized individuals, substantially increasing the risk of injury and death to people and damage to property. I hold that the allegation is sufficient to establish Boeing's duty.

Boeing next argues that its design of the cockpit doors on its "757" passenger aircraft, even if held to constitute an "unreasonably dangerous condition," was not the proximate cause of plaintiffs' injuries. Boeing argues that the criminal acts of the terrorists in hijacking the airplanes and using the airplanes as weapons of mass destruction constituted an "efficient intervening cause" which broke the "natural and continuous sequence" of events flowing from Boeing's allegedly inadequate design. [ ] Plaintiffs have the burden to prove proximate cause and, generally, the issue is a question of fact to be resolved by a jury. However, when reasonable people cannot differ, the issue becomes a question of law for the court.

The record at this point does not support Boeing's argument that the invasion and take-over of the cockpit by the terrorists must, as a matter of law, be held to constitute an "efficient intervening act" that breaks the "natural and continuous sequence" flowing from Boeing's allegedly inadequate design. Plaintiffs allege that Boeing should have designed its cockpit door to prevent hijackers from invading the cockpit, that acts of terrorism, including hijackings of airplanes, were reasonably foreseeable, and that the lives of passengers, crew and ground victims would be imminently in danger from such hijackings. Virginia law does not require Boeing to have foreseen precisely how the injuries suffered on September 11, 2001 would be caused, as long as Boeing could reasonably have foreseen that "some injury" from its negligence "might probably result."
[ ] Given the critical nature of the cockpit area, and the inherent danger of crash when a plane is in flight, one cannot say that Boeing could not reasonably have foreseen the risk flowing from an inadequately constructed cockpit door.

I. The Foreseeability Test 533

[T]he danger that a plane could crash if unauthorized individuals invaded and took over the cockpit was the very risk that Boeing should reasonably have foreseen. "Privacy" within a cockpit means very little if the door intended to provide security is not designed to keep out potential intruders.

Boeing's citation to cases in other jurisdictions, Port Authority of N.Y. and N.J. v. Arcadian Corp., 189 F.3d 305 (3d Cir. 1999), and Gaines-Tabb v. ICI Explosives USA, Inc., 160 F.3d 613 (10th Cir 1998), are distinguishable. The courts of appeals in both cases addressed the question of causation and held that defendants' actions or inactions were not the "legal proximate cause" of the injuries suffered by the victims of the 1993 World Trade Center and 1995 Oklahoma City bombings. They ruled that the manufacturers of the fertilizer products utilized in the attacks, having made lawful and economically and socially useful fertilizer products, did not have to anticipate that criminals would misappropriate ingredients, mix them with others, and make bombs to bring down a building. The bomb-making by the terrorists were found to be superseding and intervening events and were not natural or probable consequences of any design defect in defendants' products.

In re Korean Air Lines Disaster of September 1, 1983, 1985 WL 9447 (D.D.C. 1985), involved lawsuits by the legal successors of passengers who died when Korean Airlines passenger flight 007 was shot down by Russian fighter planes. The passenger plane had flown off course and over a sensitive military zone in Russia. Russian fighter pilots intercepted the plane and, instead of following international protocol for causing the plane to return to international routes over the high seas or to land at a selected landing field, shot it down. Plaintiffs sued Boeing, the manufacturer of the airplane, alleging that a product defect in its navigation systems caused it to fly off course and over Soviet territory, and that Boeing's improper and unsafe design was therefore the proximate cause of plaintiffs' damages. The court dismissed the complaint, holding that Boeing could not foresee that the Soviet Union would destroy an intruding aircraft in violation of international conventions, and had no ability to guard against such conduct. The court held, consequently, that Boeing did not owe a duty to passengers with respect to such risks, and that the actions of the Russian pilots were independent and supervening causes that broke the chain of causation.

These three cases do not offer Boeing much support in its motion. In each, the acts of the third-parties were held to be superseding causes because they were not reasonably foreseeable to the product manufacturer. In *Gaines-Tabb* and *Arcadian*, the courts of appeals held that the fertilizer manufacturers could not reasonably foresee that terrorists would mix their products with other ingredients to create explosives to cause buildings to collapse and occupants to be killed. In *KAL*, the court held that the manufacturer of airplane navigational systems could not reasonably foresee that a passenger aircraft that strayed off course would be shot down by hostile military forces in violation of international conventions. In the cases before me, however, plaintiffs allege that Boeing could reasonably have foreseen that terrorists would try to invade the cockpits of airplanes, and that easy success on their part, because cockpit doors were not designed to prevent easy opening, would be imminently dangerous to passengers, crew and ground victims.

Plaintiffs' allegations that duty and proximate cause existed cannot be dismissed as a matter of law on the basis of the record now before me. Accordingly,

I deny Boeing's motion to dismiss the complaints against it arising from the crash of flight 77 into the Pentagon [and] from the crash of flight 93 into Shanksville.

NOTES AND QUESTIONS

1. *Is the concept of a foreseeable or tortious risk adequately determinate?* According to the court, "Virginia law does not require Boeing to have foreseen precisely how the injuries suffered on September 11, 2001 would be caused, as long as Boeing could reasonably have foreseen that 'some injury' from its negligence 'might probably result.'" Is the court defining the foreseeable or tortious risk too broadly? After all, the most expansive definition is "the risk of harm," which establishes proximate cause anytime the defendant was a factual cause of the injury. This characterization of the tortious risk effectively eliminates proximate cause as an additional limitation of liability, making it too broad. On the other hand, the court is surely correct that a defendant need not foresee the precise details of the accident. After all, the most restrictive definition of a foreseeable risk includes all details of the accident, turning the tortious risk into the prospect that the particular plaintiff would suffer the particular injury at a particular time on a particular date at a particular location. This characterization effectively requires omniscience, an unrealistic behavioral obligation far more demanding than foreseeability. Between these two extremes lies the appropriate characterization of the tortious risk, something the court tried to capture in its description of the inquiry.

"No rule can be provided about the appropriate level of generality or specificity to employ in characterizing the type of harm for purposes" of establishing proximate cause. RESTATEMENT (THIRD) OF TORTS: LIABILITY FOR PHYSICAL AND EMOTIONAL HARM §29 cmt. i. Does the lack of such a rule make the inquiry inherently indeterminate, thereby preventing the foreseeability test from serving as a defensible limitation of liability? According to the U.S. Supreme Court, "If one takes a broad enough view, *all* consequences of a negligent act, no matter how far removed in time or space, may be foreseen. Conditioning liability on foreseeability, therefore, is hardly a condition at all." Consol. Rail Corp. v. Gottshall, 512 U.S. 532, 553 (1994) (emphasis in original).

Does reasonable foreseeability require sellers to expend unlimited time and resources to consider every possible way in which their products might cause harm? Is this how the court applied the concept in *September 11 Litigation*, or did foreseeability play a more meaningful role in the court's analysis of proximate cause? What about the other cases in this section?

2. *Characterizing the tortious risk.* A duty limited to the risks of foreseeable harm necessarily absolves a defendant from responsibility—and thus liability—for any harm that is entirely unforeseeable. Whether based on negligence or strict liability, the prima facie case for products liability accordingly requires proof that the plaintiff suffered some foreseeable compensable harm, like bodily injury, caused by the type of risk that rendered the product defective. In these circumstances, the defendant's "liability is limited to those harms that result from the risks that made

the [defendant's] conduct tortious," thereby satisfying the element of proximate cause. RESTATEMENT (THIRD) OF TORTS: LIABILITY FOR PHYSICAL AND EMOTIONAL HARM §29.

The appropriate characterization of the foreseeable or tortious risk accordingly depends on the safety decision implicated by the allegation of liability. In *September 11 Litigation*, the manufacturer's safety decision was whether the cockpit doors should be secured to prevent unauthorized access. Such access would create a risk of foreseeable harm only if those who entered the cockpit without authorization could somehow cause the plane to crash. The most obvious threat in this regard involves hijackers, so the tortious risk encompassed the threat that hijackers would cause injury by crashing the plane. The crash does not need to be accidental, because hijackers have intentionally harmed individuals, including themselves. Consequently, the terrorist's intentional crashing of the airplanes on September 11 was a particular instantiation of the more general tortious risk of foreseeable harm created by the alleged breach of the airplane manufacturer's duty to design secure cockpit doors.*

The duty in *Stazenski*, by contrast, presumably did not encompass the risk that someone would intentionally harm another with the defectively designed sharp edges of the machine, as in the hypothetical case of two coworkers fighting each other, with one intentionally shoving the other onto the machine. In such a case, the general risk of intentional harm would not be increased by the defect. As the court in *Stazenski* observed, "If the defendant creates no greater risk by reason of his actions, then no duty of care exists." The defendant's duty to design the machine in *Stazenski* would not encompass the coincidental occurrence of intentional harms. Consequently, an intentional injury in *Stazenski* would be unforeseeable and outside the scope of liability—the defect would not be a proximate cause of the injury—unlike the intentional injuries in *September 11 Litigation*.

3. *Easy cases and hard cases of foreseeability.* Does the behavioral formulation of the foreseeability test depend on jurors sharing identical conceptions of the "general field of danger which should have been anticipated"? Different jurors can define this "general field" differently and yet still agree about the foreseeability of a particular outcome when their different conceptions overlap. Individual differences of this type explain why a conclusion about foreseeability can be easy or obvious in some cases and controversial in others.

As a behavioral matter, the "general field of danger" that defines a foreseeable or tortious risk is comprised of the categories of accidental harms that would enable the risky actor to make meaningful predictions about the effect of the safety precaution in question. Put differently, this "general field" refers to a reference class that individuals use to compute the probability that a given outcome will occur. For example, the reference class of "coin tosses" is a set of outcomes for which the flip of the same

---

* In the interest of full disclosure, I provided legal advice on this matter for the plaintiffs, so my role in that capacity might have biased this discussion.—ED.

coin is governed by the same set of causal conditions. Based on the relative frequency of heads and tails within this reference class of causally related outcomes, one can then derive a probability assessment that any given toss will be heads or tails. The reference classes that generate probability assessments are based on causal models that employ the same type of categorical reasoning embodied in the behavioral conception of foreseeability.

The concept of reference classes helps to explain why individuals can reach the same conclusions about foreseeability, even if they do not define the associated "general field of danger" in the identical manner. To see why, consider the following example:

> In some cases, damages resulting from misconduct are so typical that judge and jurors cannot possibly be convinced that they were unforeseeable. If Mr Builder negligently drops a brick on Mr Pedestrian who is passing an urban site of a house under construction, even though the dent in Pedestrian's skull is microscopically unique in pattern, Builder could not sensibly maintain that the injury was unforeseeable.

Clarence Morris, TORTS 174-177 (1953).

The argument of Builder is a clear loser because it relies on a causal model or reference class for computing probabilities that incorporates too much detail from the case at hand. Such an excessive overfit of the data is inherently lacking in adequate predictive value: "overfitted models capture not only the relationship of interest, but also the random errors or fluctuations that inevitably accompany real world data." Edward K. Cheng, *A Practical Solution to the Reference Class Problem*, 109 Colum. L. Rev. 2081, 2092 (2009). When the causal model or reference class for predicting whether a dropped brick will hit someone on the street below depends on the microscopically unique pattern of the individual's skull, the inherent variation in that factor will produce unnecessary random errors across cases — it "makes more errors in predicting . . . than a simpler model that ignores the noise." *Id.* at 2093. Builder's argument that foreseeability depends on the unique pattern of the plaintiff's skull is easily rejected on the ground that the reasonable person would make predictions about possible harms by relying on a simpler causal model that ignores this detail.

So, too, if the plaintiff argues that foreseeability is simply defined by the occurrence of physical harm, that argument is also a clear loser for the opposite reason: It depends on a causal model or reference class that obviously underfits the data in the case at hand. "Too simple a model will fail to identify the underlying relationship and have low predictive accuracy." *Id.*

As these examples illustrate, the choice of the appropriate reference class for computing probabilities involves a trade-off "between fit and complexity"—the need to track the limited data that are available while also abstracting away from the details to simplify the causal model in the hope of enhancing predictive accuracy for future cases. *Id.* at 2093-2094. Statisticians rely on different criteria for evaluating this trade-off, and lay individuals like jurors presumably do the same. A hard or contested case of foreseeability, therefore, involves instances in which jurors disagree about the appropriate trade-off and rely on different reference classes that lead to differing conclusions about risk and foreseeability in the case at hand.

Because there is no single best method for determining the optimal specification of a reference class, the jury is particularly well suited for applying the behavioral conception of foreseeability to determine both breach and proximate cause. "[D]eciding what is reasonably foreseeable involves common sense, common experience, and application of the standards and behavioral norms of the community—matters that have long been understood to be uniquely the province of the finder of fact." A.W. v. Lancaster Cnty. Sch. Dist. 0001, 784 N.W.2d 907, 914 (Neb. 2010). The foreseeability test is not inherently indeterminate, even though "[n]o rule can be provided about the appropriate level of generality or specificity to employ in characterizing the type of harm for purposes" of establishing proximate cause. RESTATEMENT (THIRD) OF TORTS: LIABILITY FOR PHYSICAL HARM AND EMOTIONAL §29 cmt. i.

4. *Intervening causes.* For cases in which the plaintiff's harm was caused by a third-party actor, particularly one engaged in criminal behavior (like the terrorists on September 11), courts ask whether the third-party conduct was an intervening force that cuts off the defendant's causal responsibility for the harm.

> By and large external forces will be regarded as intervening if they appear on the scene after the defendant had acted unless perhaps their pending inevitability at the time of the defendant's negligent act or omission is made crystal clear. And when a new force (for which the defendant is not responsible) "intervenes" in this crude sense to bring about a result that the defendant's [tortious risk] would not otherwise have produced, the defendant is generally held [liable] for that result only where the intervening force was foreseeable. As many cases put it, a new and unforeseeable force [commonly called a "superseding cause"] breaks the causal chain.

Fowler V. Harper, Fleming James, Jr. & Oscar S. Gray, 4 HARPER, JAMES, AND GRAY ON TORTS §20.5 (3d ed. 2006-2007 & 2020 update).

For example, the third-party criminal conduct in *September 11 Litigation* was not a superseding cause because that conduct was foreseeable, whereas in our hypothetical case of a coworker who intentionally caused plaintiff's harm by smashing his head on the sharp edges of the machine in *Stazenski*, the third-party's criminal conduct would be a superseding cause that cuts off the manufacturer's liability for the defective design.

When proximate cause is determined by the foreseeability test, the concept of an intervening force does not aide the analysis—the defendant's liability is necessarily limited to the risks of foreseeable harm. The concept of an intervening force instead has independent significance for backward-looking tests that trace a direct causal sequence from the injury back to the tortious conduct.

II. BACKWARD-LOOKING TESTS

UNION PUMP v. ALBRITTON
Supreme Court of Texas, 1995
898 S.W.2d 773

OWEN, J. The issue in this case is whether the condition, act, or omission of which a personal injury plaintiff complains was, as a matter of law, too remote to constitute legal causation. Plaintiff brought suit alleging negligence, gross negligence, and strict liability, and the trial court granted summary judgment for the defendant. The court of appeals reversed and remanded, holding that the plaintiff raised issues of fact concerning proximate and producing cause. Because we conclude that there was no legal causation as a matter of law, we reverse the judgment of the court of appeals and render judgment that plaintiff take nothing.

On the night of September 4, 1989, a fire occurred at Texaco Chemical Company's facility in Port Arthur, Texas. A pump manufactured by Union Pump Company caught fire and ignited the surrounding area. This particular pump had caught on fire twice before. Sue Allbritton, a trainee employee of Texaco Chemical, had just finished her shift and was about to leave the plant when the fire erupted. She and her supervisor Felipe Subia, Jr., were directed to and did assist in abating the fire.

Approximately two hours later, the fire was extinguished. However, there appeared to be a problem with a nitrogen purge valve, and Subia was instructed to block in the valve. Viewing the facts in a light most favorable to Allbritton, there was some evidence that an emergency situation existed at that point in time. Allbritton asked if she could accompany Subia and was allowed to do so. To get to the nitrogen purge valve, Allbritton followed Subia over an aboveground pipe rack, which was approximately two and one-half feet high, rather than going around it. It is undisputed that this was not the safer route, but it was the shorter one. Upon reaching the valve, Subia and Allbritton were notified that it was not necessary to block it off. Instead of returning by the route around the pipe rack, Subia chose to walk across it, and Allbritton followed. Allbritton was injured when she hopped or slipped off the pipe rack. There is evidence that the pipe rack was wet because of the fire and that Allbritton and Subia were still wearing fireman's hip boots and other firefighting gear when the injury occurred. Subia admitted that he chose to walk over the pipe rack rather than taking a safer alternative route because he had a "bad habit" of doing so.

Allbritton sued Union Pump, alleging negligence, gross negligence, and strict liability theories of recovery, and accordingly, that the defective pump was a proximate or producing cause of her injuries. But for the pump fire, she asserts, she would never have walked over the pipe rack, which was wet with water or firefighting foam.

Following discovery, Union Pump moved for summary judgment. The question before this Court is whether Union Pump established as a matter of law that neither its conduct nor its product was a legal cause of Allbritton's injuries. Stated another way, was Union Pump correct in contending that there was no

II. Backward-Looking Tests

causative link between the defective pump and Allbritton's injuries as a matter of law?

Negligence requires a showing of proximate cause, while producing cause is the test in strict liability. Proximate and producing cause differ in that foreseeability is an element of proximate cause, but not of producing cause. Proximate cause consists of both cause in fact and foreseeability. Cause in fact means that the defendant's act or omission was a substantial factor in bringing about the injury which would not otherwise have occurred. A producing cause is "an efficient, exciting, or contributing cause, which in a natural sequence, produced injuries or damages complained of, if any." [ ] Common to both proximate and producing cause is causation in fact, including the requirement that the defendant's conduct or product be a substantial factor in bringing about the plaintiff's injuries.

Drawing the line between where legal causation may exist and where, as a matter of law, it cannot, has generated a considerable body of law. Legal cause is not established if the defendant's conduct or product does no more than furnish the condition that makes the plaintiff's injury possible. This principle applies with equal force to proximate cause and producing cause.

Even if the pump fire were in some sense a "philosophic" or "but for" cause of Allbritton's injuries, the forces generated by the fire had come to rest when she fell off the pipe rack. The fire had been extinguished, and Allbritton was walking away from the scene. Viewing the evidence in the light most favorable to Allbritton, the pump fire did no more than create the condition that made Allbritton's injuries possible. We conclude that the circumstances surrounding her injuries are too remotely connected with Union Pump's conduct or pump to constitute a legal cause of her injuries.

Accordingly, we reverse the judgment of the court of appeals and render judgment that plaintiff take nothing.

CORNYN, J., *concurring.* I concur in the Court's judgment, but for different reasons than those given in its opinion. I would hold that although the defective pump was a cause-in-fact of Sue Allbritton's injury, neither Union Pump's negligence nor the defective pump was a legal cause of her injury. Because the Court's opinion conflates foreseeability and other policy issues with its cause-in-fact analysis, I do not join its opinion. The Court's approach is not without precedent; however, I believe this expansive view of cause-in-fact obscures a proper causal analysis, and that this case presents an opportunity to clarify that analysis.

A few words about the historical development of causation analysis in American jurisprudence provide a helpful context. Throughout much of the nineteenth century, the doctrine of objective causation was the predominant theory of causation. This doctrine posited that through proper analysis, judges could scientifically determine which act in a series of events actually caused the plaintiff's injury. "Proximate cause" was one of the basic expressions of this doctrine, along with "the notion of a distinction between 'proximate' cause and 'remote' cause." [ ] Implicit was the belief that one cause would prove to be the scientific proximate cause, and the single responsible defendant would be identified and held legally accountable.

By the turn of the century, the doctrine of objective causation was subject to serious criticism. Oliver Wendell Holmes, Jr., and Leon Green, along with other members of the Legal Realist movement, argued that "because judges and jurists inevitably imported moral ideas into their determinations of legal causation, they were making discretionary policy determinations under the guise of doing science." [ ] By the 1930s, the Realists' influence was felt in American law by the innovation of a new "distinction between actual or 'but for' causation, on the one hand, and legal or proximate causation, on the other." [ ] For the Realists, cause-in-fact was a purely factual inquiry, while proximate cause was a policy determination that legal responsibility for damages should not be limitless.

Despite broad support for this approach during the first half of the twentieth century, the terminology used by Green and other Realists was not embraced by the American Law Institute in its first *Restatement of Torts*. Instead, the *Restatement* adopted a more general approach to causation under the banner of "legal cause":

> In order that a particular act or omission may be the legal cause of an invasion of another's interest, the act or omission must be a *substantial factor* in bringing about the harm and there must be no principle or rule of law which restricts the actor's liability because of the manner in which the act or omission operates to bring about such invasion.

RESTATEMENT OF TORTS §9 cmt. b (1934) (emphasis added). Under this definition, the "substantial factor" requirement served a similar role to cause-in-fact, but it was not the purely factual inquiry that the Realists had proposed. This refusal to adopt a bifurcated view paved the way for continued debate on proper causal analysis, although the leading treatise writers of the period appeared to adopt the Realist view.

More recently, the Legal Realists' bifurcated approach has itself come under attack. The primary conflict arose from the Realists' attempt to separate the fact-based cause-in-fact analysis from the policy-driven proximate cause analysis. [S]ome academics insisted that "both inquiries simply camouflage ad hoc policy decisions on ultimate liability," while others insisted that "the two inquiries are merely different steps in the ultimate attribution of responsibility based on commonsense 'causal' principles." [ ] This new generation of legal thinkers has generally sought to replace the bifurcated analysis with a flexible, single-step analysis that could be adapted to the relevant issues in any case. Even the later revisions of Prosser's famous treatise, albeit after Prosser's death, retreated from the bifurcated fact/policy analysis that Prosser had championed, and opined that the cause-in-fact determination was policy dependent, and proximate cause was, at least in part, fact-laden. These debates continue today, and the precise content and structure of the causal analysis is, to say the least, unsettled.

The foregoing discussion may help to illuminate the development of causation analysis in Texas law. In negligence, early Texas courts used the term "proximate cause" for the entire causal inquiry, in keeping with the doctrine of objective causation. More recently, this Court has used the Realists' bifurcated causal analysis in negligence law, in which proximate cause is viewed as consisting of two elements: "cause-in-fact" and "foreseeability." [ ] Even more recently, we have perhaps demonstrated the pervasive influence of post-Realist scholars, describing the cause-in-fact analysis as requiring satisfaction of both the "but for" and the "substantial factor" tests.

II. Backward-Looking Tests

This evolution of Texas law, paralleling developments throughout the United States, has caused two particular areas of uncertainty relevant to the case at hand. First, Texas law is unclear as to what degree (if any) it has retreated from the fact/policy delineation in its two-prong causal analysis. While the Court's opinion today appears to reject this bifurcated analysis, I believe that it remains an important and useful part of Texas law. Second, our cases have never clearly defined how the second prong of its proximate cause analysis in negligence cases applies to the producing cause analysis of products liability law. *The Court's opinion undertakes only one analysis, thereby implying that causation in negligence and causation in products liability are treated the same.* To the contrary, I contend that, like the limitations imposed by foreseeability in negligence law, the second part of a complete causal analysis in products liability law imposes policy-oriented limitations consistent with the underlying purposes of products liability law itself.

This case does not present a question of cause-in-fact. The pump defect clearly was a "but for" cause of Allbritton's injuries: assuming the truth of Allbritton's allegations, as we must in this summary judgment case, if the pump had not been defective, there would have been no fire, and Allbritton would have gone home uninjured at the end of her shift.

But determining that the defect was the cause-in-fact of Allbritton's injuries does not end the inquiry. We must decide whether the pump defect meets the second prong of both proximate cause and producing cause. In proximate cause, this other element is foreseeability, but it also incorporates policy driven decisions such as when subsequent events will be treated as intervening causes. In this case, the injury to Allbritton was not foreseeable. Allbritton's injuries were the result of a needlessly dangerous shortcut taken after the crisis had subsided. Holding Union Pump liable for Allbritton's failure to use proper care in exiting the area of the fire after the crisis has ended is akin to holding it liable for an auto accident she suffered on the way home, even though the accident probably would not have occurred had she left after her normal shift. Foreseeability allows us to cut off Union Pump's liability at some point; I would do so at the point the crisis had abated or at the point that Allbritton and Subia departed from their usual, safe path.

For similar reasons, Allbritton's products liability claim—which hinges on producing cause rather than proximate cause—also fails. The "other element" of producing cause limits Union Pump's liability to the types of injuries that flow naturally from the use of a defective product. Under this standard, liability for a product defect extends only to the damages occurring in a natural and continuous sequence from the use of the defective product, whether to those who use the product or those who are exposed to danger when the defect becomes manifest.

There are two potential applications of this standard to Allbritton, both of which lead to the conclusion that the product defect was not the producing cause of Allbritton's injuries. First, Allbritton's injuries did not occur in a "natural and continuous sequence" from the defect. While the fire was certainly part of such a sequence, as were the efforts to extinguish the fire, Allbritton's injuries occurred after these events had subsided. At the time of her injury, she was simply exiting the area and in doing so unnecessarily chose to take a precarious shortcut across the pipe rack. Under these circumstances, Allbritton's injuries did not flow in a natural and continuous sequence from the pump failure.

Additionally, from the facts in this record, it does not appear that Allbritton was within the scope of protection intended by products liability law. Certainly, Allbritton was within such scope when she was directly addressing problems flowing directly from the fire's existence. But when this task was completed, she re-entered the area to check a valve, completed her assignment, and was exiting the area when she was injured. When undertaking such activities, Allbritton was no longer within the scope of the protection of products liability law. Accordingly, Union Pump's liability should not extend to the injuries that she suffered.

Regardless of whether the Court agrees with my analysis of proximate and producing cause, by forcing the policy-based limitations on claims into the cause-in-fact analysis without a clear accounting of its reasoning, the Court unnecessarily perpetuates confusion in this fundamental area of the law. For these reasons, I concur in the Court's judgment but do not join its opinion.

NOTES AND QUESTIONS

1. *Causal terminology in Texas.* As the dissent explains, the court's definition of "proximate cause" in negligence cases combines both cause-in-fact with the inquiry into legal causation that limits the scope of liability to foreseeable harms. In other jurisdictions, courts would instead say that cause-in-fact is determined by the but-for or substantial-factor test, with legal or proximate cause then determined by the foreseeability test—the inquiry we addressed in the last section. Similarly, the court's definition of "producing cause" in cases of strict products liability is rather idiosyncratic; other jurisdictions would instead say that cause-in-fact is determined by the but-for or substantial-factor test, with legal or proximate cause then determined by the directness or direct-consequences test—the inquiry we now consider.

2. *The directness test.* According to the court in *Union Pump*, a producing cause is "an efficient, exciting, or contributing cause, which in a natural sequence, produced injuries or damages complained of." This formulation of legal cause is typically called the *direct consequences* or *directness test* of proximate cause. *See* David G. Owen, PRODUCTS LIABILITY LAW §12.2, at 752 (3d ed. 2015) (stating that under "the 'direct consequences test' . . . proximate cause is defined as a cause which, in natural and continuous sequence, unbroken by any efficient, intervening cause, produces the plaintiff's harm," and that a "variation on this standard is the 'natural and probable consequences' test").

For purposes of this inquiry, the defendant's tortious behavior does not directly cause injury when a force intervenes between the misconduct and the ensuing harm. "By and large external forces will be regarded as intervening if they appear on the scene after the defendant had acted unless perhaps their pending inevitability at the time" when the defendant committed the tortious act. "And when a new force (for which the defendant is not responsible) 'intervenes' in this crude sense . . . , the defendant is generally held

II. Backward-Looking Tests

[liable] for that result only where the intervening force was foreseeable. As many cases put it, a new and unforeseeable force breaks the causal chain." Fowling V. Harper, Fleming James, Jr. & Oscar S. Gray, HARPER, JAMES & GRAY ON TORTS §20.5 (3d ed. 2006-2007 & 2020 update). A new and unforeseeable intervening force that breaks the causal chain between the defendant's negligence and the plaintiff's harm is called a *superceding cause* because it negates liability by cutting off or superceding the defendant's prior tortious act. *See, e.g.*, Exxon Co., U.S.A. v. Sofec, Inc., 517 U.S. 830, 835 (1996).

3. *Conceptualizing the causal inquiry.* In effect, the directness test asks whether the plaintiff's injury can be directly traced back to the defendant's tortious conduct. A major problem with the inquiry is that it depends on terms such as directness, intervening forces, remoteness, risks coming to rest, and so on. "These terms are only conclusory labels. A reasoning and normative process is required in order to separate background causes from intervening forces and to decide which intervening forces under what circumstances are superceding, thus avoiding the liability of an actor who engaged in tortious conduct." RESTATEMENT (THIRD) OF TORTS: LIABILITY FOR PHYSICAL AND EMOTIONAL HARM §34 cmt. b. For the backward-looking inquiry required by the direct consequences test, what is the appropriate form of reasoning and normative inquiry? Does *Union Pump* provide adequate guidance on the matter?

In a subsequent case, the Texas Supreme Court abrogated its prior holding in *Union Pump* in the following respects:

> [T]o say that a producing cause is "an efficient, exciting, or contributing cause that, in a natural sequence, produces the incident in question" is incomplete and, more importantly, provides little concrete guidance to the jury. Juries must ponder the meaning of "efficient" and "exciting" in this context. These adjectives are foreign to modern English language as a means to describe a cause, and offer little practical help to a jury striving to make the often difficult causation determination in a products case.
>
> Defining producing cause as being a substantial factor in bringing about an injury, and without which the injury would not have occurred, is easily understood and conveys the essential components of producing cause that (1) the cause must be a substantial cause of the event in issue and (2) it must be a but-for cause, namely one without which the event would not have occurred. This is the definition that should be given in the jury charge.

Ford Motor Co. v. Ledesma, 242 S.W.3d 32, 46 (Tex. 2007). Does this reformulation clarify the nature of the causal inquiry? How would it have applied in *Union Pump*?

4. *Foreseeability yet again.* Under the directness test, the defendant is liable both for direct consequences, whether foreseeable or not, and for any indirect consequences (produced by intervening forces) that are foreseeable. The plaintiff, therefore, can always establish proximate cause in any jurisdiction by proving that the injury was foreseeable. Did the court in *Union Pump* persuasively explain why plaintiff's injury was not foreseeable as a matter of law?

According to the concurrence, proximate cause could not be established because the risk that injured the plaintiff was "akin to . . . an auto accident she suffered on the way home." The argument, more precisely, is that an auto accident following the fire would only be coincidentally connected to the defect, and the same is true of the plaintiff's accidental fall once the fire had been extinguished. By analogizing the auto accident to the plaintiff's slip and fall, the concurrence could persuasively argue that the risk of such harm was unforeseeable—it was something the manufacturer was not obligated to consider when making safety decisions about the pump's design.

But once foreseeability is more fully conceptualized in a behavioral manner, it becomes apparent that the plaintiff had a much stronger case than the *Union Pump* court recognized in ruling that no reasonable juror could have found the risk to be foreseeable. The plaintiff could first have argued that in considering the general risk of fire, the pump manufacturer should also consider the possibility that individuals will be injured as a result of fighting the fire. One source of injury stems from the physical and mental exhaustion inevitably caused by the firefighting effort. Tired individuals are more likely to make mistakes, resulting in injury. A good reason for pump manufacturers to adopt designs that reduce the risk of fire, therefore, is to reduce the risk that an exhausted firefighter will be less alert and vulnerable to hazards that she might otherwise be able to avoid.

The plaintiff could then argue that she was injured by such a risk. Had the plaintiff deliberated about the matter, she probably would have realized that it was not a good idea to walk in fireman's hip boots on wet pipes. But the plaintiff did not deliberate. She had just completed a full shift of work followed by two hours of firefighting, and was a trainee who was following her supervisor at the time of injury. By walking on the pipe racks, the plaintiff resorted to ordinary behavior despite the extraordinary circumstances posed by the fire. The likelihood of such behavior was arguably increased by the manner in which fighting a fire predictably causes mental and physical exhaustion. Hence the slip and fall was not coincidentally connected to the fire, yielding the conclusion that the plaintiff's injury was proximately caused by the defect. To be sure, this conclusion is debatable. But that is the point—a reasonably debatable conclusion about foreseeability ought to be resolved by the jury.

5. *Negligence versus strict liability yet again.* As illustrated by *Union Pump*, some jurisdictions rely on the directness test to determine proximate cause in cases of strict products liability, reasoning that foreseeability is relevant only for negligence and not strict liability. *E.g.*, Berkebile v. Brantley Helicopter Corp., 337 A.2d 893, 900 (Pa. 1975) ("Foreseeability is not a test of proximate cause; it is a test of negligence. Because the seller is liable in strict liability regardless of any negligence, whether he could have foreseen a particular injury is irrelevant in a strict liability case. [Once the] defective product is shown, the actor is responsible for all the unforeseen consequences thereof no matter how remote, which follow in a natural sequence of events."). For other issues such as the duty to warn, some courts as in *Green*, p. 83 *supra*, have similarly ruled that the limitation of

liability to foreseeable harms is a negligence rule and not one of strict products liability. Most jurisdictions, however, have concluded that foreseeability is an appropriate limitation of liability for claims of strict products liability. Consequently, the *Restatement (Third)* applies the foreseeability test (or "risk standard") for determining proximate cause (or "scope of liability") in both negligence and strict liability cases. *See* RESTATEMENT (THIRD) OF TORTS: LIABILITY FOR PHYSICAL AND EMOTIONAL HARM §20 cmt. l. If the directness test is not necessarily required by a rule of strict liability, what might justify this formulation of the causal inquiry?

6. *Support for the directness test.* Although the majority of jurisdictions utilize the foreseeability test for at least some aspects of the causal inquiry in claims of both negligence and strict products liability, the same is true of the directness test. "[T]he great weight of authority in this country" applies the directness test

> where the defendant has been negligent toward the plaintiff or his property (even under the restrictive [foreseeability] view of the scope of duty) and where injury has come through the very hazard that made the conduct negligent, but where because the stage is set for it the *extent* of the injury passes all bounds of reasonable anticipation. A milk deliverer, for instance, negligently leaves a bottle with a chipped lip, and this scratches a housewife's hand as she takes it in. All this is easily within the range of foresight. This particular housewife, however, has a blood condition so that what to most women would be a trivial scratch leads to blood poisoning and death.... In these and like cases of what well may be called direct consequences, the courts generally hold the defendant liable for the full extent of the injury without regard to foreseeability.

HARPER, JAMES & GRAY ON TORTS, *supra*, §20.5.

This principle for subjecting a defendant to liability for an unforeseeable extent of harm is known as the *thin-skull* or *eggshell-plaintiff* rule. According to this rule, even if the defendant could not foresee that the plaintiff had some preexisting susceptibility to physical harm (the eggshell skull), the defendant incurs responsibility for the full extent of the physical harm directly caused by the negligent conduct (a crushed skull from an impact that ordinarily would cause minor head injury).

The eggshell-plaintiff rule is nothing other than the directness test in the damages phase of the case. According to this rule, even if the defendant could not foresee that the plaintiff had some preexisting susceptibility to physical harm (the thin skull), the defendant incurs liability for the full extent of the physical harm directly caused by the tortious conduct (a crushed skull from an impact that would foreseeably cause only minor harm). As long as the tortious conduct foreseeably caused some compensable harm (a bruise or bump on the head), the extent of harm (the crushed skull) does not have to be foreseeable when directly caused by the tortious force (the blow to the head). Describing the inquiry in terms of the eggshell-plaintiff rule is certainly more evocative, but it is nothing more than a particular application of the directness test in the damages phase of the case.

This application of the directness test is not limited to cases of strict liability but also applies in negligence cases, even in jurisdictions that define proximate cause or the scope of liability in terms of the foreseeability test. How can courts coherently recognize both tests? Consider RESTATEMENT (THIRD) OF TORTS: LIABILITY FOR PHYSICAL AND EMOTIONAL HARM §29 cmt. p (recognizing that this rule is "difficult to reconcile" with foreseeability but can nevertheless be justified on the grounds that such cases "rarely arise" and it is "administrative[ly] convenien[t]" to avoid the "sometimes uncertain and indeterminate inquiry into whether the extent of the harm was unforeseeable").

7. *Foreseeability and directness combined.* Much of the difficulty posed by the element of proximate cause stems from the perceived need to choose between the foreseeability and directness tests. Rather than treating the two tests as competing conceptions of proximate cause, an alternative approach utilizes both causal rules by recognizing that each rule is the appropriate causal test for distinctive inquiries regarding proximate cause.

Causal issues are implicated by two different elements of the tort claim, and each element requires a different test for proximate cause. The foreseeability test is appropriate for defining the scope of liability with respect to the prima facie case. To recover, the plaintiff must show that he or she suffered at least some foreseeable harm encompassed by the duty. Once the prima facie case for liability has been established, the court must then determine damages. To determine the amount of damages, the court must resolve a different causal question: Did the defect cause the full extent of damages claimed by the plaintiff? The causal question for determining the extent of damages importantly differs from the causal question in the prima facie case, and that difference explains why courts continue to recognize both tests for proximate cause. The foreseeability test determines proximate cause in the prima facie case, whereas the directness test determines proximate cause in the damages phase of the case. *See* Johnson v. Ford Motor Co., 45 P.3d 86, 93 (Okla. 2002) (upholding a jury instruction which stated that "[f]or a defect in a product to be a direct cause it is necessary that some injury to a person in Plaintiff's situation must have been a reasonably foreseeable result of the defect").

Both tests are needed because tort law could not fairly determine the amount of damages by exclusively relying on the foreseeability test. Compensatory damages are limited to the amount of harm for the injury in question, even if those damages are unforeseeably low. A blow that would crush an ordinary skull, for example, could cause only minor injury to a hard-headed plaintiff, yielding a compensatory damages award substantially less than the foreseeable amount. The foreseeability test would only be operative, then, for cases in which the plaintiff suffered unforeseeably high damages (like the severe head injuries incurred by a plaintiff with an eggshell skull). The foreseeability test would prevent the defendant from paying unforeseeably high damages, while permitting the defendant to pay unforeseeably low damages—a one-sided advantage that is unfair for the plaintiff.

By contrast, the directness test more fairly determines the extent of damages. The defendant must pay for unforeseeably high damages directly caused by the tortious risk, the result attained by the eggshell-plaintiff rule for cases in which the tortious risk directly caused bodily injury. Any unfairness for the defendant in this respect is adequately offset by the requirement that compensatory damages equal the amount of harm in question, limiting the defendant's liability to actual harms that can be substantially less severe than the foreseeable harms. Unlike the foreseeability test, the directness test does not confer a one-sided advantage on either party.

The plaintiff can also suffer other harms that were indirectly caused by the tortious risk, but the defendant's liability cannot extend into the indefinite future. Lacking the limitation of direct causation, the only other defensible way for courts to limit liability is by relying on foreseeability. The extent to which the defendant's tortious conduct caused the plaintiff's damages, therefore, encompasses both direct harms and indirect, foreseeable harms — a rule corresponding to the directness test. *See In re* Kinsman Transit Co., 338 F.2d 708, 724 (2d Cir. 1964) ("The weight of authority in this country rejects the limitation of damages to consequences foreseeable at the time of the negligent conduct when the consequences are 'direct,' and the damage, although other and greater than expectable, is of the same general sort that was risked.").

The directness test, therefore, is not somehow more appropriate in cases of strict liability rather than negligence; it fairly resolves damages issues for both forms of liability. Moreover, the foreseeability test necessarily applies to the prima facie case in jurisdictions that limit the tort duty to foreseeable harms, regardless of whether the liability is fault-based or strict. *See* note 2, p. 534 *supra*. Each test has an appropriate role to play in either type of tort claim. Their distinctive roles only become clear once the element of proximate cause in the prima facie case is distinguished from the element of proximate cause in the damages phase of the case. For more extensive discussion, see Mark A. Geistfeld, *Proximate Cause Untangled*, 80 Md. L. Rev. 419, 433-455 (2021).

III. A REPRISE OF DUTY

JELD-WEN, INC. v. GAMBLE BY GAMBLE
Supreme Court of Virginia, 1998
501 S.E.2d 393

KOONTZ, J. On April 25, 1993, Anthony Kent Gamble (Gamble), then thirteen months old, fell through an open second floor window in the living room of the townhome rented by his parents after the window's screen fell out of the window frame. As a result of his fall, Gamble suffered severe, permanent injuries.

Thereafter, Gamble, by his mother and next friend, LaDonna Gamble, filed a motion for judgment against Jeld-Wen, Inc. (Jeld-Wen), the manufacturer of the window and screen. The motion for judgment asserted alternative theories of Jeld-Wen's liability, alleging both negligence in the manufacture of the window frame and screen and breach of implied warranty of merchantability.

At trial, the evidence established that this tragic incident arose under the following relevant facts. The window was approximately six feet in height and its sill was eight inches above the surface of the living room floor. The window screen was an ordinary wire mesh screen and covered the entire opening of the window. It was designed to be held in place by two fixed pins at the top and two spring-loaded pins at the lower left and right of the window frame. The left spring-loaded pin and the groove in the window frame into which the pin was intended to be inserted contained manufacturing defects that prevented the screen from being held securely in place unless light pressure was applied to the screen from the outside rather than from the inside of the window where the pin was located. While not clear from the evidence, we will assume that this pin and, thus, the screen appeared to be, but was not, secured on the day in question, resulting in a "false latch" as alleged by Gamble.

Gamble was approximately twenty-eight inches in height and weighed seventeen pounds, thirteen ounces. According to his father's testimony, Gamble was standing on the cushions of a loveseat that backed up to the window. Gamble's father had opened the blinds and raised the lower sash of the window to allow fresh air into the home and to permit Gamble to "wave good-bye" to his mother who was outside the home. When the sash began to slip down, Gamble's father left the loveseat in order to adjust it. At that point, Gamble reached out and "barely touched" the screen. The screen fell away from the window and Gamble fell through the open window, falling approximately ten feet to the concrete driveway below.

The jury awarded Gamble $15,000,000 in damages. The trial court confirmed the jury's verdict, reducing it by the amounts already received through settlement of the claims against the other defendants. We awarded Jeld-Wen this appeal.

We have not previously addressed the dispositive issue in this appeal which involves the determination, as a matter of law, of the duty of a manufacturer of an ordinary window screen that is neither designed nor manufactured to act as a body restraint to safeguard against the misuse of the screen for that purpose. Without a legal duty there can be no cause of action for an injury. We have, however, established principles that guide our analysis of this novel issue.

"A manufacturer is not required to supply an accident-proof product." [ ] Rather, "[t]he standard of safety of goods imposed on the manufacturer of a product is essentially the same whether the theory of liability is labeled warranty or negligence. The product must be fit for the ordinary purposes for which it is to be used." [ ] While a manufacturer may not be held liable for every misuse of its product, it may be held liable for a *foreseeable* misuse of an unreasonably dangerous product.

Applying these principles, we think it is clear that Jeld-Wen's duty to Gamble was to manufacture a window screen and frame "fit for the ordinary purposes for which it is to be used" and safe for a reasonably foreseeable misuse that could cause injury. Gamble concedes that the ordinary purposes of Jeld-Wen's window screen are to keep insects out while letting in light and fresh air and would not include this screen serving as a childproof restraint. Gamble asserts, however, that because the evidence supports a finding that Jeld-Wen knew or should have known of the existence of the defect that permitted the screen to have a "false

III. A Reprise of Duty

latch" appearance and that a child could make casual contact with this screen and cause the screen to fall out of the frame, Jeld-Wen should have foreseen that the child could lose his balance and fall through the open window.

The initial difficulty with Gamble's theory is that it fails to draw the necessary distinction between the foreseeability of the screen being dislodged by the child's touch and the foreseeability of the child's losing his balance and falling through the open window. Inherent in this theory is the necessary assumption that the screen was being used to provide balance and restraining support for the child's body weight, and, thus, to prevent a fall through the open window. As previously noted, this screen was not intended for this purpose, and therefore this was a misuse of the screen. Accordingly, it is not the occurrence of the "gentle touch," but the misuse of the screen to provide balance and restraining support that is the focus of our inquiry, and we must determine whether this misuse was reasonably foreseeable such that Jeld-Wen had a duty to safeguard against it.

In addition, Gamble's theory rests on the contention that because the danger of falling through open windows with screens is widely known, the "false latch" defect in Jeld-Wen's screen distinguishes this case from cases involving such falls where non-defective window screens may in fact provide a modest level of restraint. In short, Gamble is asserting that because the defect in Jeld-Wen's screen would allow it to fall away from the window more readily than a screen without a defect, it was reasonable that Jeld-Wen would have foreseen the danger of the misuse of the defective screen. We disagree.

Common knowledge of a danger from the foreseeable misuse of a product does not alone give rise to a duty to safeguard against the danger of that misuse. To the contrary, the purpose of making the finding of a legal duty as a prerequisite to a finding of negligence, or breach of implied warranty, in products liability "is to avoid the extension of liability for every conceivably foreseeable accident, without regard to common sense or good policy." [ ] In this respect, manufacturers of ordinary window screens are not charged with a duty to safeguard against the misuse of their products as body restraints as this misuse is not considered reasonably foreseeable despite, or perhaps even because of, the obvious nature of the danger the misuse presents.

It then does not logically follow that the alleged defect in Jeld-Wen's screen would impose a different or greater duty to manufacture the screen so that it would act as a childproof restraint if misused for that purpose. Although the existence of a defect is a factor in determining whether a product is unreasonably dangerous for the use to which it would ordinarily be put, it is not the dispositive factor in determining the duty, if any, to be imposed on the manufacturer to reasonably foresee a particular misuse of its product. Therefore, here it is irrelevant that, absent this defect, Jeld-Wen's screen might have provided some level of restraint, since, as we have already determined, the misuse of the screen for balance and restraining support, however modest, was not reasonably foreseeable.

For these reasons, we hold, as a matter of law, that no duty extended to Jeld-Wen to manufacture the screen in question so that it would act as a childproof restraint. Accordingly, we will reverse the judgment of the circuit court and enter final judgment for Jeld-Wen.

NOTES AND QUESTIONS

1. *Foreseeability and manufacturing defects.* For reasons discussed in prior chapters, both the duty to design and the duty to warn are limited to the risks of foreseeable harm; that is, the risk term *PL* in the risk-utility test is limited to those foreseeable harms that would be eliminated by the redesign or warning in question. How is foreseeability determined for a manufacturing defect, which does not turn on risk-utility evidence? Recall that a manufacturing defect is a deviation from the product's design. To identify the foreseeable risks threatened by the manufacturing defect, one must identify the risk-utility factors that motivated this attribute of the product design.

The defect in *Jeld-Wen* "prevented the screen from being held securely in place unless light pressure was applied to the screen from the outside rather than from the inside of the window where the pin was located." Presumably, it would be unnecessarily risky for someone to secure the screen from the outside of a window on the second floor, and if the screen were unsecured as a result, it could fall out of the window and cause injury to persons or property on the ground. For these reasons, the design of the screen enabled it to be secured by applying light pressure from the inside of the window. The defective construction of the screen accordingly created the tortious risk that someone trying to secure the screen from the outside would fall off a ladder, or that the screen would otherwise remain unsecured and fall off, harming someone or something on the ground. Based on this definition of the tortious or foreseeable risks of harm, the plaintiff's injury was not caused by the type of risk that rendered the product defective—the defect did not proximately cause the injury. *See* RESTATEMENT (THIRD) OF TORTS: LIABILITY FOR PHYSICAL HARM AND EMOTIONAL HARM §29 ("An actor's liability is limited to those harms that result from the risks that made the actor's conduct tortious.").

2. *Foreseeability and the roles of the judge and jury.* Because the issue of foreseeability limits both the element of duty and the element of proximate cause, courts can rely on either element to deny liability for an unforeseeable harm. An unforeseeable harm is not within a duty limited to the risks of foreseeable harm, which is why the court in *Jeld-Wen* denied liability on that basis. However, the unforeseeable risk also meant that the defect did not proximately cause the plaintiff's injury for reasons discussed in the preceding note. The element of duty and the element of proximate cause each provide a sufficient basis for the denial of liability, so why does it matter whether courts rely on one element rather than the other?

This question implicates the appropriate division of decision-making between the judge and the jury. Duty is a matter of law to be determined by the judge, whereas proximate cause is a jury question. In concluding that the risk was unforeseeable and outside the scope of the defendant's duty, did the court in *Jeld-Wen* conclude that the duty issue is purely a matter of law to be decided by judges, regardless of how a reasonable juror would have resolved the matter? Or did the court instead hold that no reasonable juror could have found otherwise as a matter of law? Whether an unforeseeable harm limits liability as a matter of duty or proximate cause

III. A Reprise of Duty

can determine whether the issue ought to be resolved by either judges or juries.

a. *Duty as a rule of law.* In one fundamental respect, the limitation of duty to foreseeable risks of harm is purely a matter of law. Such a legal rule is no different from any other legal rule of general application. For example, the tort of trespass on land is nothing other than a general rule obligating individuals not to "trespass on another's land." Judges then specify further legal rules defining the elements of trespass, and the jury ultimately determines how these rules apply to the case at hand. So, too, a legal rule that limits duty to foreseeable harms specifies an element of products liability that categorically applies to all product cases, which is different from its case-specific application by the jury. *See* RESTATEMENT (THIRD) OF TORTS: LIABILITY FOR PHYSICAL AND EMOTIONAL HARM §7 cmt. a (stating that duty does not depend on "factors specific to an individual case" but instead must depend on factors "applicable to a general class of cases" involving "categories of actors or patterns of conduct.").

Categorical determinations are made by judges as a matter of law. Judges have experience with a broad range of cases, enabling them to identify the general concerns of relevance for the categorical decision, unlike juries, whose comparative advantage resides in factual and evaluative judgments of case-specific matters. The scope of duty, including the limitation to the risks of foreseeable harm, is a categorical determination that applies to all tort cases; it must be made by judges as a matter of law.

However, not all duty questions involve issues of law. Whether a general or categorical duty rule applies to a particular case can depend on contested (or "adjudicative") facts. These duty issues are case specific and must be resolved by the jury. *See id.* cmt. b ("In most cases, the adjudicative facts that bear on whether a duty exists are not in dispute. When resolution of disputed adjudicative facts bears on the existence or scope of a duty, the case should be submitted to the jury with alternative instructions.").

b. *Foreseeability as a jury question.* Once the categorical issue of duty has been resolved—that is, once the tort rule defines the defendant's safety obligations in terms of categorical risks, such as the foreseeable risk of physical harm—application of that rule will be case-specific and for the jury.

> The extent of foreseeable risk depends on the specific facts of the case and cannot be usefully assessed for a category of cases; small changes in the facts may make a dramatic change in how much risk is foreseeable. Thus, . . . courts should leave such determinations to juries unless no reasonable person could differ on the matter.

Id. §7 cmt. j.

The foreseeability of any given risk is a case-specific matter that should be resolved by the jury. To be sure, an unforeseeable harm is necessarily outside of the duty, but that conclusion is a case-specific factual determination regarding the existence of duty with respect to this particular risk, making it an "adjudicative fact" that should be resolved by the jury.

c. *Policy-based limitations of duty.* Even when "reasonable minds could differ about application of the [tort] standard to a particular category of recurring facts, . . . under the rubric of duty courts [may] render a judgment about that category of cases." *Id.* cmt. i.

> [D]uty is a preferable means for addressing limits on liability when those limitations are clear, when they are based on relatively bright lines, when they are of general application, when they do not usually require resort to disputed facts in a case, when they implicate policy concerns that apply to a class of cases that may not be fully appreciated by a jury deciding a specific case, and when they are employed in cases in which early resolution of liability is particularly desirable. Duty is usefully employed when a court seeks to make a telling pronouncement about when actors may or, on the other hand, may not be held liable. Thus, the liability of social hosts for providing alcohol to their guests is best treated as a duty issue, rather than as a matter of scope of liability. On the other hand, when the limits imposed require careful attention to the specific facts of a case, and difficult, often amorphous evaluative judgments for which modest differences in the factual circumstances may change the outcome, scope of liability is a more flexible and preferable device for placing limits on liability. Its use is also consistent with the role of the jury in tort cases.

Id. §29 cmt. f.

Did the holding in *Jeld-Wen* implicate any categorical considerations that would justify a "bright line" rule of no duty? Does the holding categorically absolve all manufacturers of the obligation to design window screens to account for instances in which individuals might try to use the screen for purposes of balance or restraint? Suppose that advances in state of the art make it possible to inexpensively design screens so that they can provide enough restraining force to prevent infants and young children from falling through the screen. Would an allegation that a screen is defectively designed for not incorporating such technology be barred under *Jeld-Wen*? If such a change in facts would provide sufficient grounds for distinguishing *Jeld-Wen*, is that case sufficiently categorical to justify a holding of "no duty" as a matter of law? Would the inquiry be simplified if all instances of case-specific foreseeability were always placed within the element of proximate cause? *See id.* §7 cmt. a ("When liability depends on factors specific to an individual case, the appropriate rubric is scope of liability.").

3. *Proximate cause as an alignment of the elements.* Proximate cause is confusing and prone to controversy because it is entwined with all elements of the tort claim, ranging from duty to the determination of damages.

For purposes of strict products liability, the element of duty determines the types of harms or associated risks for which the defendant is responsible as a matter of tort law (the risk or *PL* terms in the risk-utility test). Having identified the harms or risks governed by the duty, the tort inquiry can then determine whether those risks constitute a product defect (by application of the risk-utility test). As a functional matter, the legal standard for evaluating a product defect must be defined by reference to the harms or risks for which the duty-bearer is legally responsible, explaining why the specification of duty is the first element of the tort claim.

Once a court adopts the legal rule that limits duty to the foreseeable risks of compensable harm, the jury then applies this general rule to the case at hand. It first determines whether the defendant breached the duty by commercially distributing a defective product. The inquiry at this stage is still framed in general terms. For example, the duty to warn about the flammability of perfume encompasses myriad ways in which someone might place the perfume near an open flame. Relying on this general category of foreseeable risks, the jury can find that the product was defective. The element of proximate cause then filters this more generally defined facet of the tort claim to focus on the issue of how it applies to the plaintiff's injuries in the case at hand. For example, if the plaintiff was burned because her friend poured perfume onto the candle, is that injury within the general category of foreseeable harms that motivated the duty to warn? Unless this question is answered in the affirmative, the injury suffered by the plaintiff is not encompassed within the defendant's duty, absolving the defendant of responsibility—and liability—for that particular injury as a matter of proximate cause. Properly applied, the element of proximate cause focuses the more general properties of the other tort elements onto the particulars of the case at hand.

IV. AUTONOMOUS VEHICLES AND PRODUCTS LIABILITY: PROBLEM SET 9

AV Problem 9.1

As we have found, the existing rules of strict products liability will require courts and regulators to make some difficult safety decisions. Even if they settle on performance standards for determining the conditions under which a fully functioning operating system can execute the dynamic driving task in a reasonably safe manner, they must still confront the difficult cause-in-fact issues discussed in AV Problems 8.1 and 8.2. To avoid these problems, some scholars have argued that the current liability regime ought to be discarded in favor of a regime that makes the manufacturer strictly liable for all crashes of an autonomous vehicle, regardless of whether the vehicle is defective—a regime that courts call "absolute liability."

In defending one such proposal, which they call "Manufacturer Enterprise Responsibility" (MER), Professors Abraham and Rabin argue that strict manufacturer responsibility for motor vehicle crashes "would promote deterrence and compensation more effectively than continued reliance on tort in the coming world of auto accidents. MER would be a manufacturer-financed, strict responsibility bodily injury compensation system, administered by a fund created through assessments levied on AV manufacturers." Kenneth S. Abraham & Robert L. Rabin, *The Future Is Almost Here: Inaction Is Actually Mistaken Action*, 105 Va. L. Rev. 91, 91-92 (2019) (discussing Kenneth S. Abraham & Robert L. Rabin, *Automated Vehicles and Manufacturer Responsibility for Accidents: A New Legal Regime for a New Era*, 105 Va. L. Rev. 127 (2019)). Professors Abraham and Rabin, however, do not address a problem with absolute liability that others have identified.

According to Professors Henderson and Twerski, any system of "enterprise liability" for products—that is, any system that utilizes a rule of absolute liability—is neither workable nor desirable. Their conclusion follows from their belief that any system of products liability must be anchored by a concept of fault such as that provided by the doctrines for identifying product defects. On their view, unless judges and juries are guided by the requirement of defect in their determination of liability, the products liability system could not function satisfactorily because it would be awash in legal uncertainty. *See generally* James A. Henderson, Jr. & Aaron D. Twerski, *Closing the American Products Liability Frontier: The Rejection of Liability Without Defect*, 66 N.Y.U. L. Rev. 1263 (1991). In particular, they suggest that only a but-for test of factual causation could be employed in an enterprise liability system. They rule out the possibility of a proximate-cause test on the basis that it has "no firm anchor" without a concept of product defect. *Id.* at 1281. The unsurprising conclusion is that an enterprise liability system, which purportedly can only use a but-for test of factual causation, would result in ludicrously unlimited liability. Witness their hypothetical:

> P, after eating a heavy lunch consisting of three servings of pasta accompanied by two bottles of beer, climbs the stairs to the second floor of his home to retrieve a book from his bedroom. Sleepily returning downstairs to answer the door, P trips on a roller skate left by his nine-year-old daughter, falls down the stairs, and crashes his head through the glass screen of the television in the living room. Since proof of defect is no longer required for the imposition of liability, the only question is which product(s) caused the injury. The combination of P's eating pasta and imbibing beer contributed to his being unsteady on his feet and less observant than usual. The skate helped propel him down the stairs. The stairs and the television set are similarly implicated in P's injury. With little effort, the net could be cast even more broadly. Would not the manufacturers of the vehicles that delivered the pasta, beer, television set, and stairs be but-for causes of the harm? For that matter, the book publisher also might be added to the list, especially if P had opened the book to read as he was beginning to descend the stairs.

Id. at 1280-1281.

Notice that within this hypothetical, the manufacturer of an autonomous vehicle that delivered the pasta, beer, television set, and stairs would be but-for causes of the harm subject to absolute liability. One could then generalize from this hypothetical to reach the conclusion that the system of Manufacturer Enterprise Responsibility championed by Professors Abraham and Rabin would be unworkable.

Suppose that an autonomous vehicle governed by absolute liability delivered the pasta, beer, television set, and stairs in the foregoing hypothetical. Are Henderson and Twerski correct that a rule of proximate cause cannot limit absolute liability? To answer this question, consider how the foreseeability test would apply to this problem.

IV. Autonomous Vehicles and Products Liability: Problem Set 9

Analysis of AV Problem 9.1

The foreseeability test determines proximate cause by asking whether the harm in question was reasonably foreseeable when the manufacturer made the safety decision in question. This formulation of proximate cause is easily squared with the theory of enterprise liability, which is based on the principle that when a manufacturer is absolutely liable for a product risk, it will make cost-effective investments in product safety for reducing this risk—that is, those investments that satisfy the risk-utility test. *See* Chapter 3, section I. The circumstances in which manufacturers incur absolute liability, therefore, determine the type of safety investments that would be incentivized by absolute liability. Recognizing this link between absolute liability and product safety provides a conceptual basis for applying the foreseeability test of proximate cause.

The foreseeability test defines foreseeable harms in terms of a "general field of danger" as the *Stazenski* court explained. When making safety decisions concerning the driving performance of an autonomous vehicle, manufacturers would only consider instances in which the vehicle might crash and cause injury. It is irrelevant for this purpose whether the autonomous vehicle was delivering the pasta, beer, television set, and stairs in the foregoing hypothetical. As explained in note 2, p. 528 *supra*, "Ostensibly, this [allegedly foreseeable risk] would suggest that [defendant] should have foreseen these events and, therefore, should have foreseen the need for [the safety precaution in question] at the time of manufacture. . . ." Gay v. O.F. Mossberg & Sons, Inc., 2009 WL 1743939, at *14 (Ohio Ct. App. 2009). The manufacturer of an autonomous vehicle cannot take any safety precautions that would prevent consumers from using the vehicle to deliver pasta, beer, a television set or most any other type of product (an autonomous truck would be needed to deliver the stairs). Any injury factually caused by those products would not be caused by a risk created by the autonomous vehicle; the injuries instead would be coincidental (after all, they would still have occurred if an ordinary motor vehicle had delivered the products). A coincidental harm is necessarily unforeseeable because its coincidental nature means that the manufacturer could not account for that possibility when making the safety decision.

More generally, a system of absolute liability for autonomous vehicles could define proximate cause in terms of the risks foreseeably created by operation of the vehicle. If the plaintiff's injury were caused by a risk within this general field of danger, then the vehicle would be a proximate cause of the injury. The same inquiry governs proximate cause when liability depends on a predicate finding of defect, but the requirement of defect is not necessary to apply the foreseeability test.*

Editor's Note. For more extensive discussion, see Mark Geistfeld, *Implementing Enterprise Liability: A Comment on Henderson and Twerski*, 67 N.Y.U. L. Rev. 1157 (1992).

AV Problem 9.2

According to Professors Abraham and Rabin, autonomous vehicles might pose at least two "challenging" problems of proximate cause. The first would arise when the vehicle "signaled the need for driver take-over but the operator failed to respond in a reasonable fashion and a third-party was injured. Here, questions of foreseeability (of the manufacturer) and proximate cause (assigned to the inattentive operator) would be triggered under the traditional tort framework. Proximate cause issues could conceivably arise in yet another daunting context: external hacking and corresponding disablement of safety controls in the vehicle." Abraham & Rabin, 105 Va. L. Rev. at 142 & n. 36. How would courts resolve these two scenarios under the foreseeability test?

Analysis of AV Problem 9.2

Autonomous vehicles with SAE levels 2 or 3 of automation require the driver to take over under specified conditions. As discussed in AV Problem Set 5, p. 362 *supra*, the manufacturer is obligated to design the vehicle to account for the foreseeable manner in which the autonomous operation of the vehicle will predictably lull the driver into complacency. If the vehicle signaled the need for the driver to take over and the driver failed to do so, the driver would only be able to establish a defect by proving that the vehicle should be reasonably redesigned to reduce this risk of driver error. The rationale for redesign is based on the same risk of inattention that caused the crash. Consequently, the driver's inattention would ordinarily be foreseeable, in which case the defect would proximately cause the crash.**

The same principle explains why foreseeability is not an issue for crashes caused by third-party hacking of the vehicle. The sole reason for adopting cybersecurity measures in autonomous vehicles is to reduce the foreseeable risk that a third party gains unauthorized control of the vehicle and causes it to crash. The court's proximate cause analysis in the *September 11 Litigation* fully explains why these crashes are foreseeable and do not negate the manufacturer's duty to design the vehicle's operating system to prevent its misuse by an unauthorized third party.

** *Editor's Note*. The inattentive driver's negligence would also be a proximate cause of such a crash, so these cases will involve application of the comparative responsibility rules discussed in Chapter 14, section III.

13

Damages and the Scope of Liability as Defined by the Type of Injury

To satisfy the final element of the prima facie case, the plaintiff must first prove that she has suffered a compensable injury—merely being harmed is not enough. Having established liability, the plaintiff must then prove the amount of damages to which she is entitled—proof that depends on the reasonably available evidence.

In the past few decades, that manner in which juries determine damages has been a hotly contested issue. Reasoning that there is no reliable way to determine monetary damages for the nonmonetary injuries of pain and suffering, around a dozen states have adopted tort-reform measures that cap the available amount of these compensatory damages. Punitive damages have also been a target of reform. In a line of cases, the U.S. Supreme Court has determined that the long-standing procedures used by courts to determine punitive damages can yield awards that violate the Due Process Clause of the U.S. Constitution. Like the tort-reform measures that limit compensatory damages, the Supreme Court's punitive damages jurisprudence ultimately poses difficult issues about the appropriate way to measure tort damages.

The issues involving damages are not limited to questions of quantification or measurement. Defective products often cause foreseeable injuries that are not compensable under tort law. For cases in which the defect only damages the product itself and causes foreseeable financial losses such as lost profits, most jurisdictions typically deny the plaintiff's tort claim. Most jurisdictions also ordinarily deny the plaintiff recovery when the defect causes foreseeable pain and suffering not accompanied by physical harm. Liability is usually limited to cases in which the defect causes physical harm. Why does the type of injury affect the plaintiff's ability to recover?

I. PHYSICAL HARM AND THE MEASURE OF COMPENSATION

In the event that the product defect proximately causes the plaintiff to suffer *physical harm*—bodily injury or damage to real or tangible property other than the product itself—she is entitled to receive compensatory damages for the ensuing economic harms (like medical expenses) and noneconomic harms (pain and suffering). The damages compensate the plaintiff's monetary losses, typically lost wages, medical expenses, and repair or replacement costs, in addition to the nonmonetary injuries of pain and suffering such as anxiety, grief, indignity, and the reduced ability to enjoy life. The plaintiff receives all these damages as a lump-sum award covering both past and future injuries.

The practical importance of compensatory damages is hard to overstate. In addition to remedying injuries and measuring the extent of a defendant's liability, the amount of damages drives decisions about whether it is economically worthwhile to litigate in the first instance. The computation of damages also has implications for the substantive rules of products liability. The risk-utility test requires any investment in product safety for which $B < PL$. The magnitude of loss L—the issue expressly addressed by the element of compensatory damages—is an integral component of the risk-utility test. A duty formulated in terms of the risk-utility test can be effectively and fairly enforced only if both the economic injuries and the noneconomic injuries such as pain and suffering can be translated into an appropriate monetary measure.

Determining the monetary magnitude of an economic loss is conceptually easy (although factually difficult in some cases). A plaintiff who incurs $10,000 in medical expenses as a consequence of the defective product is entitled to receive $10,000 in compensatory damages for this financial harm. Each $1 of the compensatory damages award fully repairs or compensates the associated economic loss of $1, thereby making the plaintiff "whole" for the financial harm.

What is the monetary magnitude of a noneconomic loss? Each $1 of the compensatory damages award does not clearly correspond to an associated nonmonetary loss of $1. Because monetary damages cannot fully repair nonmonetary injuries such as the loss of life's pleasures, the common law deems these injuries to be *irreparable harms*. Money improves the plaintiff's position but cannot make her "whole" in the sense that her position following receipt of the damages remedy is the same as it was before the injury had occurred.

The fact that nonmonetary injuries are irreparable harms is conveyed by jury instructions:

> No definite standard [or method of calculation] is prescribed by law by which to fix reasonable compensation for pain and suffering. Nor is the opinion of any witness required as to the amount of such reasonable compensation. [Furthermore, the argument of counsel as to the amount of damages is not evidence of reasonable compensation.] In making an award for pain and suffering you should exercise your authority with calm and reasonable judgment and the damages you fix must be just and reasonable in the light of the evidence.

California Civil Jury Instructions (BAJI) 14.13, Measure of Damages—Personal Injury—Pain and Suffering (2020 update).

I. Physical Harm and the Measure of Compensation

Although the only way to fairly compensate an irreparable injury is to determine an amount that is "just and reasonable in light of the evidence," this type of jury instruction potentially threatens the integrity of the liability rule. The risk-utility test depends on some way to quantify or monetize pain-and-suffering injuries, the same exercise required by the jury's determination of the compensatory damages award. The manner in which juries quantify damages for pain and suffering, therefore, has implications for how the jury applies the risk-utility test. If there is "no definite standard" for determining pain-and-suffering damages, then there is "no definite standard" for determining the injury costs that plug into the risk-utility test. The problem of measuring damages for pain and suffering threatens the viability of the risk-utility test.

Guidance on this matter can be derived from the nature of the duty. The manufacturer is obligated to provide a product that satisfies the reasonable safety expectations of the ordinary consumer, and those expectations can be utilized to determine the appropriate amount of damages for pain and suffering. To see why, suppose there is a 1 in 10,000 probability of accident (the term P) that would cause the average or ordinary consumer to experience the pain and suffering in question $\left(L_{pain\ and\ suffering}\right)$. The safety decision depends on how much the ordinary consumer is willing to spend (via a price increase, decreased functionality, increased precautionary efforts, and so on) to eliminate this particular risk. Suppose the reasonable (well-informed) consumer would be willing to pay no more than $10 for some product safety improvement that would eliminate the risk. Because $10 is the most the consumer would pay to eliminate the risk, the consumer must be indifferent between incurring the $10 cost or otherwise facing the risk and incurring the expected injury cost of the pain and suffering:

$$\$10 = P \bullet L_{pain\ and\ suffering}$$

$$\$10 = \left(1/10,000\right) \bullet L_{pain\ and\ suffering}$$

$$\$100,000 = L_{pain\ and\ suffering}$$

In evaluating the safety decision required by the tort duty, the reasonable consumer would monetize this particular pain-and-suffering injury at $100,000. A different injury (or even a different probability of injury) would yield a different number. The monetization of the pain-and-suffering injury does not represent the "value" of the injury or the amount of money the consumer would accept in exchange for suffering the injury with certainty. When framed in those terms, the consumer could be willing to spend everything to avoid the most severe nonmonetary injury—the loss of life's pleasures due to premature death. The value of the injury, however, is not relevant to the safety question, nor is it relevant to the damages calculation. "All agree that [full compensation for pain and suffering] does not mean the sum that the plaintiff—or anyone else—would be willing to suffer the injury for." Fowler V. Harper, Fleming James, Jr. & Oscar S. Gray, HARPER, JAMES, AND GRAY ON TORTS §20.5 (3d. ed. 2006-2007 & 2020 update). The issue is one of determining the appropriate amount of safety expenditures for eliminating a 1 in 10,000 chance of suffering the nonmonetary injury, and for this particular purpose the average or ordinary consumer would monetize the injury at $100,000.

For the same reasons, the jury can apply the risk-utility test by determining the maximum amount of money that the ordinary consumer would be willing to pay ($\$WTP$) to eliminate the entire risk in question (the full PL risk term and not merely the nonmonetary component). That determination yields a monetization of the risk $(\$WTP = \$PL)$ required by the risk-utility test. If that amount exceeds the cost or burden of the precaution (the term B), then the product is defective in this respect $(\$B < \$PL = \$WTP)$.

This method for monetizing the risk of physical injury relies on established economic methodology commonly employed by federal administrative agencies in devising regulations for the protection of human health and safety. Pursuant to executive order, federal agencies must analyze proposed regulations with a cost-benefit analysis. *See, e.g.*, Exec. Order No. 12,291, 3 C.F.R. 127 (1981), *reprinted in* 5 U.S.C. §601 (1988); Exec. Order No. 12,866, 3 C.F.R. 638 (1993), *reprinted in* 5 U.S.C. §601 (1994). To apply cost-benefit analysis to a regulation concerning human health and safety, federal agencies must quantify and monetize the impact of the regulation on bodily injuries and premature death. In 2011, for example, the U.S. Environmental Protection Agency treated the prevention of each premature death as being equivalent to a savings of $9.1 million; the Food and Drug Administration monetized the cost of premature death at $7.9 million; and the U.S. Department of Transportation "has used values of around $6 million to justify" regulations "like requiring stronger roofs on cars." Binyamin Appelbaum, *A Life's Value? It May Depend on the Agency*, N.Y. Times, Feb. 17, 2011, at A1. Federal agencies derive these measures from studies that seek to ascertain how much individuals like consumers are willing to pay to eliminate a known risk of physical harm. Under current federal regulatory practice, the WTP measure is "the standard value that is given to risk-reducing regulation." Richard L. Revesz & Michael Livermore, Retaking Rationality 76 (2008). Regulators derive the $6 million figure, for example, from empirical studies finding that consumers are willing to pay up to $6 to eliminate a 1 in 1,000,000 risk of fatal injury in a motor vehicle crash.

Courts have not expressly utilized this approach in tort cases, but it satisfies the relevant tort requirements pertaining to the calculation of these damage awards. *See generally* Mark Geistfeld, *Placing a Price on Pain and Suffering: A Method for Helping Juries Determine Tort Damages for Nonmonetary Injuries*, 83 Calif. L. Rev. 773, 796-803 (1995) (developing this approach and showing that it satisfies the relevant tort requirements pertaining to the calculation of damage awards). Compensatory damages for pain and suffering are supposed to "give to the injured person some pecuniary return for what he has suffered or is likely to suffer." Restatement (Second) of Torts §903 cmt. a. Any amount of money would provide "some pecuniary return," but presumably tort law is more demanding in this respect. Tort damages are supposed to be fully compensatory. In the prior example showing how a particular nonmonetary injury can be monetized at $100,000, a damages award for the pain and suffering equal to that amount would be fully compensatory from the perspective of the plaintiff at the time of the defendant's safety decision. To satisfy consumer expectations, the tort obligation required the defendant to monetize that injury at $100,000, and so this damages award fully compensates the plaintiff for the defendant's breach of that duty. Although the precision suggested by the example is unrealistic, recall that the plaintiff must prove the amount of damages with "as much certainty as the nature of the tort and the circumstances permit." *Id.* §912.

More fundamentally, this methodology shows that the risk-utility test can accommodate the nonmonetary injuries of pain and suffering. The monetary cost of a safety device like an airbag can be directly compared to the injury costs that would be eliminated by that precaution, including irreparable injuries such as premature death. The risk-utility test is not rendered conceptually invalid simply because it requires juries to translate the nonmonetary injuries of pain and suffering into a monetary equivalent.

II. PURE ECONOMIC LOSS

Within tort law, pure economic loss is conventionally defined as any "pecuniary or commercial loss that does not arise from actionable physical, emotional or reputational injury to persons or physical injury to property." Dan B. Dobbs, *An Introduction to Non-Statutory Economic Loss Claims*, 48 Ariz. L. Rev. 713, 713 (2006). In product cases, a pure economic loss occurs when a defect only damages the product without otherwise causing compensable physical harm—bodily injury or damage to real or tangible property other than the product itself. Instead, the defect degrades product performance in a manner that causes foreseeable economic losses, like repair costs and lost profits. Whether plaintiffs can receive tort damages for these financial harms depends on whether damage to the product itself (the defect) can serve as a predicate compensable injury that triggers tort liability for consequential economic losses.

EAST RIVER STEAMSHIP v. TRANSAMERICA DELAVEL
Supreme Court of the United States, 1986
476 U.S. 858

BLACKMUN, J. In this admiralty case, we must decide whether a cause of action in tort is stated when a defective product purchased in a commercial transaction malfunctions, injuring only the product itself and causing purely economic loss. The case requires us to consider preliminarily whether admiralty law, which already recognizes a general theory of liability for negligence, also incorporates principles of products liability, including strict liability.* Then, charting a course between products liability and contract law, we must determine whether injury to a product itself is the kind of harm that should be protected by products liability or left entirely to the law of contracts.

In 1969, Seatrain Shipbuilding Corp. (Shipbuilding), a wholly owned subsidiary of Seatrain Lines, Inc. (Seatrain), announced it would build the four oil-transporting supertankers in issue—the T.T. *Stuyvesant*, T.T. *Williamsburgh*,

---

* Federal maritime law governs cases of personal injury or property damage that occur on the high seas or in navigable waters of the United States having a significant relationship to traditional maritime activity. As illustrated by this case, the U.S. Supreme Court has developed the federal common law of maritime liability by relying on the state common law of torts.—ED.

T.T. *Brooklyn*, and T.T. *Bay Ridge*. Each tanker was constructed pursuant to a contract in which a separate wholly owned subsidiary of Seatrain engaged Shipbuilding. Shipbuilding in turn contracted with respondent, now known as Transamerica Delaval Inc. (Delaval), to design, manufacture, and supervise the installation of turbines (costing $1.4 million each) that would be the main propulsion units for the 225,000-ton, $125 million supertankers. When each ship was completed, its title was transferred from the contracting subsidiary to a trust company (as trustee for an owner), which in turn chartered the ship to one of the petitioners, also subsidiaries of Seatrain. Each charterer assumed responsibility for the cost of any repairs to the ships.

The *Stuyvesant* sailed on its maiden voyage in late July 1977. On December 11 of that year, as the ship was about to enter the Port of Valdez, Alaska, steam began to escape from the casing of the high-pressure turbine. That problem was temporarily resolved by repairs, but before long, while the ship was encountering a severe storm in the Gulf of Alaska, the high-pressure turbine malfunctioned. The ship, though lacking its normal power, was able to continue on its journey to Panama and then San Francisco. In January 1978, an examination of the high-pressure turbine revealed that the first-stage steam-reversing ring virtually had disintegrated and had caused additional damage to other parts of the turbine. The damaged part was replaced with a part from the *Bay Ridge*, which was then under construction. In April 1978, the ship again was repaired, this time with a part from the *Brooklyn*. Finally, in August, the ship was permanently and satisfactorily repaired with a ring newly designed and manufactured by Delaval.

The *Brooklyn* and the *Williamsburgh* were put into service in late 1973 and late 1974, respectively. In 1978, as a result of the *Stuyvesant*'s problems, they were inspected while in port. Those inspections revealed similar turbine damage. Temporary repairs were made, and newly designed parts were installed as permanent repairs that summer.

When the *Bay Ridge* was completed in early 1979, it contained the newly designed parts and thus never experienced the high-pressure turbine problems that plagued the other three ships. Nonetheless, the complaint appears to claim damages as a result of deterioration of the *Bay Ridge*'s ring that was installed in the *Stuyvesant* while the *Bay Ridge* was under construction. In addition, the *Bay Ridge* experienced a unique problem. In 1980, when the ship was on its maiden voyage, the engine began to vibrate with a frequency that increased even after speed was reduced. It turned out that the astern guardian valve, located between the high-pressure and low-pressure turbines, had been installed backwards. Because of that error, steam entered the low-pressure turbine and damaged it. After repairs, the *Bay Ridge* resumed its travels.

The charterers' second amended complaint contains five counts alleging tortious conduct on the part of respondent Delaval and seeks an aggregate of more than $8 million in damages for the cost of repairing the ships and for income lost while the ships were out of service. The first four counts, read liberally, allege that Delaval is strictly liable for the design defects in the high-pressure turbines of the *Stuyvesant*, the *Williamsburgh*, the *Brooklyn*, and the *Bay Ridge*, respectively. The fifth count alleges that Delaval, as part of the manufacturing process, negligently supervised the installation of the eastern guardian valve on the *Bay Ridge*. Delaval then moved for summary judgment, contending that the charterers' actions were not cognizable in tort.

II. Pure Economic Loss

The District Court granted summary judgment for Delaval, and the Court of Appeals for the Third Circuit, sitting en banc, affirmed. The Court of Appeals held that damage solely to a defective product is actionable in tort if the defect creates an unreasonable risk of harm to persons or property other than the product itself, and harm materializes. Disappointments over the product's quality, on the other hand, are protected by warranty law. The charterers were dissatisfied with product quality: the defects involved gradual and unnoticed deterioration of the turbines' component parts, and the only risk created was that the turbines would operate at a lower capacity. Therefore, neither the negligence claim nor the strict-liability claim was cognizable.

We granted certiorari to resolve a conflict among the Courts of Appeals sitting in admiralty.

We join the Courts of Appeals in recognizing products liability, including strict liability, as part of the general maritime law. Our incorporation of products liability into maritime law, however, is only the threshold determination to the main issue in this case.

Products liability grew out of a public policy judgment that people need more protection from dangerous products than is afforded by the law of warranty. It is clear, however, that if this development were allowed to progress too far, contract law would drown in a sea of tort. *See* Grant Gilmore, THE DEATH OF CONTRACT 87-94 (1974). We must determine whether a commercial product injuring itself is the kind of harm against which public policy requires manufacturers to protect, independent of any contractual obligation.

The paradigmatic products-liability action is one where a product "reasonably certain to place life and limb in peril," distributed without reinspection, causes bodily injury. *See, e.g.*, MacPherson v. Buick Motor Co., 217 N.Y. 382, 389 (1916). The manufacturer is liable whether or not it is negligent because "public policy demands that responsibility be fixed wherever it will most effectively reduce the hazards to life and health inherent in defective products that reach the market." Escola v. Coca Cola Bottling Co. of Fresno, 150 P.2d, at 441 (Traynor, J., concurring in judgment).

For similar reasons of safety, the manufacturer's duty of care was broadened to include protection against property damage. [ ] Such damage is considered so akin to personal injury that the two are treated alike.

In the traditional "property damage" cases, the defective product damages other property. In this case, there was no damage to "other" property. Rather, the first, second, and third counts allege that each supertanker's defectively designed turbine components damaged only the turbine itself. Since each turbine was supplied by Delaval as an integrated package, each is properly regarded as a single unit. The fifth count also alleges injury to the product itself. Before the high-pressure and low-pressure turbines could become an operational propulsion system, they were connected to piping and valves under the supervision of Delaval personnel. Delaval's supervisory obligations were part of its manufacturing agreement. The fifth count thus can best be read to allege that Delaval's negligent manufacture of the propulsion system—by allowing the installation in reverse of the astern guardian valve—damaged the propulsion system. Obviously, damage to a product itself has certain attributes of a products-liability claim. But the injury suffered—the failure of the product to function properly—is the essence of a warranty action, through which a contracting party can seek to recoup the benefit of its bargain.

The intriguing question whether injury to a product itself may be brought in tort has spawned a variety of answers.[3] At one end of the spectrum, the case that created the majority land-based approach, Seely v. White Motor Co., 63 Cal. 2d 9 (1965) (defective truck), held that preserving a proper role for the law of warranty precludes imposing tort liability if a defective product causes purely monetary harm.

At the other end of the spectrum is the minority land-based approach. The courts adopting this approach, including the majority of the Courts of Appeals sitting in admiralty that have considered the issue, find that the safety and insurance rationales behind strict liability apply equally where the losses are purely economic. These courts reject the *Seely* approach because they find it arbitrary that economic losses are recoverable if a plaintiff suffers bodily injury or property damage, but not if a product injures itself. They also find no inherent difference between economic loss and personal injury or property damage, because all are proximately caused by the defendant's conduct. Further, they believe recovery for economic loss would not lead to unlimited liability because they think a manufacturer can predict and insure against product failure.

Between the two poles fall a number of cases that would permit a products-liability action under certain circumstances when a product injures only itself. These cases attempt to differentiate between the "disappointed users" and the "endangered ones," and permit only the latter to sue in tort. The determination has been said to turn on the nature of the defect, the type of risk, and the manner in which the injury arose. *See* Pennsylvania Glass Sand Corp. v. Caterpillar Tractor Co., 652 F.2d 1165, 1173 93 (3d Cir. 1982) (relied on by the Court of Appeals in this case).

We find the intermediate and minority land-based positions unsatisfactory. The intermediate positions, which essentially turn on the degree of risk, are too indeterminate to enable manufacturers easily to structure their business behavior. Nor do we find persuasive a distinction that rests on the manner in which the product is injured. We realize that the damage may be qualitative, occurring through gradual deterioration or internal breakage. Or it may be calamitous. But either way, since by definition no person or other property is damaged, the resulting loss is purely economic. Even when the harm to the product itself occurs through an abrupt, accident-like event, the resulting loss due to repair costs, decreased value, and lost profits is essentially the failure of the purchaser to receive the benefit of its bargain—traditionally the core concern of contract law.

We also decline to adopt the minority land-based view. Such cases raise legitimate questions about the theories behind restricting products liability, but we believe that the countervailing arguments are more powerful. The minority view fails to account for the need to keep products liability and contract law in separate spheres and to maintain a realistic limitation on damages.

Exercising traditional discretion in admiralty, we adopt an approach similar to *Seely* and hold that a manufacturer in a commercial relationship has no duty under either a negligence or strict products-liability theory to prevent a product from injuring itself.

---

3. The question is not answered by the *Restatement (Second) of Torts* §§395 and 402A (1965), or by the Uniform Commercial Code.

II. Pure Economic Loss 565

"The distinction that the law has drawn between tort recovery for physical injuries and warranty recovery for economic loss is not arbitrary and does not rest on the 'luck' of one plaintiff in having an accident causing physical injury. The distinction rests, rather, on an understanding of the nature of the responsibility a manufacturer must undertake in distributing his products." Seely v. White Motor Co., 403 P.2d, at 151. When a product injures only itself the reasons for imposing a tort duty are weak and those for leaving the party to its contractual remedies are strong.

The tort concern with safety is reduced when an injury is only to the product itself. When a person is injured, the "cost of an injury and the loss of time or health may be an overwhelming misfortune," and one the person is not prepared to meet. *Escola v. Coca Cola Bottling Co.* at 462 (Traynor, J., concurring in judgment). In contrast, when a product injures itself, the commercial user stands to lose the value of the product, risks the displeasure of its customers who find that the product does not meet their needs, or, as in this case, experiences increased costs in performing a service. Losses like these can be insured. Society need not presume that a customer needs special protection. The increased cost to the public that would result from holding a manufacturer liable in tort for injury to the product itself is not justified. *Cf.* United States v. Carroll Towing Co., 159 F.2d 169, 173 (CA2 1947).

Damage to a product itself is most naturally understood as a warranty claim. Such damage means simply that the product has not met the customer's expectations, or, in other words, that the customer has received "insufficient product value." [ ] The maintenance of product value and quality is precisely the purpose of express and implied warranties. *See* UCC §2-313 (express warranty), §2-314 (implied warranty of merchantability), and §2-315 (warranty of fitness for a particular purpose). Therefore, a claim of a nonworking product can be brought as a breach-of-warranty action. Or, if the customer prefers, it can reject the product or revoke its acceptance and sue for breach of contract. *See* UCC §§2-601, 2-608, 2-612.

Contract law, and the law of warranty in particular, is well suited to commercial controversies of the sort involved in this case because the parties may set the terms of their own agreements. The manufacturer can restrict its liability, within limits, by disclaiming warranties or limiting remedies. *See* UCC §§2-316, 2-719. In exchange, the purchaser pays less for the product. Since a commercial situation generally does not involve large disparities in bargaining power, we see no reason to intrude into the parties' allocation of the risk.

While giving recognition to the manufacturer's bargain, warranty law sufficiently protects the purchaser by allowing it to obtain the benefit of its bargain. The expectation damages available in warranty for purely economic loss give a plaintiff the full benefit of its bargain by compensating for forgone business opportunities. Recovery on a warranty theory would give the charterers their repair costs and lost profits, and would place them in the position they would have been in had the turbines functioned properly. Thus, both the nature of the injury and the resulting damages indicate it is more natural to think of injury to a product itself in terms of warranty.

A warranty action also has a built-in limitation on liability, whereas a tort action could subject the manufacturer to damages of an indefinite amount. The limitation in a contract action comes from the agreement of the parties and the requirement that consequential damages, such as lost profits, be a foreseeable result of the breach. *See* Hadley v. Baxendale, 9 Ex. 341, 156 Eng. Rep. 145 (1854). In a warranty action where the loss is purely economic, the limitation derives from the requirements of foreseeability and of privity, which is still generally enforced for such claims in a commercial setting. *See* UCC §2-715.

In products-liability law, where there is a duty to the public generally, foreseeability is an inadequate brake. Permitting recovery for all foreseeable claims for purely economic loss could make a manufacturer liable for vast sums. It would be difficult for a manufacturer to take into account the expectations of persons downstream who may encounter its product. In this case, for example, if the charterers—already one step removed from the transaction—were permitted to recover their economic losses, then the companies that subchartered the ships might claim their economic losses from the delays, and the charterers' customers also might claim their economic losses, and so on. "The law does not spread its protection so far." [ ]

For the first three counts, the defective turbine components allegedly injured only the turbines themselves. Therefore, a strict products-liability theory of recovery is unavailable to the charterers. Similarly, in the fifth count, alleging the reverse installation of the astern guardian valve, the only harm was to the propulsion system itself rather than to persons or other property. Even assuming that Delaval's supervision was negligent, as we must on this summary judgment motion, Delaval owed no duty under a products-liability theory based on negligence to avoid causing purely economic loss. Thus, whether stated in negligence or strict liability, no products-liability claim lies in admiralty when the only injury claimed is economic loss.

We affirm the entry of judgment for Delaval.

NOTES AND QUESTIONS

1. *The majority rule.* As indicated by the discussion in *East River Steamship*, the Court adopts a rule that a strong majority of state courts had already adopted. *East River Steamship* helped to cement the majority rule. It is the "leading decision espousing the position that the nature of the loss should be the determining factor" in deciding the scope of the tort duty. RESTATEMENT (THIRD) OF TORTS: PRODUCTS LIABILITY §21 cmt. d. In particular, the rationales invoked by the Court in *East River Steamship* have influenced other courts. *See, e.g.*, Grams v. Milk Prods., Inc., 699 N.W.2d 167, 171 (Wis. 2005) ("In Wisconsin, the economic loss doctrine is based on three fundamental premises. It seeks (1) to maintain the fundamental distinction between tort law and contract law; (2) to protect commercial parties' freedom to allocate economic risk by contract; and (3) to encourage the party best situated to assess the risk of economic loss, that is, the commercial purchaser, to assume, allocate, or insure against that risk.").

2. *Revisiting the tort-contract boundary.* For reasons the Court identifies in *East River Steamship*, a tort rule governing pure economic loss returns us to the boundary between tort and contract law. In evaluating the respective roles for these two bodies of law, we have found that the appropriate rule depends on whether consumers have enough information to adequately

protect their interests by contracting. A tort duty is not justified when the ordinary consumer can make good contracting decisions and does not have frustrated safety expectations. For example, a product is not "unreasonably dangerous" and subject to strict products liability when the ordinary consumer with ordinary knowledge common to the community can make an informed risk-utility decision about the safety matter in question. *See* Chapter 5; *see also* Chapter 6, section III (discussing cases in which informed consumer choice limits liability for defective design). As applied to the issue of pure economic loss, this principle means that the tort duty should not encompass the risk of pure economic loss if the ordinary consumer has good information about the risk and can adequately protect her interests by contracting with product sellers. In justifying the economic loss rule, the court in *East River Steamship* assumed that consumers can adequately protect their interests by contracting. Is this assumption valid? If so, the Court's formulation of the economic loss rule in *East River Steamship* depends on the same contracting rationale that otherwise determines whether contract or tort law applies in product cases.

3. *A substantive contracting rationale for the economic loss rule.* To determine whether consumers have enough information to protect their purely economic interests by contracting, we need to place the contracting decision in context. Because the ordinary tort duty is based on an implied representation that the product is not defective, the consumer "has no duty to discover or guard against a product defect." General Motors Corp. v. Sanchez, 997 S.W.2d 584, 593 (Tex. 1999). Freed from the need to consider product defects that might cause physical harm, the consumer's contracting decision is limited to cases in which a defect only causes pure economic loss. Consider Trans State Airlines v. Pratt & Whitney Canada, Inc., 682 N.E.2d 45, 53 (Ill. 1997) ("[W]e believe that the incentive to manufacture safe products remains unabated under the *East River [Steamship]* approach. Where the product causes personal injury or other property damage, the manufacturer may yet be subject to liability in tort. Because no manufacturer can predict with any certainty that the damage his unsafe product causes will be confined to the product itself, tort liability will continue to loom as a possibility. Therefore, in our view, the incentive to build safe products is not diminished.").

In contracting over defects that threaten only pure economic loss, the consumer can also rely on the contractual version of the implied warranty, which guarantees that the product is not defective. U.C.C. §2-314. Although the seller can expressly disclaim the implied product warranty with clear and conspicuous language in the sales contract, *id.* §2-316(2), doing so can alert otherwise unwary consumers of the need to consider whether a defect might cause pure economic losses. The contractual transaction is further regulated in most states by consumer protection statutes that prohibit unfair and deceptive trade practices. *See* Jean Braucher, *Deception, Economic Loss and Mass-Market Customers: Consumer Protection Statutes as Persuasive Authority in the Common Law of Fraud*, 48 Ariz. L. Rev. 829, 830-831 (2006). The contractual transaction, therefore, is regulated in a manner that simplifies the consumer's decision about how to allocate liability for pure economic loss.

The amount of economic loss depends on the economic benefits that a consumer expects to receive by using the product. For example, a recording device can capture a mundane conversation or a musical performance with vast commercial potential. A defect that renders the device unable to perform the recording function would cause substantially different economic losses in the two contexts. In most cases, the manufacturer does not know how a consumer will use the product. By contrast, the consumer knows how the product will be used and has better information about the amount of financial harms, like lost profits, that could be caused by a product malfunction. This information enables the ordinary consumer to protect her interests by either contracting with the seller for warranty coverage, purchasing other types of insurance, or obtaining a supply of spare parts.

A tort duty encompassing pure economic harms, therefore, is not needed to protect the consumer interests at stake in these cases. The general duty of care protects the consumer's interest in physical security—the core concern of tort law—and the consumer can protect her pure economic interests by contracting with either the seller or other parties like insurance companies. *See generally* William K. Jones, *Product Defects Causing Commercial Loss: The Ascendancy of Contract over Tort*, 44 U. Miami L. Rev. 731, 764-767 (1990) (developing the contracting rationale for the economic loss rule).

4. *The problem of component parts.* To apply the economic loss rule, "we must first determine what the product at issue is. Only then do we find out whether the injury is to the product itself (for which recovery is barred by the economic loss rule) or to property other than the defective product (for which plaintiffs may recover in tort)." Jimenez v. Superior Court, 58 P.3d 450, 456 (Cal. 2002). "What constitutes harm to other property rather than harm to the product itself may be difficult to determine," particularly "when a component part of a machine or system destroys the rest of the machine or system." RESTATEMENT (THIRD) OF TORTS: PRODUCTS LIABILITY §21 cmt. e.

Under what appears to be the most commonly used approach, "[i]f a product was purchased as a complete whole, damage to that product caused by one of its component parts is considered damage to the product itself—rather than damage to other property—and limited to recovery in contract by the economic loss rule." Golden Spread Elec. Coop., Inc. v. Emerson, 954 F.3d 804, 809 (5th Cir. 2020). *See also, e.g.*, Trans State Airlines v. Pratt & Whitney Canada, Inc., 682 N.E.2d 45, 55-59 (Ill. 1997) (adopting this rule and citing cases from other jurisdictions in support); Saratoga Fishing Co. v. J.M. Martinac & Co., 520 U.S. 875, 884 (1997) (holding that "equipment added to a product after the Manufacturer (or distributor selling in the initial distribution chain) has sold the product to an initial User is not part of the product itself" and therefore not governed by *East River Steamship*). This definition of the "product" follows from the contracting rationale for the economic loss rule, because the integrated product typically defines the subject matter of the contractual transaction, whereas "other property" involves separate transactions. *See Golden Spread Elec. Coop.*, 954 F.3d at 809 ("Such a lack of separate bargaining can inform the determination of whether a product has damaged other property, rather than itself, but the presence of separate bargaining alone is not necessarily determinative. Replacement parts, for example, are often purchased separately from the original product [and are still part of the integrated product].").

5. *Beyond damage to the product itself.* Many courts have extended the economic loss rule to cases in which the defect also damages other property, relying on a foreseeability test. *See* Travelers Indemnity Co. v. Dammann & Co., 594 F.3d 238, 250 (3d Cir. 2010) ("The majority of jurisdictions employ some variation of a test under which tort remedies are unavailable for property damage experienced by the owner where the damage was a foreseeable result of a defect at the time the parties contractually determined their respective exposure to risk, regardless whether the damage was to the 'goods' themselves or to 'other property.'"). In Arena Holdings Charitable, LLC v. Harman Professional, Inc., 785 F.3d 292 (8th Cir. 2015), the court applied this rule to bar the tort claim that the plaintiff arena owner had filed against the manufacturer of a sound amplifier to recover damages resulting from a fire caused by a defect in the amplifier. Do cases like this involve the type of contracting problem at issue in *East River Steamship*? Is the concern about lost profits and repair costs the same as the risk that the defect will damage real or tangible property beyond the product itself?

6. *Scope of the economic loss rule.* Is the economic loss rule limited to commercial parties, or does it apply more generally to limit tort claims by ordinary consumers? *Compare* RESTATEMENT (THIRD) OF TORTS: PRODUCTS LIABILITY §21 (limiting tort recovery to cases involving bodily injury or damage to other property without any qualification concerning the type of purchaser), *with* State Farm Mutual Automobile Insurance Co. v. Norcold, Inc., 849 F.3d 328, 335 (6th Cir. 2017) ("[B]ecause the policies underlying the economic loss rule justify treating commercial and consumer transactions differently, we hold that the economic loss rule does not extend to consumer transactions."). Would an extension of the economic loss rule to cases in which the defect damages other types of property be more defensible in the commercial context, where the property in question is a business asset fully insurable by property insurance? For ordinary consumers, by contrast, real and tangible property are not merely financial assets but are often closely tied to their personal identities. Consider the difference between a commercial office space and a personal residence.

Regardless of the commercial status of the contracting parties, should the scope of the economic loss rule depend on the different reasons why plaintiffs seek tort recovery? In *East River Steamship*, the plaintiff presumably chartered the oil-transporting supertankers on the expectation that they would produce profits. Each of these ships had a defect that frustrated the plaintiff's expectations of commercial profit, the core interest protected by the Uniform Commercial Code. Do disappointed expectations of lost profit supply the only reason why plaintiffs might seek tort recovery for pure economic loss? Would any difference in this respect affect the substantive contracting rationale for the economic loss rule?

PFIZER, INC. v. FARSIAN
Supreme Court of Alabama, 1996
682 So. 2d 405

Shores, J. Garshasb Farsian sued Shiley, Inc., and its parent corporation, Pfizer, Inc. (hereinafter collectively referred to as "Shiley"), alleging, among other things, that they had fraudulently induced Farsian to receive a Bjork-Shiley heart valve implant by not revealing to Farsian certain risks and defects. Farsian alleges that when his cardiologist recommended heart surgery in 1980 he discussed with Farsian two types of heart valves. According to Farsian, the doctor recommended Shiley's valve because, the doctor said, it was an outstanding valve and would never have to be replaced. The alternative, a pig valve, would wear out in 10 or 15 years and would have to be replaced.[1] Farsian asserts that he relied on information provided by his doctor and from Shiley indicating that Shiley's heart valve was the best on the market and would last indefinitely, and that, consequently, he chose to have Shiley's heart valve implanted.

Farsian now contends that he was misled. Farsian argues that during clinical trials in 1978, Shiley's heart valve experienced the first of many strut failures.[2] Farsian alleges that Shiley told the FDA that the failure was an anomaly. As of 1990, however, Shiley had reported a total of 295 fractures, resulting in 178 deaths.[3] Farsian contends that when he received Shiley's heart valve in 1981, Shiley was engaging in fraudulent conduct by marketing the valve despite knowing of serious manufacturing problems that directly related to the fracture problem in the valve. Farsian also contends that Shiley never informed him or his physician of the fracture problem before the implantation. Farsian argues that Shiley misled physicians and the public by understating the incidence of strut fractures in a "Dear Doctor" letter in 1980 and by instructing the valve's creator not to publish any information relative to strut fracture. Shiley removed some of these heart valves from the market in 1985; Farsian alleges that it did so under pressure from the Health Research Group and the FDA. It removed all remaining valves in 1986. Farsian asserts that he would not have allowed Shiley's valve to be implanted in his heart had he known of the strut fracture risk.

Farsian sued Shiley, alleging that Shiley had made intentional, reckless, or negligent misrepresentations about the fitness of the valve; that he had relied on the representations; and that Shiley had known the representations to be false. Farsian also alleges that Shiley fraudulently concealed and withheld information from him and his medical providers regarding strut fracture with the intent to deceive, and he alleges that Shiley fraudulently induced him to have

---

1. The other major difference between the two valves is that for the rest of their lives patients in whom Shiley's valve is implanted must take medication to thin their blood, whereas patients with pig valves need not take the medication.

2. The valve is basically a disc located inside a ring that is sutured to the heart. It opens and closes rhythmically, allowing blood to flow through the heart. The disc is held in place by two wire holders called inflow and outflow struts, located on each side of the disc. The valve failure relevant to this case is caused when the outflow strut fractures. When the strut is fractured, the disc escapes from the ring, causing uncontrolled blood flow through the heart.

3. According to a congressional report, the number of reported fractures and resulting deaths "is generally agreed to be greatly understated because the distress signs of patients with common heart seizures and fracture problems are similar and autopsies are not always taken." [ ]

II. Pure Economic Loss

the Bjork-Shiley valve implanted. As a result of Shiley's conduct, Farsian contends, he has suffered damage to the extent that the implanted valve, with its higher rate of fracture and risk of death, is worth less than the valve would have been worth if it had been what Shiley represented it to be. Farsian also alleges that he has suffered mental anguish and emotional distress since he learned of Shiley's fraud. Moreover, he states that he wishes to undergo surgery to have the Shiley's valve removed and replaced, and he seeks remuneration for the expenses related to this procedure. Farsian also seeks punitive damages.

Shiley moved for a summary judgment, contending that although Farsian alleges a risk of possible future malfunction of the valve, it is uncontroverted that Farsian's valve is and has been working properly. Shiley contends that Farsian is really asserting a product liability claim. Shiley asserts that under Alabama product liability law, a cause of action regarding an implanted medical device accrues only when an "injury-producing malfunction" occurs. According to Shiley, an allegation of fraud does not relieve the consumer from having to prove an injury-producing malfunction. Because Farsian has suffered no injury-producing malfunction, Shiley argues that Farsian's claim fails.

Farsian, however, maintains that his claim is based on fraud, not product liability. Farsian contends that, in Alabama, claims against manufacturers are not governed by a product liability law that subsumes all other theories of liability. Therefore, he argues that he may recover damages on his fraud claim even if he cannot prove that his valve is not working properly.

The question certified to this Court [by the United States Court of Appeals for the Eleventh Circuit] concerns whether Farsian may maintain a fraud claim.

> [Does a heart valve implantee have a valid cause of action for fraud under Alabama law if he asserts that the valve's manufacturer fraudulently induced him to have the valve implanted when the damages that he asserts do not include an injury-producing malfunction of the product because the valve has been and is working properly?]

We conclude that he may not.

Regardless of how Farsian pleads his claim, his claim is in substance a product liability/personal-injury claim—Farsian seeks damages because of the risk that his heart valve may one day fail. Alabama courts have never allowed a recovery based on a product that, like Farsian's valve, is and has been working properly. Each of our prior cases in which fraud or other intentional conduct was alleged has involved a failure, a malfunction, or an accident that involved the defendant's products and which injured the plaintiff. [ ]

Under Alabama law, Farsian's fear that his valve could fail in the future is not, without more, a legal injury sufficient to support his claim. Although the facts as presented by the Court of Appeals indicate that the Bjork-Shiley heart valve has experienced problems with strut failures, Farsian's concern that his heart valve, which is presently functioning normally, could later malfunction is not an injury recognized by Alabama law.

Other courts have refused to recognize a cause of action in similar cases when the heart valve has not failed. [ ]

Farsian's heart valve has not failed. Instead, it has been working properly and as intended by its manufacturer, Bjork-Shiley. Although the parties see different theories of this case—Farsian relying upon Alabama fraud law, while Shiley argues in the context of product liability law—we conclude that the answer to the certified question, whether it is couched in terms of fraud law or in terms of product liability law, must be that Farsian does not now have a cause of action for damages, because the valve has not failed.

For the foregoing reasons, we answer the United States Court of Appeals' question in the negative.

NOTES AND QUESTIONS

1. *Manifestation of defect.* For cases involving a so-called *unmanifested defect*, the product has a known defect that has not yet caused physical harm. That risk, however, can cause the consumer to suffer financial harms of repair, replacement costs, or diminution in the market value of the product. Any claim seeking damages for these harms implicates the economic loss rule. Consistently with the majority rule barring recovery for pure economic loss, the majority of jurisdictions bar claims of fraud or misrepresentation based on the same subject matter governed by the implied warranty. *See, e.g.*, Wallis v. Ford Motor Co., 208 S.W.3d 153, 155-159 (Ark. 2005) (dismissing fraud claim that sought recovery for diminution in market value caused by defectively designed sport utility vehicle's increased propensity to roll over and providing extensive citation to other cases reaching the same result); *see also* Hinrichs v. Dow Chemical Co., 937 N.W.3d 37, 47 (Wis. 2020) (explaining that an exception to the economic loss rule applies under a "fraud in the inducement claim" only if the "the alleged misrepresentation was extraneous to the contract").

2. *Claims for pure economic loss and class-action suits.* "Because proof of damages is a necessary element of several claims commonly asserted in product liability actions, the individualized proof needed to establish whether and the extent to which each class member was damaged ordinarily precludes certification of product liability claims." Joseph M. McLaughlin, McLaughlin on Class Actions §5:45 (17th ed. & 2020 update). To avoid this problem, plaintiffs often pursue class-action suits seeking recovery for pure economic losses that are uniformly suffered by all owners or consumers of the defective product, such as the diminution of market value caused by the defect. Consequently, the "automotive, pharmaceutical, software, cell phone, and other industries have all recently contended with putative class actions alleging neither personal injury nor property damages, but economic loss stemming from purchase of a product with a potential but unmanifested defect." *Id.* §5:56. As *Farsian* illustrates, "[m]ost courts have taken a dim view of such classes. . . . These cases hold that diminution in resale value is not legally cognizable injury." *Id.*

3. *Different types of pure economic loss.* In evaluating claims involving unmanifested defects, courts do not distinguish between the pure economic loss caused by a diminution in market value and the pure economic loss caused by the need to repair or cure the defect. In *Farsian*, for example, the plaintiff sought recovery for both types of harm. The court dismissed the entire claim without asking whether diminished product value is substantively equivalent to the financial costs of surgery for removing the

defective heart valve and protecting the plaintiff from physical harm in the event that the defect ultimately manifests itself. Does the substantive contracting rationale for the economic loss rule draw a distinction between these two types of pure economic loss? As *Farsian* illustrates, courts regularly ignore this issue.

The distinction, however, matters for purposes of tort liability. The diminution of product value can only be a pure economic loss, because the manifestation of defect at most can only destroy the entire product value by rendering the product useless—a pure economic loss that is not a compensable harm. If the injury would not subject the defendant to tort liability when the defect becomes manifest, then obviously there should be no liability prior to the manifestation of defect. By contrast, the manifestation of defect in *Farsian* would have caused severe bodily injury for the plaintiff—a compensable tort harm. By repairing the unmanifested defect, the plaintiff would prevent a bodily injury that would undoubtedly subject the defendant to tort liability. Why should the timing of the plaintiff's claim matter? Compare Larsen v. Pacesetter Sys., Inc., 837 P.2d 1273, 1287 (Haw. 1992) (allowing recovery for defective medical implant because plaintiff "suffered actual physical injuries as a result of his replacement surgeries, distinguishing him from the general class of persons with similar implants").

In a multidistrict litigation (MDL) brought by consumers against manufacturers of airbags and vehicles containing Takata airbags that were defectively designed for containing a propellant that could cause the airbags to explode (literally) when deployed, the court rejected defendants' argument that plaintiffs seeking recovery for pure economic loss could not recover because their defects had not yet manifested:

> The crux of Plaintiffs' allegations is that the propellant used in the Takata airbags at issue is unstable. By definition, this alleged instability would mean that the airbags may not protect vehicle occupants, or it may, and it may create a more dangerous situation than having no airbag at all, or it may not. Plaintiffs allege there is no way to know whether the airbags at issue would perform satisfactorily in an accident. If Takata had installed grenades in its airbags that may or may not explode on impact, a court would not require an explosion to demonstrate manifestation of a defect. Plaintiffs have alleged essentially this scenario, explaining that occupants of vehicles equipped with the allegedly defective airbags cannot know whether their airbags will expel metal shrapnel that may kill or maim them.

In re: Takata Airbag Products Liability Litigation, 193 F. Supp. 3d 1324, 1335 (S.D. Fla. 2016). Did the defects in the airbags truly manifest themselves, or did the court instead effectively recognize that waiting for a "manifestation" of the defect makes little sense in these cases?

4. *The intermediate rule.* Recovery in a case like *Farsian* would be permitted under the "intermediate" rule discussed in *East River Steamship*, which distinguishes "disappointed users" from "endangered consumers" by permitting only the latter to sue in tort. This rule was rejected in *East River Steamship* on the ground that it is "too indeterminate to enable

manufacturers easily to structure their business behavior." Is the distinction between an endangered consumer and one with disappointed economic expectations so problematic that it justifies the rejection of tort claims in a case like *Farsian*?

Insofar as the economic loss rule is justified by a contracting rationale, could the distinction be drawn by simply looking at the substantive nature of a contractual bargain over the damages in question? Any contractual decision that is largely defined by the threat of physical harm (as in *Farsian*) involves the "endangered consumer" and is subject to the tort duty; all other contracting decisions pertain to economic expectations of lost profits and the like that could only "disappoint" users without "endangering" them, justifying the bar to recovery under the economic loss rule (as in the factual context of *East River Steamship*). In effect, the substantive nature of such a contract is defined by the substantive nature of the threatened interests the contract addresses. Would a rule that requires courts to examine the substantive nature of such a contract be too difficult to apply?

80 SOUTH EIGHTH STREET LIMITED PARTNERSHIP v. CAREY-CANADA, INC.
Supreme Court of Minnesota, 1992
486 N.W. 2d 393, amended 492 N.W.2d 256

KEITH, Chief Justice. The Federal District Court of Minnesota has certified to this court three questions of law:

1. Whether the economic loss doctrine as set forth in [ ], bars the owner of a building with asbestos-containing fireproofing from suing the manufacturer of the fireproofing under the tort theories of negligence and strict liability for the costs of maintenance, removal and replacement of the fireproofing?

2. . . .

3. . . .

The context for the certified questions is the motion for summary judgment by asbestos manufacturer W.R. Grace ("Grace") on the issue of its liability in negligence and strict liability for the costs of maintenance, removal and replacement of its Monokote fireproofing in the IDS Center located in Minneapolis, Minnesota. For purposes of presenting the above-stated questions of law to this court, the federal district court deemed Grace, the appellant, and 80 South Eighth Street Limited Partnership ("80 South Eighth"), respondent.

The IDS Center, constructed in 1970-72, is 52 stories high and is comprised of four commercial buildings: a tower and annex which includes office, retail, and common space, a hotel, a Woolworth store and underground parking. The IDS Center is used on a daily basis by tenants who lease space in the building, by maintenance and administrative staff, and by the general public.

. . .

Two types of asbestos-containing fireproofing, Firebar and Monokote, were used in the construction of the IDS Center. Firebar, manufactured by Carey Canadian Mines, Limited ("Carey"), and by the Celotex Corporation ("Celotex"),

II. Pure Economic Loss 575

was used on the first few floors of the tower and the first few floors of the annex. Carey and Celotex declared bankruptcy in October, 1990, and are no longer parties to this suit. After problems arose with the Firebar fireproofing, the decision was made to install Monokote fireproofing, manufactured by Grace, in the balance of the tower and the annex, and in the Woolworth building.

In 1986 and 1987, the Illinois Institute of Technology was employed to conduct a full survey of all floors of the IDS Center. 80 South Eighth learned from this study that asbestos-containing fireproofing was on the beams and columns on all floors of the IDS Tower, all floors of the IDS annex, and both floors of the Woolworth building. 80 South Eighth also conducted tests which showed that Monokote, even when undisturbed, will release substantial numbers of asbestos fibers. In addition, 80 South Eighth has had to institute costly maintenance procedures to keep the ceiling tiles and light fixtures in the IDS Center free from asbestos fibers.

In 1988, 80 South Eighth brought suit against Grace for compensatory damages to cover the costs of maintenance, removal and replacement of the asbestos in the Center, for punitive damages, and for costs of that suit. 80 South Eighth claims that the original owners, architects, and general contractors had intended to avoid asbestos-containing fireproofing by selecting "cementitious" fireproofing and, were not aware that the Monokote installed in the IDS Center contained asbestos. 80 South Eighth does not seek damages for personal injuries and there are no allegations of personal injuries caused by the asbestos-containing fireproofing used in the building. There are also no allegations that the Monokote has failed to perform its fireproofing function. In defense, Grace denies that the mere presence of asbestos in the building constitutes a health risk. Grace also claims that the original owners and construction team specified Monokote fireproofing and were aware of the presence of asbestos in the fireproofing. Grace further asserts that 80 South Eighth knew that Monokote was asbestos-containing fireproofing when it acquired its interest in the IDS Center.

On August 1, 1991, the federal district court certified the above-stated questions. . . . Because we answer the first certified question in the negative, we do not reach the other two questions. To answer the first question, we must examine the permissible overlap between tort and contract remedies available in Minnesota to commercial parties.

I.

Tort actions and contract actions protect different interests. Through a tort action, the duty of certain conduct is imposed by law and not necessarily by the will or intention of the parties. The duty may be owed to all those within the range of harm, or to a particular class of people. On the other hand, contract actions protect the interests in having promises performed. Contract obligations are imposed because of conduct of the parties manifesting consent, and are owed only to the specific parties named in the contract. [ ]

The economic loss doctrine provides a balance between two conflicting societal goals: that of encouraging marketplace efficiency through the voluntary contractual allocation of economic risks with that of discouraging conduct that leads to physical harm. [ ]

. . .

Here, 80 South Eighth seeks recovery for costs of maintenance, removal and replacement of the asbestos-containing fireproofing. Such a claim appears to be economic loss as defined in Minneapolis Society of Fine Arts v. Parker-Klein Associates Architects, Inc., 354 N.W.2d 816 (Minn. 1984), where plaintiff, a purchaser of bricks, sued the manufacturer in negligence and strict liability for deterioration of the bricks themselves. We said that plaintiff was barred from proceeding in tort because the claim was one for economic loss "defined as resulting from the failure of the product to perform to the level expected by the buyer and commonly . . . measured by the cost of repairing or replacing the product and the consequent loss of profits, or by the diminution in value of the product because it does not work for the general purposes for which it was manufactured and sold. . . . The damages sought in this case by [Minneapolis Society of Fine Arts] for removal and replacement of the brick and other consequential loss fall squarely within this 'economic loss' definition. As such, they were recoverable in contract, if at all." *Id.* at 820-21 (citations omitted).

We find that the rationale set forth in [ ] supports a definition of economic loss premised on a product's failure to perform as promised. The underlying assumption in [that case], as in all our cases of economic loss, is that commercial parties bring their experiences in the marketplace to the negotiations; that their reasonable contemplation is embodied in the transaction; that at the time of the contract formation they have defined the product, identified the risks, and negotiated a price of the goods that reflects the relative benefits and risks to each party. [ ]

. . .

Here, however, there is a distinguishing factor. The claim here is not that the fireproofing failed to perform satisfactorily as fireproofing. Such a claim arising from the failure of the product to meet expectations of suitability, quality and performance resulting in damages which a party to a sales contract could reasonably expect would flow from a defect in the product is a benefit of the bargain claim better addressed under contract and the Uniform Commercial Code. Rather, the claim here is that the Monokote introduced into the building asbestos which is highly dangerous to humans.

We are not persuaded by Grace's argument that cases from other jurisdictions which have allowed suits in tort for removal and replacement of asbestos-containing fireproofing were solely premised on the "other property" exception to the economic loss doctrine, which was not available in Minnesota. [ ] We simply do not believe that 80 South Eighth's claim of asbestos contamination is one for economic loss. 80 South Eighth is not seeking enforcement of the benefit of their bargain regarding the fireproofing performance of the Monokote. In seeking the costs of maintenance, removal and replacement, 80 South Eighth seeks the costs of eliminating the risks of injury and of making the building safe for all those who use and occupy this property.

Nor are we persuaded by Grace's characterization of cases of asbestos removal in governmental buildings and school districts as cases of personal injury to which the economic loss doctrine does not apply. Those cases did not turn on allegations of personal injury. [ ] Furthermore, the Uniform Commercial Code applies to a sale of goods even where the buyer is a public entity.

II. Pure Economic Loss

Instead, we find persuasive the state and federal decisions which have held that where the claim is for the contamination of the entire building with allegedly dangerous asbestos fibers, the claim is not one for economic loss. *See, e.g.,* City of Greenville v. W.R. Grace & Co., 827 F.2d 975, 978 (4th Cir. 1987) (the risk posed by materials containing friable asbestos "is not the type of risk that is normally allocated between the parties to a contract by agreement"); [ ].

II.

We believe that allowing 80 South Eighth to proceed in tort for damages relating to the maintenance, removal and replacement of asbestos-containing fireproofing advances both the rationale and public policy objectives of tort law and the Uniform Commercial Code. In the seminal economic loss case, Justice Traynor stated:

> The distinction that the law has drawn between tort recovery for physical injuries and warranty recovery for economic loss is not arbitrary and does not rest on the "luck" of one plaintiff in having an accident causing physical injury. The distinction rests, rather, on an understanding of the nature of the responsibility a manufacturer must undertake in distributing his products. He can appropriately be held liable for physical injuries caused by defects by requiring his goods to match a standard of safety defined in terms of conditions that create unreasonable risks of harm. He cannot be held for the level of performance of his products in the consumer's business unless he agrees that the product was designed to meet the consumer's demands.

Seely v. White Motor Co., 403 P.2d 145, 151 (Cal. 1965). Grace's fireproofing continues to provide fireproofing, but it does so by allegedly creating unreasonable risks of harm.

Asbestos fibers, if inhaled, can disrupt the normal functioning of the lungs and cause serious health problems. Asbestosis (a fibrous scarring of the lungs), lung cancer, and mesothelioma (a cancer of the lining of the chest or abdominal cavity) have been linked to asbestos exposure. There may be a long interval between the time of exposure to asbestos and the time when symptoms of asbestos related disease appear. [ ] It is generally accepted that mesothelioma is not dose related but can be caused by a single exposure to asbestos. [ ] One objective of tort law is to deter unreasonable risks of harm. A building owner acts reasonably in attempting to avoid or to minimize the risks of injury to the occupants of the building. Rather than waiting for an occupant or user of the building to develop an asbestos related injury, we believe building owners should be encouraged to abate the hazard to protect the public. We believe our decision today will do so.

We therefore hold that the economic loss doctrine does not bar the owner of a building with asbestos-containing fireproofing from suing the manufacturer of the fireproofing under the tort theories of negligence and strict liability for the costs of maintenance, removal and replacement of the fireproofing. Because we so hold, we do not have occasion to answer the other two certified questions of law.

NOTES AND QUESTIONS

1. *The asbestos-abatement cases.* In response to the health hazards posed by asbestos, the federal government and many states have enacted statutes requiring the removal or segregation of asbestos-containing materials from schools and public buildings. Private homeowners have also undertaken these abatement measures. The measures are quite expensive, leading property owners to seek tort compensation for the costs of abating the unreasonable risks posed by asbestos. In defending against these claims, asbestos manufacturers and suppliers have invoked the economic loss rule, maintaining that abatement costs are entirely financial.

The economic loss rule would seem to require dismissal of these claims. "In fact, most courts have done just the opposite, freely allowing property owners to sue in tort by adopting a 'liberal' definition of physical injury." Richard C. Ausness, *Tort Liability for Asbestos Removal Costs*, 73 Or. L. Rev. 505, 530 (1994). By holding that asbestos-containing material damages other property, "liberally" defined, these cases do not literally violate the economic loss rule.

The holding is unpersuasive, however, because asbestos-containing products are usually components of an integrated final product (the building). Moreover, "asbestos-containing materials do not physically alter any part of the building or impair its structural integrity." *Id.* at 532. Indeed, the building materials containing asbestos continue to perform the intended function of being fire resistant. The only reason to remove asbestos-containing materials is to reduce the risk of physical harm, not to restore the proper functioning of the building.

Consequently, the asbestos abatement cases effectively involve an exception to the majority rule on economic loss, an outcome acknowledged by the *Restatement (Third)*:

> One category of claims stands apart. In the case of asbestos contamination in buildings, most courts have taken the position that the contamination constitutes harm to the building as other property. *The serious health threat caused by asbestos contamination has led the courts to this conclusion.* Thus, actions seeking recovery for the costs of asbestos removal have been held to be within the purview of products liability law rather than commercial law.

RESTATEMENT (THIRD) OF TORTS: PRODUCTS LIABILITY §21 cmt. e at 296 (emphasis added).

By ignoring the form of damage and instead focusing on the serious health risks posed by the defect, what do the asbestos cases imply about the majority rule for pure economic loss? Consider in this regard how the reasoning in *East River Steamship* compares to the reasoning in *80 Eighth South Street*. Rather than following the majority rule, the asbestos-abatement cases effectively apply the intermediate rule that distinguishes between the disappointed consumer and the endangered consumer. As illustrated by *80 Eighth South Street*, this formulation of the economic loss rule evaluates the substantive nature of the threatened interests instead of simply looking at the form of the damages claimed by the plaintiff.

2. *Charting the "choppy" waters of the economic loss rule.* For reasons illustrated by the asbestos-abatement cases, the form of the alleged injury does not adequately define the economic loss rule across all cases. Consumers recover for the financial costs of asbestos abatement, yet are denied recovery for pure economic losses in other contexts. More generally, tort law recognizes a cause of action for pure economic loss in a wide variety of other cases, including "negligent misrepresentation, defamation, professional malpractice, breach of fiduciary duty, nuisance, loss of consortium, wrongful death, spoliation of evidence, and unreasonable failure to settle a claim within insurance policy limits." Vincent R. Johnson, *The Boundary-Line Function of the Economic Loss Rule*, 66 Wash. & Lee L. Rev. 523, 530-532 (2009) (footnotes omitted). Many of these cases pit one contracting party against another, yet plaintiffs recover tort damages for their pure economic losses. Why does contracting bar tort recovery for pure economic loss in some cases but not others involving contractual relationships? In the wake of *East River Steamship*, courts have "underscore[d] the desirability—perhaps urgency—of harmonizing the entire complex and confusing pattern of liability and nonliability for tortious conduct in contractual settings." Rardin v. T & D Mach. Handling, Inc., 890 F.2d 24, 30 (7th Cir. 1989).

The difficulty stems from the *East River Steamship* formulation of the economic loss rule, which relies on a contracting rationale that is not formulated in substantive terms. Neither the form of the alleged injury nor the form of the parties' relationship—the mere fact that they could have contracted over liability for pure economic loss—necessarily bars tort recovery across the full set of cases, so why does the contracting relationship bar tort recovery for pure economic loss in some cases but not others? The answer requires a substantive rationale for the economic loss rule that does not simply depend on the formal properties of the parties' relationship and the alleged injury, subject to a series of unexplained exceptions like those involving asbestos abatement. Unless the economic loss rule is anchored by such a substantive principle, judges will face difficulty in "chart[ing] a course in what commentators and courts across the country have referred to as the 'choppy waters' of the economic loss rule." Giddings & Lewis, Inc. v. Indus. Risk Insurers, 348 S.W.3d 729, 733 (Ky. 2011).

3. *The contracting rationale in "mixed" cases of pure economic loss.* Although a substantive contracting rationale can justify the economic loss rule in cases like *East River Steamship*, it is an open question whether that rationale applies to all cases of pure economic loss. Our prior analysis of the contracting problem for pure economic loss assumed that the product defect either causes physical harms or pure economic losses unrelated to the occurrence of physical harm, such as lost profits. *See* note 3, p. 567 *supra*. As *Farsian* and the asbestos-abatement cases illustrate, not all forms of pure economic loss satisfy these conditions. Even if the defect-related risk materializes into a pure economic loss—the financial cost of surgery to remove and replace a defective heart valve, for example—the consumer's contracting decision about that financial loss depends on a future risk of physical harm. The consumer's contracting decision over pure economic

losses is not necessarily independent from the threat of future physical harms—the two types of harms are "mixed" in this respect, unlike the harms involved in the contracting decision the court in *East River Steamship* analyzed. How does such a "mixed" case affect the substantive contracting rationale for the economic loss rule?

The general tort duty exists when the consumer does not have the information necessary for making a good contractual choice concerning the risk that the product might cause physical harm, which is why that safety decision is governed by the tort duty and not by the product contract. In our "mixed" case of pure economic loss, this informational problem still exists and can justify the tort duty, even though the plaintiff has not yet suffered physical harm and is seeking recovery only for pure economic loss.

Consider the consumer's contracting decision in a case like *Farsian*. At the time of purchase, a well-informed consumer would contractually obligate the manufacturer to pay for the costs of surgery to remove and replace a defective heart valve if those financial costs are less than the expected injury costs that the consumer would face by not removing the defective heart valve: $B_{repair} < PL_{physical}$. Hence the consumer's contracting decision is limited to the same substantive interests that are otherwise encompassed within the ordinary tort duty. The defect directly implicates the consumer's interest in physical security, not the economic interest pertaining to lost product value. The nature of the contracting decision, therefore, is substantively equivalent to the safety decision governed by the ordinary tort duty.

Due to the substantive equivalence of these two safety decisions, contracting problems that plague one decision extend to the other. Lacking both the requisite knowledge and the obligation to guard against product defects threatening physical harm, the consumer at the time of purchase cannot fairly contract over responsibility for repairing an unknown defect that only becomes manifest after purchase and threatens future physical harm. The same informational problem that justifies the ordinary tort duty extends to the consumer's contracting decision involving unknown defects that must be repaired in order to prevent future physical harms—a form of pure economic loss.

The substantive contracting rationale for the economic loss rule, therefore, only bars tort claims for defects that frustrate the consumer's economic expectations. As the court in *80 Eighth South Street* concluded, this expectancy is not implicated by a tort claim to recover the financial costs of asbestos abatement, which implicates the consumer's interest in physical security and her associated expectations of reasonably safe product performance—the interests protected by tort law. As this case illustrates, the substantive nature of the contracting decision provides a sound basis for determining whether the economic loss rule should bar tort recovery. For more extensive analysis, see Mark A. Geistfeld, *The Contractually Based Economic Loss Rule in Tort Law: Endangered Consumers and the Error of* East River Steamship, 65 DePaul L. Rev. 393 (2016).

III. THE COST OF MEDICAL MONITORING

Tort claims for the cost of medical monitoring involve product defects that have exposed plaintiff-consumers to a significant risk of suffering a disease such as cancer. In light of this risk, a plaintiff must undergo periodic, costly medical testing to determine whether she has the disease. Consequently, the plaintiff seeks tort recovery for these medical monitoring costs on the ground that the defective product foreseeably caused these expenses.

Without proof that the defect caused an existing, compensable physical harm, the plaintiff's tort claim for the financial costs of medical monitoring is a form of pure economic loss that would seem to be straightforwardly barred by the majority rule. After all, the majority formulation of the economic loss rule purportedly bars all tort claims for pure economic loss, even if the plaintiff is seeking recovery for the financial costs of preventing future physical harm. But like other liability rules that elevate form over substance, the majority rule on economic loss is most vulnerable when substantive concerns dominate the case at hand, as illustrated by the manner in which courts have effectively recognized an exception to the economic loss rule in cases of asbestos abatement. Consider whether this same dynamic influences the court's reasoning in the next case.

DONOVAN v. PHILIP MORRIS USA, INC.
Supreme Judicial Court of Massachusetts, 2009
914 N.E.2d 891

SPINA, J. The United States District Court for the District of Massachusetts, in the context of a motion to dismiss and a motion for summary judgment filed by Philip Morris USA, Inc. (Philip Morris), has certified the following question[ ] to this court: Does the plaintiffs' suit for medical monitoring, based on subclinical effects of exposure to cigarette smoke and increased risk of lung cancer, state a cognizable claim and/or permit a remedy under Massachusetts state law? We answer "Yes," to the extent the plaintiffs allege a cause of action in tort for future medical expenses.

This proposed class action was filed on December 14, 2006. The third amended complaint asserts claims on behalf of a putative class of Massachusetts residents who are fifty years of age or older, have cigarette smoking histories of twenty pack-years or more using Marlboro cigarettes,[6] currently smoke or quit smoking Marlboro cigarettes within one year of the filing of the initial complaint in this action, are not diagnosed with lung cancer or under investigation by a physician for suspected lung cancer, and have smoked Marlboro cigarettes within the Commonwealth.

---

6. A "pack-year" is the average number of packs of cigarettes smoked per day multiplied by the number of years the person has smoked. For example, two packs of cigarettes smoked per day for one year equals two pack-years.

The plaintiffs allege that Philip Morris wrongfully designed, marketed, and sold Marlboro cigarettes. They assert claims for breach of implied warranty based on design defect [and] negligent design and testing. The plaintiffs do not seek money damages or exemplary damages. They seek to compel Philip Morris to provide them with a court-supervised program of medical surveillance for early detection of lung cancer utilizing a technique known as low-dose computed tomography (LDCT) scans of the chest.

Philip Morris seeks dismissal of this action, arguing that Massachusetts law requires a plaintiff to plead and prove a present physical injury with objective symptoms to recover in tort. On this basis, Philip Morris argues that the plaintiffs' medical monitoring claims are not cognizable under Massachusetts law.

The plaintiffs proceed on the premise that Marlboro cigarettes are defectively designed. They contend that it was and continues to be wrongful conduct by Philip Morris to design, manufacture, market, and sell its Marlboro cigarettes because they deliver an excessive and unreasonably dangerous quantity of carcinogens when smoked by humans. The plaintiffs further contend that, at all relevant times, Philip Morris had available to it commercially acceptable and feasible alternative designs that would have drastically reduced the cancer-causing content of Marlboro cigarettes and, thus, the risk of developing lung cancer as a result of the prolonged and heavy use of Marlboro cigarettes. Philip Morris, it is alleged, concealed the specific product defect here at issue and kept from the public and the plaintiffs the fact that its Marlboro cigarettes contained excessive, improper, and unnecessarily high levels of carcinogens.

The plaintiffs allege that cigarette smoke from Marlboro cigarettes has caused them damage and injury to the tissues and structures of their lungs. The plaintiffs claim that cigarette smoke from Marlboro cigarettes continues to cause damage with each puff, inflicting new and additional bodily harm and substantially contributing to the risk of developing lung cancer. The plaintiffs do not allege, however, any manifest smoking-related disease resulting from their use of Marlboro cigarettes at the present time. Rather, they claim that they are at a high and significantly increased risk of developing lung cancer as a consequence of their prolonged and continuing use of Marlboro cigarettes (twenty pack-years or more) and their age (fifty years old or more).

[T]he plaintiffs allege and argue that they seek not a remedy, but a court-ordered, court-supervised program of medical surveillance for early detection of lung cancer utilizing LDCT scans. They further contend that without this program they have no adequate remedy at law, and that injunctive relief establishing such a program is necessary. We conclude that the plaintiffs have stated a claim under Massachusetts law for future medical expenses that may be satisfied by an adequate remedy at law.

Under our law of negligence, injury and damages are integrally related: there can be no invasion of the rights of another unless legal damage is caused, and for that reason nominal damages cannot be recovered. Philip Morris contends that our jurisprudence requires proof of physical harm manifested by objective symptomology as a necessary part of damages. We disagree.

There can be no doubt that an infant negligently and violently shaken by someone may recover expenses for diagnostic tests determined to be medically necessary under the standard of care to ascertain whether the child suffered a brain injury, even if those test results are negative. Similarly, a pedestrian

III. The Cost of Medical Monitoring

negligently struck by a motorist may recover expenses for diagnostic tests determined to be medically necessary under the standard of care to ascertain the existence of internal injuries absent any external injuries, even if those tests produce negative results. In those instances outward manifestations of physical harm would not be required. [ ]

Modern living has exposed people to a variety of toxic substances. Illness and disease from exposure to these substances are often latent, not manifesting themselves for years or even decades after the exposure. Some people so exposed may never develop an illness or disease, but some will. Subcellular or other physiological changes may occur which, in themselves, are not symptoms of any illness or disease, but are warning signs to a trained physician that the patient has developed a condition that indicates a substantial increase in risk of contracting a serious illness or disease and thus the patient will require periodic monitoring. Not all cases will involve physiological change manifesting a known illness, but such cases should be allowed to proceed when a plaintiff's reasonable medical expenses have increased (or are likely to increase, in the exercise of due care) as a result of these physiological changes. We leave for another day consideration of cases that involve exposure to levels of chemicals or radiation known to cause cancer, for which immediate medical monitoring may be medically necessary although no symptoms or subclinical changes have occurred. Here, the physiological changes with the attendant substantial increase in risk of cancer, and the medical necessity of monitoring with its attendant cost, may adequately establish the elements of injury and damages.

Our tort law developed in the late Nineteenth and early Twentieth centuries, when the vast majority of tortious injuries were caused by blunt trauma and mechanical forces. We must adapt to the growing recognition that exposure to toxic substances and radiation may cause substantial injury which should be compensable even if the full effects are not immediately apparent. When competent medical testimony establishes that medical monitoring is necessary to detect the potential onset of a serious illness or disease due to physiological changes indicating a substantial increase in risk of harm from exposure to a known hazardous substance, the element of injury and damage will have been satisfied and the cost of that monitoring is recoverable in tort. No particular level or quantification of increase in risk of harm is necessary, so long as it is substantial and so long as there has been at least a corresponding subcellular change. This should address any concern over false claims, yet permit a genuinely injured person to recover legitimate expenses without having to overcome insurmountable problems of proof in this difficult and complex area. In this respect, medical expenses are recoverable not only for direct treatment and diagnosis of a present injury or an injury likely to occur, but for diagnostic tests needed to monitor medically a person who has been substantially exposed to a toxic substance that has created physiological changes indicating a substantial increase in risk that the person will contract a serious illness or disease. The expense of medical monitoring is thus a form of future medical expense and should be treated as such.

In conclusion, each plaintiff must prove the following:

(1) The defendant's negligence (2) caused (3) the plaintiff to become exposed to a hazardous substance that produced, at least, subcellular changes

that substantially increased the risk of serious disease, illness, or injury (4) for which an effective medical test for reliable early detection exists, (5) and early detection, combined with prompt and effective treatment, will significantly decrease the risk of death or the severity of the disease, illness or injury, and (6) such diagnostic medical examinations are reasonably (and periodically) necessary, conformably with the standard of care, and (7) the present value of the reasonable cost of such tests and care, as of the date of the filing of the complaint.

We address a related issue. The very nature of this type of action raises the question whether the "single controversy rule," which requires a party to include in the action all related claims against the opposing party, would bar a future action for damages in the event a plaintiff subsequently contracts cancer. This rule was never intended to address the problem of toxic torts, where a disease may be manifested years after the exposure. In this context, the rule acts as a deterrent to persons seeking early detection of catastrophic disease, and it would expose both plaintiffs and defendants to far more serious consequences should the disease later manifest itself in an advanced stage. Such a result makes no sense. Finally, the single controversy rule would not apply because the subsequent cause of action would not accrue until the disease is manifested. For these reasons we conclude that, in the context of toxic torts, the single controversy rule does not bar a subsequent action for negligence if one of these plaintiffs actually contracts cancer.

We answer the certified question in the affirmative, although for the reasons stated, the cause of action is in tort, not equity.

NOTES AND QUESTIONS

1. *Another look at class certification.* Based on the court's requirements for establishing a medical monitoring claim, is there a sufficient commonality of issues to merit class certification under the Federal Rules of Evidence? In general, courts have answered this question in the negative. *See, e.g.,* Barnes v. American Tobacco Co., 161 F.3d 127, 146 (3d Cir. 1998) ("Although the general public's monitoring program can be proved on a class-wide basis, an individual's monitoring program by definition cannot. In order to prove the program he requires, a plaintiff must present evidence about his individual smoking history and subject himself to cross-examination by the defendant about that history. This element of the medical monitoring claim therefore raises many individual issues" that preclude certification under Rule 23(b)(3)). If plaintiffs are unable to pursue monitoring claims on a class-wide basis, does each individual claimant have sufficiently high damages to make the litigation economically worthwhile?

2. *A developing body of law.* The case law is closely divided on the question whether medical monitoring costs are recoverable without proof of an existing physical harm. As one court recently concluded, "While there are persuasive arguments articulated by a number of state and federal courts on both sides of the debate, neither plaintiffs nor defendants are able to demonstrate an overwhelming surge of decisions that would indicate that

III. The Cost of Medical Monitoring

there is a strong national trend one way or the other." Bell v. 3M Co., 344 F. Supp. 3d 1207, 1222–23 (D. Colo. 2018). The contradictory authority is fully reflected in Dougan v. Sikorsky Aircraft Corp., 2020 WL 5521391 (Conn. 2020), where the court first described the conflicting lines of authority and then rejected plaintiffs' claims for medical monitoring based on the *Donovan* criteria after concluding that plaintiffs had not proven that their asbestos exposures caused subcellular changes in their bodies. The court reached this conclusion by "assum[ing], without deciding, that the *Donovan* elements" create a cognizable claim under Connecticut law. *Id.* at *7.

3. *Rationales for the different rules.* In rejecting medical monitoring claims absent present physical injury, courts have expressed concern about a "potential flood of litigation stemming from unsubstantiated or fabricated prospective harms." Wood v. Wyeth-Ayerst Labs., 82 S.W.3d 849, 859 (Ky. 2002). Courts have also found monitoring claims to be problematic due to the possibility of "vast testing liability adversely affecting the allocation of scarce medical resources." Hinton v. Monsanto Co., 813 So. 2d 827, 831 (Ala. 2001). Another common criticism "is that courts use vague standards that lead to inconsistency and unpredictability in the adjudication of cases in which the plaintiff seeks medical monitoring" absent present injury. Adam P. Joffe, *The Medical Monitoring Remedy: Ongoing Controversy and a Proposed Solution*, 84 Chi.-Kent L. Rev. 663, 667 (2009).

To what extent are these concerns addressed by the court in *Donovan*? In recognizing claims for medical monitoring, the *Donovan* court required proof that the defect must have caused "subcellular changes" in the plaintiff. These "changes," however, do not amount to a compensable physical harm; otherwise the claim would be one for bodily injury that necessarily entitles the plaintiff to damages for future medical expenses. Compare Parker v. Wellman, 230 Fed. Appx. 878, 883 (11th Cir. 2007) (holding that allegations of subclinical or cellular injury are insufficient to support a claim for physical injury); Rainier v. Union Carbide Corp., 402 F.3d 608, 618-620 (6th Cir. 2005) (same). Any de minimis requirement of subcellular changes and the like instead combats the problem of frivolous or fraudulent claims.

4. *Wither the economic loss rule?* The financial costs of medical monitoring are a form of economic loss, and so absent proof of any present, compensable physical harm caused by the defect, these claims are literally barred by the majority formulation of the economic loss rule. In rejecting claims for medical monitoring, however, courts do not invoke the economic loss rule but instead limit liability for reasons discussed in the preceding note. For example, in an influential case rejecting tort claims for medical monitoring, the U.S. Supreme Court neither cited its earlier decision in *East River Steamship* nor provided any mention of the economic loss rule. See Metro-North Commuter R.R. Co. v. Buckley, 521 U.S. 424, 442-444 (1997) (rejecting plaintiffs' asbestos claim under the Federal Employers' Liability Act for a medical-monitoring remedy absent a present physical harm largely due to the concern that "tens of millions of individuals may have suffered exposure to substances that might justify some form of substance-exposure-related medical monitoring"). Why do courts not even consider

the economic loss rule when evaluating claims for medical monitoring? What implications do these cases have for the majority rule concerning pure economic loss? The intermediate rule?

Consider Seely v. White Motor Co., 403 P.2d 145 (Cal. 1965), which "is the leading state court case taking the position that damage to the product itself is economic loss and remedies for such losses are to be decided under the U.C.C. It was heavily relied upon by the [U.S. Supreme] Court in *East River Steamship*." RESTATEMENT (THIRD) OF TORTS: PRODUCTS LIABILITY §21 Rptrs' N. cmt. d. Recall that in *East River Steamship* (excerpted in section II, *supra*), the Court rejected the intermediate rule on economic loss, which distinguishes between the disappointed user and the endangered consumer. Is the intermediate rule so clearly contrary to California law as the *East River* Court had assumed? In Potter v. Firestone Tire & Rubber Co., 863 P.2d 795, 822-825 (Cal. 1993), the court recognized claims for medical monitoring absent present, compensable physical injury because (1) "there is an important public health interest in fostering access to medical testing for individuals whose exposure to toxic chemicals creates an enhanced risk of disease, particularly in light of the value of early diagnosis and treatment for many cancer patients"; (2) "there is a deterrence value in recognizing medical surveillance claims"; and (3) "the availability of a substantial remedy before the consequences of the plaintiffs' exposure are manifest may also have the beneficial effect of preventing or mitigating serious future illnesses and thus reduce the overall costs to the responsible parties." In light of this ruling, does California adhere to the majority formulation of the economic loss rule, or to the intermediate rule that distinguishes between endangered consumers and disappointed product users?

By permitting recovery for medical monitoring absent an existing compensable physical injury, courts have implicitly recognized another exception to the majority rule governing economic loss (along with the exception pertaining to the costs of asbestos abatement). As in cases of asbestos abatement, the cases that permit recovery for medical monitoring effectively recognize that the "endangered consumer" can recover for pure economic loss for expenses directly related to the reasonable prevention of future physical harm. Would this more general formulation of the rule improve upon the majority formulation that is subject to unexplained exceptions such as asbestos abatement and medical monitoring?

IV. STAND-ALONE EMOTIONAL HARMS

A product defect that does not physically harm the consumer can still cause a variety of other losses, including the foreseeable stress and emotional upset that a consumer predictably feels once she has found out that the defect might cause her to suffer debilitating disease in the near future. Is there any reason why foreseeable stand-alone emotional harms should be treated differently from

IV. Stand-Alone Emotional Harms

physical harms? Like the §402A rule of strict products liability in the *Restatement (Second)*, the liability rules governing defective products in the *Restatement (Third)* are expressly limited to physical harms. RESTATEMENT (THIRD) OF TORTS: PRODUCTS LIABILITY §1 cmt. d. The *Restatement (Third)* has a separate rule governing pure economic losses (discussed in section II), but there is no provision for the related class of stand-alone emotional harms.

As these *Restatement* provisions indicate, courts have concluded that the ordinary tort rules limiting liability for stand-alone emotional harms are also appropriate in product cases. Why is this issue governed by ordinary tort rules, whereas the economic loss rule is based on a contracting rationale distinctive to product cases? Consider in this regard the reasons that the court in the next case provides for justifying the rules governing recovery for stand-alone emotional harms. How do those rationales compare to the ones that justify the economic loss rule?

IN RE METHYL TERTIARY BUTYL ETHER ("MTBE") PRODUCTS LIABILITY LITIGATION
United States District Court, Southern District of New York, 2007
528 F. Supp. 2d 303

SCHEINDLIN, J. The plaintiffs in these cases, residents and business owners in the hamlet of Fort Montgomery, New York, live in the vicinity of two gasoline stations found or suspected to have leaked gasoline into the soil. After water from plaintiffs' private wells tested positive for contamination with methyl tertiary butyl ether ("MTBE"), a chemical compound that certain companies began adding to gasoline in 1979, plaintiffs brought these actions against the gas station owners and suppliers. Plaintiffs claim that their exposure to the contaminated water has caused them to fear that they or their family members will develop cancer or sustain other ill-health effects in the future.

Plaintiffs bring claims against the defendants for strict product liability, negligence, [and other bases of liability]. In their negligence claim, plaintiffs seek relief for the negligent infliction of emotional distress. Defendants now move for summary judgment on [this] claim[ ]. For the reasons set out below, defendants' motion is denied in [this respect].

Oil companies including [defendants] Sunoco and ExxonMobil began discussing the widespread use of MTBE as a gasoline additive in the 1980's. At that time, officials within the companies warned that because MTBE dissolved easily in water and was less likely to bind to soil than other gasoline components, it could migrate quickly and pose groundwater contamination problems in case of spills.

The health effects of MTBE remain in dispute today, and it is unclear on the record in these cases what defendants knew when they began to use MTBE in their gasoline. Several animal studies have shown that rats develop tumors and lesions after ingesting or inhaling MTBE; other studies purport to refute those results, or to show that any carcinogenicity in rats is not relevant to human carcinogenicity.

In 2000, testing revealed MTBE contamination in nearly fifty private residential wells in the hamlet of Fort Montgomery, New York. State and private investigations of the contamination centered around two gas stations near route 9W that runs through the small town as potential sources: a Sunoco station and a privately owned Mobil station. [The investigations traced the contamination to gasoline spills at these two stations.]

Plaintiffs allege that because they drank, bathed in, and otherwise were exposed to water containing MTBE, they fear that they and their family members may be at higher risk of developing cancer and other health problems. Two of the plaintiffs—Donna Boyce and Edwina Gee—testified in depositions that their worry causes them to suffer physical symptoms. Boyce, who lives directly across the road from the Mobil Station, states that her anxiety about ingesting MTBE has caused her to suffer migraines and some insomnia. Gee also states that she has suffered insomnia due to her distress about MTBE contamination. Another plaintiff, Joan Buchholz, alleges that exposure to MTBE "affected her immune system and caused her disease of melanoma." A number of other plaintiffs testified in depositions that they worry about their children's and grandchildren's exposure to MTBE.

Freedom from mental disturbance is a protected interest in New York. For most of common law history only physical injury was compensable in negligence or intentional torts, with "parasitic" damages available for emotional distress suffered as a consequence of physical injury. During the twentieth century, the law of New York developed to allow recovery for purely mental suffering absent physical harm under negligence and intentional tort theories.

Physical injury is not a necessary component of a cause of action for negligent infliction of emotional distress. Courts remain concerned, however, that unlike physical injury, emotional injury is difficult to verify objectively, and therefore have limited the scenarios under which plaintiffs can recover for emotional distress to those presenting some guarantee of the claim's "genuineness." Often the "index of reliability" of the mental suffering is in the form of "contemporaneous or consequential physical harm." [ ]

To maintain a cause of action for emotional distress caused by exposure to a toxic substance, a plaintiff must establish "both that he or she was in fact exposed to a disease-causing agent and that there is a 'rational basis' for his or her fear of contracting a disease." [ ] Courts have interpreted "rational basis" to mean "the clinically demonstrable presence of a toxin in the plaintiff's body, or some other indication of a toxin-induced disease." [ ]

In cases applying this standard, most plaintiffs are able to show that they were exposed to a disease-causing agent. Most, however, are unable to withstand summary judgment because they fail to present sufficient evidence of the presence of a toxin in their bodies and therefore cannot establish a rational basis for their fears. [ ] The stringent standard reflects the fact that "the courts of this State ... have been loathe to entertain claims for emotional damage flowing from the possibility of coming down with an illness or disease absent infection or clinical evidence of a related condition sufficient to provide a rational, nonspeculative basis for the fear." [ ]

Plaintiffs have provided sufficient evidence to allow a jury to find that they were exposed to MTBE through the well water they used in their homes for drinking, cooking, bathing and cleaning. Reports ... reveal high levels of

IV. Stand-Alone Emotional Harms

MTBE contamination in many wells at various times from 2000 through 2002. Since there is no known date for an initial release of MTBE, the duration of plaintiffs' exposure to MTBE is a fact the jury must determine at trial.

A plaintiff must also establish a physical manifestation "of a toxin in the plaintiff's body, or some other indication of a toxin-induced disease," thereby showing there is some rational basis for her fear. [ ] Defendants repeatedly point out that none of the plaintiffs have developed cancer or suffer from any medical conditions related to MTBE. In doing so they further blur the already unclear distinctions between claims for physical injury and claims for emotional distress. Plaintiffs do not assert that MTBE has caused them a compensable physical injury, nor do they need to, as physical injury is not a necessary component of a cause of action for negligent infliction of emotional distress. To interpret the legal standard for fear of *future* illness claims as requiring plaintiffs to show they *currently* suffer from that very illness would render the standard unworkable.

Instead, plaintiffs must show, through clinical evidence, some physical manifestation of their *exposure* to MTBE. The physical manifestation requirement arose in an emotional distress case where the plaintiff's exposure to asbestos was extremely limited. In its analysis of the claim, the court examined asbestos exposure cases throughout the country and found that courts permitted recovery when the plaintiff showed "clinical presence of asbestos fibers in the lung," such as "pleural or parenchymal scarring," but denied it where "there is no clinical evidence of an asbestos-related condition." Rittenhouse v. St. Regis Hotel Joint Venture, 565 N.Y.S.2d 365, 367 (Sup. Ct. N.Y. Co. 1990), *modified on other grounds*, 579 N.Y.S.2d 100 (1st Dept. 1992) ("In view of the fact that asbestos was widely used and asbestos removal now common, fear of cancer without a physical indication of disease is not reasonable.").

Substances other than asbestos may affect the body in ways that could similarly lead to illness, but often do not leave such easily identifiable markers of their presence. As the New York Supreme Court Appellate Division, Second Department has noted, "commonly in cases of this sort physical contamination cannot be demonstrated for decades, so that many causes of action to recover damages for 'fear of [developing] cancer' based upon exposure to toxins with long incubation or latency periods will be subject to summary dismissal." Wolff v. A-One Oil, Inc., 627 N.Y.S.2d 788, 789 (2d Dept. 1995) (noting that plaintiffs can later sue for damages if the disease does develop).

Plaintiffs in these cases demonstrate the presence of MTBE in the body through the testimony of their expert Dr. Myron Mehlman, who explains that MTBE molecules, when ingested or inhaled, bind to the DNA strain to form adducts on the DNA. In some cases, the presence of the adducts interferes with DNA replication, inducing mutations in newly-formed DNA. These mutations can lead to errant cell production and eventually tumors. According to Dr. Mehlman, based on data detailing the extent of plaintiffs' exposure to MTBE, plaintiffs "more probably than not experienced genetic or subcellular damage as a result of that exposure."

There is no reason why MTBE-DNA adducts should not meet the physical manifestation requirement simply because they are "subcellular." Several courts have found subcellular damage sufficient to permit emotional distress claims to proceed to trial, under similar or more stringent standards requiring physical injury or harm. [ ] The courts that have declined to recognize subcellular damage as an "injury" have done so in claims for physical injury rather than emotional distress, or emotional distress claims asserted in jurisdictions with more stringent legal standards than New York's. [ ] As the United States District Court for the District of Minnesota stated in denying summary judgment on claims for increased risk of injury and emotional distress, "this Court cannot rule as a matter of law that plaintiffs' alleged injuries are not 'real' simply because they are subcellular. The effect of volatile organic compounds on the body is a subtle, complex matter." Werlein v. United States, 746 F. Supp. 887, 901 (D. Minn. 1992), *vacated in part on other grounds*, 793 F. Supp. 898 (D. Minn. 1992) (expert testimony that plaintiffs suffered chromosome breakage created issue of fact as to whether plaintiffs had "present physical injury" as required by Minnesota law). Molecules bound to DNA are certainly "present" in the body. Further, assuming that the model of carcinogenesis Dr. Mehlman describes is valid, as I must for the purposes of summary judgment, the physical manifestation of MTBE in plaintiffs' bodies is not benign, but can be the first step in the development of the disease they claim to fear.

Testimony from experts regarding plaintiffs' subcellular damage has been sufficient evidence for plaintiffs to withstand summary judgment in other jurisdictions. [ ] For the purposes of summary judgment, I must view the facts in the light most favorable to the non-moving party and draw all inferences in favor of that party. Viewed in this manner, Dr. Mehlman's statement raises a genuine issue of material fact for trial. It is for the jury, not the court, to gauge the weight and credibility of Dr. Mehlman's testimony and determine whether MTBE adducts do in fact exist on plaintiffs' DNA, and whether plaintiffs' fear that it is likely they will cause cancer is reasonable.

Although not a required element of an emotional distress claim, courts have also evaluated the likelihood that a plaintiff's exposure will eventually lead to disease when determining whether there is a rational basis for a plaintiff's fear. Defendants argue that because no official scientific body has declared MTBE to be a human carcinogen, no reasonable juror could find that there is a rational basis for plaintiffs' fears of developing cancer.

As plaintiffs' expert states, "[i]n only a few of the many forms of cancer are the causative factors known with any degree of certainty." The lack of certainty regarding the effects of MTBE exposure should certainly be a factor for the jury when considering the reasonableness of plaintiffs' fears.

Plaintiffs offer evidence in support of the conclusion that MTBE can cause cancer. Dr. Mehlman's expert report lists several studies in which researchers found that MTBE exposure caused tumors in rats and mice, as well as many studies on adverse health effects of MTBE. Dr. Mehlman states in his expert report that "some humans exposed to MTBE are more likely than not to suffer cancers as a result of that exposure. Therefore, it is my opinion that Plaintiffs who have been exposed to MTBE or other gasoline constituents through their domestic water supplies would be reasonable to have a fear of developing future disease including cancer."

Based on this evidence, I cannot find as a matter of law that the likelihood that plaintiffs will develop disease is so low as to make their fears irrational. Plaintiffs have raised a genuine issue of material fact as to whether MTBE causes cancer, and whether plaintiffs' fears of developing cancer are reasonable. The ultimate answer to these questions is for the jury to decide.

IV. Stand-Alone Emotional Harms

For the foregoing reasons, defendants' motion [for summary judgment on the claims for the negligent infliction of emotional distress] is denied.

NOTES AND QUESTIONS

1. *Liability for stand-alone emotional harms.* Because the *Restatement (Second)* §402A rule of strict products liability is expressly limited "to liability for physical harm" caused by a defect in the product, plaintiffs with stand-alone emotional injuries must instead seek recovery for the intentional or negligent infliction of emotional distress.

Claims of intentional infliction of emotional distress require proof that the defendant either targeted the individual plaintiff or otherwise failed to incur a slight burden that would protect the plaintiff from a known risk of such harm. RESTATEMENT (THIRD) OF TORTS: LIABILITY FOR PHYSICAL AND EMOTIONAL HARM §46 cmt. h. These requirements are quite difficult to satisfy against the seller of a defective product that was widely distributed in a mass market. In a portion of the opinion not excerpted above, the court granted defendants' motion for summary judgment with respect to plaintiffs' claims for intentional infliction of emotional distress because "[p]laintiffs have submitted no evidence that, when defendants knowingly marketed a product that could cause widespread property damage and environmental harm, they also intended to cause or disregarded a substantial probability of causing severe emotional distress to the plaintiffs." 528 F. Supp. 2d at 318. *See also* Angus v. Shiley Inc., 989 F.2d 142, 147-148 (3d Cir. 1993) (rejecting claim of intentional infliction of emotional distress filed against manufacturer of allegedly defective heart valve because the alleged wrongdoing "was directed at a class of consumers rather than a particular plaintiff").

Consequently, negligent infliction of emotional distress is the most viable theory of recovery for plaintiffs who have suffered only stand-alone emotional harms, although these claims are also difficult to prove. "It has been established for over a century that a person who is placed in peril by the negligence of another, but who escapes without injury, may not recover damages simply because he has been placed in a perilous position. Nor is mere fright the subject of damages." Temple-Inland Forest Prods. Corp. v. Carter, 993 S.W.2d 88, 91 (Tex. 1999). "Without intent or malice on the defendant's part, serious bodily injury to the plaintiff, or a special relationship between the two parties, we permit recovery for mental anguish in only a few types of cases involving injuries of such a shocking and disturbing nature that mental anguish is a highly foreseeable result. This appears to be the generally accepted rule in most, if not all, American jurisdictions." *Id.* at 92.

Courts have identified three primary reasons for denying recovery of mental anguish damages to plaintiffs who have not suffered physical harm: the "special difficulty for judges and juries in separating valid, important claims from those that are invalid or 'trivial'; a threat of unlimited and unpredictable liability; and the potential for a flood of comparatively unimportant, or 'trivial,' claims." Metro-North Commuter R.R. Co. v. Buckley, 521 U.S. 424, 433 (1997).

To address these concerns, the majority of states limit liability for stand-alone emotional harms with the type of requirements described in *MTBE Products Liability Litigation*. The rules considerably vary across jurisdictions and depend on whether the defendant's tortious conduct directly threatened bodily injury to the plaintiff without actually causing such injury; whether the tortious conduct did not directly threaten physical injury but only the plaintiff's emotional tranquility; or whether the tortious conduct was directed toward a third party, such as a family member, who suffered bodily injury that in turn caused the plaintiff's emotional distress. *See* RESTATEMENT (THIRD) OF TORTS: LIABILITY FOR PHYSICAL AND EMOTIONAL HARM §§47-48.

2. *The zone-of-danger test.* Under one common formulation, plaintiffs can recover for negligent infliction of emotional distress when they "either sustain a physical impact as a result of the defendant's negligence or are placed in immediate risk of physical impact by that negligence." Consol. Rail Corp. v. Gottshall, 512 U.S. 532, 534 (1994) (adopting this rule for cases governed by the Federal Employers' Liability Act). Instances of physical impact typically involve a compensable physical harm, even if slight, and do not depart from the ordinary tort rule permitting recovery for the ensuing emotional harms. In cases lacking physical impact, the defective product must put the plaintiff "in danger of immediate bodily harm." RESTATEMENT (THIRD) OF TORTS: LIABILITY FOR PHYSICAL AND EMOTIONAL HARM §47(a). Exposure to carcinogens and other toxic substances does not satisfy this condition, absolving defendants from liability even though these consumers are foreseeably distressed by the increased likelihood that they will get cancer as a result of being exposed to the defective product. In the asbestos cases, for example, "with only a few exceptions, common-law courts have denied recovery to those who . . . are disease and symptom free." *Metro-North Commuter R.R. Co.*, 521 U.S. at 432-433.

3. *Emotional distress linked to physical injury.* In most jurisdictions, the plaintiff can recover for emotional distress if it caused her to suffer some sort of physical harm. *See* Petition of United States, 418 F.22 264, 268 (1st Cir. 1969) ("It has long been the rule that an action does not lie for negligently inflicted emotional disturbance alone. However, it is almost uniformly recognized that recovery may be had for the physical consequences of mental disturbance, at least where there is some contemporaneous physical impact also resulting from defendant's negligence."). The liability rules, however, use different definitions of the requisite physical harm. "[W]hile a frequent justification for the injury requirement is to create a principled standard for separating valid from speculative claims, there is no consistency in the courts as to how to define physical injury." Jamie A. Grodsky, *Genomics and Toxic Torts: Dismantling the Risk-Injury Divide*, 59 Stan. L. Rev. 1671, 1675 (2007).

a. *Physical harm that would otherwise be compensable.* Although the *Restatement (Second)* §402A rule of strict products liability is expressly limited "to liability for physical harm," some courts have interpreted this requirement to permit recovery when the plaintiff first suffers emotional distress that subsequently causes compensable physical harm. *See, e.g.*, Walters v. Mintec/International, 758 F.2d 73, 79 (3d Cir. 1985) (explaining why "physical

IV. Stand-Alone Emotional Harms

harm" in the *Restatement (Second)* does not have to occur within any particular causal sequence and concluding that "[t]here is no apparent reason why the policy objectives of section 402A should apply with less force when the physical harm results from emotional disturbance than when the harm results from some sort of tortious impact"). Under this approach, the physical manifestations of the mental anguish are sufficiently severe to constitute physical harm that is compensable by the ordinary rules of strict products liability (and negligence liability). As is true for many rules, application in a particular case can be difficult.

> [Emotional distress] accompanied by transitory, non-recurring physical phenomena, harmless in themselves, such as dizziness, vomiting, and the like, does not make the actor liable where such phenomena are in themselves inconsequential and do not amount to any substantial bodily harm. On the other hand, long continued nausea or headaches may amount to physical illness, which is bodily harm; and even long continued mental disturbance, as for example in the case of repeated hysterical attacks, or mental aberration, may be classified by the courts as illness, notwithstanding their mental character.

RESTATEMENT (SECOND) OF TORTS §436A, cmt. c.

b. *Physical harm that would otherwise not be compensable.* The alternative approach requires that the emotional distress must cause some sort of physical injury that would not otherwise be a compensable physical harm. The requirement serves as a screening device for distinguishing valid claims of stand-alone emotional harms from those that might be feigned. (Recall that a similar requirement applies to claims for medical monitoring.) Consequently, "[t]he term 'physical' is not used in its ordinary sense.... Rather, the word is used to indicate that the condition or illness for which recovery is sought must be one susceptible of objective determination." *Petition of United States*, 418 F.2d at 269. *See also, e.g.*, Haught v. Maceluch, 681 F.2d 291, 299 n.9 (5th Cir. 1982) (depression, nervousness, weight gain, and nightmares are equivalent to physical injury); D'Ambra v. United States, 396 F. Supp. 1180, 1183-1184 (D.R.I. 1973) ("psychoneurosis" or acute depression constitutes physical injury); Hughes v. Moore, 197 S.E.2d 214, 216, 220 (Va. 1973) (anxiety reaction, phobia, and hysteria constitute physical injury); Daley v. LaCrois, 179 N.W.2d 390, 396 (Mich. 1970) (weight loss and nervousness constitute physical injury).

c. *Proof of future compensable physical harm.* The vast majority of courts follow one of the two basic approaches described above. Both approaches were rejected by the California Supreme Court: "the physical injury requirement is a hopelessly imprecise screening device—it would allow recovery for fear of cancer whenever such distress accompanies or results in any physical injury, no matter how trivial, yet would disallow recovery in all cases where the fear is both serious and genuine but no physical injury has yet manifested itself." Potter v. Firestone Tire & Rubber Co., 863 P.2d 795, 810 (Cal. 1993). Instead, the court ruled that a plaintiff could recover for fear of cancer, in the absence of a present physical injury or illness, with proof that the defendant negligently exposed the plaintiff to "a toxic substance which threatens cancer; and the plaintiff's fear stems from a knowledge, corroborated by reliable medical or scientific opinion, that it is more likely than not that the plaintiff will develop the cancer in the future due to the toxic exposure." *Id.* Is this rule so demanding that it is tantamount to a denial of recovery in the vast majority of cases?

4. *Are product cases different?* Are the damage rules applicable to ordinary tort cases necessarily appropriate in product cases? Consider the rule barring recovery for pure economic losses caused by the product defect. The rationale for that rule is based on the contractual relationship between the parties, a rationale that obviously does not apply to all tort claims. Does the contractual relationship have implications for the rules governing claims for stand-alone emotional harms?

The general duty of care gives sellers an obligation to supply products that are reasonably safe with respect to the risk of physical harm, so liability for stand-alone emotional harms would largely serve a compensatory purpose for the consumer. Those who were exposed to the risk and subsequently suffer the physical harm are entitled to full recovery. Any recovery for those who suffer only stand-alone distress would not enable these "endangered consumers" to somehow reduce the risk of harm, unlike cases of pure economic loss seeking recovery for repair costs or medical monitoring. The damages would simply compensate stand-alone emotional harms, a form of insurance paid for by consumers via higher prices.

Individuals are willing to pay for insurance covering financial harms (health insurance, property insurance, car insurance, and so on), but do not ordinarily want to buy insurance for pain and suffering. *See* Philip J. Cook & Daniel A. Graham, *The Demand for Insurance and Protection: The Case of Irreplaceable Commodities*, 91 Q.J. Econ. 143 (1977) (providing the seminal economic analysis of the issue). A nonmonetary injury does not reduce the consumer's wealth, nor does it necessarily increase her need for (or utility of) money. For injuries of this type, the consumer would prefer to save money by not purchasing the insurance. Why spend money on an insurance premium to indemnify an injury that does not increase the need for money? If consumers are unwilling to pay for this insurance, then the ordinary consumer does not reasonably expect compensation for stand-alone emotional harms. Hence this limitation of liability can be justified by the nature of the tort duty, as in the case of the limitation governing the pure economic losses incurred by disappointed consumers.

Tort damages function as a form of insurance only when the right-holder (like a consumer) effectively pays for the tort liabilities incurred by the duty-bearer (manufacturer). For cases in which the parties are not in a contractual relationship, tort damages do not function in this manner (a pedestrian does not pay for the tort liabilities incurred by a driver). This difference explains why the rules governing stand-alone emotional harms can be more restrictive in product cases (for insurance reasons) than in other types of tort cases not involving contractual relationships (and not restricted by an insurance rationale). Consider Robert L. Rabin, *Emotional Distress in Tort Law: Themes of Constraint*, 44 Wake Forest L. Rev. 1197, 1199-1201 (2009) (identifying puzzling limitations of recovery for stand-alone emotional harms in the toxic tort cases that cannot be squared with recoveries in other tort cases unless one accounts for the different contexts in which the rules operate).

5. *A reprise of scientific uncertainty.* If one of the plaintiffs in *MTBE Products Liability Litigation* had cancer, would the scientific evidence in the case be sufficient to prove causation? *See* Chapter 11, section VI (discussing proof of causation under conditions of scientific uncertainty). After a *Daubert* hearing, the trial court decided that plaintiffs' expert "Dr. Mehlman may testify at trial that MTBE causes adducts to form on DNA, and that MTBE is a probable carcinogen." 76 Fed. R. Evid. Serv. 1129 (S.D.N.Y. 2008). To what extent do the claims for stand-alone emotional harms solve or exacerbate the problem of scientific uncertainty?

V. PUNITIVE DAMAGES

In tort cases, the plaintiff can receive punitive damages in a great majority of states, typically only when the tortfeasor has committed quite serious misconduct with a bad intent or bad state of mind such as malice. Due to the reprehensible nature of the defendant's tortious misconduct, compensatory damages no longer adequately redress the violation of the plaintiff's tort right. Does this tort inquiry pose any distinctive problems when applied to defective products?

OWENS-ILLINOIS, INC. v. ZENOBIA
Court of Appeals of Maryland, 1992
601 A.2d 633

ELDRIDGE, J. We issued a writ of certiorari in these cases [in part] to reconsider some of the principles governing awards of punitive damages in tort cases.

The plaintiffs Louis L. Dickerson and William L. Zenobia filed in the Circuit Court for Baltimore City separate complaints seeking damages for injuries resulting from exposure to asbestos, and the complaints were consolidated for purposes of trial and appeal. Both plaintiffs have pleural and parenchymal asbestosis. At the time of the trial, the plaintiffs abandoned all theories of liability except for strict liability under §402A of the Restatement (Second) of Torts.

The plaintiff Dickerson sought damages from Owens-Illinois, Inc., Eagle-Picher Industries, Inc., and Celotex Corp., all of which manufactured products containing asbestos, and from MCIC, Inc., and Porter Hayden Company, both of which supplied and installed products containing asbestos. Dickerson claimed that he was exposed to asbestos from 1953 to 1963 when he worked as a laborer both at the shipyard and at the steel mill owned and operated by the Bethlehem Steel Corporation at Sparrows Point, Maryland.

The plaintiff Zenobia sought damages from the manufacturer Owens-Illinois, Inc., and the suppliers/installers MCIC, Inc., Porter Hayden Co. and Anchor Packing Co. Zenobia alleged that he was exposed to asbestos while working as a painter for four months at the Bethlehem Steel Sparrows Point shipyard in 1948, while working as a pipe fitter for eighteen months at the Maryland Shipbuilding and Drydock shipyard in 1951 and 1952, and while employed as a cleanup man at the Carling Brewery for three months in 1968.

The jury awarded compensatory damages to the plaintiff Dickerson in the amount of $1,300,000 against all five defendants. In addition, the jury initially determined that punitive damages were warranted against certain defendants, and, subsequently the jury awarded punitive damages against Owens-Illinois in the amount of $235,000, against Porter Hayden in the amount of $2,500, and against Celotex in the amount of $372,000. The jury awarded to the plaintiff Zenobia compensatory damages in the amount of $1,200,000 against all four defendants; subsequently it awarded punitive damages against Owens-Illinois in the amount of $235,000 and against Porter Hayden in the amount of $2,500.

The compensatory and punitive damages awards were appealed to the Court of Special Appeals by Owens-Illinois, Inc., MCIC, Inc., Porter Hayden Co., Eagle-Picher Industries, Inc., and Anchor Packing, Co. The Court of Special Appeals affirmed all aspects of the awards for compensatory damages. The award of punitive damages against Owens-Illinois was affirmed, and the award of punitive damages against Porter Hayden was reversed.

Thereafter petitions and cross-petitions for a writ of certiorari were filed in this Court. The only manufacturer which filed a certiorari petition was Owens-Illinois [in part to challenge] the award of punitive damages.

[I]n recent years there has been a proliferation of claims for punitive damages in tort cases, and awards of punitive damages have often been extremely high. See 2 J. Ghiardi and J. Kircher, PUNITIVE DAMAGES LAW AND PRACTICE §21.01, at 2 (1985); D. Owen, *Problems in Assessing Punitive Damages Against Manufacturers of Defective Products*, 49 U. Chi. L. Rev. 1, 6 (1982) ("Large assessments of punitive damages may not yet be a major threat to the continued viability of most manufacturing concerns, but the increasing number and size of such awards may fairly raise concern for the future stability of American industry"); M. Peterson, S. Sarma, M. Shanley, PUNITIVE DAMAGES (Rand, The Institute for Civil Justice, 1987); J. Sales and K. Cole, *Punitive Damages: A Relic That Has Outlived Its Origins*, 37 Vand. L. Rev. 1117, 1154 (1984) ("the amount of punitive damages awarded in recent years . . . has escalated to astronomical figures that boggle the mind"). *But see* S. Daniels and J. Martin, *Myth and Reality in Punitive Damages*, 75 Minn. L. Rev. 1 (1990).

Accompanying this increase in punitive damages claims, awards and amounts of awards, is renewed criticism of the concept of punitive damages in a tort system designed primarily to compensate injured parties for harm. [ ] In Maryland the criticism has been partly fueled and justified because juries are provided with imprecise and uncertain characterizations of the type of conduct which will expose a defendant to a potential award of punitive damages.

These cases . . . directly raise the problem of what basic standard of wrongful conduct should be used for the allowance of punitive damages in negligence actions generally, and in products liability actions based on either negligence or on strict liability. [T]he plaintiffs [were required] to show by a preponderance of evidence that the defendants acted with "implied" rather than "actual" malice.

V. Punitive Damages

That is, the plaintiffs were not required to show that the defendants' conduct was characterized by evil motive, intent to injure, fraud, or actual knowledge of the defective nature of the products coupled with a deliberate disregard of the consequences. Instead, the plaintiffs were required to show only that the defendants' conduct was grossly negligent. Th[is] standard . . . requires re-examination of some of the decisions of this Court relating to punitive damages.

"The purposes of punitive damages relate entirely to the nature of the defendant's conduct." [ ] Awarding punitive damages based upon the heinous nature of the defendant's tortious conduct furthers the historical purposes of punitive damages—punishment and deterrence. Thus, punitive damages are awarded in an attempt to punish a defendant whose conduct is characterized by evil motive, intent to injure, or fraud, and to warn others contemplating similar conduct of the serious risk of monetary liability.

The irrational and inconsistent application of a punitive damages standard undermines the objective of deterrence because persons cannot predict, and thus choose to abstain from, the type of behavior that is sanctioned by a punitive damages award. Consequently we abandon the [rule permitting punitive damages in cases of implied malice]. Implied malice as that term has been used, with its various and imprecise formulations, fosters this uncertainty. [*See* D. Ellis, *Fairnesss and Efficiency in the Law of Punitive Damages*, 56 S. Cal. L. Rev. 1, 52-53 (1982) (arguing that "the law of punitive damages is characterized by a high degree of uncertainty that stems from the use of a multiplicity of vague, overlapping terms");] D. Owen, *Punitive Damages in Products Liability Litigation*, 74 Mich. L. Rev. 1257, 1283 n.135 (1976) ("any definition of the punishable conduct, such as marketing a product in 'reckless,' 'wanton,' or 'flagrant' disregard of the public safety will necessarily be quite vague").

The implied malice test has been overbroad in its application and has resulted in inconsistent jury verdicts involving similar facts. It provides little guidance for individuals and companies to enable them to predict behavior that will either trigger or avoid punitive damages liability, and it undermines the deterrent effect of these awards. Therefore, in a non-intentional tort action, the trier of facts may not award punitive damages unless the plaintiff has established that the defendant's conduct was characterized by evil motive, intent to injure, ill will, or fraud, *i.e.*, "actual malice."

"Actual malice," defined above as conduct of the defendant characterized by evil motive, intent to injure, ill will, or fraud, does not translate easily into products liability cases. "Products liability" actions are those cases in which the cause of action arises from an injury caused by a defective product. As we held above, in ordinary non-intentional tort cases, the plaintiff must prove that the defendant's conduct was characterized by an evil motive or intent to injure, or defraud the plaintiff. Nevertheless, it is not likely that a manufacturer or supplier of a defective product would specifically intend to harm a particular consumer. We agree with the academic commentary and the courts that "[t]he manufacturer of a defective product operating in vastly different circumstances, . . . will require a unique description of what specific conduct will render it liable for punitive damages." 2 Ghiardi and Kircher, PUNITIVE DAMAGES LAW AND PRACTICE, *supra*, §6.04 at 12. Some form of "knowledge" of a defect and a subsequent disregard of the danger are required for allowing an award of punitive damages in most jurisdictions. After a survey of the cases, Ghiardi and Kircher state (§6.21 at 98):

> In summary, case law establishes that a defendant must have specific knowledge of a product's defect and its potential for harm before an exemplary award is appropriate. This knowledge is usually gained through defendant's testing procedures before marketing or through postmarketing consumer accident reports and complaints received by the defendant.

We believe that in products liability cases the equivalent of the "evil motive," "intent to defraud," or "intent to injure," which generally characterizes "actual malice," is actual knowledge of the defect and deliberate disregard of the consequences. Therefore, in order for actual malice to be found in a products liability case, regardless of whether the cause of action for compensatory damages is based on negligence or strict liability, the plaintiff must prove (1) actual knowledge of the defect on the part of the defendant, and (2) the defendant's conscious or deliberate disregard of the foreseeable harm resulting from the defect.

The knowledge component, which we hold is necessary to support an award of punitive damages, does not mean "constructive knowledge" or "substantial knowledge" or "should have known." More is required to expose a defendant to a potential punitive damages award. The plaintiff must show that the defendant actually knew of the defect and of the danger of the product at the time the product left the defendant's possession or control.[23]

Furthermore, the plaintiff is required to show that, armed with this actual knowledge, the defendant consciously or deliberately disregarded the potential harm to consumers. Professor Owen suggests the term "flagrant indifference." D. Owen, *Punitive Damages in Products Liability Litigation, supra,* 74 Mich. L. Rev. at 1369. We prefer the characterization "conscious or deliberate disregard," and emphatically state that negligence alone, no matter how gross, wanton, or outrageous, will not satisfy this standard. Instead the test requires a bad faith decision by the defendant to market a product, knowing of the defect and danger, in conscious or deliberate disregard of the threat to the safety of the consumer.

The defendant Owens-Illinois and several amici argue that a theory of strict liability in tort is inconsistent with an award of punitive damages because strict liability by its nature does not require a showing of fault, and an award of punitive damages requires fault to be valid. Although a few commentators have endorsed this argument, the majority of courts which have considered the issue have found no logical inconsistency in allowing a punitive damages award in a strict liability action.

It is true that the evidence necessary to support a punitive damages award goes far beyond that required to support a compensatory damages award based on the underlying strict liability claim. In the same manner, the evidence of actual malice that will support a punitive damages award in a products liability

---

[23]. Actual knowledge, however, does include the wilful refusal to know. *See, e.g., State v. McCallum,* 583 A.2d 250, 253-55 (1991) (Chasanow, J., concurring) ("'[K]nowledge' exists where a person believes that it is probable that something is a fact, but deliberately shuts his or her eyes or avoids making reasonable inquiry with a conscious purpose to avoid learning the truth."). Therefore, a defendant cannot shut his eyes or plug his ears when he is presented with evidence of a defect and thereby avoid liability for punitive damages.

V. Punitive Damages

action based on negligence requires the plaintiff to prove much more than negligence. The defendant Owens-Illinois does not argue, however, that there is an inconsistency between a negligence cause of action and punitive damages. The showing of actual malice required for a punitive damages award is the same regardless of whether the plaintiff's claim for compensatory damages was based on strict liability or on negligence. In either case, the evidence must show malicious conduct and not simply the supplying of a defective product or negligence.

The defendant Owens-Illinois and some amici have argued that, in order for a jury to consider a punitive damages award, a plaintiff should be required to establish by clear and convincing evidence that the defendant's conduct was characterized by actual malice.

The function of the standard of proof is to allocate the risk of error between the litigants and to indicate the relative importance attached to the ultimate decision.

A growing majority of states requires that a plaintiff prove the defendant's malicious conduct by clear and convincing evidence before punitive damages can be considered. Many states have adopted the clear and convincing standard by statute. Other states have adopted the standard by judicial decisions.

Use of a clear and convincing standard of proof will help to insure that punitive damages are properly awarded. We hold that this heightened standard is appropriate in the assessment of punitive damages because of their penal nature and potential for debilitating harm. Consequently, in *any* tort case a plaintiff must establish by clear and convincing evidence the basis for an award of punitive damages.

Because the jury was not properly instructed as to the standards for allowing awards of punitive damages, we remand for a new trial of the claims for punitive damages against Owens-Illinois.

NOTES AND QUESTIONS

1. *Punitive damages and the risk-utility test.* The early common law awarded punitive damages in cases of intentional torts, resulting in a legal standard that can produce perverse results in product cases. Under California law, for example, punitive damages are available for "conduct which is intended by the defendant to cause injury to the plaintiff or despicable conduct which is carried on by the defendant with a willful and conscious disregard of the rights or safety of others." Cal. Civ. Code §3294 (West 1992 & 2020 update) (defining "malice"). This rule works well for the intentional torts—it tells jurors to impose punitive damages on a defendant who viciously punched the plaintiff in the face—but not for cases involving defective product design.

The duty to design permits the manufacturer to forego any safety improvement for which the cost or disutility exceeds the risk that would thereby be reduced. If the manufacturer did not make a design change for this reason, and a jury concludes that the product is defective in this respect, then the California standard for punitive damages is literally satisfied. By foregoing such a safety investment on the basis of cost considerations, the manufacturer "consciously disregarded" the "safety of others" as required by this standard for punitive damages. Consider Grimshaw v. Ford Motor Co., 119 Cal. App. 3d 757, 813 (1981) (affirming punitive damages award in part on ground that "[Ford] decided to defer correction of the [Pinto's] shortcomings by engaging in cost-benefit analysis balancing human lives and limbs against corporate profits. . . . There was substantial evidence that Ford's conduct constituted 'conscious disregard' of the probability of injury to members of the consuming public.").

This is a perverse result insofar as the punitive award is justified only by the manufacturer's decision to forego a safety investment because of monetary cost. What if the manufacturer was attempting, albeit erroneously in hindsight, to comply with the legal standard for design defects that does not require a safety investment if the cost or disutility is too high in relation to the risk? To avoid this type of problem, the court in *Zenobia* rejected the rules regarding punitive damages in ordinary tort cases and instead required clear and convincing proof that the defendant knew it was selling a defective product and did so in conscious disregard of consumer safety. *See also* John J. Kirchner & Christine Wiseman, Punitive Damages: Law and Practice §6.4 (2020 ed.) ("[C]ase law establishes that a defendant must have specific knowledge of a product's defect and its potential for harm before an exemplary award is appropriate. This knowledge is usually gained through defendant's testing procedures before marketing or through postmarketing consumer accident reports and complaints received by the defendant.").

2. *The deterrence rationale for punitive damages.* Why would a manufacturer sell a product that it knows to be defective? Under the risk-utility test, a product design or warning is defective only if the cost of the safety precaution is less than the expected injury costs $(B < PL)$, implying that it would be less costly for the manufacturer to make the safety investment (and pay the cost B) than to incur liability for the associated injury costs (with expected liability costs approximated by PL). This financial calculus changes, however, if the manufacturer does not expect to incur liability for every case in which a defect causes physical harm.

Suppose the manufacturer expects that only one in ten consumers with meritorious claims would actually sue and recover, perhaps because they are unable to identify the defect (like the failure to warn of a risk of cancer) as the cause of their injuries (cancer). To maximize profits, the manufacturer would make the safety decision by comparing the cost of the precaution (B) with these expected liability costs $(1/10 \bullet PL)$. The cost of the safety precaution could exceed the manufacturer's expected liability costs, creating an incentive to sell the defective product:

$$\text{Expected Liability} = 1/10 \bullet PL < B < PL = \text{Expected Injury Costs}$$

This deterrence problem can be addressed by punitive damages. If each plaintiff who recovers compensatory damages were to receive a total damages award ten times greater than the actual loss, the manufacturer's expected liability costs would equal the expected injury costs $(1/10 \bullet PL \bullet 10 = PL)$. When punitive damages are formulated in this manner, the manufacturer has a sufficient financial incentive to comply with the risk-utility test:

$$B < 1/10 \bullet PL \bullet 10 = PL$$

This reasoning motivates the conventional deterrence rationale for punitive damages. *See generally* A. Mitchell Polinsky & Steven Shavell, *Punitive Damages: An Economic Analysis*, 111 Harv. L. Rev. 869 (1998).

3. *Conscious disregard of the plaintiff's right.* Strict products liability focuses on the nature of the product and not on the defendant's conduct. Indeed, a pure rule of strict liability has no conduct requirement beyond the obligation to pay compensatory damages. By paying compensatory damages, the duty-bearer fully satisfies the tort obligation. How, then, can punitive damages be justified for cases in which a strictly liable manufacturer pays compensatory damages? In what respect would the manufacturer be acting in conscious disregard of the plaintiff's right?

The answer depends on the nature of the tort right and its correlative duty. The tort right protects the consumer's reasonable expectations of product safety by protecting the consumer from defective products. A manufacturer that sells products it knows to be defective has acted in conscious disregard of the consumer's tort right, regardless of whether the manufacturer fully expects to pay compensatory tort damages for the ensuing physical harms.

A tort rule that only entitles consumers to compensatory damages and nothing more would not adequately protect their safety expectations. The problem resides in the inherent inadequacy of the compensatory damages remedy. To see why, notice that the prior discussion assumes that the amount of the defendant's liability or damages (D) equals the legal valuation of the loss (L). This assumption is unrealistic; tort damages do not realistically make the plaintiff "whole" for serious bodily injuries. All else being equal, the prevention of serious bodily injury for the consumer is far better than an entitlement to the receipt of compensatory damages in the event that such injury occurs.

Consider a fatal product accident. Liability in a case of wrongful death is governed by a *wrongful death statute* that gives specified beneficiaries, typically immediate family members or the decedent's estate, a right to recover for their own injuries stemming from the decedent's loss of life. In the vast majority of states, however, the defendant does not have to pay damages for the decedent's loss of life's pleasures — monetary damages cannot compensate a dead person. Due to this limitation of the compensatory damages remedy, it would be "cheaper for the defendant to kill the plaintiff than to injure him." W. Page Keeton et al., PROSSER AND KEETON ON THE LAW OF TORTS, §127 at 945 (5th ed. 1984). For example, the average jury verdict in New York City from 1984 to 1993 in a case of wrongful death was over $1 million, whereas the average verdict in a case of brain damage was over $3 million. The average award for a herniated disc was over $500,000. *See* Edward A. Adams, *Venue Crucial to Tort Awards: City Verdicts Depend on Counties*, N.Y. L.J., Apr. 4, 1994, at 1, 5. Obviously, a herniated disc is not half as bad as wrongful death, yet such a relative measure of damages is routinely produced by wrongful death actions. Indeed, compensatory damages can be zero in a case of wrongful death. *E.g.*, Romo v. Ford Motor Co., 6 Cal. Rptr. 3d 793, 811 (Ct. App. 2003) (upholding a substantial punitive damages award in a wrongful death case in which the decedent's estate received no compensatory damages).

Wrongful death is the paradigmatic instance of an irreparable injury, the common-law term for a harm that cannot be fully repaired by the compensatory damages remedy. The common-law concept of an irreparable injury applies to the broader category of physical harms—bodily injury and damage to real or tangible property—governed by the general tort duty discussed in section I *supra*. *See* Mark A. Geistfeld, *The Principle of Misalignment: Duty, Damages, and the Nature of Tort Liability*, 121 Yale L.J. 142, 159-165 (2011).

In cases of irreparable injury, "judges have been brought to see and to acknowledge . . . that a remedy which *prevents* a threatened wrong is in its essential nature better than a remedy which permits the wrong to be done, and then attempts to pay for it." John Norton Pomeroy, A TREATISE ON EQUITY JURISPRUDENCE AS ADMINISTERED IN THE UNITED STATES OF AMERICA §1357, at 389 (1st ed. 1887) (emphasis in original). To prevent the irreparable injuries of physical harm, tort law can prohibit a seller from distributing products that it knows are defective, regardless of whether the seller fully expects to pay compensatory damages for the ensuing harms. This prohibition is enforced by punitive damages, yielding the type of rule the court in *Zenobia* adopted. *See also* Barrett v. Ambient Pressure Diving, Ltd., 2008 WL 4934021, at *6 (D.N.H. 2008) ("By making punitive damages available in product liability actions, Pennsylvania law discourages the sale of products known to be defective when the seller is willing to accept the payment of ordinary compensatory damages for product liability as a reasonable cost of doing business."); Man v. Raymark Indus., 728 F. Supp. 1461, 1463 (D. Haw. 1989) ("Punitive damages serve to deter manufacturers as, unlike with compensatory damages, the defendant is prevented from making the 'coldblooded calculation' that it is more profitable to pay claims than correct a defect.") (quoting Campus Sweater and Sportswear Co. v. M.B. Kahn Constr. Co., 515 F. Supp. 64, 106-107 (D.S.C. 1979), *aff'd*, 644 F.2d 877 (4th Cir. 1981)); Fischer v. Johns-Manville Corp., 472 A.2d 577, 584 (N.J. Super. App. Div. 1984) ("Were punitive damages to be withheld, those entrepreneurs who act with flagrant disregard of the public safety would be able to write off the public's injury as a cost of doing business by the payment of compensatory damages, for which there is typically insurance coverage. . . . Thus, it is only the threat of punitive damages which can ultimately induce these entrepreneurs and others to act with a reasonable modicum of responsibility."), *aff'd*, 512 A.2d 466 (N.J. 1986).

When the punitive damages award is justified by the defendant's conscious disregard of the plaintiff' tort right, is there any upper limit on the appropriate amount of damages? Should there be?

V. Punitive Damages

PHILIP MORRIS USA v. WILLIAMS
Supreme Court of the United States, 2007
549 U.S. 346

BREYER, J. The question we address today concerns a large state-court punitive damages award. We are asked whether the Constitution's Due Process Clause permits a jury to base that award in part upon its desire to punish the defendant for harming persons who are not before the court (e.g., victims whom the parties do not represent). We hold that such an award would amount to a taking of "property" from the defendant without due process.

This lawsuit arises out of the death of Jesse Williams, a heavy cigarette smoker. Respondent, Williams' widow, represents his estate in this state lawsuit for negligence and deceit against Philip Morris, the manufacturer of Marlboro, the brand that Williams favored. A jury found that Williams' death was caused by smoking; that Williams smoked in significant part because he thought it was safe to do so; and that Philip Morris knowingly and falsely led him to believe that this was so. The jury ultimately found that Philip Morris was negligent (as was Williams) and that Philip Morris had engaged in deceit. In respect to deceit, the claim at issue here, it awarded compensatory damages of about $821,000 (about $21,000 economic and $800,000 noneconomic) along with $79.5 million in punitive damages.

The trial judge subsequently found the $79.5 million punitive damages award "excessive," see, e.g., BMW of North America, Inc. v. Gore, 517 U.S. 559 (1996), and reduced it to $32 million. Both sides appealed. The Oregon Court of Appeals rejected Philip Morris' arguments and restored the $79.5 million jury award. Subsequently, Philip Morris sought review in the Oregon Supreme Court (which denied review) and then here. We remanded the case in light of State Farm Mut. Automobile Ins. Co. v. Campell, 538 U.S. 408 (2003). The Oregon Court of Appeals adhered to its original views. And Philip Morris sought, and this time obtained, review in the Oregon Supreme Court.

Philip Morris then made two arguments relevant here. First, it said that the trial court should have accepted, but did not accept, a proposed "punitive damages" instruction that specified the jury could not seek to punish Philip Morris for injury to other persons not before the court. In particular, Philip Morris pointed out that the plaintiff's attorney had told the jury to "think about how many other Jesse Williams in the last 40 years in the State of Oregon there have been. . . . In Oregon, how many people do we see outside, driving home . . . smoking cigarettes? . . . [C]igarettes . . . are going to kill ten [of every hundred]. [And] the market share of Marlboros [i.e., Philip Morris] is one-third [i.e., one of every three killed]." In light of this argument, Philip Morris asked the trial court to tell the jury that "you may consider the extent of harm suffered by others in determining what [the] reasonable relationship is" between any punitive award and "the harm caused to Jesse Williams" by Philip Morris' misconduct, "[but] you are not to punish the defendant for the impact of its alleged misconduct on other persons, who may bring lawsuits of their own in which other juries can resolve their claims. . . ." The judge rejected this proposal and instead told the jury that "[p]unitive damages are awarded against a defendant to punish misconduct and to deter misconduct," and "are not intended to compensate the plaintiff or anyone else for damages caused by the defendant's conduct." In Philip Morris' view, the result was a significant likelihood that a portion of the $79.5 million award represented punishment for its having harmed others, a punishment that the Due Process Clause would here forbid.

Second, Philip Morris pointed to the roughly 100-to-1 ratio the $79.5 million punitive damages award bears to $821,000 in compensatory damages. Philip Morris noted that this Court in *BMW* emphasized the constitutional need for punitive damages awards to reflect (1) the "reprehensibility" of the defendant's conduct, (2) a "reasonable relationship" to the harm the plaintiff (or related victim) suffered, and (3) the presence (or absence) of "sanctions," e.g., criminal penalties, that state law provided for comparable conduct. And in *State Farm*, this Court said that the longstanding historical practice of setting punitive damages at two, three, or four times the size of compensatory damages, while "not binding," is "instructive," and that "[s]ingle-digit multipliers are more likely to comport with due process." Philip Morris claimed that, in light of this case law, the punitive award was "grossly excessive."

The Oregon Supreme Court rejected these and other Philip Morris arguments. In particular, it rejected Philip Morris' claim that the Constitution prohibits a state jury "from using punitive damages to punish a defendant for harm to nonparties." And in light of Philip Morris' reprehensible conduct, it found that the $79.5 million award was not "grossly excessive."

Philip Morris then sought certiorari. It asked us to consider, among other things, (1) its claim that Oregon had unconstitutionally permitted it to be punished for harming nonparty victims; and (2) whether Oregon had in effect disregarded "the constitutional requirement that punitive damages be reasonably related to the plaintiff's harm." We granted certiorari limited to these two questions.

For reasons we shall set forth, we consider only the first of these questions. We vacate the Oregon Supreme Court's judgment, and we remand the case for further proceedings.

This Court has long made clear that "[p]unitive damages may properly be imposed to further a State's legitimate interests in punishing unlawful conduct and deterring its repetition." [ ] At the same time, we have emphasized the need to avoid an arbitrary determination of an award's amount. Unless a State insists upon proper standards that will cabin the jury's discretionary authority, its punitive damages system may deprive a defendant of "fair notice . . . of the severity of the penalty that a State may impose," *BMW, supra*, at 574; it may threaten "arbitrary punishments," i.e., punishments that reflect not an "application of law" but "a decisionmaker's caprice," *State Farm, supra*, at 416, 418; and, where the amounts are sufficiently large, it may impose one State's (or one jury's) "policy choice," say as to the conditions under which (or even whether) certain products can be sold, upon "neighboring States" with different public policies, *BMW, supra*, at 571-572.

For these and similar reasons, this Court has found that the Constitution imposes certain limits, in respect both to procedures for awarding punitive damages and to amounts forbidden as "grossly excessive." See Honda Motor Co. v. Oberg, 512 U.S. 415, 432 (1994) (requiring judicial review of the size of punitive awards); Cooper Industries, Inc. v. Leatherman Tool Group, Inc., 532 U.S.

V. Punitive Damages

424, 443 (2001) (review must be de novo); *BMW, supra,* at 574-585 (excessiveness decision depends upon the reprehensibility of the defendant's conduct, whether the award bears a reasonable relationship to the actual and potential harm caused by the defendant to the plaintiff, and the difference between the award and sanctions "authorized or imposed in comparable cases"); *State Farm, supra,* at 425 (excessiveness more likely where ratio exceeds single digits). Because we shall not decide whether the award here at issue is "grossly excessive," we need now only consider the Constitution's procedural limitations.

In our view, the Constitution's Due Process Clause forbids a State to use a punitive damages award to punish a defendant for injury that it inflicts upon nonparties or those whom they directly represent, i.e., injury that it inflicts upon those who are, essentially, strangers to the litigation. For one thing, the Due Process Clause prohibits a State from punishing an individual without first providing that individual with "an opportunity to present every available defense." [ ] Yet a defendant threatened with punishment for injuring a nonparty victim has no opportunity to defend against the charge, by showing, for example in a case such as this, that the other victim was not entitled to damages because he or she knew that smoking was dangerous or did not rely upon the defendant's statements to the contrary.

For another, to permit punishment for injuring a nonparty victim would add a near standardless dimension to the punitive damages equation. How many such victims are there? How seriously were they injured? Under what circumstances did injury occur? The trial will not likely answer such questions as to nonparty victims. The jury will be left to speculate. And the fundamental due process concerns to which our punitive damages cases refer—risks of arbitrariness, uncertainty and lack of notice—will be magnified.

Finally, we can find no authority supporting the use of punitive damages awards for the purpose of punishing a defendant for harming others. We have said that it may be appropriate to consider the reasonableness of a punitive damages award in light of the *potential* harm the defendant's conduct could have caused. But we have made clear that the potential harm at issue was harm potentially caused *the plaintiff.* [ ]

Respondent argues that she is free to show harm to other victims because it is relevant to a different part of the punitive damages constitutional equation, namely, reprehensibility. That is to say, harm to others shows more reprehensible conduct. Philip Morris, in turn, does not deny that a plaintiff may show harm to others in order to demonstrate reprehensibility. Nor do we. Evidence of actual harm to nonparties can help to show that the conduct that harmed the plaintiff also posed a substantial risk of harm to the general public, and so was particularly reprehensible—although counsel may argue in a particular case that conduct resulting in no harm to others nonetheless posed a grave risk to the public, or the converse. Yet for the reasons given above, a jury may not go further than this and use a punitive damages verdict to punish a defendant directly on account of harms it is alleged to have visited on nonparties.

Given the risks of unfairness that we have mentioned, it is constitutionally important for a court to provide assurance that the jury will ask the right question, not the wrong one. And given the risks of arbitrariness, the concern for adequate notice, and the risk that punitive damages awards can, in practice, impose one State's (or one jury's) policies (e.g., banning cigarettes) upon other

States—all of which accompany awards that, today, may be many times the size of such awards in the 18th and 19th centuries—it is particularly important that States avoid procedure that unnecessarily deprives juries of proper legal guidance. We therefore conclude that the Due Process Clause requires States to provide assurance that juries are not asking the wrong question, *i.e.*, seeking, not simply to determine reprehensibility, but also to punish for harm caused strangers.

How can we know whether a jury, in taking account of harm caused others under the rubric of reprehensibility, also seeks to *punish* the defendant for having caused injury to others? Our answer is that state courts cannot authorize procedures that create an unreasonable and unnecessary risk of any such confusion occurring. In particular, we believe that where the risk of that misunderstanding is a significant one—because, for instance, of the sort of evidence that was introduced at trial or the kinds of argument the plaintiff made to the jury—a court, upon request, must protect against that risk. Although the States have some flexibility to determine what *kind* of procedures they will implement, federal constitutional law obligates them to provide *some* form of protection in appropriate cases.

As the preceding discussion makes clear, we believe that the Oregon Supreme Court applied the wrong constitutional standard when considering Philip Morris' appeal. We remand this case so that the Oregon Supreme Court can apply the standard we have set forth. Because the application of this standard may lead to the need for a new trial, or a change in the level of the punitive damages award, we shall not consider whether the award is constitutionally "grossly excessive." We vacate the Oregon Supreme Court's judgment and remand the case for further proceedings not inconsistent with this opinion.

It is so ordered.

NOTES AND QUESTIONS

1. *The single-digit ratio.* Of the various factors that appellate courts use to evaluate the constitutionality of a punitive damages award, the most important stems from the Supreme Court's holding that "in practice, few awards exceeding a single-digit ratio between punitive and compensatory damages, to a significant degree, will satisfy due process." State Farm Mut. Auto. Ins. Co. v. Campbell, 538 U.S. 408, 425 (2003). The Court partially justified the single-digit ratio with the "long legislative history, dating back over 700 years and going forward to today, providing for sanctions of double, treble, or quadruple damages to deter and punish." *Id.* Historical practice is a defensible way to address the intractable problem of telling the jury how it can appropriately translate reprehensibility into a dollar damages award. Yet reprehensibility involves many factors, and so the Court recognizes that even higher awards can be justified, making the single-digit ratio only a presumptive requirement. *See* TXO Production Corp. v. Alliance Resources Corp., 509 U.S. 443, 459-460 (1993) (relying on potential harms rather than actual harm to affirm a punitive damages award 526 times greater than the compensatory damages award).

V. Punitive Damages

Outside of the historical practice that can justify punitive awards up to four times greater than the compensatory damages, what enables a juror to translate reprehensibility into an even greater amount of damages? The lack of guidance on this issue has predictably produced a wide range of outcomes in the lower courts. According to one comprehensive study:

> [W]hen the ratio under review has been between 4:1 and 9.9:1, a significant number of courts have rubber-stamped it as constitutionally permissible without carefully analyzing whether a further reduction might be warranted. This has led to the counterintuitive result that jury awards yielding ratios of 10:1 or more are routinely reduced to 4:1, but jury awards yielding ratios between 4:1 and 9.9:1 often withstand post-verdict review.

Lauren R. Goldman & Nickolai G. Levin, State Farm *at Three: Lower Courts' Application of the Ratio Guidepost,* 2 N.Y.U. J. Law & Bus. 509, 511 (2006). *See also* W. Kip Viscusi & Benjamin J. McMichael, *Shifting the Fat Tail of Blockbuster Punitive Damage Awards,* 11 J. Empirical Legal Stud. 350 (2014) (empirical study finding that the Court's ruling in *State Farm* has tended to reduce the size of punitive awards exceeding $100 million while also reducing the likelihood that a punitive award will exceed the single-digit ratio).

2. *Punitive damages and wrongful death.* What is the appropriate amount of punitive damages for wrongful death? Why should the measure of damages depend on its relation to a compensatory damages award that does not account for the decedent's loss of life's pleasures? Does the single-digit ratio apply in a case of wrongful death? These difficult questions were posed by the punitive award in *Williams,* which was more than ten times greater than the compensatory damages award. The Court in *Williams* was able to avoid answering these questions by concluding that the problem of nonparty harm required the case to be remanded. For discussion of how the single-digit ratio can be modified to account for the inherent limitations of wrongful-death damages, see Mark A. Geistfeld, *Punitive Damages, Retribution, and Due Process,* 81 S. Cal. L. Rev. 263 (2008) (explaining how the methodology for monetizing pain-and-suffering injuries can be employed for monetizing fatal injuries, and then using this approach to show how the $79.5 million punitive award in *Williams* could easily satisfy the presumptive constitutional requirement of a single-digit ratio).

Although wrongful death provides the paradigmatic example of an irreparable injury that cannot be adequately compensated by the ordinary damages remedy, only a slight majority of states permit recovery for punitive damages in cases of wrongful death. The early common law barred recovery altogether in these cases, making the availability of punitive damages dependent on the wrongful-death statute authorizing these claims. *See* Victoria A.B. Willis & Judson R. Peverall, *The "Vanishing Trial": Arbitrating Wrongful Death,* 53 U. Rich. L. Rev. 1339, 1362-1363 (2019) (explaining that, in 29 states, punitive damages are recoverable in cases of wrongful death; in the remainder of states, the wrongful death statute is interpreted to disallow such damages).

3. *Due process and deterrence.* Does the problem of nonparty harm foreclose the use of punitive damages for the purpose of deterrence? If, for example, the manufacturer expects to be sued by only one in ten injured consumers and decides to sell a defective product as a result, then the deterrence-based total damages award must be ten times greater than the compensatory damages recovered by the plaintiff. *See* note 2, p. 600 *supra*. Such an award would appear to involve the imposition of liability for third-party harms in contravention of *Williams*. The plaintiff, after all, is receiving damages based on the nine other injured consumers who did not pursue their claims, an apparent violation of due process according to the Court in *Williams*. Was this the type of argument made by the plaintiff's attorney in *Williams*?

The issue is highlighted in a case involving a sport utility vehicle manufactured by Ford Motor Company with a design that allegedly had a higher incidence of rollover causing 30 deaths per year as compared to another design on the market, thereby constituting a defect according to plaintiff. Based on this evidence of defect, the plaintiff's attorney made the following closing arguments to the jury:

1. "This is how Ford looks at this. That little bit of thirty people being killed every year didn't matter. Those thirty people, those thirty extra people getting killed in a year didn't matter to them because it was just a little bitty number."

2. "It does matter about those people getting killed. Those thirty people do count. Those thirty people — that's thirty more people that got killed that year. If you expect these vehicles to last about twenty years, that's six hundred more people getting killed using this vehicle as opposed to [the alternative design that was available on the market]. That's serious."

3. "And that doesn't count the paralyzed people, the quadriplegics, the people with serious injuries, the thousands of people that have been in these events because of this rollover propensity of this vehicle that they knew about, and they knew it since day one but they chose profit over safety every time because they looked at it as numbers. They didn't look at it as lives, as people."

4. "I submit to you that the evidence is that they did it because they thought it was a little, small number. . . . [T]hey did not look at it as thirty lives a year[ ], they didn't look at it as six hundred lives. That's how they should have looked at it, but that was not how they did it."

5. "They got together at the highest levels of Ford Motor Company and they made a judgment that rather than delaying and improving the [SUV in question], they were going to sell the vehicle as it was and that they were going to risk people's lives and they were going to risk serious injuries like we have here today. They were going to risk people's brains."

6. "[Plaintiff] is here today with a brain injury and six hundred other people, or however many it is, lost their lives, and numerous others have brain injuries or are paralyzed, quadriplegic, have extremely serious injuries. We believe that you should tell Ford Motor Company what you think about this kind of thing."

V. Punitive Damages

Branham v. Ford Motor Co., 701 S.E.2d 5, 21-22 (S.C. 2010). The jury awarded the plaintiff $16 million in actual damages and $15 million in punitive damages. On appeal, the Supreme Court of South Carolina overturned the punitive damages award because it was based on nonparty harms in violation of *Williams.* "It is unmistakable that the closing argument relied heavily on inadmissible evidence." *Id.* at 22. In light of this ruling, is there any type of deterrence argument that the plaintiff can make to justify an award of punitive damages?

4. *The individual tort right and deterrence.* To satisfy the federal constitutional requirement of due process, the punitive award must be wholly tied to the violation of the plaintiff's tort right. The punitive award, in other words, must vindicate the plaintiff's tort right and nothing more. "To do so, the punitive award must: (1) disgorge the defendant's expected wrongful gain in order to protect the right from within the wrongful perspective adopted by the defendant; and then (2) increase damages further to reject altogether the defendant's wrongful perspective, thereby vindicating the right in its entirety." Geistfeld, *supra* note 2, at 272-273. Such a punitive award also promotes deterrence for reasons that can be illustrated by the facts of *Williams.*

> Suppose the defendant Philip Morris estimated that it faced only a ten percent chance of incurring liability for the fraud, an estimate supported by the Oregon Supreme Court's invocation of the fact that the defendant engaged in the scheme for almost forty years. For every tortiously caused harm (L), the defendant expected to pay damages (D) in only one out of ten cases. For the tortious risk faced by each one of these individuals, including Jesse Williams, the defendant ignored the [legally] required valuation ($P \bullet L$) and instead considered only its expected liability costs, ($P \bullet D$) $\bullet$ (1/10). To eliminate this aspect of the expected wrongful gain, vindication of an individual tort right requires the defendant to incur total damages D that would equate its wrongful perspective ($P \bullet D$) $\bullet$ (1/10) with the perspective required by the tort right ($P \bullet L$):
>
> Solve for D, where $(P \bullet D) \bullet (1/10) = (P \bullet L)$.

The solution is $D = 10L$, and so the total amount of damages D must be ten times greater than the measure of full compensation L in order to account for the way in which the rights-violation involved trickery or deceit (embodied in the assumption that there was only a ten percent chance of getting caught).

[This award also promotes deterrence for a straightforward reason.] When tortious misconduct occurs in mass markets[,] vindictive damages will always further the social interest in deterrence. A mass manufacturer, for example, treats each consumer as nothing more than a member of a group—the market or those individual right-holders whose aggregate demand determines the most profitable characteristics of the product. The manufacturer's misconduct vis-à-vis the individual consumer does not differ from its misconduct toward the market in general. In these circumstances, vindicating an individual tort right necessarily protects other rights as well.

Id. at 300-301.

The punitive award in these cases does not depend on tortious harms actually suffered by nonparties to the litigation (in violation of *Williams*), but instead depends solely on evidence concerning the manner in which the defendant's safety decision reprehensibly departed from the perspective required by the plaintiff's individual tort right. In a mass market, a manufacturer's safety decision with respect to any individual consumer is often no different from its decision concerning the market as a whole, and so adequate punishment of the individual rights-violation will ordinarily deter product sellers from acting wrongfully with respect to the entire market.

5. *The hot-coffee cases.* In Liebeck v. McDonald's Restaurant, 1995 WL 360309, *vacated*, 1994 WL 16777704 (N.M. Dist. 1994) (plaintiff agreeing to new trial), plaintiff spilled scalding coffee on her lap that she had just purchased from a drive-in window at McDonald's. After proving that McDonald's failed to adequately warn about the risk, she recovered compensatory damages and $2.9 million in punitive damages. The case gained widespread notoriety as illustrating a tort system gone awry. *See, e.g.*, Debra J. Saunders, *On the Docket: Americans vs. Themselves*, Detroit Free Press, Sept. 9, 1994, at 11-A ("There was a time when only the rare American would be so shameless as to sue McDonald's if her negligence contributed to a scalding. . . . Those days are long gone. America has devolved from a country of pioneers to a nation of plaintiffs.").

Contrary to popular perception, the facts in the McDonald's case present a compelling case for punitive damages.* The plaintiff bought the coffee from a McDonald's restaurant in New Mexico, which followed corporate policy by serving coffee at a temperature of 180 to 190 degrees Fahrenheit. The plaintiff's evidence showed that the industry average was less than 148 degrees, and that the temperature achieved by a typical home brewer ranges from 140 to 150 degrees. Based on this evidence, the higher temperature of the McDonald's coffee mattered a great deal. As the plaintiff further established, coffee served at that temperature will immediately burn human skin before anything can be done. There is no margin for error. The third-degree burns suffered by the plaintiff were so severe that she was hospitalized for eight days and endured excruciating skin grafts to help repair the wounds. The industry average temperature for serving coffee, by contrast, made it far less likely that a spill would cause significant injury. Why, then, did McDonald's sell such hot coffee? It said a coffee consultant had once suggested that coffee tastes best that way, a claim contradicted by the plaintiff's evidence regarding industry practice. McDonald's also admitted that the temperature at which it sold coffee was unfit for human consumption and that corporate officials had received over 700 reports of coffee scalds in

---

* The factual description of the case was generously provided to me by (then) Chief Justice Stanley Feldman of the Arizona Supreme Court, who in 1995 had his law clerk, Dave Abney, collect the information by interviewing lawyers involved in the case. —ED. Further factual information on the case is provided in Gerlin, *A Matter of Degree: How a Jury Decided that a Coffee Spill Is Worth $2.9 Million*, Wall St. J., Sept. 1, 1994.

V. Punitive Damages

the past ten years. Nevertheless, McDonald's refused to consult a burn doctor to assess the risks, refused to turn down the coffee brewer thermostats, and refused to print any warning label on the coffee cups.

On these facts, the jury could defensibly conclude that the temperature of the McDonald's coffee was much greater than the temperature expected by the ordinary consumer, requiring a warning about the unanticipated, heightened risk of a scalding-burn injury. The jury accordingly awarded plaintiff $200,000 in compensatory damages, which was then reduced by 20 percent due to the plaintiff's contributory negligence. These facts also support the conclusion that McDonald's knew of the defect and failed to take corrective actions, despite repeated complaints by consumers who presumably had been surprised by the severity of their burn injuries. To jolt McDonald's from its corporate complacency, the jury awarded plaintiff $2.9 million in punitive damages, an amount representing the value of about two days of corporate coffee sales for McDonald's. (The trial judge subsequently reduced the award to $640,000.)

The McDonald's case only becomes troubling when considered in relation to other hot-coffee cases. A particularly instructive case involved allegations that a coffeemaker manufactured by the defendant was defective for brewing coffee at 195 degrees Fahrenheit during the brewing cycle and 179 degrees Fahrenheit as the holding temperature of a carafe on its hotplate. McMahon v. Bunn-O-Matic Corp., 150 F.3d 651, 653 (7th Cir. 1998). The alleged temperatures are within the range of those at issue in the McDonald's case. Nevertheless, the plaintiff's case was dismissed by the U.S. Court of Appeals for the Seventh Circuit:

> Warning consumers about a surprising feature that is potentially dangerous yet hard to observe could be useful, but the record lacks any evidence that 179° F is unusually hot for coffee.... [In two earlier cases,] the courts reported that the industry-standard serving temperature is between 175° and 185° F, and if this is so then the [plaintiffs'] coffee held no surprises. What is more, most consumers prepare and consume hotter beverages at home.... Until 20 years ago most home coffee was made in percolators, where the water boiled during the brewing cycle and took some time to cool below 180°. Apparently the [plaintiffs] believe that home drip brewing machines now in common use are much cooler, but the record does not support this, and a little digging on our own part turned up [the following standard adopted by the American National Standards Institute for home coffeemakers]: "On completion of the brewing cycle and within a 2 minute interval, the beverage temperature in the dispensing vessel of the coffee maker while stirring should be between the limits of 170° F and 205° F. The upper finished brew temperature limit assures that the coffee does not reach the boiling point which can affect the taste and aroma. The lower temperature limit assures generally acceptable drinking temperature when pouring into a cold cup, adding cream, sugar and spoon."... Coffee served at 180° by a roadside vendor, which doubtless expects that it will cool during the longer interval before consumption, does not seem so abnormal as to require a heads-up warning.

Id. at 655.

In light of these facts, the justification for any liability, much less punitive damages, is less clear than it appeared to be in the McDonald's case. The comparison of the two cases does not imply that the McDonald's case was wrongly decided. On its facts, the McDonald's case was rightly decided. Comparing the two cases instead illustrates how a court's decision critically depends on the litigation strategies of the parties and the evidence upon which the decision is based. Differences in litigation strategies and evidence can produce different outcomes in cases that otherwise involve comparable allegations of defect. The McDonald's jury found that the coffee required a warning, whereas the court in *Bunn-O-Matic* held as a matter of law that the coffee required no such warning. Occasional differences like this are to be expected in the case law, but they are made much more problematic by punitive damages that are formulated to change the defendant's behavior moving forward—as it did for McDonald's.

6. *Punitive damages and tort reform.* Perhaps more than any other form of tort liability, punitive damages reflect the interdependence of individual right-holders in contemporary society. When the common law first developed, the cases involved one individual wronging another, as in the case of someone punching another. Tort cases now frequently involve widespread wrongs and mass torts, as when a corporation distributes a product with a defective design or warning to large numbers of consumers. In these cases, tort liability continues to redress the violation of the plaintiff's own tort right, but each individual rights violation (cause by the defective product) is suffered or potentially faced by a large number of similarly situated right-holders (other consumers in the product market). The interdependency means that a punitive award that vindicates the individual tort right in a mass market can involve staggering sums of money.

Due to the interdependence of rights violations, the way in which a single court redresses an individual rights violation can have widespread implications. A jury verdict finding that a widely used prescription drug has a defective warning, for example, can spur a large number of similarly situated consumers to file suit. The consequences produced by a single verdict can then be extended even further with an award of punitive damages. As a practical matter, a single product case can have widespread implications that help to explain why products liability has been a focal point in the debate over tort reform.

VI. AUTONOMOUS VEHICLES AND PRODUCTS LIABILITY: PROBLEM SET 10

AV Problem 10.1

As discussed in AV Problem 9.2 and earlier problems, the wireless connections in autonomous vehicles make them vulnerable to hacking by third parties who could then gain unauthorized control of the vehicles. Over the past few

VI. Autonomous Vehicles and Products Liability: Problem Set 10

years, third parties in a number of instances have hacked into the networks of corporations and public agencies and shut down the systems, requiring that they be paid a "ransom" to make a system functional again. Suppose that a third party hacks into an autonomous vehicle and locks down the operating system unless the owner pays a "ransom" in Bitcoins. If the owner makes the payment, could she recover those damages from the manufacturer?

Analysis of AV Problem 10.1

The claim would be for pure economic loss. The malfunction (unauthorized third-party control) of the operating system only affects the performance of the vehicle; there is no bodily injury or damage to other property. The economic loss rule bars tort recovery for damages of this type, unless perhaps the damages go toward the repair of the product to prevent future physical harms (as in cases of asbestos abatement or medical monitoring). The plaintiff might argue that the damages serve this function because the manufacturer would become aware of the vulnerability in the operating system and could patch it, thereby potentially preventing future hacks in which the third party might cause the vehicle to crash and physically injure the occupants and other property. This argument is unpersuasive, however, because the "ransom" itself does not repair the vulnerability. The manufacturer could gain knowledge of the problem in the absence of tort liability in the case at hand, and so the economic loss rule would bar the plaintiff's recovery.

AV Problem 10.2

Assume instead that terrorists hacked into the autonomous vehicle and attempted to crash it, but once the vehicle began to drive erratically, backup systems took control and safely guided the vehicle off the road. The occupants of the vehicle, however, were terrorized by the experience. Could they get tort recovery from the manufacturer for their emotional distress?

Analysis of AV Problem 10.2

Ordinarily, tort claims for pure emotional distress require that the defect must cause the plaintiff to suffer some type of bodily injury. An exception, however, exists if the defect threatens the plaintiff with imminent bodily harm; that is, if the plaintiff is in the "zone of danger." *See* note 2, p. 592 *supra*. That requirement is satisfied in the case at hand. The plaintiffs' emotional distress stemmed from their fear that the vehicle would crash and cause them bodily injury. Unlike cases in which the defect only threatens future physical harm, as with exposure to toxic substances, the malfunction of the autonomous vehicle threatened imminent bodily harm, entitling the plaintiffs to recovery for their emotional distress.

AV Problem 10.3

According to some scholars, the manufacturers of autonomous vehicles might face increased exposure to punitive damages as compared to the manufacturers of other types of defective products:

> [C]ertain attributes of AVs avail themselves to significant punitive damages exposure. First, AVs powered by artificial intelligence represent an unfamiliar risk with which jurors may be uncomfortable, thereby identifying as the type of "dread" risk that are particularly susceptible to distrust and large punitive advantages awards. Second, the safety claims that AV manufacturers will and should make may present a double-edged sword. Studies and prior precedents show that jurors are particularly harsh towards products that claim to improve safety but end up harming some individuals, or where a product manufacturer makes unrestricted claims of safety. In making accurate and supportable claims about the relative safety of AVs, companies might shield themselves from exposure to punitive damages by clearly warning that, although they may be safer than other vehicles overall, AVs will be subject to occasional errors and mishaps, assuring that the company will carefully monitor for and immediately fix fleet-wide any such errors. Conversely, in making unsupported or overly broad claims of AV safety, such manufacturers are setting themselves up for punitive damage awards in the events where AVs are involved in injury-producing accidents, which will inevitably occur.

Gary Marchant, Rida Bazzi, *Autonomous Vehicles and Liability: What Will Juries Do?*, 26 B.U.J. Sci. & Tech. L. 67, 117 (2020).

To what extent is this argument supported by the doctrinal rules of products liability? Explain.

Analysis of AV Problem 10.3

The various factors identified by Professors Marchant and Bazzi all explain why a jury might be more inclined to find that an autonomous vehicle is defective as compared to other types of products. For example, if jurors impute a "dread risk" into their risk-utility analysis of an AV's design or warning, they might impose safety requirements more demanding than required by ordinary cost-benefit analysis. *See* Chapter 6, section II.B. Similarly, the manufacturer's representations of safe product performance shape consumer expectations. If those representations lead consumers to expect that AVs will not crash, then such a crash will be a malfunction subject to strict liability. *See* AV Problem 1.2, p. 151 *supra*. Because a manufacturer must first incur liability in order to be potentially subject to punitive damages, the various factors that enhance a finding of defect will necessarily increase exposure to punitive damages.

Whether AV manufacturers will actually be hit with punitive damages for these reasons is another question. In the majority of jurisdictions, the plaintiff can receive punitive damages only by proving that the manufacturer knew that the product was defective. None of the factors that Professors Marchant and Barzi discuss are relevant to this issue. In the remaining jurisdictions such

VI. Autonomous Vehicles and Products Liability: Problem Set 10   615

as California, however, AV manufacturers might be particularly vulnerable to punitive damages awards that only require "conscious indifference" to the plaintiff's tort right. In particular, AV manufacturers that rely on cost-benefit analysis might incur punitive damages for that reason alone. Although these states are only a minority, their imposition of punitive damages could shape the conduct of AV manufacturers in the national market for reasons illustrated by the hot-coffee cases.

14

Defenses Based on Consumer Conduct

Even if the plaintiff proves all elements of a prima facie case, the defendant may be able to avoid or reduce liability by establishing an affirmative defense. The primary defenses—contractual limitations of tort liability, assumption of risk, and contributory negligence or product misuse—involve different types of consumer conduct, requiring consideration, once again, of the interplay between consumer choice and tort liability.

I. CONTRACTUAL LIMITATIONS OF LIABILITY

A contractual limitation of tort liability—commonly called a *disclaimer* or *waiver*—"is so inimical to the public good as to compel an adjudication of its invalidity." Henningsen v. Bloomfield Motors, Inc., 161 A.2d 69, 95 (N.J. 1960). Courts do not enforce contractual waivers of products liability because "[i]t is presumed that the ordinary product user or consumer lacks sufficient information and bargaining power to execute a fair contractual limitation of rights to recover." RESTATEMENT (THIRD) OF TORTS: PRODUCTS LIABILITY §18 cmt. a. Disclaimers and waivers return us to the recurring issue of whether consumers have enough information to adequately protect their interests by contracting over product safety.

A disclaimer or waiver operates against a tort duty, which in turn exists only when the ordinary consumer is unable to make an informed risk-utility decision about the safety matter in question. *See* Chapter 5, section III. The plaintiff, who presumably has the characteristics of the ordinary consumer, therefore presumably lacks the requisite risk-utility information to contract over the appropriate scope of liability for defective products. Insofar as there is no reliable way to determine whether the plaintiff differs from the ordinary (uninformed) consumer in this respect, the presumption cannot be rebutted; the court must conclude that the plaintiff did not have the risk-utility information needed to execute a fair contractual limitation of the tort right. Waivers and disclaimers accordingly violate the substantive rationale for the tort duty—a form of public policy—rendering them unenforceable.

Other policy reasons further explain why disclaimers are not enforceable. At the time of purchase, the consumer knows that the seller has completed its investments in product safety. The threat of tort liability at this point could not induce the seller to make any further safety investments, giving each consumer an incentive to waive liability in exchange for a reduction in product price. If these waivers were enforceable, product sellers could predict that consumers would routinely waive their tort rights at the point of sale. The resultant lack of liability would remove the financial incentive for product sellers to comply with the tort obligation in the first instance. Contracting, therefore, can yield unreasonably dangerous products when courts permit consumers to disclaim or waive a seller's tort liability. *See generally* Abraham L. Wickelgren, *The Inefficiency of Contractually Based Liability with Rational Consumers*, 22 J.L. Econ. & Org. 168 (2006).

Contractual disclaimers or waivers of liability potentially encompass *all* tort claims that the consumer could file against the seller, a contracting problem that is quite difficult due to the large number of risk-utility trade-offs inherent in almost any product. The issue is considerably simplified for discrete safety decisions involving a single risk-utility choice—the issue addressed by assumption of risk.

II. ASSUMPTION OF RISK

According to the doctrine known as *assumption of risk* or the *assumed-risk rule*, an individual right-holder who voluntarily chooses to face a known risk bears responsibility for her ensuing injuries, thereby reducing or eliminating the liability that a duty-bearer might otherwise incur with respect to the risk. Individuals can expressly assume a risk by contract—the issue discussed in the last section. Alternatively, individuals can make choices that evince their assumption of the risk, a doctrine known as *implied assumption of risk*.

> The traditional assumption of risk rule was sometimes expressed in terms of the maxim *volenti non fit injuria* [a person is not wronged by that to which she consents] or under the name of incurred risk. However formulated, the essential idea was that the plaintiff assumed the risk whenever she impliedly did so by words or conduct, just as would be true if she did so expressly. . . . Courts began to think that conduct implied consent whenever the plaintiff had specific knowledge of the risk posed by the defendant's negligence, appreciated its nature, and proceeded voluntarily to encounter it nonetheless. By focusing on the plaintiff's knowledge of the risk as if that were an agreement to relieve the defendant of liability, courts sometimes allowed the negligent defendant to escape all responsibility for his misconduct even though the plaintiff acted quite reasonably and never signaled any intent to relieve the defendant from responsibility. The Second Restatement and more modern theory added that the risk was assumed only if the plaintiff's conduct in encountering the risk manifested the plaintiff's willingness to accept responsibility for the risk.

II. Assumption of Risk

Dan B. Dobbs, Paul T. Hayden & Ellen M. Bublick, THE LAW OF TORTS §235 (2d ed. & 2020 update).

Like virtually every other aspect of strict products liability, the role of assumed risks in product cases has been heavily influenced by official comments accompanying §402A of the *Restatement (Second)*, in this instance comment n:

> Since the liability with which this Section deals is not based upon negligence of the seller, but is strict liability, the rule applied to strict liability cases applies. Contributory negligence of the plaintiff is not a defense when such negligence consists merely in a failure to discover the defect in the product, or to guard against the possibility of its existence. On the other hand the form of contributory negligence which consists in voluntarily and unreasonably proceeding to encounter a known danger, and commonly passes under the name of assumption of risk, is a defense under this Section as in other cases of strict liability. If the user or consumer discovers the defect and is aware of the danger, and nevertheless proceeds unreasonably to make use of the product and is injured by it, he is barred from recovery.

To establish the affirmative defense of assumption of risk, the defendant must prove that the plaintiff (1) made a voluntary choice (2) with sufficient knowledge of the risk. At the time when the *Restatement (Second)* was promulgated, this defense barred recovery altogether. Whether the defense bars recovery today depends on the rules of comparative responsibility that are discussed in section III.

A. Voluntary Choice

CREMEANS v. WILLMAR HENDERSON MFG. CO.
Supreme Court of Ohio, 1991
566 N.E.2d 1203

DOUGLAS, J. Michael Cremeans ("Cremeans") and his wife, appellees, filed an amended complaint in the Court of Common Pleas of Union County naming as defendants, inter alia, Sohio Chemical Company ("Sohio") and Willmar Henderson Manufacturing Company, a Division of Waycrosse, Inc. ("Willmar"), appellant. Cremeans alleged that on November 30, 1983, he was injured while operating a loader during the performance of his required job duties as an employee of Sohio. Cremeans alleged that the loader was manufactured and/or designed by Willmar and was purchased by Sohio without a "protective cage" manufactured by Willmar as a separate component for use with the loader. Further, Cremeans alleged that the loader was defective and dangerous due to the absence of a protective cage.

In his amended complaint, Cremeans sought recovery against Willmar for products liability based upon theories of strict liability and negligence. Additionally, Cremeans sought recovery against Sohio for an intentional tort.

Cremeans's job duties required him to drive a front-end loader manufactured by Willmar into fertilizer bins, "scoop" (or retrieve) a load of fertilizer, back out of the bin, and then haul the fertilizer to another location. The Willmar loader Cremeans used to perform his job duties was not equipped with any type of protective cage or structures although the structures were a standard feature for the loader. Had the structures been affixed to the loader, the loader could not have been used in the fertilizer bins as entry into the bins would have been impossible, given the dimensions of the protective structures and the height of the entrance to the bins. Willmar sold the loader to [Sohio] without protective structures. Willmar had been advised that the loader could not be operated in [Sohio's] building (bin) had the structures been affixed to the loader. Willmar was also advised regarding [Sohio's] proposed uses for the loader. As part of the sales agreement, Willmar apparently demanded and [Sohio] apparently agreed that [Sohio] would assume any liability arising from the removal of the protective structures and the invoice for the sale of the loader prepared by Willmar reflects that agreement.

On the day of the accident giving rise to the present appeal, Cremeans drove the Willmar loader into a fertilizer bin and retrieved fertilizer. As Cremeans was exiting the fertilizer bin, an avalanche of the fertilizer occurred within the bin and some of the fertilizer landed on the front end and scoop of the loader. As a result, Cremeans was injured when the rear wheels of the loader lifted off the ground, causing Cremeans to be wedged between the seat of the loader and either the doorway to the bin or a support bar within the bin. Had the loader been equipped with protective structures, Cremeans would not have sustained his injury.

Cremeans was aware that fertilizer avalanches had occurred prior to his injury; however, to his knowledge, no one had ever been injured by the avalanching of the fertilizer. Cremeans admitted that prior to the occurrence, he was concerned by the fact that the Willmar loader was not equipped with protective structures or a protective cage since an operator of the machine would be unprotected in the event of an avalanche of the fertilizer stored in the bins. Nevertheless, Cremeans continued to operate the loader in the fertilizer bins even though he was aware of the potential for an avalanche. Cremeans continued to operate the loader because it was his job.

With the foregoing evidence before it, the trial court granted Willmar summary judgment with respect to all of Cremeans's claims against Willmar finding that Cremeans had assumed the risk of his injuries. In its judgment entry, the trial court specifically found "no just reason for delay," leaving Cremeans's claim against Sohio for intentional tort liability to be adjudicated.

Cremeans and his wife appealed. The court of appeals reversed the judgment of the trial court, finding that a genuine issue of material fact exists as to whether Cremeans assumed the risk of his injury, and the extent, if any, to which Cremeans's conduct contributed to his injury.

The cause is now before this court pursuant to the allowance of a motion to certify the record.

The first issue presented by this appeal is whether the defense of assumption of risk bars Cremeans from recovery on his products liability claim against Willmar based upon strict liability in tort. Cremeans will be barred from recovery on his claim if he voluntarily and unreasonably assumed a known risk posed by the defective product manufactured by Willmar.

The defense of assumption of risk is a product of laissez-faire economics and evolved in master and servant cases. At common law, an employer's liability was shielded by defenses such as assumption of risk based upon an economic theory that there was complete mobility of labor, and that the supply of work was

II. Assumption of Risk

unlimited. Prosser & Keeton, LAW OF TORTS §80 (5th ed. 1984). Therefore, a worker was viewed as an entirely free agent not compelled to enter into a particular employment relationship. Thus, a person who entered into an employment relationship was deemed to accept all the usual and known risks of the chosen trade, thereby relieving the employer of any duty to protect the employee from the dangers of employment.

In more recent years, the doctrine of assumption of risk has been sharply criticized in its application to claims based upon injuries sustained in the workplace. Dean Prosser has recognized that the limitation of an employer's responsibility at common law was judicially created upon the basis of old industrial conditions, and a social philosophy and attitude toward labor which are "long since outmoded." Prosser & Keeton, *supra*, at 568. According to Prosser, the view that an employee assents to relieve his employer of liability based upon the theory that an employee is completely free to forgo the employment entirely disregards "[t]he economic compulsion which left . . . [the employee] no choice except starvation." Many courts in recent years have moved away from the strict common-law application of the doctrine of assumption of risk in the employment context by realizing that an employee does not voluntarily or unreasonably assume the risks of employment simply by accepting employment or by performing required job duties. [ ]

With the foregoing discussion in mind, we believe that the time has come for Ohio to realize that the days of laissez-faire economics are long gone, and that the industrial revolution is no longer with us. Today, an employee must either accept the dangers of his or her job or face the prospect of finding new employment in an economic setting where the supply of work has become increasingly limited. Ohio should now move into the Twentieth Century and join the ranks of the growing number of state and federal courts that have ruled on the question. The trend in this country set by the jurisdictions which have carefully analyzed the issue is that the defense of assumption of risk in the employment setting is no longer valid. [ ] Accordingly, common sense dictates, and we so hold, that an employee does not voluntarily or unreasonably assume the risk of injury which occurs in the course of his or her employment when he or she must encounter that risk in the normal performance of his or her required job duties and responsibilities. We realize that our holding "abolishes" assumption of risk in the employment setting in the sense that the defense of assumption of risk is unavailable for certain claims arising from work-related injuries.

The record in this case demonstrates that Cremeans encountered the risks associated with the use of the Willmar loader because he was required to do so in the normal performance of his job duties and responsibilities and that Cremeans was injured during the execution of such duties and responsibilities. Therefore, his assumption of the risk was neither voluntary nor unreasonable and, hence, . . . Cremeans is not barred from recovery on his products liability claim based upon strict liability in tort. This is so regardless of the fact that it was Cremeans's employer, and not Willmar, who required Cremeans to perform the particular job duty which resulted in the injury. Given the facts of this case, to wit, that Willmar knew that the loader it was selling to Sohio was not equipped with a necessary safety device and, in fact, demanded indemnity from Sohio before agreeing to make the sale, the issue is even clearer.

Willmar suggests that Comment b to Section 496E of the *Restatement (Second) of Torts* (1965), supports its position that Cremeans's decision to encounter the risk associated with the use of the Willmar loader was voluntary.

We disagree. Section 496E provides:

> (1) A plaintiff does not assume a risk of harm unless he voluntarily accepts the risk.
>
> (2) The plaintiff's acceptance of a risk is not voluntary if the defendant's tortious conduct has left him no reasonable alternative course of conduct in order to
>
> > (a) avert harm to himself or another, or
> >
> > (b) exercise or protect a right or privilege of which the defendant has no right to deprive him.

Comment b to Section 496E provides in part:

> The plaintiff's acceptance of the risk is to be regarded as voluntary even though he is acting under the compulsion of circumstances, *not created by the tortious conduct of the defendant*, which have left him no reasonable alternative. *Where the defendant is under no independent duty to the plaintiff, and* the plaintiff finds himself confronted by a choice of risks, or is driven by his own necessities to accept a danger, the situation is not to be charged against the defendant. . . . (emphasis added)

With regard to the first sentence in Comment b, we have determined that the compulsion of Cremeans's circumstances was, to some degree, attributable to Willmar. Willmar provided Cremeans's employer with a defective product which made it possible for Cremeans to encounter the risk. With regard to the second sentence in Comment b, Willmar certainly had an independent duty to Cremeans not to place a dangerously defective product into the stream of commerce, thereby placing Cremeans at risk. Furthermore, in our judgment, Cremeans's decision to encounter the risk posed by Willmar's product was clearly "not voluntary" within the meaning of Section 496E(2).

The judgment of the court of appeals is affirmed and this cause is remanded for further proceedings consistent with this opinion.

NOTES AND QUESTIONS

1. *Whose choice?* The loader in *Cremeans* was allegedly defective because it did not have a protective cage that was available as an optional safety feature. The plaintiff's employer decided not to purchase the cage because it would have rendered the loader unusable for scooping fertilizer. The employer, more precisely, concluded that the cost or burden of the cage (B_{cage}) exceeded the extent to which it would reduce risk (PL_{cage}). Should this risk-utility decision ($B_{cage} > PL_{cage}$) foreclose an allegation that the design was defective because it did not incorporate the protective cage ($B_{cage} < PL_{cage}$)? Does it matter for this purpose that the employer made the choice, not the plaintiff employee? *See* Chapter 6, section III.C (discussing rule that renders a product nondefective with respect to an optional safety

II. Assumption of Risk

feature, even if the choice to forego the option was made by an employer rather than the plaintiff employee).

2. *The problem of patent dangers.* Was the defendant's argument in *Cremeans* any different from the argument that the plaintiff's choice to face a patent danger negates liability? Unless properly formulated, the assumed-risk rule could effectively revitalize the patent-danger rule, a problematic outcome given the widespread rejection of that rule. To be functionally different from the patent-danger rule, assumption of risk cannot be established simply because the plaintiff decided to use a product with a patent danger.

3. *Which choice?* The plaintiff employee, of course, made a voluntary choice that left him vulnerable to the risk in question: He could have quit. The question is whether the plaintiff made a voluntary choice of the right type for establishing assumption of risk. Did the court in *Cremeans* adequately explain why the choice that had been made by the plaintiff was not "voluntary"?

Consider the nature of the decision made by the plaintiff employee with respect to the risk of injury posed by the product defect. According to the allegation of defective design, the cost of the protective cage is less than its safety benefit:

$$B_{cage} < PL_{cage}$$

How does this risk-utility decision compare to the plaintiff employee's choice to face the risk? The plaintiff either could have used the defective machine or quit the job, the only other way for him to avoid the risk. In making this choice, the plaintiff presumably considered the cost or burden of quitting the job as compared to the risk of being harmed by the loader lacking a cage. Insofar the cost of changing jobs would be substantial, the plaintiff made a reasonable decision to face the risk:

$$B_{quit} > PL_{cage}$$

The plaintiff's reasonable choice to face the risk was based on a risk-utility decision different from the one implicated by the allegation of defect. The plaintiff's voluntary choice to stay working, therefore, did not mean he voluntarily chose to face the risk of being injured by the defective product—the two choices are fundamentally different. Why should the plaintiff's reasonable choice to face the risk make him entirely responsible for the unreasonable risk created by the defective product?

As the *Cremeans* court observed when invoking *Restatement (Second)* §496E(2), the plaintiff's choice to face a known risk is not "voluntary" if "the defendant's tortious conduct has left him no reasonable alternative course of conduct in order to . . . exercise or protect a right or privilege of which the defendant has no right to deprive him." The defendant had no right to deprive the plaintiff of his job, nor did the plaintiff have any reasonable alternative for avoiding the risk. The plaintiff's reasonable decision to stay on the job—to exercise that right—did not absolve the defendant from the independent duty to provide a nondefective product.

Hence the plaintiff's choice to face the risk was not "voluntary" for purposes of the assumed-risk rule.

Would the outcome be different if the plaintiff had been given the opportunity to use the loader with a protective cage, but decided to remove the cage to make it easier to use the loader? Consider Kenneth W. Simons, *Assumption of Risk and Consent in the Law of Torts: A Theory of Full Preference*, 67 B.U. L. Rev. 213, 238 (1987) (showing why assumption of risk should apply only when the plaintiff's "chosen course of action was based on a full and true preference, i.e., made with knowledge of all the alternatives that defendant had a duty to offer, including that alternative which plaintiff claims defendant tortiously failed to offer"). Would such a bar to liability be any different from the one based on the employer's decision not to purchase the cage as an optional piece of safety equipment, discussed in note 1 *supra*?

4. *"Voluntary" choices outside of the workplace.* To what extent does the foregoing analysis of a "voluntary" choice depend on the limited options that employees have in the workplace? Consider David G. Owen & Mary J. Davis, 1 OWEN & DAVIS ON PRODUCTS LIABILITY §13:15 (4th ed. 2014 & 2020 update) (identifying workplace accidents and rescues as "two contexts in which courts have been especially open to challenges to the voluntariness of risk encounters"). In the workplace context, a plaintiff can clearly face a "choice of evils": Use the defective product or quit the job. But outside of the workplace, consumers also routinely face that same type of constrained choice. For example, it would be reasonable for a consumer to drive an automobile that is defectively designed for not incorporating airbags ($B_{airbag} < PL_{airbag}$): The lost benefits of not being able to use the automobile substantially exceed the risk posed by the absence of airbags ($B_{lost\ use} > PL_{airbag}$). For the same reasons that the plaintiff employee's choice was not "voluntary" in *Cremeans*, the consumer's choice to use the defectively designed automobile would not be "voluntary" for purposes of the assumed-risk rule. Consumers have the right to use the product in a reasonable manner, and their exercise of that right does not absolve the manufacturer from the independent duty to provide a nondefective product. Compare Dan B. Dobbs, Paul T. Hayden & Ellen M. Bublick, THE LAW OF TORTS §236 (2d ed. & 2020 update) ("The court that finds consent when the plaintiff is confronting a known risk in a reasonable way is limiting the plaintiff's freedom to act reasonably."). Properly applied, the "voluntariness" requirement is no different in the workplace than outside of the workplace.

To what extent is this reasoning dependent on the reasonableness of the plaintiff's decision to use the product in light of its patent danger? What if the plaintiff's decision was unreasonable? Does the plaintiff necessarily assume the risk in these circumstances? Consider RESTATEMENT (SECOND) OF TORTS §402A cmt. n ("If the user or consumer discovers the defect and is aware of the danger, and nevertheless proceeds unreasonably to make use of the product and is injured by it, he is barred from recovery.").

WANGSNESS v. BUILDERS CASHWAY, INC.
Supreme Court of South Dakota, 2010
779 N.W.2d 136

SEVERSON, J. Tanner Wangsness (Wangsness) brought this strict products liability action against Builders Cashway, Inc. (Builders Cashway), alleging the bi-fold door his grandfather purchased from Builders Cashway was defective. Wangsness's strict products liability action against Builders Cashway proceeded to trial. After hearing the evidence, the jury rendered a verdict, and the circuit court entered a judgment in favor of Builders Cashway. We affirm.

Builders Cashway, Inc. is a hardware store and lumberyard in Miller, South Dakota. Wangsness, Inc. is a farming and ranching operation located southwest of Miller, South Dakota, and operated by Darrell Wangsness and his brother, Mark. In 1991, Wangsness, Inc. sought to replace the sliding door on its Quonset building, which was originally built in the 1950s. Mark Wangsness selected and purchased a bi-fold door from Builders Cashway. The door was manufactured by Schweiss Chicken Pluckers (Schweiss) and was installed by Builders Cashway employees.

The bi-fold door purchased by Wangsness, Inc. utilized a horizontal hinge system that allowed the door to fold into two halves. When opened, the door folded outside the building, thereby providing overhead clearance inside the building. The door was set in motion by a switch box connected by a cord to the bi-fold door's motor. This switch box was not mounted in a stationary position but sat on a work bench near the door. A rotating shaft and cable mechanism, located on the bottom left-hand side of the door, winched the door upward. The door rose as the cable wrapped around a rotating shaft. The point at which the cable wrapped around the shaft was plainly visible.

On August 4, 2003, fifteen-year-old Wangsness and his grandfather, Darrell, arrived at the Quonset building shortly after lunch. The two planned to work on a vehicle in the building. Darrell first went to the nearby house to make a phone call. Meanwhile, Wangsness opened the bi-fold door to the Quonset building. Shortly thereafter, Wangsness appeared at the door of the nearby house, displaying serious injuries to his hands. Wangsness had set the bi-fold door in motion and an incident occurred, amputating the four fingers of his left hand. No one other than Wangsness was present, and Wangsness maintains he does not remember the incident.

Prior to the summer of 2003, Wangsness was living and working on the Wangsness, Inc. farm. He spent a little more than ten hours per week working for Wangsness, Inc. He primarily assisted by mowing grass and moving vehicles around the farm. He also worked on cars in and around the Quonset building. He therefore regularly observed the operation of the bi-fold door on the building, particularly in the summer. He operated the door himself on at least two occasions prior to the accident. Wangsness never received any specific instruction on the use of the door, because, as Darrell testified, the door "is so simple" that no instruction on its operation is necessary.

Wangsness initiated this lawsuit against Builders Cashway. [The manufacturer had filed for bankruptcy.] He alleged the bi-fold door was defective due to (1) the unguarded nature of the rotating shaft and cable and (2) the lack of adequate warning as to the door's use. After hearing the evidence, the jury rendered a verdict, and the circuit court entered a judgment in favor of Builders Cashway. Wangsness appeals.

Wangsness argues the circuit court erred by instructing the jury on the doctrine of assumption of the risk. It is well established in South Dakota that assumption of the risk is a defense to a claim of strict products liability. A plaintiff assumes the risk when he is "aware the product is defective, knows the defect makes the product unreasonably dangerous, has reasonable opportunity to elect whether to expose himself to the danger, and nevertheless proceeds to make use of the product." [ ] "A person is deemed to have appreciated the risk if it is the type of risk that no adult of average intelligence can deny."[1] [ ]The plaintiff must have knowledge of the specific defect and risk posed rather than simple generalized knowledge that he has entered a zone of danger. [ ]

Evidence relevant to the doctrine of assumption of the risk was presented at trial. Wangsness worked on cars in and around the Quonset building. He regularly observed the operation of the bi-fold door, particularly in the summer. He also operated the door himself on at least two occasions prior to the accident. The rotating shaft and cable were open and obvious. Wangsness understood that failing to keep his hands away from the rotating shaft and cable mechanism on the bi-fold door could result in serious injury. Likewise, Wangsness's experts testified that a reasonable person could appreciate the visible danger of the rotating shaft and cable mechanism. The evidence presented was sufficient to submit the issue of assumption of the risk to the jury.

Builders Cashway requested a special verdict form that would have specifically identified the basis for the jury's decision. However, Wangsness objected and requested a general verdict form. The circuit court sustained his objection and provided the jury with a general verdict form. A special verdict form would have made clear what effect the instruction on the doctrine of assumption of the risk had on the jury's ultimate determination. As it stands, we cannot know which theory the jury accepted, so we must assume the jury decided the case on a proper theory. The jury's verdict should be affirmed as there exist valid bases for the general verdict in favor of Builders Cashway.

Affirmed.

ZINTER, J. (concurring in part and concurring in result in part). I join the opinion of the Court on all issues except assumption of the risk. On that issue, I concur in result. In my view, there was insufficient evidence for an assumption of the risk instruction. Nevertheless, because of the general verdict form, Wangsness has not established reversible error.

---

1. Because Wangsness was fifteen-years-old at the time of the accident, the circuit court instructed the jury on the standard of care applicable to minors:

> Generally, a minor is not held to the same standard of conduct as that of an adult unless he engages in an activity normally only undertaken by adults. The objective standard of the reasonably prudent person does not apply to a minor, but rather a special subjective standard of care is used which takes into account his age, intelligence, maturity, experience, and capacity. In other words, the standard of conduct of a minor is what is reasonable to expect of children of like age, intelligence, maturity, capacity, and experience.

The majority misapplies the rule that in order for a plaintiff to have assumed the risk, "it [must be] the type of risk that no adult of average intelligence can deny." Although the majority is correct that the circuit court provided a "standard of care" instruction applicable to juveniles, the instruction related to contributory negligence rather than assumption of the risk. In distinguishing the two defenses, this Court [in a prior case] has specifically pointed out that such standards of conduct relate to questions of negligence, but the question in assumption of the risk is knowledge of the danger and intelligent acquiescence in it. Yet in this case, the circuit court's instruction on a juvenile standard of conduct did not advise the jury that a fifteen-year-old is not bound by an adult's mental capacity and a juvenile must have fully recognized and intelligently acquiesced in assuming the specific risk. [Wangsness] may have appreciated the nature and risk of opening a large bi-fold door, but there was no evidence he had an adult's appreciation of the specific defect and risk posed by the unshielded drum and cable mechanism. Therefore, the circuit court erred in giving the instruction.

NOTES AND QUESTIONS

1. *Objective or subjective consent?* The court in *Wangsness* evaluated the plaintiff's conduct by reference to an objective standard of knowledge. However, a "plaintiff did not assume the risk unless she knew of the risk itself as well as the facts that gave rise to it and 'really' assumed the risk. This kind of statement implied what many cases substantiated, that the plaintiff's subjective consent was required." Dan B. Dobbs, Paul T. Hayden & Ellen M. Bublick, THE LAW OF TORTS §236 (2d ed. & 2020 update) (footnotes omitted). If subjective consent is required for purposes of the assumed-risk rule, why did the court invoke objective consent?

In product cases, objective consent is defined by the reasonable risk-utility choices that are made by the ordinary consumer. When the ordinary consumer can make an informed risk-utility decision to face the risk in question, then the product in this regard is not more dangerous than expected by the ordinary consumer with ordinary knowledge common to the community. This attribute of the product is not "unreasonably dangerous" for purposes of §402A, eliminating the seller's duty with respect to that particular safety decision. *See* Chapter 5, section III. Objective consent, therefore, provides a limitation of liability different from the assumed-risk rule based on subjective consent.

To be sure, considering the plaintiff's choices in relation to the ordinary consumer's reasonable or objective choices can reduce or bar recovery on other grounds. However, "[n]egligence analysis, couched in reasonable man hypotheses, has no place in the assumption of the risk framework. When one acts knowingly, it is immaterial whether he acts reasonably." Kennedy v. Providence Hockey Club, Inc., 376 A.2d 329, 333 (R.I. 1977). Subjective consent provides a limitation of liability that is independent from the reasonable or objective choices that define contributory negligence. By analyzing the plaintiff's behavior in terms of objective consent, did the court in *Wangsness* apply the defense of contributory negligence or assumption of risk? Consider Thomas v. Holliday, 764 P.2d 165, 169 (Okla. 1988) (observing that the "[t]ouchstone" of the assumed-risk rule is "consent to harm and not heedlessness or indifference").

2. *Assumption of risk or contributory negligence?* If the court in *Wangsness* had concluded that plaintiff was only contributorily negligent, he would have received full recovery. *See* Berg v. Sukup Mfg. Co., 355 N.W.2d 833, 835 (S.D. 1984) (holding that the "defense of contributory negligence is not available to bar recovery in a strict liability case"). Did the concurring opinion adequately flag this issue?

When the *Restatement (Second)* was promulgated, assumption of risk and contributory negligence barred the plaintiff's recovery altogether, although comment n of §402A limits the relevance of contributory negligence to assumed risks: "If the plaintiff acts unreasonably in making his choice, he may be barred from recovery . . . by his assumption of risk . . . in failing to exercise reasonable care for his own safety." Today, contributory negligence only reduces the plaintiff's recovery under the principles of comparative responsibility, whereas assumption of risk can completely bar recovery, depending on the jurisdiction. As *Wangsness* fully illustrates, the appropriate characterization of the plaintiff's conduct can determine whether the plaintiff is able to recover any damages at all—an issue we further explore in Section III *infra*.

3. *A voluntary choice?* In *Wangsness*, the alleged defect still left the plaintiff with a reasonable alternative for avoiding the risk—the exercise of reasonable care would have kept his hand away from the exposed moving parts of the door. Due to this reasonable alternative course of conduct, the *Wangsness* court concluded that the plaintiff's choice to face the risk was "voluntary" and barred recovery. Other courts reach the same conclusion. *See* Dan B. Dobbs, Paul T. Hayden & Ellen M. Bublick, THE LAW OF TORTS §236 ("Courts that continue to use implied assumption of risk to bar a claim entirely adhere to this rule."); *see also* RESTATEMENT (SECOND) OF TORTS §496E cmt. d ("If the plaintiff acts unreasonably in making his choice, he may be barred from recovery . . . by his assumption of risk . . . in failing to exercise reasonable care for his own safety.").

Did the plaintiff intentionally place his hand into the exposed moving parts of the folding door? If not, in what respect did he "voluntarily" choose to face the risk? Compare Campbell v. ITE Imperial Corp., 733 P.2d 969, 976 (Wash. 1987) (rejecting claim that a defendant electrician assumed the risk of being shocked by defendant's product on the ground that "[t]o conclude that [plaintiff] was aware of the specific defect in this configuration would be tantamount to believing that he intended to commit suicide").

For reasons discussed in the notes following *Cremeans*, to fully evaluate the issue of whether the plaintiff made a "voluntary" choice to face a risk, the court must consider how that choice relates to the defendant's independent duty to provide a nondefective product. In a case like *Wangsness*, the product posed a patent danger, and the plaintiff alleges that a design change (such as a guard covering exposed moving parts) is more effective than the consumer's exercise of reasonable care (to keep his hands away from the exposed moving parts). The same issue is implicated by the rule that determines whether a warning can substitute for a design change. A warning makes a risk apparent to the user. Even if the plaintiff could have avoided injury by following a warning about safe use, she can still prove that the risk should have been eliminated by a reasonable alternative design, thereby subjecting the manufacturer to liability for the defective product. *See* Chapter 8. By holding that the manufacturer is subject to liability in these cases, courts have recognized that the duty to design is not eliminated simply because the consumer had a reasonable alternative for avoiding the risk—comply with the safety instructions supplied by the warning.

Consequently, the plaintiff's unreasonable choice to face the risk in *Wangsness* was not "voluntary" for purposes of the assumed-risk rule. Any choice he made to expose his hands to the moving parts of the machine did not absolve the defendant from the independent duty to adopt a reasonable alternative design to eliminate the patent danger, and so the situation should "be charged against the defendant." RESTATEMENT (SECOND) OF TORTS §496E cmt. d. By barring the plaintiff's recovery, the *Wangsness* court effectively adopted a formulation of the assumed-risk rule that permits a manufacturer to rely on a patent danger (or product warning) instead of adopting a reasonable alternative design that would eliminate the need for users to avoid the patent danger by exercising reasonable care (or complying with the warning).

4. *Failure to use a readily available safety device.* "[C]ourts are likely to be sympathetic to defendants offering the assumption of risk defense . . . when the plaintiff does not use a readily available safety device." Marshall S. Shapo, SHAPO ON THE LAW OF PRODUCTS LIABILITY §20.03[J][1] (7th ed. 2017 & 2020 update). These cases illustrate proper application of the assumed-risk rule.

For example, suppose that the plaintiff employee removed the protective guard from a machine. In making this decision, the plaintiff presumably concluded that the guard did not make sense for him. Having made an informed risk-utility choice to forego use of the guard in favor of the less safe alternative, the plaintiff did not actually or reasonably expect the greater safety offered by the protective guard, eliminating the seller's duty with respect to that particular safety decision. The plaintiff's informed choice to face the risk ($B_{guard} > PL_{guard}$) accordingly absolves the defendant of responsibility to design the machine with a guard that cannot be removed ($B_{guard} < PL_{guard}$). The plaintiff's risk-utility choice manifested the requisite willingness to assume responsibility for the associated risk-utility decision, explaining why the plaintiff "voluntarily" assumed the risk. When applied in this manner, the assumed-risk rule bars recovery for the same reasons inherent in the patent-defect rule that bars recovery under the tort version of the implied warranty. *See* Chapter 5, section II.

B. Knowledge of Risk

TRAYLOR v. HUSQVARNA MOTOR
United States Court of Appeals, Seventh Circuit, 1993
988 F.2d 729

POSNER, J. Ronnie Traylor and his wife appeal from the dismissal of their products liability suit, a diversity suit governed by Indiana law. The case was tried before a magistrate judge by consent of the parties and the jury brought in a verdict for the defendants, whom we refer to collectively as Omark.

A maul, the agent of the injury that gave rise to the suit, is a long-handled striking tool the steel head of which has an axe blade on one side and a flat, sledgehammer-like surface on the other. One day in 1986 Ronnie Traylor and his friend Dierking were splitting logs on Traylor's property. Each had a maul—Dierking a maul that had been manufactured by Omark. Each maul had been sold with a warning not to strike one maul against another, because chipping could occur and cause an eye injury, and not to use a maul without safety goggles. Traylor's maul got stuck in a log he was splitting. With the axe head embedded in the log, the flat surface of the head facing up, and the handle of the maul sticking out sideways, the two men set about to free the axe head. Traylor—who was not wearing safety glasses—crouched down, holding the handle of his maul to steady it, his unprotected face only a couple of feet from the head of the maul. Dierking gave the flat surface of Traylor's maul a whack with the flat surface of *his* maul. When Dierking's maul struck, it chipped, and the chip shot into Traylor's right eye and put the eye out.

Dierking had noticed before the accident that the flat surface of the head of his maul was chipped, cracked, and misshapen. There was considerable although not conclusive evidence that this was not due just to normal wear and tear—rather, that Dierking's maul was defective in two respects. First, it had an unusually narrow bevel around the flat surface of the head. A bevel is an angled as distinct from a right-angled edge. The larger the bevel, the less likely a surface is to chip. Second, the steel in the head, which had been manufactured in China, was of uneven hardness, which made it more likely that the head would chip when it was struck against another hard surface. The fact that a product is of low quality does not make it defective merely because higher-quality products are likely to be safer, safety being a dimension of quality. But Omark, while denying that its maul was defective, has not argued that the plaintiffs were trying to hold it to a standard of safety appropriate only to a more expensive maul.

Besides denying that the maul was defective, Omark raised affirmative defenses of misuse and "incurred risk," the latter a synonym for assumed risk. [ ] The common law tort defense of "open and obvious danger" used to be available to defendants in products liability cases as in other personal injury cases in Indiana. [ ] Then the Indiana legislature as part of a general overhaul of products liability law decided in effect to replace the defense of open and obvious danger (a much-criticized defense . . .) which the legislature abolished in products liability cases, with another common law defense, which the legislature proceeded to codify for those cases—that of assumed or incurred risk. [ ] The products liability statute defines the defense as follows: "It is a defense

II. Assumption of Risk

that the user or consumer . . . knew of the defect and was aware of the danger and nevertheless proceeded unreasonably to make use of the product and was injured by it." Ind. Code §33-1-1.5-4(b)(1).

The doctrine of incurred risk, more familiarly assumption of risk, teaches that a person who proceeds in the face of what he knows to be a risk of a certain consequence cannot complain if the consequence materializes. Dierking may well have known that *his* maul was defective, so if he had been injured by it we may assume that he could not recover damages against Omark. But there is little or no evidence that *Traylor* knew that Dierking's maul was defective. He probably knew that striking a maul against another maul can cause one of the mauls to chip. The instructions that came with his own maul expressly warned him of this danger and he is (or at least was, before his accident) a factory worker who wore safety goggles at work to protect his eyes from metal chips. But to assume the risk of an eye injury from a flying maul chip is not the same thing as assuming the risk of an eye injury caused by a chip from a *defective* maul. These could be risks of different orders of magnitude.

The difference is well illustrated by Moore v. Sitzmark Corp., 555 N.E.2d 1305 (Ind. App. 1990), which involved safety binders for skis. A safety binder is designed to release the ski from the skier's boot when lateral force is applied to the binder, so that the boot (and the foot in it) won't be twisted by the ski. Anyone who skis knows that even the best safety binders are fallible, so that there is still a nontrivial risk of breaking one's leg. But of course if the safety binder is defective and therefore *highly* unlikely to release the ski in a fall, the danger of breaking one's leg is much greater. *Moore* holds that merely by going skiing and thus assuming some irreducible risk of being injured, the purchaser of safety binders does not assume the greater, hidden risk due to the defect in the particular binders he bought. If, however, he had known about the defect and had decided to take his chances, he would have assumed the specific risk of a defective binder and the doctrine of incurred risk would bar him from recovering damages if he was injured as a result of the defect.

It is the same here. If Traylor knew that Dierking's maul was defective and decided to take his chances, the incurred-risk statute bars recovery. But if he merely knew that striking two mauls together can cause one of them to chip even if neither is defective, that knowledge would not bar recovery. This is provided of course that the accident was due to the defect. If the accident would have occurred anyway, there would be no prima facie liability and the defense would not come into play.

All this is background to the question whether the nature of the incurred-risk defense was adequately explained to the jury. Instruction 20 explains that if the plaintiff "disregarded an adequate warning . . . he incurred the risk of the injury he sustained," for "the doctrine of incurred risk is based upon the proposition that one incurs all the ordinary and usual risks of an act which he voluntarily enters, if those risks are known and understood by him." Instruction 21 explains that the "essential elements" of the defense are that Traylor knew either "of the danger associated with using a maul without adequate eye protection" or "of the danger associated with striking a maul with another maul," and that knowing these things he voluntarily exposed himself to the danger and was injured as a proximate result. These are the only instructions that deal with incurred risk. Nowhere do they state that the relevant knowledge is knowledge of the *defect*.

The reference to "adequate warning" and to the two dangers associated with the use of a maul is a giveaway that the magistrate judge thought the defense applicable whenever the plaintiff knows that the use of the product in a particular way creates a danger of injury. That is not Indiana law, and would in fact strip plaintiffs of virtually all protection against hidden product defects.

The judgment is reversed with directions to grant the plaintiffs a new trial to be conducted in conformity with this opinion.

NOTES AND QUESTIONS

1. *How much knowledge is enough?* To prove assumption of risk, the defendant must show that "plaintiff had actual knowledge of the specific danger posed by the defect in design, and not just general knowledge that the product could be dangerous." Jackson v. Harsco Corp., 673 P.2d 363, 366 (Colo. 1983). In Wilson Sporting Goods Co. v. Hickcox, 59 A.3d 1267 (D.C. 2013), plaintiff was an umpire of Major League Baseball games who was injured by a foul fall that struck his "traditional umpire's mask" manufactured by defendant. Plaintiff alleged that the mask was defective because the throat guard could have been designed to deflect an oncoming ball rather temporarily trapping it and "concentrating the ball's energy at the point of impact." Defendant argued that plaintiff had assumed the risk. He "was an experienced umpire who knew that participating in sports creates the risk of injury, that no face mask can guarantee safety, and that injury is more likely without protective equipment." The court rejected this argument because the defendant "needed evidence that [plaintiff] knew that the throat guard's acute, forward angle had a tendency to concentrate energy and increase the risk of injury." In the absence of such evidence, "the trial court did not err by declining to give an assumption-of-risk instruction." *Id.* at 1274.

Under what conditions would a plaintiff have adequate knowledge of the specific defect?

> "Risk" implies a degree of want of appreciation of the forces that are at work in a given factual setting, since if one knew and understood all these forces he would know that injury was certain to occur or that it was certain not to occur. Thus the expression "fully appreciated the risk" may seem to be a self-contradiction.

Robert E. Keeton, *Assumption of Risk in Products Liability Cases*, 122 La. L. Rev. 122, 124 (1961).

2. *Conceptualizing the knowledge requirement.* The knowledge requirement can be developed by reference to the rationale for the assumed-risk rule. According to the *Restatement (Second)* §402A rule of strict products liability, assumption of risk completely bars the plaintiff's recovery. A complete bar to recovery is defensible if the plaintiff voluntarily chose to face a risk after making the same risk-utility decision involved in the allegation of defect, and so the knowledge requirement must pertain to *all* factors required by that risk-utility decision.

II. Assumption of Risk

In deciding to use the maul, the plaintiff in *Traylor* presumably concluded that the burden of not using the maul exceeded the associated risk that the maul would chip and injure him ($B_{lost\ product\ use} > PL_{chip}$). The specific risk that a *defective* maul would chip ($PL_{chip\ from\ defect}$), however, substantially exceeds the general risk that an *ordinary* nondefective maul would chip ($PL_{chip\ from\ defect} > PL_{chip}$). These relationships, in turn, allow for the possibility that if he had known of the defect, the plaintiff would not have used the maul for this purpose:

$$PL_{chip\ from\ defect} > B_{lost\ product\ use} > PL_{chip}$$

Under these circumstances, the plaintiff's risk-utility decision (involving the risk term PL_{chip}) is not identical to the one implicated by the alleged defect (involving the risk term $PL_{chip\ from\ defect}$). The knowledge requirement confirms that assumption of risk only applies when the plaintiff made an informed choice based on the same risk-utility factors implicated by the allegation of defect.

3. *Is knowledge of risk sufficient?* Would the knowledge requirement be satisfied if the plaintiff knew of the risk but not of the different methods for reducing it? To have knowledge of *defect*, the plaintiff must know that the product in this respect does not conform to the risk-utility test ($B < PL$), requiring knowledge of both the risk (PL) and the reasonably available method for reducing it (with a cost or burden B). Knowledge of the specific defect therefore means that the plaintiff knows about the risk-utility factors that render the product defective; mere knowledge of risk is not enough. *See* Chapter 5, section II (distinguishing patent dangers from patent defects). An informed *voluntary choice*, in turn, requires the plaintiff to make such a risk-utility decision identical to the one implicated by the allegation of defect.

C. Primary Assumption of Risk

Some courts evaluate assumed risks by distinguishing between primary and secondary assumption of risk. A plaintiff who primarily assumes a risk relieves the defendant of the legal duty to protect the plaintiff from that particular risk of harm. In a case of secondary assumption of risk, the defendant first breached a duty owed to the plaintiff, and the plaintiff then made an informed choice to face the tortious risk.

FORD v. POLARIS INDUS., INC.
Court of Appeal, First District, California, 2006
43 Cal. Rptr. 3d 215

REARDON, J. Susan Ford sustained severe orifice injuries after falling off the rear of a two-seater Polaris personal watercraft. The jet-powered nozzle propelled a high-pressure stream of water that tore apart her internal organs. Today she uses a colostomy bag, she urinates through a catheter, and her lower right torso and leg are numb from nerve damage. Susan and her husband sued the manufacturer and distributor of the watercraft on a strict products liability theory.

This appeal frames the question whether the doctrine of primary assumption of risk applies to the manufacturer of the personal watercraft so as to preclude the injured jet skier from raising a defective design claim. We conclude that the trial court properly ruled that primary assumption of the risk did not bar plaintiff's suit.

In April 2001 Steve and Laura Nakamura bought two 2-seater Polaris SLH-700 personal watercraft. On September 9, 2001, the Fords and Nakamuras and various family members went to Lake Berryessa for a picnic. Laura took Susan for a ride on the watercraft. Susan was wearing a one-piece swimsuit and a life jacket. This was her first time riding a personal watercraft. Susan held onto Laura's waist. After about five minutes, Laura stopped to tell Susan she was holding on too tight and to hold onto the grips behind her instead. Susan looked around; all she saw were the grab handles. She had to lean back and could only hook a couple fingers into each handle. They started out again in a straight line. The jet ski was "bumping up and down." Susan lost her grip, was lifted off the seat and fell backward off the rear of the watercraft. As Susan hit the water she felt "a lot" of pain and vomited. Laura saw Susan floating in a pool of blood. Paramedics rushed Susan by helicopter to University of California Davis Medical Center.

Susan sustained a severe hernial and rectal injury [that required multiple surgeries and caused severe, ongoing urological complications]. As well, Susan is numb from her right kneecap to her waist; her buttocks and pelvic area are also numb. She can no longer engage in such activities as playing softball and dancing. And, because of loss of sensation and the physical limitations she endures, Susan and Anthony's sex life has suffered. Susan used to work at Raley's Superstore but was unable to keep up with her responsibilities after she returned to work. She now takes care of her father-in-law.

[As to the cause of the accident,] Michael Burleson, an industrial engineer and safety professional with extensive experience on personal watercraft concerns, testified that the jet nozzle is centrally positioned in back of the Polaris watercraft and protrudes two and five-eighths inches beyond the rear deck. The position of the jet increases the chance of high-pressure exposure should a passenger be ejected to the rear of the watercraft. Susan landed less than a foot from the back of the jet nozzle.

When a watercraft is accelerating and encounters a wave, the passenger can "get some lift" off the seat, and if the passenger is not well coupled to the craft he or she may lose balance and roll off. When there is a rearward ejection into the stream of water thrust by a jet nozzle such as occurred with Susan, the high pressure of the water penetrates the body, causing internal injuries.

Burleson explained that because it is important that nothing interfere with the operator's ability to control a personal watercraft, a passenger cannot always hold onto the operator. Sometimes passengers pull more than is comfortable for the operator. In some situations it may not be feasible to hold on, for example if the operator stands up to move around. As well there may be social constraints to holding onto the operator. A significant difference in size may also militate against holding on.

In Burleson's opinion there was a defect in the design of the SLH Polaris watercraft because this particular craft lacked adequate design safeguards to protect against a rearward ejection injury. In other words, there was no easily identifiable alternative means for the passenger to hold on when it was not feasible to hold onto the operator.

Several feasible design features were available to Polaris to protect against rear ejections. A seatback is one alternative to prevent the passenger from "coming off" the back. Another solution would be recognizable and accessible handgrips that the passenger can "grasp completely." For fifty cents at most, a simple seat strap that goes around the seat would provide a secure handhold for passenger stability. Several models in the Polaris manual for this machine had a seat strap, and there were bolt holes for such a strap on the craft but it had not been installed. Had the machine been equipped with a seat strap, Burleson did not think the accident would have occurred.

Dr. Edward Karnes was the Fords' human factors engineer. That discipline concerns the evaluation of human factors involved in the design and use of products, including how people understand risks and respond to warnings. He described the hazard in this case as falling off the rear of the watercraft and being struck by the jet thrust. The manufacturer's job is to identify and evaluate hazards and make decisions about remedies according to a safety hierarchy. The first tier on the hierarchy is to design out the hazard. If that cannot be accomplished, the next tier would be to provide some type of guard to prevent access to the hazardous situation. Warning—the last tier—is an appropriate remedy only if the hazard cannot be eliminated by design or guard.

Polaris's solution to orifice injuries was to admonish participants to wear protective clothing. The rear and front on-craft labels for the SLH warned that the passenger must wear a wetsuit or equivalent protective clothing to avoid orifice injuries. The owner's manual reproduced the rear decal, in bigger typeface, as well as the front warning label, and instructed elsewhere to wear protective clothing for body or orifice protection. Susan did not notice the warning decal and, being a guest, she never saw the owner's manual.

In Dr. Karnes's opinion, warnings alone were not an appropriate remedy for the hazard that creates the risk of orifice injury. He regarded the cost of compliance—or the effort required to comply with warning—as high for wearing a wetsuit. First, they are not comfortable when worn in warm weather conditions. Second, the likelihood that owner-operators would have wetsuits on hand for recreational passengers such as friends or family members is "going to be about nil." Third, the person at greatest risk—the passenger—is also the person least likely to have read the vehicle warning label.

Polaris designated Daniel Schroepher as the employee most qualified to address safety features on the SLH such as rear passenger seating, safety testing and safety studies. He testified that Polaris designed the SLH in-house. By the time of the 1996 model year, the label warned against orifice injuries. Polaris did not conduct tests to distinguish the risk of falling off the back of the craft as opposed to the side.

Schroepher identified several design features intended to prevent the passenger from sliding off the back. The driver's seat and handgrips were of non-slippery material so the driver could stay put as well as the passenger who was hanging on. The foot pad was also of grippy material, and there was a spot where the passenger could put his or her heels. Grab handles were an option to stay on board if there was discomfort with holding onto the operator. Schroepher testified that Polaris had been aware of the possibility of falling off the watercraft and the nature of injuries that could be sustained, and had done everything it could to address the situation.

Schroepher was not sure if Polaris ever provided seat straps for the two-person SLH. They were not offered as an optional feature because there was "no safety need" and "engineering got busy and was never able to get it done."

By 2001 Polaris was aware that the thrust of the jet pump would be dangerous to someone who fell off the rear of a moving watercraft. Yet the Polaris safety video did not refer to the risk of orifice injury. Schroepher offered as a rationale for this omission that Polaris "wanted to provide adequate information but not drag out the video so it's so long so people won't watch it." Therefore, the video "hit the highlights" such as wearing proper gear, avoiding collisions and the most common injuries. "And if you do those things, then it would avoid orifice injuries...."

In September 2002 the Fords filed suit, alleging causes of action for "products liability" against Polaris and negligence against Laura Nakamura. Polaris cross-complained against Laura for equitable indemnity.

Laura moved for summary judgment asserting that the doctrine of primary assumption of risk barred the Fords' action against her. Laura argued that she owed no duty to eliminate, or protect Susan against, "the risk of falling while the water craft was engaged in its maneuvers[,] as those maneuvers constitute a risk inherent in, if not the very purpose of, the sport itself." The Fords did not oppose the motion but Polaris did, arguing that Laura failed to communicate to Susan the instructions and warnings provided by the company, and wrongfully instructed her to ride the watercraft in an unsafe manner.

Granting the motion and directing that judgment be entered in Laura's favor, the trial court concluded that the activity that Laura and Susan were engaged in was subject to the doctrine of primary assumption of the risk. As to Polaris's claims, the court ruled that although Laura did not communicate to Susan the Polaris warning to wear protective clothing, and told her to hang onto the handles, contrary to Polaris instructions and warnings, these lapses at most amounted to mere negligence. Therefore under the doctrine of primary assumption of the risk Laura owed Susan no duty of care.

Polaris also moved for summary judgment, arguing that under principles of collateral estoppel, the court must apply primary assumption of the risk to the Fords' claims against it. Denying the motion, the trial court explained that reliance on the ruling in favor of Laura was misplaced because the Fords' allegations against Polaris concerned its duty to provide products free of design defects, a duty that did not attach to Laura. Moreover, while the court acknowledged that primary assumption of the risk may be applied to the activity of jet skiing, there was no finding that "rearward ejection jet thrust injuries" were inherent in the sport.

The jury returned a special verdict against Polaris on the design defect claim, awarded Susan $382,024 in economic losses and $3,262,500 in noneconomic losses, and awarded Anthony $115,000 for loss of consortium. The jury also found that Susan was not comparatively negligent. This appeal followed.

II. Assumption of Risk

[T]he heart of [defendant's] argument is that the court erred in deciding the lawsuit did not fall within the doctrine of primary assumption of the risk.

[I]n Knight v. Jewett, 834 P.2d 696 (Cal. 1992), involving coparticipants in a game of touch football, our Supreme Court differentiated between cases involving primary assumption of the risk—where, in view of the nature of the activity and the parties' relationship to it, the defendant owes no legal duty to protect the plaintiff from a particular risk of harm—and those involving secondary assumption of the risk, in which the defendant owes a duty of care but the plaintiff knowingly encounters the risk. In the former situation, the absence of a duty operates as a complete bar to recovery whereas in the latter, the [conduct is a form of contributory negligence subject to rules of apportionment governing that defense].

The determination whether the defendant owes a legal duty to protect the plaintiff from a particular risk of harm turns on *the nature of the activity in which the defendant is engaged and the relationship of the defendant and the plaintiff to that activity.* As to any given active sport, "defendants generally have no legal duty to eliminate (or protect a plaintiff against) risks inherent in the sport itself, [although] defendants generally do have a duty to use due care not to increase the risks to a participant over and above those inherent in the sport." This passage from *Knight* reflects a policy that in a sports setting it is not appropriate to "recognize a duty of care when to do so would require that an integral part of the sport be abandoned, or would discourage vigorous participation in sporting events." [ ] Further, because the duty question also hinges on the role of the defendant whose conduct is at issue, duties with respect to the same risk may vary depending on whether the defendant is a coparticipant, coach, recreation provider, manufacturer, and the like.

Polaris's refrain on appeal, expressed in various ways throughout the briefs, is as follows: Falling off a watercraft and coming into contact with the surface of water are inherent risks of the sport of jet skiing. As well, suffering orifice injuries is an inherent, but rare, risk of the sport. Polaris owed Susan no duty to eliminate or protect against these risks and therefore primary assumption of the risk absolves it of any liability.

Defining the risks inherent in a particular sport is integral to determining whether a particular defendant owes a duty of care. "Inherent" means "involved in the constitution or essential character of something: belonging by nature or habit: intrinsic." Merriam-Webster's Collegiate Dict., p. 600 (10th ed. 2001). The court in Freeman v. Hale, 30 Cal. App. 4th 1388, 1394-1395 (1994), articulated the test this way: An inherent risk is one that, if eliminated would fundamentally alter the nature of the sport or deter vigorous participation.

Here, the general risk of falling and coming into contact with water is inherent in jet skiing. However, Polaris asks us to evaluate its potential for liability under a rubric that includes the specific risk of suffering orifice injuries within the inherent risks of jet skiing, thereby eliminating its duty of care. The trial court specifically declined to find that such injuries are inherent in the sport. We agree.

Orifice injuries and the conduct that causes them do not belong to the "fundamental nature or habit" of the sport. Such injuries occur by way of rearward ejection into a very dangerous, defined space, namely the high-pressure stream of water thrust by the jet nozzle of the watercraft. Polaris's role with respect to the sport of jet skiing is as the manufacturer and designer of the Polaris SLH-700 personal watercraft. The Fords asserted that the watercraft was defective because Polaris did not consider or utilize appropriate alternative designs that would reduce the chances of rearward ejection into the jet propulsion. The norm in jet skiing is to hold on. Providing an alternative to hanging on while jet skiing in circumstances where holding onto the operator is not feasible would not alter the fundamental nature of the sport or deter vigorous participation. Moreover, the evidence does not support Polaris's proposition: Its own expert testified that "roughly half" of watercraft sold have seat straps, and roughly half do not!

[I]n a case such as this where the asserted design defect is the failure to incorporate protection against a serious injury into the design of the recreational equipment, the manufacturer's duty to design non-defective products could be rephrased as a duty to take reasonable steps to minimize inherent risks without altering the nature of the sport, at least under circumstances where the risk poses the gravest danger. Here, the trial court determined that a finding of a design defect would in itself establish that Polaris increased the risk of harm inherent in jet skiing. We agree. The inherent risk is falling into the water. The Fords' theory was that the Polaris SLH-700 watercraft was defectively designed because it did not provide a way for the passenger to hang on securely when it was not feasible to hold onto the operator. We have concluded that the asserted design defect did not attack an inherent risk of the sport because protecting against rearward ejection into the jet stream, thereby preventing orifice injury, would not alter the sport or deter vigorous participation. The very nature of the defect necessarily increased the likelihood that a passenger would fall rearward and suffer the extreme harm of orifice injuries. Thus as a matter of law the defect escalated the risk of harm beyond the inherent risk of falling into the water.

The judgment is affirmed.

NOTES AND QUESTIONS

1. *Review.* Can you explain why the plaintiff's proof sufficiently showed that the proposed design modifications were a reasonable alternative to the warning instruction? *See* Chapter 8 (discussing relation between the duty to warn and the duty to design). Can you also explain why the plaintiff's choice in *Ford* was not "voluntary" for purposes of the assumed-risk rule? Does this analysis bolster the *Ford* court's conclusion about the matter?

2. *Primary assumption of risk in product cases.* Unless the product is utilized for recreational purposes as in *Ford*, courts typically do not recognize primary assumption of risk in product cases. *E.g.*, Rose v. Brown & Williamson Tobacco Corp., 809 N.Y.S.2d 784, 791 (N.Y. Sup. Ct. 2005) (declining to apply primary assumption of risk to products liability claim brought by smoker against tobacco company because "[i]n cases where the [New York] appellate courts have applied primary assumption of the risk to activities that were not, strictly speaking, sporting or recreational activities, the

activities involved were physical activities, the elevated risks involved were clear, and the immediate risks of physical harm ended when the activity ended"). Is there any reason why a consumer cannot primarily assume a product risk outside of recreational activities?

When an individual right-holder primarily assumes a risk, her choice to engage in a risky activity, such as downhill skiing, makes her responsible for the risks inherent in the activity. In these cases, the ordinary rightholder (skier) has enough information to make an informed decision that the benefits of engaging in the activity (skiing) outweigh the inherent risks, thereby relieving the duty-bearer (a ski resort) of responsibility for the risks that are inherent in the sport. *See, e.g.*, Sajkowski v. Young Men's Christian Ass'n of Greater N.Y., 702 N.Y.S.2d 66, 67 (N.Y. App. Div. 2000) ("[I]f the risks of an activity are fully comprehended or perfectly obvious, one who participates in the activity is deemed to have consented to the risks."). These considerations are also quite relevant in product cases, yet courts do not recognize the defense unless the product is utilized for recreational purposes. Why limit the doctrine in this manner?

Primary assumption of risk and categorical liability both involve inherent risks, either in the activity itself (skiing) or in the relevant product category (those risks that cannot be eliminated by a reasonable redesign or by safe use). Courts reject categorical liability because the ordinary consumer has made an informed risk-utility decision that the total utility of using a product within the relevant category outweighs the inherent risks necessarily shared by all products within the category. *See* Chapter 6, section III.A. That informed risk-utility choice makes consumers responsible for these inherent risks. As in the case of primary assumption of risk, consumer right-holders who make informed, voluntary choices to face inherent product risks are responsible for the consequences of those choices, making it unnecessary for courts to recognize primary assumption of risk as a distinct affirmative defense. This rule limits the duty to "minimize inherent risks without altering the nature of the sport," as the *Ford* court put it, which generalizes to a duty to adopt reasonable alternative designs that minimize the inherent risks of a product category without otherwise altering the nature of that category.

3. *Is there any role for assumption of risk?* Because primary assumption of risk negates the element of duty and moots the issue of defect, the only remaining cases that implicate the assumed-risk rule are those involving secondary assumption of risk. In these cases, the defendant first breaches the duty by distributing a defective product that threatens injury to the plaintiff, who then has a subsequent choice of whether to face the risk. If the plaintiff decided to use the product despite the known defect and was injured as a result, her tort claim against the seller is potentially subject to the affirmative defense of secondary assumption of risk.

In these cases, the plaintiff's conduct will always be a form of contributory negligence. To see why, compare the legal outcomes that occur under the two forms of informed consent—objective consent as defined by the informed choices of the ordinary consumer, and subjective consent as defined by the informed choices of the plaintiff:

ORDINARY CONSUMER	PLAINTIFF	OUTCOME
Consent	Consent	No liability (no duty)
Consent	No consent	No liability (no duty)
No consent	No consent	Liability
No consent	Consent	Contributory negligence/ assumption of risk

Objective consent negates duty, regardless of the plaintiff's own choice (row 2) — the same outcome achieved by the doctrine of primary assumption of risk. Secondary assumption of risk requires subjective consent and is potentially dispositive of the tort claim only for cases in which the duty exists because the ordinary consumer would not consent to the risk (row 4). Because the ordinary, well-informed (reasonable) consumer would not use the defective product, the plaintiff's choice to do so, by definition, is unreasonable. This form of assumed risk is a species of contributory negligence, making it possible to evaluate the plaintiff's conduct entirely in terms of contributory negligence. Compare RESTATEMENT (SECOND) OF TORTS §402A cmt. n (limiting the assumed-risk rule under strict products liability to cases in which the plaintiff "voluntarily and *unreasonably* proceeds to encounter a known danger") (emphasis added).

III. CONTRIBUTORY NEGLIGENCE AND COMPARATIVE RESPONSIBILITY

In product cases, contributory negligence typically involves the plaintiff's misuse of a defective product. To serve as an affirmative defense, contributory negligence must apply to cases in which the defendant would otherwise be fully liable, and so the defect must have proximately caused the plaintiff's injury. Contributory negligence, in turn, requires proof showing that the plaintiff's misuse of the product proximately caused the injury. These cases accordingly involve two tortious causes — the defect and the contributory negligence — that were each independently sufficient to cause the injury.

Prior to the adoption of comparative responsibility, the plaintiff's contributory negligence barred recovery altogether. During this era, tort law employed the concept of "objective causation" to identify a single cause of the accident. *See* Union Pump v. Albritton, 898 S.W.2d 773, 777-779 (Tex. 1995) (Cornyn, J., concurring) (excerpted in Chapter 12, p. 539 *supra*). Ordinarily, the plaintiff's unreasonable behavior was deemed to be the "sole" cause of an accident, thereby exculpating the defendant from liability. The concept of objective causation has since been abandoned. Today, the vast majority of jurisdictions recognize that an accident can be proximately caused by both the defect and the plaintiff's unreasonable behavior, making it possible to apportion liability between the plaintiff and defendant under principles of comparative responsibility.

III. Contributory Negligence and Comparative Responsibility

A. *Product Misuse Without Comparative Responsibility*

The *Restatement (Second)* §402A rule of strict products liability was promulgated at a time when the plaintiff's contributory negligence barred recovery altogether, and so its provisions regarding unreasonable consumer conduct must be interpreted accordingly.

BEXIGA v. HAVIR MFG. CORP.
Supreme Court of New Jersey, 1972
290 A.2d 281

PROCTOR, J. This is a products liability case. Plaintiff John Bexiga, Jr., a minor, was operating a power punch press for his employer, Regina Corporation (Regina), when his right hand was crushed by the ram of the machine, resulting in the loss of fingers and deformity of his hand. His father, John Bexiga, Sr., brought this suit against Havir Manufacturing Corporation (Havir), the manufacturer of the machine, for damages in behalf of his son and individually Per quod. The action was grounded in negligence, strict liability in tort and breach of warranty of fitness of purpose. The trial court dismissed the action at the close of the plaintiffs' case. The Appellate Division affirmed, and this Court granted plaintiffs' petition for certification.

The machine which caused the injuries was a 10-ton punch press manufactured by Havir in 1961 and sold that same year to J.L. Lucas & Son, Inc., a dealer, and, at its direction, shipped to Regina. With the exception of a guard over the flywheel there were no safety devices of any kind on the machine when it was shipped. Plaintiffs do not contend that the accident resulted from defective materials, workmanship or inspection. Rather, their theory is that the punch press was so dangerous in design that the manufacturer was under a duty to equip it with some form of safety device to protect the user while the machine was being operated.

In June of 1966, plaintiff John Bexiga, Jr., 18 years of age and a junior in high school, had been employed by Regina at its Rahway plant for about two months, working nights after school. During his employment he operated punch presses and drilling machines for 40 hours per week.

On June 11, 1966, John, Jr. reported for work at 5:00 P.M. and was assigned to operate a drilling machine. He worked on this machine until the 9:30 break, after which the foreman directed him to work on the Havir punch press (which he had never before operated) and instructed him in its use. Thereafter he operated the machine unattended. He testified that the punch press was approximately six or seven feet high with a ram, die and foot pedal.

The particular operation John, Jr. was directed to do required him to place round metal discs, about three inches in diameter, one at a time by hand on top of the die. Once the disc was placed on the die it was held there by the machine itself. He would then depress the foot pedal activating the machine and causing the ram to descend about five inches and punch two holes in the disc. After this operation the ram would ascend and the equipment on the press would remove the metal disc and blow the trimmings away so that the die would be clean for the next cycle. It was estimated by John, Jr. that one cycle as described above would take approximately 10 seconds and that he had completed about 270 cycles during the 40 minutes he operated the machine. He described the accident as follows:

> Well, I put the round piece of metal on the die and the metal didn't go right to the place. I was taking my hand off the machine and I noticed that a piece of metal wasn't in place so I went right back to correct it, but at the same time, my foot had gone to the pedal, so I tried to take my hand off and jerk my foot off too and it was too late. My hand had gotten cut on the punch, the ram.

Plaintiffs' expert, Andrew Gass, a mechanical engineer, testified that the punch press amounted to a "booby trap" because there were no safety devices in its basic design and none were installed prior to the accident. He added that the accident would probably never have occurred had the machine been properly designed for safety. The only literature accompanying the sale of the machine was a service manual which made no mention of safety devices in the operation of the machinery with the exception of a reference to the guard on the flywheel which was unrelated to the accident. He said there should have been more stress put on the factor of safety but that he did not know what recommendations should be made.

Gass described two "basic types" of protective safety devices both of which were known in the industry at the time of the manufacture and sale. One was a push-button device with the buttons so spaced as to require the operator to place both hands on them away from the die area to set the machine in motion. The other device was a guardrail or gate to prevent the operator's hands from entering the area between the ram and die when the machine was activated. These and other safety devices were available from companies specializing in safety equipment.

[The court then concluded that the plaintiffs' evidence of defect was sufficient to withstand a motion for dismissal, contrary to the conclusions reached by the lower courts.]

Because of our disposition of the case it is necessary to consider defendant's contention that John, Jr. was contributorily negligent as a matter of law. Neither court below decided this issue. Contributory negligence may be a defense to a strict liability action as well as to a negligence action. However, in negligence cases the defense has been held to be unavailable where considerations of policy and justice dictate. And in [a prior case] this Court said that undoubtedly the defense will be unavailable in special situations within the strict liability field. We think this case presents a situation where the interests of justice dictate that contributory negligence be unavailable as a defense to either the negligence or strict liability claims.

The asserted negligence of plaintiff—placing his hand under the ram while at the same time depressing the foot pedal—was the very eventuality the safety devices were designed to guard against. It would be anomalous to hold that defendant has a duty to install safety devices but a breach of that duty results in no liability for the very injury the duty was meant to protect against. [ ] We

III. Contributory Negligence and Comparative Responsibility

hold that under the facts presented to us in this case the defense of contributory negligence is unavailable.

The judgment of the Appellate Division is reversed and the cause is remanded for a new trial.

NOTES AND QUESTIONS

1. *Limiting contributory negligence in order to recognize the duty regarding foreseeable misuse.* If the manufacturer could always avoid liability in cases of contributory negligence, it would effectively owe no duty to reduce the foreseeable risks of product misuse; any form of misuse would be a form of contributory negligence that would bar recovery, effectively negating the duty. Like the *Bexiga* court, others have limited contributory negligence to ensure that the duty regarding foreseeable forms of misuse can be enforced. Does this objective provide a way to determine which forms of misuse should bar recovery?

Under one formulation, "[m]isuse, to bar recovery, must be a use or handling so unusual that the average consumer could not reasonably expect the product to be designed and manufactured to withstand it—a use which the seller, therefore, need not anticipate and provide for." Findlay v. Copeland Lumber Co., 509 P.2d 28, 31 (Or. 1973). If a form of product misuse is unforeseeable, a court could limit liability on the alternative ground that the seller's duty does not encompass unforeseeable risks. This formulation accordingly limits contributory negligence to cases in which there otherwise is no duty, thereby ensuring that manufacturers remain fully responsible for the foreseeable risks of misuse encompassed by the duty. How does this formulation of contributory negligence compare to the one adopted in *Bexiga*?

2. *An outdated rule?* To what extent does the holding in *Bexiga* depend on the manner in which a finding of contributory negligence barred plaintiff's recovery altogether? If contributory negligence would instead merely reduce plaintiff's recovery—the outcome permitted by comparative responsibility—would the court's reasoning in *Bexiga* still justify a finding of no contributory negligence on the facts of that case?

B. Product Misuse in a System of Comparative Responsibility

Beginning in the 1970s, states increasingly adopted comparative responsibility under common-law principles or statutory authorization. Except for a few southeastern states, every jurisdiction in the United States (like many other countries around the world) has adopted some form of comparative responsibility. Within such a system, contributory negligence (now often called *comparative negligence*) does not necessarily bar recovery. For example, the jury can compare and then apportion liability between a comparatively negligent plaintiff and a negligent defendant, leaving the plaintiff with less than full recovery. Can liability be apportioned between a plaintiff who misused the product and a defendant subject to strict liability for the product defect? Does comparative responsibility apply to strict products liability?

DALY v. GENERAL MOTORS CORP.
Supreme Court of California, 1978
575 P.2d 1162

RICHARDSON, J. In the early hours of October 31, 1970, decedent Kirk Daly, a 36-year-old attorney, was driving his Opel southbound on the Harbor Freeway in Los Angeles. The vehicle, while travelling at a speed of 50-70 miles per hour, collided with and damaged 50 feet of metal divider fence. After the initial impact between the left side of the vehicle and the fence the Opel spun counterclockwise, the driver's door was thrown open, and Daly was forcibly ejected from the car and sustained fatal head injuries. It was equally undisputed that had the deceased remained in the Opel his injuries, in all probability, would have been relatively minor.

Plaintiffs, who are decedent's widow and three surviving minor children, sued General Motors Corporation, Boulevard Buick, Underwriter's Auto Leasing, and Alco Leasing Company, the successive links in the Opel's manufacturing and distribution chain. The sole theory of plaintiffs' complaint was strict liability for damages allegedly caused by a defective product, namely, an improperly designed door latch claimed to have been activated by the impact. It was further asserted that, but for the faulty latch, decedent would have been restrained in the vehicle and, although perhaps injured, would not have been killed. Thus, the case involves a so-called "second collision" in which the "defect" did not contribute to the original impact, but only to the "enhancement" of injury.

At trial the jury heard conflicting expert versions as to the functioning of the latch mechanism during the accident. Plaintiffs' principal witness testified that the Opel's door was caused to open when the latch button on the exterior handle of the driver's door was forcibly depressed by some protruding portion of the divider fence. It was his opinion that the exposed push button on the door constituted a design "defect" which caused injuries greatly in excess of those which Daly would otherwise have sustained. Plaintiffs also introduced evidence that other vehicular door latch designs used in production models of the same and prior years afforded substantially greater protection. Defendants' experts countered with their opinions that the force of the impact was sufficiently strong that it would have caused the door to open resulting in Daly's death even if the Opel had been equipped with door latches of the alternative designs suggested by plaintiffs.

Over plaintiffs' objections, defendants were permitted to introduce evidence indicating that: (1) the Opel was equipped with a seat belt-shoulder harness system, and a door lock, either of which if used, it was contended, would have prevented Daly's ejection from the vehicle; (2) Daly used neither the harness system nor the lock; (3) the 1970 Opel owner's manual contained warnings that seat belts should be worn and doors locked when the car was in motion for "accident security"; and (4) Daly was intoxicated at the time of collision, which evidence the jury was advised was admitted for the limited purpose of determining

III. Contributory Negligence and Comparative Responsibility

whether decedent had used the vehicle's safety equipment. After relatively brief deliberations the jury returned a verdict favoring all defendants, and plaintiffs appeal from the ensuing adverse judgment.

In response to plaintiffs' assertion that the "intoxication-nonuse" evidence was improperly admitted, defendants contend that the deceased's own conduct contributed to his death. Because plaintiffs' case rests upon strict products liability based on improper design of the door latch and because defendants assert a failure in decedent's conduct, namely, his alleged intoxication and nonuse of safety equipment, without which the accident and ensuing death would not have occurred, there is thereby posed the overriding issue in the case, should comparative principles apply in strict products liability actions?

In Li v. Yellow Cab Co., 532 P.2d 1226 (Cal. 1975), we announced the adoption of a "pure" form of comparative negligence which, when present, reduced but did not prevent plaintiff's recovery. We held that the defense of assumption of risk, insofar as it is no more than a variant of contributory negligence, was merged into the assessment of liability in proportion to fault. Within the broad guidelines therein announced, we left to trial courts discretion in the particular implementation of the new doctrine.

Those counseling against the recognition of comparative fault principles in strict products liability cases vigorously stress, perhaps equally, not only the conceptual, but also the semantic difficulties incident to such a course. The task of merging the two concepts is said to be impossible, that "apples and oranges" cannot be compared, that "oil and water" do not mix, and that strict liability, which is not founded on negligence or fault, is inhospitable to comparative principles. The syllogism runs, contributory negligence was only a defense to negligence, comparative negligence only affects contributory negligence, therefore comparative negligence cannot be a defense to strict liability. [ ] While fully recognizing the theoretical and semantic distinctions between the twin principles of strict products liability and traditional negligence, we think they can be blended or accommodated.

The inherent difficulty in the "apples and oranges" argument is its insistence on fixed and precise definitional treatment of legal concepts. In the evolving areas of both products liability and tort defenses, however, there has developed much conceptual overlapping and interweaving in order to attain substantial justice. The concept of strict liability itself arose from dissatisfaction with the wooden formalisms of traditional tort and contract principles in order to protect the consumer of manufactured goods. Similarly, increasing social awareness of its harsh "all or nothing" consequences led us in *Li* to moderate the impact of traditional contributory negligence in order to accomplish a fairer and more balanced result. We acknowledged an intermixing of defenses of contributory negligence and assumption of risk and formally effected a type of merger. "As for assumption of risk, we have recognized in this state that this defense overlaps that of contributory negligence to some extent." [ ] "[T]o wit, where a plaintiff unreasonably undertakes to encounter a specific known risk imposed by a defendant's negligence, plaintiff's conduct, although he may encounter that risk in a prudent manner, is in reality a form of contributory negligence. We think it clear that the adoption of a system of comparative negligence should entail the merger of the defense of assumption of risk into the general scheme of assessment of liability in proportion to fault in those particular cases in which the form of assumption of risk involved is no more than a variant of contributory negligence." *Li*, 532 P.2d at 1240-1241.

Furthermore, the "apples and oranges" argument may be conceptually suspect. It has been suggested that the term "contributory negligence," one of the vital building blocks upon which much of the argument is based, may indeed itself be a misnomer since it lacks the first element of the classical negligence formula, namely, a duty of care owing to another.

We think, accordingly, the conclusion may fairly be drawn that the terms "comparative negligence," "contributory negligence" and "assumption of risk" do not, standing alone, lend themselves to the exact measurements of a micrometer-caliper, or to such precise definition as to divert us from otherwise strong and consistent countervailing policy considerations. Fixed semantic consistency at this point is less important than the attainment of a just and equitable result. The interweaving of concept and terminology in this area suggests a judicial posture that is flexible rather than doctrinaire.

We pause at this point to observe that where, as here, a consumer or user sues the manufacturer or designer alone, technically, neither fault nor conduct is really compared functionally. The conduct of one party in combination with the product of another, or perhaps the placing of a defective article in the stream of projected and anticipated use, may produce the ultimate injury. In such a case, as in the situation before us, we think the term "equitable apportionment or allocation of loss" may be more descriptive than "comparative fault."

A second objection to the application of comparative principles in strict products liability cases is that a manufacturer's incentive to produce safe products will thereby be reduced or removed. While we fully recognize this concern we think, for several reasons, that the problem is more shadow than substance. First, of course, the manufacturer cannot avoid its continuing liability for a defective product even when the plaintiff's own conduct has contributed to his injury. The manufacturer's liability, and therefore its incentive to avoid and correct product defects, remains; its exposure will be lessened only to the extent that the trier finds that the victim's conduct contributed to his injury. Second, as a practical matter a manufacturer, in a particular case, cannot assume that the user of a defective product upon whom an injury is visited will be blameworthy. Doubtless, many users are free of fault, and a defect is at least as likely as not to be exposed by an entirely innocent plaintiff who will obtain full recovery. In such cases the manufacturer's incentive toward safety both in design and production is wholly unaffected. Finally, we must observe that under the present law, which recognizes assumption of risk as a complete defense to products liability, the curious and cynical message is that it profits the manufacturer to make his product so defective that in the event of injury he can argue that the user had to be aware of its patent defects. To that extent the incentives are inverted. We conclude, accordingly, that no substantial or significant impairment of the safety incentives of defendants will occur by the adoption of comparative principles.

A third objection to the merger of strict liability and comparative fault focuses on the claim that, as a practical matter, triers of fact, particularly jurors, cannot assess, measure, or compare plaintiff's negligence with defendant's strict liability. We are unpersuaded by the argument and are convinced that jurors are able to undertake a fair apportionment of liability.

III. Contributory Negligence and Comparative Responsibility

We note that the majority of our sister states which have addressed the problem, either by statute or judicial decree, have extended comparative principles to strict products liability. [ ]

Having examined the principal objections and finding them not insurmountable, and persuaded by logic, justice, and fundamental fairness, we conclude that a system of comparative fault should be and it is hereby extended to actions founded on strict products liability. In such cases the separate defense of "assumption of risk," to the extent that it is a form of contributory negligence, is abolished. While, as we have suggested, on the particular facts before us, the term "equitable apportionment of loss" is more accurately descriptive of the process, nonetheless, the term "comparative fault" has gained such wide acceptance by courts and in the literature that we adopt its use herein.

We conclude that, for reasons of public policy and the reasonable expectations of the parties to this action and litigants generally, the principles herein expressed shall apply to all cases in which trial has not begun before the date this opinion becomes final in this court. In the event of retrial, however, the principles herein announced will, of course, apply.

[The court then concluded that the trial court had admitted evidence that constitutes prejudicial error.]

The judgment is reversed.

NOTES AND QUESTIONS

1. *The impact of comparative responsibility on the* Restatement (Second) §402A *rule of strict products liability.* In a system of comparative responsibility, product misuse no longer bars recovery altogether, but instead reduces the plaintiff's recovery. Having altered the rule in this regard, should courts alter their approach for deciding whether a form of product misuse constitutes comparative negligence?

> Section 402A of the *Restatement (Second) of Torts*, recognizing strict liability for harm caused by defective products, was adopted in 1964 when the overwhelming majority rule treated contributory negligence as a total bar to recovery. Understandably, the Institute was reluctant to bar a plaintiff's products liability claim in tort based on conduct that was not egregious. Thus, §402A, Comment *n*, altered the general tort defenses by narrowing the applicability of contributory negligence and emphasizing assumption of risk as the primary defense. Since then, comparative fault has swept the country. Only a tiny minority of states retain contributory fault as a total bar.
>
> A strong majority of jurisdictions apply the comparative responsibility doctrine to products liability actions. Courts today do not limit the relevance of plaintiff's fault as did the *Restatement (Second) of Torts* to conduct characterized as voluntary assumption of the risk.

RESTATEMENT (THIRD) OF TORTS: PRODUCTS LIABILITY §17 cmt. a.

2. *The exercise of comparison.* When a comparatively negligent plaintiff recovers under strict products liability, how can the *fault* of the plaintiff be compared to the *strict liability* incurred by the defendant? The difficulty

exists only if one assumes that apportionment is based on "comparative fault" rather than "comparative responsibility." The rule of strict products liability makes the defendant responsible for injuries *caused* by the defective product. Can liability be apportioned by comparing the relative causal contribution of each party to the accident in question?

> Factors for assigning percentages of responsibility to each person whose legal responsibility has been established include
> (a) the nature of the person's risk-creating conduct, including any awareness or indifference with respect to the risks created by the conduct and any intent with respect to the harm created by the conduct; and
> (b) the strength of the causal connection between the person's risk-creating conduct and the harm.

RESTATEMENT (THIRD) OF TORTS: APPORTIONMENT OF LIABILITY §8.

What does it mean to evaluate the "strength of the causal" connection of the plaintiff and defendant? To be subject to liability, the defect for which the defendant is responsible must have proximately caused the plaintiff's injury. For the plaintiff's comparative negligence to reduce damages, her unreasonable conduct must also have proximately caused the injury in question. Each party caused the harm, so how can liability be apportioned on that basis?

One way to determine the relative strength of the causal connection is by reference to the relative amount of tortious risk for which each party is responsible. Tortious risk is defined by reference to the liability rule, whether it is one of negligence or strict liability. The amount of risk created by the plaintiff's unreasonable conduct, therefore, can be compared to the amount of risk created by the defect, making it possible to apportion liability on this basis. Consider RESTATEMENT (THIRD) OF TORTS: PRODUCTS LIABILITY §16 cmt. f ("The seriousness of the plaintiff's fault and the nature of the product defect are relevant in apportioning the appropriate percentages of responsibility between the plaintiff and the product seller.").

3. *Comparative responsibility and the apportionment of damages.* Once the jury has determined the comparative responsibility of the parties, the impact of that finding on the apportionment of liability depends on the form of comparative responsibility.

> The applicable rules of apportionment of responsibility vary among jurisdictions. Some states have adopted "pure" comparative fault, which allocates responsibility to each actor purely in proportion to the actor's percentage of total fault. Others follow some variant of "modified" comparative fault, in which actors' responsibilities are adjusted according to predetermined thresholds of responsibility. For example, in many modified jurisdictions the plaintiff is totally barred if found more than 50 percent at fault.

RESTATEMENT (THIRD) OF TORTS: PRODUCTS LIABILITY §17 cmt. b.

4. *Multiple tortfeasors subject to joint and several liability.* Under the common law, the rule of joint and several liability applies to multiple tortfeasors

III. Contributory Negligence and Comparative Responsibility

who independently caused the plaintiff's injury. In product cases, any commercial distributor of the defective product is legally responsible for injuries proximately caused by the defect, subjecting each one to joint and several liability. "[T]he injured person may sue for and recover the full amount of recoverable damages from any jointly and severally liable person." RESTATEMENT (THIRD) OF TORTS: APPORTIONMENT OF LIABILITY §10. The plaintiff can sue any one or all of the jointly and severally liable parties. Consequently, if one or more of those parties is insolvent, the plaintiff can get full recovery from the solvent tortfeasor(s). A defendant subject to joint and several liability, in turn, can seek contribution or indemnity from the other tortfeasors, a right that is meaningless if those other tortfeasors are insolvent. Hence "[j]oint and several liability imposes the risk that one or more tortfeasors liable for the plaintiff's damages is insolvent on the remaining solvent defendants." *Id.* cmt. a.

After adopting comparative responsibility, courts extended the rule to apportion liability among multiple tortfeasors based on the factors discussed in note 2: "If one defendant and at least one other party or settling tortfeasor may be found by the factfinder to have engaged in tortious conduct that was a legal cause of an indivisible injury, each such party and settling tortfeasor is submitted to the factfinder for assignment of a percentage of comparative responsibility." *Id.* §A19.

5. *Multiple tortfeasors subject to several liability.* Beginning with the tort-reform movement in the 1980s, most states have abolished joint and several liability in favor of several liability. *Id.* §17, at 151-159. This reform limits "the comparative share of the plaintiff's damages assigned to that defendant by the factfinder." *Id.* §B18. For example, if the jury determines that Defendant 1 is 20 percent comparatively responsible for the injury and that Defendant 2 is 80 percent comparatively responsible, then several liability limits the plaintiff's recovery from Defendant 1 to 20 percent of the damages. Can you see why the adoption of several liability shifts the risk of insolvency onto the plaintiff?

By shifting the risk of insolvency onto the plaintiff, does several liability potentially create any deterrence problems?

> Imagine a driver injured by a collision in which his airbag fails to inflate because of a product defect. The driver suffers enhanced physical injuries valued at $100,000. If the cause of the car accident was not negligence, perhaps bad weather, the driver might recover in full from the manufacturer. If the accident was instead caused by another driver's negligent act, perhaps looking away from the roadway, the driver might recover a portion of the damages from the manufacturer, perhaps 50%, or $50,000. Yet if the accident was caused by a drunk driver, a large percentage of responsibility, perhaps 90%, might be assigned to the drunk. Consequently, the victim might recover only one tenth of any enhanced injury from the manufacturer. In each case, the manufacturer created the same defective product which resulted in the same enhanced injury to the victim. In each case, the victim acted without fault. And yet, the victim of the drunk driver, by virtue of being the victim of both a reckless and a negligent actor, becomes tort-proof vis-à-vis the manufacturer.

Ellen M. Bublick, *The Tort-Proof Plaintiff: The Drunk in the Automobile, Crashworthiness Claims, and the* Restatement (Third) of Torts, 74 Brook. L. Rev. 707, 713 (2009).

DONZE v. GENERAL MOTORS, LLC
Supreme Court of South Carolina, 2017
800 S.E.2d 479

JUSTICE HEARN. This case concerns the applicability of comparative negligence to strict liability and breach of warranty claims in a crashworthiness case brought by Plaintiff Reid Harold Donze against Defendant General Motors ("GM"). [The evidence showed that plaintiff and a friend had been smoking synthetic marijuana prior to the crash involving plaintiff's pickup truck while it was being driven by his friend. The truck "burst into flames," badly injuring plaintiff and killing his friend. Plaintiff alleged that the truck was defectively designed because it placed the gasoline tank outside of the truck's frame. He sought damages "only for his enhanced burn injuries." The federal district court certified two questions to the South Carolina court, asking whether comparative responsibility applies to crashworthiness cases and whether the state's "public policy bar[s] impaired drivers from recovering damages in a crashworthiness case when the plaintiff alleges claims of strict liability and breach of warranty?"] We hold the defense of comparative negligence does not apply in crashworthiness cases, and that South Carolina's public policy does not bar a plaintiff, allegedly intoxicated at the time of the accident, from bringing a crashworthiness claim against the vehicle manufacturer.

I. COMPARATIVE NEGLIGENCE IN CRASHWORTHINESS CASES

Donze argues comparative negligence is inapplicable in crashworthiness cases where the plaintiff is only seeking recovery of the enhanced injuries caused by the alleged defect. In particular, Donze asserts that in crashworthiness cases, the damages from the initial collision and those caused by the alleged design defect are divisible. In other words, according to Donze, the enhanced injuries are a subsequent and separate event, the sole cause of which is the manufacturer's defective design. Therefore, any negligence on the part of the plaintiff in causing the initial collision is irrelevant. We agree for the reasons set forth below, and therefore answer this first certified question, "no."

. . .

Although South Carolina has not yet addressed whether comparative negligence may be raised as a defense in crashworthiness cases, a number of other jurisdictions have considered this question and reached differing results. We are aware of twenty-two states which have resolved this issue either statutorily or through case law. Of those, sixteen states permit a comparative fault analysis to reduce a plaintiff's recovery in crashworthiness cases and six do not. [ ]

Most states espousing the majority view have statutes which require application of comparative fault analysis in *all* personal injury actions, regardless of

III. Contributory Negligence and Comparative Responsibility

the cause of action or the theory of liability under which they are brought. [ ] However, some state courts have themselves extended comparative fault principles to crashworthiness claims. For example, the Supreme Court of California held in Daly v. General Motors Corp., 575 P.2d 1162 (Cal. 1978), that comparative negligence principles apply in strict products liability actions such that evidence of a plaintiff's intoxicated misuse of a vehicle was admissible in a crashworthiness case. . . .

On the other hand, a minority of states have declined to recognize comparative negligence as a defense in strict liability crashworthiness cases. In some states the legislature resolved the question. [ ] Still other jurisdictions, including Nevada, New Jersey, and the District Court for the District of South Carolina, have reached the same conclusion—that comparative negligence is incompatible with strict liability crashworthiness claims—based upon their interpretation of the crashworthiness doctrine. . . .

[In Green v. General Motors Corp., 709 A.2d 205, 211-212 (N.J. App. Div. 1998)], the court reasoned that

> When GM placed this vehicle on the market, it certainly knew that it would be driven at lawful speeds up to fifty-five miles per hour and in some states sixty-five miles per hour. It also knew that the vehicle might collide with another vehicle similarly operated. . . . We see, therefore, that if GM was required to design a reasonably safe vehicle for its intended and reasonably foreseeable use, it should, if possible, have designed a vehicle that could reasonably withstand a crash at considerably higher speeds than in this case.

Thus, the court held that "[i]nsofar as [the] plaintiff's injuries were caused solely by the product defect," any negligence on the part of the plaintiff in causing the collision was irrelevant. *Id.* at 212.

. . .

Unlike many states who have taken the alternative view, South Carolina has no statutory mandate to apply comparative negligence in crashworthiness cases based upon theories of strict liability and breach of warranty. . . . Additionally, the underlying premise of the crashworthiness doctrine—that manufacturers are only liable for enhanced damages caused by a design defect when the defect does not cause the initial collision—is already taken into account through the concept of enhanced injuries. [ ] In other words, the doctrine of crashworthiness itself divides and allocates fault to a manufacturer for damages it alone caused, so it would be incongruous to allow comparative negligence to apply to further reduce the manufacturer's liability or shift that responsibility to another party. . . . Regardless of the theory under which a plaintiff chooses to bring a crashworthiness claim, the heart of the crashworthiness doctrine remains the same—manufacturer liability for enhanced injuries following a foreseeable collision. [ ] . . . Accordingly, we answer the first certified question, "no."

[The court then rejected the defendant's statutory-based public policy arguments against impaired driving barring plaintiff's recovery. "The General Assembly is both capable of and willing to create statutory consequences for drug and alcohol abuse when it sees fit. This Court has repeatedly declined to create or expand public policies which the General Assembly could have adopted had it chosen to do so, and we decline to deviate from that practice now."]

NOTES AND QUESTIONS

1. *Rationale for not applying comparative responsibility to enhanced injury cases.* Are you persuaded by the court's reasoning that the defect in crashworthiness cases is the sole proximate cause of the enhanced injuries? If the plaintiff and his friend had not been intoxicated, the crash would not have occurred, thereby establishing factual causation under the but-for test. Why weren't the enhanced injuries also proximately caused by the intoxication of plaintiff and his friend? Consider whether it was foreseeable to the plaintiff that the truck might be defectively designed and would burn in a crash. If a defect were always unforeseeable for purposes of contributory negligence, would there be *any* cases in which contributory negligence proximately causes an injury that was also proximately caused by the defective product?

In support of its ruling, the *Donze* court cited to a number of other cases in which other courts had concluded that the reason for a crash is irrelevant when the manufacturer's duty is to design the vehicle in a manner that would reasonably protect the occupants from enhanced injury in the event of a crash. Is this type of rationale any different from the court's reasoning in *Bexiga*, p. 641 *supra*? If the purpose of a safety precaution is to protect consumers from injuries foreseeably caused by product misuse, does it make sense to reduce the plaintiff's recovery in cases involving such misuse? The result in cases like *Bexiga* has survived the adoption of comparative responsibility in New Jersey. *See* Green v. Sterling Extruder Corp., 471 A.2d 15, 20 (N.J. 1984) (affirming that comparative responsibility is no defense when the asserted negligence of the plaintiff "was the very eventuality the safety devices [required by the reasonable alternative design] were designed to guard against").

2. *Comparative responsibility, deterrence, and fairness across consumers.* A minority of jurisdictions continue to rely on the *Restatement (Second)*'s narrow formulation of contributory negligence that is limited to voluntary assumption of risk, reasoning that "[t]he deterrent effect of imposing strict product liability standards would be weakened were we to allow actions based upon it to be defeated, or recoveries reduced by [comparative] negligence concepts [introduced by comparative responsibility]." Kimco Dev. Corp. v. Michael D's Carpet Outlets, 637 A.2d 603, 607 (Pa. 1993). To what extent is this problem addressed by punitive damages? Consider Chapter 13, section V (discussing rule that a defendant is subject to punitive damages for selling a product it knows to be defective).

Product misuse implicates an issue of fairness across consumers. The individual plaintiff's vindication of her tort right can also protect other consumers with respect to defects that threaten other consumers in the market. The elimination of such defects works to the benefit of all consumers, providing a defensible reason not to reduce recovery because the plaintiff misused the product. The damages award, however, also increases the product price for all other consumers, including those who do not misuse the product. "A major policy reason which courts articulate for accepting comparative responsibility is that allowing a victim's negligence to be irrelevant to her recovery is unduly unfair because it makes careful product users bear the costs created by the careless users of products." William J. McNichols, *The Relevance of the Plaintiff's Misconduct in Strict Tort Products Liability, the Advent of Comparative Responsibility, and the Proposed* Restatement (Third) of Torts, 47 Okla. L. Rev. 201, 242 (1994).

3. *Other limitations on comparative responsibility.* Some forms of consumer conduct are exempt from comparative responsibility. Consumers, for example, have no duty to inspect the product for defects and therefore cannot be contributorily negligent in that respect. *See, e.g.,* Star Furniture Co. v. Pulaski Furniture Co., 297 S.E.2d 854, 862-862 (W. Va. 1982) ("The plaintiff's negligence must be something more than failing to discover a defect or to guard against it. Strict liability assumes that products which are placed in commerce are safe. If not, liability attaches if they result in damage or injury. Thus, there is no reason why a consumer should be expected to inspect products for defects or to guard against them. We therefore hold that comparative negligence is available as an affirmative defense in a cause of action founded on strict liability so long as the complained of conduct is not a failure to discover a defect or to guard against it."); *see also* David G. Owen, PRODUCTS LIABILITY LAW §13.3, at 803-804 (3d ed. 2015) (concluding that "almost every court that has considered the matter has chosen to shield consumers from all responsibility for their failure to watch for product defects").

C. Forms of Product Misuse

A plaintiff who misused the defective product has acted unreasonably. To determine whether such conduct is governed by comparative responsibility, one must be careful to distinguish the various ways in which misuse can affect the tort claim.

"Misuse" is at the center of a rich vocabulary, which includes "abnormal use," "intended use doctrine," and the conventional doctrines of contributory negligence and assumption of risk. The concept of misuse is also linked to the general question of whether a product is defective. It is difficult to extract working general principles from the precedents, since the term has such a chameleon character.

Marshall S. Shapo, THE LAW OF PRODUCTS LIABILITY ¶21.01 (7th ed. & 2020 update).

STATES v. R.D. WERNER CO.
Colorado Court of Appeals, 1990
799 P.2d 427

PIERCE, J. In this product liability action, plaintiffs, Lloyd Dean States, Myrna States, and Niagara Fire Insurance Co., appeal the trial court's judgment entered on a jury verdict finding in favor of defendant, R.D. Werner Co., Inc. We affirm.

Plaintiff Lloyd States fell from a step ladder at a construction site. He had positioned the front feet of the ladder (those with the rails in which the ladder's steps are mounted) on a sidewalk and had placed the rear feet on the surface of an unfinished parking lot that was six to nine inches below the level of the front feet. This positioning was contrary to instructions for the proper use of the ladder which were affixed to the ladder itself.

He then climbed the ladder and turned on the steps with his back to them and leaned over toward the building to attempt to affix a sign to the building with a power wrench while the sign was being held in place by an overhead crane. He pressed against the sign with one hand and used his other to apply pressure on the power wrench. As he did so, the ladder moved away from him and he fell. Plaintiffs alleged that the cause of the accident was a defect in the aluminum rivets which secure the spreader bars that connect the front legs to the back legs of the ladder.

Plaintiffs brought this action under theories of strict products liability, breach of warranty, and negligence.

The strict liability claim was based on the alleged product defectiveness. Plaintiffs contend that the trial court erred in instructing the jury that defendant could not be held legally responsible for Lloyd's injuries if his misuse of the ladder, rather than a defect, was the cause of his injuries. We disagree.

Colorado adopted the doctrine of strict products liability as set forth in Restatement (Second) of Torts §402A (1965). Misuse of a product by the injured person is a recognized defense to a Restatement §402A action. *Id.* cmt. h. The concept of misuse concerns an issue of causation and provides a complete defense to liability, regardless of any defective condition, if an unforeseeable and unintended use of the product, *and not the alleged defect*, caused the plaintiff's injuries.

Plaintiffs argue that the concept of comparative negligence is to be applied in all product liability actions. Depending on the facts of the case, the injured person's misuse of the product could constitute comparative fault which would reduce the plaintiff's recovery. However, if the injured person's misuse of the product is the sole cause of damages, and thus, the alleged defect was not a cause thereof, then the plaintiff cannot recover under strict liability theory. [ ]

Here, the instruction given to the jury provided that if Lloyd's misuse of the ladder, rather than a defect, caused Lloyd's injuries, defendant could not be held legally responsible for those injuries. We conclude that the trial court did not err in giving this instruction.

Judgment affirmed.

NOTES AND QUESTIONS

1. *Misuse, comparative responsibility, and causation.* The defense of comparative fault is relevant only if the plaintiff has first proven the prima facie case for liability, including proof that the defect was a cause-in-fact of plaintiff's injury. In some cases, the product misuse was the sole cause of the injury—that is, even if the product had not been defective, the injury still would have occurred because of the misuse. What facts in *States* supported the jury verdict that the plaintiff's misuse was the sole cause of the injury? In cases like this, does it matter whether the misuse was foreseeable?

III. Contributory Negligence and Comparative Responsibility

2. *Product alteration as a form of misuse that negates defect-related causation.* In Brown v. United States Stove Co., 484 A.2d 1234 (N.J. 1984), plaintiff was extensively burned by a propane gas heater manufactured by defendant. The plaintiff's employer had extensively modified the heater, and plaintiff argued that the manufacturer should have redesigned the product to reduce the risk of misuse by making it more difficult to modify the product. According to the court, "the foreseeable misuse of a product that proximately causes injury is analogous to a foreseeable subsequent alteration of the product, and generates the same legal consequences in terms of strict products liability." *Id.* at 1241. The court concluded that the plaintiff had created a jury question concerning his allegation of defective design. Nevertheless, the court dismissed the plaintiff's claim for causal reasons:

> In this case, the asserted defect was that the safety device was too easily removeable. In terms of its causal relationship to the accident, however, the only evidence produced by plaintiff was that its proposed alternative design would probably have made it "more difficult" to have altered the original safety feature. No evidence was proffered to indicate that with a proper design the removal of the heater's safety features probably could not have been accomplished or even rendered so substantially difficult as to be unlikely. Rather, the record discloses that the heater was deliberately altered for the specific purpose of operating it beyond its safe capacity and, further, it was wilfully, persistently and intensively misused in this fashion for an extraordinarily long period of time, perhaps for as long as fifteen years. In the face of this chronic misconduct, the inference to be drawn is that even were the original design modified in accordance with the plaintiff's proposal, it would not realistically or likely have deterred or obstructed these subsequent abusers of the product or have prevented the kind of injury that resulted from the misuse.

Id. at 1244.

3. *Product misuse as the failure to follow a warning.* Could the court in *States* have barred recovery on the ground that plaintiff's failure to follow the warning was an unforeseeable misuse? If the failure to follow a warning were necessarily a form of unforeseeable misuse, then manufacturers could always avoid design defect liability by simply instructing consumers on how safe use of the product would eliminate the risk. To enforce the rule that such warnings do not always substitute for design changes, courts must recognize that the failure to follow a warning can be a foreseeable misuse of the product. *See* Chapter 8 (discussing rule that warnings do not always substitute for design changes). Nevertheless, courts sometimes appear to require evidence showing that this form of misuse was foreseeable. *See* Kampen v. American Isuzu Motors, Inc., 157 F.3d 306, 310-311 (5th Cir. 1998) (rejecting proposition "that an adequate warning will *always* be dispositive of reasonably anticipated use," but requiring plaintiff to prove that "the manufacturer should have reasonably expected users to disregard the warning").

4. *Unforeseeable product misuse and proximate cause.* In addition to negating liability for reasons of factual causation, an unforeseeable misuse can

also negate liability for reasons of proximate cause under the foreseeability test. Is the rationale for this limitation of liability altered by the adoption of comparative responsibility?

EXXON COMPANY, U.S.A. v. SOFEC, INC.
United States Supreme Court, 1996
517 U.S. 830

THOMAS, J. In this case we affirm that the requirement of legal or "proximate" causation, and the related "superseding cause" doctrine, apply in admiralty notwithstanding our adoption of the comparative fault principle.

I

This case arises from the stranding of a tanker, the Exxon *Houston,* several hours after it broke away from a Single Point Mooring System (SPM) owned and operated by the HIRI respondents and manufactured by respondent Sofec, Inc. The *Houston* was engaged in delivering oil into HIRI's pipeline through two floating hoses, pursuant to a contract between Exxon and respondent PRII, when a heavy storm broke the chafe chain linking the vessel to the SPM. As the vessel drifted, the oil hoses broke away from the SPM. The parting of the second hose at approximately 1728 nautical time was designated below as the "breakout." The hoses were bolted to the ship, and a portion of the second hose remained attached to the ship. So long as the hose was attached to and trailing from the ship, it threatened to foul the ship's propeller, and consequently the ship's ability to maneuver was restricted.

During the 2 hours and 41 minutes following the breakout, the captain of the *Houston,* Captain Coyne, took the ship through a series of maneuvers. . . . [By] 1830, the *Houston* had successfully avoided the peril resulting from the breakout. [ ] The ship had "reached a safe position," [ ] and was "heading out to sea and in no further danger of stranding" [ ].

Many of Captain Coyne's actions after 1830 were negligent, according to the courts below. Most significant was his failure to have someone plot the ship's position between 1830 and 2004. . . . Without knowing his position, Captain Coyne was unable to make effective use of a navigational chart to check for hazards. The courts found that this failure to plot fixes of the ship's position was grossly and extraordinarily negligent. [ ] The District Court found that "Captain Coyne's decisions were made calmly, deliberately and without the pressure of an imminent peril." [ ] His failure to plot fixes after 1830 "was entirely independent of the fact of breakout; he voluntarily decided not to plot fixes in a situation where he was able to plot fixes." [ ]

At 1956, Captain Coyne initiated a final turn toward the shore. Because he had not plotted the ship's position, Captain Coyne was unaware of its position until he ordered another crew member to plot the fix at 2004. Upon seeing the fix on the chart, the captain apparently realized that the ship was headed for a reef. Captain Coyne's ensuing efforts to avoid the reef came too late, and moments later the ship ran aground, resulting in its constructive total loss.

III. Contributory Negligence and Comparative Responsibility

The District Court found that Captain Coyne's decision to make this final turn "was not foreseeable." [ ]

Exxon filed a complaint in admiralty against the HIRI respondents and respondent Sofec for, *inter alia*, the loss of its ship and cargo. The complaint contained claims for breach of warranty, strict products liability, and negligence. . . .

Following a 3-week bench trial in admiralty, the District Court found that Captain Coyne's (and by imputation, Exxon's) extraordinary negligence was the superseding and sole proximate cause of the *Houston*'s grounding. [ ] The court entered final judgment against Exxon with respect to the loss of the *Houston*, and Exxon appealed. [The Ninth Circuit affirmed.]

II

Exxon makes four arguments for the reversal of the judgment below: (1) that the superseding cause doctrine does not or should not apply in admiralty; (2) that respondents' breaches of warranty were causes in fact of the loss of the *Houston* and hence respondents should be liable for that loss; (3) that the lower courts' finding that Captain Coyne's extraordinary negligence was the sole proximate cause of the loss of the Houston was in error; . . .

Exxon's primary argument is that the proximate causation requirement, and the related superseding cause doctrine, are not or should not be applicable in admiralty. In particular, Exxon asserts that the lower courts' refusal to allocate any share of damages to parties whose fault was a cause in fact of Exxon's injury conflicts with our decision in United States v. Reliable Transfer Co., 421 U.S. 397 (1975).

We disagree. In *Reliable Transfer* we discarded a longstanding rule that property damages in admiralty cases are to be divided equally between those liable for injury, "whatever the relative degree of their fault may have been," [ ], and adopted the comparative fault principle in its stead. The proximate causation requirement was not before us in *Reliable Transfer*, and we did not suggest that the requirement was inapplicable in admiralty. (Nor, for that matter, did we consider whether the injury had been proximately caused by the defendant in that case.)

There is nothing internally inconsistent in a system that apportions damages based upon comparative fault only among tortfeasors whose actions were proximate causes of an injury. Nor is there any repugnancy between the superseding cause doctrine, which is one facet of the proximate causation requirement, and a comparative fault method of allocating damages. . . .

Indeed, the HIRI respondents assert that of the 46 States that have adopted a comparative fault system, at least 44 continue to recognize and apply the superseding cause doctrine. [ ] Exxon does not take issue with this assertion and concedes that it is not aware of any state decision that holds otherwise. [ ]

Exxon also argues that we should in any event eschew in the admiralty context the "confusing maze of common-law proximate cause concepts"; a system in which damages are allocated based upon the degree of comparative fault of any party whose act was a cause in fact of injury is "fairer and simpler," it says. [ ] It is true that commentators have often lamented the degree of disagreement regarding the principles of proximate causation and confusion in the doctrine's application, [ ], but it is also true that proximate causation principles are generally thought to be a necessary limitation on liability, [ ]. Indeed, the system Exxon apparently proposes either would let proximate causation principles, with all of their complexity, creep back in as one factor in the "comparative fault" analysis itself, [ ], or would produce extreme results. . . .

In ruling upon whether a defendant's blameworthy act was sufficiently related to the resulting harm to warrant imposing liability for that harm on the defendant, courts sitting in admiralty may draw guidance from, inter alia, the extensive body of state law applying proximate causation requirements and from treatises and other scholarly sources. [ ]

B

Exxon's argument that the District Court erred in rendering judgment against Exxon on its breach of warranty claims fares no better. . . . We agree with the Ninth Circuit that where the injured party is the sole proximate cause of the damage complained of, that party cannot recover . . . from a party whose breach of warranty is found to be a mere cause in fact of the damage. . . .

C

The legal question that we took this case to address is whether a plaintiff in admiralty that is the superseding and thus the sole proximate cause of its own injury can recover part of its damages from tortfeasors or contracting partners whose blameworthy actions or breaches were causes in fact of the plaintiff's injury. As we have held above, the answer is that it may not. Apparently anticipating that this legal issue would not likely be resolved in its favor, Exxon devotes a large portion of its briefs to arguing that the findings by the lower courts that Captain Coyne's extraordinary negligence was the sole proximate cause of Exxon's injury were in error. The issues of proximate causation and superseding cause involve application of law to fact, which is left to the factfinder, subject to limited review. . . . Without necessarily ratifying the application of proximate causation principles by the courts below to the particular facts here, we decline to reconsider their conclusion.

. . .

The judgment is affirmed.

NOTES AND QUESTIONS

1. *Admiralty law and tort law.* Recall that in *East River Steamship*, p. 561 *supra*, the Court held that the common law of strict products liability applies in admiralty actions. The Court's ruling in *Sofec* further illustrates the interplay between these two bodies of law. As indicated by the Court's discussion, admiralty law has long recognized that the apportionment of damages can be appropriate when two ships negligently collided into one another. Since the early nineteenth century, admiralty law has divided damages equally among all tortfeasors. In the cited *Reliable Transfer* case, the Court rejected this rule due to "the patent harshness of an equal division of damages in the face of disparate blame." 421 U.S. at 406. The divided-damages rule, though harsh in some cases, did show that apportionment

III. Contributory Negligence and Comparative Responsibility

is possible and helped to persuade courts that liability could also be apportioned in ordinary tort cases based on the principles of comparative responsibility.

2. *Unforeseeable product misuse as a bar to recovery.* Can you more fully explain why an unforeseeable misuse bars recovery under comparative responsibility? How does such a bar accord with the idea of fairness that each party should bear liability in proportion to its comparative responsibility?

3. *Unforeseeability in the case at hand.* The *Sofec* case provides an interesting comparison with *Union Pump v. Albritton*, p. 538 *supra*, in which the court held, as a matter of law, that a fire caused by a defective pump did not proximately cause the plaintiff's injury she incurred while walking on wet pipes after the fire had been put out. Can you see why the Court's analysis in *Sofec* casts doubt on the court's reasoning in *Union Pump*? Consider the discussion in note 3 following *Union Pump*.

D. Assumption of Risk and Comparative Responsibility

Recall that in cases of secondary assumption of risk, the plaintiff's decision to face the risk is always a form of contributory negligence. *See* Note 3, p. 639 *supra*. Does the adoption of comparative responsibility necessarily turn every instance of assumption of risk into a form of comparative responsibility requiring apportionment? Should it?

ANDREN v. WHITE-RODGERS CO.
Court of Appeals of Minnesota, 1991
465 N.W.2d 102

SHORT, J. This products liability action arises from a liquid propane gas explosion in Robert Andren's cabin. On appeal from a grant of summary judgment, Andren argues the trial court erred in deciding his lighting of a cigarette in a basement filled with gas was a legal bar to recovery. We disagree and affirm.

Andren owned a lake cabin which was heated by liquid propane (LP) gas. A line ran from an LP tank outside the cabin to a space heater in the basement. Andren bought the space heater in used condition in 1982 and installed it himself. The heater operated for several winters without problems.

In January of 1985, Andren went to check on the cabin. When he entered the basement, he noticed the smell of LP gas. After turning on the basement light, Andren discovered the smell of gas grew stronger as he walked further into the basement. Believing the pilot light on the heater had blown out, Andren sent his daughter upstairs to find matches to use to light the heater later. Andren then tried to open the basement windows to air out the room.

Because the basement windows were jammed shut, Andren decided to get a screwdriver from his car to pry them open. Before Andren left the basement, he stopped just inside the door and lit a cigarette. The LP gas exploded and the basement began to burn. Andren's hands, face and head were severely burned.

Although Andren had no formal training regarding LP gas appliances, he had installed over 100 LP gas heaters. Andren had also used LP gas appliances all of his life. He knew LP gas was dangerous and could explode if exposed to a spark or an open flame. Andren specifically knew not to smoke or to light a match when the smell of LP gas was in the air.

Andren claims a defective regulator in the gas heater allowed LP gas to leak into the basement. He sued the manufacturer, White-Rodgers Company, and the retailer, Sears, Roebuck & Co., alleging strict liability, breach of warranty and negligence. The manufacturer brought Flexan Corporation into the lawsuit by alleging it provided the defective regulator part. The manufacturer moved for summary judgment and agreed, for purposes of the motion, the valve in the LP gas heater was defective. The trial court granted summary judgment against Andren and held Andren's claims were barred because he primarily assumed the risk of injury.

Minnesota law recognizes two types of assumption of the risk. "Primary assumption of the risk arises where parties have voluntarily entered a relationship in which plaintiff assumes well-known, incidental risks. As to those risks, the defendant has no duty to protect the plaintiff and, thus, if the plaintiff's injury arises from an incidental risk, the defendant is not negligent." [ ] Conversely, secondary assumption of the risk "is a type of contributory negligence where the plaintiff voluntarily encounters a known and appreciated hazard created by the defendant without relieving the defendant of his duty of care with respect to such hazard." [ ] The elements of both primary and secondary assumption of the risk are whether a person had (a) knowledge of the risk; (b) an appreciation of the risk; and (c) a choice to avoid the risk but voluntarily chose to chance the risk. The manifestations of acceptance and consent dictate whether primary or secondary assumption of the risk is applicable in a given case. The wisdom and reasonableness of the plaintiff's actions are not factors in the determination.

The doctrine of primary assumption of the risk defines the limits of a defendant's duty to the plaintiff. By voluntarily entering into a situation where the defendant's negligence is obvious, the plaintiff accepts and consents to it and agrees "to undertake to look out for himself and relieve the defendant of the duty." W. Keeton, D. Dobbs, R. Keeton & D. Owen, PROSSER AND KEETON ON TORTS, §68 at 485 (5th ed. 1984) (hereinafter W. Keeton).

The three elements of both primary and secondary assumption of the risk are present in this case. First, Andren demonstrated his knowledge of the risk by testifying he knew LP gas was dangerous and was specifically aware that lighting a cigarette in a room filled with LP gas would cause an explosion. Second, the record shows appellant appreciated the risk because he recognized the smell of LP gas in the basement, and knew he should not light a cigarette while he was in the basement. Finally, the evidence is clear Andren had a choice to avoid the danger by not smoking, yet he voluntarily chose to light the cigarette.

Andren's lighting of a cigarette in a gas-filled room was a voluntary acceptance of a known danger. The volitional act constituted consent to relieve respondents of their duty to protect Andren from harm. That Andren lighted the cigarette without considering its consequences makes his act no less volitional, because it is clear a reasonable person in his position must have understood the danger. In essence, respondents were relieved of their duty to protect Andren because Andren was in an equal position to protect himself. *See* W. Keeton, *supra*, §68 at 490-91.

III. Contributory Negligence and Comparative Responsibility

Further, the smell of gas in this case alerted Andren to the need to use extreme caution in the basement. In any products liability case, the plaintiff must establish a causal relationship between the defect and the injury. Here, the issue of causation did not require jury determination where the obvious danger of Andren's activities eliminates the alleged defective valve as the substantial cause of the accident. Under these circumstances, the trial court properly granted summary judgment for respondents.

Affirmed.

NOTES AND QUESTIONS

1. *The duty question.* Is it possible to avoid issues of assumption of risk within a system of comparative responsibility? Insofar as assumption of risk negates duty, what is the legal basis for imposing *any* liability on the defendant?

The need to establish duty is supposed to be captured by the difference between primary and secondary assumption of risk, with the former denying all recovery (no duty) and the latter permitting reduced recovery (breach of duty plus comparative negligence based on the plaintiff's unreasonable choice to face the risk). *See* section II.C *supra*. Why does the assumed risk negate duty in one set of cases but not the other? What justifies the treatment of secondary assumption of risk as a form of comparative responsibility that permits some recovery on the basis of a breached duty?

Consider these questions in relation to *Andren*. Secondary assumption of risk involves a breach of duty followed by the plaintiff's consent to face the risk. Under the established definition, a defendant does not violate the plaintiff's tort right—and fully breach the correlative duty—unless the defective product proximately caused the plaintiff to suffer physical harm. Any consent prior to the occurrence of injury, therefore, constitutes consent prior to breach, explaining why the plaintiff's assumption of risk in *Andren* (prior to injury) relieved the defendant of any further duty with respect to that particular risk. When that risk subsequently materialized and caused injury, the plaintiff had already consented, eliminating the duty and any basis for apportionment.

By this same reasoning, however, secondary assumption of risk should *always* negate duty. To secondarily assume the risk, the plaintiff must first be exposed to the defect and then voluntarily choose to face it. The consent at this point eliminates the duty moving forward (as in cases of primary assumption of risk). Consequently, duty is negated *before* the risk materializes and causes injury, eliminating the duty and any legal basis for subjecting the defendant to liability for the subsequent injury. For this reason, "some decisions hold that a plaintiff's assumption of the risk is a complete defense to a products liability action, not merely a basis for apportionment of responsibility." RESTATEMENT (THIRD) OF TORTS: PRODUCTS LIABILITY §17 cmt. d.

Although some courts have reached this conclusion, most have concluded that secondary assumption of risk is merely a form of unreasonable behavior that reduces plaintiff's recovery in a system of comparative responsibility. *See id.* ("The majority position is that all forms of plaintiff's failure to conform to applicable standards of care are to be considered for the purpose of apportioning responsibility between the plaintiff and the product seller or distributor."). How can the majority rule be squared with the conclusion, illustrated by *Andren,* that a plaintiff who secondarily assumes a risk has relieved the defendant of any duty with respect to that risk, thereby eliminating any possibility of apportionment?

2. *Did the plaintiff in* Andren *assume the risk?* In principle, secondary assumption of risk can bar recovery altogether. A plaintiff who knew of the defect and made the requisite voluntary choice to face that unreasonable risk of physical harm presumably did so because her resolution of the risk-utility decision differs from the ordinary consumer's resolution. Subjective consent is an established ground for limiting the duty in an ordinary tort case, and that same principle can limit duty in a product case. As the *Andren* court explained, "The wisdom and reasonableness of the plaintiff's actions are not factors in the determination."

Nevertheless, this approach is problematic for reasons illustrated by *Andren.* When properly applied, the assumed-risk rule only bars recovery when the plaintiff's choice is based on the same risk-utility factors implicated by the allegation of defect. Was this requirement satisfied in *Andren?* Insofar as the plaintiff made a risk-utility decision, he presumably concluded that the burden of waiting to smoke outweighed the risk of explosion ($B_{delayed\ smoking} > PL_{explosion}$). The defect involved a faulty gas regulator, one posing a risk of explosion that would be eliminated by a nondefective regulator ($B_{regulator} < PL_{explosion}$). The plaintiff's safety decision did not involve the same risk-utility factors implicated by the allegation of defect, so the plaintiff did not assume the risk merely because he made some choice (to smoke) with knowledge of the risk. (Can you explain why the court effectively applied the now-discredited version of the patent-danger rule to bar plaintiff's recovery?)

3. *The majority rule and the avoidance of legal error.* As illustrated by *Andren* and other cases in this chapter, courts often misapply the assumed-risk rule. This potential for error is avoided by the majority rule, which relies on the simpler inquiry asking whether the plaintiff's conduct was unreasonable. Would a reasonable person light a cigarette in the circumstances faced by the plaintiff in *Andren?* That inquiry is much more straightforward than the one required by proper application of the assumed-risk rule.

Even if courts always limit the assumed-risk rule to the appropriate circumstances in which the plaintiff made a safety choice based on the same risk-utility factors implicated by the allegation of defect, proper application of the assumed-risk rule is still quite difficult. For the risk-utility choices to match up in the requisite manner, the plaintiff must have made a well-informed choice to use the defective product despite having had the option of using a nondefective version of the product (e.g., a plaintiff who chooses to remove a safety guard from a machine). This behavior differs from the behavior of the ordinary consumer in every relevant respect, and it is exceedingly difficult to determine reliably whether there truly is such a difference.

III. Contributory Negligence and Comparative Responsibility

For the duty to exist, the ordinary consumer must be unable to make a well-informed choice to face the risk. What, then, enabled the plaintiff to make an informed choice? Does extensive prior experience or professional expertise necessarily mean that the plaintiff assumed the risk?

Someone who has extensively used a product without suffering injury can make poor safety decisions by relying on the mental shortcut known as the *availability heuristic*. Such an individual's perception of risk is based on easily available data. Without a readily identifiable adverse outcome produced by the decision to face a risk, the easily available data indicate that the activity is safer than it actually is, causing individuals to engage in excessively risky behavior. *See* Eldad Yechiam, Ido Erev & Greg Barron, *The Effect of Experience on Using a Safety Device*, 44 Safety Science 515 (2006). "People also tend to have an overly rosy sense of optimism and control when making decisions about their own behavior. Most drivers are *overconfident* in their abilities, thinking that they are better than average drivers, and consumers tend to think that they are less likely than others to be harmed by products." Jennifer K. Robbennolt & Valerie P. Hans, THE PSYCHOLOGY OF TORT LAW 44 (2016). Hence prior experience with the product can translate into more knowledge, mere complacency, or unjustified overconfidence. How can the court reliably determine which factor explains the plaintiff's conduct?

And even if the ordinary consumer were well informed, she would use the nondefective version of the product. What, then, explains why the plaintiff instead selected the defective version? A difference in preferences or a mistake attributable to poor information, mere complacency, or unjustified overconfidence? As revealed by these evidentiary questions, a court will have a hard time reliably determining whether the plaintiff truly assumed the risk and properly absolved the defendant of any responsibility for the injury, or instead simply used the product in an unreasonably dangerous manner.

These evidentiary problems are avoided if the court instead evaluates the plaintiff's conduct relative to the conduct of the ordinary consumer. The ordinary consumer, upon being informed of the risk, would choose not to face the risk by using the defective product. Insofar as this is the sole reliable evidence, it only supports the conclusion that the plaintiff's decision to face the risk—to use the defective product rather than the nondefective alternative—was an unreasonable form of product misuse. Evidentiary limitations, therefore, explain why courts can defensibly treat secondary assumption of risk as a form of comparative negligence that does not negate duty but merely reduces the plaintiff's recovery.

4. *The ordinary consumer as the benchmark of behavior.* By merging secondary assumption of risk into comparative responsibility, the majority rule effectively defines the legal standard by reference to the conduct of the ordinary consumer. For cases in which the ordinary consumer can make an informed risk-utility decision, the seller is absolved of any duty with respect to that decision. This doctrine goes by various names (like the rule against categorical liability), but ultimately is no different from primary assumption of risk. *See* section II.C *supra*. Because the duty exists only when

the ordinary consumer would not assume the risk threatened by the product defect, the choice by an individual plaintiff to use the defective product instead of its nondefective alternative is necessarily unreasonable (secondary assumption of risk). In principle, such subjective consent negates the duty, but due to the difficulty of reliably determining whether the plaintiff differs from the ordinary consumer in the relevant respects, courts instead treat the conduct as a form of comparative negligence based on the plaintiff's failure to conform to the conduct of the reasonable consumer. For both the assumed-risk rule and comparative negligence, the affirmative defense depends on a legal standard defined by the behavior of the ordinary consumer.

IV. AUTONOMOUS VEHICLES AND PRODUCTS LIABILITY: PROBLEM SET 11

AV Problem 11.1

When autonomous vehicles are first commercially distributed, they will be operating on public roads alongside of conventional vehicles with human drivers behind the wheel. "In its current state, AV technology struggles to reliably predict the behavior of other road users and communicate with other road users." For example, a particularly difficult problem occurs when an AV attempts to make a left turn against oncoming traffic.

> One reason why left turns have proved so challenging is that merging into rapidly flowing lanes of traffic is a delicate task that often requires eye contact with oncoming drivers. Engineers are experimenting with different signals that could be broadly understood. But it would be difficult to convey anything more than the simplest messages. AVs would also often need to determine that their messages have been received as well. As with behavior prediction, local knowledge and culture can complicate the communication problem.

Matthew Wansley, *The End of Accidents*, 55 U.C. Davis L. Rev. (forthcoming 2021) (footnotes and quotation omitted), https:/.ssrn.com/abstract=3816158.

The problem, more generally, is that the operating system of an AV does not have a sophisticated "theory of mind"—that is, the "ability to extrapolate from our own internal mental states to estimate what others are thinking, feeling, or likely to do." Harry Surden & Mary-Anne Williams, *Technology Opacity, Predictability, and Self-Driving Cars*, 38 Cardozo L. Rev. 121, 124 (2016). Unable to interpret the behavioral signals sent by a human driver, the operating system can have a difficult time navigating through traffic, as illustrated by the problem of left turns.

A detailed study of reported crashes involving AVs being tested on public roadways (two crashes in Arizona and 210 in California) found that in the vast majority of cases, the AV was rear-ended by a human driver. Why are these crashes so common?

IV. Autonomous Vehicles and Products Liability: Problem Set 11

AVs may be behaving in unpredictable ways that make them more vulnerable to being rear-ended. AVs are programmed to follow the speed limit, which will make them drive more slowly than the speed of traffic in many situations. AVs also may be more likely to decelerate or stop abruptly when a vehicle, cyclist, or pedestrian stops ahead or moves closer to the roadway. AVs' limited capacity to predict behavior and communicate with other road users may contribute to this problem. If an AV can't accurately predict where a pedestrian walking up to a curb will move next, it might be risk-averse and stop where a human driver wouldn't stop, surprising the human driver behind it.

Wansley, *supra*, at 29.

However, even if a rear-end collision was caused by the AV's unpredictable behavior, the manufacturer might be able to avoid liability. "In a tort case, there's no rule of law that makes the driver doing the rear-ending liable and the driver being rear-ended not liable. But in practice, the rear-ender is usually liable." *Id.* at 26. Based on this practice, the AV manufacturer "would avoid some or all liability as long as the company could raise a comparative negligence defense." *Id.* at 44. According to Professor Wansley, the reduced liability will reduce the manufacturer's incentives to adopt an operating system that minimizes the risk of crashing with conventional vehicles, leading him to conclude that the manufacturer or commercial operator of an AV should be strictly liable anytime an AV comes into contact with another vehicle or third party such as a bicyclist or pedestrian. *See generally id.*

Are there counterarguments to Professor Wansley's thesis? To evaluate this question, assume the human driver in a rear-end collision with an AV can prove that the operating system was defectively designed because it caused the vehicle to drive in an unpredictable manner that caused the crash in question. Would the doctrine of comparative responsibility necessarily mean that the manufacturer's liability is reduced by the contributory negligence of the human driver in rear-ending the AV? Would any such reduction of liability unduly dilute the manufacturer's financial incentives for adopting a reasonably safe operating system?

Analysis of AV Problem 11.1

The plaintiff, a human driver, has shown that the operating system is defective or unreasonably dangerous because it causes the AV to drive in unpredictable manner that can foreseeably cause a human driver to become confused and rear-end the AV. As the court in *Bexiga v. Havir Mfg. Corp.* explained, "The asserted negligence of plaintiff—placing his hand under the ram while at the same time depressing the foot pedal—was the very eventuality the safety devices were designed to guard against. It would be anomalous to hold that defendant has a duty to install safety devices but a breach of that duty results in no liability for the very injury the duty was meant to protect against." This same reasoning applies in the case at hand.

To be sure, the *Bexiga* court was discussing a complete bar to recovery, whereas today contributory negligence would only reduce the plaintiff's recovery. But the rationale for not recognizing the defense of contributory negligence in these cases remains sound. Why make the plaintiff responsible for the very same behavior that the reasonable design was supposed to anticipate and prevent? Moreover, letting the plaintiff recover full damages does not raise an issue of fairness across consumers of the defective product—a major reason that courts rely on to justify comparative responsibility. In ordinary product cases, full recovery means that those who use the product carefully incur the injury costs of those consumers who are contributorily negligent. In the case at hand, the product injures a bystander—the driver of the conventional motor vehicle. The only question of fairness, therefore, is whether the consumers of the AV should bear the injury costs of human drivers who are confused by the AV's driving performance. For the reasons discussed above, allocating those injury costs to the AV is quite defensible. Indeed, a minority of jurisdictions continue to permit full recovery in these cases even under a system of comparative responsibility.

Even if the jurisdiction decides to apply comparative negligence to the human driver, the reduction in liability would not necessarily dilute the financial incentives for AV manufacturers to adopt reasonably safe operating systems. The plaintiff would still get some recovery for compensatory damages, reduced by his or her share of comparative responsibility. If the plaintiff then proves that the AV manufacturer knew its operating system was defectively designed due to its unpredictable driving behavior, the plaintiff could recover punitive damages in an amount that, in theory, could restore the manufacturer's financial incentives for adopting reasonably safe operating systems.

Editor's Note. As a practical matter, such proof might not be so difficult for plaintiffs to procure. A plaintiff can see how the manufacturer has responded to prior instances in which a human driver rear-ended the AV. Did the manufacturer seek to remedy the problem, or did it ignore the problem? The latter pattern of behavior establishes the "willful ignorance" that satisfies the standard for punitive damages. Consider in this regard the process of how the software engineers are supposed to respond to instances in which the AV crashes or almost crashes with another vehicle.

> AV software is being continuously updated. Engineers frequently review data from on-road testing. This includes autonomous driving on public roads and in private closed-course facilities, where more risky scenarios can be tested. Engineers also review the results of computer simulations that model how the AV software will behave in a larger set of traffic scenarios.
> ... Crashes or near misses in real-world testing and in simulation reveal "edge cases"—scenarios that occur infrequently but need "specific design attention to be dealt with in a reasonable and safe way." They also reveal corner cases—"combinations of normal operational parameters" that can become edge cases if the combination "produces an emergent effect."
> The software development process is iterative. New edge cases are identified from testing or simulation. New algorithms or fixes to existing algorithms are proposed. The proposed solutions undergo regression testing—simulations that assess whether the new software might perform worse in known traffic scenarios than earlier versions did. If the fix passes regression testing, it goes into the next software release and is evaluated on the road. If it fails, the engineers go back to the drawing board. The process then repeats itself. If the process works, the on-road performance of the company's AVs should improve over time.

Wansley, *supra*, at 11-12.

15

The Scope of Strict Products Liability as Defined by the Nature of the Transaction

The *Restatement (Second)* §402A rule of strict products liability expressly applies to "[o]ne who *sells* any *product* in a defective condition unreasonably dangerous to the user or consumer or to his property." Whether a transaction is governed by strict products liability accordingly depends on how courts define "sales" and "products."

These rules can raise difficult issues. Is a formal sales transaction always required? Even when the requirement of a sales transaction is satisfied because nonmanufacturing entities, such as wholesalers or retailers, sold the defective product to another party, why subject them to strict liability if they did not create the defect or were not otherwise negligent? If policy reasons exempt a commercial seller from strict liability, can the exemption be adequately implemented by characterizing the transaction as one that involves the provision of a *service* not subject to strict *products* liability? Resolution of these issues depends on the underlying substantive rationale for strict products liability, providing another opportunity for us to address this foundational question.

I. DISTRIBUTOR AND RETAILER LIABILITY

The rule of strict products liability applies both to the manufacturer of the defective product and "to any wholesale or retail dealer or distributor, and to the operator of a restaurant." RESTATEMENT (SECOND) OF TORTS §402A cmt. f. In these cases, the rule truly is one of strict liability. "Liability attaches even when . . . nonmanufacturing sellers or distributors [of defective products] do not themselves render the products defective and regardless of whether they are in a position to prevent defects from occurring." RESTATEMENT (THIRD) OF TORTS: PRODUCTS LIABILITY §1 cmt. e. What is the rationale for strict liability in these cases?

GODOY v. ABAMASTER OF MIAMI, INC.
Supreme Court of New York, Appellate Division, Second Department, 2003
754 N.Y.S.2d 301

TOWNES, J. In this products liability action, the issue, which appears to be one not previously presented to this court, is whether the distributor of a defective product is entitled to indemnification from an importer/distributor of the product which is higher in the chain of distribution, where both are strictly liable in tort to the plaintiff.

The plaintiff commenced this action to recover damages for the loss of all four fingers on her right hand, an injury sustained while she was operating a manually fed, electrically-powered commercial meat grinder. The plaintiff commenced the instant action against the retailer that sold the meat grinder, Mike's Restaurant Equipment Corp. (hereinafter Mike's Restaurant Equipment), Abamaster of Miami, Inc., and Abamaster, Inc. (hereinafter collectively referred to as Abamaster), a wholesale distributor of restaurant equipment in Miami, Florida, that sold the meat grinder to Mike's Restaurant Equipment, and Carfel, Inc. (hereinafter Carfel), an importer/distributor, also based in Miami, that sold the meat grinder to Abamaster.

Abamaster and Carfel interposed separate answers denying the plaintiff's allegations and asserting affirmative defenses and cross claims against one another. Abamaster cross-claimed for contribution and indemnification, while Carfel sought only contribution from Abamaster. A default judgment on the issue of liability was entered against Mike's Restaurant Equipment. It is Abamaster's cross claim against Carfel for indemnification which is the subject of this appeal.

Carfel attempted to commence a third-party action against, *inter alia*, Aroma Taiwan Machinery Company, the manufacturer of the meat grinder. Carfel was not able to obtain jurisdiction over the third-party defendants. Thus, the manufacturer is not a party to this action. Carfel settled with the plaintiff before trial for the sum of $350,000.

At a jury trial on the issue of liability, the plaintiff introduced the deposition testimony of Epifanio Capote, the president of Abamaster. Capote testified that Abamaster was a wholesale seller of restaurant equipment. Abamaster ordered the meat grinder from Carfel, and sold the meat grinder to Mike's Restaurant Equipment. Carfel directed that a metal plate showing Abamaster's name be affixed to the meat grinder at Abamaster's request. Called as a witness for Abamaster at trial, Capote testified that Abamaster had nothing to do with the manufacture or design of the meat grinder, that Abamaster received meat grinders from Carfel in sealed cartons, and that Abamaster shipped them to buyers in the same sealed cartons without having opened them.

Abamaster introduced the deposition testimony of Fannie Hanono, vice president of Carfel. Hanono testified that Carfel had offices in Taiwan and that some of Carfel's products were manufactured there because of inexpensive production costs. Hanono further testified that Abamaster placed orders for meat grinders, including the one at issue, with Carfel's Miami office, which in turn placed orders with Carfel's Taiwan office. Carfel's Taiwan office then placed the orders with a vendor in Taiwan. Carfel did not design or manufacture the meat grinder. Instead, it was designed and manufactured by Aroma Thunderbird, a company with manufacturing facilities in Taiwan. Aroma Thunderbird regularly

I. Distributor and Retailer Liability

shipped meat grinders to Carfel in Miami via Carfel's Taiwan office. When they were received in Miami, the meat grinders were immediately shipped to Abamaster without being inspected or even removed from the cartons in which they were shipped.

At the close of the plaintiff's case, the defendant Carfel, which had previously settled with the plaintiff, made an application to dismiss Abamaster's cross claim for indemnification. The Supreme Court deferred decision on the application until the close of the proof and subsequently, until the verdict was rendered on the issue of liability. The jury, which had been charged on strict products liability, found that the meat grinder in question was defective in design and that the defect was a substantial factor in causing the plaintiff's injury.

The jury further found that the product was designed and/or manufactured by a Taiwanese company, that both Carfel and Abamaster were distributors of the product, and that the design defect existed at the time the product left their respective hands. The jury apportioned fault in the happening of the accident as follows: 40% to the plaintiff, 50% to Abamaster, and 10% to Carfel.

After the verdict, Abamaster sought a determination of its cross claim for common-law indemnification against Carfel, and Carfel renewed its application to dismiss the cross claim. Carfel argued that the jury's assignment of 50% of the fault in the happening of the accident to Abamaster, and only 10% to it, reflected that the jury found Abamaster more culpable than Carfel, and that Carfel should not be compelled to indemnify the more culpable defendant. Abamaster argued, on the other hand, that the proof presented in the case allowed only one conclusion, that the product was designed and manufactured by a Taiwanese company not a party to this action and that both Carfel and Abamaster were mere sequential distributors who passed the product along the distribution chain without knowledge of the defect. The Supreme Court ruled that Abamaster was not entitled to indemnification because Abamaster and Carfel were found by the jury to be joint tortfeasors.

In strict products liability, a manufacturer, wholesaler, distributor, or retailer who sells a product in a defective condition is liable for injury which results from the use of the product "regardless of privity, foreseeability or the exercise of due care." [ ] The plaintiff need only prove that the product was defective as a result of either a manufacturing flaw, improper design, or a failure to provide adequate warnings regarding the use of the product, and that the defect was a substantial factor in bringing about the injury. Distributors and retailers may be held strictly liable to injured parties, even though they may be innocent conduits in the sale of the product, because liability rests not upon traditional considerations of fault and active negligence, but rather upon policy considerations which dictate that those in the best "position to exert pressure for the improved safety of products bear the risk of loss resulting from the use of the products." [ ] Strict products liability is not vicarious liability, but like vicarious liability, it creates an exception to the usual rule which limits one's liability to one's own wrongdoing.

Here, the jury was charged solely on strict products liability. The answers on the verdict sheet indicate that it found that the meat grinder was defectively designed and/or manufactured by Aroma Taiwan Machinery Corp., a nonparty, and that the defect was a substantial factor in bringing about the plaintiff's injury. As to Carfel and Abamaster, the jury expressly found that each was a distributor of the defectively designed meat grinder. Indeed, the proof presented at trial did not support the conclusion that either defendant was anything more than an innocent conduit in the sale of the defective product. There was no proof to support a finding that either Carfel or Abamaster was actively negligent in designing the meat grinder, or that they committed any independent tort which caused or contributed to the plaintiff's injury.

Carfel and Abamaster stand in similar shoes vis-à-vis the plaintiff—they each moved the product through the stream of commerce without knowledge of the design defect which caused the plaintiff's injury. Neither committed a primary nor affirmative act of negligence, and Abamaster was no more or less active in moving the product toward retail sale than was Carfel. Under these circumstances, there was no basis for the Supreme Court to instruct the jury to apportion fault in the happening of the accident between Carfel and Abamaster. Instead, the Supreme Court should have determined the issue of Abamaster's entitlement to indemnification as a matter of law at the close of the proof. At that point in the trial, it was evident that the proof did not support the conclusion that either of these parties was more actively negligent than the other.

Here, both Carfel and Abamaster are liable to the plaintiff, not because they were negligent, but "only by imputation of law." [ ] Thus, "there is no rational way to apportion the damages between them." [ ] And, precisely because they are liable only by imputation of law, there is no right of contribution between them. Contribution is available where "two or more tortfeasors combine to cause an injury and is determined in accordance with the relative culpability of each such person." [ ] Where, as here, liability is not based upon culpability, the appropriate concept is indemnification, rather than contribution.

One who is liable for an injury "by imputation of law may seek common-law indemnity from a person primarily liable for the injury." [ ] Where an entity "has discharged a duty which is owed by it but which as between it and another should have been discharged by the other," a contract to reimburse or indemnify is implied by law. [ ] Thus, it is well settled that a seller or distributor of a defective product has an implied right of indemnification as against the manufacturer of the product. In the instant case, both Carfel and Abamaster have the benefit of the implied right of indemnification as against the manufacturer of the defectively designed meat grinder. Unfortunately, the manufacturer is not amenable to the jurisdiction of the Supreme Court. In the absence of the manufacturer, we must determine whether, as Abamaster contends, the importer/distributor, Carfel, as the party closest to the negligent manufacturer, should indemnify the distributor lower in the commercial chain of distribution of the product.

In New York, strict products liability evolved as an exception to the usual rule limiting liability to one's own wrongdoing for policy reasons related to the allocation of the risk of loss and deterrence. Manufacturers are in the best position to know when products are suitably designed and properly made, as well as to diffuse the cost of safety in design and production. The rule imposing strict liability upon retailers and distributors advances the policy of encouraging improved product safety because, by reason of their continuing relationships with manufacturers, sellers and distributors are in a position to exert pressure on them to produce safe products. Of those in the chain of distribution, the distributor or importer closest to the manufacturer (at the top of the chain of

I. Distributor and Retailer Liability

distribution) is in the best position to further the public policy considerations underlying the doctrine of strict products liability. Here, the upstream distributor, Carfel, selected the Taiwanese manufacturer and dealt exclusively with it through Carfel's offices in Taiwan. Carfel is in a better position to exert pressure on the Taiwanese manufacturer to make a safer product and, thus, to eliminate the danger posed by the meat grinder at issue in this case. Carfel is also in a better position to seek indemnification from the Taiwanese manufacturer for the loss, thereby shifting the cost of the loss to the entity best able to distribute the cost to all users of the product. Thus, the Supreme Court should have granted judgment as a matter of law to Abamaster on its cross claim for indemnification.

ORDERED that judgment is granted as a matter of law to the defendant Abamaster of Miami, Inc., on its cross claim for indemnification as against Carfel, Inc.

NOTES AND QUESTIONS

1. *Another manifestation of the deterrence rationale for strict products liability.* In the landmark opinion that first applied strict products liability to retailers and distributors, the California Supreme Court justified strict liability in terms of its ability to promote product safety:

> In some cases the retailer may be the only member of [the overall producing and marketing] enterprise reasonably available to the injured plaintiff. In other cases the retailer himself may play a substantial part in insuring that the product is safe or may be in a position to exert pressure on the manufacturer to that end; the retailer's strict liability thus serves as an added incentive to safety.

Vandermark v. Ford Motor Co., 391 P.2d 168, 171-172 (Cal. 1964) (Traynor, J.). "Support for the rule is widespread." RESTATEMENT (THIRD) OF TORTS: PRODUCTS LIABILITY §1 Rptrs' N. cmt. e.

In the global economy, manufacturers are often located in foreign countries and not subject to the jurisdiction of a U.S. court. The retailer of a defective product, however, is usually "reasonably available to the injured plaintiff." Strict liability permits the plaintiff to recover from the retailer. The retailer often has a contractual right to be indemnified for these liabilities by the immediate wholesaler. The wholesaler can then seek indemnity from its upstream supplier, and so on. And for the reasons the court in *Godoy* provides, tort law also permits indemnity actions not based on contract. A rule of indemnity shifts the entire liability incurred by a jointly and severally liable downstream seller to an upstream seller, unlike a rule of contribution that would apportion liability among the parties. When all members of the producing and marketing enterprise are solvent, the indemnity actions will pass the entire liability along to the party responsible for the defect, thereby creating the correct safety incentives. Of course, an upstream distributor or the manufacturer can be insolvent, leaving a nonmanufacturing seller without recourse. That prospect, however, gives sellers an incentive to deal with financially sound distributors and manufacturers.

To the extent that a seller is concerned about incurring liability, it also has an incentive to engage in independent product testing, a practice adopted by many large retailers of products manufactured by foreign firms. *See* Matt Pottinger, *Outsourcing Safety Tests*, Wall St. J., Nov. 26, 2004, at B1. Similarly, large retailers can require suppliers to adopt safety standards. *See* William Neuman, *Costco Urges Stricter Safety Measures on Cantaloupes*, N.Y. Times, Sept. 29, 2011, at B3 (discussing efforts of a larger retailer "regarded as a leader in requiring food safety measures from its suppliers").

2. *Limitations of the deterrence rationale.* Although the rule of strict liability for nonmanufacturing retailers and distributors can promote product safety, this justification is problematic in some respects. Even if the retailer can be indemnified, it must incur substantial legal costs to achieve this outcome. Why permit the plaintiff to sue the retailer when recovery is available from the manufacturer? Inclusion of the retailer in the suit merely raises the cost of distribution (and product price) without providing any safety benefit. Moreover, a small business like the corner deli can sell hundreds of products from different manufacturers and distributors. Does a small business really have the ability to exert any pressure on its upstream distributors and manufacturers with respect to issues of product safety?

3. *Tort reform.* At least 17 states have enacted tort-reform statutes limiting the liability of nonmanufacturing product sellers. "[T]he statutes generally provide that the nonmanufacturing seller or distributor is immunized from strict liability only if: (1) the manufacturer is subject to the jurisdiction of the court of plaintiff's domicile; and (2) the manufacturer is not, nor is likely to become, insolvent." RESTATEMENT (THIRD) OF TORTS: PRODUCTS LIABILITY §1 cmt. e. In these circumstances, the plaintiff can obtain full recovery from the manufacturer under strict products liability, so she ordinarily has no reason for attempting to establish negligence liability against a nonmanufacturing seller. Consequently, the nonmanufacturing sellers typically avoid the unnecessary legal expenses they would otherwise incur if they were subject to strict liability.

II. THE "SALE" OF A PRODUCT

Restatement (Second) §402A applies to "one who *sells* a product in a defective condition." (emphasis added). Are the policies of strict products liability only furthered in cases involving a completed sales transaction?

DELANEY v. TOWMOTOR CORP.
United States Court of Appeals, Second Circuit, 1964
339 F.2d 4

FRIENDLY, J. Defendant Towmotor Corporation is a manufacturer of fork lift trucks, often described as hilos, which it marketed in New York City through a

II. The "Sale" of a Product

sole distributor, A. A. Moore, Inc. It developed a new model, containing an overhead guard manufactured by the third-party defendant, Marine & Industrial Equipment Co. On the instructions of Towmotor's New York service manager, one of the new lifts, owned by Towmotor, was delivered to T. Hogan & Sons, a stevedore, "as a demonstrator for them to try it out and get acquainted with our newer type of equipment." Delaney, an employee of Hogan, operating the hilo on a North River pier seven weeks later, was injured when the overhead guard collapsed.

This action against Towmotor in the District Court for the Southern District of New York followed, federal jurisdiction being based on diverse citizenship. Delaney alleged both negligence in design and manufacturer's strict liability. Towmotor impleaded Marine & Industrial and Hogan. Delaney's action against Towmotor was tried to Judge Wyatt and a jury. His case rested on a claimed defect in the manner in which the overhead guard was affixed. In the new hilo, as in its predecessors, whereas the rear portions of the uprights were attached by U-bolts which permitted movement, the forward portions allegedly were welded to the horizontal plate of an angle iron and this was held rigidly against the front of the hilo. An expert metallurgist testified that this construction would have the result that vibrations would cause metal fatigue and consequent fracture. The jury found for Towmotor on the claim of negligence in design but for Delaney on the claim of strict liability. Towmotor appealed.

Towmotor's argument is that a manufacturer's liability is for breach of an implied warranty and that there can be no such warranty where as here, there has been no sale. The transaction between it and Hogan, says Towmotor, was a gratuitous bailment and the only duty of the bailor in such a case is to give "warning or notice of those defects, if any, of which it had knowledge and which in reasonable probability would imperil those using" the subject of the bailment.

[We disagree. W]e are convinced that New York is among those enlightened jurisdictions that no longer regard "an obligation which the law imposes irrespective of the intention of the parties or even in direct contravention of their expressions as in the same category as a contractual warranty, express or fairly implied." *See* Prosser, *The Assault Upon the Citadel (Strict Liability to the Consumer),* 69 Yale L.J. 1099, 1124-1134 (1960). New York regards the liability of the manufacturer of an article as arising from "having invited and solicited the use," [ ]; "strict tort liability [is] surely a more accurate phrase" to identify this new concept than breach of warranty. [ ] We realize that the latest version of the section of the *Restatement (Second) of Torts* dealing with a manufacturer's liability, §402A(1) (Tent. Draft No. 10, 1964), speaks of "one who sells any product in a defective condition." But we think the Court of Appeals would regard this, as we would, as a description of the situation that has most commonly arisen rather than as a deliberate limitation of the principle to cases where the product has been sold, intentionally excluding instances where a manufacturer has placed a defective article in the stream of commerce by other means. We can see no sensible reason why Delaney's rights against Towmotor should be less extensive on the facts here than if Towmotor had first sold the hilo to its distributor, or than if it had sold the machine to Hogan, for a nominal down payment, subject to return if Hogan was not satisfied after a trial period. Since we can see no such reason, we must assume the New York Court of Appeals would be equally unable to perceive one.

Affirmed.

NOTES AND QUESTIONS

1. *Sales transactions and beyond.* For reasons underscored by the demise of the privity rule, the tort duty does not depend on the requirements of contract law, enabling courts to conclude that a completed sale is not required in order to subject a defendant to strict products liability. But once the formalities of a sales transaction are no longer required, how should courts determine whether a particular transaction is subject to strict products liability?

Consider lease transactions, which "are an increasingly common method by which consumers take possession of the products they put to daily use, such as cars, trucks, cranes, and other chattels that are likely to be dangerous if defective." David G. Owen & Mary J. Davis, 2 OWEN & DAVIS ON PRODUCTS LIABILITY §17:3 (4th ed. 2014 & 2020 update). When first confronted with cases involving leases, courts had little difficulty in extending the rule of strict products liability to these transactions.

> Rather than stretching to call these transactions "sales," courts simply declared that the same policy objectives that supported strict liability in the sales context supported strict liability in other contexts. The first significant extension involved commercial product lessors. Although title does not pass in lease transactions, courts have reasoned that the same policy objectives that are served by holding commercial product sellers strictly liable also apply to commercial product lessors. Over time, courts have extended strict products liability to a wide range of nonsale, nonlease transactions.

RESTATEMENT (THIRD) OF TORTS: PRODUCTS LIABILITY §20 cmt. a. To what extent does this reasoning apply to other types of transactions?

2. *Bailments.* The transaction in *Delaney* involved a bailment. "A bailment arises when one party delivers property to another for some purpose after which the property will be returned to the original party." Golt by Golt v. Sports Complex, Inc., 644 A.2d 989, 992 (Del. Super. Ct. 1994) (concluding that a bailment subject to strict products liability occurred when defendant amusement park operator allowed child to drive a go-cart in exchange for a ticket). "Traditionally, product leases were regarded as 'bailments for hire.' In modern practice, lease transactions often are set forth in formalized contracts, whereas product bailment transactions normally are much more casual." 2 OWEN & DAVIS ON PRODUCTS LIABILITY LAW, *supra*, §17:4 at 1068. Due to the functional overlap of leases and bailments, courts extended strict products liability to these transactions.

The functional overlap is not complete, however, when the bailment is for a short time and is otherwise unrelated to the defendant's business. In these cases, courts often scrutinize the nature of the transaction to determine whether the defendant is subject to strict products liability:

> Bailments typically involve short-term transfers of possession. Several categories of cases are fairly clear. When the defendant is in the business of selling the same type of product as is the subject of the bailment, the seller/bailor is subject to strict liability for harm caused

by defects. Thus, an automobile dealer who allows a prospective customer to test-drive a demonstrator will be treated the same as a seller of the demonstrator car. Even when sale of a product is not contemplated, the commercial bailor is subject to strict liability if a charge is imposed as a condition of the bailment. Thus, a laundromat is subject to strict liability for a defective clothes dryer, and a roller rink that rents skates is treated similarly. When products are made available as a convenience to customers who are on the defendant's premises primarily for different, although related purposes, and no separate charge is made, strict liability is not imposed. Thus, bowling alleys that supply bowling balls for customer use and markets that supply shopping carts are not subject to strict products liability for harm caused by defects in those items. Similarly, doctors who use medical devices while treating patients are not considered distributors of those products.

RESTATEMENT (THIRD) OF TORTS: PRODUCTS LIABILITY §20 cmt. f.

The case law in this area is difficult to synthesize. Why is the provision of bowling balls by a bowling alley not subject to strict liability, given that strict liability applies to the provision of roller skates by a roller rink? Why does a separate charge matter? Even though bowling alleys do not charge separately for bowling balls, the cost of the balls is nevertheless incorporated into the price of bowling. As these questions reveal, the case law in this area is hard to synthesize. Is the problem related to the attenuated deterrence rationale for nonmanufacturer liability?

NEW TEXAS AUTO AUCTION SERVICES, L.P. v. GOMEZ DE HERNANDEZ
Supreme Court of Texas, 2008
249 S.W.3d 400

BRISTER, J. Auctioneers are usually neither buyers nor sellers, but agents for both. While they are obviously engaged in sales, the only thing they sell for their own account is their services; the items they auction are generally sold for others. In this case, the court of appeals held an auto auctioneer could be liable in both strict liability and negligence for auctioning a defective car. But product-liability law requires those who place products in the stream of commerce to stand behind them; it does not require everyone who facilitates the stream to do the same. Accordingly, we reverse.

The 1993 Ford Explorer at issue here was repossessed by a finance company, who consigned it for sale in Houston by Big H Auto Auction. Big H took title to the car and sold it at auction on October 17, 2000 for $3,100 to Houston Auto Auction, which auctioned the car a week later to Progresso Motors, which sold it three days later to Jose Angel Hernandez Gonzalez in Progresso, Texas. About a year later, Gonzalez was killed in a rollover accident in Mexico.

Twelve plaintiffs (Gonzalez's wife, parents, children, and six others whose relationship to him is unclear) filed suit in Hidalgo County against the car manufacturer (Ford Motor Co.), tire manufacturer (Bridgestone/Firestone

Corp.), Progresso Motors, and the two auto auctioneers. The trial court granted summary judgment for Big H and severed that claim. The court of appeals reversed, finding Big H was not entitled to summary judgment on the plaintiffs' strict liability or negligence claims. We address each claim in turn.

Modern American product-liability law is derived primarily from section 402A of the *Restatement (Second) of Torts*, "the most influential section of any Restatement of the Law on any topic," and perhaps in all of tort jurisprudence. [ ] From the beginning, section 402A did not apply to everyone. By its own terms, section 402A limits strict liability to those "engaged in the business of selling" a product.

Like many other short statements of legal doctrine, this one has been construed through the years to mean both more and less than what the plain words appear to say. For example, although section 402A appears to limit recovery to users or consumers of a defective product, we long ago extended it to innocent bystanders as well. Similarly, section 402A explicitly applies only to those whose business is "selling" a product, but from the outset we have applied it more broadly. Thus, we held strictly liable a distributor who handed out free samples, reasoning that the samples were distributed with "the expectation of profiting therefrom through future sales." McKisson v. Sales Affiliates, 416 S.W.2d 787 (Tex. 1967). Since then, we have applied strict liability to manufacturers, distributors, lessors, bailors, and dealers. [ ]

On the other hand, we have limited the scope of those "engaged in the business of selling" to those who actually placed a product in the stream of commerce. [ ] "Imposition of strict liability demands more than an incidental role in the overall marketing program of the product." [ ] An advertising agency that provides copy, a newspaper that distributes circulars, an internet provider that lists store locations, and a trucking business that makes deliveries all might be "engaged" in product sales, but they do not themselves sell the products. Since *McKisson*, we have applied strict liability only to businesses that are "in the same position as one who sells the product." *McKisson*, 416 S.W.2d at 792.

The reason for this limitation arises from the justifications for strict liability itself, namely: (1) compensating injured consumers, (2) spreading potential losses, and (3) deterring future injuries. Businesses that play only an incidental role in a product's placement are rarely in a position to deter future injuries by changing a product's design or warnings. If required to spread risks, they must do so across far more products than the one that was defective. And while many businesses may be able to pay compensation, consumers normally expect a product's manufacturer to be the one who stands behind it.

The *Restatement (Third) of Torts* adopted in 1998 recognized these developments in products law, expanding strict liability to those "engaged in the business of selling or otherwise distributing products," and defining those terms as a business that either "transfers ownership" or "provides the product." RESTATEMENT (THIRD) OF TORTS: PRODUCTS LIABILITY §20 (1998). In a comment, the *Restatement (Third)* specifically excluded auctioneers:

> Persons assisting or providing services to product distributors, while indirectly facilitating the commercial distribution of products, are not subject

II. The "Sale" of a Product

to liability under the rules of this Restatement. Thus, commercial firms engaged in advertising products are outside the rules of this Restatement, as are firms engaged exclusively in the financing of product sale or lease transactions. *Sales personnel and commercial auctioneers are also outside the rules of this Restatement.*

Id. cmt. g (emphasis added).

Nevertheless, the court of appeals held section 402A applied to auctioneers because Texas law "requires only that the defendant be responsible for introducing the product into the stream of commerce." It is true we have sometimes referred to strictly liable defendants as "introducing" products into the stream of commerce although more often we have referred to them as "placing" them in that current as has the Legislature. [ ] But both concepts were intended to describe producers, not mere announcers like an auctioneer or an emcee at a trade show who "introduces" a product to a crowd but has nothing to do with making it.

Courts in other jurisdictions have consistently held that auctioneers are not subject to section 402A. [ ] We agree, and hold that because Big H was not in the business of selling automobiles for its own account, it cannot be held strictly liable.

The plaintiffs alleged Big H was negligent in failing to replace the tires on this Explorer pursuant to a recall issued a few weeks before the auction took place. We agree with the trial court that Big H had no such duty on the facts here.

Unquestionably, ignoring a recall may run the risk of severe injury. But there are a huge number of recalls, and the risks they involve varies widely. Federal law generally places the duty on manufacturers of products to report potential defects, notify the public, and make necessary repairs. [ ]

By contrast, imposing a duty on auto auctioneers to discover and repair defects would require them to go into a side business other than their own. The evidence establishes that Big H auctions about 1,000 vehicles each week, with many of them moving on and off the premises in a matter of hours. It does not inspect or repair vehicles unless a customer specifically requests and pays for such services. Many of the cars sold at its auctions need repairs, and some have to be towed on and off the auction block. Moreover, Big H's knowledge is clearly inferior to that of the car and tire manufacturers the plaintiffs sued for these same defects, and there is no indication that Big H had any control over how those manufacturers made their products.

Additionally, Big H made no warranties of its own at the auction, serving merely as a conduit for warranties made by sellers. The car here was sold under a red light, indicating the car was being sold "as is." Generally, those who buy a product "as is" accept the risk of potential defects, and thus cannot claim a seller's negligence caused their injuries. Imposing a different duty here would effectively prohibit car dealers from selling cars "as is." And as one federal court has pointed out, imposing such a duty on auctioneers would seem to require imposing it on every person who ever sold a used car, as there is "no sensible or just stopping point." [ ] We decline to impose so sweeping a duty.

We reverse the court of appeals' judgment and reinstate the trial court's take-nothing judgment for Big H.

NOTES AND QUESTIONS

1. *Used products.* In most jurisdictions, the nonmanufacturing seller of a used product is ordinarily subject only to negligence liability. "[A] buyer does not have the right to expect a used product in obviously used condition to present the same defect-related risks as if the product were new, [but] the buyer at least has the right to expect the used-product seller to exercise reasonable care." RESTATEMENT (THIRD) OF TORTS: PRODUCTS LIABILITY §8 cmt. b.

Why does the *Restatement (Third)* rely on consumer expectations to justify this rule, even though it does not invoke consumer expectations to justify most other liability rules? Is the implicit premise that consumers reasonably expect a seller to incur liability only when doing so would promote product safety? Consider Peterson v. Superior Court, 899 P.2d 905, 915 (Cal. 1995) (emphasizing the absence of "risk reduction" as the reason for ordinarily immunizing the seller of used goods from strict liability); Tillman v. Vance Equipment Co., 596 P.2d 1299, 1304 (Or. 1979) (holding that the seller of a used crane on an "as is basis" was not subject to strict liability because "any risk reduction which would be accomplished by imposing strict liability on the dealer in used goods would not be significant enough to justify our taking that step").

In some cases, the buyer's reasonable safety expectations can justify subjecting the seller of used products to strict liability. For example, the seller of a used product is subject to strict liability for manufacturing defects if the "seller's marketing of the [used] product would cause a reasonable person in the position of the buyer to expect the used product to present no greater risk of defect than if the product were new." RESTATEMENT (THIRD) OF TORTS: PRODUCTS LIABILITY §8(b). The seller of a used product is also subject to strict products liability for any type of defect if the used product had been "remanufactured by the seller or a predecessor in the commercial chain of distribution of the used product," or the used product does not otherwise comply with an applicable safety statute or regulation. *Id.* §§8(c)-(d). "Reconditioning or remanufacturing a product is different from servicing or repairing the item. Reconditioning extends the useful life beyond what was contemplated at the point of manufacture and effectively creates a new product." Malen v. MTD Prods., Inc., 628 F.3d 298, 306 (7th Cir. 2010). Do any of these exceptions apply to *New Texas Auto Auction Services*, or would subjecting auctioneers to strict liability instead lack the requisite safety rationale?

2. *After-market product alterations.* If the owner alters a product by incorporating a so-called after-market component not produced by the original manufacturer, can that manufacturer nevertheless be liable if the component is defective? In what respect, if any, did the original manufacturer "sell" the defective component? Confronting this question, the court in Ellingsworth v. Vermeer Mfg. Co., 949 F.3d 1097 (8th Cir. 2020), dismissed the claims of Robert Ellingsworth, who was injured by a defective winch that was added as an after-market component to a wood chipper manufactured by defendant Vermeer:

> The record shows that Vermeer did not manufacture the winch attachment that injured Ellingsworth. It is uncontested that Vermeer

II. The "Sale" of a Product

offers no after-market winch attachments for sale and that the wood chipper that injured Ellingsworth did not have a winch when Vermeer manufactured it. At most, the evidence suggests that the winch was constructed by a third party out of mostly Vermeer parts, but Ellingsworth's suit is not about the quality of the winch parts. He alleges that Vermeer manufactured the winch itself. Because the record forecloses that argument, the district court correctly granted Vermeer summary judgment. We affirm.

Id. at 1101.

3. *From auctions to online marketplaces?* In Inman v. Technicolor USA, Inc., 2011 WL 5829024 (W.D. Pa.), plaintiff sued 20 defendants, including eBay Inc., for commercially distributing electronic vacuum tubes containing mercury that allegedly caused the plaintiff to suffer from "acute mercury poisoning." Plaintiff purchased the tubes from defendant sellers via the online marketplace hosted by defendant eBay. Defendant eBay moved to dismiss the claims against it, arguing that it was not a "seller" for purposes of strict products liability. Its online User Agreement stated in part:

> [W]e are not a traditional auctioneer. Instead our sites are venues to allow anyone to offer, sell and buy just about anything . . . in a variety of pricing formats and locations, such as stores, fixed price formats and auction-style formats. We are not involved in the actual transaction between buyers and sellers.

The court granted eBay's motion, largely relying on cases concluding that auctioneers and brokers are not "sellers" for purposes of strict products liability but instead merely facilitate transactions. The court also emphasized that the plaintiff

> has not alleged that eBay ever had physical possession of the products, that they were moved or stored in a facility owned by eBay, or any other facts to suggest that holding eBay responsible would incentivize safety, that eBay is the only member of the marketing chain available, or that eBay is in a better position than Inman to prevent the circulation of such defective vacuum tubes.

Id. at *6. If the plaintiff had made allegations of this type, would eBay be a "seller" for purposes of strict products liability, even though it never held title to the goods sold on its online marketplace?

BOLGER v. AMAZON.COM, LLC
California Court of Appeal, 2020
267 Cal. Rptr.3d 601

GUERRERO, J. Plaintiff Angela Bolger bought a replacement laptop computer battery on Amazon, the popular online shopping website operated by defendant Amazon.com, LLC. The Amazon listing for the battery identified the seller as "E-Life," a fictitious name used on Amazon by Lenoge Technology (HK) Ltd. (Lenoge). Amazon charged Bolger for the purchase, retrieved the laptop battery from its location in an Amazon warehouse, prepared the battery for shipment in Amazon-branded packaging, and sent it to Bolger. Bolger alleges the battery exploded several months later, and she suffered severe burns as a result.

Bolger sued Amazon and several other defendants, including Lenoge. She alleged causes of action for strict products liability, negligent products liability, breach of implied warranty, breach of express warranty, and "negligence/negligent undertaking." Lenoge was served but did not appear, so the trial court entered its default.

Amazon moved for summary judgment. It primarily argued that the doctrine of strict products liability, as well as any similar tort theory, did not apply to it because it did not distribute, manufacture, or sell the product in question. It claimed its website was an "online marketplace" and E-Life (Lenoge) was the product seller, not Amazon. The trial court agreed, granted Amazon's motion, and entered judgment accordingly.

Bolger appeals. She argues that Amazon is strictly liable for defective products offered on its website by third-party sellers like Lenoge. In the circumstances of this case, we agree.

As a factual and legal matter, Amazon placed itself between Lenoge and Bolger in the chain of distribution of the product at issue here. Amazon accepted possession of the product from Lenoge, stored it in an Amazon warehouse, attracted Bolger to the Amazon website, provided her with a product listing for Lenoge's product, received her payment for the product, and shipped the product in Amazon packaging to her. Amazon set the terms of its relationship with Lenoge, controlled the conditions of Lenoge's offer for sale on Amazon, limited Lenoge's access to Amazon's customer information, forced Lenoge to communicate with customers through Amazon, and demanded indemnification as well as substantial fees on each purchase. Whatever term we use to describe Amazon's role, be it "retailer," "distributor," or merely "facilitator," it was pivotal in bringing the product here to the consumer.

Strict products liability "was created judicially because of the economic and social need for the protection of consumers in an increasingly complex and mechanized society, and because of the limitations in the negligence and warranty remedies." [ ] It "arose from dissatisfaction with the wooden formalisms of traditional tort and contract principles in order to protect the consumer of manufactured goods." [ ] The scope of strict liability has been expanded, where necessary, to account for "market realities" and to cover new transactions in "widespread use . . . in today's business world." [ ]

The structure of Amazon's relationship with Lenoge, on one hand, and Bolger, on the other, presents just such a new transaction now in widespread use. We must therefore return to the principles underlying the doctrine of strict products liability to determine whether it applies. [ ] Those principles compel the application of the doctrine to Amazon under the circumstances here. As noted, Amazon is a direct link in the chain of distribution, acting as a powerful intermediary between the third-party seller and the consumer. Amazon is the only member of the enterprise reasonably available to an injured consumer in some cases, it plays a substantial part in ensuring the products listed on its website are safe, it can and does exert pressure on upstream distributors (like Lenoge) to enhance safety, and it has the ability to adjust the cost of liability between itself and its third-party sellers. Under established principles of strict liability, Amazon should be held liable if a product sold through its website turns out to be defective. *See* Vandermark v. Ford Motor Co., 391 P.2d 168, 171-72 (Cal. 1964). Strict liability here "affords maximum protection to the injured plaintiff and works no injustice to the defendants, for they can adjust the costs of such protection between them in the course of their continuing business relationship." *Id.* at 263.

We further conclude Amazon is not shielded from liability by title 47 United States Code section 230. That section, enacted as part of the Communications Decency Act of 1996 [ ], generally prevents internet service providers from being held liable as a speaker or publisher of third-party content. It does not apply here because Bolger's strict liability claims depend on Amazon's own activities, not its status as a speaker or publisher of content provided by Lenoge for its product listing.

We therefore reverse the trial court's judgment in favor of Amazon. On remand, the court shall vacate its order granting Amazon's motion for summary judgment and enter an order granting the motion in part and denying it in part, as discussed more fully below.

. . .

NOTES AND QUESTIONS

1. *Amazon's litigation experience.* Until recently, "every court to consider the question of Amazon's liability has concluded that Amazon is not strictly liable for defective products sold on its marketplace." Eberhart v. Amazon. Com, Inc., 325 F. Supp. 3d 393, 399 (S.D.N.Y. 2018). These decisions typically emphasize that Amazon does not take title to the products of third-party vendors marketed on its website, nor does it exercise physical control over those products, making it analogous to auctioneers for purposes of strict products liability. *See, e.g.*, Erie Insurance Co. v. Amazon.com, Inc., 925 F.3d 125, 141 (4th Cir. 2019) ("We . . . find no indication that the term 'seller,' as used in Maryland's products liability law, should be understood in any manner other than its ordinary meaning. And the ordinary meaning of 'seller' is 'one that offers [property] for sale,' with 'sale' defined as 'the transfer of ownership of and the title to property from one person to another for a price.'"). Did the case law discussed early in this chapter focus on these formalities of the transaction? *Bolger* illustrates the more recent trend subjecting Amazon to strict products liability for defective products purchased on its online marketplace. *See, e.g.*, State Farm Fire & Casualty Co. v. Amazon.com, Inc., 390 F. Supp. 3d 964 (W.D. Wis. 2019) (holding that Amazon is not a "peripheral entity like an auctioneer" but an "integral part of the chain of distribution more akin to [a] lessor"); State Farm Fire & Casualty Co. v. Amazon.Com Services, Inc., 137 N.Y.S.3d 884 (N.Y. Sup. Ct. 2020).

2. *Safety problems in the Amazon marketplace.* Because Amazon was not subject to strict products liability until recently, reputational concerns and other competitive pressures of the free market largely dictated the quality of products sold on its marketplace. In this type of environment, are

there sufficient financial incentives to ensure product safety? One investigation "found 4,152 items for sale on Amazon.com Inc.'s site that have been declared unsafe by federal agencies, are deceptively labeled or are banned by federal regulators—items that big-box retailers' policies would bar from their shelves." Alexandra Berzon, Shane Shifflet & Justin Scheck, *Amazon Has Ceded Control of Its Site. The Result: Thousands of Banned, Unsafe or Mislabeled Products*, Wall St. J., Aug. 23, 2019. Faced with bad publicity and the increasing threat of tort liability, Amazon recently announced that it probably will need to "spend billions of dollars in the future to prevent the sale of counterfeit goods, expired food or dangerous products on its platforms." Tripp Mickle, *Amazon Ready to Pour Billions Into Policing Products on Its Site*, Wall St. J., Oct. 22, 2019. To what extent does this market dynamic illustrate the safety rationale for subjecting the nonmanufacturing commercial distributors of defective products to strict liability?

3. *The safety rationale for strict products liability.* In the portions of the *Bolger* opinion not excerpted above, the court at considerable length explains why Amazon is well positioned to promote product safety. To sell products on the Amazon marketplace, a third-party vendor must enter into a services agreement with Amazon. This agreement gives Amazon the exclusive authority to supervise vendors, impose price constraints, provide the exclusive means for communication between customers and third-party vendors, regulate the quality of customer services, and then bill for sales. The agreement also requires the vendor to indemnify Amazon for any liabilities stemming from the vendor's product, and if the vendor meets a sales threshold, it must obtain general commercial liability insurance listing Amazon as an additional named insured. Finally, Amazon in its sole discretion can remove unsafe products from its website. 267 Cal. Rptr. 3d at 616. As another court concluded, "imposing strict liability upon Amazon would be an incentive to do so." Oberdorf v. Amazon.com Inc., 930 F.3d 136, 146 (3d Cir. 2019), *reh'g granted, opinion vacated*, 936 F.3d 182 (3d Cir. 2019), *certification question accepted*, 237 A.3d 394 (Pa. 2020).

4. *Consumer expectations.* In another portion of the *Bolger* opinion not excerpted above, the court relied on consumer expectations to further justify the imposition of strict products liability on Amazon. "Because Amazon customers have an expectation of safety—and Amazon specifically encourages that expectation—it is appropriate to hold Amazon strictly liable when a defective product is sold through its website." 267 Cal. Rptr. 3d at 618. Do consumers have different expectations about products purchased on the Amazon online marketplace as compared to those they buy at brick-and-mortar retail stores, all of which are clearly subject to strict products liability? Consider State Farm Fire and Casualty Co., 137 N.Y.S. 3d at 889 ("The consumer goes to Amazon's website to look for a product in the same manner one would walk into a Lowes, Home Depot, or a neighborhood True Value, or order from one of those entities' website. . . . Amazon seeks to have all the benefits of the traditional brick and mortar storefront without any of the responsibilities.").

5. *Reframing the liability rule.* Whereas *Restatement (Second)* §402A defines the liability rule in terms of a product "seller," *Restatement (Third)* §1 formulates the general liability rule differently: "One engaged in the business of

selling or otherwise distributing products who sells or distributes a defective product is subject to liability for harm to persons or property caused by the defect." Does a focus on "commercial distribution" better characterize the inquiry that the courts actually employ? Consider *id.* §20 ("One otherwise distributes a product when, in a commercial transaction other than a sale, one provides the product to another either for use or consumption or as a preliminary step leading to ultimate use or consumption. Commercial non-sale product distributors include, but are not limited to, lessors, bailors, and those who provide products to others as a means of promoting either the use or consumption of such products or some other commercial activity.").

III. THE SALE OF A "PRODUCT"

Because the liability of nonmanufacturing product sellers is truly strict, cases involving defendants of this type can turn on the issue of whether the defendant sold a "product" governed by the rules of strict products liability. If the transaction instead involved the provision of a service, the defendant typically is subject only to negligence liability. Unless the plaintiff can prove negligence, a defendant can avoid liability altogether if the court concludes that the transaction is more appropriately characterized as the provision of a service rather than the sale of a defective product.

GORRAN v. ATKINS NUTRITIONALS, INC.
United States District Court, Southern District of New York, 2006
464 F. Supp. 2d 315

CHIN, J. Plaintiff Jody Gorran, a 53-year old businessman, went on the popular low-carbohydrate Atkins Diet (the "Diet") in the spring of 2001. Six months earlier, his cholesterol level was only 146 and he had a "very low risk" of heart disease. After just two months on the Diet, however, his cholesterol level shot up to 230. Nonetheless, he remained on the Diet until October 2003, when he experienced severe chest pain. As a consequence, he had an angioplasty—a surgical procedure—to unclog one of his coronary arteries, and a stent was placed into the artery to help keep it open.

Gorran now sues defendants Atkins Nutritionals, Inc. ("ANI"), and Paul D. Wolf, co-executor of the Estate of Robert C. Atkins, M.D. (the "Estate"), for products liability . . . under Florida law. Gorran contends that the Diet is dangerous because it calls for a high-fat, high-protein, low-carbohydrate diet that increases the risk of coronary heart disease, diabetes, stroke, and certain types of cancer. He alleges that products sold by defendants—books, food products, and nutritional supplements—are "defective and unreasonably dangerous."

Defendants move for judgment on the pleadings dismissing the complaint. Defendants argue that Gorran has failed to state a products liability claim because (1) the food products are not defective or unreasonably dangerous, and (2) the Book is not a "product" for purposes of product liability. I address each argument in turn.

Even assuming the food products here could be considered unreasonably dangerous over an extended period of time, Gorran alleges only that he purchased $25 worth of defendants' products. Gorran's consumption of $25 worth of protein bars, pancake mix, and pancake syrup was not sufficient, as a matter of law, to have caused his arterial blockage. To the extent plaintiff's products liability claim is based on food products sold by defendants, it fails.

Gorran's products liability claim is also deficient to the extent it is based on the Book, for the Book is not a "product." Products liability law focuses on "the tangible world." Winter v. G.P. Putnam's Sons, 938 F.2d 1033, 1034 (9th Cir. 1991); Restatement (Third) of Torts §19(a) (1998) (defining product as "tangible personal property distributed commercially for use or consumption"). Thus, a defect in a book's tangible qualities—the cover, pages, and binding—could potentially give rise to a products liability action. *See* Cardozo v. True, 342 So.2d 1053, 1056 (Fla. 2d Dist. Ct. App. 1977) (distinguishing between tangible and intangible aspects of a book). The intangible qualities of a book, however—the ideas and expressions—are not products for purposes of products liability law. Winter, 938 F.2d at 1034; RESTATEMENT (THIRD) OF TORTS: PRODUCTS LIABILITY §19(a) cmt. d (noting that books are "intangible personal property"). Imposing liability for physical injuries caused by the ideas contained in a book would "inhibit those who wish to share thoughts and theories," for no author would write on a topic that could potentially result in physical injury to the reader. Winter, 938 F.2d 1033, 1035; *see, e.g.*, Jones v. J.B. Lippincott Co., 694 F. Supp. 1216, 1217 (D. Md. 1988) (dismissing products liability action against medical textbook publisher where student suffered injury after taking enema described in textbook, and stating that "[n]o case has extended Section 402A to the dissemination of an idea or knowledge in books"). Here, too, because the intangible expressions contained in the Book are not products, Gorran's products liability claim, to the extent it is based on the Book, also fails.

For the foregoing reasons, defendants' motions for judgment on the pleadings are granted, and the complaint is dismissed in its entirety.

NOTES AND QUESTIONS

1. *Definition of a "product."* As the New York Court of Appeals recently recognized, "when considering whether strict products liability attaches, the question of whether something is a product is often assumed; none of our strict products liability case law provides a clear definition of a 'product.'" Matter of Eighth Jud. Dist. Asbestos Litig., 129 N.E.3d 891, 896 (N.Y. 2019). The court then recognized that "intertwined with our analysis of whether something is a product is the more central question of whether the defendant manufacturer owes a duty" in the case at hand.

> To that end, although the criteria for determining whether a duty should attach to a seller may be tied to the nature of the given transaction, our case law emphasizes governing factors such as a defendant's control over the design of the product, its standardization, and its

III. The Sale of a "Product"

superior ability to know—and warn about—the dangers inherent in the product's reasonably foreseeable uses or misuses.

Id. at 897. How would this analysis apply in *Gorran,* which was also governed by New York law? Is the tangible/intangible distinction a better method for differentiating products from services?

2. *The tangible/intangible distinction.* Strict products liability is largely limited to the "tangible world," although a few types of intangible goods have been subject to strict products liability. Intangible goods are deemed to be products when "the context of their distribution and use is sufficiently analogous to the distribution and use of tangible personal property that it is appropriate to apply the rules [of product liability]." RESTATEMENT (THIRD) OF TORTS: PRODUCTS LIABILITY §19(a).

A good example is provided by electricity, an intangible form of energy. Most courts have concluded that once electricity has been distributed to the consumer through the meter, it is subject to strict products liability. "Plaintiffs in the post-delivery cases typically complain of unexpected drops or surges in voltage, resulting in personal injury or property damage. Those claims seem better governed by principles of strict liability for physical deviations from intended design." *Id.* cmt. d.

By contrast, intangible property in the form of information is not deemed to be a product as illustrated by *Gorran.* "Although a tangible medium such as a book, itself clearly a product, delivers the information, the plaintiff's grievance in such cases is with the information, not with the tangible medium." *Id.* False or misleading information arguably departs from intended design (the truth), but courts are concerned "that imposing strict liability for the dissemination of false and defective information would significantly impinge on free speech." *Id.*

Hence a policy concern about strict liability can lead courts to conclude that a particular transaction does not involve the sale of a "product" to avoid application of strict products liability. To what extent is the nature of this policy decision obscured by an inquiry that simply asks whether the transaction involved a "product"? Consider again the reasoning of the New York Court of Appeals in note 1.

3. *Software.* There still is no firmly established body of case law recognizing that a manufacturer incurs a tort duty for defective software. *See* Alan Butler, *Products Liability and the Internet of (Insecure) Things: Should Manufacturers Be Liable for Damage Caused by Hacked Devices?,* 50 U. Mich. J.L. Reform 913, 915-916 (2017) ("Despite the fact that discussions of liability for defective software go back more than forty years, very few cases have addressed the issue outside the financial services context."). In general, the tort duty for software designers can be limited for various reasons, most notably the economic loss rule that limits consumers to contractual remedies for intangible forms of intellectual property that have been designed for a specific purpose. Frances E. Zollers et al., *No More Soft Landings for Software: Liability for Defects in an Industry That Has Come of Age,* 21 Santa Clara Computer & High Tech. L.J. 745, 758-760, 764 (2005). Relying on the policy rationales for strict products liability, others have argued that these reasons for limiting the tort duty should not apply to defective software

that foreseeably causes physical harms. *See, e.g.*, Butler, *supra* (arguing that the tort duty can be justified in cases of third-party hacking because the risk of property damage is foreseeable, software defects can be remedied by remote updates, and "holding manufacturers liable for downstream harms caused by their insecure devices is well aligned with the purposes of products liability law"); Zollers et al., *supra* at 782 (concluding that "the policy reasons underlying strict [products] liability are congruent with the application of the doctrine to software"). Is the rationale for the tort obligation more straightforward when the defective software determines the performance of a tangible product in a manner that causes bodily injury or damage to other property? Consider in this regard a surge of electricity that causes a computer to catch fire.

In Graves v. CAS Medical Systems, Inc., 735 S.E.2d 650 (S.C. 2012), plaintiff parents alleged that the software design of a baby monitor, which they used to track the breathing and heart rates of their prematurely born baby, was defective and caused the alarm to fail, thereby causing the baby's death. The plaintiffs relied on expert testimony to establish that the software design was defective. The court granted summary judgment to the defendant manufacturer after ruling that the plaintiffs' computer experts did not identify a specific defect in the software of the baby monitor:

> Although we use computers in some form or fashion almost every day of our lives, the design and structure of the software they run is beyond the ordinary understanding and experience of laymen. Hence, the [plaintiffs' must support their allegations with expert testimony, and without it, their claims are subject to dismissal.

Id. at 659. Why didn't the court instead dismiss the claim on the ground that software is an "intangible" service not governed by strict products liability? Does that argument seem nonsensical in a case like this? *See also* Gen. Motors Corp. v. Johnston, 592 So.2d 1054, 1056 (Ala. 1992) (affirming jury verdict for plaintiffs based on claim "that a programmable read only memory chip" in the fuel delivery system of a new pickup was defectively designed, which caused the vehicle to stall in an intersection, where it was then hit by an oncoming truck).

Even if the software were deemed to be a service that is embedded in a tangible product, the entire transaction would still be a hybrid product/service transaction governed by the rules discussed in the next set of materials. Consider whether these rules shed further light on the issue of whether defective software can be subject to strict products liability.

CAFAZZO v. CENTRAL MEDICAL HEALTH SERVICES, INC.
Supreme Court of Pennsylvania, 1995
668 A.2d 521

MONTEMURO, J. In this case of first impression, we are presented with the question of whether a hospital and a physician can be held subject to strict liability

III. The Sale of a "Product"

under the *Restatement (Second) of Torts* §402A, for defects in a product incidental to the provision of medical services.

In 1986, appellant Albert Cafazzo underwent surgery for implantation of a mandibular prosthesis. In 1992, some time after it was discovered that this device was defective, a complaint was filed against appellees, the physician who performed the surgery and the hospital where the operation took place, claiming that "all defendants sell, provide or use certain prosthetic devices," and that they should be held strictly liable as having "provided, sold or otherwise placed in the stream of commerce products manufactured by Vitek, Inc., known as Proplast TMJ Implants." The complaint alleged that the prosthesis was defectively designed, unsafe for its intended use, and lacked any warning necessary in order to ensure safety.

Appellees' preliminary objections in the nature of a demurer were granted by the trial court which concluded that appellant had failed to state a claim cognizable under Pennsylvania law, and the Superior Court affirmed. We granted allocatur to determine whether liability will attach under the circumstances of this case.

Whether appellees are sellers for the purposes of 402A is the central issue in this matter, and, therefore, appellants' assertion that appellees are in fact, sellers, need not be accepted out of hand. Moreover, even if the central question is answered in the affirmative, the corollary issue arises as to whether appellees, by virtue of their position as providers of health care, are exempted from the consequences of having so acted.

This Court finds that the answer to the initial question is a negative, and further holds that even if appellees could be shown to have "marketed" the prothesis, strict liability does not apply.

While we do not slavishly adhere to the language of 402A, the rule enunciated there, as with other non-statutory declarations, is a common law pronouncement by the court, which "always retains the right and the duty to test the reason behind a common law rule in determining the applicability of such a rule to the facts before it." [ ] What appellants would have us do is to apply the rule while ignoring the facts of this case, after having accepted as a "fact" the central issue which must be resolved in order to determine whether application of the rule is proper. Such a procedure makes a mockery of the idea behind strict liability, i.e., that it inheres only in situations where a defective product has been provided by a seller "engaged in the business of selling such a product."

In Musser v. Vilsmeier Auction Co., 562 A.2d 279 (Pa. 1989), this Court observed that "the broadened concept of 'supplier,' for purposes of predicating strict liability, is not without practical limits. The limits obtain in the purposes of the policy. When those purposes will not be served, persons whose implication in supplying products is tangential to that undertaking will not be subjected to strict liability for the harms caused by defects in those products." *Id.* at 281. The policy behind strict liability is "to insure that the costs of injuries resulting from defective products are borne by the manufacturers who put such products on the market rather than by the injured persons who are powerless to help themselves" [ ], and to further insure that defective products are removed from the market.

In this instance, the manufacturer is in bankruptcy, and unable to sustain liability. Thus, an alternative, and solvent, payor was sought. All other considerations were subordinated to this objective, hence the unequivocal necessity, in appellants' view, for appellees to be designated as sellers irrespective of the actual facts of this matter. However, to ignore the ancillary nature of the association of product with activity is to posit surgery, or indeed any medical service requiring the use of a physical object, as a marketing device for the incorporated object. This is tantamount to deciding that the surgical skills necessary for the implantation of, e.g., mandibular prostheses, are an adjunct to the sale of the implants. Moreover, under such a theory, no product of which a patient in any medical setting is the ultimate consumer, from CT scanners to cotton balls, could escape the assignment of strict liability. Clearly, the relationship of hospital and/or doctor to patients is not dictated by the distribution of such products, even if there is some surcharge on the price of the product.

The thrust of the inquiry is thus not on whether a separate consideration is charged for the physical material used in the exercise of medical skill, but what service is performed to restore or maintain the patient's health. The determinative question becomes not what is being charged, but what is being done [citing cases from other jurisdictions in which strict liability was not applied to hospital for failure of hip prosthesis; to hospital which supplied epidural kit containing defective needle; to hospital for defective pacemaker; and to dentist whose drill broke during use on patient].

The cases cited above have been labelled by some the exponents of a "service exception" to 402A. However, the very term "service exception" is misleading, since it presupposes that the distinction drawn where medical personnel/hospitals are involved is an artificial one. The cases, however, make clear that provision of medical services is regarded as qualitatively different from the sale of products, and, rather than being an exception to 402A, is unaffected by it.

This distinction is made clearer by the fact that case law also supports the application of 402A where what has been provided is not medical service or products connected with diagnosis and treatment, but rather materials related to mechanical or administrative functions [citing cases in which court held that hospital strictly liable where hospital gown ignited when lighted match fell on it; hospital would be found liable where not engaged in activities integrally related to primary function of providing medical services, e.g., defective product sold in gift shop].

In this connection, it must be noted that the "seller" need not be engaged solely in the business of selling products such as the defective one to be held strictly liable. An example supporting this proposition appears in comment f of the *Restatement (Second) of Torts* §402A and concerns the owner of a motion picture theater who offers edibles such as popcorn and candy for sale to movie patrons. The analogue to the instant case is valid in one respect only: both the candy and the TMJ implant are ancillary to the primary activity, viewing a film or undergoing surgery respectively. However, beyond that any comparison is specious. A movie audience is free to purchase or not any food items on offer, and regardless of which option is exercised the primary activity is unaffected. On the other hand, while the implant was incidental to the surgical procedure here, it was a necessary adjunct to the treatment administered, as were the scalpel used to make the incision, and any other material objects involved in performing the operation, all of which fulfill a particular role in provision of medical service,

III. The Sale of a "Product"

the primary activity. Once the illness became evident, treatment of some kind became a matter of necessity to regain health.

We find, consistent with the decisions cited above which distinguish medical services from merchandising, that in the first instance, appellees are not sellers, providers, suppliers or distributors of products such as to activate 402A.

Then, even assuming that providers of medical services could reasonably be termed sellers, in examining the test relied upon by appellants to "prove" their major premise, the policy reasons for strict liability are not present.

The test was posited by this Court in Francioni v. Gibsonia Truck Corp., 372 A.2d 736 (Pa. 1977), to determine whether a particular supplier of products, whose status as a supplier is already determined, is to be held liable for damages caused by defects in the products supplied. It was first concluded that a lessor of hauling equipment could properly be considered a supplier after the application of a four part inquiry, which focuses initially on which members of the marketing chain are available for redress; then asks whether imposition of liability would serve as an incentive to safety; whether the supplier is in a better position than the consumer to prevent the circulation of defective products; and, finally, whether the supplier can distribute the cost of compensation for injuries by charging for it in his business.

Appellants, ignoring the precondition necessary for application of this analysis, that is, establishment of the appellees as sellers, would nevertheless apply it. Even were we to do so, appellees would not be found liable.

First, as to the availability of some entity for redress, medical personnel and hospitals are already subject to liability, albeit only where the quality or quantity of the services they provide may be called into question. It is perfectly reasonable to assume, for example, that a physician or hospital possesses the necessary skill and expertise to select a product for use in medical treatment which is fit for its intended purpose. An error of choice might indeed be attributed to negligence or ignorance. However, no allegation has been made that the selection of the Vitek TMJ was made either carelessly or intentionally despite knowledge of its defects. To assign liability for no reason other than the ability to pay damages is inconsistent with our jurisprudence. Where the liability is sought to be imposed on a party which is not a seller under 402A, such liability would indeed be assigned for no reason at all.

Next comes the matter of whether applying strict liability would provide an incentive to safety. As the Superior Court correctly pointed out, the safety of the product depends on the judgment of those connected to the research, development, manufacture, marketing and sale of the product. Moreover, the safety testing and licensing for use of medical devices is a responsibility specifically undertaken by the federal government. Therefore, imposing liability for a poorly designed or manufactured product on the hospitals and doctors who use them on the assurances of the FDA is highly unlikely to effect changes of this sort. Again, selection of the wrong product becomes a matter of professional negligence for which recovery is available.

As to the related matter of restricting circulation of defective products, appellees and those similarly situated have no control over distribution. In Musser v. Vilsmeier Auction Co., 562 A.2d 279 (Pa. 1989), this Court noted that the "[control] factor implies the existence of some ongoing relationship with the manufacturer from which some financial advantage inures to the benefit of the latter and which confers some degree of influence on the [putative seller]." *Id.* at 282.

The influence described is that of the putative seller, i.e., doctor/hospital, on the manufacturing process. *Id.* However, in finding the relationship between auctioneer and product too tenuous to justify assignment of liability, the *Musser* Court notes that the catalogue of items for sale listed more than ninety different tractors, for each of which the auctioneer would have to be held strictly liable were 402A applied in the auction context. The list is easily comparable to the many items employed in surgery, which includes but is not limited to surgical instruments, medical devices such as the implant, anesthesia machine and accoutrements, drugs, bandages and dressings, surgical apparel and operating suite furniture, such as the table on which the procedure is performed.

The implications of the ruling espoused by appellants extend far beyond responsibility for a defective TMJ, and thus bring into sharp relief the problems surrounding any notion that it is enumerated products which should be exempted from the application of 402A. The difficulties inherent in such a course are obvious; particularly in medicine, the changes in technology are such that even definitional problems may arise. As an example, for purposes of 402A, is gene therapy a drug, and thus exempt under comment k, or a device or something else altogether? Who is to determine such exemptions, and at what time intervals?

The fourth question posed is whether the supplier of the product can distribute the cost of compensating for injuries resulting from defects by spreading the charges therefor. The Superior Court, in addressing this element in conjunction with redress for potential plaintiffs, notes that the only considerations for extending strict liability, ability to pay plaintiffs and ability to charge others, would result in absolute rather than strict liability, and further observed that relying on cost factors alone without a logical basis would confine the focus of the 402A principle to the search for a deep pocket. The net effect of this cost spreading would further endanger the already beleaguered health care system. As a practical matter costs would merely be absorbed by the insurers of physicians and hospitals, whose charges would reflect the increase in policy rates without corresponding improvement to any aspect of the health care system. Rather, research and innovation in medical equipment and treatment would be inhibited. The Supreme Court of Wisconsin in Hoven v. Kelble, 256 N.W.2d 379 (Wis. 1977), has observed, albeit in a slightly different context, that on balance, the peculiar characteristics of medical services outweigh any of the reasons which might exist to assign strict liability in the medical setting. These include the tendency to be experimental, which would certainly be adversely affected if 402A were applicable; a dependence on factors beyond the control of the professional; and a lack of certainty or assurance of the desired result. *Id.* at 390-393. In short, medical services are distinguished by factors which make them significantly different in kind from the retail marketing enterprise at which 402A is directed.

Finally,

> [B]efore a change in the law is made, a court, if it is to act responsibly must be able to see with reasonable clarity the results of its decision and to say with reasonable certainty that the change will serve the best interests of society.

Id. at 391.

III. The Sale of a "Product"

The consequences of a step such as appellant would have us take are of such magnitude, and of such potentially negative effect as to require more examination than has yet been afforded this issue. It is, for example, not clear enough that strict liability has afforded the hoped for panacea in the conventional products area that it should be extended so cavalierly in cases such as the present one.

For these reasons, the order of the Superior Court is affirmed.

CAPPY, J., *dissenting*. I am deeply troubled by the majority's opinion and therefore must respectfully dissent. In analyzing the *Francioni* test, the majority has presented a muddled view of the test's purpose and an imperfect application of the test's prongs.

The first prong of *Francioni* requires this Court to examine whether the defendant is in the marketing chain of the product. The majority, ostensibly applying this test, concludes that the defendants are not amenable to strict liability because "medical personnel and hospitals are already subject to liability, albeit only where the quality or quantity of the services they provide may be called into question." This answer is a non-sequitur; the majority has sidestepped, rather than answered, the pertinent query of whether doctors and hospitals are in the marketing chain of this prosthesis. Furthermore, the majority's new version of the first *Francioni* prong is no improvement on the old test. This new test will not advance our analysis as to whether a certain defendant is amenable to strict liability, but instead will thwart it. The majority's test will exclude from strict liability those defendants which may be amenable to causes of action other than strict liability; it seems not to matter to the majority whether the plaintiff in the case before the court actually has that "other" cause of action available to it. I find this "test" perplexing for I can think of no entity which would not be excluded under the test fashioned by the majority. Thus, what purpose would this new "test" serve other than to eradicate strict liability?

Second, the majority also distorts the *Francioni* prong which directs the Court to ascertain whether this defendant is in a better position than the consumer to prevent the circulation of defective products. The majority commences its analysis of this point by recognizing that the focus of this inquiry is on whether there is "some ongoing relationship with the manufacturer from which some financial advantage inures to the benefit of the latter and which confers some degree of influence on the [putative seller]." Musser v. Vilsmeier Auction Co., 562 A.2d 279, 282 (Pa. 1989). The majority, however, rapidly loses sight of its objective. It deduces that since the defendants here have an extensive list of products at their disposal, as did the defendant in *Musser*, then the defendants here should also be held immune from strict liability as was the defendant in *Musser*. This distortion of *Musser* could have frighteningly far-reaching implications. Such reasoning would lead to the absurd result that a department store, with an inventory of tens of thousands of items, would be less likely to be held strictly liable than the local, family-run convenience store with its modest inventory. Such a "test" does not advance the goals of strict liability, but rather perverts them.

I am gravely concerned that the majority's opinion will have an unwanted and adverse impact on our strict liability law. In an effort to reach its result in the area of medical services, the majority has failed to advance with caution. I agree with the majority that this area deserves "more examination than has yet been afforded this issue." Unfortunately, such an examination has not been presented and I am, therefore, compelled to dissent.

NOTES AND QUESTIONS

1. *Rationales for distinguishing products from services.* One who provides a service is still subject to negligence liability. Why not instead apply strict liability to the provision of services?

> To explain their refusal to apply implied warranties to service contracts, some courts have focused on the fact that warranties that relate to the promisor's conduct or to the quality of the service are identical to a negligence standard. Where the plaintiff has sought an implied warranty of results, rather than conduct, courts have simply held that implied warranties are inapplicable outside the context of transactions in goods. Courts have also contended that it is inappropriate to impose implied warranties on service providers because services frequently are not susceptible to the level of definition and certainty that characterizes goods.

Ellen Taylor, *Applicability of Strict Liability Warranty Theories to Service Transactions*, 47 S.C. L. Rev. 231, 269 (1996) (arguing that courts should recognize an implied warranty when "the goal of the contractual relationship is capable of enough specification and definition").

If strict liability does not apply to services only because they "are not susceptible to the level of definition and certainty that characterizes goods," why wouldn't strict liability always apply to transactions involving the provision of a service and the sale of a product when liability is based on a defect in the product—a source of liability "capable of enough specification and definition"?

2. *Nature of the inquiry.* "In sales-service hybrid cases, most courts search for the 'essence' of the transaction to ascertain whether the sale or service aspect dominates. If the transaction predominantly involves a product sale, then strict liability principles are appropriate; if service aspects dominate the transaction, then negligence alone should be applied." David G. Owen & Mary J. Davis, 2 OWEN & DAVIS ON PRODUCTS LIABILITY §17:9 (4th ed. 2014 & 2020 update).

Is an inquiry into the "essence" of the transaction likely to produce clear guidance on whether a hybrid transaction involves the sale of a product or provision of a service? Consider the issue of whether a movie theater should be strictly liable for selling popcorn that was contaminated through no fault of its own.

> It is not necessary that a commercial seller or distributor be engaged exclusively or even primarily in selling or otherwise distributing the type of product that injured the plaintiff, so long as the sale of the product is other than occasional or casual. Thus, the rule applies to a motion-picture theater's routine sales of popcorn or ice cream, either for consumption on the premises or in packages to be taken home.

RESTATEMENT (THIRD) OF TORTS: PRODUCTS LIABILITY §1 cmt. c. Is the consumption of popcorn part of the essence of the movie-going experience for the ordinary consumer? Does the consumer's need for the product persuasively distinguish the sale of popcorn from the distribution of the

III. The Sale of a "Product"

medical implant in *Cafazzo?* Consider *id.* §20 cmt. f ("When products are made available as a convenience to customers who are on the defendant's premises primarily for different, although related purposes, and no separate charge is made, strict liability is not imposed. Thus, bowling alleys that supply bowling balls for customer use and markets that supply shopping carts are not subject to strict products liability for harm caused by defects in those items. Similarly, doctors who use medical devices while treating patients are not considered distributors of those products."). Can these varied rules be readily understood in relation to the "essence" of the transaction?

Is the problem adequately resolved by the following inquiry described by the *Restatement (Third)?*

> *Sales-service combinations.* When the same person provides both products and services in a commercial transaction, whether a product has been sold may be difficult to determine. When the product and service components are kept separate by the parties to the transaction, as when a lawn-care firm bills separately for fertilizer applied to a customer's lawn or when a machinery repairer replaces a component part and bills separately for it, the firm will be held to be the seller of the product. This is especially true when the parties to the transaction explicitly characterize the property aspect as a sale.
>
> When the parties do not clearly separate the product and service components, courts differ in their treatment of these so-called "sale-service hybrid transactions." These transactions tend to fall into two categories. In the first, the product component is consumed in the course of providing the service, as when a hair dye is used in treating a customer's hair in a salon. Even when the service provider does not charge the customer separately for the dye, the transaction ordinarily is treated as a sale of the material that is consumed in providing the service. When the product component in the sale-service transaction is not consumed or permanently transferred to the customer—as when defective scissors are used in the hair salon—the transaction ordinarily is treated as one not involving a sale of the product to the customer. But while the salon is not a seller, all commercial sellers in the chain of distribution of the scissors, from the manufacturer through the retailer who sold them to the salon, are clearly sellers of the scissors and are subject to liability to the salon customer under the rules of this Restatement. *It should be noted that, in a strong majority of jurisdictions, hospitals are held not to be sellers of products they supply in connection with the provision of medical care, regardless of the circumstances.*

RESTATEMENT (THIRD) OF TORTS: PRODUCTS LIABILITY §20 cmt. d (emphasis added).

The question remains: Why is a movie theater strictly liable for selling contaminated popcorn, unlike a health-care provider who sells a defective medical product?

3. *An exception for medical care?* According to the *Restatement (Third),* transactions in which a product is "consumed" are governed by strict products liability. *Id.* Medical products are "consumed" in the course of the transaction, yet "hospitals are held not to be sellers of products they supply in connection with the provision of medical care, regardless of the

circumstances." The rule extends to medical care in general: "courts have broadly refused to apply strict liability rules to doctors, dentists, hospitals, and other health care providers." 2 OWEN & DAVIS ON PRODUCTS LIABILITY, *supra*, §17:10. For some reason, transactions involving the provision of medical care are exempt from the ordinary rules that determine whether strict products liability governs the transaction.

As illustrated by *Cafazzo*, courts have had a hard time justifying this exemption. For example, some courts have concluded that health care deserves exceptional treatment because of the professional nature of the services rendered. *Compare* Magrine v. Krasnica, 227 A.2d 539, 543 (N.J. 1967) (holding that dentist was not subject to strict liability for treatment involving a defective syringe needle: "A dentist or physician offers, and is paid for, his professional services and skill. That is the essence of the relationship between him and his patient."), *with* Newmark v. Gimbel's Inc., 258 A.2d 697, 702-703 (N.J. 1969) (holding that defendant beautician was subject to strict liability for applying a defective permanent wave solution to plaintiff's hair: "The beautician is engaged in a commercial enterprise; the dentist and doctor in a profession."). This rationale has been sharply criticized for "embrac[ing] elitist distinctions based on . . . professional status . . . and, thereby, draw utterly contradictory conclusions regarding the significance of this status. Contradictions aside, professionalism has nothing to do with the central question to be answered here." Murphy v. E.R. Squibb & Sons, Inc., 710 P.2d 247, 258 (Cal. 1985) (Bird, C.J., dissenting). Other than "professional" status or the "essence" of the transaction, is there any other basis that courts could rely on to explain why health-care providers are exempt from strict liability?

4. *Policy analysis.* Many courts have recognized that the product/service inquiry requires a policy analysis to determine whether the transaction is appropriately governed by strict products liability. As illustrated by *Cafazzo*, policy analysis does not conclusively resolve the matter if there is disagreement about the policy rationales for strict products liability.

Recall that the policy rationales for exempting a product from strict liability are contained in the "unavoidably unsafe product" exemption afforded by comment k of the *Restatement (Second)* §402A rule of strict products liability. *See* Chapter 9. Based on this provision, many courts have concluded that pharmaceuticals and other medical products are "unavoidably unsafe" under comment k. This conclusion implies that the nonmanufacturing sellers of these "unavoidably unsafe" medical products are also exempt from strict liability. Would it be better if courts expressly invoked the "unavoidably unsafe" rationale instead of the product/service distinction to exempt these sellers from strict liability? Consider *Murphy*, 710 P.2d at 261 (Bird, C.J., dissenting) ("The opinions cited by the majority [in support of its holding that the sale of a prescription drug by a pharmacy involves the provision of a service] rely heavily on comment k to section 402A of the *Restatement Second of Torts*. Each interprets comment k as exempting prescription drugs from strict liability for design defects on the theory that all such drugs are unavoidably unsafe products which are useful to society.").

To be sure, the product/service distinction appears to be quite different from the issue of whether a product is "unavoidably unsafe" for purposes of comment k. As a substantive matter, however, the doctrines implicate the same set of policy reasons, making it possible to consider how each doctrine would resolve the issue in question.

In the context of medical care, the product/service distinction requires courts to adopt untenable distinctions as emphasized by the dissenting opinion in *Cafazzo*. For example, if the sale of a medical device involves a "service," why doesn't the sale of popcorn at a movie theater also involve a "service"? In each case, the "essence" of the transaction involves a service, so this express reason for exempting the medical product from strict liability ought to exempt the sale of popcorn from strict liability. Is the relevant difference that the seller in one case is a "professional" whereas a movie theater is just an ordinary commercial enterprise? Rather than draw untenable distinctions, courts can instead rely on the policy rationale for exempting "unavoidably unsafe" products from strict liability. As comment k establishes, a product should be exempt from strict liability if that form of liability could disrupt a market essential to public health and safety, producing a self-defeating safety outcome. *See* Chapter 9. This rationale clearly explains why health-care providers are exempt from strict liability, unlike movie theaters that sell popcorn. The comment k rationale would avoid the unfortunate precedential effects or policy implications that might otherwise be created by the opaque inquiry that courts employ to draw the product/service distinction. Compare *Newmark*, 258 A.2d at 702-703 (justifying the conclusion that a beautician is subject to strict products liability for having used a defective product while rendering a "non-professional" or "commercial" service, whereas doctors and dentists render "professional" services not subject to strict products liability because "the nature of the[se] services, the utility of and need for them, involving as they do, the health and even survival of many people, are so important to the general welfare as to outweigh in the policy scale any need for the imposition . . . of the rules of strict liability in tort").

IV. AUTONOMOUS VEHICLES AND PRODUCTS LIABILITY: PROBLEM SET 12

AV Problem 12.1

Most manufacturers of conventional motor vehicles (so-called original equipment manufacturers, or OEMs) are developing autonomous vehicles. Under one approach, an OEM partners with a different firm that has the software and technological expertise necessary for fully automating the vehicle. In 2016, for example, the Munich-based auto manufacturer BMW entered into an alliance with the U.S. chip manufacturer Intel and the Israeli software company Mobileye.

Suppose that this alliance is able to bring a fully autonomous vehicle to the market. Suppose also that the operating system is defective for one of the various reasons identified in earlier problem sets, and that the defect causes the vehicle to crash. Because the defect is embodied in the software supplied by Mobileye, some have questioned whether products liability would govern such a tort claim. In the event that the victims of the crash sued BMW, could BMW defend on the ground that the allegedly defective software is a "service" not subject to strict products liability?

Analysis of AV Problem 12.1

Arguably, Mobileye provided a "service" to BMW when it conveyed the software coding that comprises the operating system of the autonomous vehicle. BMW, however, incorporated that software into a tangible product—a motor vehicle. The software then determines how the tangible product performs, and so any defect in the software will be treated as a "product" for various reasons.

For example, electricity is intangible and so the transmission of electricity is treated as a "service" until it passes through the customer's meter. Once electricity has been distributed to the customer through the meter, however, it is subject to strict products liability. "Plaintiffs in the post-delivery cases typically complain of unexpected drops or surges in voltage, resulting in personal injury or property damage. Those claims seem better governed by principles of strict liability for physical deviations from intended design." RESTATEMENT (THIRD) OF TORTS: PRODUCTS LIABILITY §19 cmt. d. Like electricity, software is intangible (a series of instructions that generate electrical charges arranged in patterns). But once this intangible good becomes converted into a physical environment where a defect causes bodily injury or property damage—as with surges in electricity that damage electrical appliances—it is a "product" for purposes of tort liability.

Indeed, a defective operating system presents an easier case for products liability. Unlike surges of electricity that have a physical impact, the operating system of an autonomous vehicle actually controls the safety performance of a tangible product. Whether the operating system is defective, therefore, depends on how it affects the safety performance of a tangible product. The liability inquiry in these cases is no different from any other product case in which the allegation of defect requires the court to evaluate the safety performance of a tangible product. This explains why courts did not even consider the product/service distinction in the few cases in which defective software caused tangible products to perform in an unreasonably dangerous manner.

AV Problem 12.2

If the victims of the crash in the previous problem sued Mobileye rather than BMW, could Mobileye defend on the ground that its provision of software to BMW was merely a "service" not subject to strict products liability?

Analysis of AV Problem 12.2

Even if the transaction between Mobileye and BMW involves the provision of a "service," the question is whether Mobileye effectively provided a "product" to the users of the BMW vehicles driven by the Mobileye operating system. A component supplier's liability, like the liability of any commercial distributor, is limited by the requirement of foreseeability. Mobileye actually knew that the software would be used for this purpose, and it was foreseeable that a defect in the operating system would cause the motor vehicle to crash. The analysis at this point is no different from the one applicable to claims against BMW discussed in the prior problem. Consequently, Mobileye would be subject to strict products liability.

AV Problem 12.3

Suppose BMW incurred full liability for the injuries discussed in Problem 12.1 above. Could BMW get full indemnification for those liabilities from Mobileye?

Analysis of AV Problem 12.3

The transaction between Mobileye and BMW might involve the provision of a "service" for certain purposes, but the inquiry in the indemnity action tracks the inquiry in the underlying tort litigation. For purposes of those tort claims, Mobileye provided a "product" subject to strict products liability. Allowing BMW to be fully indemnified for the liabilities would further the policy rationale of strict products liability by shifting the full cost of injury to the party responsible for the defect, which in this instance is Mobileye. This dynamic is illustrated by the *Godoy v. Abamaster* case.

16

Bystander Liability

By focusing almost exclusively on the consumer—the purchaser or user of the product—our approach so far reflects the orientation of products liability. The consumerist orientation stems from the implied warranty, which is the primary rationale for strict products liability in the *Restatement (Second)*. *See* Chapter 2, section I. One who distributes a product in the market makes an implicit representation of product safety to the foreseeable users of the product. The product transaction does not create an implied representation of safety to someone who does not use the product—a bystander. Consequently, the *Restatement (Second)* "expresses no opinion" whether strict products liability applies "to harm to persons other than users or consumers." §402A, caveat (1).

I. THE EXTENSION OF STRICT PRODUCTS LIABILITY TO ENCOMPASS BYSTANDERS

GIBBERSON v. FORD MOTOR CO.
Supreme Court of Missouri, 1974
504 S.W.2d 8

MORGAN, J. Plaintiffs sued defendant to recover for damages allegedly suffered by them in an automobile accident on May 6, 1969, in the City of Springfield, Missouri. Liability of defendant was premised on the assertion that it had "manufactured and sold" an automobile with a "defective engine" which had exploded under "normal usage" and that such "tortious conduct" was the proximate cause of the accident in question. The trial court sustained defendant's motion to dismiss for failure to state a cause of action, and plaintiffs appealed. We reverse and remand.

Plaintiffs alleged in their petition that defendant had sold the city a certain automobile; that on the date mentioned it was being driven by a police officer in a line of traffic wherein plaintiff (husband) was driving; that the motor in the automobile sold by defendant exploded; that said explosion created a dense cloud of steam, smoke and gas which restricted visibility of other drivers to such an extent that a multiple automobile collision occurred.

The parties agree as to the existing law in this state reference the rule of strict liability in tort in the area of products liability, and they submit only one question, i.e., should the rule be made applicable to a bystander who was not a purchaser or user of the defective chattel?

In a case factually comparable to that here, the Supreme Court of California in Elmore v. American Motors Corporation, 70 Cal. 2d 578 (1969), first noted, that: "The authors of the restatement have refrained from expressing a view as to whether the doctrine of strict liability of the manufacturer and retailer for defects is applicable to third parties who are bystanders and who are not purchasers or users of the defective chattel. (*Restatement (Second) of Torts* §402A cmt. o)," and thereafter concluded . . . that:

> If anything, bystanders should be entitled to greater protection than the consumer or user where injury to bystanders from the defect is reasonably foreseeable. Consumers and users, at least, have the opportunity to inspect for defects and to limit their purchases to articles manufactured by reputable manufacturers and sold by reputable retailers, whereas the bystander ordinarily has no such opportunities. In short, the bystander is in greater need of protection from defective products which are dangerous, and if any distinction should be made between bystanders and users, it should be made, contrary to the position of defendants, to extend greater liability in favor of the bystanders.
>
> An automobile with a defectively connected drive shaft constitutes a substantial hazard on the highway not only to the driver and passenger of the car but also to pedestrians and other drivers. The public policy which protects the driver and passenger of the car should also protect the bystander, and where a driver or passenger of another car is injured due to defects in the manufacture of an automobile and without any fault of their own, they may recover from the manufacturer of the defective automobile.

The Court of Appeals of Arizona in Caruth v. Mariani, 463 P.2d 83 (1970), extended the rule to include a "bystander" and commented, that: "All states which have adopted the theory of strict tort liability have extended the theory to the bystander when called upon to do so." [ ]

More recently, the Supreme Court of Wisconsin brought the bystander within the protection of the rule, and observed that: "The prevailing reason for the extension has been the feeling that there is no essential difference between the injured user or consumer and the injured bystander. The reasons for the initial adoption of strict liability are uniformly felt to apply equally to the bystander. Some have gone much further by suggesting that because of his inability to 'kick the tires' the bystander is in need of more protection than the user or consumer." [ ]

From all of the authorities noted it is apparent that regardless of the different legal theories upon which different courts have extended protection to the bystander, the same underlying philosophy dictated the result in each, i.e., that one controlling the making and inspection of a product should be held responsible for damage caused by defects in that product. The logic of placing the burden on the one with the best opportunity of avoiding the distribution of a defective product cannot be questioned, and we find no legitimate legal barrier

I. The Extension of Strict Products Liability to Encompass Bystanders

to doing so. In fact, no additional burden is thereby placed on the maker of the product, for the reason that the same precautions required to protect the buyer or user would generally do the same for the bystander. Therefore, we extend any rights flowing from the "rule of strict liability in tort" . . . to include a bystander.

Of necessity, we do mention that the trial court cannot be charged with anticipating the conclusion reached herein.

The judgment is reversed and the cause is remanded for further proceedings consistent with this opinion.

NOTES AND QUESTIONS

Extending the liability rule from consumers to bystanders. Does the reasoning of the court in *Gibberson* show that for purposes of strict products liability, there is never any "essential difference between the injured . . . consumer and the injured bystander"? Consumers pay for product safety, unlike bystanders. Does that make a difference? To what extent does the court's conclusion depend on the assumption that "the same precautions required to protect the buyer or user would generally do the same for the bystander"?

HORST v. DEERE & CO.
Supreme Court of Wisconsin, 2009
769 N.W.2d 536

GABLEMAN, J. [T]he main question before us is whether Wisconsin has adopted or should adopt a "bystander contemplation test." We hold that the consumer contemplation test, and not a bystander contemplation test, governs all strict products liability claims in Wisconsin, including cases where a bystander is injured. While bystanders may recover when injured by an unreasonably dangerous product, the determination of whether the product is unreasonably dangerous is based on the expectations of the ordinary consumer.

The facts of this case are horrific. On the afternoon of May 2, 2004, the Horst family returned home from an overnight trip to Wisconsin Dells. Two-year-old Jonathan and his older brother went to play outside in the yard. Jonathan's mother, Kara, was planning to watch Jonathan as she hung laundry on an outdoor clothesline, but stopped to use the restroom first. Before Kara arrived outside, Jonathan's father Michael decided to mow the lawn using their John Deere LT160 riding lawn mower. As Michael began to cut the lawn, he decided to mow in reverse along the rear of the house, looking over his right shoulder. Jonathan, however, had moved behind the lawn mower to Michael's left, out of Michael's line of sight. As Michael proceeded backwards, he saw Jonathan's shoe come out the other side. Michael screamed, realizing that he had severed both of Jonathan's feet. Kara called 911, and Jonathan was flown to Children's Hospital. There he received multiple surgeries, and now wears prosthetics on both legs.

The John Deere LT160 mower Michael was using came equipped with a no-mow-in-reverse safety feature that stops both the engine and mower blades when an operator begins to travel in reverse while the mower blades are engaged. However, the lawn mower also had what amounts to an override feature, the Reverse Implement Option ("RIO"), which allows an operator to mow in reverse with the mower blades in operation.

To implement the RIO feature, an operator must depress the brake pedal and press the RIO switch. Once engaged, the RIO system allows an operator to mow in reverse without stalling either the engine or the mowing device. When reverse mowing is complete, the operator can continue to mow forward without shutting off the mowing device. When the operator begins mowing forward again, the lawn mower returns to its default position, which requires the operator to manually engage the RIO device again to mow in reverse.

Michael Horst engaged the RIO device twice before the accident in this case. He first engaged the RIO to mow toward the Horst home along his gravel driveway. He then moved forward along the back of the house. He engaged the RIO device again to mow in reverse along the back of the house. That is when Jonathan was injured.

The LT160 lawn mower operator's manual contained numerous warnings relating to mowing in reverse and mowing in the presence of children or bystanders. The parties agree that Michael read but disregarded these warnings, choosing to mow in reverse in the presence of his young children.

Following the accident, the Horsts filed a lawsuit against Deere & Company ("Deere") in Washington County Circuit Court, bringing negligence and strict products liability claims. On the strict products liability claim, the Horsts argued that designing a mower to operate in reverse is unreasonably dangerous and that the mower should have had an alternative design. The Horsts asserted that the lawn mower should not have been equipped with the RIO, thus preventing an operator from ever mowing in reverse. The Horsts also sought punitive damages, alleging that the design demonstrated a deliberate disregard for safety.

At trial, the Horsts requested that Wisconsin Jury Instruction-Civil 3260, which does not mention bystanders, be supplemented to reflect the availability of recovery for bystanders. They specifically proposed that the instruction include the phrase "or bystander" following most occurrences of "user" and "consumer" in the standard instruction. The circuit court denied the Horsts' proposed instructions, choosing to give the standard instructions supplemented with the following statement: "The law in Wisconsin imposes a duty on a manufacturer to a bystander, if the bystander is injured by a defective product, which is unreasonably dangerous to the ordinary user or consumer."

The jury ultimately found both Michael and Kara Horst, but not Deere, negligent in the injury to their son, Jonathan. The jury also found that the lawn mower in question was not in a defective condition so as to be unreasonably dangerous to a prospective user or consumer. Accordingly, Deere was not strictly liable for Jonathan's injuries. This case asks us to evaluate the sufficiency of the circuit court's jury instructions.

No one in the case at bar disputes that bystanders may recover if a product is unreasonably dangerous. The issue in this case is the proper legal standard for determining whether a product is unreasonably dangerous when a bystander is injured.

I. The Extension of Strict Products Liability to Encompass Bystanders

The Horsts argue that the jury instructions in this case, which asked whether the lawn mower was unreasonably dangerous based on the expectations of the ordinary user or consumer, were incorrect as a matter of law. They maintain that the law in Wisconsin is, or should be, what they call a "bystander contemplation test." The bystander contemplation test asks exactly the same question as the consumer contemplation test, but replaces the expectations of the user or consumer with the expectations of an ordinary bystander. Accordingly, the Horsts assert that "when a bystander is injured by a product, the question is whether the product was as reasonably safe as an ordinary bystander would contemplate or expect, not whether the user or consumer understood and appreciated the risk." Like the consumer contemplation test, the bystander contemplation test is an objective test and not dependent on an injured party's knowledge. The bystander contemplation test, according to the Horsts, applies when a bystander is injured and "where a manufacturer designs and sells a product that poses a unique risk of bodily harm to bystanders alone." They submit that the consumer contemplation test is still proper when a bystander is injured and when the danger is present for both the user or consumer and the bystander.

The Horsts further contend that the bystander contemplation test is not only the law, but that it is necessary to provide meaningful protection to bystanders. They argue that bystanders need greater protections than users and consumers because they have less information about the product, and less access to warnings and instructions.

No Wisconsin Supreme Court case directly answers the question before us. Our holding today clarifies the law related to the consumer contemplation test; it impinges on no precedent and does not require us to overturn or modify the holding of any prior cases. We reject the proposed bystander contemplation test and reiterate that the consumer contemplation test is the proper standard for all strict products liability cases.

At its root, the bystander contemplation test is inherently unworkable. While an ordinary consumer or user of a product can be said to have some objective expectations regarding a product, the same cannot be said of bystanders. The consumer contemplation test was developed in recognition of the fact that it is reasonable for users and consumers of products to hold certain expectations regarding the products they use and the products they buy. *See* Rebecca Korze, *Dashing Consumer Hopes: Strict Products Liability and the Demise of the Consumer Expectations Test*, 20 B.C. Int'l & Comp. L. Rev. 227, 232 (1997) ("[T]he consumer expectations test is the natural, logical outgrowth of strict products liability as the extension of implied warranty law."). Thus, the concept of an "ordinary consumer" has some reasonably objective content. But bystanders may have no familiarity with a product. This is especially so in complex design defect cases. What does a bystander expect of the technical design and reasonably available safety features of a product he or she does not buy, does not use, and may not even be aware of?

In addition, it is difficult, if not impossible, to discern who an "ordinary" bystander is and what they know. To illustrate, if a bystander is injured by a combine on a farm, is the "ordinary" bystander a neighboring farmer or a life-long urbanite who cannot tell you what a combine does? In short, the notion of an "ordinary bystander" is a concept without content.

The Horsts' suggested application of the bystander contemplation test is equally puzzling. They argue it applies only when the threat of injury is to a bystander alone. It is difficult to conceive of a situation where a product is dangerous to a bystander, yet poses no danger to a user or consumer. The Horsts say that is the case here, but surely there is some danger to the user of a riding lawn mower who is driving in reverse. Undoubtedly, the risk of danger is much lower than the danger of running over an unsuspecting child, but it does exist. This means that, under the Horsts' proposal, the bystander contemplation test would not be appropriate here, and may never be.

Additionally, a user or consumer's expectations regarding a product will often include safety expectations relating to bystanders. That is, users and consumers do not just have expectations regarding their own safety; they expect that a product will be reasonably safe for bystanders as well. Juries can certainly take this into account in their deliberations and evaluation of whether a product is unreasonably dangerous.

The Horsts also argue that our holding today impermissibly delegates the duty to make a product safe to the user or consumer. But this is begging the question; it assumes a product is unreasonably dangerous. If a product is not unreasonably dangerous (based on consumer expectations), the user or consumer has no duty to make the product safe for bystanders because, by definition, it is sufficiently safe for strict products liability purposes. Users and consumers simply have a duty to use the potentially, but not unreasonably dangerous product with the appropriate standard of care toward their fellow citizens, as they do in all of life.

This truly was a tragic injury, but we cannot simply invent legal theories to make the manufacturer pay for the injuries. This was a horrible accident caused by the negligent use of the lawn mower and negligent supervision of the boy by his parents. At the end of the day, as has been noted elsewhere in a case involving almost precisely the same legal claims, a lawn mower is a lawn mower—it is dangerous, and accidents happen. [ ] A bystander contemplation test is a creative, but ultimately unsupported, unwise, and unfair attempt to create liability where none exists.

The decision of the court of appeals is affirmed.

NOTES AND QUESTIONS

1. *Consumer expectations and bystander interests.* According to the court in *Horst*, "a user or consumer's expectations regarding a product will often include safety expectations relating to bystanders. That is, users and consumers do not just have expectations regarding their own safety; they expect that a product will be reasonably safe for bystanders as well." Was this statement true in the case at hand? Is there anything particular about those facts that might not generalize to other cases?

First consider the concept of the consumer.

> *User or consumer.* In order for the rule stated in this Section to apply, it is not necessary that the ultimate user or consumer have acquired the product directly from the seller, although the rule applies equally

if he does so. He may have acquired it through one or more intermediate dealers. It is not even necessary that the consumer have purchased the product at all. He may be a member of the family of the final purchaser, or his employee, or a guest at his table, or a mere donee from the purchaser. The liability stated is one in tort, and does not require any contractual relation, or privity of contract, between the plaintiff and the defendant.

RESTATEMENT (SECOND) OF TORTS §402A cmt. l.

Why does the rule of strict products liability formulate consumer expectations in terms of the interests of both the purchaser and users of the product? The purchaser pays for the safety precautions and guarantees of injury compensation via the associated price increases. One who buys a product frequently contemplates that it will be used by others, typically family members or friends. In making the purchase decision, the buyer presumably gives equal consideration to the welfare of these other users. The interests of these parties coincide, making it defensible to conceptualize the consumer as including both the buyer and any reasonably foreseeable user of the product.

The same reasoning applies to products that are purchased by employers for use by employees. In a well-functioning labor market, the employer must compensate the employee for any job-related risks. Rather than paying the employee a higher wage to face a particular risk, the employer could instead pay for a safety precaution that eliminates the risk. The employer's decision accordingly involves a comparison of the cost posed by the risk with the cost of the safety precaution that would eliminate the risk, the same comparison made by the product purchaser.

The definition of the "consumer," therefore, implies that the consumer expectations test can be defined in terms of the full range of interests that would influence the safety decisions of the ordinary purchaser. The purchaser would be concerned about any product risk that threatens injury to friends or family members, regardless of whether they are using the product. Hence the consumer expectations test could justify a finding of defective design in a case like *Horst* that involves an injury suffered by a family member who was merely a bystander not using the product.

Is this formulation of consumer expectations adequately conveyed by the jury instructions in *Horst*, which defined "a defective product" as one that is "unreasonably dangerous to the ordinary user or consumer"? *See Horst*, 769 N.W.2d at 561-564 (Walsh Bradley, J., dissenting for this reason).

2. *The duty to warn, the protection of bystanders, and human rights violations in global supply chains.* As *Horst* illustrates, warnings about safe product use can protect bystanders rather than consumers. If the warning is inadequate in this respect and the bystander is injured, the bystander can recover for the defective warning. Due to this attribute of the duty to warn, products liability has the potential to ameliorate the troubling problem of human-rights violations in global supply chains.

Many consumers in developed countries have a lower willingness-to-pay for products produced by global supply chains that systemically subject foreign workers to egregiously dangerous working conditions in gross violation of their human rights. This attribute of consumer demand provides a basis for subjecting the supply "chain leader"—the manufacturer or commercial seller of the finished product—to domestic tort liability for the bodily injuries suffered by these foreign workers. Chain leaders, like other product sellers, are obligated to warn about foreseeable safety risks that are not known by consumers and would be material to their decision whether to purchase or use a product. The tort duty also requires sellers to instruct consumers about the ways in which the purchase or use of the product might foreseeably harm third parties. A domestic seller that is the chain leader of a global supply chain would breach this duty by not warning domestic consumers that the product is produced by foreign workers who are systemically subjected to working conditions that are so unsafe as to amount to a gross violation of their human rights. Because the purchase of the product foreseeably exposes foreign workers to this ongoing risk of physical harm, they are protected by the tort duty and can recover for its breach. *See* Mark A. Geistfeld, *The Law and Economics of Tort Liability for Human Rights Violations in Global Supply Chains*, 10 J. Eur. Tort L. 130 (2019).

3. *An impermissible delegation of the duty to consumers?* In purchasing or using products, consumers can altruistically consider the interests of others, such as foreign workers in global supply chains. Indeed, consumers regularly account for the interests of bystanders such as family and friends. Consumers will also indirectly account for the interests of total strangers when the defect threatens injury to both the consumer and bystanders, as in *Gibberson*. According to the court in *Horst*, "It is difficult to conceive of a situation where a product is dangerous to a bystander, yet poses no danger to a user or consumer." If such a situation were to exist and consumers did not otherwise altruistically consider bystanders, would the consumer expectations test impermissibly delegate the safety decision to the consumer, resulting in a product that is reasonably safe for the consumer but unreasonably dangerous for bystanders?

II. CONFLICTS BETWEEN CONSUMERS AND BYSTANDERS

GAINES-TABB v. ICI EXPLOSIVES, USA, INC.
United States Court of Appeals, Tenth Circuit, 1998
160 F.3d 613

EBEL, J. Individuals injured by the April 19, 1995, bombing of the Alfred P. Murrah Federal Building ("Murrah Building") in Oklahoma City, Oklahoma, filed suit against the manufacturers of the ammonium nitrate allegedly used to create the bomb. The plaintiffs' complaint set forth [different theories of liability including] theories of manufacturers' products liability. The district court dismissed the complaint for failure to state a claim upon which relief may be granted, and the plaintiffs appealed. We affirm.

On April 19, 1995, a massive bomb exploded in Oklahoma City and destroyed the Murrah Building, causing the deaths of 168 people and injuries to hundreds

II. Conflicts Between Consumers and Bystanders

of others. On May 10, 1995, plaintiffs filed this diversity action, on behalf of themselves and all persons who incurred personal injuries during, or may claim loss of consortium or wrongful death resulting from, the bombing, against ICI Explosives ("ICI"), ICI's parent company, Imperial Chemical Industries, PLC, and another of Imperial Chemical's subsidiaries, ICI Canada.

ICI manufactures ammonium nitrate ("AN"). Plaintiffs allege that AN can be either "explosive grade" or "fertilizer grade." According to plaintiffs, "explosive-grade" AN is of low density and high porosity so it will absorb sufficient amounts of fuel or diesel oil to allow detonation of the AN, while "fertilizer-grade" AN is of high density and low porosity and so is unable to absorb sufficient amounts of fuel or diesel oil to allow detonation.

Plaintiffs allege that ICI sold explosive-grade AN mislabeled as fertilizer-grade AN to Farmland Industries, who in turn sold it to Mid-Kansas Cooperative Association in McPherson, Kansas. Plaintiffs submit that a "Mike Havens" purchased a total of eighty 50-pound bags of the mislabeled AN from Mid-Kansas. According to plaintiffs, "Mike Havens" was an alias used either by Timothy McVeigh or Terry Nichols, the two men tried for the bombing. Plaintiffs further allege that the perpetrators of the Oklahoma City bombing used the 4000 pounds of explosive-grade AN purchased from Mid-Kansas, mixed with fuel oil or diesel oil, to demolish the Murrah Building.

Plaintiffs assert that ICI is strictly liable for manufacturing a defective product. We read their complaint as alleging both that the AN was defectively designed because, as designed, it was more likely to provide explosive force than an alternative formula, and that ICI failed to issue adequate warnings to Mid-Kansas that the AN was explosive grade rather than fertilizer grade so that Mid-Kansas could take appropriate precautions in selling the AN.

As the basis of their defective design claim plaintiffs contend that ICI could have made the AN safer by using an alternate formulation or incorporating additives to prevent the AN from detonating. Plaintiffs' suggestion that the availability of alternative formulas renders ICI strictly liable for its product contradicts Oklahoma law. "Apparently, the plaintiff would hold the manufacturer responsible if his product is not as safe as some other product on the market. That is not the test in these cases. Only when a defect in the product renders it less safe than expected by the ordinary consumer will the manufacturer be held responsible."[ ]; *see also* Woods v. Fruehauf Trailer Corp., 765 P.2d 770, 775 (Okla. 1988) ("[T]he evidence that the tank could have been made 'safer' does not establish that it was less safe than would be expected by the ordinary consumer."). The "ordinary consumer" is "one who would be foreseeably expected to purchase the product involved." *Woods*, 765 P.2d at 774. As plaintiffs acknowledge, the ordinary consumer of AN branded as fertilizer is a farmer.[10] There is no indication that ICI's AN was less safe than would be expected by a farmer. *See* Duane v. Oklahoma Gas & Elec. Co., 833 P.2d 284, 286 (Okla. 1992) ("A product is not defective when it is safe for normal handling and consumption. . . .").

Similarly, plaintiffs have failed to state a claim regarding ICI's alleged failure to warn Mid-Kansas that the AN was explosive grade rather than fertilizer grade.

---

10. We recognize that Oklahoma has indicated that manufacturers' products liability principles extend to protect bystanders. The bystander plaintiff, however, must still prove that the product was less safe than expected by an "ordinary consumer" of the product. [ ]

Interpreting Oklahoma law, this court has held that the duty to warn extends only to "ordinary consumers and users of the products." [ ] Under this rationale, defendants had no duty to warn the suppliers of its product of possible criminal misuse. *See* Port Authority of N.Y. and N.J. v. Arcadian Corp., 991 F. Supp. 390, 408-410 (D.N.J. 1997) (under New York and New Jersey law, manufacturers of ammonium nitrate had no duty to warn distributors, retailers, dealers, or other suppliers of possibility that product could be criminally misused).

We AFFIRM the dismissal of plaintiffs' complaint for failure to state a claim upon which relief may be granted.

NOTES AND QUESTIONS

1. *The inherent limitation of the implied warranty rationale for strict products liability.* In an analogous case involving the 1993 bombing of the World Trade Center, plaintiffs claimed that the same type of fertilizer at issue in *Gaines-Tabb* was defective because defendants failed to use an alternative formulation of the fertilizer that would "deter the criminal use of ammonium nitrate fertilizer in bombs" and "could be accomplished at nominal cost." Port Authority of N.Y. and N.J. v. Arcadian Corp., 991 F. Supp. 390, 397 (D.N.J. 1997). If the explosive qualities of the fertilizer could be eliminated at nominal cost, why wouldn't manufacturers adopt that design change? Would the ordinary consumer of the fertilizer—a farmer—significantly benefit from the reduced risk? If not, would the ordinary consumer be willing to pay the "nominal cost" for the enhancement of product safety?

To be sure, the court in both cases concluded that the risk was unforeseeable. *See id.* at 401 (finding, "as a matter of law, that the World Trade Center bombing was not reasonably or objectively foreseeable"); *Gaines-Tabb*, 160 F.3d at 621 ("[W]e hold that as a matter of law it was not foreseeable to defendants that the AN that they distributed to the Mid-Kansas Co-op would be put to such a use as to blow up the Murrah Building."). Unfortunately, the use of fertilizer for this purpose has become more common. For example, "Taliban fighters in southern Afghanistan . . . use homemade explosives fashioned from ammonium nitrate fertilizers," leading the Afghan government to ban "the use, production, storage or sale of ammonium nitrate." Yochi J. Dreazen, *Afghan Bombs Grow, Forcing Troops to Adapt*, Wall St. J., Mar. 20-21, 2010, at A9. But even if the risk of bombing today is foreseeable and could be eliminated by reformulating the fertilizer at nominal cost, the design would still not be defective under the consumer expectations test for the reasons given by the court in *Gaines-Tabb*.

As these cases illustrate, the interests of concern to the purchaser of a product do not always adequately account for the interests of total strangers. A product can be reasonably safe with respect to consumer interests while being unreasonably dangerous for strangers.

2. *The negligence rationale for the risk-utility test.* Because the implied warranty exclusively focuses on consumer expectations, it might not adequately protect bystanders. In these cases, the negligence-based risk-utility test in the *Restatement (Third)* correctly specifies the liability inquiry for

allegations of defective designs or warnings. Its negligence-based risk-utility test encompasses "foreseeable risks of harm" not limited to consumers. RESTATEMENT (THIRD) OF TORTS: PRODUCTS LIABILITY §§2(b)-(c). Due to this extension of the duty, the negligence-based risk-utility test is not wholly defined in terms of consumer interests, and so "consumer expectations do not define an independent standard for judging the defectiveness of product designs." *Id.* cmt. g. Although this formulation of the liability rule can be problematic for cases involving consumers, the *Restatement (Third)* provides the appropriate framework for cases involving bystanders.

By not drawing any distinction between consumers and bystanders, the *Restatement (Third)* remedies the type of problem illustrated by *Gaines-Tabb*. As compared to the implied warranty, the *Restatement (Third)* undoubtedly "takes a more progressive view, and far more realistic approach" for resolving design-defect claims involving bystanders. Berrier v. Simplicity Mfg., Inc., 563 F.3d 38, 54 (3d Cir. 2009). Reasoning that these cases "underscore and highlight the deficiencies" of the consumer expectations test, some have also argued that this limitation merits "redress" by a wholesale rejection of strict products liability in favor of the liability rules in the *Restatement (Third)*. Horst v. Deere & Co., 769 N.W.2d 536, 559-560 (Wis. 2009) (Gabelman, J., dissenting). But by rejecting the more narrowly defined consumer expectations test based on the implied warranty, has the *Restatement (Third)* adopted an overly general negligence-based approach that does not adequately distinguish between consumers and bystanders in other contexts?

MCCARTHY v. OLIN CORP.
United States Court of Appeals, Second Circuit, 1997
119 F.3d 148

MESKILL, J. On December 7, 1993, Colin Ferguson boarded the Long Island Railroad's 5:33 P.M. commuter train departing from New York City and opened fire on the passengers. Six people, including Dennis McCarthy, were killed and nineteen others, including Kevin McCarthy and Maryanne Phillips, were wounded in the vicious attack. Ferguson was armed with a 9mm semiautomatic handgun, which was loaded with Winchester "Black Talon" bullets (Black Talons). The injuries to Dennis and Kevin McCarthy and Maryanne Phillips were enhanced by the ripping and tearing action of the Black Talons because, unfortunately, the bullets performed as designed.

The Black Talon is a hollowpoint bullet designed to bend upon impact into six ninety-degree angle razor-sharp petals or "talons" that increase the wounding power of the bullet by stretching, cutting and tearing tissue and bone as it travels through the victim. The Black Talon bullet was designed and manufactured by Olin Corporation (Olin) through its Winchester division and went on the market in 1992. Although the bullet was originally developed for law enforcement agencies, it was marketed and available to the general public. In November 1993, following public outcry, Olin pulled the Black Talon from the public market and restricted its sales to law enforcement personnel. Colin

Ferguson allegedly purchased the ammunition in 1993, before it was withdrawn from the market.

Plaintiffs brought this action against Olin, Sturm, Ruger & Company Inc., the manufacturer of the handgun used by Ferguson, and Ram-Line Inc., the manufacturer of the fifteen round capacity magazine used with the handgun, in New York State Supreme Court to recover for the injuries of Kevin McCarthy and Maryanne Phillips and the death of Dennis McCarthy. The complaint was based on various theories of negligence and strict liability. The action was subsequently discontinued with prejudice against Sturm, Ruger and Ram-Line.

Olin moved to dismiss the complaint for failure to state a claim upon which relief can be granted. The district court granted the motion.

Plaintiffs appeal the dismissal of their complaint, claiming that the issue of whether they will ultimately prevail is a matter to be determined on a factual basis and not merely on the pleadings. In the alternative, plaintiffs request that because the complaint is based on novel theories of liability under New York law, we certify the questions raised in this case to the New York Court of Appeals.

Although the New York Court of Appeals has not addressed the issue of ammunition manufacturer liability, existing precedents in New York law provide us with sufficient guidance to analyze the district court's dismissal of this case. Therefore, we decline to certify any questions of law to New York's highest court. We will now address the merits of plaintiffs' appeal.

Appellants' first argument is that Olin should be held strictly liable for their injuries because the Black Talon ammunition was defectively designed and the design and manufacture of the bullets were inherently dangerous.

A manufacturer who places into the stream of commerce a defective product which causes injury may be held strictly liable. Appellants argue that the Black Talons were defectively designed because the expansion mechanism of the bullets, which causes ripping and tearing in its victims, results in enhanced injuries beyond ordinary bullets. The district court rejected this argument because the expanding of the bullet was an intentional and functional element of the design of the product. We agree.

To state a cause of action for a design defect, plaintiffs must allege that the bullet was unreasonably dangerous for its intended use. "[A] defectively designed product is one which, at the time it leaves the seller's hands, is in a condition not reasonably contemplated by the ultimate consumer." [ ] "This rule, however, is tempered by the realization that some products, for example knives, must by their very nature be dangerous in order to be functional." [ ] The very purpose of the Black Talon bullet is to kill or cause severe wounding. Here, plaintiffs concede that the Black Talons performed precisely as intended by the manufacturer and Colin Ferguson.

"As a matter of law, a product's defect is related to its condition, not its intrinsic function." [ ] The bullets were not in defective condition nor were they unreasonably dangerous for their intended use because the Black Talons were purposely designed to expand on impact and cause severe wounding.

Appellants next argue that under the risk/utility test analysis applied by New York courts, appellee should be held strictly liable because the risk of harm posed by the Black Talons outweighs the ammunition's utility. The district court properly held that the risk/utility test is inapplicable. "There must be 'something wrong' with a product before the risk/utility analysis may be applied in determining whether the product is unreasonably dangerous or defective." [ ]

II. Conflicts Between Consumers and Bystanders

The purpose of risk/utility analysis is to determine whether the risk of injury might have been reduced or avoided if the manufacturer had used a feasible alternative design. However, the risk of injury to be balanced with the utility is a risk not intended as the primary function of the product. Here, the primary function of the Black Talon bullets was to kill or cause serious injury. There is no reason to search for an alternative safer design where the product's sole utility is to kill and maim. Accordingly, we hold that appellants have failed to state a cause of action under New York strict products liability law.

Appellants also argue that Olin should be held strictly liable because the Black Talon ammunition is "unreasonably dangerous per se." According to the appellants' theory, a product is unreasonably dangerous per se if a reasonable person would conclude that the danger of the product, whether foreseeable or not, outweighs its utility. As the district court held, this is essentially a risk/utility analysis, which we have refused to apply. Under New York's strict products liability jurisprudence, there is no cause of action for an unreasonably dangerous per se product. Thus, this claim was properly dismissed.

On appeal, appellants do not appear to pursue their negligent manufacturing claim but rather focus their argument on Olin's negligent marketing of the ammunition. New York courts do not impose a legal duty on manufacturers to control the distribution of potentially dangerous products such as ammunition. Accordingly, although it may have been foreseeable by Olin that criminal misuse of the Black Talon bullets could occur, Olin is not legally liable for such misuse. To impose a duty on ammunition manufacturers to protect against criminal misuse of its product would likely force ammunition products—which legislatures have not proscribed, and which concededly are not defectively designed or manufactured and have some socially valuable uses—off the market due to the threat of limitless liability. Because Olin did not owe a legal duty to plaintiffs to protect against Colin Ferguson's horrible action, appellants' complaint does not state a cause of action for negligence and the claim was properly dismissed.

Accordingly, we affirm the judgment of the district court.

CALABRESI, J., *dissenting.* In cases that are dramatic and involve "hot" issues, there is a tendency for the parties to describe themselves as raising new issues that are remarkable in their legal context. But in fact, such cases are usually best looked at in the most traditional of ways. Courts must see how these cases fit into old categories before considering whether it is either necessary or proper to expand those old categories or to create new ones. And so it is with the case before us.

The requirements for strict products liability in New York are not markedly dissimilar from those for negligent products liability: (a) a duty is needed; (b) that duty must be breached by the defendant's manufacture or sale of a defective product; (c) the plaintiff must suffer an injury; and (d) the defect must be the cause of the plaintiff's injury.[25] The primary difference between the two causes of action is that a plaintiff may recover in strict products liability

---

25. These are not the elements of a cause of action in strict products liability. Those elements are much more specific, and depend on the theory of liability being asserted. Rather, these are the basic requirements for any cause of action in tort for products liability, regardless of the particular theory of recovery.

without showing that the defendant's conduct was wrongful, so long as its product was defective.

There is no doubt that, in order for strict products liability to apply, there must be a defect, *i.e.* "something wrong with the product, and if nothing is wrong there will be no liability." [ ] But a large number of jurisdictions have held that there is something wrong with *any* product that is unreasonably dangerous, "even though it comports in all respects to its intended and obvious design." [ ] In other words, these jurisdictions employ a risk/benefit calculus to establish a design defect. "Under this approach, a product is defective as designed if . . . the magnitude of the danger outweighs the utility of the product," that is, if "the harmful consequences in fact from intended and reasonably foreseeable uses resulting from the way the product was designed and marketed up to the time of plaintiff's injury outweigh[ ] the benefits in terms of wants, desires, and human needs served by the product." W. Page Keeton et al., Prosser and Keeton on the Law of Torts §99, at 699 (5th ed. 1984).

Nonetheless, the fact that a product fails the risk/utility test may not be sufficient to give rise to strict liability. This is so because, as the majority notes, New York law has appeared to require that the plaintiff also show a reasonable alternative design before she will be permitted to recover in strict liability for a defectively designed product.

In the instant case, however, a possible alternative design does exist. It consists of the elimination of the extra-destructive "talons." The proposed RESTATEMENT (THIRD) OF TORTS: PRODUCTS LIABILITY (Tentative Draft No. 2, 1995), contains a remarkably relevant discussion:

> Several courts have suggested that the designs of some products are so manifestly unreasonable, in that they have low social utility and high degree of danger, that liability should attach even absent proof of a reasonable alternative design. In large part the problem is one of how the range of relevant alternative designs is described. For example, a toy gun that shoots hard rubber pellets with sufficient velocity to cause injury to children could be found to be defectively designed within the rule of §2(b). Toy guns that do not produce injury would constitute reasonable alternatives to the dangerous toy. Thus, toy guns that project ping pong balls, soft gelatin pellets, or water might be found to be reasonable alternative designs to a toy gun that shoots hard pellets. However, if consideration is limited to toy guns that are capable of causing injury, then no reasonable alternative will, by hypothesis, be available. In that instance, the design feature that defines which alternatives are relevant-the capacity to injure-is precisely the feature on which the user places value and of which the plaintiff complains. If a court were to adopt this characterization of the product, it could conclude that liability should attach without proof of a reasonable alternative design. The court would condemn the product design as defective and not reasonably safe because the extremely high degree of danger posed by its use or consumption so substantially outweighs its negligible utility that no rational adult, fully aware of the relevant facts, would choose to use or consume the product.

Id., §2 cmt. d.

It is worth noting that courts and commentators have been wrestling with the questions of what is a relevant safer alternative design, and whether entire categories of products can be deemed defective in the absence of an alternative

II. Conflicts Between Consumers and Bystanders

design, with increasing frequency in recent years. *See generally* Symposium on Generic Products Liability, 72 Chi.-Kent L. Rev. 1 (1996). The New York Court of Appeals has yet to confront the issue, and should be given the opportunity to do so here.

I do not know whether the New York Court of Appeals would allow a cause of action for negligence or strict liability to proceed in this case. Nor do I know whether that Court *should* allow such liability. What I do know is that these questions are not for *this* Court to decide. [The majority, however, decided not to certify these questions for resolution by the New York Court of Appeals.] And for that reason, I respectfully dissent.

NOTES AND QUESTIONS

1. *Consumer choice, categorical liability, and third-party harms.* Did the majority in *McCarthy* adequately explain why an "ordinary bullet" is not a reasonable alternative design of the Black Talon bullet? Consider Chapter 6, section III.B (discussing difficulty of determining whether the plaintiff is inappropriately trying to rely on one product category as a reasonable alternative design for products in another category). Did the dissenting opinion by Judge Calabresi persuasively explain why a claim of categorical liability could be appropriate in this case, even if it is not otherwise defensible in the ordinary product case involving an injured consumer?

The reasoning of the majority in *McCarthy* is reflective of the approach taken by courts in other cases seeking to impose tort liability on gun manufacturers. As a product category, guns impose substantial risks on third-party bystanders. "According to the National Crime Victimization Survey, 467,321 persons were victims of a crime committed with a firearm in 2011. In the same year, data collected by the FBI show that firearms were used in 68 percent of murders, 41 percent of robbery offenses and 21 percent of aggravated assaults nationwide." National Institute of Justice, *Gun Violence in America* (Feb. 26, 2019), https://nij.ojp.gov/topics/articles/gun-violence-america. Despite the substantial risk that handguns pose to bystanders, the products liability claims filed on behalf of gunshot victims against gun manufacturers have been uniformly rejected by courts because plaintiffs could not show that the handguns were defectively designed. *See generally* SUING THE GUN INDUSTRY: A BATTLE AT THE CROSSROADS OF GUN CONTROL AND MASS TORTS (Timothy D. Lytton ed., 2005).

Absent an identifiable defect, courts would have to impose categorical liability on handguns—an obviously controversial proposition that is best addressed by the legislature, subject to any federal constitutional constraints. The plaintiffs in *McCarthy*, however, were only seeking to impose categorical liability on a particularly destructive type of bullet. Deeming that entire category to be defective would drive the Black Talon bullet off the market, but guns users could still use ordinary bullets.

The judicial resistance to categorical liability would be understandable for claims brought by consumers, because the general rule against categorical liability stems from the desirability of fostering consumer choice across product categories. *See* Chapter 6, section III.B. But *McCarthy* involves bystander injuries, with the plaintiffs effectively alleging that consumers should not be given the choice to purchase Black Talon bullets. By relying on the general rule against categorical liability to dismiss these claims, the majority in *McCarthy* failed to recognize that products can be unreasonably dangerous for the innocent third parties who suffer the injurious consequences of consumer product choices. In his dissenting opinion, Judge Calabresi did not make this point, but instead relied on the formulation of categorical liability in the *Restatement (Third)* that draws no distinction between claims brought by bystanders and those brought by consumers.

2. *Bystanders on the highway.* Like handguns, motor vehicle crashes cause a large number of bystander injuries (to the occupants in other automobiles, pedestrians, and others on or near the road). With respect to the design of motor vehicles, do consumer expectations give the manufacturer an adequate incentive to account for the injuries that could be suffered by the occupants in another vehicle?

According to one government study, the design of sport utility vehicles (SUVs) in 1999 was causing nearly 1,000 "unnecessary deaths a year in other vehicles." Keith Bradsher, *Carmakers to Alter S.U.V.'s to Reduce Risk to Other Autos*, N.Y. Times, March 21, 2000, at A1.

> SUVs impose excessive collision damage because the height differential creates a mismatch between their structures and the protective structures of vehicles with lower ride-heights. In frontal collisions or collisions on a tangent, SUVs often override a passenger car's front bumper and frame, driving the engine or other relatively soft metal components into the passenger compartment. In frontal collisions between large SUVs and passenger cars, the SUV can ride up onto the car's hood and crush it, striking the base of the windshield and causing devastating damage to the car's passenger compartment and its occupants. This height differential is even more lethal in side-impact collisions.

Howard Latin & Bobby Kasolas, *Bad Designs, Lethal Profits: The Duty to Protect Other Motorists Against SUV Collision Risks*, 82 B.U. L. Rev. 1161, 1201-1202 (2002) (paragraph structure omitted).

In the first reported case involving the allegation that an SUV design posed an unreasonable override risk for occupants of other cars, the plaintiff was injured when a Range Rover crashed into the side of her passenger vehicle and penetrated the passenger compartment. *See* de Veer v. Land Rover North America, Inc., 2001 WL 34354946 (Cal. Ct. App. 2001) (unpublished opinion). The plaintiff's expert testified that the Range Rover could have been redesigned to reduce the likelihood that it would override another vehicle in a manner that would not have reduced the utility of the SUV. In support, the expert pointed to designs that SUV manufacturers had subsequently adopted to reduce the risk of override. After observing that the Range Rover's "bumper height, stiffness coefficient, and weight are comparable to similar SUV makes and models" that were manufactured in the same model year, the California Appellate Court affirmed dismissal of the plaintiff's claim for negligent design:

II. Conflicts Between Consumers and Bystanders

> The law does not impose an obligation on automobile manufacturers to make homogenous vehicles, but takes into account, in determining liability, the unique designs of a vehicle. For example, in *Dreisonstok v. Volkswagenwerk, A.G.,* . . . the Fourth Circuit considered the unique design of a minibus, concluding that the manufacturer did not violate a duty of care. While its minibus design did not afford the same protection to its passengers as compared with a conventional passenger car, it had the design advantage of maximizing cargo space. . . . Just as in *Dreisonstok*, accepting [plaintiff's] theory of liability fails to consider the unique features of a special class of vehicles that are designed to perform off road and carry more and heavier cargo.

Id. at *5.

This case further illustrates how courts have invoked a consumer-choice doctrine to dismiss the tort claims of a bystander. Recall that the *Dreisonstok* case, p. 211 *supra*, establishes that the informed consumer choice of one product category (like a microbus) over another (an ordinary passenger vehicle) eliminates the seller's duty with respect to that particular risk-utility decision. Why should this reasoning apply to the claims of a bystander?

In a case involving bystander injury, a consumer-choice doctrine does not provide an appropriate limitation of liability. A well-informed consumer choice of SUV design predictably leads to an "arms war" on the highway. To protect themselves from the increased override risk posed by SUVs, consumers rationally purchase an SUV for themselves. But as one empirical study found, when "drivers shift from cars to light trucks or SUVs, each crash involving fatalities of light-truck or SUV occupants that is prevented comes at a cost of at least 4.3 additional crashes that involve deaths of car occupants, pedestrians, bicyclists, or motorcyclists." Michelle J. White, *The "Arms Race" on American Roads: The Effect of Sport Utility Vehicles and Pickup Trucks on Traffic Safety*, 47 J.L. & Econ. 333, 334 (2004). The implications of these consumer choices were summed up by the Administrator of the National Highway Traffic Safety Administration: "The theory that I'm going to protect myself and my family even if it costs other people's lives has been the operative incentive for the design of these vehicles, and that's just wrong." Danny Hakim, *Regulators Seek to Make S.U.V.'s Safer*, N.Y. Times, Jan. 30, 2003, at C1 (quoting Dr. Jeffrey W. Runge). Consumer choices can create incentives for sellers to adopt product designs that are unreasonably dangerous for bystanders. By summarily dismissing a bystander's claim based on consumer-choice doctrines, courts enshrine the operative incentive that ignores bystander interests.

Due to this pronounced safety problem, regulators pressured the auto industry into redesigning motor vehicles. The effort has been largely successful. For the models marketed after these regulations, "the death rates for occupants of cars are virtually the same whether the vehicle is hit by another car, or an SUV of similar weight." Joseph B. White, *SUVs Get Less Deadly: Design Changes Cut Fatality Rates in Collisions With Cars*, Wall St. J., Sept. 28, 2011 (quoting Joseph N. Nolan, a co-author of an empirical study reaching these conclusions). Without this regulatory pressure — something lacking for most products—would these SUVs have been redesigned if governed by liability rules of the type applied in *McCarthy*?

The regulations, in turn, provide a basis for bystander recovery. For trailers and semitrailers on trucks manufactured since January 26, 1998, federal safety regulations require rear-impact guards that must meet minimally specified performance standards to prevent other vehicles from underriding the trailer in the event of a crash. For cases in which these "ICC bumpers" did not meet regulatory standards, plaintiffs who were injured in rear-end crashes with the semi truck have been able to use the violation of the federal regulatory standard as proof that the bumper was defectively designed. *See* Karney v. Leonard Transp. Corp., 561 F. Supp. 2d 260 (D. Conn. 2008). Can you see why liability in these cases straightforwardly follows from the statutory violation?

3. *Whither negligence liability?* The limitation of the risk-utility test in terms of consumer-choice doctrines effectively defines the safety decision in terms of the preferences of the ordinary consumer. Is that result consonant with the principle of negligence liability? Consider RESTATEMENT (SECOND) OF TORTS §283 cmt. e (stating that reasonable care requires "that the actor give . . . an impartial consideration to the harm likely to be done to the interests of the other as compared with the advantages likely to accrue to his own interests, free from the natural tendency of the actor, as a party concerned, to prefer his own interests to those of others"). To satisfy this obligation, the manufacturer must give "impartial consideration" to the interests of bystanders, treating them no differently from its own interest in satisfying consumer demand for the product. How would this rule apply in a case like *McCarthy*?

III. NEGLIGENCE LIABILITY AND THE PROTECTION OF BYSTANDERS

PASSWATERS v. GENERAL MOTORS CORP.
United States Court of Appeals, Eighth Circuit, 1972
454 F.2d 1272

LAY, J. This is an appeal from a directed verdict granted the defendant General Motors Corporation against Donald Passwaters suing on behalf of himself and his injured daughter, Susan (hereinafter designated as plaintiff). The amended complaint pleaded both negligent design and strict liability. The accident occurred in the State of Iowa and both parties agree that Iowa law controls. Plaintiff asserts that she was a passenger on a Honda motorcycle being operated on a public highway which collided with a 1964 Buick Skylark automobile. She claims her left leg came into contact with a wheel cover on the rear wheel of the car. She asserts that the wheel cover consisted of unshielded metal flanges or flippers which protruded outward from the base of the cover. These spun when the wheel rotated rapidly. When her leg contacted these metal protrusions as a result of the accident, the suit alleges she received a severe mangling type laceration to her lower calf.

III. Negligence Liability and the Protection of Bystanders

The district court directed a verdict at the close of *all* of the evidence. The court ruled: (1) that the State of Iowa has not adopted the rule of strict liability, (2) that the defendant was not accountable to the injured party for negligent design since there was no foreseeable duty of care extending to her, and (3) that the collision between the motorcycle and the auto constituted an intervening cause thereby insulating the conduct of the manufacturer. We reverse and remand the cause for a new trial.

The collision took place on May 23, 1967, on the open highway near Webster City, Iowa. The driver of the Buick was proceeding in the same direction behind the motorcycle on which plaintiff was a passenger. The evidence shows as the automobile passed the motorcycle the car's right rear side came into contact with the handlebar of the cycle. It is plaintiff's claim that this collision caused her left leg to be thrown into the opening of the rear wheel well containing the protruding spinning blades of the hubcap. She received a severe lacerating injury to the outside of the lower leg just above the ankle. Her doctor described the injury as a "Mangling type injury with multiple lacerations of the foot." The bone was so severely severed that only some soft tissue held her leg together. Her father came to the scene of the collision and discovered the Buick's right rear hubcap with human flesh and blood on it. The highway patrolman verified the blood on the hubcap.

The wheel cover was designed with the two ornamental blades protruding some three inches from the base of the cover itself. The flippers serve only the purpose of aesthetic design. These spinners or flippers were recessed two and one-eighth inches within the outer perimeter of the car's body shell. Within the five square feet of the car's rear wheel well there was no covering or protection from the blades. When the vehicle moved at a speed of 40 m.p.h. the blades revolved at 568 r.p.m. or nine and one-half revolutions per second. Plaintiff's expert witness, who held a Ph.D. in agricultural engineering and theoretical applied mechanics, testified that the protruding blades moving at high speeds in an unshielded area constituted an unsafe design to persons who might come within their vicinity. Defendant's design experts testified to the contrary observing that the area was recessed within the body shell of the vehicle and therefore not considered dangerous.

A manufacturer's liability for negligent design has generally been extended to persons outside privity and to nonusers. This court long ago observed: "The rule is now established that a manufacturer owes *to the public* a duty, irrespective of contract, to use reasonable care in the manufacture of an automobile. . . ." (Emphasis ours.) [ ] And as we more recently observed: "We can perceive of no significant difference in imposing a common law duty of a reasonable standard of care in design the same as in construction." [ ] In dealing with the plaintiffs' claims of negligence against the manufacturers the court [in these cases] relied on the *Restatement (Second) of Torts* §398 (1965). The Restatement speaks of the manufacturer being liable for the "failure to exercise reasonable care in the adoption of a safe plan or design." More importantly, subsumed within the negligence concept expressed in §398 is the rule of foreseeability. Section 398 reads in part: "liability to others whom he [the manufacturer] should expect . . . to be endangered by its [the product's] probable use. . . ." This language would encompass plaintiffs who are outside the distributive chain. For example, the manufacturer of an automobile should expect the users of the highways to be endangered by a negligently designed brake system or steering system. [Another] court [has referred] to §398 as the "modern and proper rule." [ ]

The trial court held that a manufacturer's liability against negligent design should only be extended to the persons classified in the status of the general public by legislative enactment. This statement misconstrues the general rule relating to foreseeable harm. Although the specific injury and the manner in which it occurred may have been difficult to foresee, nevertheless the unshielded operation of propeller-like blades on the four wheels of an automobile created a high risk of foreseeable harm to the general public. The use of the highways by pedestrians, the frequency of travel by unprotected persons riding on bicycles, motorbikes and motorcycles is a common occurrence. We think it now settled that a manufacturer does have the responsibility to avoid design in automobiles which can reasonably be foreseen as initially causing or aggravating serious injury to users of the highway when a collision occurs. RESTATEMENT (SECOND) OF TORTS §395 cmt. i. A vehicle cannot be made "accident free," but it is now recognized that a manufacturer does hold a duty to exercise a reasonable degree of care to make the car itself inherently "danger free." We thus conclude there was sufficient evidence to submit the question of negligent design to the jury.

We turn to the issue of the manufacturer's duty under strict liability. Accepting the fact that strict liability is now the rule in Iowa we must judge its applicability to the instant case. The focal issue presented has not been passed on by the Iowa Supreme Court, i.e., whether a user of a highway, within a class of persons who are neither users or consumers of the product may sue the automobile manufacturer under the doctrine of strict liability.

Strict liability is generally viewed as a tort doctrine. It is distinguishable from concepts of negligence in that a plaintiff need not prove whether the defendant had exercised reasonable care under the circumstances. The acceptance of strict liability is based on policy considerations of spreading the risk to the manufacturer as the party financially best able to afford the cost of injuries.

We conclude in the present case that the Iowa court would apply the doctrine of strict liability to a person in plaintiff's status. First, the Iowa court in adopting strict liability relies on cases from California, Illinois and New Jersey, which have been key states in early application of the doctrine in product cases. [ ] Justice Traynor's opinion in the *Greenman* case is considered by many to be the foremost authority explicating the doctrine of strict liability. In amplifying the rule pronounced in Greenman v. Yuba Power Prods. Corp., 377 P.2d 897 (Cal. 1962), the California Supreme Court has recognized liability to bystanders in a position similar to plaintiff's; likewise, New Jersey, and by federal decision, Illinois, have extended strict liability coverage to bystanders. [ ] Clearly, the plaintiff would be covered as a person within the vicinity of the use of the product under the test of foreseeability which is operative in these strict liability cases.

Second, when a federal court is faced with the problem of determining state law without decisions of the state directly controlling, the court may be guided by the law which in its opinion provides the most just and reasoned analysis. We find the reasoning of the California Supreme Court persuasive in this regard [citing Elmore v. American Motors Corp., 451 P.2d at 88-89].

Under the circumstances, we hold plaintiff is entitled to have her case submitted to the jury under Iowa law governing both negligent design and strict liability.

Reversed and remanded for a new trial.

III. Negligence Liability and the Protection of Bystanders 719

NOTES AND QUESTIONS

1. *Categorical liability and bystander interests.* The hubcaps at issue in *Passwaters* may have been inspired by the chariot wheels used by Roman gladiators in the hugely popular movie *Ben-Hur* (Metro-Goldwyn-Mayer 1959). But unlike the chariot wheels, the hubcaps served only an aesthetic purpose. This consideration, however, does not alter the risk-utility analysis. "A car is not a strictly utilitarian product. We believe that a jury properly may consider aesthetics in balancing the benefits of a challenged design against the risk of danger inherent in the design." Bell v. Bayerische Motoren Werke Aktiengesellschaft, 105 Cal. App. 4th 1108, 1131 (Ct. App. 2010); RESTATEMENT (THIRD) OF TORTS: PRODUCTS LIABILITY §2 cmt. f (stating that aesthetic considerations are relevant to the risk-utility analysis of product design).

The hubcap in question was an optional feature, and the purchaser presumably made an informed decision that the aesthetic benefits of the hubcap exceeded the risks posed by the design. Why didn't the consumer's informed risk-utility decision about the matter render the design non-defective as a matter of law? Is a finding of defective design in *Passwaters* tantamount to categorical liability? Consider Chapter 6, section III.B (discussing various rules, including those governing categorical liability and optional safety equipment, that rely on consumer choice to limit liability for defective design).

In concluding that the plaintiff's defect claim was sufficient to support a finding of liability by the jury (which had not yet decided the matter), the court in *Passwaters* never considered categorical liability or the related doctrines involving consumer choice. The court presumably found these doctrines to be entirely inapposite, as indeed they are. The consumer may have made a well-informed choice to purchase a hubcap with propeller-like blades. The consumer's choice, though, does not provide a good reason for limiting the duty of the automobile manufacturer. The consumer's decision was made "only for the purpose of aesthetic design," a reason that pales in comparison to the risk that a bystander would be injured by the rapidly rotating blades. The consumer chose a wheel cover having a "manifestly unreasonable design" with "low social utility and a high degree of danger," the requirements for categorical liability. *See* RESTATEMENT (THIRD) OF TORTS: PRODUCTS LIABILITY §2 cmt. e.

When the product risk largely threatens injury to bystanders, categorical liability can be defensible. Consumer choice ordinarily is desirable and properly promoted by the limitation of the seller's duty with respect to categorical liability. But in cases of bystander injury, the plaintiff is alleging that the consumer should not be given the choice in question. The purchaser of the Buick Skylark with rotating blades in the wheel well presumably made an informed choice and does not have frustrated safety expectations. Nevertheless, this product choice was unreasonably dangerous for the third-party bystander who suffered the injurious consequences. In these cases, duty does not have to be limited to foster consumer choice, explaining why "[s]everal courts have suggested that the designs of some products are so manifestly unreasonable, in that they have low social utility and high degree of danger, that liability should attach even absent proof of a reasonable alternative design." *Id.* The *Restatement (Third)*'s formulation of this rule, however, does not clearly distinguish between consumers and bystanders, creating the type of problems illustrated by *McCarthy*, p. 709 *supra.*

2. *Optional safety features and product misuse.* In Bohnstedt v. Robscon Leasing L.L.C., 1993 P.2d 135 (Civ. App. Okla. Div. One 1999), the plaintiff claimed that the "back up alarm system [in defendant John Deere's road grader] was defective because John Deere was aware that these back up alarms were frequently disconnected and did not attempt . . . to make the safety device tamper resistant." *Id.* at 136. Why wasn't the consumer's choice to disable the safety device a sufficient reason for negating the seller's duty? Isn't that choice equivalent to the consumer's decision to forego the purchase of optional safety equipment, which ordinarily forecloses the plaintiff from alleging that the design is defective for not incorporating that equipment?

In thinking about this issue, consider who incurs the burden of the safety device (the loud beeping) and who benefits from it. Does a user's self-interest in reducing noise explain why the design must account for this particular risk of misuse? Compare Scarangella v. Thomas Built Buses, Inc., 717 N.E.2d 679, 683 (N.Y. 1999) (holding that a bus was not defectively designed for making a back-up alarm an optional safety feature in part because "plaintiff made no factual showing to the contrary that school children, other pedestrians or occupants of other vehicles were exposed to any hazards of the operation of [these] buses in reverse, without back-up alarms") (excerpted in Chapter 6, p. 228 *supra*). If consumer choice does not limit design defect liability in these cases, should consumer choice bar other allegations of defective design involving bystanders?

3. *Bystander liability, the negligence principle, and the distinctive character of strict products liability.* Did the court in *Passwaters* adequately explain why bystanders are protected both by negligence liability and strict products liability? As we have found, the negligence principle can justify the rule of strict products liability. According to this justification, strict liability should apply to malfunctioning products, like soda bottles that explode, because of the evidentiary difficulties that would be faced by a plaintiff who had to prove that the seller unreasonably failed to discover the defect. *See* Chapter 2, section II. These evidentiary difficulties are the same for all plaintiffs, regardless of their status as a consumer or bystander. The evidentiary rationale for strict liability, therefore, justifies the extension of strict products liability to bystanders.

For products that do not malfunction, however, the implied warranty and the negligence principle can reach different outcomes when the product design creates a conflict between consumer expectations and the reasonable safety of bystanders. Once situated within its appropriate normative framework, strict products liability necessarily has a limited scope. When defective products injure bystanders, the tort issue is not wholly defined by the protection of consumer expectations—the distinctive normative attribute of the implied warranty. Bystander cases instead turn on the general principles of tort law, which justify a negligence-based framework in product cases that is normatively different from the implied warranty rationale for strict products liability.

For cases involving consumers, by contrast, the more narrow focus of the implied warranty frames the liability inquiry in the normatively appropriate manner, giving the regime of strict products liability a decisive analytic advantage over the negligence-based framework of the *Restatement (Third)* across the distinctive elements of the tort claim—duty, breach (or defect), and causation. Rather than posing an intractable problem for the consumer expectations test, bystander injuries fully reveal the normative structure of strict products liability.

The normative focus of strict products liability has only become more important over time. "The consumer expectations test intrinsically recognizes a manufacturer's central role in crafting the image of a product and establishing the consumer's expectations for that product—a portrayal which in turn motivates consumers to purchase that particular product." Aubin v. Union Carbide Corp., 177 So.3d 489, 507 (Fla. 2015). Manufacturers and other sellers now have the unsurpassed ability to portray their products in a manner that is most appealing to the consumer. Mining the user data generated by mobile phones and other products connected to the Internet of Things, businesses can appropriate "human experience as free raw material for translation into behavioral data." Shoshana Zuboff, THE AGE OF SURVEILLANCE CAPITALISM 8 (2019). As a consequence of competitive pressures within this emergent system of "surveillance capitalism," businesses engage in "an increasingly complex and comprehensive 'means of behavioral modification.'" The objective, of course, is "to shape our behavior in ways that favor surveillance capitalists' commercial outcomes." *Id.* at 19. Holding these commercial enterprises strictly responsible for their implied representations of product quality—the rationale for strict products liability—has never been more important than it is today.

IV. AUTONOMOUS VEHICLES AND PRODUCTS LIABILITY: PROBLEM SET 13

AV Problem 13.1

To "teach" the operating system of an autonomous vehicle how to drive, programmers run the software through myriad traffic simulations and specify the "correct action" or desired outcome for each situation. The machine-learning algorithm in the operating system then employs statistical analysis to determine the best way to achieve the desired outcomes. What constitutes the "correct action" for situations in which the autonomous vehicle will inevitably crash and could injure either passengers (consumers) or others on the road (bystanders)? How should the vehicle's operating system be instructed to execute actions that can protect one party at the expense of another?

A study involving millions of people from 233 countries around the world found the strongest preferences for safety decisions that spare the most lives in a crash, even if doing so kills the occupants of the vehicle. *See* Edmond Awad et al., *The Moral Machine Experiment*, 563 Nature 59, 60 (2018). A different study similarly found that most participants approved of designs that would sacrifice the occupants of an autonomous vehicle to save others, although they would prefer not to ride in such vehicles and would be less willing to purchase one as a result. *See* Jean-François Bonnefon et al., *The Social Dilemma of Autonomous Vehicles*, 352 Science 1573, 1574 (2016).

Suppose that to satisfy this pocket of consumer demand, the manufacturer of a level 4 DAS autonomous vehicle provided two different versions of the operating system. One specified the "correct action" for the vehicle to treat passengers and bystanders equally in the event of an unavoidable crash; the other operating system was designed to always protect passengers at the expense of bystanders. As is true for other types of autonomous vehicles, sensors in these vehicles can identify the number of passengers in the vehicle along with the number of nearby pedestrians. The manufacturer marketed the vehicle on this basis, emphasizing that consumers could choose a passenger-protective design instead of one that might injure passengers to protect bystanders. In addition to its marketing materials, the manufacturer also provided an adequate warning about this aspect of the vehicle's performance. Finally, suppose that the manufacturer's marketing campaign was extraordinarily successful, resulting in the widespread commercial distribution of the vehicle with the passenger-protective operating system.

Consider the liability question for a case in which such a fully functioning autonomous vehicle could not avoid crashing into an oncoming car going 10 miles-per-hour on an urban street. Consequently, the autonomous vehicle executed the dynamic driving task by veering onto a crowded sidewalk to protect the vehicle's single occupant. In the ensuing wrongful-death suits brought on behalf of the fatally injured pedestrians, how would a court that has adopted the relevant rules in the *Restatement (Third)* resolve a claim that the passenger-protective operating system is defectively designed, with the plaintiffs' proposed reasonable alternative design being the identical operating system that specifies the "correct action" so that it treats passengers and pedestrians equally in the event of an unavoidable crash?

Analysis of AV Problem 13.1

Because the manufacturer widely marketed this aspect of the vehicle's performance and provided an adequate warning about the matter, consumers made an informed choice to purchase or use the passenger-protective operating system precisely because it protects them instead of others. Under the *Restatement (Third)*, this attribute of consumer demand places the design in a product category different from the alternative design proposed by plaintiffs. The *Restatement (Third)* recognizes categorical liability only in exceptional cases involving products that are "manifestly unreasonable" and not "widely and commonly" distributed. By applying this liability rule, the court would dismiss the plaintiffs' claims: The commercial success of the passenger-protective operating

IV. Autonomous Vehicles and Products Liability: Problem Set 13

system has made it "widely and commonly" distributed and therefore not an appropriate candidate for categorical liability. In effect, the same feature that makes the vehicle appealing to consumers and highly profitable for the manufacturer also immunizes the manufacturer from liability, regardless of its impact on bystanders. For more extensive discussion of these rules and concepts, see Chapter 6, section III.B.

AV Problem 13.2

How would a court resolve a claim under the implied warranty that the passenger-protective operating system is defectively designed, with the proposed alternative design being the identical operating system that specifies the "correct action" so that it treats passengers and pedestrians equally in the event of an unavoidable crash?

Analysis of AV Problem 13.2

In effect, the two different versions of the operating system provided consumers with different safety options. Both types of operating systems were available when the allegedly defective vehicle was purchased, and the ordinary consumer could make an informed risk-utility choice between them. Consequently, the plaintiffs' proposed alternative design is based on the same set of risk-utility factors that consumers relied on in rejecting that design in favor of the passenger-protective system, and so the claim would be barred under the patent-defect rule. *See* Chapter 5, section II. The design of the passenger-protective system fully satisfies consumer expectations and is not "unreasonably dangerous" under §402A.

AV Problem 13.3

How would a court resolve an ordinary negligence claim that the operating system is defectively designed, with the proposed reasonable alternative design being the identical operating system that specifies the "correct action" so that it treats passengers and pedestrians equally in the event of an unavoidable crash?

Analysis of AV Problem 13.3

Instead of protecting consumer expectations, the negligence duty of reasonable care requires the contracting parties to perform their obligations in a manner that is reasonably safe for strangers to the transaction. As someone who would be foreseeably threatened by operation of the vehicle, a bystander is encompassed within the manufacturer's duty to exercise reasonable care in designing the operating system. To satisfy this obligation, the manufacturer must give impartial consideration to the interests of bystanders, treating them no differently from its own interest in satisfying consumer demand for the product.

The manufacturer, therefore, must initially code or teach the operating system of an autonomous vehicle so that the "correct action" treats consumers and bystanders equally.

In the case at hand, the autonomous vehicle had sensors indicating that it was occupied by one person and would crash into a group of nearby pedestrians. The "correct action" in this context requires equal treatment of consumers and bystanders, which would have caused the vehicle to avoid veering onto the crowded sidewalk, even though doing so would threaten injury to the lone passenger who would have crashed into the oncoming vehicle going 10 miles per hour. To avoid liability, the manufacturer must design the operating system of the autonomous vehicle to minimize the expected injuries from any given crash whether the potential victims are occupants or bystanders.

Editor's Note. In addition to the operating system, the manufacturer must design other aspects of the vehicle to reasonably account for bystander interests. The manufacturer, for example, may have to design the autonomous vehicle so that it can adequately communicate with other vehicles or pedestrians, signaling the driving behavior that they can expect. *See* Harry Surden & Mary-Anne Williams, *Technological Opacity, Predictability, and Self-Driving Cars*, 38 Cardozo L. Rev. 121, 163-174 (2016) (discussing how "the activities of autonomous vehicles . . . can be made more predictable through deliberate technological design decisions").

17

Comparative Products Liability

Comparative products liability ordinarily connotes the study of products liability laws across different countries, although the term also applies to the United States, where there is not one uniform law of products liability, but rather the varying laws of the individual states. What do these differences teach us about products liability more generally?

Comparative study helps to identify how important differences among the laws of different jurisdictions are subject to pressures that produce a certain degree of harmonization. For example, the laws of a particular state, such as California, often influence the laws of other jurisdictions, a process that is then facilitated by projects like the *Restatement of Torts*. In addition to "law borrowing" among states, uniformity is produced by market competition.

> [M]anufacturers are normally unable to tailor the price or quality of the products sold in a particular state to that state's liability laws. Apart from the difficulty of calculating the cost of potential liability in different states, differential pricing creates a market for middlemen. Intermediate purchasers will buy the products in the states with low prices and resell in the states with high prices, at once reducing the manufacturer's revenue for its product and increasing its liability exposure. The threat of this interstate arbitrage compels manufacturers to sell their products at uniform prices that reflect average liability levels across states.

Bruce L. Hay, *Conflicts of Law and State Competition in the Product Liability System*, 80 Geo. L.J. 617, 618-619 (1992).

A large jurisdiction like California will have a disproportionately large impact on a manufacturer's "average" liability costs, creating an incentive for manufacturers to comply with California laws, even if the laws of other jurisdictions are less demanding. However, a product seller that consciously disregarded the more demanding law of any particular state would be subject to punitive damages in cases governed by that law. The threat of punitive damages could induce product sellers to comply with the most demanding liability rule in the country, even if that state otherwise comprises only a small share of the national market.

Both economic and jurisprudential forces accordingly promote uniformity in mass markets, a dynamic that now operates across the global economy. The study of comparative products liability requires attention both to the differences in laws across countries and the forces of harmonization that tend to reduce those differences.

Outside of the United States, Europe has played the leading role in the development of products liability. Consider how the historical development of tort (also called delict) in Western Europe since 1850 compares to the experience in the U.S.

> [I]n the middle of the nineteenth century, the contractual approach predominated, drawing essentially on Roman law typology and offering two sorts of remedy: first, liability arising in sales law from failure to adhere to an express contractual undertaking in respect of the qualities of the good sold; and the well-known latent defect warranty, subject to short limitations rules. Contract law was however in many ways an unsatisfactory remedial tool, particularly due to limitations engendered by the privity rule. Delict offered another route, due to the general delictual provisions found [in the French Civil Code]. Utility of such provisions was initially restricted due to the prerequisite of showing fault of the manufacturer or supplier of the defective product. Piecemeal exceptions did start to emerge however to these restrictive rules, driven by the need to protect consumers through the occurrence of mass injuries due to increased industrialization.
>
> In the twentieth century, it was not until the 1960s onwards that the topic of products liability coalesced as a distinct conceptual area of the law, and one which might require tailor-made solutions. Comparative law influenced the doctrinal writing, in particular but not solely taking US law as a reference point.

Duncan Fairgrieve & Richard Goldberg, PRODUCT LIABILITY 14–15 (3d ed. 2020) (footnotes omitted) (summarizing THE DEVELOPMENT OF PRODUCT LIABILITY (Simon Whittaker ed. 2010)).

The reform of products liability within Europe was prompted by major health disasters. "[T]he prescription drug disaster of Thalidomide, which had particularly hit Britain and Germany in the early 1960s," was "the original impetus for products liability law reform in Europe." Jane Stapleton, *Liability for Drugs in the U.S. and EU: Rhetoric and Reality*, 26 Rev. Lit. 991, 1001 (2007). The products liability rules adopted by European countries were not uniform, however, creating a problem for the member states of the European Economic Community, the precursor to the European Union.

> The European Community ("EC"), seeking to unify its laws of products liability, promulgated a directive in 1985 that was greeted with a chorus of praise. The EC had long aspired to reconcile the many national laws on the subject. In a stance familiar to American readers of the Restatements of common law, the Council of the Community eschewed explicit movement away from existing rules. It described its task as rather one of approximation: to derive an ideal law of products liability from the traditions of the twelve nations that make up the European Community.
>
> Titled "On the approximation of the laws, regulations and administrative provisions of the Member States concerning liability for defective products,"

the Directive is known as a strict liability measure, although the phrase "strict products liability" or "strict liability" does not appear in it. Instead, "liability without fault on the part of the producer" signals its message. The Directive contains a detailed Preamble that announces its goals and explains its substantive choices, later detailed in specific articles. Major provisions include a "development risks" defense (the exoneration of manufacturers for damage caused by defects unknowable to them at the time of production), as well as definitions of "producer" and "defective product," and a cap on damages. The Commission has applied a familiar but ambiguous term, "harmonization," to this effort. . . .

According to its Preamble, the Directive is needed for harmonization of the laws of the member nations, because "the existing divergencies may distort competition and affect the movement of goods" within the Community. In an ideal Community, goods would be distributed throughout the Common Market, without the barriers of divergent laws. The EC has maintained that economic progress will result when national barriers are removed. Predicted benefits include a rational division of labor within the Community, lower production costs, and larger-scale production with a resultant increase in productivity and wages.

Anita Bernstein, *L'Harmonie Dissonante: Strict Products Liability Attempted in the European Community*, 31 Va. J. Int'l L. 673, 673-674, 681 (1991).

"Eventually, the Council Directive of 1985 became the foundation of modern product liability in the European Community where all member states now have special products liability regimes." Mathias Reimann, *Product Liability in a Global Context: The Hollow Victory of the European Model*, 11 Eur. Rev. Private L. 128, 128 (2003).

According to article 6 of the Directive, "[a] product is defective when it does not provide the safety which a person is entitled to expect." Europe has adopted the consumer expectations test, which in turn has influenced other countries.

> The vast majority of jurisdictions with a special product liability regime are in line with the European model and thus rely on reasonable consumer expectations rather than employing a cost-benefit test. This is true in Europe as well as in countries as diverse as Australia, Brazil, China, Japan, Korea, Malaysia, Peru, the Philippines, Quebec and Taiwan.
>
> One might thus conclude that the influence of the European model has caused a worldwide trend towards a uniform definition of defectiveness under a consumer expectation test. While this is by and large true, it is also somewhat misleading because it underrates the role of American law in this context. To get the full picture, one must take into account that the earlier American product liability regime, as formulated in §402A of the Second Restatement in 1966, also assumed a uniform concept of defectiveness and also judged it according to consumer expectations. . . . Thus it is more accurate to say that most jurisdictions in the world have followed the approach that *once* dominated in the United States . . . and eschewed, or simply overlooked, the American refinements of the last two decades.

Reimann, *supra*, at 140-141.

The consumer expectations test in the *Restatement (Second) of Torts* has become the majority rule across the globe, not the risk-utility test adopted by the

Restatement (Third). This global development, not surprisingly, has been sharply criticized by proponents of the risk-utility test:

> the consumer expectations test for defect adopted recently in Europe and Japan has been thoroughly discredited in the United States as a way to decide classic product design cases. Adoption of this standard will not threaten the economic well-being of industrialized nations around the world. But if the American experience is any guide, judges in those countries applying that standard are going to face conceptual difficulties trying to make sense of it in "classic design cases."

James A. Henderson, Jr. & Aaron D. Twerski, *What Europe, Japan, and Other Countries Can Learn From the New American Restatement of Products Liability*, 34 Tex. Int'l L.J. 1, 20 (1999).

In the following case, the court analyzes a range of issues involving contaminated blood under the European Products Liability Directive as implemented in the United Kingdom. In reading the case, consider how you would analyze the issues by applying the rules from the *Restatement (Third)*. Is the analysis easier or harder? If so, what might explain the difference?

A v. NATIONAL BLOOD AUTHORITY
English and Wales High Court of Justice, Queen's Bench Division, 2001
3 All E.R. 289

BURTON, J. This trial has concerned the claims of 114 Claimants for recovery of damages arising out of their infection with Hepatitis C from blood and blood products through blood transfusions from 1 March 1988. The 114 Claimants received blood transfusions or blood products usually in the course of undergoing surgery, whether consequent upon having suffered an accident or otherwise, or immediately after childbirth or in the course of treatment for a blood disorder.

The claims that are the subject matter of this trial are not in negligence, but are put against the Defendants by way of "strict" or "objective" liability by virtue of the Consumer Protection Act 1987 ("CPA"), which implemented in the United Kingdom the European Union (then the EEC) Product Liability Directive of 1985, being a Council Directive of 25 July 1985 ("the Directive"). The Directive is not, in any event in this action, said to be directly enforceable against the Defendants by the Claimants, who rely for their cause of action on the CPA. However, it is apparent from the judgment of the European Court, reported as *European Commission v. United Kingdom* [1997] AER (EC) 481, that, there not at that stage having been any decisions of the English courts, whatever be the precise terms of the CPA, the United Kingdom would so implement and construe the CPA as to be consistent with the Directive. Consequently both parties have during this trial almost exclusively concentrated on the terms of the Directive. As will be seen, the arguments were directed mainly to the true and proper construction of Article 6 of the Directive (the equivalent being Section 3 of the CPA) and Article 7(e) (the equivalent being Section 4(1)(e)), and consequently it is with those Articles, and not the relevant Sections, with which this judgment will be primarily, if not exclusively, concerned.

It is conceded for the purpose of these proceedings that the blood or blood products by which the Claimants were infected are products within the meaning of the CPA and the Directive, and that the Defendants' production of blood was, for the purpose of the Directive, an industrial process.

The National Health Service bodies responsible for the production and supply of blood and blood products prior to 1 April 1993 in England (and also covering northern Wales) were fourteen regional blood transfusion centres ("RTCs"), controlled and administered by Regional Health Authorities. From that date, [legal responsibility for blood transfusions was transferred to other governmental authorities]. I shall refer in this judgment to "the Defendants" without taking into account the various changes of identity and responsibility.

Organised blood transfusion began in England and Wales in 1921. The practice (unlike in the United States, where donors were paid until the 1970s) was of donation by unpaid volunteers.

Hepatitis simply means "inflammation of the liver." It can result from a number of different causes, including self-inflicted substance abuse. It has been known since the 1940s that Hepatitis can be transmitted by transfusions of blood and plasma. It quickly became apparent that there was a distinction between what was then called infectious Hepatitis (now known as Hepatitis A) and serum Hepatitis (now known as Hepatitis B). However by 1975 an agent other than Hepatitis A or B was recognised to be causing Post-Transfusion Hepatitis ("PTH"), and it was found that by 1985 PTH still occurred in 7% to 12% of blood transfusion recipients in the United States. The condition caused by this unknown agent was described as Non-A Non-B Hepatitis ("NANBH"). The virus which caused NANBH was eventually first identified in Spring 1988. The virus was hurriedly itself christened, perhaps inevitably, as Hepatitis C.

As appears above, there was neither identification of the NANBH virus nor, consequently, development of any screening test or assay so as to eliminate such virus from blood donations prior to their use, in the years up to 1988. There was however, considerable research and academic discussion in the medical journals about the problem of PTH, particularly in the United States, which was still suffering from the aftermath of paid donors, and at all times appears to have had a much higher incidence of PTH than Europe.

The claims in this trial have been that, pursuant to the CPA, those who received blood or blood products infected by Hepatitis C subsequent to 1 March 1988, when the Act came into effect, are entitled to recover damages: that is notwithstanding that: the Hepatitis C virus itself had not been discovered or identified at the date when the claims commence on 1 March 1988; no screening test to discover the presence of such virus in a donor's blood was even known of, certainly not available, until Spring/Summer 1989; it is not sought to be alleged (at least not in this trial) that the UK blood authorities for whom the Defendants are responsible were negligent in not introducing the screening tests until they did on 1 September 1991 (or now, as a result of the agreed concession, 1 April 1991) nor that they were negligent in not having introduced surrogate tests. The case which is put is that they are liable irrespective of the absence of any fault, under the Directive and the CPA.

The parties before me agreed to number what are in the published Directive an otherwise unnumbered set of nineteen recitals. The significant ones for the purpose of these proceedings have been as follows:

[1] Whereas approximation of the laws of the Member States concerning the liability of the producer for damage caused by the defectiveness of his product is necessary because the existing divergences may distort competition and affect the movement of goods within the common market and entail a differing degree of protection of the consumer against damage caused by a defective product to his health or property;

[2] Whereas liability without fault on the part of the producer is the sole means of adequately solving the problem, peculiar to our age of increasing technicality, of a fair apportionment of the risks inherent in modern technological production;

[3] Whereas liability without fault should apply only to movables which have been industrially produced; whereas, as a result, it is appropriate to exclude liability for agricultural products and game, except where they have undergone a processing of an industrial nature which could cause a defect in these products;

[6] Whereas, to protect the physical well-being and property of the consumer, the defectiveness of the product should be determined by reference not to its fitness for use but to the lack of the safety which the public at large is entitled to expect; whereas the safety is assessed by excluding any misuse of the product not reasonable under the circumstances;

[7] Whereas a fair apportionment of risk between the injured person and the producer implies that the producer should be able to free himself from liability if he furnishes proof as to the existence of certain exonerating circumstances;

[11] Whereas products age in the course of time, higher safety standards are developed and the state of science and technology progresses; whereas, therefore, it would not be reasonable to make the producer liable for an unlimited period for the effectiveness of his product; whereas, therefore, liability should expire after a reasonable length of time, without prejudice to claims pending at law;

[13] Whereas under the legal systems of the Member States an injured party may have a claim for damages based on grounds of contractual liability or on grounds of non-contractual liability other than that provided for in this Directive; insofar as these provisions also serve to attain the objective of effective protection of consumers, they should remain unaffected by this Directive; whereas, in so far as effective protection of consumers in the sector of pharmaceutical products is already also attained in a Member State under a special liability system, claims based on this system should similarly remain possible;

[16] Whereas, for similar reasons, the possibility offered to a producer to free himself from liability if he proves that the state of scientific and technical knowledge at the time when he put the product into circulation was not such as to enable the existence of a defect to be discovered may be felt, in certain Member States, to restrict unduly the protection of the consumer; whereas it should therefore be possible for a Member State to maintain in its legislation or to provide by new legislation that this exonerating circumstance is not admitted; whereas, in the case of new legislation, making use of this derogation should, however, be subject to a Community stand-still procedure, in order to raise, if possible, the level of protection in a uniform manner throughout the Community.

17. Comparative Products Liability

It is not in dispute between the parties that the Directive can and must be construed by reference to its recitals and indeed to its legislative purpose, insofar as it can be gleaned otherwise than from the recitals.

The relevant Articles are as follows:

> 1. The producer shall be liable for damage caused by a defect in his product.
>
> 4. The injured person shall be required to prove the damage, the defect and the causal relationship between defect and damage.
>
> 6.1 A product is defective when it does not provide the safety which a person is entitled to expect, taking all circumstances into account, including: (a) the presentation of the product; (b) the use to which it could reasonably be expected that the product would be put; (c) the time when the product was put into circulation.
>
> 6.2 A product shall not be considered defective for the sole reason that a better product is subsequently put into circulation.
>
> 7. The producer shall not be liable as a result of this Directive if he proves: (a) that he did not put the product into circulation; or (b) that, having regard to the circumstances, it is probable that the defect which caused the damage did not exist at the time when the product was put into circulation by him or that this defect came into being afterwards; or . . . (d) that the defect is due to compliance of the product with mandatory regulations issued by the public authorities; or (e) that the state of scientific and technical knowledge at the time when he put the product into circulation was not such as to enable the existence of the defect to be discovered; . . .
>
> 8.1 Without prejudice to the provisions of national law concerning the right of contribution or recourse, the liability of the producer shall not be reduced when the damage is caused both by a defect in product and by the act or omission of a third party.
>
> 8.2 The liability of the producer may be reduced or disallowed when, having regard to all the circumstances, the damage is caused both by a defect in the product and by the fault of the injured person or any person for him the injured person is responsible.
>
> 9. For the purpose of Article 1, "damage" means: (a) damage caused by death or by personal injury. . . .
>
> 12. The liability of the producer arising from the Directive may not, in relation to the injured person, be limited or excluded by a provision limiting his liability or exempting him from liability.
>
> 15.1 Each Member State may . . . (b) by way of derogation from Article 7(e) maintain or . . . provide in its legislation that the producer shall be liable even if he proves that the state of scientific or technical knowledge at the time when he put the product into circulation was not such as to enable the existence of a defect to be discovered. . . .

The Claimants allege that, upon the basis of a proper construction of the Directive and the agreed factual common ground, the blood was defective under Article 6 and the Defendants have no escape within Article 7(e), without need for further consideration of the facts.

I turn then to consideration of Article 6. The question to be resolved is the safety or the degree or level of safety or safeness which persons generally are entitled to expect. The test is not that of an absolute level of safety, nor an absolute liability for any injury caused by the harmful characteristic. In the assessment of that question the expectation is that of persons generally, or the public at large. The safety is not what is actually expected by the public at large, but what they are entitled to expect. There are some products, which have harmful characteristics in whole or in part, about which no complaint can be made. The examples that were used of products which have obviously dangerous characteristics by virtue of their very nature or intended use, were, on the one hand knives, guns and poisons and on the other hand alcohol, tobacco, perhaps foie gras. This does not of course amount to an exemption for such a product from the Article, but simply an explanation of how the Article operates. Drugs with advertised side-effects may fall within this category. The Defendants point out that, with other such products also, the known dangerous characteristics need not be the desired ones—e.g., carcinogenicity in tobacco.

As to Article 6, the Claimants assert that, with the need for proof of negligence eliminated, consideration of the conduct of the producer, or of a reasonable or legitimately expectable producer, is inadmissible or irrelevant. Therefore questions of avoidability cannot and do not arise: what the Defendants could or should have done differently: whether there were any steps or precautions reasonably available: whether it was impossible to take any steps by way of prevention or avoidance, or impracticable or economically unreasonable. Such are not "circumstances" falling to be considered within Article 6. Insofar as the risk was known to blood producers and the medical profession, it was not known to the public at large (save for those few patients who might ask their doctor, or read the occasional article about blood in a newspaper) and no risk that any percentage of transfused blood would be infected was accepted by them.

The Defendants assert that the risk was known to those who mattered, namely the medical profession, through whom blood was supplied. Avoiding the risk was impossible and unattainable, and it is not and cannot be legitimate to expect the unattainable. Avoidability or unavoidability is a circumstance to be taken into account within Article 6. The public did not and/or was not entitled to expect 100% clean blood. The most they could legitimately expect was that all legitimately expectable (reasonably available) precautions—or in this case tests—had been taken or carried out. The Claimants must therefore prove that they were legitimately entitled to expect more, and/or must disprove the unavoidability of the harmful characteristic. There would need to be an investigation as to whether it was impossible to avoid the risk and/or whether the producers had taken all legitimately expectable steps. Insofar as there was thus an investigation analogous to, or involving similar facts to, an investigation into negligence, it was not an investigation of negligence by the individual producer and was necessary and, because it was not an investigation of fault, permissible. If, notwithstanding the known and unavoidable risk, the blood was nevertheless defective within Article 6, then it is all the more necessary to construe Article 7(e) so as to avail those who could not, in the then state of scientific and technical knowledge, identify the defect in a particular product so as to prevent its supply.

The Claimants respond that Article 7(e) does not apply to risks which are known before the supply of the product, whether or not the defect can be identified in the particular product; and there are a number of other issues between the parties in respect of Article 7(e) to which I shall return later.

In the establishment of the level of safety, Article 6 provides that the Court (on behalf of the public at large) takes into account *all circumstances*. There is no dispute between the parties that consideration of the fault of the producer is excluded; but does consideration of "all circumstances" include consideration of the conduct to be expected from the producer, the level of safety to be expected from a producer of that product? The parties agree that the starting point is the particular product with the harmful characteristic, and if its inherent nature and intended use (e.g., poison) are dangerous, then there may not need to be any further consideration, provided that the injury resulted from that known danger. However, if the product was not intended to be dangerous, that is the harmful characteristic was not intended, by virtue of the intended use of the product, then there must be consideration of whether it was safe and the level of safety to be legitimately expected.

If, the Defendants contend, the producer did not use obviously available safety processes or precautions, then that itself must be a factor to be taken into account against him, just as it would be in his favour if all available safety precautions were adopted. They accept that the investigation of what level of safety the public is entitled to expect may involve consideration of factual issues which would also be relevant in a negligence enquiry, but they say that this would be a matter of overlap rather than duplication, and inevitable and acceptable.

The Claimants contend that any consideration of the method or processes of production, including the safety precautions taken or not taken, is irrelevant. They assert that it is necessary only to look at the product itself (including comparison with similar or identical products on the market), which would involve its expected or intended use, without considering what more could have been done (and how easy or difficult or cheap or expensive it would have been to have done it). The safeness even of a scrid must be considered by reference to examination of such a product and its intended or foreseeable use, not its method of manufacture.

In any event, however, the Claimants make a separate case in relation to the blood products here in issue: namely that they are what is called in the United States "rogue products" or "lemons," and in Germany "*Ausreisser*"—escapees or "off the road" products. These are products which are isolated or rare specimens which are different from the other products of a similar series, different from the products as intended or desired by the producer. Other more attractive or suitable descriptions were canvassed, and I have firmly settled on what I clearly prefer, namely the "non-standard" product. Thus a standard product is one which is and performs as the producer intends. A non-standard product is one which is different, obviously because it is deficient or inferior in terms of safety, from the standard product: and where it is the harmful characteristic or characteristics present in the non-standard product, but not in the standard product, which has or have caused the material injury or damage. Some Community jurisdictions in implementing the Directive have specifically provided that there will be liability for "non-standard" products, i.e., that such will automatically be defective within Article 6: Italy and Spain have done so by express legislation, and [a leading authority] considers that that is now the position in Belgium also as a result of the implementation of the Directive.

Were the infected bags of blood in this case non-standard products? The Claimants say yes—99 out of 100 are safe and uninfected as intended. The Defendants say no—all blood, derived as it is from a natural raw material, albeit then processed, is inherently risky. But the Claimants assert that persons generally are entitled to expect that all blood and blood products used for medical treatment are safe, and that they will not receive the unsafe 1 in 100. The Claimants say that this will only not be the case if the public does know and expect that blood, like cigarettes or alcohol, is or may be defective, not because the public's expectation is limited to an expectation that legitimately expectable safety precautions will have been taken.

United States tort law has developed a difference between manufacturing defects, design defects and instruction defects, (the last category being irrelevant for our purposes). This was worked through in case law, though it did not appear in the Second Restatement, published in 1965, but it has been expressly incorporated into the Third Restatement, published in 1998 (section 2(a)(b)(c): Categories of Product Defects). There is almost a separate jurisprudence for manufacturing defects as opposed to design defects. The Claimants say that, in terms of that dichotomy, the infected blood here is a manufacturing defect—an error in production has led to a one-off. The Defendants say that, if a defect at all, it is a design defect, because the process as designed leads inevitably to the occasional failure as a result of an inherent defect in the raw material. In this context, so far as the academics are concerned, the Claimants appear to have the better of it. However, notwithstanding that there was some use of these American terms in the *travaux preparatoires* [the official record of negotiations resulting in the Directive], there is no place for them in the Directive. After some discussion in the course of the hearing, I am satisfied, and indeed neither Counsel contended to the contrary, that no assistance can be gained from the categorisation, of defects in this regard for the purpose of construction of the Directive, or the determination of any of the issues before me. Whether it is appropriate to define the one infected bag of blood in one hundred as a manufacturing defect, or as an inevitable result of a chosen design process which cannot guarantee uniformity of product, the issue is still the same, namely whether the safety was provided which the public was entitled to expect in respect of that product.

There is nothing much to assist in the *travaux preparatoires*, save for the rejection of the express US approach and risk-utility analysis.

I turn to consider the few court decisions in Europe in which the Directive, or these issues under the Directive, have been considered or touched upon.

In what has been called the "German Bottle Case" the Bundesgerichtshof, (BGH), the German Federal Supreme Court, gave judgment on 9 May 1995, allowing an appeal by a Claimant injured as a result of an exploding mineral water bottle, resulting from a very fine hairline crack, not discovered notwithstanding what was found to be a technical and supervisory procedure in the Defendant's factory in accordance with the very latest state of technology (including seven different inspections). Although the BGH dealt at some length with the questions under Article 7(e), to which I shall refer below, it had no difficulty, after what was obviously detailed consideration, in concluding that the harmful characteristic was a defect within Article 6 (or the German statute implementing it). The BGH concluded (translated from the German):

> The Court of Appeal [was] correct in law to assume that pursuant to [Article 6] a product is defective if it does not guarantee the degree of safety which may be expected when taking all circumstances into account. The Court of Appeal

also [assumed] correctly that a consumer expects a mineral water bottle to have no obvious or even microscopic damage which might lead it to explode. The fact that it is not technically possible to detect and repair such defects in the bottle does not alter the consumer's expectations.

The Defendants accept that the crack in that case was plainly a manufacturing defect, capable of being described, as the BGH expressly did, as a rogue product ("*Ausreisser*") and do not contend that the decision of the BGH was wrong. They submit however that this logic does not apply to a bag of blood, which they submit to share the same characteristics as all blood, namely in that all blood bears—or bore—the 1% risk of being infected. (The BGH also rejected the producer's arguments under Article 7(e), to which I shall return.)

The County Court of Amsterdam, Holland (not an appellate court) gave a judgment on 3 February 1999 in the case of *Scholten v. The Foundation Sanquin of Blood Supply*. In this case the claimant received blood infected with HIV, after the introduction of HIV screening tests in that country, because of the (infinitesimal) risk in that case from blood which had been so screened but must have been given by a donor who had only just contracted HIV, such that his infection could not be detected by a test during what has been called "the window period." The Court appears to have looked at the facts in that case with some care. The claimant was pointing out that the Foundation's leaflet suggested that the chance of being infected with HIV was so small that one should consider that one would not be infected. The defendants pointed out that the media had paid a great deal of attention to the fact that blood products always carried a risk of transmitting infections, and the defendants contended that (paragraph 6 as translated from the Dutch):

> the Foundation carefully carried out investigations of the blood and followed the correct and relevant Guidance, so that one is not able to expect a greater safety of the blood product than that which can be offered by the proper compliance with the relevant regulations.

The Court concluded, in finding for the claimant in respect of Article 6 (or the Dutch implementing equivalent), as follows:

> The Court agreed with Scholten that, taking into account the vital importance of blood products and that in principle there is no alternative, the general public expects and is entitled to expect that blood products in the Netherlands have been 100% HIV free for some time. The fact that there is a small chance that HIV could be transmitted via a blood transfusion, which the Foundation estimates at one in a million, is in the opinion of the Court not general knowledge. It cannot therefore be said that the public does not or cannot be expected to have this expectation. The fact that the Foundation acted in accordance with the relevant Guidance, and that the use of an HIV-1 RNA test at the time could not have detected the HIV virus does not have any bearing on this.

The Defendants contend that this decision of the County Court of Amsterdam, which is obviously not in any way binding upon me, was wrong: but further or in the alternative they contend that the decision which the Court then went on to make which resulted in Scholten's claim failing by reference to Article 7(e) (to which I shall return below) was right.

I repeat, for the sake of convenience at this stage, Article 7(e):

The producer shall not be liable as a result of this Directive if he proves . . . that the state of scientific and technical knowledge at the time when he put the product into circulation was not such as to enable the existence of the defect to be discovered.

Must the producer prove that the defect had not been and could not be discovered in the product in question, as the Defendants contend, or must the producer prove that the defect had not been and could not be discovered generally, i.e., in the population of products? If it be the latter, it is common ground here that the existence of the defect in blood generally, i.e., of the infection of blood in some cases by hepatitis virus notwithstanding screening, was known, and indeed known to the Defendants. The question is thus whether, in order to take advantage of the escape clause, the producer must show that no objectively assessable scientific or technical information existed anywhere in the world which had identified, and thus put producers potentially on notice of, the problem; or whether it is enough for the producer to show that, although the existence of the defect in such product was or should have been known, there was no objectively accessible information available anywhere in the world which would have enabled a producer to discover the existence of that known defect in the particular product in question. The Claimants say that once the defect in blood is known about, as it was, it is a known risk. A known but unavoidable risk does not qualify for Article 7(e). It may qualify for Article 6, not because it was unavoidable (see their contentions set out in paragraph 35 above) but if it could be shown that, because the risk is known, it was accepted, and lowered public expectations—like poison and alcohol.

The BGH in the German Bottle Case concludes that Article 7(e) applies only to design defects, and not manufacturing defects. But in my judgment there is no need nor call for differentiation between manufacturing and design defects in the construction of the Directive, and the BGH appears to have been working on the assumption that rogue or non-standard products are always manufacturing defects; and the relevant conclusion, as I see it, was that set out at II(bb) in the judgment (as translated from the German) namely: "such rare and inevitable [production] defects ('*Ausreisser*') are not defects for the purposes of Article 7(e) of the . . . Directive . . . simply because they are inevitable despite all reasonable precautions. The purpose of the [Directive] is merely to exclude liability for so called development risks." This proposition plainly supports the Claimants. The BGH continues (again in translation): "Liability should only be excluded when the potential danger of the product could not be detected because the possibility to detect it did not (yet) exist at the time of marketing." As "the potential danger of re-usable bottles filled with carbonated drinks has been known for a long time" the Article 7(e) defence was not available. In those circumstances the perhaps unnecessary repetition by the BGH of the words "unavoidable production risks do not constitute development risks" seems to me to be set into context. What the BGH was primarily saying is that if the risks are known, unavoidability of the defect in the particular product is no answer.

In Scholten, after resolving the Article 6 defence in favour of the Claimant, the County Court of Amsterdam reached a conclusion supportive of the Defendants on Article 7(e). The Court's conclusion on Article 7(e) (as translated from the Dutch) is based upon the submission by the Foundation that it was not liable because it was impossible to detect the infection of the blood with HIV in the window phase, and that the new PCR test was technically not yet fully developed to achieve such detection; it stated, "Given the state of scientific and technical knowledge at the time of the blood donation and the transfusion to Scholten, this leads to the conclusion that it was, practically speaking, not possible to use the [PCR] test as a screening test in order to detect HIV contamination in blood products. This could therefore not have been expected of the Foundation." The Claimants, while supporting the Court's decision on Article 6, do not agree with its decision on Article 7(e), and the Defendants' position is the reverse. It does seem to me however, on consideration of the judgment alone that reference by the Court in that passage to "expectation" seems to me inapt. The expectation test is relevant only to Article 6, which had been resolved in favour of the claimant. It [also] is not clear whether the point in issue before me, and resolved against the producer in the German Bottle Case, was argued.

I do not consider it to be arguable that the consumer had an actual expectation that blood being supplied to him was not 100% clean, nor do I conclude that he had knowledge that it was, or was likely to be, infected with Hepatitis C. It is not seriously argued by the Defendants that there was any public understanding or acceptance of the infection of transfused blood by Hepatitis C. Doctors and surgeons knew, but did not tell their patients unless asked, and were very rarely asked. It was certainly, in my judgment, not known and accepted by society that there was such a risk.

In my judgment it is impossible to inject into the consumer's legitimate expectation matters which would not by any stretch of the imagination be in his actual expectation. He will assume perhaps that there are tests, but his expectations will be as to the safeness of the blood. In my judgment it is as inappropriate to propose that the public should not "expect the unattainable"—in the sense of tests or precautions which are impossible—at least unless it is informed as to what is unattainable or impossible, as it is to reformulate the expectation as one that the producer will not have been negligent or will have taken all reasonable steps.

In this context I turn to consider what is intended to be included within "all circumstances" in Article 6. I am satisfied that this means all relevant circumstances. It is quite plain to me that the Directive was intended to eliminate proof of fault or negligence. I am satisfied that this was not simply a legal consequence, but that it was also intended to make it easier for claimants to prove their case, such that not only would a consumer not have to prove that the producer did not take reasonable steps, or all reasonable steps, to comply with his duty of care, but also that the producer did not take all legitimately expectable steps either.

I conclude therefore that avoidability is not one of the circumstances to be taken into account within Article 6. I am satisfied that it is not a relevant circumstance, because it is outwith the purpose of the Directive, and indeed that, had it been intended that it would be included as a derogation from, or at any rate a palliation of, its purpose, then it would certainly have been mentioned.

This brings me to a consideration of Article 7(e) in the context of consideration of Article 6. Article 7(e) provides a very restricted escape route, and producers are unable to take advantage of it, unless they come within its very restricted conditions, whereby a producer who has taken all possible precautions (certainly all legitimately expectable precautions) remains liable unless that producer can show that "the state of scientific and technical knowledge [anywhere and anyone's in the world, provided reasonably accessible] was not such as to enable the existence of the defect to be discovered." The significance seems to be as follows. Article 7(e) is the escape route (if available at all) for the producer who has done all he could reasonably be expected to do (and more); and yet that route is emphatically very restricted, because of the purpose and effect of the Directive.

Further, in my judgment, the infected bags of blood were non-standard products. I have already recorded that it does not seem to me to matter whether they would be categorised in US tort law as manufacturing or design defects. They were in any event different from the norm which the producer intended for use by the public. I do not accept that all the blood products were equally defective because all of them carried the risk. That is a very philosophical approach. It is one which would be equally apt to a situation in which one tyre in one million was defective because of an inherent occasional blip in the strength of the rubber's raw material. The answer is that the test relates to the use of the blood bag. For, and as a result of, the intended use, 99 out of 100 bags would cause no injury and would not be infected, unlike the one hundredth. However, in any event, I do not accept that the consumer expected, or was entitled to expect, that his bag of blood was defective even if (which I have concluded was not the case) he had any knowledge of any problem. I do not consider that he was expecting or entitled to expect a form of Russian roulette. That would only arise if, contrary to my conclusion, the public took that as socially acceptable.

Accordingly I am quite clear that the infected blood products in this case were non-standard products (whether on the basis of being manufacturing or design defects does not appear to me to matter). Where, as here, there is a harmful characteristic in a non-standard product, a decision that it is defective is likely to be straightforward, and I can make my decision accordingly. However the consequence of my conclusion is that "avoidability" is also not in the basket of circumstances, even in respect of a harmful characteristic in a standard product.

I conclude that the following are not relevant:

i. Avoidability of the harmful characteristic, i.e., impossibility or unavoidability in relation to precautionary measures;
ii. The impracticality, cost or difficulty of taking such measures;
iii. The benefit to society or utility of the product: (except in the context of whether—with full information and proper knowledge—the public does and ought to accept the risk).

The purpose of the Directive, from which Article 7(e) should obviously not derogate more than is necessary (see Recital 16) is to prevent injury, and facilitate compensation for injury. The Defendants submit that this means that Article 7(e) must be construed so as to give the opportunity to the producer to do all he can in order to avoid injury: thus concentrating on what can be done in relation to the particular product. The Claimants submit that this will rather be achieved by imposing obligation in respect of a known risk irrespective of the chances of finding the defect in the particular product, and I agree.

The purpose of Article 7(e) was plainly not to discourage innovation, and to exclude development risks from the Directive. Hence it protects the producer in respect of the unknown. But the consequence of acceptance of the Defendants' submissions would be that protection would also be given in respect of the known.

Unknown risks are unlikely to qualify by way of defence within Article 6. They may however qualify for Article 7(e). Known risks do not qualify within Article 7(e), even if unavoidable in the particular product. They may qualify within Article 6 if fully known and socially acceptable.

The blood products in this case were non-standard products, and were unsafe by virtue of the harmful characteristics which they had and which the standard products did not have. They were not ipso facto defective (an expression used from time to time by the Claimants) but were defective because I am satisfied that the public at large was entitled to expect that the blood transfused to them would be free from infection. There were no warnings and no material publicity, certainly none officially initiated by or for the benefit of the Defendants, and the knowledge of the medical profession, not materially or at all shared with the consumer, is of no relevance. It is not material to consider whether any steps or any further steps could have been taken to avoid or palliate the risk that the blood would be infected.

In those circumstances the Claimants recover against the Defendants because their claim succeeds within Article 4, the blood bags being concluded to be defective within Article 6, and Article 7(e) does not avail.

NOTES AND QUESTIONS

1. *Consumer expectations redux.* Does *National Blood Authority* confirm the claim that the Directive's adoption of the consumer expectations test will inevitably cause the European courts to confront the same conceptual difficulties previously encountered by U.S. courts? The case implicates virtually the entire spectrum of difficult problems posed by the consumer expectations test:

- What is the relation between the safety expectations of consumers based on actual knowledge and their reasonable safety expectations based on constructive knowledge—what they are "entitled to expect."? *See* Chapter 3, section III (discussing the issue).
- Does the consumer expectations test provide any reason to distinguish among the different types of defects? *See* Chapter 3, section III (discussing how consumer expectations can justify strict liability for manufacturing defects and negligence liability for design and warning defects); Chapter 4, section II (explaining why the process of production does not define the design against which a manufacturing defect is measured); Chapter 5, section I and Chapter 6, section I.C (discussing case law in California that first rejected any differentiation among defects

and then evolved into a consumer expectations test formulated in risk-utility terms for design and warning defects).
- How are consumer expectations influenced by considerations pertaining to cost or the avoidability of risk? *See* Chapter 3, section III.B (showing why consumers reasonably expect that product designs and warnings conform to the safety requirements embodied in the risk-utility test).
- What does the consumer expectations test require with respect to unforeseeable risks? *See* Chapter 7, section II (discussing issue in context of duty to warn).
- Does blood or any other product having a primary purpose of promoting health and safety necessarily "malfunction" and frustrate consumer expectations simply because it causes injury? *See* Chapter 9, section II (discussing the issue).
- Do transactions involving blood or other forms of health care involve the sale of a product or service? *See* Chapter 15, section III (discussing majority approach of treating these cases as being exempt from strict products liability because they primarily involve the provision of a service).
- Is the social value of a product irrelevant for purposes of consumer expectations? *See* Chapter 9 (discussing the exemption from strict products liability for "unavoidably unsafe" products).

2. *The Products Liability Directive.* Detailed study of the Products Liability Directive is beyond the scope of our present concerns. For example, whether the United Kingdom's withdrawal from the European Union—Brexit—affects the relevance of the Directive within the United Kingdom depends on a host of factors. Brexit does not invalidate the Consumer Protection Act, the most important source of domestic law governing products liability in the United Kingdom. The Act arguably represents "the truest implementation" of the Directive "as compared with French and German law." Duncan Fairgrieve & Richard Goldberg, PRODUCT LIABILITY 215 (3d ed. 2020). For this reason, products liability law in the United Kingdom could continue to develop in parallel with the Products Liability Directive governing the remaining members of the European Union, even though the United Kingdom is no longer a member.

3. *The dearth of reported cases in England and Wales.* The opinion in *A v. National Blood Authority* has been called a "monumental judgment." Wilkes v. DePuy International Ltd., [2016] EWHC 3096 (QB), 2016 WL 07048503. Aside from the power of the court's reasoning, the case stands out due to the "dearth of reported cases in England and Wales," which "contrasts with continental countries, such as France, Austria, Germany, and Italy, where application of the implemented Directive is a commonplace occurrence." Contributing factors to this disparity involve "access to justice issues in England and Wales." Fairgrieve & Goldberg, PRODUCT LIABILITY at 185. As this comparison reveals, the practice of products liability is driven by a host of factors other than the substantive liability rules—an issue discussed at greater length below.

4. *Consumer expectations and the risk-utility test.* In *Wilkes,* Judge Hickinbottom held that the issue of defect is potentially affected by the

cost and "practicability of producing a product of risk-benefit equivalence." The court also observed that the inquiry is "holistic."

> The standard of safety which people are entitled to expect across the whole range of these products is incapable of precise definition in a framework document such as the Directive; but, of course, more assistance and guidance could have been given than is found in that document. As Professor Stapleton has said, as it is left, the definition of "defect" used is at best circular, and at worst empty, because "what a person is entitled to expect is the very question a definition of defect should be answering" [ ] However, those responsible for the Directive clearly, and deliberately, declined to give better particulars. Indeed, in the report commissioned by the European Union in 2003 [ ], the possibility of defining "defect" to clarify controversial issues was mooted; but, the authors of the report understood that this might fetter the ability of judges to deal with such matters on a case-by-case basis. The report envisaged that a body of case law would develop that would give guidance with regard to the concept. However, no such body of law has yet developed.

To what extent has the U.S. experience informed this dynamic? "In view of the experience of the American courts in grappling with issues of design defectiveness over many years and the views of commentators, there has been a spectrum of opinion within a European context on the relevance of a risk-benefit test." Fairgrieve & Goldberg, PRODUCT LIABILITY at 400.

5. *Ongoing assessment of the Directive.* Under the terms of the Directive, it must be evaluated periodically by the European Commission. These reports provide a useful perspective on the evolving nature of the Directive. How does this dynamic compare to the evolution of strict products liability in the United States?

SECOND COMMISSION REPORT OF 31 JANUARY 2001 ON THE APPLICATION OF DIRECTIVE 85/374 ON LIABILITY FOR DEFECTIVE PRODUCTS (COM (2000) 893 FINAL)

During the first reading of Directive 99/34, the European Parliament called for a substantial revision of the existing product liability system. Although the Commission did not share this view, it promised to open a wide discussion with all interested parties in the form of a Green Paper, which would prepare the second report on the application of Directive 85/374.

The present application report considered the information and observations received to the Green Paper as well as any other relevant information available.

2.1.2 *The position of European businesses vis-à-vis their foreign competitors*

It seems that the Directive does not weaken the position of European businesses in the global context. Foreign companies selling their products on the European market must also respect Community provisions. In their assessment of third countries, European industry notes that they don't encounter difficulties in those countries the product liability legislation of which follows the principles introduced by the Directive (such as Australia, Japan, Switzerland, Norway and others).

The situation in the United States is considered to constitute a particular case and to have an important impact on European businesses. The answers confirm the way in which the legal framework of which US product liability law forms part—the trial by juries, the "no win, no fee" principle, the awarding of high punitive damages, the possibility of class action—are elements that encourage victims to go to court. This is claimed to create a climate of unpredictability of the outcome for producers. Due to this different situation, European companies, namely small and medium-sized ones, claim that they refrain to some extent from exporting their products to the United States. Another consequence is that they have to pay higher insurance premiums and to face a considerably higher level of litigation. According to figures presented by the Belgian industry, the US legislation renders exports from Europe to the United States two times (for textiles and steel), five times (for food stuffs) and ten times (for pharmaceuticals) more expensive than exports to other countries. These figures have not been assessed and verified by the Commission.

2.2. *Protection of public health and safety*

The first question addressed by the Green Paper in this respect concerned the compensation of victims. It is said that product liability cases have been mostly dealt with under traditional systems and much less under the legislation transposing the Directive. In Finland, the Consumer Complaint Board registered between 1.1.1993 and 22.11.1999 71 cases; 46 cases were decided on the basis of the Product Liability Act and 25 cases on the basis of the Finnish Consumer Protection Act. In Portugal, 200 claims were made since the date of the Directive's implementation; their legal basis is not indicated. In the UK, the number of cases is low.

There are only few reported Court cases based on the Directive: a recent case in Ireland, 2 cases in Italy, 3 cases in the UK, 3 or 4 cases in Belgium, Sweden and Finland, 20 to 25 decisions in Austria, some 30 decisions in Germany, 19 judgments in Portugal, no decision yet in France, Greece and Luxembourg.

The number of product liability cases seems to be relatively low. In the vast majority (90%, according to the German and Dutch insurers) these claims are settled out of court, in particular when the facts (i.e. the defect, the damage and the causal link) are clear. Business recognises the benefits of settling genuine, validated claims by avoiding the length and costs of litigation. In these cases, liability is not an issue and all that remains to discuss is compensation. While some consider the out-of-court settlement a mechanism which functions well, consumer organisations criticise it since the details of the settlement often remain confidential and because producer and insurers have an inequitably advantageous position.

Given the high number of out-of-court settlements, it is said that victims are compensated in general quickly and efficiently. With regard to cases brought before the national courts, the question of a swift solution is more a question of the speed and efficiency of the national systems of civil procedure than of the adequacy of the substantive law. Spanish procedural law is said to be very formal and strict concerning the submission of evidence.

Another question of the Green Paper concerned the impact of the Directive on the victim's interests. The number of claims based on defective products seems not to have increased. It is stated that the level of product safety increased considerably since the Directive was adopted in 1985. This situation results from the existence of a high safety level ensured by a strict regulatory framework, namely in certain product sectors, such as pharmaceuticals, chemicals, machinery, electrical equipment, while the other sectors are covered by the Directive 92/59 on General Product Safety. Industry is said to take into account these safety features in design, production, labelling and post-marketing systems and uses extensively good practice standards. The replies confirm that the Directive on Product Liability has a deterrent effect on manufacturers and suppliers and gives them a strong incentive, alongside the obligations under the aforementioned safety regulations, to improve the safety level.

The view of industry is that the Directive found the right balance between the protection of victims and the interests of producers. Consumer organisations disagree on this point and call for several changes.

3.2 *Issues for a possible future reform*

Earlier political discussions, stakeholders and experts have highlighted several aspects of the directive as deserving special analysis with a view to possible reform.

3.2.2 *Development risks*

Under Directive 85/374 a producer is exempt from liability when he proves the existence of certain facts. One of the exemptions concerns the so-called "development risks." The European Court of Justice interpreted the relevant provision in the following way: the producer of a defective product is absolved of liability if he can establish that the objective state of technical and scientific knowledge, at its most advanced level, at the time when he put the product into circulation was not such as to enable the existence of the defect to be discovered. If it is to be a valid argument against the producer, the relevant knowledge must have been available when the product was put into circulation.

Given the controversial debate, the Community legislator in 1985 did not settle this issue definitely, but provisionally: exemption was possible for a period of ten years, and the Member States had the option of abolishing it unilaterally. Under Article 15(3) of the Directive, it had been agreed that the Commission would assess the effect that rulings by the courts as to the application of Article 7(e) and of Article 15(1)(b) have on consumer protection and the functioning of the internal market. In the light of this assessment it was to be decided whether producers should be liable for "development risks" after the transition period.

After implementation, in some Member States the producer is liable also in case of development risks. In Luxembourg and Finland the scope of liability concerns all types of products. Other countries limited this liability to specific product sectors: Spain in the case of food and pharmaceutical products and France for products derived from the human body and for those marketed before May 1998. In Germany the producer's liability in cases of development risks existed since 1978 in the area of pharmaceutical products.

In this context, the Green Paper asked whether and how liability for development risks involves insurmountable consequences for producers at the

European level, by discouraging them from innovation, especially in the sector of pharmaceuticals, and whether it would be feasible to insure this kind of risk in the insurance market.

Industry's replies put forward a number of arguments in favour of maintaining the exemption based on development risks. In their view this kind of liability would prevent scientific progress, the development and innovation of new products. Linked to the specific features of the pharmaceutical sector, the product launch of innovative bio-tech products could be delayed or prohibited. The degree of unforeseeable risk in so-called "orphan drugs," i.e. those designed to treat rare diseases, would be comparatively higher than with other medicines because the clinical testing is limited to a small number of patients. Introducing such a liability could lower the standard of care to which the pharmaceutical industry works since producers could be made liable notwithstanding the fact that they have applied the highest existing level of scientific knowledge.

Insurers stress the difficulties which will result in pricing a product liability insurance that covers development risks. Given the unforeseeable and unknown risk, it would be very difficult to cover it and insurers might exclude it in their policies.

Other replies, namely those from consumer organisations, stress the fact that strict liability is based on the recognised principle under which the person taking benefits from a dangerous activity should compensate the disadvantage of other persons. Consequently, the producer should be held liable also in case of damages due to any undetectable risk.

Some information is available with regard to the five Member States where, partially or in general, the producer is liable for development risks.

Finland: The Government regarded cases of development risks as very rare and introduced producer liability in this case since there was no justification for consumers having to bear these risks. In practice, the level of insurance premiums increased, the additional costs being negligible. At a public hearing organised by the Ministry of Justice in November 1999, it had been noted that there had been no cases of development risks.

Luxembourg: Case law existing before the Directive was adopted made producers also responsible for development risks. The option had been used to maintain this situation. Specific problems due to this system are not known.

Spain: Introducing liability for development risk for foodstuffs and pharmaceuticals is explained by the fact that these sectors are of greatest public sensitivity and the occurrence of these risks is likely in this area. The financial impact on industry (insurance premiums) is not known.

France: Under the traditional liability system, an undetectable defect was not grounds for exonerating the producer. Owing to ethical considerations, the transposing law made the producer liable for development risks with regard to the elements and products of the human body. Although it is known that insurance companies had difficulties with this provision, no specific data is available.

Germany: Strict liability including development and production risks with regard to pharmaceutical products had already existed before the adoption of the Directive. Given the direct impact on the human body medicines have, the Law on Pharmaceuticals provided for this solution. The inclusion of liability for development risks is combined with financial ceilings (liability is limited to 500,000 DM in any individual case and 200 million DM for each pharmaceutical or 12 million DM for each product per year in the case of annuities). No data on the practical impact is available and very little case law exists.

Very little data is available on what practical impact the introduction of producer liability in case of development risks would have for industry and insurers. No detailed research on the rulings of national courts with regard to the application of the exemption clause related to development risks exists. The few cases known seem to indicate that in practice it is not so easy for the producer to prove that the defect could not be detected on the basis of the knowledge that was available when the product was marketed and, thus, waive his liability. The occurrence of damages due to a development risk seems to be most likely in the following sectors: pharmaceutical products, chemical substances, genetically modified organism and foodstuffs.

THIRD REPORT ON THE APPLICATION OF COUNCIL DIRECTIVE ON THE APPROXIMATION OF LAWS, REGULATIONS AND ADMINISTRATIVE PROVISIONS OF THE MEMBER STATES CONCERNING LIABILITY FOR DEFECTIVE PRODUCTS (COM (2006) 496 FINAL), SEPTEMBER 2006

In accordance with Article 21 of Directive 85/374[1] ("the Directive"), the Commission must review the efficiency of the product liability legal framework on a regular basis.

4. FURTHER WORK

Certain aspects of the Directive concerning the protection of consumers and the functioning of the Internal Market require continued monitoring and could even be subject to further clarification. Differences on the interpretation of these concepts by national courts can sometimes lead to disparities in the judicial application of certain aspects of this Directive from one Member State to another, but there is little evidence that those disparities create significant barriers to trade or distortions to competition in the EU.

- *the concept of defect* (Art. 6)

The Directive prescribes an "expectations" test for defect—that is, a product is said to be defective if it does not provide the safety that a person is entitled to expect. The subjective nature of the "expectations" test means that this principle is incapable of precise definition. This leads to some very practical questions about matters such as whether it is appropriate for a court to undertake a risk/benefit analysis when assessing what a person is entitled to expect, and the extent to which the actual conduct of a producer (such as the degree of care taken, or not taken) is ever relevant in this context. These questions have arisen in reported cases but have yet to be finally resolved by the courts in any Member State. For example, in *A and Others v. National Blood Authority*, the English High Court said that the conduct of the defendant is not a factor to be taken into account when considering whether a product is defective. However, in the subsequent case *of Sam Bogle and others v. McDonald's Restaurants Ltd.*, the English High Court cited . . . the steps taken by McDonalds to train its staff in relation to the safe service of hot drinks to customers.

Uncertainty also surrounds the question of what is required to prove "defect." In some cases, courts seem to have decided that it is sufficient that the claimant merely prove that the product failed and that such failure resulted in injury. In a case decided by the Tribunal de grande instance of Aix en Provence in France, the claimant was injured when a glass window in a fireplace exploded in circumstances where the precise cause was unknown. The Tribunal said that the intervention of the product at the time of the harm was sufficient and that the claimant did not have to prove the precise cause of the accident to prove that the product was defective.

In a similar case in Belgium involving an exploding soft drink bottle the claimant was not required, under the Directive, to prove "the exact nature of the defect, in particular as regards all its technical aspects."

This is in contrast to the approach of the courts of the United Kingdom in *Richardson v. LRC Products Ltd* (which involved a condom that broke during use) and *Foster v. Biosil* (which involved a silicone breast implant that ruptured in situ). In both of these cases, the product failed, but the cause of the failure was unknown. Unlike the decisions in France and Belgium, the United Kingdom court in each case decided that, under the Directive, the claimant bore the onus of proving the nature of the alleged defect, and not merely that the product had failed. As the claimants were not able to prove what had caused the failure, the claims were unsuccessful.

- *the development risks defence* (Art. 7(e))

Member States, by Article 15(1)(b), have had the option to exclude the defence in their implementing legislation, but only Finland and Luxembourg have chosen to do so. Although the Court of Justice has provided some explanation of the scope of the defence, its precise scope remains uncertain. Indeed, there appears to have been only one reported example of where the defence has been used successfully, namely the *Sanquin Foundation* case in the Netherlands. In this case, suppliers of blood contaminated with HIV were able to rely on the defence in circumstances where there was not a reliable screening test available to them at the time of supply. It is interesting to note, however, that a court of the United Kingdom [*A v. National Blood Authority*] decided in a subsequent case that the defence was not available in similar circumstances.

FOURTH REPORT ON THE APPLICATION OF COUNCIL DIRECTIVE 85/374/EEC (COM (2011) 547), 8 SEPT. 2011

. . .

The data collected for the drafting of this report show that some Member States, including Austria, France, Germany, Italy, Poland and Spain, recorded an increase in the number of product liability cases brought under national laws transposing the Directive. In some of the Member States, there was both an increase in the absolute number of cases brought on the grounds of product liability in the last few years and an increase in the relative use of the Directive against cases brought on the grounds of civil or contractual liability.

The increase in the number of product liability cases brought in recent years is thought to be mainly due to external factors such as greater consumer awareness and better organisation of consumer groups or improved means of accessing information. In contrast, it would seem that the costs of the action discourage this type of proceedings in some Member States, for example the United Kingdom.

This having been said, the swift resolution of a case brought before the national courts depends on the thoroughness and effectiveness of national systems of civil law. In cases where liability is not called into question (i.e. the defect, damage and causal link are clear), these claims are settled out of court, which contributes to the injured party being compensated quickly for the damages sustained [ ].

. . .

Using the same methodology as for the third report, the Commission invited the national authorities and interested parties who are members of the informal advisory groups to express their opinions on the application and effectiveness of the Directive during the reference period. The task was to assess the practical impact of the Directive and the issues raised in the previous report, the different interpretations of which by national courts could at times lead to differences in the application of the Directive from one Member State to another.

. . .

Consumers emphasise the difficulty, in particular due to the economic costs, of furnishing proof of the defect of certain highly technical products as well as proving the causal link between the defect and the damage when such damage is complex in nature. In order to better guarantee consumer protection, they believe the burden of proof should be reversed.

As for the producers and insurers, they believe that the requirement to prove the causal link between the damage and the product's defect is fundamental to the balance between producers' interests and consumer interests guaranteed under the Directive. They also believe that relaxing the rules for the burden of proof would encourage consumers to take legal action for minor damage. According to legal practitioners, plaintiffs are able to establish the causal link between the defect and damage on the basis of the rules of evidence in the various Member States. This is proved by the increasing number of claims for compensation arising from a defective product.

- Defence of regulatory compliance (Article 7(d)).

Directive 85/374/EEC establishes that the producer shall not be liable if he proves that the defect is due to compliance of the product with mandatory regulations issued by the public authorities. On the basis of the information available, the Commission notes that there is very little case law on this ground of defence.

CONCLUSION

Directive 85/374/EEC is not aimed at fully harmonising all aspects of legislation on liability arising from defective products in the EU. Moreover, the Court of Justice of the European Union, through its case-law, makes a key contribution towards defining the scope of this Directive and ensuring its correct and uniform implementation.

In the light of the information available, the situation regarding the application of Directive 85/374/EEC is similar to that stated in the previous report. . . . In general, the Directive is seen as achieving a balance between consumer protection and the producers' interests.

EUROPEAN COMMISSION, FIFTH REPORT ON THE APPLICATION OF COUNCIL DIRECTIVE ON THE APPROXIMATION OF LAWS, REGULATIONS AND ADMINISTRATIVE PROVISIONS OF THE MEMBER STATES CONCERNING LIABILITY FOR DEFECTIVE PRODUCTS (85/374/EEC) (COM/2018/246 FINAL), 7 MAY 2018

1. INTRODUCTION

For more than three decades, the Product Liability Directive ('the Directive') has ensured that producers take responsibility for defective products vis-à-vis consumers. When it was adopted in 1985, the Directive was a bold and modern instrument that required substantial adaptations of Member States' civil codes.

The Directive was one of the first pieces of EU legislation that explicitly aimed to protect consumers. It introduced the concept of strict liability, where producers are responsible for defective products, regardless of whether the defect is their fault. The Directive also aims to contribute to economic growth by providing a stable and legal environment of equal competition that allows companies to place innovative products on the market.

The Directive complements EU product safety legislation and what is known as the 'New Approach' to product safety. Introduced at the same time as the Directive, the 'New Approach' aims to prevent accidents by setting common safety rules that allow the single market for goods to function smoothly and to reduce administrative burden. The Directive is the safety net for instances when accidents nevertheless occur.

2018 is not 1985. The EU and its rules on product safety have evolved, as have the economy and technologies. Many products available today have characteristics that were considered science fiction in the 1980s. The challenges we are facing now and even more acutely in the future—to name but a few—relate to digitisation, the Internet of Things, artificial intelligence and cybersecurity.

Exponential growth in computing power, the availability of data and progress in algorithms turn are making especially artificial intelligence (AI) in particular into one of the most important technologies of the 21st century. The Commission adopted its Communication on 'Maximising the benefits of Artificial Intelligence' to ensure a coherent policy response that also addresses legal challenges. Product safety and liability—should there be damage—are one essential aspect in finding of a policy response that enables European societies, businesses and consumers to benefit from artificial intelligence.

Given that the Directive has never been evaluated since its entry into force and in the light of these recent technological developments, the Commission carried out an evaluation of the Directive to assess its performance. The evaluation includes consideration of recent technological developments. More specifically, it analysed whether the Directive: (i) continues to be effective in meeting its original objectives; (ii) is efficient; (iii) is consistent with the relevant EU rules; (iv) remains relevant by embracing recent technological changes; and (v) whether EU product liability legislation continues to provide added value to businesses and injured persons.

The evaluation also looked at whether the Directive in its current form still serves its purpose. Does it adequately address the challenges of increasingly autonomous devices and cybersecurity? What about sustainability and reaching a circular economy? Does the Directive unnecessarily discourage producers from placing innovative products on the market? Or conversely, does it deter manufacturers from placing faulty and unsafe products on the market? Does it still protect injured persons in a changing world?

The evaluation has shown that even though products are much more complex today than in 1985, the Product Liability Directive continues to be an adequate tool.

However, we need to clarify the legal understanding of certain concepts (such as product, producer, defect, damage and the burden of proof) and look closely at certain products such as pharmaceuticals, which may pose a challenge to the performance of the Directive.

In addition, on emerging digital technologies, a preliminary analysis on how these affect the functioning of the Directive, has raised a number of open questions. In light of these findings, the Commission will consult broadly to reach a common understanding with all stakeholders. The aim is to draw up comprehensive guidance on how to apply the Directive today. In addition, it will assess to what extent emerging digital technologies can be adequately addressed by the current Directive. This guidance and the assessment will help us to pave the way forward for a product liability framework fit for the digital industrial revolution.

Our goal is to ensure that: (i) the EU continues to have a product liability regime that fosters innovation; (ii) products placed on the EU market are safe; and (iii) people who suffer injury because of defective products are able to claim compensation when accidents occur. We have a responsibility both to businesses and to people who suffer injury. This is our compass. We need to navigate the coming technological changes carefully and sensibly so as to respect either objective.

. . .

3. IMPLEMENTATION OF THE DIRECTIVE

. . .

The findings of the evaluation suggest that most product liability claims between 2000 and 2016 were actually settled out of Court. 46% of cases were settled in direct negotiation, 32% in Court, 15% through alternative dispute settlement mechanisms, and 7% were resolved through other means such as through the insurer of the responsible party. The external study commissioned for the evaluation identified 798 claims based on product liability rules from 2000 to 2016. It is, however, likely that the real number of cases was higher, and not all cases were included in the public and private databases consulted. The products most concerned are raw materials (21.2% of cases), pharmaceuticals (16.1%), vehicles (15.2%) and machinery (12.4%). The types of damage identified relate to the characteristics of each product.

6. CONCLUSION: A FOURTH INDUSTRIAL REVOLUTION—A PRACTICAL APPROACH TO LIABILITY

The problems we face today differ to some extent from those we had in the largely analogue world of 1985. We are undergoing another technological revolution. The economy and products themselves are increasingly becoming interconnected, digital, autonomous and intelligent. We need a coherent and global response to these challenges, as outlined in the Artificial Intelligence Initiative [ ].

The Directive has until now covered a broad range of products and technological developments. In principle, it is a useful tool for protecting injured persons and ensuring competition in the single market, by harmonising rules for injured persons and businesses in the aspects that it covers. It is an area where EU level rules provide a clear added value. Having EU level rules for product liability is uncontested.

This does not mean that the Directive is perfect.

Its effectiveness is hampered by concepts (such as 'product', 'producer', 'defect', 'damage', or the burden of proof) that could be more effective in practice. As the evaluation has also shown, there are cases where costs are not equally distributed between consumers and producers. This is especially true when the burden of proof is complex, as may be the case with some emerging digital technologies or pharmaceutical products.

To remain relevant for the future, the Directive would benefit from clarification to address such issues. The Directive covers a broad range of products and possible scenarios. Guidance can help to make these concepts more effective and highlight their continued relevance.

Our objective is to continue ensuring a fair balance of the interests of consumers and producers for all products.

Some of the concepts that were clear-cut in 1985, such as 'product' and 'producer' or 'defect' and 'damage' are less so today. Industry is increasingly integrated into dispersed multi-actor and global value chains with strong service components. Products can increasingly be changed, adapted and refurbished beyond the producer's control. They will also have increasing degrees of autonomy. Emerging business models disrupt traditional markets. The impact of these developments on product liability needs further reflection. At the end of the day, a producer is and needs to be responsible for the product it puts into circulation, while injured persons need to be able to prove that damage has been caused by a defect. Both producers and consumers need to know what to expect from products in terms of safety through a clear safety framework.

Conversely, the development of a strong single market in cybersecurity products and services will be hampered by problems over the attribution of damage for businesses and supply chains and failure to address these issues, as highlighted by the Commission in its Communication on 'Resilience, Deterrence and Defence: Building strong cybersecurity for the EU' [ ]. Again, consumers and businesses need to be aware of the security levels they can expect, and they need to know who to turn to if a failing in cybersecurity leads to material damage.

Recent large-scale cross-border issues affecting many consumers across the EU, such as the 'Dieselgate' scandal, have had a negative impact on consumer trust in the single market. In its 'New Deal for Consumers', the Commission proposes—among other measures—to modernise redress systems and make it easier for consumers to obtain their rights [ ]. To make sure that the single market lives up to its full potential we need to reassure consumers that their rights will be respected.

Other wider aspects require similar attention. This is particularly relevant in the context of a more sustainable economy in which products are refurbished, patched and reused. Who will be the manufacturer of such products, e.g. in the case of repair, reuse and refurbishment? Also, is the fact that all preliminary rulings of the Court of Justice concerned pharmaceutical and medical devices indicative of specific characteristics in this sector?

The Commission has launched an expert group on liability to explore the effect of these developments in detail. The group has two configurations. One is composed of representatives from Member States, industry, consumer organisations, civil society and academia: this group will assist the Commission in interpreting, applying and possibly updating the Directive, including in light of developments in EU and national case-law, the implications of new and emerging technologies and any other development in the field of product liability. The expert group's other configuration, composed solely of independent academic experts and practitioners, will assess whether the overall liability regime is adequate to facilitate the uptake of new technologies by fostering investment stability and consumer trust.

As the Commission, we aim to put in place a positive and reliable framework for product liability that fosters innovation, jobs and growth while protecting consumers and the safety of the general public. We will issue guidance on the Directive as well as a report on the broader implications for, and potential gaps in and orientations for, the liability and safety frameworks for AI, Internet of Things and robotics in mid-2019. If necessary, the Commission will update certain aspects of the Directive, such as the concepts of 'defect', 'damage', 'product' and 'producer'. However, the overall principle of strict liability will remain intact.

A coherent, technology-neutral safety framework should prevent accidents as far as possible. However, when accidents do happen, our liability framework should ensure that those who suffer injury are compensated.

NOTES AND QUESTIONS

1. *Harmonization?* The European Union's Directive on Products Liability has required courts to address numerous substantive questions identical to the ones faced by courts in the United States. A common set of recurring issues helps to explain the commonality of products liability rules around the world.

> On a global level there is... a partial convergence towards some fundamental rules and principles as well as a remaining diversity in matters large and small. The convergence is explained mainly by the successive impact of two leading models. [F]rom the late 1960s through the early 1980s, the American approach became widely influential, especially in Western Europe. Then, since the mid-1980s, the modified European regime, as enshrined in the EC-Directive of 1985, provided the blueprint for the special product liability rules not only of the EU member states, but of many countries in Eastern Europe, the Far East, Latin America, and other parts of the world as well. Unsurprisingly, where national laws followed these models, the respective rules are often quite similar both in general outline and in many details. The persistent diversity is due primarily to a combination of two factors. First, the two leading models (American and European) are not completely identical but diverge in several regards. Second, the influence of these models was by and large limited to the special product liability regimes recently created by many countries. It rarely affected the remedies existing under general tort or contract law, and these traditional remedies are often quite varied.

Mathias Reimann, *Liability for Defective Products at the Beginning of the Twenty-First Century: Emergence of a Worldwide Standard?*, 51 Am. J. Comp. L. 751, 761-762 (2003).

2. *Diversity in application.* Any uniformity regarding the black-letter law of products liability does not necessarily translate into uniform application. Consider the number of cases decided in Europe over the past decade as compared to the United States. Multiple factors influence the actual impact of products liability law, making the comparative study of products liability "a dangerous business." Jane Stapleton, *Product Liability in the United Kingdom: The Myths of Reform*, 34 Tex. Intl. L.J. 45, 46 (1999).

As compared to the U.S., countries in the European Union have less tort liability supplemented by more extensive administrative regulation and government-provided insurance. *See* Julie A. Davies & Paul T. Hayden, GLOBAL ISSUES IN TORT LAW 13 (2008). Tort law is one institution of many that protect individuals from physical harm, making the practice of tort law contingent on the full range of complementary institutions. Consider Dana A. Kerr, Yu-Luen Ma & Joan T. Schmit, *A Cross-National Study of Government Social Insurance as an Alternative to Tort Liability Compensation*, 76 J. Risk & Insur. 367 (2009) (using data from 24 countries over a 12-year period to find "a strong negative relationship between the government social spending and the size of liability costs as measured by insurance premiums," thus supporting "the hypothesis that generous social programs have influenced the development of litigation as a means to compensate injured parties").

The most important factor influencing the practical impact of products liability laws appears to be the rules regarding procedures and damages. As compared to the U.S., both types of rules make it substantially harder for consumers in other countries to pursue a products liability claim.

> In civil law countries, there is simply nothing at all like a pre-trial discovery process. A party must essentially put the initial case together

without any cooperation from the other side. Once in court, he or she can ask the judge to request certain documents from the opponent, to subpoena witnesses, or to allow examinations, but without an explicit order by the court, neither the opponent nor third parties are normally under an obligation to assist the plaintiff. Under this approach, it is obviously very difficult, if not impossible, for a victim or her lawyer to investigate a product liability case. To be sure, in some jurisdictions with a civilian procedural system, recent reforms have somewhat strengthened the parties' rights to obtain evidence from the other side, as in Japan, Germany, and Spain. But these measures do not even approach an American-style discovery regime, and it remains to be seen whether they will have much of an impact in practice.

Reimann, *supra*, 51 Am. J. Comp. L. at 817-818.

Damage awards in the U.S. are also much higher than elsewhere, particularly with respect to nonmonetary (pain and suffering) and punitive damage awards. "[A] really high award even in rich countries like Japan or Germany is a few hundred thousand dollars, in the United States it is tens of millions." *Id.* at 809.

The amount of damages available to successful claimants has a feedback effect on their ability to procure legal representation in the first instance, a particular problem in the vast majority of countries that do not permit a plaintiff's lawyer to take the case on a contingency-fee basis. "In short, how products liability law functions in practice depends in no small part on the rules and realities of legal representation." *Id.* at 822.

The practical importance of strict products liability in any given country undoubtedly depends on various factors other than the liability rules themselves, but "[w]hen the focus is on legal argument, a grasp of comparative materials yields its richest intellectual rewards for the practitioner and judge because 'it is arguments that influence decisions.'" Jane Stapleton, *Benefits of Comparative Tort Reasoning: Lost in Translation*, 1 J. Tort L., issue 3 article 6 (2007). How one country has addressed the conceptual difficulties posed by strict products liability can influence judges in another country. Due to the global reach of the consumer expectations test, one's ability to comprehend consumer expectations in all respects, including its relation to the risk-utility test, should prove to be a highly valuable skill in the twenty-first century.

Table of Cases

Principal cases are in italics.

80 South Eighth Street Limited Partnership v. Carey-Canada, Inc., 574, 578, 580

A v. National Blood Authority, 728, 739, 740, 745
Abel v. Eli Lilly & Co., 474
Ackerman v. Wyeth Pharms., 445, 455
Adamo v. Brown & Williamson Tobacco Corp., 221
Adelman-Tremblay v. Jewel Companies, Inc., 273
Air & Liquid Systems Corp. v. DeVries, 286, 326
Ake v. Gen. Motors Corp., 129, 187, 198
Allen v. Grafton, 131
Allex v. Rodgers Mach. Mfg., 118
Allison v. Merck & Co., 388
Althen v. Secretary of Health & Human Servs., 509
Altria Group, Inc. v. Good, 409
Amchem Products Inc. v. Windsor, 11
American Safety Equip. Co. v. Winkler, 41
American Tobacco Co., Inc. v. Grinnell, 288, 290, 291, 292, 294, 301
Anderson v. Owens-Corning Fiberglass Corp., 257, 260, 262, 264, 270
Anderson v. Van Doren, 166
Andren v. White-Rodgers Co., 659, 661, 662
Angus v. Shiley Inc., 591
Arena Holdings Charitable, LLC v. Harman Professional, Inc., 569
Asbestos Products Liability Litigation, In re, 286
Aspinall v. Phillip Morris Cos., Inc., 255
Aubin v. Union Carbide Corp., 77, 147, 721
A.W. v. Lancaster Cnty. Sch. Dist. 0001, 537

Banks v. ICI Americas, Inc., 76
Barker v. Deere & Co., 247
Barker v. Lull Engineering Co., 94, 161, 190, 191, 260
Barnes v. American Tobacco Co., 584
Barrett v. Ambient Pressure Diving, Ltd., 602
Barron v. Abbott Labs., Inc., 318

Baxter v. Ford Motor Co. (12 P.2d 409), *449*, 452, 453, 454
Baxter v. Ford Motor Co. (35 P.2d 1090), *451*, 456
Beatty v. Trailmaster Prods., Inc., 404
Bell v. 3M Co., 585
Bell v. Bayerische Motoren Werke Aktiengesellschaft, 719
Belle Bonfils Mem'l Blood Bank v. Hansen, 385, 390
Bennett v. Pilot Prods. Co., 273
Berg v. Sukup Mfg. Co., 628
Berkebile v. Brantley Helicopter Corp., 544
Berrier v. Simplicity Mfg., Inc., 709
Beshada v. Johns-Manville Prods. Corp., 263, 264
Bexiga v. Havir Manufacturing Corp., 641, 643, 652, 665
Bifolck v. Phillip Morris, Inc., 102, 106, 165, 178
Boatland of Houston v. Bailey, 238, 243
Bohnstedt v. Robscon Leasing L.L.C., 720
Bolger v. Amazon.com LLC, 679, 681, 682
Borel v. Fibreboard Paper Products Corp., 5, 7, 8, 11, 12, 19, 22, 243, 255, 287
Brandenburger v. Toyota Motor Sales, U.S.A., Inc., 113
Brandt v. Rokey Realty Co., 273
Branham v. Ford Motor Co., 77, 101, 178, 179, 348, 609
Brewer v. Paccar, Inc., 234
Brody v. Overlook Hosp., 125, 384
Broussard v. Continental Oil Co., 318, 322
Brown v. Bowen, 431
Brown v. Superior Court, 366, 371, 476, 478, 488
Brown v. United States, 655
Bruesewitz v. Wyeth LLC, 370, 415
Burke v. Spartanics, Ltd., 301, 302
Burningham v. Wright Medical Tech., 380
Butler v. Daimler Trucks North American LLC, 418, 686

Cafazzo V. Central Medical Health Services, Inc., 125, 686, 693, 694, 695
Calles v. Scripto-Tokai Corp., 185

Camacho v. Hondo Motor Co., 79, 83, 113, 118, 228, 233, 234
Campbell v. Boston Scientific Corp., 226
Campbell v. ITE Imperial Corp., 628
Campos v. Firestone Tire & Rubber Co., 277, *323*, 324, 325, 326
Campus Sweater & Sportswear Co. v. M.B. Kahn Constr. Co., 602
Carlin v. Superior Court, 455
Caronia v. Phillip Morris USA, Inc., 482
Carrel v. National Cord & Braid Corp., 262
Carroll Towing Co., United States v., 64, 309
Carroll v. Otis Elevator Co., 205
Carson v. Monsanto Co., 518
Cepeda v. Cumberland Engineering Co., *161*, 164, 166, 169, 187
Cipollone v. Liggett Group Inc., *107*, 153, 439
Clinkscales v. Carver, 397
Codling v. Paglia, 113
Coffman v. Keene Corp., *442*, 444, 445, 447
Cole v. Goodwin & Story, *60*, 61
Collins v. Eli Lilly Co., 479, 492
Colon ex rel. Molina v. BIC USA, Inc., 190
Colter v. Barber-Greene Co., 454
Commonwealth v. *See name of opposing party*
Compaq Computer Corp. v. Lapray, 452
Concrete Pipe & Prod. v. Construction Laborers Pension Trust, 431
Conn. Interlocal Risk Management Agency v. Jackson, 473
Consol. Rail Corp. v. Gottshall, 534, 592
Cooley v. Public Serv. Co., 65
Corbin v. Coleco Indus., 169
Corder v. Ethicon, Inc., 164
Crawfordsville Town & Country Center v. Cordova, 277, 278
Cremeans v. Willmar Henderson Manufacturing Co., *619*, 622, 623, 624, 628
Cronin v. J.B.E. Olson Corp., *154*, 157, 161, 164, 170, 185
Crossfield v. Quality Control Equip. Co., 244
Crossley v. General Motors Corp., *424*, 427, 429, 433, 440
Cunningham v. MacNeal Mem'l Hosp., 384
Cushing v. Rodman, 63

Daley v. LaCrois, 593
Daly v. General Motors Corp., *644*
D'Ambra v. United States, 593
Dansak v. Cameron Coca-Cola Bottling Co., 143
Daubert v. Merrell Dow Pharms., Inc. (43 F.3d. 1311), *433*, 436, 437, 438, 440, 475, 520
Daubert v. Merrell Dow Pharms., Inc. (509 U.S. 579), 435, 500, 501, 502, 517
Davol, Inc/C.R. Bard, Inc., Polypropylene Hernia Mesh Products Liability Litigation, In re, 221, 243, 313
Dawson v. Chrysler Corp., *200*, 204

de Veer v. Land Rover N. Am., Inc.-602, 714
Delaney v. Deere & Co., 76, 349
Delaney v. Towmotor Corp., *672*, 674
Denny v. Ford Motor Co., *89*, 93, 94
DePuy Orthopaedics, Inc. Pinnicale Hip Implant Product Liaibility Litigation, In re, *217*, 221, 222
Donovan v. Philip Morris USA, Inc., *581*, 585
Donze v. General Motors, LLC, *650*, 652
Dougan v. Sikorsky Aircraft Corp., 585
Dreisonstok v. Volkswagenwerk, A.G., *211*, 213, 214, 216, 222, 232, 715

Eagle-Picher Indus. Inc. v. Balbos, 428
East River Steamship v. Transamerica Delavel, *561*, 566, 567, 568, 569, 573, 574, 578, 579, 580, 585, 586, 658
Eberhart v. Amazon.Com, Inc., 681
Egbert v. Nissan Motor Corp., 468
Eghnayem v. Boston Scientific Corp., 226
Eighth Jud. Dist. Asbestos Litig., Matter of, 684
Ellingsworth v. Vermeer Mfg. Co., 678
Elmore v. Owens-Illinois, Inc., 248
Engle v. Liggett Group, Inc., 295
Eric Insurance Co. v. Amazon.com, Inc., 681
Escola v. Coca Cola Bottling Co., 36, 39, 40, 41, *56*, 59, 61, 62, 65
Evans v. General Motors Corp., 207
Evans v. Lorillard Tobacco Co., 185, 455, 456
Exxon Co., U.S.A. v. Sofec, Inc., *543*, *656*, 658, 659

Farias v. Mr. Heater, Inc., 277, 278
Farkas v. Addition Mfg. Techs., LLC, 166
Farmer v. International Harvester Co., 79
Fasolas v. Bobcat of New York, Inc., 234
Feldman v. Lederle Labs., 264
Findlay v. Copeland Lumber Co., 643
Finn v. G.D. Searle & Co., 326
Fischer v. Johns-Manville Corp., 602
Ford Motor Co. v. Ledesma, 543
Ford Motor Co. v. Reese, 335
Ford Motor Co. v. Trejo, 77
Ford v. Polaris Industries, Inc., *633*, 638, 639
Foster v. Biosil, 746
Frankel v. Lull Eng'g Co., 454
Freeman v. Hoffman-La Roche, Inc., *372*, 378, 380, 381
Frye v. United States, 500

Gaines-Tabb v. ICI Explosives, USA, Inc., *706*, 708, 709
Gardiner v. Gray, 35
Gay v. O.F. Mossberg & Sons, Inc., 529, 555
Geier v. American Honda Motor Co., 414, 416, 417, 418, 419

Table of Cases 757

General Motors Corp. v. Johnston, 686
General Motors Corp. v. Saenz, 440, 441
General Motors Corp. v. Sanchez, 567
Genie Indus. v. Matak, 243
Gibberson v. Ford Motor Co., 699, 701, 706
Giddings & Lewis, Inc. v. Indus. Risk Insureres, 579
Godoy v. Abamaster of Miami, Inc., 668, 671, 697
Golden Spread Elec. Coop., Inc. v. Emerson, 568
Goldman v. Johns-Manville Sales Corp., 473
Golonka v. General Motors Corp., 445
Golt by Golt v. Sports Complex, Inc., 674
Gordon v. Axtec Brewing Co., 39
Gorran v. Atkins Nutritionals, Inc., 683, 685
Graff v. Beard, 153
Graves v. CAS Medical Systems, Inc., 686
Gray v. Badger Mining Corp., 281
Great Northern Insurance Co. v. Honeywell Int'l, Inc., 329, 333
Green v. Smith & Nephew AHP, Inc., 76, *83,* 87, 93, 94, 179, 248, 262, 544
Green v. Sterling Extruder Corp., 652
Greenman v. Yuba Power Prods., 39, 42, 74, 157, 180
Greiner v. Volkswagenwerk Aktiengesellschaft, 523
Grimshaw v. Ford Motor Co., 194, 195, 600
Grinnell v. Charles Pfizer & Co., 388
Grogan v. Garner, 431
Grubb v. Smith, 309
Grubbs v. Walmart Stores, Inc., 179

Halliday v. Sturm, Ruger & Co., 76, *80,* 82, 87, 93, 94, 95, 160, 161
Hammontree v. Jenner, 15, 18, 19, 22
Harned v. Dura Corp., 394, 397, 398, 399, 406
Haught v. Maceluch, 593
Henningsen v. Bloomfield Motors, Inc., 40, 41, 42, 617
Henry v. General Motors Corp., 278
Hernandez v. Tokai Corp., 171
Hickerson v. Yamaha Motor Corp., 347, 348
Hinrichs v. Dow Chemical Co., 572
Hinton v. Monsanto Co., 585
Hoffman v. Houghton Chemical Corp., 282, 285
Hood v. Ryobi America Corp., 324, 325, 326, *358,* 361, 362
Hopkins v. Dow Corning Corp., 500
Horst v. Deere & Co., 701, 705, 706, 709
House v. Armour of Am., Inc., 215
Howard ex rel. Estate of Ravert v. A.W. Chesterton Co., 428
Hubbard-Hall Chem. Co. v. Silverman, 277
Huff v. White Motor Corp., 207
Hughes v. Moore, 593
Huset v. J.I. Case Threshing Mach. Co., 50
Hyjek v. Anthony Industries, 244, 247, 318
Hymowitz v. Eli Lilly & Co., 479, 482, 492

Iliades v. Dieffenbacher North America Inc., 303
In re. *See name of party*
Indian Brand Farms, Inc. v. Novartis Crop Protection, Inc., 210
Inman v. Technicolor USA, Inc., 679
Izzarelli v. R.J. Reynolds Tobacco Co., 111

Jackson v. Harsco Corp., 632
Jacob E. Decker & Sons v. Capps, 27, 31, 41, 63
Jeld-Wen, Inc. v. Gamble by Gamble, 547, 550, 552
Jimenez v. Superior Court, 568
Johnson & Johnson Talcum Powder Prod. Mktg., Sales Prac. & Liab. Litig, In re, 452
Johnson Insulation, Commonwealth v., 46
Johnson v. American Standard, Inc., 266, 270, 272, 279
Johnson v. Ford Motor Co., 546
Johnson v. Johnson Chem. Co., Inc., 322
Jones v. Amazing Products, Inc., 311, 313
Jones v. Hittle Serv., Inc., 404
Jones v. Just, L.R., 35
Jones v. Nordictrack, Inc., 209

Kampen v. American Isuzu Motors, Inc., 655
Karney v. Leonard Transp. Corp., 716
Kennedy v. Providence Hockey Club, Inc., 627
Kim v. Toyota Motor Corp., 198, 199, 236, 237
Kimco Dev. Corp. v. Michael D's Carpet Outlets, 652
Kinnett v. Mass. Gas & Elec. Co., 473
Kinsman Transit Co., In re, 547
Kirkbride v. Terex USA, 445
Klein v. Sears, Roebuck & Co., 344, 347, 348, 349
Klopp v. Wackenhut Corp., 344, 349, 350
Koutsoukos v. Toyota Motor Sales, U.S.A., Inc., 147

LaPlante v. American Honda Motor Corp., 195, 198, 199
Larsen v. Pacesetter Sys., Inc., 573
Liebeck v. McDonald's Restaurant, 610, 612
Linegar v. Armour of America, 222, 225, 226, 232
Lipitor (Atorvastatin Calcium) Mktg., Sales Practices and Prods. Liabl. Litig., In re, 519
Liriano v. Hobart Corp., 295, 429, 431, 433, 435, 436, 439, 440
Livingston v. Marie Callender's Inc., 271, 272, 302
Longmeid v. Holliday, 50
Lovick v. Wil-Rich, 288, 333
Luque v. McLean, 158, 161, 165, 166, 169, 175, 184

MacDonald v. Ortho Pharmaceutical Corp., 313, 315, 317, 318, 322, 377, 440, 441
MacPherson v. Buick Motor Co., 51, 54, 55
Magrine v. Krasnica, 694

Malen v. MTD Prods., Inc., 460, 678
Man v. Raymark Indus., 602
Martin v. Abbott Labs., 476, 479
Matter of. *See name of matter*
May v. Portland Jeep, 465, 467
McCabe v. American Honda Motor Corp., 147
McCabe v. L.K. Liggett Drug Co., 80, 177
McCann v. Atlas Supply Co., 136
McCarthy v. Olin Corp., 709, 713, 714, 716, 720
McCarty v. Pheasant Run, Inc., 192
McCathern v. Toyota Motor Corp., 76
McGee v. S-L Snacks Natl., 452
McGregor v. Scotts Co., 130
McKenzie v. SK Hand Tool Corp., 126, 129, 144
McMahon v. Bunn-O-Matic Corp., 611, 612
Medina v. Louisville Ladder, Inc., 275, 277, 278
Merrill v. Beaute Vues Corp., 275
Methyl Tertiary Butyl Ether ("MTBE") Products Liability Litigation, In re, 587, 591, 592, 595
Metro-North Commuter R.R. Co. v. Buckley, 585, 591, 592
Metropolitan Property & Casualty Co. v. Deere & Co., 137, 143, 144
Micallef v. Miehle Co., 113, 165
Mikolajczyk v. Ford Motor Co., 77, 101
Miles Labs. v. Doe, 389
Mitchell v. Volkswagenwerk, AG, 463
Moberly v. Secretary of Health & Human Servs., 505
Moran v. Faberge, Inc., 303, 308, 316, 324, 325, 326, 528
Mulcahy v. Eli Lilly & Co., 490
Murphy v. E.R. Squibb & Sons., Inc., 475, 476, 478, 488, 694

Nease v. Ford Motor Co., 190
Neurontin Mktg., Sales Practices, & Prods. Liab. Litig., In re, 510
New Texas Auto Auction Services, L.P. v. Gomez de Hernandez, 675, 678
New York Cent. R.R. Co. v. White, 62
New York City Asbestos Litigation, Matter of, 262
Newmark v. Gimbel's Inc., 694, 695
Niedner v. Ortho-McNeil Pharm., Inc., 221
Norfolk & Western Railway Co. v. Ayers, 11

Oberdorf v. Amazon.com Inc., 682
O'Brien v. Muskin, 185
Ortiz v. Fibreboard Corp., 11
Owens-Illinois, Inc. v. Zenobia, 260, 595, 600, 602

Palmer v. A.H. Robins Co., 199
Parish v. Jumpking, Inc., 210, 216
Parker v. Wellman, 585

Parks v. Ariens Co., 232
Passwaters v. General Motors Corp., 716, 719, 720
Pavildes v. Galveston Yacht Basin, Inc., 255, 312
Pelman v. McDonald's Corp., 255, 256
Perez v. Wyeth Labs., Inc., 377
Peterson v. Lamb Rubber Co., 39
Peterson v. Superior Court, 678
Petition of United States, 592, 593
Pfizer, Inc. v. Farsian, 570, 572, 573, 574, 579, 580
Philip Morris USA v. Williams, 603, 607, 608, 609, 610
Phillips v. Kimwood Mach. Co., 19
Pliva, Inc. v. Mensing, 286
Port Auth. of N.Y. & N.J. v. Arcadian Corp., 708
Potter v. Chicago Pneumatic, 76, 97, 100, 101, 106, 115, 147
Potter v. Firestone Tire & Rubber Co., 586, 593
Precise Eng'g, Inc. v. LaCombe, 316
Pritchett v. Cottrell, Inc., 177

Rainier v. Union Carbide Corp., 585
Ramirez v. Plough, Inc., 400, 404, 406
Randi W. v. Muroc Jt. Unified Sch. Dist., 264
Rardin v. T & D Mach. Handling, Inc., 579
Reliable Transfer; United States v., 658
Reyes v. Vantage S.S. Co., 432
Reyes v. Wyeth Labs., 378
Rhone-Poulenc Rorer, Inc., In re, 384
Rice v. Santa Fe Elevator Corp., 414
Richardson v. LRC Products Ltd, 746
Rider v. Sandoz Pharmaceuticals Corp., 494, 501, 503, 510, 520
Riegel v. Medtronic, Inc., 414, 415
Rivera v. Philip Morris, Inc., 446
R.J. Reynolds Co. v. Marotta, 295
Robinson v. Brandtjen & Kluge, Inc., 117, 247
Robinson v. McNeil Consumer Healthcare, 317
Rodriguez v. Suzuki Motor Corp., 76
Rogers v. Miles Labs, Inc., 381, 387, 388, 389
Romo v. Ford Motor Co., 602
Rose v. Brown & Williamson Tobacco Corp., 638
Roundup Products Liability Litigation (358 F. Supp. 3d 956), *514*
Roundup Products Liability Litigation (385 F. Supp. 3d 1082), 517
Roundup Products Liability Litigation (390 F. Supp. 3d 1102), *510*, 513, 520
Rutherford v. Owens-Ill. Inc., 428

Sajkowski v. Young Men's Christian Ass'n of Greater N.Y., 639
Salazar v. Wolo Manufacturing Group, 208, 209, 531
Sam Bogle and others v. McDonald's Restaurants Ltd., 746
Saratoga Fishing Co. v. J.M. Martinac & Co., 568
Scarangella v. Thomas Built Buses, Inc., 228, 232, 234, 720
Schafer v. American Cyanamid Co., 370

Table of Cases 759

Schafer v. JLC Food Systems, Inc., 132
Scholten v. The Foundation Sanquin of Blood Supply, 735, 746
Seely v. White Motor Co., 586
Seixas & Seixas v. Woods, 32
September 11 Litigation, In re, 531, 534, 535, 537, 556
Sexton v. Bell Helmets, Inc., 117
Shanks v. Upjohn Co., 378
Sharpe v. Bestop, Inc., 445
Sigler v. American Honda Motor Co., 144, 146
Simler v. Dubuque Paint Equip. Servs., 531
Simonetta v. Viad Corp., 310
Sindell v. Abbott Laboratories, 469, 473, 474, 475, 476, 478, 483, 486, 488, 489, 491, 492
Skyhook Corp. v. Jasper, 342, 343, 344, 347, 350, 357
Smith v. Eli Lilly & Co., 479, 481, 483
Smith v. E.R. Squibb & Sons, Inc., 453
Smith v. Louisville Ladder Co., 193
Soule v. General Motors Corp., 94, 146, *180,* 184, 185, 190
Sowell v. American Cyanamid Co., 279, 280, 281, 285
Spaur v. Owens-Corning, 490
Sprietsma v. Mercury Marine, 417
Star Furniture Co. v. Pulaski Furniture Co., 653
State Farm Fire & Casualty Co. v. Amazon.com, Inc., 681
State Farm Fire & Casualty Co. v. Amazon.com Services, Inc., 681, 682
State Farm Mut. Auto. Ins. Co. v. Campbell, 606, 607
State Farm Mut. Auto. Ins. Co. v. Norcold, Inc., 569
States v. R.D. Werner Co., *653,* 654
Stazenski v. Tennant Co., 526, 528, 529, 530, 531, 535, 555
Sternhagen v. Dow Co., 87, 113, 262
Stevens v. Secretary of Department of Health & Human Services, 505, 509, 510
Stinson v. DuPont de Nemours and Co., 273
Story Parchment Co. v. Paterson Parchment Paper Co., 463, 465, 467
Strauss v. Belle Realty Co., 20, 22, 54
Summers v. Tice, 473, 483, 484, 485, 486, 488, 492

Takata Airbag Prod. Liab. Litig., In re, 573
Tatham v. Bridgestone Americas Holding, 146
Temple-Inland Forest Prods. Corp. v. Carter-499, 591
Tersigni v. Wyeth, 378
T.H. v. Novartis Pharm. Corp., 287
The T.J. Hooper, 236
Thing v. La Chusa, 308
Thomas v. Hoffman-LaRoche, Inc., 446, 448, 455
Thomas v. Holliday, 628
Thomas v. Winchester, 47, 49, 50
Tillman v. Vance Equip. Co., 678
Tincher v. Omega Flex, Inc., 96, 118
Todd v. Societe BIC, S.A., 322

Trans State Airlines v. Pratt & Whitney Can., Inc., 567, 568
Transue v. Aesthetech Corp., 385, 387, 388
Travelers Indemnity Co. v. Dammann & Co., 569
Traylor v. Husqvarna Motor, 630
Trull v. Volkswagen of America, Inc., 457, 460, 461, 463, 465, 467, 468
Trust v. Arden Farms Co., 39
Tune v. Synergy Gas Corp., 444
TXO Production Corp. v. Alliance Resources Corp., 606

Union Pump v. Albritton, 538, 542, 543, 544, 640, 659
Uniroyal Goodrich Tire Co. v. Martinez, 351
United States v. *See name of opposing party*

Van Bracklin v. Fonda, 24, 26
Vandermark v. Ford Motor Co., 671
Vassallo v. Baxter Healthcare Corp., 105, *261,* 263
Veysey, United States v., 436
Voss v. Black & Decker Mfg. Co., 153

Wagner v. International Harvester Co., 233
Wallis v. Ford Motor Co., 572
Walters v. Mintec/International, 592
Wangsness v. Builders Cashway, Inc., 625, 627, 628, 629
Watkins v. Ford Motor Co., 93, *253,* 255, 453
Webb v. Special Elec. Co., 281
Whiteford by Whiteford v. Yamaha Motor Corp., 526, 530, 531
Wilkes v. DePuy International Ltd., 740
Williamson v. Mazda Motor of America, 410, 416, 417, 418, 419
Willis Mining, Inc. v. Noggle, 168
Wilson Sporting Goods Co. v. Hickox, 148, 190, 632
Winterbottom v. Wright, 2, 4, 5, 8, 13, 22, 47, 49, 50, 54, 55
Wood v. Wyeth-Ayerst Labs., 585
Woods v. A.R.E. Accessories, LLC, 207
Wright v. Brooke Group Ltd., 76, 118
Wysocki v. Reed, 483

Yates v. Ortho-McNeil-Janssen Pharmaceuticals, Inc., 317, 318, 377

Zimmer, NextGen Knee Implant Products Liability Litigation, In re, 377
Zuchowicz v. United States, 432
Zurbriggen v. Twin Hill Acquisition Co., 148
Zypexa Prods. Liab. Litig., In re, 408

Index

Absolute liability, 19, 119-120, 260, 554-555
Accidents, 13-19. *See also* Automobile accidents
Actual versus constructive knowledge, 110
Admiralty law, 561-569, 656-659
Affirmative defenses. *See also* Defenses
   assumption of risk. *See* Assumption of risk
   bulk supplier defense, 281-285, 291
   commonly known risks, 288-295, 301-302
   contributory negligence. *See* Contributory negligence
   misuse of products. *See* Misuse of products
   prima facie case and, 291
   sophisticated user defense, 270, 291
   unavoidably unsafe products, 380-381
"Age of statutes." *See* Legislation and regulations
AIDS epidemic, 382
Airbags, 147-149
Allergic reactions, 271-275
Alteration of products, 655, 675-676
Alternative design requirement, 76, 106, 116-117, 186-192. *See also* Design defects
Alternative liability doctrine, 473-474, 483, 486-487
Amazon, 679-683
American Law Institute, 42, 75. *See also* Restatement *(Second) of Torts*; Restatement *(Third) of Torts*
Animal studies, 503-504
Artificial intelligence, 249-251
Asbestos cases
   abatement cases, 574-580
   bare metal defense, 286
   bellwether cases, 221
   duty to warn, 5-13
   factual causation, 428, 461-462, 492
Assumed risk rule. *See* Assumption of risk
Assumption of risk
   overview, 618-619
   categorical liability and, 639
   comparative responsibility and, 659-664
   contributory negligence and, 628
   elements of, 619
   implied, 618, 628
   objective versus subjective consent, 627-628, 640
   primary assumption of risk, 633-640, 661-664
   readily available safety devices, failure to use, 629-633
   recreational activities and, 638-639
   secondary assumption of risk, 633, 639-640, 661-664
   unreasonably dangerous products and, 175
   voluntary choice, 619-630
Auctions, 675-679
Automobile accidents. *See also* Autonomous vehicles
   airbags, 147-149
   bystander liability and, 714-716
   crashworthiness doctrine, 456-468, 650-653
   negligence liability and, 15-18
   rear-end crashes with autonomous vehicles, 664-666
   rollovers as malfunctions, 93-94
   strict products liability and, 19
Automobiles, 113, 334-335, 456-468
Autonomous vehicles
   artificial intelligence, 249-251
   bystander liability and, 721-724
   contributory negligence, 664-666
   damages, 612-615
   defective products, 150
   defenses, 664-666
   design defects, 173-175, 248-251, 362-364
   development of, 172-173
   driver-assistance systems, 172-173
   factual causation, 521-524
   negligence liability and, 149-152
   preemption, 418-421
   proximate cause, 553-556
   rating of technology used for, 173
   scope of liability, 695-697
   tort law changed by, 19
   unavoidably unsafe products, 390-392
   warnings, 336-339, 362-364
Availability heuristic, 204-205, 663

Bailments, 672-675
Bare metal defense, 286
Bellwether cases, 221

Index

Best available explanation, 438
Blood and blood products, 381-385, 728-741
Blood shield statutes, 384-385
Breach of warranty. *See* Express warranty; Implied warranty
Bulk supplier defense, 281-285, 291
Burden of proof
  design defects, 190-192
  enhanced injury, 468
  factual causation, 465
  globally, 747
  heeding presumption standard for warning cases, 446
  medical products, 380-381
But-for test, 424-440
Bystander liability
  automobile accidents and, 714-716
  autonomous vehicles and, 721-724
  categorical liability and, 719-720
  choice and, 714-715
  conflicts between consumers and bystanders, 706-716
  consumer expectations test, 704-705
  extension of coverage to, 699-706
  implied warranty and, 708
  negligence liability and, 716-721
  unreasonably dangerous products, 716-720

Carcinogens. *See* Asbestos cases; Toxic tort cases
Categorical liability. *See also* Optional safety equipment
  assumption of risk and, 639
  bystander liability and, 719-720
  choice by consumers and, 222-226, 719
  consumer expectations test and, 221-222
  design defects and, 210-228, 248-249
  duty, 227-228
  guns, 713-714
  Restatement (Third) of Torts, 216-222, 228, 719, 722-723
  unreasonably dangerous products, 227
  warnings and, 215
Causation
  factual causation. *See* Factual causation
  foreseeability of risk, 311
  globally, 746
  scope of liability. *See* Proximate cause
  sufficiency of evidence, 129
Caveat emptor, 23-24, 32-42
Chain leaders, 705-706
Chemical structure, biological activity and, 504
Choice by consumers. *See also* Assumption of risk
  bystander liability and, 714-715, 720
  categorical liability and, 222-226, 719
  design defects, 207-235
  optional safety equipment, 199-200, 228-235, 622-623
  patent-defect rule, 215

  value of, 111-118
  warnings and, 222, 253-256, 287-288
Circumstantial evidence, 126, 137
Class actions, 572, 584
Coding errors, 150-151
Coffee cases, 610-612
Coincidental harm, 530-531
Comment k. *See* Unavoidably unsafe products
Commercial availability, 242-243
Commonly known risks, 288-295, 301-302
Comparative products liability
  blood and blood products, 728-741
  consumer expectations test, 727-728, 739-740
  consumer expectations test and, 727-728
  defined, 725
  globally, 726-727, 740
  uniformity and market competition, 725-726
Comparative responsibility
  overview, 640-641
  alteration of products, 655
  assumption of risk and, 659-664
  crashworthiness doctrine and, 650-653
  enhanced injury, 649-652
  misuse of products
    forms of, 653-659
    system for, 643-653
    without system for, 641-643
  superseding causes, 656-659
  warnings, failure to follow, 655
Compensatory damages, 558, 560. *See also* Damages; Punitive damages
Component part suppliers, 243-244, 285-286, 568-569
Conclusive presumption, 432-433
Conflict preemption, 414
Constructive versus actual knowledge, 110
Consumer, defined, 45
Consumer choice. *See* Choice by consumers
Consumer expectations test. *See also* Unreasonably dangerous products
  autonomous vehicles, 151
  basis of, 147-148
  bystander liability and, 704-705
  categorical liability and, 221-222
  complex products, 146
  constructive versus actual knowledge, 110
  defects and, 46, 115
  duty and, 171-172
  factual causation, 455
  foreseeability and, 87
  global application of, 727-728, 739-740, 745-746
  implied warranty and lack of, 95-96
  incomplete design, 136-137
  limits of, 94
  manufacturer intentions versus, 149
  negligence and, 69-70
  online marketplace, 682

Index

as opaque, 94
patent defects and dangers and, 168-171
product malfunctions, 87-88, 178-179, 185
Restatement (Third) of Torts, 137, 149
risk-utility test and, 79-96, 100-121, 126, 178-186
types of expectations, 109-111
unreasonably dangerous products. *See* Unreasonably dangerous products
used products, 678
warning defects, 521
Consumer Product Safety Commission (CPSC), 335-336
Consumers, meaning of, 704-705
Contaminated or unwholesome food, 24-32, 63, 131-137
Contract law
implied warranty compared, 31
implied warranty under UCC, 92-93
privity requirement, 4, 40-41, 47-55
pure economic loss and, 566-568, 579-580
reformation, 31-32
tort liability and, 2-5, 19-22
waivers of liability, 617-618
Contributory negligence. *See also* Comparative responsibility
overview, 640-641
assumption of risk and, 628
autonomous vehicles, 664-666
foreseeability of risk, 311
misuse of products, 643
secondary assumption of risk as, 639
Controlled studies, 494, 503
Cost considerations, 96, 116, 407, 417
Cost-benefit analysis. *See also* Risk-utility test
design defects, 599-600
insurability of risk and, 264-265
negligence liability and, 63-64
regulations, 560
Council Directive 85/374/EEC
application diversity issues, 752-753
beginnings of, 726-727
consumer expectations test, 745-746
development risks, 262, 743-745, 746
fifth report on, 748-751
fourth report on, 746-748
harmonization issues, 751-752
influence of *Restatement* on, 46
litigation risk, 742
second report on, 741-745
settlements, 742, 747, 749-750
third report on, 745-746
COVIC-19 pandemic, 371
CPSC (Consumer Product Safety Commission), 335-336
Crashworthiness doctrine, 456-468, 650-653
Crowding out effect, 322
Customary practices, 235-244

Damages
overview, 557
autonomous vehicles, 612-615
comparative responsibility and, 648
compensatory damages, 558, 560
economic loss rule, 561-580, 585-586
enhanced injury and, 462-465
fraud and, 570-572
globally, 752-753
intentional infliction of emotional distress, 591
intermediate rule, 573-574
irreparable harms, 558
medical monitoring, 581-586
mental anguish, 591
physical harm and, 558-561
punitive damages. *See* Punitive damages
pure economic loss, 561-580, 612-613
stand-alone emotional harms, 586-595, 613
types of, 558
unmanifested defects, 570-574
warranty cases, 452
DAS (driver-assistance systems), 172-173
Daubert standard, 189-190, 500-503
Deceptive trade practices, 255-256
Defect per se, 396-398, 406
Defective products. *See also* Design defects; Manufacturing defects; Warning defects
autonomous vehicles, 150
categories of, 67-70
circumstantial evidence supporting inference, 70-71
limits of, 46
Restatement (Second) of Torts, 44, 46, 66-67
Restatement (Third) of Torts, 66-72
Defenses
assumption of risk. *See* Assumption of risk
autonomous vehicles, 664-666
bare metal defense, 286
bulk supplier defense, 281-285, 291
commonly known risks. *See* Commonly known risks
comparative responsibility. *See* Comparative responsibility
contractual limitations of liability, 617-618
contributory negligence. *See* Contributory negligence
misuse of products. *See* Misuse of products
regulatory compliance defense, 399-409, 414-417, 747
sophisticated user defense, 270, 291
DES cases, 469-493
Design defects. *See also* Autonomous vehicles
alternative design requirement, 76, 106, 116-117, 186-192
approaches to, 178-186
burden of proof, 190-192
categorical liability, 210-228, 248-249
choice by consumers and, 207-235

Design defects *(continued)*
  circumstantial evidence supporting inference, 70-71
  commercial availability, 242-243
  component part suppliers, 243-244
  consumer expectations test, exclusive reliance on, 178-179
  cost-benefit analysis, 599-600
  customary practices, 235-244
  duty, 207-208, 235-248, 341-344, 550
  elements of, 171
  factual causation, 455-456
  food products, 136
  foreseeable misuse, 209-210
  foreseeable product use, 207-210
  incomplete design, 136-137
  jury instructions, 206, 328
  limits on duty, 235-248
  manufacturing defects, 177
  optional safety equipment, 199-200, 228-235
  patent dangers and, 178-179
  product malfunctions and, 161, 177
  production process as definition, 130
  public policy, 75-76
  Restatement (Third) of Torts and, 68-69, 75, 76, 225-226, 235-238
  Restatements compared, 73-74
  risk/benefit test, 74-76
  risk-utility test. *See* Risk-utility test
  scope of liability, 177
  social value, 210-211
  state of the art, 235-248
  subsequent remedial measures, 244-248
  technological feasibility, 235-248
  theories of, 74-76
  warning defects and, 344-351
  warning duty and, 341-344
Deterrence
  accidents and, 18
  distributors and retailers, 671-672
  due process and, 608-609
  individual tort right and, 609-610
  public policy and, 482
  punitive damages and, 600-601, 666
  scientific uncertainty and, 519-520
Development risks, 262, 743-745, 746
Direct evidence, 126
Directive 85/374. *See* Council Directive 85/374/EEC
Directness test of proximate cause, 542-547
Disappointed users versus endangered consumers, 564, 573-574, 594
Disappointment theory, 88-89
Disclaimers, 617-618
Discovery, globally, 752-753
Distributors and retailers, 667-672
Divided-damages rule, 658-659. *See also* Comparative responsibility

The Doctrinal Unity of Alternative Liability and Market-Share Liability (Geistfeld), 483-490
Driver-assistance systems (DAS), 172-173
Drugs. *See* Medical products
Due process, deterrence and, 608-609
Duty. *See also* Design defects; Proximate cause; Risk-utility test
  assumption of risk. *See* Assumption of risk
  categorical liability, 227-228
  consumer choice and, 170-171
  consumer expectations test and, 171-172
  defined, 153-154
  design defects, 207-208, 235-248, 341-344, 550
  emotional harms, 594-595
  to exercise reasonable care, 529
  foreseeability of risk, 310, 529-530
  general tort duty, 580
  implied warranty and lack of, 172
  proximate cause and, 547-553
  Restatement §402A, 153-154
  as rule of law, 551
  unreasonably dangerous requirement and, 171
  to warn. *See* Warning defects
  warnings versus design, 341-344

Economic loss rule, 561-580, 585-586
Efficiency versus fairness, 77-78
Eggshell-plaintiff rule, 545
Endangered consumers versus disappointed users, 564, 573-574, 594
Enhanced injury, 456-468, 649-652
Enterprise liability, 78-79, 553-555
Epidemiologic evidence, 494, 502-503
Europe, 726. *See also* Comparative products liability
European Economic Community, 726-727. *See also* Comparative products liability
European Union, 46-47, 262, 752. *See also* Comparative products liability
Evidence
  assumption of risk, 663
  bystander liability and, 720
  causation, 129
  Daubert standard, 189-190, 500-503
  direct versus circumstantial, 126
  expert witnesses, 129, 189-190
  negligence pleaded to allow bad conduct evidence, 135-136
  product malfunctions, 137-149
  spoliation, 143
  subsequent remedial measures, 247
  warning defects, 263-264
Evidential grouping, 485, 489-491, 492
Excessive liability, 22, 54-55
Expected liability costs (PL), 63-64
Expert witnesses, 129, 189-190. *See also Daubert* standard
Exploding bottle cases, 36-39, 55-60, 130

Index

Express preemption, 413-414
Express warranty, 41-42, 46

Factual causation
  overview, 423-424
  alternative liability doctrine, 473-474, 483, 486-487
  autonomous vehicles, 521-524
  best available explanation, 438
  but-for test, 424-440
  counterfactual hypothesis, 427
  deterrence and, 519-520
  elements of, 427
  enhanced injury, 456-468
  epidemiologic evidence, 494, 502-503
  evidential grouping, 489-491, 492
  flexible approach to scientific uncertainty, 502-505
  heeding presumption standard for warning cases, 442-448, 454, 523-524
  identity of tortfeasor uncertain, 469-493
  indivisible injuries, 460-461
  inherent product risks and, 447-448
  liability grouping, 485
  liberal rule of but-for causation, 431-433, 435-440, 446-447
  market-share liability, 469-493
  multiple tortfeasors, 460-461, 468
  multiple tortious causes, 428
  negligence liability, 448, 453-454, 456
  objective standard for warning cases, 441
  ordinary evidentiary standard, 429-433
  preponderance-of-the-evidence standard, 431
  product safety and, 482
  relative plausibility theory of proof, 438-439
  scientific uncertainty, 493-521
  statistics or probabilities to show, 436-437, 485-486
  subjective standard for warning cases, 440-441
  substantial factor test, 428-429
  substantial share requirement, 473-476
  toxic tort cases, 461-462, 493-521
  warning defects, 440-449, 454
  warranty cases, 448-456
Fairness, 77-78, 652-653, 666
Fairness in Asbestos Injury Resolution Act (FAIR), 10-11, 13
False advertising, 255-256
False positives versus false negatives, 431
Federal Rule 407, 247
Federalism, 12-13, 415-416, 418. *See also* Preemption
Field preemption, 414
Finland, 744. *See also* Council Directive 85/374/EEC
Flexible approach to scientific uncertainty, 502-505, 510
Food products
  contaminated or unwholesome food, 24-32, 63, 131-137
  design defects, 136
  implied warranty for, 23-24, 35
  manufacturing defects, 131-137
Ford Bronco II, 93-94, 253-255, 608-609
Ford Pinto case, 194-195
Foreseeability test of proximate cause, 526-537, 543-553, 555-556, 655-659
Foreseeable misuse, 209-210
Foreseeable product use, 207-210
France, 744. *See also* Council Directive 85/374/EEC
Fraud, 570-572

Geistfeld, Mark A., 111-118, 483-490
General acceptance test, 495
General causation, 427
General field of danger, 535-537
Germany, 744-745. *See also* Council Directive 85/374/EEC
Global supply chains, 705-706
Glyphosate (Roundup) cases, 510-521
Green Paper. *See* Council Directive 85/374/EEC
Guns, 709-716

Heeding presumption standard for warning cases, 442-448, 454-455, 523-524
Heuristics, 204-206, 663
Hindsight bias, 204-205
Hot coffee cases, 610-612

IARC (International Agency for Research on Cancer), 512-513, 519
Illiteracy, 278
Imminently dangerous requirement, 51-54
Implied assumption of risk, 618, 628. *See also* Assumption of risk
Implied preemption, 414, 415-418
Implied warranty
  overview, 23-24
  bystander liability and, 708
  caveat emptor compared, 23
  consumer expectations test and, 95-96, 110
  contaminated or unwholesome food, 24-32
  contract law compared, 31
  controversy over, 73-79
  cost considerations, 96
  duty and, 172
  extension to products that do not malfunction, 111
  factual causation, 448-456
  food products, 23-24, 35
  negligence standard compared, 120
  non-food products, 32-42, 51-54
  patent defects and, 165-166
  pure economic loss and, 567-568
  reliance and, 452-454

Implied warranty *(continued)*
   role in product liability, 106, 112
   strict products liability compared, 46
   theories of, 26, 31-32, 40-41
   tort rationale for, 110
   UCC and, 92-93
Impure blood, 381-385, 728-741
Inadequate warnings or instructions. *See* Warning defects
Incomplete design, 136-137
Indemnification, 671-672, 697
Individualized causation, 427
Industrialization, impacts of, 13-19, 25
Infliction of emotional distress, 591-592
Information cost, 313, 325-326
Information overload, 325-326
Informed decision-making. *See* Choice by consumers; Consumer expectations test
Inspection, implied warranty and lack of, 35
Instructions. *See* Warning defects
Insurance
   ordinary verus tort, 119-120
   pain and suffering, 594-595
   as rationale for strict products liability, 18
   rising costs of, 11-12
   warning defects, 264-265
Intangible versus tangible goods, 683-685, 696
Intensity of expression of warnings, 400-407
Intentional infliction of emotional distress, 591
Intermediate rule for damages, 573-574
International Agency for Research on Cancer (IARC), 512-513, 519
Intervening causes, 537-547
Irrebuttable presumption, 432-433
Irreparable harms, 558-561

Joint and several liability, 460-461, 468, 648-649, 671-672
Judges, role of, 550-551
Jurors
   foreseeability of risk and, 535-537
   framing of problem, 205
   heuristics used by, 204-206
   point of view considerations, 205-206
   polycentricity, 328-329
   risk-utility test, application by, 193-195
   role of, 550-551
Jury instructions
   design defects, 206, 328
   irreparable harms, 558
   warning defects, 327-329, 333

Language issues, 275-278, 400-407
Latent defects versus patent defects, 167
Learned intermediary doctrine, 286-287, 372-381, 454-455
Legal cause. *See* Factual causation; Proximate cause

Legislation and regulations
   overview, 393
   blood shield statutes, 384-385
   negligence per se, 394-399
   preemption. *See* Preemption
   regulatory compliance defense, 399-409, 747
   responses to tort liability, 10-12, 256
   safety and, 743
   statutory violations as proof of defect, 394-399, 716
Liability, scope of
   overview, 667
   alteration of products, 675-676
   auctions, 675-679
   bailments, 672-675
   bystander liability. *See* Bystander liability
   damages. *See* Damages
   distributors and retailers, 667-672
   indemnification and, 671-672, 697
   leases, 674
   online marketplace, 679-683
   products, what constitutes, 683-695
   proximate cause. *See* Proximate cause
   remanufactured products, 678
   sales transactions, what constitutes, 672-683
   services versus products, 683-697
   used products, 675-679
Liability crisis, 11-12
Liability grouping, 485
Liability insurance, 11-12
Liberal rule of but-for causation, 431-433, 435-440, 446-447
Litigation risk, 742
Loss-spreading, 125
Luxembourg, 744. *See also* Council Directive 85/374/EEC

Machine learning, 249-251
Malfunction doctrine. *See* Product malfunctions
Manufacturer Enterprise Responsibility (MER), 553-555
Manufacturer expectations rationale, 76
Manufacturing defects. *See also* Strict products liability
   autonomous vehicles, 150-152
   circumstantial evidence supporting inference, 70-71
   design defects and, 177
   food products, 131-137
   incomplete design and, 136-137
   medical products, 381-390
   production process as definition, 130
   proof of, 126-131
   quality control measures, 95-96, 115-116, 124
   rationales for strict liability, 123-126
   Restatement (Second) of Torts designed for, 96
   Restatement (Third) of Torts and, 67-70, 75, 115-116, 123-125, 126

Index

warning defects compared, 264-265
wholesalers and retailers, 124
Market equilibrium, 236
Market-share liability, 469-493
Mass torts, 12, 221
Material misrepresentations, 452
Material representations, 452
Materiality, 311
MDL (multidistrict litigation), 221
Media attention, 256
Medical monitoring, 581-586
Medical products
   blood and blood products, 381-385
   burden of proof, 380-381
   heeding presumption standard for warning cases, 454-455
   learned intermediary doctrine, 286-287, 372-381, 454-455
   manufacturing defects, 381-390
   orphan drugs, 744
   product malfunctions, 381-390
   reasonable physician standard, 378-379
   regulatory compliance defense, 408-409
   sales versus service, 693-694
   scientific uncertainty, 493-521
   thalidomide, 379-380
   vaccines, 369-371, 388-389, 505-510
Mental anguish damages, 591
MER (Manufacturer Enterprise Responsibility), 553-555
Mesothelioma. *See* Asbestos cases
Misrepresentation, 570-572
Misuse of products
   alteration of products, 655
   bystander liability and, 720
   comparative responsibility and, 641-653
   contributory negligence, 643
   design defects and, 209-210
   fairness and, 652-653
   foreseeable, 209-210
   forms of, 653-659
   warning defects and, 361-362
Motor vehicles. *See* Automobile accidents; Automobiles; Autonomous vehicles
MTBE cases, 587-595
Multidistrict litigation (MDL), 221
Multilingual warnings, 275-278, 400-407

National Childhood Vaccine Injury Act, 369-370
National Highway Traffic Safety Administration (NHTSA), 334-335
National Vaccine Act, 505-510
Negligence liability
   automobile accidents, 15-18
   autonomous vehicles, 149-152
   beginnings of, 4-5
   bystander liability and, 716-721

contributory negligence. *See* Contributory negligence
demise of privity and, 47-55
design defects and, 178-179
evidentiary rationale for strict liability and, 60-65
factual causation, 448, 453-454, 456
foreseeability of risk, 544-545
imminently dangerous requirement, 51-54
implied warranty compared, 120
infliction of emotional distress, 591-592
negligence per se, 394-399
privity requirement and, 4, 47-55
products liability and, 8
proof of, 55-60
public policy and, 5
Restatement (Third) of Torts and, 55, 65-72, 120
risk-utility test and, 94, 708-709
unavoidably unsafe products, 135-136
warning defects and, 257-265
workers' compensation and, 62
Net benefit of products, 287-288. *See also* Risk-utility test
NHTSA (National Highway Traffic Safety Administration), 334-335

Obvious risks, 82, 301-302
Obvious-danger rule, 301-302
Occupational diseases, 5-13. *See also* Asbestos cases
OEMs (original equipment manufacturers), 695
Online marketplace, 679-683
Operating systems, 249-250
Optional safety equipment, 199-200, 228-235, 622-623, 720
Original equipment manufacturers (OEMs), 695
Orphan drugs, 744
Overconfidence, 663

Pasteur rabies vaccine, 388-389
Patent defects, patent dangers compared, 165-170
Patent-danger rule
   assumption of risk and, 623
   design defects, 178-179
   obvious risks and, 302
   patent defects compared, 165-170
   risk-utility test and, 164-165
   unreasonably dangerous products, 154-165
   warning and, 341-344
Patent-defect rule, 166-171, 173-175, 215, 226-227
Pattern jury instructions, 206
Pinto case, 194-195
Pleading rules, 135-136
Polycentricity, 328-329
Post-sale duty to warn, 329-336

Preemption
   overview, 393-394, 409-418
   autonomous vehicles, 418-421
   federalism and, 415-416, 418
   prescription drugs, 286-287
   regulatory compliance defense and, 414-417
   types of, 413-418
   vaccines, 369-370
PREP (Public Readiness and Emergency Preparedness) Act, 370-371
Preponderance-of-the-evidence standard, 431
Prescription drugs. *See* Medical products
Primary assumption of risk, 633-640, 661-664
Private law, 423-424
Privity requirement, 4, 40-41, 47-55
Probabilities or statistics to show causation, 436-437, 485-486
Product defects. *See* Design defects; Inadequate warnings or instructions; Manufacturing defects; Product malfunctions; Warning defects
Product Liability Directive. *See* Council Directive 85/374/EEC
Product malfunctions. *See also* Design defects; Manufacturing defects
   autonomous vehicles, 150-152
   bystander liability and, 720
   consumer expectations test, 87-88, 178-179, 185
   design defects and, 161, 177
   medical products, 381-390
   proof of, 137-149
   Restatement (Second) of Torts, 79-80, 83, 88
   Restatement (Third) of Torts, 149
   unreasonably dangerous products, 154-158
   vehicle rollovers as, 93-94
   version 1.0 of strict products liability and, 95
   warnings and, 348
   what constitutes, 179
Product net benefit, 287-288. *See also* Risk-utility test
Products, what constitutes, 683-695
Products liability
   controversy over liability rule, 73-79
   defined, 1
   federalism and, 12-13
   negligence liability and, 8
   politicized nature of, 12
   Restatement rules. *See Restatement (Second) of Torts*; *Restatement (Third) of Torts*
   strict products liability. *See* Strict products liability
   types of, 75
Profit motive, 195-199
Programming errors, 150-151
Proportional liability, 481-482
Prosser, William, 59-60

Proximate cause. *See also* Comparative responsibility; Contributory negligence
   overview, 525-526
   autonomous vehicles, 553-556
   coincidental harm and, 530-531
   directness test of, 542-547
   duty and, 547-553
   elements and, 552-553
   foreseeability of risk, 526-537, 543-553, 555-556, 655-659
   general field of danger and, 535-537
   intervening causes, 537-547
   misuse of products, 653-654
   reference classes and, 535-537
   thin-skull rule, 545
   zone of risk, 529
Public law, 423-424
Public policy
   design defects, 75-76
   deterrence, 482
   disclaimers, 617-618
   heeding presumption standard for warning cases, 445-446
   negligence liability and, 5
   sales versus service, 694
Public Readiness and Emergency Preparedness (PREP) Act, 370-371
Punitive damages
   amount of, 603-612
   autonomous vehicles, 614-615
   comparative products liability and, 725
   conscious disregard of plaintiff's rights, 601-602
   deterrence and, 600-601, 666
   hot coffee cases, 610-612
   nonparty harms, 603-612
   post-sale duty to warn, 334
   problems with, 595-602
   profit motive, 199
   ratio for, 604, 606-607
   risk-utility test and, 599-600
   tort reform and, 612
   wrongful death, 607
Pure economic loss, 561-580, 612-613

Quality control measures, 95-96, 115-116, 124

Radical proof doctrine, 462
Reasonable alternative design, 186-197, 210-214, 216-222, 235-238
Recalls, 329-336
Reference classes, 535-537
Reformation of contracts, 31-32
Regulations. *See* Legislation and regulations
Regulatory compliance defense, 399-409, 414-417, 747
Relative plausibility theory of proof, 438-439
Reliance, 451-454

Index

Remanufactured products, 678
Remedial measures in design, 244-248
Res ipsa loquitur, 55-60, 124, 137-144
Restatement (Second) of Torts. *See also* Medical products
   assumption of risk, 619, 624, 628, 632, 640
   bystander liability, 699
   comparative responsibility and, 647
   compensatory damages, 560
   consumers, meaning of, 704-705
   contributory negligence, 628, 641, 652
   damages, 465
   defect in, 166
   defective products not appropriately covered by, 66-67
   distributors and retailers, 667
   elements of tort claim, 171
   express warranty, 46
   factual causation, 428-429, 467
   global influence of, 46-47
   Greenman case and, 180
   heeding presumption standard for warning cases, 445
   implied warranty. *See* Implied warranty
   infliction of emotional distress, 592-593
   manufacturing defects, 96
   patent-defect rule and, 167-168
   product malfunctions, 79-80, 83, 88
   reasonable care standard, 64-65
   regulatory compliance defense, 399
   Restatement (Third) of Torts compared, 71-74, 117-118
   risk-utility test, 186, 348
   safety standards, 397
   stand-alone emotional harms, 591
   strict products liability rule. *See* Strict products liability
   unavoidably unsafe products, 365
   unreasonably dangerous products. *See* Unreasonably dangerous products
   warning defects, 265
   warning duty and, 347-348
Restatement (Third) of Torts
   application of strict products liability, 667
   asbestos abatement, 578
   assumption of risk, 661
   bailments, 674-675
   blood and blood products, 385
   burden of proof, 468
   bystander liability, 709
   categorical liability, 216-222, 228, 719, 722-723
   comparative responsibility, 647-648
   component part suppliers, 244, 568-569
   consumer expectations test, 137, 149
   customary practices, 236
   design defects, 68-69, 75, 76, 225-226, 235-238. *See also* Risk-utility test
   development of, 96-97
   directness test, 546
   distributors and retailers, 667, 672
   duty, 551
   epidemiologic evidence, 502-503
   factual causation, 424, 428, 433, 448, 502-503, 510
   flexible approach to scientific uncertainty, 510
   foreseeability of risk, 529, 545
   foreseeable product use, 208-209
   growth from earlier *Restatement*, 1
   infliction of emotional distress, 591-592
   intensity of expression of warnings, 322
   intervening causes, 543
   joint and several liability, 460-461, 649
   learned intermediary doctrine, 372-381
   leases, 674
   manufacturing defects, 67-70, 75, 115-116, 123-125, 126
   multiple tortious causes, 428
   negligence foundation of, 55, 65-72, 120
   obvious risks, 82
   post-sale duty to warn, 329, 333, 334, 336
   product malfunctions, 149
   proof of negligence, 55
   proximate cause, 528, 534-535, 537, 543, 545, 546
   reasonable alternative design, 186-197
   reasonable foreseeability of harm, 309
   reasonable physician standard, 378-379
   regulatory compliance defense, 399, 405
   res ipsa loquitur, 142-143
   Restatement (Second) of Torts compared, 71-74, 117-118
   risk standard, 529, 545
   risk-spreading properties of strict liability, 88
   risk-utility test. *See* Risk-utility test
   safety standards, 394-399
   sales, what constitutes, 682-683
   sales versus service, 692-693
   scope of liability. *See* Proximate cause, above
   stand-alone emotional harms, 587
   state of the art, 235
   tangible versus intangible goods, 685
   unreasonably dangerous products, 720
   used products, 678
   waivers of liability, 617
   warning defects, 68-69, 262, 316, 322, 327, 329, 334, 336. *See also* Warning defects
   warning duty and, 522-523
Retailers, liability for manufacturing defects, 124
Retailers and distributors, 667-672
Risk/benefit test, 74-76
Risk-risk trade-offs, 199-207
Risk-utility test. *See also* Assumption of risk; Damages
   adoption of, 97, 116
   application of, 193
   autonomous vehicles, 174-175, 250-251

Risk-utility test *(continued)*
   consumer expectations test and, 79-96, 100-121, 126, 178-186
   cost considerations, 96, 116, 195-199
   defining consumer expectations with, 106-121
   design defects
      balancing factors in, 192-207
      combination of consumer expectations with, 180-186
      exclusive reliance on, 179-180
      product malfunctions, 185
      profit motive, 195-199
      reasonable alternative design, 186-197, 210-214, 216-222, 235-238
      risk-risk trade-offs, 199-207
   design warnings and, 351-362
   globally, 727-728
   incentives to obtain optimal safety, 112
   incorporation into strict products liability, 97-106
   inherent dangers, 170
   macro-balancing, 187
   monetizing risk of physical injury, 559-561
   negligence and, 94, 708-709
   obvious risks and, 82
   patent defects and, 166-167
   patent-danger rule and, 164-165, 168-169
   punitive damages and, 599-600
   rationale for, 146
   Restatement (Third) of Torts on, 109, 172, 186
   Wade-Keeton test, 187
   warning defects, 278, 281, 323-329
   warnings and design and, 351-362
Roundup (glyphosate) cases, 510-521

Safety. *See also* Risk-utility test
   factual causation and, 482
   incentives to obtain, 112
   online marketplace, 681-682
   optional safety equipment, 199-200, 228-235, 622-623, 720
   quality control measures, 95-96
   regulatory framework and, 743
   statutes or regulations, 190
   strict products liability increasing, 65, 682
   workers' compensation and, 78-79
Safety standards, 203, 394-399. *See also* Legislation and regulations; Preemption
Sales transactions, what constitutes, 672-683
Scientific uncertainty, 493-521
Scope of liability. *See* Liability, scope of; Proximate cause
Secondary assumption of risk, 633, 639-640, 661-664
Services versus products, 683-695
Settlements, 742, 747, 749-750
Several liability, 649-650. *See also* Joint and several liability
Signature diseases, 504. *See also* Asbestos cases; DES cases
Single-digit ratio, 604, 606-607
Social value, 19-22, 210-211, 371
Software, 685-686, 695-697
Sophisticated user defense, 270, 291
Spain, 744. *See also* Council Directive 85/374/EEC
Specific causation, 427
Spoliation, 143
State of the art, 235-248
Statistics or probabilities to show causation, 436-437, 485-486
Statutes or regulations. *See* Legislation and regulations
Stewart, Larry S., 74-76
Strict Liability for Defective Product Design (Stewart), 74-76
Strict products liability. *See also* Asbestos cases
   absolute liability compared, 19, 260
   application of, 667
   automobile accidents, 19
   beginnings of, 5-13, 22, 42
   comparative responsibility. *See* Comparative responsibility
   consumer, defined, 45
   consumer choice, 111-118
   consumer expectations test. *See* Consumer expectations test
   design defects. *See* Design defects
   doctrinal foundations for, 23-72
   enterprise liability, 78-79
   equitable rationale for, 88
   evidentiary rationale for, 60-65, 144
   exploding bottle cases, 36-39, 55-60, 130
   implied warranty. *See* Implied warranty
   implied warranty compared, 46
   insurance rationale for, 15-19
   manufacturers, 8
   manufacturing defects. *See* Manufacturing defects
   medical products. *See* Medical products
   negligence principle, 47-72
   normative focus of, 720-721
   product-caused injuring leading to, 14-15
   rationale for, 389-390, 720-721
   Restatement rules. *See Restatement (Second) of Torts*; *Restatement (Third) of Torts*
   risk-spreading properties of, 88, 125
   risk-utility test. *See* Risk-utility test
   safety improved by, 65, 682
   scope of liability. *See* Liability, scope of
   Traynor's influence on, 39-40
   unavoidably unsafe products, 135-136
   unreasonably dangerous products, 44-45, 46
   user, defined, 45
   version 1.0, 79-96
   version 2.0, 96-121, 171

Index

warning defects. *See* Warning defects
workers' compensation as, 62
Subsequent remedial measures, 244-248, 317-318
Substantial factor test, 428-429
Substantial number requirement, 271-275
Substantial share requirement, 473-476
Superseding causes, 537-547, 656-659
Supremacy Clause, 409
Surveillance capitalism, 721

Tangible versus intangible goods, 683-685, 696
Technological feasibility, 235-248, 407, 417
Tesla. *See* Autonomous vehicles
Thalidomide, 379-380
Theory of mind, 664
Thin-skull rule, 545
Tobacco litigation, 292-295
Tort liability
  consent and, 111
  contractual relationship, limitation to, 2-5, 19-22
  legislative responses to, 10-12, 256
  products liability as departure from, 1
  public versus private law, 423-424
  punitive damages and, 612
  pure economic loss and, 566-567
  purposes of, 77-78
Tort reform
  asbestos cases and, 9-10, 12
  damages and, 557
  distributor and retailer liability, 672
  joint and several liability and, 468
  punitive damages and, 612
  several liability, 649-650
Toxic tort cases, 437, 461-462, 493-521
Transaction types, liability and. *See* Liability, scope of

Unavoidably unsafe products, 135-136, 380-381, 390-392, 694-695. *See also* Medical products
Uniform Commercial Code (UCC), 89-92, 452
United Kingdom, 740. *See also* Council Directive 85/374/EEC
Unmanifested defects, 570-574
Unreasonably dangerous products. *See also* Consumer expectations test
  alternative design and, 214-215
  assumed risk rule and, 175
  bystander liability and, 716-720
  categorical liability, 227
  commonly known risks, 291
  differing interpretations of, 154-165
  obvious risks and, 82
  patent dangers and, 154-165
  patent defects and, 167, 170
  product malfunctions and, 154-158
  Restatement §402A, 44-45, 46, 74, 114-115, 154
  warnings, 347-348
Unwholesome or contaminated food, 24-32, 63, 131-137
U.S. Constitution, 409
Used products, 675-679
User, defined, 45

Vaccines, 369-371, 388-389, 505-510
The Value of Consumer Choice in Strict Products Liability (Geistfeld), 111-118
Vehicles. *See* Automobile accidents

Wade-Keeton test, 187
Waivers, 617-618
Warning defects
  adequacy of disclosure, 311-323
  allergic reactions, 271-275
  asbestos cases, 5-13
  bare metal defense, 286
  bulk supplier defense, 281-285, 291
  commonly known risks, 288-295, 301-302
  component part suppliers, 285-286
  consumer choice and, 222, 253-256, 287-288
  consumer expectations test, 521
  content and format of disclosure, 311-323
  deceptive trade practices and, 255-256
  design defects and, 344-351
  design duty and, 341-344
  duty, 550
  factual causation, 440-449, 454
  false advertising and, 255-256
  foreseeability of risk, 302-311
  illiteracy, 278
  information cost and, 313, 325-326
  inherent risks, 300-301
  intensity of expression of warnings, 322
  intermediaries and, 279-287
  jury instructions, 327-329, 333
  learned intermediary doctrine, 286-287, 372-381, 454-455
  manufacturing defects compared, 264-265
  media attention on, 256
  multilingual warnings, 275-278, 400-407
  obvious risks, 301-302
  post-sale duty, 329-336
  product net benefit and, 287-288
  reasonable foreseeability of harm, 302-311
  Restatement (Third) of Torts and, 68-69, 262, 316, 322, 327, 329, 334, 336
  Restatements compared, 73-74
  risk-utility test, 278, 281, 323-329
  safe product use, 300
  sophisticated intermediaries, 281
  sophisticated user defense, 270, 291
  state-of-the-art knowledge and, 263-264
  subsequent remedial measures, 317-318

Warning defects *(continued)*
  substantive basis of liability for, 257-265
  suppliers, 281-285
  tobacco litigation, 292-295
  types of risk to disclose, 287-311
  unforeseeability of risk, 264-265
  to whom
    overview, 265
    average or ordinary consumers, 266-278
    intermediaries and, 279-287
    sophisticated users, 270, 291
    substantial number requirement, 271-275
Warnings. *See also* Warning defects
  autonomous vehicles, 336-339, 362-364
  bystander liability and, 701-706
  categorical liability and, 215
  consumer choice and, 117, 222
  deliberate product misuse, 361-362
  not followed by consumers, 249-251, 361, 363
  product malfunctions and, 88
  product misuse as failure to follow, 655
  scientific uncertainty, 520-521
Warranty cases
  express warranty, 41-42, 46
  factual causation in, 448-456
  implied warranty. *See* Implied warranty
  reliance, 451-454
Wholesalers, liability for manufacturing defects, 124
Willful ignorance, 666
Workers' compensation, 62, 78-79
Writ system, 4
Wrongful death, 601-602, 607

Zone of risk, 529
Zone-of-danger test, 592